W9-AST-862

DICTIONARY OF AMERICAN HISTORY
CSS

DICTIONARY OF

AMERICAN HISTORY

VOLUME V

DICTIONARY OF AMERICAN HISTORY

JAMES TRUSLOW ADAMS

Editor in Chief

R. V. COLEMAN

Managing Editor

VOLUME V

NEW YORK

CHARLES SCRIBNER'S SONS

1940

Printed in the United States of America

A

Advisory Council

DICTIONARY OF AMERICAN HISTORY

Sabbath, The — Zwaanendael Colony

Sabbath, THE, in the United States is generally understood to refer to Sunday, or the First Day. Stemming as it did from English and Scottish Puritanism, its observance was originally proverbially strict, "a day for a man to afflict his soul."

Despite the presumptive aid of the law, the post-revolutionary period saw increasing laxity due particularly to the war itself, the French Revolution and certain rationalistic principles of the day.

Sabbatarian efforts helped arrest the profanation somewhat, yet the first half of the 19th century saw new patterns in desecration constantly being introduced, and the older ones did not fade. Sunday travel was an excellent example. Not only were stages, canal boats, steamboats and mails rolling the Sabbath into oblivion, but a new mode of transportation, the railroad[qqv], was catching the public fancy. It was apparent that the growing trade and commerce were centered in the city where almost all kinds of business were carried on upon the Sabbath, often by virtue of necessity. The Sunday newspaper reappeared. Moreover, the urban trend toward divertissement showed no abatement, an attitude greatly influenced by the immigrant. Meanwhile, on the frontier, missionaries reported that very often there was no observance at all. The Civil War merely accentuated these trends.

Of course, the "claims of the Christian Sabbath" still continued to exert a considerable influence on the American people. But the path was being, and continued to be, increasingly trod away from the Sunday of ascetic self-denial to one of "recklessness of the law" and rest and recreation.

[F. L. Bronner, Observance of the Sabbath in the United States, 1800-1865, an unpublished ms. deposited at the Harvard University Library.]

FREDERICK L. BRONNER

Sabbath-Day Houses were small buildings where members of the congregation, who had come from a distance, would take refuge between the morning and afternoon church service. Considered typical of colonial New England, somewhat similar conditions saw their revival in the West and, at least in Texas, they lasted into the 20th century.

[A. M. Earle, *The Sabbath in Puritan New England.*]

FREDERICK L. BRONNER

Sabine Crossroads, Battle at. During his raid up the Red River[qv] Valley in the spring of 1864, Gen. Banks (U.) was unable to get his fleet above Grand Écore, near Natchitoches. He then marched overland toward Shreveport, but was met and defeated by Confederate forces under Gen. "Dick" Taylor in the battle of Sabine Crossroads (or Mansfield), about forty miles south of Shreveport, on April 8, 1864, thus ending the advance upon Shreveport and causing the abandonment of the campaign.

[C. A. Evans, ed., *Confederate Military History*, Vol. X; J. K. Hosmer, *Outcome of the Civil War, 1863-1865.*]

WALTER PRICHARD

Sabine River, as Boundary. *See* Neutral Ground; Louisiana Purchase, Boundaries of the.

Sable, Isle of, about 150 miles east of Halifax, was of interest to colonial New Englanders and Acadians as a place to obtain walrus, seal, wild horses and black foxes. Attempts to make settlements there failed.

[Harold St. John, Sable Island, in Boston Society of Natural History, *Proceedings*, Vol. 36, No. 1.]

ROBERT E. MOODY

Sabotage. This term first came into general use in the United States early in the 20th century. It was borrowed from the syndicalist movement of southern Europe, and introduced here by the Industrial Workers of the World[qv] to describe one phase of its fundamental strategy of "direct action." This strategy, having a class-struggle^qv animus and a revolutionary air, involved repudiation of political action and disdain for collective bargaining^qv. Sabotage tactics represented a means of harassing the avowed class enemy, capitalist employers, without foregoing wage-income as in strikes^qv.

The practice of sabotage involves injury, in some way, of the employer's property, as by surreptitiously mixing a little sand in lubricating oil. While the methods of sabotage are myriad and need not in all cases involve violence, or destruction of plant equipment, the aim is invariably vexation and pecuniary loss to the employer. Methods of somewhat similar import, such as "soldiering on the job," had long been familiar and are still regularly practised by conservative unionists simply as an incident of effective bargaining procedure: giving as little as need be for as much as can be obtained. But the general terroristic strategy of the I. W. W. made little appeal to American labor and sabotage never became established here, as a concerted, persistent tactic in the labor struggle.

[S. B. Mathewson, *Restriction of Output among Unorganized Workers;* T. Veblen, *Absentee Ownership.*]

MYRON W. WATKINS

Sacco and Vanzetti Case, THE, involving two Italian aliens, convicted of murdering a paymaster and his guard at South Braintree, Mass., April 15, 1920, became one of the most famous criminal cases of the century; produced violent anti-American demonstrations abroad; and in the minds of many people who knew little of the facts and still less of criminal law, became a symbol of the class struggle^qv. At the original trial the defense had introduced the radicalism of the defendants as an explanation of certain actions alleged to show "consciousness of guilt." The harsh questioning of the prosecutor, some questionable remarks by the judge, and certain weaknesses in the evidence combined to create a widespread belief that the defendants were being punished for radicalism rather than murder. Defense funds were raised and propaganda conducted. In the meantime, for six years the case dragged its way through a series of dilatory motions and appeals, until in 1927 all legal resources were exhausted and the death sentence again was imposed. A special investigating commission, appointed by Gov. Fuller, after elaborate review declared the trial had been fair and the conviction just; clemency was refused; and Sacco and Vanzetti were executed Aug. 22, 1927.

[The complete transcript of the record has been published in five volumes. There is a voluminous periodical literature on the subject readily accessible through the *Readers' Guide to Periodical Literature.*]

W. A. ROBINSON

Sachem is a term of Algonkin^qv origin appearing in colonial writing about 1625. In New England the sachem was the chief, or leader, of two or more allied tribes. Later the term was used as synonymous with chief. Sagamore, from the Abnaki^qv name for chief, had a similar meaning, but came to be used for chiefs of inferior rank to sachems. In government and territorial distinctions, sachemship signified the territory and jurisdiction of a chief. The Tammany Society^qv adopted the title sachem for its head men, as Grand Sachem, Sachem, etc.

[Lewis H. Morgan, *League of the Iroquois.*]

CLARK WISSLER

Sackett's Harbor, Operations at. In the War of 1812^qv the importance of naval control on Lake Ontario made the Sackett's Harbor naval base, near its foot, a hive of shipbuilding activity. Here seamen, shipwrights, and stores were assembled for Commodore Isaac Chauncey's flotilla, and in 1814 some six hundred workers were building two immense three-deckers of over one hundred guns. The base underwent two British attacks, the first, July 19, 1812, being limited to an ineffective two-hour naval bombardment. The second, May 27–29, 1813, was a combined operation by Commodore Yeo's squadron and over one thousand British regulars and Indians under Gov. Gen. Sir George Prevost. Although the base was well fortified and manned by equal forces, the New York militia fled at the first landing of British troops. As the British approached the blockhouse and barracks, however, they were held up by sharp fire from regulars and artillery. Gen. Jacob Brown, in chief command, rallied the militia, and at this reinforcement the British retreated to their boats. Losses were about equal, numbering for the British 48 killed and 208 wounded. Stores valued at $500,000 were burned to prevent capture, but two ships on the stocks escaped with slight damage.

[Theodore Roosevelt, *The Naval War of 1812.*]

ALLAN WESTCOTT

Sackville, Fort. *See* Knox, Fort.

Sackville-West Incident. In September, 1888, Lord Sackville-West, the British minister at Washington, received a letter, signed Charles F. Murchison, saying that the writer was a naturalized Englishman who desired advice as to how he should vote in the coming election. Without suspecting that the letter was only a decoy and that he was being made the victim of a hoax, the minister replied that he thought Cleveland more friendly to England than Harrison. The Republicans promptly published the correspondence, expecting that the incident would turn the Irish vote away from Cleveland. Sackville-West's explanations only made matters worse. When Lord Salisbury refused to call him home, he was dismissed.

[Allan Nevins, *Grover Cleveland, A Study in Courage.*]

THOMAS L. HARRIS

Saco Bay, The Settlement of, proceeded from various grants made by the Council for New England[qv]. In 1630 Richard Vines, by a grant of Feb. 12, 1629, O.S., to John Oldham and himself, began a settlement south of the Saco River; and in 1631 Thomas Lewis and Richard Bonython, by a grant of the same date, began a settlement north of the river. Farther east Thomas Cammock, in 1633, took possession of 1500 acres granted Nov. 1, 1631; and beyond that was the Trelawney[qv] and Goodyear grant (Dec. 1, 1631), of which John Winter took possession in 1632, driving out George Cleeve and his partner, Richard Tucker. The majority of the settlers came as employees of, or as settlers under, the proprietors. The settlements were contemporaneously known as Winter Harbor (Biddeford Pool); Saco (Saco and Biddeford), about four miles up the river where Vines, Lewis and Bonython had their dwellings; Blue Point (Pine Point); Black Point (Prout's Neck); Spurwink (Cape Elizabeth); and Richmond's Island, the main seat of the Trelawney plantation. Andrew Alger, who came with Winter, and his brother Arthur settled Dunstan (a village of Scarborough), claiming under Indian deed. Fishing, farming, lumbering and trading were the means of livelihood. All these settlements were abandoned during King Philip's War[qv] in 1675.

[W. D. Spencer, *Pioneers on Maine Rivers.*]

ROBERT E. MOODY

Sacramento, Battle of (Feb. 28, 1847). To defend Chihuahua city, the Mexicans under Gen. José A. Heredia erected fortifications on the Sacramento River, fifteen miles north. Although superior in number, they were routed with heavy losses by Col. Alexander W. Doniphan's Missouri mounted volunteers, whose casualties were only two killed and seven wounded.

[G. R. Gibson, *Journal of a Soldier under Kearny and Doniphan.*]

RALPH P. BIEBER

Saddle Bag Banks. Under the "Free Bank Laws" passed by Middle Western states in 1851–53, any one purchasing state bonds up to a given amount or higher might start a bank and issue notes in a commensurate sum. Smart promoters "organized" many such banks, giving as their location remote, unknown (sometimes purely imaginary) hamlets, the object being to keep the notes in circulation and make it difficult for any noteholder to collect their face value from the "bank of issue"—often just a crossroads merchant or blacksmith, the promoter's agent, holding a small sum in cash to take care of any notes that might come in.

[William Graham Sumner, *A History of Banking in the United States;* Alvin F. Harlow, *Old Waybills.*]

ALVIN F. HARLOW

Saddles, American. Saddles for men have been of three principal types: (a) "English"—a flat tree with low pommel and cantle, introduced into America during the early colonial period and still (in 1939) the popular style throughout the Eastern states; (b) "army"—first fully developed during the Civil War and, in this initial form (the McClellan), an English tree modified by heightening pommel and cantle, dishing the seat and lengthening the stirrup leathers; (c) "stock," interchangeably termed also "cowboy," "cow," "Mexican," "Western" or "range."

The progenitor of the stock saddle was brought to Mexico by Cortez in 1519. Of the same pattern as that which the Moors carried into Spain during their 8th-century invasion, it was a deeply dished tree with wall-like pommel and cantle. The rider sat in it, rather than on it. Upon the pommel of the Cortez saddle Mexican *vaqueros* presently attached a vertical protuberance (the "horn") to which the lariat could be fastened. This Mexican saddle was adopted by western Americans when in 1823 they began ranching. It became, and is today, the standard saddle of the West. By permitting lariat throwing from horseback, riding of bucking broncos and traveling great distances, it hastened the spread of civilization throughout the plains.

Women at the outset of the colonial period used a pillion (a pad fastened behind the saddle occupied by a rider) on which they sat facing sideways. Soon the pillion was supplanted by the "side saddle"—in its ultimate form, a copy of the man's English tree altered by omitting the right-hand stirrup and adding hooked-shaped pommels which imprisoned the horizontally bent right knee and prevented the left foot from losing its stirrup. When, in approximately 1900, eastern women commenced visiting western ranches where they had to ride astride—few broncos would tolerate a side saddle—the side saddle began everywhere to disappear.

Pack saddles for conveyance of goods were of two sorts, the wooden "crossbuck" and the leathern *aparéjo*. These originated in Spain and came without change of form by way of Mexico into the United States.

[S. Dunbar, *History of Travel in America;* J. A. Garland, *The Private Stable;* P. A. Rollins, *The Cowboy.*]

PHILIP ASHTON ROLLINS

Safety First Movement. Massachusetts pioneered, in 1877, regarding factory safeguards, and, in 1886, in the reporting of accidents. Voluntary efforts of leading corporations, particularly those of the steel industry in 1907, accelerated the efforts to reduce accidents*qv*. The greatest incentive, however, came with the passage of workmen's compensation*qv* laws after 1910. Many national and international organizations, as well as governmental agencies, have rendered valuable service in promoting safety in industry. The Iron and Steel Engineers' Association studied the safety problem in 1911, and in 1913 organized The National Safety Council which organization carries on research in the development and standardization of safety methods and devices, and collects and disseminates data pertaining to safety activities. The American Standards Association promulgates safety codes which are used by increasing numbers of administrative bodies.

At first the safety movement emphasized adequate mechanical safeguards, but gradually the personal or human factor is receiving more careful consideration. Leading companies employ safety engineers to educate and supervise the superintendents, foremen, and employees in safety work. It has been demonstrated that the high-accident toll can be greatly reduced by intelligent and sincere co-operation between management and employees.

[U. S. Bureau of Labor Statistics, Bulletin No. 602, *Industrial Accidents and Diseases;* John R. Commons and John B. Andrews, *Principles of Labor Legislation;* W. H. Heinrich, *Industrial Accident Prevention.*]

JOSEPH H. FOTH

Safety Fund System. By way of abating some of the abuses that prevailed in the field of banking in New York State, a plan was formulated in 1829 for the mutual insurance of the debts of banks. This plan came to be called the Safety Fund System. Each bank incorporated in New York was required to contribute each year to a common fund—the "safety fund"—administered by the State Comptroller, an amount equal to one half of 1% of its capital stock, until such contributions aggregated 3% of its capital stock. Whenever a bank failed, after its assets had been fully utilized, this fund was to be used in settlement of its debts. Should this safety fund be drained by a succession of bank failures, the State Comptroller was empowered to levy on the banks for additional contributions. As experience with bank failures accumulated, the need became clear for giving the holders of the notes (somewhat similar in form and appearance to National Bank Notes*qv*) of a defunct bank priority in the distribution of its assets, and the state laws were changed accordingly.

[Robert E. Chaddock, *The Safety-Fund Banking System in New York State, 1829-1866.*]

FRANK PARKER

Sag Harbor, Long Island, was one of the leading colonial whaling*qv* ports. During the Revolution it was, for a time, used by the British as a depot for military stores. In the spring of 1777 the Americans, angered by the destruction of Danbury*qv* by Tryon, planned a raid on Sag Harbor, and on May 23 Lt. Col. Meigs with 234 men in thirteen whale boats crossed the Sound, made a surprise attack, destroyed the military supplies at Sag Harbor and took ninety prisoners.

By the middle of the 19th century the increasing use of petroleum*qv* began seriously to affect the whaling industry. The fleet of Sag Harbor dwindled, and it is said that the last whaling ship, the *Myra,* sailed out of the harbor in 1871.

[B. F. Thompson, *History of Long Island.*]

A. C. FLICK

Sagadahoc is the alternative ancient Indian name for the Kennebec*qv* region and river, especially that stretch of the stream from Merrymeeting Bay south to the Atlantic. The first recorded English settlement in New England was made at the mouth of the Sagadahoc, by Popham*qv*, in 1607. The region was remarkably rich in fish and furs, and many of the first settlers were fishermen or traders with the Indians. Settlements were established along this waterway at Georgetown, Merrymeeting Bay, Bath and Arrowsic, near the middle of the 17th century. The river was the scene of bitter fighting in the century of Indian warfare.

[Wilbur D. Spencer, *Pioneers on Maine Rivers.*]

ROBERT P. TRISTRAM COFFIN

Sage Plains were encountered by California-bound emigrants turning south at Fort Boisé*qv*, Idaho, to Malheur and Pitt rivers, after which the sage plains intervened on the way to Sacramento. The journey was so disastrous that after 1844 it was given the name of Death Route.

[K. Coman, *Economic Beginnings of the Far West.*]

CARL L. CANNON

Saginaw, Fort (1822–23). In 1822 soldiers from Fort Howard*qv*, led by Maj. Daniel Baker, established Fort Saginaw, in the heart of modern Saginaw, Mich., to overawe the troublesome neighboring Chippewa[qv]. An epidemic of fever the following summer utterly prostrated the garrison; the survivors were taken to Detroit in October; and the fort was permanently abandoned.

[James C. Mills, *History of Saginaw County, Michigan.*]

M. M. QUAIFE

Saginaw Treaty. On Sept. 24, 1819, Lewis Cass negotiated a treaty with the Chippewa Indians[qv] at Saginaw (Michigan Territory) in which a large land cession, located chiefly in Michigan Territory, was obtained from the tribe. There were sixteen reservations to the tribe within the lands ceded and several other smaller reserves for specified individuals. For the cession the United States agreed to pay annually forever $1000 in silver and to convert all previously promised annuities into payments in silver. The United States promised to furnish the natives with a blacksmith, cattle, farm tools, and persons to aid them in agriculture, in return for the privilege of building roads through their country.

The sequel throws much light on the history of Indian Land Cessions[qv]. On June 16, 1820, at Saulte de St. Marie, Michigan Territory, the Chippewa tribe ceded to the United States sixteen square miles of land on St. Marys River. On July 6, 1820, at L'Arbre Croche and at Michilimackinac, the Chippewa and Ottawa tribes ceded the St. Martin Islands in Lake Huron. At Chicago, Aug. 29, 1821, the Chippewas surrendered more of their lands to the Federal Government. Again on Aug. 19, 1825, at the Treaty of Prairie du Chien[qv] the Chippewas, together with several other tribes, ceded lands to the United States. Another treaty was secured from the Chippewas at Butte des Morts[qv] on Aug. 11, 1827, in which additional lands were secured by the National Government.

[C. J. Kappler, *Indian Affairs, Laws, and Treaties,* Vol. II; *American State Papers, Indian Affairs,* Vol. II.]

GEORGE D. HARMON

***Saginaw's* Gig, Cruise of the,** was undertaken to bring rescue to the officers and seamen of the U. S. S. *Saginaw,* Lt. Commander Montgomery Sicard, U. S. N., wrecked by a reef near Ocean Island in mid-Pacific, on Oct. 29, 1870. A party of five men volunteered to navigate the ship's gig to Honolulu and secure relief. The party consisted of Lt. John G. Talbot, the *Saginaw's* executive officer; William Halford, coxswain; Peter Francis, quartermaster; and John Andrews and James Muir, seamen. They left Ocean Island on Nov. 18, 1870, and after a voyage of thirty-one days, during which they encountered many dangers and endured much privation and suffering, they arrived on Dec. 19 off the island of Kauai, one of the Hawaiian group. They had previously lost their oars in a storm, and in attempting to land without them the gig was upset, William Halford alone surviving to reach the shore with Commander Sicard's despatches. The Hawaiian government immediately sent a steamer, the *Kilauea,* with supplies, to rescue the men left on Ocean Island. The *Kilauea* reached them Jan. 4, 1871. The American minister to Hawaii, Henry A. Pierce, also chartered a schooner, the *Kona Packet,* to assist in the rescue, which reached the island Jan. 5. The *Saginaw's* gig is now permanently on display at the United States Naval Academy[qv].

[*Annual Report,* Secretary of the Navy, 1871; G. H. Read, *Last Cruise of the Saginaw.*]

LOUIS H. BOLANDER

Sailor's Creek, Battles at (April 6, 1865). After Five Forks[qv], Lee (C.) abandoned Petersburg and Richmond, eluded Meade (U.) at Jetersville, and fled westward, his remnant of an army sleepless, fatigued and hungry. Near Sailor's Creek, Union pursuers overtook Gordon, Anderson and Ewell, protecting the trains. Humphreys' II Corps (U.) drove Gordon toward the Appomattox. Sheridan's Cavalry Corps (U.) struck from the south and demolished Anderson on the road from Rice's Station. In the center at Sailor's Creek, Wright's VI Corps (U.) charged Ewell's ridge position, outflanking left and rear from the northeast as Sheridan sent cavalry against its right. Ewell surrendered. Anderson's and Gordon's reduced commands escaped toward Appomattox[qv].

[A. A. Humphreys, *The Virginia Campaign of 1864 and 1865.*]

ELBRIDGE COLBY

Sailor's Snug Harbor, a home for retired seamen on Staten Island, N. Y., was created by the will of Robert R. Randall in 1801, but its beginning was delayed by litigation until 1831. Randall's farm in mid-Manhattan was the nucleus of the trust, and the rentals from the land now make this one of the world's wealthiest charities.

[I. N. Phelps Stokes, *Iconography of Manhattan Island.*]

ALVIN F. HARLOW

St. Albans (Vt.) Raid (Oct. 19, 1864), by Lt. Bennett H. Young of the Confederate Army, with about thirty men not in uniform, from Canada, was in retaliation for depredations of Sheridan in Virginia (*see* Shenandoah Campaign). Three banks were looted of over $200,000, but an attempt to burn the town failed. One citizen was killed. The raiders escaped into Canada, where Young and twelve of his men were captured and held by the Canadian authorities, who released them in December.

[J. B. McMaster, *A History of the People of the United States during Lincoln's Administration.*]

CHARLES H. COLEMAN

St. Anthony, The Falls of, were named after his patron saint, St. Anthony of Padua, by Father Hennepin^qv^, the first white man known to arrive there (1680). Later came Jonathan Carver, Zebulon M. Pike^qqv^ and other explorers. Attracted by their water power, settlements grew up on either side of the Falls (St. Anthony and Minneapolis), uniting under the latter name in 1872. First lumber and then flour industries were developed. Threatened with destruction in 1869, the Falls were saved with emergency cofferdams. Later a great dike and apron preserved them as they are today, the seat of world-famous flour mills.

[Father Louis Hennepin, *A New Discovery of a Vast Country in America*, edited by Reuben G. Thwaites; W. W. Folwell, *A History of Minnesota.*]

RUTH THOMPSON

St. Antoine, Fort, was a French military post built by Nicolas Perrot, in 1686, on the southeast shore of Lake Pepin (a widening of the Mississippi), and named for Antoine de la Barre, governor of New France. There in May, 1689, Perrot staged a ceremony of taking possession for France of the upper Mississippi and the Sioux country. The fort was abandoned in 1690.

[L. P. Kellogg, *French Régime in Wisconsin and the Northwest*, pp. 241-242.] LOUISE PHELPS KELLOGG

St. Augustine, Fla., was founded by Pedro Menéndez^qv^ in September, 1565, to establish Spanish authority on the mainland, protect shipping in the Bahama Channel and demolish the French settlement at Fort Caroline^qv^. Menéndez hoped to make St. Augustine the center of an ambitious expansion, a dream never realized, but it remained the garrisoned settlement, generally poor and needy, from which radiated mission enterprise to the south, west and north. As the colonial rivalry of England and Spain developed, it was attacked by British corsairs and by expeditions from the southern colonies. It was defended by San Marco (now Fort Marion^qv^), begun in 1672 and completed in 1756.

When Florida became British (*see* Paris, Treaty of, 1763), St. Augustine was the government seat of East Florida^qv^ and although most of the inhabitants left, the town shared the plantation prosperity of the region. Restoration to Spain turned it into a sleepy, unprogressive, little garrison town, for Spain's interests lay elsewhere; but it was still the administrative seat of East Florida and, as such, the object of attack by the "Patriots" in 1812 (*see* East Florida, Attempted Seizure of). It was also one of three Spanish forts when the United States purchased the Floridas (*see* Adams–Onís Treaty).

During early territorial days, St. Augustine was the leading eastern town connected with Pensacola^qv^ by the new national road. It developed a reputation as the leading winter resort, a position held until the opening of south Florida. During the 1820's the orange industry, first fostered by the British, reached importance, and by 1834 the harbor of St. Augustine was filled with fruit boats trading with northern markets. The great freeze of 1835 and the purple scale sent the groves farther south, the Seminole War^qv^ frightened away settlers and the growth of Jacksonville proved a successful rival. Between 1830 and 1839, the population dropped nearly 50%. When the question of statehood arose, St. Augustine headed the movement to divide Florida into two states, expecting to be the capital of one.

Contemporary St. Augustine retains the lure of its age. Since 1937 a program of historical restoration has been progressing under the auspices of the Carnegie Institution of Washington^qv^ and other research organizations.

[J. T. Connor, The Nine Wooden Forts at St. Augustine, in *Fla. Hist. Qu.*, Vol. IV; George R. Fairbanks, *St. Augustine;* Charles B. Reynolds, *Old St. Augustine.*]

KATHRYN T. ABBEY

St. Castin's Trading House was situated at the French Pentegoët, the present Castine, Me. Jean Vincent, Baron de St. Castin, gentleman adventurer, came to the Penobscot about 1667, and, adopting the habits of the Indians, one of whom he married, amassed a fortune in trade, particularly after the fort at Pentegoët came into his hands (1676). Anxious to be neutral, he was alternately in difficulties with both French and English. The seizure of his trading-house in 1688 by Governor Andros^qv^ was believed by the people of New England to be the cause of the war which broke out in 1689 (*see* King William's War). Castin probably returned to France in 1701, leaving the trade in charge of his son.

[Maine Historical Society, *Collections*, Ser. 1, Vol. VII.]

ROBERT E. MOODY

St. Charles, Fort, was established in 1732 by the Sieur de la Vérendrye^qv^ on the southern shore of the Northwest Angle Inlet of the Lake of the Woods^qv^, in what is now Minnesota. It served as a base for the earlier explorations of the Northwest made by LaVérendrye, his sons, and his nephew LaJemeraye; and it was occupied by the French for more than two decades. In 1908 Jesuits from St. Boniface College discovered its ruins.

[L. J. Burpee, ed., *Journals and Letters of Pierre Gaultier de Varennes de la Vérendrye and His Sons;* T. C. Blegen, Fort St. Charles and the Northwest Angle, in *Minnesota History*, September, 1937.]

T. C. BLEGEN

St. Clair, Fort, a stockade for storage purposes, was built by American troops (1791–92) during the expeditions against the northwestern Indians. Constructed by a detachment of James Wilkinson's troops a mile north of the present Eaton, Ohio, it constituted a lesser link in the chain of communications erected between Fort Washington*qv* (Cincinnati) and the Lake Erie region.

[E. O. Randall, Fort St. Clair, in *Ohio Archæological and Historical Society Publications*, XI.]

FRANCIS PHELPS WEISENBURGER

St. Clair's Defeat (Nov. 4, 1791). Gen. Harmar's failure*qv* to subdue the northwestern Indians compelled the American Government to send a second army against them. President Washington obtained from Congress authority to raise an army of 3000 men, and appointed Gov. Arthur St. Clair to command it.

Plans were made to have the army in readiness at Fort Washington*qv* (Cincinnati) by July 10, whence it was to march to Fort Wayne*qv* and conquer the hostile Indian confederacy. From beginning to end, however, everything went wrong. October had arrived before as many as 2000 men could be assembled. Considered as an army, their quality was deplorable. The supplies provided were poor; the commissary department was both corrupt and incompetent; the commander was sick and incapable; the soldiers themselves (apart from two small regular regiments) were "wretched stuff," consisting of raw militia and six-months' levies "purchased from prisons, wheelbarrows and brothels at two dollars a month."

Thus composed, the army stumbled northward through the Ohio wilderness; about sunrise of Nov. 4, it was furiously assailed in its camp at present-day Fort Recovery*qv*, and after two hours the survivors fled madly back to Fort Jefferson*qv*, twenty-two miles away. Two thirds of the army —900 men—had been killed or wounded. Efforts to make St. Clair a scapegoat for the sins of others proved unavailing; responsibility for the disaster rested squarely upon the Government and the American public in general, which entered upon a difficult war without troubling to undertake the preparations essential for success. (*See also* Wayne Campaign.)

[B. J. Griswold, *The Pictorial History of Fort Wayne;* Elmore Barce, *The Land of the Miamis;* W. H. Smith, ed., *The St. Clair Papers.*]

M. M. QUAIFE

St. Croix Falls, Battle of (*ca.* 1770). A powerful war party of Foxes and Sioux*qqv* encountered 300 LaPointe (Wis.) Chippewa*qv* under Waubojeeg on the portage trail at St. Croix Falls (Wis.). A fierce battle ensued, begun by the Foxes and assumed by the Sioux. The Chippewa, receiving reinforcements, virtually annihilated the Foxes, and badly defeated the Sioux.

[William W. Warren, *A History of the Ojibway Nation.*]

WILLOUGHBY M. BABCOCK

St. Croix River, The. After the extinction of the short-lived St. Croix Settlement*qv*, its precise location was lost sight of. There are two sizeable rivers which flow into Passamaquoddy Bay, and a third smaller stream. European map-makers during the 17th and 18th centuries named now one and now another of these streams as the St. Croix, without really knowing which was the river discovered and named by Champlain. The British and the American negotiators of the preliminary articles of the Definitive Treaty of Peace*qv* used John Mitchell's Map of North America*qv* of 1755, which designates the eastern of the two larger streams as the St. Croix; and the treaty placed the boundary of the United States at the St. Croix River. After the treaty was ratified, the British and American governments disputed the identity of the St. Croix. Great Britain claimed it was the western stream, locally known as the Schoodiac; the United States contended for the eastern stream, called the Magaguadavic. Some 2,000,000 acres of coastal land were involved. By Jay's Treaty*qv* of 1794 the identity of the true St. Croix River was left to a mixed commission, which in 1798 fixed on the westernmost stream (Schoodiac), traced through its northeastern branch, and placed a monument there.

[John Bassett Moore, *International Adjudications*, Vols. I, II, The St. Croix River Arbitration; Hunter Miller, *Treaties and Other International Acts of the United States*, Vols. I, IV. For a Mitchell's Map set over a present-day map, to show discrepancies, see Samuel Flagg Bemis, *A Diplomatic History of the United States.*]

SAMUEL FLAGG BEMIS

St. Croix Settlement, The (1604–5). Sieur de Monts sailed for Acadia, April 7, 1604, with two vessels. His claim extended from Cape Breton to Pennsylvania with a monopoly of the fur trade and authority to convert the Indians. With Samuel de Champlain, a Catholic priest, a Protestant minister and more than a hundred others, he "entered a river almost half a league in breadth at its mouth" and came to an island. "This place was named by Sieur de Monts Saint Croix Island." While de Monts returned to France, Champlain explored the coast, and workmen prepared winter quarters. During the long and severe winter with scarcity of fresh food and water, scurvy[qv] developed among them. Thirty-five persons perished. Finding the island unsuited for permanent settlement, the survivors moved to Port Royal[qv]. Two years later they returned to France, and their buildings were completely destroyed in 1613 by the English from Virginia.

[W. D. Williamson, *The History of the State of Maine; Collections* of the Maine Historical Society; *Sprague's Journal of Maine History; Tercentenary of De Monts' Settlement at Saint Croix Island.*]

THOMAS MORGAN GRIFFITHS

St. Denis' Expedition. In 1714 Juchereau de St. Denis led a French expedition from the present Natchitoches[qv], La., into Spanish Texas. Though captured by Spaniards and sent to Mexico City, he secured his release by winning the friendship of the Spanish viceroy. This expedition, and another which St. Denis made in 1716, resulted in establishing a profitable trade between the French post of Natchitoches, of which he was commandant from 1722 to 1744, and the Spanish territory to the southwest.

[Charles Gayarré, *History of Louisiana;* Alcée Fortier, *History of Louisiana.*]

WALTER PRICHARD

St. Francis, Rogers' Expedition against. In September, 1759, because of the activities of the St. Francis Indians against Gen. Amherst's army while it lay at Crown Point[qv], Maj. Robert Rogers, commander of Rogers' Rangers[qv], proposed to Amherst that he be allowed to attack and destroy St. Francis (on the St. Francis River, three miles above its confluence with the St. Lawrence). Amherst agreed, and Rogers left Crown Point on Sept. 13, 1759, with 17 whaleboats and a force of 220 Rangers, among them several Stockbridge Indians and Mohawks. Two days later forty members of the expedition returned to Crown Point, ostensibly because of sickness. The remainder rowed on, arriving in Missisquoi Bay, at the northern end of Lake Champlain, on Sept. 23. The detachment hid its boats and set off through the forest for St. Francis. On Sept. 25 the boats were discovered and burned by French and Indians, leaving Rogers without a base. He sent a messenger to Gen. Amherst asking that supplies be deposited at the juncture of the Lower Ammonoosuc and Connecticut rivers; then went on. For nine days Rogers and his men marched through a spruce bog, sleeping at night in the branches of felled trees. On Oct. 5 the detachment, reduced to 142 men, sighted St. Francis; and at dawn on Oct. 6 Rogers attacked, burning the town, killing 200 Indians, releasing 5 whites who had been held captive, and keeping 5 Indian children as prisoners. An hour after the attack he commenced his homeward trip with no provisions but dried corn. His second-in-command, Capt. Amos Ogden, had been shot through the body, but contrived to keep up. On Oct. 14, near Lake Memphremagog, the detachment ran short of food. Rogers divided his force into "small companies," so that they might live off the country, and ordered them to rendezvous at the mouth of the Ammonoosuc. On Oct. 16 one of the companies was ambushed by French and Indians, and destroyed. Several days later Rogers arrived at the mouth of the Lower Ammonoosuc to find that Amherst had sent provisions as requested, but that they had been taken away a few hours before his arrival. He built a raft and on Oct. 27 set off down the Connecticut to get supplies for his starving men. With him went Capt. Ogden, another Ranger, and one of the Indian boys captured at St. Francis. On Oct. 28 the raft was wrecked at White River Falls. Too weak to swing a hatchet, Rogers obtained logs for another raft by burning down trees, saved it from destruction at Wattoquitchey Falls with his last reserve of strength, and on Oct. 31 arrived at the fort at Number 4[qv] (Charlestown, N. H.). He returned at once to the mouth of the Ammonoosuc with food for the survivors of the expedition. Lt. Samuel Stephens, the Ranger officer who had gone with provisions to the mouth of the Ammonoosuc but failed to wait, was court-martialed and found guilty of neglect of duty. Of the 142 men who attacked St. Francis, 93 returned to Crown Point.

[Kenneth Roberts, *Northwest Passage,* Appendix to Special Edition.]

KENNETH ROBERTS

St. Francis Xavier. *See* Green Bay.

Ste. Genevieve Lead Mining District. One of the earliest references to lead in Missouri was made by Father Gravier in an account of his trip in 1700. Later in the same year, an expedition headed by LeSueur was sent up the Mississippi from its mouth for the special purpose of investigating minerals in the valley. The report was inadequate, but it mentioned that the savages in the Merrimac River (Mo.) area had lead mines.

LeMoine d'Iberville was interested in the report to the extent that he asked the French government, in 1701, for the exclusive right of lead mining and fur trading in the Missouri area, but died before the petition was granted. The

French authorities gave a similar but enlarged grant to Anthony Crozat[qv] in 1712. Crozat's governor, de la Motte Cadillac, investigated the lead producing area, but little was done in the way of developing lead production until Crozat's successor to the grant of the monopoly, John Law, of the Company of the Indies[qv], commissioned Philip Renault in 1723 as director general of mining operations. A rapid development followed, and lead was carried to Kaskaskia[qv] to be shipped down the Mississippi. By 1735 the activities of the lead miners and fur traders had become so general on the west side of the river that Ste. Genevieve was established and became the shipping point for the lead-mining district of the hills a few miles to its west.

The French, like the Indians, continued to use the primitive shallow-pit method of mining until Moses Austin moved to the district in 1798 and developed shaft mining and other tendencies toward modern methods. With the building of a railroad connecting the "Lead Belt" with St. Louis, Ste. Genevieve lost its lead-shipping industry. Flat River became the most important of a number of mining towns in St. François County which continues to be one of the greatest lead-producing areas in the world.

[Louis Houck, *History of Missouri;* Ruby Johnson Swartzlow, Early History of Lead Mining in Missouri, in *Missouri Historical Review,* Vols. XXVIII and XXIX.]

W. J. HAMILTON

St. Germain-en-Laye, The Treaty of, signed March 19/29, 1631/2, was the general settlement between England and France which followed the Treaty of Susa (1629). Its American section provided for the return by England to France of all places occupied by England in New France, Acadia and Canada—including particularly Port Royal[qv], Quebec and Cape Breton. The following summer Quebec was restored to the United Company, and Port Royal to the Company of New France.

[F. G. Davenport, ed., *European Treaties Bearing on the History of the United States and Its Dependencies to 1648.*]

ROBERT E. MOODY

St. Ignace, Mission of. Father Charles Dablon, superior of the Jesuit missions[qv] of the Upper Lakes, began on Mackinac Island[qv] in the winter of 1670–71 a mission named for St. Ignatius. In the spring of 1671 came Father Marquette with his Huron flock from the upper end of Lake Superior. Whether they settled at once on the island or on the promontory on the mainland north of the straits does not appear; in any case, Dablon's Mission of St. Ignace was soon, very probably in 1672, being conducted at the latter location with Father Marquette in charge. Here the mission, surrounded by a fort, a French village, a village of Hurons and one of the Ottawa, was maintained until 1706, when difficulties occasioned by the brandy trade and the withdrawal of most of the Indians to Detroit or elsewhere caused its suspension. Reopened about 1712, it was moved, probably in 1741, to a site on the mainland south of the island, where Jesuits were in charge until 1765.

[E. O. Wood, *Historic Mackinac;* A. I. Rezek, *History of the Diocese of Sault Ste. Marie and Marquette.*]

GILBERT J. GARRAGHAN

St. John, Fort (also called St. Jean, San Juan and Spanish Fort), built by France on Lake Pontchartrain[qv] at the mouth of Bayou St. John to protect New Orleans in the rear, was occasionally garrisoned by Spaniards between 1776 and 1803; held by American troops during the British attack upon New Orleans[qv] in 1814–15; occupied by Confederate forces at outbreak of Civil War; and since abandoned.

[J. S. Kendall, *History of New Orleans;* Charles Gayarré, *History of Louisiana.*] WALTER PRICHARD

St. Johns, Siege of (1775). The newly fortified position of St. Johns, on the Richelieu River, was the first important obstacle encountered in the American invasion of Canada[qv] in 1775. It was held by a garrison of about 650 men, chiefly regulars, commanded by Maj. Preston. After two initial movements against it had failed, the post was invested on Sept. 17, 1775, and bombardment began on Sept. 25. The American guns, however, were few and small, supplies were short, and the besieging army was depleted by sickness; there were probably never more than 2000 effectives before St. Johns. The surrender of Fort Chambly[qv] (Oct. 18), however, provided the Americans with ammunition and provisions; new batteries were established; and on Nov. 2, Preston, with food running short in the fort, signed a capitulation providing for the surrender of his force with the honors of war. With this surrender, the majority of the British regulars in Canada fell into American hands, and the way to Montreal and Quebec was open; nevertheless, the delay of seven weeks occasioned by the siege of St. Johns had been of great value to the defenders of Canada.

[A. L. Burt, *The Old Province of Quebec;* Justin H. Smith, *Our Struggle for the Fourteenth Colony.*]

C. P. STACEY

St. Johns College, established in 1696 at Annapolis, Md., as King Williams School, became a college in 1784. Four hundred books from King William of England are in the library. A treaty with the Susquehannock Indians^qv^, Lafayette's visit in 1824, and graves of French soldiers in the American Revolution distinguish the campus as historic. Fairfax and Lawrence Washington were students at the college.

[J. H. MacCracken, *American Universities and Colleges.*]

FRANK MARTIN LEMON

St. Johns River, Huguenot Massacre on. *See* Florida, French in.

St. Joseph, Fort. St. Joseph, near modern Niles, Mich. (close by the St. Joseph-Kankakee rivers portage), was one of the earliest centers of French activity in the Great Lakes area. Here LaSalle^qv^ (1679) and uncounted other travelers passed; here Father Allouez labored and died (1689); here for sixty years (*ca.* 1700–1760) French soldiers kept guard; here a British garrison was destroyed (1763), a Spanish army raided (1781), an American Army sojourned (en route to establish Fort Dearborn^qv^ in 1803); here lived the French officer whom George Washington "assassinated" in 1754, and the brother who promptly compelled the latter to surrender a few days later (*see* Great Meadows).

Yet St. Joseph's story still remains unwritten; precise dates for the establishment of both mission and garrison are unknown; until recent years even capable historians were ignorant of the true location of the fort. During the Revolution in the Northwest, St. Joseph was a British outpost whose possession was disputed by the rival armies. Since the massacre of 1763 (*see* Pontiac War) the place had remained ungarrisoned, although it was under constant British control, exercised from Detroit and Mackinac. In July–August, 1779, a British force occupied it several weeks, awaiting a threatened rebel invasion which did not materialize. In December, 1780, a band of raiders from Cahokia^qv^ plundered the place, and, retreating, was itself overtaken and destroyed near Michigan City. In January, 1781, the Spanish governor at St. Louis dispatched a small army against St. Joseph. It ascended the Illinois River to Peoria in boats and from there made a midwinter march across 300 miles of wilderness. St. Joseph was occupied on Feb. 12, and for twenty-four hours the flag of Spain floated over it.

The army then retired, having laid the foundation for the claim, advanced by Spain in the peace negotiations at Paris (*see* Definitive Treaty of Peace, 1783), to the ownership of the Old Northwest^qv^. Following the Revolution, British and American traders dominated the life of the ancient settlement until the arrival of American settlers in the 1830's.

[M. M. Quaife, *Chicago and the Old Northwest;* The St. Joseph Baptismal Register, in *Miss. Val. Hist. Rev.*, XIII; monographs on Spanish capture of St. Joseph by C. W. Alvord in *Mo. Hist. Rev.*, Vol. II, and by F. J. Teggart, *ibid.*, Vol. V.]

M. M. QUAIFE

St. Joseph, Mo., originally known as "Blacksnake Hills," was founded by Joseph Robidoux as a trading post in 1826. The town was platted in 1843 and incorporated in 1845. Population jumped from 964 in 1846 to 2257 in 1853. St. Joseph's economic growth, particularly in grain and livestock, was stimulated by outfitting Oregon and California immigrants^qqv^ and furnishing supplies to military posts. In 1859 the Hannibal and St. Joseph Railroad^qv^ was completed; in 1860 the Pony Express^qv^ linked St. Joseph with California. During the Civil War decade population increased from 8932 to 19,565: thereafter the construction of stockyards^qv^, the completion of the Missouri River bridge and the extension of the railroad accelerated St. Joseph as a grain and cattle mart.

[F. S. Popplewell, St. Joseph, Missouri, As a Center of the Cattle Trade, in *The Missouri Historical Review*, Vol. 32; *Missouri Historical Review*, Vol. 19.]

WILLIAM J. PETERSEN

St. Lawrence River, THE, was explored by Jacques Cartier in 1535 as far as the island of Montreal, Cartier having discovered the Gulf of St. Lawrence in his voyage of the previous year. The name was first given by the explorer to a bay on the gulf, and later extended to the gulf and river. In 1541 Cartier carried his exploration to the second rapid above Montreal. It is not certain who first ascended the river from there to Lake Ontario, but it is known that the missionary Simon LeMoyne traveled to the villages of the Onondagas south of Lake Ontario in 1653 and returned the following year by way of the upper St. Lawrence. The St. Lawrence River, with its tributary the Ottawa, and with the Great Lakes^qv^ which geographically are part of the same river system, formed the main water thoroughfares from the sea to the interior of the continent. From Quebec or Montreal set forth explorers, missionaries and fur traders, bound for the west or the southwest; Champlain up the Richelieu to Lake Champlain, and by the Ottawa to Lake Huron; LaSalle, Marquette and Jolliet to the Mississippi^qqv^; Radisson, DuLhut and Allouez to Lake Superior^qqv^ and the country south of it; LaVérendrye^qv^ to the plains of Manitoba, the Missouri and the Yellowstone. Fur-trading brigades of the North West Company^qv^ left Montreal bound for Mackinac^qv^, Grand Portage^qv^, Lake Winnipeg, the Saskatchewan and the

Columbia^{qv}. Trading goods came from overseas up the St. Lawrence to Montreal, and thence in canoes to the west; and furs came down to Montreal and over to the London market. The colonial wars, the Revolutionary War and the War of 1812^{qqv} each found the use or mastery of the St. Lawrence waterways a factor to be striven for. Shipping developed on the Great Lakes as communities grew up about their shores and beyond; canals were built and channels deepened in the connecting rivers and the St. Lawrence; and grain and other commodities were brought down to Montreal, from both the Canadian and American West, for shipment to Europe and elsewhere. Ocean vessels of limited draft made their way up from the sea through the St. Lawrence and the Lakes to Toronto, Cleveland, Detroit or Chicago; and, with the completion of a deep channel from the head of the lakes down to Lake Ontario, and from Montreal to the sea, a movement grew in the United States and Canada for the removal of the only remaining barrier, between Lake Ontario and Montreal. (*See also* Great Lakes–St. Lawrence Waterway Project.)

[S. E. Dawson, *The St. Lawrence Basin;* G. W. Browne, *The St. Lawrence River.*] LAWRENCE J. BURPEE

St. Louis, British Attack on (May 26, 1780), was part of the British strategy of the Revolutionary War, and the successful defense of this village is generally accounted a victory for the United Colonies. It shared with King's Mountain^{qv} the sum total of victories over the British in 1780. Instructions had been received by the British Gen. Haldimand on June 16, 1779, to reduce the Spanish and Illinois posts. In consequence he organized a force of Indian bands including Menominee, Sauk, Fox, Winnebago and Sioux^{qqv}, under Emmanuel Hesse, together with some Canadians, traders, and their servants. Sent by various routes, these combined into a body of about 1200 for a surprise attack upon St. Louis^{qv}. It was generally supposed that Cahokia^{qv}, about five miles farther south, was the first British objective, but the garrison at St. Louis had some warning the previous day that they would be first attacked. In consequence the British, who had planned a surprise attack, were themselves astonished. The village was successfully defended by 50 soldiers and 280 townsmen, including a small reinforcement from Ste. Genevieve, with a loss of 104 men. The attackers were so badly demoralized and delayed that the whole expedition collapsed and the British menace from the West entirely removed.

[Stella M. Drumm, The British-Indian Attack on Pain Court (St. Louis), in *Journal of the Illinois State Historical Society*, Vol. 23.] STELLA M. DRUMM

St. Louis, Fort (1682–91), was intended to be the principal defense of LaSalle's^{qv} Illinois colony. An inclosure of palisades and log houses, it was built on Starved Rock^{qv} in the winter of 1682–83 by LaSalle and Tonti. Nine years later it was abandoned in favor of Fort Pimitoui^{qv}, but Tonti and others used it intermittently for a decade. St. Cosmé found it deserted in 1699, and Charlevoix saw only its ruins in 1721.

[Sauer, Cady and Cowles, *Starved Rock State Park and Its Environs;* Francis Parkman, *LaSalle and the Discovery of the Great West.*] PAUL M. ANGLE

St. Louis, Mo., was founded Feb. 15, 1764, by Pierre Laclede Ligueste, a Frenchman commonly known as Laclede. He was at the time commander of an armed force and commercial enterprise organized in New Orleans to take over for a period of eight years the exclusive privilege to "trade with the savages of the Missouri and all nations residing west of the Mississippi River." This monopoly was granted in 1762 by the French Director-General of Louisiana. When placed at the head of his "considerable armament," Laclede moved his outfit, containing a large quantity of merchandise and supplies, up the Mississippi to Ste. Genevieve and thence across the river to Fort Chartres^{qv}, where he found temporary housing. After searching the west bank of the Mississippi above this point to the mouth of the Missouri for a suitable place to build his establishment, Laclede found, in December, 1763, the best location at the present site of St. Louis: perched on a limestone bluff forty feet high and two miles long, backed up by terraces of higher ground around which the river flowed in the shape of a bow. Here he blazed with his own hands a number of trees to mark the place, and returned to Fort Chartres. There he announced that he had chosen a spot which, on account of its many natural advantages, would become one of the finest cities in America. The following February Laclede sent a party of thirty, including "two dependable men," with Auguste Chouteau to clear off the trees and begin necessary buildings on the chosen ground. In April, 1764, Laclede followed, selected the spot for his own dwelling and laid out the exact plan of the village, which he named St. Louis in honor of the patron saint of Louis XV, reigning King of France. St. Louis early became the center of the fur trade^{qv} and the starting point of most expeditions and trails into the western country. Here they outfitted and gathered supplies for their journeys and from here *voyageurs,* trappers[qqv], traders and soldiers plied their labored way along the streams into the wilderness.

In 1762 in the secret treaty of Fontainebleau[qv], France ceded to Spain all of the territory of Louisiana west of the Mississippi River and also New Orleans, but it was several years before local authorities knew of the transaction, and the first Spanish governor was driven away. Even after 1770 when Spanish Lt. Gov. Pedro Piernas came into command at St. Louis, the village continued to be predominantly French. It was not incorporated until 1808. Soon after the Purchase of Louisiana[qv] from France by the United States, the town was overrun by a large number of speculative New Englanders, who launched a very considerable boom. In course of time a new town grew up beside the old one. Here began almost perceptibly a line of cleavage between the new industrial speculative type and the old conservatives, which ultimately divided the city into two groups of different social and political caste. Racial changes in the course of time greatly altered the character of the population. Many Virginians, Kentuckians and North Carolinians moved into Missouri in the Spanish days and also after the Purchase. These settled largely in rural districts but a goodly number settled in St. Louis and participated in the early fur trade, Santa Fé and Oregon expeditions as well as local merchandising. These people mixed well with the French, were accustomed to African slavery and found no antagonism in the native trend. In the early days the slaves numbered about one third of the total population.

With the advent of the steamboat St. Louis rose very rapidly in both population and wealth. From 1811 to 1882 the assessed valuation of real estate in St. Louis was multiplied about fifteen hundredfold. With a great river at her feet, and near to the outlets of many other rivers there came to her wharf river craft of every shape and kind from the many boatable tributaries of the Mississippi. Iron, lead and zinc from near-by mines; bituminous coal from across the river; farm and garden products from rich valleys nearby; hemp, cotton and sugar from the South; all contributed to make St. Louis the great river capital of the West and the second largest railroad center of the United States.

In the late 1820's a German by the name of Duden wrote many letters and stimulated considerable immigration from his native land. This influx was followed by another and larger German immigration in 1848–49. Most of these German immigrants were industrialists and became strongly allied with the New Englanders. They opposed slave labor as a kind of aristocratic paternalism, a menace to free labor and a phase of social life to which they had never been accustomed. When the sectional war excited by the crusaders against slavery was seen to be approaching, large numbers of privately drilled, unofficial German military bodies early joined in a movement to suppress the militia and block the legislative and executive departments of the state. Thus identified with the Union cause and constituting a large portion of the victorious element in the Civil War, the German population of St. Louis increased rapidly in numbers and political power.

[Auguste Chouteau, Journal of the Founding of St. Louis, in *Missouri Historical Society Collection,* Vol. III; Louis Houck, *History of Missouri;* William Hyde and Howard L. Conard, *Encyclopedia of the History of St. Louis.*]

STELLA M. DRUMM

St. Louis Missouri Fur Company should not be confused with the Missouri Fur Company (*see* below). Manuel Lisa[qv] persistently spoke of the former as the "Missouri Fur Company," and historians have thus been led astray. St. Louis Missouri Fur Company was the first enterprise of its kind. Formally organized through articles of co-partnership dated March 7, 1809, its purposes were to launch and conduct hunting and trading expeditions on the Upper Missouri River and tributaries for a term of three years; a subordinate enterprise was the return of Shehaka and his family to their village on the Upper Missouri. He was the Mandan chief whom Lewis and Clark[qv] persuaded to join them on their return to Washington to visit President Jefferson. The Government paid the Company $10,000 for the safe conduct home of these guests of the nation on this last part of their journey. The partners were Benjamin Wilkinson, Pierre Chouteau, Manuel Lisa, Auguste P. Chouteau, Reuben Lewis, William Clark, Sylvestre Labaddie, Pierre Menard, William Morrison and Andrew Henry, who by the articles of agreement were each required to accompany the expedition, or else provide a substitute agreeable to the other partners. William Clark was detailed to manage the headquarters at St. Louis. The first expedition left St. Louis in June, 1809, with 172 men and nine barges loaded with goods worth $4269, including $165 worth of whiskey. Because of desertions and sickness they had only 153 men when they left Fort Osage[qv] on July 10, 1809; the main party reaching the Big Horn about Nov. 1. A profitable trading and trapping campaign ensued, but two of the partners suffered very severe losses, through treachery of the Blackfeet, when they set out in the spring for the Three Forks of the Missouri. Many of the men were killed and all of their horses, guns, traps and furs were taken (*see* Manuel's Fort). In spite of these losses, the returns from the posts that were not attacked saved the original capital and a small profit besides. A relief expedition was launched Sept. 10, 1810, with Manuel Lisa (who returned with Menard in July, 1810) in charge. The other partners and some of the men did not return until the following summer. The company was reorganized Jan. 14, 1812, with the surviving partners excepting Morrison. The capital was fixed at $50,000 and the time limitation 1818. William Clark was made president and Manuel Lisa and Sylvestre Labaddie directors. An expedition with two barges, leaving in May, 1812, yielded a profit of $9000. Fort Manuel (not to be confused with Manuel's Fort[qv]), near present Kenel, S. D., and probably Fort Lisa[qv], near Omaha, were established on this expedition. After six months' liquidation the company was dissolved Jan. 17, 1814.

The Missouri Fur Company, as distinguished from the St. Louis Missouri Fur Company, was a partnership formed by Manuel Lisa and Theodore Hunt in July, 1814. For this company Lisa conducted expeditions up the Missouri from 1814 to 1817. On June 14, 1817, the cargo of fur brought in was valued at $35,000. This company expired by limitation the following month, and another Missouri Fur Company was organized by Lisa in April, 1819. The new partners were Joshua Pilcher, Thomas Hempstead, Joseph Perkins, Andrew Woods, Moses B. Carson, John B. Zenoni, Andrew Drips and Robert Jones. Their principal establishment, like those of the former companies from 1813 on, was at Fort Lisa. Manuel Lisa died in 1820 and Pilcher was made president of the company. Lucien Fontenelle, William Vanderburg and Charles Brent were added to the partnership. This firm carried on until about 1830.

[Walter B. Douglas, ed., Thomas James, *Three Years among the Indians and Mexicans;* Ms. Missouri Historical Society; John C. Luttig, *Journal of a Fur Trading Expedition on the Upper Missouri, 1812-1813.*]

STELLA M. DRUMM

St. Louis of Texas. When LaSalle[qv] landed on the shore of Matagorda Bay in Texas in 1685 he founded a temporary fort, near the mouth of a river which he called LaVaca but which has been identified as Garcitas Creek, to house his colony of more than 180 persons. Later, the fort was moved to a more suitable location five or six miles up the creek. This permanent fort, which he named St. Louis in honor of the French king, consisted of one large building and a number of smaller ones, the whole being surrounded by a palisade, and cannon being mounted at the corners. It was from this place that LaSalle set out on his three futile efforts between 1685 and 1687 to find the Mississippi[qv]. All the while, sickness, accidents and desertions were reducing the number of his colonists until there were only about thirty left after he departed on his last journey. Most of these were massacred by the Indians early in 1689. A few months later, the Spanish searches for LaSalle[qv] came to an end when DeLeon found the ruins of the fort. On his next expedition in 1690, DeLeon burned the buildings.

[H. E. Bolton, The Location of LaSalle's Colony on the Gulf of Mexico, in *Southwestern Historical Quarterly,* XXVII; C. E. Castaneda, *The Finding of Texas.*]

C. T. NEU

St. Louis World's Fair. *See* Louisiana Purchase Exposition.

St. Marks on Apalache, Fla., was fortified by the English early in the 18th century and also served as a trading post. When the Treaty of Paris[qv] fixed the western boundary of British Florida[qv] at the Apalachicola River, British troops occupied St. Marks. By the Definitive Treaty of Peace[qv] it was transferred to Spain, the British trading firm of Panton, Leslie & Co.[qv] being permitted to remain (*see* Spanish Indian Relations). In 1788 Bowles[qv] threatened an attack and in 1792, and again in 1800, he burned the Panton Leslie store. In 1818 Jackson occupied the post (*see* Arbuthnot and Ambrister, Case of). After the Florida cession (*see* Adams-Onís Treaty) St. Marks became United States territory (*see* Forbes Purchase). During the Civil War it was used by the Confederates as a blockade-running and salt-[qqv]making center. The fort was destroyed by a Federal naval raiding party, June 15, 1862, but was rebuilt. The salt works were destroyed on Feb. 17, 1864.

[M. F. Boyd, The Fortification at San Marcos de Apalache, in *Florida Historical Quarterly,* Vol. XV; H. G. Cutler, *History of Florida.*]

THOMAS ROBSON HAY

St. Martin's Stomach. When Alexis St. Martin, young French-Canadian *voyageur,* was wounded accidentally in the stomach by a shotgun on Mackinac Island, June 6, 1822, he was cared for by Dr. William Beaumont, post surgeon. Miraculously the patient recovered, but the hole in his stomach would not close. At length a fold of the stomach's coats filled the orifice, forming a lid which could be pushed aside by a finger.

The invitation to experiment actuated Dr. Beaumont in May, 1825, to begin testing the time particular foods required to digest by introducing pieces tied to threads into the stomach and withdrawing them at intervals. He continued making other experiments, with interruptions and changes of locality, until the end of 1833. His observations and conclusions he published in a book entitled: *Experiments and Observations on the Gastric Juice, and the Physiology of Digestion,* Plattsburg, 1833. Sir William Osler has set forth eight particulars that Dr. Beaumont contributed to the science of digestion which were unknown or not reliably confirmed before the appearance of this volume. Dr. Victor C. Vaughn called it the "greatest contribution ever made to the knowledge of gastric digestion." Dr. Harvey Cushing declared that Dr. Beaumont's work left only a single factor in gastric digestion to be discovered—pepsin.

Dr. Beaumont left army service in 1840 and practised successfully in St. Louis until his death in 1853. St. Martin, who had married, became the father of seventeen children, farmed a little, "hired" out his stomach to at least one other physician for experiments, and exhibited himself to the public. He died at St. Thomas, Quebec, in 1880, being between seventy-six and eighty-three years old.

[Introduction to Dr. Beaumont's book; J. S. Myer, *Life and Letters of Dr. William Beaumont.*]

HOWARD H. PECKHAM

St. Marys, the first settlement in Maryland, was founded, March 27, 1634, on the north bank of the Potomac not far from its mouth, in accordance with instructions from Cecil Calvert, proprietor and founder of Maryland.

[B. C. Steiner, *Beginnings of Maryland and other Maryland Studies.*]

RAPHAEL SEMMES

St. Marys, The Treaty of (June 16, 1820), was negotiated with the Chippewas[qv] by Lewis Cass, territorial governor of Michigan. The Indians ceded to the United States a 4-mile-square tract at the Sault on which Fort Brady was erected in 1822. The treaty, negotiated under dramatic circumstances, marks the first real assertion of American authority in the Lake Superior area.

[U. S. *Stat. at Large*, Vol. VII; M. M. Quaife, From Detroit to the Mississippi in 1820, in *Burton Hist. Coll. Leaflet*, VIII.]

M. M. QUAIFE

St. Marys Falls Ship Canal, opened in 1855, is an artificial waterway on the St. Marys River connecting Lake Superior with Lake Huron. In 1797 the North West Company[qv] of Montreal constructed a small canal and lock on the north shore of the rapids of St. Marys River, where the water of Lake Superior descends some twenty-one feet to the level of Lake Huron. An American canal was projected by Michigan in 1837. It became imperative after the commencement of copper and iron mining[qqv] in the next decade. Congressional aid was sought, and in 1852 a land grant of 750,000 acres was provided for this purpose (*see* Canal Lands). The state contracted with an eastern corporation to construct the works, and the canal was ready for use in June, 1855. Tolls were charged, but they were inadequate for the maintenance and necessary improvement of the waterway. In 1869 the legislature invited Federal operation. This was effected in 1881, when the state ceded the canal to the United States, which abolished tolls and assumed maintenance and control. The War Department is in charge and through the U. S. Engineer Corps[qv] has enlarged the canal and locks, the largest of which are 1350 feet long. The tonnage on this route considerably exceeds the combined tonnage passing through the Panama[qv] and Suez canals.

[*St. Marys Falls Semicentennial, 1905;* Annual Reports of St. Marys Falls Ship Canal, per U. S. Engineers, War Dept.]

L. A. CHASE

St. Mihiel, Operations at (Sept. 12–16, 1918). The front between the Moselle River and the Argonne forest having been selected as the field for American operations, after the successful Aisne-Marne offensive[qv], in which many American divisions participated, the American 1st Army was organized, Aug. 10, and immediately began gathering its troops between the Moselle and Verdun. Marshal Foch and Gen. Pershing planned that this army should direct its first blow against the German salient at St. Mihiel. Nine American divisions, numbering 550,000 men, and four French divisions under Pershing's command, numbering 70,000, were assembled. Seven American divisions were placed on the south face of the salient, two American and two French divisions on the west face, and two French divisions around its tip. The Germans held this front with nine divisions of the Gallwitz Army Group, under Fuchs (about 60,000 men).

On the morning of Sept. 12, after a violent artillery bombardment, the 1st Army advanced into the salient and by midnight the southern attack had penetrated to an average depth of five miles. Just after daylight, Sept. 13, the 1st Division, from the south, and the 26th Division, from the west, met at Vigneulles-les-Hattonchatel, trapping 16,000 Germans in the point of the salient. Altogether 443 guns were captured. By Sept. 16 the salient was entirely obliterated. American losses had aggregated 7000.

[DeChambrun and DeMarenches, *The American Army in the European Conflict;* J. M. Hanson, History of the American Combat Divisions, in *The Stars and Stripes.*]

JOSEPH MILLS HANSON

St. Paul, Minn. *See* Twin Cities, The.

St. Philip, Fort, Surrender of. *See* Mississippi, Opening of the (1861–63).

St. Stephens, Ala., was begun about 1789 as a fortification on the site of a former French post at the head of navigation on the Tombigbee*qv* River by the Spaniards after their conquest of West Florida*qv*. It was a severe blow to Spain when this outpost was found to be on the American side of the demarcation line of 1798 (*see* Southern Boundary, Survey of the). The settlement was surrendered to Lt. John McClary, who marched from Natchez*qv* in 1799, but who moved his troops on to Fort Stoddert*qv*, nearer the international boundary. St. Stephens, however, survived as a town and became the seat of the government factory*qv*, established by Joseph Chambers in 1803 and made famous by George Strother Gaines. For twenty-five years it remained the center of American influence among the Choctaws*qv*.

[Dunbar Rowland, *Mississippi.*]

JAMES W. SILVER

Salaries as distinguished from wages are a result of social rather than economic classification. The common distinction is between white-collar and overall workers. The former, as a rule, obtain their income from clerical and administrative work; today this includes not only the humblest employee but the high-paid officials. Certain groups of professional people also come within this classification, as with teachers, and, in certain occupations, lawyers, doctors, engineers. In short, a salaried worker is an employee and in this respect is in the same category with artisans and common laborers. The historical course of salaries has been much the same as that of wages*qv*, except that in recent years the spread between the low and the high income has become much greater with salaries than with wages. The early accounts of salaries are not very informative and comparisons are difficult. In Massachusetts, about 1640, schoolmasters in the various towns received from £20 to £30 a year; this pay increased only slowly until after the Revolution. A doctor's fee in Boston in 1780 was said to have been "very modest." The charge for the ordinary visit was from one shilling sixpence to two shillings. Higher rates were charged only for those who were in "high life." Even then, charging "what the traffic will bear" seems to have been common practice. In 1782 a club of leading physicians fixed the charge for ordinary visits at fifty cents, and for consultations $1.00. "Capital operations" commanded from ten to twenty times as much. In the early days of the development of industrialism, up to and beyond 1860, businesses were relatively small, usually in the form of partnerships, with a growing intermingling of corporations; the enterprise was operated by the owner. He usually classified his return as profit. Technical skill was conspicuous by its absence. The "bookkeeper" was usually the most important clerical man; he was frequently cashier, collector and credit man. As late as 1880 he was fortunate to receive $75.00 a month. The growth of the colossal corporation*qv* has caused a rather wide division and specialization of labor in the salaried class. Along with this has gone a rapid advance in the compensation for top executives, and a considerable rise for all others. Notably in the large industrial corporations, in railroads and in the larger city banks salaries may range from $25,000 to over $200,000 a year. In some cases the payment of bonuses has added to the compensation of such officials. Since 1930 considerable popular criticism has been directed against large salaries; upon occasion the Federal Government has enacted laws to reveal not only incomes, but salaries. Meanwhile, over the last forty years, the salaries of technical experts have advanced rapidly.

[*Statistical Abstract of the United States; Reports* of the Security Exchange Commission.]

ISAAC LIPPINCOTT

Salary Grab was the popular name for a congressional act for boosting specified Federal salaries. It was originally designed to benefit the President only, whose compensation was considered too small. As finally passed during the closing hours of the 42nd Congress, March 3, 1873, the bill provided increases of salary for the President from $25,000 to $50,000, for the Chief Justice from $8500 to $10,500, for the Vice-President, Cabinet members, Associate Justices and Speaker of the House from $8000 to $10,000, and for Senators and Representatives from $5000 to $7500. A last-minute amendment made the advance for the members of Congress retroactive for the preceding biennium, thus enabling them to return home with a bonus in "back pay" of $5000 each. Coming at a time when Congress was in disfavor because of the Crédit Mobilier*qv* and the exposure of other scandals, the "Salary

Grab" and the "Back Pay Steal" became issues in all the elections of that year. In most of the state platforms both parties denounced the act openly. Consequently, most congressmen, for political or other reasons, either refused to accept the increased compensation or, having received it, returned it to the Federal treasury or donated it to charity. In January, 1874, the 43rd Congress repealed the legislation except for those provisions affecting the salaries of the President and the Justices.

[E. P. Oberholtzer, *A History of the United States since the Civil War*, Vol. III.]

ASA E. MARTIN

Salem, Mass., was founded by John Endecott and the colonists sent out by the Massachusetts Bay Company[qv] in the ship *Abigail.* They reached Salem Sept. 6, 1628, with a copy of the charter, which superseded the rights of the Dorchester Company[qv] under the Sheffield Patent in the area now Massachusetts. A few settlers of the defunct Dorchester Company had moved up from Cape Ann and built some huts on the peninsula of Salem as early as 1626. In 1629 came the ministers Skelton and Higginson, and there was founded on Aug. 6 the first Puritan Congregational Church modeled to a large extent on the Separatist Church at Plymouth. Roger Williams was minister of the church in 1633–35, and was forced out by the magistrates of Boston over the protests of the Salem people for political reasons. The famous Hugh Peter was the next minister, and was instrumental in starting the fisheries[qv], on the products of which a foreign trade with Spain, Portugal and the West Indies was built up, which largely accounted for the prosperity of Salem for the next 150 years.

John Winthrop and his fleet (*see* Great Migration) landed at Salem on June 12, 1630, and then proceeded to Boston Bay, around which they settled later in the summer.

In 1692 a wave of the witchcraft[qv] delusion, which had spread all over Europe, reached Salem, and an hysterical outburst of accusations occurred, chiefly at Salem Village (now Danvers). The accused were tried in Salem, and eighteen persons were hanged. All the convictions and executions occurred between June and September, 1692. The jury and most of the judges not long afterward made public confession of their error.

The town aided vigorously in all the colonial wars, and Benjamin Pickman was a dominant factor in promoting the crusade against Louisburg[qv] in 1745. The capital of Massachusetts was twice transferred to Salem; under Gov. Burnet in 1728, and under Gov. Gage in 1774. The first provincial congress was organized there in October, 1774, and the first armed resistance to the British troops occurred at the North Bridge on Feb. 26, 1775. A Salem ship, the *Quero,* carried the first news of the Battle of Lexington[qv] to England, and another, the *Astrea,* brought the first news of the treaty of peace to America. About one tenth of the privateers[qv] of the Revolution, some two hundred or more, were sent out of Salem Bay.

After the Revolution for forty years Salem ships sought out trade in every corner of the world, and actually began the foreign trade with more different ports than all other American ports combined.

[J. B. Felt, *Annals of Salem;* J. D. Phillips, *Salem in the 17th and 18th Centuries;* J. B. F. Osgood and H. M. Bachelder, *Sketch of Salem.*]

JAMES DUNCAN PHILLIPS

Sales Tax. Four types of general sales tax are recognized by students of public finance. They are, first, a manufacturers' excise tax; second, the retail sales tax—a tax paid by the consumer on his purchases from retail stores; third, the "gross sales" tax on sales of commodities by manufacturers or merchants; and fourth, the "gross income" tax, which applies to the sales of services as well as commodities.

Probably the first tax in the United States resembling closely a sales tax was a merchants' license tax, measured by gross sales, imposed by Pennsylvania in 1821. Two other merchants' license taxes, both measured by purchases, in Virginia in 1887 and Delaware in 1906, also resembled the modern sales tax, but the real sales tax movement began with a gross sales tax law in West Virginia in 1921.

Gross sales tax laws were next adopted in Georgia and Mississippi in 1929, and Kentucky initiated the retail sales tax by the adoption of a law in 1930. The depression, which began in 1929, soon brought pressure to bear on many states for means of obtaining additional revenue and in 1933 twelve states adopted sales tax laws as an emergency device to offset the decline in revenue from other sources.

Since 1933 the number of states adopting the sales tax has grown and by the summer of 1937 twenty-six states had some type of sales tax law. Passed in most cases as emergency measures, these laws appear to be becoming a part of the permanent tax structure of many of the states employing them. Of the laws in effect in 1937, six applied purely to retail sales, while twelve others included retail sales as well as other items.

Similar to the sales tax are the taxes many states have adopted on a limited number of commodities, such as the relief tax on liquor and the state tax on cigarettes in Pennsylvania and the state taxes on gasoline in practically all states.

The imposition of general sales taxes has been confined to the states and municipalities, although such a tax has at times been recommended as a source of revenue for the National Government. Most of the retail sales taxes bear a rate of 2%, although a few have a 3% rate and some have graded rates. Payment of retail sales taxes is made in some states with metallic tokens, in some with tickets, and in some with the smallest United States coin, the cent. (*See also* Taxation.)

[W. J. Shultz, *American Public Finance.*]
FREDERICK A. BRADFORD

Salesman, Traveling. When the early factories had supplied local markets it became necessary to solicit orders in more distant places. As early as 1803 the pioneer textile manufacturers, Almy and Brown, sent the junior partner to New York, Baltimore, Philadelphia, Alexandria, and towns in the neighborhood of each city, where he persuaded merchants to take small lots on trial. Large importers who sent out collectors also appear to have had them solicit orders for merchandise. Previous to about 1845, however, the traveling salesman for an American manufacturer or merchant was practically unknown. A seller's market existed and buyers made semiannual trips to the seaboard wholesale markets where they were met and solicited by representatives of various firms.

With the growth of the factory system and improvements in transportation the number of business solicitors increased. Some states passed laws requiring these early commercial travelers to obtain licenses before they were permitted to do business. In 1860 there were perhaps a thousand commercial travelers in the United States. In 1870 there were 7262 people who followed this occupation, and in 1900 the number reached 92,919.

The development of a buyer's market in the latter part of the 19th century caused more aggressive methods to be used in selling. It was said that salesmen used "high pressure" methods. Generally there were more sellers than buyers. Attention was given to improving the technique of salesmanship. In this John Patterson of the National Cash Register Company was the leader. Mr. Patterson was manufacturing a product for which no great need was felt. Accordingly he searched for the best technique of salesmanship and in this technique he trained his salesmen.

As competition became more intense, firms with a force of salesmen whose chief assets were a glib tongue, a stock of stories intended to entertain and a code of uncertain business ethics discovered that profits were more and more difficult to earn. Increased attention began to be given to training salesmen. Hundreds of books on salesmanship were published and courses in the subject were offered in the business schools. This training encouraged better ethics among salesmen and improved their knowledge of their products and services. In 1930 there were 223,-732 commercial travelers in the United States. The number had more than doubled since 1900 in spite of many adverse economic factors.

[E. P. Briggs, *Fifty Years on the Road;* R. W. Johnson and R. W. Lynch, *The Sales Strategy of John H. Patterson;* Fred M. Jones, *Middlemen in the Domestic Trade of the United States, 1800-1860.*]
FRED M. JONES

Salmon Falls, Attack on (March 18, 1690). Frontenac, Governor of New France[qv], sent out three expeditions against the English settlements in the winter of 1690. The smallest, of about fifty men, half French and half Abenaki Indians[qv], led by François Hertel, reached Salmon Falls, N. H., after a hard winter journey of two months from Three Rivers. At daybreak they attacked the fortified house and two stockades, completely surprising the settlers and finding no opposition. The buildings and near-by farms were burned, and about thirty-four persons killed. Fifty-four were made prisoners, of whom several were later cruelly killed, and the others taken to Canada. A force from Portsmouth caught up with the raiders but was repulsed.

[Francis Parkman, *Frontenac and New France;* Jeremy Belknap, *History of N. H.*]
HERBERT W. HILL

Salmon Fisheries. Of the total value of canned fishery products, salmon represents about half, i.e., 40 million dollars annually, all of this pack originating in the Pacific states and Alaska. Commercial fishing began in the Columbia and smaller coastal streams of Oregon in the early 1880's, the Chinook being the leading catch of six varieties taken. By 1899 investment in the salmon industry had grown to 5 million dollars, value of vessels and fishing equipment not included; the value of the annual pack was about 6 million dollars. In the next decade, Alaska outstripped the states in this industry and has since held first rank as a salmon producer, maintaining its place partly by aid of careful regulation. Japanese poaching has caused some friction. Alaska employed in 1936 some 30,400 persons in the industry, racially divided: 56% white;

23% Indian; 12% Filipino; 4% Japanese, and 5% all others.

[*Annual Report Gov. of Alaska;* Publs. of Bureau of Fisheries, Dept. of Commerce.]

ROBERT G. RAYMER

Saloons. During the heyday of the saloon from 1870 to 1900, one could be found on nearly any corner. Its windows were heavily curtained but once inside the swinging doors of the front entrance one crossed the sawdust-covered floor to a long hardwood bar. In front of this was a brass footrail, behind it a huge gilded mirror topped by a nude Venus or a brawny John L. Sullivan. Though reputedly the home of "demon rum" the standard drinks were straight corn or rye whiskey and beer. Fancier drinks were on display but seldom sold. Cocktails were known, but not shaken until the prohibition era. The free lunch consisted of salty foods to stimulate thirst. The saloon's alliance with gambling and prostitution contributed to its downfall. In 1880 the ratio of saloons to population in the United States was 1 to 735; by 1910 it was 1 to 1350. Many towns, e.g., Lafayette, Ind., in the 1880's, had one saloon for every 200 people; as local option[qv] grew many had none. Elegant bars like the Sazerac in New Orleans, the Waldorf in New York or Righeimer's in Chicago and the wild wide-open saloons of mining boom towns like Deadwood and Tombstone will be best remembered in our social history.

[George Ade, *The Old Time Saloon.*]

HARVEY L. CARTER

Salt was important in the domestic economy of the colonists, who, in the absence of refrigeration and canning processes[qqv], employed it not only to preserve fish and meat for home use, but for commercial manufacture when an active trade developed with the West Indies (*see* Cod Fisheries). Salt making was one of the earliest industries attempted in Virginia, New York and New England, and was carried on with varying vigor and success under the impetus of monopolies or bounties throughout the colonial period. The fishermen cured their fish chiefly, however, with salt imported from the Barbadoes, West Indies and Southern Europe, taken usually in ballast.

The interruption of foreign trade by the Revolution occasioned distressing scarcity of salt, and produced numerous small establishments along the shore from Cape Cod to Georgia. The states, urged by the Continental Congress, encouraged the industry by offering bounties[qv] and by some ventures at state salt works.

As the western country opened up after the Revolution, salt was carried over the mountains at great expense by pack horses. Saline springs and salt "licks"[qv] in many parts of the Mississippi Valley awaited capital for development. The Onondaga salines in New York were worked only after 1787, though they had been known through Jesuit priests since 1652, and remained the chief source for the West until 1810 when the strong salt of the Kanawha[qv] Valley in western Virginia offered strong competition. The famous wells in southwestern Virginia remained undeveloped until about 1782.

The discovery of salt wells in Michigan on the eve of the Civil War was opportune, for the Mississippi Valley had been depending chiefly on the Kanawha salt and on foreign importations at New Orleans. So active was Michigan competition with New York salt that the price in the North averaged 87½ cents a bushel, while in the South it soared to $35 and more. (*See* Salt in the Confederacy.)

In the last half century the United States has become the world's greatest producer of salt. The great "domes" of rock salt of Louisiana, the beds in Texas, as well as the salt lagoons along the coast, and the sheets of rock salt found in New York and Michigan, have been exploited. Discovery of a salt field in Kansas, while boring for natural gas, was fortunate for the packing industry in the vicinity. The solar system of evaporation has proved practicable on the shores of the Great Salt Lake and on San Francisco Bay. Manufacturing processes have been greatly improved and the production increased by the demand for salt in chemical manufactures and ore reduction plants. Since 1892 the country has produced more than it has consumed.

[J. L. Bishop, *A History of American Manufactures;* Victor S. Clark, *History of Manufactures in the United States;* Katherine Coman, *The Industrial History of the United States;* E. E. Sparks, Salt in Early American History, in *The Chautauquan,* July, 1900.]

ELLA LONN

Salt in the Confederacy. There were few salines in the South, notably the wells at Saltville, Va., in southern Alabama and in northern Louisiana. When the blockade[qv] shut off the outside supplies and the price of salt soared to $35 a bushel, individuals exploited the weakest brines and planters drove hundreds of miles to the nearest salt wells or to the seacoast. States and counties became manufacturers of salt; even the central government conducted works along the coast, especially on the Gulf coast of Florida (*see* St. Marks). The destruction of these enterprises became an objective of Federal naval attack. Research reveals that the states alone poured out $5,500,000 to produce this humble item. Time, energy and men were thus diverted from the first objective of war—the winning of battles.

[Ella Lonn, *Salt as a Factor in the Confederacy.*]

ELLA LONN

Salt Lake City. Originally laid out in 10-acre squares with streets 132 feet wide, following the plan of the "City of Zion" prepared in 1833 by Joseph Smith, Salt Lake City was founded by Brigham Young and the Mormons[qv] in 1847. The city is the headquarters of the Church of Jesus Christ of Latter-Day Saints, or Mormons, and is noted for its many fine structures, including the Mormon Temple and Tabernacle[qv]. The Temple is of Utah gray granite from the Wasatch Mountains and was forty years in course of construction (1853–93).

[*Documentary History of the Mormon Church;* O. F. Whitney, *History of Utah.*]

JOSEPH FIELDING SMITH

Salt Licks. *See* Licks.

"Salt River," or "Up Salt River," is a term used to describe political defeat, which has its origin in an incident occurring during the presidential campaign of 1832 on the Salt River, a Kentucky branch of the Ohio. Henry Clay, as the National Republican candidate against Jackson, hired a boatman to row him up the Ohio to Louisville, where he was to make a speech; but the boatman, said to be a Jackson man, rowed Clay, by mistake or by design, up the Salt River instead, and Clay failed to reach Louisville in time for his speech. His defeat for the Presidency brought later derisive references to this incident, and Representative Alexander Duncan (Ohio), gifted in coining apt terms, probably first used the expression, "they have been rowing up Salt River," in a speech in the House in 1839, to describe the futility of the opposition party.

[Carl Scherf, Slang, Slogan and Song in American Politics, in *Social Studies*, Vol. 25, pp. 424-430.]

CLARENCE A. BERDAHL

Salt Springs Tract, The, consisted of 24,000 acres of land along the Mahoning River, near Niles, Ohio, granted (1788) by Connecticut (*see* Western Reserve) to Gen. Samuel H. Parsons. Parsons visited his lands (1788) but, returning home, was drowned in the Beaver River. At first the Parsons claim was disregarded by the Connecticut Land Company, but later parts of two townships were given to his heirs and assigns. The springs, used by the Indians for salt making, were known to pioneers at least by 1755 (Lewis Evans Map[qv]), were visited by Pennsylvania's salt makers during the Revolution, were used, later, by settlers in the region, but were never developed commercially.

[*Historical Collections of the Mahoning Valley;* C. L. Shepard, *Connecticut Land Company and Accompanying Papers;* Charles Whittlesey, *Early History of Cleveland.*]

HAROLD E. DAVIS

Salt War, The (1877), was a disturbance in El Paso County, Texas, over the free use of the salt lakes east of San Elizario. The salt question became involved in politics and a feud developed between Louis Cardis, backed by the Mexicans, and Charles H. Howard, supported by the Americans. Howard killed Cardis and the bitter feeling that followed culminated in a riot at San Elizario in which Howard and two other men were slain by a mob of Mexicans from both sides of the Rio Grande. Later some Mexicans were killed by Texas rangers[qv] and a sheriff's posse, but most of the rioters escaped to Mexico.

[W. P. Webb, *The Texas Rangers;* H. H. Bancroft, *North Mexican States and Texas.*]

C. T. NEU

Saluda, Treaty at (July 2, 1755), was made with the Cherokee Indians[qv] by Gov. James Glen of South Carolina at a great meeting on the border of that colony. By it the Indians nominally ceded all their lands to the British crown, and made it possible for the provincial government to build Fort Loudoun[qv], on the Little Tennessee River, to hold the country against the French. The cession amounted to nothing, for the Cherokees a few years later repudiated the English alliance and captured and destroyed Fort Loudoun.

[D. D. Wallace, *History of South Carolina.*]

R. L. MERIWETHER

Salvaging of Ships. The first large American salvage job was that performed in 1687 by William Phips of Maine, who located the wreck of a Spanish ship sunk off the Bahamas forty-three years before and recovered £300,000 in treasure from her. For this he was knighted by James II, and later made governor of Massachusetts. A noted 19th-century case of this sort was that of the steamship *Golden Gate,* sunk off Manzanillo, Mexico, in 1862, with $1,577,760 in California gold aboard. About $1,000,000 was recovered in 1863, and several vain efforts have been made since to find the remainder. Little raising of sunken vessels was done until the last quarter of the 19th century, when wrecking apparatus was greatly improved and there were several companies in the large seaboard cities which could raise the wooden ships then used, if not too large and in not too deep water. A famous instance of ship raising was that of the battleship *Maine*[qv], sunk by explosion in Havana harbor Feb. 15, 1898. In 1910–11 the hulk was raised, partly to rid the harbor of a nuisance, partly to solve the mystery of the explosion. It was a difficult job, costing the United States Government more than a million dollars. The after half was finally cut off, taken to sea and resunk, and the forward part raised separately. Some of the most remarkable feats have been done in the raising of Navy submarines[qv]. The *S51*, sunk in 1925, of 993 tons burden, was raised by sinking eight submersible pontoons alongside her and pumping them and the wreck itself full of air. When the *F4* sank in 304 feet of water off Honolulu in 1915, divers made several descents to the boat before she was raised—the deepest diving on record.

[A. Gowans Whyte and R. L. Hadfield, *Deep Sea Salvage.*]

ALVIN F. HARLOW

Salvation Army, THE, founded in London in 1865 by William Booth, first appeared in the United States in 1880. It gained but little foothold until 1889, when an organizer, George Scott Railton, was sent from England, and the work spread rapidly. It was incorporated in New York in 1899. With its horns and drums, its pseudo-military organization and the doggerel songs which it sang in its early days, it was at first an object of ridicule and was criticized as making a travesty of religion; but as years passed, its work among the "down-and-outs," among prisoners and ex-convicts, gradually won general respect. It established low-priced lodging houses (mostly for men, though later some for women were set up), workrooms, children's homes, hospitals and dispensaries. During the World War, the Salvation Army carried on work in all the army camps in America, and sent 150 workers, male and female, to France. It maintained 50 "huts" in France and 34 ambulances. It also established rest rooms and hostels for soldiers and sailors in France and the United States. In 1896 Ballington Booth—a son of William Booth—and his wife Maud (both former Salvation Army workers) established in New York a rival and similar organization, the Volunteers of America, which has grown to a considerable size.

[Anon., *Where the Shadows Lengthen: a Sketch of the Salvation Army's History in the United States of America.*]

ALVIN F. HARLOW

Salzburgers in Georgia. In 1734 a group of seventy-eight Salzburgers, who had been driven out of their European home by the Bishop of Salzburg, landed in the new colony of Georgia[qv]. They were settled by James Oglethorpe up the Savannah River at a place which they called Ebenezer. Being dissatisfied with their original location, they were moved to a more convenient spot on the river itself, bringing the name Ebenezer with them. By 1741 twelve hundred Salzburgers were living in Georgia, mostly in Ebenezer and the surrounding territory, but a few had settled on St. Simons Island. Lutheran in religion and German in language, they were largely ruled over by their ministers.

[C. C. Jones, Jr., *The History of Georgia;* W. B. Stevens, *A History of Georgia;* C. C. Jones, Jr., *The Dead Towns of Georgia;* P. A. Strobel, *The Salzburgers and Their Descendants.*]

E. MERTON COULTER

Sam Houston, Fort. From 1715, when it was known as the mission of San Antonio de Valero, San Antonio, Texas, has held military garrisons, either under French, Spanish, Mexican, Texan, Confederate or American flags. It includes the famous "Alamo"[qv] and from the close of the Mexican War[qv] was used as an American troop garrison. In 1865 the post of "San Antonio" was established and in 1890 it was redesignated Fort Sam Houston to honor Gen. Sam Houston. It is today our largest army post, functioning as Corps Area and Divisional headquarters.

[*Circular No. 4*, Surgeon General's Office, 1870; *Circular No. 8*, Surgeon General's Office, 1875; *Description of Military Posts and Stations of the United States*, compiled by the Inspector General, R. B. Marcy, 1872; *General Orders of the War Department.*]

ROBERT S. THOMAS

"Sam Slick" was the pen name of Thomas Chandler Haliburton (1796–1865), a Canadian humorist. Though a native of Nova Scotia, Haliburton achieved his fame as a portrayer of the typical New England Yankee. In several volumes of sketches Haliburton carries "Sam Slick" through numerous adventures in America and England.

[V. L. O. Chittick, *Thomas Chandler Haliburton, Sam Slick: a Study in Provincial Toryism.*]

E. H. O'NEILL

Samoa. American interest in Samoa—an archipelago consisting of some fourteen islands lying in the southwest Pacific with a total area of some 1200 square miles—was first aroused by the visit of Commodore Charles Wilkes[qv] in 1839. Thirty-three years later, with the greater development of transpacific commerce, the navy dispatched Commander Richard W. Meade to the islands with orders to secure the harbor of Pago Pago as a naval base and coaling station. The agreement he negotiated to this effect with the Samoan chiefs was not ratified, but a later treaty ceding Pago Pago and granting the United States certain commercial and extraterritorial^qv^ privileges won senatorial approval in 1878. Similar ambitions on the part of Great Britain and Germany, however, soon led to international friction and were also the cause of continuing quarrels among the different factions in the islands. In order to forestall the establishment of a protectorate by any one of the three interested powers, a conference was held in Washington in 1887, but no acceptable agreement could be reached. Soon thereafter German intrigue led to the establishment in Samoa of a controlled administration, civil warfare among the natives, and actual intervention by Germany in behalf of her candidate for the kingship.

With naval forces of the three powers concentrated at Samoa in dangerous proximity, a calming influence was unexpectedly exerted on this troubled situation by a sudden storm which in March, 1889, completely wrecked the foreign vessels then in the harbor of Apia^qv^. Bismarck had already proposed a further conference, to be held in Berlin; and with Germany in a more conciliatory frame of mind a tripartite agreement, the Berlin Act of 1889, was successfully reached. The neutrality and independence of Samoa were guaranteed through what virtually amounted to a three-power protectorate.

Difficulties in administration, however, led to further dissensions in Samoa; the death of the king created new rivalries, and continuation of the existing system became plainly impossible. A proposal for the division of the islands was finally advanced by Germany in 1899, and in the ensuing negotiations an agreement for carrying it out was successfully reached. In return for concessions elsewhere, Great Britain relinquished her Samoan claims and the convention, signed on Dec. 2, 1899, provided that the United States should take over the island of Tutuila with the harbor of Pago Pago; and Germany, the islands of Upolo and Savii. As a result of the World War, German rights in Samoa were transferred to New Zealand as mandatory power, but American Samoa has remained the naval outpost of the United States in the southwest Pacific.

[George H. Ryden, *The Foreign Policy of the United States in Relation to Samoa.*]

FOSTER RHEA DULLES

Samplers originated as a means of keeping samples of stitches used in embroidering tablecloths, napkins, towels, pillow cases and other household articles before books of patterns existed.

The earliest-known mention of a sampler was in 1505, when Elizabeth of York paid 8d for "an elne of lynnyn for a sampler for the queen." The will of Mary Thompson, dated 1546, reads: "I gyve to Alys Pinchebeck my sampler with semes." By the middle of the century samplers had become the fashion in England, and in the early part of the next, English women were making them in New England.

The early type was long and narrow. The earliest example in this country (now in the Essex Institute, Salem) was worked by Anne Gower in 1610, and brought by her to America; the first sampler known to have been made in America (now in Pilgrim Hall, Plymouth) was the work of Laura Standish, daughter of Myles.

Not infrequently the creation of children as young as five, the American samplers surpass all others in originality, invention and decorative quality. In the mid-18th century Adam and Eve were popular subjects. Later "family trees," shepherds and shepherdesses, the maker's house, and sometimes whole villages, were depicted, the designs becoming increasingly freer. In the early 19th century the American eagle often appeared. After 1830 the art of sampler making deteriorated and gradually disappeared.

[Ethel S. Bolton and Eva J. Coe, *American Samplers.*]

KATHARINE METCALF ROOF

Sampling Referenda. The precursor of the modern scientific sampling referendum was the straw poll, which was first developed near the turn of the century. Among the earliest to begin using the straw-poll technique as an indicator of public opinion were the *New York Herald* (1904), the *Columbus Dispatch* (1906) and the *Cincinnati Enquirer* (1908). It remained for the *Literary Digest,* however, to bring the technique to the attention of the whole country. Beginning in 1920 the *Digest* periodically conducted nationwide canvasses on such questions as prohibition and the soldiers' bonus, and on presidential candidates. Owing to a faulty choice of cross section which failed to include poor voters in sufficient numbers, the *Digest* forecast the 1936 presidential election incorrectly.

The year 1935 saw the appearance of surveys of public opinion by the American Institute of Public Opinion and by *Fortune* magazine. These surveys differ in two respects from earlier efforts. First, they are conducted continuously—every month by *Fortune* and virtually every week by the Institute. Second, they use techniques more advanced and more scientific than those of the *Literary Digest* straw poll, whose greatest flaw was nonselectivity.

The basic principle of scientific sampling is that, by sounding the opinions of a relatively small number of persons, proportionate to each population group and in every section of the country, the opinions of the whole voting population can be determined.

The secret of this new type of opinion sampling is not numbers. Statisticians have repeatedly demonstrated that a few thousand voters correctly selected will reflect faithfully the views of an electorate of millions of voters. The secret is in the cross section—the way voters for the sample are selected. To be a reliable indicator of public opinion the sample must include views of members of all political parties, and of rich and poor, old and young, men and women, farmers and city dwellers, persons of all religious faiths—in short, voters of all types from every state in the land. Moreover, it must include these types numerically in the sample in approximately the same proportion as they exist in the voting population. It must, in effect, select a miniature electorate that is representative of the views of the larger whole. When this sampling process is executed with statistical skill, the voters in the miniature electorate will divide into opinion blocs in virtually the same way as all the voters would divide if their views were canvassed.

Both the American Institute of Public Opinion and *Fortune* conduct their surveys by the personal interview method, using field investigators who interview voters in the home, on the street, in offices and on farms.

Accuracy depends chiefly on two kinds of skill: skill in selecting people to be interviewed so that they will constitute a representative cross section, and skill in preparing ballot questions which go to the heart of an issue in such a way that replies will reflect basic convictions of the public rather than surface judgments.

The greatest usefulness of the sampling referendum lies not in forecasting elections—a process valuable chiefly as a test of accuracy—but in measuring the trends of opinion on important public issues between elections. Sampling referenda make the masses articulate on these issues, thereby helping to interpret to the leaders the wishes of the group. These referenda also gauge the strength of specific pressure groups[qv] that seek to influence legislation. Legislators and political leaders have for years been close students of public opinion; through sampling referenda they are in a position to obtain a truer measure of national public sentiment than they have had in the past.

Sampling referenda are also powerful tools for the social scientists who endeavor through research to lay down the rules that govern group life. Scholars are now able to examine the opinions of farmers, city dwellers, old people, young people, Republicans, Democrats, Catholics, Protestants, men, women, members of labor unions and so on, either singly or in combinations. Moreover, these referenda can be taken at short intervals, enabling the student to relate opinion changes with contemporary events.

[Claude E. Robinson, *Straw Votes*, and Recent Developments in Straw Poll Field, in *Public Opinion Quarterly*, July and October, 1937.]

GEORGE GALLUP

Sampson–Schley Controversy, The, arose primarily from the fact that when the Battle of Santiago[qv] began, July 3, 1898, Admiral William T. Sampson in his flagship *New York* was seven miles to eastward, in distant signal range, but unable to participate effectively. Largely because of his more affable treatment of press correspondents, Commodore Winfield S. Schley—second in command and formerly Sampson's senior—received popular credit for the victory. The resultant controversy raged bitterly in press and Congress, halted promotion of both officers and raised criticism of Schley's conduct earlier in the campaign. In 1901 a court of inquiry requested by Schley condemned the much-discussed outward turn of his flagship *Brooklyn* at Santiago and his "dilatoriness" earlier while commanding the "Flying Squadron." Upon final appeal, President Theodore Roosevelt declared Santiago "a captains' battle," in which "technically Sampson commanded" and movements followed standing orders. Both officers received routine promotion to permanent rear admiral in 1899.

[Record of Schley Court of Inquiry, *House Doc. 485*, 57 Cong., 1st Sess.]

ALLAN WESTCOTT

San Antonio, Texas, was founded in 1718 by the establishment of a mission and *presidio*[qv], or military camp. Some of the soldiers were married, and their families formed the nucleus of a village, or civil settlement. Several years later a chain of missions was established in the valley below San Antonio, and in 1731 the village was reinforced by a small colony from the Canary Islands. The settlement thus became the civil and military capital of Texas during the Spanish-Mexican regime.

The prominence of San Antonio in state and regional life and literature is derived chiefly from its historic past. During the Texas revolution, it was first captured from its strong Mexican garrison by siege (December, 1835) and later recaptured by Santa Anna in the tragic assault on the Alamo (March, 1836), only to be regained by the Texans as a result of their victory at San Jacinto (April, 1836), which practically established the independence of the Republic of Texas^qqv^. As the largest settlement on the southern and western frontier, San Antonio was exposed to raids from Mexicans and Indians. During 1842 it was twice occupied by Mexican raiders and was the scene of desperate fighting in which a considerable proportion of the Comanche leaders were massacred after having assembled for a council to discuss terms of peace. Soon after the annexation of Texas^qv^ by the United States, San Antonio became the chief military post in a line of forts that the Federal Government established to guard the southern and western frontier; and today it is the center of vast military- and air-training activities.

Prior to the development of ranching on the west Texas plains, in the early 1880's, San Antonio was the headquarters of the Texas cattle industry^qv^.

[William Corner, *San Antonio de Bexar;* F. Chabot, *The Alamo;* The Bexar Archives at the University of Texas.]

E. C. BARKER

San Antonio Missions, so named because they lie in and near San Antonio, Texas, were founded by the Spanish Franciscans^qv^ between 1718 and 1731, and formed the center of activity in Texas during the 18th century. The one in San Antonio, the present much-visited Álamo, is the oldest. Best known of the other four erected along the San Antonio River are Mission Purísima Concepción and, the most beautiful of all, Mission San José, which was founded in 1720 by Ven. Antonio Margil.

[C. E. Castañeda, *Our Catholic Heritage in Texas.*]

FRANCIS BORGIA STECK

San Diego, Calif., named after Didacus de Alcalá, a Franciscan saint, was founded in 1769 by Gaspár de Portolá, governor of Lower California. A military post until 1835, it occupied the site known today as Old Town, while Mission San Diego lay five miles up so-called Mission Valley. Being a seaport and close to the Mexican border, San Diego loomed large in the disturbances following Mexico's emancipation from Spain and in the later conflict between Mexico and the United States (*see* California, The Conquest of). Though a civil government was established in 1835, the town had in 1840 only 150 inhabitants. It was practically extinct when eight years later California became a state. The present metropolis, three miles below Old Town, was founded in 1867 by A. E. Horton, a merchant prospector of San Francisco. At San Diego in 1846 the United States flag was officially raised for the first time on California soil.

[H. H. Bancroft, *History of California.*]

FRANCIS BORGIA STECK

***San Felipe-Correo* Affair.** The *Correo de Méjico,* a Mexican revenue cutter, on Sept. 1, 1836, attempted to capture the *San Felipe,* which was allegedly laden with munitions for the coming Texan revolt^qv^. The Texans not only resisted capture; but attacked and captured the cutter, thus stirring Mexico City to punitive action which committed the Texans to war.

[Jim Dan Hill, *The Texas Navy.*]

JIM DAN HILL

San Francisco, Calif. In 1769 during the course of Spain's settlement of Alta California, Gaspár de Portolá, while exploring northward from the first Spanish settlement of San Diego^qv^, discovered San Francisco Bay. Subsequent expeditions revealed the landlocked harbor's great size, safety and strategic value, and in 1776 Spain occupied the peninsula site of the present city. On Sept. 17 settlers brought from Sonora by Juan Bautista de Anza founded a *presidio*^qqv^, and the mission San Francisco de Asís was dedicated on Oct. 9. Following California's transfer to Mexico with the latter's independence from Spain in 1822, the village of Dolores was formed near the mission. Three miles away, the small trading settlement of Yerba Buena (changed to San Francisco in 1847) grew up on the beach, beginning in 1835.

United States interest in the region was early apparent. With the turn of the century, New England whalers^qv^ used the Bay as a provisioning and refitting station, and American traders largely dominated Yerba Buena, except for a short period of Hudson's Bay Company^qv^ control. After vain endeavors by President Tyler to purchase the Bay region, Capt. John B. Montgomery of the United States Navy at length established American rule on July 9, 1846, during the Mexican War.

With the discovery of gold^qv^, San Francisco mushroomed from a quiet village of about 900 people in early 1848 to a bustling cosmopolitan town of at least 10,000 in September, 1849. Six great fires between December, 1849, and May, 1851, swept away the community's makeshift tents and buildings, causing damage estimated at nearly $25,000,000, uninsured, but resulting in the city's erection on a more substantial basis. Lawlessness^qv^ was an even greater problem. The government's failure to deal effectively with the large vicious element led in 1851 and 1856 to the organization of citizens' "vigilance committees"[qv], which rid the city of many criminals. Politics largely continued to be corrupt, however, until 1906, when a sweeping graft investigation, halted temporarily by the great earthquake and fire (*see* San Francisco Earthquake and Fire) of that year, brought about the victory of a reform party.

Following the decline of gold production and the resultant depression of the late 1850's, San Francisco developed rapidly as a center of industry, finance and world trade. Threatened in the 1870's by a severe financial crash, largely the product of overspeculation in Nevada mining stocks, the city's position was assured by the completion of the transcontinental railroad in 1869 and the Panama Canal in 1913[qqv].

[Z. S. Eldridge, *The Beginnings of San Francisco;* C. C. Dobie, *San Francisco: A Pageant.*]

CHARLES EDWARD CHAPMAN
ROBERT HALE SHIELDS

San Francisco de los Tejas, the first Spanish mission established in eastern Texas, was founded in 1690 west of the Neches River, near the present village of Weches. Pestilence and Indian hostility led to its abandonment in 1693. In 1716 it was re-founded farther inland near the present town of Alto, where it was called San Francisco de los Neches. Three years later it was again abandoned, but Aguayo[qv] re-established it in 1721. It was never successful, because the Indians could not be induced to accept mission life. It was moved from eastern Texas in 1730 and re-founded the next year at San Antonio[qv], under the name of San Francisco de la Espada.

[F. W. Hodge, *Handbook of American Indians.*]

C. T. NEU

San Francisco Earthquake and Fire (April 18, 1906). San Francisco experienced several earthquakes and major fires prior to 1906, but none approaching the catastrophe of that year. The first and heaviest shocks came early on the morning of April 18, being followed by minor tremors lasting three days. Serious damage was produced in an area about 450 miles long and fifty miles wide. In San Francisco, buildings crumpled, streets on filled ground buckled and settled, and gas and water mains ruptured. Fire, however, caused the heaviest damage, raging through the central business and residential districts for three days before being controlled. Some 497 city blocks were razed, or about one third of the city. With the water-supply system disrupted, dynamite and artillery were used to check the holocaust.

The property loss has been estimated at between $350,000,000 and $500,000,000. There were about 500 deaths, and some 250,000 homeless refugees flooded the streets, the Presidio and Golden Gate Park, or went to neighboring cities. To meet the emergency, martial law was declared.

The tragedy excited nationwide and international sympathy and, through the medium of the Red Cross, money and supplies poured in from American, Asiatic and European contributors. Under stringent building regulations, reconstruction progressed rapidly and within three years a new city arose upon the ruins of the old.

[F. W. Aitken and E. Hilton, *A History of the Fire and Earthquake in San Francisco;* Calif., State Earthquake Investigation Commission, *The California Earthquake of April 18, 1906.*]

CHARLES EDWARD CHAPMAN
ROBERT HALE SHIELDS

San Gabriel, Battle of (Jan. 8–9, 1847). The opening of this two-day conflict saw about 600 American soldiers, sailors and volunteers, commanded by Commodore Robert F. Stockton and Gen. Stephen W. Kearny, pitted against some 500 Californians (Mexicans) under Col. José María Flores, Andrés Pico and José Antonio Carrillo, at Paso de Bartolo on the San Gabriel River, a little north of present-day Whittier, Calif. The Californians were dislodged from their position on Jan. 8, after about two hours of fighting. As the American forces continued their advance toward Los Angeles next day, the Californians, reduced in numbers, attacked them on both flanks, near the Los Angeles River, in the southern part of modern Los Angeles. This action, known also as the Battle of La Mesa, was the last conflict in the American conquest of Mexican California, and resulted in the retreat of Flores' command. On Jan. 10 the Americans reoccupied Los Angeles and three days later the Californians surrendered to Lt. Col. John C. Frémont at Rancho Cahuenga[qv], ending hostilities in California.

[R. G. Cleland, *A History of California: The American Period.*]

RUFUS KAY WYLLYS

San Ildefonso, Treaty of. By this treaty, executed in preliminary form on Oct. 1, 1800, and made effective on Oct. 15, 1802, Louisiana[qv] was re-ceded (*see* Fontainebleau, Treaty of) by Spain to France in return for an Italian kingdom of Etruria.

Sovereign over Louisiana only since the French and Indian War[qv], Spain had developed neither economic profit nor colonial attachment, but in surrendering the province, the king of Spain ignored vital issues of strategy and national prestige. He negotiated without the knowledge of his minister, Manuel Godoy, who, on learning the facts, was shocked by the levity with which an empire had been alienated. Godoy's chagrin equaled the elation of Lucien Bonaparte, Napoleon's brother, who assumed much credit for the French success. While Spain was losing a vast but unprofitable domain beyond the Mississippi, Napoleon believed himself restorer of the colonial empire lost so ignominiously by his Bourbon predecessors.

Rumors of the pending transfer rekindled Thomas Jefferson's interest in the Mississippi Valley and motivated the dispatch of James Monroe to France in 1803 and the resultant purchase of Louisiana[qv].

[Edward Channing, *A History of the United States*, Vol. IV; Charles E. Hill, *Leading American Treaties*.]

LOUIS MARTIN SEARS

San Jacinto, Battle of (April 21, 1836). On March 11, 1836, five days after the Alamo[qv] debacle, Gen. Sam Houston took command of 374 men at Gonzales and two days later began his retreat from Santa Anna's advance. Extermination of forces under Fannin[qv] and King left Houston's band the sole body under arms in the republic. Difficulties were increased by the flight of the government and of the civil population toward the United States border and the Gulf ports. For thirty-seven days Houston retreated, adding to the force he held together by the exercise of personal authority, while Santa Anna divided his army in pursuit. With 800 men, on April 20, Houston intercepted Santa Anna, with 910, at a ferry over the San Jacinto. Brushing aside a Mexican reconnaissance in force, Houston waited for 540 men under Cos to join Santa Anna the following morning, in order, he later said, not "to take two bites of a cherry." Then, cutting down a bridge protecting his own as well as the Mexicans' avenue of retreat, Houston formed up under a screen of trees and attacked. Santa Anna's surprise was complete. A thinly held barricade protecting his camp being quickly overrun, organized resistance was at an end in twenty minutes. The rest was slaughter. Texan figures on enemy casualties—630 killed, 208 wounded, 730 prisoners—are inexact, the total representing 200 more men than Santa Anna had on the field. Texan losses were 16 killed, 24 wounded including Gen. Houston. Santa Anna, a prisoner, signed armistice terms under which the other divisions of his army immediately evacuated Texas (*see* Texas Revolution).

[Marquis James, *The Raven, a Biography of Sam Houston.*]

MARQUIS JAMES

San Juan, Seizure of (July, 1859). San Juan Island, important for its position midway in the Straits of Juan de Fuca, became the object of jealousy between American settlers in Washington Territory and the Hudson's Bay Company[qv], with headquarters at Victoria. Americans colonized the island in 1854, though the company had previously established a stock ranch there. The alleged shooting of a pig by an American and his threatened removal to Victoria for trial provided the necessary "incident." Within a month 500 American soldiers invaded the island and two British warships took up a menacing position. The American and British governments settled the dispute by arranging for joint occupation, March, 1860.

[Hugh L. Keenleyside, *Canada and the United States.*]

RICHARD W. VAN ALSTYNE

San Juan Country, THE, in southwestern Colorado, includes rich ranching land, the Mesa Verde Park and the famous gold and silver mines around Creede, Durango, Ouray, Rico, Silverton and Telluride. After discovery of rich ore in the San Juan mountains in 1870 and 1871 the region flourished until the silver collapse in 1893, although mining for gold and other minerals has steadily continued. The region includes such famous mines as Camp Bird (opened by Thomas F. Walsh), Smuggler-Union, American Nettie, Silver Lake, Liberty Bell, etc. The American Smelting and Refining Company has a large smelter at Durango.

[T. A. Rickard, Across the San Juan Mountains, in *Engineering and Mining Journal*, 1903; Charles W. Henderson, Mining in Colorado, in U. S. Geological Survey *Professional Paper 138;* James J. Gibbons, *In the San Juan, Colorado.*]

MALCOLM G. WYER

San Juan Hill and El Caney. After the withdrawal of Spanish outposts from Las Guasimas, the key points defending Santiago against Gen. Shafter's advance, June, 1898, were along the line San Juan Hill, northeasterly to El Caney. The former was directly in the path of the American advance; the latter protected the city from envelopment by the American right wing.

On July 1 the Americans attacked along the entire line. Lawton's division, on the right, carried El Caney. The attack against San Juan Hill was not so well timed. Kent's division and the dismounted cavalry, including the Rough Riders[qv], advancing as much from desperation as by design, captured San Juan. This placed the American Army in control of high ground overlooking the city, and in position to isolate the city. Admiral Cervera, alarmed by possibilities of American artillery on hills overlooking the bay in which his fleet was anchored, sought safety, July 4, in a dash to sea—and destruction. Santiago[qv] surrendered July 17.

[Walter Millis, *The Martial Spirit*.]

JIM DAN HILL

San Lorenzo el Real Treaty. *See* Pinckney's Treaty.

San Marco, Fort. *See* Marion, Fort.

San Pascual, Battle of (Dec. 6, 1846). Eighty mounted Californians (Mexicans) under Capt. Andrés Pico, at San Pascual, forty miles northeast of San Diego[qv], Calif., disputed the advance of 160 United States cavalry coming from Santa Fé, N. Mex., under Gen. Stephen Kearny, who had been reinforced by Capt. Archibald Gillespie's relief party of forty men from San Diego. Kearny's men, worn by their long journey, found themselves at a disadvantage, and the Californians broke through their lines. Nineteen Americans were killed, and an equal number were wounded, while the Californian loss is said to have been only twelve wounded. But Pico received no reinforcements and had to give way, so that Kearny, with the aid of 200 of Commodore Stockton's marines, reached San Diego safely on Dec. 12.

[H. H. Bancroft, *History of California*, Vol. V; R. G. Cleland, *A History of California: The American Period;* I. B. Richman, *California under Spain and Mexico, 1535-1847;* J. H. Smith, *The War with Mexico.*]

RUFUS KAY WYLLYS

Sanborn Contracts. President Grant's Secretary of Treasury, W. A. Richardson, in collusion with Representative Benjamin F. Butler of Massachusetts, gave to John D. Sanborn of Boston contracts to collect large sums of overdue Federal internal revenue taxes. Since little effort had been made to secure payment, Sanborn easily collected $427,000 at a commission of 50%. On May 4, 1874, the House Ways and Means Committee exposed the fraud. Richardson resigned and Butler was defeated for re-election.

[*House Executive Documents*, 43rd Cong., 1st Sess., No. 132.]

GEORGE D. HARMON

Sanctions. The Covenant of the League of Nations[qv] provided for the imposition of certain sanctions (coercive action) against violators of the Covenant. Rejection of the Treaty of Versailles[qv] and of the League left the United States uncommitted to any obligation of sanctions.

The first attempt of the League to apply sanctions was when Italy was adjudged to have violated the Covenant by her aggressions on Abyssinia in 1935. A rather mild restriction of trade to Italy was imposed by the League, which proved ineffective. At the time it was argued that the absence of the United States from concerted sanctions would frustrate any serious effort to use this weapon. Nevertheless, the President of the United States, after proclaiming (Oct. 5, 1935) the new neutrality law of Aug. 31, 1935[qv], went beyond the law and declared, on executive responsibility, that: "In these specific circumstances I desire it to be understood that any of our people who voluntarily engage in transactions of any character with either of the belligerents do so at their own risk." Little trade was possible, of course, except to Italy. This executive statement has been interpreted as notice to the world that the United States would not protest any sanctions—for example, blockade—by the League even though they might interfere with neutral commerce. This interpretation is fortified by the fact that the administration openly discouraged trade with the belligerents in contraband[qv] beyond "arms, ammunition and implements of war," the exportation of which was forbidden by the neutrality law. In 1934 when the League voted to embargo the export of arms to Paraguay, in an effort to end the Chaco War, the United States by Act of Congress embargoed shipments of arms, ammunition and implements of war to *both* belligerents, but rejected the League's request to apply the embargo only to the recalcitrant power, Paraguay. This neutral embargo in 1934 and the informal discouragement of trade in contraband in 1935 are as close as the United States has ever come to participation in international sanctions. It was the tendency of the F. D. Roosevelt administration to desire to have neutrality legislation so drafted as to permit the executive to co-operate with international sanctions when the President thought wise. So far (1939) this has successfully been opposed by opinion which contends this would unnecessarily entangle the country in non-American power-politics.

SAMUEL FLAGG BEMIS

Sand Creek Massacre, The, is the most controversial subject in Colorado history. Following repeated Indian raids and depredations in 1864, giving the Indians control of all lines of travel between Denver and the Missouri River, thus cutting off supplies, and with the Government unable to render effective defense because of the Civil War, local military authorities decided that punitive measures were necessary. Col. J. M. Chivington, commanding the District of Colorado, on Nov. 29, 1864, with about 900 soldiers made a surprise attack at Sand Creek near Fort Lyon on a camp of Cheyennes and some Arapahoes[qqv], containing about 200 warriors and about 500 women and children. Estimates of Indians killed range from 150 to 500 with a loss of 10 soldiers. Controversy still rages over whether these Indians were peaceful or hostile; whether they considered themselves under protection; justification for killing women and children; responsibility for the attack and other points.

[Frank Hall, *History of the State of Colorado;* Irving Howbert, *The Indians of the Pikes Peak Region;* George B. Grinnell, *The Fighting Cheyennes.*]

MALCOLM G. WYER

Sandbar Duel (Sept. 19, 1827). Thomas H. Maddox and Samuel Levi Wells met on a sandbar in the Mississippi River, opposite Natchez, to duel with pistols. Accompanying feudists entered into a deadly fight, and among them James Bowie killed his enemy with a knife that gave both the affair and himself fame (*see* Bowie Knife).

[Walter Worthington Bowie, *The Bowies and Their Kindred.*]

J. FRANK DOBIE

Sandusky (spelled also Sandoské, and with other variations from the original Huron "Otsaandosti," or "cool water") was a name applied to the river, bay and Indian villages in this section of northern Ohio. Wyandots (Hurons[qv]) from Detroit occupied the region by 1740 and permitted English traders to erect a post on the northern side of the bay in 1745. The French displaced the English and built "Fort Sandoski" (1751), but soon evacuated it and erected Fort Junandot (1754) on the east side of the mouth of the Sandusky River, retaining it until the fall of Fort Duquesne[qv]. An English blockhouse was built and occupied in 1761 by Ensign Pauli (or Paully) and fifteen men, but the garrison, except Pauli, was wiped out in Pontiac's uprising[qv]. Col. Bradstreet's expedition[qv] later encamped up the river at present Fremont to treat with the Indians. Both Lower Sandusky (Fremont) and Upper Sandusky[qv] were important Indian centers during the American Revolution. By the Treaty of Greenville[qv] the former became a government military reservation, two miles square. In the War of 1812 Fort Stephenson[qv], located here, was attacked unsuccessfully by British and Indians. In 1816 an act of Congress created the town of Croghanville in the reservation which later became Lower Sandusky, and finally was renamed Fremont. The present city of Sandusky on the bay was settled in 1817.

[E. O. Randall and D. J. Ryan, *History of Ohio;* Lucy E. Keeler, Old Fort Sandoski of 1745 and The Sandusky Country, in *Ohio Archæological and Historical Society Publications,* XVII.]

EUGENE H. ROSEBOOM

Sandwich Islands. *See* Hawaii.

Sandy Creek, Battle of (May 30, 1814). Driven into Big Sandy Creek, Lake Ontario, while transporting guns and cables from Oswego to Sackett's Harbor, Master Commandant Melancthon Woolsey ambuscaded with riflemen and captured six pursuing British boats, inflicting a loss of 18 killed, 40 wounded and about 130 surrendered. One American was wounded.

[E. S. Maclay, *A History of the United States Navy.*]

ALLAN F. WESTCOTT

Sandy Hook, N. J., a low, narrow, sandy peninsula, six miles long, at the entrance to New York Bay, has been recognized as of strategic importance in the defense of New York Harbor since the 17th century. Turned landward at the outer end in the shape of a hook, and so called (*hoek*) by the Dutch, it was known to most of the early explorers of the Atlantic coast, while the region surrounding it was described by Verrazzano in 1524. Gen. Clinton retreated to Sandy Hook after the Battle of Monmouth[qv], and on July 5, 1778, the British army established headquarters there. During the War of 1812[qv] British squadrons off the Hook sought to blockade New York City. On the northern end are Fort Hancock, the Sandy Hook Proving Ground for heavy ordnance and Sandy Hook Light, erected in 1764, the only colonial lighthouse now in use without exterior alteration.

[I. N. P. Stokes, *The Iconography of Manhattan Island;* G. R. Putnam, *Lighthouses and Lightships of the United States.*]

STANLEY R. PILLSBURY

Sandy Lake, Battle of (*ca.* 1725). During their westward movement early in the 18th century, a strong force of Chippewa[qv] from the Great Lakes bands, reputedly under Bi-aus-wah, marched against the Dakota or Sioux[qv] village at Sandy Lake (Minn.). In a fierce battle, the Chippewa, with firearms, routed their enemies and took permanent possession of the region.

[William W. Warren, *A History of the Ojibway Nation.*]

WILLOUGHBY M. BABCOCK

Sangre de Cristo Grant, THE, one of the famous Mexican land grants, was given by the Mexican government in 1844 to Narciso Beauv[b]ien and to Stephen Louis Lee. On the death of the two grantees, Carlos Beauv[b]ien secured possession and his ownership was confirmed by the United States Government in 1860. Patents were issued in 1871. The grant contained more than one million acres in the San Luis Valley of southern Colorado and in New Mexico, embodying the waters of the Trinchera, Culebra and Costilla rivers. Some of the earliest Colorado settlements were started on these rivers and the first water rights in the state were established in 1852. The grant was sold by Carlos Beauvien in 1864 to Gov. William Gilpin, who disposed of it to an English company. Later the grant was divided into two parts: the Trinchera Estates, 490,000 acres, comprising the northern half and the Costilla Estates, 510,000 acres, the southern half. These two estates remain practically intact today (1939) and have been in the possession of various development companies, who have colonized, established settlements, constructed irrigation systems, and engaged in large-scale ranching and grazing operations. The Trinchera Ranch, comprising nearly 300,000 acres of the Trinchera Estates, was purchased in February, 1938, by Mrs. Ruth Hanna McCormick Sims. The Costilla Estates, 350,000 acres, is now owned by the Costilla Land Company.

[L. R. Hafen, Mexican Land Grants in Colorado, *The Colorado Magazine*, May, 1927.]

MALCOLM G. WYER

Sanitary Commission, The United States, was created by the United States Government in June, 1861, under the presidency of Rev. H. W. Bellows, a noted Unitarian divine, who had been active in organizing war-relief work. Its purpose was to assist in the care of sick and wounded soldiers and of their dependent families. It was supported mainly by private contributions. Most of the local Aid Societies, active since the very first days of the war, immediately affiliated as branches of the national organization. (*See also* Christian Commission.)

The Commission developed an elaborate organization and at times employed as many as five hundred agents. Its work covered almost every conceivable form of aid, such as field and hospital medical inspection, field ambulance and hospital service, and hospital cars and steamers. It also maintained feeding stations and soldiers' lodges, and supplied assistance to dependent families. Funds were raised by churches, private contributions, and especially by Sanitary Fairs. Camp life was much improved by its work.

[E. D. Fite, *Social and Industrial Conditions in the North;* C. J. Stillé, *History of the U. S. Sanitary Commission.*]

JOHN COLBERT COCHRANE

Sanitation, the preservation of health, has grown from the taking of simple precautions against epidemics[qv] during early American history to the complex regulations of the present. In colonial and later times, health officers were stationed at the Atlantic ports to inspect incoming ships. Subject to yellow fever[qv] particularly, coastal towns adopted elaborate precautions to prevent the introduction of disease. The dearth of scientific information, however, led to many regulations which seem ridiculous in the light of subsequent knowledge. As late as 1797 a Pennsylvania law regulating the "importation of Germans" provided that the ship at sea weekly burn charcoal or tobacco between decks and wash down the ship with vinegar. On the other hand, we get both a respect for the medical profession and a picture of the American city from a letter written by the College of Physicians of Philadelphia to the governor of the state, suggesting measures to be taken to mitigate the yellow-fever menace. It was proposed that the city be cleaned up, that sewers be closed and that filth be quickly removed.

Satisfactory precautions could not usually be taken against disease until the nature of disease itself was known. These precautions followed Pasteur's discoveries. The simplest measures would be obtaining a constant water supply, sewage disposal and refuse collection. It was only with regard to the first that American cities made any noticeable progress before 1880. Boston had a water-pipe system as early as 1652. The emphasis in the water-supply systems, however, was on quantity instead of quality. Although sand filters were introduced in Poughkeepsie in 1885, as late as 1908 few other cities had followed its example. As more sewer systems contaminated the rivers, New York and other large cities began to pipe their water from uninfected sources.

American cities were frequently swept by epidemics. With the exception of vaccination for smallpox[qqv], introduced into this country in 1799, the precautions taken in all cases were too late, consisting of efforts to confine diseases within communities by means of quarantine laws and within the communities themselves by means of pesthouses. It was an epidemic of unusual severity in Memphis in 1879 which focused national attention on sewage disposal. Over 5000 people died of yellow fever. Congress acted; a National Board of Health was set up which investigated conditions in the city. The nation was shocked at the conditions exposed. Shortly after (1887) the Massachusetts Board of Health undertook a systematic study of methods of sewage disposal. Septic tanks proved a failure. Around 1915 Milwaukee and Cleveland developed the aerated sludge system by which sewage was nitrified and purified by means of aerating in series of tanks.

Too expensive for cities with population under 25,000 people, its cost was subsequently reduced by making the purified sewage available as fertilizer.

Garbage removal was a third basis of better sanitation. At first garbage was dumped in waste lands, where it provided a breeding place for flies and rats. The first garbage furnace was built by Lt. H. I. Reilly of the United States Army in 1885 on Governors Island, New York Harbor. Slowly municipal incinerators have been making progress against dumping grounds. Cleveland reclaimed some of the cost by selling the residue as a low-grade fertilizer. One other improvement was the use of covered cans for garbage collection.

Control of epidemics, pure water supply, sewage disposal and garbage removal constitute only a beginning in public sanitation. Demand for drugs of a decent standard led in the 1840's to appointment of drug inspectors at the ports and to the subsequent Pure Food and Drugs Acts[qv] of 1906 and 1938. Publicity attending the information on the large number of deaths caused by adulterated meats in the Spanish-American War (*see* Embalmed Beef) together with Upton Sinclair's *The Jungle* led to the Meat Inspection Act[qv] of 1906. Since the turn of the century two factors have enlarged the scope of sanitary regulations: more accurate information on the origin and spread of diseases, and increased communal activities. With regard to the first, sanitary regulations are designed to rid the country of disease carriers. With regard to the second, great industries have developed which have taken the place of small-scale or home activity in the past. Milk distribution, bread making and meat packing are only a few. Amusements have been commercialized with the result that swimming pools, tourist camps and theaters, for example, must be controlled for cleanliness and ventilation. The relation between noise and the health of city dwellers is also receiving increased attention. (*See also* Health, Public.)

[C. E. Ehlers and E. W. Steel, *Municipal and Rural Sanitation;* J. J. Cosgrove, *History of Sanitation;* The Progress of Sanitation, in *Monthly Journal of the Engineers' Club,* Vol. 6, pp. 115-127.]

HENRY BURNELL SHAFER

Santa Elena. *See* Port Royal.

Santa Fé. Abandoning their first settlement in New Mexico[qv], on the Rio Chama, the Spaniards selected for their capital a more suitable site twenty-five miles to the southeast. Here in 1609 Gov. Peralta founded the present city of Santa Fé. In 1630 the town numbered about 1050 inhabitants, of whom 250 were Spaniards. It suffered severely during the Pueblo Revolt[qv] in 1680 and was always exposed to Navaho and Comanche raids. After the reconquest (1693) and during the first half of the 18th century, Santa Fé with its 1500 inhabitants was the objective of Mexican traders from Chihuahua and of French traders from the Mississippi Valley, whose activities after 1763 were continued by the Americans over the famous Santa Fé Trail[qv]. During the first decades of the 19th century and the later troubles between the United States and Mexico it was often the scene of political disturbances (*see* Mexican War). Gen. Kearny[qv] occupied the city in 1846 and suppressed the revolt that broke out the next year. Santa Fé remained the capital when, in 1850, Congress organized New Mexico into a territory and in 1912 made it a sovereign state. Being the second oldest white settlement in the United States, Santa Fé has a special attraction for the historian and antiquarian.

[H. H. Bancroft, *Arizona and New Mexico;* F. W. Hodge in *The Memorial of Fray Alonso de Benavides,* Ayer translation with Notes.]

FRANCIS BORGIA STECK

Santa Fé Railroad. *See* Atchison, Topeka and Santa Fé Railway.

Santa Fé Trail, THE, famed in history and fiction, was an important commerce route for the fifty-nine years between 1821 and 1880. Since the greater extent of its 780 miles lay across the plains[qv] and avoided the rivers, wagons could easily traverse it. As the trail was extended south from Santa Fé[qv] for an additional thousand miles through El Paso, Chihuahua and Durango, wagon masters continued to find natural roads the entire distance.

Prior to the opening of the trail, Santa Fé was supplied with goods brought by mule back at great expense from the Mexican seaport of Vera Cruz, over a roundabout path, the last 500 miles of which were infested with Apaches[qv], whose very name signifies robber. Thus, while Santa Fé was rich in silver, wool and mules, she lacked the simplest manufactured articles. News of this condition came to the Mallet Brothers[qv] of Canada, who crossed the plains to Santa Fé in 1739. In succeeding years more Frenchmen passed at intervals from the Missouri or from Arkansas Post[qv] to the Rio Grande. Zebulon M. Pike[qv], American Army lieutenant, arriving in 1807, met two Americans, Baptiste LaLande and James Purcell, who had preceded him to Santa Fé in 1804 and 1805 respectively.

American attempts at Santa Fé trade met with summary action by Spanish authorities, who arrested twelve St. Louisans in 1812 and imprisoned them for nine years, and arrested A. P. Chouteau's St. Louis fur brigade in 1815 for merely trapping on the Upper Arkansas. Chouteau's property, valued at $30,000, was confiscated, but he was released after forty-eight days. Information that Mexico had overthrown Spanish rule and that traders were welcome in Santa Fé came to three Indian traders on the plains late in 1821. First of the three to arrive was William Becknell[qv], of Arrow Rock, Mo., who reached Santa Fé Nov. 16 and sold his Indian trade goods at from ten to twenty times higher than St. Louis prices. Thomas James of St. Louis and Hugh Glenn, Osage Indian trader, arrived later and also were welcomed. There was no well-defined Santa Fé Trail prior to Becknell's journey. The Mallets, LaLande and Purcell followed the Platte River part way to the mountains. Chouteau and Glenn traversed the Osage trail from southwest Missouri to the Arkansas. James crossed the present Oklahoma and Arkansas from the Mississippi.

Becknell, father of the trail, started from the steamboat landing of Franklin, Mo., followed the prairie divide between the tributaries of the Kansas and the Arkansas to the Great Bend of the Arkansas[qv], then followed the Arkansas almost to the mountains before turning south to New Mexico. His route became the Santa Fé Trail of history. All early travelers transported their goods by pack horse. In 1822 Becknell, on his second journey, carried part of his merchandise in wagons. After that wagons were generally employed. The Missouri River terminus was first Franklin, then Independence and finally Westport[qqv] (now Kansas City). At the western end the trail turned south to Santa Fé from the Arkansas by three different ways. The Taos Trail[qv] diverged from the Arkansas at the Huerfano River. A middle course branched from the Arkansas west of the mouth of Purgatory River to cross Raton Pass[qv]. The shortest and in later times the most-traveled route was the Cimarron Cutoff, leaving the Arkansas near the present Cimarron, Kans. (this crossing varied), and proceeding southwest across the Cimarron Valley.

Merchants traveled in caravans, the wagons moving in parallel columns so that they might be quickly formed into a circular corral, with livestock inside, to repel Indian attacks. Indians seldom risked battle with well-organized caravans. Such phrases as "the trail was red with blood" or "bleached bones marked the trail" are pure romance. Up to 1843 Gregg reported the Indians killed but eleven men on the trail. Losses were greatest from 1864 to 1869, the bloodiest year being 1868 when seventeen stagecoach passengers were captured and burned at Cimarron Crossing. In that year Gen. Custer's *Wild Life on the Plains* lists forty-five deaths on or near the trail.

Santa Fé trade brought to the United States much-needed silver, gave America the Missouri mule and led to the conquest of New Mexico in the Mexican War[qv]. Here are comparative figures as to westward-bound traffic on the trail at three different periods: Gregg reported that 350 persons transported $450,000 worth of goods at St. Louis prices in 1843, the largest year up to that time. Lt. Col. Gilpin's register shows 3000 wagons, 12,000 persons and 50,000 animals in twelve months of 1848–49, a large part of the number being bound for California (*see* California Gold Rush). The register at Council Grove, Kans., in 1860 showed 3514 persons with 2567 wagons, 61 carriages and stagecoaches, 5819 mules, 478 horses and 22,738 oxen. Federal mail service by stagecoach was instituted in 1849. Completion of the last section of the railroad from Topeka to Santa Fé in 1880 ended the importance of the wagon road (*see* Atchison, Topeka and Santa Fé Railway).

[Herbert E. Bolton, French Intrusions into New Mexico, in H. Norse Stephens, ed., *The Pacific Ocean in History;* R. L. Duffus, *The Santa Fe Trail;* Josiah Gregg, *Commerce of the Prairies.*]

BLISS ISELY

Santa Maria. Under this name Columbus' flagship headed the fleet of three vessels that reached the New World on Oct. 12, 1492 (*see* America, Discovery of). Two months later, on Christmas eve, it ran aground off the coast of Hispaniola. From the wreckage Columbus had a fort erected at La Navidad before he left for Spain. He found it destroyed and its garrison murdered when he returned the next year.

[R. H. Major, *Select Letters of Christopher Columbus;* John Fiske, *The Discovery of America.*]

FRANCIS BORGIA STECK

Santa Rosa Island, Battle on (Oct. 8, 1861). On Jan. 10, 1861, Lt. Adam Slemmer withdrew Federal troops from Pensacola to Fort Pickens[qv] on Santa Rosa, leaving the navy yard and mainland forts to the Confederates. By April 13 reinforcements reached Pickens and two months later volunteer forces (*see* Powhatan Incident). By midsummer (1861) Pensacola was blockaded. In September Federals burned the dry docks and schooner *Judah.* Confederates under Gen. Richard H. Anderson retaliated by a night attack (Oct. 8, 1861) on Santa Rosa. They surprised and burned the Federal camp, driving the troops to the fort. At daylight Anderson withdrew to the mainland. Both sides claimed victory.

[William Watson Davis, *The Civil War and Reconstruction in Florida.*] KATHRYN T. ABBEY

Santanta's Wars ranged from Texas to Kansas in the period following the Civil War. An accomplished warrior and an adept at the art of deception, the Kiowa[qv] chief caused trouble for Custer, Sheridan and Sherman in numerous raids. Cattlemen and settlers also felt his heavy hand. He was at the Battle of Adobe Walls[qv] (1874). After imprisonment in Texas, he was paroled, raided again in Texas, was reimprisoned, and finally killed himself rather than serve a life sentence. At the Medicine Lodge Treaty in 1867 Santanta stated the case of the irreconcilables in the following words:

"I love the land and the buffalo and will not part with it. I want the children raised as I was. I don't want to settle. I love to roam over the prairies. A long time ago this land belonged to our fathers; but when I go up the river I see camps of soldiers on its banks. These soldiers cut down my timber; they kill my buffalo; and when I see that it feels as if my heart would burst with sorrow."

[W. S. Nye, *Carbine and Lance.*]
CARL L. CANNON

Santee Canal, THE, connecting the head of navigation on the Cooper River with the Santee in South Carolina, was a work of private enterprise, begun in 1792 and completed in 1800 at a cost of about $750,000. The channel was twenty-two miles long, thirty-five feet wide and four feet deep, containing thirteen locks and capable of carrying vessels of twenty-two tons burden. Projected as a means of cheapening the transportation of foodstuffs from the interior of the state to the low-country plantations, the enterprise was never a financial success, especially after the introduction of cotton[qv] into the up country. With the building of railroads its business gradually declined until permanently abandoned about 1858.

[F. A. Porcher, *History of the Santee Canal;* U. B. Phillips, *History of Transportation in the Eastern Cotton Belt.*] JAMES W. PATTON

Santiago, Blockade and Battle of (*see* Spanish-American War). Ten days after Cervera's four armored cruisers arrived in Santiago de Cuba on May 19, 1898, they were blockaded by Sampson and Schley with the battleships *Massachusetts, Iowa, Indiana, Oregon* and *Texas,* and by the armored cruisers *New York* and *Brooklyn.* At nine o'clock on the morning of July 3 Cervera dashed out to avoid being caught in a trap by the army encircling the city (*see* San Juan Hill and El Caney). As the flagship, *Infanta Maria Teresa,* headed westward, followed by the *Vizcaya, Colon* and *Oquendo,* the blockaders quickly closed in and concentrated on the *Teresa,* which within fifteen minutes was set on fire and three quarters of an hour later driven ashore, as was also the *Oquendo.* By eleven o'clock the *Vizcaya* was crippled and beached, and at one o'clock the *Colon,* a new and fast ship, already under fire from the 13-inch guns of the *Oregon*[qv], lowered her colors and turned shorewards. Meanwhile the *Gloucester* had forced the Spanish destroyer *Pluton* ashore, where she soon blew up. Another Spanish destroyer, the *Furor,* was sent to the bottom by a heavy shell from the *New York.*

The greater Spanish loss, 600 killed, as compared with one American killed and one seriously wounded, was due primarily to the American rapid-fire guns, which swept the decks, ignited the woodwork and drove the gunners from their stations. The victory removed all chance of Spanish naval resistance in the New World, and greatly increased the respect which Europe held for the American Navy.

Schley, second in command, had been on the *Brooklyn* in the very forefront of the engagement, so close indeed that when the *Teresa* turned toward the *Brooklyn* as if to ram, Schley circled back and narrowly avoided a collision with the other ships. As Sampson was not within firing distance during most of the fight, having gone in the *New York* for a conference with Gen. Shafter, a controversy arose as to who should receive the chief credit for the victory (*see* Sampson-Schley Controversy).

[H. W. Wilson, *Battleships in Action,* Vol. I; U. S. Navy Department, *Naval Operations of the War with Spain.*] WALTER B. NORRIS

Santiago de Chile Inter-American Congress. The fifth Inter-American Congress was held at Santiago in 1923 (*see* Pan-American Conferences). Mexico, unrecognized by the United States, was absent. Peru, at odds with Chile over the Tacna-Arica dispute[qv], did not attend, nor did Bolivia, involved in the same controversy. The principal achievements of the Conference were the adoption of the Gondra Convention, and a projected reform of the Pan American Union[qv] at Washington. The Gondra Convention for international conciliation is a multilateral "cooling off" device for preservation of peace similar to the bilateral Bryan conventions (*see* Bryan Treaty

Model) previously negotiated by the United States.

[*Report of Delegates of the United States of America to the Fifth International Conference of American States*, Washington, 1934.]

SAMUEL FLAGG BEMIS

Santo Domingo. *See* Dominican Republic.

Santo Domingo, Secret Mission to (1846). The Republic of Santo Domingo having separated from Haiti, it became necessary for Secretary of State James Buchanan to investigate its social stability and resources, preliminary to according recognition. In May and June, 1846, two navy lieutenants, David D. Porter and William E. Hunt, accomplished the work on a secret mission. Porter traveled through the little-known interior of the island while Hunt in the brig *Porpoise* surveyed its coast. The reports being favorable, friendly relations between the United States and Santo Domingo were shortly established.

[R. S. West, Jr., *The Second Admiral.*]

RICHARD S. WEST, JR.

Sarah Constant, THE, flagship of the three vessels conveying the founders of the first successful English settlement in the New World, sailed down the Thames for Virginia[qv] Dec. 20, 1606 (O.S.). She (100 tons) and her consorts, the *Goodspeed* (40 tons) and the *Discovery* (20 tons), were under the command of Christopher Newport. Delayed off the coast by contrary winds until February, Newport followed the southern route via the West Indies. Arriving at the entrance of the Chesapeake Bay, a landing was made April 26, 1607 (O.S.), at the cape which was named Henry. After sailing well up the Powhatan, or James, River in order to have better protection against attacks by Spaniards, the colonists established themselves upon "an extended plaine and spot of earth, which thrust out into the depth and middest of the channel." Here the *Sarah Constant* and her sister ships were "moored to the trees in six fathoms of water," and the site was named James-Forte or Jamestowne[qv].

[L. G. Tyler, *Narratives of Early Virginia.*]

MATTHEW PAGE ANDREWS

Saratoga, N. Y. In the summer of 1767 Sir William Johnson, suffering from a wound received in the French and Indian War, was taken by the Mohawks to bathe in the healing waters at High Rock Spring. Washington, as the result of a visit in 1783, considered the purchase of a tract of land to include "the mineral spring at Saratoga." At first little or no attempt was made to exploit the spring. Accommodations were scarce and many visitors came in wagons equipped with beds in which they slept. In 1801, however, Gideon Putnam opened the Grand Union Hotel. The popularity of the springs increased rapidly. An English visitor in 1828 stated that "1500 visitors have been known to arrive in a week." In 1830 the famous United States Hotel was built. Saratoga was declared to be a "resort of wealth, intelligence and fashion—a political observatory." Madam Jumel, Van Buren, Douglas, DeWitt Clinton, Webster, Joseph Bonaparte and other celebrities were frequent visitors. Lavish display became the order of the day. The size and number of the trunks of the visitors became a fashionable feature. The medicinal properties of the springs ceased to be of importance to the thousands of pleasure seekers. During the decade of the 1860's the Civil War profiteers discovered Saratoga. Drilling was started on six new springs; several new hotels were opened; Congress Park was completed; and the first races were run on the Travers track.

[W. L. Stone, *Reminiscences of Saratoga.*]

A. C. FLICK

Saratoga, Surrender at (Oct. 17, 1777). After his defeat at the second battle of Freeman's Farm[qv] on Oct. 7, Gen. John Burgoyne with his 4500 men slowly retreated northward. He neglected to crush a detachment of 1300 Continental militia commanded by Gen. John Fellows, which had been posted to block his retreat, but instead took up a strong position near Old Saratoga (now Schuylerville, N. Y.). The British troops were dead tired, and their supplies were running low. The American forces under Gen. Horatio Gates now consisted of about 5000 regulars and more than 12,000 militia. Gates almost made a fatal mistake by ordering an attack against the British position on Oct. 11 under the misconception that it was defended only by a rear guard, but he finally changed his mind, perhaps at the suggestion of Col. James Wilkinson.

Burgoyne could not decide what to do, though a prompt and complete retreat was the only logical course left open to him. While he hesitated, Gates surrounded his position. Burgoyne finally asked for terms on Oct. 13. Gates at first demanded an unconditional surrender but on Oct. 15 weakly accepted Burgoyne's "convention," which provided that the British troops should be returned to England on condition that they would take no further part in the war (*see* Convention Army). Burgoyne, having heard that Sir Henry Clinton had captured the Continental forts near

West Point (*see* Highlands, 1777–81) and was sending an expedition against Albany, now tried to delay the surrender. The negotiations came to resemble a comic opera, but on the afternoon of Oct. 16 Burgoyne accepted the inevitable, and the formal laying down of arms took place on the next day. Burgoyne, with a graceful bow, said, "The fortune of war, General Gates, has made me your prisoner," and Gates courteously replied, "I shall always be ready to testify that it has not been through any fault of your Excellency." This event marked the turning point of the American Revolution, since France now decided to enter the war as an ally of the thirteen United States (*see* Franco-American Alliance).

[Hoffman Nickerson, *The Turning Point of the Revolution.*]
EDWARD P. ALEXANDER

Saturday Evening Post. The most prosperous magazine in America claims its beginning in the *Pennsylvania Gazette*[qv], established in 1728 in Philadelphia. For many years the *Gazette* was owned and published by Benjamin Franklin. His partners took it over in 1766 and their successors issued it until 1815. In 1821 the *Saturday Evening Post* was first published by Samuel C. Atkinson, one of the partners in the defunct *Gazette,* and Alexander. For four decades the magazine flourished as a semiliterary weekly, with some of the best known authors in America and an occasional foreign writer as contributors—among them Harriet Beecher Stowe, J. Fenimore Cooper, Bayard Taylor, Nathaniel P. Willis, G. P. R. James and Edgar Allan Poe. After the Civil War the periodical declined in prosperity and was on the verge of dissolution when it was bought by Cyrus H. K. Curtis in 1897. Under the editorship of George Horace Lorimer (1899–1937), the *Post* became the largest magazine in circulation in America (today over 3,000,000) and virtually a national institution. Long regarded by authors' agents as in a class by itself, demanding in its stories high literary skill, careful construction and accurate detail, it has maintained a high entertainment level in its fiction and has published some stories of great literary merit by the country's most distinguished contemporary writers. The magazine's factual articles have established an enviable reputation for timeliness.

[F. L. Mott, *A History of American Magazines; A Short History of the Saturday Evening Post.*]
ALVIN F. HARLOW

Saturday Night. The significance of Saturday night is twofold, economic and social. Saturday is pay day for the wage earner and before the night is over much of his money is again in circulation. It is the farmer's night in town. The farmer's wife buys for the coming week. All retail establishments stay open for business; in some cases banks are open until 9 P.M. On Saturday and Saturday night from one third to one half of the volume of business for the entire week is transacted. In groceries it is nearer one half. Towns ranging from one to fifty thousand may be called Saturday-night towns.

The weekly bath, still taken by many in a washtub beside the kitchen stove, is a traditional preliminary to the relaxation and diversion sought on Saturday night. Country people go to town; townspeople go to the city; city people go to the country clubs, all in pursuit of relief from the monotony of ordinary existence. Night clubs, dance halls, restaurants, bars, ice-cream parlors, movies, poolrooms are crowded, yet the streets are lined with others who talk and look. Young men and girls are on the lookout for company. The ideal spot from which to observe a cross-section of America is the main corner of a Saturday-night town.

HARVEY L. CARTER

Saugus Furnace was erected on Saugus Creek near Lynn, Mass., in 1645 by British and colonial proprietors to smelt bog ores found in the vicinity. This furnace, which had a capacity of seven or eight tons a week, cast cannon and hollow ware directly from the ore as well as "sowe" or pig iron. A finery and forge attached to the works refined the latter into bars "as good as Spanish." The enterprise was not very profitable but remained in operation with interruptions for more than a hundred years when neighboring ore and timber were exhausted. Specimens of its castings are still preserved (*see* Bog Iron Mining).

[James M. Swank, *History of Iron in All Ages.*]
VICTOR S. CLARK

Sauk Indians. This tribe of Algonquian[qv] stock was first known to the French near Saginaw Bay, Mich. In the middle of the 17th century they retreated to Wisconsin and built villages on the shores of Green Bay and Lake Michigan. After uniting with the Fox Indians[qv] during their wars on the French, the Sauk retreated to the Wisconsin River, where they built a large village on Sauk Prairie, which Jonathan Carver[qv] described in 1766. After the American Revolution the Sauk retired to the mouth of Rock River and hunted on the western side of the Mississippi in Iowa. Tricked into a treaty in 1802, they sold all their land east of the Mississippi, but in 1832 one of their warriors, Black Hawk[qv], began a border war. At its close the Sauk retired to Iowa, and thence to Kansas and Oklahoma. A small refugee band went to northern Minnesota and gave their name to place names in that region. United with the Fox they now number over 800 in Iowa and Oklahoma.

[F. W. Hodge, *Handbook of American Indians.*]

LOUISE PHELPS KELLOGG

Sauk Prairie (1778). In the southeastern part of Sauk County, Wis., a large and fertile prairie stretches along the Wisconsin River, rimmed by the bluffs of the Baraboo range. On this prairie the Sauk Indians[qv] settled about the middle of the 18th century, after having been driven from the shores of Green Bay[qv] by the French. The first British officer in Wisconsin, who occupied Fort Edward Augustus at Green Bay, 1761–63, made a treaty of alliance with the Sauk chiefs, who professed their friendship for the British newcomers. When Jonathan Carver[qv] in 1766 passed along the Fox-Wisconsin waterway[qv] he found a large and prosperous village of the Sauk Indians on their prairie, and noted that the loss of the friendship of this large tribe would be disastrous for the British cause in the West. This was tested after the outbreak of the American Revolution, when in 1777 Capt. Charles de Langlade, of the British Indian department, sent his nephew, Charles Gautier de Verville, to arouse the Wisconsin Indians for auxiliaries in Canada, to assist in repelling the American invasion. Gautier arrived at the Sauk village in Sauk Prairie in May, 1778, only to find that he had been preceded by a "rebel belt," that is, by a messenger from the tribes of Eastern United States to engage the Western Indians to come to the support of Washington's army. At the same time a Spanish messenger from St. Louis arrived bidding for the Sauk trade and alliance.

Thus in the heart of Wisconsin was heard the repercussion of the contest being waged between the British and the colonies, with the outlying support of the Spanish officials. Gautier succeeded in securing a number of Sauk for Langlade's party; but the tribe began moving to the Mississippi near the mouth of Rock River in order to approach the Spanish and the Americans of the Illinois settlements, which were captured by Clark[qv] in July, 1778. Thereafter the Sauk forsook for a time their British alliance for that of Clark and the Americans.

[L. P. Kellogg, *British Régime in Wisconsin and the Northwest.*]

LOUISE PHELPS KELLOGG

Sault Ste. Marie, French Mission and Trading Post at. The sault or rapids of St. Marys River, which discharges the waters of Lake Superior into Lake Huron, were a favorite rendezvous in colonial days for Indians and traders. The limitless supply of excellent whitefish to be found in the rapids was a lure to the Indians, who, moreover, if they came from the North, had to pass through this locality on their trading trips to the lower St. Lawrence. The designation, Sault Ste. Marie (St. Marys Falls or Rapids), originated with the Jesuit missionaries[qv]. The first white man to reach the Sault appears to have been Etienne Brulé, *ca.* 1622, followed in 1634 by Jean Nicolet[qv], and in 1641 by the Jesuits, St. Isaac Jogues and Father Charles Raymbaut, who gave the place its first distinct mention in the records. In 1668 Father Jacques Marquette opened on the south (American) side of the rapids, at their foot, a mission post around which grew up the earliest settlement of whites in Michigan. He is generally taken to be the founder, as he was the first chronicler, of Sault Ste. Marie.

The Jesuit mission was in 1670 a square enclosure of cedar posts twelve feet high with chapel and residence within. The Indian population of the Sault numbered some 2000 souls, among them the Chippewa[qv] or Saulters, so called from their customary habitat at the rapids. As a trading center and crossroads the place began early to decline, owing, among other causes, to the enterprise of the Hudson's Bay Company[qv], which directed much trade to the North, and to Cadillac's policy of concentrating the Indians at Detroit[qv]. Later came a revival, the North West Company, and afterward the American Fur Company[qqv], maintaining important posts at the Sault. The mission also declined toward the end of the 17th century, the last resident pastor, Father Albanel, dying in 1696, after which date there was no resident clergyman of any denomination at Sault Ste. Marie until 1831.

[L. P. Kellogg, *The French Régime in Wisconsin and the Northwest;* Stanley Newton, *The Story of Sault Ste. Marie.*]

GILBERT J. GARRAGHAN

Sault Ste. Marie, Great Pageant at (1671). Jean Talon, Canada's "Great Intendant," cherished a dream of French imperial expansion into midcontinental North America. His first step toward realizing it was to annex the illimitable and altogether unknown "country of the West" (*pays de l'Ouest*) to the French crown by proclamation, and this he did by staging, through his agent, the Sieur Daumont de St. Lusson, a dramatic ceremony at Sault Ste. Marie, June 14, 1671. The French colors were displayed and St. Lusson thrice cried aloud that he took possession, in the name of Louis XIV, of Sault Ste. Marie, Lakes Huron and Superior, the Island of Caientoton (Manitoulin[qv]) and "of all other countries, streams, lakes and rivers contiguous and adjacent, as well discovered as to be discovered which are bounded on one side by the seas of the North and of the West, and on the other side by the South Sea, and in all their length and breadth." An official record of the proceedings was drawn up, signed by nineteen of the witnesses present and affixed with the French arms to a tree, while Father Allouez, the Jesuit[qv], made an address to the Indians who had been summoned in numbers from far and near for the historic occasion. St. Lusson's *prise de possession* ignored standing Spanish and English claims to the territory in question or parts of it.

[R. G. Thwaites, ed., *Jesuit Relations*, LV; J. Winsor, *The Pageant of St. Lusson;* E. Gagnon, *Louis Jolliet;* F. Parkman, *LaSalle and the Discovery of the Great West.*]

GILBERT J. GARRAGHAN

Sault Ste. Marie, Mich., Lock Canal. *See* St. Marys Falls Ship Canal.

Savage Station, Battle at (June 29, 1862). McClellan (U.), having abandoned his base on the Pamunkey (*see* Stuart's Ride), left Sumner's and Franklin's corps to guard a temporary issue depot at Savage Station while the rest of the army retreated across White Oak Swamp[qv]. Magruder (C.), pursuing, attacked the Federals during the afternoon, momentarily expecting Jackson to assail them from the north. Jackson not arriving, Sumner repulsed Magruder's attacks. After destroying vast quantities of supplies and leaving 2500 sick and wounded in field hospitals, the Federals after nightfall retired unmolested.

[Matthew F. Steele, *American Campaigns; Official Records, Union and Confederate Armies*, Vol. XI.]

JOSEPH MILLS HANSON

Savannah was the first settlement in the colony of Georgia. Having made friends with the Yamacraw Indians who occupied the site, James Oglethorpe on Feb. 12, 1733, landed his colonists and immediately laid out a town with numerous squares breaking the monotony of the streets —a plan adhered to in the subsequent growth of the city. The principal thoroughfare was named Bull for William Bull, a South Carolinian, who aided the settlers in the early days. Each colonist was given five acres for a building lot, a garden and land to cultivate on the outskirts of the city. Though other settlements were made, Savannah continued for the next century to be the principal town in the colony and state. It became the seat of the local governmental division (called first Christ Church Parish and after 1777 Chatham County) and it remained the capital city until 1786. The first commercial house carrying on foreign trade was Harris & Habersham, founded in 1744, and the first printing press was set up here by James Johnston in 1763, which began the same year to publish the *Georgia Gazette,* the first newspaper in the colony. The Anglicans, Presbyterians and Jews early established congregations and erected houses for worship, the first-named being served during 1736 and 1737 by John Wesley.

Savannah was the center of opposition to British authority as the Revolution drew near. During the exciting years of 1765–66, Liberty Boys[qv] spiked royal cannon and rolled them down the river banks, burned in effigy the royal governor, drove out the stamp agent, and forced the removal of the stamps (*see* Stamp Act). A Council of Safety (*see* Committees of Safety) was appointed in 1775, and here the various provincial congresses met preparatory to driving out of the colony in 1776 the royal governor Sir James Wright. In December, 1778, the British seized the city and held it until 1782, making it again the capital of the royal government and in the meantime beating off in October, 1779, a furious attack by the French and Americans (*see* Savannah, Siege of, 1779).

In 1786 Savannah ceased to be the capital, losing the prize to Augusta. Its growth in population and trade though steady was never spectacular. In 1810 it had a population of about 5000; twenty years later it had about 7700; in 1850 there were 14,000; and at the end of the Civil War it was 24,000. Its exports in 1773 were valued at about $380,000; in 1788 the first bale of cotton[qv] was shipped out; in 1800 its exports, coastwise and foreign, amounted to over $2,000,000, which had increased in 1860 to $18,000,000.

The city has been visited by two disastrous fires, 1796 and 1820, the latter being the greatest conflagration to strike any American city up to that time. In antebellum times the city was visited by two yellow-fever[qv] epidemics, 1820 and 1854.

Early in the Civil War the city's outer defenses (Fort Pulaski[qv]) fell, and in December, 1864, Gen. Sherman captured the city (*see* Savannah, Siege of, 1864). After the war its growth was marked, though its prosperity has been somewhat marred by the decline in its naval stores[qv] and cotton exports.

[F. D. Lee and J. L. Agnew, *Historical Records of the City of Savannah;* C. C. Jones, Jr., *History of Georgia;* W. Harden, *A History of Savannah and South Georgia;*

C. C. Jones, Jr., O. F. Vedder, and F. Welden, *History of Savannah.*]

E. MERTON COULTER

Savannah, Siege of. In September, 1779, Count d'Estaing with about 4500 soldiers, joined by Benjamin Lincoln with about 2100 Americans, sought to wrest Savannah from the British, who had about 2500 defenders. After a siege of three weeks, on Oct. 9 a general assault was made which resulted in a disastrous failure. More than a thousand of the attacking forces were killed, including Count Pulaski and Sergeant Jasper of Fort Moultrie[qv] fame. Lack of co-ordination and understanding between the French and Americans was held responsible for the defeat.

[E. M. Coulter, *A Short History of Georgia;* C. C. Jones, Jr., *The Siege of Savannah in 1779, as Described in Two Contemporaneous Journals of French Officers in the Fleet of d'Estaing.*]

E. MERTON COULTER

Savannah, Siege of (December, 1864). On Dec. 10, Sherman (U.) began to invest Savannah (*see* Sherman's March to the Sea). A skilful Confederate defense at Honey Hill kept the railroad open to Charleston, but Fort McAllister[qv], commanding the southern water approach, was captured and connection established with the Federal supply fleet. Greatly outnumbered but his line of escape still open, Hardee, the Confederate commander, after a brief defense, on the night of Dec. 20, withdrew into South Carolina (*see* Carolinas, Sherman's March through the). Sherman telegraphed Lincoln: "I beg to present you, as a Christmas gift, the City of Savannah" with "plenty" of guns, ammunition and cotton.

[*Battles and Leaders of the Civil War*, Vol. IV.]

THOMAS ROBSON HAY

***Savannah Steamship*, THE,** was the first ship to cross the Atlantic Ocean, propelled or aided by steam. Built in New York as a sailing ship with auxiliary steam power, it was bought by a shipping company in Savannah, Ga., whence it sailed for Liverpool on May 22, 1819, arriving twenty-nine days later.

[M. S. Anderson et al., *Georgia: A Pageant of Years;* E. M. Coulter, *A Short History of Georgia;* J. F. Reigart, *The Life of Robert Fulton.*]

E. MERTON COULTER

Savings Banks. *See* Banks, Savings.

Sawmills. In 1634, or earlier, a sawmill was in operation on the Piscataqua River—where there were seventy in 1706—and another, driven by wind, was reported on Manhattan Island. A primitive type had a single sash saw pulled downward by a water wheel and upward by an elastic pole, but more usually the saw was moved both up and down by water power. A few colonial mills already had gangs, or parallel saws, set in one frame so as to cut several boards simultaneously. Muley saws, with a lighter guiding mechanism, were also used. Sawmills multiplied but were not greatly improved in colonial times. They handled principally soft timber of moderate dimensions and were considered satisfactory if they cut a thousand board feet a day.

Shortly before 1810 Oliver Evans' wood-burning high-pressure steam engines began to be installed in sawmills and made it possible to manufacture lumber where water power was not available, as in the forested flatlands of the South. Indeed, the portable engine owes its development in America partly to its usefulness for sawing timber. Circular saws, introduced about the middle of the 19th century, increased mill capacity on account of their higher speed. Band saws, though invented earlier, were not introduced in America until after the Civil War. They are now used extensively because they are faster, economize timber by their narrower "kerf" or cut, and can handle logs of the largest size. Some modern mills cut up to half a million feet a day.

These giant mills developed for the most part in the great forest regions west of the Appalachians—in the white-pine belt of the Great Lakes Basin, in the yellow-pine area of the South, and in the fir and redwood forests of the Pacific Northwest.

[Albert S. Bolles, *Industrial History of the United States;* Eleanor L. Lord, *Industrial Experiments in the British Colonies of North America;* Victor S. Clark, *History of Manufactures in the United States.*]

VICTOR S. CLARK

Saybrook, Conn. On the basis of the Warwick Patent (*see* Connecticut, The Old Patent of) John Winthrop, Jr., was appointed on July 7, 1635, "governor of the river Connecticut" for one year and commissioned to establish a settlement and fort there. He arrived in Boston on Oct. 6 and sent Lt. Gibbons with about twenty men who began the settlement of Saybrook on Nov. 24. They were soon joined by Lion Gardiner, an expert in fortifications. Thus a Dutch undertaking to occupy the place was forestalled by a few days.

After entering into an agreement with the settlers of the River Towns[qv] in March, Winthrop reached Saybrook in the late spring of 1636. About the same time George Fenwick, now one of the patentees, appeared. Neither stayed long, so Gardiner was in charge until Fenwick returned in 1639, bringing his wife. Meanwhile Saybrook had been the center of the Pequot War[qv]. In 1643 Fenwick became a magistrate of the Connecticut Colony and on Dec. 5, 1644, sold the fort and land at Saybrook to Connecticut.

[C. M. Andrews, *Colonial Period of American History*, Vol. II; G. C. Gates, *Saybrook.*]

GEORGE MATTHEW DUTCHER

Saybrook Platform, THE, was a revision of the ecclesiastical polity of the colony of Connecticut, drawn up by a synod meeting at the call of the legislature in Saybrook, Sept. 9, 1708. Its chief feature was an accentuation of the principle of "consociation" or rule by councils, away from the independency of early Congregationalism[qv]. The Platform was the outcome of a wide feeling in conservative circles that the Cambridge Platform[qv], which gave to synods a right merely to "advise" individual churches, did not furnish adequate authority for keeping all churches in line. At Saybrook the churches were organized into county associations, ruled by a council of ministers and lay delegates, which was given extensive disciplinary powers over erring congregations, and supervision over the choice of new pastors; county associations then sent delegates to an annual assembly which regulated the whole colony. A similar movement in Massachusetts, resulting in the ministerial Proposals of 1705, failed because of a lack of legislative support and the attacks of John Wise; in Connecticut, governmental support of the Platform effectively transformed the polity of the 18th century into a centrally administered unit, making the church practically a form of Presbyterianism[qv].

[Williston Walker, *The Creeds and Platforms of Congregationalism.*]

PERRY MILLER

Scab. At a trial in Philadelphia in 1806, of eight workingmen for intimidation of non-union men, a journeyman shoemaker testified that, when he came to America from England in 1794, he was notified that he must either join the shoemakers' union or be considered a "scab" and forbidden to work with union men (*see* Philadelphia Cordwainers' Case). To the latter, the epithet thereafter came to mean one who took the job of a union man during a strike. The word did not come into public notice until about 1885–86, when unions were coagulating into great national organizations. Its meaning had to be explained to a congressional committee in the latter year.

[Trade Unionism in Its Infancy, in *Lippincott's Magazine*, March, 1876; Mary Ritter Beard, *The American Labor Movement.*]

ALVIN F. HARLOW

Scalawag was a term of opprobrium used by the conservative whites in the South after the Civil War for the class of native whites who accepted the radical Reconstruction[qv] measures of Congress and who associated themselves with carpetbaggers[qv] and Negroes in dominating the state governments. The most probable original meaning of the word was an undersized, ill-favored member of a herd of cattle or of a flock of sheep. Before Reconstruction times it was applied to any low, mean, disreputable person.

[James Ford Rhodes, *History of the United States, 1850-1877*, Vol. VI.]

C. MILDRED THOMPSON

Scalping and Scalp Bounties. Among many tribes of American Indians the scalp proper, a circular patch of skin and hair at the crown of the head, was allowed to grow long and abundant as a conspicuous ornament. The remainder of the hair was shaved or cut short. Before contact with the white man, the only Indian tribes to scalp their foes were the Iroquois, Muskhogean Choctaws, Chickasaws and Creeks[qqv]. The process was extremely painful but not always fatal. A circular incision was made about the scalp lock, and it was alternately pulled and cut from the head. If taken as a trophy, nearly the whole scalp might be peeled off, stretched on a hoop, cleaned and dried, painted on the underside and fastened to a short pole.

The white frontiersmen quickly adopted the Indian custom, and British, French, Colonial and United States governments all came to offer rewards for the taking of enemy scalps. It was customary to justify the bounties by pointing to "the Cruel & Barbarous Practice of Scalping our Inhabitants" followed by the enemy Indians and to the "absolute necessity in Retaliation to Pursue the same Methods." Scalps of grown men usually brought about twenty-five to fifty dollars (though the colony of Massachusetts once offered as much as £100), and those of women and children half that amount. Occasionally a humane provision of the bounty laws offered double the scalp bounty for prisoners, but, of course, scalps could usually be transported more easily than prisoners. Urged on by the bounties, which were still offered during the Indian wars of the 19th century, and by thousands of "scalping knives" given or sold by traders and government agents, the gruesome practice of scalping spread among the Indians of the central and western United States.

[A. C. Parker, *The Indian How Book.*]

EDWARD P. ALEXANDER

Schechter v. U. S. (1935). This case and that of U. S. v. Schechter arose out of alleged violations of the "Code of Fair Competition for the Live Poultry Industry" of metropolitan New York, which code was established under provisions of the National Recovery Act^qv^ of June 16, 1933. The Schechters, owning two plants doing a wholesale poultry business in New York City and Brooklyn, were indicted and convicted in a Federal district court on nineteen counts for violation of the code. The Circuit Court of Appeals reversed the lower court on two counts, holding that the Federal Government had no constitutional right to regulate hours of work and wages. The conviction on the other seventeen counts was sustained, however.

Thereupon both the Government and the Schechters appealed to the Supreme Court which on May 27, 1935, unanimously ruled the code to be unconstitutional. Rejecting the emergency justification, the Court declared that the code-making authority conferred on the President by Section III of the National Industrial Recovery Act was "an unconstitutional delegation of legislative power."

Granting that Congress had authority to regulate not only interstate commerce^qv^ but also those activities which directly affected such commerce, the highest tribunal insisted that codes could not regulate activities which only indirectly affected commerce among the states.

[295 U. S. 495; T. R. Powell, Would the Supreme Court Block a Planned Economy?, in *Fortune*, Vol. XII.]

ERIK McKINLEY ERIKSSON

Schenectady, N. Y. In 1661 the great flat upon the Mohawk River, seventeen miles west of Fort Orange (*see* Albany), was purchased from the Indians by Arendt Van Corlaer and fourteen associates. Stuyvesant confirmed the grant in 1662, and in 1664 the lands were surveyed and laid out. The settlement embraced an area of four lots, each having a frontage of 400 feet. Although its location on the Mohawk River, the only natural east-west passage through the Appalachian barrier, pointed to its growth as a trading center, Schenectady (because of the Albany monopoly) was forbidden to engage in the fur trade^qv^, and so developed first as an agricultural community. In 1690 came one of those devastations which harried the Mohawk Valley until after American independence. One of three raiding parties of French regulars and Indians, sent out by Frontenac, fell on Schenectady on Feb. 8 and burned it to the ground. Sixty-three houses and a church were destroyed. A number of inhabitants were killed or taken prisoner. The terrified survivors fled to Albany. The village was rebuilt and continued to grow slowly. It became the center of a prosperous farming community, land in the vicinity being so fertile as to sell commonly for £45 per acre.

During the Revolution the district committee in Schenectady was most active. Complete records are extant which show the election of members, sending of representatives to confer with the Albany committee, arrest of Tories^qv^, guarding of the western passage and efforts to placate the Mohawks^qv^.

[Nelson Greene, *History of the Mohawk Valley.*]

A. C. FLICK

Schenk v. United States (249 U. S. 47, 1919). The Espionage Act^qv^ of 1917 penalized any attempt to cause disloyalty in the army or navy or to obstruct recruiting. Schenk, secretary of the Socialist party^qv^, circulated leaflets encouraging resistance to the draft. He was convicted and the act was sustained in an opinion in which Justice Holmes made his famous statement that "the words used" in every case must tend "to create a near and present danger" of substantive evils which Congress has a right to prevent.

HARVEY PINNEY

Schlosser, Fort, Attacked (1813). On the morning of July 5, a British detail composed of thirty-four officers and men of the militia, Volunteer Thompson and Ensign Winder with six privates of the 49th Regiment, under the command of Lt. Col. Thomas Clark, crossed the Niagara River in three boats arriving at Schlosser a little after daybreak. Surprising the small guard at the public storehouse, they captured and removed to Canada a large amount of arms, ammunition, equipment, provisions, two bateaux and a gunboat. As they were embarking from Schlosser with the booty, twelve or fifteen men came to the beach and fired twenty shots of musketry. There were no casualties.

[E. Cruikshank, *Documentary History of the Campaign upon the Niagara Frontier in the Year 1813*, pt. 2.]

ROBERT W. BINGHAM

Schoenbrunn (beautiful spring) was a mission of the Moravian^qv^ Brethren, established by David Zeisberger and five families of Delawares^qv^ in 1772 near present New Philadelphia, Ohio. John Heckewelder and other missionaries joined him and several little missions were organized along the Tuscarawas for Christian Delawares and Mohicans from Pennsylvania. During the troubles of the Revolution Schoenbrunn was abandoned for Lichtenau, but in 1779 a new Schoenbrunn was set up across the river from the old, only to be destroyed in the bloody year of 1782 (*see* Gnadenhutten).

[Edmund DeSchweinitz, *Life and Times of David*

Zeisberger; E. O. Randall and D. J. Ryan, *History of Ohio*, Vol. II.]

EUGENE H. ROSEBOOM

Schomburgk Line, THE, was an initial survey made in 1840 by Sir Robert Schomburgk, English-German geographer, in an attempt to establish a boundary between British Guiana and Venezuela[qv]. The latter repudiated the survey and the boundary remained an open question until President Cleveland forced an arbitration, 1897. The Schomburgk survey was of primary importance in the negotiations.

[George L. Burr, The Search for the Venezuela-Guiana Boundary, in *American Historical Review*, Vol. IV.]

JIM DAN HILL

School, District. As indicated in the general article on Education[qv] the original form of school in the American colonies was, in New England and New York, the town school, and in the South, the private or charity (church) school[qqv]. With the increase of population, improvement of roads and transportation, and the removal of Indians and wild animals, the population scattered over the area of the towns. Most New England towns contained several villages as well as a scattered farm population. The school was supported in whole or in part by a town tax. In order to have this tax voted, the school must be made accessible to those who paid the tax; hence first came the moving school, where the teacher went to the pupils; this developed into the divided school, where the school went for a portion of the year to a village. When these short school terms were made permanent, the school district was formed. This was made legal in Massachusetts in 1769. Later Massachusetts gave the power of school support and school control to these districts, and still later (1820) made mandatory the formation of such districts by the towns.

The district school developed very early. Short terms, poorly equipped and poorly paid teachers, unruly conduct of school children, bad hygienic conditions, a multiplicity of textbooks, too many pupils or too few pupils, an impossibly long program of recitations for the teacher and lack of discipline were the leading evils of the district system. Yet the district school was probably the only basis on which democracy could build up a public-school system[qv].

While the district-school system of the early 19th century has been called the lowest point reached by the American school system, it at least made possible the development of a school system controlled and supported by the public that patronized it. It was against the evils of the system that Horace Mann in Massachusetts (1838–49) and Henry Barnard in Connecticut (1838–42) and in Rhode Island (1843–49) labored in their educational reforms. However, the district-school system was carried from New England into nearly all the new states west of the Alleghenies. Thomas Jefferson advocated it as an ideal form of government along with the town[qv] political organization. The district system after the middle of the 19th century was modified in most Western states by the superimposing of the township system or the county system, or both, on the district system. With the middle of the 19th century the union school appeared in New York (1853), in Massachusetts (1869), and in Connecticut (1889). By the close of the century, good roads made possible the consolidated school[qv] which has gradually replaced the one-room, ungraded district school throughout most of the country.

[G. H. Martin, *The Evolution of the Massachusetts State School System;* E. P. Cubberley, *State and County Education Organization;* Cubberley and Elliott, *State and County School Administration*, Vol. II; H. Suzzalo, *The Rise of Local School Supervision in Massachusetts;* F. H. Swift, *Federal and State School Finance;* H. Updegraff, *The Origin of the Moving School in Massachusetts.*]

PAUL MONROE

School Lands. When Congress created new states out of the Public Domain[qv] it reserved to itself the management and disposal of the public land within their boundaries. However, it granted land to the states for various purposes, chief of which was to aid the development of elementary schools. Beginning with 1803, Congress granted one section in each township for school purposes to the new states as they were admitted into the Union; in 1850 the grant was increased to two sections in each township and in 1896 it was again increased to four sections in each township. Twelve states received one section, thirteen states received two sections and four states received four sections in each township.

The pressure of public opinion prevented these lands being held for high prices and induced the legislatures to take early action for this disposal. Ohio, the first public-land state[qv], tried a number of experiments in managing its school lands, among them being short-term leases, perpetual leases for 12 cents per acre, 99-year leases at 6% of appraised valuation, one-year leases and sale at a minimum price of $5 per acre. Some states, like Ohio, held the lands and proceeds from them as trustees for the townships while others, like Indiana, turned them over to the townships. Local management generally led to favoritism, careless administration and reckless use of the funds derived from the sale. State management frequently played into the hands of large speculator groups as in Wisconsin where individuals acquired as much as 57,000 acres of school lands. Wisconsin and Nebraska loaned their school-land funds to individuals, taking mortgages on the lands of these persons as security and when payments were delayed were forced to foreclose. The more common procedure was to require that the school funds should be invested in state bonds paying 6% interest. Despite the haste in selling, the mismanagement of the funds and the actual diversion of receipts by some of the states the lands did aid materially in making possible elementary schools in communities where the tax base was insufficient to permit the establishment of schools or where school taxes were opposed.

Management of school lands in the newer states of the Far West during the last seventy-five years has been more successful than it was in Ohio, Illinois or Wisconsin, partly because Congress attempted to prescribe more fully the conditions under which the lands should be sold and partly because the states have been more prudent in their administration of them. Such states as Minnesota, North Dakota and Washington, to cite only a few, have accumulated large funds from their school lands, the income from which comprises a substantial part of the state contribution to the public schools[qv]. The newer states have been slower in disposing of their lands and still retain about 60,000,000 acres. Of this amount 38,000,000 acres are leased and thus provide a steady addition to the public-school funds.

[G. W. Knight, *History and Management of Land Grants for Education in the Northwest Territory;* M. N. Orfield, *Federal Land Grants to the States with special reference to Minnesota.*]

PAUL WALLACE GATES

Schoolbooks, Early. Since education was a handmaid to religion in colonial America, the Catechism, the Testament, the Psalter and the Bible[qv] were the most commonly used books of elementary instruction, although a few small texts and hornbooks[qv] of English origin were imported. Various primers were adapted to American schools, but *The New-England Primer*[qv] (1690), "the little Bible of New England" among Calvinists and Lutherans until 1800, remained pre-eminent as the guide to rudiments of spelling and religion. Thomas Dilworth's *New Guide to the English Tongue* (1740), a British work, dominated spelling and reading instruction until Noah Webster's *A Grammatical Institute of the English Language* appeared. These three books, a speller (1783), a grammar (1784) and a reader (1785), Revolutionary-born and perfervidly patriotic, demanded a native literature in the American language; the author proceeded to compile *Webster's Dictionary*[qv]. *Webster's Spelling Book*[qv] enjoyed phenomenal success until 1915; with the dictionaries it standardized spelling in America. Other early books to attain wide circulation were Ezekiel Cheever's *Latin Accidence* (1650), Jedidiah Morse's *Geography* (1784), Nicholas Pike's *Arithmetic* (1788), Caleb Bingham's *American Preceptor* (1794), Lindley Murray's *Grammar* (1795) and Charles A. Goodrich's *History of the U. S.* (1822). As the public-school system[qv] expanded after 1834, publications multiplied, but in each subject the books followed similar patterns until about 1900. In the teaching of grammar, more than elsewhere, methodology and books changed. Until 1825 the memorizing of rules and exceptions was universal; between 1825 and 1850 parsing became popular; between 1850 and 1890 structural analysis lent a bridge-building interest to syntactical study; after 1890 a strong tendency set in to eliminate formal grammar instruction and to substitute "good English." In recent years "functional grammar" has won many adherents, although a conservative majority has urged a return to formal instruction combining parsing and analysis. English composition as a separate subject was introduced in the 1840's, yet the earliest textbook was G. P. Quackenbos' *First Lessons in Composition* (1851). Although practised in conjunction with catechetical and conversational instruction, oral composition did not achieve a separate place until 1880 nor attain its present importance until 1920. History texts tended to stress political and military events, and, with the aid of sharp criticisms of monarchy and royalty, to extol American representative democracy. Civics was taught as a part of the work in history or reading. Books of reading selections varied little in type, yet two series became especially popular. In 1827 Samuel G. Goodrich, "Peter Parley,"[qv] introduced a friendly narrator and extensive pictorial illustrations as teaching devices in his many books for children. William Holmes McGuffey's *Readers*[qv] (1836) captivated the whole Middle West and gave a foundation for cultural pursuits on the frontier. In general it may be said that the contents of textbooks remained haphazard in choice and arrangement until about 1825, when Pestalozzian principles redirected educational activity toward observation, investigation and discussion rather than memorization and rote recitation. In recent years careful research has assisted in reorganizing content and presentation to achieve a psychological order and an adaptation to pupil interest.

[G. E. Littlefield, *Early Schools and Schoolbooks of New*

England; Clifton Johnson, *Old-Time Schools and School-Books;* A. M. Earle, *Child-Life in Colonial Days;* C. F. Heartman, *American Primers . . . and Other Non-New-England Primers;* E. A. Cross, *Fundamentals in English.*]

HARRY R. WARFEL

Schools. *See* Education.

Schools, Consolidation of. For more than a century educators have agreed that the best solution of rural district-school problems—pedagogical and administrative inefficiency arising from ungraded schools, short terms, inadequate equipment, ill-paid and poorly trained teachers, unnecessary units and control by jealous, nonprofessional local boards—is consolidation of contiguous districts which, surrendering autonomy, unite in community, township, or county units to support graded schools with adequate plants, well-trained teachers, enriched curricula and public transportation of pupils. James G. Carter (1820's) and Horace Mann (1840's) advocated consolidation for Massachusetts, and New York (1853) and Massachusetts (1869) passed laws permitting it. Little was done until the 1890's when agrarian unrest elevated problems of rural education and led to further permissive state legislation. In 1897, when the National Education Association's Committee of Twelve on Rural Schools unequivocally espoused consolidation, state and Federal authorities supported it. By 1900 consolidation began, especially in states where town or county units of school administration and good roads prevailed. After 1910 many states promoted it by grants-in-aid[qv]. From 1912 to 1929 the number of consolidated schools rose rapidly: to 7500 in 1917 (nearly half organized in the preceding three years); to 11,890 in 1920; and to 17,004 in 1928. By 1929 consolidations were increasing by about 1000 per year, the movement being strong particularly in New England, the South and the Far West. Growth was retarded after 1929, and though the number remained above 17,000, it included less than one fifth of the total rural-school population.

[Lee L. Driver, The Consolidation of Rural Schools, in *Addresses and Proceedings of the National Education Association,* LX; James F. Abel, Recent Data on Consolidation of Schools and Transportation of Pupils, in *U. S. Bureau of Education Bulletin,* 1925, No. 22; *Biennial Survey of Education, 1916-18,* Department of Interior, Bureau of Education, Bulletin, 1919, No. 88; *Report of the Committee of Twelve on Rural Schools,* 1897.]

RAYMOND P. STEARNS

Schools, Private, may be defined as those "dependent on private initiative for [their] inception and maintenance, not wholly or in part dependent on public taxation." Such schools were established almost simultaneously with the settlement of most of the English colonies.

The Collegiate School of New York, established by the Dutch in 1638, which still continues as a local day school, may well claim to be the oldest private school in the United States. The Latin Grammar School of England, an outgrowth of the Reformation, was early transplanted to New England (*see* Latin Schools). The Roxbury Latin School, established in 1645 by John Eliot, missionary to the Indians, remains a private school today of the country day type.

The first private foundation for education in the United States was established in 1657 by the bequest of Edward Hopkins, an uncle of Elihu Yale, and one-time governor of Connecticut, who had amassed a fortune in the West Indian trade. The Hopkins Grammar School of New Haven, established in 1660, survives as a private country day school.

Lt. Gov. Dummer of Massachusetts in 1761 left an endowment for a grammar school which soon after became an academy[qv] and has recently been revived as a college preparatory school. The two Phillips, uncle and nephew, following the Revolution, established academies at Andover and Exeter. Academies, initiated by local groups to provide a broad secondary education, spread from New England westward and south and reached their maximum number in the 1850's when there were upward of 7000. In northern New England many still survive, some taken over as local high schools or transformed into modern preparatory schools.

The first church school on the English model, St. James, was established at Hagerstown, Md., in 1842, and followed by St. Paul's, Concord, N. H., in 1855.

The first country day school originated with the Gilman Country Day School in 1897 at Baltimore, Md. Ten years later, there were three. Today almost every well-to-do city has one or more. Many other schools, private and public, have adopted the characteristic features of afternoon supervised study and play.

Roman Catholic schools have existed in Maryland and Louisiana since the 18th century. The recent increase has been rapid. Catholic secondary schools increased in number from 2500 in 1915 to 5000 in 1934. About 10% of the children in this country attend Catholic schools, about 1% attend non-Catholic private schools.

A total of 16,577 private schools are listed in the printed report for the year 1935–36 by the U. S. Office of Education. Of these, 9992 are elementary, 3327 secondary, 2099 private commercial schools; 1159 are private or nontax-supported colleges. No final count of private schools can be made. If those listed in local telephone books and newspapers under schools of beauty culture, radio, aviation, engineering, costume design and laboratory technique were included the number would run over 30,000. As many as 17,000 music schools have been counted.

[Porter Sargent, *A Handbook of Private Schools*, editions 1915-40.] PORTER SARGENT

Schools, Public. This term is generally used in the United States to designate that part of the state school system that is public in support and control, nonsectarian, universal, open and free to all the educable children and youth without tuition charges. Formerly it designated the first six, seven or eight grades in the course of study in the public schools, or those grades above the kindergarten and those below the so-called high (secondary) school. Since the development of secondary education as a function of the state, the term may very properly be used to designate the public high school[qv] as well as the elementary school.

Among the forces that served to advance the idea of the common school was nationalism, which gained strength in the late 18th century and the early 19th century, in the United States and also in the major European countries. Under the influence of nationalism education has come increasingly to be employed as an instrument for the promotion of patriotism and for the achievement of national ends. And nationalism has continued as a definite purpose of the common school, whether in democracies or authoritarian states. In the late 18th century and the early 19th century leaders almost everywhere commonly said that popular education was the foundation on which the welfare of the people must be preserved and advanced. In European countries "class" schools generally formed, but in the United States the "ladder" system developed. This has come to be considered a distinctive feature of the common school in this country. Other forces that promoted the idea of the common school were the industrial revolution, the growth of the factory system and the awakening of a class consciousness among the laboring people in industrial centers, the frontier and the westward migration, humanitarian movements, Jacksonian democracy, and the removal of property qualifications for voting and the extension of the suffrage[qqv]. Under these and other influences, including the work of many humanitarians and educational leaders, the element of "charity," which had so long attached to the education of the underprivileged, was removed and elementary education slowly came to be considered a proper function of government. Interest in education as a responsibility of the state developed slowly, but it may be said that by 1870 (although an exact date cannot be fixed) the principle of civil responsibility for elementary education had been very widely accepted, even if it had not passed universally into practice in the United States. "Rate bills," for example, under which practice local school officers in many American states admitted indigent children to school and charged the cost of their instruction to those parents in the district who were able to pay it, seem not to have been abolished in Indiana until 1852, in Ohio in 1853, in Illinois in 1855, in Iowa in 1858, in Kansas in 1861, in Vermont in 1864, in New York in 1867, in Connecticut, Rhode Island and Pennsylvania in 1868, in Michigan in 1869 and in New Jersey in 1871. In Delaware, Maryland and most of the Southern states completely free elementary education was not provided until after the Civil War. Since the dispute and final decision in the Kalamazoo case[qv] in the State of Michigan in the early 1870's, and similar decisions in other states later, the principle that local and state governments had the right to levy taxes for education above the elementary school was established. By 1900 this principle had been widely accepted in practice, except in the Southern states, where common high-school education, at public expense, did not develop until the first and second decades of the 20th century. There the selective idea in education persisted longer than in some other parts of the country.

[Edgar W. Knight, *Education in the United States;* Edward H. Reisner, *The Evolution of the Common School.*] EDGAR W. KNIGHT

Schoolteachers, Early. Teachers were scarce in early colonial days. In 1624 Gov. Bradford wrote: "Indeed, we have no common school for want of a fit person or hitherto means to obtain one." Pains were taken in New England to avoid employing masters who "have manifested themselves unsound in the faith, or scandalous in their lives." In general the parish pastor reviewed the candidate's qualifications, but by the beginning of the 19th century the schools had passed from the care of the church to that of the state.

The simple rudiments were taught at mother's knee; gifted women sometimes drew their own and neighbors' children into a little circle, or girls of sixteen or older conducted "dame schools"[qv]. The colonial master seldom received as much as a third of the sum paid a pastor. His qualifications were few; often he was required to possess no more than "the knack to continue in the schoolroom the discipline of the kitchen, and to be a good mender of quill pens." Ignorance, incompetence, ill temper, intemperance, boorishness and laziness were commonly mentioned as characteristics of teachers, yet among the wielders of the ferule were many men and women whose idealism fostered intellectual ambitions in callow frontier lads.

Four classes of teachers existed: preachers who conducted parish or grammar schools (*see* Latin Schools); young college graduates who taught school while preparing for professional careers in law, medicine and divinity; indentured servants[qv] who earned their freedom by teaching; and men and women who dedicated their lives to education and remained for many years in charge of common and grammar schools. One of the most famous of the last class was Ezekiel Cheever, author of *Latin Accidence,* a famous colonial book (*see* Schoolbooks, Early). At twenty-three he began a twelve-year service in New Haven; he then taught at Ipswich for eleven years and at Charlestown for nine; and at fifty-six he was called to Boston, where he remained thirty-eight years, dying in harness at ninety-four.

Girls were generally excluded from colonial public schools; but private schools[qv] made progress in educating women. After the Revolution girls were admitted to a few academies[qv], but in the main received advanced education at such schools as Miss Sarah Pierce's at Litchfield, Conn. Some of the graduates of these seminaries were pioneers in establishing women's colleges. Upon the opening of normal schools[qv] women replaced men as teachers in the lower schools, and gradually advanced into higher institutions.

[W. H. Small, *Early New England Schools;* E. E. Slosson, *The American Spirit in Education;* E. W. Knight, *Public Education in the South;* R. G. Boone, *Education in the United States.*]

HARRY R. WARFEL

Schooner, THE, in its pure form, originated at Gloucester, Mass., in 1713–14. It is a fore-and-aft-rigged vessel, originally small (50- to 100-ton), with two masts, designed for coastwise trade, but developed in the 1880's and 1890's to vessels of two or three thousand tons, having 4, 5 and even 6 masts, engaged also in foreign trade. Only one 7-master was attempted (1901–2), the *Thomas Lawson,* 368 feet long, of 5200 tons.

The schooner has always stood as the favorite and distinctive rig of American waters.

[Winthrop L. Marvin, *The American Merchant Marine;* S. E. Morrison, *Maritime History of Massachusetts;* Babson, *History of Gloucester.*]

WILLIAM LINCOLN BROWN

Schooner *Exchange* v. McFaddon (7 Cranch 116, 1812). The nonsuability of a governmental instrumentality of a foreign state or sovereign was here established. The title of Napoleon to the schooner *Exchange,* used as a ship of war, "demeaning herself in a friendly manner" in our ports, could not be questioned in our courts whatever the grounds. Public vessels cannot be subjected to forfeiture.

HARVEY PINNEY

Schuyler, Fort. *See* Stanwix, Fort.

Schuylkill Fishing Company, claiming to be the oldest English-speaking social club in the world, was founded by twenty-seven gentlemen of Philadelphia in 1732, one of whom was James Logan, scholar, bibliophile and secretary for William Penn. The club's first quarters, called the Court House, was erected in 1748 on the west bank of the Schuylkill. William Warner donated the land to the Colony in Schuylkill (the club's original name) and was then made Baron by the "citizens," his socage fee being three sun perch carried to him on the Penn Platter each June. In 1781 the Colony in Schuylkill merged with St. David's Fishing Company and changed its name to the State in Schuylkill. The Court House was moved in 1812, in 1822, in 1843 and in 1887, when it was removed to Andalusia on the Delaware. Washington and many other famous men have enjoyed the hospitality, including the celebrated Fish House Punch, of this most exclusive and most distinguished of American social clubs.

[William Milnor, Jr., *History of the State in Schuylkill,* 1830; *History of the State in Schuylkill,* 1888.]

JULIAN P. BOYD

Schwenkfelders, THE, were followers of Caspar Schwenkfelder, 16th-century German religious reformer. Persecuted as sectarians, they emigrated to Pennsylvania in 1734. There are now six churches and 1800 members, with headquarters at Pennsburg, Pa.

[H. E. Kriebel, *Schwenkfelders in Pennsylvania.*]

AUGUSTUS H. SHEARER

Science Service is an institution for the popularization of science, organized in 1921 as a nonprofit corporation with trustees nominated by the National Academy of Sciences, the National Research Council, the American Association for the Advancement of Science, the E. W. Scripps estate and the journalistic profession. Disseminating scientific information to the public through services to newspapers, magazines, books, radio, etc., it is the liaison agency between scientific circles and the world at large.

WATSON DAVIS

Scientific Management. *See* Industrial Management.

Scientific Schools comprise those institutions of university grade whose educational programs are devoted to the sciences underlying engineering and industrial processes. Such schools have kept pace in their development with the growth of science itself. Under the stimulus of Avogadro's exposition of the structure of the molecule in 1811 and the publication of Dalton's *New System of Chemical Philosophy* in 1808, professorships in chemistry became active at Princeton and Yale colleges. A professorship of chemistry had already been endowed at Harvard in 1791. Such was the state of the sciences from which scientific schools had their origins.

Rensselaer School (later Polytechnic Institute) was founded in 1824 for the purpose of instructing persons to apply "science to the common purposes of life," the principal object being "to qualify teachers for instructing the sons and daughters of farmers and mechanics . . . in the application of experimental chemistry, philosophy and natural history to agriculture, domestic economy, the arts and manufactures."

Rensselaer School was reorganized in 1849 to become chiefly a school of civil engineering, with a curriculum modeled after the courses in the *École Centrale des Arts et Manufactures* of Paris. In 1847 the Lawrence Scientific School was established at Harvard, Sheffield Scientific School at Yale and an engineering school at the University of Michigan, formal engineering courses being offered in all three about 1852. In addition strong divisions of engineering have since been developed at other large universities, especially Columbia, Pennsylvania, Johns Hopkins and Stanford.

The Morrill Act[qv] of 1862 gave rise to state colleges of mechanic arts, many of which, notably Iowa (1862), Cornell (1865), Wisconsin (1867), Illinois (1867), Minnesota (1868), California (1868), Ohio (1870), Purdue (1874) and Texas (1881), have risen to a high level of scientific endeavor.

The same economic factors which stimulated the growth of the foregoing institutions gave rise to certain privately endowed schools, strongly scientific in character, such as Massachusetts Institute of Technology (chartered 1860, opened 1866), Lehigh University (1866), Carnegie Institute of Technology (1900) and California Institute of Technology (1910). The recognized colleges of engineering in the United States now number about one hundred.

All such institutions were essentially schools of applied science until early in the 20th century. In 1903 the Engineering Experiment Station was founded at the University of Illinois, and since that time experiment stations or research institutes have been established at all leading technological schools. They and the research laboratories in industry which they engendered have had a notable effect in implanting in engineering[qv] much of the investigative spirit which characterizes its present methodology.

[W. E. Wickenden, *A Comparative Study of Engineering Education in the United States and in Europe.*]

CLEMENT C. WILLIAMS

Scioto Company. In July, 1787, through the agency of Manasseh Cutler, the Ohio Company's[qv] representative, a group of New York speculators, headed by William Duer, Secretary of the Treasury Board, secured from Congress an option to a great tract of land lying north and west of the Ohio Company purchase and extending to the Scioto River on the west. As later surveyed, it contained 4,901,480 acres. Payment was to be made in six installments at 66⅔ cents an acre, the first payment due six months after the boundary had been surveyed. A number of New York and Massachusetts speculators divided the thirty shares among themselves with Duer, Royal Flint and Andrew Craigie acting as trustees, and Richard Platt as treasurer. Joel Barlow was sent to France as their agent and organized, with William Playfair, an unscrupulous Englishman, the Compagnie du Scioto to sell the Scioto lands. Although sales were active at first, little cash came in and the French company presently collapsed. The financial panic of 1792 swept away the fortunes of the leading American partners, and the Scioto Company defaulted on its contract with the Government. Gallipolis[qv] was the only settlement resulting from its efforts.

[E. O. Randall and D. J. Ryan, *History of Ohio*, Vol. II; A. B. Hulbert, *Records of the Ohio Company, Marietta College Historical Collections*, Vol. I.]

EUGENE H. ROSEBOOM

Scioto Gazette (Chillicothe, Ohio), established by Nathaniel Willis, April 25, 1800, later in the year absorbed *Freeman's Journal,* successor to the *Centinel of the North-Western Territory*[qqv], and thus claims lineage from the first newspaper in the Old Northwest[qv]. Published continuously, with little change of name, it was originally Democratic Republican, later Whig, and eventually Republican in politics.

[O. C. Hooper, *History of Ohio Journalism, 1793-1933.*]

EUGENE H. ROSEBOOM

Scioto Trail, The, followed the Sandusky and Scioto valleys almost due south from Sandusky Bay to the Ohio River and southward through

Kentucky to Cumberland Gap[qv]. A branch ran southeast from the Scioto along the divide west of the Hocking River to the mouth of the Great Kanawha River, which it followed into Virginia. The main trail was used both for the fur trade and as a warpath by northern Indians to reach the Cherokee and Catawba country, and during the American Revolution for invasions of Kentucky by the Ohio tribes. Part of the trail near Cumberland Gap, known as "Warrior's Path," was used for Boone's Wilderness Road[qqv].

[A. B. Hulbert, *Historic Highways of America*, Vol. II.]
EUGENE H. ROSEBOOM

Scopes Trial, THE. A Tennessee statute of March 21, 1925, forbade any educational institution supported by public funds "to teach the theory that denies the story of the divine creation of man as taught in the Bible." In a test case, John T. Scopes, a teacher of biology in the public schools of Dayton, Tenn., was tried in the following July for violation of the act, the trial attracting world-wide attention. Clarence Darrow and other distinguished counsel volunteered their services for the defendant, and William J. Bryan represented the state. The latter's appearance on the witness stand as an expert on the Bible constituted the climax of what the state supreme court afterward characterized as "this bizarre case." Scopes was convicted, but while the state supreme court upheld the constitutionality of the statute, sentence was set aside inasmuch as the trial court imposed a fine in excess of its authorized maximum. Further appeal was thereby prevented, but the trial not only added to the gaiety of nations, but undoubtedly led to the withdrawal of similar legislative projects in other states.

[There is a voluminous periodical literature accessible through the *Reader's Guide.*]
W. A. ROBINSON

Scotch-Irish, THE, in the American colonies and the United States emanated from the Scottish Protestants who were transplanted to Ulster, Ireland, chiefly during the 17th century, and from their descendants. The migrations from Scotland to Ulster, begun during the years from 1607 to 1609 under the sponsorship of James I, continued intermittently throughout the century. The settlers in their new environment naturally tended to adjust themselves and modify their customs. By the close of the century, however, adverse economic conditions and political and religious disabilities arose to create in them a desire to leave Ireland. Their farms were owned by absent English landlords who demanded high rentals; parliamentary regulation, 1665–80, seriously impaired their cattle-raising industry; the Woolens Act of 1699, which forbade the exportation of wool from Ireland, rendered sheep raising unprofitable; an act of Parliament in 1704, excluding Presbyterians from holding civil and military offices, denied them a voice in government; and the government taxed them to support the Anglican Church in which they did not worship. Consequently, thousands of these people from Ulster, with their Scotch heritage, with their experience in colonization, and with their Presbyterian faith, came to the American colonies.

The Scotch-Irish began to arrive in the American colonies as early as the middle of the 17th century, if not before, and continued to come in small numbers until about 1715. This influx was greatly accelerated after 1717, however, because of the efforts of English landlords to increase the rentals upon farms which had been held under long-term leases in Ulster and which expired in that year. Thereafter, a steady stream of Scotch-Irish poured into American ports, as many as ten thousand, reputedly, arriving in Pennsylvania within a single year. The total number of these immigrants to America has never been definitely ascertained but various studies indicate that probably 7% of the total population of the United States in 1790, or approximately 225,000 people, were Scotch-Irish or of Scotch-Irish extraction.

Upon their arrival in America, they scattered themselves throughout the colonies and established clusters of settlement in every colony. Their tendency was to penetrate to the frontiers[qv], however, following the main channels of migration to the fertile lands along the streams and in the valleys of the mountains of the back country. While some Scotch-Irish immigrants arrived in nearly every port along the Atlantic seaboard, Baltimore and Philadelphia were the chief ports of entry. From Baltimore many of these settlers followed the Potomac River westward to the Shenandoah Valley and turned southward into the back counties of Maryland, Virginia and the Carolinas or went westward to the Monongahela country in southwestern Pennsylvania; others went northward along the Susquehanna River and into the valleys between the mountain ranges in Pennsylvania. From Philadelphia, many followed the Delaware River to the north or went westward to the frontier. Thus, while Scotch-Irish settlers were found in every colony, the frontier regions of Pennsylvania and the southern colonies received the greater contingents. As the frontiers moved westward across the continent, the Scotch-Irish and their descendants, usually among the vanguard of settlers, migrated to the newer regions. While they may now be found in every state in the Union, they settled in greater numbers in Tennessee, Kentucky, Missouri, Ohio, Indiana and Illinois.

The Scotch-Irish contributions to the development of the United States have been great. Rugged and fearless, they made fine settlers on the more extended frontiers; their educated ministers gave an effective intellectual leadership and stimulated the founding of many institutions of higher learning; and their qualities for leadership and their inclination for politics produced from among them fine political leaders in every generation.

[Henry Jones Ford, *The Scotch-Irish in America.*]

R. J. FERGUSON

Scott, Fort, on the Marmaton River in Bourbon County, Kans., was established in 1842 as an intermediate post on the military road from Fort Leavenworth to Fort Gibson[qqv], which had been constructed to facilitate the protection of the Southwest from hostile Indians. It was abandoned as a post during 1853 and 1854. In 1855 the Government sold its substantial frame buildings at public auction, and shortly thereafter the present town of Fort Scott came into existence.

[T. F. Robley, *History of Bourbon County, Kansas.*]

RALPH P. BIEBER

Scott-Pillow Quarrel, THE (1847–48). Maj. Gen. G. J. Pillow, commanding Scott's Third Division in the Mexican War[qv], was a political appointee of President Polk. After the battle of Contreras[qv] he claimed, in his official report, undeserved credit for the victory. Scott courteously asked revision of the report. Pillow caused publication in the New Orleans *Delta* of an anonymous and vainglorious account of his military prowess, exasperating Scott. Arrested for insubordination and disrespect, he appeared before the same court that investigated Scott's conduct. Both were exonerated, but Pillow was discredited by the army.

[Justin H. Smith, *The War with Mexico;* C. W. Elliott, *Winfield Scott, The Soldier and the Man.*]

CHARLES WINSLOW ELLIOTT

Scottsboro Case, THE. In March, 1931, in the court at Scottsboro, Ala., eight of nine Negroes, charged with the rape of two white women, were convicted and sentenced to death. This case remained in the courts for six years, creating nationwide attention and arousing much racial prejudice. In November, 1932, the Supreme Court of the United States ordered a new trial, on the ground that the defendants had been denied adequate counsel. In 1934, the case having been retried twice in the meantime, the Supreme Court ordered a new trial, on the ground that Alabama excluded Negroes from jury service. Finally, in 1938 the Supreme Court denied new trials to four of the defendants, one of whom in their last trial had received the death sentence and three of whom had received long prison sentences. The other defendants had been released in 1937.

HUGH T. LEFLER

Scouting on the Plains. Fur trappers who penetrated the West before the advent of civilization acquired a remarkable knowledge of the geography and savage tribes of the country which fitted them to be scouts and guides in the later military campaigns on the plains. Such celebrated scouts as Kit Carson, Jim Bridger, Bill Williams, Charlie Reynolds, Billy Comstock, Sharp Grover and others were former fur trappers, while others including Billy Dixon and W. F. (Buffalo Bill) Cody were in the allied occupation of buffalo[qv] hunting.

For all the skill of these white frontiersmen, however, the army would have been seriously handicapped had it not been for friendly Indian scouts. Thus, Osage guides led Custer's march in the Washita campaign[qv] of 1868; the Pawnee battalion under Frank and Luther North took Carr to the Cheyenne village at Summit Springs in 1869, Mackenzie to Dull Knife's[qv] camp on the Crazy Woman in 1878, and did much scouting and fighting elsewhere; Tonkawa, Delaware, Seminole and other scouts guided Miles, Mackenzie and other officers in the Indian Territory uprising of 1874 (*see* Red River Indian War); Shoshone, Crow and Arickaree warriors did the trailing and much of the fighting for the commands of Custer, Crook and Miles in the Sitting Bull Sioux war[qv] of 1876–77; and Cheyennes and Sioux performed important services in the Ghost Dance[qv] uprising of their own people in 1890–91.

In the Southwest, friendly Apache, Mojave, Papago and other Indian scouts actually bore the brunt of many campaigns against hostile Apaches, notably in the Geronimo wars[qv]. Scouting on the plains required rare qualities of endurance, plainscraft, courage and wisdom, so that a military commander could be said to have been no more successful than the excellence of his body of Indian and white scouts permitted.

[George Bird Grinnell, *Two Great Scouts and the Pawnee Battalion;* Paul I. Wellman, *Death on the Prairie.*]

PAUL I. WELLMAN

Scurvy. Writing to his wife in England who was preparing to join him in Massachusetts,

John Winthrop cautioned her (1631): "Remember to bringe juice of lemons to sea with thee, for thee and thy company to eate with your meate as sauce." John Josselyn published (1674) a warning to New England voyagers to provide themselves with the "juice of Lemons well put up to cure, or prevent the scurvy." Scurvy afflicted the crew of Sebastian Vizcaino when he explored the coast of California (1602); it decimated the companions of California's first physician, Don Pedro Prat (1769); and it ravaged the passengers who came to California by boat during the Gold Rush (1848–53). The captains admitted to an indignant health officer that the shipowners would not permit them to stop on the way to take fresh vegetables on board. The calamity of sailors, and the scourge of settlers, fatal scurvy continued to flourish while the simple remedy for its control was definitely known. The first in the United States to describe night-blindness (1842) as one of the symptoms of scurvy was Edward Coale, who noted that, due to the fact that so many men of the frigate *Columbia* could not see after sundown, deck work had to be discontinued. Since the recognition of scurvy as a disorder of metabolism due to deficiency of the antiscorbutic vitamin (Vitamin C), scurvy has ceased to be a major problem in the public health[qv] of America.

[Alfred Fabian Hess, *Scurvy, Past and Present.*]

VICTOR ROBINSON

Sea Fencibles, THE, were the first organization of the United States Army charged exclusively with coast defense. By act of Congress of July 26, 1813, ten separate companies were organized to be employed "as well on land as on water for the defense of the ports and harbors." Each company consisted of a captain, first lieutenant, second lieutenant, third lieutenant, boatswain, six gunners, six quarter-gunners and ninety privates; in aggregate 1070 men. The fencibles were discharged June 15, 1815. Their most notable service was at the defense of Fort McHenry[qv], Sept. 13, 1814, where the companies of Captains M. Simmones Bunbury and William H. Addison formed part of the garrison, which also included the "Baltimore Fencibles," one of several volunteer companies of the same class of troops.

[Francis B. Heitman, *A Historical Register and Dictionary of the United States Army;* Benson J. Lossing, *The Pictorial Field-Book of the War of 1812.*]

DON RUSSELL

Sea Otter Trade. Europeans and Americans first came to the North Pacific coast of America for sea otter skins. While beaver trapping was drawing furmen from the Atlantic seaboard into the interior of North America, the sea otter trade caused mariners to push into the North Pacific, where they established bases whence they ran the coast from the Aleutian Islands to Lower California. In China sea otter furs were exchanged at good profit for prized oriental goods.

Russia and Spain were the pioneer nations to engage in this trade. After the Bering expeditions of the early 18th century, *promishleniki* (fur traders) pushed eastward until in 1784 the first permanent Russian settlement in America was established on Kadiak Island[qv]. In the same year Spain organized a sea otter trade between California and China. The great fur rush to the Northwest coast was caused by published accounts of Capt. Cook's[qv] last Pacific voyage, 1776–80. English and American vessels led the drive, but within a decade the former had practically withdrawn. At the opening of the 19th century American and Russian traders entered the California sea otter fields where in the face of strong opposition they poached throughout the Spanish period. After 1821 the liberal commercial policy of independent Mexico stimulated the California otter trade, and many Americans became Mexican citizens in order to participate in the business.

The number of skins obtained in the sea otter trade can only be estimated. From 1804 to 1807 it was reported that 59,346 furs were taken by American vessels, while the period 1808 to 1812 yielded 47,962. The greatest number of skins known to have been taken from the California coast in any one year was 10,638 in 1811. By 1818 the number decreased to 4500.

The sea otter trade came to an end when ruthless hunting, intensified by the introduction of firearms, exterminated the animals. In general, the fur areas were exhausted in the order in which they were opened, and at approximately the following dates—Kamtchatka and the westernmost Aleutian Islands, 1790; Kadiak, 1805; Sitka to Nootka Sound, 1820; and California, 1840.

[H. H. Bancroft, *History of California* and *History of the Northwest Coast;* C. J. DuFour, E. O. Essig, Adele Ogden, *The Russians in California;* F. A. Golder, *Russian Expansion on the Pacific, 1641-1850;* K. W. Porter, *John Jacob Astor, Business Man.*]

ADELE OGDEN

Sea Power. Although the influence of sea power has been known to historians since Thucydides, it was Alfred T. Mahan who first impressed it on the modern world. His definition includes in sea power all those forces in na-

Sea Power

tional life which tend to give a nation strength on the sea—military and merchant navies, naval and commercial bases, advantageous position in relation to trade routes, good harbors, a seafaring population, and a political system which allows sufficient concentration of authority to administer large fleets. In the New World these factors have been present in some measure from the first, for its very discovery and colonization depended on maritime enterprise. Only a nation strong on the sea, like England, could ever permanently colonize North America. By 1763 French inferiority at sea had lost her all her possessions on the mainland, and Spanish galleons bringing home the wealth of Mexico and Peru were at the mercy of English seamen such as Drake, Blake and Rodney.

The causes of many American wars have been connected with control of the sea and of the commerce it carries. The triangular trade[qv] of the American colonies was so lucrative that when George III interfered, revolt soon appeared. Our wars with France and the Barbary States were the result of interference with our rapidly developing commerce, and the War of 1812 had as its most prominent causes impressment and the restrictions on our trade as neutrals which were produced by British Orders in Council and French Decrees[qqv]. The United States entered the World War[qv] primarily because German submarines destroyed American ships and lives by operating in defiance of the accepted rules of international law regarding neutral shipping.

It has been said that seven out of the eight wars in which the United States has engaged have been won by sea power. This is true of the Revolutionary struggle in that French assistance was vital to American success. The French naval threat in Europe kept many British ships at home and thus enabled needed supplies and a French army to reach American shores. When DeGrasse with his French fleet off the Chesapeake capes forced the British admiral Graves to abandon his attempt to relieve Cornwallis, the decisive victory at Yorktown[qv] was assured.

In the War of 1812 the small American navy on the Atlantic had to succumb to superior British forces and could win only isolated engagements of little strategic value. But on the inland waterways hastily improvised fleets demonstrated the advantages of sea power. Perry's capture of the British squadron on Lake Erie enabled Gen. Harrison to transport his troops across the lake and defeat Tecumseh at the battle of the Thames[qqv]. On Lake Champlain Macdonough[qv] prevented an invasion of New York and saved the northern boundary in the peace negotiations a few months later.

The Civil War was won indirectly by the blockade[qv] instituted by the navy. This cut off the South from the war supplies she could not manufacture and prevented the export of cotton, her chief economic support abroad. When the capture of Fort Fisher[qv] at Wilmington stopped blockade running[qv], lack of arms, munitions, clothing, medicines and even food, soon brought Lee's surrender. The threat of intervention by France or England was met by the building of iron monitors[qv] superior to any ships Europe could send to our shores. Also in the World War the navy, by protecting troops and supplies against the German submarine menace, safeguarded the vital needs of the Allies.

American foreign commerce, always an important element in the national strength, has developed under the protection of sea power. British sea power sheltered it in colonial times and gave it many advantages. Against the Barbary pirates and the pirates of the West Indies the navy waged successful wars. In the decades preceding the Civil War commercial sea power was as important an activity as the settlement of the West, due largely to the demands of Europe for wheat, cotton and lumber, and to the discovery of gold in California (*see* Clipper Ships). In 1860 the American merchant marine[qv] was virtually equal to Great Britain's. Its decline was caused in about equal measure by British development of the iron steamship, the activities of Confederate raiders such as the *Alabama*[qv], and by American absorption in the West and in manufacturing, by that time a better investment for American dollars.

In carrying out the chief policies of the United States as a "world power"—a position for which the naval victories of Manila Bay and Santiago[qqv] were mainly responsible—especially the protection of the Philippines, the Panama Canal and our commercial interests in Latin America and the Far East, sea power has become a necessary reliance. The navy has become the nation's first line of defense. With the increase of these needs it has grown from insignificance to parity with Great Britain. When opportunities for commercial and political expansion shifted to the Pacific, the American fleet was transferred to that area and Hawaii made our chief naval and military outpost.

Proposals and treaties for the limitation of naval armaments have been only partially successful because sea power has been recognized as so important that no nation wishes to tie its hands in this respect (*see* Naval Limitation Conferences). As long as the United States is committed to the defense of distant possessions, the Panama Canal, the Monroe Doctrine, and its rights to trade in peace and war, it will continue to maintain the advantages of sea power.

[A. T. Mahan, *The Major Operations of the Navies in the War of American Independence; Sea Power in Its Relations to the War of 1812; Lessons of the War with Spain;* Krafft and Norris, *Sea Power in American History;* H. C. Bywater, *Sea Power in the Pacific.*]

WALTER B. NORRIS

Seal, Great, of the Confederate States of America. Ordered by the Confederate Congress[qv], April 30, 1863, and decreed to depict Crawford's esquestrian statue of Washington in Richmond with the date Feb. 22, 1862, and the motto *Deo Vindice,* the seal was cut in solid silver by Joseph S. Wyon of London. It was about four inches in diameter, cost about $600 and, with its ivory handle, weighed about four pounds. It reached Richmond in September, 1864, but was never affixed to any document. After a romantic career it came into the custody of the Confederate Museum at Richmond, Va.

[Gaillard Hunt, *Harper's Weekly*, Sept. 21, 1912.]

JOHN C. FITZPATRICK

Seal, Great, of the United States. The day the Continental Congress[qv] declared the United States an independent nation it appointed a committee to devise a great seal with which to authenticate its formal, official documents. The necessity was obvious; but after more than six weeks the committee could suggest only a weird jumble of impossible heraldic detail and biblical legend. It took Congress six years more to obtain a satisfactory design. The obverse of the seal finally adopted was the design of Secretary Charles Thomson. William Barton's idea was selected for the reverse. Both obverse and reverse are pictured on the United States one-dollar note (series of 1935). The Great Seal is kept by the Secretary of State and is affixed only on the signed order of the President. A circle of special white paper, with serrated edge, is attached to the document, and the seal impressed through both by a metal die. From 1856 to 1869 a special wax impression (about 6 inches in diameter), enclosed in a gold or silver box, was attached to treaties by silken cords. Although recut three times (1841, 1883 and 1902) to improve its artistic appearance the Great Seal has always been precisely as decreed by the Continental Congress, June 20, 1782.

[Gaillard Hunt, *History of the Seal of the United States.*]

JOHN C. FITZPATRICK

Seal Fisheries. Walrus sealing, in Arctic waters, began in connection with whaling[qv] early in the 17th century. Several varieties of smaller seals began to be hunted actively late in the 18th century. They are found all the way from near the White Sea to Greenland, Newfoundland and Labrador. In those regions Norwegians, Canadians and Americans still capture more than half a million young male seals each year, leaving the cows and the mature bulls for breeding purposes. A somewhat similar though less fruitful situation exists in Antarctic waters.

American interest, however, centers largely in the fur seal herd of the Pribilof Islands[qv], St. Paul and St. George, in Bering Sea. The herd is not stationary, the seal being migratory, its movements determined by the temperature of sea water; but those islands contain the "rookeries" or breeding grounds to which the herd returns, from far south, every spring. There the young are born and grow strong enough to endure the winter migration which takes them to the latitude of California and Mexico.

This Bering Sea herd was discovered on Bering's second Alaska voyage, in 1741, and was described by Steller, the German naturalist of the expedition. For more than half a century thereafter the chaotic Russian fur trade of Alaska threatened the complete destruction of the herd, but it was saved when the business of seal catching came to be regulated by the monopolistic Russian-American Company[qv]. Under that company's wise management the herd increased, though with some fluctuations, and when the United States bought Alaska[qv] in 1867 it was of considerable consequence.

Alaska at that time was by many considered worthless. But the tiny seal islands were a valuable estate. The Government in 1869 leased them to the Alaska Commercial Company[qv] for $55,000 per year. In addition the company agreed to pay $2.62½ for every seal skin shipped from the islands and an additional $.55 per gallon for all seal oil made. It was licensed to kill 100,000 male seals over one year old.

The latter provision was too generous and in consequence the herd declined. Scientists at a later time maintained that no male under three years of age should be killed, or the proper proportion between breeding males and females would be injuriously affected. The Government tried the plan of obtaining expert opinion from time to time and limiting the kill accordingly. Experts, however, were sometimes too liberal and the company was always under the temptation to make its annual operations for the year show a good profit. So the herd continued to decrease. A new contract in 1890 gave the Government better returns: $60,000 for rental, $2.00 per skin revenue charge and $7.62½ for every seal killed.

But, by that time the herd seemed to be doomed through the activity of pelagic or deep-sea sealers. Land killing could be regulated; but since several different nationalities—the Americans, Canadians, Mexicans, Russians and Japanese—preyed upon the herd at sea, sometimes aggregating in a single year more than 100,000 seals, it was a serious problem what could be done to save a remnant of the herd.

At that point James G. Blaine, then Secretary of State, set up the theory that Bering Sea was *Mare Clausum*[qv] (a closed sea) which the United States Government had a right to police. To be sure, many seals were killed in the Pacific also, but the greatest destruction was caused during the period when the young were being fed by their mothers on the islands, for the killing of mother seals visiting the cod banks for food meant the death of an equal number of pups on the rookeries.

When several Canadian vessels were seized Blaine's theory was tested and in 1893 an arbitration tribunal at Paris pronounced it untenable. For years it seemed as if the herd was doomed, but finally a treaty signed by Britain, Russia, Japan and the United States outlawed pelagic sealing. The Government tightened its regulations about killing seals. Consequently the herd is increasing. In 1925 the number of males killed was 19,860, in 1937 it was 55,180. Thus did conservation justify itself.

[*Investigation of the Fur Seal Industry of Alaska*, Washington, 1914; *Annual Reports of the Governor of Alaska;* J. Schafer, *The Pacific Slope and Alaska.*]

JOSEPH SCHAFER

Sealers, Town, are officers chosen by the New England town meeting for annual terms to test and certify the accuracy of weights, scales and measures. Their services are frequently called for in disputes involving the weight of hay, coal, livestock, etc. Payment is usually by fee.

[J. S. Garland, *New England Town Law.*]

W. A. ROBINSON

Search, Right of. *See* Visit and Search; also Unreasonable Searches and Seizures.

Seceded States, Representation of the, at Washington (1861–64). With the exception of five representatives from the northwestern counties of Virginia, none of the seceded states was represented in the House of Representatives after May, 1861. Individuals elected by "rump" conventions and legislatures in North Carolina and northern Virginia (the Alexandria government) applied for admission, but they were denied their seats. Under Lincoln's direction, loyal governments were organized in 1864 in Tennessee, Arkansas and Louisiana, each of which sent senators and representatives to Washington, but both houses of Congress refused to seat the aspiring legislators. Two senators, elected by the loyal part of the Virginia legislature, were admitted by the Senate in July, 1861. Andrew Johnson, of Tennessee, however, was the only regularly elected senator from one of the seceded states who retained his seat in the United States Senate. He continued his senatorial duties until he was appointed military governor of Tennessee in March, 1862.

[W. A. Dunning, *Reconstruction, Political and Economic;* J. C. McGregor, *The Disruption of Virginia; The Congressional Globe*, 37th, 38th Congresses.]

RICHARD E. YATES

Secession, The Ordinance of, was the enactment in legal form by which eleven Southern states withdrew from the Union in 1860–61. According to the compact theory[qv] of union, sovereign states had entered the partnership by ratifying the Constitution of the United States. Secession, therefore, was achieved by a repeal of the act of ratification. This was accomplished in each state by a convention, elected for the purpose, as the instrumentality of government most nearly expressive of the sovereign will.

[D. L. Dumond, *The Secession Movement, 1860-1861.*]

C. MILDRED THOMPSON

Secession, The Right of. The Southern states of the American Union were advancing no new theory when they appealed to and exercised the right of secession[qv] in 1860. Publicists and statesmen had championed the right from the beginning of American independence. The right of a people to establish, alter and abolish their government, and to institute a new one if their safety and happiness demanded it was a fundamental principle of the American Revolution (*see* Declaration of Independence). This idea was the basis of the threat of both Vermont (*see* Haldimand Negotiations) and Kentucky (*see* Spanish Conspiracy; Western Separatism) to separate from the Confederation[qv] and set up independent governments, or to ally with some foreign power, during the 1780's.

More specifically the right of secession was based upon the doctrine of state sovereignty and the compact theory[qqv] of the Union. James Madison stated this theory very clearly when he wrote: "Our governmental system is established by *compact,* not between the Government of the United States and the State *Governments* but between the STATES AS SOVEREIGN COMMUNITIES, *stipulating* EACH with THE OTHER. . . ."

The first serious threat of secession came in 1798 when the Democratic Republicans (*see* Republican Party, Jeffersonian), smarting under Federalist[q.v.] legislation, talked of separation. John Taylor of Caroline openly advocated secession but the more moderate views of Jefferson prevailed, and Virginia and Kentucky adopted their Resolutions[q.v.] condemning the legislation as unconstitutional, null and void, and proclaiming the right of the states to interpose or nullify such acts. Jefferson's purpose was to appeal to the people in the election of 1800, rather than ...pply either nullification or secession.

...fter Jefferson's victory in 1801 the New Eng...d Federalists sought a remedy against Demo...tic domination. Sen. Timothy Pickering said ...at "the principles of our Revolution point to ...e remedy—a separation." The purchase of ...ouisiana[q.v.] further antagonized the Federalists and the Essex Junto[q.v.] planned a new confederacy composed of New England and New York, "exempt from the corrupt . . . influence and oppression of the aristocratic democrats of the South." Alexander Hamilton blocked their efforts but Josiah Quincy still maintained in 1811 that the admission of Louisiana would dissolve the Union. The disgruntled Federalists of New England resorted to treasonable action in opposing "Mr. Madison's war," and in 1814 met in the Hartford Convention[q.v.] behind closed doors and in utmost secrecy. There is little doubt that their object was the dissolution of the Union and the formation of a New England Confederacy if their program of constitutional reform failed. Fortunately the news of the peace treaty prevented action.

The next rumblings of discontent were heard in the Southern states. Threats of separation were made over both the Missouri question (*see* Missouri Compromise) and the Indian controversy (*see* Cherokee Nation v. Georgia), and the tariff issue brought these threats to the very threshold of action. South Carolina nullified the tariff acts of 1828 and 1832 and signified her intention of seceding if the Federal Government attempted to coerce her (*see* Nullification).

Slavery[q.v.] in the territories caused both North and South to threaten to secede. John Quincy Adams thought the free states would secede if Texas[q.v.] were annexed, and the Southern leaders threatened separation if slavery were excluded from the Mexican cession[q.v.]. This controversy culminated in the assembling of the Nashville Convention of 1850[q.v.] and of state conventions in several Southern states. These conventions reluctantly accepted the Compromise of 1850[q.v.] and secession was halted. The abolitionists[q.v.] called a convention of all the free states to meet at Cleveland in 1857 to consider separation, but the depression prevented the meeting.

The threat of secession had been the last resort of the minority to protect its interests under the Constitution, and had been constantly present from the Revolution to the Civil War.

[H. V. Ames, *State Documents on Federal Relations;* C. R. Brown, *The Northern Confederacy According to the Plans of the Essex Junto;* Edward Channing, *History of the United States;* E. W. R. Ewing, *Northern Rebellion and Southern Secession;* P. M. Hamer, *The Secession Movement in South Carolina;* C. W. Harris, *The Sectional Struggle;* D. W. Howe, *Political History of Secession;* E. P. Powell, *Nullification and Secession in the United States.*]

FLETCHER M. GREEN

Secession of Southern States. Upon Lincoln's election the governor of South Carolina recommended and the legislature called a state convention (that being the method by which the Constitution of 1787 was ratified) which met amidst great excitement and on Dec. 20, 1861, by a unanimous vote, passed an ordinance dissolving "the union now subsisting between South Carolina and other States." The convention issued a "Declaration of Immediate Causes," expressing the state rights[q.v.] view of the Union, and appointed commissioners to other Southern states and to Washington. By many who favored further efforts to secure constitutional rights (through an all-Southern convention, appeals to the North, or compromise through Congress) this action seemed precipitate. But South Carolina had assurances that other states would follow, and many thought that better terms might be made out of the Union than in it. Overriding minorities, six other states by conventions passed ordinances of secession: Mississippi, Jan. 9 (84 to 15); Florida, Jan. 10 (62 to 7); Alabama, Jan. 11 (61 to 39); Georgia, Jan. 19 (164 to 133); Louisiana, Jan. 26 (113 to 17); and Texas (over the opposition of Gov. Houston), Feb. 1 (166 to 8), thus completing the secession of the lower South. Nearly all who voted against secession did so because they doubted its expediency, not the right.

Buchanan, believing secession unconstitutional but considering himself without authority to coerce, and anxious not to give the upper South cause for secession, was determined not to risk war by an overt act in protecting Federal property (forts, arsenals, post offices, etc.) and sustaining the operation of Federal laws. The South

Carolina commissioners, sent to negotiate with Buchanan for the peaceful division of property, debts, etc., demanded that Maj. Anderson, then occupying Fort Sumter*qv* in Charleston harbor, evacuate that post as inconsistent with the sovereignty of South Carolina. This he refused. Meanwhile Congress, despite an address from some Southern members saying that "All hope of relief in the Union, through the agency of committees, Congressional legislation, or constitutional amendments, is extinguished," was sifting compromise proposals. Of these the Crittenden Compromise, involving the extension of the Missouri Compromise*qqv* line, was the more hopeful, but it failed to get the support of the Republican leaders, as did Crittenden's suggestion for a national referendum. More certain was the failure (because opposed by the extremists on either side) of the Washington Peace Conference (Border Slave State Convention*qv*) which, two months later, presented proposals similar to Crittenden's.

With compromise failing and with Buchanan taking a firmer attitude as he became less hopeful of peace and union (he sent the *Star of the West*qv to reinforce Sumter) representatives from the seceded states met at Montgomery*qv* (Feb. 4, 1861) to organize a new nation. Lincoln's inaugural promise "to hold, occupy, and possess the property and places belonging to the government," coupled with his assertion that "Physically speaking, we cannot separate," seemed none the less threatening by his assurance that "The government will not assail you." Peaceful secession seemed remote after Lincoln's fateful decision to relieve Fort Sumter, the firing on the fort and Lincoln's call for volunteers. This practical state of war compelled the states of the upper South to make a reluctant choice between the Confederacy*qv* and the Union.

One month after Lincoln's inauguration the Virginia convention voted against secession (88 to 45), preferring a conference of the border states*qv* and further discussions with Lincoln. But two days after the call for volunteers the convention (April 17) adopted the ordinance of secession (88 to 55) which was ratified by popular vote on May 23, although the convention had entered into a military league with the Confederacy on April 24. In Arkansas opinion was very evenly divided (a popular referendum had been set for Aug. 5), but the governor rejected Lincoln's call for militia and on May 6 the convention passed the secession ordinance (65 to 5). Tennessee, like Virginia, had large nonslaveholding sections where many people for geographic, economic or social reasons did not feel that their interests would be served by the Confederacy. The legislature on Jan. 19 provided for a popular vote for delegates to a convention and for the convention itself which was rejected (69,675 to 57,798). After the firing on Fort Sumter and the threat of coercion, the legislature ratified a league with the Confederacy (May 7) and authorized the governor to raise a force of 55,000 men. On June 8 the people voted for secession (104,913 to 47,238). The opposition to secession in western Virginia led to the formation of a separate state (*see* West Virginia); a like movement in eastern Tennessee proved abortive. The unanimous vote for secession by the convention of North Carolina, the last state to secede (May 20), was clearly the result of Lincoln's proclamation. The border slave states of Kentucky, Maryland, Delaware and Missouri did not secede and Kentucky's attempted neutrality failed.

[D. L. Dumond, *The Secession Movement, 1860-1861*.]

R. H. WOODY

Secret Protocol, The. During the conversations preceding the signature of the Lansing-Ishii Agreement of Nov. 2, 1917, Secretary of State Lansing had striven to include in the agreement the following statement: "They [the Governments of the United States and Japan] will not take advantage of the present conditions to seek special rights or privileges in China which would abridge the rights of subjects or citizens of other friendly states." This was precisely what the Japanese negotiator did not wish to accept, because it was Japan's real policy to take advantage of the conditions which existed in China in order to secure a special position there. With the express approval of President Wilson, this formula was relegated to a secret protocol signed simultaneously with the public agreement. But the language of the secret protocol sounds more like an epitaph for the formula than a confirmation of it, because it records that: "Upon careful examination of the question, it was agreed that the clause above quoted being superfluous in the relations of the two Governments and liable to create erroneous impressions in the minds of the public, should be eliminated from the declaration. It was, however, well understood that the principle enunciated in the clause which was thus suppressed was in perfect accord with the declared policy of the two Governments in regard to China."

[*War Memoirs of Robert Lansing; The Lansing Papers, 1914-1920,* Dept. of State Publication, 1421.]

SAMUEL FLAGG BEMIS

Secret Service, The, is a division of the United States Treasury intrusted with the detection of crime of those who attempt to defraud the United States Treasury. Though not originally established by law nor recognized by Congress with special appropriations, it was established in 1864 with a brigadier general of volunteers as its chief officer. When it was organized, its special function was the detection and arrest of counterfeiters, moonshiners and smugglers[qqv].

Since Lincoln's death the Secret Service has detailed trained men to guard the person of the President at the White House and to accompany him when he is away from Washington. President McKinley's death in 1901 caused the Secret Service to increase its vigilance in protecting the life of the President. Not only must it protect the President and his family but also the person elected to be President and his family as well. Besides protecting the chief executive of the nation, the Secret Service sends men to foreign countries to watch for smugglers; others to the Appalachian Mountains to spy on moonshiners, and still others to watch for income-tax evasions.

After the Civil War, for nearly a half century, the chief work of the Secret Service was the swift detection and punishment of counterfeiters. Such work required men of nerve, bravery and wit. During the World War the Secret Service was active in uncovering plots designed to destroy or otherwise interfere with the manufacture and shipping of war munitions by aliens resident abroad.

It is also the duty of the Secret Service "to investigate matters relating to the Treasury Department and the several branches of the public service under its control as directed by the Secretary of the Treasury." As a consequence collections of pictures of international crooks were started in 1875. They were pasted in albums after 1888. By 1901 over 3000 pictures had been collected.

The War Department also employs men to obtain information of various kinds; the Post Office Department has an inspection department to protect the public against frauds through the mails; and the Department of Justice has the Federal Bureau of Investigation[qv].

[R. W. Rowan, *The Story of Secret Service.*]

FRANK MARTIN LEMON

Secret Societies. These organizations found in rudimentary form even among primitive peoples and appearing in all lands and ages have been especially numerous and active in the United States. Organized, in most instances, for the social and moral welfare of their members and to promote good-fellowship and patriotism, they have apparently met a deep-seated psychological need in the American people. In addition they have done an enormous amount of charitable and educational work which has been of advantage to the general community. The Masonic order whose ritual and philosophy have influenced many similar organizations, was introduced from Great Britain about 1730, the Independent Order of Oddfellows from the same country in 1819. A roster of indigenous societies would reach encyclopædic proportions. A few well-known ones are the Knights of Pythias founded in 1864, the Benevolent and Protective Order of Elks, 1866, the Knights of Columbus[qv], 1882, the Loyal Order of Moose, 1887.

For a decade following 1826 there was a strong popular prejudice against secret orders. While directed primarily against the Masons, even college fraternities were under popular disfavor and an extensive literature of exposure and denunciation poured from the press. The movement soon subsided, Masonry[qv] quickly revived, new societies were formed and ritual and secrecy were effectively used to promote a wide variety of causes—temperance, liquor control, agricultural improvement, life insurance, the betterment of underprivileged racial and economic groups. Local societies have occasionally shown vigilante proclivities, pursuing alleged evildoers with tar and feathers, birch rods, or even more lethal weapons.

The subversive and revolutionary secret society, so common in European countries, has had an unfruitful field in America although the pre-Revolutionary activity of the Sons of Liberty and the disloyal operations of the Knights of the Golden Circle[qqv] during the Civil War are somewhat analogous. Antiforeign and anti-Catholic prejudice produced the secret Know-Nothing party[qv] in the 1850's and history repeated itself seventy years later in the similar activities of the Ku Klux Klan[qv]. For the most part American secret societies have avoided direct participation in politics, but the mere existence of large and cohesive bodies of brethren has made them a factor to be considered by the astute party leader. Predictions that the increasing urbanization of American life, the radio, the automobile, popularity of sports[qqv], etc., would be adverse to societies seem to have been unfounded although they have always shown a marked shrinkage in periods of depression, that following 1929 being especially serious.

[Charles W. Ferguson, *Fifty Million Brothers.*]

W. A. ROBINSON

Sectionalism. The older American historians were inclined to regard the sectional struggles that culminated in the Civil War and Reconstruction[qqv] as essentially a contest between freedom and democracy on the one hand and slavery and oligarchy on the other. But a later and more dispassionate generation of scholars, whose historical philosophy has been given classic expression in the later writings of Frederick Jackson Turner, look upon sectionalism as the permanent product of climate, soil, geography, race and natural resources. The basic factors of sectionalism being thus regarded as permanent, sectional conflict within the United States is frankly recognized as not having begun with the slavery issue nor as having come to an end with emancipation. Indeed sectionalism has been accepted as a continuing reality in American life.

While the United States is divided into several natural regions, politically these areas have usually aligned themselves into three or four sections. Before 1860, in a general sense, these groupings were the East, the South and the West. The social and economic interests of the dominant groups of the East centered in commerce, industry and finance, while the dominant groups as well as the masses of the South and West were engaged in agriculture[qv]. The East desired a protective tariff, a national bank, internal improvement[qqv] at national expense, and it opposed territorial expansion and free lands for settlers—until it became clear that the settlers might become political allies. The South asked little of the National Government in domestic affairs, but was imperialistic[qv] in foreign affairs. It favored territorial expansion and free land[qv] until it became apparent that such lands would be settled by immigrants unfriendly to the South. It opposed a protective tariff—except in 1816 while still under the shadow of the War of 1812; it objected to a national bank and internal improvements at national expense. In fact the South opposed the entire program of the East. The West was agreed with the South on all save two items: it wanted internal improvements at national expense and it was not averse to a protective tariff. An alliance between the South and West was, therefore, a natural consequence of the near identity of interests of the two sections. When it is recalled that the majority of the inhabitants of the Old Northwest[qv] were of Southern origin or descent as late as 1850 it will be even more obvious that a political alliance between South and West was the normal thing until the end of the first half of the 19th century.

The combination of South and West was not made—or if made was not strong enough to gain control of the National Government—until the election of 1800. During the preceding twelve years the East through the medium of the Federalist party[qv] had controlled the Federal Government and had put much of its program into operation to the supposed detriment of the rest of the country. After the Jeffersonian party came into power in 1801 (*see* Campaign of 1800), the combination of South and West, with three exceptions, elected the President and usually held a majority in Congress until 1860. It is a mistake, however, to say that the South controlled the National Government during this time. Perhaps it is not incorrect to say that the South determined the selection of President, and that it usually had more influence with the President than did the Western or the Eastern Democrats. But the South did not control Congress—nor the judiciary[qv] until after John Marshall's death. Despite the ability of the South to designate the presidential nominee and despite the fact that Congress more often than not had a majority of Democrats, the South had no control over Congress on issues of a sectional nature. Turner has made a microscopical study of sectionalism from 1820 to 1850 and he has found that political lines broke down in the face of sectional issues, so that Eastern and Western Whigs and Democrats often voted side by side against Southern Whigs and Democrats.

Reconstruction, following upon Civil War, was an attempt to form an alliance between the East and South by means of the Negro vote and the disfranchisement of the white leaders. This alliance was successful only long enough to place Grant and Hayes in the White House. Its aftermath was the Solid (white) South[qv] and the virtual disfranchisement[qv] of the Negro race. Perhaps an unexpected result of Reconstruction was the creation of a Republican West which remained the steadfast ally of the East for many years.

One of the issues that transcended sectional and party alignments was slavery[qv]. While the South before the Missouri Compromise[qv] agreed in the abstract with the other sections that slavery was an evil, after that event and under the attack of the radical abolitionists[qv], it reversed its position and defended slavery on principle (*see* Proslavery). Since the extension of slavery into the territories involved the balance of power between the East and the South, if not between the slave and free states, it was inevitable that the slavery issue should be injected into politics. The moral and religious fervor which the radical abolitionists added to the political controversy over slavery made it inevitable that slavery should become a sectional rather than a party issue, and it was the mutual hostility aroused in the West and the South over the right of extension of slavery into the territories that finally destroyed the political alliance of those two sections and contributed powerfully to the creation of the East-West combination that brought the Republican party[qv] into power, and precipitated the secession[qv] of the South. However, it is not meant to state positively that slavery was the cause of secession and the Civil War. It was, without much doubt, the most potent single cause; but the conflicting economic and social interests that had characterized the sections, and had created sectionalism before the slavery issue became important, were even greater in 1860 than ever before, and furnished the underlying causes for the South's attempted withdrawal from the Union.

While the East has been the dominant power since Reconstruction—usually symbolized by Wall Street[qv]—the other sections of the country have not failed to fight for what they considered their own interests. The Greenback Movement, the Granger laws, the Populist party, the Interstate Commerce Commissions, Free Silver, the Federal Reserve Banking System, the Agricultural Adjustment Administration programs and the Antitrust Laws[qqv] were moves of the hinterland sections against the dominant East.

[Frederick Jackson Turner, *The Rise of the New West*, *The United States, 1830-50*, and *The Significance of Sections in United States History;* William E. Dodd, *Expansion and Conflict.*]
FRANK L. OWSLEY

Securities and Exchange Commission (S.E.C.). In attempts to eliminate the evils in the sale of stocks and other securities, Congress in 1933 passed the Federal Securities Act and, in 1934, supplemented this with the Securities Exchange Act. The administration of the first act was entrusted to the Federal Trade Commission[qv], but, when the 1934 act was passed, a new organization, known as the Securities and Exchange Commission, was set up to administer both laws.

The Commission, composed of five members, has several important functions. One is to protect the public against fraud and to see that no deception is practised in the sale of securities. Another is to require the registration of all proposed issues of stocks or bonds and to insist that true and sufficient information shall be furnished regarding such issues so that investors may know just what they are buying. In general, it supervises the activities of all stock exchanges[qv]. Congress, in 1938, authorized the Commission to extend its supervision to "over the counter" stock sales.

[Charles H. Meyer, *Securities Exchange Act of 1934 Analyzed and Explained.*]
ERIK McKINLEY ERIKSSON

Sedgwick, Fort (Colo.), was established by the United States Army in August, 1864, at the junction of Lodge Pole Creek with the South fork of the Platte River. In January, 1865, it was attacked by the Sioux. It served to check the Sioux, Cheyenne and Arapaho[qqv] until the close of the Civil War released troops for policing the plains. It was abandoned in 1871.

[H. H. Bancroft, *History of Nevada, Colorado and Wyoming.*]
CARL L. CANNON

Sedition Acts. Twice in the history of the United States national laws have been passed to prevent sedition. The first instance was the Sedition Act of 1798, passed by a Federalist Congress to silence derogatory criticism of the Government and of public officers and to strengthen the hand of the Government in an impending war with France (*see* Franco-American Misunderstanding). The second occurred in 1918 when Congress enacted an amendment to the Espionage Act[qv] of 1917 designed to prevent attempts to obstruct the efforts of the Government to bring the World War to a successful conclusion.

The Sedition Act of 1798 was denounced by Jefferson as contrary to the First Amendment to the Constitution. When he became President in 1801 Jefferson issued pardons to all persons who had been convicted under the act, and Congress eventually repaid all the fines. The 1918 act was but one evidence of wartime hysteria. It was paralleled by similar acts passed by state legislatures.

Sedition and criminal syndicalism[qv] acts are defended as necessary adjuncts to governmental authority in time of war. They are vigorously attacked by others as threats to freedom of speech and freedom of the press[qqv], particularly if not repealed at the close of hostilities. Many of the statutes enacted during the World War are still effective and are often used for purposes not consistent with their original object.

[Zechariah Chaffee, Jr., *Freedom of Speech.*]
HARVEY WALKER

Seigniorage is the difference between the face and bullion value of short-weight metallic money. In the case of United States coins, other than copper pieces, seigniorage first appeared in the short-weight silver 3-cent pieces coined under the law of March 3, 1851, and in all subsidiary coins from 1853 (Act of Feb. 21) to the time of the Civil War. After the silver dollar was demonetized in 1873, it became a short-weight coin and has since borne seigniorage varying in amount with the market price of silver, as have subsidiary silver and minor coins. The amount of seigniorage in the silver dollar at present (1939) is about 68.5 cents.

[N. Carothers, *Fractional Money.*]

FREDERICK A. BRADFORD

Seizin, or Seisin. This word, coming through the French, meant in ancient times, and still does, possession, and is used, ordinarily as a verb in the past tense, in connection with property left by a decedent. The legal statement, "he died seized of the following," etc., is the formal way of saying that "he died possessed of," and came from this old Latin or French word. The usual expression involving the concept in question was "livery of seisin," or in more modern language, the "delivery" of seisin, which meant simply the delivery of possession. Since it nearly always was used in connection with land, a ceremony of transfer was required, such as the presence of witnesses, and as a symbol of the transfer a literal delivery of a clod of earth, or other similar token, was taken as evidence that the transaction was completed. A record, or memory, perhaps even a tradition, that this ceremony had been performed was sufficient to decide a dispute at law. This ceremony was known in England as early as the time of Henry II. The "livery of seisin" appears to have been a means whereby the transfer of real property was made a matter of public knowledge. As written documents came into general use, the ceremony was discarded. The ceremony, "livery of seisin," was never used to any extent in America, and as a practice is now obsolete. (*See also* "Turf and Twig".)

[Kenelm E. Digby, *History of the Law of Real Property;* William F. Walsh, *A Treatise on the Law of Property.*]

BENJAMIN HORACE HIBBARD

Selden Patent, THE, was the first and most bitterly contested of all the automobile patents. The original application for a patent on a vehicle propelled by an internal combustion engine was filed in 1879 by George B. Selden, a lawyer of Rochester, N. Y., but was kept pending while Selden attempted to interest capital in his ideas, and the patent (No. 549,160) was not issued until 1895. First purchased by the Pope Manufacturing Company, several shifts in control finally brought the rights into the possession of the Electric Vehicle Company. In 1900 this concern began a vigorous enforcement of its patent rights by filing suit against the Winton Motor Carriage Company. The case dragged along for three years, only to be abandoned when Winton and nine other companies organized themselves into the Association of Licensed Automobile Manufacturers and agreed to pay royalties.

Henry Ford, however, refused to take part in the agreement and in 1903 an infringement suit was filed against him. Outstanding legal talent was engaged for both sides of the controversy, and the amazing case was spun out for eight years, amassing thirty-six large volumes of testimony. A principal argument made by the defense was that the Selden patent contemplated use of the Brayton two-cycle motor, and not the Otto four-cycle engine then being used in practically all cars. This argument was strengthened by a contemptuous entry in Selden's diary characterizing the Otto motor as "another of those damned Dutch engines." The lower court upheld the claim of infringement but the court of appeals, which ruled in Ford's favor, stated that although the patent was valid, it was not being infringed by manufacture of vehicles using the Otto type motor.

[James Rood Doolittle, *The Romance of the Automobile Industry.*]

RICHARD W. TUPPER

Selective Service. *See* Draft.

Selectmen. From the earliest times the New England town meeting[qv] has chosen these executive officers. Their performances are interwoven with the literature and history of the region. The usual number has been three, although five to nine in some larger communities, and annual election has been the prevailing rule. The selectmen constitute an executive committee for the town and handle its administrative affairs. In the earlier period they were vested with police and educational functions now usually transferred to other authorities. Their general functions are determined by state law, and while varying in different states, usually involve the preparation of the warrant for annual or special meetings, supervision of local highways, valuation and assessment of property, election control, issuance of licenses, poor relief, etc. Special duties not otherwise provided for may be authorized by the town meeting. The office has served as a training school for local political leadership and administration.

[J. F. Sly, *Town Government in Massachusetts;* J. S. Garland, *New England Town Law.*]

W. A. ROBINSON

Self-Serve Stores came into prominence with the Piggly Wiggly Stores, Inc., the first of which was opened in Memphis, Tenn., on Sept. 12, 1916, by Clarence Saunders. About this time the first "Grocerteria" was opened in Inglewood, Calif. The name suggests that the idea was taken from the cafeterias, which had been popular for some years. The self-serve method had been partially used for many years previously by the variety chains, where the customer selected his purchases from open tables, clerks being used largely for making collections and guarding against theft. The self-serve stores grew in the sale of packaged goods, especially groceries, for two reasons: lower prices made possible by a reduction in the number of people required to operate a store; and freedom of customers to select goods without urging by salesmen. The method seems especially suited to large stores which, under the name of "super-markets"[qv], became popular after 1930.

P. D. CONVERSE

Seminole Indians, The, now consisting of 3200 persons in Oklahoma and 580 in Florida, were Lower Creeks who began their movement into Florida soon after the invasions of that area by Col. James Moore of South Carolina in 1702 and 1704, during which much of the native Indian population was wiped out.

The newcomers, who took the name of Simanoli (Semanole), meaning in the Creek language runaways or separatists (sometimes renegades), combined with or absorbed the remnants of the native red population. Their movement into Florida was slow and their beginning as a separate people did not occur until about 1750.

During and even before the American Revolution there were other Indian migrations to Florida, perhaps the chief of which was the Mickasuki from Georgia. Many Upper Creeks came after Jackson broke their power during the War of 1812. All of these became one resisting element, taking the general name of Seminole during the Seminole Wars[qv]. In the struggle of 1835–42 they were pushed into far Southern Florida and were there joined by the remnant of the ancient Caloosa tribe on the lower west coast.

Of the composite Seminole group 3824 were removed to the west of the Mississippi during the war of 1835–42, and more than 150 others were sent west between 1850 and 1859.

The descendants of those taken from Florida occupy an area of about 365,000 acres in Oklahoma at the present time. The Seminoles of Florida live mainly in unoccupied parts of the Everglades and in the Big Cypress. The Oklahoma Seminoles are decreasing in population, while those in Florida have more than doubled since 1880.

[Daniel G. Brinton, *The Floridian Peninsula;* John R. Swanton, *Early History of the Creek Indians; Senate Document 314,* 71st Congress, 3d Session.]

W. T. CASH

Seminole Wars (1816–18, 1835–42). The Seminole Indians[qv], living in Spanish Florida adjacent to the United States, became a haven for runaway slaves and a victim of international rivalries. United States troops seeking escaped slaves blew up "Negro Fort" on the Apalachicola River in 1816, leading to retaliation by Negro and Seminole raiders. Andrew Jackson led an expedition against the latter in 1818, executed two British subjects, Arbuthnot and Ambrister[qv], and routed the Seminoles. His arbitrary seizure of Spanish posts helped frighten Spain into signing the Adams-Onís Treaty[qv] of 1819 which included the cession of East Florida[qv] to the United States.

In 1832 and 1833 the treaties of Payne's Landing[qv] and Fort Gibson provided for the removal of the Seminoles westward. The Seminoles resisted, especially when their leader Osceola was arrested and imprisoned after a conference in 1835. Following his release they killed many troops and settlers, including Indian Agent Wiley Thompson and Maj. Francis L. Dade[qv]. Osceola was captured by deception in 1837, and later died in prison. The Second Seminole War then degenerated into a process of harassing, bargaining with and seizing Indian groups, who were deported to Oklahoma. The last hostile body was removed in 1842. (*See also* Indian Removal.)

[John R. Swanton, *Early History of the Creek Indians and Their Neighbors;* Marquis James, *Andrew Jackson, the Border Captain;* Grant Foreman, *Indian Removal.*]

PHILIP COOLIDGE BROOKS

Senate, The. *See* Congress, The United States.

Senatorial Courtesy. *See* Courtesy of the Senate.

Senators, Election of. Until 1866 the state legislatures determined their own procedure for electing United States senators, in some cases the chambers voting separately, in others in joint session. Frequent deadlocks and other unsatisfactory conditions led Congress in that year to prescribe uniform procedure under which both branches first voted separately by roll call and in case of disagreement were required to meet in joint session and continue voting daily until a candidate secured a majority. In the meantime there was a growing demand for popular election as uniform procedure failed to create a satisfactory system. By use of the direct primary[qv] for nominating senatorial candidates, and exaction of pledges from state legislators to support the popular choice, the old system of election was being rapidly nullified when in 1913, by the

Seventeenth Amendment*qv* it was formally transferred to the electorate.

[Allen Johnson and W. A. Robinson, *Readings in Recent American Constitutional History;* G. H. Haynes, *The Election of Senators;* Lindsay Rogers, *The American Senate.*]

W. A. ROBINSON

Seneca Falls Convention, the first modern woman's rights*qv* convention, called through the initiative of Lucretia Mott and Elizabeth Cady Stanton, was held in the Wesleyan Chapel at Seneca Falls, N. Y., July 19 and 20, 1848. At the gathering a Declaration of Sentiments, listing the many discriminations existing against women, was read, and a series of eleven resolutions, one of them calling for woman suffrage*qv*, were adopted. This convention launched the organized modern woman's rights movement*qv*.

[Inez Haynes Irwin, *Angels and Amazons;* E. C. Stanton, S. B. Anthony and M. J. Gage, *The History of Woman Suffrage.*]

MARY WILHELMINE WILLIAMS

Seneca Indians, The, constituted the most populous division of the Iroquois Confederacy*qv*, when discovered, occupying the region about Seneca Lake westward to or nearly to the Genesee River. They were divided into eight clans and had eight civil chiefs, ranking with the Mohawks*qv* as "Elder Brothers." The group was warlike and engaged in many raids against surrounding tribes not affiliated with their league. Their warriors were largely responsible for the destruction of the Huron confederacy and Erie and Neutral tribes*qqv*, the survivors of which they largely adopted (1648–54), giving the captives special consideration and ultimate political equality. The Senecas sided with the British in most of the colonial conflicts with the French and later suffered heavily for their espousal of the British cause in the American Revolution. About 3200 survive in New York and Ontario.

[Arthur C. Parker, *Analytical History of the Senecas;* F. W. Hodge, ed., *Handbook of American Indians.*]

ARTHUR C. PARKER

Separation of Powers. *See* Powers, Separation of.

Separatist Movement. *See* Western Separatism.

Separatists, or Independents, were radical Puritans*qv* who refused to wait for a Puritan reformation within the Church of England, but set up churches outside the established order. Robert Browne gathered the first Separatist church at Norfolk in 1581; later Separatists were dubbed "Brownists"*qv*, but the groups did not constitute an organized movement. As with the Scrooby congregation in 1602, a Separatist church resulted whenever a number of earnest Puritans concluded that the true Biblical polity had to be achieved "without tarying for anie." In the main, Separatists proposed a Congregational*qv* or "Independent" form of church polity, wherein each church was to be autonomous, founded upon a formal covenant, electing its own officers and restricting the membership to visible saints. Separation was held a major offense by the regular Puritans as well as by Anglicans*qv* and royal authorities; yet the Puritans who settled Massachusetts Bay*qv* already believed that Congregationalism rather than Presbyterianism*qv* was the polity of the New Testament, and when founding churches at Salem and Boston, 1629 and 1630, sought advice from the Separatists at Plymouth. In England during the 1640's the minority wing of the Puritan party maintained Congregationalism against the majority in the Westminster Assembly and the Parliament, and were known as "Independents," but the multitude of sects which arose out of the disorders of the time also took unto themselves the title of Independents, so that the term came to be a vague designation for opponents of Presbyterianism. Orthodox New England Puritans, although practising a Congregational discipline, always denied that they were either Separatists or Independents.

[Henry M. Dexter, *The Congregationalism of the Last Three Hundred Years;* Williston Walker, *The Creeds and Platforms of Congregationalism;* Perry Miller, *Orthodoxy in Massachusetts;* William Haller, *The Rise of Puritanism.*]

PERRY MILLER

Sequoia, The, averaging 275 feet in height, with specimens over 70 feet taller and trunks from 25 to 35 feet in diameter, these greatest of all American forest trees are found only in a belt of ten groves, at an altitude of from 5000 to 7000 feet, on the west slope of the Sierra Nevada Mountains in California. Their wood is soft, light and of a reddish color that darkens on exposure. Sentinels of the ages, they probably first became known to the white man when John Bidwell took shelter among them in 1841. A. T. Dowd is credited with discovering the Calavaris grove in 1852.

[Charles Sprague Sargent, *The Silva of North America.*]

JOHN FRANCIS, JR.

Sequoyah, Proposed State of, was to include the lands of the Indian Territory*qv*. Its constitution was drafted by a convention of 182 delegates from the Five Civilized Tribes*qv*, which met at Muskogee in the late summer and early autumn of 1905. This was ratified by a vote of the people of Indian Territory, but Congress refused to consider the admission of Sequoyah to the Union. The movement is significant because its leaders became leaders of the Oklahoma constitutional convention the following year.

[E. E. Dale and J. L. Rader, *Readings in Oklahoma History;* Roy Gittinger, *The Formation of the State of Oklahoma.*]

EDWARD EVERETT DALE

Sequoyah's Alphabet (1821), named for its inventor, a half-breed Cherokee, made it possible to put the Cherokee language into writing. The *Cherokee Phoenix and Indian Advocate* (1828–35), edited by Elias Boudinot, first made use of Sequoyah's alphabet.

[Grant Foreman, *Sequoyah.*]

THOMAS ROBSON HAY

Sermons have had an influential part in moulding American life. Since in Protestant worship the sermon has the central place it was particularly important throughout the colonial period and especially in New England. Habitually based on a Scripture text the typical New England sermon averaged about an hour in its delivery, though on special occasions it was apt to be of greater length. The importance of the sermon, aside from religion, in early New England is well illustrated by John Cotton who did not hesitate to treat matters of government in the pulpit and frequently his pulpit pronouncements were effective in shaping governmental policies. Matters of educational, social and even economic interest were often treated in the pulpit. Sermonic literature constituted the major output of the early colonial press, and throughout the whole period sermons frequently appeared in large editions and were widely read. Benjamin Franklin's press printed the sermons of George Whitefield and they were spread broadcast throughout the country. The election, fast day and thanksgiving sermons of the New England clergy were influential factors in propagating the revolutionary philosophy. John Adams is authority for the statement that the clergy of Philadelphia, of all denominations, "thunder and lighten" every Sunday on public issues. On the frontier, in scattered communities the Sunday sermon and the prayers were often the means of disseminating the news of the neighborhood.

The revivalistic sermon achieved its greatest importance in America. In this type of sermon the appeal was primarily to the emotions and the conscience. Perhaps the greatest of American preachers have been of this kind, from Jonathan Edwards to Henry Ward Beecher. The American temperance movement[qv] was inaugurated by a series of sermons on temperance preached by Lyman Beecher in 1826 and has been carried to a large degree by pulpit propaganda. The patriotic sermon has been an effective means of stirring patriotic fervor in all the wars the United States has waged.

[Moses Coit Tyler, *A History of American Literature during the Colonial Period,* and *Literary History of the American Revolution;* Arthur S. Hoyt, *The Pulpit and American Life;* Ray H. Abrams, *Preachers Present Arms;* Alice M. Baldwin, *The New England Clergy and the American Revolution;* Phillips Brooks, *Lectures on Preaching;* J. A. Broadus, *Preparation and Delivery of Sermons;* W. B. Sprague, *Annals of the American Pulpit,* 9 vols.]

WILLIAM W. SWEET

Sesqui-Centennial International Exposition, THE, was held in League Island Park and environs, South Philadelphia, Pa., from May 31 to Nov. 31, 1926. It was designed to celebrate one hundred and fifty years of American independence and to show the progress of the American people in many fields since the centennial celebration of 1876[qv]. Two notable features were: the reproduction of High Street, Philadelphia's main street of 1776, and the Pennsylvania State Building. The architecture was classical and conventional. Sixteen foreign nations participated. The total cost of the Exposition was almost $19,000,000; the subsequent deficit was not the most important feature of one of America's most unsuccessful expositions.

FRANK MONAGHAN

Settlement of War Claims Act (1928). *See* War Claims Act.

Settlement Work. *See* Social Settlements.

Seven Cities of Cíbola. *See* Cíbola.

Seven Days' Battles (June 25–July 1, 1862) were the succession of battles in which Lee's (C.) army forced that under McClellan (U.) to abandon its threatening position east of Richmond[qv] and retreat to the James River.

McClellan had pushed his right wing, 30,000 strong, under Porter, northward across the Chickahominy, hoping that McDowell's corps would join it from Fredericksburg. Aware that Porter was separated from McClellan's main force of 75,000, Lee ordered Jackson, with 18,500 men from the Shenandoah Valley, to fall upon Porter's right and rear. Simultaneously Lee with 40,000 of his 68,000 troops, crossing the Chickahominy north of Richmond, would assail Porter in front.

Lee attacked at Mechanicsville[qv] (June 26) but,

Jackson not arriving, was repulsed. Porter withdrew to Gaines' Mill[qv], where next day the Confederate Army, including Jackson's command, drove him across the Chickahominy. The Federal base on the Pamunkey River was now exposed, but McClellan transferred it by water to Harrison's Landing on the James, and marched his army thither. June 29 his covering troops repulsed Confederate attacks at Savage's Station[qv]. Discovering that his adversary was retiring on the James, Lee hurried columns to Frayser's Farm[qv]. Here his desperate assaults on June 30 failed to interrupt McClellan's retreat, while at White Oak Swamp[qv] Jackson was equally unsuccessful in crushing his rear guard. McClellan, continuing his retirement, occupied Malvern Hill[qv], where (July 1) Lee's final attack suffered decisive repulse. McClellan now fortified his army at Harrison's Landing, having lost 16,000 men in total casualties, while Lee had lost 20,000.

[*Battles and Leaders of the Civil War*, Vol. II; Douglas S. Freeman, *R. E. Lee*, Vol. II; *Official Records, Union and Confederate Armies*, Vol. XI.]

JOSEPH MILLS HANSON

"Seven Pillars," THE, were the seven men who entered into the covenant founding the first church at New Haven[qv], Aug. 22, 1639; they were John Davenport the minister, Theophilus Eaton, Robert Newman, Mathew Gilbert, Thomas Fugill, John Ponderson and Jeremy Dixon. Since the leaders of the New Haven colony had moved beyond Massachusetts Bay[qv], in part because they thought even that community too lax and worldly by their standards, they took exceptional care that the founders of their church should be men of indubitable righteousness. The seven gave themselves an extremely severe examination and applied equally rigorous criteria to later candidates for membership.

[Isabel MacBeath Calder, *The New Haven Colony*.]

PERRY MILLER

Seven Pines. *See* Fair Oaks.

Seven Ranges, Survey of the. As Connecticut had not ceded the Western Reserve[qv] and since the Pennsylvania boundary had not been run north of the Ohio, the first surveys under the Ordinance of 1785[qv]—the Seven Ranges—were made south of the Geographer's Line[qv] (*see* Public Lands, Survey of). Not for fifteen years were lines run north of this base. The survey was begun Sept. 23, 1785, but hostile Indians, disease, bad weather and other hazards interposed such obstacles that only four ranges were surveyed along the outside lines of the townships by February, 1787. They were placed on sale later in the year. As section lines had not been surveyed but merely marked on township plats, difficulties developed, particularly where the windings of the Ohio River were little known. Also no allowance was required to be made for the convergence of meridians, while crude instruments, a difficult terrain and poor pay—$2 per mile—caused other irregularities. Geographer Hutchins numbered the sections in a township from south to north beginning at the southeast corner, thus giving the first row numbers from 1 to 6, the second from 7 to 12, and so on. Only the Ohio Company[qv] tract and the land between the Miamis are similarly numbered. The Seven Ranges formed a triangle with a western boundary 91 miles in length, a northern one of 42 miles and the Ohio River as the third side.

[C. E. Sherman, Original Ohio Land Subdivisions, in *Ohio Cooperative Topographic Survey, Final Report*, Vol. III; W. E. Peters, *Ohio Lands and Their History*.]

EUGENE H. ROSEBOOM

Seven Years' War. *See* French and Indian War.

Seventeenth Amendment. Demand for popular election of United States senators appeared in the fourth decade of the 19th century but the prestige and general effectiveness of the upper chamber were then such that little headway was made until after the Civil War. Popular belief that the Senate had deteriorated, recurrent cases of buying election from venal legislatures, corporate influence in selecting candidates, and other unsatisfactory features of the existing system gave a tremendous impetus to the movement. A proposed amendment to the Constitution, making direct election possible, passed the House several times but it was not until 1912 that the Senate finally accepted the inevitable. Ratification followed and the amendment became effective May 31, 1913. (*See also* Senators, Election of.)

[G. H. Haynes, *The Election of Senators;* Lindsay Rogers, *The American Senate*.]

W. A. ROBINSON

Seventh-day Adventists, successors to the Millerites[qv], believers in Ellen G. White as leader and prophetess, and maintainers of the immutability of the decalogue, organized their general conference in 1863. They stress promotional endeavors through education, medicine, evangelism and publication, and teach the personal, imminent second advent without date setting, immersion as true baptism, immortality through Christ, death as an unconscious state and the destruction of Satan and his followers at the millennium's end. As an international organization, they number approximately 450,000, including 165,924 in the United States, active in 649 tongues and 378 countries.

[M. E. Olsen, *A History of the Origin and Progress of the Seventh-day Adventists; Religious Bodies, 1926*, II; *Seventh-day Adventist Year Book;* G. D. Hagstotz, *Seventh-day Adventists in the British Isles, 1878-1933;* A. W. Spaulding, *Pioneer Stories of the Second Advent Message.*]

G. D. HAGSTOTZ

Severn, Battle of the (March 25, 1655), was an engagement between Puritan settlers in Maryland and the forces of Lord Baltimore's Protestant governor, Thomas Stone. About 125 men fought on each side, the Puritans assisted by two armed ships. Both parties lost about fifty men, but Stone was defeated and four of his men executed. For three years the Puritans practically controlled the colony.

[W. B. Norris, *Annapolis: Its Colonial and Naval Story.*]

WALTER B. NORRIS

"Seward's Folly." *See* Alaska; Alaska, The Purchase of.

Sewing Machine, The. American sewing machines developed with explosive suddenness about 1850 from inventions perfecting ideas previously current in America and Europe. These were recorded in patents by Elias Howe, John Bachelder, Allen B. Wilson, I. M. Singer, W. O. Grover, James Gibbs and others between 1846 and 1860. A flood of improvement patents followed. In the early 1850's three companies were manufacturing machines for the general market. In 1856 the "Albany Agreement" pooling the principal patents[qv] was concluded by leading makers. Under this, 130,000 machines were sold within three years. The industry's rapid expansion and quick success in creating a popular market were possible because automatic machinery and standardized parts were already familiar in America. Sewing machine factories soon ranked among the country's largest manufacturing establishments. By 1870 the annual output had reached half a million machines. In 1929 the product was valued at more than $45,000,000. Sewing machines not only lightened the work of the home but revolutionized the making of clothing, footwear, harness and other articles of popular consumption. They have been extensively exported, but manufacture for foreign markets has largely passed into the hands of affiliated firms abroad, some of which bear the name of the parent company.

[Albert S. Bolles, *Industrial History of the United States;* Chauncey M. Depew, *One Hundred Years of Commerce.*]

VICTOR S. CLARK

Sex Relations. In the Puritan colonies great emphasis was placed on the premarital contract to marry. While the courts consistently punished fornication in both 17th and 18th centuries, they usually regarded illicit sexual relations subsequent to betrothal but prior to marriage as much less serious than fornication without benefit of contract. None the less the notoriety attendant upon premature childbirth combined with the general tendency of the times to report one's neighbor's delinquencies resulted in numerous prosecutions of married couples for illicit relations prior to marriage. The Congregational churches required married couples who had a child seven months after the nuptials to make a public acknowledgment before the congregation on pain of having baptism refused the infant.

Closely related to the special liberties accorded engaged couples was the peculiar custom of bundling[qv], practised in most colonies, but more conspicuously in New England. In order to obviate the necessity of the suitor's having to make the long journey home on a cold winter night, he would be permitted to "bundle" in the same bed or couch with the maiden upon whom he was calling. The parties were expected to sleep with some or all of their clothes on, and often a precautionary board was wedged between them. The practice, explainable in part by bed shortages and doubtless in the interest of fuel economy, was, needless to say, a great strain upon human nature, as court and church records abundantly attest. Among the New England Puritans adultery was punished capitally for a very short time, but subsequently whipping and the wearing of the capital letters "AD" was substituted. During the crime wave of 1642, bestiality was punished capitally.

In all the colonies fornication was a criminal offense, and prosecutions a regular part of routine court business. In rape and fornication matters the court minutes attest, both North and South, to the frankest descriptions of intimate sexual matters in language often of the coarsest vulgarity. In 17th-century Massachusetts indictments for illicit sexual relations probably exceeded in number indictments for crimes against property. In the South fornication was punished by fine or whipping, sometimes by public penance in the church, and adultery was regarded as twice as sinful being punished by twice the penalty. In one Virginia case an adulteress was dragged through the water behind a boat passing between two previously designated points. In this region many fornication cases involved servants; members of the upper classes were far more able to keep such cases out of court. None the less, care had to be exercised to prevent indentured servitude of young girls from being perverted into white slavery. In one case the master was ordered to appear in the parish church in a white sheet, while the guilty woman received a sound whipping. Harsh penalties were exacted against miscegenation[qv]. Heavy extra service was required of servant women who had illegitimate children during their term of service. In Virginia, for example, where the master was the putative father of the child, the mother was to be sold for two years' extra service, the money to go to the parish.

In all the colonies prosecutions for bastardy were systematic and thorough, the chief objective being, not the punishment of the putative father, but the holding of him liable "to save the Parish harmless" in the matter of supporting his offspring. In Virginia, for instance, the mother might be whipped and the father ordered to pay the cost of building a bridge across one of the creeks situated in the county. Illegitimate children could be bound out by the justices or the church wardens in order to minimize the expense to the parish. A marked increase in illegitimacy was recorded in New England between 1730 and 1770 and the county court records of the South also reveal a heavy load of actions in this category during the same period.

In more recent history the courts have been relatively far less concerned with illicit sexual activity than in colonial days. This is by no means conclusive of a higher moral standard today, but indicative of a general feeling that the courts have not proven themselves the best instruments in dealing with this perpetual problem. In the 19th century the church and family were still responsible for maintaining that traditional sex attitude, often called "Victorian," and closely bound up with the maintenance of the "clinging vine" tradition of womanhood. With the turn of the century civic crusaders attacked prostitution in such cities as New York and Chicago with the resultant breaking up of "red-light districts" in many cities. A further check on organized prostitution[qv] was the enactment in 1910 of the White Slave Traffic Act, imposing severe penalties on the transport in interstate or foreign commerce of women or girls for immoral purposes.

With the advent of the World War long-established sex tabus were uprooted. In this revolutionary social change industrialism played an important role: the transfer of economic functions from the home to the factory and the consequent economic emancipation of women, the decline of parental authority and the introduction of the automobile, all contributed to a growing laxity of sex standards. The periodical literature of this period expressed an increasingly favorable attitude toward birth control, easy divorce and extramarital sex relations. Lurid magazines, newspapers and motion pictures came to emphasize sex "thrills," promiscuous "petting" and seminudity. In the year 1932, by way of example, 45% of the motion pictures dealing with sex subjects indicated approval of adultery or other sexual irregularities on the part of leading characters. The "divorce mills" in such states as Nevada and Arkansas and the airing of theories of "companionate marriage" helped foster a casual attitude toward matrimony.

By the early 1930's this trend seemed to have largely spent itself, but there survived a more realistic attitude toward the social consequences of sexual conduct. More widespread sex education, a nationwide campaign led by the Federal Government against venereal disease, and greater self-discipline and social consciousness on the part of the motion picture and radio industries were manifestations of this new realism in matters of sex.

[A. W. Calhoun, *Social History of the American Family*, Vol. I; G. E. Howard, *History of Matrimonial Institutions*, Vol. II; H. R. Stiles, *Bundling;* President's Research Committee on Social Trends, *Recent Social Trends in the United States*, Vol. I, 414-23; H. Woolston, *Prostitution in the United States.*] RICHARD B. MORRIS

Seybert, Fort, The Massacre at (April 28, 1758), was an incident in the French and Indian War[qv]. Despite the score or more defenses built and maintained by Col. George Washington in and about the valley of the South Branch of the Potomac River, a party of Indians led by Killbuck, a Delaware chieftain, attacked Fort Seybert (in present Pendleton County, W. Va.), murdered seventeen of its occupants and carried others into captivity. On the previous day this same party had attacked near-by Fort Upper Tract and killed all the occupants, twenty-two in number.

[Alexander S. Withers, *Chronicles of Border Warfare;* Oran F. Morton, *History of Pendleton County, West Virginia.*] C. H. AMBLER

Shackamaxon, Treaty of. Traditionally known as the "Great Treaty," much doubt still remains about the details. There is no doubt, however, that William Penn met the Indians in 1682 at Shackamaxon (now Kensington), the chief village of the Delawares[qv], and entered into negotiations with them for friendly relations and good feeling. On June 23, 1683, several agreements were signed with the Indian chiefs granting to Penn and his heirs land in southeastern Pennsylvania. All of these were duly witnessed by both whites and Indians. The leading representative of the Indians was Tammanen (Tammany). No valid reason exists for rejecting the traditional story of Penn's meeting the Indians seated under a large elm. This event has been made familiar by Benjamin West's painting and Voltaire's allusion as "the only treaty never sworn to and never broken." Penn described the seating arrangements of a meeting with the Indians in a letter to the Free Society of Traders[qv] written on Aug. 16, 1683.

[*Pennsylvania Archives*, 1st Series, Vol. I, p. 62 ff.; Wayland F. Dunaway, *History of Pennsylvania;* Howard M. Jenkins, ed., *Pennsylvania, Colonial and Federal*, Vol. I.]

J. PAUL SELSAM

"Shades of Death." This name, given the densely wooded northern part of the Great Swamp lying some twelve miles from Wilkes-Barre, Pa., toward Easton, and shown on maps previous to 1778, acquired added significance from being the refuge of many fleeing from the Wyoming Massacre[qv].

FRANCES DORRANCE

Shadrach Fugitive Slave Case (1851). While being held for examination under the Fugitive Slave Act of 1850[qv], Shadrach was allowed to walk out of a Federal Court in Boston and escape into Canada. The incident added to the growing controversy between antislavery and proslavery forces.

[W. H. Siebert, *The Underground Railroad in Massachusetts*, and *The Underground Railroad from Slavery to Freedom; The Atlantic Monthly*, 1897.]

WILBUR H. SIEBERT

Shakers, The American Sect of, officially known as the United Society of Believers in Christ's Second Appearing, was founded by (Mother) Ann Lee of Manchester, England, who came to this country in 1774. Its origin was in the Quaker[qv] church, but its tenets were those of a distinctive social-religious culture. The Shakers believed in a dual Deity and Messiahship; in confession, celibacy, sex equality, separation from the world, consecrated labor and common property. Between 1787–94 eleven communities were established in New York and New England, and in the first quarter of the 19th century, seven more in Ohio, Kentucky and Indiana. These societies were divided into "families" and grouped into bishoprics, a central ministry at New Lebanon, N. Y., directing affairs through subordinate ministers, elders, eldresses and trustees. As fine agriculturists and mechanics, as moral purists or perfectionists[qv] and as successful communists, the Shakers exerted considerable influence in 19th-century America. Numbering about 6000 in 1840, less than 100 members remain (1939) in the five extant colonies.

[Charles Nordhoff, *Communistic Societies of the United States.*]

EDWARD DEMING ANDREWS

Shalam, Land of, was a communistic, agrarian, humanitarian and vegetarian colony established near Doña Ana, N. Mex., by Andrew M. Howland, a Boston philanthropist, under the influence of Dr. John B. Newbrough, a religious mystic who had written a new bible, entitled "Oahspe." The colony, incorporated in 1885 under the name "First Church of the Tae," was composed largely of orphan children. Howland sunk his fortune into excellent buildings, stock and equipment, but financial failure wrecked the colony, which finally broke up in 1901.

[G. B. Anderson, The Land of Shalam, in *Out West*, XXV, 414-424, 1906.]

P. M. BALDWIN

Shanty Towns as an American social phenomenon first appeared during the lag in reemployment after the World War, rising on dump heaps or wastelands within or at the edges of large industrial cities. Later such communities flowered in the depression of the early 1930's, when they received the indulgence if not the approval of officials. The shanties were constructed and occupied by single men who had fitted into an economy of abundance as transient workers. Forced to stay in one place they built crude homes of any free material available: boxes, waste lumber, tin cans. Some occupied abandoned boilers, box cars, caves. They continued to take odd jobs when jobs could be found, living on them with the extra aid of social agencies.

CHARLES J. FINGER

Share Cropper is the general term used, particularly in the South, to describe the type of tenant farmer[qv], white or black, owning neither tools nor working stock, who receives a share of the crop—usually half—in return for the labor of himself and his family. While varying in detail, the landlord generally provides the land, a cabin, fuel, tools, working stock, and feed for stock, the seed and half the fertilizer. Since few croppers can maintain themselves until the crops are gathered they must have credit. A landlord may keep a "commissary" from which a few staple articles of food and clothing are issued in limited amounts; or credit to a fixed sum is secured from a merchant, who is protected, more or less, by a lien on the tenant's share of the growing, or even the unplanted crops. When the crop—cotton or tobacco—is gathered, all these advances, and half the cost of ginning and fertilizer, are deducted from the tenant's share. With unfavorable weather conditions or a low price for the product all concerned are likely to lose. The best estimate of the number of share croppers is about 750,000, representing over three and a half million persons, and this form of tenancy seems to be increasing.

[R. B. Vance, *Human Factors in Cotton Culture;* C. S. Johnson, E. R. Embree and W. W. Alexander, *Collapse of Cotton Tenancy.*]

HOLLAND THOMPSON

Share-the-Wealth Movements in the United States. At the lowest ebb of the great depression, in the winter of 1932–33, two impressions were stamped on the popular mind by the publicity concerning "Technocracy"qv. They were, first, a prophecy of impending doom and, second, a promise of potential utopia. "The nation stands at the threshold of what is simultaneously opportunity and disaster," announced the foremost "Technocrat." These two ideas together with the acute distress of the unemployed, the insecurity of the middle class and the deepening plight of the aged, formed the common basis of appeal for the great mass organizations that sprang into existence in the South and West between 1933 and 1936. Among those declaring their purpose to be the redistribution of wealth were the Townsend Plan, Father Coughlin's National Union for Social Justice, Sen. Long's Share-Our-Wealth Clubs, William Lemke's Union party and Upton Sinclair's EPICqqv.

Differing widely in their proposals, these organizations joined in disclaiming any desire to destroy the capitalistqv order, and all, except the EPIC, depended fundamentally upon a core of inflationist doctrine. Following American middle-class traditions of utopianism, mingled with religious zeal, they adopted such new techniques as national radio "hook-ups," skilled publicity methods of pressure politics, huge mass meetings, or "conventions," swayed by frenzied emotionalism, and blind trust in spectacular individual leaders rather than in the slow education of a party. Moving in and out of alliance with the New Dealqv and with one another, according to the whims or mutual jealousies of their leaders, they ran the gamut of reform tactics: the whirlwind drive for power of an individual leader, the attempt to capture an old party, the trial of the third party method, disciplined backing of congressional candidates of either old party who pledged support of "the plan," and finally sporadic drives to perfect schemes within single states. Revealed in all these movements was the anxious disillusionment, the distress, the experimental frame of mind of the lower middle class and the complete unreality of party divisions in the United States.

C. VANN WOODWARD

Sharps Rifle, The, one of the earliest successful breech-loaders, was invented by Christian Sharps about 1850. It first attracted wide attention during the Kansas Border Warqv (1855–56) when some 900 of them, often called "Beecher's Bibles," were used by the Free State party. About half of these were supplied by officers of the New England Emigrant Aid Companyqv. These rifles gave the Free State side a moral, if not a military, superiority throughout the conflict. They probably saved Lawrence from attack during the Wakarusa Warqv, and were undoubtedly a factor in provoking the Proslavery men to acts of violence. Later they were used by Montgomery in the border war and by John Brown at Harpers Ferryqv. The Sharps rifle was considered for adoption by the United States Army in 1856, and though not finally adopted, some 80,000 were used by the North during the Civil War. It had a high reputation for range and accuracy.

[W. H. Iseley, The Sharps Rifle Episode in Kansas History, in *American Historical Review*, Vol. XII.]

SAMUEL A. JOHNSON

Sharpsburg. *See* Antietam, The Battle of.

Sharpshooters are a select corps of skilled marksmen used in skirmishing and outposts. The word apparently was not used before the first decade of the 19th century, but the principle is to be found in the Riflemen of Abercrombie, in Capt. Fraser's Body of Markmen at Saratogaqv and in the regiment of "expert riflemen" commanded by Daniel Morgan. Jackson's Kentucky and Tennessee riflemen and the light infantry of that period performed similar services. In the Civil War numerous organizations of volunteer Sharpshooters were organized, being regarded as almost a separate branch of service. The most famous of such organizations was the First Regiment of United States Sharpshooters, commanded by Col. Hiram Berdan, which served with distinction in the campaigns of the Army of the Potomac. In the World War the term "snipers" was used. In army and navy qualification with the rifle (since 1907) sharpshooter rates above marksman and below expert rifleman.

[C. A. Stevens, *Berdan's United States Sharpshooters in the Army of the Potomac; Small Arms Firing Manual, United States Army, 1913;* J. G. W. Dillon, *The Kentucky Rifle;* E. B. O'Callaghan, ed., *Orderly Book of Lieut. Gen. John Burgoyne.*]

DON RUSSELL

Shawmut was the Indian name of the peninsula upon which the town of Boston, Mass., was planted. The name fell into disuse very early, long before urban growth effaced the three hills (Tremont) and the narrow isthmus, frequently awash, which joined it to the mainland at the south.

[N. B. Shurtleff, *Topographical and Historical Description of Boston.*]

C. K. SHIPTON

Shawnee, THE (a term meaning Southerners), were the southernmost of the Algonquian Indian[qv] tribes, and are first recognized by anthropologists as inhabiting the Cumberland basin in what is now Tennessee with an outlying colony on the Savannah in South Carolina. The latter group was the first to abandon its southern hunting grounds in a migration lasting from about 1677 to 1707, caused by friction with the near-by Catawba[qv] who were favored by the whites. Their new homes were in the valleys of the Susquehanna and Delaware rivers, but congestion soon caused them to remove to the waters of the upper Ohio Valley in a migration lasting from about 1725 to the years of the French and Indian War[qv] (1754–63). The Shawnee on the Cumberland began retreating north as the result of friction with the Cherokee and Chickasaw[qqv] about 1710 and began to merge with their brethren from the east in a group of villages on the Ohio River from what is now Tarentum, Pa., to the mouth of the Scioto in Ohio—hunting in the forests on both sides of the river.

The Shawnee were the spearhead of resistance to advancing settlement in that period of frontier warfare lasting from 1755 to 1795, supporting and being supported, first by the French and then by the English. By 1795 their homes were in the valley of the upper Miami, and the Treaty of Greenville[qv] of that year forced them to retreat to the Au Glaize. A movement for confederated Indian regeneration and resistance to further white expansion developed under the leadership of the Shawnee brothers, Tecumseh and The Prophet, but met disaster in the battle of Tippecanoe[qv] in 1811. The loss to the Indians of British support, as the result of the War of 1812[qv], hastened the rapid dispersion of the Shawnee. The main body is now incorporated with the Cherokee in Oklahoma where they number about 1500 souls.

[F. W. Hodge, *Handbook of American Indians.*]

R. C. DOWNES

Shawnee and Delaware Migration to the Ohio Valley (*ca.* 1720–53). This migration from the Susquehanna and Delaware river valleys was important in the prelude to the French and Indian War[qv]. It not only brought Indian life and power to a French area that had been uninhabited, but it diminished English influence through the loss of those tribes. Moreover, in the Ohio region the eastern Shawnee[qv] merged with their western brethren who had migrated from the Cumberland Valley.

The migration was caused by the encroachment of whites, by such aggravations as the Walking Purchase[qv] of 1737, by the decline of hunting and knowledge of better hunting grounds[qv] in the West, by the probability that the Iroquois[qv] would not be able to keep them out of the new grounds and by encouragement from both French and English traders. In the competition for the furs of the new region the English got the lion's share. But the fact that the English trade was accompanied by uncontrolled rum selling and unpunished fraud caused many Shawnee and Delaware[qv] to prefer the French, with whom their leaders were in touch from the beginning of migration. They were well disposed toward French expansion, which culminated in the occupation of the Forks of the Ohio (1753) and the erection of Fort Duquesne[qqv]. The English, first through the Pennsylvania colonial government and later through the Iroquois overlords of the Shawnee and Delaware, sought in vain to bring the migrants back to English protection. Although the Iroquois scolded their dependents, they went no farther; and the failure of the Pennsylvania government to establish an Indian department impressed the Indians with the inability of the English to make their traders behave.

During the French and Indian War when the western Shawnee and Delaware, supporting the French, sought to wipe out the interior Pennsylvania settlements, the status of those remaining in the East was imperiled. The reassertion of English supremacy caused most of these to join the western tribesmen. After 1763 (*see* Paris, Treaty of, 1763) all were again under English influence.

[Randolph C. Downes, *Indian Relations in the Ohio Valley.*]

R. C. DOWNES

Shawomet, R. I., was purchased in 1642–43 from the Indians by Samuel Gorton, a contentious religious leader, and his followers. Soon after they built at Shawomet they became involved with Massachusetts Bay[qv] and that colony sent an armed force which captured the settlement in September, 1643, and took Gorton and his chief men prisoners to Boston. Upon his release Gorton returned to Narragansett Bay, obtained from the Narragansett Indians[qv] an act of submission to the king and took this to England, where his rights to Shawomet were upheld and Massachusetts Bay forced to withdraw. Gorton renamed the settlement Warwick in honor of the Earl of Warwick. (*See also* Gortonites.)

[O. P. Fuller, *History of Warwick, R. I.*]

HOWARD M. CHAPIN

Shaw's (Col. John) Explorations, as reported in his reminiscences, indicate one of the earliest attempts to reach New Mexico from Missouri. He claimed that in the spring of 1809, with two companions, he left Cape Girardeau, Mo., and penetrated to the neighborhood of the Colorado mountains. It is not certain that he intended to reach Santa Fé and the inaccuracy of his statements in some instances throws doubt on others. There is no contemporary evidence to support his contention except his own memoirs in the Wisconsin State Historical Society.

[W. J. Ghent, *Early Far West.*]

CARL L. CANNON

Shays' Rebellion (August, 1786 to February, 1787), in western and central Massachusetts, was the outstanding manifestation of the discontent widespread throughout New England during the economic depression following the Revolution. Many small property holders in Massachusetts were losing their possessions through seizures for overdue debts and delinquent taxes; many faced imprisonment for debt. Town meetings and county conventions petitioned for lightening of taxes (disproportionately burdensome to the poorer classes and western sections), sought suspension, abolition or reform of certain courts, as well as revision of the state constitution, and especially urged the issue of paper money[qv], but were stubbornly opposed on most points by the legislature. Lacking, in many cases, property qualifications for voting and thus unable to look for relief through the ballot, the malcontents, beginning at Northampton, Aug. 29, resorted to massed efforts to intimidate and close the courts to prevent action against debtors. Fearful they might be indicted for treason or sedition by the supreme court at Springfield, in September, they appeared there in armed force. Daniel Shays, Revolutionary veteran and local officeholder of Pelham, emerged as leader, demanding that the court refrain from indictments and otherwise restrict its business. A clash with neighborhood militia under Maj. Gen. Shepard was avoided when both bands agreed to disperse. The court adjourned.

In January the insurgents returned to Springfield for supplies from the Confederation[qv] arsenal there, a move foreseen by state and Federal authorities. Federal preparations for arsenal defense were masked by announcement that requisitioning of forces was necessitated by menacing Indians on the frontier. Adequate government funds were not forthcoming for either Federal or state troops, but Gen. Lincoln secured for the latter some $20,000 from private individuals. Shepard's forces repulsed the Shaysites' attack on the arsenal (Jan. 25); Lincoln's men dispersed a near-by insurgent force under Luke Day. Marching to Petersham through a blinding snowstorm Lincoln surprised and captured most of the remaining insurgents early in February, and the rebellion soon collapsed. Shays escaped to Vermont; eventually, with about a dozen others condemned to death, he was pardoned. Bowdoin, governor during the insurrection, was defeated at the next election; reforms in line with the Shaysites' demands were soon made, and amnesty granted with few exceptions. Alarmed by "this unprovoked insurrection" of "wicked and ambitious men" some conservatives despaired of republican institutions. Far greater numbers viewed the rebellion as proof of need for a stronger general Government, capable of suppressing such uprisings, or, better still, preventing them by improving economic conditions throughout the United States. Thus, indirectly, the rebellion strengthened the movement culminating in the adoption of the Federal Constitution[qv].

[G. R. Minot, *The History of the Insurrections in Massachusetts;* J. T. Adams, *New England in the Republic;* J. P. Warren, The Confederation and the Shays Rebellion, in *American Historical Review,* October, 1905.]

LOUISE B. DUNBAR

Sheep, domesticated, were introduced into the Americas by European colonists—into Mexico by the Spanish, into Virginia (1609) and Massachusetts (1629) by the English, into New York (1625) by the Dutch and into New Jersey (1634) by the Swedes. These animals were unimproved.

In colonial times sheep were raised as a part of self-sufficient agriculture to supply wool for homespun clothing and not for commercial purposes. Because of wolves[qv], improper care and English competition, the number of sheep remained relatively few and the quality and quantity of the wool poor. The industry improved somewhat during the Revolution, but slumped after peace and the resumption of British trade.

The first decades of the 19th century witnessed a marked change. Two events of importance occurred: the introduction of Merino sheep, and the exclusion of English competitors from the American market by the various nonintercourse acts and the War of 1812[qqv]. The first Merinos were imported in 1801–2 from France and from Spain. With the passage of the Embargo Act[qv] (1807), native mills increased, wool prices skyrocketed and the demand for fine-wool sheep was insatiable. A Merino craze followed. Merino wool sold for $2 a pound and the early importers sold sheep for $1000 a head. In the midst of this craze the Napoleonic armies broke the Spanish restrictions on the exportation of Merinos, and between 1808–11 approximately 24,000 Merinos were imported into the United States. Sheep raising entered its commercial phase.

After 1815 British woolen importations again depressed the industry. The growth of the factory system and the tariff of 1828 revived it. Woolen manufactures (*see* Wool) doubled in a decade, the price of wool went up and eastern flocks increased tremendously. In the 1830's 60% of American sheep were in New England and the Middle Atlantic states. After 1840, because of westward migration, improved transportation facilities, easy access to cheap western land and an increase in the prices of foodstuffs, the center of sheep raising shifted westward. By 1850 it was in the Ohio Valley.

The Civil War produced a second Merino craze. After the war, sheep raising continued to travel West to the Rocky Mountains and Pacific coast states. In 1935, 60% of all the sheep in the United States were in the western states. Meanwhile the animals were improved. Through importations of European breeds and selective breeding, the average weight per fleece increased from 2 pounds in 1840 to 7.9 pounds in 1935. Its quality also improved.

Progressively as the Far West shifted to wool production, the East under the stimulus of growing urban markets turned to mutton production. English mutton breeds were introduced—the Leicesters, Southdowns, Shropshires and similar breeds. After 1890 even the Far West placed more emphasis on dual-purpose sheep and mutton production; lamb feeding developed in this area.

[L. G. Connor, A Brief History of the Sheep Industry in the United States, in *American Historical Association, Annual Report*, 1918; C. W. Wright, *Wool-Growing and the Tariff;* H. F. Wilson, The Rise and Decline of the Sheep Industry in Northern New England, in *Agricultural History*, Vol. IX.]

ROBERT G. DUNBAR

Sheep Wars, Western. Spanish colonists introduced the sheep industry to the West when they occupied New Mexico, Arizona, Texas and California. But not until long after the intrusion of the Anglo-Americans were there causes for range wars. After the Homestead Act[qv] of 1862 the free prairie range rapidly diminished and three decades later range wars had begun. The average cowboy[qv] looked with scorn upon the drab routine of the lowly shepherd (*pastor*). But this did not lead to conflict; the causes for trouble were more tangible. The sharp hoofs of feeding sheep destroyed the turf and a range was often made barren after months of occupancy. Moreover, cattle would not drink from watering places of sheep. Thus the sheepmen had a natural advantage in range controversies. And when the *pastores* were driven from a favorite range by their enemies because of superior numbers, they could usually find a redress of grievances in near-by courts.

By 1875 clashes between these natural rivals occurred along the New Mexico-Texas boundary. New Mexicans drove their flocks upon the Canadian range of Col. Charles Goodnight. But Goodnight's cowhands drove more than four hundred sheep into the Canadian River and drowned them. Later a New Mexican court found judgment in favor of the sheepmen. In 1876 Goodnight and the sheepmen agreed on a division of a Staked Plains range. The shepherds were allowed the range of the Canadian Valley and Goodnight was to graze undisturbed the Palo Duro canyon.

Other range controversies ended in bloodshed. In Colorado, Nevada, Idaho, Wyoming and Montana thousands of sheep were killed in the bitter wars, and shepherds and cowboys were slain. During the 1880's and 1890's sheepmen controlled the Arizona range from Ashfork to Seligman, and threatened to drive the cowmen from other choice ranges. This led to the Graham-Tewksbury feud in which twenty-six cattlemen and six sheepmen lost their lives. During this period also Wyoming cowmen attacked shepherds who had invaded their ranges and drove more than 10,000 sheep into the mountains to be eaten by coyotes and mountain lions. Another clash near North Rock Springs was won by the cowmen who then destroyed 12,000 sheep by driving them over a cliff. But rivalries subsided with the occupation of the country by landowners and the fencing[qv] of the range.

[William MacLeod Raine, *Famous Sheriffs and Western Outlaws;* J. Evetts Haley, *Charles Goodnight;* E. P. Snow, Sheepmen and Cattlemen, in *Outlook*, LXXIII.]

C. C. RISTER

Shelby's Mexican Expedition (1865). After the downfall of the Confederacy in 1865, Gen. Joseph O. Shelby, one of the ablest Southern cavalry commanders, rather than surrender, called on his men to follow him into Mexico and there enlist in the army of the Emperor

Maximilian, then precariously maintaining his throne.

With 1000 men, including many Confederate notables, such as Generals E. Kirby-Smith, John B. Magruder, T. C. Hindman, C. M. Wilcox, and Governors Murrah of Texas, Morehead of Kentucky and Allen of Louisiana, Shelby crossed the Rio Grande to Piedras Negras from Eagle Pass, Texas, burying the Confederate flag in the river on July 4, 1865. At Piedras Negras, four cannon were exchanged for gold to buy supplies, and Shelby's expedition began fighting its way across northern Mexico toward Monterrey, being impeded by guerrillas supporting Benito Juarez, the Mexican Republican leader who was fighting Maximilian (*see* Mexico, French in).

At Monterrey, the expedition broke up into several sections, parts going to Canada, British Honduras, Sonora, and even joining the French army in Mexico. Shelby, with the remnant of his men, marched to Mexico City. The vacillating Emperor Maximilian, however, refused the offer of Shelby's sword, fearing the displeasure of the United States, and the Confederates attempted to establish a colony on land given them by the Empress Carlotta[qv]. The overthrow of Maximilian and his execution, June 19, 1867, however, made the colony untenable, and most of the Confederate exiles returned to the United States or went elsewhere.

[John N. Edwards, *Shelby's Expedition to Mexico.*]

PAUL I. WELLMAN

Shenandoah, THE. *See* Dirigibles.

Shenandoah, THE, was the last armed cruiser to carry the Confederate flag and, next to the *Alabama,*[qv] was the most destructive to United States shipping. Purchased in England September, 1864, the *Sea King* sailed to Madeira, where Capt. James Waddell equipped her as an armed cruiser and named her the *Shenandoah.* The cruiser was a fast, well-armed vessel of 790 tons register, powered with steam and sail. From Madeira, she began a cruise to the Pacific by way of the Cape of Good Hope and Australia, which resulted in the capture of nearly forty prizes valued at about $1,400,000. On August 2, 1865, Capt. Waddell learned from a British ship that the war had ended. He then sailed for Liverpool by way of Cape Horn, reaching the English port in November, 1865. The British government transferred the cruiser to the United States, by whom it was sold to the Sultan of Zanzibar. Later it was lost at sea. (*See also* Alabama Claims.)

[Cornelius E. Hunt, *The Shenandoah; or the Last Confederate Cruiser.*]

RICHARD E. YATES

Shenandoah Campaign, THE (1864). Coincident with Grant's advance (*see* Wilderness, Battles of the) Federal forces in western Virginia, under Sigel, moved eastward to clear the Shenandoah Valley and cut Lee's supply communications. After engagements at Cloyd's Mountain, New Market and Piedmont, the Federal columns under Hunter, Sigel's successor, were united for an advance on Lynchburg. To meet this threat, Lee detached Early's corps with instructions to defeat Hunter, move down the Valley into Maryland and threaten Washington. Early drove Hunter into the mountains, crossed the Potomac, defeated Lew Wallace at Monocacy[qv] and on July 11, 1864, halted before the defenses of Washington. Too weak to do more than threaten, he withdrew into the Valley. Prompted by Federal division of force and uncertainty of leadership, Early, late in July, again crossed into Maryland, interrupted railroad traffic, destroyed vast supplies, burned Chambersburg, Pa.,[qv] and then safely withdrew.

Alarmed by Early's successes, Grant consolidated all Federal troops in the Valley under Gen. P. H. Sheridan, whose force greatly outnumbered Early's. A month of maneuver followed. On Sept. 19 Sheridan, with a three to one superiority, defeated Early at Opequon and at Fisher's Hill[qv]. Instead of destroying his opponent, Sheridan spent several weeks burning crops, provisions, factories, farm property, etc., after which he took position along Cedar Creek. Cavalry raids (*see* Tom's Brook, Engagement at) and foraging expeditions occupied the ensuing weeks. On Oct. 19 Early attacked during Sheridan's absence and was at first successful (*see* Cedar Creek, Battle of), but for lack of numbers and because of Sheridan's energetic leadership (*see* Sheridan's Ride), the Confederate Army was again defeated and again retreated up the Valley. By mid-December, 1864, both Early and Sheridan had been recalled to Virginia.

Early had saved Lynchburg, threatened Washington, interrupted important communication lines, collected immense supplies, diverted a large force from Grant's army and preserved Lee's western line of supply. Sheridan, in spite of his great superiority, had gained little from a military point of view. He did not leave the Valley and never seriously interfered with Lee's defense of Richmond (*see* Petersburg, Siege of).

[*Battles and Leaders of the Civil War,* Vol. IV.]

THOMAS ROBSON HAY

Shenandoah Hunting Path. *See* Virginia Path, The.

Shenandoah Valley, THE, is that part of the great valley between the Allegheny and the Blue Ridge Mountains extending from the Potomac River at Harpers Ferry south to the watershed of the James River a few miles southwest of Lexington. There are three parts of the Shenandoah Valley: the lower, extending from the Potomac forty miles south, settled chiefly by English immigrants from tidewater Virginia; the middle, from near Strasburg to the vicinity of Harrisonburg, settled almost wholly by Germans; and the upper, from Harrisonburg to the waters of the James, originally more wooded than the middle and lower valley. This last was the part chosen by the Scotch-Irish[qv] immigrants, most of whom came down from Pennsylvania.

There were travelers into the Valley at least fifty years before Gov. Spotswood's expedition of the Knights of the Golden Horseshoe[qv] in 1716 and the larger movement of Germans led by Joist Hite in 1732 and of Scotch-Irish led by John Lewis in the same year. Bona fide settlers were known near Shepherdstown in 1717; Adam Miller had settled in the present Page County by 1726; and there were settlers near Luray in 1727.

The lower valley became the seat of slavery and tobacco, and adhered to the Church of England, while the middle valley, Lutheran in religion, marked by large barns and rolling meadows, was settled by quiet home-loving "Valley Dutch" people. The upper valley, Presbyterian in its life, Scotch-Irish in its politics, was known for its fierce democracy, its exploring hunger for land, and its Indian wars. The lower valley was linked closely with tidewater[qv] Virginia geographically and socially; George Washington served in the House of Burgesses as delegate from Frederick County before he represented Fairfax. The middle valley was largely self-contained. The upper valley, including the famous Augusta County[qv], extended to "the Great South Sea, including California" and held its county court at times near Fort Duquesne[qv], the present Pittsburgh.

[Samuel Kercheval, *History of the Valley of Virginia.*]

JAMES ELLIOTT WALMSLEY

Sheridan-Warren Controversy, THE (1865f.), grew out of Sheridan's dissatisfaction with Gen. G. K. Warren's handling of his troops at the Battle of Five Forks[qv]. In spite of conflicting orders, Warren won a valuable victory, but to his astonishment and that of his subordinates and others, Sheridan relieved him of his command. Warren made repeated requests for a board of inquiry, but it was not until 1879 that one was ordered. Warren was fully exonerated, the court criticizing the manner of his relief.

[E. G. Taylor, *Gouverneur Kemble Warren: The Life and Letters of an American Soldier, 1830-1882.*]

THOMAS ROBSON HAY

Sheridan's Ride. During the Shenandoah Campaign[qv] of 1864, Gen. Early (C.) attacked Sheridan's army (U.) at dawn on Oct. 19, along Cedar Creek[qv] near Strasburg. Two Federal corps, awakened from sleep, were quickly thrown into panic. Other troops, however, rallied and resisted the Confederate advance, though they were slowly forced back. Gen. Sheridan, returning from a visit to Washington, had stopped at Winchester on the night of the 18th. Awakened next morning by the distant sound of artillery firing, he left for the front, and soon began to meet the routed commands, who told him that all was lost. He reached the battlefield about 10:30 A.M. and his presence quickly restored confidence. By mid-afternoon the Confederates were in retreat, losing heavily in artillery and supplies. A poem written several months later by T. Buchanan Read, with its refrain, "And Sheridan twenty miles away" (in reality, the distance was less than fifteen), fixed his ride in the public mind as one of the heroic events of history.

[*Personal Memoirs of P. H. Sheridan; Battles and Leaders of the Civil War.*]

ALVIN F. HARLOW

Sherman Act of 1890, THE, was the upshot of political higgling. At the time this bill was laid before Congress, a certain group was anxious to enact the McKinley Tariff Bill[qv], and the advocates of silver currency were urging the enactment of a bill providing for the free coinage of silver[qv]. While the silver advocates had a majority in the Senate, powerful enough to force the House into line, they were advisedly fearful that President Harrison would veto a free coinage bill even if it were attached as a rider to a tariff bill which he otherwise favored. As a practical solution to this dilemma the "Silver" senators determined to adopt not a free coinage measure but the nearest possible approach to it, namely, the Sherman Act of 1890, which became a law July 14, 1890. The act provided for the issuance of legal tender notes sufficient in amount to pay for 4,500,000 ounces of silver bullion each month at the prevailing market price. Then enough silver dollars were to be coined from the bullion purchased to redeem all the outstanding Treasury notes issued in this manner. The notes were made full legal tender except where otherwise expressly stipulated in the contract, and were made redeemable on demand either in gold or silver coin at the discretion of the Secretary of the Treasury, although the act went on to declare it to be "the established policy of the United States to maintain the two metals on a parity with each other upon the present legal ratio or such ratio as may be established by law."

With the passage of the Sherman Act of 1890 there were three kinds of currency, substantial in amount, which the Federal Government had to keep at par with gold, namely, greenbacks, silver certificates and Treasury notes*qqv*. The direct effect of the Sherman Act was twofold: First, it increased the circulation of redeemable paper currency in the form of Treasury notes by $156,000,000, and second, it accentuated the drain on the Government's gold reserves by requiring the Treasury notes to be redeemed in gold as long as the Treasury had gold in its possession. The financial crackup in Argentine and the resultant liquidation in Great Britain, involving the failure of Baring Brothers, eventually forced an exportation of gold from the United States to Great Britain, and this exodus, coupled with an extraordinary stringency in the money market induced by unusually heavy demand for funds evoked by the industrial activity in the West and South, created a situation bordering on panic in the latter part of 1890.

Some respite from this taut financial situation was gained by the extraordinary grain crop of 1891 in the United States and the European crop shortage, as a consequence of which the exports of gold were transformed into imports, which in turn made bank reserves ample and the money market easy. However, this respite was short-lived. The arbitrary issues of Treasury notes again began to undermine public confidence. The Treasury's already precarious position ensuing from a policy of increased governmental expenditures, the marked growth of our indebtedness to foreign nations, the reduction in custom receipts brought about by the McKinley Tariff Law, was aggravated by the additional drain upon the Treasury's resources which the redemption of the Treasury notes entailed. The cumulative effect of the foregoing factors culminated in the Panic of 1893*qv* which was characterized by a fear of the abandonment of the gold standard*qv* due to the depletion of the Government's gold reserve. The panic was checked in the autumn of 1893 by the repeal of the Sherman Act.

[W. Jett Lauck, *The Causes of the Panic of 1893.*]

FRANK PARKER

Sherman Antitrust Law, THE, has been one of the great landmarks in the relation of American Government to business. Hostility to monopoly*qv* has been traditional among English-speaking people. Some centuries ago laws in England existed against forestalling, monopolizing and regrating. The tradition has taken firm root here. Combination activity which finally induced the passage of the Sherman law began on a considerable scale in the decade from 1870 to 1880. The first Standard Oil*qv* trust was formed in 1879, and revised in 1882. This stimulated combination in like form among other growing businesses. The so-called trust movement has developed through a number of stages —pools, simple business trusts, holding companies, combinations in the form of amalgamations and mergers, and finally combinations of nonrelated businesses. Active legislation against the "trusts"*qv* started in several states about 1885. These acts culminated in the Federal law of 1890, now known as the Sherman Antitrust law. Only one specific kind of combination was named in the act—"trusts"—but a blanket phrase covered all others, whether present or future. Thus the first line of the law reads, "Every contract, combination in the form of trust or otherwise, or conspiracy, in restraint of trade or commerce among the several States, or with foreign nations, is hereby declared to be illegal." The act contains eight sections and is a model of brevity and clarity, wherein are stated methods of procedure and penalties for violation. But some years passed before the Government obtained notable success with the law. Resort of business to the holding company*qv* device under the General Corporation Act of New Jersey (1899), which made possible organization of a pure finance company under a general statute, temporarily provided a means of escape. One of the first major successes was the dissolution of the American Tobacco Company and of the Standard Oil Company*qqv* (1911). The "unscrambling" of combinations presented many difficulties. The device employed with the two companies just named was to dissolve the old organizations into a number of competing units. The properties of the old companies were transferred to the new. The stock was distributed ratably among the stockholders. Complete consolidation put many companies on firmer ground, since it could be maintained that the various divisions of the organization did not compete and consequently were not contrary to the law. Subsequently, the methods of attack were relaxed under the application of the rule of reason*qv*, and in some cases by consent decrees.

In 1938–39 the Government was proceeding with an extensive monopoly investigation for the purpose of clarifying the monopoly idea and in some cases the revamping of the structure of some organizations. A new policy seemed to be in the process of formation the lineaments of which appear to be to permit combination in mass production industries which contribute to industrial efficiency, to tolerate concerted action on the part of competitors in the process of orderly marketing and to restore competition where monopolistic practices have dislocated certain groups of industries.

[W. Z. Ripley, *Trusts, Pools, and Corporations;* William S. Stevens, *Industrial Combinations and Trusts.*]

ISAAC LIPPINCOTT

Sherman's March to the Sea. With a vivid and daring imagination and against Grant's judgment, Gen. W. T. Sherman conceived the plan of marching across Georgia from Atlanta to Savannah. His purpose was to destroy the food supplies of a region on which Lee largely depended and to break the will of the people to continue the war. On Nov. 15, 1864, he burned Atlanta[qv], preparatory to setting out on his march the next day. With four army corps and 5000 cavalrymen, in all numbering 62,000 men, he pointed his course toward Milledgeville, Sandersville, Louisville, Millen and Savannah. Gen. O. O. Howard commanded his right wing; Gen. H. W. Slocum, his left, which Sherman, himself, accompanied; and H. J. Kilpatrick led the cavalry force. The army was spread out sufficiently to cover a course sixty miles wide through the state.

Cutting all communications, Sherman lived off the country through which he marched. His regularly organized raiding parties ranged widely, returning at the end of each day heavily laden with food, livestock, vehicles of various kinds and a great deal of nondescript property secured through pillage. Within a week the left wing reached Milledgeville but not in time to capture the fleeing state officials. In keeping with the general picnic spirit of the march, the soldiers held here a mock session of the legislature in which they repealed the secession ordinance. On Dec. 10 the army drove in the pickets before Savannah[qv], and after a ten-day siege forced the Confederates to flee across the Savannah River into South Carolina. Sherman sent his famous message to President Lincoln giving him the city for a Christmas present. As Gen. Hood at the outset of the march retreated into Tennessee, Sherman had no opposition except the ineffectual raiding of Gen. Joe Wheeler. Sherman estimated that he had inflicted damages amounting to $100,000,000–$80,000,000 being "simple waste and destruction."

[J. F. Rhodes, *History of the Civil War, 1861-1865; Memoirs of General William T. Sherman*, Vol. II; J. D. Cox, *The March to the Sea—Franklin to Nashville;* H. Hitchcock, *Marching with Sherman.*]

E. MERTON COULTER

Shiloh, Battle of (April 6–7, 1862). Grant's capture of Forts Henry and Donelson[qqv] opened the Cumberland and Tennessee rivers to Union water traffic and pierced the center of the Confederate far-flung defensive line so that Columbus, Ky., had to be evacuated. Buell could occupy Nashville, Tenn., with the Army of the Ohio, and Halleck on March 1 could order C. F. Smith with 30,000 troops of the Army of the Tennessee by water up that river to concentrate at Pittsburg Landing twenty-five miles north of the Confederates under Albert Sidney Johnston at Corinth, Miss. Grant arrived and assumed command on March 16. Buell's 25,000 were to join by marching overland from Nashville preparatory to a vigorous combined thrust southward as the next logical step in the campaign for the conquest of the Mississippi Valley.

On April 3 Johnston moved out of Corinth, 50,000 strong, to strike Grant's force before the junction could be effected. On April 6, after a slow massed march, undetected by Grant, Johnston made a sudden surprise attack early in the morning against the unfortified and incompletely covered Union position. Vigorous Confederate attacks drove in Grant's outlying units, shattered the hastily formed lines in all day fighting, costly for both sides, and pushed the Union troops against the river.

Grant personally was absent when the massed assault struck. He hurried to the scene, approved arrangements McPherson had made in his stead, co-ordinated the defense, concentrated rear units, and—Buell arriving by night—counterattacked next morning. The Confederates were disrupted and confused by their own violent attacks and the death of their commander, Johnston. Grant's stroke, with the fresh troops of Buell and Lew Wallace, aided by portions of Sherman's and McClernand's commands, swept them from the field toward Corinth[qv].

[A. L. Conger, *The Rise of U. S. Grant;* J. Fiske, *The Mississippi Valley in the Civil War;* J. C. Ropes, *Story of the Civil War.*]

ELBRIDGE COLBY

Shimonoseki Expedition (1864). The opening up of Japan to foreign intercourse and particularly the treaties of 1858 with foreign powers, made in the name of the Shogun, aroused the opposition of the Japanese nobles who capitalized popular hostility to foreigners as a means of overthrowing the Shogun and setting up another regime under the Mikado, or Emperor. After insults, murder and commotion, those antagonistic to the foreign element fired on French, Dutch and American ships. Secretary of State Seward permitted a small American chartered armed ship to take part with nine British, four Dutch and three French warships in a punitive bombardment of Shimonoseki, in the feudal domain of one of the hostile noblemen. The United States returned to Japan its share of the indemnity of $3,000,000 extracted from Japan after this reprisal.

[Payson J. Treat, *Diplomatic Relations between the United States and Japan, 1853-1895.*]

SAMUEL FLAGG BEMIS

Shin Plasters is a term which has been applied in this country at various times to privately issued fractional paper currencies or to those issued by other than the regularly constituted authorities, although, less frequently, it is applied to all fractional paper money. The term, which goes back to Revolutionary times, is used here in the narrower sense. It is, of course, impossible to know just how much of such currency has been issued or at just what times, because of lack of any official data on the subject. Since the establishment of the National Government, however, it seems likely that the three or four years prior to the passage of the coinage act of 1853 (*see* Coinage, Subsidiary), when much of the fractional silver disappeared from circulation, and in 1862, before the postage stamp currency and fractional paper notes were used (*see* Fractional Currency), represent the two instances in which shin plasters circulated most widely. It is probable that more than $15,000,000 of such currency was issued in the latter period.

[N. Carothers, *Fractional Money.*]

FREDERICK A. BRADFORD

Shipbuilding was one of the first industries established by the colonists, who needed ships for their transatlantic and coastwise commerce and particularly for their fishing operations. Its real beginning as a commercial enterprise dates from the launching of Gov. Winthrop's small thirty-ton sloop, the *Blessing of the Bay*[qv], in 1631.

The prosperity of this industry has always been dependent upon the prosperity of the American merchant marine[qv]. The latter flourished until the Civil War, and shipbuilding in the United States prospered in direct proportion. During this period, many shipowners were financially interested in shipyards and many shipbuilders operated ships for their own account or at least retained an interest in them. American shipbuilders possessed many economic advantages over foreign competitors. The United States possessed large supplies of excellent cheap timber suitable for the construction of wooden vessels and its supply of shipbuilding labor was plentiful and highly skilled. Mass production methods could be employed because vessels were mostly of standard design. As a result, construction costs were low and vessels were sold throughout the world. Indeed, it was common for merchant traders to sell both their ships and cargo in foreign ports. Shipbuilding yards were located mostly along the North Atlantic coast.

After the Civil War, shipbuilding along the coast declined and this condition continued almost uninterruptedly until the entrance of the United States into the World War. The substitution of the metal steamship for the wooden sailing vessel gave British shipbuilders a construction advantage. The American foreign trade merchant marine, handicapped by higher capital and operating costs, declined and the United States Government failed to follow other maritime nations in adequate subsidization of its shipping. It also failed to build up its navy for a period of twenty years after the Civil War. Finally, the United States became engaged in its internal development on a large scale and its interest in foreign trade declined. The shipbuilding industry could not overcome these handicaps even though there was an increasing demand for ships to carry the growing commerce along the coast and on the Great Lakes.

The World War marked the beginning of an extraordinary period of shipbuilding activity. The transportation of war supplies, the destruction of merchant vessels, the withdrawal of most of the German merchant tonnage and that of the Allied nations from normal peacetime routes, and the entry of the United States into the conflict, brought about a tremendous shortage of shipping. Whereas, only 225,122 tons were constructed in 1915, over 12,000,000 tons were built between 1917 and 1922 inclusive.

This notable increase in tonnage enlarged the merchant marine of the United States so greatly that there was little demand for new tonnage during the postwar period. Naval construction was also reduced by the international disarmament agreements. In 1929 only 128,976 tons of merchant shipping were built. The Mail Subsidy Act of 1928 (*see* Merchant Marine Acts) temporarily increased the amount of new construction, but in 1935, only 62,919 tons were built, a new low since 1830. However, the Ship Subsidy Act of 1936 (*see* Maritime Commission) resulted in the construction of a number of new merchant ships and the European political crisis has stimulated the construction of many naval vessels. These developments have increased shipbuilding activity once more in the United States.

[E. R. Johnson and collaborators, *History of Domestic and Foreign Commerce of the United States;* R. W. Kelly and F. J. Allen, *The Shipbuilding Industry; Merchant Marine Statistics,* Department of Commerce.]

HOBART S. PERRY

Shipping, Ocean. Trade with the early American colonists was conducted originally by chartered companies[qv] which, for economic and political reasons, were given trade monopolies over particular areas on the Atlantic coast. These companies were organized primarily for profit and, in return for their extraordinary privileges, were required to colonize the area and administer it in the interests of the Government. They were created because mercantilism[qv] was the dominant principle in international trade and this policy compelled the governments to regulate foreign commerce strictly. Furthermore, it was realized that co-operative efforts were necessary to establish the new colonies since they required large amounts of capital and they would not return a profit for many years. These chartered companies proved unprofitable and retired from the field within a short time.

The merchant trader, who owned both the ship and the cargo, replaced these companies, and reigned supreme until the early part of the 19th century. The trader was primarily a merchant and the ship was part of his business capital and equipment. His cargo was bought, sold and traded for his account in a foreign port and frequently he sold his ship as well. Occasionally, merchandise belonging to other individuals was carried for a charge.

Economic and political circumstances and conditions favored the growth and development of this transportation agency. Industry and commerce were conducted on a small scale and small ships were satisfactory. Capital was not available in large amounts. The demand for goods was highly irregular and producers were not in close communication with distant markets. International commerce was conducted at great risk and largely on a barter basis. Piracy[qv] was common and there were several long wars which compelled those engaged in foreign trade to proceed with secrecy.

Government legislation was also important in developing the colonial and American merchant marine[qv] during the merchant traders' era. Prior to the Revolutionary War, the British Navigation Acts[qv], by excluding foreign vessels from intercolonial trade and commerce between England and her colonies, gave colonial shipping an advantage in fishing and in its trading with Africa, Spain, Portugal and the West Indies[qv]. Some American colonies also enacted legislation in order to assist their merchants to build up a direct commerce with foreign markets in their own ships. The creation of a centralized government in 1789 helped the industry still more. Among Congress' first enactments were those which virtually excluded foreign tonnage from the coastwise trade[qv], and granted preference in customs duties to foreign goods carried in American vessels in the ocean trade. However, between 1815 and 1828, Congress abandoned the policy of protecting ocean shipping because it believed the industry to be in such a strong position that it could do without the help of discriminating import and tonnage taxes and that the abandonment of these aids would remove foreign discriminations and therefore benefit shipping and foreign commerce. This policy of shipping reciprocity compelled United States foreign trade ship operators to shift for themselves, and as economic conditions were favorable to the industry, their vessel tonnage continued to expand, although the relative proportion of the value of foreign trade carried in American bottoms gradually declined from 92.3% in 1826 to 66.5% in 1860.

The years following the War of 1812 saw the decline of the merchant trader and the beginning of the common carrier, a new type of water transportation agency in the United States foreign trade. The latter differed from the former in that it did not own the cargo it transported. Trading and transportation were conducted by separate interests. At first this trend was gradual, but as economic conditions changed, the common carrier became more important until it handled most of the world's commerce.

Two types of carriers were organized—line and chartered or tramp. The former was begun for the first time in the United States with the inauguration of the Black Ball Line[qv] in 1816. The latter, while it had existed on a small scale ever since the early days of maritime commerce, did not become important until after the middle of the 19th century. Several causes led to the development of these two types of common carriers. Foreign trade increased substantially and many merchants desired to enter into this type of commerce without engaging in shipping. The risk of loss had decreased because ships were better designed and constructed, piracy had been eliminated, and the world was at peace once more. The flow of commerce became more regular and there arose a demand for fast, regular and frequent passenger and mail services. The construction of the metal steamship permitted the building of large vessels which could transport cargoes more cheaply than the small wooden merchant trading ship. Finally, the development of the cable[qv] permitted rapid, world-wide communication which altered the methods by which business was transacted.

The beginning of the Civil War marked the end of the United States merchant marine's supremacy in its foreign trade operations. In 1861 it transported 65.2% of the value of the United States foreign trade, and by 1865 this proportion had declined to 27.7%. A slight recovery was made during the next six years, but by 1911 this figure had dropped almost steadily to 8.7%. Economic conditions were no longer favorable to the development of an American merchant marine and the United States Government did not support it properly during this critical period. The substitution of steam propulsion for sail and of iron and steel for wood gave Great Britain's shipbuilders a decided advantage over the American. In 1858 the United States withdrew its financial support of American shipping and while this aid was renewed in 1891, it was inadequate. The Civil War, coming at a critical time in the evolution of shipping organization and shipbuilding, had a disastrous effect on the merchant marine, as it was heavily taxed and subject to capture by Confederate privateers[qv] which were outfitted by the British who were the United States' most important shipping competitors. Congress burdened the industry after the war by refusing readmission to American registry of those American vessels which had transferred to foreign registry during the conflict, by not exempting shipbuilding materials imported for the purpose of repairing or constructing wooden vessels engaged in the foreign trade until 1872, and for metal vessels until 1890. It took no steps to modernize the outmoded wooden naval vessels until 1885, thus delaying the modernization of the country's shipyards and the development of a technical group of marine engineers and naval architects. Labor costs in the United States rose sharply and increased ship operating and capital costs. Finally, the United States became interested in its internal economic development and turned its attention away from the relatively unprofitable shipping industry.

The advent of the 20th century witnessed the development of the private or industrial carrier, a vessel owned by large industrial and mercantile organizations. Most of these ships transport bulk freight, but many carry general cargo and their business operations are such as to strongly resemble the merchant trader. This type of carrier was developed by industry to provide specialized equipment in order to stabilize and reduce transportation costs and provide a more efficient transportation service, to adjust vessel operations to fit their commodities' characteristics, and to better control competition where transportation conditions affect such control.

Whereas the Civil War marked the beginning of the decline of the United States' foreign trade shipping, the World War furnished the impetus for the revival of this trade. Foreign commerce increased enormously because of the Allied nations' demand for supplies (*see* Trade, Foreign). The German merchant marine was virtually withdrawn from service because of the blockade and the Allied nations' merchant ships were diverted to war-time needs. When the United States entered the conflict it needed ships to transport its troops and supplies and as a result it built many more vessels than were ever constructed during a similar period of time (*see* Shipping Act of 1916). At the conclusion of the war, many of these ships were scrapped or burned, but the remainder were either sold to American shipping companies or operated by private interests for the Government's account. The result of this policy was to increase the value of the country's foreign trade carried by American vessels from 9.7% in 1914 to 42.7% in 1920. Increasing competition from foreign vessels caused this proportion to decline to 32.2% by 1926, but additional governmental support, especially the Mail Contract Act of 1928 (*see* Merchant Marine Acts), increased this figure to 35.7% in 1936. The Ship Subsidy Act of 1936 (*see* Maritime Commission) was enacted to provide a more satisfactory type of government aid for the purpose of further developing a modern American merchant marine in both foreign and domestic commerce.

[J. Russell Smith, *The Ocean Carrier;* E. R. Johnson and collaborators, *History of Domestic and Foreign Commerce of the United States;* E. L. Bogart, *Economic History of the American People;* E. R. Johnson, G. G. Huebner and A. K. Henry, *Transportation by Water.*]

HOBART S. PERRY

Shipping Act of 1916, THE, created the Shipping Board[qv] empowered to construct or buy vessels for use in commerce or as naval and military auxiliaries and to operate them or lease or sell them to American citizens. In time of emergency the transfer or sale of American-flag ships to foreign registry or ownership was restricted and the President was given power to conscript vessels. Various practices, including deferred rebates, were declared unfair and prohibited to ocean common carriers. (*See also* Merchant Marine Acts; Emergency Fleet Corporation.)

[*The Shipping Act of 1916 . . . and other laws relating to the United States Maritime Commission,* Washington, 1936.]

FRANK A. SOUTHARD, JR.

Shipping Board, United States, created by the Shipping Act of 1916[qv], controlled the Emergency (later Merchant) Fleet Corporation[qv], and carried out American World War and postwar merchant marine policy. It was superseded in 1933 by the United States Shipping Board Bureau of the Department of Commerce which, in 1936, gave way to the Maritime Commission[qv]. (*See also* Merchant Marine.)

[*Annual Reports,* United States Shipping Board.]

FRANK A. SOUTHARD, JR.

Ships-of-the-line, or line-of-battle ships, were the 18th and early 19th century counterparts of modern first-class battleships, ships fit to engage the most formidable enemy ships in battle line. As planned for the United States Navy, they were about 190 feet long, of about 2600 tons displacement, mounted at least 74 guns on three decks, though the largest, the *Pennsylvania,* mounted 120 guns. Our first ship of this type, the *America,* was launched at Portsmouth, N. H., Nov. 5, 1782, and was given to our French allies. Congress authorized six "Seventy-fours" in 1799, but none were built, and again in 1813 authorized four more. These were named the *Franklin, Independence, Washington* and *New Orleans.* The latter, built at Sackett's Harbor[qv] on Lake Ontario, was never launched. The *Franklin* was converted into a steamer in 1854, the *Washington* was broken up in 1843 and the *Independence* served as a naval receiving ship until her sale in 1913.

In 1816 Congress authorized nine more ships-of-the-line. They were the *Columbus, Ohio, Pennsylvania, Vermont, Virginia, Delaware, Alabama, New York* and *North Carolina.* The *Virginia* and *New York* were never completed. The *Pennsylvania, Columbus* and *Delaware* were burned at the Norfolk Navy Yard, April 20, 1861. The *Vermont, North Carolina* and *Ohio* were long used as receiving ships at navy yards; and the *Alabama,* renamed the *New Hampshire* in 1864, and the *Granite State* in 1904, was used as a training ship by the New York Naval Militia until 1921. None of these ships was ever engaged in battle. The introduction of steam, explosive shells and armor plate rendered them obsolete before they could be used in actual warfare.

[G. F. Emmons, *The Navy of the United States, from the Commencement, 1775 to 1783;* Louis H. Bolander, Ships-of-the-line of the Old Navy, in *U. S. Naval Institute Proceedings,* October, 1938.]

LOUIS H. BOLANDER

"Shirt-Sleeve Diplomacy." Of a note written by Secretary of State Gresham in 1895, to the British government during the Seal Fisheries controversy[qv], a British editor, alleging its crudeness and tactlessness, remarked caustically that the Secretary would appear to have written it in his shirt sleeves. American Secretaries of State and diplomats had for years been accused by Europeans (and by some Americans as well) of ineptitude, unnecessary bluntness, even truculence at times—the result of appointing inexperienced men to such positions. Many Americans professed to accept the British editor's quip as a compliment, as picturing a diplomacy less verbose, more frank and honest than the old sort.

[David Starr Jordan, *Democracy and World Relations.*]

ALVIN F. HARLOW

Shoe Manufacturing in the United States began with the first permanent European settlement. In pioneer communities it was a part of the regular household work, but increasing density of settlement and improvement of transport facilities brought successively the itinerant craftsman, the one-man village shop and (around Boston, New York and Philadelphia) the merchant contractor who hired home workers and also maintained a central cutting and shipping room.

A few operations had been done by power machinery prior to 1860, but the most important step in mechanization was the introduction, in the 1860's and 1870's, of the McKay machine for sewing soles to uppers. Subsequent inventions such as the Goodyear stitcher and the lasting machine virtually completed the mechanization of processes. As shoemaking processes, one by one, were mechanized, they were brought in to the proprietor's "central shop," which thus evolved into the modern integrated shoe factory.

The nonstaple character of the product, the tardy introduction of factory methods, the considerable degree of manual skill required and the fact that most of the machinery has always been leased rather than bought, are interrelated factors helping to explain why shoe factories are often small, poorly financed and short-lived. Instability has been characteristic especially of the manufacture of women's shoes, where the style element necessitates small-scale and highly seasonal production in localized districts affording a supply of trained labor. Labor troubles have naturally been more acute in that branch of the industry, and have led in recent years to considerable transfer of operations to smaller towns.

The interregional distribution of the shoe industry has been determined in the main by labor supply and access to markets. Factories were at first concentrated in eastern New England and to a lesser extent around New York City and Philadelphia; but the partial replacement of skill by machinery and the westward movement of population have steadily extended shoe manufacturing through the Middle West. The chief focal points in that region are St. Louis, Chicago, Milwaukee, Columbus and Cincinnati.

There are about a thousand shoe factories in the United States, with an average of about two hundred employees each. The largest firm in the industry (1939) controls about one thirtieth of the factories, one eighth of the employees and one ninth of the output. Recently there has been an important movement toward integration of control between manufacturers and retailers.

[Blanche E. Hazard, *The Organization of the Boot and Shoe Industry in Massachusetts before 1875;* Charles H. McDermott, ed., *A History of the Shoe and Leather Industries;* Victor S. Clark, *A History of Manufactures in the United States;* Edgar M. Hoover, Jr., *Location Theory and the Shoe and Leather Industries.*]

EDGAR M. HOOVER, JR.

Shooting Match, THE, reached its apex of popularity in the backwoods of the South during the first part of the 19th century. The prize might be a turkey, a cow, etc. For a beef valued at $20, contestants paid the owner twenty-five cents a shot, eighty shots to be purchased. Any entrant could buy any number of shots. The best shot took the hide and tallow; second and third best shots, a hindquarter each, etc. A shooting match was likely to be an all-day festival, women talking, quilting and providing food, and everybody dancing through the night.

[David Crockett, *Tour to the North and East.*]

J. FRANK DOBIE

Shop Committee, THE, or works council movement, was a phase of intensified efforts of employers shortly before and during the World War to allay labor unrest and reduce industrial friction. The distinctive feature of the shop committee was joint representation of employers and employees upon a single body, but other features generally found in this type of organization were restriction of jurisdiction to one establishment and of powers to the settlement of grievances.

The War Labor Board was an active sponsor of shop committees and secured their establishment in over 600 plants. During the 1920's the movement gradually died down, and the committees were either abandoned or else transformed into employee-representation plans or company unions.

[C. E. French, *The Shop Committee in the United States.*]

MYRON W. WATKINS

Short Ballot. *See* Ballot, The.

"Shot Heard Round the World," THE. This phrase from Emerson's poem, written for the dedication of the monument at Concord Bridge in 1836, and carved on the base of Daniel Chester French's Minute-Man statue erected there in 1875, has been accepted by the American public as expressing the patriotism which, risking everything in an immediate crisis, began the war which led to American independence.

By the rude bridge that arched the flood,
Their flag to April's breeze unfurled,
Here once the embattled farmers stood
And fired the shot heard round the world.

ALLEN FRENCH

Showboats. William Chapman, an English actor, had a small floating theater built at Pittsburgh in 1828, and with his family of six as the entire company, toured the Ohio and Mississippi rivers until his death in 1839. Mrs. Chapman then managed the boat until 1847, when she sold it to Sol Smith, a popular midwestern low comedian of the period. Other boats appeared on the Ohio-Mississippi river system before the Civil War, including two circus craft, those of Spalding & Rogers and Dan Rice's Floating Palace. John Robinson's circus also traveled the rivers through one season as a boat show. Meanwhile, Henry Butler had in 1836 placed a boat on the Erie Canal[qv] system—by day a "museum" with a few stuffed animals and wax figures, by night a theater. A fleet of three boats on the Pennsylvania canals[qv], lashed alongside each other at night with the sides removed, became one auditorium, where a vaudeville performance was given. The Civil War damaged the showboat business, but it revived again in the 1870's. Capt. A. B. French launched the boat, *French's New Sensation,* one of the most famous of its kind, on the Ohio in 1878. French at times owned two or three boats. He died in 1902 and his wife managed the *New Sensation* for four years before selling it. The Menke brothers, noted river showmen, owned it later, as they did also the *Golden Rod.* In 1890 Capt. C. F. Breidenbaugh launched the *Theatorium,* the finest boat yet seen on the rivers. W. P. Newman's Great American Water Circus, which carried forty horses and fourteen parade wagons, appeared on the Ohio in 1901. Two big barges side by side with hulls filled with earth and a canvas top overhead, supplied the ring. In 1925 there were fourteen showboats on the midwestern rivers and one touring Chesapeake Bay and the North Carolina sounds.

[Wesley W. Stout, Tonight on the River Landing, in *Saturday Evening Post*, Oct. 31, 1925.]

ALVIN F. HARLOW

Shreveport Rate Case, THE, was a landmark in the extension of the power of the Federal Government to regulate commerce within the individual states. It grew out of a complaint by jobbing interests of Shreveport, La., against the authority of the Texas Railroad Commission to fix rates on freight shipments wholly within the State of Texas, which rates were lower than those on comparable shipments between Louisiana and Texas. In 1911 the Railway Commission of Louisiana acting at the direction of the Louisiana legislature placed the complaint before the Interstate Commerce Commission[qv], which decided against the discriminatory rates. The case was appealed to the Federal courts, and in a momentous decision (Houston, E. & W. T. R. Co. v. U. S.) the Supreme Court held that Congress through such an agency as the Interstate Commerce Commission may step in and override rates prescribed by a state within its borders, if such rates impose an "undue burden" upon interstate commerce as a whole, or if they unduly discriminate against persons and localities shipping in interstate commerce.

[23 I. C. C. Reports 31; 41 I. C. C. 83; 48 I. C. C. 312; 205 Fed. 380; 234 U. S. 342, 34 Sup. Ct. 833.]

S. H. ACHESON

Siberian Expedition. In the summer of 1918 the United States, with the other Allied powers approving, joined Japan in military action to aid friendly Russians and Czechoslovak soldiers in eastern Siberia against dangers from the Russian Soviet government. In August the 27th and 31st United States Infantry regiments, with auxiliary troops, left Manila, P. I., and landed at Vladivostok. This American Expeditionary Force in Siberia, eventually reinforced from the United States to a strength of about 9000, was commanded by Maj. Gen. William S. Graves, though the Japanese commander in chief, Gen. Kikuzo Otani, was in supreme command of the allied Japanese, American and Chinese forces.

The Americans garrisoned Vladivostok and served in detachments as railway guards on certain sections of the Trans-Siberian and Chinese-Eastern railways. These sections totaled 316 miles and included one, from Verhnudinsk to Mysovaya, near Lake Baikal, which was 1700 miles west of Vladivostok. While performing their duties thirty-six American soldiers were killed in conflicts with armed partisans. The American forces were withdrawn from Siberia early in 1920, the last troops leaving Vladivostok for Manila, April 1, 1920.

[W. S. Graves, *America's Siberian Adventure, 1918-1920.*]

JOSEPH MILLS HANSON

Sibley Expedition to Dakota. *See* Dakotas, Expeditions of Gen. Sibley and Gen. Sully in.

Sibley Expedition to the Rio Grande. *See* Rio Grande, Sibley's Operations on (1861–62).

"Sic semper tyrannis" (thus ever to tyrants), Latin motto of Virginia from 1776, recommended by George Mason, its probable originator, is popularly associated with Lincoln's assassination[qv], April 14, 1865, in Ford's Theater, Washington, by the deranged John Wilkes Booth, who shouted *"Sic semper tyrannis!* The South is avenged!" as he fired.

[G. E. Shankle, *State Names, Flags, Seals, Songs, Birds, Flowers and other Symbols;* Stanley Kimmel, *The Mad Booths of Maryland.*]

IRVING DILLIARD

Sideling Hill, rising to an elevation of 2195 feet, is located approximately seventeen miles west of Fort Loudon, Pennsylvania. It is now crossed by the Lincoln Highway[qv] (U. S. Route 30) and was formerly considered one of the more difficult grades of the Forbes[qv] or Pennsylvania Road. Its chief claim to historical significance stems from the attack made there by the Black Boys[qv] upon a convoy of eastern goods on its way to the Indian country beyond Fort Pitt[qv].

In order to open the Illinois country to military occupation and trade, the Indian Department determined to send George Croghan[qv], famous trader, with presents of ammunition, dry goods and liquor to the Indians. With this shipment to Croghan at Fort Pitt was included a large consignment from the firm of Baynton, Wharton and Morgan[qv]. Incensed at a series of Indian depredations during and after Pontiac's Conspiracy[qv], and convinced that these much-needed supplies would be followed by another period of Indian raids, the people of the Conococheague Valley determined to prevent the delivery of the goods, particularly arms that might be used against them. When appeals to turn back went unheeded, Col. James Smith collected ten of his Black Boys and ambushed the pack train on Sideling Hill in March, 1765, and burned those goods they did not take. The Black Boys continued to patrol the road and permitted no goods to pass without their inspection.

[Albert T. Volwiler, *George Croghan and the Westward Movement;* J. Pritts, comp. *Mirror of Olden Time Border Life.*]

R. J. FERGUSON

Sign Language, The, a method of gesture communication in general use among Indians of the Great Plains area, developed because of the nomadic existence of the interior tribes which, following the buffalo[qv], frequently met other tribes with alien tongues. Largely manual, it became a remarkable *lingua franca,* so universal that a Blackfoot from the Canadian border could freely exchange ideas with a Comanche from the Staked Plains although neither understood the other's spoken language.

Expert "sign talkers" can converse by signs as rapidly and fluently as they can speak orally. Signs originally were pantomimic but many have been conventionalized. Thus the sign for "wolf" —the upraised hand with the first two fingers pointing up, the thumb and other fingers touching tips—may mean the animal, a member of the Pawnee or "wolf" tribe, or the abstract idea of sagacity, a quality ascribed to the coyote. Basic simplicity made the sign language not difficult to learn and many white men have been proficient in it.

[W. P. Clark, *The Indian Sign Language.*]

PAUL I. WELLMAN

Signal Corps, U. S. Army. A signal officer was first appointed in our army in 1860; on March 3, 1863, the Signal Corps was created but it ceased to exist with the termination of the Civil War. Our present organization dates from July, 1866. This body, with a dwindling number of troops assigned to it, operated until the Spanish-American War, when, in 1898, a temporary Volunteer Signal Corps was created and incorporated in the regular establishment.

In 1908 the corps purchased its first heavier-than-air flying machine and, in 1914, there was formed the "Aviation Section, Signal Corps." By executive order of May 20, 1918, the Signal Corps was divorced from all duties connected with the army's aerial activities, as this order created the "Division of Military Aeronautics" and the "Bureau of Aircraft Production." Thus, in the Signal Corps, lies the genesis of our present Air Corps.

The Signal Corps is responsible for the use and maintenance of all signal and communication devices—telephone, telegraph, pigeons, radio and cable. It conducts a school at Fort Monmouth, N. J.; operates an extensive radio net; conducts a pictorial section; and is closely allied, as the communications agency, with every activity of the army.

[Col. John W. Wright, *The Signal Corps and Air Service,* W. D. Document 1109, July 1, 1922; *Reports of the Chief Signal Officer*—War Department.]

ROBERT S. THOMAS

Silhouettes, or black profile portraits cut out of paper or painted on card, were used as wall decorations during the first half century of the republic. William M. S. Doyle (1769–1830) and Henry Williams (1787–1830) worked in Boston; and William Bache (1771–1845) was an itinerant. Another itinerant was the boy silhouettist Master Hubard who cut profiles in twenty seconds. August Edouart (1789–1861) was a French visitor who cut full-length silhouettes. William Henry Brown (1808–83), who was born at Charleston, S. C., likewise cut full-length silhouettes and published a *Portrait Gallery of Distinguished American Citizens* in 1855.

[E. S. Bolton, *Wax Portraits and Silhouettes;* A. Van L. Carrick, *Shades of Our Ancestors;* F. N. Jackson, Contemporary Silhouette Portraits of George Washington, in *Connoisseur,* January, 1932.]

THEODORE BOLTON

Silk Culture and Manufacture. Public encouragement was offered silk growers in America in colonial times and later. Some silk was exported from Louisiana and Georgia during the 18th century. Between the Revolution and the Civil War otherwise idle family labor was occasionally employed raising and manufacturing silk in households. During the 1830's a short-lived *morus multicaulis* craze swept the country when thousands of mulberry trees were planted and many cocooneries were built. Despite considerable propaganda, however, silk raising never became more than an amateur occupation.

Manufacturing imported raw silk succeeded better. About 1810 small mills making thread, trimmings and ribbons existed in New England. Thirty years later the industry entered the factory stage. Most establishments were in Connecticut and the Paterson-Philadelphia area accessible to imported raw materials and to metropolitan markets for their products. About 1850 sewing machines caused the invention of sewing twist which became an important branch of American manufacture. Broad goods were not woven extensively until after the Civil War, when luxury tariffs gave the silk industry a spurt of prosperity. In the 1880's silk spinning and throwing mills began to move to Pennsylvania mining towns to secure cheap operatives.

The industry has depended on tariff protection and on labor-saving machinery[qqv], mostly invented or improved in this country. Economical power manufacturing requires strong pure-silk yarns and discourages adulteration, so that American fabrics usually excel in strength and durability. Since 1900 silk hosiery has become an important item of manufacture. The raw silk used in America comes mostly from the Orient, especially Japan. Between 1870 and 1936 imports of raw silk rose from $1.3 million to $67.6 million, while imports of silk manufactures fell from $28.6 million to $8.6 million. Between 1929 and 1935, however, the total value of silk and rayon[qv] goods made in America (not separately reported) fell from $738 million to $308 million; but while all-silk broad goods declined from $386 million to $70 million, all-rayon broad goods increased from $35 million to $141 million.

[L. P. Brockett, *The Silk Industry in America;* V. S. Clark, *History of Manufactures in the United States; Statistical Abstract of the United States, 1937.*]

VICTOR S. CLARK

Sill, Fort, established by Gen. Philip H. Sheridan as Camp Wichita, Jan. 6, 1869, near the foot of the Wichita Mountains in the Indian Territory, was later renamed in honor of Gen. Joshua W. Sill. From the first the post was important in the Indian wars, many campaigns starting from it, and in negotiations with the hostile tribes among which it was a center. Agency headquarters for the Comanches[qv], Kiowas[qv] and Wichitas were established near the fort (*see* Washita, Sheridan's Operations on).

At different times many famous officers made their headquarters at Fort Sill, including Generals Sheridan, W. T. Sherman, R. S. McKenzie, G. A. Custer and B. H. Grierson. The troops stationed at the post from 1869 to 1877 were in an almost constant state of activity due to the Indian troubles.

After the subjugation of the hostile tribes Fort Sill became an artillery school. Remnants of Geronimo's Apache[qv] band were held there as prisoners of war from 1897 to 1912. During the World War, Camp Doniphan, an important cantonment, was erected on the Fort Sill military reservation.

[W. S. Nye, *Carbine and Lance.*]

PAUL I. WELLMAN

Silver as Money. *See* Bimetallism; Bland-Allison Act; Dollar, Silver; Fractional Currency; Free Silver; Money; Pittman Act; Sherman Act of 1890; Silver Legislation; Silver Purchase Act of 1934; Token Money; Trade Dollar.

Silver Certificates were first authorized (by the act of Feb. 28, 1878) to be issued in denominations of not less than ten dollars. The act of Aug. 4, 1886, authorized one-, two- and five-dollar denominations, and the act of March 14, 1900, limited denominations of over ten dollars to 10% of the total. Silver certificates were made full legal tender by the Joint Resolution of June 5, 1933. The Gold Reserve Act[qv] of 1934 authorized the President to issue silver certificates against deposited silver bullion as well as coined silver dollars.

[Bureau of the Mint, *Monetary Systems of the Principal Countries of the World.*]

FREDERICK A. BRADFORD

Silver Democrats was a term used at various times after 1878 to distinguish those members of the Democratic party who were active advocates of free coinage of silver at the 16 to 1 ratio[qv]. More general use followed the inauguration of President Cleveland in 1893 and the special session of Congress called by him to repeal the Sherman Act of 1890[qv]. This proposal split the party wide open, with silver Democrats in opposition to the administration, which in turn used every means at its command to force Democrats in Congress to support the administration's plan. From that time until the national convention of July, 1896, the silver Democrats were a large faction of the party at odds with the official leadership. That convention was a test of strength between the administration and the silver Democrats, and had the latter lost, undoubtedly many of them would have joined the other free-coinage factions in support of a fusion candidate. Its complete victory in the convention made the silver Democrats the regulars beyond question and the term tended to fall into disuse. This result was encouraged also by the disappearance of the issue from politics. Nevertheless the platform of 1900 was a silver-Democratic document, and only in 1904 was free coinage repudiated by the party's candidate, A. B. Parker.

[J. F. Rhodes, *History of the United States;* Mark Sullivan, *Our Times.*]

ELMER ELLIS

Silver Dollar, THE. *See* Dollar, Silver.

Silver Grays was a name given to the conservative minority who, approving of the conciliatory policies of President Fillmore, bolted the Whig state convention of 1850 in New York when the radical antislavery attitude of Sen. Seward was endorsed by the convention. It was so called because of the color of the hair of Francis Granger, one of the bolters. A few weeks later the Silver Grays called a convention of their own.

[A. C. Flick, ed., *History of the State of New York*, Vol. VI.]

A. C. FLICK

Silver League, THE, was a term which was applied to various prosilver propaganda organizations. Especially it described the American Bimetallic League, which was organized in 1892, and under the leadership of A. J. Warner was the most active agitator of the silver cause. In 1895 it consolidated with its principal competitor, The National Bimetallic Union, which was under the direction of Edwin B. Light. The new organization, The American Bimetallic Union, was exceedingly active in 1896 in spreading the free-coinage doctrine, and in attempting to bring about a union of all silver factions in national politics.

[W. J. Bryan *Papers*, in the Library of Congress.]

ELMER ELLIS

Silver Legislation may be deemed to refer to the totality of American legislation which in any way involved silver coinage. Or it may be considered to refer only to monetary statutes passed in the interests of silver as a metal and silver miners as a class. Both types of legislation have loomed large in American history. The details of the specific statutes of both types will be found under their appropriate titles. Silver legislation is here considered from the general standpoint of its place in American history.

It was the intention of the founders of the nation to establish a genuine bimetallism*qv*. From the dollar to the tiny "half-disme" silver coins had free coinage and were unlimited legal tender*qqv*. It has been generally accepted by historians that this policy was based upon the theory, actually offered by Hamilton in his *Mint Report,* that under bimetallism there is a more plentiful supply of money. An equally cogent reason was the fact that the principle of subsidiary silver coinage*qv* was unknown to science or to history, and bimetallism was a necessity if small silver was to be coined.

The bimetallic system was a failure. Revision of the legal ratio in 1834 and 1837 created an adequate gold coinage but drove out the limited silver coinage in circulation. From 1834 on, American silver coins as standard money ceased to play a part in the life of the nation. The establishment of subsidiary silver coinage in 1853 confirmed this situation legally. By an accident, fraught with dire consequences for the country, the silver dollar*qv* was overlooked in 1853. It was left a standard coin, at a ratio of 16 to 1, although the market ratio continued to make its coinage impossible. In a revision of the statutes in 1873 the unknown piece was dropped (*see* Crime of 1873).

In 1873 the world market ratio of silver to gold fell below 16 to 1, for the first time in history. This decline coincided with the opening of rich silver mines in the West, with the post-Civil War deflation, and with a deep depression which sorely afflicted the country (*see* Panic of 1873). The consequence was a political movement, promoted by the silver interests and embraced by the agrarian and inflationary elements, for the restoration of bimetallism. The pressure has never ceased, though it has been relaxed in prosperous periods. Eventually there developed in the Senate and less definitely in the House a non-partisan "silver bloc," made possible by the meager population and mine-owner control of the silver states of the West.

In the 1870's and the 1890's, as well as in 1933, the unceasing labors of this pressure group, reinforced by the popular clamor for inflation*qv*, almost achieved bimetallism. Just failing in this endeavor, they have at intervals extracted from Congress legislation which gave a cash subsidy of some sort to the producers of silver. Among the measures were the creation of the trade dollar*qv* in 1873, with a "joker" in the statute making it legal tender; the coinage of a wholly superfluous 20-cent silver piece in 1875; the passage of a premature resumption of silver coinage act in 1875; the Bland-Allison Act of 1878 (passed over Hayes' veto); the Sherman Act of 1890 (approved by Harrison and repealed on the insistence of Cleveland); the Pittman Act of 1918 (approved by Wilson); the Silver Purchase Act of 1934*qqv* (approved by F. D. Roosevelt); and the presidential proclamations from 1933 to 1938 which gave subsidies to domestic silver miners. Reference should be made also to illegal or unauthorized Treasury action in connection with silver coinage, which had the effect of aiding the silver interests. Such action was taken by Treasury secretaries from 1853 to 1862, by Richardson in 1873, by Bristow in 1875 and by Sherman in 1876.

All the measures referred to were condemned by economists and financial experts practically unanimously. All of them resulted in damage to our money system and economic loss to the country.

[A. B. Hepburn, *History of the Currency;* J. L. Laughlin, *Bimetallism;* N. Carothers, *Fractional Money.*]

NEIL CAROTHERS

Silver Prospecting and Mining. The discovery of silver within the United States goes back to an early date. Extensive mining for gold and silver in the Southwest had been done by the Spaniards. It was against the enslavement in the mines that the Pueblo Indians^qv^ revolted and drove the Spanish off the Rio Grande in August, 1680. The same year, San Franciscan monks discovered and worked a silver mine at El Paso. These mines were sealed and hidden by them for 100 years. Other discoveries were made at Santa Rita, N. Mex. (1769), Olazal, Calif. (1802), in New Hampshire (1828), in Virginia and Tennessee (1832–34). But the real era of silver mining did not begin until about a decade after the gold excitement of 1849 and 1859. There are several reasons for this. The first gold discoveries were pure gold in placer^qv^ deposits. Its recovery was simply a matter of washing it from the debris. Silver seldom is found in this form. Silver usually occurs in lodes or veins which run to great depth underground. Again, silver occurs most frequently in combination with other metals such as gold, lead and copper, which many prospectors could not recognize, and, if they did, would not have the necessary fuel or smelters accessible. Finally, silver mining had to await the building of concentrating mills and smelters in the mining districts. The first successful smelter was built at Blackhawk, Colo., in 1868, and by 1871 Col. David Buell of Nevada had successfully smelted the silver-lead ores of Utah.

The discovery of the most famous silver mine was a direct result of the California Gold Rush^qv^. Prospectors from that region spread eastward prospecting the Rocky Mountain region. In 1859 Peter O'Reiley and Patrick McLaughlin discovered gold and staked the Ophir mine, Nevada, known as the Comstock lode^qv^; this gold mine turned out to be the most famous silver mine. Rich silver strikes were made at Georgetown, Colo., in 1864 and in 1869 at the Caribou mine in Boulder County, Colo., whose silver bricks paved the entrance to the Teller House at Central City, Colo., for President Grant's visit. Chance frequently comes to the aid of the prospector, as when W. M. Kellogg's donkey stepped on an outcropping of quartz and thereby disclosed the Bunker Hill and Sullivan mines in the Cœur d'Alene Mountains of Idaho. Because the donkey belonged to a partner, O. O. Peck, who had left him two weeks earlier, the courts awarded the absent ex-partner a share. At Silver Reef, Utah, in 1873, John Barker discovered melted silver oozing from the sandstone where he had built a campfire.

If the ore contains native silver it is crushed in a stamp mill and passed over copper plates coated with mercury. The silver amalgamates with the mercury and can be separated by volatilization in a retort. But many silver ores are complex ores, i.e., the silver is found in combination with other metals. Then intricate metallurgical processes are necessary for their recovery. The silver extracted from the copper ores of Butte have put Montana near the top in silver production. Lead-silver ores made Leadville a great city after the gold placers had played out. In 1872 the tellurides of gold and silver were discovered in the Red Cloud mine at Gold Hill, then in the San Juan Mountains, and in 1893 in the richest gold field—Cripple Creek, Colo.

The United States Bureau of the Mint estimates that from 1848 to 1935 the United States produced 3,322,807,933 fine ounces of silver, which is approximately one third of the world's total. Over 98% of the United States silver has been produced in the western half of the United States.

[W. R. Crane, *Gold and Silver;* T. A. Rickard, *Journeys of Observation; United States Minerals Yearbook.*]

PERCY S. FRITZ

Silver Purchase Act of 1934, passed on June 19, had for its objectives a government subsidy to silver, the establishment of a hybrid monetary standard of mixed gold and silver, and the issue of silver certificates^qv^ to swell the currency. During the depression beginning in 1929 the price of silver fell to unprecedented levels. A flood of proposals for subsidies to silver were urged upon Congress. The futile 1933 World Economic Conference^qv^ at London enacted, under pressure of United States members, an agreement for stabilizing silver, under cover of which, by presidential proclamation, the United States paid from 64.64 cents to 77 cents per ounce for domestic silver whose value was 45 cents. Unable to achieve bimetallism^qv^ at 16 to 1 (the market ratio was 70 to 1), even with the provisions of the Thomas Amendment^qv^, the silver interests finally forced the passage of the Silver Purchase Act. It provided for the nationalization of domestic stocks of silver and the purchase of silver by the Treasury until the price should reach $1.2929 per ounce or the amount held should equal one third of the value of the government gold holdings. The immediate effect was a speculative rise of silver to 81 cents an ounce, which destroyed the currency systems of China and Mexico.

Under the act the Treasury has bought approximately a billion dollars worth of silver from foreign countries, at prices well above its market value, and paid for it with irredeemable paper money in the form of silver certificates. Since the people refuse to accept silver dollars[qv] in circulation, the bullion has been deposited in government vaults, especially at West Point, where it remains an inert mass, without present or apparent future use. Despite the fictitious value of $1.29 per ounce assigned bullion worth 45 cents, the large increase in gold holdings has prevented the proportion of silver holdings from reaching the one-third proportion, and at the end of 1938 nearly a billion ounces remain to be purchased.

[R. B. Westerfield, *The Silver Debacle;* N. Carothers, *Silver in America;* Herbert M. Bratter, The Silver Episode, in *Journal of Political Economy*, October, December, 1938.]

NEIL CAROTHERS

Silver Republican Party, THE, was formed by the delegates who bolted the Republican convention of 1896 after the adoption of the gold plank (*see* Campaign of 1896). They later issued an indorsement of Bryan and called upon all Republicans who believed in bimetallism[qv] to support him. State organizations were set up in the West, which usually fused with the Democrats or Populists[qv] in local politics. In 1900 the party met in its first and only national convention (*see* Campaign of 1900). The leaders hoped to secure a common ticket with the Democrats, but failed when the latter refused to accept a Silver Republican as the vice-presidential candidate. Thereafter the rank and file of the Silver Republicans favored a separate vice-presidential nomination, but their leaders prevented this by postponing action. The national committee later accepted the Democratic nominee. In March, 1901, the party's members of Congress joined in an address urging all supporters to unite with the Democratic party.

[Elmer Ellis, The Silver Republicans in the Election of 1896, *Mississippi Valley Historical Review*, XVIII, March, 1932, 519-534.]

ELMER ELLIS

Silversmithing was popular in the colonies as early as 1650, as it offered a secure way of preserving capital. Its quality, evident in the earliest pieces, was due to the adoption of the European apprenticeship system with its attendant seven years' indenture. The centers of the craft in the 17th century were Boston and New York. The output consisted of beakers, tankards, caudle cups and porringers for secular use, as well as beakers, cups and baptismal basins for ecclesiastical usage. In Boston these were based upon the current English styles and are marked by their vigorous simplicity. The early artisans there were English-trained Robert Sanderson and his partner John Hull. The early 18th century, with the introduction of luxuries, ushers in the golden age of American silversmithing with the richly ornamented standing salts, chocolate pots, sugar boxes and imposing loving cups by the American-trained Jeremiah Dummer (1645–1718), John Coney (1656–1722) and Edward Winslow (1669–1753). By the second quarter of the century the studied simplicity of the English Queen Anne style is reflected in the work of Jacob Hurd (1702–58). The popularity of tea drinking added to variety of form. The exuberant rococo and its succeeding reserved classic styles of the last half of the 18th century are best seen in the work of Paul Revere (1735–1818).

The origin of the New York style is a combination of Dutch and French as reflected in the names of the early artisans: Cornelius Vanderburg (1653–99), Jacob Boelen (1654–1729) and his son Henricus (1697–1755), Jacobus Vanderspiegel (1668–1708), Bartholomew LeRoux (*ca.* 1688–1713) and his sons John and Charles (1689–1745), as well as Simeon Soumain (1685–1750). Surfaces were more richly ornamented and a high standard set. After 1750 styles were anglicized. In the early 18th century Newport and Philadelphia became important centers, Samuel Vernon (1683–1737) in Newport, and the Richardson and Syng silversmithing dynasties in Philadelphia, where silversmithing reached its peak *ca.* 1790. In the early 19th century Baltimore had its group of craftsmen, among them Samuel Kirk (1793–1872), whose firm still (1940) flourishes. In Boston George C. Gebelein is carrying on the early traditions. The most comprehensive public collections are those of the Museum of Fine Arts, Boston; The Metropolitan Museum of Art; Museum of the City of New York; Philadelphia Museum of Art; Baltimore Museum of Art; and the Mabel Brady Garvan Collection, Gallery of Fine Arts, Yale University.

[C. Louise Avery, *Early American Silver;* F. H. Bigelow, *Historic Silver of the Colonies and Its Makers;* E. Alfred Jones, *The Older Silver of American Churches.*]

JOHN MARSHALL PHILLIPS

Singing School, THE, was to be found in every part of the United States at some time, but was especially common in the rural districts of the South and West during the greater part of the 19th century. It was usually conducted by an itinerant teacher of music who collected a small fee from each student enrolled. A session commonly continued from two to four weeks with a meeting held each evening. Nominally formed to teach singing, it was actually largely a social institution. Books either with "round notes" or "shape notes" were used. In the latter the note could be determined by the shape without any regard to its position on the staff. Each evening was spent in group singing interspersed from time to time with instruction from the teacher. As a social, and often a matrimonial agency, the singing school was quite successful, but it is doubtful if many of the so-called students learned much of music. Yet it did serve to stimulate an interest in music and no doubt created confidence and gave some helpful knowledge.

[W. J. Baltzell, A Picture of Community Music Work Eighty Years Ago, in *The Musician*, Vol. XXII, No. 12.] EDWARD EVERETT DALE

Single Tax, THE, plan of Henry George was set forth in his famous work *Progress and Poverty*[qv] published in 1879. In place of all other taxes George advocated a single tax which would appropriate for government use all of the economic rent of land. His proposal was intended as much more than a mere fiscal device. It was set forth as an engine of social reform.

On the ground that land was a gift of nature, not a product of man's effort, George condemned private property in land which he considered the cause of economic and social ills. Land values, he held, were due to social or community causes. The State, therefore, and not the individual, should be the beneficiary of these values and any increases therein. "What I, therefore propose," he wrote, "as the simple yet sovereign remedy, which will raise wages, increase the earnings of capital, extirpate pauperism, abolish poverty, give remunerative employment to whoever wishes it, afford free scope to human powers, lessen crime, elevate morals, and taste, and intelligence, purify government, and carry civilization to yet nobler heights, is—to appropriate rent by taxation."

Henry George was undoubtedly influenced in his views by his years in California, where he had observed the speculation in land and the rapid rise in land values following the gold rush of 1849[qv]. He was not content merely to expound his views in writing. He endeavored to secure their adoption through the campaign for his election as mayor of New York City in 1886.

The single-tax program has had but limited acceptance in the United States despite vigorous attempts to promote it through political campaigns, legislative action and general education. The single-tax cause has been aided in these several directions through the Joseph Fels fund. In California on seven occasions between 1912 and 1936 the question was before the voters. Each time it was rejected. Agitation for the single tax, or for a partial application of it, has been carried on in such other widely separated states as Oregon, Washington, Colorado, Missouri, New York, Pennsylvania and Texas.

[M. H. Hunter, *Outlines of Public Finance;* Fagan and Macy, *Public Finance.*] MARVEL M. STOCKWELL

Singleton Peace Plan. In the winter and spring of 1865 James Washington Singleton, a native of Virginia, was the bearer of confidential messages between President Lincoln and Confederate authorities, at first in the interest of peace, but later with respect to the restoration of the South. His mission was ended by Lincoln's death.

[M. P. Andrews, *Virginia, the Old Dominion.*] MATTHEW PAGE ANDREWS

Sinking Fund, National. Early in the 19th century the sinking-fund plan was highly extolled as a means of providing for the gradual extinction of a nation's debt. While a national sinking-fund plan may take on a variety of forms, the following procedure is illustrative: the Government guarantees an annual appropriation to the sinking fund, as for example 2% of the principal of the debt, and this sum is then used to repurchase a part of the debt outstanding in the investment market. Ordinarily the bonds so purchased are not destroyed but placed in the sinking fund and continue to draw interest. The interest on the bonds deposited in the sinking fund the first year, plus the second year's cash appropriation, is used to redeem and retire bonds purchased in the open market the second year. By this procedure, the Government in time acquires possession of all of its own bonds of that particular issue, which presumably are then destroyed and the debt expunged. The mechanics of the sinking-fund plan are comparatively simple, but there are practical difficulties which obstruct or defeat it. In the first place, the Government may not always have the money available to make this stipulated appropriation to the sinking fund; in the second place the purchase of bonds in the open market may not be warranted because the premium on the government's credit may have pushed their market prices far above par; and in the third place the unissued bonds lying in the sinking fund present a persistent temptation to the government's administrative officers in times of fiscal emergency, real or fancied.

The untoward circumstances and the administrative vagaries to which national sinking funds are subject are clearly illustrated by the fiscal history of the United States Government. A national sinking fund for the retirement of the Federal Government's debt was inaugurated informally in 1790 by Alexander Hamilton, when it was provided that the proceeds of the sales of public lands[qv] were to be used solely for the redemption of the outstanding debt. Although a regular sinking fund was established by the Act of May 8, 1792, its career has been plagued by all the quirks of circumstance that are likely to affect a nation's treasury. As the net revenues of the Federal Government expanded, statutory commitments to the sinking fund were made by Congress which could not be lived up to when expenditures exceeded receipts. Even when the national sinking fund contained large surpluses they could not be expediently used for the retirement of the Federal debt because of the premium on government bonds. Despite a succession of statutory changes in the procedure for managing the sinking fund, it may be said to be an institution more observable in its breach than in its performance. The fiscal history of the United States is dotted with periods in which there was no debt cancellation and other periods in which debt cancellation proceeded rapidly, just as the balance of revenues and expenditures permitted, rather than in conformity with the stipulated procedure of the sinking fund. Apparently Congress and the Treasury Department have been satisfied by the course of events which up to 1930 accounted for an aggregate debt reduction far greater than that contemplated by the law.

[William J. Shultz and M. R. Caine, *Financial Development of the United States.*]

FRANK PARKER

Sino-Japanese War. The conflict in the Far East in 1894 concerned the United States only indirectly: our Asiatic policy had not yet been crystallized by Secretary Hay's pronouncement on the Open Door[qv]. A treaty with Korea, however, pledged the United States to exert its good offices in the event of a dispute with foreign powers and efforts were consequently made to induce Japan and China to withdraw their troops from that country. At the same time the United States rejected British overtures for foreign intervention to avert the war, and during the subsequent hostilities warned Japan that if she did not follow a moderate policy "other Powers having interests in that quarter may demand a settlement not favorable to Japan's future security and well-being." As the war proceeded the United States extended its good offices in favor of peace and was instrumental in bringing Japan and China together for the final peace negotiations.

[Tyler Dennett, *Americans in Eastern Asia.*]

FOSTER RHEA DULLES

Sioux-Chippewa Council (June 10–11, 1850). In an attempt to end the Sioux-Chippewa warfare[qv], Gov. Alexander Ramsey of Minnesota Territory, ex-officio superintendent of Indian affairs, convened 400 of these tribesmen at Fort Snelling[qv] on June 10, 1850. After lengthy speechmaking, with the customary Indian recriminations, an existing treaty of 1843 between the Sioux and Chippewa, agreeing to maintain peace and pay damages for murders by individuals out of tribal annuities, was renewed, the governor to enforce the treaty at his discretion.

[William W. Folwell, *A History of Minnesota,* Vol. I.]

WILLOUGHBY M. BABCOCK

Sioux-Chippewa War. For nearly two centuries, prior to 1858, the Sioux and the Chippewa[qqv], of different linguistic stocks, battled for control of the northern Wisconsin and Minnesota hunting grounds, as the latter tribe moved slowly westward along the Great Lakes. By the aid of firearms secured from French traders, the Chippewa disastrously defeated a Sioux-Fox alliance near St. Croix Falls (Wis.) and then destroyed the Sioux villages at Sandy Lake and Mille Lacs (Minn.)[qqv]. The withdrawal of the Sioux to southern Minnesota and their receipt of firearms after 1750 produced a territorial stalemate, and the intertribal war became a series of retaliatory raids like the battle of Crow Wing[qv], punctuated by truces. The Government vainly laid down a boundary line between the two in 1825.

The establishment of the Indian agency at Fort Snelling[qv] in 1819, readily accessible from the Mississippi and St. Croix rivers, constantly drew the Chippewa deep into Sioux territory and conflicts were inevitable. In 1827 Sioux treacherously murdered Chippewa just outside the fort. The battles of Rum River[qv] and Stillwater in 1839 resulted from a Chippewa ambush, and the Lake Pokegama Sioux raid of 1841 produced the Kaposia battle[qv] of 1842. The sharp fight near Shakopee (Minn.), May 27, 1858, closed the long and bloody series of ambushes and scalp raids, with a final stalemate.

[Samuel W. Pond, Indian Warfare in Minnesota, in *Minnesota Historical Collections,* Vol. III; Willoughby M. Babcock, Sioux versus Chippewa, in *Minnesota History,* Vol. VI.]

WILLOUGHBY M. BABCOCK

Sioux Claims Commission, The (1863). Following the Minnesota Sioux Outbreak of 1862[qv], Congress by law, Feb. 16, 1863, abrogated all

Minnesota Sioux treaties, declared forfeit their lands and annuities, appropriated $200,000 from such funds for damages to whites, and established a claims commission, which after hearings awarded 2635 claimants $1,370,374, an amount duly paid by appropriation.

[William W. Folwell, *A History of Minnesota*, Vol. II; Claims for Depredations by Sioux Indians, *House Executive Documents, 58, serial 1189*, 38 Congress, 1 session.]

WILLOUGHBY M. BABCOCK

Sioux Council (July 26–Aug. 6, 1889). During the 1880's there was ever-increasing pressure for the reduction of the so-called Great Sioux Reservation, an area roughly extending from Nebraska's northern line to the 46th parallel and from the Missouri west to the 104th degree of longitude. Several attempts to negotiate with the Sioux by commission failed. A law of March 2, 1889, provided for the setting aside of certain specified areas for seven reservation groups in Dakota Territory[qv] and the opening of the balance for sale to whites, the amounts received to be credited to Indian funds. But before the law became operative it required the consent of three fourths of the adult Indians. A three-man commission, after visiting several agencies concerned, began its most important council at Standing Rock (Dak. Terr.), July 26, 1889. Indian opposition, headed by John Grass, stressed failure to observe the Laramie Treaty of 1868[qv], particularly payments, schools, etc. In successive sessions the commissioners patiently explained the provisions of the act and, by minor concessions, met the objections. Indian agent James McLaughlin in private conferences finally convinced Grass and Chief Gall of the wisdom of accepting the act, and the formal signing followed on Aug. 3, after Sitting Bull had failed to stampede the council. The compensation was estimated at upwards of $7,000,000.

[Sioux Commission Report in *Senate Executive Document 51, serial 2682*, 51 Congress, 1 session; James McLaughlin, *My Friend the Indian*.]

WILLOUGHBY M. BABCOCK

Sioux Indians is the name commonly used to designate the Dakota confederacy of Siouan tribes which played an important role in western history. The word Sioux is abbreviated from Nadowessioux, a French spelling of a Chippewa word meaning "snake," hence enemy. Dakota, Nakota or Lakota, depending on whether the pronunciation is in Santee, Yankton or Teton dialect, means "allies."

The Sioux numbering about 30,000, were the most numerous of the plains people, comprising many loosely confederated bands ranging from the Minnesota lake country to the Powder River Valley and from the Canadian border to south of the Platte. Three major divisions are listed: the Santees, including the Mdewakanton, Wahpekute, Wahpeton and Sisseton groups which occupied the most easterly hunting grounds along the upper Mississippi and Minnesota rivers; the Yanktons and Yanktonais, the middle group, living in what is now eastern South Dakota; and the Tetons, subdivided into Oglalas, Brules, Sans Arcs, Minneconjous, Hunkpapas and some lesser bands, who hunted in the high plains, the western end of the Sioux range.

The Sioux are mentioned as early as 1640 in the Jesuit Relations[qv]. They were continuously at war with the Chippewas[qv], who, supplied by the French with firearms, drove the Sioux westward where they collided with other tribes already in the country and whom they successively defeated. During the Revolution and the War of 1812, the Dakotas aided the British. Lewis and Clark[qv] passed through their country in 1804–5, encountered most of their tribes, and described their habitat.

The Sioux were among the most determined of all Indians in resisting white encroachment in the West, the series of Sioux wars[qv] extending, with intervals of peace, over more than thirty years. They developed a number of celebrated chiefs whose names became well known, including Red Cloud, Little Crow, Spotted Tail, Crazy Horse, Gall and Sitting Bull. Chiefs ordinarily rose to power through demonstration of fitness for leadership, but their power consisted largely of the weight of their personal influence.

Early writers universally pay tribute to the Sioux for their great courage and skill with weapons and in horsemanship. Their women were chaste, their men exceptionally honorable considering their savage state. Mentally and physically they were among the finest of all the American Indians.

[Stanley Vestal, *Sitting Bull;* Chief Standing Bear, *My People the Sioux;* George E. Hyde, *Red Cloud's Folks;* J. P. Dunn, *Massacres of the Mountains*.]

PAUL I. WELLMAN

Sioux Treaties. Negotiations and treaties with the Sioux Indians[qv] covered a period of some eighty-five years, from 1805 to 1889, and a geographical area extending from Fort Snelling (Minn.) and Portage des Sioux (Mo.) on the Mississippi to Fort Laramie in Wyoming. The terms of these treaties reflect in a general way the growth of American power as settlement crossed the upper Mississippi and advanced into the Great Plains country (*see* Westward Movement).

On Sept. 23, 1805, Lt. Zebulon M. Pike[qv], at

Pike's Island (Minn.), purchased from the Minnesota Sioux for $2000 in goods a tract roughly nine miles square at the mouth of the Minnesota River for a military post (the later Fort Snelling[qv]), to inaugurate the series of treaties. Termination of the War of 1812 necessitated peace treaties with England's Indian allies, and between 1815 and 1817 a series of peace agreements acknowledging the sovereignty of the United States were negotiated by Gen. William Clark and others at Portage des Sioux and St. Louis with various Siouan tribes.

The extension of fur trading operations up the Missouri River by Ashley[qv], and the movement of troops up that stream under Gen. Atkinson (*see* Yellowstone River Expeditions) produced friction with the Sioux and other tribes of the Missouri, some fighting, and then, in 1825, several treaties such as that of Fort Lookout (S. D.), providing for peaceful relations and the admission of traders to the country. The same year witnessed the great treaty council of Prairie du Chien[qv] (Wis.), where on Aug. 19 the Sioux and other warring tribes, by treaty under governmental supervision, agreed upon mutual boundary lines and the maintenance of intertribal peace. The treaty of July 15, 1830, negotiated likewise at Prairie du Chien, was concerned with peace measures between the Sauk and Fox Indians[qqv] and the Minnesota Sioux and allied groups, but attempted to attain such results by setting up a block of neutral territory between tribal enemies.

By the Treaty of Washington of Sept. 29, 1837, the Sioux began the sale of their Minnesota lands, and the assignment of treaty funds to settle debts to traders. By the time the agreements of Traverse des Sioux[qv] and Mendota of 1851 and Washington in 1858 had been completed, they retained only a ten mile wide strip in that state. The Sioux uprising in Minnesota[qv] (1862) had its Dakota phases, and eventually the great treaties of Fort Laramie[qv] in 1868 attempted to end the Indian wars by setting up a vast Sioux reserve west of the Missouri River and promising certain annuities and payments. The Indians were to withdraw opposition to the building of railroads through their country.

The act of March 3, 1871 (*see* Indian Policy, National) prohibited further treaty making with Indian tribes, but in order to secure Indian acceptance of laws applicable to them, periodic councils for ratification were held, of which those in the summer of 1889 with the Sioux[qv] are typical. Although similar to treaty councils, the Indians in these assemblies acted as individuals, not as agents for semi-independent tribal entities.

[Charles J. Kappler, ed., *Indian Affairs, Laws and Treaties;* Commissioner of Indian Affairs, *Reports, passim;* William W. Folwell, *A History of Minnesota,* Vols. I and II.]

WILLOUGHBY M. BABCOCK

Sioux Uprising in Minnesota (1862). Concentration upon upper Minnesota River reservations, without hunting areas, following the cession of their lands (*see* Traverse des Sioux, Treaty of), resulted in semistarvation for the Sioux[qv]. After wanton murders near Acton, Minn., on Aug. 17, the outbreak came at the Redwood Agency the following day, and for two weeks raiding bands swept through southwestern Minnesota, murdering and pillaging. Despite the loss of twenty-four soldiers from Fort Ridgely[qv], ambushed at the Redwood Ferry late Aug. 18, the successful defense of New Ulm[qv] and Fort Ridgely (Aug. 19–24) against Little Crow's warriors, permitted the movement up from Fort Snelling[qv] of troops under Col. H. H. Sibley. The white victory at Wood Lake Sept. 23, following the Birch Coulee[qqv] defeat Sept. 2, crushed the uprising, except for sporadic incidents like the Dustin murders[qv]. The Sibley and Sully expeditions in the Dakotas[qv] freed the frontier. Thirty-eight Sioux were executed at Mankato Dec. 26, 1862. The uprising cost about 450 lives.

[W. W. Folwell, *A History of Minnesota,* Vol. II.]

WILLOUGHBY M. BABCOCK

Sioux Wars (1854–91). The Sioux were accounted warlike from earliest times but the first military clash with Americans occurred Aug. 19, 1854, when Lt. J. L. Grattan and eighteen men were killed near Fort Laramie[qv], Wyo. The next year Gen. W. S. Harney, in retaliation, attacked a camp of Brulé Sioux, Sept. 3, near Ash Hollow[qv], Nebr., killing about one hundred.

Treaty dissatisfaction led primarily to the Sioux uprising[qv] in Minnesota under Little Crow (Chetan Wakan Mani), beginning Aug. 18, 1862.

Troops pursuing fugitive Santees out on the plains spread excitement among the Teton Sioux. Not until 1865, however, were the Tetons generally hostile, when they aided the Cheyennes[qv] in raiding the stage lines and in the Platte Bridge fight[qv], July 25–26 (*see* Powder River Campaign). The Government's decision to erect forts along the Bozeman Trail[qv] aroused the Sioux in 1866. Under Red Cloud (Mahkpiya-luta) they harassed the trail and hampered construction at Fort Phil Kearny and Fort C. F. Smith[qqv]. Capt. William Fetterman[qv] and eighty men were killed near Fort Phil Kearny, Dec. 21, 1866, Fort C. F. Smith was unsuccessfully attacked Aug. 1, 1867, and the following day Capt. James Powell defeated the Sioux in the Wagon Box fight[qv]. The so-called Red Cloud War[qv] was terminated by the Treaty of Fort Laramie in 1868[qv], by which the Government abandoned the trail and forts.

Discovery of gold in the Black Hills[qv], S. D., in 1874, caused a rush of prospectors, although the Laramie Treaty of 1868 guaranteed the hills to the Sioux. Fearing trouble, the Government ordered the wild Teton bands to come in to the agencies. The principal chiefs, Sitting Bull (Tatanka y Yotanka) and Crazy Horse (Tashunka Witko) refused and Gen. George Crook, in March, 1876, failed to drive them in.

Crook, Col. John Gibbon and Gen. Alfred Terry each led columns into the Sioux country in June, 1876. Crook fought the hostiles on the Rosebud River, June 17, and was compelled to fall back. On June 25, Gen. George A. Custer, with a detachment from Terry's force, encountered the Sioux on the Little Bighorn River[qv], suffering one of the greatest disasters in Indian warfare. Custer and 264 officers and men were killed.

The Sioux separated after the Custer fight. Crook defeated American Horse's band at Slim Buttes[qv], Sept. 9; Dull Knife's Cheyenne village was destroyed in Crazy Woman Canyon by Col. Ranald S. Mackenzie, Nov. 25; and Sitting Bull was chased into Canada by Gen. Nelson A. Miles. Crazy Horse, defeated by Miles at Wolf Mountain, Jan. 7, 1877, surrendered with most of the hostiles the following spring, ending the Sitting Bull War.

The final Sioux uprising was due to religious excitement during the ghost dance[qv] craze of 1889–91 (*see* Messiah War). Sitting Bull was killed by Indian police, Dec. 15, 1890, and approximately 200 fanatical Sioux were slain by troops at the so-called Wounded Knee fight[qv], Dec. 29.

[George E. Hyde, *Red Cloud's Folks;* Stanley Vestal, *Sitting Bull.*]

PAUL I. WELLMAN

Sit-down Strikes. *See* Strikes, Sit-down.

Six Nations. *See* Iroquois League.

Six-Power Consortium in China. *See* Consortiums in China.

Six Shooter. *See* Colt Six Shooter.

Sixteen to One. *See* Bimetallism.

Sixteenth Amendment. When the Supreme Court invalidated the income tax[qv] of 1894 the decision (*see* Pollock v. Farmers Loan and Trust Co.) aroused widespread disapproval on the ground that as long as tariff duties and excises constituted the main source of Federal revenue, those best able to pay were escaping a fair share of the load. It was argued, furthermore, that Federal outlays were bound to increase in the future, emergencies like war could not be disregarded, and additional taxing power was needed. In view of the limitation imposed by the Supreme Court, a constitutional amendment empowering Congress to lay income taxes without apportionment among the states, was the only way out of an impasse. In 1908 the Democratic platform endorsed such an amendment, and it was widely supported by the progressive wing of the Republican party. President Taft eventually recommended submission of an amendment to the states and the necessary resolution passed both Houses by overwhelming majorities in July, 1909. The necessary ratifications were forthcoming and the amendment was declared effective Feb. 25, 1913.

[E. R. A. Seligman, *The Income Tax;* A. C. McLaughlin, *Constitutional History of the United States.*]

W. A. ROBINSON

Skinners. *See* Cowboys and Skinners.

Skyscrapers. The term skyscraper was applied very early to the high buildings that appeared shortly after the development of the passenger elevator[qv]. Five-story buildings almost immediately leaped to eight and ten stories. The first office structure using elevators was the Equitable Life Insurance Building (New York, 1871). Exterior walls of the early skyscrapers were of solid masonry and floors were supported on cast iron columns with beams of wrought iron or heavy timber. Notable examples of this period, both of them by Burnham and Root, were the Rookery (Chicago, 1885), which standardized office building planning, and the Monadnock block (Chicago, 1890), a *tour de force* in functional architecture completely without ornament. In New York the *Sun* and *Tribune* buildings on Park Row are typical examples. These masonry skyscrapers were for the most part truthfully and sensibly designed, using, after 1880, either the Romanesque features made fashionable by H. H. Richardson, or the still more popular Queen Anne or Free Classic style.

A new era dawned with the Home Insurance Building in Chicago (1884). The architect, Maj. William LeBarron Jenney, endeavoring to obtain more light for the offices, took the floor load from the exterior masonry piers by inserting cast iron columns, thereby making it possible to reduce their width. These he bound together at each floor by iron girders and lintels. The iron "skeleton," as he called it, supported not only the floors but the exterior walls as well, and Jenney is therefore commonly called the father of skeleton construction. Other claimants for the honor were Holabird and Roche, architects of the Tacoma Building (Chicago, 1887), who used the same principle in a more highly developed state and also first expressed architecturally the skeleton of steel within; and L. S. Buffington of Minneapolis, who took out a patent in 1888 for a system of skeleton construction.

Skeleton construction was introduced to Boston by the Ames Building (1889), and to New York by the Tower Building (1889). The skeleton of steel, supplanting masonry walls and piers, removed practically all limits to building heights. The country entered its richest period in the science of building, which lasted until the World War, and the business districts of our cities were transformed. Æsthetically, the skyscrapers attempting classic proportions and adorned for the most part with classic ornament were inferior to those of the 1880's. Cass Gilbert's Woolworth Tower (New York, 1911–13), 792 feet high, introduced the "super-skyscraper." In 1916 New York zoning ordinances imposed setback regulations which became popular throughout the land and still further advanced the cause of the picturesque mass and sky line. However, the real revolution in the æsthetics of the skyscraper was caused by Eliel Saarinen's second-prize design in the Chicago *Tribune* competition of 1922. His formula, based perhaps on the theories of Louis Sullivan, has been accepted universally for new skyscrapers.

The fate of the skyscraper is now in the balance. More are being torn down today than are being erected, and it is possible that such buildings as the Empire State, eighty-four stories and 1250 feet high (New York, 1929), and Rockefeller Center (New York, 1931) will never be repeated.

THOMAS E. TALLMADGE

Slade's Girls was a term applied to the young women sent West as teachers in the middle of the 19th century by the Board of National Popular Education. Founded in 1847 under home missionary impulses, this organization, of which former Gov. William Slade of Vermont was general agent, had by 1857 sent more than four hundred women from New England and New York to western states and territories.

[Annual *Reports* of Board of National Popular Education, 1847-57.]

COLIN B. GOODYKOONTZ

Slang, American. Slang is ingenious and amusing language of a highly picturesque and often metaphorical nature, generally of temporary popularity and of wide colloquial dispersion. It differs from cant, a term of depreciation describing insincere repetition of meaningless or hollow phrases, particularly by religious sectaries; from jargon, the vocabulary of a science, art, trade, sect, or specialized group intelligible only to initiates; from argot, the language of thieves; from vulgarism, a word outside the pale of accepted speech; from colloquialism, an expression permissible in conversation but not in formal writing; and from standard language, that vocabulary and its idiomatic usage which have gained general acceptance in the writings of representative authors. These gradations are frequently difficult to distinguish, for language is a living entity, coming to birth and dying with vicissitudes similar to those of human beings. Not all picturesque language is slang: *like greased lightning* is picturesque, but is sound English; *blockhead* is acceptable English, but *bonehead* is slang. *Nice, buncombe, to show off, to put it over, to chisel, bootlegger, racketeer, poppycock* and *O.K.* have risen from slang into standard English.

Slang originates from an individual's effort to replace a faded, stale, or worn-out expression with a pungent, descriptive and often satiric term. Little slang was invented in America before the great westward movement[qv] began after the War of 1812. Freed from the conventionality of the eastern settlements, the pioneers[qv] expressed their exuberant optimism and individualism in dazzling extravagances. David Crockett, whose books in the 1830's amused the East with western tall-tales (*see* Stories, Tall) and tall-talk, described himself as "fresh from the backwoods, half-horse, half-alligator, a little touched with the snapping turtle; can wade the Mississippi, leap the Ohio, ride upon a streak of lightning, and slip without a scratch down a honey locust; can whip my weight in wildcats." The humorous literature of the Old Southwest introduced such terms as *sockdolager, to hornswoggle, rambunctious, skedaddle, shebang, some punkins, galoot, to go the whole hog, stagger-soup, tonsil-paint, pie-eyed, stewed, woozy.* Mark Twain's books are rich repositories of the slang of the mid-19th century Middle and Far West. In recent years most American slang of national currency has been invented by cartoonists[qv] or columnists (*see also* Comic Strips and Funny Papers); the syndication of their work in many newspapers has rapidly spread its use. Radio comedians on national hookups similarly introduce new coinages. From such sources have come *boloney, whoopee, high-hat, belly-laugh, Reno-vated* (for divorced), *storked, blessed-event* (birth of a child), *dumb Dora, schnozzle, apple-sauce, skiddoo, the cat's pajamas* and *punch-drunk*. Teachers of English habitually decry the use of slang on the ground that "alert minds create slang; lazy minds repeat slang." France creates as much slang as the United States, but only Americans employ slang joyously in every possible speech situation.

[M. M. Mathews, *The Beginnings of American English;* H. L. Mencken, *The American Language*, 4th Ed.; Walter Blair, *Native American Humor; American Speech: A Quarterly of Linguistic Usage.*]

HARRY R. WARFEL

Slang, Money, is nearly always half jocular and half satirical, the expression *Almighty dollar*, used by Washington Irving, being an example. Money slang also springs from such obvious comparisons as *cartwheel* for a silver dollar, and *sawbuck* for a ten-dollar bill, the suggestion coming from the Roman numeral X. As soon as a separate American coinage was established American slang terms replaced the familiar designations brought from England, and money was referred to as *hickory leaves, wampum* and *Roanoke*. Humor asserts itself in the term *booby head* for an inartistic penny coined in 1839, and contempt for small money is exemplified by *chicken feed, shot* and *picayunes*. The term *bit*[qv] deriving from the Spanish real, or Mexican shilling, is a well-established equivalent of 12½ cents. Current money slang springs largely from the argot of criminals and gamblers, being a part of their secret language, but as detective-story writers and newspapermen reveal these secrets to the public the terms pass into common usage. An example is *G* or *Grand* for a thousand dollars.

[*New York Public Library Bulletin*, September, 1937, pp. 688-689.]

W. J. BURKE

Slaughter House Cases, The (1873), are considered as the Supreme Court's first interpretation of the due process clause[qv] of the Fourteenth Amendment and the most important decision of that Court since the Dred Scott case. In 1869 the carpetbag[qv] legislature of Louisiana, probably under corrupt influences, granted a monopoly of the slaughtering business within the city limits of New Orleans in favor of a single corporation, thereby depriving some thousand persons of their occupation. This monopoly was challenged in the courts mainly as a violation of the Fourteenth Amendment particularly with reference to the "privileges and immunities" clause, the denial by the state of the equal protection of the laws, and a deprivation of property under the due process clause. Justice Miller, delivering the majority opinion of the Court, declared that the "one pervading purpose" of the Amendment was the protection of the Negro freedman[qv] and not that of transferring the control over the entire domain of civil rights from the states to the Federal Government. This decision was in flagrant violation of the intent of the Radical Republican[qv] framers of the Amendment, who had desired to bring about Federal protection of corporations and other businesses from discriminating state legislation, as well as to achieve social guarantees for the Negro. The Slaughter House Cases are significant as a temporary reversal in the strong trend of Federal centralization[qv] evident since the Civil War.

[C. Warren, *The Supreme Court in U. S. History.*]

HARVEY WISH

Slave Codes, emanating from specific enactments to meet current problems, took the form of general police laws based upon cumulative experience, supplemented periodically by additional legislation as new issues arose. The Barbadian assembly passed a series of acts beginning in 1644 which were brought together in a general law of 1688. After experimenting with specific statutes, South Carolina in 1712 adopted much of the Barbadian law, but added further regulations in 1740 following a servile revolt. Georgia adopted the South Carolina system in 1770, Florida drew upon the Georgia code in the 1820's, and other states utilized the same sequential sources. Several 17th-century Virginia acts culminated in a general police law of 1680, subsequently drawn upon by neighboring colonies and western slaveholding states. In Louisiana the liberal Code Noir[qv] of 1724 served throughout the French and Spanish eras, but was subjected to material changes in the American period. Northern colonial legislatures enacted laws regulating slave status, and all, whether North or South, passed acts affecting Indian slavery[qv].

Negro slave codes, designed to protect property rights and white society, varied in character but certain provisions were common to many. These restrained freedom of assembly, trade, transit and the bearing of arms; provided for the return of absconders and penalties for theft and homicide; forbade any one to instruct them in reading and writing, or to sell them liquor without the owners' consent; specified compensation for slaves executed for capital crimes; and permitted testimony in court only in cases involving other slaves. Occasionally an act guaranteed adequate clothing and rations, limited working hours, or prevented separate sale of mothers and small children. Codes were severest in the West Indies, harsher on the rice coast than in the tobacco area; everywhere enforcement was lax. Except in Delaware and the North, a Negro was presumed to be a slave.

[U. B. Phillips, *American Negro Slavery;* H. T. Catterall, ed., *Judicial Cases concerning American Slavery and the Negro.*]

WENDELL H. STEPHENSON

Slave Insurrections. It is difficult to estimate the extent of slave unrest leading to attempted insurrections in the United States, because of the obvious policy of silence regarding such events, the difficulty of distinguishing between personal crimes and organized revolt, and the quick spread of baseless rumors. A unique record of slave convictions in Virginia, 1780–1864, shows out of a total of 1418, 91 for insurrection and conspiracy and 346 for murder. Fifty-three cases of slave ship mutinies, 1699–1808, have been listed. In 17th-century Virginia two or three plots involving white servants and slaves were discovered. In the early 18th century there were a good many scares in Virginia and South Carolina—the outbreak at Stono, S. C., 1740, probably being the most formidable. The New York outbreaks of 1712 and 1741 (*see* "Negro Plot" of 1741) were both "more notable for the frenzy of the public than for the formidableness of the menace."

The insurrections in San Domingo growing out of the French Revolution led to a new series of plots in Virginia, South Carolina and Louisiana. Gabriel's uprising[qv] near Richmond in 1800 was marked by a real plan and followed by numerous plots and rumors from Virginia to Louisiana (with one in York, Pa., in 1803), lasting to about 1816. The plot of Denmark Vesey (Charleston, 1822), for able maturing of plan, faithfulness of leaders to one another and variety of Negro types involved, is probably the most noteworthy of revolts. Nat Turner's insurrection[qv] in 1831 led to another wave of plots and rumors. In Louisiana especially a succession of plots, 1835–40, was followed by a succession of reports finally proved baseless. In 1856, connected in Southern minds with the rise of the Republican party, there was believed to be a widespread conspiracy covering the whole South. Harpers Ferry[qv] was followed in 1860 by reports of arson and poison plots from Texas to Virginia. In 1861 the question became important in the North and throughout the war the possibility of a slave insurrection figured prominently in Northern policies and politics.

The plots were marked naturally by poor planning, participation of some whites and free Negroes, betrayal by some slave. Each episode brought a new crop of repressive legislation often relaxed and evaded when fears subsided. Negro historians tend to stress the amount of slave unrest and Phillips admits that the actual revolts and plots "were sufficiently serious to produce a very palpable disquiet from time-to-time and the rumors were frequent enough to maintain a fairly constant undertone of uneasiness."

[U. B. Phillips, *American Negro Slavery;* Harvey Wish, American Slave Insurrections before 1861, in *Journal of Negro History,* Vol. XXII; Joseph C. Carroll, *Slave Insurrections in the United States, 1800-1865.*]

LAURA A. WHITE

Slave Representation. *See* Compromises of the Federal Constitution, The.

Slave Ships, which brought slaves from Africa to America, sailed under the flags of all nations—but Dutch, Spanish and English were most active in the trade. As the New England colonies developed, their vessels entered the trade also.

The ships were usually sloops or schooners of fifty to one hundred tons burden with a deck three feet below the regular deck on which the slaves were crowded, unable to stand erect.

They carried a crew of eight to fifteen men in addition to the captain. The crew received wages and the captain received a commission and frequently the right to transport and sell for his own profit.

On the voyage to Africa the ship was loaded with hogsheads of rum and trinkets for trading. On its return all available space below deck was filled with slaves. The horrors of "the middle passage,"[qv] as the trip to America was called, beggar description. Slaves were kept shackled. They suffered from the tropic heat, overcrowding and seasickness. Epidemics of scurvy and smallpox decimated them. Often food and water ran short and the death rate was high.

However, the slave ship was a profitable investment and owners of such vessels made fortunes out of the trade.

[U. B. Phillips, *American Negro Slavery.*]

HALLIE FARMER

Slave States, more properly slaveholding states, were those states which permitted slavery[qv]. In 1776 slavery was permitted in all of the states, but by 1860 had been abolished in the territory north of a line formed by the Mason-Dixon Line[qv], the Ohio River and the southern boundary of Missouri. At that time the slave states were: Alabama, Arkansas, Delaware, Florida, Georgia, Kentucky, Louisiana, Maryland, Mississippi, Missouri, North Carolina, South Carolina, Tennessee, Texas and Virginia.

[Jesse Macy, *The Antislavery Crusade.*]

HALLIE FARMER

Slave Trade, The American. The beginning of traffic in Negro slaves is lost in antiquity but the modern trade dates from 1444, when a Portuguese trader imported ten Negro slaves from Africa. Two years later a trading company was organized and the trade soon became systematized. Columbus brought the first Negro to America in 1492 and the trade in Negro slaves to America was recognized ten years later. Charles V granted Lorenzo deGomenot the exclusive right to supply the West Indian Islands with 4000 Negro slaves in 1518. This was done at the suggestion of Las Casas and others to lighten the burden of the red men. John Hawkins, the first Englishman to engage in the African slave trade, brought a cargo of Negroes from Sierra Leone and sold them in Hispaniola in 1562.

The first Negro slaves introduced into the English continental colonies were landed at Jamestown[qv] by a Dutch vessel in 1619. They seem to have been sold as indentured servants[qv] for life. The importation of slaves for a number of years thereafter was occasional and incidental. At first there was little demand for slaves and in 1650 they numbered only about 300. As tobacco[qv] culture became more profitable the demand for slaves increased, and in 1661 slavery was given legal recognition. Between that date and the chartering of the Royal African Company[qv] in 1672 several shiploads of slaves were imported into Virginia. Slavery was introduced into Massachusetts from the West Indies in 1636 and given legal status in 1641. Importation of slaves increased rapidly during the latter half of the 17th century and slavery[qv] was given legal recognition in all the English colonies in America.

Much of the slave trade during the early part of the 17th century was a secondary one from the West Indies, and was largely carried on by the Dutch. The Royal African Company was given a monopoly of the English slave trade in 1672 and entered largely into the traffic. Between 1680 and 1688 this company sent out some 249 ships which landed 46,396 slaves in America. The importance of this company declined after 1688 when it lost its privileged position. The Asiento[qv] of 1713 between Spain and England gave the latter a monopoly of the Spanish slave trade for thirty years. Under this agreement England was to supply the Spanish colonies with 144,000 slaves at the rate of 4800 per year. The first colonial ship to engage in the trade was built at Marblehead in 1636. The trade became very profitable to the shipping colonies and Massachusetts, Rhode Island, Connecticut and New Hampshire had many ships in the triangular trade[qv]. Rhode Island alone had 150 vessels engaged in this traffic in 1770. The largest number of English vessels engaged in the trade in any one year was 192 in 1771. Reports indicate that the horrors of the middle passage[qv] were more unbearable in New England than in English ships.

Rapid growth of slave population during the 18th century led the colonial assemblies[qv] to place restrictions on the trade. Opposition to the increase of slavery in the planting or southern colonies was based upon fear of slave insurrection[qv], while the argument that slave labor was unprofitable was largely used in the farming or middle colonies. The moral argument against slavery arose early in the New England shipping colonies but it could not withstand the profits of the trade and soon died out. Most colonial laws restricting the trade were disallowed by the king in council because of the advantages of the trade to England. The trustees of Georgia at first forbade slavery, but the settlers clamored for Negro laborers and slave trade and slavery were legalized in that colony in 1750.

The total number of slaves imported into the thirteen English colonies can never be known, but the Negro population in 1776 has been estimated at 502,132. Negro slaves were distributed as follows: 15,000 in New England; 32,000 in the middle colonies; and the remainder in the South: 16,000 in Georgia, 75,000 in North Carolina, 110,000 in South Carolina and 165,000 in Virginia.

Upon the outbreak of the American Revolution the colonies were able to restrict the slave trade. Virginia forbade importation of slaves from England in 1768 and was shortly followed by the other colonies. In 1774 the Continental Association also forbade importation from England. Reasons for this action may be summarized as follows: slavery was economically unprofitable in the northern colonies; the southern colonies feared slave insurrections; the American market was overstocked; traders feared their ships would be captured by the English; human bondage was incompatible with the natural rights[qv] philosophy of the period; and, it was believed that nonimportation[qv] would force England to redress colonial grievances. Jefferson condemned the slave trade in the original draft of the Declaration of Independence[qv] but the New England traders joined the planters of Georgia and South

Carolina to strike out the clause. The Articles of Confederation[qv] made no mention of the slave trade but the Constitution[qv] prohibited Congress from interdicting the trade before 1808. All the states, however, ended the importation of foreign slaves before 1803. South Carolina removed her restrictions in 1804 and some 40,000 slaves were imported into that state during the next four years. In 1808 Congress exercised the power bestowed on it by the Constitution and forever put an end to legal importation of slaves.

Both the New England traders and southern planters opposed the action of Congress and smuggling[qv] soon became a profitable enterprise. It is estimated that up to 1816 more than 15,000 slaves were annually smuggled in. Barataria and Amelia Island[qqv] were important centers for this illicit trade. Drake, a famous smuggler, had a depot in the Gulf of Mexico where he at one time had a supply of 1600 Negroes awaiting a purchaser. More than 10,000 slaves were smuggled into New Orleans in one year alone. Congress at first made little attempt to enforce the law, but after 1820, when the slave trade was made piracy, an agency was set up to enforce it. It is worthy of note, however, that no person was executed under this act until the outbreak of the Civil War. The price of slaves mounted in the 1850's and southern planters began to agitate the reopening of the foreign slave trade. As a result of the agitation smuggling rapidly increased in the years just preceding the war. The *Wanderer*[qv], last slave ship to land a cargo of African Negroes in the United States, was owned by Georgia planters. Stephen A. Douglas estimated that 15,000 slaves were imported in 1858, and 85 vessels are reported to have sailed from New York in 1859–60 to engage in the trade. The Confederate Constitution[qv] forbade the foreign slave trade in spite of the interest of the planters to reopen it.

A local domestic trade developed soon after slavery was introduced into America. All purchasers could not buy direct from the shipper and a local market was established. When a planter abandoned his business for any reason or a slaveholder died without heirs the slaves had to be disposed of. Some slaveholders had no need for the natural increase of their slaves and the surplus had to be sold. Planters had no hesitancy in advertising the sale of slaves at public auction before the county courthouse or at their residence. The early trade was chiefly confined to American-born slaves but not entirely restricted to such, for planters often desired to sell refractory Africans. The trade was small in the beginning but reached sizable proportions in the last quarter of the 18th century. Partly casual and partly systematic it became a well-organized business by 1800. The close of the African slave trade in 1808 was a potent factor in the increase of the domestic trade between the Upper and the Lower South. As the new lands of the Southwest were opened to settlers the demand for slaves on the part of the cotton and sugar planters increased by leaps and bounds. The only source of supply was the domestic trade. Slavery was becoming less profitable on the worn-out lands of the old tobacco belt and the profits to be derived from the trade were sufficiently large to induce many men to engage in it. As a rule, however, there was a stigma attached to the business.

In the towns of the Upper South, there were many local dealers and brokers who bought surplus Negroes to sell either direct to planters who came to the local market, or to the long-distance trader who shipped slaves to the markets of the Southwest. Local dealers were often employed as regular agents of the shipping firms. With the rise in prices some planters of the Upper South deliberately encouraged a rapid birth rate among the breeding Negroes.

The long-distance trade was systematically organized. Trading companies had assembling headquarters in the Upper South and distributing markets in the Southwest. In addition to purchasing from the local dealer the shippers had field agents who combed the countryside for slaves. They advertised widely in local papers offering to pay cash prices for likely or prime Negroes. Some traders used the local jail, taverns, or warehouses for assembling their slaves, others owned their pens and stockades.

Franklin and Armfield, one of the best-known firms, owned an assembling plant in Alexandria, and sold in the markets at Natchez and New Orleans. The Alexandria plant was equipped with brick office and residence, two whitewashed stockades or courts for men and women, eating quarters, a hospital and sleeping barracks. All were clean and sanitary. Armfield was in charge of the plant. Isaac Franklin, who became a wealthy and respected planter as well as slave dealer, disposed of the purchases in the Southwest markets.

Slaves were transported to market by boat around the Florida peninsula and through the Gulf, or down the Mississippi after being driven overland from Alexandria. Some were transported in hired ships, others in ships owned by the trader. Some slaves were driven in coffles all the way to New Orleans. Some of these might be sold at local markets or to individual planters along the route. Slaves were well-fed and cared for in transit so that they might be in good or prime condition when they reached the market. Slaves generally dreaded being sold down the river not only because it meant breaking family ties but also because the institution was less patriarchal in the Southwest.

The public auctions, whether local or general, exhibited all the worst features of the trade. Auctioneers, usually coarse, cruel fellows, had little or no sympathy with the finer feelings of the slave. Human beings were placed on the block to be examined by the prospective purchaser as if they were mere livestock. The markets and auctions were found in all the chief towns of the Old South but centered in Alexandria, Richmond, Charleston, Savannah, Mobile, New Orleans, Natchez, Memphis, Louisville and Lexington. There were, of course, markets in some inland towns.

All the Southern states made some effort to regulate and restrict the domestic trade. Laws were passed prohibiting the export of slaves from the state, but Delaware alone really enforced the law. Other laws forbade the importation of slaves for sale and prohibited the sale of young children away from their mothers. Most such laws were ineffective. Congress forbade the trade in the District of Columbia as a part of the Compromise of 1850[qv].

The volume and value of the domestic slave trade cannot be fixed with any degree of accuracy since no statistics of the trade were kept. Virginia, Maryland, Kentucky, Missouri and the Carolinas were almost exclusively exporting states; Texas, Florida and Arkansas were exclusively importing states; and Georgia, Alabama, Mississippi, Louisiana and Tennessee were both importing and exporting states. The latter group chiefly imported up to 1850 but exported considerable numbers to the newer states in the decade of the 1850's. During the period from 1830 to 1860 Virginia exported about 220,000 slaves. Mississippi imported about 102,000 in the fourth decade and exported about 1000; the figures for the fifth decade are 58,000 and 3000; and for the sixth decade of the century 56,000 and 8000. For the decade of the 1850's the estimate for all the states is an annual turnover of about 80,000 valued at $59,000,000.

[Frederic Bancroft, *Slave Trading in the Old South;* H. T. Catterall, *Judicial Cases concerning American Slavery and the Negro;* W. H. Collins, *The Domestic Slave Trade of the Southern States;* Elizabeth Donnan, *Documents Illustrative of the History of the Slave Trade to America;* W. E. B. DuBois, *Suppression of the African Slave Trade to the United States;* U. B. Phillips, *American Negro Slavery;* J. R. Spears, *The American Slave Trade;* W. H. Stephenson, *Isaac Franklin: Slave Trader and Planter of the Old South.*]

FLETCHER M. GREEN

"Slavers" was the name popularly given in the 1840's to long, low, black wagons sent out by New England factories harassed by labor shortage to entice girls from northern New England to work in the mills of the large industrial cities of Massachusetts and near-by states. The "commanders" of the "slavers" represented to the girls that once in the mill towns they could dress in silks and spend half their time in reading, whereas in reality disillusioned girls, unable to return to their distant homes, were obliged to work from twelve to fourteen hours a day of speeded-up labor, often for as little as one dollar a week and board.

[N. J. Ware, *The Industrial Worker, 1840-1860.*]

STANLEY R. PILLSBURY

Slavery. Chattel slavery had practically disappeared from Europe before the discovery of America; serfdom was declining and had already been destroyed in England, but the expansion of European states in the 16th century, and of England during the following century, resulted in the revival of the institution of slavery in their colonial possessions and of serfdom in a modified form. In the North American colonies of England the unsatisfactory attempts to enslave the Indians were followed by the use of white indentured servants[qv], men and women who contracted to serve and to subject themselves to their masters for a period of years, thus supplying a small population with what was considered a necessary type of labor for a new, undeveloped country. "Redemptioners,"[qv] convicts and political prisoners constituted the source of this labor, and each colony received its share. As late as 1818 a cargo of "redemptioners" was landed in Philadelphia. The opportunities offered by a new country encouraged indentured servants to jump their contracts, while a general disinclination and physical inability to perform the kind of labor demanded in the Southern colonies resulted in the exploitation of another source.

The development of the plantation system[qv] in Virginia, and its spread to other Southern colonies during the 17th century led to the introduction and adaptation of Negro slave labor for the agricultural industry, and a corresponding experimentation in the provinces to the north. It was not, however, until the first quarter of the 18th century that a rapid development is noted, and the lively trade direct to Africa transformed Newport and Bristol (R. I.) to flourishing centers of the traffic.

By 1776 some 500,000 slaves, out of a total population of 2,500,000, were distributed along the Atlantic seaboard, their treatment and occupation differing according to section. In the New England colonies they were generally employed in trades and domestic duties; in the Middle Atlantic region far more were used in agriculture; and in the South, where they were present in the largest numbers and agriculture was the chief occupation, the institution became basic to the social and economic system. This new element in colonial society led first to the modification of the laws regulating indentured servants to meet the needs of the community, and then to positive legislation defining the legal, political and social status of Negroes in a white society. When the American Revolution broke out Virginia led the group with 200,000 slaves, South Carolina 100,000, Maryland and North Carolina, 70,000 each, New York, 25,000, Georgia, 10,000, New Jersey and Pennsylvania, 6000 each, Connecticut and Massachusetts, 5000 each, Rhode Island, 4000, New Hampshire, 700, with no data for Delaware. (These figures, which are necessarily estimates, are based on J. F. Jameson, *The American Revolution Considered as a Social Movement*. For a different estimate *see* article on the Slave Trade, in which the figures are based on J. D. B. DeBow, *Industrial Resources of the South and West*.)

New England farmers grew no produce which found a ready and widespread market to encourage the enlargement of their agricultural units and the industries found slave labor too expensive and too difficult to train for the skilled trades, and, according to John Adams, the white laborers disliked competition with the Negro slaves. Moral and economic considerations promoted antislavery sentiment in the Middle Atlantic provinces. Colonial leaders were aware of the inconsistency of the doctrines of natural rights[qv] and the enslavement of a half million Negroes and scarcely needed to be reminded by Lord Mansfield that slavery was "so odious that nothing could be suffered to support it but positive law." Humanitarians[qv] who attacked the institution were found in every section, John Usselinx, James Edward Oglethorpe, Roger Williams, John Eliot, Anthony Benezet, John Woolman, Henry Laurens and Thomas Jefferson, for example, were voices crying against it from 1624 to 1776. Indeed, the official attitude of the English government had been far less liberal than that of many of the colonies. Massachusetts, Connecticut, Rhode Island, Pennsylvania and Virginia attempted to abolish the slave trade only to find that such action interfered with the Royal African Company and was nullified by royal disallowance[qqv]. The First Continental Congress (1774) approved a nonimportation agreement prohibiting the slave trade, and by 1786 all of the states, except Georgia (in 1798), abolished the foreign trade. Antislavery societies were organized on the eve of the Revolution, the first by Philadelphia Quakers, to curb slavery and to promote manumission. Many of these organizations were found in the South.

Emancipating the slaves in the Northern colonies was comparatively easy, since they were few in proportion to the whites, and were not deemed essential to the economic system. Where there were considerable numbers, emancipation was gradual. By legislative action Rhode Island freed her slaves in 1774; Vermont, by her constitution (1777); court decisions in Massachusetts (1781) and New Hampshire (1783) put an end to slavery there; Pennsylvania (1780), Connecticut (1784), New York (1799) and New Jersey (1804) adopted gradual emancipation laws, the latter two requiring until 1827 and 1846 respectively to effect complete abolition. The Southern states debated the problem, but the large number, the force of custom, the race question and the economic value of the system to agriculture prevented emancipation. More liberal manumission laws were passed, however, with the result that Virginia freed more slaves by private action than there were in Massachusetts, Rhode Island and New Hampshire combined. From 1790 to 1860 there was an actual decline in the number of slaves in Delaware and Maryland, and two thirds of all the free Negroes in the South in 1860 were in these two states and Virginia. Jefferson's proposal to exclude slavery from the Old Northwest Territory found its way into the Ordinance of 1787[qv]. The framers of the Federal Constitution[qv] of 1787 regarded the question of emancipation as a state matter, and their concern with a general framework of government excluded such a consideration as much as the relations between an employer and his clerk. Nevertheless, the congressional powers over commerce, the three-fifths clause, the mutual obligations of states as members of the Union, and congressional powers in the territories were potential sources of controversy (*see* Compromises of the Federal Constitution).

The invention of the cotton gin[qv] by Eli Whitney (1793) and the introduction of sea-island cotton (1784) relieved the depressed South Atlantic states, revived slavery, and showed the value of the Negro to the industry. It was cotton[qv] more than any other staple that gave new strength to a moribund institution. The Negro seemed perfectly adapted to its growth, and women and children could be utilized in numerous ways. Established, embryonic and aspiring planters moved into the southern piedmont[qv], swung south and westward, and each decade thereafter saw a growth in the number of slaves, the bales of cotton, and a corresponding diminution in the southern liberality of 1776.

Climatic and geographical factors divided the South into four zones of staple production—(1) Tobacco: Maryland, Virginia, Kentucky and North Carolina; (2) Cotton: South Carolina, Georgia and the Gulf states; (3) Sugar cane: Georgia and Louisiana; (4) Rice: South Carolina and Georgia. Slavery sought its climatic and geographical level, being found even in the southern portions of the free states along the Ohio River. Slavery was unevenly distributed, its irregularity following that of the plantation belts, and nearly one half of all slaves in 1860 were found in the cotton states. Of the total white population of that area, namely over 8,000,000, only 383,000 owned slaves, less than one third of that number owned over 10 slaves each, while only 2292 owned 100 or more each. Less than one half the whole area of the South was in the cotton zone, and less than one half its people were engaged in its production.

The Southern farm and plantation had an almost equal division of slaves, and on both they were classified as field hands and house servants. The latter took pride in their privileged position and were the envy of their less fortunate brethren. The industrial and social life of the field hands was strictly regulated: they lived in quarters, received regular rations of food and clothes, labored in gangs, usually, under the supervision of an overseer[qv] or the owner, and were not allowed to leave the premises without a pass. Overseers were given detailed instructions as to the administration of the plantation, the industrial direction of the slaves, and even their punishment. The degree of regimentation depended upon the size of the plantation or farm, the staple grown and the locality. While house servants by no means enjoyed full freedom, their lot was far better than that of the field hands, and they were not subject to such strict control.

Family life was encouraged among the slaves, and the majority of the adults were apt to be married. Cast-off furniture and ornaments found their way to the quarters, articles of slave manufacture, gardens and perhaps a few chickens gave an air of domesticity to the little cabins. Medical attention was given by the master's physician, and on the large plantations a hospital might be found. Generally, the slaves were well-fed, even if the food was coarse, reasonable rest periods were observed, and while the hours of labor were long, there was no systematic exploitation of the workers. Slaves represented capital, and no owner would risk its loss any more than the owner of a valuable horse or a registered bull. Moreover, most of the slave-owners were fully aware that their property were human beings and treated them accordingly, such treatment being commensurate with the character, temper and intelligence of the master. Religious instruction was given at regular intervals on the large plantations, and frequently the slaves attended their master's church. Truancy, sullenness, the refusal to obey orders, etc., brought punishment, usually whipping, the degree being in proportion to the nature of the offense.

Slaves were employed to some extent in industry, but experimentation with slave labor in cotton mills and railroad construction proved unsatisfactory. Some worked as stevedores, carpenters, masons, plasterers and mechanics, furnishing a mobile labor supply, and were hired out frequently to individuals desiring such workers, the profits accruing to the owner.

The nature of the institution, antislavery sentiment, latent and active, in the North, and political expediency injected the issue into national politics and made the course of our territorial expansion difficult. The first important controversy came over the application of Missouri for admission as a state in 1818. Some politicians from the Middle Atlantic states, tired of the rule of the Virginia Dynasty[qv], saw an opportunity to break its hold on the Republican party (Jeffersonian)[qv] through the slavery question, by presenting it in such a way as to force the South to set the bounds to its expansion, and consequently lose political power in the National Government, or reject it, and thus alienate the northern wing of the party. James Tallmadge[qv], of New York, introduced an amendment in the House (1819) excluding slavery from Missouri, and so heated were the arguments in Congress that such leaders as John Adams and Thomas Jefferson were thoroughly alarmed. The settlement of the question would be a precedent for other states carved from the major part of the Louisiana Purchase[qv] of 1803. The compromise of 1820, admitting Missouri with slavery but excluding it from the territory north of 36° 30′, removed the question from public arenas for some time (*see* Missouri Compromise).

Geographical proximity, the activities of land speculators, and the expansion of the southern frontier resulted in the settlement of the Mexican state of Texas by Americans, and its successful revolution in 1836 raised the question of annexation to the Union. Slavery existed in Texas, and if admitted to the Union the political advantage would be to the South. The Panic of 1837[qv] postponed the matter, but subsequent debates and sharp political division kept it in the foreground. In general the majority of the Democrats favored annexation, the majority of the Whigs opposed. By the end of 1844 it seemed impossible to secure the necessary two thirds of the Senate to annex Texas by a treaty, so a joint resolution of Congress was adopted in 1845, the offer rushed to Texas just before the Tyler administration retired, and Dec. 29, it was admitted as a state. The annexation of Texas led directly to the War with Mexico[qqv] (1846–48), and again political expediency was fateful in its results. David Wilmot[qv] (Pa.) introduced the famous proviso to an appropriation bill (1846) calling for the exclusion of slavery from any territory acquired from Mexico. It passed the House of Representatives, was defeated in the Senate, and the passions thus aroused, aggravated by Abolitionist[qv] demands for the emancipation of slaves and the abolition of the slave trade in the District of Columbia, with the counter demand of Southerners for an equal share in the territories and a better fugitive slave law, led to an organized secession movement in the South[qqv]. Conservatives and moderates in Congress adopted the Compromise of 1850[qv] which admitted California as a free state (its constitution forbade slavery), organized Utah and New Mexico as territories with no reference to slavery, abolished the slave trade in the District of Columbia, and provided a more stringent fugitive slave law. The Southern Convention meeting at Nashville[qv] (Tenn.) in 1850 accepted the Compromise as a permanent solution of the question, but warned that any future interference with slavery in the states or the domestic slave trade, or the refusal by Congress to admit a state because of slavery would be met with resistance even to the point of secession.

As things stood in 1850, every square inch of territory had been divided between slavery and freedom; the Missouri Compromise took care of the Louisiana Purchase and the northern part of Texas; that of 1850, California and New Mexico; Oregon did not feature in the dispute. The great majority, North and South, took this as the final settlement, and the elections of 1852 and 1856 seemed to prove that the country was weary of the controversy.

The contest was raised again by the Kansas-Nebraska Act[qv] of 1854. Stephen A. Douglas (Ill.), chairman of the Senate committee on the territories, was highly desirous of organizing a territorial government for the region so as to facilitate the construction of a transcontinental railroad to the Pacific. Jefferson Davis (Miss.) and others planned a similar project from New Orleans and following the southern route to the Pacific, the line passing through a territory already organized. Others favored a line running north of Kansas. The result was the reporting of a bill organizing both regions. Sen. Archibald M. Dixon (Ky.) proposed an amendment repealing the Missouri Compromise[qv], and all efforts to have him withdraw the motion failed. The bill passed. This put the slavery issue, politically, where it was in 1819. The doctrine of popular, or "squatter" sovereignty[qv], advocated by Douglas and Lewis Cass (Mich.), left Kansas to be controlled by the first groups arriving, and the struggle that ensued over the framing of the constitution and the control of the government was a prelude to the Civil War (*see* Border War). The Republican party[qv] was organized on this issue.

The decision of the Supreme Court of the United States on March 6, 1857, in Dred Scott v. Sanford[qv] was an effort to suppress the dispute and take the question out of politics. The right of Congress to prohibit slavery in a territory was denied, and the Missouri Compromise was pronounced unconstitutional and void. This seemed to be an approval of Calhoun's doctrine that slavery followed the flag into the territories.

The controversy was settled, after an appeal to arms, by a victorious North standing unquestioned over a prostrate South. The Thirteenth Amendment[qv] to the Constitution, legally abolishing slavery, passed Congress in 1864, and Secretary of State William H. Seward announced Dec. 18, 1865 that the requisite number of states had ratified, including eight states of the former Confederacy.

[U. B. Phillips, *Life and Labor in the Old South;* R. S. Cotterill, *The Old South;* W. B. Hesseltine, *A History of the South, 1607-1936.*]

RALPH B. FLANDERS

Slavery, Attitude of the Churches to. All the larger colonial churches accepted slavery[qv] without question. The Society for the Propagation of the Gospel[qv] instructed its missionaries to give attention to the religious instruction of slaves, but did not condemn slavery as such. Prominent New England ministers owned slaves and respectable New England citizens were interested in the slave trade[qv]. Several of the smaller German sects as Mennonites and Dunkers opposed slavery and the Quakers[qqv] had taken steps to eliminate slaveholding members by 1787.

The first antislavery movement[qv] came from two main sources: the increased humanitarian impulse coming out of the 18th century revivals[qv]; the revolutionary philosophy embodied in the Declaration of Independence[qv], which states that "all men are created equal." Responding to these influences the American churches during the last quarter of the 18th and the first quarter of the 19th centuries became increasingly antislavery. It was during this period that the Northern states rid themselves of slavery. New England Congregationalism[qv] became actively antislavery under the leadership of Samuel Hopkins; the Methodists[qv] passed antislavery legislation at their organizing conference in 1784; the Presbyterians[qv] took strong antislavery positions in 1787 and 1818; and various Baptist[qv] associations took similar action.

The churches began to recede from this strong antislavery position after 1830, due to the influences arising out of the agricultural revolution taking place at the South and the rise of the rabid abolition movement[qv] in the North. Slaveholding church members and even slaveholding ministers became an accepted fact at the South, while at the North, condemnation of slaveholding church members came to be increasingly virulent.

The general church officials, having in charge national church bodies, attempted to keep down controversy within the church, fearing for its unity, and until 1840 they generally occupied a moderate position and condemned abolitionism. William Lloyd Garrison at first found considerable support for his radical movement among church people, but his violent methods soon alienated them and after 1840 his movement found little church support. As a result, Garrison developed an anticlerical and antichurch obsession, and he and his disciples were responsible for the legend that the American churches were the chief bulwarks of American slavery.

After about 1836 a new antislavery movement began among church people led by Theodore Dwight Weld and a group of Oberlin graduates, which swept throughout central and western New York, Ohio, western Pennsylvania and Michigan. This Oberlin movement[qv] was particularly strong among New School Presbyterians, slavery having been one of the causes leading to the Old School-New School division in 1837. The Weld influence was largely responsible for sending the first antislavery members to Congress, and for a time Weld acted as an extremely effective lobbyist. Growing differences over the slavery issue divided Methodists and Baptists in 1844–45 into Northern and Southern bodies, the Northern section of the churches becoming increasingly antislavery, the Southern bodies increasingly proslavery. Roman Catholics and Episcopalians[qqv] generally avoided all agitation of the question and thus avoided a slavery schism.

[W. W. Sweet, *The Story of Religion in America;* Gilbert H. Barnes, *The Antislavery Impulse, 1830-1844;* Albert Barnes, *An Inquiry into the Scriptural Views of Slavery*, and *The Church and Slavery;* J. G. Birney, *The American Churches the Chief Bulwarks of American Slavery;* J. N. Norwood, *The Schism in the Methodist Episcopal Church, 1844: A Study of Slavery and Ecclesiastical Politics;* A. C. Thomas, The Attitude of the Society of Friends toward Slavery, etc., *Papers of the Am. Society of Church Hist.*, Series I, Vol. VIII; F. Stringfellow, *Scriptural and Statistical Views in Favor of Slavery.*]

WILLIAM W. SWEET

Slaves, Fugitive. *See* Fugitive Slave Acts.

Slavocracy, THE, in its broader sense refers to those persons or interests in the ante-bellum South representing slavery[qv] and using their influence to preserve or advance their peculiar institution. In a more restricted sense the word may be regarded as synonymous with the "Slave Power," a term of reproach used, principally in the North, during the 1850's to designate a group of Southern expansionists supposedly united in a vast and aggressive plot to extend slavery into the territories, and possibly into Mexico, Cuba and Central America, thereby creating a great "slave empire," from which it was feared not even the free states would be safe. That certain Southern imperialists were interested in extending slave territory is no doubt true, but that the majority of Southern slaveholders were engaged in, or even acquainted with, such a scheme as was imagined by the Northern abolitionists has been discredited by modern historical scholars.

[Theodore C. Smith, *Parties and Slavery;* Chauncey S. Boucher, *In re* That Aggressive Slavocracy, in *Mississippi Valley Historical Review*, VIII.]

JAMES W. PATTON

Sleeping-cars. *See* Pullmans.

Sleepy Hollow. About three quarters of a mile north of Tarrytown, N. Y., lies Sleepy Hollow, famous for its old Dutch church (1699) and for its associations with the writings of Washington Irving. About this narrow ravine or valley, through which flows the Pocantico River, cluster legends connected with Irving's classic tale of Ichabod Crane, who fled wildly across the bridge to escape the "Headless Horseman." This region Irving visited in early youth, probably for the first time in 1798, and he now lies buried in the cemetery behind the church. Romantic memories of Sleepy Hollow recur in Irving's essays (e.g., *Wolfert's Roost*), and attain most complete and delightful expression in "The Legend of Sleepy Hollow," originally published in Number VI of *The Sketch Book,* on Dec. 29, 1819.

STANLEY T. WILLIAMS

Sleighs. Because of the long New England and New York winters, snow vehicles were very nearly as important in the Northeast in early days as those with wheels. They conveyed not only the passenger, but in village and country, did nearly all the commercial and industrial hauling during the winter. Detachable runners were in every barn, ready to replace the wheels on wagons and buggies when the first snow fell. Straw rides in these emergency wagon-bed sleighs were a popular winter amusement. Sleighs varied widely in design, from the rough sled for wood-hauling, through the homemade pung with its homely box bed, where was space for several passengers and no little freight, to the graceful cutter for town driving, seating only two persons comfortably. For pleasure driving, sleighs were used in America earlier than wheeled vehicles. Sleigh racing, often on frozen rivers, was a favorite 19th century, New England winter sport. In cities like New York, certain streets were speedways on Sundays and holidays, where the owners of noted trotters drove to and fro in cutters and had impromptu brushes with each other. One small town, East Hampton, Conn., produced practically all the sleigh bells used in America in the 19th century, and still does so.

[Edwin Valentine Mitchell, *Horse and Buggy Days.*]

ALVIN F. HARLOW

Slidell's Mission to Mexico. John Slidell, a Democratic congressman from Louisiana, was sent to Mexico by the Polk administration in November, 1845, to secure a boundary adjustment between the two nations (*see* Texas, Annexation of). His flexible instructions included cancellation of Mexican claims and a liberal bonus for the Rio Grande as the boundary of Texas. Five millions would be none too much for the cession of New Mexico. A line to the Pacific yielding San Francisco to the United States would merit even twenty millions; while a line to Monterey might call for twenty-five.

Notwithstanding previous pledges, the Mexicans did not receive Slidell officially. After the formal rejection of his proposal, on Dec. 21, 1845, the minister withdrew to Jalapa, where he remained till April, 1846, cultivating the auxiliary purposes of his mission as an observer and a martyr, striving "to place us in the strongest moral position before our own people and the world by exhausting every means of conciliation." Failure of the mission presaged war with Mexico[qv].

[Louis Martin Sears, *John Slidell.*]

LOUIS MARTIN SEARS

Slim Buttes, Battle of (Sept. 9, 1876). After the disastrous battle of the Little Big Horn[qv] troops under Crook and other commanders pursued and scattered the Indians. His rations nearly exhausted, Crook finally abandoned pursuit and marched for the Black Hills[qv] settlements. At Grand River, Capt. Mills with 150 cavalrymen on the strongest horses pushed ahead for supplies, and twenty miles south, at Slim Buttes, discovered a Sioux village of fifty lodges, containing 100 warriors under American Horse. At daybreak Mills rushed the village and captured it. A messenger to Crook brought up the main body by noon and American Horse, mortally wounded and at bay in a cave, surrendered. Crazy Horse, arriving tardily with a large force chiefly of Oglala Sioux, attacked but was repulsed, and the troops reached the Black Hills safely.

[Cyrus Townsend Brady, *Indian Fights and Fighters;* Charles King, *Campaigning with Crook.*]

JOSEPH MILLS HANSON

Slocum, General, THE, a steamboat carrying an excursion party from St. Mark's Lutheran Evangelical Church, New York City, was destroyed by fire in the East River on June 15, 1904, with a loss of 955 passengers and two of the crew. This disaster led to a congressional investigation, revision of steamboat inspection laws and stricter discipline on excursion boats throughout the United States.

[H. D. Northrop, *New York's Awful Steamboat Horror.*]

STANLEY R. PILLSBURY

Slogans in Electoral Campaigns. The statement that slogans are catch phrases which serve as convenient substitutes for thought is certainly true of those employed in politics. Their purpose is usually to distract attention from the real issues, and to center it upon emotional aspects of the current scene. The idea emphasized by the slogan may be quite irrelevant, but it may nevertheless be extremely effective in developing group loyalty among the supporters of a candidate, or a common bond of contempt for the opposition. Examples are: "Tippecanoe and Tyler Too" (1840); "Fifty-four Forty or Fight" (1844); "A House Divided Against Itself Cannot Stand" (1860); "Full Dinner Pail" (1896); "The Big Stick" (1904); "He Kept Us Out of War" (1916); "The Forgotten Man" (1932).

The informal nicknames of candidates have frequently acquired a currency not easily distinguishable from that of the slogans: "Old Hickory"; "Honest Abe"; "The Great Commoner"; "Teddy"; "Cautious Cal" and many others. Similarly, certain tunes adopted for campaign songs have become intimately associated with candidates, such as: "There'll Be a Hot Time in the Old Town Tonight" (Theodore Roosevelt, 1904); "I Didn't Raise My Boy to be a Soldier" (Wilson, 1916); "The Sidewalks of New York" (Smith, 1928).

[Joseph B. Bishop, *Presidential Nominations and Elections*; Emerson D. Fite, *The Presidential Campaign of 1860;* Frederick E. Lumley, *Means of Social Control;* Carl Scherf, Slang, Slogan and Song in American Politics, in *Social Studies*, December, 1934; Mark Sullivan, *Our Times.*]

W. BROOKE GRAVES

Sloop, THE, was a naval vessel, generally ship-rigged and three-masted, with all its guns on the open spar deck. In the War of 1812 sloops like the *Wasp*[qv] won many famous actions. Last and strongest were the wooden screw sloops, *Hartford,* 22 guns, *Niagara, Brooklyn,* and *San Jacinto,* of the Civil War. The only one now remaining (1939) is the *Hartford*[qv].

[H. I. Chapelle, *History of American Sailing Ships;* F. M. Bennett, *The Steam Navy of the United States.*]

WALTER B. NORRIS

Slums. As cities began to grow in the colonies, there were inevitably low and undesirable areas where the dwellings of the poor congregated. In New York, the lower East Side slum area had been established before 1795. Half a dozen streets southeast of Chatham Square were then unpaved, marshy, filthy, bordered with ramshackle houses which became partly buried by erosion from the neighboring slopes; and there poverty-stricken immigrants, then mostly German and Irish, lived in cellars, attics, single rooms, often lying upon the bare floor or a few shavings. Pestilences broke out here and in similar slums along the North River almost yearly and carried off hundreds. The great influx of unrestricted immigration in the first half of the 19th century, when European countries emptied their poorhouses, asylums and prisons upon our shores, built up the slums enormously; thousands of the immigrants went almost directly from the ship to the slums or to some charitable institution. Between 1825 and 1855—when it was somewhat ameliorated—the Five Points in New York probably exceeded in degradation, criminality and horror any other area in the world. The slums naturally became breeding places of crime, and those of New York became notorious for their gangs, at first of political or mere ruffianly tendency, but becoming more and more addicted to robbery, graft and murder by contract. They had always political alliances, and supplied thuggery and illegal votes on election days. Streets were uncleaned and hogs ran at large (in New York until 1867). The tenements were enormously profitable to the landlord, and were built with little or no consideration for comfort or sanitation.

In 1894 Carroll D. Wright, Commissioner of Labor, submitted a report to President Cleveland upon the slums of New York, Philadelphia, Baltimore and Chicago. He found the slum population of New York (then embracing Manhattan only) to be 360,000; of Philadelphia, 35,000; Chicago, 162,000; Baltimore, 25,000. In Chicago only 2.83% of all families and in New York only 2.33% had bathtubs with water connection. In New York 6576 out of 28,000 families lived in windowless rooms. One thirty-two-acre sanitary district in New York on June 1, 1894, showed an average of 986.4 persons per acre. The world's next most densely populated area was one in Bombay, India, where the average was only 759.66 on each of 46 acres. Efforts at reform were made for decades, but it came slowly. A large "model" tenement building was privately erected in New York in 1879–81, and another in Brooklyn in 1890. A Tenement House Act for New York in 1895 was superseded by that of 1901 which has served as a model for most tenement house legislation in America since that time. It provided for plumbing, fireproofing, light, ventilation, inspection and rigid enforcement. Nevertheless, in 1939 there still remained in New York many "old law tenements," though they were then rapidly disappearing. Boston handled her slum problem most creditably among all American cities. In 1936 yard privies were still widely used in the slum districts of all large cities of the United States save Boston. In Boston, more than 99% of the tenement families then had water connection, while in New York many still used hall sinks and hall toilets. Private capital has built a number of model tenements in New York and elsewhere since 1920. The Federal Government took a hand in housing reform during Hoover's administration with the Reconstruction Finance Corporation[qv], and after 1933 the F. D. Roosevelt administration went in for it on a large scale, though it was found difficult to create self-supporting tenements which could be rented cheaply enough for the poorer families to afford.

[James Ford, Katherine Morrow and George N. Thompson, *Slums and Housing;* Alvin F. Harlow, *Old Bowery Days.*]

ALVIN F. HARLOW

Smallpox. The finding of America was followed by a sinister exchange of disease: the Indians gave syphilis to the Spaniards, and the Spaniards gave smallpox to the Indians. The early settlers, while deploring their own mortality, derived considerable satisfaction from the fatal effects of the smallpox upon the aborigines, and the suggestion was made that they be exterminated altogether by spreading smallpox among those tribes that had hitherto escaped. The only medical publication in the colonies during the 17th century was the broadside by the clergyman, Thomas Thacher, *A Brief Rule to Guide the Common-People of New-England how to order themselves and theirs in the Small Pocks, or Measels* (1677/8). Signed, "a well wisher to the sick," this single sheet—a double-columned poster, printed on one side of the paper, fifteen and a half inches long and ten inches across—is significant as the origin of American medical literature, and as the first attempt in this country to control the most fatal of diseases.

The next step was likewise made by a theologian. The dominating Cotton Mather, who committed infinite mischief with his medical theories, which included the searching for witch marks, has definitely to his credit the introduction of inoculation into America. In the midst of his voluminous reading, coming across the Turkish method, he urged the Boston physician, Zabdiel Boylston, to put variolation into practice. Boylston first inoculated his youthful son, Thomas (June 27, 1721), two Negroes and such patients as were willing to submit. Cotton Mather, and his father, Increase Mather, defended the innovation in their usual forceful manner; active opposition developed, led by a Scotch and a French physician in America. Satan was declared the first inoculator (inoculation of Job); mobs carrying a halter searched for Boylston, who was compelled to visit his patients at night and in disguise.

The discovery of vaccination[qv] was introduced into this country by another Boston physician, Benjamin Waterhouse, who followed Boylston in first vaccinating his own son, Daniel Oliver Waterhouse (July 8, 1800). That the malignancy of smallpox could be rendered not only innocuous, but protective, by passing it through the cow, was the first miracle of immunity. Waterhouse forwarded some of the vaccine to Thomas Jefferson, the presidential hand vaccinating his family and his neighbors. Jefferson's letter (Monticello, May 14, 1806) to Jenner is an historic document: "Medicine has never before produced any single improvement of such utility. Harvey's discovery of the circulation of the blood was a beautiful addition to our knowledge of the ancient economy; but on a review of the practice of medicine before and since that epoch, I do not see any great amelioration which has been derived from that discovery. You have erased from the calendar of human afflictions one of its greatest. Yours is the comfortable reflection that mankind can never forget that you have lived; future nations will know by history only that the loathsome smallpox has existed, and by you has been extirpated."

Jefferson's prophecy has been nullified by carelessness. In "the banner health year in the history of the United States" (1938), all communicable diseases dropped to new minima, with two exceptions: smallpox and measles were unusually prevalent, thus again reminding us of America's earliest publication in medicine.

[Essay on Edward Jenner, in Victor Robinson's *Pathfinders in Medicine.*]

VICTOR ROBINSON

Smelters. Smelting is a method of separating gold, silver and other metals from their ores with fire and heat intense enough to melt the ores. A Spanish law (Aug. 22, 1584) required a government smelter to be established in every mining district and required all miners to bring their gold and lead-silver there. Ruins of crude smelters have been noted in southern California.

In 1750 coal, and in 1830 anthracite coal, was first used as a fuel for smelting, and by 1860 smelters had attained practically their present form. But the era of improved metallurgical and chemical processes had scarcely begun. Colorado's gold sulphide ores defied recovery until a professor of chemistry, Nathaniel P. Hill, after conducting experiments at Swansea, Wales, and Freiburg, Germany, built the Boston and Colorado smelter at Blackhawk, Colo., in 1868. Its successor, the Argo smelter at Denver, under management of Richard Pearce, began the smelting of copper ores in reverberatory furnaces, and up to 1900 was the only one to smelt gold and silver ores to matte exclusively in reverberatories. Discovery of lead carbonates at Leadville caused the erection of a dozen large smelters there, like the Arkansas Valley smelter which is still operating (1938).

The main change in smelters has been their rapid growth in size. The Blackhawk smelter had only one small calcining and one small reverberatory furnace. In 1888 Meyer Guggenheim, who had been sold some silver mines at Leadville, decided that he would make more profit if he smelted his own ores. Accordingly he built the Philadelphia smelter at Pueblo, Colo., with six great furnaces with a capacity of sixty tons of ore each daily. In 1893 the largest smelters in the United States were at Denver, Pueblo and Salt Lake City. The Washoe smelter of the Anaconda Copper Mining Company at Anaconda, Mont., has a smoke stack 300 feet high and 30 feet inside diameter. Leading up the hillside to the base of this stack are 1234 feet of flue sixty feet wide. Toward the close of the 19th century cutthroat competition between the smelters led to combination. On April 4, 1899, the American Smelting and Refining Company brought together eighteen of the country's largest smelting companies. In 1901 the Guggenheims, the largest of the independents, joined and obtained control of the American Smelting and Refining Company.

[W. Davis, *The Story of Copper;* H. F. Collins, *The Metallurgy of Lead and Silver*, Part II; G. Williams, *William Guggenheim.*]

PERCY S. FRITZ

Smith, Fort (Ark.), an early frontier military post, was established in 1817 by Maj. Stephen H. Long at the confluence of the Arkansas and Poteau rivers. It was named for Col. Thomas A. Smith of the United States Army. The original walls were made of pickets with blockhouses at the corners. Inside the enclosure were barracks and officers' quarters. Founded to preserve order among the near-by Indian tribes and to defend the frontier, it became an important border post during the Civil War.

[A. H. Abel, *The American Indian as Participant in the Civil War;* J. B. Thoburn, *History of Oklahoma.*]

EDWARD EVERETT DALE

Smith, Fort C. F., named for Gen. Charles Ferguson Smith, was established Aug. 12, 1866, by Lt. Col. N. C. Kinney at the Big Horn River crossing of the Bozeman Trail*qv*, in southern Montana, ninety-one miles north of Fort Phil Kearny*qv*. It was built of logs and adobe.

During most of its existence it was virtually besieged by hostile Sioux. On Aug. 1, 1867, Indians attacked hay makers and their soldier escort in a meadow three miles northeast of the fort (*see* Wagon Box Fight). By agreement with the Sioux, the fort was abandoned early in August, 1868, at the conclusion of Red Cloud's War*qv*.

[G. R. Hebard and E. A. Brininstool, *The Bozeman Trail.*]

PAUL I. WELLMAN

Smith, Fort, Council of, met early in September, 1865, to make peace with the Five Civilized Tribes*qv* and other smaller tribes of Indian Territory that had joined the Southern Confederacy (*see* Indian in the Civil War). The commissioners from the United States were important civil or military officials, while the Indian representatives included the ablest leaders of the various tribes. The work of the Council was complicated by the fact that the Cherokee had two groups of delegates. One of these, led by John Ross, represented the faction that had repudiated the former treaty with the Confederacy and declared allegiance to the United States. The other was led by Stand Watie, head of the southern branch of the tribe. The Indians were told that by joining the Confederacy they had made themselves liable to a forfeiture of all the rights guaranteed them in former treaties with the United States. They were given the general terms of new treaties they must sign in order again to receive the favor and protection of the United States. The various tribes then signed an agreement as to peace and amity with the United States in which they further agreed to send commissioners to Washington the following year to negotiate these new treaties.

[A. H. Abel, *The American Indian under Reconstruction;* M. L. Wardell, *A Political History of the Cherokees.*]

EDWARD EVERETT DALE

Smith Explorations. Jedediah Strong Smith (1799–1831) joined the Ashley expedition*qv* at St. Louis, 1822, ascended the Missouri River, and in the spring of 1824 headed the first party of Americans to travel through South Pass*qv*. In the summer of 1826 he led a party from Salt Lake to southern California—the first Americans to reach the Spanish settlements by an overland route (*see* Cajon Pass). In June, 1827, he and two companions returned to Salt Lake by the central route—the first white men to pass that way. Shortly afterward he set out again for California with eighteen men, ten of whom were massacred by Mojaves on the Colorado. In 1828 he traveled up the Pacific coast to Fort Vancouver on the Columbia*qv*, losing all but two of his men by massacre on the Umpqua River. During the following year he explored the Snake River country, and in 1830 returned overland to St. Louis. In the spring of 1831 he set out with a wagon train for Santa Fé[qv], and while seeking water for his party was killed by Comanches[qv] on the Cimarron River, southwestern Kansas, May 27, 1831.

[H. C. Dale, *The Ashley-Smith Explorations and the Discovery of the Central Route to the Pacific;* Maurice S. Sullivan, *The Travels of Jedediah Smith* and *Jedediah Smith, Trader and Trailbreaker;* John G. Neihardt, *The Splendid Wayfaring.*]

JOHN G. NEIHARDT

Smith-Hughes Act, The (1917), a landmark in the advance of Federal centralization as well as in vocational education, created a Federal Board for Vocational Education for the promotion of training in agriculture, trades and industries, commerce, home economics and the teaching of vocational subjects. This is a form of Federal grant-in-aid[qv] to be matched by state or local contributions, or both. Supplementary acts have extended the original activities to vocational rehabilitation with socially important experimental aspects.

[W. P. Sears, *The Roots of Vocational Education.*]

HARVEY WISH

Smith-Lever Act, The (1914), provided for an elaborate system of agricultural extension work conducted through a field force of specialists with the assistance of a Federal grant-in-aid[qv] system based on equal state contributions. Students not attending colleges obtained the instructions and demonstration work in agriculture and home economics, and thus enjoyed indirectly the benefits of the agricultural colleges and experimental stations[qqv]. Like other forms of grants-in-aid, the Smith-Lever Act gave significant additions of local activities to the Federal Government.

[W. H. Shepardson, *Agricultural Education in the United States.*]

HARVEY WISH

Smithsonian Institution, The. James Smithson, an Englishman, dying in Genoa in 1829, bequeathed about $600,000 to the United States of America "to found at Washington, under the name of the Smithsonian Institution, an establishment for the increase and diffusion of knowledge among men."

Congress provided in 1846 that the President, the Vice-President, the Chief Justice, and the members of the Cabinet should be the "establishment." It should be governed by a Board of Regents, partly ex officio, partly selected by Congress, and a secretary chosen by the regents.

In 1846 the regents elected as secretary the eminent electrical investigator, Joseph Henry. Under his guidance the Institution took shape. The work of the Smithsonian has, besides its well-known museum activities, consisted, in the main, of original investigation and the publication of memoirs, of publications and correspondence of a more popular nature; of the free distribution of publications to important libraries throughout the world; of initiating or taking part in expeditions for collections or investigations; of providing apparatus or making grants of money to worthy investigators; and of co-operating with government departments in the advancement of scientific work.

In 1850 Spencer Fullerton Baird, a distinguished naturalist, was elected assistant secretary of the Institution. After Henry's death, in 1878, he succeeded him as secretary, and continued in that office until his own death in 1887.

An opportunity to secure collections, never to come again, was presented at this time in the opening up of the great West. Baird seized the opportunity and made the most of it. He was himself an indefatigable student of the collections, but even more, he trained an able school of young men. With Henry, Baird organized the system of international exchange of publications. He promoted and organized the United States Fish Commission, and was its commissioner from its foundation until his death. The Bureau of American Ethnology was established during Baird's secretaryship.

The third secretary, 1887–1906, was Samuel Pierpont Langley. He established the Astrophysical Observatory at the Smithsonian Institution, 1890. Langley made careful investigations at the Institution of the physics of mechanical flight, and as early as 1896 built large models with which he conducted flights of nearly a mile (*see* Aviation). He promoted the establishment of the National Zoological Park, 1890.

The fourth secretary, 1907–27, the distinguished paleontologist, Dr. Charles Doolittle Walcott, had been in the service of the Geological Survey for over a quarter of a century, and from 1891 its director. During Secretary Walcott's administration the National Gallery of Art, 1906 (now termed the National Collection of Fine Arts), and the Freer Gallery, 1920, were added as branches of the Smithsonian Institution.

Dr. Charles Greeley Abbot was elected to the secretaryship on Jan. 10, 1928. He has been engaged principally in research on the sun, and has established and maintained several observatories on high desert mountains for these studies. Besides directing the Astrophysical Observatory, he is the active director of the Division of Radiation and Organisms, which he established in 1929 for the study of the effect of light on plant and animal life.

[*The Smithsonian Institution, 1846-1896; Smithsonian Scientific Series*, Vols. 1-12; *Smithsonian Reports*, published annually, 1846-1937.]

CHARLES GREELEY ABBOT

Smoky Hill Trail, THE, came into importance with the Pikes Peak Gold Rush[qv], though Frémont had traversed part of it in 1844. Its route was up the Kansas, or Kaw, River and the Smoky Hill fork to its source, thence westerly to and along the Big Sandy, then to and down Cherry Creek to its mouth at Denver. A party of gold seekers broke the trail in the fall of 1858. Others who followed suffered from lack of water and food. Once there was cannibalism. Such difficulties discouraged use of the route, though it was the shortest to the gold country. In 1860 Leavenworth City employed W. G. Russell, discoverer of gold in Colorado, to survey and mark this trail in an effort to divert emigration over it and through the sponsoring city. This had little effect. The Butterfield Overland Despatch was established on this trail in 1865, competing with Holladay's Overland Mail[qqv]. Minor variations of route developed. The stage service was displaced by the railroad in 1870. Highway U. S. 40 now follows rather closely the old Smoky Hill Trail.

LEROY R. HAFEN

Smoot-Hawley Tariff. *See* Hawley-Smoot Tariff.

Smuggling began very early in colonial times (*see* Smuggling, Colonial) and has never ceased. When the nation became independent, several of the states enacted revenue laws, and there was much smuggling of foreign goods along the Atlantic coast, usually by small vessels which met larger merchantmen at sea and brought the goods by night into shallow creeks and inlets. In 1789–90 Congress passed laws placing these matters under Federal jurisdiction, limiting the smallness of vessels in which goods might be brought, making rigid provisions as to manifests and dutiable goods and authorizing search, when necessary, within four leagues of the shore. Secretary of the Treasury Gallatin is found in 1808 asking for additional revenue cutters, the deeply serrated coast of Maine, Cape Cod, Buzzards Bay, Long Island Sound and the lonely sounds and inlets of the Carolinas being particularly vulnerable to smugglers. Liquors, silks, West Indian tobacco and cigars were favorite contraband articles in those days, though the smuggling of Negro slaves[qv] was a large industry. Around 1800 a small army of smugglers practically ruled the Louisiana coast; Jean Lafitte became their leader shortly after 1810 (*see* Barataria). Internal smuggling began very early, with the forbidding by the colonies, one after another, of the selling of liquor to Indians. In the 19th century illicit selling of firearms and whiskey to the Indians was a major problem in the West. Outward-bound smuggling began very early in that century with the secret supplying of arms to Mexican revolutionists, and continued later with gun-running to Cuba and to Central and South American countries; and this continued into the 20th century (*see* Filibustering). The blockade running of foreign and Confederate, and even of Northern vessels, into and out of Southern ports during the Civil War may be considered an episode in this chronicle (*see* Blockade Runners, Confederate). The opium habit was introduced by Chinese immigrants, and in the latter 19th century opium[qv] smuggling, as well as that of other drugs, had reached disquieting proportions. Heroin, originated in Germany, became a still more dangerous item after 1900, and so continues. After the enactment of Chinese exclusion acts[qv], the secret entry of Chinese into the United States began and is still carried on, mostly through Mexico and the West Indies. With the rapid increase of our national wealth, the desire for jewels arose, and they—especially diamonds and pearls—have ever since been persistent items in individual smuggling, enormous ingenuity being exercised in concealing them from customs officers. So efficient was our Revenue Cutter Service that there was no great amount of smuggling *in bulk* along our seacoasts between 1900 and 1917, though it was admitted that "Along the borders there is still more or less smuggling of Chinese persons, opium and spirits." But with the Prohibition[qv] era there came an enormous flood of smuggled liquor from abroad. Several states had voted out liquor before the Eighteenth Amendment[qv], but were unable to stop the secret shipping of liquor into their territory from "wet" states. Early smuggling had its good effects; as for example, it improved our seamanship and the build of our vessels.

[A. Hyatt Verrill, *Smugglers and Smuggling;* William E. Masterson, *Jurisdiction in Marginal Seas.*]

ALVIN F. HARLOW

Smuggling, Colonial. The extent of smuggling and its effect upon the imperial relationship offer one of the most perplexing problems of colonial history. That smuggling existed there can be no doubt. Parliament was surprisingly negligent in providing for the enforcement of the Navigation Acts[qv]. It provided regulations in

1660 and 1663 governing exportations and importations. But not until 1673 did it create officials to enforce them, and not until 1696 did it give them the powers granted customs officers in England. The colonial charters complicated problems of enforcement already made complex by natural geographic conditions. The lengthy coastline, numerous sheltered coves, afforded tempting opportunities for clandestine activities. Accounts of tobacco packed in flour barrels and foreign wine masquerading as New England rum, of the connivance of officials, forgery of certificates, and tarring and feathering of informers, all show that violations occurred.

A quantitative analysis of colonial trade, however, throws a clearer light on the extent of smuggling. Although obviously no statistical records of surreptitious activities exist, official records showing the great volume of tobacco and other enumerated products[qv] moving in legal channels and the quantities of European manufactures coming to the colonies from England as the laws prescribed demonstrate that the bulk of the trade with Europe was legitimate. Any other assumption would greatly exaggerate colonial productive and consumptive capacities. Violations of the Molasses Act[qv], however, were a different matter. The amount of rum[qv] produced in the Northern colonies demonstrates that a flourishing illicit trade existed with the foreign West Indies. It is more difficult to estimate the extent of smuggling during the revolutionary period, but the probabilities seem to be that it was held in check by increased enforcement activities.

Many elements were required to precipitate the American Revolution, and smuggling did more than add spice to the formula. The very fact that the European clauses of the laws were reasonably well enforced, left the colonists with an unfavorable balance of trade in the Old World. The monopolistic advantages enjoyed by the English factors kept Southern planters in a state of continual indebtedness which served to intensify any irritation aroused by other causes. After the Molasses Act, illicit trade with the foreign West Indies was an economic necessity. Its treasonable aspect during the French and Indian War aroused British resentment, and subsequent attempts to restrain it awakened such active opposition in the colonies as to warrant John Adams' remark that "molasses was an essential ingredient in American independence."

Equally important, the other commercial reforms which Britain initiated at the same time attempted too much. The new duties in America and the decreased drawbacks on goods which the colonists were obliged to acquire in England either tended to increase smuggling or added economic grievances to political irritation. The rearrangement of the duties on tea[qv], which offered a legal supply at lower prices, aroused smugglers whose profits were threatened, while the demand for bonds even when shipping nonenumerated articles, the burdensome restrictions on the coasting trade, and worst of all arbitrary adherence to the letter of the law injured even the "fair trader." At first the merchants expressed their resentment in the form of nonimportation agreements[qv], but such attempts at peaceful coercion soon led to acts of "riot and rebellion."

[C. M. Andrews, *The Colonial Period;* G. L. Beer, *British Colonial Policy*, 1754-1763; E. Channing, *History of the United States;* L. A. Harper, *English Navigation Acts;* V. D. Harrington, *The New York Merchant on the Eve of the Revolution;* A. M. Schlesinger, *Colonial Merchants and the American Revolution.*]

LAWRENCE A. HARPER

Smuggling of Slaves. The importation of African Negroes into the United States was not made illegal until 1808, because of a constitutional provision which forbade congressional interference until that year. Most states, however, had already by then passed laws prohibiting the trade. Federal action was subsequently taken, cruisers and revenue cutters were authorized to make captures, and courts were directed to try offenders. These national measures generally emphasized the punishment of smugglers rather than the prevention of smuggling. The traffic became a very profitable business, supported by Northern capital and dovetailing into the domestic slave trade[qv] in the South. Illicit cargoes of Negroes were either infiltrated into the South through secluded rivers and inlets, or baldly unloaded at ports of entry where public apathy or the connivance of local authorities permitted the business. Between 1808 and 1860 at least 250,000 Negroes were thus imported. Cargoes of captured bootleg slaves were occasionally returned to be colonized in Sierra Leone or Liberia[qv]. More frequently, however, they were sold at auction in the Southern slave market to cover the costs of capture and prosecution, thus paradoxically defeating the original purpose of the laws.

International co-operation to suppress the slave traffic was generally ignored or rejected by the United States until 1842, although the Treaty of Ghent[qv] contained a statement condemning the trade. In the Webster-Ashburton Treaty in 1842[qv] the United States agreed to send a squadron with eighty guns to the African coast, but subsequently failed to provide its full quota.

More effective was the belated Anglo-American treaty of June 7, 1862, which granted a limited mutual right to search merchant vessels for smuggled slaves, and which established three international courts (at Sierra Leone, Cape of Good Hope and New York) to try the smugglers. Finally, the Thirteenth Amendment[qv] in 1865, by abolishing domestic slavery, at the same time gave the final blow to the slave trade.

[W. E. B. DuBois, *The Suppression of the African Slave-Trade . . ., 1638-1870; Annual Reports* of Secretary of Interior, Nov. 30, 1861, Nov. 29, 1862; U. S. Statutes at Large, II, 426-30, III, 450-53, 532-34, 600-601.]

MARTIN P. CLAUSSEN

Smyth v. Ames (169 U. S. 466, 1898) is the leading precedent upon the rate-making power of legislatures, as well as of administrative tribunals to which legislatures may under certain conditions delegate that power, in the regulation of public utilities[qv]. The specific principle for which the case stands is known as "the rule of fair value." By this is meant that the rates imposed upon a public utility (in the instant case, a railway) by a regulatory body acting under the "police power"[qv] may not (under the Fourteenth Amendment to the Constitution) be such as to impair the "fair value" of the property used by the utility in the public service. Several elements "to be considered" in the determination of "fair value" were enumerated in the opinion of the court. These included, for example, "original cost," market value of the securities of the utility corporation, and "reproduction cost." But it was explicitly denied that the elements listed could be regarded as exhaustive of all the factors "to be considered."

The so-called rule of Smyth v. Ames has been criticized, accordingly, for its indefiniteness. It has been even more severely criticized as being self-contradictory, that is, as comprehending incompatible elements. It certainly gave rise to a long course of expensive and vexatious litigation over the constitutional limits of rate regulation, which after forty years appears to have brought the courts little nearer to a solution of the problem.

[John Bauer, *Effective Regulation of Public Utilities;* J. C. Bonbright, *Valuation of Property.*]

MYRON W. WATKINS

Snagboats were twin-hull steamboats designed especially for use in removing snags from western rivers. Operating during low water, when snags were visible above or immediately below the surface, the heavy iron-plated beam connecting the two hulls, below the water line, was run under the snag to loosen it from its moorings, after which it was hauled aboard and disposed of. As steamboat traffic increased, snag losses were heavy, mounting to $1,362,500 between 1822 and 1827. Congress was petitioned to remove this menace in 1820, but no action was taken until 1827, when Capt. Henry Miller Shreve, the most prominent of the snagboat operators, was appointed Superintendent of Western River Improvements. Between 1829 and 1841 Shreve removed most of the snags from the Ohio and Mississippi. (*See also* Red River Raft.) Other men continued his work, the need for which constantly decreased with the disappearance of timber from the river banks in the progress of settlement.

[E. W. Gould, *Fifty Years on the Mississippi;* Caroline S. Pfaff, Henry Miller Shreve: A Biography, in *Louisiana Historical Quarterly*, Vol. X; J. Fair Hardin, The First Great Western River Captain: A Sketch of the Career of Captain Henry Miller Shreve, in *Louisiana Historical Quarterly*, Vol. X.]

WALTER PRICHARD

Snake Dance. The Hopi Indians[qv] in Arizona maintain a men's cult which still performs a ritual to invoke the gods controlling rain and crops. One concept in the complex is that snakes are messengers to the unseen world where these gods reside. Accordingly, a large number of snakes are gathered, taken to the kiva, or ceremonial chamber, where they are kindly treated. On the last day of the ceremony the members of the cult dance in the open with snakes held in their mouths, hence the name. Then the snakes are turned loose to report to the gods. Snakes of several species are used, including rattlers, but so skilfully handled that the dancers do not become ill. The ceremony is prehistoric in origin and though not practised by other tribes in the United States, had parallels in Mexico, suppressed by the Spanish conquerors.

[John G. Bourke, *The Snake-Dance of the Moquis of Arizona.*]

CLARK WISSLER

Snake (or Shoshonean) Indians. The term Snake Indians was incorrectly applied by early explorers and fur traders, ignorant of native language, dialectic variations, cultures and political organizations, to groups of the Shoshonean family residing chiefly in the Snake River Valley of southern Idaho, and in contiguous areas of Montana, Wyoming, Utah, Nevada and Oregon. Among these Indians were the Wihinasts (along the Boise River), the Sheepeaters, the Lemhis, the Diggers, the "Dog-Ribs" (of Irving's *Astoria*) and the Bannocks. The confusing term was employed for over a century, but today the groups which formerly resided in southern Idaho are scientifically designated as Shoshoni and Northern Paiutes. The origin of the name "Snake" is obscure. Contrary to frequent assertions that Lewis and Clark[qv] conferred it upon a native group in 1805, modern research discloses that it was used by Upper Missouri River fur traders prior to 1770.

[Cornelius James Brosnan, *History of the State of Idaho;* Julian H. Steward, *Linguistic Distributions and Political Groups of the Great Basin Shoshoneans.*]

CORNELIUS JAMES BROSNAN

Snake River, or Shoshone, the 900-mile stream looping about southern and western Idaho, was followed by Lewis and Clark[qv] from the mouth of the Clearwater to the Columbia in 1805. Astor's expedition to Astoria[qv] in 1811 attempted to float down the turbulent river and suffered great hardships. The Rocky Mountain Fur Company and the Hudson's Bay Company[qqv] battled each other in the fur-trapping business up and down the stream through the early 19th century. From Fort Hall the Oregon Trail[qqv] paralleled the river closely for some 400 miles. In the 20th century the river's mighty waterfalls became great agencies for water power and irrigation.

[C. J. Brosnan, *History of the State of Idaho.*]

ALVIN F. HARLOW

"Snap Convention," The, was a name given to a New York state convention called by David B. Hill for Feb. 22, 1892, to control the election of delegates to the Chicago Democratic national convention. To oppose the solid Hill delegation, the "Anti-Snappers" called a convention and sent a protesting delegation to Chicago. Hill's action was resented by Cleveland's friends in the state.

[Allan Nevins, *Grover Cleveland, A Study in Courage.*]

A. C. FLICK

Snelling, Fort, was established in 1819 by Col. Henry Leavenworth as part of a general plan of frontier defense. Its site, at the junction of the Mississippi and Minnesota rivers, was originally selected in 1805 by Lt. Zebulon M. Pike. It was at first called Fort St. Anthony, but in 1825 its name was changed to Fort Snelling in honor of Col. Josiah Snelling, who became commandant in 1820 and erected permanent buildings and fortifications. The fort was the headquarters for the Indian agency, of which Maj. Lawrence Taliaferro had charge for twenty years; and it served to protect the headquarters of the American Fur Company[qv], located across the Minnesota River at Mendota, and the pioneer settlers of Minnesota. It was never the scene of a hostile demonstration. It was abandoned in 1858 and reoccupied in 1861.

[M. L. Hansen, *Old Fort Snelling;* W. W. Folwell, *History of Minnesota,* Vol. I.]

T. C. BLEGEN

Snowshoes. Archæological specimens of snowshoes are known both in the Old and New Worlds. However, the highest development in snowshoes seems to have been among the Indians of Canada and the northern United States. The French traders and immigrants adopted them, as did the adventurous trappers and traders in New England and the North Atlantic states. These shoes facilitated winter travel and made winter Indian attacks upon outposts possible, as in the case of Schenectady (1690) and York, Maine (1692)[qqv].

[D. S. Davidson, Snowshoes, in *Memoirs, American Philosophical Society,* 1937.]

CLARK WISSLER

Snug Harbor. *See* Sailor's Snug Harbor.

Soap Making was encouraged in colonial America by abundant raw materials. Much soap was made in households. Soap boilers' shops were numerous and their products were an item in intercolonial trade. The art of making Castile soap was brought from Portugal to Rhode Island before 1750. By the War of 1812 the industry had pushed westward to St. Louis. Later chemical progress and steam boiling revolutionized methods of manufacture, diversified production and encouraged larger establishments. By 1860 one firm made about one hundred varieties of soap ranging from scented toilet cakes to bulk soap used in manufacturing. The next generation saw floating and scouring soaps introduced, to be followed by packaged soap powders.

This industry reveals two lines of development. One started with specialized establishments of which Colgate & Company is probably the oldest and largest representative. The other was associated with the packing industry which has incorporated most manufactures employing fats including vegetable oils. Cincinnati was an important soap-making center in the early 19th century and Ohio still leads the industry, followed by New York, Illinois, California and Pennsylvania. The annual output, which was valued at 18 million dollars in 1860 and 44 million dollars in 1890, reached 310 million dollars in 1929.

[Chauncey M. Depew, *One Hundred Years of Commerce;* United States Census Reports.]

VICTOR S. CLARK

Social Compact. *See* Compact Theory.

Social Democratic Party. The Social Democracy of America as an organization was formed at Chicago during June 15–18, 1897, of sections of the American Railway Union, the Socialist Labor party clubs and various religious and trade-union groups. The "colonization" plan of Eugene V. Debs provided that the Socialists concentrate their forces upon a state such as Colorado, wherein unemployment was to be abolished and co-operative industry fostered. This scheme of "colonization" was repudiated in June, 1898, by a group of Socialists led by Debs himself, Victor Berger and Jesse Cox to form the Social Democratic party of America. That year they were able to send two members to the Massachusetts legislature and elect the mayor of Haverhill; during the presidential election of 1900 their candidate, Debs, polled 96,878 votes. The subsequent fusion in 1901 of anti-DeLeonites in the Socialist Labor party[qv] and the Social Democratic party led to a new party designation, the Socialist party[qv] of America.

[N. Fine, *History of Farmer and Labor Parties in the U. S.*]

HARVEY WISH

Social Gospel, THE, is an emphasis in American Protestant Christianity which has developed since the Civil War. The rise of labor organizations and the resulting labor disturbances of the 1880's brought the accusation from labor that the church was more sympathetic with capital than labor. This stirred liberal church leaders to a study of the implications of the teachings of Jesus on social and economic questions. Among the early leaders in this movement were Washington Gladden, Walter Rauschenbusch and Shailer Mathews. Their teachings and writings were soon exercising widespread influence, and a lively social consciousness was created in all the major denominations which has led to their adoption of definite social programs.

[Shailer Mathews, *The Church and the Changing Order;* Walter Rauschenbusch, *Christianity and the Social Crisis;* Washington Gladden, *Tools and Man: Property and Industry under the Christian Law,* and *Applied Christianity.*]

WILLIAM W. SWEET

Social Legislation has aimed to substitute collective action for individual action in providing protection for wage earners and other economically insecure persons against the risks of accident, illness, invalidity, premature old age, premature death and unemployment. Such protection is known as *social insurance.*

Workmen's compensation laws[qv], the first form of social insurance established by law in the United States, were enacted because of the wage earner's inability to carry the financial burden of occupational accidents and diseases and the failure of common-law rules of employers' liability[qv] to safeguard the injured workman and his dependents. Precedent for compulsory insurance against accidents was found in such countries as Germany (1885), Austria (1887), Norway (1894) and Great Britain (1897). Opposition to such laws in the United States was based upon fear of enhanced costs of production, adverse effects upon competition, the possible danger of habitual malingering, and the alleged socialistic nature of these measures. Accident compensation laws were, however, passed in Maryland (1902), Montana (1910) and New York (1910), but all were declared unconstitutional by state courts as holding the employer liable without fault, depriving him of property without due process[qv] of law, and denying to employers and employees the right of trial by jury.

State constitutional amendments paved the way for remedial action. New York amended its constitution and in 1914 enacted a compulsory workmen's compensation law. In upholding the constitutionality of the New York, Iowa and Washington laws the United States Supreme Court (1917) declared this type of legislation a valid exercise of the police power[qv] in behalf of public welfare and denied that it is arbitrary and unreasonable class legislation. By 1920 similar laws were on the statute books of forty-three states, and of Alaska, Hawaii and Puerto Rico. By 1939 only two states (Arkansas and Mississippi) were without workmen's compensation legislation. The Federal Government enacted such laws for all Federal civilian workers (1916), for longshoremen and harbor workers (1927), for civil employees of the Government and for private employees in the District of Columbia (1928). As yet unprovided for are interstate transportation employees and seamen. Occupational diseases are gradually being included in accident compensation laws.

The first attempt in the United States to provide, through law, assistance to the dependent aged was made in Massachusetts (1903), but without success. Arizona (1914) was the first state to enact such a measure, but the state supreme court held the law unconstitutional. Alaska (1915) was the first to put such a law into effect. By May, 1937, largely as a result of the enactment of the Federal Social Security Law[qv] (1935), all the states except Virginia had laws dealing with old-age security.

Although unemployment[qv] is generally regarded as an uninsurable risk, advanced industrial nations have followed the leadership of Great Britain (1911) in providing unemployment compensation. Wisconsin was the first American state to pass an unemployment insurance law (1932). When the Federal Social Security Act was passed in 1935 the movement was greatly accelerated. Influential, also, was the favorable attitude of the United States Supreme Court which, by a five to four decision in May, 1937, upheld the constitutionality of the tax provisions of Title IX of the act (Stewart Machine Co. v. Davis, 57 Sup. Ct. 993).

The Federal Social Security Act also provided Federal grants-in-aid[qv] to states for assistance to dependent children, the needy blind, maternal and child-welfare activities, crippled children, vocational rehabilitation of the physically disabled and extension of state and local health services.

Except for blindness[qv], nonindustrial disabilities have not received legislative attention in the United States, but many of the states have recognized the problem. As early as 1875 the State of New York authorized the Department of Charities of the City of New York to give financial assistance to the blind. Ohio was the first state to enact a general pension law for the blind (1898). Illinois followed in 1903 and Wisconsin in 1907. By 1939 approximately one half of the states had pension laws providing for the blind.

Aid to dependent mothers and children was first provided through legislation in Missouri (April, 1911). Illinois passed a similar mothers' aid law in 1911, and Colorado in 1912. The movement spread rapidly and by 1920 thirty-nine states and the territories of Alaska and Hawaii had enacted such legislation. By 1939 all states except Georgia and South Carolina had passed similar laws. As already indicated, the Federal Social Security Act of 1935 also provided financial assistance to the states in caring for dependent mothers and children.

[Paul H. Douglas, *Social Security in the United States;* Harry A. Millis, *Sickness and Insurance.*]

GORDON S. WATKINS

Social Security. Though social-security programs had long been in effect in European countries, little progress had been made in the United States in the promotion of such a program, prior to 1935. In 1934 President F. D. Roosevelt created a committee to study the matter. On Jan 17, 1935, he sent to Congress a special message, accompanied by the committee's report, and urged the speedy enactment of legislation. Finally, on Aug. 14, 1935, the National Social Security Act was added to the statutes of the United States. On Jan. 1, 1940, important amendments adopted in 1939 became effective.

This law, which is divided into eleven titles, may be considered under four heads: assistance for the aged, unemployment insurance, miscellaneous promotion of social welfare and administration.

Under the first head is the provision for Federal subsidization of state programs for old-age[qv] assistance. The Federal subsidy amounts to one half the total amount paid each eligible person, up to $40.00 per month. By Aug. 15, 1939, about 1,875,000 people, or approximately 27% of all persons sixty-five years of age or over in the United States, were receiving old-age assistance.

Another form of aid for the aged, administered entirely by the Federal Government, is the old-age annuity system provided by Titles II and VIII. Funds to retire workers at the age of sixty-five, beginning in 1940, or to pay "survivor" benefits, are raised by compulsory "income" taxes on wages and "excise" taxes on pay rolls. Seven classes of employees are exempted from the plan. Altogether, by July, 1939, about 45,500,000 persons had applied for "account numbers" under this part of the law. The constitutionality of the Federal old-age annuities plan was upheld by the Supreme Court, on May 24, 1937, by a 7 to 2 decision.

Unemployment insurance[qv] is provided by Titles III and IX. The act levies an "excise" tax on wages paid by employers of eight or more persons. An "offset" or credit of 90% of this tax is granted employers in states which set up their own unemployment insurance plan, as all did by the middle of 1937. Though there are seven exempted classes, about 27,500,000 persons had been made eligible for benefits by the middle of 1939. A total of $396,342,074 had actually been apportioned to unemployed persons during 1938. The constitutionality of the state and Federal unemployment insurance plans was upheld by the Supreme Court on May 24, 1937, in two 5 to 4 decisions.

Social welfare is further promoted by miscellaneous provisions of the law. Title IV provides for Federal subsidies to aid the states in furnishing assistance to dependent children. Title V, as amended, specifies that $5,820,000 shall be apportioned annually among the states to promote the health of mothers and infants; $3,870,000 for aid to crippled children; $1,500,000 for the care of homeless children "and children in danger of becoming delinquent"; and $4,000,000 (after 1939) for the promotion of vocational rehabilitation. Under Title VI, as amended, $11,000,000 is made available annually to aid the states "in establishing and maintaining adequate public health services." Finally, Title X of the law makes provision for Federal subsidies to the states in supplying aid to the blind[qv].

General administration of the National Social Security Act is vested in a National Social Security Board of three members. In addition, the Secretaries of the Treasury and of Labor, the

Chief of the Children's Bureau, the Surgeon General of the Public Health Service and the Bureau of Internal Revenue all have administrative duties in connection with the act.

Supplementing the general social-security legislation are special laws of 1937 and 1938, providing for old-age retirement benefits and unemployment insurance for railroad employees.

[Paul H. Douglas, *Social Security in the United States;* Maxwell S. Stewart, *Social Security.*]

ERIK McKINLEY ERIKSSON

Social Settlements. The settlement-house movement was the most important American reaction to the basic social problem represented by the labor unrest of the 1870's, the revolutionary socialism of the 1880's, the isolation of "colonies" of immigrants in congested tenements, unemployment, and the progressive lowering of the standard of living, factors furnishing rich soil for unscrupulous politicians. In 1886 Stanton Coit and Charles B. Stover, following the example of Toynbee Hall, London, established the Neighborhood Guild (later University Settlement) in New York, "to cultivate friendly relations between the educated and the uneducated and thus uplift the latter."

Others followed: College Settlement, New York, 1889 (Vida D. Scudder and Jean G. Fine); Hull House, Chicago, 1889 (Jane Addams); East Side House, New York, 1891; Northwestern University Settlement, 1891 (Harriet Vittum); South End House, Boston, 1892 (Robert A. Woods); Henry Street Settlement, New York, 1893 (Lillian Wald). Economic distress brought rapid increase after 1893, especially: Hudson Guild, New York, 1895 (John L. Elliott); University of Chicago Settlement, 1894 (Mary McDowell); Chicago Commons, 1894 (Graham Taylor); Hiram House, Cleveland, 1896 (George A. Bellamy); Greenwich House, New York, 1902 (Mary Kingsbury Simkhovitch). Although new houses continued to be established until the World War, few were established thereafter. A national federation, organized 1911, had 160 members in 1930. Of 300 nonmember houses, most were church-supported. About twenty houses were supported by Catholics (1922) and twenty-eight by Jews. The Y. M. C. A., Y. W. C. A. and other national agencies carried on similar work.

The greatest single service of the settlements has been in Americanization[qv]. In addition, they have sponsored group study of music, art, literature and handicrafts; provided clinics, visiting nurses, classes in cooking and child care, playgrounds, summer camps, employment bureaus; revived national festivals, and helped inspire the Little Theater Movement[qv].

[Jane Addams, *Twenty Years at Hull-House,* and *Second Twenty Years at Hull-House;* A. C. Holden, *Settlement Idea;* R. A. Woods and A. J. Kennedy, *Handbook of Settlements,* and *The Settlement Horizon.*]

HAROLD E. DAVIS

Social Work. Although the late 18th century produced a few pioneers like Dr. Benjamin Rush and Thomas Eddy, modern social service in the United States had its beginning in organizations like the Society for Prevention of Pauperism (New York, 1818) and the Associations for Improving the Condition of the Poor of the 1840's. Early workers were philanthropic merchants and professional men, or members of their families. The Charity Organization Movement[qv] of the late 1870's, although chiefly dominated by volunteer workers, brought the first conscious development of social service as a profession.

Multiplication of social-service institutions after 1880 brought specialization of work. Relief of poverty became social case work, or family work, producing the "case worker." Social settlements[qv] aroused interest in housing, community betterment and slum[qv] clearance, producing such specializations as group workers and settlement workers, and led to work in community organization. Educational and preventive social work introduced teachers, recreational and playground directors, visiting nurses, social medical workers and legal-aid officers. Psychiatrists and housing experts were called into service. Social case work was the most important and characteristic, and best represented the principles of scientific sociology, biology and psychology. It marked clearly the departure from the spirit of early 19th-century reform with its exclusive interest in saving individuals. The new purpose was to analyze and change the environment deemed responsible for the individual's or family's plight.

In 1873 the National Conference of Charities and Corrections (now National Conference of Social Work) was founded. A National Council of Charity Officers soon followed. By the end of the 19th century expansion and specialization of agencies had created a demand for more specialized training than that provided by study of the "economic aspects of altruism" in the college sociology classes of the day. The New York School of Philanthropy was established (1904); and by 1939 there were thirty-seven schools, members of the American Association of Schools of Social Work (established, 1919). Enrollment in 1938 exceeded 7000 students, 83% women. Volunteer work continued to characterize private charities through the World War, but the tendency toward professionalization became marked after

1920. Mary Richmond's book *Social Diagnosis* (1917) blazed the trail. The Russell Sage Foundation[qv] gave liberal encouragement to the study of the problems of social work, and the American Association of Social Workers (1922) enhanced professional prestige.

[E. T. Devine, *Social Work;* P. R. Lee, Social Work: Cause and Function, in *Proceedings of National Conference of Social Work,* 1929; G. B. Mangold, *Organization for Social Welfare.*]

HAROLD E. DAVIS

Socialist Labor Party. In July, 1874, several New York sections of the Socialist International organized the Workingmen's party of the United States. By December, 1877, this group, profiting by industrial unrest (*see* Railroad Strike of 1877), became the first American Socialist party on a national scale and designated themselves the Socialist Labor party. A temporary alliance in 1880 with the Greenback party[qv] proved unsatisfactory, and in 1892 the socialists chose a presidential candidate of their own who polled 21,164 votes. During the 1890's, the party fell under the domination of the revolutionary philosophy of Daniel DeLeon, who considered that the primary function of unionism was to serve as a weapon for the overthrow of capitalism[qv]. The party attained its greatest strength during the congressional elections of 1898 but declined steadily thereafter, particularly after 1899 when an anti-DeLeon element seceded to join the less militant Socialist party[qv] of Eugene V. Debs. The followers of DeLeon have uncompromisingly opposed craft unionism, propagandizing for the victory of socialism within a syndicalist[qv] structure of industrial unionism (*see* Congress of Industrial Organizations).

[F. E. Haynes, *Social Politics in the United States.*]

HARVEY WISH

Socialist Movement, The. Socialism may be defined as a system of philosophy which requires that the instruments of production, distribution and exchange shall be owned, controlled and operated by society co-operatively for the advantage of all rather than privately and competitively for the benefit of a few. (*See also* Communism.) It necessarily involves the abolition of private wealth, except perhaps in consumption goods.

During the early 19th century, there were many experiments in the United States based upon the theories of such utopian reformers as the Welshman, Robert Owen, and the Frenchmen, Etienne Cabet and Charles Fourier. Among Americans interested in these new movements were Albert Brisbane, Horace Greeley, William Cullen Bryant, Charles A. Dana and Nathaniel Hawthorne. Brook Farm, Cabet's Icarian colony and Owen's New Harmony[qqv] were typical of many utopian communities. (*See also* Fourierism.)

Modern socialism, however, is identified with Karl Marx and Friedrich Engels. Their fundamental theories were incorporated first in the *Communist Manifesto* (1848). Marx and Engels concerned themselves with an analysis of industrial conditions, economic tendencies and social forces which, they believed, would destroy capitalism[qv] and lead to socialism. Their doctrines included the economic interpretation of history, which attributes to economic forces the predominant role in determining historical development; the class struggle[qv], which posits an irreconcilable conflict between the possessing and the propertyless classes; the theory of value and surplus value, which holds that labor[qv] creates all value and produces a surplus that is expropriated by the capitalist; and the law of capitalist development, according to which capitalism is digging its own grave through the concentration of capital, recurring economic crises, increasing unemployment, disappearance of the middle class, and increasing misery of the masses. The inevitable overthrow of the capitalistic system through social revolution is predicted.

The American socialist movement, from the organization of the Socialist Labor party[qv] in 1874, has embraced these doctrines. The Social Democracy of America was formed in 1897. Unwilling to accept its utopian aims, Eugene V. Debs and Victor Berger organized the Social Democratic party[qv] of America. In 1901 the Socialist party[qv] came into existence, and ever since has championed opportunistic socialism. Debs retained leadership until his death in 1926, and was succeeded by Norman Thomas.

From the beginning, the movement has suffered from internal dissension, relentless opposition by adherents of capitalism, the relatively high status of American wage-earners, and the conservatism of trade unionism. Reflecting the Russian Revolution (1917), it split into three distinct groups. The opportunists remained in control of the Socialist party; the extreme left wing formed the Communist party; and the center-left wing organized the Communist-Labor party. Because of violent differences and internal strife, the collectivist movement has become (1940) hopelessly divided.

[H. W. Laidler, *A History of Socialist Thought.*]

GORDON S. WATKINS

Socialist Party, The. During June, 1897, a group of middle-western socialists met at Chicago to form the Social Democracy of America. A "colonization plan" fostered by Eugene V. Debs of Terre Haute, Ind., proposed that the socialists capture a western state such as Colorado for the introduction of a socialist regime. A year later the "anti-colonizers" seceded to organize the Social Democratic party[qv] and after successes won in state and local elections merged in 1901 with the moderate wing of anti-DeLeonites in the Socialist Labor party[qv] to create the new Socialist party. Debs remained the presidential candidate from 1900 to 1912, and again in 1920, while in Atlanta penitentiary on a wartime espionage charge, receiving 897,011 votes in 1912 and 919,799 votes in 1920, but subsequent candidates were less fortunate. The secession in 1919 of a revolutionary element, later the Communist party[qv] of America, on the issue of a future "dictatorship of the proletariat," left the Socialist party almost entirely reformist in character, hoping for a peaceful transformation of capitalist society into a socialist commonwealth. The Socialist party, frequently serving as an outlet for the American protest vote registered against the major parties, has been notably successful in municipal elections, particularly in Milwaukee and in certain sections of New England, where the tendency has been to emphasize "good government" rather than revolutionary tactics. The Socialist platform of 1936 proposed the immediate socialization of the "banks, mines, railroads, the power industry, and all key industries," the abolition of "the usurped power of the Supreme Court to declare social legislation unconstitutional," and other measures designed to establish a thirty-hour week for labor, a drastic increase in the income tax, farm relief, guarantees of civil liberty and pacifism[qqv].

[N. Fine, *Labor and Farmer Parties in the United States.*]

HARVEY WISH

Socializing Tendencies in American history may be considered from the standpoint of spontaneous movements among the people and from that of governmental intervention. The first prepares the ground for the second.

With the failure of the communal experiments in Jamestown and Plymouth and the change from working for the "common stock" to each person working for himself, the traditional "rugged individualism" began. This often misused term embraced the ideas of private property, of being unhampered, and of having the chance of going as far as each individual could, but it did not preclude that of social co-operation which has always been strongly characteristic of Americans. They early learned to work together and for each other, in such matters, at first, as house-raisings, husking and quilting bees[qqv], making of roads or bridges, and so on. In the communities of a simpler day voluntary organization preceded governmental responsibility, as in volunteer fire companies[qv]. The early militia, with its training days[qqv] and elective officers, was essentially social and democratic. Throughout almost all its history the labor union movement[qv] has developed from the people without government aid. Among many other evidences of popular socializing tendencies we may mention the rise of the business corporation from the end of the 18th century, the development of mutual savings banks, insurance companies and building and loan associations[qqv]. Without a state church and state endowments, the many denominations working freely have played their part. The social spirit has also been extraordinarily marked in private gifts and the endowments of museums, schools, colleges, libraries, hospitals, foundations[qqv] and other institutions for public welfare. We may likewise note the great number of fraternal organizations[qv], such as the Grange, Rotary, veterans' societies and many others. "Rugged individualism" has not prevented the American from becoming the greatest "joiner" in the world. In fact he seems to be almost incapable of working outside a committee or group. The political party system[qv], unprovided-for in the scheme of government or the Constitution, arose spontaneously among the people as a socializing tendency.

If the "rugged individual" naturally coheres into small or large groups for mutual aid he also has not hesitated to call in the aid of government, local or Federal, when it suited him. The two tendencies—to be unhampered and to use government help—are represented by the two philosophies of strict or loose construction[qqv] of the Constitution as originally enunciated by Jefferson and Hamilton. It is, however, a mistake to consider these as continuing schools of thought to which people and the leading two parties consistently adhere. Historically, the truth is that both persons and parties shift from one to another whenever interest or expediency seem to call for it. Naturally the broad construction view gives a wider scope to socializing tendencies; and government, both local and Federal, has immensely and almost continuously increased its social functions, although there have been periods of setback, such as that after Jackson's veto of the Maysville Road Bill[qv].

Among the earliest aids which government gave to socializing tendencies was the legislation in the Massachusetts colony establishing free education, at least nominally, for the poor. From that small beginning has developed the vast educational system of the present, with all its adjuncts, such as free food, clinics, playgrounds and other paternalistic projects. As population increased and spread, many activities which had been carried on by the people were taken over by governments. The early decades of the 19th century witnessed an outburst of public improvements in the building of roads, such as the Cumberland, and canals, such as the Erie[qqv]. Toll roads and bridges[qqv] gradually came to be operated by public authority, and free. Later with the rise of the West came the government aid to the railways in the form of great land grants[qv]. The manufacturers received their aid in the shape of protective tariffs[qv]. As population concentrated, more and more services, such as fire and police protection, sewerage, health, museums, libraries and much else have passed to a large extent naturally and almost unnoticed to public instead of private control and maintenance.

The more government has done, the more it is taken for granted it will do. For example, the pension system for war veterans has now developed into the colossal system of old-age and unemployment benefits[qqv]. The comparatively simple early public works have developed into such vast projects as the Panama Canal[qv], the great dams in the West and the Tennessee Valley Authority[qv], which last is undertaking to recast the life of a whole section.

There has also been an increasing demand for regulation, either state or Federal, and we have the railway and public utility commissions, such laws as the Sherman Antitrust Act, the Pure Food Law, the Wagner Act for labor and the Securities Exchange Commission[qqv]. The greatest development took place under the New Deal[qv] subsequent to 1933. Scores of boards or commissions undertook to help or regulate almost all industry, including farming, shipping, security trading, banking and manufacturing. Taxation, especially in such forms as the graduated income tax, the graded inheritance tax and the undivided profits tax were used not merely to provide for the expense of government, but as means of social change.

Nevertheless, the two strains in the American character, the two streams of our political philosophy, still persist side by side—the desire to be let alone and the desire to use the aid of government. The history of our thought and legislation depicts a constant effort to reconcile the two.

JAMES TRUSLOW ADAMS

Society for Propagating the Gospel. *See* Gospel, The Society for the Propagation of the, in Foreign Parts.

Society for the Prevention of Cruelty to Animals. The American society, the first of its kind in the United States, was organized in New York City in 1866 by Henry Bergh. He also secured the first effective animal protective legislation that same year. The movement was quickly copied until in 1938 there were over 500 such societies scattered through the forty-eight states.

In 1877 the American Humane Association was organized as a federation of animal protective societies. It is now their clearinghouse with headquarters at Albany, N. Y. It prints a large amount of humane literature, assists local societies with field workers and holds an annual meeting in a different section of the country each year.

Animal protective societies are incorporated as humane societies, anticruelty societies, animal rescue leagues and societies for the prevention of cruelty to animals. They specialize in securing and enforcing laws for the protection of animals. Nearly all of them promote humane education in the schools. They are united in a campaign to reduce cruelty in the transportation of livestock, in the trapping of fur bearers, in the use of draft animals and in the inspection of all places where animals are housed and used. Particular attention is devoted to the small animal population. Many societies maintain animal shelters and look after the pound work in their respective localities. Several have animal hospitals and clinics especially designed to care for the animals of the poor. All of them are supported by membership and contributions.

[Sydney H. Coleman, *Humane Society Leaders;* Files of the *National Humane Review* and *Our Dumb Animals;* Early *Annual Reports* of the American Society for the Prevention of Cruelty to Animals; The *Directory* of the American Humane Assn.]

SYDNEY H. COLEMAN

Society for the Prevention of Cruelty to Children. In April, 1874, Mrs. Etta Angell Wheeler, a New York social worker, brought a mistreated child to the attention of Henry Bergh, head of the Society for the Prevention of Cruelty to Animals[qv], and suggested a similar agency for the protection of children. Bergh agreed, and on Dec. 15, 1874, organized such a society for New York, which was incorporated in 1875. At that time, it was said that there were 10,000 homeless boys in New York City. Elbridge T. Gerry, attorney for the S.P.C.A., assisted in organizing the S.P.C.C., and in 1879 became its president. For twenty-two years thereafter, he directed its policies, and was so closely identified with it that it was popularly known as the "Gerry Society." In 1880 the society installed its first shelter for children in need of protection. Similar societies were organized in other cities and states, and in 1882 an English visitor was so impressed by the work that he founded one in Liverpool, the first of many to appear in foreign countries as years went on. The society sponsored child labor[qv] legislation, and its activities were often unpopular, but it successfully resisted nearly all moves to curb its power.

[Sydney H. Coleman, *Humane Society Leaders in America;* American Humane Association, *The Story of Mary Ellen.*]

ALVIN F. HARLOW

Society of Colonial Wars, composed of the General Society and constituent state societies (now twenty-eight), was established in 1892 to perpetuate the memory of events of colonial history from the settlement of Jamestown, Va. (1607), to the Battle of Lexington (1775), by membership, preservation of records, commemorations and memorials. Membership is eligible to male lineal descendants, in male and female lines, of men who, in colonial and British military, naval and civil positions, assisted in the establishment, defense and preservation of the American colonies.

[Constitution of the General Society of Colonial Wars.]

FRANCES DORRANCE

Sod House, THE (1830–1910), appeared when settlement began on the prairies away from the streams where timber was obtainable. The plains Indians had long made their permanent winter homes from dirt, and the white man adapted the Indian habitation to his needs. In the early days in the area beyond the Missouri River, in many counties, 90% of the people at one time or another lived in sod houses.

In building a sod house, the settler plowed half an acre of ground. The thick strips of turf were cut into three-foot bricks with a spade. These bricks were then hauled to the building location and laid up like a brick wall. The first layer was laid side by side around the base except where the door was to be. The cracks were then filled with dirt and two more layers were placed on these. The joints were broken as in bricklaying. Every third course was laid crossways to bind the sods together. A doorframe and two window frames were set in the wall and sods built around them at the proper time. Sometimes hickory withes were driven down into the walls for reinforcement.

The gables were built of sod or frame according to the means of the builder. Poorer settlers built a roof in the crudest manner. A forked pole set in each end of the cabin furnished support for the ridge pole. The rafters were made of poles and the sheeting consisted of brush covered with a layer of prairie hay. Over this a layer of sod was placed. Those who could afford it sometimes used lumber sheeting covered with a light layer of sod. The cracks were filled with fine clay. In a short time growths of sunflowers and grass appeared on the roof. Sometimes the inside was plastered with ashes and clay. Often the outside was hewn smooth. The dirt floor was sprinkled in dry weather to keep down the dust. In wet weather the water-soaked roof dripped constantly, making puddles on the floor. The whole structure was built for less than five dollars. These little cabins often housed a dozen people. The three-foot walls were warm in winter and cool in summer but the houses were illy ventilated and dark. As soon as possible the family moved into a frame structure, leaving the old house to the stock.

[Everett Dick, *The Sod House Frontier;* Cass G. Barnes, *The Sod House.*]

EVERETT DICK

Soda Fountains followed a demand created when a Philadelphia perfumer began to serve soda water with fruit syrups soon after 1800. In 1832 John Mathews started in New York the manufacture of apparatus for generating and dispensing soda water. Improvements soon appeared and about 1855 the marble fountain was invented and patented by a Boston maker. An American fountain was exhibited in Paris in 1867 and a popular concession at the Centennial Exposition[qv] at Philadelphia in 1876 marked it as a national institution. Today there are said to be about 100,000 in the United States as compared with 1000 in all Europe.

[Chauncey M. Depew, *One Hundred Years of Commerce.*]

VICTOR S. CLARK

"Soft" Currency is naturally the opposite of hard currency based on specie[qv]. The term originated about 1876 when the Greenback party[qv] drew from the Republicans and Democrats those whom we would now call inflationists. They opposed the resumption[qv] of specie payments and the issue of notes by banks. They thought that the currency should be a government paper one, given value by government edict, not by being redeemable in specie. Later the Populists[qv] held similar views.

[D. R. Dewey, *Financial History of the United States.*]

JAMES D. MAGEE

Soil is the covering, a mantle, of the rocks which make the earth's foundation. Geologists have described soil as mainly derived from the basic rocks themselves, through the process of weathering. This they call *residual* soil. They recognize also a type of *derivative* soil—material which may have been created elsewhere and carried to its present locale by glaciers, by floodwaters, or by wind. Wind-borne derivative soil is called *loess*. The theory is that, with some exceptions, the soil of a given area is what the basic rock strata made it.

That theory no longer satisfies soil scientists. They hold that it has so little relation to the facts as revealed by the actual study of the soils themselves as to be quite misleading. In place of the geologic theory, which would make the soils of the country as multitudinously diverse as are the basic rocks, they contend for a soil geography that shall divide the country into a very few great soil regions.

Soil physics and soil chemistry have furnished the clues for the new classification. The Federal Government was already 110 years old, and population had so spread over its entire length and breadth as to abolish the frontier when in 1899 the soil survey was begun. In the course of a generation so many localities had been studied in so many different states that scientists were in possession of soil facts enabling them to make new generalizations.

They found that soils are created by a variety of forces which develop qualities quite independent of the "parent" rock underlying them. These qualities are determined mainly by the related influences of climate and vegetation, under which soils evolve, "and by the land forms they occupy."

The most general division is into nonlime-accumulating soils and lime-accumulating soils, and on that basis the country can be practically halved by a line running nearly due north and south from northwestern Minnesota to Corpus Christi, Texas, on the Gulf of Mexico. Soils of the eastern division do not accumulate lime in their subsoil principally because of the way these soils were built, under forests and the tall grass association, and because the relatively abundant rainfall of that portion of the United States serves to leach the lime away, even in the subsoil.

In other words, the physical quality of the soils, due to their origin, and the operation of climatic forces, has induced a chemical quality which is distinctive of the region in general.

It will now be apparent why the western half of the United States has soils which—with extensive exceptional areas intermingled, especially in the mountain and Pacific coast districts—are lime-accumulating. In the first place, most of those lands were not forested, and the grass covering provided by nature grew lighter as rainfall decreased westward. The physical quality of the soils therefore differs from that of those described above. In the second place, the rainfall being light, it carried the soluble elements down to only a slight depth where the lime therefore accumulated in the subsoil.

American history fortunately began where the soils were strong, built through ages of leaf-mold accumulation under deciduous forests. That made farming successful from southern Georgia to the north half of Maine and New Hampshire. Pine forest land of northern New England, the Adirondacks and the Great Lakes states of Michigan, Wisconsin and Minnesota, has poor, acid soils. South of that pine belt are the "Graybrownerths," mantling most of the Middle West and the eastern states to below the Potomac, also portions of Kentucky and West Virginia; below these are the "Red-yellowerths" of the southern states, extending west through Louisiana and parts of Arkansas. Florida and southern Georgia have the so-called "Feruginous Laterites"; and there is also a "Prairieerth" belt embracing southern Minnesota, Iowa, most of Illinois, parts of Missouri, Arkansas, Texas and eastern Oklahoma, Kansas and Nebraska.

This outlines the historic small farming and planting region of the United States. The "Blackerths" of the plains belt have proved their worth for wheat and corn growing. Beyond these, westward, are the "Chestnuterths," the "Brownerths" and the "Grayerths," progressively less moist and lighter covered, the last-named being the actual deserts.

In its land management the Federal Government has not yet learned how to deal with the three last-named great belts of soil. Nor has it a definite policy for dealing with the forested mountain areas. The sorriest failure has been in dealing with the subarid high plains, Chestnuterths and Brownerths, which should be devoted to pasturage in large tracts, say 5000 to 25,000 acres, instead of to homesteads of 160 acres. (*See also* Soil Exhaustion.)

[Louis A. Wolfanger, *The Major Soil Divisions of the United States;* R. T. Ely, *A National Policy for Land Utilization;* R. T. Ely and others, *The Foundations of National Prosperity;* Cyril G. Hopkins, *Soil Fertility and Permanent Agriculture;* U. S. Dept. of Agriculture, Bul. G-54, *Soil Conservation*, 1936; *House Doc. 195*, 67th Cong. 2d Sess., 1922, p. 111ff.]

JOSEPH SCHAFER

Soil Conservation and Domestic Allotment Act of 1936 was enacted by Congress to accomplish what the judicially invalidated Agricultural Adjustment Act of 1933[qv] had sought, namely, control of agricultural production in order to prevent the recurrence of unmarketable surpluses, and thereby restore "the ratio between the purchasing power of the net income per person on farms and the income per person not on farms" that had prevailed from 1909–14. Indirect production-control replaced the system of direct control set up in the earlier act, by making such control *incidental* to soil conservation. Five hundred million dollars a year was placed at the disposition of the Secretary of Agriculture, to be used chiefly in payments to farmers for voluntarily co-operating with the Government in the work of soil conservation, especially in shifting some 30,000,000 acres from cultivation of soil-depleting crops, which had been chiefly responsible for the troublesome surpluses, to soil-conserving crops or soil-building uses. For seven crops (cotton, tobacco, peanuts, sugar cane, sugar beets, flax and rice) payments were based upon poundage or bushels; in the case of other crops, upon acreage. Responsibility for carrying out the plan was divided between the Federal Department of Agriculture, designated state agencies and local control committees. Important amendments were added by the Agricultural Adjustment Act of 1938[qv]. (*See also* Soil Erosion Act.)

[*49 U. S. Statutes at Large*, 1148-1152; *Report of the Secretary of Agriculture*, 1936, pp. 11-21; *ibid.*, 1937, pp. 8-15; H. A. Wallace, Outlines of the New Farm Program, in *N. Y. Times*, March 6, 1936; H. A. Wallace, America's Choice, *U. S. News*, May 18, 1936, p. 18; F. A. Ogg and P. O. Ray, *Introduction to American Government.*]

P. ORMAN RAY

Soil Erosion. The United States Department of Agriculture, in Bulletin G-54 (1936), stated that, "Recent surveys of the extent of soil erosion in this country indicate that approximately 50,000,000 acres of once fertile land have been essentially ruined for practical cultivation. Another 50,000,000 acres are in a condition almost as serious. About 100,000,000 acres still in cultivation have been seriously impoverished by the loss of soil; and about 100,000,000 more of cultivated land are being depleted of productive soil at an alarming rate."

The situation is ominous because the forces of soil degradation operate with the inevitability of fate. If man should do as little to conserve the nation's soil resources in the next two or three centuries as he has done thus far, it can safely be predicted that the American people, at the end of that time, would be living in a poor country instead of one of the richest countries.

More than a century ago John Randolph of Roanoke, in Congress, referred bitterly to Virginia's "galled and gullied hillsides." From that day to the present not only has gullying proceeded with slight hindrance, but what is called sheet erosion, a still more destructive process, has carried away each year millions of tons of the precious topsoil, the main guarantee of fertility. In addition, flood waters have destroyed hundreds of thousands of acres, and in the great plains area wind erosion has shifted the topsoil from cultivated fields to new locations, sometimes hundreds of miles away.

Defenses against heavy downpours of rain, falling on sloping fields, are still in the main what they were a hundred years ago—deep plowing or subsoiling, contour plowing and terracing. But the favorite plan now recommended is to refrain from using steep slopes for open row crops and to keep them as much as possible in grass or legumes. Many slopes once cultivated are being reforested to check runoff, and existing gullies are being eliminated by means of dams, or by direct filling.

The problem of flooding is bound up with the prevention of erosion on the watersheds. Dams in the rivers can prevent flooding only temporarily, until the process of silting up renders the dams useless. If the watersheds could be made to yield their surplus water to the streams more slowly and free from accumulations of soil, floods could be eliminated permanently. Otherwise, their effects can only be palliated.

Wind erosion can never be fully controlled. It has gone on for ages and will continue indefinitely. It impoverishes some regions but fortunately enriches others as districts having a loess soil prove. A covering of grass instead of cultivated crops helps to hold the soil; so do windbreaks of trees and brush. But there is no sure defense against the high winds (*see* Dust Bowl).

[Charles Richard Van Hise, *The Conservation of National Resources.*]

JOSEPH SCHAFER

Soil Erosion Act, THE, was passed by Congress in April, 1935, following widespread devastation and distress wrought by flood[qv] and sandstorms (*see* Dust Bowl). The act declared it to be "the policy of Congress to provide permanently for the control and prevention of soil erosion and thereby to preserve natural resources, control floods, prevent the impairment of reservoirs, maintain the navigation of rivers and harbors, protect public health and public lands, and to relieve unemployment." The act became the basis of the Soil Conservation and Domestic Allotment Act of 1936[qv].

[*49 U. S. Statutes at Large*, 163-164; Great Plains Committee, The Future of the Great Plains, *House Doc.* No. 144, 75th Congress, 1st Session, 1937; L. C. Speers, Erosion is Ruining Tremendous Area, *N. Y. Times*, June 14, 1936; W. Gard, America's Desolate Acres, *Current History*, June, 1935; A. D. Carlson, Dust Blowing: Why the Storms, *Harper's Mag.*, July, 1935; The Future of the Great Plains: Grasslands or Waste Lands?, *U. S. News*, Aug. 31, 1936; S. Chase, *Rich Land, Poor Land.*]

P. ORMAN RAY

Soil Exhaustion has not been confined to any particular region of the United States, though it has been more evident in the South and has generally been associated with that section. It made its appearance in colonial times in Virginia and Maryland, and by 1820 it had become a major calamity to the tidewater[qv] regions of those states. It followed closely on the heels of the plantation system[qv], and by the outbreak of the Civil War, worn-out fields were a common sight as far west as Texas.

Depletion of the fertility of the soil arose from various causes, but basically it grew out of the one-crop system of agriculture and cheap land. Other factors were the migratory disposition of the American people, the sparsity of population, slavery and the high labor costs it entailed, the overseer system[qv], the desire of the people for quick wealth, and agricultural practices which induced soil erosion[qv]. Tobacco[qv] was the first great offender in the one-crop practice, being responsible for the woes which overtook Maryland and Virginia. Cotton[qv] came later and its effects were much more widespread. As new land was easy to acquire, the typical planter wore out the soil and moved on—always taking from the soil but restoring nothing. In New England and other parts of the North where the population was denser, intensive agriculture was the practice, with the consequent attempts to build up the soil. It was long the custom in the North to charge to slavery alone soil exhaustion in the South, though in reality it was the high cost of slave labor and not the system that led the planter to skim the fertility and pass on. Where the custom of paying the overseer with a percentage of the crop, or of making his wages depend on the amount he raised, prevailed, like results could be expected. Erosion induced by ridge culture and shallow plowing not only carried away the fertility but the soil itself.

Intelligent planters soon saw the destructive effects of soil exhaustion on their whole economic order. They issued their warnings and preached their cures. Abandoning the one-crop system and restoring to diversified agriculture were widely advocated, as was also deep subsoil plowing. Some advised the use of various fertilizers; Edmund Ruffin of Virginia favored marl. John Taylor of Caroline believed that the solution lay in planting crops which would catch certain ingredients from the air and restore them to the soil, and Thomas Spalding of Sapelo believed a proper balancing of one crop against another would preserve nature's reservoir of soil fertility, which one crop alone must certainly exhaust. These preachments were producing results, for by 1860 much of the worn-out lands in Virginia and other regions were coming back into productivity through diversified farming.

Since the Civil War science has been applied to agriculture with pronounced effect. The United States Department of Agriculture, various state agencies and many agricultural colleges have turned their attention to restoring soil fertility, and with the coming of the New Deal a determined campaign has been made against soil exhaustion and erosion. The South still remains, however, the land of vanishing soil fertility.

[L. C. Gray, *A History of Agriculture in the United States to 1860;* U. B. Phillips, *American Negro Slavery;* Avery Craven, *Edmund Ruffin, Southerner*, and *Soil Exhaustion as a Factor in the Agricultural History of Virginia and Maryland;* H. H. Simms, *Life of John Taylor.*]

E. MERTON COULTER

Solar Compass, THE. The Ordinance of 1785[qv] provided for a rectangular system of land survey[qv] based on astronomical lines, in place of the older plan of indiscriminate location of lands. In the early 1830's William A. Burt of Michigan, a surveyor, became convinced that the magnetic needle could not be relied upon for accuracy, and his reflections led to the invention of the Solar Compass (patented 1836), by whose use the true meridian is determined from an observation of the sun. Burt's invention has proved of incalculable benefit, being used, substantially unchanged, by most civilized nations.

[John Burt, *History of the Solar Compass;* articles on Burt in *Mich. Pioneer and Hist. Colls.*, Vols. V, XXVIII and XXXVIII.]

M. M. QUAIFE

"Sold Down the River" refers to the punishment meted out to unruly slaves in the border slave states in ante-bellum days. The belief was prevalent that labor on Louisiana sugar plantations and great cotton estates of the lower South was exceedingly severe; and the mere threat of being "sold down the river" usually changed the conduct of unruly slaves.

[F. Bancroft, *Slave Trading in the Old South;* W. H. Stephenson, *Isaac Franklin.*]

WALTER PRICHARD

Soldier Vote. This phrase, common in American politics since the Civil War, has been applied to the ex-soldiers of our principal wars whose votes could be attracted by appeals to their patriotism or to their group interests. Politicians assumed that the wishes of the veterans were announced in the resolutions of their principal organizations, such as the Grand Army of the Republic, the Spanish War Veterans, the American Legion, or the Veterans of Foreign Wars, and often acted accordingly. Much legislation was enacted in response to the activities of the high-pressure lobbies of these bodies, which, without this driving force, would not have been adopted. The weight of the soldier vote has been thrown in favor of higher pension expenditures; veteran preference in the civil service; Northern sectionalism after the Civil War; "one hundred percent Americanism" after the World War, including opposition to radical or subversive doctrines and to the teaching of such doctrines, resulting in the criminal syndicalism laws of the 1920's and teachers' loyalty oaths; and other similar measures.

Cleveland's vetoes of pension bills aroused the hostility of the veterans and this contributed to his defeat in 1888. Between this time and the World War the pension system developed into a system of social security for veterans only, which was criticized as class legislation and as a source of great expense. After the World War the carefully devised system of compensation for the armed forces, adopted in 1917, was gradually broken down and supplanted by the pension system[qv]. In 1937 the Veterans of Foreign Wars demanded jobs or pensions for all ex-service men. Meanwhile the same forces had obtained the enactment of the still more expensive bonus[qv] legislation of 1924 and 1936.

[W. H. Glasson, *Federal Military Pensions in the United States;* M. Duffield, *King Legion;* K. Mayo, *Soldiers, What Next?*]

DONALD L. MCMURRY

Soldiers and Sailors Conventions (1866) were episodes in the political campaign between President Andrew Johnson and the Conservatives against the Radical Republicans[qv] seeking to influence the fall elections. Meeting at a National Union Convention[qv], in Philadelphia, Aug. 14, former Federal and Confederate officers joined in support of the President, and the gathering became known as "the Arm-in-Arm Convention."

Meeting in Cleveland, Sept. 17, Conservative Federal veterans, led by Generals Thomas Ewing, Jr., Gordon Granger, Custer, McClernand of Illinois and Steedman of Ohio, urged support of the Johnson policies. The venerable Gen. Wool, who presided, denounced the Abolitionists[qv] as "revengeful partisans with a raging thirst for blood and plunder." Many leaders joined in a round robin attacking Edward M. Stanton, Secretary of War.

The Radicals countered at Pittsburgh with a Soldiers and Sailors Convention (Sept. 25). Gen. Jacob D. Cox, of Ohio, was permanent president. The resolutions, drafted by Benjamin F. Butler, "the hero of Fort Fisher," endorsed the Fourteenth Amendment[qv] as "wise, prudent and just," and denounced the Johnson policies.

[G. F. Milton, *The Age of Hate.*]

GEORGE FORT MILTON

Soldiers' Homes. The National Home for Disabled Volunteer Soldiers was created to meet conditions developed during the Civil War. As the sick and wounded began to return from the war, relief stations had been organized and operated in several localities north of the Mason and Dixon Line, largely through the efforts of patriotic women, but as the war progressed, the numbers requiring aid increased until these stations would no longer meet the demands made upon them.

With this condition it was recognized that the care of disabled veterans was a governmental rather than a local obligation and in March, 1865, Congress created a corporation of high-ranking officers of the Government and public-spirited citizens to furnish relief and care for disabled veterans.

In March, 1866, an amendment to that act established a board of managers to provide "The National Asylum for Disabled Volunteer Soldiers."

This board immediately set about establishing homes and within a year three—at Dayton, Ohio (the central), Milwaukee, Wis., and Augusta, Maine, respectively—were in operation. Eight others were added as need developed, as follows: Hampton, Va., Leavenworth, Kans., Los Angeles, Calif., Marion, Ind., Danville, Ill., Johnson City, Tenn., Hot Springs, S. Dak., and Bath, N. Y.

These homes, located in extensive grounds, provided medical and domiciliary care, recreational and religious facilities, as well as all necessary utilities, each practically a self-sustaining community.

The administration was in keeping with military practice, the commanding officer being designated as governor, and the members organized into companies and housed in barracks.

From the establishment of the Home and its branches, a gradual increase in membership culminated in 1906 with a peak of 21,105 Civil War members, followed by a steady decrease of Civil War members, the membership later being augmented by Spanish-American War veterans and still later greatly increased by World War veterans.

In July, 1930, the National Home, the Pension Bureau and the Veterans' Bureau were consolidated to form the present Veterans' Administration, the Government's agency for all phases of veteran relief.

The Veterans' Administration, with the Central Office in Washington, D. C., maintains and operates 86 facilities, of which 11 are veterans' homes providing domiciliary and hospital care; 75 are hospitals, with 37 of which regional office functions are combined; also 15 separate regional offices and 2 supply depots. Insular offices are also maintained at Honolulu, T. H., Manila, P. I., and San Juan, P. R.

Since the establishment of the Veterans' Administration, the name of the Home at Hampton, Va., has been changed to Kecoughtan; the former Milwaukee Home is now called Wood, that at Augusta, Maine, is known as Togus, and Leavenworth, Kans., is now named Wadsworth. The Homes at Marion, Ind., and Danville, Ill., have been converted for hospital use, and two new homes have been provided at Biloxi, Miss., and Bay Pines, Fla., respectively.

FRANK T. HINES

Solid South, The Democratic Party in the. During Reconstruction[qv] the Negroes were given the ballot and a large part of the Southern whites were disfranchised. Consequently the Republican party, composed of Negroes, carpetbaggers and scalawags[qqv], secured control of the state governments. Determined to secure home rule[qv] and to maintain white supremacy, the conservative white Democrats resorted to a mixture of intimidation, force and fraud to eliminate the Negro from politics. Secret organizations like the Ku Klux Klan[qv] very effectively frightened the Negroes and violently and forcefully kept many from the polls. White Democrats stuffed the boxes with fraudulent ballots to counterbalance the Negro votes which were cast. State after state was redeemed from Negro-carpetbag rule, and when President Hayes withdrew the troops from the South in 1877 every Southern state fell under Democratic[qv] control. In the presidential election of 1880 Democratic solidarity of the South was established, for the five border states joined the eleven seceded states in a solid Democratic phalanx.

Incipient revolt against the restricted program of state Democratic administrations arose in several states, but the Republican party made little effort to win the independents. In fact the Republican party of big business had little to offer the democratic agrarian and labor classes of the South. The Republicans preferred to work through the Negro element and the Democratic leaders held the independents in line with the cry of "Negro rule." The Republican party in the South exists largely for Federal patronage and minor offices, although it occasionally elects a governor or a congressman. Except for minor appointments the rewards have been slight in Federal affairs, although Presidents Hayes, Garfield, Theodore Roosevelt, Taft and Hoover appointed one or more Southerners to their Cabinets. An occasional seat on the Supreme Court has also been given a Southerner. The Republican machine has been able to control a "solid block" of Southern delegates to the national convention. These delegates were the deciding factor in the renomination of Taft in 1912 and were, therefore, partly responsible for the split in the Republican party (*see* Campaign of 1912).

The South has elected practically solid Democratic delegations to Congress since 1880. By reason of their long service these congressmen gained key positions on committees and whenever their party gained the ascendancy they dominated congressional committees. Under President Wilson Southerners headed 42 of 59 House committees and all 10 of the important Senate committees. Southern Democrats have also figured prominently as Speakers of the House, Cabinet members, and in diplomatic posts under Democratic administrations. Southern congressmen have been generally a conservative group and have opposed social legislation[qv] and an expanding National Government. And yet the South supported the Wilson program and the F. D. Roosevelt New Deal[qv] more wholeheartedly than any other section.

It looked as if the Solid Democratic South would be broken when in 1896 Kentucky cast one electoral vote for McKinley, but with slight defections in the border states and the defection of Tennessee in 1920, it remained unshaken until 1928. In that year Protestantism and prohibition split the Solid South and Hoover carried Virginia, North Carolina, Florida, Tennessee and Texas, as well as the border states. All were back in the fold in 1932, however, and, except for the border states, Tennessee is the only doubtful Southern state.

[P. H. Buck, *The Road to Reunion;* Virginius Dabney, *Liberalism in the South;* H. A. Herbert, *Why the Solid South;* W. H. Skaggs, *The Southern Oligarchy;* Holland Thompson, *The New South.*]

FLETCHER M. GREEN

Somers, The Mutiny on the (1842). The U. S. brig *Somers* was en route from the African coast to New York when, on Nov. 26, 1842, the purser's steward reported to Commander A. S. Mackenzie, that Acting-Midshipman Spencer had attempted to induce him to aid in seizing the ship, murder the officers and turn pirate. Two seamen were also named as Spencer's accomplices. The three men were held prisoner, and a court of inquiry was convened which adjudged them guilty. Commander Mackenzie caused them to be hanged on Dec. 1. Subsequently Mackenzie was tried by court-martial for his act, but was acquitted.

[J. F. Cooper, *Proceedings* of the Naval Court-Martial in the Case of Alexander Slidell Mackenzie; G. R. Clark and others, *A Short History of the United States Navy.*]

LOUIS H. BOLANDER

Somers Isles. *See* Bermudas, The.

Somers' Voyage to Virginia. In 1609 the Virginia Company[qv], having secured a new charter and subscriptions to a large joint stock fund, placed Sir George Somers in command of the greatest expedition set forth for purposes of English settlement in America at any time prior to 1630. Leaving Blackwell on May 15 with six ships, he sailed from Plymouth on June 2, with "eight good shippes and one Pinnace," 600 "land men" and a possible total of 800 prospective colonists of all sorts. Seven weeks out on a course that left the Canary Islands 100 leagues to the east and then ran directly westward for Virginia, the *Sea Adventure*, carrying Somers, Sir Thomas Gates and Capt. Christopher Newport, the three men most important to the execution of the company's plans, was separated from its consorts in a severe storm and foundered off the Bermudas[qv] on July 28. All passengers were saved, and in two small vessels constructed of Bermuda cedar Somers brought his company to Jamestown[qv] on May 24, 1610. The remainder of the fleet had reached Virginia safely the preceding summer. The settlement of Bermuda by a group of Virginia adventurers in 1612 was a direct outgrowth of Somers' experiences there.

[C. M. Andrews, *Colonial Period of American History*, Vol. I; W. F. Craven, *Introduction to the History of Bermuda.*]

WESLEY FRANK CRAVEN

Somme Offensive (Aug. 8–Nov. 11, 1918). Three American divisions, the 33rd (Bell), 27th (O'Ryan) and 30th (Lewis), participated in the Somme offensive under the British 4th Army (Rawlinson). Elements of the 33rd Division aided in capturing Hamel, July 4, Chipilly Ridge and Gressaire Wood, Aug. 9, and Etinehem Spur, Aug. 13.

The 27th and 30th Divisions constituted the American 2nd Corps (Read). After serving in the Ypres-Lys operation[qv] in August, Read's corps entered the line east of Peronne. In the 4th Army attack, Sept. 29, the corps assaulted and broke through the Hindenburg Line at the Bellicourt Canal Tunnel. Alternating in attack with the Australian Corps (Monash), the Americans between Oct. 9 and Oct. 21 captured Brancourt-le-Grand, Premont and Vaux-Andigny, crossed the Selle River, Oct. 17, conquered Ribeauville, Mazinghien and Rejet-de-Beaulieu, and nearly reached the Sambre River. When relieved Oct. 21, the two divisions had advanced 11½ miles against resistance and lost 3414 killed and 14,526 wounded.

[*Order of Battle of the United States Land Forces in the World War;* J. M. Hanson, History of the American Combat Divisions, *The Stars and Stripes;* J. J. Pershing, *My Experiences in the World War.*]

JOSEPH MILLS HANSON

Songs, Popular. These are to be distinguished from "art songs" or the better type of vocal compositions, and on the other hand from folk songs[qv], with no known composer; but these classes sometimes overlap. Popular songs, especially recently, have been written for popular consumption, with hopes of large sales, commercially pushed. Frequently "catchy" for whistling or singing, they do not have to be learned. Thousands of good songs never became popular, and sometimes only chance turned a failure into a success. Sometimes a too great popularity ran a song into the ground ("Bei mir bist du schön"). Sometimes a song reappeared after many years ("Man on the flying trapeze," 1867, 1933). Radio and movies have helped revive some songs, but these agencies have also had a partially destructive effect on popular songs.

The earliest American popular songs appeared about the time of the American Revolution. Then followed some sentimental songs, some Negro and some pseudo-Negro. Political campaigns brought songs as early as the Harrison campaign of 1840[qv] (Log Cabin songs). Visits of foreign singers (Jenny Lind[qv], Adelina Patti) popularized some higher class songs. Temperance[qv] songs had a vogue from the 1850's. Traveling troupes like the Hutchinson family (1840's–1860's) helped popularize a group (like "The Battle Cry of Freedom"). Stephen Foster (1826–64) with 185 songs was the most permanently popular (e.g., "Old Folks at Home," "My Old Kentucky Home," "Oh, Susanna"[qqv]). Septimus Winner (pseudonym Alice Hawthorne) wrote "Listen to the Mocking Bird" and many others in the 1860's. After the Civil War popular songs were comic, especially Irish (Harrigan and Hart's "Mulligan Guards," 1873); Irish heroic; some "coon" songs; some sentimental; some sepulchral, "Violet from Mother's Grave," 1881; some dude comics, "Captain Jinks."

The publishing promoters appeared in the 1880's and 1890's (some hits, "Comrades," 1887; "Banks of the Wabash," 1897) and "plugged" waltz songs like "Daisy Bell," 1892, "Sidewalks of New York," 1894. Tin Pan Alley[qv], resort of song writers, began in this decade; also W. W. Delaney's song-sheets (1890–1911) helped popularize songs. Also came the first of the ragtime, "Take your clothes and go," 1897, "All coons look alike to me," 1896. The sob ballad included Paul Dresser's "She's more to be pitied than censured," 1898. The minstrels, Christy's in the 1850's, Carncross and Dixey, and Dumont in Philadelphia, Primrose and West, and Dockstader in New York, helped popularize songs; and so did the musical comedies in the 1900's. The World War checked song production except for war songs. After the war, jazz appeared, 1917 (Ben Harney), and in 1920 symphonic jazz (Paul Whiteman, Gershwin).

Mention should be made of cowboy songs[qv] (collected by John A. Lomax), coster songs (Albert Chevalier), Erie Canal songs, sea chanties, sectional songs (Southern mountains, collected by Cecil Sharp), railroad songs ("Casey Jones," 1909), drinking songs ("Bohemia Hall," "Stein on the Table"), ribald parodies, often hard to find in print, wisecracking songs ("Hurray for Baffin's Bay," 1903). College songs have in some cases become generally popular, as Amherst's "Lord Jeffrey Amherst," Harvard's "Fair Harvard," Yale's "Boola," Cornell's "Far above Cayuga's water," Rutgers' "On the banks," Dartmouth's "Winter song."

Every war has brought forth some songs: the Revolution, "Yankee Doodle"; the War of 1812, "The Star-Spangled Banner." The Civil War brought a great number, many still sung, as Julia Ward Howe's "Battle Hymn of the Republic," "Dixie," "Marching Through Georgia," "John Brown's body," all of George F. Root's ("Tramp, tramp, tramp). The Spanish-American War had only one hit, Metz's "Hot Time in the Old Town tonight" (written fifteen years before). In the World War, many songs were written, but some seemed forced and did not sweep the country. However, "Over there," 1917, "Long, Long Trail," 1915, "Pack up your troubles," 1915, are popular examples.

[E. B. Marks, *They all Sang;* Sigmund Spaeth, *Read 'em and Weep*, and *Weep Some More, My Lady;* Carl Sandburg, *American Song Bag.*]

AUGUSTUS H. SHEARER

Sons of Liberty (Civil War) was a secret "Copperhead"[qv] order, strongest in the Northwest, formed in 1864 by reorganization of the Order of American Knights[qv] with C. L. Vallandigham[qv] of Ohio, exile in Canada, as supreme commander. The 300,000 members were sworn to oppose unconstitutional acts of the Federal Government and to support states' rights[qv] principles. They opposed the draft[qv] and discouraged enlistments. Confederate agents in Canada attempted unsuccessfully to promote a Northwest Conspiracy[qv], using the order to form a Northwestern Confederacy. Six members were arrested and tried for treason at Indianapolis in September and October, 1864. Three were condemned to death but never executed.

[E. J. Benton, *The Movement for Peace without a Victory during the Civil War.*]

CHARLES H. COLEMAN

Sons of Liberty (Revolutionary) was organized in the American colonies at the time of the Stamp Act[qv] controversy. Societies sprang up simultaneously in scattered communities, an indication that while leadership was an important factor in agitating American independence, there existed among the people a considerable discontent which had been aggravated by parliamentary interference. New York and Boston had two of the most energetic and spirited chapters. The Sons of Liberty constituted the extralegal enforcement arm of the movement for colonial self-government. Members circulated patriotic petitions, tarred and feathered[qv] violators of patriotic decrees, and intimidated British officials and their families. They stimulated a consciousness of colonial grievances by propaganda. They conducted funerals of patriots killed in street brawls. They promoted picnics, dinners and rallies, drank toasts to the honor of historic leaders of liberty, sang songs, denounced British tyranny and hanged unpopular officials in effigy. Upon discovery of governmental impotency they issued semiofficial decrees of authority, and impudently summoned royal officials to Liberty Trees[qv] to explain their conduct to the people. Notwithstanding faults, the organization was a vigorous recrudescence in man's age-long struggle to improve his economic and political conditions.

[Ellen Chase, *The Beginnings of the American Revolution.*]

LLOYD C. M. HARE

Sons of the American Revolution, National Society of the, is a patriotic hereditary organization. The Sons of Revolutionary Sires was organized in San Francisco, Oct. 22, 1875, and on April 30, 1889, combined with certain members of the Society of the Sons of the Revolution[qv] to organize in New York City the Sons of the American Revolution, with membership restricted to lineal descendants of those who saw actual military or naval service during the Revolutionary War[qv]. The society was incorporated in 1906.

[W. Seward Webb, *Historical Notes of the Organization of Societies of Sons of the American Revolution.*]

ALVIN F. HARLOW

Sons of the Revolution, Society of the, patriotic and hereditary, was organized in New York City, Feb. 22, 1876, and reorganized in 1883. Its membership consists of male lineal descendants of those who actively participated in procuring American independence during the Revolutionary War[qv], whether as soldiers, sailors or otherwise. The society became active in preserving and marking historic spots, especially in the vicinity of New York City. The New York City chapter restored and has its headquarters in Fraunces Tavern[qv], where Washington bade farewell to his officers in 1783.

[E. H. Hall, *History of the Movement for the Union of the Societies of the Sons of the American Revolution and Sons of the Revolution.*]

ALVIN F. HARLOW

Sons of the South, THE (1854), sometimes called "Blue Lodges,"[qv] "Social Bands" and "Friends Society," was a secret society recruited largely from Missourians to make Kansas a slave state. Organized in bands, it encouraged emigration and protected proslavery settlers in Kansas, and in numerous other ways, sometimes illegally and violently, tried to counteract the advertised influences of Northern emigrant aid societies[qv].

[*Reports* of the House of Representatives, 34 Cong., 1 Sess., No. 200.]

HENRY T. SHANKS

Soo Canal, THE. *See* St. Marys Falls Ship Canal.

"Sooners" were those persons who illegally entered certain lands in the Indian Territory[qv] prior to the date that had been set for the opening of the lands to settlement. The term was first used in connection with the settlement of the "Oklahoma Lands,"[qv] which occurred at noon, April 22, 1889. A proclamation issued thirty days earlier by President Benjamin Harrison had set this date and hour for these lands to be settled and had forbidden any person to enter them earlier. Those who did so came to be called "Sooners." The term was also used at later openings of Indian Territory lands to settlement.

[J. S. Buchanan and E. E. Dale, *A History of Oklahoma;* J. B. Thoburn, *History of Oklahoma*, Vol. II.]

EDWARD EVERETT DALE

Sorghum Making. In the 1840's the seed of sorghum was imported from Liberia and grown in the United States with a view to manufacturing sugar commercially from its juice. All attempts proved futile, since glucose is the only saccharine matter in the plant. Col. Isaac Hedges of Missouri was the greatest promoter of the product. During the Civil War when Southern molasses was shut off, sorghum became a popular product in the Upper Mississippi Valley. Most sorghum today is still produced on the farm. The stalks, while standing in the field, are stripped of their leaves by hand, with large wooden knives. When cut and hauled to the neighborhood mill, they are run between rollers to extract the juice, which is then boiled to the proper consistency in large vats. Great quantities of this "long sweetening" were made and used as a substitute for sugar on the prairie frontier.

[Wm. M. Ledbetter, Isaac Hedges' Vision of a Sorghum Industry in Missouri, in *Missouri Historical Review*, Vol. 21.]

EVERETT DICK

Sound Dues. By "immemorial prescription" Denmark claimed the right to collect dues on ships passing through the Sound (between Denmark and Sweden). American vessels paid the dues until 1854 when Secretary of State Marcy informed Denmark that as we had not helped to create the dues and had never received any benefit from them, we intended to stop paying them. Denmark in 1855 invited an international congress to meet in Copenhagen to discuss the problem. The United States refused to send delegates. The congress met, however, and in February, 1856, decided to redeem the dues at a figure satisfactory to Denmark, 35,000,000 rix-dollars. Each nation was to pay an amount based on the proportion of its trade through the Sound. Although the United States had not taken part in the congress, she agreed by a treaty (1857) to pay her share, 717,829 rix-dollars ($393,011). Denmark agreed to keep up the lighthouses, buoys and other improvements of the Sound.

[S. P. Fogdall, *Danish-American Diplomacy, 1776-1920;* C. E. Hill, *The Danish Sound Dues and the Command of the Baltic.*]

S. P. FOGDALL

South, Civilization of the Old. Covering a vast area, from the Mason-Dixon Line[qv], the

Ohio and Missouri rivers, to the Gulf of Mexico and the Rio Grande, with the greatest variety of soil and climate, the South in 1860 was the most clearly defined section of the country. Geographical factors fostered the production of staple crops for world markets, which led to the development of the plantation system[qv], while the adaptation of Negro slave labor to the industry created a lasting race problem. The eight million whites, with only about 13% of the total foreign-born of the nation, formed a homogeneous population of basically Anglo-Saxon stock, belonged mainly to the Presbyterian, Methodist and Baptist churches, and insisted upon the protection of states' rights[qqv]. These factors, plus the entire complex of social relationship in the presence of two totally different races, gave the distinctive color and flavor to the customs, manners, habits, institutions and thought of the "Land of Dixie."

While the large planters constituted only a small group of society, they dominated the entire life of the region and controlled its politics. The middle class, smaller planters, professional men and merchants with whom planting was frequently a side line, was closely allied with the planters and furnished the most vigorous expounders and defenders of Southern civilization. The small slave-owners, small farmers, small tradesmen and skilled workers made up a stratum devoted to the evangelical churches and Jeffersonian doctrines, willing to give political support to the ruling order, and which sanctioned the existing social system. At the bottom was found an element collectively poverty-stricken, shiftless, devoid of ambition, "the poor whites,"[qv] inhabiting the pine barrens of the low country and the sand hills farther inland. Hatred of the ruling class was second only to their enmity for the Negro, which impelled them to support the institution of slavery as an alternative to competition with the Negroes. The white inhabitants of the mountains of Tennessee, Virginia, the Carolinas and Georgia (*see* Mountain People), with little or no contact with slavery, formed a class entirely separate from all the others. The Negroes, 4,088,765 in 1860, were mainly slaves, although about 250,000, living in the upper southern states, were free. Even slave society had its definite grades: field hands, house servants and skilled workers. No rigid caste system prevailed, and, except for the Negro, the social wheel moved easily, advancing many in the process, but always geared to the ideals of the plantation system.

Agriculture was the chief interest of the South, and in that industry the production and sale of cotton[qv] was of tremendous importance in the development of the social and political economy of the section. Even though a minority was involved, this staple determined the standards, conditions and patterns of society. Only 7.8% of the population lived in towns of 4000 and over, and even these were focal points for the agricultural communities.

The homes of the wealthy planters were sufficiently splendid to give substance to a tradition, but the majority of citizens lived in conditions ranging from comfort to squalor. Richmond, Charleston, Savannah, Mobile and New Orleans, with their lovely homes, flowers, trees, and men and women of grace, quiet elegance and courtly manners, drew praise from Michael Chevalier, John S. Buckingham, Achille Murat and even Harriet Martineau, but they and other travelers reserved comments of a different nature for the major portion of the South. Natural conditions and the way of living engendered physical courage, pride of section and quick tempers, fused by racial and economic considerations into a temperament peculiarly sensitive to outside criticism.

Free public education was decidedly limited in the Old South. Academies of high-school grade were numerous (private institutions, occasionally with some public financial support) and in 1860 there were 425,600 children in school in the cotton states alone, and 25,000 students in colleges. Indeed, the decade before the Civil War saw attendance in almost all the colleges doubled. The state universities of Virginia, the Carolinas, Georgia, Alabama, Mississippi and Louisiana attracted to their faculties scholars of the caliber of Francis Lieber, political scientist, Joseph and John LeConte, scientists, Joseph C. Nott, ethnologist, and J. D. B. DeBow. Medical colleges were founded in Charleston, Mobile and New Orleans. Wisdom and theology might be learned at denominational colleges: Furman University (S. C.), Mercer University (Ga.) and Howard College (Ala.), Baptist institutions, and Randolph-Macon (Va.) and Emory College (Ga.), Methodist. William H. Ruffin (Va.), Calvin S. Wiley (N. C.), William L. Yancey and Dr. Basil Manly (Ala.) were educational reformers of no mean ability, who had doubts of the efficacy of a classical curriculum alone.

College literary societies encouraged a native love of the art of language, and the florid oratory, with its classical allusions and flowing phrases, was as inseparable from the Southern politician as the mint julep from the Kentucky colonel. A large number of periodicals of every kind were published (721 in 1850), but insufficient financial support made the majority short-lived. Southern journalism ranked with the best, as the names Duff Green, Thomas Ritchie, Francis P. Blair, Sr., Robert Barnwell Rhett, John C. Rives, Amos Kendall, George D. Prentice and C. E. Bartlett prove. The Richmond *Whig* and *Enquirer,* the Charleston *Mercury,* the Augusta *Constitutionalist,* the Mobile *Advertiser,* the New Orleans *Bee* and *Picayune* and the Louisville *Journal* were powerful in developing sectional concepts and opinions.

Romanticism detracted from the originality of literature generally, but William Gilmore Simms, Henry Timrod, Paul Hamilton Hayne and Richard Henry Wilde, poets, and Augustus Baldwin Longstreet, Joseph G. Baldwin, William Tappan Thompson and Joseph P. Kennedy, writers, deserve their place in American letters. In scientific achievement this agrarian section earned a place of distinction. Crawford W. Long's pioneer work in anæsthesia[qv], Ephraim McDowell's contribution to surgery are especially noteworthy and M. F. Maury, oceanographer, Edmund Ravenel, conchologist, Henry W. Ravenel, mycologist, Edmund Ruffin, soil chemist, and J. J. Audubon are distinguished representatives of a large group. Joseph Le Conte's scientific investigations at the University of South Carolina pointed to a theory of the origin of the species which gave Darwin his reputation.

Slavery[qv] and the decades of controversy over it directed the intellectual activity of many into channels less productive of ultimate achievement. The progressive sweep of the cotton kingdom revived slavery, apparently moribund in 1776, and abolition[qv] attacks moved men to the disagreeable task of repudiating the humanitarianism of Jefferson. Ridicule of the equalitarian doctrines by John Randolph and John Marshall of Virginia paved the way for the William and Mary College professor, Thomas R. Dew, who marshaled history, Christianity and economics to prove that slavery was sound at every point (*see* Proslavery). William Harper, George Fitzhugh, James H. Hammond and John C. Calhoun expanded Dew's thesis, while newspapers and a multitude of pamphlets popularized a social philosophy which justified inequality and bondage, and the right of minority rule. It is not surprising that a politically minority section, with a social and economic system peculiarly its own, should have developed political and constitutional theories and have insisted upon their recognition in national circles. Political and governmental practices in the Old South reveal the practical application of the theory of the right of minority rule, which men like Calhoun shaped to meet the needs of their day. Indeed, in his exposition of the doctrine of concurrent minorities, the South Carolinian made a contribution to political thought (*see* Calhoun's *Disquisition on Government*). National development moved steadily in the direction of an industrial state, but Southern leaders preferred to follow the High Priest of agrarianism, John Taylor of Caroline.

[R. S. Cotterill, *The Old South;* William E. Dodd, *The Cotton Kingdom;* W. S. Jenkins, *Pro-Slavery Thought in the Old South.*]

RALPH B. FLANDERS

South America, United States Commerce with, originated in the intercourse of the Thirteen Colonies with ports in the Spanish Indies. Shortly after the United States acknowledged the independence of the Spanish-American republics, she began to negotiate treaties of commerce with them (*see* Latin-American Republics, Recognition of the). The treaty signed on Oct. 3, 1824, between Colombia and the United States regulated trade between that country and northern South America for many years.

During the period from 1825 to 1850 large quantities of cotton goods were exported from the United States to Colombia, Chile and Brazil. South America sent to the United States hides, wool, sugar, guano and copper. During the year ending June 30, 1850, the United States imported $15,856,701 of produce from South American countries, while she exported to them goods amounting to $7,050,767. After 1850, because of the Civil War and the increasing competition from European countries, the export trade of the United States with South American nations declined. Although in 1867 the United States made purchases of coffee and rubber from Brazil and of sugar, spices, fruits, chemicals and woods from other nations of South America amounting to $88,408,119, yet her sales of manufactured goods to these countries amounted to scarcely one third of the total of her purchases from them.

Meantime a brief experiment was made with reciprocity. The McKinley Tariff Act[qv] of Oct. 1, 1890, authorized the President to reimpose the duties on sugar, molasses, coffee, tea and hides, which were on the free list, whenever he deemed that the duties imposed on products of the United States by nations exporting those articles were "reciprocally unjust or unequal." Secretary of State Blaine accordingly negotiated reciprocity agreements with Brazil, Guatemala, Honduras, Nicaragua, Salvador and the Dominican Republic. However, these reciprocity agreements were all ended by the Wilson Tariff^qv in 1894.

During the years from 1900 to 1914 a marked development took place in the commerce of the United States with South American nations. In particular, there was an increase in the volume of imports from Argentina, Brazil, Chile, Peru, Colombia and Venezuela. Imports into the United States from Argentina increased from $105,078,714 in 1900 to $273,821,496 in 1914. The United States was the second largest importer from Chile, while the amount of her exports to that country was exceeded only by those of England and of Germany.

During the World War leading nations of South America sent larger shares of their products to the United States and purchased more manufactured goods in this country. Imports into the United States from South America in 1916 were nearly 100% in excess of those in 1914, while exports from the United States to that continent showed a gain of 140% during the two-year period, 1914–16. By 1917 the United States enjoyed about one half of the total trade of South America.

The years immediately following the World War were distinguished by a great expansion of commercial life in South America. In 1913 Colombia and Venezuela purchased $10,000,000 of goods from the United States; in 1927 they purchased $90,000,000. After the construction of the Panama Canal^qv, the trade of the United States with countries on the west coast of South America increased considerably. The chief exceptions to this tendency were countries in the basin of La Plata River, where the staple products were the same as those of the United States. Import duties levied by the United States tariff on wheat as well as the stringent application of sanitary regulations to meat provoked resentment in Argentina, resentment which made them turn more and more toward English marts and markets.

[American Commerce: *Commerce of South America, Central America, Mexico, and the West Indies, with Share of the United States and Other Countries Therein, 1821-1898;* W. S. Robertson, *Hispanic-American Relations with the United States.*]

WILLIAM SPENCE ROBERTSON

South as a Conscious Minority. From the formation of the Federal Constitution in 1787 until the stroke for Southern independence in 1861, Southern political thought was devoted to evolving an adequate philosophy of protection to minority interests^qv in the Federal system. Until 1820 chief reliance was placed upon the principle of local self-government, involving such a distribution of powers between the central Government and the state governments as would, in the words of Thomas Jefferson, "make us one nation as to foreign concerns, & keep us distinct in Domestic ones." But unforeseen use of the "sweeping clauses" of the Constitution, through which the powers of the central Government were expanded at the expense of the states, led to a shift during the middle decades to the principle of the concurrent voice, embracing, according to its chief advocate, John C. Calhoun, "such an organism of the government . . . as will, by dividing and distributing the powers of government, give to each division or interest, through its appropriate organ, either a concurrent voice in making and executing the laws, or a veto on their execution." To apply this principle, plans were advanced for establishing an effective Southern check through a reorganization of the executive, the judicial and the legislative departments. The last hope of success, however, went glimmering with the loss of sectional equality in the Senate through the admission of California into the Union in 1850.

Thereafter, for a decade, Southern political thinkers turned to the principle of constitutional guarantees to test the efficacy of a written fundamental law as an effective restraint upon the power of a numerical majority. The Constitution, asserted Alexander H. Stephens, protects slavery^qv in the states and the territories, and those in control of the Government cannot evade that solemn obligation except by the support of that extra-majority vote required for constitutional amendments. But by 1860 the rising tide of immigration and the expanding number of free states foreshadowed the abolition of Negro slavery by constitutional amendment. Hence the final resort to the principle of Southern independence based in part upon a concept of the nature of the Union, which permitted secession as a constitutional right (*see* Secession, Right of), and in part upon a theory of natural rights^qv transcending constitutional limitations and drawn largely from colonial experience. The Confederate Constitution^qv of 1861, though modeled largely upon the Federal instrument, presumably embodied the necessary innovations for the successful application of this minority philosophy of the ante-bellum South.

[J. T. Carpenter, *The South as a Conscious Minority.*]

JESSE T. CARPENTER

South Carolina was first visited by Spaniards in 1521, and temporarily settled by them under

Ayllon[qv] in 1526. In 1562 the French Protestant, Jean Ribaut, attempted to establish a colony on Parris Island, but was thwarted by Spaniards (*see* Port Royal). England claimed the region also, but the charter granted to Sir Robert Heath[qv] in 1629 was allowed to lapse, and in 1663 Charles II granted Carolina (including the present North Carolina) to eight of his favorites (*see* Carolina Proprietors). By a second charter (1665) the grant was extended to include the territory from 29° on the south to 36° 30′ on the north and stretching from "sea to sea." Under the government of the Proprietors, chief of whom was called the Palatinate, legislation was to be "by and with the advice, assent and approbation of the freemen," and religious freedom was permitted but not required. In 1669 a plan of government was prepared by John Locke in the elaborate and unworkable Fundamental Constitutions (*see* Carolina, The Fundamental Constitutions of). The first permanent settlement (Albemarle Point[qv], April, 1670) was later (1680) moved across the Ashley River to the present site of Charleston[qv].

Almost from the first the colony prospered, partly because of the excellent harbor and the advertising ingenuity of the Proprietors, and partly because of the influx of English Dissenters and French Huguenots[qv]. During the proprietary rule (1663–1719) there were wars with Spain (1686, 1702–4) and France and Spain (1706), as well as with the troublesome pirates (1718) and the native Indians in the bloody Yamasee War[qv] (1715). Internally there was friction between the absentee Proprietors and the people who feared the effects of the Fundamental Constitutions and who were loath to pay the quitrents[qv]. In 1693 the commons house won the right to initiate legislation equally with the governor and council. A religious controversy, resulting in the establishment of the Church of England (1706–78), together with the failure of the Proprietors to approve needed legislation and to protect the colonies, served to further weaken the hold of the Proprietors, and in 1719 the commons house usurped control of the colony. The Privy Council[qv] took this opportunity to appoint a royal governor, and in 1729 Parliament provided for the purchase of the Proprietors' land titles. In 1730 a preliminary boundary was fixed between the two Carolinas which had been separately governed except for one period (1691–1712).

The period of royal control (1719–1776), with the increased export of skins, rice and indigo, and with the flourishing Indian trade, was an era of prosperity. Also important were the growing influence of the commons house and the decline of the authority of the governor and council, who found the commons peculiarly stubborn in the contests for control of the purse and for "constitutional rights."

Unhappy experiences with the men and methods of royal control and a desire for local self-government brought resistance to the Stamp Act[qv] and delegates were sent to the Stamp Act Congress[qv] (1765). Subsequent British legislation fanned the flame, and in July, 1774, a provincial congress elected delegates to the Continental Congress[qv] and practically assumed the government of the colony. On Sept. 15, 1775, the royal governor fled, and on March 26, 1776, a constitution was signed.

The British hope of taking Charleston and uniting with the Tories[qv] of the upcountry was dashed at the battle of Fort Moultrie[qv] (June 28, 1776), and it was not until 1780 that the city fell (*see* Charleston, Capture of). The sporadic attacks of the partisan leaders, Sumter, Marion and Pickens, served to keep alive the patriot cause, and the victories of King's Mountain (Oct. 7, 1780) and Cowpens[qqv] (Jan. 17, 1781) put some restraint upon the British, although Charleston was not evacuated until December, 1782.

The economic and political difficulties of wartime gradually gave way to a revival of trade and extensive internal improvements. The social and economic cleavage between the small-property, democratic upcountry, and the aristocratic, slaveholding, high-church planters of the low country resulted in the removal of the capital to Columbia in 1790. In 1808 a constitutional amendment reapportioned representation on a basis of population and wealth, the upcountry and the low country dividing control of the general assembly. Until 1865 there were dual state offices in Charleston and Columbia.

Strongly nationalistic through the War of 1812[qv], South Carolina began to exhibit states' rights[qv] leanings in the 1820's. Simultaneously there was an economic decline, with a cessation in immigration, a large emigration into the West and Southwest and a fall in the price of cotton and a reduction in exports. In 1828 Calhoun drew up his Exposition[qv] demanding tariff reform and close adherence to the Constitution. On Nov. 24, 1832, the ordinance of Nullification[qv] was passed, but Jackson's threat of armed force, together with the compromise tariff[qv] of 1833, brought an adjustment. But the gathering force of the abolition movement[qv] united the Unionists and Nullifiers and in 1850–52 a secession movement failed only because no other state was ready to co-operate. The state was the first to adopt (unanimously) an ordinance of Secession[qv] (Dec. 20, 1860), and the war began with the firing on Fort Sumter[qv] in Charleston Harbor (April 12, 1861).

The defeat of war was crowned by the march of Sherman through the state (February–March, 1865, *see* Carolinas, Sherman's March through the) and the burning of Columbia[qv] (Feb. 17, 1865). The social upheaval and economic ruin were made more distressing by the refusal of Congress to accept the re-established civil government (December, 1865). Under congressional Reconstruction[qv] the grant of Negro suffrage[qv] and the disfranchisement of many whites meant the establishment (under the constitution of 1868) of a government of "carpetbaggers," "scalawags" and Negroes[qqv]. Then followed eight years of fraud and corruption until the white Democrats "redeemed" the state (1876). The disfranchisement[qv] of the Negro through the white Democratic primary and the constitution of 1895 ensured white supremacy[qv] but did not eliminate political rivalry between the whites (*see* Tillmanism).

[D. D. Wallace, *History of South Carolina;* Edward McCrady, *History of South Carolina;* W. A. Schaper, *Sectionalism and Representation in South Carolina;* J. G. Van Deusen, *Economic Basis of Disunion in South Carolina;* F. B. Simkins and R. H. Woody, *South Carolina during Reconstruction;* F. B. Simkins, *The Tillman Movement in South Carolina.*]

R. H. WOODY

South Carolina, Proposed Nobility in (1671–1718). The Fundamental Constitutions (*see* Carolina, The Fundamental Constitutions of) designed at once a government agreeable to Charles II and a safeguard against a "numerous democracy." They reserved two fifths of the land for an hereditary nobility, whose estates should be inalienable and indivisible. Some Proprietors functioned locally, and twenty-six landgraves and thirteen caciques acquired estates and seats in the governor's council. One title passed through three generations, and baronies survive as tracts of land. Although no manor or manorial jurisdiction was created or exercised, social and political preferments were enjoyed. Proprietary efforts to transfer English law and practice to America produced a half century of conflict.

[Edward McCrady, *South Carolina under the Proprietary Government;* C. M. Andrews, *The Colonial Period of American History,* Vol. III.]

O. C. SKIPPER

South Carolina, Spanish Expeditions against. French attempts to gain a foothold along the southern Atlantic coast prompted the Spaniards to capture Fort Caroline[qv] (Fla.) and found St. Augustine[qv] (1565). In the same year Spaniards from Cuba burned Ribaut's abandoned Charlesfort at Parris Island (*see* Port Royal). Spaniards from St. Augustine fortified the island and held the region from 1566 to 1586. In August, 1670, Spanish vessels from St. Augustine appeared before Charleston[qv], but retired without attacking. South Carolinians trespassed among Spanish Indians; in 1686 the Spanish in retaliation destroyed Stuart's Town, a Scotch settlement near Port Royal, and raided to the northward. Spanish Indians retaliating for the 1702 attacks on St. Augustine and on the region of Tallahassee and eastward were crushed by South Carolina traders and Indians. Gov. Moore ravaged the region Tallahassee and eastward December–January, 1703–4 (*see* Ayubale). In 1706 a Franco-Spanish naval attack on Charleston failed disastrously. The tradition that the Spanish inspired the Yamasee War[qv] seems groundless, although they harbored the defeated Yamasees. Forces from St. Augustine, seeking to avenge a Georgia-South Carolina attack (1740), were defeated by Oglethorpe (1742) at Bloody Marsh[qv], Ga., and abandoned their planned attack on South Carolina.

[V. M. Crane, *Southern Frontier;* E. McCrady, *South Carolina under the Proprietors,* and *South Carolina as a Royal Province;* J. T. Lanning, *Spanish Missions in Georgia;* D. D. Wallace, *History of South Carolina.*]

D. D. WALLACE

South Carolina, Tea Party of (1773). *See* Tea Parties.

South Carolina, The State Bank of (1812–68), was a commercial, state-owned institution located in Charleston with branches in Columbia, Camden and Abbeville. The state deposited its funds in the bank, accepted its notes and limited its debt-contracting power. The size, the security and the distribution of its loans among representative districts were regulated by statute. It made loans to the state without interest, managed and from its profits retired a large part of the state's debt. However, C. G. Memminger and J. H. Hammond charged it with favoritism and with possessing dangerous powers, but its connections and the sectional controversy saved it.

[D. D. Wallace, *History of South Carolina,* Vol. II.]

O. C. SKIPPER

South Carolina Canal, THE, between the Santee and Cooper rivers, was proposed by Chancellor Rutledge in 1786. One hundred shares of stock of indefinite value were subscribed, the legislature granted the charter, and operations were begun in 1792. In 1795–96 a lottery was resorted to in order to provide funds. Dug mostly by Negroes, the canal, four feet deep and thirty-five feet wide at the surface, was completed in 1800. In 1858, after railroads were established, the canal was abandoned.

[U. B. Phillips, *Transportation in the Eastern Cotton Belt.*]

CHARLES B. SWANEY

South Carolina Interstate and West Indian Exposition, THE, held at Charleston from Dec. 1, 1901, to June 1, 1902, was designed to promote closer commercial relations between the United States and the seventy principal West Indian islands. The exposition cost $1,250,000 and covered 160 acres, including 20 acres of midway attractions. It included a complete display of West Indian resources and products, but the emphasis was chiefly upon American manufactures and exports.

FRANK MONAGHAN

South Carolina Railroad, THE, was chartered as The South Carolina Canal and Railroad Company in 1827. It was organized and promoted by Charleston merchants and business interests for the prime purpose of reviving the economic condition of that city. The road was completed from Charleston to Hamburg (a village across Savannah River from Augusta, Ga.) in October, 1833. It was 136 miles long and was at that time the longest in the world.

In 1843 the South Carolina Canal and Railroad Company was merged with the Louisville, Cincinnati and Charleston Railroad Company to form the South Carolina Railroad Company. In 1842 the Louisville, Cincinnati and Charleston Railroad Company had completed a line from Branchville, a station on the Charleston and Hamburg road, to Columbia as a part of its ambitious but futile scheme to build a trunk line from Charleston to Cincinnati. This branch of 66 miles became the property of the new company. In 1848 a branch of 37 miles was constructed from Kingville on the Branchville-Columbia line to Camden. This constituted the total mileage of the railroad.

The company remained intact until 1878 when it was forced into bankruptcy and sold to a group of New York capitalists. The new company was known as The South Carolina Railway Company. In 1894 the road was again sold as a result of bankruptcy and became the South Carolina and Georgia Railroad Company. In 1899 the Southern Railway Company[qv] acquired control of the company and has since operated the lines as a part of the Southern System.

[S. M. Derrick, *Centennial History of South Carolina Railroad.*]

S. M. DERRICK

South Dakota, consisting of the southern half of Dakota Territory[qv], was admitted as a state on Nov. 2, 1889. The state is divided by the Missouri River into two sections of about equal size. East of the river is rolling prairie, which has developed as agricultural land: general farming, wheat growing and grazing. West of the Missouri River the land is rougher, culminating in the Badlands and the Black Hills[qqv].

When the state was admitted all of the area west of the Missouri River, except the lands between the Forks of the Cheyenne River (which included the Black Hills), consisted of the Great Sioux Reservation, created by the Treaty of Laramie in 1868[qv]. On the east side of the Missouri were the Yankton, Wahpeton and Sisseton reservations. In all 25,000 Indians, mostly of Sioux stock, lived on these reservations under the jurisdiction of the Federal Government.

In 1890, 3,840,000 acres of the Great Sioux Reservation were opened to white settlement, and the Indians limited to reservations within the former territory, as follows: Pine Ridge Reservation, Rosebud Reservation, Lower Brule Reservation, Cheyenne River Reservation and Standing Rock Reservation.

In the same year (1890) came the Messiah War, caused by religious frenzy and culminating in the battle of Wounded Knee[qqv].

In 1892 the Sisseton Indian Reservation, consisting of 384,000 acres, was opened to white settlement pursuant to an agreement ratified by act of Congress. Twelve years later (1904) 416,000 acres of the Rosebud Reservation, along the south line of the state west of the Missouri, were opened to settlement by previous registration, priority determined by lot. One hundred and six thousand persons entered these lands. The succeeding years saw a rush of homesteaders to the trans-Missouri territory, and, side by side with this rush of settlement, went extensions of the railroads across the state—into the Black Hills in 1908 and through the northern part of the state the following year. In 1909 the Cheyenne River and Standing Rock reservations were opened to settlement west of and adjoining the Missouri River.

Today (1940) there remain in South Dakota only five Indian reservations representing a total of 8147 square miles. Although under Federal supervision and living within reservations supervised by the Federal Government, the Indians enjoy full citizenship and vote in the state and Federal elections. The present Indian population is in the neighborhood of 28,000.

Throughout its history South Dakota has been subject to alternate periods of drouth and favorable crop conditions. Doubtless this has contributed to some experiments in state business, such as those which allowed the state to mine coal, manufacture cement and enter into other economic and social obligations which have, in the main, proved disastrous.

Within recent years the minerals of the state have attracted particular attention and several important discoveries, such as bentonite, manganese and feldspar, have been made.

[Doane Robinson, *Encyclopedia of South Dakota*, 1925; *Report* South Dakota Planning Board, 1937; South Dakota Historical *Collections*, Vol. III.]

DOANE ROBINSON

South Improvement Company, The, was utilized by John D. Rockefeller and associates (*see* Standard Oil Company) in their first attempt (1871–72) to secure a monopoly of the petroleum industry by means of exclusive rebates*qv* from the railroads of the oil region. Resistance from producers, public indignation and annulment of its charter defeated the scheme.

[Ida M. Tarbell, *The History of the Standard Oil Company.*]

CHESTER McA. DESTLER

South Mountain, Battle of (Sept. 14, 1862). Compelled by McClellan's (U.) rapid pursuit from Frederick (*see* Lost Order, Lee's) to concentrate his scattered army and cover Jackson's (C.) investment of Harpers Ferry*qv*, Lee (C.) posted D. H. Hill's division at Turner's and Fox's gaps, protecting the roads to Boonsboro and Sharpsburg. Five miles south Cobb (C.) with three brigades held Crampton's Gap, shielding Jackson's operations.

Burnside (U.), commanding two corps, about 9 A.M. attacked Hill. Desperate fighting continued until after dark. Longstreet (C.) reinforced Hill, but Burnside captured the gaps, the Confederates retiring toward Sharpsburg. Meantime Franklin's (U.) corps had carried Crampton's Gap by assault, driving the Confederates westward into Pleasant Valley, where next morning they held so strong a line that Franklin would not attack it.

[*Battles and Leaders of the Civil War*, Vol. II.]

JOSEPH MILLS HANSON

South Pass. This is the most celebrated of the passes in the Rocky Mountains, because over it passed the great emigrant trail to Oregon and California. It is located in Wyoming at the southern end of the Wind River Mountains. The approach to the pass is so easy and gradual that, to use the words of John C. Frémont, "the traveller, without being reminded of any change by toilsome ascents, suddenly finds himself on the waters which flow to the Pacific Ocean." There are claims that John Colter discovered the South Pass in 1807 or 1808, and that Robert Stuart and the returning Astorians*qv* crossed it in 1812, but both claims are disputed. It is certain that the effective discovery was made in 1824 by Thomas Fitzpatrick, a fur trader. Capt. Bonneville*qv* first took wagons over the pass in 1832, and a few years later it became the mountain gateway through which passed the Oregon Trail*qv*.

[Hiram M. Chittenden, *The American Fur Trade of the Far West;* E. W. Gilbert, *The Exploration of Western America, 1800-1850;* W. J. Ghent, *The Road to Oregon.*]

DAN E. CLARK

South Platte Route, The, a branch of the Overland Trail*qv*, led to Denver. Leaving the main trail at Julesburg, where the Overland crossed the South Platte River and headed northwest toward Fort Laramie*qv*, the branch route followed the right bank of the South Platte River all the way to Denver. An important stage and freight route, it was attacked by Cheyenne*qv* war parties early in 1865 (*see* Powder River Campaign), Julesburg being looted twice and burned the second time, and ranches destroyed up and down the river, so that traffic was suspended for a considerable period.

[George Bird Grinnell, *The Fighting Cheyennes.*]

PAUL I. WELLMAN

South Sea Expedition (1838–42). *See* Wilkes Exploring Expedition.

Southampton, Long Island, the oldest English town in the State of New York, was settled in the summer of 1640. The settlers came from Lynn, Mass., and the emigration was one of the early examples of the "swarming" from the original hive on the shore of New England, which carried New England influence to the Pacific. The Dutch claimed all of Long Island and had peopled the west end, but in settling Southampton, Southold and Easthampton the English established their claim to the east end. The settlers, under the leadership of Edward Howell, received title to the land under grant from the so-styled "Earl of Stirling" and the local Indian tribes. Southampton's early connections were almost wholly with Connecticut but after the English conquest of New Amsterdam it took its place among the other small communities of the proprietary of the Duke of York[qv], which soon became the royal colony of New York[qv].

[J. T. Adams, *History of the Town of Southampton.*]

JAMES TRUSLOW ADAMS

Southampton Insurrection. *See* Nat Turner's Rebellion.

Southern Boundary, Survey of the (1798–1800), was begun, after long delay, on March 29, 1798, by Andrew Ellicott[qv], United States commissioner, and Thomas Freeman, surveyor, in company with Stephen Minor and Sir William Dunbar, Spanish commissioners. The line surveyed extended from the Mississippi River eastward along the 31st parallel to its intersection with the Chattahoochee (*see* Dunbar's Line), thence down that river to its junction with the Flint, thence direct to the head of St. Marys River and down that stream to the Atlantic Ocean (*see* Pinckney's Treaty). Accompanied by military escort, the survey party cut through virgin forest and dense cane brake, forded swamps, bayous and rivers, suffered Indian attacks and was delayed by Spanish "crooked talk" and procrastination. Supplies, baggage and instruments had to be transported, and disease and sickness combated. The work was laborious and frequently interrupted. Over two years were required for completion.

[B. A. Hinsdale, The Southern Boundary of the United States, in *Report* American Historical Association, 1893.]

THOMAS ROBSON HAY

Southern Campaigns (1780–81). These years were marked by a vigorous effort of the British to reduce the Carolinas and Georgia. On Dec. 26, 1779, Sir Henry Clinton and Lord Cornwallis sailed from New York with 8000 men, and landed at Savannah. They presently invested Gen. Lincoln, American commander in the South, in Charleston[qv] and compelled his surrender on May 12, 1780. The only American regiment not in Charleston was destroyed at the Waxhaws[qv], leaving no organized American force in the three states. But partisan leaders such as Thomas Sumter, Francis Marion, Andrew Pickens and others raised troops of patriots and pursued a guerrilla warfare. Washington sent 2000 men under De Kalb to the aid of South Carolina, but DeKalb was superseded by Horatio Gates, who promptly lost most of his army at the Battle of Camden[qv], and again the Carolinas seemed conquered. Cornwallis detached Ferguson with 1200 men to recruit in the highlands, but this force was annihilated at King's Mountain, and another detachment under Tarleton was destroyed at the Cowpens[qqv]. Nathanael Greene succeeded Gates in December, 1780, and, with Morgan's aid, lured Cornwallis into North Carolina and dealt him a crippling blow at Guilford Court House[qv], after which the British commander retired to Wilmington, N. C., and then marched into Virginia. Benedict Arnold[qv] had been sent into Virginia with 1600 men by Sir Henry Clinton, and Baron von Steuben was detailed on the American side to watch him, but Arnold did nothing of consequence. Greene, ignoring Cornwallis, returned to South Carolina, and though theoretically losing engagements at Hobkirk's Hill, Ninety-Six and Eutaw Springs[qqv], nevertheless conducted his campaign with such masterly strategy that he won his objectives, and by Dec. 10, 1781, had driven the only remaining British force in the South into a state of siege at Charleston. Meanwhile, Cornwallis had been cornered and taken at Yorktown[qv].

[John Fiske, *The American Revolution;* George Washington Greene, *Life of Major-General Nathanael Greene.*]

ALVIN F. HARLOW

Southern Commercial Conventions. The most notable gatherings to which this name applies were the sessions of the so-called Southern Commercial Convention, which met successively at Baltimore, Memphis, Charleston, New Orleans, Richmond, Savannah, Knoxville, Montgomery and Vicksburg between December, 1852, and May, 1859.

The original object of the Southern Commercial Convention was to devise remedies for Southern "decline." The South was not keeping pace with the North in population, manufacturing, railroad building, shipping and other lines of economic development. This was galling to the pride of loyal Southerners. It was taken as proof that the section was not prospering as it should. Thoughtful Southerners felt that the industrial and commercial dependence of their section resulted in Southern earnings being drained away to build up the North. The superior population and wealth of the free states were giving them an advantage in the bitter struggle over slavery[qv]. The convention canvassed a wide variety of proposed remedies, such as, building a railroad to the Pacific by a southern route, promotion of trade with Latin America, direct importation of European goods and encouragement of Southern manufactures by bounties or by discriminatory taxation of Northern-made articles.

Although in effect mass meetings, the earlier sessions of the convention were representative of all parts of the South and all shades of opinion. As time went by and the convention failed to produce tangible results moderate men ceased to attend, and the sessions came to be dominated by the secessionists of the lower South, who contended that the Union was an obstacle to Southern economic development. Finally a question was injected which threatened seriously to divide the disunionists themselves, namely the desirability of reopening the foreign slave trade[qv]. Secessionists leaders then exerted themselves to bring the convention to an end. The net result of the gatherings was to promote Southern sectionalism[qv].

Similar to the Southern Commercial Convention, and forerunners of it, were the "direct-trade" conventions held in Augusta and Charleston, 1837–39, and in Richmond and Norfolk, 1838, and the Southwestern Convention in Memphis, 1845.

[R. R. Russel, *Economic Aspects of Southern Sectionalism, 1840-1861;* H. W. Wender, *Southern Commercial Conventions, 1837-1859.*]

R. R. RUSSEL

Southern Exposition, The, was first opened at Louisville, Ky., in the summer of 1883 and was successfully revived each year through 1887. The one principal exhibit building covered fifteen acres. After the first year the educational exhibits disappeared and industry and amusement clearly dominated the exposition designed to "save the city of Louisville from falling into the commercial lethargy overcoming other and larger cities."

FRANK MONAGHAN

Southern Literary Messenger, The (1834–64), was a magazine published at Richmond, Va., which was devoted especially to literature and the fine arts. It was outspoken in 1842 against England's search of American ships suspected of carrying African slaves (*see* Slave Trade, The American). Its most famous editor was Edgar Allan Poe. Usually it reflected the thought of the Southern country gentleman who owned slaves. From January, 1846, until December, 1847, while Benjamin Blake Minor was editor and proprietor, it was known by the more ambitious title, *Southern and Western Monthly Magazine and Review.* Other editors were Thomas W. White, John Reuben Thompson, George William Bagby and Frank H. Alfriend. It ceased publication in 1864 because of the fighting around Richmond.

[David Kelly Jackson, *The Contributors and Contributions to the Southern Literary Messenger;* Edward Ingle, *Two Southern Magazines.*]

FRANK MARTIN LEMON

Southern Nationalism. *See* South as a Conscious Minority.

Southern (or Butterfield) Overland Mail, The, first land mail to California in competition with the ocean route, came after a long struggle in Congress. The act of March 3, 1857, provided a semiweekly service on a 25-day schedule at $600,000 per year. Postmaster General Brown, Tennessean, chose a southern route, running from St. Louis and Memphis by way of Fort Smith[qv], El Paso and Tucson to San Francisco. John Butterfield, W. G. Fargo and others were the contractors. After a year's preparation, service began Sept. 15, 1858, with four-horse coaches; passenger fare $100 to $200 each way. The schedule was successfully maintained until the outbreak of the Civil War, when the line was moved to the Central route (*see* Overland Mail and Stagecoaches).

[L. R. Hafen, *The Overland Mail, 1849-1869.*]

LeRoy R. Hafen

Southern Pacific Railroad Company. From 1865 to 1884 local connecting railway lines were being built and mergers were being formed to provide through service from San Francisco to New Orleans (*see* Gadsden Purchase). The California legislature chartered the Southern Pacific Company on Dec. 2, 1865. But the Panic of 1873[qv] and the general lack of finances so retarded construction that it did not reach the eastern boundary of the state until May, 1877, and then only by buying up shorter lines and effecting a consolidation. For this reason, Congress allowed it to amend its route so that it would not include San Diego as provided in its original charter.

The Southern Pacific of Arizona then built eastward to the New Mexico line via the Gila River route, and by 1882 the Southern Pacific of New Mexico formed a junction with the Texas and Pacific[qv] at Sierra Blanca, ninety-two miles east of El Paso. Between these two towns the Southern Pacific and Texas and Pacific operated the line jointly, each paying one half the maintenance cost, and the Texas and Pacific paying in addition $10,000 per mile. And from Sierra Blanca eastward the Southern Pacific carried out still another merger. Short Texas lines were bought to provide through service from El Paso to New Orleans via San Antonio, Houston and Galveston by February, 1883. Then finally, in 1884, C. P. Huntington, Leland Stanford and others created a holding company which took over all the local lines of the southern route and provided a consolidated Southern Pacific from New Orleans to San Francisco.

[Lewis H. Haney, *A Congressional History of Railways in the United States, 1850-1887;* R. N. Richardson and C. C. Rister, *The Greater Southwest.*]

C. C. RISTER

Southern Railroad Route. A southern route of travel from New Mexico to California via the Gila River (through southern New Mexico and Arizona) was well known prior to the Mexican War. But during the war, when Col. Stephen W. Kearny[qv] made his well-known expedition from Leavenworth, Kans., to San Diego, Calif. (1846), it was reported as a desirable railroad route. Kearny was accompanied by Lt. W. H. Emory[qv], whose notes and sketches were the basis for the proposal. The Gadsden Purchase[qv] guaranteed an all-American right-of-way. In 1853 Congress had appropriated $150,000 for Pacific railway surveys, and one of these was made soon thereafter over the southern approach (*see* Southern Pacific Railroad Company). That part of it east of El Paso was surveyed by Capt. John Pope and that farther west by Lt. J. G. Parke.

[J. R. Perkins, *Trails, Rails, and War;* Lewis H. Haney, *A Congressional History of Railways in the United States, 1850-1887;* R. N. Richardson and C. C. Rister, *The Greater Southwest.*]

C. C. RISTER

Southern Railway, THE, was organized in 1894 to take over about thirty Southern railroads, large and small, which had been weakened by the Panic of 1893[qv], the Richmond & Danville being the original nucleus. In rapid succession, the new corporation acquired at foreclosure sales the Charlotte, Columbia & Augusta; the Columbia & Greenville; the East Tennessee, Virginia & Georgia (1265 miles); the Georgia Pacific and others; and by Sept. 1, 1894, was operating 4429 miles of rail. It continued to grow, acquiring by lease the Queen & Crescent system—Cincinnati to New Orleans and Shreveport—and another line giving it entrance to St. Louis, and in 1939 controlled 7895 miles of track.

[Slason Thompson, *A Short History of American Railways.*]

ALVIN F. HARLOW

Southern Rights Movement. Though as old as the Union, the movement for Southern rights during the ante-bellum period is particularly associated with aggressive efforts during the late 1840's and the 1850's to solidify the South for the protection of its interests expressed chiefly in the institution of Negro slavery[qv]. The movement took various forms and was sponsored by men of varying beliefs. Influenced by John C. Calhoun, Southern congressmen in Washington in 1848 and again in 1850 issued addresses to the Southern people praying for "unity among ourselves"; at the same time various Southern state legislatures resolved "to act with resolution, firmness and unity of purpose." Southern commercial conventions[qv] worked for economic independence, while certain politicians were interested in the formation of a sectional political party. William L. Yancey organized a League of United Southerners, and later favored committees of safety which at the proper moment could "precipitate the cotton states into a revolution." Among the lesser lights were a group of self-syled secessionists *per se* who had always advocated a Southern Confederacy in preference to any possible means of protection within the Union. It was this group which became the nucleus of the movement for Southern independence after the election of Lincoln in 1860[qv].

[J. T. Carpenter, *The South as a Conscious Minority.*]

JESSE T. CARPENTER

Southern Unionists during the Civil War. Considering the fifteen slave states[qv] as making up the South, the border states[qv] of Missouri, Kentucky, Virginia, Maryland and Delaware were the greatest strongholds of Unionism. Their desire to remain in the Union is evident, for if war came they saw themselves made the battlefield; and with their economic and social connections north and south, they could better weigh the advantages of a united country. In all these states except Virginia, they were able to prevent secession[qv], and of the latter state that part joining free territory broke away and formed the State of West Virginia[qv]. In the Confederacy[qv] itself there were many people who remained loyal to the Union, or who soon returned to their former loyalty. They lived mostly in the upcountry, especially in the mountains (*see* Mountain People), or in the pine barrens[qv] and other less fertile regions. East Tennessee was the outstanding storm center of Unionism within the Confederacy. Fundamental love for country, opposition to the ante-bellum leadership of the slaveholders who were now identified with the Confederacy and who were merged in the Democratic party, and, as the war progressed, dislike of conscription[qv] and of Confederate revenue measures—these things made Unionists. It has been estimated that almost 300,000 Southerners fought in the Union armies.

[C. C. Anderson, *Fighting by Southern Federals;* T. Speed, *The Union Cause in Kentucky, 1860-1865;* E. M. Coulter, *William G. Brownlow, Fighting Parson of the Southern Highlands;* G. L. Tatum, *Disloyalty in the Confederacy;* E. Lonn, *Desertion during the Civil War.*]

E. MERTON COULTER

Southold, Long Island, was purchased and settled under the authority of New Haven Colony[qv], in the summer of 1640. The settlement was commenced in combination with New Haven, but was made over to Southold in 1649. It was admitted to the jurisdiction of Connecticut on Oct. 9, 1662, but was obliged to submit to the Duke of York's[qv] government in 1665.

[E. R. Lambert, *History of the Colony of New Haven; New Haven Colonial Records*, Vol. I; *Public Records of Connecticut.*]

MORTON PENNYPACKER

Southwest, Old. In contrast with the historical concept of the territorial limits of the Old Northwest[qv], the Old Southwest was never so exact. The term came to be applied first to the region embraced in the present states of Tennessee and Kentucky, but it was extended to include also primarily Alabama and Mississippi, and sometimes vaguely Louisiana and Arkansas. In colonial times it came within the limits of Virginia, North Carolina, South Carolina and Georgia, but no attempt was ever made to extend an active government over this region. The Proclamation of 1763[qv] reserved it "under the sovereignty, protection, and dominance of the king" and forbade further colonial grants to settlers.

Colonial adventurers and land speculators paid little attention to this proclamation. In 1769 various settlers, mostly from Virginia, began their Watauga[qv] venture in what is now East Tennessee and three years later made for themselves a framework of government; in 1775 Richard Henderson was instrumental in organizing the Transylvania Company[qv], which made a settlement at Boonesborough in a region later to become Kentucky; and near the end of the Revolution, Nashborough in the Cumberland Valley of Tennessee was founded. Internal commotion in the Kentucky region led Virginia to stamp out the Henderson venture, while other settlements were promoted which led to the organization of the State of Kentucky in 1792. Watauga grew into the State of Franklin[qv], which North Carolina suppressed, and the settlements here, with those in the Nashborough region, developed into the State of Tennessee, admitted in 1796.

After the treaty of peace in 1783, fixing the western limits of the United States at the Mississippi, a movement sprang up promoted by the landless states to force the states with western lands[qv] to cede them to the central Government. Virginia reserved her Kentucky region and gave it her permission to become a state; North Carolina in 1789 gave up her Tennessee region to the Federal Government; South Carolina ceded her shadowy claims to a twelve-mile-wide strip south of Tennessee; but Georgia refused to make terms which Congress would accept.

Claims to the Georgia western lands were varied and confused. The Federal Government denied the validity of the Georgia claims and Spain declared all lands south of 32° 28′ her own, re-enforcing her claim by continuing to occupy the Natchez region. To add to the complication, powerful tribes of Indians (Creeks, Cherokees, Choctaws and Chickasaws) held actual control of most of the region. In 1789 Georgia sought profit from the confusion by selling most of it to three Yazoo companies[qv]. The first Federal control over any part of the Old Southwest came with the organization of the Southwest Territory[qv] in 1790.

[Archibald Henderson, *The Conquest of the Old Southwest;* Constance L. Skinner, *Pioneers of the Old Southwest*, Vol. 18 in The Chronicle of America Series; T. P. Abernethy, *Western Lands and the American Revolution.*]

E. MERTON COULTER

Southwest, THE, may be roughly defined as the southwestern quarter of the United States, though any distinct delimitation of the area is necessarily arbitrary. So considered, it includes Oklahoma, Texas, New Mexico, Arizona, the southern half of California and the southern portions of Kansas and Colorado. With the exception of most of Kansas and Oklahoma, which formed part of the Louisiana Purchase[qv], all of this region was a part of the possessions of Spain, and later of Mexico, well into the 19th century and so has, historically, a background that is distinctly Spanish. Kansas[qv] is a "marginal state," since its history is partially bound up with that of the Southwest and in part with that of the central prairie states. Oklahoma and Texas[qqv] each has a history essentially its own. The former was for more than half a century a great Indian territory forbidden to settlement by whites. The Five Civilized Tribes[qv], occupying much of it, formed small commonwealths or republics, each with its own government and laws. Texas, settled largely by Anglo-Americans, won its independence of Mexico in 1836. After nearly ten years' existence as a republic, it was annexed to the United States in 1845. The remainder of this southwestern region, except the little Gadsden Purchase[qv], became a part of the United States in 1848 with the signing of the Treaty of Guadalupe Hidalgo[qv] with Mexico.

The influence of the Southwest upon the political history of the United States began early in the 19th century. The Louisiana Purchase boundary line[qv], which had been the subject of much controversy, was drawn in 1819, leaving Texas to Spain (*see* Adams-Onís Treaty). Later the question of the annexation of Texas[qv] became an important political issue. After annexation the dispute over the boundary helped to precipitate the War with Mexico[qv]. Disputes over the organization of the new territory acquired from Mexico by this war ended in the much-debated Compromise of 1850[qv]. Four years later came the Kansas-Nebraska Act[qv] and the violent controversies following it attracted the attention of the entire nation.

Significant as this region has been in the political history of the United States, its importance in our economic history is even more apparent. The discovery of gold in California[qv] and later in Colorado (*see* Pikes Peak Gold Rush) brought about one of the most picturesque movements in all American history. The settlement of the Pacific coastal region and the increased production of gold stimulated industry, caused the building of the Pacific railways and created demands for a Panama Canal[qqv].

Texas, which had early developed as a great pastoral empire, poured a stream of cattle northward from 1866 to 1890 (*see* Cattle Drives) to stock ranges on the central and northern plains, and so was the chief factor in the formation of the "cow country"[qqv]. The production of petroleum and natural gas in California and in the great midcontinent field lying largely in Oklahoma and Texas has been of enormous significance in the economic life of the nation[qqv]. The fruit-growing industry[qv] of southern California, Arizona and the lower Rio Grande Valley of Texas has also been of great importance to the country as a whole. The production of wheat and cotton[qqv] in this area adds materially to the nation's crop of these two staples. The manufacture and distribution of motion pictures[qv] centering in southern California is an industry of world-wide importance. Its influence upon the people of America can hardly be estimated.

Culturally the Southwest has not been without some importance since it has produced many writers and a regional literature of considerable significance. Much of the development of this area has come since the beginning of the 20th century, and it seems that its influence upon the country as a whole may be even greater in the future than it has been in the past.

[R. N. Richardson and C. C. Rister, *The Greater Southwest;* C. C. Rister, *The Southern Plainsmen.*]

EDWARD EVERETT DALE

Southwest Boundary. *See* Louisiana Purchase, Boundaries of the; Adams-Onís Treaty; Mexican Boundary.

Southwest Fur Company. As part of his scheme to dominate the American fur trade, John Jacob Astor, chief proprietor of the American Fur Company and the Pacific Fur Company[qqv], organized the Southwest Fur Company, which in 1811 bought out the British-owned Michilimackinac (Mackinaw) Company at Michilimackinac[qv]. This move was designed to give him control of the fur trade of the Great Lakes and the upper Mississippi[qqv], for his associates agreed to sell their stock in the Southwest to him in five years.

Unfortunately his partners were British subjects and directors of the North West Company[qv] of Canada. In the War of 1812 the North West's traders occupied the trading forts of the Southwest Company. After the war Astor dissolved the Southwest Company, regained its scattered properties, merged them with the American Fur Company as its Northern Department and placed a loyal American, Ramsay Crooks, in command.

[Hiram Martin Chittenden, *The American Fur Trade of the Far West;* Washington Irving, *Astoria.*]

BLISS ISELY

Southwest Point (Kingston), where the Clinch and Holston rivers form the Tennessee, was on the Cumberland Road and was the western outpost of the State of Franklin[qqv]. In 1792 United States troops were stationed there to protect settlers on the road to Nashville[qv] and in the surrounding territory. The land, formally ceded by the Tellico treaty, Oct. 27, 1805, was tentatively designated as the state capital.

[James Phelan, *History of Tennessee.*]

THOMAS ROBSON HAY

Southwest Territory. This is the short title applied to the region officially set up and denominated in 1790, "The Territory of the United States, south of the River Ohio." It consisted in fact of only the future State of Tennessee, though in theory it embraced the twelve-mile strip which South Carolina had ceded, and possibly the Georgia western lands. The actual government was applied only to Tennessee. With the exception of certain conditions made by North Carolina in her cession of 1789, the government of this territory was similar to that set up for the Northwest Territory[qv]. William Blount was appointed governor and superintendent of Indian affairs and he served in this capacity the entire life of the territory. When Tennessee became a state in 1796, the government fell into abeyance, but it may be said to have taken life again in 1798 when the Mississippi Territory was erected.

[F. L. Paxson, *History of the American Frontier, 1763-1893;* C. E. Carter, ed., *The Territory South of the River Ohio, 1790-1796,* Vol. IV in The Territorial Papers of the United States; Thomas Donaldson, *The Public Domain.*]

E. MERTON COULTER

Sovereigns of Industry was a form of co-operative movement, active in the 1870's, which was concerned with the distribution of the necessities of life. It grew out of the Patrons of Husbandry[qv] and at one time numbered 40,000 members. It maintained a number of co-operative stores, some on the Rochedale system and at one time absorbed some trade unions. It began to decline after 1875.

[J. R. Commons and others, *History of Labor in the United States.*] CARL L. CANNON

Sovereignty, The Doctrine of, is a legal concept which attempts to explain the final location and source of the political authority in the modern state. It is the "hallmark" of legality.

Sovereignty may be defined as that supreme authority which is externally independent and internally paramount (T. E. Holland), and a sovereign nation as a political community without a political superior (Abraham Lincoln).

There are two aspects of sovereignty. One is *de facto,* subject to the test of its actual use as shown by the exercise of authority, and the other is *de jure,* or its legal justification. While the subject of much controversy among lawyers and political theorists, sovereignty on the one hand is usually considered to be indivisible. On the other hand the administration or use of sovereign powers may be delegated to various subordinate administrative authorities. In accordance with this theory, sovereignty lies in the people of the United States (*see* "We the People . . .") who have created a National Government and delegated to it certain sovereign powers. But "the powers not delegated to the United States by the Constitution, nor prohibited by it to the States, are reserved to the States respectively or to the people" (Amendment X). Therefore the forty-eight American states are not sovereign, but subject to the sovereignty of the people of the entire nation as such.

[T. E. Holland, *Jurisprudence;* C. E. Merriam, *American Political Theories.*] WILLIAM STARR MYERS

"Sow Case," THE (1643–44), famous in Massachusetts history because of its far-reaching consequences, began as a controversy between a poor woman named Sherman and a well-to-do shopkeeper, Keayne, over the ownership of a sow. Lower courts decided in favor of Keayne, but Mrs. Sherman, encouraged by popular sympathy, appealed to the General Court[qv]. In that body, the majority of assistants or magistrates supported Keayne; and the deputies the woman. Although up to this time the assistants and deputies had sat in one body, the former claimed a negative voice[qv] on the action of the latter. Their attempt to exercise that negative in the sow case against the sympathies of the deputies brought the conflict to a crisis, the outcome of which was the division of the General Court into two houses (*see* Bicameral Legislatures).

[C. M. Andrews, *The Colonial Period of American History,* Vol. I.] VIOLA F. BARNES

Spanish-American Relations. Until Spain lost the last remnant of her American empire in 1898 her relations with the United States were generally characterized by a mutual antagonism which was already strong in the 17th century. Spain resented the establishment of the English colonies in America as a challenge to her monopoly of territory, trade and navigation in the New World; and the colonists, as Englishmen and Protestants, believed in the "Black Legend" of the faithlessness, tyranny and bigotry of Spain.

The American Revolution changed the conditions of this rivalry, and aggravated the potential danger to Spain. She tried to meet it by making secret loans to the United States and joining France in the war against England, at the same time that she withheld direct military aid from the United States and opposed the recognition of its independence. This conduct, together with controversies over the international boundary and the navigation of the Mississippi[qv], sharpened the antagonism of the American people toward Spain. In the negotiations of John Jay[qv] in Spain (1780–82) and with the Spanish envoy Gardoqui at New York (1785–88) futile efforts were made to settle the dispute. It dragged on until Spain, faced by grave dangers in both Europe and America, yielded in the Treaty of San Lorenzo[qv] (Oct. 27, 1795), by which the United States made good its long-standing claims to the free navigation of the Mississippi River and the thirty-first parallel as its southern boundary[qv], and also obtained the right of deposit[qv] and a liberal definition of neutral maritime rights; and each power agreed to restrain the Indians within its borders from attacking the citizens or subjects of the other power. By promoting American commerce and settlement in the Mississippi Valley, this treaty led to the retrocession of Louisiana by Spain to France (*see* Ildefonso, Treaty of), which then sold it to the United States in 1803 (*see* Louisiana Purchase).

The latter transaction gave rise to a bitter controversy between the United States and Spain which lasted until 1821. Spain first protested that the sale was illegal. Under French pressure she withdrew the protest (1804); but in the War of 1812[qv] and at the Congress of Vienna she renewed her efforts to recover Louisiana. When these failed, she finally resigned herself to the loss. Of longer duration was the controversy over the boundaries of Louisiana[qv], which were vaguely described in the treaty of 1803. Instead of clarifying the question the French foreign minister Talleyrand merely advised the United States to make the most of its noble bargain—advice which was hardly needed by Jefferson and Madison. They claimed that Louisiana included Texas to the Rio Grande and West Florida to the Perdido River. Spain disputed both claims. The controversy led to tortuous dealings with Napoleon, was related to the Burr Conspiracy[qv] and brought the United States to the brink of war with Spain. Diplomatic relations were suspended during the French invasion of Spain (1808–14). In this period the United States seized a part of West Florida (Baton Rouge[qv]) and the desire of expansionists to annex the rest of the two Floridas was one of the causes of the War of 1812; but all they gained was Mobile[qv]. After the renewal of diplomatic relations Spain, hoping for support from Russia and England, followed a dilatory course until Andrew Jackson invaded Florida in pursuit of marauding Indians whom Spain had not restrained as the treaty of 1795 obligated her to do (*see* Arbuthnot and Ambrister, Case of), and Secretary of State Adams bluntly pointed the moral: Spain might as well sell all Florida, since she was sure to lose it anyway. On Feb. 22, 1819, the so-called Florida treaty was signed by Adams and the Spanish envoy Onís, the former regarding it as one of the greatest achievements of his life (*see* Adams-Onís Treaty). By its terms the United States obtained the Floridas and Spain's claim to the territory on the Pacific coast north of the 42nd parallel, but relinquished its own claim to Texas[qv]. It also agreed to pay Spain $5,000,000, but this sum was earmarked for the satisfaction of spoliation claims of American citizens against Spain. After a long delay, caused partly by Spain's effort to obtain the United States' pledge not to recognize the Spanish-American revolutionists, ratifications of the treaty were finally exchanged on Feb. 22, 1821. When the United States took the first step toward recognition of the new Spanish-American states (March, 1822) Spain was resentful but too weak to retaliate (*see* Latin-American Republics, Recognition of the); and when the Monroe Doctrine[qv] was proclaimed (December, 1823) His Catholic Majesty did not even bother to read it.

With Spain's elimination from the American continent the most important of the familiar sources of friction disappeared. Another of equal importance—the Cuban question—was raised a quarter of a century later under the impulse of filibustering, proslavery interests and the idea of Manifest Destiny[qqv]. It produced the extraordinary Ostend Manifesto[qv] (1853); but domestic opposition to the annexation of slaveholding Cuba[qv] prevented the United States from pushing the issue to the breaking point. During our Civil War, Spain reconquered Santo Domingo and attacked Peru, but retired in 1865, partly because of pressure from Washington. In the Cuban Ten Years' War for independence (1868–78) the sympathy of the United States for the insurrectionists was restrained by many considerations, one of which was that recognition of their belligerency would have weakened the case of the United States in its current *Alabama* claims[qv] controversy with England. It acted with prudent moderation in the sensational *Virginius* case[qv]. Rejecting the United States' tender of its good offices to end the war in Cuba, Spain brought it to a close with the promise of far-reaching reforms. These were not fully carried out.

The Cuban war for independence was renewed in 1895. Suffering caused by recent tariff changes by the United States was partly responsible for the revolt and it was aided by *juntas* of Cuban refugees in the United States. Cleveland and for a time McKinley sought to avoid interference in it; but the rising tide of public opinion and the procrastination of Spain made this impossible. Although the United States had long had a considerable economic stake in Cuba, there seems to be no ground for the widespread belief that businessmen were responsible for our intervention; many of them actively opposed it. In other respects, social and political conditions were favorable to the development of interventionism and the war spirit. These were promoted by stories of Spanish atrocities which were broadcast by the Hearst and Pulitzer newspapers and revived the "Black Legend" of Spanish cruelty; by the new navalism of A. T. Mahan; by a new and popular version of Manifest Destiny, which stressed the civilizing mission of the United States and its obligations as a world power; and by the sinking of the *Maine*[qv] at Havana, the responsibility for which is still uncertain but which was widely attributed to Spain. In the indignation caused by this tragic affair, Congress gave little weight to the fact, mentioned by McKinley's message of April 11, 1898, that Spain had just made most of the concessions previously urged by the United States. By a joint resolution of April 20 the independence of Cuba was made one point in an ultimatum to Spain, and when this was not accepted Congress declared war (April 25). The "short and glorious" war (*see* Spanish-American War), which lasted only three months, was marked by Commodore Dewey's victory over one Spanish fleet at Manila, by Admiral Schley's victory over another at Santiago de Cuba[qqv] and by the relatively minor but spectacular activities of Lt. Col. Theodore Roosevelt in Cuba (*see* Rough Riders). In the Teller Amendment[qv] to the resolution of April 20 Congress had disclaimed any intention of annexing Cuba. In the treaty of peace (signed at Paris[qv], Dec. 10, 1898) the United States obtained Puerto Rico, Guam and the Philippines[qqv] (paying Spain $20,000,000 for the latter), and established a protectorate over Cuba. The war also hastened the acquisition of Hawaii and part of Samoa[qqv] by the United States. It marked both the end of the Spanish empire in Asia and America and also the first important stage in the oversea expansion of the United States in the Pacific as well as the Caribbean (*see* Imperialism). Although before the outbreak of hostilities Spain had received some support from England as well as from Germany and other European powers, developments during the war and the peace negotiations inaugurated in the United States a new era of friendship toward England and suspicion toward Germany.

[S. F. Bemis, *Diplomatic History of the United States;* J. F. Rippy, *Latin America in World Politics;* A. K. Weinberg, *The Idea of Manifest Destiny.*]

A. P. WHITAKER

Spanish-American War, THE, was the outgrowth of the Cuban insurrection against Spanish rule, which began in February, 1895, and was waged with ruthlessness for three years by both Spanish and insurgents. American investments in Cuba (estimated at $50,000,000) suffered, and the destruction of the sugar and tobacco crops by the insurgents reduced the trade between Cuba and the United States to the vanishing point. Many commercial firms along the Atlantic and Gulf coasts of the United States desired intervention to stop the war, but business interests in general were opposed to interference by the United States. Humanitarian or sentimental sympathy with the Cuban people in their struggle for independence, and popular indignation at the cruelty of the Spanish methods of warfare, were inflamed by a one-sided picture of the Cuban war presented in the sensational press. A large section of the religious press, also, preached the sacred duty of intervention to put an end to Spanish misrule.

President Cleveland (1893–97) resisted all pressure for intervention, and so at first did his successor, President McKinley (1897–1901). In Spain the Liberal Sagasta ministry, assuming control in 1897, abandoned the more objectionable military methods in Cuba and offered a limited autonomy to the Cubans. A peaceful settlement seemed in prospect, but the destruction of the United States battleship *Maine*[qv] in Havana harbor (Feb. 15, 1898) led to a new outburst of anti-Spanish feeling in the United States. Though advised by the United States minister in Madrid that the Spanish government was making all the concessions which public opinion would permit, McKinley sent to Congress (April 11, 1898) a message asking authority to end the civil war in Cuba. Congress promptly (April 19) passed resolutions recognizing the independence of Cuba, demanding that Spain withdraw from the island, and authorizing the President to use the armed forces of the United States to effect those ends. A fourth resolution disclaimed all purpose of annexing Cuba (*see* Teller, or Fourth, Resolution). Spain at once severed diplomatic relations, and on April 25 Congress declared the existence of a state of war, retroactive to and including April 21.

A blockade of Cuban ports was instituted April 22, but the first dramatic event of the war occurred in the Far East. On the morning of May 1, Commodore George Dewey, commanding the U. S. Asiatic Squadron, entered Manila Bay[qv] in the Philippine Islands and completely destroyed the antiquated Spanish fleet which defended it. Dewey's squadron remained in Manila Bay and before the end of July was reenforced by an army of some 10,000 men under Gen. Wesley Merritt. The city of Manila was occupied Aug. 13.

Meanwhile, Spain's Atlantic fleet, under Admiral Cervera, had entered the harbor of Santiago[qv], Cuba, on May 19, and was there blockaded by an American fleet under Rear Admiral W. T. Sampson. The capture or destruction of this Spanish fleet now became the immediate military objective of the United States. An army of 18,000 regulars and volunteers, assembled at Tampa, Fla., was transported to the Cuban coast east of Santiago before the end of June. Commanded by Gen. W. R. Shafter, it stormed the heights overlooking Santiago in the battles of El Caney and San Juan Hill[qv], July 1. The Spanish position in Santiago now became untenable. Cervera was ordered by Capt. Gen. Blanco to lead his fleet out of the harbor. His sortie on July 3 resulted in the total destruction of his squadron by the blockading fleet.

The destruction of Cervera's fleet practically ended the war. The city of Santiago was surrendered July 16. On July 25 an army under Gen. Nelson A. Miles landed in Puerto Rico^qv^ and occupied that island almost unopposed. The Spanish government now initiated peace negotiations through the French ambassador in Washington, and on Aug. 12 hostilities were terminated by a protocol under which Spain relinquished Cuba^qv^, ceded to the United States Puerto Rico and one of the Ladrone Islands (later fixed as Guam^qv^), and agreed to the occupation of Manila by the United States until the disposition of the Philippine Islands^qv^ should be determined by the definitive treaty of peace. This was to be negotiated by commissioners meeting in Paris. The treaty, signed in Paris^qv^ Dec. 10, 1898, and approved by the Senate Feb. 6, 1899, supplemented the above terms by providing for the cession of the Philippines to the United States, the payment of $20,000,000 by the United States to Spain and the retention by Spain of liability for the Cuban debt.

The war had cost the United States about $250,000,000 in money and over 5000 lives. Of the dead, however, fewer than 400 had been killed in battle or died of wounds. The balance represented the toll of disease. At this cost the United States had acquired a colonial empire of 120,000 square miles and some 8,500,000 people and had risen suddenly to a position of prominence in world affairs, particularly in the Caribbean and the Far East (*see* Imperialism).

[S. F. Bemis, *Diplomatic History of the United States;* F. E. Chadwick, *The Relations of the United States and Spain: The Spanish-American War;* W. Millis, *The Martial Spirit;* J. W. Pratt, *Expansionists of 1898.*]

JULIUS W. PRATT

Spanish-American War, The Navy in. Unlike the American Revolution, War of 1812 and Civil War^qqv^, the conflict with Spain saw the brunt of the fighting borne by the navy and not by the army. Further, the war was unique in the widely separated zones of operations. At once, on the declaration of the existence of a state of war, a blockade of western Cuba was announced, with the purpose of isolating Havana. But all seemed insignificant in comparison with the battle, fought ten days after the beginning of hostilities, which virtually ended Spanish dominion in the Far East. Commodore George Dewey, commanding the American Squadron in Asiatic waters, had received a cable to capture or destroy the Spanish naval force in the Philippines. This, he accomplished May 1, 1898, in Manila Bay^qv^. He had delayed his arrival off the entrance to the bay until about midnight preceding, and then attempted to steal past the fortifications at Corregidor and El Fraile. Three shots fired by the Spanish showed that they were aware of his movements, but the channel proved not to be mined. Shortly after dawn, the American squadron attacked the Spanish squadron, commanded by Admiral Montojo, anchored off Cavite. Dewey confused the Spanish gunners by leading his ships over an elliptical course constantly altering the range. Not alone in gunfire, however, but in all particulars, the Spanish squadron proved inferior, and before noon their ships were in flames and the defenders were fleeing to Cavite.

Meanwhile on the Atlantic coast of the United States there was considerable nervous tension, caused by the Spanish fleet under Admiral Cervera which had assembled at the Cape Verde Islands and sailed for the west. Thus the American navy was called upon to protect the Atlantic coast, patrol the approaches to the West Indies, maintain the blockade of Cuba and hold a force prepared to engage the enemy on his being found. When authoritative information disclosed that Cervera had entered the deep and well-fortified harbor of Santiago^qv^, Rear Admiral W. T. Sampson commanding the Naval Force, North Atlantic Station, proceeded to blockade it. On the evening of June 3, Lt. R. P. Hobson with a small volunteer crew guided the collier *Merrimac*^qv^ into the narrow channel and sank her. He did not succeed in blocking the passage, but he made egress more difficult. Four days later, 600 American marines effected a landing at Guantanamo, and the army began slowly to close in on Santiago. Cervera's force, on Sunday morning, July 3, sought to escape by coming out and fleeing to the west. A running battle followed, in which one Spanish battleship, three cruisers and two torpedo boat destroyers were opposed to four American battleships, two cruisers and a converted yacht. The losses were all on one side. Within fifteen minutes after clearing the entrance the *Maria Teresa* (the Spanish flagship) had caught fire and was run ashore. Other ships of the Spanish squadron fared no better, and when the *Colon* was beached at one o'clock the last was destroyed. The battle of Santiago virtually ended the war.

[F. E. Chadwick, *The Relations of the United States and Spain: The Spanish-American War.*]

CARROLL S. ALDEN

Spanish and Spanish-American Influence in United States. The long French-Spanish-English contest for North America, and United States' 19th-century expansion into Spanish America were bound to leave an impression on American history, geography and life. Two thirds of the area of continental United States, exclusive of Alaska, once belonged to Spain. The small Spanish colonial population of this area, reinforced by subsequent immigration, grew by 1930 to be a substantial American population element of nearly two million persons, largely concentrated in Texas, California, Arizona, New Mexico and Colorado. The map of the United States is eloquent of these historical facts. Physical features carry Spanish names (sierras, cordilleras, mesas). The memory of Christian saints is perpetuated in melodic Spanish in the names of rivers and towns. State names in the Southwest and thousands of American place names are reminiscent of early Spanish occupation or of the Mexican and Spanish-American wars.

Spaniards laid the basis of American agriculture. A royal order of 1532 required all ships sailing for the Indies to carry plants, seeds and domesticated animals. Early Spanish explorers in Florida and the Southwest brought horses (*see* Horse, The Spanish), cattle[qv], swine, wheat, barley, pomegranates, figs, oranges and grapes. Wild swine of the Gulf Plain, Spanish in origin, became an important source of food for English settlers in the 17th century as far north as Jamestown[qv]. The first English settlers in South Carolina bought from the Indians pork derived probably from Spanish mission stock. Wild horses and cattle provided the basis for the 18th-century ranching industry in Georgia, and for the 19th-century development in Texas and the western plains. The best American asses, mules and Arabian horses are of Spanish origin. Alfalfa[qv], sugar cane and ginger owe their American origin to Spain, and the various American varieties of tobacco[qv] were first developed by Spaniards in the Caribbean area.

Spaniards were the pioneers in mining in the United States, and their methods, including the Mexican invention of the patio (amalgam) process, dominated until well into the 19th century. Spain's New World production of precious metals made the Spanish Dollar, or "piece of eight,"[qv] the most universal coin in the Americas during the colonial period. It became the monetary unit of the United States (1786), as of all the other nations of America. The expression "two bits" (*see* Bit) is reminiscent of this Spanish origin of the dollar.

Mexican ranching, adopted in the western plains, produced the popular American idol, the cowboy[qv]. When not actually a Mexican, he adopted the vocation, equipment and jargon of the Mexican "buckaroo" (*vaquero*). He rode a "bronc," a "mustang,"[qv] or "caballo," controlled by a hackamore (*jáquima*), wore a sombrero and "chaps" (*chaparejos*), carried a quirt and a lariat (*la reata*) to lasso cows and horses. The rodeo[qv] or annual roundup gradually became a popular American fiesta. Spanish words such as "savvy" (*sabe*), *mañana,* "hoosegow" (*juzgado*) and "calaboose" (*calaboza*) found their way into the cowboy's ordinary vocabulary, and into the songs he sang to his *chiquita.*

In addition to this regional and colloquial vocabulary, Spanish influence on American language (a good indication of cultural influence) is measured in thousands of words, many of them of Spanish-American origin. Words like alligator, alpaca, banana, barbecue, cockroach, corral, pampa, quinine, tapioca, hammock, vanilla, cannibal, mosquito, tomato, tobacco and pickaninny are so thoroughly anglicized that Americans are scarcely conscious of their foreign origin. Spanish words, idioms and folklore give special flavor to the works of Dana, Bret Harte, Clemens, Mary Austin, Harold Bell Wright, Gertrude Atherton and Willa Cather.

Spanish law influenced the legal systems of Texas, Arizona, New Mexico and California in the fields of property, mining, obligations, the range, irrigation and property rights of married women. Early elimination of the distinction between common law and equity, and the simplification of pleading in these states are due in part to Spanish influence. The Roman-French-Spanish civil code of Louisiana (1805) exercised an important formative influence on the law of the states formed from the Louisiana Purchase[qv].

Spanish missions, scattered from Georgia to California, are principally responsible for "Spanish" architecture in the United States, with houses designed around a central patio, roofs of "tapered mission" or other roofing tile, walls of yellow or pink stucco, interiors lacking in symmetry, and walls and tile floors of brilliant hues. Decorative tiles, elaborate stone and wood carvings of Moorish feeling, wrought-iron grills, furniture combining wood with wrought iron, and the "hip joint" chair are Spanish influences in interior decoration.

Spanish horses, cattle and swine made the Indians herders. Spanish products found their way into the agriculture of Indians of the Southeast and Southwest. A particularly radical change was effected in the economy of the plains Indians with the adoption of the horse. Spanish missions exerted a lasting influence on the Indians of the Southwest, adding many products to their agriculture, Christianizing them and teaching them Spanish so effectively that many still prefer it to English.

The American diet owes to Spanish-American influence the banana, pineapple, mango, orange, lemon, lime, avocado, tomato, tamale and various varieties of beans and nuts, not to mention the Texas *chili con carne*. Cuba set the American taste in cigars. The American taste in coffee is South American, if not Spanish American, coming principally from American predilection for the Brazilian coffee bean.

The Southwest, where every important city has its "Spanish Quarter," abounds in Mexican folk songs, fiestas, customs and tales of old Spanish mines and buried Spanish treasure. A by-product of the Mexican influence in this region was the racial antagonism which developed after the Mexican War, and more particularly after 1890–1900, when American settlers began to outnumber the natives. Elsewhere, too, Spanish-American cultural influence was felt, especially after the World War brought increased American economic interests in Latin America. Mexican painting achieved a great vogue after 1920. Latin-American popular music, dances and dance bands grew in favor. Intellectual contacts, however, and the exchange of ideas and publications developed very slowly. The work of American students extended American acquaintance with Spanish-American literature, but the latter exercised little influence on American letters.

[H. W. Bentley, *A Dictionary of Spanish Terms in English;* Harry Bernstein, Spanish Influence in the United States, *Hispanic American Historical Review*, XVIII; L. C. Gray, *History of Agriculture in the Southern United States;* Nina Otero, *Old Spain in Our Southwest;* R. W. Sexton, *Spanish Influence in American Architecture and Decoration;* L. P. Sherman, *Roman Law in the Modern World;* A. P. Whitaker, The Spanish Contribution to American Agriculture, *Agricultural History*, III.]

HAROLD E. DAVIS

Spanish Capture of British Posts on the Mississippi and Gulf (1779–81) comprised the final stage in Spain's participation in the American Revolution[qv]. Between 1776 and 1779 Spain had secretly supported the war against England, in order to weaken her imperial rival. Money and war materials were sent through intermediary merchants (*see* Spanish Military Supplies from New Orleans, 1776–79; Pollock's Aid to the Revolution), and American privateers with prizes were protected in Spanish ports. In June, 1779, Spain renewed the Bourbon family compact[qv] and joined France in hostilities against England. She did not, however, explicitly guarantee the independence of the United States, because of the fear, as expressed by Floridablanca, Spanish foreign minister, that a successful republican insurrection in North America might inspire her own colonies to revolt and might create a new power, the United States, to threaten the Spanish Empire.

Spain's military operations in America were conducted along the Anglo-Spanish frontier on the Mississippi and the Gulf. Under the leadership of Bernardo de Galvez, governor of the province of Louisiana, the posts at Fort Manchac, Baton Rouge and Natchez[qqv] were easily taken from the British late in 1779. Next Fort Charlotte[qv] (Mobile) was captured March 17, 1780, and Fort George (Pensacola[qv]) surrendered May 9, 1781, after a long naval siege combined with a land attack. Thus were East and West Florida[qqv] assured for Spain, although her claim to control also the navigation of the Mississippi was defeated in the Definitive Treaty of Peace of 1783[qv].

[J. F. Yela Utrilla, *España ante la independencia de los Estados Unidos;* J. W. Caughey, *Bernardo de Galvez in Louisiana, 1776-1783.*]

MARTIN P. CLAUSSEN

Spanish Conspiracy, The, was a series of more or less closely related intrigues, between Spain and certain western Americans, which began in 1786 and continued for a score of years thereafter. The main purpose of Spain was to defend Louisiana and Florida by promoting the secession of the West from the United States through bribery, the manipulation of commerce on the Mississippi River (over which Spain retained some control until 1803), and the exploitation of sectional antagonism between East and West. Before the United States obtained the free navigation of the Mississippi by the Pinckney Treaty of 1795[qv], some of the American conspirators were probably sincere in their profession of secessionist aims; but after 1795 their sole purpose and at all times their main purpose seems to have been to advance their own personal interests by obtaining from Spain money, commercial privileges, support for colonization schemes, and other advantages. The first intrigue, a short-lived one begun in 1786 by Diego de Gardoqui and James White, was related to the Muscle Shoals Speculation[qv]. (*See also* D'Arges Colony.) The central figure in these intrigues, however, was James Wilkinson and their focal point was in Kentucky. In 1786 great indignation was aroused in the West by the decision of Congress not to press the United States' claim to the free navigation of the Mississippi[qv]; and in 1787 Wilkinson, who had won a prominent place in Kentucky politics, went to New Orleans to try his hand at direct negotiation with the Spanish officials of Louisiana. The upshot was that he won some commercial privileges for the Western people and more for himself, took an oath of allegiance to the Spanish crown and became the principal agent of Spain in its secessionist intrigue, with a pension of $2000 a year (later raised to $4000), which was paid to him at intervals for many years after he became an officer in the United States Army (1791). Benjamin Sebastian, Harry Innes and a few other influential Kentuckians joined in the intrigue; but they often worked at cross-purposes with Wilkinson, Spain and each other. The existence of the conspiracy was widely suspected almost from the beginning, some partial revelations of it were made in the 1790's, and many of the details were exposed in 1806 by the *Western World* (a Kentucky newspaper) and in 1809 by Daniel Clark's *Proofs of the Corruption of . . . Wilkinson* (*see* Burr Conspiracy); but full legal proof was lacking. Wilkinson retained his commission in the army and continued to enjoy the apparent confidence of Presidents Jefferson and Madison as he had that of Presidents Washington and Adams. The exposure did, however, put an end to the conspiracy which had long since become a farce. The secessionist plan was never put into action. What few advantages the conspiracy yielded were reaped by the Americans, and Spain footed the bill.

[A. P. Whitaker, *Spanish American Frontier*, and *Mississippi Question;* I. J. Cox, James Wilkinson, in *Dictionary of American Biography.*]

A. P. WHITAKER

Spanish Dollar, THE, first coined in 1728 to replace the old "piece of eight,"[qv] circulated throughout the commercial world, and became recognized and accepted as a reliable medium of exchange. It served as the metallic basis of the monetary system of the British colonies prior to the American Revolution; and because of its wide acceptance and familiarity, Congress adopted it in 1786 as the basis of our coinage system, the first American silver dollars[qv] containing approximately the same silver content as their Spanish counterparts.

[Davis Rich Dewey, *Financial History of the United States;* John Parke Young, *Central American Currency and Finance;* John Bach McMaster, *History of the People of the United States.*]

WALTER PRICHARD

Spanish-Indian Relations (1783–1803). During 1782–83 Spain formulated a plan to handle Indian affairs east of the Mississippi through Lt. Gov. Gilbert Antoine de St. Maxent who should also monopolize the Indian trade. To provide the necessary merchandise, direct trade with France was permitted by a *cédula* of Jan. 22, 1782. Maxent failed to fulfil his contract and Gov. Estevan Miró had to buy presents from Panton, Leslie & Co.[qv] for the Creeks who attended the "congress" in Pensacola at which Miró negotiated the treaty of May 31–June 1, 1784. By this treaty the Creeks accepted Spanish protection and promised to exclude all but Spanish traders. Their chief, Alexander McGillivray, became Spanish commissary at a salary of fifty dollars per month. At another "congress" at Mobile in July the Choctaws and Chickasaws[qqv] came under Spanish protection.

Through McGillivray's influence Panton, Leslie & Co. obtained the Creek trade through Pensacola with the privilege of importing goods from England. Mather and Strother, who obtained the trade of the other Indian nations through Mobile, were unable to please the Indians and, to check the Americans who were undermining Spanish influence, Panton's company was given that trade in 1788. Thereafter, the company was one of the mainstays of Spanish-Indian policy.

Without consulting his protectors, McGillivray sent the Creeks against the Georgians in 1786. Miró, nevertheless, supplied guns and ammunition until stopped in 1787 by orders from Spain. Munitions were furnished again in 1789 to offset the influence of the adventurer Bowles[qv]. Insufficient support, however, was a major factor in causing McGillivray[qv] to agree to the Treaty of New York in 1790. Miró's successor, Carondelet[qv], with Panton's help and the offer of a larger pension, won McGillivray back to Spanish influence, but his supineness in dealing with Bowles' second expedition (1791–92) caused Carondelet to send another commissary to the Creeks in 1792. McGillivray died the next year.

Meanwhile Carondelet was working to create a confederation of all the Southern Indians and to establish Spanish domination west of the Alleghenies. His subordinate, Gayoso de Lemos, built a fort at Nogales (Walnut Hills) in 1792 and in October, 1793, negotiated the Treaty of Nogales[qv] establishing the confederation. The next year Fort Confederation[qv] was built on the Tombigbee and Fort San Fernando at Chickasaw Bluffs[qv] in 1795. Carondelet was then stopped by the Treaty of San Lorenzo[qv]. He tried to evade it but was able only to delay the final results. Early in 1798 all Spanish garrisons retired below the 31st parallel (*see* Southern Boundary, Survey of the).

Spain and the United States had scarcely composed their differences when Bowles, returning in 1799, threw the Lower Creeks into confusion. Through the co-operation of the agents of both nations he was captured in 1803.

[A. P. Whitaker, *The Spanish-American Frontier, 1783–1795,* and *The Mississippi Question, 1795–1803;* John Caughey, *McGillivray of the Creeks;* Charles Gayarré, *History of Louisiana.*]

DUVON CLOUGH CORBITT

Spanish Military Supplies from New Orleans (1776–79). When armed hostilities began between England and her North American colonies in 1775, commercial intercourse with the mother country was suspended, and British fleets blockaded Atlantic ports to prevent importation of munitions and other supplies from foreign countries. In this emergency the colonists turned to Spanish New Orleans as a source of needed supplies, since Spain was a traditional enemy of England and was eagerly watching developments, in the hope of recovering territory and prestige lost to the British in the French and Indian War (*see* Paris, Treaty of, 1763). Spain resented British West Florida[qv] trade with Louisiana, and wished to end this menace. Spain was also jealous of British expansion and increasing influence over the Indians west of the Alleghenies, which endangered Spanish control of Louisiana.

The Spanish government was exceedingly cautious to avoid war with England; and Unzaga, Spanish governor of Louisiana, reflected this caution in his dealings with American agents sent to New Orleans in 1776. However, through the influence of Oliver Pollock[qv], these agents were permitted to purchase guns, gunpowder, blankets and medicines, especially quinine, from Spanish sources in that port. These supplies were rowed up the Mississippi in boats carrying the Spanish flag, to prevent their seizure by British authorities at West Florida posts above New Orleans (*see* Gibson-Linn Episode).

Bernardo de Galvez, who succeeded Unzaga as governor of Louisiana in 1777, was bolder than his predecessor in assisting American agents in New Orleans, since he was unperturbed by the prospect of war with England in consequence of such unneutral acts. Through Galvez's assistance the traffic in supplies up the Mississippi from New Orleans went on apace, and from this source the Americans procured the sorely needed supplies which enabled George Rogers Clark to defeat the British in the Old Northwest in 1778 and 1779 (*see* Clark's Northwest Campaign).

The chief obstacle to this trade was the lack of colonial funds to purchase supplies available in New Orleans, the treasuries of the central and state governments being chronically empty. Pollock extended his credit to the limit to finance this trade and became bankrupt through tardiness of the revolutionary governments concerned in repaying the advances made by him in their behalf. When France joined the United States in the war in 1778 (*see* Franco-American Alliance), her fleets landed supplies at Atlantic ports, thus reducing the dependence upon the New Orleans trade; and after Spain entered the war against England in 1779, secrecy was no longer necessary in this up-the-river trade.

[James A. James, *Oliver Pollock;* James A. James, *The Life of George Rogers Clark;* Charles Gayarré, *History of Louisiana;* François Xavier Martin, *History of Louisiana;* Alcée Fortier, *History of Louisiana;* James A. James, Spanish Influence in the West during the American Revolution, in *Mississippi Valley Historical Review,* IV.]

WALTER PRICHARD

Spanish-Missouri Fur Company, THE, was organized May 5, 1794, as "Spanish Commercial Company for the Exploration of the Country West of the Misuri." The articles of agreement were signed by Laurent Durocher, Antoine Reihle, Joseph Robidou, Hyacinthe St. Cyr, Charles Sanguinette, Louis Chauvin, Louis Dubreuil, Joseph Motard, Benito Vasquez and Jacques Clamorgan. The Spanish government granted this company the exclusive trade of the Upper Missouri above the Ponca Indian villages. Jacques Clamorgan was the chief director. The company sent three expeditions up the river: the first in July, 1794, the second in April, 1795, and the third in July or August, 1795. The first two expeditions were commanded by Jean Baptiste Truteau and the third by James Mackay. The business of the company was not successful; the members of the company became suspicious of and dissatisfied with Clamorgan and gradually fell away. Clamorgan succeeded in interesting Andrew Todd in the company and it was with money advanced by him that the last expedition was outfitted. Clamorgan, Loisel and Company seem to have taken over the business of the Commercial Company. In addition to trading and the discovery of nations hitherto unknown, the company undertook to discover a route to the South Sea. To stimulate the successful accomplishment of this endeavor, the King of Spain offered to pay $3000 to the first Spaniard who should penetrate, by way of the Missouri River, to the Russian settlements which had been established on the shores of the Pacific Ocean. The great majority of the merchants of St. Louis, including the Chouteaus and Charles Gratiot, held aloof from this company.

[Louis Houck, *Spanish Regime in Missouri;* Trudeau's Journal, in *South Dakota Historical Collections,* Vol. VII; *Missouri Historical Society Collections,* Vol. IV.]

STELLA M. DRUMM

Spanish Posts on the Mississippi, Surrender of (1797–98). *See* Guion's Expedition; Southern Boundary, Survey of the.

Spanish Succession, War of the. *See* Queen Anne's War.

Spanish Trail, The, an important overland route between Santa Fé, N. Mex., and Los Angeles, Calif., dates from 1775–76, during the Spanish occupation. Two Franciscan monks first traversed most of it, Father Garcés traveling its westerly section in 1775–76, and Father Escalante its eastern portion in 1776[qqv]. Jedediah Smith[qv] came up the western half of the trail but the first American to cover its full length was William Wolfskill, a Kentuckian, who led a company of trappers over it in 1830–31. From that period annual caravans passed over it in trade, the trail being sufficiently far north to avoid most Apache incursions while finding water across the desert. It later was an important immigrant route, and the Mountain Meadows Massacre[qv] took place on it in 1857.

The Spanish Trail led from Santa Fé up the Chama River through Durango, and followed the Dolores. It crossed the Grand and Green rivers, passed through the mountains up the Sevier Valley, followed the line of the Santa Clara and Virgin rivers southwest, and cut across the desert to the Mojave River, thence over the mountains to Los Angeles.

[George Douglas Brewerton, *Overland with Kit Carson*, edited by Stallo Vinton.] PAUL I. WELLMAN

"Speak-easy," also known as a "blind pig" or "blind tiger," is an illicit or unlicensed establishment dispensing intoxicating liquor. The "speak-easy" had been part of the American scene for at least thirty years before the passage of the Volstead Act[qv] (1920), but reached its heyday during national prohibition[qv]. At the height of their popularity in 1924–33, "speak-easies" were generally either bars or restaurants, to which admission was gained by personal introduction or by presenting a card, although often without any formality. In social class they ranged from smart restaurants to underworld dens, but were uniformly influential in establishing a single drinking-standard for both men and women. Before prohibition appearance in a public bar had been unknown for women of repute.

[S. Walker, *The Night Club Era;* C. F. Ware, *Greenwich Village, 1920-1930.*] STANLEY R. PILLSBURY

Speaker of the House of Representatives. The Constitution provides that "the House of Representatives shall choose their Speaker and other officers." Early American precedents furnish evidence that the colonial speaker was not a mere moderator but an active political force; the office under the Constitution has developed in that tradition. Custom has long decreed that the Speaker be a member of the House. Formal rules, tradition, custom and politics have combined to direct the development of the speakership. The Speaker is formally elected by the House at the opening of each Congress; actually he is selected at a party caucus[qv] or conference held prior to the session. Length of congressional service, experience, parliamentary ability, the existing political situation and geographical support are usually the determining factors in the decision of the caucus.

The office has a dual character; its occupant is both a presiding officer and a political figure. In the former capacity, he is the "organ of the House" and its executive head. He enforces the rules of the House, preserves order, answers inquiries and decides questions of parliamentary law. He also performs certain duties as the impartial representative of the House in its collective capacity and in its relations to other agencies. The political influence and power of the Speaker from 1811 to 1911 were the result of slow but steady growth.

By 1861 the political character of the office was clearly recognized, although its significance was occasionally lessened under the guidance of mediocre Speakers. From the Civil War to 1910, the office increased in importance and in power, especially under the speakership of Blaine, of Randall, of Carlisle, of Reed and of Cannon, respectively. Many of the partisan struggles in the House were prolonged and bitter. To get the awkward parliamentary machine to function it was necessary to dictate the procedure and to control the time of the body. Thus, party government became more essential, more powerful, and the party machine, led by the Speaker, more arbitrary. The rules and precedents developed in accordance with the necessities of party discipline and for the purpose of rendering a minority powerless to defeat the will of a majority of the House. As agents of party strategy to insure order and efficiency in law making, the various Speakers of the period 1889–1909 were highly efficient, if not somewhat despotic.

The chief sources of the Speaker's political power were three. He appointed, 1790–1910, the standing committees of the House, with due regard to geographical distribution, to seniority and to party regularity. He also named select committees and conference committees, and does today. He was a member and dominant factor of the powerful Committee on Rules, 1859–1910, and could thereby utilize the power of his office to execute the majority program. The Speaker, and the chairmen, respectively, of the Ways and Means Committee and of the Appropriations Committee frequently formed the majority of the committee and constituted a very effective steering committee. The important power of recognition, enjoyed by the Speaker since 1789, was a powerful factor in his domination of the House. These also developed a system of rewards and punishments under which new members, by party discipline, could be brought to prominence or kept in obscurity. Under the circumstances it was inevitable that sentiment against the Speaker should develop. The personal characteristics of Speaker Cannon (1903–11) and the wide belief that he represented reaction and entrenched privilege were instrumental in arousing strong public sentiment against the Speaker and his centralized power.

The rise of the Insurgent Republicans brought to the House, chiefly from the West, a formidable minority opposed to the rule of Cannon. A combination of Democrats and Insurgents, united in a bipartisan parliamentary but not a political alliance, in the so-called Revolution of March, 1910, revolted against the Speaker and so amended the rules as to remove him from his membership on the Committee on Rules, increasing that body to ten and vesting in the House of Representatives the power to appoint it. In 1911 the Democratic majority further amended the House rules as to provide for the formal election of all committees by the House itself, with the Speaker ineligible for membership on the Committee on Rules. As a consequence, the Speaker lost two of his great powers. The recognition power has been retained, although in modified form. The Speaker actually presides over the House only about one fourth of the time, while other rules and precedents of the House have given priority of recognition in certain parliamentary situations, such as unanimous consent and special orders of business.

Thus, the speakership since 1911 has been syndicated. Power is still exercised, but responsibility is now diffused and divided, with the Speaker merely one of several leaders.

[M. P. Follett, *The Speaker of the House of Representatives;* C. W. Chiu, *The Speaker of the House of Representatives since 1896;* D. S. Alexander, *History and Procedure of the House of Representatives;* C. R. Atkinson, *The Committee on Rules and the Overthrow of Speaker Cannon;* P. D. Hasbrouck, *Party Government in the House of Representatives;* G. R. Brown, *The Leadership of Congress.*]

THOMAS S. BARCLAY

Specie Circular, THE (1836). In pursuance of the Jackson administration policy of making specie the chief form of money in circulation, several circulars were issued by the Treasury Department. The first of these, issued on Nov. 5, 1834, ordered collectors of customs and receivers of public money not to receive, after Jan. 1, 1835, any form of money not described in a congressional resolution of April 30, 1816. The order was designed specifically to exclude the drafts of the branches of the Bank of the United States[qv]. On April 6, 1835, a second circular was issued directing collectors and receivers, after March, 1836, to receive only gold and silver for all dues under ten dollars.

These actions were preliminary to the issuance of the specie circular on July 11, 1836. This was addressed to the receivers of public money and to the deposit ("pet") banks[qv] and directed that, after Aug. 15, 1836, nothing but gold or silver should be accepted in payment for public land[qv]. Until Dec. 15, 1836, however, "actual settlers or *bona fide* residents in the State" where the sales were made could, as before, use paper money in paying for government land. By curbing land speculation the specie circular probably hastened the Panic of 1837[qv].

[Davis Rich Dewey, *Financial History of the United States.*]

ERIK McKINLEY ERIKSSON

Specie Payments, Suspension and Resumption of. Until 1934 the general rule was that fiduciary money should be redeemed on request in standard money (called specie when monetary standard is metallic) by the issuing authority. Thus, when the country was on a gold-coin standard[qv], all its moneys were ultimately redeemable in gold coin. There were several exceptions to the rule, of which the following are noteworthy. (1) The Government as well as the national banks assumed responsibility for the national bank notes[qv]. (2) Banks might redeem in legal tender[qv], which included some paper money after 1862. (3) Even before this, state banks[qv] often refused to redeem their notes in specie knowing that the only penalty would be having the notes pass at a discount. (4) Silver certificates[qv], first issued in 1878 and legally redeemable only in silver dollars, in practice have been redeemed in gold to keep them at a parity.

Specie payments have been wholly or sectionally suspended in the United States during eight emergency periods, 1814–17, 1819–22, 1837–38, 1839–42, 1857–58, 1861–78, 1917–19, 1933–34. All banks except those of New England suspended specie payments after the capture of Washington[qv], Aug. 24, 1814. The banks' recent unregulated credit expansion as well as the war was responsible. Resumption took place Feb. 20, 1817. During the depression years, 1819–22, most banks in the South and West refused to pay specie (*see* Panic of 1819).

The decade following 1825, notable for westward expansion and internal improvements, culminated in a period of land speculation[qqv]. The Treasury's "specie circular"[qv] of July 11, 1836, permitting agents to accept only specie for public lands[qv], embarrassed many banks. On May 10, 1837, New York City banks led in a widespread suspension of specie payments (*see* Panic of 1837). Resumption on Aug. 13, 1838 was premature: Pennsylvania banks suspended again Oct. 9, 1839, followed by those of other states. Resumption occurred gradually, by regions, throughout 1842.

The decade of the 1850's witnessed railroad expansion and industrial development on a large scale. Overspeculation, European depression, and finally the bankruptcy of the Ohio Life Insurance and Trust Company in August of 1857 caused all but one New York City bank (the Chemical) to suspend payments on Oct. 13 (*see* Panic of 1857). Nearly all banks elsewhere followed. Resumption took place slowly between November and February.

The suspension of specie payments during the Civil War began in New York City, Dec. 30, 1861. It was caused by the unfavorable course of the war, the *Trent* affair[qv], and Secretary Chase's increasing use of demand treasury notes and his failure to recommend an adequate tax program to Congress (*see* Civil War, Financing Problems of, Federal). It was not owing to issues of United States notes, "greenbacks"[qv], which began Feb. 25, 1862, but the suspension was prolonged because of them. By 1865 there were about $735,000,000 in various kinds of money in circulation, $431,000,000 being greenbacks. The gold value of $100 in currency averaged $49.50 that year. Several methods of resumption were suggested. Under the Funding Act of April 12, 1866, greenbacks in circulation were gradually reduced to $356,000,000 on Feb. 4, 1868, when further retirement was stopped. The amount was temporarily raised to $382,000,000 by 1872. In 1874 Grant vetoed the Inflation Bill, intended to raise the greenback circulation permanently to $400,000,000. On Jan. 14, 1875, a Republican lame-duck Congress passed Sen. George Edmunds' Resumption Act[qv], providing that greenbacks be reduced to $300,000,000 and resumption begin Jan. 1, 1879. Delay in accumulating a gold reserve, the free silver[qv] threat and Congress' halting the greenback reduction at $346,681,000 on May 31, 1878, made resumption on time seem unlikely for a while. Thanks to Secretary Sherman's efforts the premium on gold disappeared Dec. 17, 1878, and resumption took place as scheduled (*see* Silver Legislation). In summary, resumption was accomplished partly by retiring greenbacks. Of at least equal importance, however, was the fact that during this period the country's business needs grew up to the larger currency supply.

Attention in passing is called to the panics of 1893 and 1907[qqv] when specie payments were entirely suspended at clearinghouses and partially so in banks in New York City for several weeks. The years, 1893–95, are memorable because the Treasury barely managed to obtain enough gold to redeem the treasury notes presented.

Our entry into the World War caused President Wilson to issue orders on Sept. 7 and Oct. 12, 1917, placing an embargo on gold exports. Although this did not result in a formal suspension of specie payments by the Federal Reserve Banks[qv], the unnecessary use of gold coin was officially discouraged. It is usually regarded as a *de facto* suspension of the gold standard. All restrictions were removed June 9, 1919.

The last suspension resulted from the depression following the Panic of 1929[qv]. In 1930–32 there were 5102 bank failures[qv], a new record; England abandoned the gold standard in September, 1931, and gold flowed out of the United States on net balance every month of 1932 from January to July. These large gold exports and the publicity of the Reconstruction Finance Corporation's[qv] loans to banks frightened the public. The first "banking holiday" was declared in Nevada, Oct. 31, 1932. Public confidence declined further that winter. On Feb. 14 Gov. W. A. Comstock of Michigan declared a bank holiday (*see* Banking Crisis of 1933). Other states followed, New York on Saturday, March 4. On March 6 President F. D. Roosevelt announced a four-day nation-wide banking moratorium. Congress met on the 9th and hastily passed the Emergency Banking Act (*see* "Emergency" Legislation). The President imposed a temporary embargo on gold exports and ordered every one to turn gold in to the Government for other money (*see* Gold, Federal Expropriation of). By March 29, 12,800 out of about 18,000 banks had been licensed to open on an unrestricted basis, but specie payments were not resumed. On April 20 a second presidential embargo on gold exports signalized the indefinite abandonment of the gold-coin standard (*see* Public Faith).

The Gold Reserve Act[qv] and presidential order of Jan. 30–31, 1934, established a new dollar of 13.71 grains of fine gold, and made it possible, with the approval of the Treasury, to obtain gold bullion for making international payments. It remains impossible at this writing

(1939) to get any money redeemed in gold for domestic use.

[D. C. Barrett, *The Greenbacks and Resumption of Specie Payments;* F. A. Bradford, *Money and Banking;* D. R. Dewey, *Financial History of the United States;* J. B. McMaster, *History of the People of the United States;* A. D. Noyes, *Forty Years of American Finance, 1865-1907,* and *The War Period of American Finance, 1908-25;* R. C. Catterall, *The Second Bank of the United States.*]

DONALD L. KEMMERER

Specific Duties. *See* Duties, Ad Valorem and Specific.

Spelling Match (or Bee), The. An exaggerated importance has been attached to correctness in spelling, for it is erroneously assumed that spelling is an index to general intellectual capacity. Partly the cause and partly the result of this prejudice, the spelling match arose as a teaching device. As often as twice a day and never less than once a week, students spelled out loud for the head position in the class. Rivalry led to the division of classes into two parties. The game took the form of a competitive examination in which candidates attempted to spell such words as were submitted by an examiner. Prizes were awarded to the successful contestants. Various rules marked the game; generally a single failure eliminated a contestant from a match. Since amusement went hand in hand with improvement, the sternest moralist could not object to this game. By the 1840's Middle Western communities held spelling matches as part of an evening entertainment, and the widespread popularity of the game began in the West. The term "spelling bee" was first used in Edward Eggleston's *The Hoosier Schoolmaster* (1871), although Caroline M. Kirkland in *Western Clearings* (1845) described the contest as the "spelling school." In 1875 London imported the game. The spelling match never lost its popularity in rural areas; it became the fashion in the cities in the 1930's, when local and national contests were sponsored by radio stations and educational organizations.

[Mark Sullivan, *Our Times,* Vol. II; E. M. Stone, *Life and Recollections of John Howland;* Warren Burton, *The District School as It Was.*]

HARRY R. WARFEL

Spencer Rifle, The, a self-loading, repeating weapon, was patented by Christopher M. Spencer in 1860, and shortly thereafter adopted by the United States Army. It was the first effective and widely used magazine repeater; 106,667 pieces in rifle and carbine form were bought by the Government from Jan. 1, 1861 to June 30, 1866, for $2,861,024.38. Many officers of the Civil War declared it to have been the best arm of its time. The magazine capacity was 9 rounds, rimfire cartridges of .56 caliber. Sixteen shots per minute could be fired. Eight Spencer patents were obtained during the years 1860–73. The weapon had a weakness in its tendency to explode shells carried in the magazine.

[H. B. C. Pollard, *A History of Firearms;* John Metschl, *The Rudolph J. Nunnemacher Collection of Projectile Arms;* Charles W. Sawyer, *Our Rifles.*]

CARL P. RUSSELL

Spermaceti Trust. The manufacture of sperm candles in America began in Rhode Island about 1750. In 1761 Richard Cranch & Company proposed the forming of a "union" or trust for the entire country, and enlisted all manufacturers save one in Newport and some in Philadelphia. The nine members of the "United Company of Spermaceti Candlers," mostly in New England, agreed on a maximum buying price for whale "head-matter," commissions for factors and selling prices for candles, and the members pledged themselves to do all in their power by fair and honorable means to prevent any increase in competition. They also began to build up a whaling[qv] fleet of their own. The sperm-candle-making process had been kept a trade secret, but by 1772 the Nantucket Islanders had learned it and begun to start factories. The steady spread of the knowledge and the founding of other factories gradually broke the power of the trust.

[Alexander Starbuck, *History of American Whale Fishing.*]

ALVIN F. HARLOW

Spies, or secret agents employed by a government to secure military information from an enemy, have played a dramatic role in American history. Little documentary evidence exists concerning their work, as the nature of their activities made the keeping of written records an additional and unnecessary hazard. The young American spy, Nathan Hale[qv], who was hanged by the British in New York, Sept. 22, 1776, was, doubtless, the most noted spy of the Revolution[qv]. Another spy, the Quakeress Lydia Darrah, is credited with once saving Washington's army, and another spy, Charles Morgan, penetrated Lord Cornwallis' lines at Yorktown[qv] in 1781 and secured valuable military secrets for Lafayette. On the British side the most notable spy was Maj. John Andre[qv], captured in civilian clothes with despatches from Gen. Benedict Arnold and hanged Oct. 2, 1780. Spying for the British government on the Continent were the Americans, Dr. Edward Bancroft, Benjamin Franklin's supposed friend; Paul Wentworth, who directed an intricate espionage system on the Continent; the Rev. John Vardill, once assistant minister of Trinity Church, New York; and Capt. Joseph Hynson, a Maryland seaman, who stole despatches destined for the Continental Congress^{qv}.

During the Civil War large numbers of men and women, North and South, performed heroic service as spies, a few of whose names stand out: Allan Pinkerton, who organized the United States Secret Service^{qv}; his agent, Timothy Webster, captured and hanged in Richmond; Emma Edmonds, army nurse, who penetrated the Confederate lines eleven times; Lafayette C. Baker, who entered Richmond as an itinerant photographer; Harry Young, Gen. Philip H. Sheridan's chief spy; and Elizabeth L. Van Lew, Gen. U. S. Grant's most valued spy in Richmond. On the Confederate side, Belle Boyd, Walter Bowie, Mrs. Rose O'Neal Greenhow and many others supplied Lee's army with invaluable military information.

Maj. Gen. D. E. Nolan, Chief of Intelligence of the American Expeditionary Force, or of the G-2, directed a vast espionage service during the World War that secured information on German troop movements and concentrations, forthcoming attacks and the state of enemy morale among the troops and at home. The identity of the spies engaged in this work has never been revealed. (*See also* Military Intelligence.)

[Lewis Einstein, *Divided Loyalties, Americans in England during the War of Independence;* W. G. Beymer, *On Hazardous Service, Scouts and Spies of the North and South;* T. M. Johnson, *Our Secret War, True American Spy Stories;* L. C. Baker, *History of the United States Secret Service.*]

LOUIS H. BOLANDER

Spinning Inventions. *See* Loom, The.

Spirit Lake Massacre. During 1856 five cabins were erected by white settlers on the Okoboji lakes and one on Spirit Lake. The following winter was bitter cold, Indians and settlers alike suffering from hunger and exposure. On March 7, 1857, a small band of Sioux Indians^{qv} under Inkpaduta held a war dance on the lakes. The following day the massacre began at Rowland Gardner's cabin: Gardner was shot in the back, Mrs. Gardner, Mrs. Luce and three children were beaten to death and fourteen-year-old Abbie Gardner taken captive. Between March 8–13, the same scenes were enacted at the other cabins. Thirty-two men, women and children were brutally slain, and four women carried off captive. After an unsuccessful attack on Springfield, Minn., Inkpaduta fled westward. Two captive women were killed, one released through the mediation of friendly Indians, and Abbie Gardner (who wrote a harrowing account of her experience) was also finally ransomed. A relief expedition set out from Fort Dodge under Maj. William Williams on March 24, suffered frightful privations, but succeeded only in burying the dead. A detachment from Fort Ridgely^{qv} in Minnesota also failed to overtake Inkpaduta, who died a natural death years later. On July 25, 1895, the State of Iowa dedicated a monument in memory of the Spirit Lake Massacre.

[T. Teakle, *The Spirit Lake Massacre.*]

WILLIAM J. PETERSEN

Spirit of St. Louis, Flight of the. *See* Lindbergh Flies across the Atlantic.

"Spirit of '76." This famous painting was made by Archibald M. Willard, a carriage painter of Wellington, Ohio. The original sketch, made in 1874 or 1875, was intended only as a humorous presentation of a Fourth of July celebration and was entitled "Yankee Doodle." The patriotic spirit which swept the country prior to the Centennial celebration^{qv} at Philadelphia was responsible for the change from comic to the deadly serious picture which we now know. For his characters in the revised picture, Willard chose his own father, a Baptist minister, as the central figure; for the fifer he took his friend Hugh Mosher, a former soldier; and for the drummer-boy he took the thirteen-year-old son of Col. John H. Devereux. The painting, which was of heroic size, was prominently exhibited at the Centennial Exposition where it attracted such wide attention that after the close of the Exposition it was exhibited at Boston, at Washington, D. C., at Chicago, at San Francisco and a number of other cities. In 1880 it was purchased by Col. Devereux and by him presented to his native town of Marblehead, Mass., where it now hangs in the town hall (known as "Abbot Hall") and is viewed annually by thousands of tourists.

The painting is a simple and not too theatrical appeal to the spirit of that patriotism which rises to confront a warlike emergency. The little drummer-boy, looking with confidence to the old man who, beating his drum and with the fire of youth in his eyes, steps sturdily forward, together with the man of middle age, wounded but giving the cadence with his fife, all three advancing while the battle-clouds loom—these seem to mean that in any crisis, whether martial or civil, the citizens of all ages should rise in defense of liberty. Even the many political caricatures of the painting cannot disguise nor cheapen its significance, while on the other hand, the picture has often been used as a moving appeal to public spirit. It has long satisfied the idealism of the American people.

[*Publications*, Ohio Archæological and Historical Society, Vol. 39, pp. 471-78.] ALLEN FRENCH

Spiritualism, the belief that the spirits of the dead may and do manifest themselves to the living, originated in the United States in 1846 at the home of John D. Fox in Hydesville, N. Y. Fox's three daughters claimed to have heard persistent rappings which proved to be a code of communication with the spirit world (*see* Rochester Rappings). The sisters became the first mediums. An alleged confession charged to one of them that the knockings were fraudulent was later repudiated. Great excitement was created, and a cult appeared and grew rapidly. It at first became complicated with mesmerism, or as renamed, hypnotism, and developed various manifestations—trances, occultism, prophecy, table tipping, crystal gazing, etc. Scores of Spiritualist papers and periodicals were launched. Learned men studied its phenomena, some declaring them fraudulent, some being baffled, some becoming converts. The National Spiritualists' Association was organized in 1893, but in the 20th century, the believers had become divided into four cults. The *Scientific American* and the American Society for Psychical Research have persistently challenged Spiritualism and exposed much deception. Eusapia Palladino, a famous medium who had puzzled Europe, visited America in 1909–10, but was alleged to have been detected in trickery by Prof. Hugo Münsterberg. The noted magician, Harry Houdini, exposed many alleged psychic phenomena and duplicated several by physical means.

[A. Conan Doyle, *The History of Spiritualism;* J. A. Hill, *Spiritualism: Its History, Phenomena and Doctrine.*] ALVIN F. HARLOW

Spoils System. "To the victor belong the spoils," is the slogan of the spoilsmen, coined in 1832 by Sen. William L. Marcy of New York. The spoils system makes loyalty and service to a party the chief qualification for appointment to a public office. Under the system officeholders are ruthlessly removed to make room for those who have been faithful to the victorious party. These removals are justified on the ground that rotation in office*qv* is a proper principle to apply under a democratic system. The theory is that one person is as well qualified as another to perform the duties of an office. In its worst form the spoils system is characterized by the assessment of officeholders to raise money for the party's expenses (*see* Political Assessments). The system makes possible the building up of a party machine*qv* ready to do the bidding of the leaders. It makes impossible a career in public service and so discourages the best qualified citizens from seeking governmental offices.

When the Government of the United States began functioning under the Constitution, it could hardly be said that the spoils system was a new phenomenon. Ancient as well as modern history abounds with examples of it. But it is under a two-party system*qv* such as has prevailed in this country that the spoilsmen operate most effectively.

President Washington, at the beginning of his first administration, made loyalty to the Constitution the chief qualification for appointment to office. Later, after the rise of the party system, he made appointments on the basis of faithfulness to the Federalist party*qv*. Certainly, his successor, President John Adams, made appointments on a purely partisan basis as was illustrated by his 1801 "midnight appointments"*qv*. President Jefferson went even farther. While professing to make fitness for office the test for appointments, he was careful to select men of his own party. Nor did he hesitate to remove Federalists to make room for loyal Democratic-Republicans (*see* Republican Party, Jeffersonian).

Since the three Presidents who followed Jefferson were of the same party they had little occasion to disturb the officeholders, so few removals were made. Meanwhile the spoils system was firmly established in some of the states, notably in New York and Pennsylvania. When President Jackson assumed office in 1829 the situation was favorable for a wholesale introduction of the system into national politics. Jackson's followers confidently expected him to sweep the offices clean and to appoint to the vacancies men who had helped him achieve his triumph at the polls. In his inaugural address he encouraged this expectation by alluding to "reform" as inscribed "on the list of Executive duties, in characters too legible to be overlooked."

Historians have been prone to accept, without examining the record, the charge that Jackson introduced the spoils system into national politics. He did make partisan removals; he placed his own followers in offices, including some unfit for their positions; and he took advantage of the Four Year Act of 1820 to replace incumbents when their four-year terms expired. Jackson believed in the theory of rotation in office and he used officeholders in developing an effective party machine. The charge that officeholders were assessed for party purpose during his administration has, however, never been proved but merely asserted. In the final analysis, Jackson was not a wholehearted spoilsman. During the period when he was alleged to have made a clean sweep of the officeholders, he and his subordinates actually replaced 919 or one eleventh of the whole number. Not over one fifth of those whom he found in office were replaced during his eight years in the Presidency. The worst that should be said of President Jackson is that his administration merely marked another step toward the establishment of the spoils system. He hardly deserved any more blame than President Jefferson for its introduction. Each removed about the same proportion of officeholders and each filled vacancies on a partisan basis.

When the Whigs[qv] came into power in 1841 they proceeded to make the clean sweep that Jackson has been falsely accused of making. Thereafter, with each change of administration, officeholders were removed wholesale and were replaced by faithful supporters of the successful candidate.

The spoils system continued to operate without hindrance until after the Civil War. Though feeble attempts were made to secure reform, no substantial success was achieved until 1883 when Congress passed the Federal Civil Service Act[qv]. Under this act successive Presidents have extended the civil service classified list until approximately three fourths of the regular civil service employees of the Federal Government fill offices, eligibility for which is determined by examinations. But outside the classified list are thousands of officeholders whose positions are still considered as political spoils. The need of genuine reform still exists in the national as well as in the state and local governmental fields.

[Erik McKinley Eriksson, The Federal Civil Service under President Jackson, in *Mississippi Valley Historical Review*, XIII; C. R. Fish, *The Civil Service and the Patronage*.]

ERIK McKINLEY ERIKSSON

Spokane Expedition. *See* Yakima Indian Wars (1855–58).

Spokane House was built by the North West Company[qv], a British fur-trading company, in 1810–11, at Spokane Falls about ten miles north of the present city of Spokane, Wash. It was the center of the Columbia, Kootenay and Flathead trade, was later taken over by the Hudson's Bay Company[qv] and was abandoned in 1826 for Fort Colville.

[E. Voorhis, *Historic Forts and Trading Posts.*]

CARL L. CANNON

Spoliation Claims. *See* French Spoliation Claims.

Sponge Fisheries. Florida sponge beds, containing about 9300 square miles, extend from Key West to St. Marks Light near Apalachicola; they are 10 to 130 feet deep and reach 1 to 50 miles from shore. Sponge fishing appeared in Key West, and rose to a small industry by 1861. During the 1870's it spread to St. Marks, Apalachicola and Anclote Key (Tarpon Springs). Here John K. Cheyney and associates developed the industry in the 1890's. The Spanish-American War made Tarpon Springs the center of the fisheries.

Originally all sponges were "hooked" at depths not exceeding thirty feet. In 1905 divers from Greece and the Aegean Islands were introduced to harvest richer varieties. Sponge-diving boats are small cruisers making voyages of a few weeks to several months—until a cargo is collected. The number of divers carried depends on the depth to be searched. Tarpon Springs alone employs around 600 men and about 73 boats.

Sponges are sold at the "Sponge Exchange," a co-operative supported by small fees on gross sales. It has about twenty-five members, selling on commission besides their own crop. At Tarpon Springs Exchange auctions total over $1,000,000 annually and private transactions about $50,000.

[*Florida Second Biennial Report, 1836;* I. P. Stockbridge and J. H. Perry, *So This Is Florida.*]

KATHRYN T. ABBEY

Sports, Organized, came into existence in the United States only shortly before the Civil War. In the colonial period and in the opening decades of the 19th century, informal rural sports associated with farm festivals, militia musters and election days were virtually all that the country knew in the way of athletic activities. Horse races[qv], rowing and yachting[qv] regattas, so-called "pedestrian races," and occasional prize fights[qv] (strictly forbidden by law) were in the 1830's and 1840's presaging the growth of what are now termed spectator sports, but otherwise the field of organized athletics was completely undeveloped. Many commentators on the national scene singled out this lack of interest in sports as responsible for a marked deterioration in American health.

The growth of cities and creation of a new class of factory operatives as a result of the gradual industrialization of the country made the need for some substitute for the rural pastimes of the agricultural era increasingly imperative. An unconscious demand arose for organized sports as an antidote to the confining life of the new city dwellers, and as they were successively introduced, they were taken up eagerly by vast numbers of people. In every instance the new sports were first adopted as a diversion of the more leisured and wealthy members of society, but the prevailing spirit of democracy combined with increasing leisure for the working class to give them a continually broadening popular appeal.

Baseball[qv] was the first of these organized sports, being played in New York in virtually its modern form by the 1840's, and its rapid growth in popularity had assured its permanence as an important feature of American recreation before 1860. After the Civil War it was played throughout the country, both by organized teams which were heading slowly toward professionalism and modern big-league baseball, and by men and boys who asked nothing more than a bat, a ball and a vacant lot. It became a national game. At the same time, the introduction of croquet and lawn tennis, a revival of archery, and the invention of roller skating brought about a national craze for sports which could be enjoyed by both men and women and gave a special significance to the first post-war decade. When bicycling[qv] was added to these outdoor activities, the rise of sports was fully under way with immense value to the nation as a whole. Sports provided not only the means for healthy exercise necessary in what had now become a predominantly urban civilization, but an important escape valve for the restlessness engendered by the pace of modern city life.

The colleges also took up athletics with a new interest and the development of intercollegiate football[qv] from English rugby in the 1870's, which later received great impetus from the coaching of Walter Camp at Yale, added a distinctive game to sporting recreation. Rowing found fresh favor, both college and professional, and amateur athletics, with field and running events, were organized, the National Association of Amateur Athletes of America being formed in 1879. The year 1891 saw the introduction of the one distinctly American sport, basketball[qv], which was invented by James Naismith, a student at the Springfield (Mass.) Y.M.C.A. Training School. Among other sports to enliven the American scene, golf also made its way across the Atlantic before the close of the century and while it did not immediately attain the more democratic basis of these other games, it won wide popularity.

The further growth of sports was fostered by many different agencies which brought about first local and then national organization. The baseball leagues, amateur athletic organizations, schools and colleges, the Y.M.C.A., individual national associations which brought together local golf and tennis clubs, such organizations as the League of American Wheelmen, all contributed to a highly elaborate system of organized sports. The newspapers devoted increasing space to these activities in the 1880's and 1890's and sporting magazines multiplied. With the 20th century, municipal governments further encouraged sports by provision of the necessary public facilities and definite recreation programs.

Professional sports—baseball, football, hockey, prize fighting—have continued to draw immense crowds of spectators, but the less publicized participant sports—sand-lot baseball, the new game of softball, amateur basketball, bowling, tennis and golf—more regularly reach even larger numbers of people. Organized sports in a hundred different forms have become in less than a century one of the most prominent features of American life.

[John A. Krout, *Annals of American Sports.*]

FOSTER RHEA DULLES

Spotswood's Expedition (1716). *See* Knights of the Golden Horseshoe.

Spotswood's Iron Furnaces were erected by Gov. Spotswood of Virginia soon after 1716 at Germanna on an extensive land grant about twenty miles above the falls of the Rappahannock. He began the work with German miners and ironworkers who had been brought to Virginia by a Swiss promoter and left stranded there. Before long, however, he was using Negro slaves in all except a few skilled positions. The original enterprise was a charcoal smelting furnace which cast sowe iron from the neighboring rock ores and had a capacity of twenty tons a week. He later built an air furnace at Massaponax, fifteen miles distant, which remelted sowes to cast hollow ware, chimney backs, andirons, mortars and other utensils in local demand. Spotswood was also interested in a third smelting furnace at Fredericksville, a now extinct town thirty miles southwest of Fredericksburg. British as well as colonial capital was engaged in these undertakings. Ships brought English coal for remelting iron, limestone for flux, and clay for furnace linings to Spotswood's wharf and took abroad his surplus pig iron for the British market. These works were very prosperous shortly before the Revolution but soon thereafter record of their operation ceases.

[William Byrd, *A Progress to the Mines in the Year 1732;* Kathleen Bruce, *Virginia Iron Manufacture in the Slave Era.*]

VICTOR S. CLARK

Spotsylvania Courthouse, Battle of (May 8–21, 1864). Warren's (U.) 5th Corps, leading Grant's southward march from the Wilderness[qv], was stopped northwest of Spotsylvania Courthouse by Kershaw's (C.) division, leading Anderson's corps. Sedgwick's (U.) 6th Corps joined Warren's left and late in the afternoon these corps assaulted Anderson, but were repulsed. During May 9 Ewell's (C.) and Hill's (C.) corps extended Anderson's line northeast to McCool's house and thence south to Spotsylvania Courthouse, entrenching a front four miles long. Hancock's (U.) 2nd Corps joined the 5th and 6th, while Burnside's (U.) 9th Corps, marching from Fredericksburg, approached Hill at Spotsylvania. At McCool's, Ewell's corps occupied a salient separating Burnside from the three corps of the Federal right. May 10 the latter three corps, assaulting Anderson and Ewell, suffered another repulse. On the 12th Hancock attacked and captured Ewell's salient but was driven back to the outside of the entrenchments. Hancock being reinforced by Wright and Burnside, the opposing masses fought all day hand-to-hand at this, the "Bloody Angle"[qv]. About midnight Ewell retired to an inner line. Thereafter for some days Grant gradually withdrew his right and pushed his left southward and on May 20 marched toward Hanover Courthouse. At the North Anna River[qv], however, Lee again blocked him. Grant's losses at Spotsylvania were 17,000; Lee's, 8000.

[D. S. Freeman, *R. E. Lee;* Matthew F. Steele, *American Campaigns*, Vol. I.]

JOSEPH MILLS HANSON

Spring Hill, Engagement at (Nov. 29, 1864). On Nov. 28 Hood (C.) and Schofield (U.) faced each other at Columbia, Tenn. (*see* Hood's Tennessee Campaign). During the night Hood moved northward to get across Schofield's line of retreat. Wilson, commanding Schofield's cavalry, reported Hood's movement and urged prompt retreat to Nashville. Schofield delayed. Hood's troops gained position about Spring Hill along the line of retreat. After dark Schofield's troops marched hurriedly northward within sound of Hood's army. For some reason, never clearly established, no attack was ordered. By daylight Schofield had passed safely northward. Hood's best opportunity had passed. The battle of Franklin[qv] followed.

[Thomas Robson Hay, *Hood's Tennessee Campaign.*]

THOMAS ROBSON HAY

Spring Wells, The Treaty of, was made near Detroit, Sept. 8, 1815, between the United States and seven Indian tribes of the Northwest[qv]. With the Chippewa, Ottawa and Potawatomi[qqv] it restored prewar relations, as had been specified by the Treaty of Ghent[qv]; for the Seneca, Delaware, Miami and Shawnee[qqv] it confirmed a treaty made at Greenville the preceding year, and gave an amnesty for Indian misdeeds since that time. William Henry Harrison was the head of the United States delegation to negotiate the treaty. At the same time the British, at Malden, were holding a similar council with some of the same tribes for a similar purpose, and considerable friction resulted between Harrison and the British officials.

[*American State Papers, Indian Affairs,* Vol. II, pp. 15-25; C. J. Kappler, ed., *Indian Affairs, Laws and Treaties,* Vol. II, pp. 117-119.]

R. S. COTTERILL

***Springbok* Admiralty Case,** The, elaborated the principle of the continuous voyage[qv]. The *Springbok,* English owned both as to vessel and contraband cargo, was captured by a Federal cruiser, June 29, 1862. The neutral port of Nassau was her destination.

The American admiralty courts held that the character of the cargo and manifests indicated the contraband was never intended to be broken up and become a part of the common stock of Nassau, but in reality was for immediate transshipment through the blockade[qv] on a vessel better designed for that perilous voyage; that the ultimate destination of the cargo and not of the ship should govern; and that the *Springbok* should be released but the cargo confiscated.

The English Foreign Office accepted this decision. Its principle was often invoked against American cargoes (1914–17) intended for Germany via a neutral port.

[John Bassett Moore, *International Law Digest.*]

JIM DAN HILL

Springer v. U. S. (102 U. S. 586). In this decision the Supreme Court, in 1881, unanimously upheld the validity of a Federal income tax[qv]. On the basis of earlier precedents it declared that direct taxes, within the meaning of the Constitution, were capitation and real-estate taxes. An income tax was not a direct tax and could therefore be levied on individuals without apportionment among the several states.

W. A. ROBINSON

Springfield, Mo., Battle of. *See* Wilson's Creek, Battle of.

Springfield, N. J., Battle of (June 23, 1780). When Sir Henry Clinton received rumors of mutiny (*see* Pennsylvania Troops, Mutinies of) in Washington's army at Morristown he invaded New Jersey with over 5000 men, simultaneously threatening West Point. At Springfield, Maj. Gen. Greene, with 1000 troops, contested his advance. So vigorous was Greene's defense of the bridge before that town that Clinton proceeded no farther and, after burning the village, returned to Staten Island.

[S. G. Fisher, *The Struggle for American Independence*, Vol. II.]

C. A. TITUS

Springs. Nothing determined the location of so many homes, even villages in pioneer days, as the natural supply of drinking water. Except in the low ground along the coast, a settler's cabin was almost invariably located close to a spring. So were all forts and blockhouses—though as the spring was usually in a low spot, it was almost inevitably outside the palisade, and therefore a hazard. The heroism of the women of Bryan's Station[qv], Ky., who, at dawn of a morning in 1782, when the garrison had become aware that a force of Indians lay in the surrounding woods, went to the spring at some distance down the slope and brought a supply of water, is commemorated by a stone wall monument around the spring, and a tablet. The distilleries of western Pennsylvania and Kentucky all chose large, never-failing springs of pure limestone water as their places of location, and the larger and more famous of them cherished their springs with particular care ever afterwards. The hundreds of place names containing the word "spring," such as Springfield, Springville, Springdale, Spring Hill, Spring Valley, Spring Run, Springs, Rock Springs, Green Springs and many others indicate the importance of the spring in the mind of the early settler. Many large cities cover the sites of springs which in some cases aided in their founding. There were once many springs on Manhattan Island, some of which still flow through hidden conduits into sewers. Mineral springs[qv] gave birth to some of our oldest and largest vacation resorts. In the drier portions of the West, the rare fresh-water spring or water hole became of even greater importance, inasmuch as many springs in such areas were apt to be bitter, strongly alkaline, unpotable. Trails and roads detoured in order to pass good springs, stage and express stations were established there, wagon trains and emigrants made them night stopping places (*see* Water Holes).

ALVIN F. HARLOW

"Spurlos Versenkt." A German phrase, meaning "sunk without a trace being left," used by Count Luxburg, the German chargé d'affaires at Buenos Aires, in telegrams of May 19 and July 9, 1917, to the foreign office in Berlin. He advised that Argentine ships be spared by German submarines or else "sunk without a trace being left." These telegrams and many others, which were sent through the Swedish legation in Buenos Aires, were made public in the United States on Sept. 8, 1917, and in consequence the Count was given his passports by the Argentine government.

[*The Times' History of the War*, Vol. XV.]

BERNADOTTE E. SCHMITT

"Square Deal," THE, was a picturesque phrase used with political significance by Theodore Roosevelt while he was President, to symbolize his personal attitude toward current topics of the period. He first used the phrase in Kansas while on a tour of the western states as he explained the principles later to be embodied in the platform of the Progressive party[qv]. The "square deal" included Roosevelt's ideals of citizenship, the dignity of labor, nobility of parenthood, great wealth, success and the essence of Christian character. Later it was applied to industry. The phrase was extremely popular in 1906.

[Theodore Roosevelt, *A Square Deal.*]

FRANK MARTIN LEMON

Squatter Sovereignty. *See* Popular Sovereignty.

Squatters' Societies. *See* Claim Associations.

Squaw Campaign (February, 1778). Gen. Edward Hand, who had been sent by Washington to defend the western frontier, ordered out Westmoreland County (Pa.) militia to seize some military stores at Sandusky. The troops were hindered by wet weather from reaching their objective, and, in what is now eastern Ohio, fell upon two small camps of Indians which were composed mainly of Delaware[qv] women and children. One or two squaws were killed, and two captured who were later sent back to their tribe. The expedition proved a failure.

[R. G. Thwaites and L. P. Kellogg, *Frontier Defense on the Upper Ohio.*]

LOUISE PHELPS KELLOGG

Squaw Man. The Algonkin[qv] tribes in Massachusetts called a woman a *squaw*. The term appears in colonial English early in 1600, quickly becoming the universal designation for an Indian woman. Later when frontiersmen married Indian women they were given the class designation *squaw men*. However, this term seems not to have become common until after 1830, or when the reservation system developed west of the Mississippi, and white men taking Indian wives were permitted to acquire Indian lands. Their residence among Indians and their special economic status sharply differentiated them as a class. The tendency was to look upon such white men as having gone Indian, or as having debased themselves. The term is now obsolete and rarely met with in contemporary literature.

[Clark Wissler, *The Indian Cavalcade.*]

CLARK WISSLER

Squier Treaty, or Squier-Zepeda Treaty (Sept. 3, 1849), was signed by Ephraim George Squier, diplomatic agent of the Taylor administration, with Nicaragua[qv] with the object of promoting the construction of a ship canal. It differed in detail from its unapproved predecessor, the Hise Treaty[qv], but was only a degree less challenging to England in that it recognized Nicaraguan sovereignty over Mosquito[qv]. Though disapproved and discarded in favor of the Clayton-Bulwer Treaty[qv] with England, Squier's Treaty was nevertheless symptomatic of the new, though premature, American determination not only to have a canal, but to make good the Monroe Doctrine[qv]. It was one of a series of incidents which focused Anglo-American rivalry in the Caribbean on Nicaragua. (*See also* Panama Canal.)

[Samuel Flagg Bemis, *The American Secretaries of State and Their Diplomacy,* Vol. VI.]

RICHARD W. VAN ALSTYNE

"Squirrel Hunters," THE. This term originated in 1862 when Cincinnati was in imminent danger of attack by Confederate troops (*see* Kentucky, Invasion of). Gov. Tod called for help, asking the men to bring their own arms. The response was largely from rural districts, and the equipment that of men accustomed to squirrel hunting.

[N. E. Jones, *The Squirrel Hunters.*]

HARLOW LINDLEY

Stabilization Fund. The Gold Reserve Act of 1934[qv] provided for the creation of a stabilization fund of $2,000,000,000 out of the profit from the devaluation[qv] of the dollar (*see also* Gold, Federal Expropriation of). The fund was for the purpose of stabilizing the exchange value of the dollar, but any portion not needed for this purpose might be invested in United States securities. The fund was to have a life of two years, but might be terminated before that time or extended a year by the President. On Jan. 10, 1936, the President extended the operation of the fund for the year permitted. On Jan. 23, 1937, Congress extended it to June 30, 1939, and on July 6, 1939, again extended its operation to June 30, 1941.

[F. A. Bradford, *Money and Banking;* J. Donaldson, *The Dollar.*]

FREDERICK A. BRADFORD

Stafford v. Wallace (258 U. S. 495, 1922). The Packers and Stockyards Act[qv] of 1921 gave to the Secretary of Agriculture the authority to regulate the operations of the livestock dealers and commission men. In a case, T. F. Stafford et al, brought against Secretary Wallace, the act was challenged on the ground that such businesses were not in interstate commerce, but were purely local in character. In the decision handed down May 1, 1922, Chief Justice Taft declared that the stockyards and commission houses "are but the throat through which the current [of interstate commerce] flows," and that such regulation was a proper exercise of Federal power under the Constitution.

[R. A. Clemen, *The American Livestock and Meat Industry.*]

ERNEST S. OSGOOD

Stagecoach Lines of the Greater Southwest. The California gold discovery[qv] (January, 1848) and the consequent rush of the "Forty-niners" made necessary transcontinental stagecoach lines. In the summer of 1849 stage service was provided between Independence, Mo., and Santa Fé[qqv], N. Mex.; and two years later another was instituted between Independence and Salt Lake City[qv]. Coaches over the central route made monthly runs. But a more satisfactory service was provided in 1857 between San Antonio and San Diego via the Gila route (1475 miles) when semimonthly coaches were used on an approximate thirty-day schedule.

Within the next decade thousands of miles of stage lines were in use. John Butterfield and associates began the Southern Overland Mail[qv] in September, 1858, over the long "ox-bow" route from Tipton, Mo., to San Francisco via Fort Smith, Ark., across the Choctaw Nation, the frontier of Texas, and thence by El Paso, Tucson and San Diego (2795 miles). Memphis, Tenn., was made one of the eastern termini when a branch line made connection with the other at Fort Smith. A Colorado gold discovery (1858) also made possible another line, the Leavenworth and Pikes Peak Company[qv]. Then Ben Holladay[qv] entered the field (1862) with his extensive operations, taking over the interests of Majors, Russell and Waddell[qv]. One of his lines extended from Atchison, Kans., to Denver (687 miles); another from Denver to Salt Lake City, passing over the Rockies at Bridger's Pass; and a triweekly line from Salt Lake City to the Dalles in northern Oregon (950 miles). A branch line connected Virginia City, Mont., with the main line at Fort Hall*ᵠᵛ*. Then from Denver Holladay ran a subsidiary line to Central City, Nev. He sold his interests in 1866 to Wells Fargo*ᵠᵛ*.

[LeRoy Hafen, *The Overland Mail;* C. C. Rister, *Southern Plainsmen.*]
C. C. RISTER

Stagecoach Robberies occurred in Eastern and Middle Western America, but the dramatic character of Western holdups, together with the large amounts of booty secured, make them more important historically. Of these the California robberies stand out because of the movement of gold ore through the express companies who used stagecoaches to transport it. The first robbery of importance was in 1852 when Reelfoot Williams' gang took $7500 from the express strong box. The work was carried on by "Rattlesnake Dick" Barter whose gang robbed the Wells Fargo*ᵠᵛ* mule team of $80,000 in gold dust in 1855, and Rhode and Lusk's express of $26,000 in 1856. He was succeeded by Tom Bell, "gentleman highwayman." In 1856 the Bell gang tried to take $100,000 in gold from the Marysville stage, but were fought off almost singlehanded by the armed messenger. Following this attempt Bell was captured and hanged. In fifteen years of operation ending in 1869 Wells Fargo Express Company had suffered 313 stage robberies. A second era of stage holdups followed the discovery of gold in the Black Hills*ᵠᵛ* of South Dakota. The Wall-Blackburn gang operated in 1877 and 1878. Since the treasure on some of the coaches amounted to as much as $140,000 there were frequent attempts but not many successful large robberies, as the stage lines supplied the best guards that could be found.

[A. F. Harlow, *Old Waybills;* J. Brown and A. M. Willard, *Black Hills Trails.*]
CARL L. CANNON

Stagecoach Travel. The first successful stagecoach lines in the United States were established in the northern colonies in the two decades before the Revolution, most of them running to near-by places from the three largest cities, Boston, New York and Philadelphia. The only lines connecting large cities were those between Boston and Providence, between New York and Philadelphia, and between Philadelphia and Baltimore. In each instance a short land journey was substituted for a long water passage. No stagecoaches ran south of Annapolis in colonial times.

These lines were halted by the Revolution, but most of them were again in motion before the treaty of peace was signed. They were aided financially and clothed with greater public interest when, in 1785, Congress first provided for the carrying of the mail by stagecoach over roads where it had grown too heavy for horse and rider. Slowly the mail stage network widened, the Post Office*ᵠᵛ* encouraging and frequently, through its mail contracts, giving financial assistance to proprietors who established lines through new territory. Such assistance resulted in 1803 in the first line connecting the Central Atlantic states with the Carolinas and Georgia. The Ohio Valley was first penetrated by a line established to Pittsburgh in 1804. Rapid development of stagecoach facilities west of the Alleghenies did not take place until the Jacksonian era when Post Office subsidies became heavy. The mileage of mail stage lines tripled between 1828 and 1838, the latter date representing approximately the peak of staging activity east of the Mississippi River.

As lines were thrust westward with the advancing frontier, service on the older roads in the East grew more rapid and more frequent, and additional local routes were established until there were few villages that did not have a stagecoach arriving and departing several times a week. On the busier roads stagecoach companies ran both "limited" mail coaches, taking but a few passengers through rapidly at higher fares, and "accommodation" coaches which traveled more slowly, stopped more frequently along the way, and allowed the full resting time at night. Landlords of taverns*ᵠᵛ* where the stages stopped were usually partners in the line, a community of interest along the road being thus established. Stages of rival lines stopped at rival taverns. Eventually, large stagecoach companies controlled the paying lines in certain areas, and these companies in turn formed working agreements with each other. The Post Office because of its interest in efficiency and smooth connecting arrangements generally tolerated these large combinations of interest. (*See also* Post Roads.)

After railroads invaded the heaviest routes of travel the stage lines became extensions of advancing railheads or feeders from fertile tributary areas. The amount of staging, all told, did not necessarily decline at once, for the railroads encouraged travel and shipping and often furnished the stages with more business than they had previously known. Ultimately, however, when the railroads had completed their trunk lines and built branches into the more profitable tributary regions, the stagecoach was forced back to a marginal fringe which it did not pay the railroads to develop. In mountainous regions in both East and West it lingered, serving isolated valleys and villages, until the coming of the motor bus[qv].

[Seymour Dunbar, *History of Travel in America.*]
OLIVER W. HOLMES

Stages, Fishing, were high wooden platforms built on the shore upon which to dry fish. Less specifically, the term is also used for the place whereon the land operations—cleaning, curing, oil extraction, etc.—connected with fishing were carried on. The most famous American stages were those along the Newfoundland, Nova Scotia and New England coasts. A picture of one taken from an old woodcut may be found in D. W. Prowse, *History of Newfoundland.*

ROBERT E. MOODY

Staked Plains, THE (*Llano Estacado*), is the name applied to the high level part of northwest Texas and eastern New Mexico which lies above the Cap Rock escarpment. Coronado[qv] led the first expedition of white men across it and later other Spaniards visited it. It was so named, perhaps, because one such expedition drove stakes at intervals by which to retrace their route. The fierce Comanche Indians[qv] occupied it until about 1880, and the whites did not consider it worth wresting from them. Within the decade 1880–90 the buffaloes[qv] were extinguished, the Comanches were expelled, the Fort Worth and Denver Railroad was built across the region, and the huge XIT Ranch was being formed by the Capitol Syndicate out of the three million acres which were granted to it by the State of Texas. The region soon became a cattle country and later, in part, a dry farming[qv] section.

[Fred W. Allsop, *Albert Pike;* J. E. Haley, *The XIT Ranch.*]
L. W. NEWTON

Stalwarts was a term applied to certain conservative Republican leaders led by Sen. Roscoe Conklin of New York. They opposed the Southern policy and the civil-service reform program of Hayes' administration and dubbed his adherents "Halfbreeds"[qv]. Though the Stalwarts were unsuccessful in securing Grant's nomination for a third presidential term in 1880, one of their henchmen, Chester A. Arthur, was awarded the vice-presidential nomination. After Conklin's retirement from politics in the 1880's the designation soon passed out of use.

[E. P. Oberholtzer, *A History of the United States since the Civil War,* Vol. III.]
ASA E. MARTIN

Stamp Act, THE (1765). By 1763 British and colonial arms had driven French power from Canada (*see* Paris, Treaty of, 1763). The extension of colonial empire raised new and serious problems. The conquest of Canada brought under British rule disaffected French and hostile Indians. In 1763 the Indians, under the leadership of Pontiac[qv], fearing British rule and colonial encroachment on their land, fell upon the frontier settlements in a devastating attack. Clearly it was necessary to station garrisons on the long border to guard the colonists against Indian attack and the Indians against predatory whites. It was equally clear that the control of frontier affairs could no longer be left to the separate colonies with their conflicting interests. Frontier problems became more than ever a matter of common concern to be met and solved by the British government as the central authority.

The garrisoning of the border meant a heavy expense, and at once the financial question became a decisive factor. The estimates fixed £320,000 as the cost of supporting an American army of ten thousand men for defense in the mainland colonies and the West Indies. Where should this financial burden fall? The French war had doubled the British national debt, bringing it to the sum of £130,000,000 with a yearly interest charge of £4,500,000. In addition to the support of a colonial military force, increased estimates were necessary to maintain British naval supremacy. So heavy was the strain upon the British taxpayer that the ministry decided to call upon the colonies to share the expense of the American army. This decision once made, another decisive question arose. Should the colonial share be levied by the several colonial representative bodies or by the British Parliament? In the past, Parliament had not taxed the colonies for revenue purposes. In time of imperial wars, royal requisitions were sent to the colonies to raise and pay troops to co-operate with the British forces. But the realities of the late war plainly showed that the requisition system was inefficient and unfair. A general lack of vigorous co-operation impaired military operation. The military burden was not equitably distributed, a few colonies responded loyally, some half-heartedly, others far short of their abilities. This conduct led during the war to proposals to tax the colonies by act of Parliament. The Indian uprising under Pontiac further revealed that the colonies could not be depended upon for adequate frontier defense nor would they share the burden equitably.

These facts decided the British ministry to resort to the levy of a parliamentary tax upon the colonies. The first step was the passage of the Sugar Act[qv] of 1764. The old severe duties on colonial trade with the foreign West Indies were reduced in the hope that it would yield some revenue, probably £45,000. This was held to be less than the colonial share, and Sir George Grenville, Chancellor of the Exchequer, proposed a stamp tax upon the colonies. He deferred the plan a year to give the colonies an opportunity to suggest means more to their liking. They protested strongly against a stamp act and suggested nothing more than taxation by the colonial assemblies[qv] as of old. Grenville conferred with the colonial agents[qv] in London, among them Benjamin Franklin of Pennsylvania and Jared Ingersoll of Connecticut. The agents pleaded for the old method of raising revenue in the colonies. To this Grenville countered by asking if the colonies could agree on the quotas each should raise and whether it was certain every colony would raise its quotas. In the light of past experience, the agents had no answer to these questions. And so Parliament proceeded to the passage of the famous Stamp Act of 1765 with a heavy majority. The use of stamps was required on all legal and commercial papers, pamphlets, newspapers, almanacs, cards and dice. The law provided for a Stamp Office in London, an inspector for each of the colonial districts, and a stamp distributor for each colony. The estimated yield from stamps ranged from £60,000 to £100,000, collected in both mainland colonies and the West Indies. The combined revenues of the Sugar and Stamp Acts, £105,000 to £145,000, would meet less than half the cost of the American garrison forces.

Few in England realized the significance of the stamp tax. Parliament, in harmony with the rule not to receive petitions against revenue bills, did not heed the colonial protests. The ministers and Parliament felt that the law was a fair solution of a pressing problem. Even the colonial agents failed to understand the colonial temper. Franklin nominated a stamp distributor for Pennsylvania and Ingersoll accepted the post for Connecticut. News of the Stamp Act blew up a colonial storm. Parliamentary taxation for revenue was an innovation which threatened the very foundation of colonial self-government and outraged the precious right of Englishmen[qv] to be taxed only by their consent. Colonial opposition nullified the Stamp Act.

[C. H. Van Tyne, *The Causes of the War of Independence;* G. L. Beer, *British Colonial Policy, 1754-1765;* Edward Channing, *History of the United States;* L. H. Gipson, *Jared Ingersoll.*]

WINFRED T. ROOT

Stamp Act Congress, THE (1765). The Stamp Act[qv] and other recent British statutes menaced self-rule in all the colonies and thus furnished a principle of union. The House of Representatives of Massachusetts, appreciating the value of united effort, issued in June a call to all the colonies to send delegates to New York. Nine colonies responded and a total of twenty-seven delegates met in the City Hall in October. They framed resolutions of colonial "rights and grievances" and petitioned king and Parliament to repeal the objectionable legislation. They held that taxing the colonies without their consent violated one of the most precious rights of Englishmen[qv]. Since distance precluded colonial representation in the British Parliament, they could be taxed only by their local assemblies (*see* Colonial Assemblies) in which they were represented. The Congress is significant in that parliamentary threats to colonial self-control fostered the movement which slowly brought to maturity the spirit and agencies of national unity.

[C. H. Van Tyne, *Causes of the War of Independence;* Edward Channing, *History of the United States.*]

WINFRED T. ROOT

Stamp Act Riot in New York City. On Nov. 1, 1766, as a part of the agitation against the Stamp Act[qv], the Sons of Liberty[qv] erected a sham gallows on the Common in New York and hung thereon effigies of Gov. Colden with the Devil whispering in his ear. They marched to the fort, threw bricks and stones at it and taunted the soldiers. They seized the lieutenant governor's coach and burned it, together with the gallows and effigies, in front of the fort. Next they broke into another British official's house, gutted it and burned the furnishings in the street. Their secretly promulgated threats of vengeance effectually blocked the use of the stamps.

[Mrs. Martha J. Lamb, *History of New York City.*]

ALVIN F. HARLOW

Stampedes were the most dramatic, hazardous and disastrous events of roundups and cattle drives[qqv]. Oxen, horses, buffaloes, all might stampede, but the frantic flight which *rancheros* called *estampida* was especially characteristic of Longhorns[qv]. A great herd peacefully bedded down might, with the instantaneity of forked lightning, be on its feet and then with hoofs, hocks and horns knocking together, the ground shaking from the impact, thunder away in headlong flight. The only way to check them was to circle the leaders and thus swing the mass into a "mill." Causes of stampedes were many—the whirr of a rattlesnake near the head of some snoring steer, the flirt of a polecat's tail, the jump of a rabbit, the smell of a lobo or Indian, the flash of a match by some careless cowboy lighting a cigarette, any unexpected sound such as the shaking of an empty saddle by a horse. Cowboy songs[qv] were not so much to soothe cattle as to afford a barrier against surprises. The best preventives were bellies full of grass and water.

Western artists like Remington, Russell and Frank Reaugh have pictured the stampede. Popular ballads like "Lasca" (by Desperez) and "When Work's All Done This Fall" have dramatized it. The most powerful story yet written on any Western subject—*Longrope's Last Guard,* by Chas. M. Russell—translates it fully. Yet, human fatalities from stampedes were rare, and a great mass of writing about them is balderdash. The worst results were to the cattle themselves—animals trampled to death, horns and legs broken, and more "tallow run off" in a night than could be restored by a month of grazing.

[J. Evetts Haley, *Charles Goodnight, Cowman and Plainsman;* W. M. Raine and W. C. Barnes, *Cattle;* C. M. Russell, *Trails Plowed Under.*]

J. FRANK DOBIE

Standard Oil Company, an Ohio corporation, was incorporated in January, 1870, with a capital of $1,000,000, the original stockholders being John D. Rockefeller (2667 shares); William Rockefeller (1333 shares); Henry M. Flagler (1333 shares); Samuel Andrews (1333 shares); Stephen V. Harkness (1334 shares); O. B. Jennings (1000 shares); and the firm of Rockefeller, Andrews & Flagler (1000 shares). It took the place of the previous firm of Rockefeller, Andrews & Flagler, whose refineries were much the largest in Cleveland and probably the largest in the world. Important extensions were immediately made. Thanks partly to these, partly to superior efficiency, and partly to the threat of the South Improvement Company[qv], the Standard early in 1872 swallowed practically all rival refineries in the Cleveland area. The roster of stockholders on Jan. 1, 1872, was slightly increased, and the capital raised to $2,500,000. Coincidentally with the conquest of Cleveland, the Standard began reaching out to other cities. In 1872 it bought the oil-transporting and refining firm of J. A. Bostwick & Co. in New York; the Long Island Oil Company; and a controlling share of the Devoe Manufacturing Company on Long Island. In 1873 it bought pipelines, the largest refinery in the oil regions, and a half-interest in a Louisville refinery. The acquisition of the principal refineries of Pittsburgh and Philadelphia was carried out in 1874–76, while in 1877 the Standard in a terrific war defeated the Pennsylvania Railroad[qv] and the Empire Transportation Company, taking possession of the pipelines and refineries of the latter. Another war with the Tidewater Pipeline resulted in a working agreement which drastically limited the latter's operations. By 1879 the Standard, with its subsidiary and associated companies, controlled from 90% to 95% of the refining capacity of the United States, immense pipeline and storage-tank systems, and powerful marketing organizations at home and abroad. Under Rockefeller's leadership it was the first company in the world to organize the whole of a huge, complex and extremely rich industry. In 1875 the stock of the Standard was increased for the last time to a total of $3,500,000, the million dollars of new stock being taken by Charles Pratt & Co., Warden, Frew & Co., and S. V. Harkness. In 1879 there were thirty-seven stockholders, of whom John D. Rockefeller, with 8984 shares, held nearly three times as much as any other man.

While the Standard Oil of Ohio remained legally a small company with no manufacturing operations outside its state, practically it was the nucleus of an almost nation-wide industrial organization, the richest and most powerful in the country. Its articles of incorporation had not authorized it to hold stock in other companies or to be a partner in any firm. It had met this difficulty by acquiring stocks not in the name of the Standard of Ohio, but in that of some one prominent stockholder as trustee. Henry M. Flagler, William Rockefeller, J. A. Bostwick and various others served from 1873 to 1879 as trustees. Then in 1879 the situation was given more systematic treatment. All the stocks acquired by the Standard and held by various trustees, and all the properties outside Ohio in which the Standard had an interest, were transferred to three minor employees (George H. Vilas, Myron R. Keith, George F. Chester) as trustees. They held the stocks and properties for the exclusive use and benefit of the Standard's stockholders, and distributed dividends in specified proportions. But while this arrangement was satisfactory from a legal point of view, it did not provide sufficient administrative centralization. On Jan. 2, 1882, therefore, a new arrangement, the Standard Oil Trust Agreement, set up the first trust[qv] in the sense of a monopoly in American history. All stock and properties, including that of the Standard Oil proper as well as of interests outside Ohio, were transferred to a board of nine trustees, consisting of the principal owners and managers, with John D. Rockefeller as head. For each share of stock of the Standard of

Ohio, twenty trust certificates of a par value of $100 each were to be issued. The total of the trust certificates was therefore $70,000,000, considerably less than the actual value of the properties. The Standard's huge network of refineries, pipes, tanks and marketing systems was thus given a secret but for the time being satisfactory legal organization, while administration was centralized in nine able men with Rockefeller at their head.

This situation lasted until 1892, the Standard constantly growing in wealth and power. Then as the result of a decree by the Ohio courts the Standard Oil Trust dissolved, and the separate establishments and plants were reorganized into twenty constituent companies. But by informal arrangement, unity of action was maintained among these twenty corporations until they could be gathered into a holding company (Standard Oil of New Jersey). Then in 1911 a decree of the Federal Supreme Court forced a more complete dissolution (*see* Standard Oil Co. of New Jersey v. U. S.). Rockefeller remained nominal head of the Standard until 1911, but after 1895 he had surrendered more and more of the actual authority to his associates, with John D. Archbold as their chief.

[Ida M. Tarbell, *History of the Standard Oil Company;* John T. Flynn, *God's Gold;* Gilbert H. Montague, *The Rise and Progress of the Standard Oil Company.*]

ALLAN NEVINS

Standard Oil Co. of N. J. v. U. S. (1911), originated in 1906 when the Government filed a suit against more than seventy corporations and individuals alleging that they were conspiring "to restrain the trade and commerce in petroleum . . . in refined oil, and in other products of petroleum" in violation of the Sherman Antitrust Act of 1890. In 1909 the Circuit Court of the United States for the Eastern District of Missouri upheld the charge. The court's decree held that the combining of the stocks of various companies in the hands of the Standard Oil Company of New Jersey in 1899 constituted "a combination in restraint of trade and also an attempt to monopolize and a monopolization under Sec. 2 of the Antitrust Act." The New Jersey corporation was forbidden to control thirty-seven subsidiary companies or to vote their stock. In other words, thirty-eight ostensibly independent companies were to be formed. On May 15, 1911, the decree was upheld by the Supreme Court which, however, declared that applications of the Antitrust law should "be determined by the light of reason."

This decision, confirming the dissolution of the so-called Standard Oil "Trust," has often been erroneously confused with a 1907 decree by District Judge Kenesaw M. Landis, fining the Standard Oil Company of Indiana a total of $29,240,000 for receiving "an unlawful secret rate" from a railroad in violation of the Elkins Act[qv] of 1903. This decree, reversed in 1908 by the Seventh Circuit Court of Appeals, was not reviewed by the Supreme Court.

[221 U. S. 1; *Political Science Quarterly*, December, 1911.]

ERIK McKINLEY ERIKSSON

Standard Time. *See* Time.

Standards, The Bureau of, grew out of the problem of standardizing weights and measures for facilitating trade and contractual relations, local, national and international. The Secretary of the Treasury was early charged with maintaining standards in custom houses and the work remained under his supervision until 1903. A separate agency was recognized by law in 1882. In 1901 an act of Congress laid the basis of the present institution and assigned the name National Bureau of Standards. In 1903 the Bureau was transferred to the newly formed Department of Commerce and Labor and in 1913 became part of the Department of Commerce[qv].

The Bureau rapidly expanded into one of the largest institutions for scientific research in the world. Various branch plants were established, as at Seattle for testing the cement used in constructing Grand Coulee Dam[qv]. The Bureau works out standard methods of testing materials and processes. It attempts to improve the quality of products and to promote economy of production through simplified practice for eliminating needless types, sizes and varieties of products. It emphasizes research in new fields, especially such as seem likely to provide a basis for new industries. It makes tests and formulates specifications for use by consumers, but consumers' interests are served directly only in the case of tax-supported purchasing agencies.

[G. A. Weber, *The Bureau of Standards;* U. S. Department of Commerce, *Department of Commerce: Condensed History, Duties and Practical Operation of the Department and Its Several Bureaus and Offices, Together with Laws Relating Specifically Thereto;* American Academy of Political and Social Science, *The Annals*, Vol. 173, pp. 125-157.]

WITT BOWDEN

Standards of Living. Real wages quadrupled in the United States between 1791 and 1931, although the improvement was neither uniform nor continuous. Rapid increases accompanied eras of falling prices which generally succeeded wars (1799–1805, 1814–17, 1865–71, 1918–23) while extreme declines came with the wars themselves, with periods of actual or anticipated credit overexpansion (1853–57, 1862–64, 1915–17), and with inflationary threats (1873–79, 1893–94, 1896). The result was standards of living higher than the world ever knew.

In spite of the famous but indefinable "American standard of living," great variations in modes of living among social classes have existed throughout American history. Congress fixed the President's salary originally at $25,000 a year, an amount which probably represented lavish living at that time and which contrasted sharply with average annual wages (1817) for manual and skilled workers—$200 and $400 respectively. A minimum of $600 was considered necessary in 1835 to provide a family of four in New York City with an "adequate" living. In many instances undoubtedly produce and service income supplemented money income so that no widespread suffering took place; at least organized and permanent charity was unknown at the time. Even more marked discrepancies appeared with industrialization (1850). There were probably not more than six fortunes of five million dollars or more in 1860; in 1921 there were 649. The Bureau of Labor Statistics in 1921–22 estimated an urban budget for minimum health and decency for five people required from $2000 to $2500, yet 86% of the American people had incomes of $2000 or less. An increased dependence upon money income was illustrated by the necessity for widespread relief in the depression years immediately following 1929.

Our high standards have been responsible for the greater part of the immigration to this country and for the subsequent problems of assimilation[qqv]. The great differences in standards combined with fluctuations in them have accounted partially for the development of our labor movement, for social legislation, for crime, slum and pauper problems, for inheritance and income taxes, and for many other attempts to ameliorate the effects of a maldistribution of wealth and income[qqv].

[W. I. King, *The National Income and Its Purchasing Power;* M. Leven and others, *America's Capacity to Consume;* R. Tucker, Real Wages under Laissez-faire, in *Barron's*, Oct. 23, 1933; C. A. Beard and M. R. Beard, *The Rise of American Civilization;* F. A. Shannon, *Economic History of the People of the United States.*]

W. B. LOCKLING

Standing Order. For nearly two centuries New England was dominated by a close association of the clergy, the magistrates and the well-to-do, which consciously controlled political, economic, social and intellectual life. This control rested on popular acceptance, a limited suffrage and the special legal position of the Congregational church[qv], and was so firmly established as to win the name of the Standing Order. Its members were aristocratic and intensely conservative, and failed to hold out against the growing democracy of the early 19th century.

[H. Adams, *History of the United States.*]

HERBERT W. HILL

"Standpatters." The term came into political parlance in connection with the cleavage in the Republican party during Taft's administration over the Payne-Aldrich tariff, the Ballinger-Pinchot affair, and "Cannonism"[qqv]. The insurgent Republicans, styling themselves "progressives"[qv], called the conservatives "standpatters" and denounced them as satisfied with the present social order, against reform, and devoted to the vested interests. This factional difference contributed to the election of a Democratic House of Representatives in 1910 and led to the Republican split of 1912 (*see* Campaign of 1912).

[J. A. Woodburn, *Political Parties and Party Problems in the United States;* Mark Sullivan, *Our Times*, Vol. IV.]

GLENN H. BENTON

Stansbury Exploration, The, made by Capt. Howard Stansbury of the U. S. Army in 1852, had for its object a survey of the valley of Great Salt Lake, an inspection of the Mormon[qqv] colony, and an examination of a new route through the mountains. These were all accomplished in the face of difficulties, and Stansbury's illustrated report and accompanying atlases make it one of the most interesting and valuable explorations ever made under government auspices.

[H. Stansbury, *Expedition to Valley of Great Salt Lake.*]

CARL L. CANNON

Stanton, Fort (N. Mex.), was established by the U. S. Army in Lincoln County in 1856 to hold the Apache[qv] in check. In 1871 the Mescalero tribe of this people was placed on reservation there, and became the center of stealing and murder, with charges and countercharges by Indians and whites. The fort was abandoned Aug. 17, 1896.

[C. C. Rister, *Southwestern Frontier.*]

CARL L. CANNON

Stanwix, Fort. In 1758 the old fort at the Oneida carrying place, which had been destroyed by Gen. Webb after the French captured Oswego[qv] in 1756, was rebuilt and named Stanwix after its builder, Gen. John Stanwix. Its strategic location between the upper Mohawk and Wood Creek made it an important point of defense during the colonial period and a center of

Indian trade and treaties. After the conclusion of peace with the French in 1763 (*see* Paris, Treaty of, 1763) it was allowed to fall into disrepair, and at the beginning of the Revolution was found to be untenable. It was rebuilt and for a time called Fort Schuyler in honor of Gen. Philip Schuyler. It was here that in 1777 St. Leger was held back on his way to Albany (*see* British Campaign of 1777). With the conclusion of peace the usefulness of the old fort was over. Immigrants from New England swarmed into the region. A village, the present city of Rome, was founded on the site of the fort.

[J. A. Scott, *Fort Stanwix and Oriskany.*]

A. C. FLICK

Stanwix, Fort, Second Treaty of (1784). The powerful Iroquois Indians[qv] had been greatly weakened by the vigorous campaigns of Sullivan and Brodhead[qqv] during the Revolutionary War and their leaders recognized the futility of further resistance to the white advance. Consequently at Fort Stanwix in October, 1784, they ceded a small tract of land in western New York, and all that part of Pennsylvania north and west of the Indian boundary line established by the first Treaty of Fort Stanwix in 1768[qv] (constituting about one fourth of the area of the state). They also relinquished their claim to land west of the Ohio River—a claim, however, which was disputed by other tribes.

[Charles C. Royce, *Indian Land Cessions in the United States*, Eighteenth Annual Report of the Bureau of American Ethnology, Pt. II.]

DAN E. CLARK

Stanwix, Fort, Treaty of (1768). At the time of the Proclamation of 1763[qv] it was evidently intended that another Indian boundary line farther west than the Proclamation Line would be established by means of treaties with the Indian tribes. This plan was forgotten until late in 1767 when Lord Shelburne received letters from America warning him of dangers of Indian warfare unless something were done. The Lords of Trade and the Privy Council[qqv] discussed the matter and Shelburne was authorized to instruct the two Indian superintendents (*see* Indian Policy, Colonial) in America to negotiate with the Indians with a view to establishing a boundary line.

Upon receipt of these instructions Sir William Johnson summoned the Iroquois Indians[qv] and their allies to meet him at Fort Stanwix in September, 1768. Twenty boatloads of presents were alluringly displayed before the covetous eyes of the Indians, who were told that all these attractive goods would be theirs if they would make a grant of land to the king. The prospect, together with well-placed private gifts, won the desired result late in October. The Iroquois agreed to cede their claims to lands east and south of a line which was indicated in detail in the treaty. This line ran from the vicinity of Fort Stanwix on the upper Mohawk southward to the Delaware, then in a general southwestwardly direction across and along both branches of the Susquehanna to the Allegheny River, and down that stream and the Ohio to the mouth of the Tennessee. The extension of the line to the Tennessee River was an afterthought, and was apparently included because of the intrigues of certain traders, although the Iroquois themselves requested permission to cede land south of the Ohio in order to prove their claims to the region as against the Cherokees[qv].

The Indian boundary line was continued southward by treaties made by John Stuart, the most important being those made at Hard Labor in 1768 and Lochaber in 1770[qqv], by which the Cherokees ceded their claims to lands in the present State of West Virginia. These two treaties have a close connection with the Treaty of Fort Stanwix, for between them they opened to settlement large areas of land in southwestern Pennsylvania and in the region back of Virginia. Whether the British authorities intended the making of these treaties to authorize settlement west of the Proclamation Line is not clear, but American settlers indicated their own interpretation by moving in large numbers into the country between the two lines.

[Clarence W. Alvord, *The Mississippi Valley in British Politics;* Max Farrand, The Indian Boundary Line, in *American Historical Review*, Vol. X; Albert T. Volwiler, *George Croghan and the Westward Movement.*]

DAN E. CLARK

Staples, Colonial. The continental British-American colonies had three important staple crops—tobacco, rice, indigo[qqv]. Tobacco was a major crop in Virginia, Maryland and parts of North Carolina. Tobacco was an enumerated product[qv] and found its chief market in England and Scotland where it was graded, processed and shipped to the various markets of the world. Rice was mainly grown on the lowlands of South Carolina and Georgia. It found its chief market in England, the West Indies and in Southern Europe. As England could not use the entire crop it was permitted to be marketed in Europe south of Cape Finisterre. Indigo was produced only in South Carolina and some of the West Indies. It had to have rich soil and special treatment. It was encouraged by British bounties and was marketed almost entirely in England. In the British West Indies, especially in Barbados, sugar[qv] was another important staple crop. This product, like the others, was enumerated and was shipped largely to England where it was refined and marketed throughout the British Empire and Europe. Molasses[qv] was an important by-product of this industry and was used directly by the rum[qv] distilling industry in England and America.

The staple industries had several things in common. Each tended to become a plantation type of crop where the labor was almost exclusively done by slaves. Such single-crop types of farming tended to develop irregular production, absentee landlords and dependence upon foreign financing and foreign markets. All, except indigo, were bulky and required extensive shipping to carry them to England.

[George Louis Beer, *The Old Colonial System.*]

O. M. DICKERSON

***Star of the West*, THE**, was an unarmed merchant vessel which President Buchanan, influenced by Unionist Cabinet members, secretly dispatched on Jan. 5, 1861, with troops and supplies, to reinforce Maj. Anderson at Fort Sumter[qv]. Reaching Charleston harbor on Jan. 9, the vessel was fired upon by the batteries on Morris Island and Fort Moultrie[qv]. Neither Anderson nor the vessel returned the fire, and the latter sailed away only to be captured by Confederate forces on April 20, 1861.

[S. W. Crawford, *Genesis of the Civil War;* F. E. Chadwick, *Causes of the Civil War.*]

FLETCHER M. GREEN

Star Route Frauds. Star Routes were roads, principally in the West, where mail was carried under contracts by wagons or horses and not by railroad or steamboat. Extensive frauds in the Post Office Department[qv] caused great financial losses to the Government. Departmental officials, contractors, sub-contractors and an ex-senator were in conspiracy. This "gang" demanded more congressional appropriations for starting new and useless routes; fraudulent and padded petitions supported their demands for money to expedite old routes; worthless bonds and securities were imposed on the Department; and contractors exacted fines and profits from sub-contractors. One $90,000 contract was let on the affidavit of one contractor. Another route with $761 income annually was expedited in speed and number of trips at a cost of $50,000, although for thirty-nine days no papers or letters were carried over that road. Analysis of the specifications of John M. Peck, one contractor, showed requirements that each horse had to travel twenty hours daily and the rider forty hours daily! Congressional investigations, special agents, Pinkerton detectives and attorneys brought about more than twenty-five indictments. Trials in 1882 and 1883 proved frauds on ninety-three routes. But no convictions resulted and the Government was defrauded of about $4,000,000.

[*House Reports*, 1st Sess., 48th Congress, VII, Doc. 2165.]

LOUIS PELZER

"Star-Spangled Banner," THE, was inspired by the British attack on Fort McHenry[qv] in the War of 1812. On the night of the attack, Francis Scott Key, a young Baltimore lawyer, together with a group of friends had gone to the British admiral to seek the release of a prominent physician who had been captured by the British. Because of plans for the attack, Key and his companions were detained on ship in the harbor and spent the night watching the British bombard the fort. Key felt sure that the attack had been successful, but when dawn disclosed the flag still flying Key's emotions were so stirred that he wrote the words of "The Star-Spangled Banner" on the back of an envelope, adapting them to a then popular drinking song, "To Anacreon in Heaven." The original version was printed as a handbill the next day; a week later it appeared in a Baltimore newspaper. Later Key made a complete draft which is now in a private collection in Baltimore. The song soon became in fact the national anthem, but it was not until 1931 that Congress officially recognized it as such. Despite its prominence there are few people who know more than the first stanza of the "Star-Spangled Banner" and even fewer who can sing the difficult melody. Numerous attempts have been made to simplify the music, but none have been generally accepted.

[John Tasker Howard, *Our American Music.*]

E. H. O'NEILL

Stare Decisis denominates the practice of English and American courts of deciding present cases on the basis of past precedent. In its favor, it may be said that this is a time-saving device, that it utilizes the experience of the past, and that it gives stability and continuity to the law. Critics object to what they regard as its rigidifying influence, and to the fact that it induces judges to look backward rather than forward. The adherence of American courts to this doctrine does not mean, however, that decisions once made may not be modified or reversed; they have been in the past, and they doubtless will be in the future. For example, the Supreme Court followed the doctrine in dealing with child labor. It had decided in United States v. E. C.

Knight Sugar Refining Company[qv] (156 U. S. 1, 1895) that manufacturing was production, and not commerce, on the ground that the former involved a change of form, the latter a change of place. This doctrine was affirmed in Hammer v. Dagenhart[qv] (247 U. S. 251, 1918), in which the Court declared unconstitutional a child-labor act based on the commerce clause, and in Bailey v. Drexel Furniture Company[qv] (259 U. S. 20, 1922), in which it declared unconstitutional an act of similar purpose based on the tax power. It followed precedent in one recent minimum-wage case, and then abandoned the reinforced precedent in a third decision, handed down within a year's time. The original decision, Adkins v. Children's Hospital[qv] (261 U. S. 525, 1923), declared invalid a District of Columbia law, on the ground that it violated the worker's freedom of contract. Thirteen years later, relying largely on precedent, it declared invalid a New York law, carefully drafted in the effort to avoid the objections which the Court had raised to the first law (Morehead v. New York, 298 U. S. 587, 1936). The following year it upheld a very similar Washington statute in West Coast Hotel Company v. Parrish[qv] (300 U. S. 379, 1937). It thus appears that the decisions of the Court in a given type of case depend not only upon precedent, but upon the personnel of the Court at the time, existing conditions, the trend of public opinion and other factors.

[Charles K. Burdick, *The Law of the American Constitution;* Albert Kocourek and Harold Koven, Renovation of the Common Law through *Stare Decisis*, in *Illinois Law Review*, April, 1935; Andrew C. McLaughlin, *Constitutional History of the United States;* Burke Shartel, *Stare Decisis*—a Practical View, in *Journal of the American Judicature Society*, June, 1933; James B. Thayer, *Legal Essays;* W. W. Willoughby, *Constitutional Law of the United States.*]

W. BROOKE GRAVES

Stars, The Falling of the (Nov. 12, 13, 1833), was the most sublime heavenly phenomenon in American history. At about eleven o'clock in the evening, eastern time, the number of falling meteors began to attract attention. The meteors descended as numerous as snowflakes in the most severe storm and with lightning speed. At Niagara Falls a luminous table appeared above the falls emitting streams of fire. At Fort Leavenworth, Kans., soldiers could read ordinary print at the darkest hour of night. Sailors far out on the Atlantic and trappers in the Rockies as far as man had ventured reported the spectacular display. Many religious people interpreted the phenomenon as a sign of the end of the world. The meteoric storm continued until it was rendered invisible by the light of day.

[Denison Olmstead in *American Journal of Science*, Vol. XV, pp. 363 ff.]

EVERETT DICK

Stars and Bars. *See* Confederate Flag, The.

Stars and Stripes. *See* Flag of the United States.

Starved Rock, which rises abruptly 125 feet above the river level, is located on the south side of the Illinois River nearly opposite the town of Utica in LaSalle County. Three sides of the rock, the top surface of which approximates an acre, are almost sheer; on the fourth side the ascent is difficult. Near the rock Jolliet and Marquette found the Great Village of the Illinois[qv] in 1673; on it LaSalle and Tonti erected Fort St. Louis[qv] in 1682–83.

Known to French explorers simply as *le rocher,* Starved Rock received its present name from a tradition to the effect that about 1770 a band of Illinois Indians was besieged on its summit by tribal enemies, starved into submission and then exterminated. No evidence to support the tradition is known to exist, but the story is popularly believed and cherished.

[Sauer, Cady and Cowles, *Starved Rock State Park and Its Environs;* Francis Parkman, *LaSalle and the Discovery of the Great West.*]

PAUL M. ANGLE

"Starving Time" is the term used to refer to the food shortage at Jamestown[qv] in the spring of 1609. There was a similar shortage of food at Plymouth in the spring of 1622. The Jamestown starving time was relieved by the arrival of a ship from England, that at Plymouth by the arrival of a fishing vessel via Virginia.

[L. G. Tyler, *England in America;* Wm. Bradford, *History of Plymouth Plantation.*]

MATTHEW PAGE ANDREWS

State, Department of. Before the Constitution[qv], control of the foreign relations of the United States was exercised by the Congress, meeting at first under no written agreement, and from March 1, 1781, under the Articles of Confederation[qv]. Subject to that control, the management of foreign affairs was from time to time in the hands of committees of Congress. The Department of Foreign Affairs and the office of Secretary for Foreign Affairs were created on Jan. 10, 1781. The first Secretary for Foreign Affairs was Robert R. Livingston, who served from Oct. 20, 1781, until June 4, 1783. His successor was John Jay, who took office on Dec. 21, 1784; during the remaining period of the Articles of Confederation Jay was Secretary for Foreign Affairs; and, after the setting up of the Government under the Constitution (March 4,

1789), he continued to act in a similar capacity, though without further appointment, until Thomas Jefferson, who was commissioned as the first Secretary of State on Sept. 26, 1789, took office on March 22, 1790.

At the first session of the first Congress under the Constitution (March 4 to Sept. 29, 1789) three executive departments were established: Foreign Affairs, War and Treasury. The act of July 27, 1789, which created the Department of Foreign Affairs, is still the organic law of the Department of State. The head or principal officer of the Department is thereby charged to "perform and execute such duties as shall from time to time be enjoined on or intrusted to him by the President of the United States, agreeable to the Constitution, relative to correspondence . . . or to such other matters respecting foreign affairs, as the President of the United States shall assign to the said department."

During that session of Congress it was proposed to establish a Home Department for the conduct of numerous domestic affairs the administration of which was obviously and admittedly essential; but the sentiment of Congress was against the creation of a fourth executive department, chiefly on the ground of expense; so there followed the act of Sept. 15, 1789, which changed the name of the Department of Foreign Affairs to Department of State and the title of Secretary for Foreign Affairs to Secretary of State.

The result was that the Department of State for some decades administered all "home affairs" except those under the jurisdiction of the War Department, the Treasury and the Postmaster General[qqv]. The Territories, the Patent Office and the Censuses[qqv] up to and including that of 1840 were among the many domestic responsibilities of the Department of State. It may properly be said that, at least until the establishment of the Department of the Interior[qv] in 1849, and to some degree even thereafter, the Secretary of State was secretary for foreign affairs and for home affairs.

Some few domestic matters still remain within the Department of State, such as publication of the Statutes at Large, and the certification of amendments[qv] to the Constitution; and the Secretary of State has certain duties in connection with electoral votes; but all these are now relatively insignificant; the essential function of the Department of State is the conduct of the foreign affairs of the United States under the direction of the President.

The Secretary of State is the ranking member of the President's Cabinet and is first in the presidential succession after the Vice-President; he has the custody of the Seal of the United States[qv]; he is *ex officio* a member of the Governing Board of the Pan American Union[qv], and Chairman of the National Munitions Control Board; and he is also a member of the National Emergency Council.

When Jefferson took office as first Secretary of State, the staff of the Department consisted of five clerks; there were two diplomatic agents of the United States abroad and only four foreign governments were represented in the United States.

The growth of the Department was slow; in 1820 the personnel came to only fifteen; and the early organizational history of the Department is one of insufficiency, both at the capital and abroad. Instances are not lacking of the sending of original papers to the Senate for want of copies; documents in foreign languages were left untranslated; American diplomats often had to pen their own despatches; answers thereto were delayed or even omitted; Secretary of State Clayton could write in 1850 that he hoped his successor would have enough clerical assistance to enable him not to be a slave; and until 1853 when the office of Assistant Secretary of State was created, the ranking officer in the Department under the Secretary was the Chief Clerk.

Thereafter there was a turn toward betterment of conditions, and, beginning with the tenure of Secretary of State Hamilton Fish (1869–77), notable improvement.

The vast increase in the influence, power and activities of the United States in world affairs, dating from events of 1898, and, more importantly, from 1914, necessarily multiplied times over the work of the Department of State at Washington and of the foreign service abroad, and brought corresponding recasting of organization.

At the present time the officers of the Department whose appointments by the President require confirmation by the Senate are the Secretary, the Undersecretary, the Counselor, three Assistant Secretaries of State and the Legal Adviser. Under various titles there are advisers to the Secretary on political, economic and other questions; in general the organization of the Department is by divisions, offices and bureaus, each with a chief; of these there are more than thirty. Four of the divisions called "regional" (European, Far Eastern, Near Eastern and American Republics) are concerned with relations with foreign countries; and among the varied charges of other divisions may be mentioned treaties, trade agreements, arms and munitions control, Philippine affairs and international conferences. The total personnel of the Department (1940) is about 1020.

Strictly, the foreign service[qv] of the United States is distinct from the Department of State; but realistically the two are a unit in the conduct of foreign affairs.

There were secret agents of the Continental Congress[qv] in Europe before July 4, 1776. The earliest commissions to diplomatic officers of the United States were two issued on Sept. 28, 1776; one of these was to Benjamin Franklin, the first American diplomat in more senses than one. A consul in France was appointed in 1781 and one at Canton in 1786.

The number of diplomatic and consular representatives abroad naturally augmented with increasing foreign interests and foreign commerce. The list includes many famous and notable Americans; and there are instances of long tenure; one consul at Naples, for example, served continuously from 1809 to 1861; but under the spoils system[qv] turnover in office and political misfits not infrequently gave our consular service a bad name; the evil was recognized and obviated by placing the consular service on a merit basis in 1906.

Since the Rogers Act of May 24, 1924, the foreign service has been a conjoined staff of both diplomatic and consular officers. Below the grade of minister, officials of the foreign service may be appointed as diplomatic or as consular officers or as both, or may be assigned for a limited period to serve in the Department of State; entry into the foreign service, except for an occasional transfer from the Department, is limited to those who are successful in stiff written and oral examinations (from the former, foreign service clerks are exempt after five years); and promotion is, by statute, on the basis of merit. Moreover, in the grades of ambassador and minister nearly half the present incumbents are career men.

There are now (1940) fifty-six American diplomatic missions to fifty-eight countries; of the chiefs of those missions, twenty have the rank of Ambassador[qv] and the others (with two exceptions, one Minister Resident and Consul General and one Diplomatic Agent and Consul General) that of Envoy Extraordinary[qv] and Minister Plenipotentiary. Of the fifty-six diplomatic missions, thirty-five perform consular as well as diplomatic duties. The number of consular offices is 250, including twenty-five agencies; and the total staff of the foreign service, including clerks and employees of all kinds, is some 4127.

The Department of State is the oldest of the executive departments; it is also the smallest; the annual appropriation for the Department of State is less than one fourth of 1% of the national budget.

[Publications of the Department of State, particularly *The Department of State of the United States;* Gaillard Hunt, *The Department of State of the United States, Its History and Functions;* Tracy H. Lay, *The Foreign Service of the United States;* Graham Stuart, *American Diplomatic and Consular Practice;* Wilbur J. Carr, The American Consular Service, in *American Journal of International Law*, Vol. I, No. 4.]

HUNTER MILLER

State-aid Plan in the Good Roads Movement. The term "state-aid" may be used with reference to grants paid by the Federal Government to the states, or with reference to grants paid by the states to their political subdivisions. Both types of grant have affected the movement for good roads. In the first, there is a matching of Federal grants by the states, in a prescribed ratio, and Federal supervision and control over the use of the whole amount. When the first Federal Aid Road Act was passed in 1916 (*see* Rural Post Roads Act), sixteen states had no functioning highway departments. As a result of this and subsequent acts such departments were soon established, and they have grown steadily in importance. The grants were long made on a fifty-fifty basis, but the terms have been more generous to the states in recent years, because of the value of highway projects as public works to which the unemployed might be assigned.

In the second type, aid has been extended by states to local units in several different ways: by the state incorporating, in the state system, certain highways which otherwise would remain as county or township roads; by the state assuming responsibility for the maintenance of rural roads; by direct state appropriations for road purposes to local units; by agreements between the state and local units affecting distribution of receipts from the liquid fuels tax.

[V. O. Key, *The Administration of Federal Grants to States;* Austin F. Macdonald, *Federal Aid;* Henry J. Bitterman, *State and Federal Grants-in-Aid.*]

W. BROOKE GRAVES

State Bank of Indiana, THE, was created in 1834 as a closely organized federation of banks under control of a central board at Indianapolis. The central board had power to fix the rate of dividend, make inspections, control issues and order receiverships. Each of the ten branches originally established was mutually liable for the debts of the whole system and a minimum fund was required to be reserved from profits as a surplus. The state owned one half of the stock and elected the president and some members of the central board.

On account of the soundness of basic principles and conservative management, this institution was one of the few successful state banks of the period. By limitation of its charter it went into a two-year liquidation period in 1857 and expired in 1859. It had withstood the panics of 1837 and 1857[qqv], however, paid high dividends and turned over to the common-school fund several millions of dollars.

[L. C. Helderman, *National and State Banks: A Study of their Origins.*] LEONARD C. HELDERMAN

State Banking. State investment in banks was common before the Panic of 1837[qv]. Sometimes the state was sole owner, as in South Carolina, more commonly it was part owner, as in Indiana (*see* South Carolina, The State Bank of; State Bank of Indiana). State ownership was due to the speculative mania of the period. The idea was frequent that bank profits would lead to abolition of taxes. In some cases the ventures were profitable, in others they were disastrous.

In Illinois, where the state owned $3,600,000 of stock, there was failure, and in 1843 divorce of bank and state. In Mississippi, Arkansas and Florida, where the investment was nearly $12,000,000, the result was repudiation of a debt which has never been paid (*see* Repudiation of State Debts). In Louisiana, where the bonds issued to aid banks amounted to $19,000,000, there was collapse and reform under the Specie Reserve System of 1842 (*see* Louisiana, Specie Reserve, Banking System).

Among the successful state-owned banks, the State Bank of Missouri was the most important. It continued in operation through the panics of 1837 and 1857 and in 1862, when it entered the national system (*see* Banks, National) as a private bank, the state sold its stock for a premium. The State Bank of Indiana passed through the panics and emerged in 1857, when its charter expired, with a net profit to the state of over $2,000,000, still the basis of the school fund. The Bank of the State of South Carolina also withstood the panics and continued through the Civil War as one of the strongest institutions in the country.

Whether banks were sound or wildcat[qv] did not depend on whether they were privately or publicly owned. Rather, it depended on conservatism of management and legal regulation. In general, however, banking became private after the Panic of 1837.

[L. C. Helderman, *National and State Banks: A Study of Their Origins.*] LEONARD C. HELDERMAN

State Banks, chartered by states but privately owned, existed from the early national period. The earliest type were those with special legislative charters. Except for a few "perpetual charter banks" these usually had charters expiring in twenty years. This type was superseded in the Jacksonian period by banks chartered under general incorporation laws—the "free banks." Occasionally large banks with branches and closely supervised by a general board were chartered by special act.

Before the Panic of 1837[qv] only two states had achieved any degree of uniformity. In Massachusetts the Suffolk System[qv], centering in the Suffolk Bank of Boston, came into effective operation in 1825. This became the most important system in New England before the National Bank Act (*see* Banks, National). The system was entirely extralegal. With a common fund of $300,000, the Suffolk Bank and other large Boston banks bought up the notes of country banks and presented them for specie redemption. Clearing country notes daily, they forced country banks to keep large deposits and redemption balances in Boston. This system operated effectively until 1858 when it was superseded by the Bank of Mutual Redemption organized by country banks to perform the same service.

The first important legally organized system was the New York Safety-Fund system[qv] of 1829. Supervised by a central board, all member banks contributed to a fund equal to 3% of their capital. This fund was used to pay the debts of insolvent banks. The fund proved inadequate for both deposit and note liability and was superseded by the bond-security principle of the Free Bank System of 1838[qv]. The safety-fund principle exerted no influence on the National Bank System but was adopted by Canada in 1890.

Another type of legally organized systems was the Louisiana Specie Reserve System of 1842[qv]. In 1845 Ohio adopted a system with principles drawn from Louisiana, New York, Massachusetts and Indiana, and her banks were of unusual strength. In 1855 Indiana created the Bank of the State (not to be confused with the State Bank of Indiana described above), a specially chartered institution under close supervision of a central board. It was from the presidency of this bank that Hugh McCulloch came to Washington as first Comptroller under the National Banking System.

[L. C. Helderman, *National and State Banks: A Study of Their Origins.*] LEONARD C. HELDERMAN

State Birds, Flowers, Mottoes, Names, Nicknames, Songs and Trees. State emblems such as birds, flowers, songs and trees must be adopted officially by action of the legislative bodies of the respective states to which they belong before one properly may designate them as such.

Twenty-two of the states have official state avian emblems. The thirteen birds adopted and the state or states having selected each are as follows: Alabama, the yellowhammer; Arizona, the cactus wren; Arkansas, Florida, Tennessee and Texas, the mockingbird; California, the California valley quail; Colorado, the lark bunting; Idaho, the mountain bluebird; Illinois, Indiana, Ohio and Kentucky, the cardinal; Iowa and New Jersey, the eastern goldfinch; Maine, the chickadee; Michigan, the robin redbreast; Missouri, the bluebird; Montana, Nebraska and Wyoming, the western meadow lark; and Pennsylvania, the ruffed grouse.

Forty-one states have official state flowers. With few exceptions, these floral emblems are indigenous to the states which have selected them. The state flower of Ohio, the scarlet carnation, a cultivated plant, was adopted as "a token of love and reverence for the memory" of President William McKinley because he loved that flower more than he did any other. Tennessee has two floral emblems: the passion flower, or the wild apricot, and the iris, the latter being a cultivated flower. The following states have no official state floral emblems: Delaware, Mississippi, New York, North Carolina, Rhode Island, Washington and Wisconsin.

The state mottoes are expressed in seven languages; namely, American Indian, English, French, Greek, Italian, Latin and Spanish. The motto of the State of Washington is the American Indian word, *Alki,* signifying By and bye. Twenty-six states have mottoes delineated in the English language. The French language supplied the motto of Minnesota, *L'Etoile du Nord,* meaning The Star of the North. The Greek word, *Eureka,* is the motto of California. One of the mottoes of Maryland is the Italian statement, *Fatti Maschii, Parole Feminine,* signifying Deeds are males, words are females. Twenty-three states have Latin mottoes. Most of these were taken from standard classical Latin writers. Arkansas, Missouri, Wisconsin and Wyoming have both an English and a Latin motto. The Spanish phrase, *Oro y Plata,* signifying Gold and Silver, is the motto of Montana. New Hampshire is the only state which has no motto.

The names of the various states were derived from words, roots, stems and suffixes belonging to the eight languages: American, American Indian, Anglo-Saxon, Dutch, French, Greek, Latin and Spanish. The number of state names supplied by each is as follows: American, one; American Indian, twenty-six; Anglo-Saxon, one; Dutch, one; French, three; Greek, one; Latin, eleven and Spanish, four.

Georgia, Louisiana, Maryland, North Carolina, South Carolina, Virginia and West Virginia were named after kings and queens. Delaware, The District of Columbia, New York, Pennsylvania and Washington were named after noted personages other than kings and queens. British localities supplied the names of New Hampshire and New Jersey.

Each of the states has one sobriquet or more. The inhabitants of forty-four of the states also have nicknames; but the people of Montana, North Dakota, South Dakota and Wyoming have no sobriquets. New Jersey has nine nicknames and Kansas has eight. Four other states have seven; nine have six; fourteen have five; nine have four; two have three; eight have two and The District of Columbia has one.

Alabama, Arizona, Arkansas, Colorado, Delaware, Florida, Georgia, Idaho, Illinois, Indiana, Iowa, Kentucky, Louisiana, Maryland, Nevada, New Mexico, North Carolina, Oklahoma, Oregon, Tennessee, Texas, Virginia and Washington, each has an officially adopted state song.

Six states have adopted trees officially; namely, Idaho, the white pine; Illinois, the native oak; Indiana, the tulip tree; Oklahoma, the red bud; Pennsylvania, the hemlock; and Texas, the pecan.

[George Earlie Shankle, *State Names, Flags, Seals, Songs, Birds, Flowers and Other Symbols.*]

GEORGE EARLIE SHANKLE

State Boundary Disputes. *See* Boundary Disputes between the States.

State Chairman is the chairman of the state committee of a political party. The committee itself is now subject to statutory regulation in most states, and in a half dozen states the chairman is given a special position by being elected independently of the committee, by the state convention, by the party nominees, or at the party primary. In most states, however, he is chosen by the state committee from its own membership, and acts for the committee in raising money, organizing party campaigns and managing party affairs. The position carries with it a great deal of political prestige and sometimes important patronage.

[Edward M. Sait, *American Parties and Elections;* C. N. Fortenberry, Legal Regulation of Political Party Organization in the United States, a manuscript deposited in University of Illinois Library.]

CLARENCE A. BERDAHL

State Constitutions. The precipitate departure of royal governors, the flight of royal councillors and the acceptance of responsibility for government by revolutionary conventions, congresses or assemblies inaugurated a period of intensive constitution-making in the original states (*see* Revolutionary Committees). During the years 1776–80 every state but Connecticut and Rhode Island provided itself with a new instrument of government. These two states possessed royal charters which were democratic in form and which were deemed by their people adequate to their needs. The Continental Congress[qv] when asked by several colonies to advise on procedure adopted a resolution presented by John Adams urging those colonies which had no adequate governments to form them.

The first two documents, those of New Hampshire and South Carolina, were hastily drawn. The former became effective Jan. 5, 1776, and the latter on March 26. Virginia and New Jersey also acted prior to the Declaration of Independence, but prepared constitutions which were carefully drawn and designed to serve as permanent bases of government. The Virginia document was adopted June 29 and New Jersey's Provincial Congress directed the drafting of a constitution by a resolution adopted on June 21. The Declaration of Independence[qv] hastened action in the remaining states. Before the end of the year, work on the new documents was completed in Delaware, Maryland and Pennsylvania. But New York, Georgia and North Carolina, due to war conditions, did not complete their constitutions until 1777. Massachusetts kept its colonial charter until 1780 when a constitution, drafted by the first body which could rightfully be called a constitutional convention, was approved by the people.

The work of constitution-making was done by the revolutionary legislatures in South Carolina, Virginia and New Jersey. In seven other states special elections were held for the choice of members of the bodies which were to draft the instruments of government. But in every case these groups were also to act as legislative bodies. None of these ten earliest constitutions was submitted to a vote of the people. They were all put into effect immediately after their approval by the bodies which drafted them.

In drafting the first state constitutions the outstanding men in each state took part. Loyalists[qv] were excluded but the patriot group had in every state distinguished leadership. Many of these men were well read in English history and law and in the political theory then current. John Adams, Thomas Paine and others stated their views on constitution-making in pamphlets which enjoyed a wide circulation. Those documents first prepared, such as that of Virginia, exerted a profound influence on the form and contents of all which followed.

The sources of the details on which the first state governments were based are numerous. The most important, of course, were the colonial charters[qv]. No state made any violent changes in the form of government to which it had become accustomed as a colony. In the main only those changes were made which were necessary to adapt familiar institutions to the conditions resulting from the separation from the English crown. For example, Pennsylvania and Georgia, which had used unicameral legislatures before 1776, were the only two states to insert provisions for such legislative bodies in their first constitutions.

Besides the colonial charters, there were a number of colonial documents, such as the Mayflower Compact and the Fundamental Orders of Connecticut[qqv], which formed links in the chain of state constitutional development. The works of the then recent and contemporary writers on politics were carefully read by many of the members of the constitution-drafting bodies. That they were familiar with the works of John Locke, Jean Jacques Rousseau, the Baron Montesquieu, Aristotle, Plato and Polybius there seems little reason to doubt. Most of them were educated men in a day when education and the classics were synonymous.

The form of organization then used in the Established Church also played its part in suggesting machinery for the new states. The determination to separate church and state was not so strong as to prevent an appreciation of the benefits of experience in the development of successful governmental forms. The church had had such experience, and it was close to the people. In contrast, the government of the mother country itself suggested few desirable points. Only in the realm of local government was there much borrowing from English precedents. And here, much of the copying had occurred long before the constitutions were formed. It was not surprising that the colonists could see little good in the governmental institutions which had precipitated the conflict in which they then found themselves.

But their love of liberty and their fierce desire to establish a government which should perpetuate that freedom for which they fought not only to themselves but to their children's children led them to consult in the preparation of their bills of rights that series of milestones in English history including Magna Carta[qv] (1215), the Petition of Right (1628), the Habeas Corpus Act (1679), the English Bill of Rights (1689), and others which marked out the rights of Englishmen against arbitrary action by their government. (*See* Common Law.)

The constitutions thus prepared and promulgated did not long endure. Some of the earlier ones, which had been hastily drawn, were soon revised. The Federal Constitution drafted in 1787 had a profound effect and served as a model. Pennsylvania and Georgia abandoned their unicameral legislatures for bodies on the Federal pattern. Connecticut found it necessary in 1818 to prepare a state constitution to take the place of her royal charter. Rhode Island kept her charter until 1842, but it had become so obsolete that it caused a rebellion (*see* Dorr's Rebellion) before it was changed. Of the original thirteen states only Massachusetts has avoided the necessity of wholesale revision of her constitution. Her 1780 document, while extensively amended, still serves her. In every other case one or several complete revisions have been required although, on each occasion, many of the articles and sections of the old document were carried forward.

The influence of the constitutions of the original states upon those which have been admitted to the Union since 1789 has been extensive. A favorite method of constitution drafting on the frontier was to assemble a collection of the earlier constitutions and select articles and sections without too much regard to experience with the provision chosen. It is small wonder that extensive tinkering with state constitutions has been a continuous necessity.

The rise of Jacksonian democracy[qv] was the occasion for much constitutional change. The earlier states entered the union with a strong legislature. The governor and judges were chosen by the legislative body. In only one of the original states, Massachusetts, was the governor given a veto. Today only one, North Carolina, denies it. The period from 1820 to 1840 saw the adoption of many new state constitutions in which a separately elected executive and elected judges established for the first time a basis for a separation of powers. A long list of elected executive officers in addition to the governor was also provided at that time. A voting privilege which began in the manhood suffrage limited by property qualifications has been modified by numerous amendments and revisions to the present near-universal form (*see* Franchise, The).

The Civil War led to a new wave of constitution writing. New social and economic conditions in the Southern states led to new constitutions during the period of the war and reconstruction[qv]. In many cases there were as many as three attempts at the framing of new documents before the Southern states could win readmission to representation in Congress. This period left its scars, which can be seen today.

Since 1870 state constitutional development has proceeded without spectacular spurts. The principal changes have lain first in the increasing suspicion of state legislatures, leading to denial by the people of the power to pass special legislation and later to a considerable lengthening of the constitutional documents, removing more and more subjects from legislative competence. A second tendency has been toward greater democracy in local government through constitutional grants to the residents of cities of the right to frame, adopt and amend their own city charters. Third, may be noted a gradual assumption by the people of the right to propose legislation through the initiative[qv] or to have legislation passed by the legislature referred to popular vote through the referendum[qv]. Even constitutional amendments have been opened to initiative in fourteen states.

New inventions, changed social conditions, a world war and many other factors have required constant adaptation of state constitutions to new situations. The greater detail of state constitutional documents makes frequent changes even more necessary than in the Federal sphere. This development occurs in several ways. The most obvious is through the process of formal amendment. Three methods exist in the states for the initiation of formal changes: proposal by the legislature; constitutional conventions; and the initiative. In every state but Delaware such proposals require approval by popular vote. A second method of change is through judicial interpretation. This is not as important in the states as in the Federal Government, as state constitutions are limitations of power and are strictly construed. A third method of constitutional elaboration is by statute. Many provisions of state constitutions are not self-executing and hence require enabling legislation before they can be put into effect. And finally, state constitutions are expanded through custom and usage. These devices enable our states to continue, over long periods of time, to use constitutions which otherwise would be quickly outgrown.

[Allan Nevins, *The American States during and after the Revolution, 1775-1789;* W. C. Webster, *State Consti-*

tutions of the American Revolution, Annals of the American Academy, 1897; Harvey Walker, *Law Making in the United States*.]

HARVEY WALKER

State Debts, except for issues of paper money, were unimportant until the 1820's. The first funded debts were incurred in a wave of borrowing touched off by New York's success in financing the Erie Canal*qv*, completed in 1825. Immediately thereafter Maryland, Pennsylvania, Ohio and other states embarked upon programs of canal and, a little later, railroad building*qqv*. Several Southern states borrowed heavily to establish banks (*see* State Banking). Borrowing was general except in New England, Georgia and North Carolina. Aided by a widespread demand for transportation facilities, a period of prosperity, and state bank inflation, the states, by 1839, had borrowed, mostly from Europe, over $175,000,000, of which $60,000,000 were for canals, $53,000,000 for railroads and $43,000,000 for banks. In the ensuing depression eight states and one territory (Florida) with debts of approximately $122,000,000 defaulted. After trying various financial expedients, the defaulting states, except Arkansas, Florida, Michigan and Mississippi, which repudiated their debts in whole or in part, levied additional taxes to pay their debts (*see* Repudiation of State Debts). Interest payments were resumed in 1845–48. Soon thereafter the defaulting states began to dispose of their canal and railroad holdings, taking heavy losses.

As a result of these experiences nineteen states, before the Civil War, amended their constitutions to curb the borrowing power of their legislatures. A second wave of borrowing started about 1850; Missouri, North Carolina, Tennessee and Virginia borrowed more than $80,000,000, mainly for railroads. The gross debts of all states in 1860 was $257,406,950.

During the Civil War, Northern states borrowed, mainly for the payment of bounties*qv*, over $100,000,000, while the war debts of Southern states, partly in paper money, were almost as great. The Southern debts were repudiated at the end of the war (*see* Confederate Debt). During Reconstruction*qv*, debts approximating $110,000,000 were imposed upon Southern states, largely on the pretext of aiding railroads. The bonds were sold far below par, some as low as 15 or 20 cents on the dollar. When native white rule was re-established (*see* Home Rule, Restoration of) these debts were either repudiated or drastically scaled down; some prewar debts were also reduced. The principal amount of such repudiations and scalings was near $120,000,000. In the North, Minnesota repudiated $5,000,000 of bonds, but later recognized their validity and made a compromise settlement. After the war states—other than those in the South—reduced their debts steadily. From a peak of over $350,000,000, the total of all state debts was reduced to a low point of about $225,000,000 in the early 1890's. New York completely repaid a debt of over $30,000,000. Just before 1900 another borrowing movement began, this time for canals and highways. New York converted the Erie into a barge canal (*see* New York Barge Canal) at a cost, to 1916, of $118,000,000. California, Maryland, Massachusetts and New York owed over $105,000,000 for highways in 1916 (*see* Roads). The total of net state debts was then $465,139,000.

After the World War the states began borrowing, principally for highways and for bonuses*qv* to World War veterans, on a scale never before approached. For the years 1919–36 the total borrowed was over $3,500,000,000 of which $1,590,000,000 was for highways and $440,000,000 for bonuses or loans to veterans. Three states—Minnesota, North Dakota and South Dakota—borrowed some $225,000,000 for rural credit systems, which have produced heavy losses. Borrowing for unemployment relief*qv*, begun in 1932, amounted to $438,000,000. The net debts of all states amounted to $935,544,000 in 1922, $2,360,958,000 in 1932 and $3,117,000,000 in 1936. New York was first in 1936 with $485,000,000. With four others—Illinois, California, Arkansas and Louisiana in the order named—it accounted for 47% of the total. The ten states (New York, Illinois, California, Arkansas, Louisiana, North Carolina, Pennsylvania, Missouri, New Jersey and Minnesota) with debts of over $100,000,000 owed 70% of the total.

In the depression beginning with 1929 several states had difficulties with debts but only one defaulted. In 1927 Arkansas began an ambitious program of borrowing for highways, state institutions and pensions for Confederate veterans. By 1932 the debt amounted to $160,000,000 and in 1933 the state defaulted. In 1934 the debt was refunded and payments were resumed. The state in 1936 had the highest per capita net debt—approximately $80—and also the largest debt in relation to wealth and income of any state in the Union. Other states with heavy debts in relation to resources were: Louisiana, North Carolina, South Dakota and West Virginia.

Constitutional debt limitations have been extended until now they are found in all except seven states. In eighteen states debts can be incurred only by constitutional amendment, while in seventeen others proposals to borrow must be approved by a referendum vote. In the remaining six states legislatures borrow within limits established by constitutions.

The latest development, primarily to evade constitutional debt limitations, has been extensive borrowing by state institutions, commissions and special authorities. These agencies sell revenue bonds which are not obligations of the state and use the proceeds to build bridges, buildings and highways. The bonds are serviced from fees, tolls and other revenues collected by the agencies and from special state taxes. The courts have generally held that such debts are not covered by constitutional limitations. The next wave of state borrowing may develop along this line.

[Henry C. Adams, *Public Debts;* Reginald C. McGrane, *Foreign Bondholders and American State Debts;* Evans Clark, ed., *The Internal Debts of the United States;* John F. Fowler, *Revenue Bonds;* Edna Trull, *Borrowing for Highways*, and *The Resources and Debts of the Forty-eight States.*]

B. U. RATCHFORD

State Fairs. The first state fair of continued existence was held in Syracuse, N. Y., in 1841. By 1860 eighteen states had established fairs. Permanent sites near urban centers were the rule by 1900. In 1937 thirty-four state fairs were held, the largest being Minnesota with 635,000 in attendance. At the second largest, Wisconsin, 240,000 glasses of milk and 360,000 of beer were sold. This fair is exceptional in two respects: it pays its own way and it has abolished the midway. State fairs have aided in improving livestock, popularizing new inventions and providing a gala day on which rural and urban people intermingle. (*See also* County Fairs.)

[W. C. Neely, *The Agricultural Fair;* E. D. Ross, The Evolution of the Agricultural Fair in the Northwest, in *Iowa Journal of History and Politics*, XXIV.]

HARVEY L. CARTER

State Government. The constituent units of the American federal system are popularly known as states. Their government is the product of an evolution whose origins are older than the first state; even older than the first colony or settlement. While there was no exact English counterpart for the governmental units known as states in this country, many of the fundamental principles of state government rest on English models. The bills of rights (*see* Bills of Rights, State) which appear in each state constitution are direct descendants of the Magna Carta[qv], the Petition of Right and the writings of 17th and 18th century British political philosophers. The judicial system, with its primary reliance on the justice of the peace, the sheriff and the coroner as local representatives of the law, is traceable to British patterns. The reliance by the new states on the integrity of legislative assemblies, popularly chosen, was a reflection of the growing power of the House of Commons *vis à vis* the crown. Even French and Dutch influences may be noted. The writings of Montesquieu were known to the architects of the new states and they played an important role in the construction of the governmental theory of the Revolutionary period. But perhaps the most pervasive and long-continued influence was that afforded by the charters granted to the powerful trading companies[qv] which were authorized to carry on commerce with America and, incidentally, to colonize and to govern any colonies which were deemed necessary to facilitate this trade.

The Virginia colony received a charter in 1621 which was virtually a counterpart of the charter of the Virginia Company of 1609[qqv]. Massachusetts Bay[qv] was governed during its early years under a royal charter issued primarily for the promotion of commerce. As the populations of the colonies grew and the king began to realize how important it was to retain a control over them, many of the charters which had been granted to proprietors were revoked and instruments of government were issued direct from the crown. Royal governors[qv] emulated in the colonies the petty tyrannies and royal prerogatives of their master.

With the outbreak of the American Revolution[qv] the royal governors fled. The legislative bodies were purged of loyalists[qv] and the remaining members carried on the government and prosecuted the war. On the recommendation of the Continental Congress[qv] each state but Connecticut and Rhode Island drafted a new constitution. The two states mentioned merely repudiated the authority of the king and continued under their colonial charters as state constitutions. They were already more democratic than those of most of the other colonies. The constitutions framed by the other eleven states made few changes in the institutional life of the people. Only such alterations were made as were necessary to make the processes of government democratic, as the selection of the governor and council (formerly nominated by the crown) and the introduction of a theory known as the separation of powers[qv]. Strangely enough, the legislature was in most states given power to select both governor and judges, thus negating any effort at real division of authority.

The states which were erected as a result of

the successful revolt against British rule were bound together by their own consent first into a confederation under the Articles[qv] (1783–89) and later into a federal state under the Constitution[qv] (effective 1789). To the original thirteen states, thirty-five have been added. The constitutions of these new states have been copied in large part from the instruments framed by the original states, either directly or indirectly (*see* State Constitutions). This has tended to create in the United States a system of state government which displays remarkable uniformity. Each state has a governor, now popularly elected, an independent judiciary and a popularly chosen legislative body. In every state but Nebraska (which has but one house) the legislature consists of two houses and their concurrence is required in the making of law. In every state but North Carolina a law must be approved by the governor.

Under the Constitution (Amendment X) "the powers not delegated to the United States by the Constitution nor prohibited by it to the states, are reserved to the states respectively, or to the people." This has the effect of saving to the states a vast domain of responsibility which is reflected in their ever-increasing administrative tasks. The growing complexity of state governmental structure is reflected in increasing detail in constitutions. Also the people seem to be evidencing a distrust of state legislative bodies which leads to more prohibitions on their actions. There is a trend toward centralization[qv] of authority in the National Government, largely fostered by the power over the purse. But a large domain still remains for cultivation by the states.

[W. B. Graves, *State Government and Administration in the United States;* A. W. Bromage, *State Government in the United States.*] HARVEY WALKER

State Governments, Council of the. *See* New England Council.

State Laws, Uniform. The movement for uniform state legislation began in 1889 when, under the leadership of the American Bar Association, the National Conference of Commissioners on Uniform State Laws was organized. Since that time the progress of the movement has been steady but slow, and in view of the great need, grossly inadequate. The efforts of the Conference have been supplemented by those of numerous other agencies, most of them working in specialized fields.

At the first conference, nine states were repre-

TABLE I

Section	Name	Number of Acts Proposed	Total Number of Adoptions
I	Commercial	11	192
II	Property	10	108
III	Public Laws	12	101
IV	Social Welfare	7	35
V	Corporations	3	4
VI	Torts and Criminal Laws	9	99
VII	Civil Procedure	16	165
	Totals	68	704

TABLE II

Number	Name	Year Proposed	Section	Adoptions
1	Bills of Lading Act	1909	I	29
2	Limited Partnership Act	1916	I	20
3	Sales Act	1906	I	34
4	Warehouse Receipts Act	1906	I	48
5	Negotiable Instruments Act	1896	II	53
6	Stock Transfer Act	1909	II	25
7	Aeronautics Act	1922	III	22
8	Narcotic Drug Act	1932	VI	27
9	Declaratory Judgments Act	1922	VII	25
10	Proof of Statutes Act	1920	VII	25
11	Veterans' Guardianship Act	1928	VII	33
	Total			341

sented; since 1912, all the states, territories, and the District of Columbia have been regularly and officially represented. The Conference is composed of three commissioners from each state, chosen usually by the governor, from the legal profession, to serve without compensation. An elaborate organization of regular and special committees has been developed; these are concerned with a wide variety of subjects coming within the jurisdiction of the state governments. Two short tables are presented for the purpose of indicating, in a general way, the scope and nature of the subject matter considered by the Conference. In the first table are listed the seven sections into which the Conference has been divided, the number of uniform acts proposed by each, as of 1936, and the number of adoptions of these acts, as of the same year. In the second table are listed the eleven acts of the Conference which have received twenty or more adoptions each, together with the number of the section sponsoring each act, the year of its submission, and the number of adoptions as of 1936.

It thus appears that the commercial acts and those relating to matters of civil procedure have been the most successful in securing adoptions. The eleven acts which received twenty or more adoptions each—about one sixth of the total number proposed—account for about one half of the total number of individual adoptions. Other organizations active in furthering uniformity, in one way or another, include the American Law Institute, the American Legislators Association, the Council of State Governments and associated organizations and various other public and private groups. Among the former are the nationwide groups of state officers in the various administrative departments.

[Emerson D. Fite, *Government by Cooperation;* W. Brooke Graves, *Uniform State Action: a Possible Substitute for Centralization*, and Uniform State Regulation and Control of Commerce, in *Harvard Business Review*, Spring, 1936; Richard Hartshorne, Inter-Governmental Cooperation—the Way Out, in *New Jersey Law Review*, January, 1936; John Hemphill, The Uniform Laws Craze, in *American Mercury*, May, 1925; National Conference of Commissioners on Uniform State Laws, *Handbook*, annually; Rodney L. Mott, Uniform Legislation in the United States, in *Annals* of the American Academy of Political and Social Science, January, 1940.]

W. BROOKE GRAVES

State-making Process. The original thirteen states had their origin as colonies of Great Britain and, following their successful war for independence, they formed the original United States of America. The Constitution[qv] of the United States went into effect in 1789 following its ratification by conventions in eleven of the states (*see* Constitution, Ratification of the). North Carolina and Rhode Island were included soon after. The State of Vermont[qv] may possibly be considered as belonging to the same class of original states since its people formed a constitution and declared themselves independent in 1777, and the state was admitted into the Union in 1791 by act of Congress. Kentucky[qv], originally a part of the State of Virginia, was formed into a county of that state in 1776. The people of this district asked Virginia to consent to the creation of a new state. The consent was given in 1789 and Kentucky was admitted as a state in 1792. Also, North Carolina originally included the territory comprising the State of Tennessee[qv]. This latter was transferred to the Union and was admitted as a state in 1796. All creations of states and admissions to the Union were, of course, authorized by act of Congress.

By virtue of the Definitive Treaty of Peace of 1783[qv], with Great Britain, the territory of the United States was extended to the Mississippi River. Further annexations of lands during the succeeding years, such as the purchase of Louisiana[qv] and Florida (*see* Adams–Onís Treaty) and the cessions from Mexico added to this wide extent of national possessions (*see* Guadalupe Hidalgo, Treaty of; Gadsden Purchase). The State of Texas was originally an independent nation from 1836–45 (*see* Texas, Republic of), having successfully won its independence from Mexico. It was annexed to the Union by joint resolution of Congress in 1845 (*see* Texas, Annexation of). With the exception of Texas and the State of Maine[qv] which was separated from Massachusetts in 1820 the remainder of the states were carved out of the public lands (*see* Public Domain) owned by the United States as the result of the various cessions and annexations.

Immediately following the American Revolution the Continental Congress[qv] took the first steps in organizing the then western lands[qv] with a view to preparing the inhabitants for local self-government and organization into territories not only for this purpose but also with the objective of their final admission as states into the Union. The famous "Northwest Ordinance" or "Ordinance for the Government of the Territory of the United States Northwest of the River Ohio," was passed on July 13, 1787 (*see* Ordinances of 1784, 1785 and 1787). It contained three very important provisions: first, there was a grant to the inhabitants of the ter-

State-making Process

ritory of those fundamental political and personal rights which are presumed to be the basis of American liberty; second, there was a statement of a plan for the immediate government of a territory; and third, there was a statement of the policy of the Federal Government with regard to the final status of such a territory. This ordinance was the basis upon which all public lands and even foreign possessions of the United States have been organized in various degrees for their administration during the succeeding one hundred years.

For the immediate government of an organized territory all powers were vested in a governor, a secretary and a court of three judges, all of whom were to be appointed by the Continental Congress. At first there was to be no legislature but the above officials had the authority to adopt and promulgate the laws of the already existing states as they considered them best suited to the needs of the territory. While these laws were to be reported to Congress they were supposed to go into effect unless disallowed by that body. This concentration of executive and legislative power in the same hands was a violation of fundamental American ideas of free government, but was justified on the grounds of temporary expediency. A more complete government was to be substituted as soon as there were five thousand free male inhabitants in any one of the territories, then or in the future to be created. There was to be a legislative body consisting of a house of representatives on a certain arbitrary numerical basis of apportionment and an upper house or council of five members to be chosen by Congress upon nomination of the lower house of the legislature. The governor and legislature under a delegation of power by act of Congress were to pass all laws needed for local government, but there was no provision for a veto by the governor. A further provision required that the two houses of the legislature in joint session should elect a delegate to Congress who should have a seat in that body with a right to participate in debate but no vote. This plan as contained in the Ordinance of 1787 forms the basis upon which has been built up since that time in the various stages of development the system of government for the future states of the United States. The first United States Congress under the new Constitution passed an act on May 26, 1790, which provided that a like plan of government should be created for the Southwest Territory[qv] which lay south of the Ohio River. Ohio, the first state to be founded under the Northwest Ordinance, was admitted to the Union in 1803.

As soon as an organized territory had maintained self-government under these conditions and had grown in population to a position sufficient to justify, in the varying public opinion of the times, its admission as a state, the United States Congress has passed a specific enabling act[qv] under which the people of the territory have chosen delegates to a territorial constitutional convention. The general procedure has been for this convention to draw up a constitution for the prospective state which usually was modeled upon the constitutions of the original or other early states already in the Union (*see* State Constitutions). Upon adjournment of the convention this constitution was submitted to the people of the territory for their ratification and generally has been accepted by them. The prospective state has then applied to Congress for admission to full status in the Union. Congress has usually passed the necessary enabling act and upon a like acceptance by the people and government of the territory a new state has been formally admitted into the Union. When finally admitted, each new state acquires complete equality with all the other states and a like possession of all reserved powers[qv] not specifically delegated to the National Government according to the provisions of the United States Constitution.

In the course of time new problems of social and political importance have arisen and these have on various occasions caused Congress to impose certain restrictions upon the states in the form of mandatory requirements of provisions in their constitutions before an enabling act for their admission is passed. This procedure in reality began in the original provision in the Ordinance of 1787 which forever prohibited slavery within territories soon to be organized. Also, when the Southern states were "readmitted" to the Union in the years following the Civil War, Congress required the inclusion in their respective constitutions of certain provisions, among which the abolition and future prohibition of slavery were the most important.

In illustration of the above may be given the procedure in the admission of Utah[qv] to the Union. Congress refused to pass the enabling act until Utah included in its constitution a provision prohibiting polygamy[qv] within the prospective state, which then was admitted in 1896. Also in 1910 the territories of New Mexico and Arizona were given congressional permission to frame constitutions and apply for admission to the Union. This procedure was completed by the territories within the next year but, due to the inclusion in the proposed Arizona constitution of a provision for the popular recall[qv] of judges, admission of the territories was refused. For political reasons, the case of New Mexico was included with that of Arizona. In the year 1912 the Arizona constitution had been amended to exclude the clause to which there was objection and both states were admitted to the Union. This completed the full number of forty-eight states. Such territories as Hawaii and Alaska and the "insular possessions"[qv] of Puerto Rico have from time to time demanded that the process of admission be applied to them but as yet no real movement for this purpose has been undertaken.

[W. F. Willoughby, *Territories and Dependencies of the United States;* James Bryce, *The American Commonwealth*, Vol. I.]

WILLIAM STARR MYERS

State Sovereignty as a doctrine appeared shortly after 1776. "Among the first sentiments expressed in the first Congress," said James Wilson in the Convention of 1787[qv], "one was that Virginia is no more, that Pennsylvania is no more, etc. We are now one nation of brethren. We must bury all local interests and distinctions. This language continued for some time. No sooner were the State governments formed than their jealousy and ambition began to display themselves. Each endeavored to cut a slice from the common loaf, to add to his morsel, till at length the confederation became frittered down to the impotent condition in which it now stands." So intolerable had the evils of particularism become by 1787 that Henry Knox wrote: "The State systems are the accursed things which will prevent our becoming a nation. The democracy might be managed, nay, it would be a remedy itself after being sufficiently fermented; but the vile State governments are sources of pollution, which will contaminate the American name for ages—machines that must produce ill, but cannot produce good."

There was sound reason for the display of state loyalty in 1787. State governments were known and trusted; they had carried the people through the war with Great Britain while the impotent Congress of the Confederation[qv] had been unable to achieve the objects for which it was created. It followed that not only did men distrust a national government, but they also failed to understand that two jurisdictions largely co-ordinate could work toward a similar end. They imagined that co-ordination meant antithesis, and feared lest the surrender of a portion of the power wielded by the states would end in the destruction of personal liberty. It could therefore be argued that the National Government must rest in part on the states.

The part the states should play in the American political system was the subject of prolonged debate in the Convention of 1787. Hamilton, who wanted the states reduced to "corporations for local purposes," was poles asunder from members who argued for the complete sovereignty of the states. As he listened to the debate, Dr. William Samuel Johnson of Connecticut remarked that "the controversy must be endless whilst gentlemen differ in the grounds of their arguments; those on one side considering the states as districts of people composing one political society; those on the other considering them as so many political societies." Finally, a compromise was reached whereby the states were secured against encroachment by the National Government through their equal representation in the Senate (*see* Connecticut Compromise).

The problem of sovereignty remained unsolved when the government under the Constitution[qv] was inaugurated in 1789. The prevalent opinion was that somehow sovereignty had been divided between the states and the Union. This view was staunchly maintained by James Madison and was enunciated by the Supreme Court in Chisholm v. Georgia[qv] (1793). Up to the time when the theory of Calhoun became influential, the characteristic American doctrine was that in the United States the sovereignty had been divided into several portions without the destruction of its life principle.

Calhoun, in insisting that sovereignty in the United States is indivisible, returned to the issues debated in the Federal Convention. He declared that to the people of the several states sovereignty devolved upon the separation from Great Britain, and it was through the exercise of this sovereignty that the state constitutions[qv] as well as the Constitution of the United States were created. In other words, the Constitution of the United States was ordained and established by the people of the several states, acting as so many sovereign political communities, and not by the people of the United States, acting as one people, though within the states.

The accepted statement of the states' rights[qv] doctrine was set forth by Calhoun[qv] in his *Disquisition on Government* and his *Discourse on the Constitution and Government of the United States*. The influence of Calhoun is without question; his political theories became the dogma of the states' rights party and found expression in the constitution of the Confederate States[qv].

The nationalist theory of the Union was de-

States, Relations between

fended by Daniel Webster[qv], who insisted that the Constitution is an agreement among individuals to form a national government. "It is established," he said, "by the people of the United States. It does not say by the people of the several States. It is as all the people of the United States that they established the Constitution." Between the party of Calhoun and that of Webster the division of opinion was identical with that observed by Dr. Johnson in the Federal Convention. State sovereignty was made to rest upon the idea that the people of the United States constitute a number of political societies among whom a treaty or agreement was made to form a national government. The Constitution was not, as the nationalists maintained, a fundamental law ordained and established by the whole people of the United States. The controversy remained for the clash of arms to settle, but the victory of Grant at Appomattox[qv] settled the question in favor of the defenders of nationalism.

[C. E. Merriam, *History of American Political Theories.*]

WILLIAM S. CARPENTER

States, Relations between the. The Constitution (Article IV, Section 2) makes definite provision for interstate rendition of fugitives from justice. Nevertheless, this clause has occasioned much friction between the states, since the duty of determining who is a fugitive from justice rests upon the governor to whom the request is made. While the Supreme Court has held that the clause includes every offense punishable by the law of the state in which it was committed, governors have sometimes been unwilling to act upon this principle. If the governor decides that the so-called fugitive is not a fugitive—that the evidence against him is inadequate to establish a presumption of guilt, or that the offense is not of a sufficiently serious nature—there is nothing that can be done about it, for Congress has provided no remedy. The Supreme Court, in Kentucky v. Dennison (24 Howard 66, 1860), decided that the clause is not mandatory. Therefore, a Federal court will not issue a mandate to compel a governor to accede to such a request. The decision undoubtedly weakened the intent of the Constitution, but it avoided the exceedingly troublesome question of the coercion of a state.

Article IV, Section 1 of the Constitution provides that "full faith and credit shall be given in each State to the public acts, records, and judicial proceedings of every other State." This provision is mandatory, but it has been somewhat weakened by judicial interpretation. The intention was to make sure that the constitution, acts and records of each state, properly proved and authenticated, should have full effect in the courts of the other states. It has been held that it establishes a rule of evidence and not of jurisdiction; its application is especially apt to become an issue in connection with the use in one state of the records of judicial proceedings in another, as in divorce proceedings (*see* Atherton v. Atherton, 181 U. S. 155, 1900, and Sistare v. Sistare, 218 U. S. 11, 1910).

The constitutional provision respecting interstate citizenship (Article IV, Section 2) asserts that "citizens of each State shall be entitled to all privileges and immunities of citizens in the several States." This provision was extended by the Fourteenth Amendment[qv]. It has been interpreted frequently by the courts, notably in Corfield v. Coryell (4 Wash. C. C. 371, 1825) and Crandall v. Nevada (6 Wallace 35, 1867). It means "that citizens may move freely about the country and settle where they will, with the assurance that as newcomers they will not be subjected to discriminatory taxation, that they will be permitted to carry on lawful occupations under the same conditions as native residents, and that they will not be prevented from acquiring and using property, or denied the equal protection of the laws, or refused access to the courts." Other items coming within the scope of privileges and immunities include the right of a citizen "to come to the seat of government, to transact any business he may have with it, to seek its protection, to share its offices, to engage in administering its functions. He has the right of free access to its seaports, through which all operations of foreign countries are conducted, to the sub-treasuries, land offices, and courts of justice in the several states."

The Constitution (Article I, Section 10) forbids a state to enter into "any treaty, alliance, or confederation," and it prohibits any "agreement or compact" between states, or between a state and a foreign power, except with the consent of Congress. Between 1789 and 1932, inclusive, sixty-two such agreements were made, to which the consent of Congress was specifically given. Forty-five of these were adopted within the present century. Between 1789 and 1932 sixteen agreements were negotiated to which Congress did not consent, only three of these being after 1900. Twenty-three have dealt with the settlement of boundary disputes[qv]; others were concerned with jurisdiction over interstate waters, water supply, cession of territory, criminal jurisdiction and interstate or international bridges. Recently there has been a revived confidence in the usefulness of interstate compacts[qv] in connection with labor and other controversial subjects. In order to avoid delay after the completion of negotiations, Congress on several occasions has been induced to authorize certain types of compacts while negotiations were still in progress.

The types of interstate relationships cited above are based on provisions of the Federal Constitution. The social and economic growth of the nation has given rise to other types, such as the movement for uniform state legislation; greater co-operation between administrative officers in a given field, in different states; state commissions on interstate co-operation; and interstate organizations devoted to a particular problem, some on a national and some on a local scale.

The co-operation of administrative officers in charge of similar services in the several states antedates the efforts to secure uniformity through legislative means (*see* State Laws, Uniform), and offers greater promise of substantial achievement. The National Convention of Insurance Commissioners was organized in 1878, the National Board of Dental Examiners in 1883 and seven more such groups were organized and functioning prior to the establishment of the National Conference of Commissioners on Uniform State Laws in 1892. Since then few years have passed without the organization of one or more associations of state administrative officers. The Governors' Conference, organized in 1908, has held annual sessions which always attract considerable attention. There is a long list of associations of state officers in the fields of agriculture, banking and securities, civil service, commerce, conservation, education, health, etc. Finally, there is the Council of State Governments, organized in 1935 for the purpose of furthering interstate co-operation. The movement for the establishment of state commissions on interstate co-operation was an outgrowth of the work of the Council. By the summer of 1938, such commissions were provided for in thirty-six states. Their function is to study all questions involving interstate relations, and to try to devise methods of effective co-operation.

Certain problems are common to all the states. The tax problem was the first to be dealt with through the agency of an interstate commission. In February, 1933, the American Legislators' Association was responsible for the meeting in Washington of a national conference on this subject; out of its deliberations grew the Interstate Commission on Conflicting Taxation, which has carried on research leading to many valuable suggestions for the elimination of frictions resulting from tax conflicts. The Interstate Commission on Crime, similarly organized, functions on a national basis. The same technique has been used for the particular problems of some two or more adjacent states, for example, the Interstate Commission on the Delaware River Basin (Incodel); the Interstate Commission on the Ohio River Basin (Incohio); the Port of New York Authority; the Palisades Interstate Park Commission; the Lake Champlain Bridge Commission; the Delaware Bridge Commission; and many others. Some of these organizations have been functioning for years, rendering significant service to the people of the co-operating states.

[George C. S. Benson and Marshall E. Dimock, *Interstate Compacts;* Charles K. Burdick, *The Law of the American Constitution;* Jane Perry Clark, *The Rise of a New Federalism;* Council of State Governments, *Book of the States,* and *Interstate Compacts, 1789-1936;* Northcutt Ely, *Oil Conservation through Interstate Agreement;* Emerson D. Fite, *Government by Cooperation;* Governors' Conference, *Proceedings;* W. Brooke Graves, *American State Government,* and *Uniform State Action, a Possible Substitute for Centralization;* Richard Hartshorne, Inter-Governmental Cooperation—The Way Out, in *New Jersey Law Review,* January, 1936; James B. Scott, *Judicial Settlement of Controversies between States of the American Union;* W. W. Willoughby, *Constitutional Law of the United States.*]

W. BROOKE GRAVES

States' Rights. As a political or constitutional principle states' rights is an outgrowth of colonial particularism. The spirit of particularism or states' rights manifested itself during the Revolution and the Confederation, and presented a major problem to the Constitution makers of 1787[qqv]. The classic and constitutional basis of states' rights, as maintained under the Constitution, may be found in the Tenth Amendment adopted in 1791: "The powers not delegated to the United States by the Constitution, nor prohibited by it to the States, are reserved to the States respectively, or to the people" (*see* Reserved Powers of States).

In practice, states' rights has meant different things at different times. As originally formulated by Jefferson it was hardly more than a rule of strict construction[qv] applied to the powers of the central government, jealously reserving undelegated powers to the states. In recent years this form or construction of states' rights has vigorously reasserted itself, especially among those opposed to the rapidly expanding functions of the Federal Government under the so-called New Deal[qv].

At times states' rights has meant state sovereignty[qv] expressing itself in various ways. It has meant the right of nullification[qv]. Jefferson and Madison formulated this conception in the Kentucky and Virginia Resolutions[qv] of 1798 and 1799; the conception was utilized by New England in opposing the embargo and the War of 1812[qqv]; and was actually applied by South Carolina in nullifying the tariff laws of 1828 and 1832. In effect other states and sections have resorted to this theory, as in the case of Georgia in defying the Federal Executive and the Supreme Court in her Indian troubles of 1825–35 (*see* Cherokee Nation v. Georgia; Worcester v. Georgia), and of certain Northern states in passing personal liberty laws[qv] which nullified the Federal Fugitive Slave Act of 1850[qv]. By 1860 states' rights, considered as state sovereignty, meant to the Southern states the constitutional right to secede from the Federal Union (*see* Secession, The Right of). Because of the tragic nature of the ensuing struggle states' rights has become indissolubly associated with the Lost Cause[qv].

In one form or another states' rights has been asserted in every section and in practically every state east of the Mississippi River. The constant factor seems to be economic and material interests. Whenever these interests have been thought jeopardized, the section or state affected has resorted to the cry of states' rights.

At one time or another every major political party in American history has championed states' rights. First associated with Jefferson and the Republican party (Jeffersonian)[qv], the arguments of states' rights were employed by the Federalists[qv] after the Republicans had taken over the government. The Democrats and the Whigs[qqv] each raised the cry in the middle period when the other was in power. The new Republican party[qv] of Lincoln, associated with a larger nationalism in the struggle to save the Union, has since the Civil War, when out of power, and more particularly in the last decade, reverted to the time-honored shibboleth.

It may be assumed that states' rights, conceived as state sovereignty, affording the right of nullification or secession is dead. However, conceived as a constitutional device with which to restrict the activity of the party in power, states' rights continues to manifest itself in American political thought and practice.

[Alexander H. Stephens, *A Constitutional View of the War between the States;* Arthur M. Schlesinger, The State Rights Fetish, in *New Viewpoints in American History.*]

HAYWOOD J. PEARCE, JR.

States' Rights, Effect of, on the Confederate Conduct of the Civil War. The doctrine of states' rights, which was developed in the South as the defense mechanism of a minority section within the Federal Union, was productive of disastrous results when it was applied by extremists to the Confederate government during the Civil War. Led by Gov. Joseph E. Brown of Georgia, Gov. Zebulon B. Vance of North Carolina and Vice-President Alexander H. Stephens, they attacked conscription[qv] as unconstitutional and impeded its operation even after favorable decisions by the courts. The army was crippled by the insistence on the right of states to appoint officers, and by the policy of some states withholding men and arms from the Confederate government and themselves maintaining troops. On similar grounds the states' rights faction opposed suspension of the writ of habeas corpus[qv], so that the government was able to employ this valuable military weapon for periods aggregating less than a year and a half. Under the theory of states' rights the impressment of supplies for the army was broken down; likewise the laws were repealed which had given the government a monopoly in foreign trade by means of which it had exported cotton and brought in war supplies through the blockade[qv].

States' rights hampered the government at every turn and in the end contributed to its downfall.

[Frank Lawrence Owsley, *State Rights in the Confederacy;* Louise Biles Hill, *State Socialism in the Confederate States of America.*]

LOUISE BILES HILL

Statue of Liberty, properly "Liberty Enlightening the World," on Bedloe's Island, New York harbor, was conceived by Frederic Auguste Bartholdi, Alsatian sculptor, who built it in Paris during the 1870's and early 1880's. A gift to the United States from the people of France, costing approximately a million francs, raised by subscription, the colossal copper figure was shipped in sections in 1885, and unveiled Oct. 28, 1886. Cleveland accepted it in a belated commemoration of a century of American independence. The statue with its upraised torch, standing 152 feet above the pedestal and 300 feet above sea level, forthwith became the symbol of welcome to immigrating thousands.

[F. A. Bartholdi, *The Statue of Liberty Enlightening the World;* Frances Rogers, *Big Miss Liberty.*]

IRVING DILLIARD

Statutes at Large, a collection of all public and private acts and concurrent and joint resolutions passed by Congress. For many years, two volumes—one containing public acts and resolutions, and a second, private acts, concurrent resolutions, treaties and presidential proclamations —were published at the end of each Congress; beginning in 1937 they have been issued at the close of each session. By 1937 the collection numbered fifty volumes.

[*Code of the Laws of the United States.*]

P. ORMAN RAY

Statutory Law includes all laws made by the Federal Congress or by the state legislatures through the usual legislative processes; also state laws enacted directly by the people through the initiative[qv]. It excludes constitutions, treaties and executive and local ordinances as well as the common law.

Law in the United States is arranged in an hierarchical form as follows: (1) The Constitution of the United States, (2) Acts of Congress, (3) Treaties, (4) Executive Rules and Ordinances, (5) State Constitutions, (6) Acts of State Legislatures, (7) Executive Rules and Ordinances (under state law), (8) Common Law, (9) Municipal Ordinances.

Each type takes precedence, in case of conflict, over all those below it in the list except Acts of Congress and Treaties, where the latest in point of time governs.

[Harvey Walker, *Law Making in the United States.*]

HARVEY WALKER

Stay and Valuation Acts. As a result of the Panic of 1819[qv], many citizens of the new western states were unable to meet obligations they had incurred in the time of expansion and prosperity of the previous years. Foreclosures and forced sales at ruinous prices became common. In addition to establishing inflationist banking schemes operated by the state, the states of Illinois, Missouri, Kentucky and Tennessee adopted stay and valuation laws.

A stay law provided for a moratorium or extension of time for meeting a debt obligation. The extensions ranged from three months to two and one half years.

The stay law usually applied an unpleasant alternative to the case of a creditor who would not agree to the valuation laws. Property sold at forced sales was bringing only a small fraction of its normal value, and to protect the frontier debtors from such heavy losses, valuation laws provided for the appointing of a local board to set a fair value upon property offered in satisfaction of debt, usually a price much above that which would be secured at forced sale. If the creditor would not accept this overvalued property in satisfaction of his debt, he was forced to defer collection for the duration of the period provided by the accompanying stay law.

The state courts were accused of sympathy with creditors when they declared both varieties of relief laws unconstitutional. Missouri attempted to curtail the power of her courts, and Kentucky was plunged into chaotic conditions when her legislature voted the state supreme court out of existence and established a new pro-relief court in its place (*see* Old Court–New Court Struggle).

[N. S. Shaler, *History of Kentucky;* W. J. Hamilton, The Relief Movement in Missouri, 1820-22, in *Missouri Historical Review*, Vol. XXII.]

W. J. HAMILTON

Steam Power. The first successful steam engine in the American colonies was put into operation in 1755 at the Schuyler Copper Mines, near Newark, N. J., for pumping water from the mines. The engine, a Newcomen model, was built by the Hornblowers, an English firm of engine builders. It was in operation until the eve of the American Revolution when work at the mines was abandoned except for surface digging. In 1792 the engine again operated, but only for a short period. Before 1775 several English engines were imported into New England and a few built in the colonies. They were not successful.

During the last part of the 18th century when Watt and others in England were pushing their inventions from an experimental to a practical stage, Henry, Colles, Fitch, Rumsey, Evans, Donaldson, Latrobe, Kinsey, Voight, Thornton, Hall and others were experimenting with steam power in this country. Many were interested in applying steam to navigation. As early as 1787 John Fitch[qv] demonstrated a steamboat on the Delaware River before members of the Constitutional Convention, but not until Robert Fulton's *Clermont* (*see* Fulton's Folly) appeared on the Hudson River in 1807 was the success of the steamboat assured. Oliver Evans and others led attempts to apply steam power also to land conveyances, but success was delayed until the introduction of steam railroads[qv].

The development of steam power for driving machinery was retarded in the United States largely by the abundance and cheapness of water power. In 1800 there were only six engines in successful operation. They were designed on the Boulton and Watt plan, but most of the parts were made here. The high-pressure engine perfected by Oliver Evans opened the way for utilizing steam for driving machinery. By 1812 at least ten engines of this type provided power for sawmills, gristmills, sugar mills and textile mills. In the following decades New England slowly adopted the steam engine, but still relied to a large extent upon water power. In the rest of the country, especially in the Pittsburgh region and in the growing West, the introduction of the stationary steam engine made more rapid progress. In the period following the Civil War steam power was in general use, industrially.

Among the inventors who improved the steam engine in the United States, the name of George H. Corliss ranks high. The most important of his many inventions was his "drop cut-off" mechanism. A great Corliss engine provided power for all the machinery at the Philadelphia Centennial Exposition in 1876[qv]. Another American inventor, Charles E. Curtis, combined the ideas of Gustaf de Laval, a Swedish engineer, and Charles A. Parsons, an English engineer, in producing an improved steam turbine.

The steam engine has been one of the greatest inventions of modern times. It has provided the motive force for the industries that have produced modern civilization. During the past thirty years, electric power and power produced by internal-combustion engines have shown more rapid development than steam power, but steam still contributes much of the mechanical power used today.

[V. S. Clark, *History of American Manufactures, 1608-1928;* William Nelson, *Josiah Hornblower and the First Steam Engine in America;* The History of the Steam Engine in America, *Journal of the Franklin Institute,* Vol. 72, pp. 253-268.]

ARTHUR C. BINING

Steamboat Monopolies were granted by states on a number of rivers. The procedure on the Hudson was typical. Fulton's successful trip secured for his company a monopoly on the Hudson for twenty years (*see* Fulton's Folly). Others who desired to operate steamboats were required to secure a license from the Fulton company.

There were three reasons for the monopoly's failure. First, team-boats were constructed. They were twin boats with a wheel between them to protect it from floating ice. Eight horses walked in a circle on a heavy plank platform which rested on the two boats. No licenses were required to run such boats. Second, the controversy between New York and New Jersey led to disputes. New York courts declared that New York could control navigation on the Hudson River just as it could slavery or the transportation of infectious goods. The New Jersey courts denied the contention of New York courts.

This controversy led Chancellor Kent of the New York supreme court to advise that the case be carried to the United States Supreme Court. In the case of Gibbons v. Ogden[qv], Webster, the foremost lawyer of his time, and Attorney General Wirt supported the antimonopolists. Webster argued that it was the right of any steamship, when properly registered, to go anywhere on any United States river. Respondent attorneys, Oakley and Hamett, argued the right of a state to grant monopolies. The decision of Chief Justice Marshall destroyed all monopolistic rights enjoyed by the Fulton company. This decision determined the outcome in all pending steamship monopoly cases. In one, Heirs of Livingston and Fulton v. Reuben Nichols and Steamboat *Constitution,* the United States District Court for Eastern District of Louisiana declared against the steamship monopoly on the Mississippi River in Louisiana.

[James Alton James, *Readings in American History,* pp. 311-314; 9 Wheaton 1; Charles Warren, *The Supreme Court in American History.*]

CHARLES B. SWANEY

Steamboat Racing reached its zenith in 1870 when the *Robert E. Lee* raced from New Orleans to St. Louis in three days, eighteen hours, fourteen minutes, defeating the *Natchez* by over three hours. All America was agog, telegraphic reports were flashed to Europe, and more than a million dollars in bets is said to have changed hands. Although editorials denounced the practice as dangerous, fast boats were popular with travelers and shippers. Moreover, few explosions occurred while boats were racing, for engineers were more alert. Many races were against time, captains endeavoring to break records between ports. By 1840, when steamboats were attaining a high standard in marine architecture, the average speed was about six miles per hour upstream, and ten to twelve miles per hour downstream. Fast boats could average better than ten miles per hour upstream. Thus, in 1844 the *J. M. White* ran from New Orleans to St. Louis in three days and twenty-three hours, a record that stood for years. In 1815 the *Enterprise* churned from New Orleans to Louisville in twenty-five days; by 1853 the *Eclipse* had reduced this time to four days, nine hours, thirty minutes. The *Cataract* raced from St. Louis to LaSalle, Ill., in 1854, in twenty-three hours, forty-five minutes. The *James H. Lucas* ran from St. Louis to St. Joseph on the Missouri in 1856 in two days, twelve hours, fifty-two minutes; and the *Hawkeye State* sped from St. Louis to St. Paul in 1868 in two days and twenty hours. On a short run from St. Louis to Alton in 1853 the *Altoona* made twenty-five miles in one hour and thirty-five minutes.

[E. W. Gould, *Fifty Years on the Mississippi.*]

WILLIAM J. PETERSEN

Steamboating on Western Waters was inaugurated by the *New Orleans*[qv] in 1811. Scarcely a dozen steamboats were built by 1817, but in the next two years over sixty were launched for traffic on the Mississippi, the Missouri and the Ohio. By 1834 there were 230 steamboats, aggregating 39,000 tons, on western waters. Of the 684 steam craft constructed by the close of 1835, the Pittsburgh district contributed 304, the Cincinnati district 221 and the Louisville area 103. So phenomenal was the growth that steam tonnage on western waters soon exceeded steam tonnage in the British merchant marine. The cost of running the 1190 steamboats on western waters in 1846 was estimated at $41,154,194. At that time fully 10,126,160 tons of freight valued at $432,621,240 were transported annually. This was nearly double the United States foreign commerce. Pittsburgh, Cincinnati and Louisville were great Ohio ports, while New Orleans dominated the Lower Mississippi. In 1854 New Orleans and St. Louis ranked second and third respectively in enrolled steam tonnage in the United States. Six years later St. Louis recorded 1524 steamboat arrivals from the Upper Mississippi, 767 from the Lower Mississippi, 544 from the Illinois, 277 from the Ohio, 269 from the Missouri, 35 from the Cumberland, 31 from the Tennessee and 7 from the Arkansas.

The first steamboat navigated the Missouri in 1819, the Tennessee in 1821, the Upper Mississippi in 1823 and the Illinois in 1828. Before the Civil War, over forty tributaries of the Mississippi system had been navigated by steamboat. Captain-ownership was followed by the formation of powerful corporations such as the Cincinnati and Louisville Mail Line, the Anchor Line on the Lower Mississippi, the Northern Line on the Upper Mississippi and the Union Packet Line on the Missouri. The attempts of "tramp" boats or new lines to enter a profitable trade led to cutthroat competition and ruinous rates. River towns collected staggering wharfage fees but failed to provide adequate terminal facilities. Expensive litigation, unbusinesslike methods, uncertain rates and the limited season of navigation were additional handicaps. The Civil War ruined steamboating on the Lower Mississippi and contributed to the decline on the Ohio River, already locked in a death struggle with the railroads[qv]. Corporations were re-established on the Lower Mississippi after the Civil War, and St. Louis advertised lines to the Arkansas, the Red, the Ouachita, the Tennessee and other streams. But the halcyon days were soon gone: not even the race of the *Natchez* and the *Robert E. Lee* in 1870 could revive them (*see* Steamboat Racing). The Mississippi was paralleled by rails and trussed with bridges that were frequently hazardous to navigation. The iron horse reached St. Joseph on the Missouri in 1859, Council Bluffs in 1867, Bismarck in 1872. Most river improvements came after steamboating had virtually died. The gradually increasing tonnage on the Ohio and Mississippi since the World War reflects the persistence of steamboating on western waters.

[E. W. Gould, *Fifty Years on the Mississippi;* C. H. Ambler, *Transportation in the Ohio Valley;* H. M. Chittenden, *Early Steamboat Navigation on the Missouri River;* W. J. Petersen, *Steamboating on the Upper Mississippi;* J. T. Scharf, *History of Saint Louis;* F. H. Dixon, *A Traffic History of the Mississippi River System.*]

WILLIAM J. PETERSEN

Steamboats. The idea of steam-powered boats intrigued men before the days of James Rumsey, John Fitch and Robert Fulton[qqv]. Practical steamboat experiments began with the double-acting engine in 1782; both Rumsey and Fitch operated their boats before Washington's inauguration. Successful commercial navigation, however, is usually dated from the voyage of Fulton's *Clermont* in 1807. Thereafter steamships were launched for deep-sea passage; steamboats for the swift streams of the tidewater and Mississippi Valley whose tortuous curves and shallow sand-bar studded waters required high-powered, light draft boats. The first steamboat on western waters, the *New Orleans*[qv], was built from Fulton-Livingston patents in 1811. She was a 300-ton, two-masted sidewheeler with boiler, engine and vertical stationary cylinder placed in her open hold. The bow was reserved for freight—the cabins were aft of the machinery. In 1813 Daniel French launched the twenty-five-ton *Comet,* a stern-wheeler featuring vibrating cylinders. The *New Orleans* and *Comet* served as models until 1816, when Henry Shreve built the *Washington,* the first real steamboat on western waters. Shreve contributed three ideas to his 403-ton craft: he placed the machinery and cabin on the main deck, used horizontal cylinders with vibrations to the pitmans, and employed a double high-pressure engine. Subsequent marine architecture simply improved on these features.

A generation passed before the floating palaces of the Mark Twain era evolved. Steamboats increased in tonnage, boasted ornate cabins and private staterooms, bars and barber shops, bands and orchestras, steam whistles and calliopes. Steam was used to work the capstan, handle the spars, or swing the stage. An auxiliary engine, or doctor, pumped water into the boiler. Coal gradually replaced wood, the electric searchlight was substituted for the wood-torch. Spacious decks with promenades were built high above the main deck —the "Texas" (for the crew) and the pilot house being placed high above all. In 1843 the second *J. M. White* was launched at Pittsburgh. She was 250 feet long, 31 feet beam, 8½ feet hold, had seven boilers, 30-inch cylinders and a 10-foot stroke. In 1878 the third *J. M. White* was built at Louisville at a cost of over $200,000. She was 325 feet long, 50 feet beam and 11½ feet hold. She had ten boilers 34 feet long and her cylinders were 43 inches in diameter with an 11-foot stroke. The main cabin was 260 feet long. She could carry 8500 bales of cotton. The record load of 9226 bales of cotton was carried by the *Henry Frank* in 1881. It would have taken a season of hard work for the *New Orleans* to carry this amount.

[E. W. Gould, *Fifty Years on the Mississippi;* W. J. Petersen, *Steamboating on the Upper Mississippi.*]

WILLIAM J. PETERSEN

Stedman, Fort, Assault on (March 25, 1865). South of the Appomattox River Gordon's corps held the left of the Confederate defenses before Petersburg[qv]. In his front the Federal Fort Stedman was 200 yards distant. Strongly reinforced, before dawn Gordon assaulted this work with about 11,000 men. The garrison was surprised and the fort captured easily. But further advance was smothered by the fire of adjacent Federal batteries, while heavy counterattacks soon developed. By 8 A.M. the Confederates were driven to their own lines, having lost 2783 prisoners and many killed and wounded.

[Douglas S. Freeman, *R. E. Lee*, Vol. IV; *Official Records, Union and Confederate Armies*, Vol. XLVI.]

JOSEPH MILLS HANSON

Steel. *See* Iron and Steel Industry.

Steel Strikes (1892, 1901, 1909, 1919, 1937). In 1891 the Amalgamated Iron and Steel Workers was the strongest union up to its time. Negotiations over the renewal of an agreement between the Carnegie Company and the union led to a strike in June, 1892 (*see* Homestead Strike). The strike spread to other plants but was lost. Unionism in the steel industry was weakened by this failure. After the organization of the U. S. Steel Corporation[qv] in 1901 the Amalgamated, which declined steadily after 1892, endeavored to re-establish itself in the industry. A general strike ensued in August; results were again disastrous. In 1909 the last of the unionized mills of the U. S. Steel Company adopted an open-shop[qv] program, and in June, the Amalgamated again called a strike; Pennsylvania, West Virginia, Ohio and Indiana plants were struck. Despite the support of organized labor the strike ended in complete failure.

After the World War a renewed effort was made to organize steel. Headed by the American Federation of Labor[qv], a group of twenty-four unions in 1918 established a Committee for Organizing the Steel Industry. The campaign gained many members. Efforts to negotiate with the companies failed; a strike to force recognition began in September, 1919. The entire industry was affected. The strike continued for several months, but had generally failed by January, 1920.

The 1937 strike proceeded from a different background. The U. S. Steel Company in March, 1937, yielded recognition to the Steel Workers Organization Committee (*see* Congress of Industrial Organizations), but Little Steel[qv], including independent companies, refused to recognize the union. Strikes (led by the Steel Workers Organizing Committee), demanding recognition, failed.

[J. R. Commons and associates, *History of Labor in the United States*, Vol. IV; Lois MacDonald, *Labor Problems and the American Scene;* Industrial Relations Section, Princeton University, F. H. Harbison, *Collective Bargaining in the Steel Industry*, 1937.]

HERBERT MAYNARD DIAMOND

Steel Trap, THE. In *Book 14, Orders and Wills of York County, 1709–1716* (Williamsburg, Va.), Capt. Daniel Taylor's inventory of personal property includes "steele traps." This is probably the earliest record of the steel trap in America. By the middle of the 18th century it was in use wherever Europeans traded for furs with the Indian. The records of the British trade are especially revealing in this respect, and there are a few dated traps of this period in American collections. The *Sir William Johnson Papers* contain a requisition of 1764 for 5000 beaver traps valued at ten shillings each. British and French traps were carried far into the interior, and by 1797 were in use on the Lower Red River. In October, 1804, the Lewis and Clark[qv] party found steel traps in use by the Mandan Indians[qv], who explained that they had been obtained from the French.

The British traders of Canada and the Pacific Northwest imported from England or manufactured locally a trap of distinctive design, which found use in India as well as in America. The Hudson's Bay Company[qv] factors recognized the American-made trap as superior to this British product and obtained it as occasions permitted. By 1853 the Newhouse trap made by the Oneida Community[qv] was recognized throughout America as standard for design and quality, although it had competitors. One of the best collections of traps in the United States is possessed by the Bucks County Historical Society, Doylestown, Pa.

[A. R. Harding, *Steel Traps;* J. S. Campion, *On the Frontier.*]

CARL P. RUSSELL

Steele's Bayou Expedition. During Grant's (U.) advance on Vicksburg[qv] in 1863, flanking expeditions were set afoot, to get into the rear of the city. One of these was an effort by Gen. Sherman and Admiral Porter with gunboats (March

14–27) to reach the Sunflower and Yazoo rivers via Steele's Bayou. Falling streams and Confederate obstructions foiled the movement.

[*Battles and Leaders of the Civil War.*]

ALVIN F. HARLOW

Steering Committee is a committee in a legislative body whose principal functions are to select the measures to be taken up at any session and to determine the priority of their consideration. Such a committee was appointed in the English House of Commons as early as 1571, and, sometimes under the name of sifting committee, has been commonly used in our state legislatures, especially toward the end of a session. In Congress the steering committee is a strictly party committee, apparently established in the 1890's. At first a committee of the majority only, there has for some time been a steering committee for each party in each house, the minority committee becoming essentially a committee on party policy rather than a committee to steer the legislative program. Originally a small committee (usually seven members, under the chairmanship of the Floor Leader^qv^), it was dominated by the party leaders, but was changed by the Democratic majority in the House in 1933 to a large committee of nineteen, four being party leaders *ex officio* and fifteen being elected from as many geographical groups into which the Democratic membership was divided. The steering committee became therefore much more representative in character and to some extent a check on the party leaders instead of an instrument for carrying out their desires.

[Robert Luce, *Legislative Procedure;* George Rothwell Brown, *The Leadership of Congress;* Paul D. Hasbrouck, *Party Government in the House of Representatives.*]

CLARENCE A. BERDAHL

Stephenson, Fort, Defense of (Aug. 1, 2, 1813). When Proctor failed to dislodge Harrison from Fort Meigs^qv^ July, 1813, he withdrew down the Maumee and proceeded up the Sandusky to Fort Stephenson at Upper Sandusky (now Fremont, Ohio). Major George Croghan, the commander, twenty-one years old, had about 160 men and one cannon. Disregarding orders of Gen. Harrison to evacuate if attacked in force, he resisted the assaults of some twelve hundred British and Indians, equipped with light artillery, inflicting heavy losses upon them while his own losses were one killed and seven wounded. Proctor withdrew on Aug. 3 and made no further attempt to invade Ohio.

[E. O. Randall and D. J. Ryan, *History of Ohio,* Vol. III.]

EUGENE H. ROSEBOOM

Sterling Iron Works (N. Y.), one of the oldest iron and steel producing plants in the United States, located in the Ramapo Mountains at Sterlington, Orange County, dates from 1738, when Cornelius Board who discovered the ore in 1730 built the first furnace. Purchased in 1740 by Henry Townsend, the tract remained in that family until 1864 when the Sterling Iron and Railway Company acquired it. The superiority of Sterling iron made this the preferred source of munitions during the Revolution. Anchors and farm implements were manufactured here from the middle of the 18th century until 1891.

[Macgrane Coxe, *The Sterling Furnace and the West Point Chain.*]

PAULINE K. ANGELL

Steuben, Fort, built on the present site of Steubenville, Ohio, was an early American fortification against the Indians. Its immediate purpose was protection for the surveyors of the "Seven Ranges"^qv^ west of the Ohio River. Begun in 1786 by Col. John Francis Hamtramck it was completed the next year and was garrisoned by United States troops, 1786–87. It consisted of four blockhouses set diagonally on the corners with lines of pickets forming the sides. Apparently it burned to the ground in 1790.

[*Ohio Archaeological and Historical Publications,* Vol. VI; Joseph B. Doyle, *20th Century History of Steubenville and Jefferson County, Ohio.*]

FRANCIS PHELPS WEISENBURGER

Stevens' Indian Treaties (1854–59). Gov. Isaac I. Stevens of Washington Territory was also superintendent of Indian affairs for his territory. Late in 1854 and continuing into 1855 he negotiated a number of important treaties with the Indian tribes north of the Columbia River and west of the Cascade Mountains. Joel Palmer, the superintendent of Indian affairs for Oregon, cooperated with Stevens in the joint negotiation of some of the most important of these treaties and the general policy for the treaties followed the one worked out by Palmer in Oregon. This plan was to concentrate the Indians on a few reservations and pay for their lands with useful goods and instruct them in farming. The Medicine Creek Treaty, signed Dec. 26, 1854, by sixty-two chiefs and headmen representing the Puget Sound tribes, accepted the reservation policy. In 1855 three added treaties with the Canoe Indians of the Sound region were signed.

The great council for the interior was opened in the Walla Walla Valley in May, 1855, and the treaty was proclaimed June 12, 1855. It accepted the reservation policy for the powerful tribes of the interior. The outbreak of a series of Indian wars, and friction between the Indian agents and Federal military officers delayed the ratification of these Walla Walla treaties by the Federal Government until March 8, 1859.

[Charles H. Carey, *A General History of Oregon prior to 1861.*]
ROBERT MOULTON GATKE

Stevens' Railroad Survey. Isaac I. Stevens of Massachusetts in 1853 was appointed as governor of the newly created Washington Territory and given two important added duties, that of Superintendent of Indian Affairs for the Pacific Northwest and director of the survey to find a route for a Northern railway to the Pacific. Stevens was a trained army engineer and excellently qualified for his job. Capt. George B. McClellan, assigned to assist in the active direction of the survey, was directed to explore the Cascade Mountains for a practicable pass. Stevens' personal command, while on the overland trip to the coast, explored the passes in the Rocky and Bitter Root mountains. The Marias Pass, later used by the Great Northern[qv], was missed by Stevens' exploring parties although they were searching especially for it because Indians had told them of its existence.

The location of a suitable pass into the Puget Sound region (across the Cascades) proved the most difficult problem of the survey. McClellan was instructed to explore the Naches Pass but failed because he was too easily convinced it was impassable. A. W. Tinkham received orders at Walla Walla to attempt passage of the Snoqualmie Pass, and with the aid of two Indian guides made the trip through it and discovered grades practicable for a railway. Between Oct. 7, 1853, and Feb. 1, 1854, Tinkham covered some 1164 miles of new country. McClellan long stubbornly contested the practicability of the route discovered by Tinkham but it was accepted by Stevens.

[George W. Fuller, *A History of the Pacific Northwest.*]
ROBERT MOULTON GATKE

Stillwater, Battle of. *See* Freeman's Farm, Battles of.

Stillwater Convention (1848). When Wisconsin was admitted to the Union in 1848, a large part of what is now eastern Minnesota was excluded from the new state. A demand for a territorial government by the people of this unorganized area led to a public meeting on Aug. 4, 1848, and a "convention" on Aug. 26, both held at Stillwater. Sixty-one delegates, including most of the prominent men in the Minnesota country, signed memorials to Congress and to the President recommending the "early organization of the Territory of Minnesota." To further that purpose, the convention named Henry H. Sibley a delegate to "visit Washington and represent the interests of the proposed territory." In October, acting upon the assumption that the Territory of Wisconsin was still in existence, the people of the excluded area elected Sibley as delegate to Congress, and in January, 1849, to his great surprise, he was seated.

[W. W. Folwell, *A History of Minnesota*, Vol. 1; William Anderson and A. J. Lobb, *A History of the Constitution of Minnesota.*]
T. C. BLEGEN

Stimson Nonrecognition Doctrine, The. *See* Nonrecognition Policy.

Stock Companies, Colonial, required a large capital. One person or a few could not meet the financial demand. It called for a combination of the capital of many men willing to invest in a venture likely to yield a profit. The answer to the problem was the joint-stock company familiar to the history of English oversea expansion. A few illustrations will suffice. The Virginia Company of London[qv] of 1606 lacked capital adequate to launch a successful colony in Virginia. Under the charter of 1609 a joint-stock company was organized which solicited subscriptions to the stock at £12 10s a share from all who wished to invest. New capital was secured and Virginia took a new start. Plymouth Colony[qv] followed a similar pattern. The Pilgrims wished to colonize but lacked money. They entered into an agreement with seventy English merchants who provided the capital to the extent of £7000. A joint stock was formed at £10 a share to run for seven years. To the stock the merchants paid in money, the colonists in service. Another example is that of the Dorchester Company[qv] of 1623 consisting of 110 investors who advanced a total of £3000 to found a fishing station at Cape Ann, Mass. When profits failed to come, it was succeeded by the New England Company[qv] of 1628, composed of ninety members. Stock was sold and settlers were dispatched to Salem, Mass., to produce profits.

[C. M. Andrews, *The Colonial Period of American History*, Vols. I-III; W. R. Scott, *English Joint Stock Companies to 1720;* H. L. Osgood, *American Colonies in the Seventeenth Century*, Vols. I-III.]
WINFRED T. ROOT

Stock Market, The, is the market for securities. In this country, trading of considerable volume started with the formation of the Bank of the United States in 1791, the refunding of the Federal debt, and the assumption of the state debts[qqv], and then in the stocks of banks and insurance companies. Tradition says that the New York brokers met in the shade of an old buttonwood tree on Wall Street. There is an agreement about commissions signed by a group of twenty-four brokers on May 17, 1792. The growth of business caused by the War of 1812 led to a formal organization on March 8, 1817. By this time state and municipal securities were also dealt in. The next large group of securities came with the development of canals and railroads from 1830 on. Petroleum and mining stocks came in the 1850's. The Civil War brought increased business. After the war, railroads expanded tremendously and there were fights for control by such operators as Gould, Fisk, Drew and Vanderbilt. The next group of securities were the industrial and utilities and the combinations into trusts, particularly in the late 1890's and early 1900's. The World War brought activity and speculation in "war babies," stocks which benefited by the war. The war and the purchase of foreign bonds in the 1920's added greatly to the foreign list on the exchange. There was a crash in 1920 and then the start of the long upward movement which culminated in the Panic of 1929[qv].

On June 30, 1937, there were twenty-two national security exchanges registered with the Securities and Exchange Commission[qv], the stock exchanges of Baltimore, Boston, Chicago, Cincinnati, Cleveland, Detroit, Los Angeles, New Orleans, New York, Philadelphia, Pittsburgh, St. Louis, Salt Lake, San Francisco, Washington (D. C.), and Board of Trade of the City of Chicago, Chicago Curb, New York Curb, New York Real Estate Securities, San Francisco Curb, San Francisco Mining Exchanges and the Standard Stock Exchange of Spokane. In the year July 1, 1936 to June 30, 1937, the total market value of all sales on registered exchanges was $28,052,500,-834. Of this the New York Stock Exchange accounted for $24,241,188,872 and the New York Curb Market for $2,638,146,721. The Boston Exchange is an important market for mining stocks and the Chicago Exchange has an important list both local and national.

Membership in the New York Exchange is called a "seat" although there are no seats on the trading floor. By telephone, telegraph and cable orders come from all over the United States and Europe to the brokers on the floor. When they have bought or sold, the transaction is carried by the ticker all over the country. The settling for the sales of securities is facilitated by the Stock Clearing Corporation started in 1920. Settlement is now made the second business day after the transaction. The corporation enables the members to deliver or receive the net amount of shares he owes or is to receive. Also one check is received or drawn for the net amount of money owed or due the member.

The stock market break in 1929 brought many complaints. It was said that pools manipulated prices of stocks, selling them at high prices to outsiders and then withdrawing their support and letting the prices fall. Margin buyers, it was claimed, usually lost everything when a reaction came. The specialists, the brokers who handle orders which are above or below the market, were accused of using the knowledge for their own profit and even of acting as pool managers in the stock in which they specialized.

These complaints led to the regulation of stock exchanges by the Federal Government through the Security and Exchange Act of June 6, 1934. The enforcement is by the Securities and Exchange Commission, composed of five members. The law gave the Federal Reserve Board[qv] control over margins. Wash sales, matched orders and manipulation are all prohibited. No puts, calls or straddles are allowed. The Commission may segregate the functions of brokers and dealers and regulate the specialists. The borrowing of members is limited. If exchanges do not force their members to obey the rules, the Commission may close them.

The possibility of selling securities at once makes them good collateral for loans at the banks. The stock market facilitates the process of investment since more people will invest if they know that they can get their money back if they need it.

The New York Curb market formerly met in the open street. It has now moved indoors. It deals with newer securities and the securities of some companies which do not wish to give the information required by the New York Stock Exchange.

[J. E. Meeker, *The Work of the Stock Exchange.*]

JAMES D. MAGEE

Stock Ticker, The, is a printing telegraph system by which records of transactions are sent from the Stock Exchange as they occur and are printed at once on a tape at each place where a ticker is located. It was introduced into the New York Stock Exchange in 1867. Since then it has been greatly improved in speed. A modern variant reproduces the tape on a screen so more can see it at the same time.

[J. E. Meeker, *The Work of the Stock Exchange.*]

JAMES D. MAGEE

Stocks, The, were a device for punishing petty offenders, consisting of a frame in which the culprit's hands, or hands and feet, were confined while he was kept in a sitting posture. Required by law in some of the American colonies, they were to be found in practically every English town in which a court or magistrate dispensed justice. The theory behind the use of the stocks was that the public exposure humiliated offenders known to the villagers, and gave honest citizens an opportunity to become acquainted with the faces of vagrants. When the offense was one which displeased the public, the onlookers adjusted the punishment by throwing things at the culprit, by pulling the stool from beneath him, or by tipping him over backwards so that he hung head down. Of course there was much malicious baiting of the victims; as late as the beginning of the 19th century American gentlemen sometimes amused themselves in this manner.

C. K. SHIPTON

Stockton-Kearny Quarrel, THE (1846–47), arose from a dispute over rank. Commodore R. F. Stockton had aggressively extended Sloat's conquest to the south, precipitating revolt among the Californians. When Gen. S. W. Kearny, under orders to take possession of California and to set up a temporary civil government, arrived at San Diego, he found Stockton unwilling to relinquish his command. Strained relations existed until the middle of January, 1847, when Stockton passed the governorship over to J. C. Frémont[qv], who was in turn superseded by Kearny, early in March.

[H. H. Bancroft, *History of California*, Vol. V; R. G. Cleland, *California: The American Period.*]

ROBERT J. PARKER

Stockyards. Travelers along the Cumberland Road[qv] and other highways leading into the West of the 1820's and 1830's were accustomed to the familiar sight of droves of cattle fattened on the frontier farms of the Middle West on their way to the markets of the Eastern seaboard cities. The extension of the railroads[qv] into the West in the two succeeding decades changed all this, so that by the outbreak of the Civil War, livestock[qv] had become one of the chief freight items of the western roads. This change in the marketing of livestock resulted in new business methods. At the various western termini, accommodations for holding livestock, commission firms to handle the consignments for the shipper, and packing plants to process a portion of the shipments appeared as component parts of a great business community.

The early stockyards in these terminal cities were either private yards or yards owned and operated by the railroads. As the traffic increased, need for a consolidated yard became clear to all. On Christmas Day, 1865, the Union Stockyards in Chicago were opened. Under a charter granted by the Illinois legislature, a company, known as the Union Stockyard and Transit Company, was formed with a capital of one million dollars. The railroads running into Chicago took most of the stock and on the Board of Directors were to be found officials of most of the roads. As the trade in Western cattle grew, yards were opened in other cities: Kansas City in 1871, St. Louis in 1872, Cincinnati in 1874, Omaha in 1884 and St. Paul and Denver in 1886.

The rise of Chicago to a position of supremacy in this business was due to its favorable location, the convergence of nine important railroad lines there, the advantage of an early start given it by the concentration of supplies for the Northern armies during the Civil War, and the enterprise of its citizens in furnishing those factors indispensable for the efficient marketing of livestock: commission houses, stockyards and packing plants. With the concentration of the packing business in Chicago—Nelson Morris in 1859, Armour in 1867 and Swift in 1875—and the mounting flood of cattle pouring in from the Western ranges (*see* Cattle Industry), Chicago became the greatest livestock center in the world.

In and around the "Yards" in the various cities, there grew up distinctive communities. The great packing[qv] companies built their plants near by and around them sprawled the "Packingtowns" made famous in Upton Sinclair's *Jungle*. In the "Yards" were to be found a lusty crowd of commission men, cattle and horse buyers, railroad men, reporters of stock news, cattlemen and their cowboys from the Western ranges and stock detectives representing Western livestock associations. They formed a vigorous, distinctive and colorful group in the business community of the West.

[R. A. Clemen, *The American Livestock and Meat Industry;* W. J. Grand, *The Illustrated History of the Union Stockyards;* Louis F. Swift, *The Yankee of the Yards: The Biography of Gustavus Franklin Swift.*]

ERNEST S. OSGOOD

Stoddert, Fort, was a stockaded work constructed by Capt. Bartholomew Shaumberg in July, 1799, near the junction of the Alabama and Tombigbee rivers about fifty miles above Mobile[qv]. Named for the Acting Secretary of War, Benjamin Stoddert, it became a thriving settlement and military post, as well as a port of entry, the seat of a court of admiralty[qv], and the revenue headquarters of the district of Mobile. The fort acted as a check on ambitious frontiersmen anxious to take Spanish Mobile (*see* Kemper Raid). Here Aaron Burr was kept prisoner in 1807 and here the first newspaper was published within the present limits of Alabama.

With the taking of Mobile in the War of 1812, Fort Stoddert lost its importance and was abandoned.

[Peter Hamilton, *Colonial Mobile.*]
JAMES W. SILVER

Stone Fleets, THE, consisted of small sailing-vessels loaded with stone, which the Navy Department purchased in Baltimore, New York, New Bedford, New London and other Northern ports, and sank at the entrances of Southern harbors in the hope of closing the channels to blockade-runners[qv]. Three such vessels were sunk in Ocracoke Inlet, N. C., Nov. 18, 1861; sixteen in the main entrance to Charleston Harbor[qv], Dec. 20, 1861; and twenty in Maffitt's Channel, another entrance to Charleston Harbor, Jan. 26, 1862. The work accomplished nothing as marine worms ate away the ships' timbers and the stones sank in the mud.

[J. R. Spears, *The Story of the New England Whalers; Records of the Union and Confederate Navies in the War of the Rebellion*, Series I, Vols. VI, XII.]
LOUIS H. BOLANDER

Stone Mountain, Confederate War Memorial at. *See* Borglum's Colossal Sculptures.

Stone River, Battle of. *See* Murfreesboro, Battle of.

Stonewall, THE, a Confederate ironclad ram[qv], was built in France, sold to Denmark, and purchased from that country by Confederate agents. The vessel was 172 feet long and 33 feet in breadth of beam. Under the command of Capt. T. J. Page, the *Stonewall* sailed from Copenhagen Jan. 6, 1865, and, after a futile attempt to draw two United States warships into combat, crossed the Atlantic to Cuba. After the war ended, it was delivered to the United States and subsequently sold to Japan.

[J. Thomas Scharf, *History of the Confederate States Navy.*]
RICHARD E. YATES

Stoney Creek, Battle of (June 6, 1813). Generals Chandler and Winder with about 1400 Americans encamped on June 5, at Stoney Creek, near the British camp at Burlington Heights, Ontario. The following morning, shortly before daybreak, Gen. Vincent with about 700 British regulars attacked the Americans and heavy casualties were suffered on both sides. The two American commanders, eighteen other officers and eighty men, as well as ordnance, were captured. Fearing a renewal of the attack the American army withdrew (*see* Niagara Campaigns).

[Louis L. Babcock, *The War of 1812 on the Niagara Frontier.*]
ROBERT W. BINGHAM

Stonington, The Bombardment of. On Aug. 9, 1814, four British vessels, detached from the squadron blockading New London, under Commodore Sir Thomas Hardy appeared off the borough of Stonington and gave warning of one hour for removing noncombatants before bombarding the town. Though the attack continued at intervals until noon on the twelfth, no buildings were destroyed, though many were damaged, and no persons were killed and only a few were wounded. The citizens, assisted by the militia of the vicinity, offered effective resistance and prevented any attempt to make a landing. The action was probably intended as a preliminary to a British attack on New London.

[J. W. Barber, *Connecticut Historical Collections;* R. A. Wheeler, *History of the Town of Stonington.*]
GEORGE MATTHEW DUTCHER

Stony Point, Capture of (July 16, 1779). This rocky peninsula on the west bank of the Hudson was connected with Verplanck's Point on the east shore by King's Ferry, a link between two main traveled roads leading from New England to Pennsylvania. On May 31 the British occupied the two points and began to fortify them strongly. Washington himself carefully reconnoitered Stony Point. Deciding that a surprise of the position was practicable, he chose "Mad Anthony" Wayne and the American Light Infantry, a picked corps of 1300 men, for the attack. "I'll storm Hell if you'll plan it," Wayne is reported to have told him. The attack took place at midnight. While a small detachment in the center fired noisily to divert the attention of the defenders, two silent columns, their empty muskets surmounted by bayonets, swarmed over the fortifications to kill and wound 123 men and to take 575 prisoners. Though Washington abandoned the works on July 18, the expedition had done much for the morale of his army.

[H. B. Dawson, *The Assault on Stony Point.*]
EDWARD P. ALEXANDER

Store, General. The small self-sufficing population of the early settlements was fertile soil for the growth of a retail store which catered to a variety of needs as does the general store. The demand for any one class of merchandise was too small to permit specialization. In 1625 Virginia had forty-nine stores to supply a white population of 1232.

For over two hundred years the general store continued to be the typical retail store in the United States, but as demand and sources of supply increased in size the specialty stores began to take the place of the general stores. This specialization was recognized when it was determined to gather statistics on retail stores for 1839 as a part of the census of 1840. The census reported 57,565 "retail dry goods, grocery and other stores" with a capital of $250,301,799. Most of these stores in all likelihood were general stores.

Since early times the general store, often the location of the village post office, has been a social center as well as a trading center, and the changes in its business methods have been relatively few and small. In 1935 there were 1,653,961 retail stores in the United States of which only 95,410 were general stores.

[Paul Nystrom, *The Economics of Retailing;* Fred M. Jones, *Middlemen in the Domestic Trade of the United States, 1800-1860.*]

FRED M. JONES

Store Boats. Each year from about 1800 to the time of the Civil War there descended the Ohio and Tennessee rivers with the spring floods numerous flatboats*qv* fitted out as store or trading boats. The part of the craft dedicated to trade was outfitted with shelves and counters. Since they served as the department stores of the rivers they carried large stock of groceries, liquors, dry goods and hardware. They carried a calico flag to indicate their character and responded to a hail from dwellers on the banks, or tied up near a plantation or hamlet too small to afford a store. Their arrival was announced by a blast on a tin horn, and the inhabitants with money to spend or goods to barter flocked to the landing. Enterprising traders made the voyage every year, and the immigrant often made his way to his new home, selling goods as he drifted.

[Leland D. Baldwin, *Keelboat Age on Western Waters.*]

LELAND D. BALDWIN

Stories, Tall, is a term used in America to denote a comic folk tale characterized by grotesque exaggeration. Although not confined to America, the tall tale has flourished here as nowhere else and is thoroughly characteristic of the popular psychology which resulted from the rapid expansion of the United States in the 19th century (*see* Westward Movement). As an English traveler in 1869 observed, "The immensity of the continent produces a kind of intoxication; there is a moral dram-drinking in the contemplation of the map. No Fourth of July orator can come up to the plain facts in the land commissioner's report."

The subjects of the tall tales were those things with which the tellers were familiar: weather, fauna, topography, adventure. Long before the nation became "dust-bowl conscious," plainsmen told of seeing prairie dogs twenty feet in the air digging like hell to get back to the ground. In the Southern Highlands such astounding tales arose as that of the two panthers who climbed each other into the sky and out of sight. David Crockett used to save powder by killing coons with his hideous grin. Once when the varmint failed to fall, Crockett discovered that he had mistaken a tree-knot for a coon; he had, however, grinned all the bark off the knot. Tony Beavers, southern lumberman, took a day out of the calendar by arresting the rotation of the earth. A northern lumberman, Paul Bunyan, with his blue ox, Babe, snaked whole sections of land to the sawmills. Mike Fink, king of keelboatmen*qv*, used to ride down the Mississippi River dancing Yankee Doodle on the back of an alligator. Freebold Freeboldsen, having left his team in his Nebraska field while he went for a drink, returned to find his horses eaten up by the grasshoppers*qv*, who were pitching the horses' shoes to determine which should get Freebold. Kemp Morgan built an oil derrick in the Mid-Continent field so high that an axe which fell from the crown wore out nineteen handles before it hit the ground. Pecos Bill eared down a Texas mountain lion, mounted him, and rode away quirting him with a rattlesnake.

Unless they were deliberately imposing upon tenderfeet, tall liars did not expect to be believed. Sometimes they lied as a defense against assumptions of superiority; sometimes they lied through modesty; sometimes, finding that the truth was not believed, they lied to regain their reputations for veracity; sometimes they lied with satiric intent; but mostly they lied because they were men of imagination and resource and knew how to make the time pass pleasantly. And in lying, they gave America some of its most characteristic folklore*qv*.

[Walter Blair and Franklin J. Meine, *Mike Fink, King of Mississippi Keelboatmen;* Mody C. Boatright, *Tall Tales from Texas;* Roark Bradford, *John Henry;* Esther Shepherd, *Paul Bunyan.*]

MODY C. BOATRIGHT

Stourbridge Lion, THE, was the first steam locomotive to run on a track in America. The Delaware and Hudson Canal Company*qv* built a railroad line between its mines at Carbondale, Pa., and its canal terminus at Honesdale, and had four locomotives built in England, of which one, the Stourbridge Lion, was tested at Honesdale on Aug. 8, 1829. It weighed seven tons, whereas the company had specified only three. The company's engineer bravely drove it over trestles which trembled under its weight, but that first trip was its last; it was discarded as being too heavy for any bridge. What became of the other three engines is unknown.

[*A Century of Progress: History of the Delaware & Hudson Company.*] ALVIN F. HARLOW

Straight Ticket. Most partisan ballots are so arranged as to permit the voter, by a single cross mark, to vote for all of the candidates of one party. This is known as straight ticket voting. By minimizing the voter's effort and aiding him through party emblems^qv^ at the head of a party column to vote straight, such voting is encouraged. The adoption of the Massachusetts or office block ballot without party emblems in place of the Indiana or party column type with party emblems often is urged as a needed reform.

[E. M. Sait, *American Parties and Elections.*] HARVEY WALKER

Strangite Kingdom. The death of Joseph Smith, founder and prophet of Mormonism^qv^, in June, 1844, left a numerous religious sect which had been taught to obey blindly a prophet in the flesh, bereft of such a leader. A struggle over the vacant succession ensued, and among the aspiring prophets who attracted a considerable following was James J. Strang. With the aid of angelic visitations, unearthing of golden plates, and other phenomena characteristic of the Mormon sect, Strang developed the holy city of Voree, near modern Burlington, Wis., in the years 1844–49, and attracted a considerable following of Saints scattered throughout the country.

Before long, Prophet Strang's attention was diverted to the Beaver Islands in Lake Michigan, where in 1849 the city of St. James was founded as his new holy city. A year later (July, 1850) the Kingdom of God on Earth was formally proclaimed, with Strang as God's vicegerent who should establish his rule in this world. Strang was an able orator, and a man of much native shrewdness, who for six years dominated the several thousand people who composed his kingdom. At length he was murdered by disgruntled conspirators (June, 1856), and his followers were plundered and driven into exile by a frontier mob. A tiny body of zealots still adheres to the Strangite faith.

[M. M. Quaife, *The Kingdom of St. James.*] M. M. QUAIFE

Stratford Hall, in Westmoreland County, Va., about a mile from the Potomac, was built by Thomas Lee in the 1720's. It consisted of a Great House with its dependencies and gardens. The central mansion was H-shaped—the two wings, each topped by four grouped chimneys, were connected by a Great Hall. "Home of the Lees," until sold in 1822, it suffered neglect and by the second century of its completion stood "bleak and gaunt." In 1929 it was acquired by the Robert E. Lee Foundation and restored.

[Ethel Armes, *Stratford Hall, The Great House of the Lees.*] LEONARD C. HELDERMAN

Stratosphere, a region of the upper air from six to thirty miles above the earth consisting mainly of nitrogen, whose study was made possible by a hermetically sealed gondola invented by a Swiss, Prof. Auguste Piccard, has been explored successfully on five different occasions in America in the decade, 1930–40. A balloon ascent to the stratosphere was made Nov. 11, 1935, when Capt. Albert W. Stevens and Capt. Orvil Anderson (U. S. A.), piloting the National Geographic Society–U. S. Army Air Corps balloon "Explorer II" over Rapid City, S. D., reached an altitude of 13.71 miles. Small, unmanned balloons equipped with instruments have ascended as high as 17.42 miles. These stratosphere flights have been made to study cosmic rays, stratosphere temperature and barometric pressure, ozone concentration, and speed and direction of the winds.

[C. G. Philp, *Exploring the Stratosphere;* A. W. Stevens, Man's Farthest Aloft, in *National Geographic Magazine,* January, 1936.] LOUIS H. BOLANDER

Strauder v. West Virginia (1880). The Supreme Court declared that a West Virginia statute restricting jury service to whites violated the Fourteenth Amendment^qv^ because it denied Negroes equal protection of the laws; and upheld the Civil Rights Act^qv^ provision for removal of cases to the Federal courts when equal rights were denied in state courts.

[Charles Warren, *The Supreme Court in United States History.*] RANSOM E. NOBLE. JR.

Straw Votes. *See* Sampling Referenda.

Strawberry Bank. Thomson's settlement on the Piscataqua (*see* New Hampshire) was taken over in 1630 by the Laconia Company^qv^ which sent two ships under Walter Neale. He carried on some fishing and trading and explored as far as the White Mountains. John Mason^qv^, the most active member of the company, secured more colonists in 1631 who moved the settlement to the west bank of the upper harbor and named it "Strawbery Banke" for the many wild strawberries. The company sent, in all, about eighty persons, spent £3000, failed, and divided its assets in 1634, leaving Mason to work alone until his death in 1635. Deserted by his heirs, and outstripped by the settlement at Dover, the slowly growing Bank formed its own government and elected Francis Williams governor, until 1641. It then placed itself under Massachusetts, which claimed the region, reserving for its Anglican inhabitants the right to vote. Under the new rule, with more security and protection, the town grew; town meetings provided for ferries, roads, a highway to Boston and a fort. In 1652 it was allowed to elect representatives to the Massachusetts General Court, and in 1653 it changed its name to Portsmouth.

[Ralph May, *Early Portsmouth History.*]

HERBERT W. HILL

Streamlined Trains were the outgrowth of years of effort by the railroads to attain lighter weight, higher speed and greater operating economy. Stainless steel or aluminum bodies and an improved Diesel engine were the answers to the problem. One of the first trains "streamlined" to offer the least possible air resistance was a two-car unit built for short run service on the Texas & Pacific[qv] in 1933. Two Diesel electric streamlined trains—each of three cars, articulated, including the locomotive-mail-baggage car—were launched by the Union Pacific and Burlington roads[qqv], respectively, early in 1934. In a test, the Burlington's "Zephyr" ran from Denver to Chicago, 1017 miles, in 785 minutes, without a stop and without changing engines. In October, 1934, the Union Pacific's second streamliner, a six-car (including engine) train, was pulled by one locomotive from Los Angeles to New York in 56 hours, 55 minutes—an average speed of slightly under 60 miles per hour. Other roads rapidly took up the new idea. Yet others clung to steam, though streamlining locomotives and trains. Early in 1935 the Chicago, Milwaukee & St. Paul[qv] installed oil-burning, streamlined steam locomotives capable of 120-mile an hour speed. The New York Central, Baltimore & Ohio[qqv] and other roads adopted similar types.

ALVIN F. HARLOW

Street Cleaning. As large cities sprang up in the wake of the Industrial Revolution[qv], medical, commercial and esthetic considerations demanded more systematic street cleaning. The 19th century American city presented an appalling scene. Cans of refuse lined the curbs. Filth covered the streets. Droppings from the horses which hauled most of the traffic abounded. Medical boards or police departments had failed to enforce cleanliness. Beginning with New York City in 1881, cities established departments of street cleaning or sanitation. By 1915 all large cities had such departments. Borrowing methods of street sanitation from European cities and from each other, they achieved, by 1920, reasonable cleanliness from medical and commercial points of view.

Apparatus, too, grew more complex. For example, in 1860 the squeegee was a hand-powered device consisting of a handle and rectangular board used to push dirt into the gutter or into a receptacle. By 1900 it had become a horse-drawn machine with a tank of water surmounting a rubber roller. Today it has been displaced by a motor-driven tank used for flushing. Despite mechanical advances, "white wings," so-called after George Waring of New York City in the late 1890's equipped street-cleaners with white uniforms, continued in service. Originally employed to clean up horse-droppings and litter, they have been retained mainly to pick up litter.

Several factors have revolutionized street cleaning. Garbage-collection has eliminated refuse. Paving and night-flushing have made possible cleaner streets. The internal combustion engine, however, has effected the most far-reaching changes. It has minimized the use of horses in traffic; its almost universal adoption has necessitated more paved streets; finally, it has made greater speed available in cleaning the streets.

Cleaner streets have been achieved by these factors. Coercive methods failed in New York City in 1915. Cleveland set an example in an educational program in the schools. Today all cities are attempting to inculcate in their citizenry the ideal of urban cleanliness. Success has attended the removal of the medical and commercial problems. The esthetic problem of unkempt, littered streets alone remains.

[W. P. Capes and J. D. Carpenter, *Municipal Housecleaning;* G. A. Soper, *Modern Methods of Street Cleaning.*]

HENRY BURNELL SHAFER

Street Railways. The first street railway in America was laid on the Bowery and Fourth Avenue, from Prince Street to Murray Hill, New York City, in 1832–33. A portion of it was put into operation in June, 1833. The horse-drawn cars had bodies like stagecoaches, and two passengers might ride on the dickey, or driver's seat. This road met much opposition because its rails were slotted so deeply that they damaged the wheels of other vehicles. It was a financial failure, and not until 1836 was another car line attempted, this one in Boston. Thereafter, little was done in street railways until about 1850; between that date and 1855, six new lines were built in various cities. In 1855 the Boston line tried a rail with a slot only seven-eighths inch deep, and in the following year, the modern type of streetcar rail was designed for a Philadelphia line, which greatly accelerated the development of the business. Between 1855 and 1860 thirty new lines were built; between 1860 and 1880 eighty more came into being. By 1890 there were 769 such railways in the principal cities of the country.

As cities grew larger and distances greater, horses became too slow for the longer lines. Beginning in the 1870's, steamcars were tried in some cities, but they were highly objectionable. The continuous cable, running in a slot under the surface, the cars attaching themselves to it by a clutch or grip, next became the most popular form of rapid transit. The first such line was completed in San Francisco in 1873, and was found well adapted to the steep hills of that city. During the next fifteen years most of the larger cities had one or more cable lines, but such systems were very costly—about $100,000 per mile. Electric cars, introduced between 1880 and 1890 (*see* Railways, Electric), rapidly superseded all other systems. In 1912 there were 41,065 miles of electric railways in the United States, but the rapid development of the automobile and then the motor bus[qqv] was already beginning to threaten their existence. By 1920 street railways in most places were losing money heavily. Fares—which had always been five cents for almost any length of ride—were being raised practically everywhere save in New York City, but this only increased competition. After 1930 the railway lines began to disappear more and more rapidly and to be replaced by motor buses.

ALVIN F. HARLOW

Strict Construction. This principle of constitutional interpretation has played an important part in American politics since 1789. Its fundamentals were stated by Thomas Jefferson in opposing the incorporation of the United States Bank[qv] in 1791. Such a project was not authorized by the enumerated powers[qv] of Congress, the "general welfare clause"[qv] conferred no power but merely authorized taxation for the general welfare, and the "necessary and proper clause" meant *necessary,* not merely useful and convenient. Strict construction could be made a bulwark for minority groups or sectional interests[qqv] whose social and economic philosophy called for a limited exercise of national power, and was resolutely upheld by the slaveholding states as a guaranty for the survival of their "peculiar institution"[qv]. (*See also* Loose Construction.)

[B. J. Hendrick, *Bulwark of the Republic;* A. C. McLaughlin, *Constitutional History of the United States.*]

W. A. ROBINSON

Strike, Sympathetic, is a cessation of work by wage earners in a given plant, trade, occupation or industry having no special grievance with their employers, in order to assist workers on strike[qv] in another plant, trade, occupation or industry. Such strikes usually occur where the workers are unionized on a craft basis, as in the building industry. The principal purpose of the sympathetic strike is to increase the mass power of unionized labor in compelling adjustment of its grievances with a given union or group of unions. In the United States the sympathetic strike has generally been condemned by the courts. The judiciary holds that sympathetic strikes are unreasonable and inexcusable because they are called against an employer or employers with whom the workers involved have no dispute.

[J. R. Commons and J. B. Andrews, *Principles of Labor Legislation.*]

GORDON S. WATKINS

Strikes. Comparatively little is known about the origin of strikes in American industry. The first strike of which there appears to be any record occurred in New York City in 1741, presumably among the journeymen bakers. For a half century thereafter, not much is heard about industrial unrest. In 1792 the journeymen shoemakers of Philadelphia developed a rather strong organization and called a strike in each of the years 1796, 1798, 1799. In 1805 these same workers again called a strike in support of further demands for higher wages, but were unsuccessful. The masters brought charges of conspiracy against the leaders in the Mayor's Court of the city of Philadelphia on the grounds that the workers' association was an unlawful conspiracy to raise wages. The three-day trial, in which the defendants were found guilty and fined eight dollars each, commanded considerable public attention (*see* Philadelphia Cordwainers' Case). That modern trade union methods were used is evident from the testimony of employers who complained of their inability to fulfill contracts, the refusal of members of the journeymen's association to work with nonmembers, the threatened and actual beating of those who disobeyed the association's orders, and the application of a boycott[qv]. By 1809 such terms as "scab," "strike" and "general turn-out" were in common usage.

The celebrated trial of the journeymen cordwainers of New York City in 1810 and other cases of prosecution of unions as conspiracies indicate that unionism and its chief weapon, the strike, were increasingly effective. Groups of sailors, printers, shipbuilders, hat workers, spinners and weavers called strikes in this period, but they were relatively few to 1835, and not of serious consequence. Despite the claim of the New York *Daily Advertiser* that "Strikes are all the fashion," investigation has proved that in all the years prior to 1835 there were about twenty-four strikes of which records have been kept. Most of these had to do with wages, and about one half of them apparently were successful. From 1835 to 1870 there was a marked increase in the number of strikes, a consequence of active reform movements in the interest of labor and the development of stronger unionism. Some three hundred strikes took place in this period, most of them caused by disputes over wages and hours of labor. Relatively few were successful.

The decade of the 1870's ushered in significant changes. The increasing complexity of our industrial system and the growth of powerful labor organizations resulted in strikes that were wider in scope and more serious in their effects. The railroad strikes[qv] of 1877 were violent and widespread. These struggles, which began over a 10% reduction in wages, were the first strikes on a national scale. They seriously impaired the business of the nation, and state militia and Federal troops were called out to suppress violence and safeguard life and property.

Rather complete statistics of strikes are available for the United States since 1881. Following that year the number of strikes increased steadily to an extraordinary level during the World War[qv] and the years following. The average number of strikes per year from 1881 to 1885 was 500, while from 1916 to 1921 the annual average was 3500. In the years of depression and prosperity from 1921 to 1929, there was a marked decline in the annual average. Temporary recovery from the depression of 1929 was accompanied by a revival of industrial strife, and in 1937 there were 3420 strikes, involving 1,650,000 persons, and causing a loss of 40,000,000 workdays. Industrial unrest continued in accentuated form through 1938 and 1939.

Unionists view the strike as a basic right, guaranteed under the Thirteenth Amendment[qv] to the Constitution, which precludes slavery and involuntary servitude. The courts do not share this conception completely, there being only one state (California) in which all strikes, regardless of purpose, are held lawful. In general, the legality of strikes is determined by their purpose and method of execution. Strikes for higher wages and reduced hours are lawful. The courts are divided on the legality of strikes for recognition of the union and the discharge of nonunion workers, that is, for the so-called closed shop[qv]. Sympathetic strikes[qv] are held invalid by most jurisdictions, and sit-down strikes[qv] have been declared illegal by the Supreme Court. Strikes against nonunion materials are regarded in many jurisdictions as illegal boycotts, although some courts take a different position. With regard to the conduct of strikes, the courts are in agreement. In seeking the co-operation of other workers, and of customers, strikers are within the law when they use persuasion (*see* Picketing). If, however, they use threats, coercion, intimidation, or violence, their actions are judged unlawful. It is evident that in the United States the law of strikes is confused and inconsistent, being for the most part judge-made and commission-made law (*see* National Labor Relations Board), which accounts for the prevalence of conflicting decisions. Interpretation of purpose and method rests with judges and commissioners who have not been able to agree on any universally applicable criteria of legality.

Wage earners have won about one third of their strikes, employers about one third, and one third are compromised. No general quantitative measurement of the beneficial effects of strikes is available. Unionists insist that labor has gained infinitely more than it has lost through strikes, since this is the only effective weapon possessed by the laboring class. Labor economists are inclined to agree that the advance of collective bargaining[qv] and the economic gains of labor would not have been so great in the absence of the strike. To employers and the public no such gains accrue, hence the general opposition to strikes as a method of industrial conflict.

[P. H. Douglas, An Analysis of Strike Statistics, in *Journal of the American Statistical Association*, September, 1923; Dale Yoder, *Labor Economics and Labor Problems*, 2nd edition, 1939, especially Chapter IV; Louis Adamic, *Dynamite, The Story of Class Violence in America;* E. T. Hiller, *The Strike.*]

GORDON S. WATKINS

Strikes, Sit-down, were first used on a wide scale in Italy following the World War, until suppressed by Mussolini and his Fascists. During 1936 sit-down strikers made their appearance in France. In the fall of that year, the sit-down method was introduced into the United States by the United Automobile Workers and other industrial unions affiliated with the Congress for Industrial Organizations^qv^. Labor leaders favoring this method, whereby strikers took possession of a plant, claimed that the sit-down strike was legal because it was "the most effective and least costly way" for workers to protect their right to their jobs. Those opposed asserted that the use of the method was a "legal wrong" and that it was "revolutionary."

National attention was focused on sit-down strikes in January, 1937, when the method was used to force a complete suspension of activity in the General Motors plant at Flint, Mich. Instead of permitting the forcible ejection of the "sit-downers," the governor of the state sent national guardsmen to the scene to prevent any action pending negotiations between company officials and union leaders. Federal officials refused to condemn the sit-down method or to intervene, though Secretary of Labor Perkins did confer with leaders of both sides. She made it clear that she was in "doubt" regarding the legality of sit-down strikes.

In contrast to the Michigan procedure, the police, early in 1937, removed discharged sit-down strikers from the factory of the Fansteel Metallurgical Corporation plant in North Chicago, Ill. Later the National Labor Relations Board^qv^ ordered the reinstatement by the company of these workers, including thirty-seven who had been convicted of violating the laws of Illinois by seizing and detaining property. The Circuit Court of Appeals refused to enforce this order whereupon the case of National Labor Relations Board v. Fansteel Metallurgical Corporation was carried to the Supreme Court. On Feb. 27, 1939, the highest tribunal, in a 6 to 2 decision, emphatically declared the sit-down strike to be "illegal in its inception and prosecution," and a "high-handed proceeding without shadow of legal right." The employees had a right to strike "but they had no license to commit acts of violence or to seize their employer's plant." The employer had "the right to discharge the wrongdoers from its employ." Following this sweeping decision, sit-down strikes practically ceased in the United States.

[55 S. Ct. 490; Herbert Harris, *American Labor.*]

ERIK MCKINLEY ERIKSSON

Strip, THE. *See* Cherokee Strip, The.

Stuart's Ride (June 12–15, 1862). As Lee (C.) prepared to resist McClellan's (U.) attempt to capture Richmond (*see* Seven Days' Battles), it was necessary to know the exact position of the Federal right (*see* Jackson's Valley Campaign). On June 13 Stuart's (C.) cavalry accomplished this. Then, Stuart decided to ride around McClellan's army, because he thought such a movement would be unexpected. On June 14 Stuart was in McClellan's rear; on June 15 the cavalry rode into Richmond, having traveled over one hundred miles. As a result of Stuart's ride McClellan changed his supply base to the James River; Lee was supplied with the information he required. The moral value of the ride was tremendous; from a military viewpoint its value was questionable.

[John W. Thomason, *Jeb Stuart.*]

THOMAS ROBSON HAY

Students, Foreign Exchange. American students going abroad have pursued their studies principally in France, Germany, the British Isles, Italy, Scandinavia and Belgium. Few have gone to Latin America and the Orient.

The migration of students to the United States began in 1784, from Latin America. From China, Yung Wing came to Yale, graduating in 1854. Joseph Neesima of Japan began his American studies in Phillips Andover Academy, later graduating from Amherst College; returning to Japan in 1874, he founded Doshisha University. In 1904 the U. S. Bureau of Education reported a total of 2673 students from seventy-four foreign countries. According to a census compiled by the Friendly Relations Committee of New York, the total registration of foreign students in the United States in the college year 1939–40 was 6498 men and 1777 women, a total of 8275. When to this total are added the students from Hawaii and United States born Orientals, the grand total is 12,773. One hundred and two different countries were represented. Canadians, Chinese and Puerto Ricans led in registration, with 2213, 893 and 573 respectively.

Notable contributions to foreign student exchange have been made by educational foundations. The Rockefeller Foundation^qv^ first granted fellowships to Chinese in 1914; to Europeans in 1919. Since 1922 The Institute of International Education has provided fellowships for 2079 American students going abroad and for 1638 foreign students coming to the United States.

Between 1917 and 1938 Barbour Scholarships have been granted at the University of Michigan to 175 women students from the Orient. Between 1920 and 1940 the Belgian American Educational Foundation has provided scholarships for 223

Americans in Belgium, and in the United States for 452 coming from Belgium. The Commonwealth Fund had appointed 403 Fellows from Great Britain between 1925 and 1940.

Under the auspices of The American-Scandinavian Foundation 238 American students had been sent to Norway, Sweden and Denmark, and 636 Scandinavians have been brought to this country up to 1940.

[Friendly Relations Committee, *Unofficial Ambassadors.*]

RALPH CLELAND SCOTT

Stump-Speakers. Jackson's heavy popular vote in the national elections of 1824 first apprised the Eastern seaboard of the potential power, as well as peculiar prejudices, of the backwoods voters beyond the Alleghenies. However, local politicians had already gauged the fierce, often cantankerous, dislikes of the independent pioneers: their distrust of the townsman, his money power, his suave manners and effete learning and his easy, "degenerate" life. Campaigning among the scattered settlements, the successful candidate for town, county, or state office, mounting a stump in a clearing, stressed the things that would appeal to his farmer, woodsman, village-storekeeper hearers. His oratory was of the florid, spread-eagle variety wherein freedom, the flag, the right to do and acquire as one pleased were mixed with violent denunciations of bankers, manufacturers and Philadelphia lawyers. It was a guarantee of victory could he impugn his opponent as Eastern-educated, foppish, in sympathy with the rich. Promises were freely made and liquor as freely, though a trifle more discreetly, dispensed. The candidate dressed for the part and professed the democratic dogma that he was but the humble equal of the roughest-dressed of the horny-handed nobles before him. Thus was the pattern set for all later appeals to the rural vote; and "stumping" retained its usage long after the decaying tree stumps of the pioneer settlements gave way first to the platform under the trees and, in our own day, to the private train and the automobile equipped with loud-speakers. Stumping became a national phenomenon in the gaudy presidential campaign of 1840[qv], when Harrison himself, though descended from Virginia aristocrats, played the part of a rough Westerner in coonskin cap and spoke from stumps as well as platforms in his tour through the former Northwest Territory[qv].

CHARLES J. FINGER

Sturges v. Crowninshield (4 Wheat. 122, 1819). This case examined at length (1) the respective powers of state and Federal governments over bankruptcy, and (2) what constitutes that "impairment of the obligation of contract" which the Constitution forbids. The Court concluded that the power of Congress to enact "uniform laws on the subject of bankruptcies" was supreme but not exclusive until Congress, by legislation, makes it so; that the obligation of contract[qv] lies in the law which makes the contract binding at the time it is made, and provides the remedy in case of breach; and that the New York bankruptcy law here involved was invalid because it applied retroactively to contracts made prior to its enactment.

[Charles Warren, *The Supreme Court in United States History.*]

HARVEY PINNEY

Sublette's Cut-Off (1841–69) was a dry branch of the Oregon Trail[qv] between South Pass and Bear River, Wyoming, fifty-three miles shorter than the better watered Fort Bridger[qv] detour. Part of the cut-off was used in 1832 for pack mules by William Sublette, hair-trigger fur man and congressional aspirant. Capt. Bonneville's wagon train followed the route in 1832. Others took the same general course. Father DeSmet crossing South Pass (1841) ahead of the Oregon migration found two trails, one bearing south, the other west across the desert. One became the Oregon Trail. The other—Sublette's—was also called Meek's, Greenwood's or Hedspeth's cut-off. Both were traveled extensively until 1869.

[H. M. Chittenden, *The American Fur Trade;* Archer B. Hulbert, ed., *Crown Collection of American Maps;* Washington Irving, *Adventures of Captain Bonneville;* R. G. Thwaites, ed., *DeSmet's Letters;* Edwin Bryant, *Rocky Mountain Adventures;* Richard J. Oglesby: Forty-Niner, *Papers in Illinois History, 1938,* Ill. State Hist. Soc.]

JAY MONAGHAN

Submarine and International Law, THE. The perfection of the submarine as an instrument of naval warfare before the outbreak of the World War in 1914 introduced a new factor in the application of traditional concepts of international law. Traditional practice had accepted the right of a belligerent warship to visit and search[qv] a merchant ship on the high seas, in order to establish its identity, belligerent or neutral; if found to be belligerent[qv], to capture it for condemnation at prize court; if neutral[qv], to send it in to prize court[qv] for adjudication if suspected of violating international law. If impossible to send in a belligerent merchant ship to a prize court, practice permitted the destruction of the vessel, after first providing for the safety of passengers, crew and ship's papers. During the World War the opposing belligerents developed a structure of confessedly illegal "retaliations"^{qv} against each other, for the initiation of which it is impossible to locate the original spot of sin. Submarines of Germany and her allies began to torpedo enemy merchant ships without warning. Great Britain and her allies armed their merchant ships with instructions to fire on enemy submarines that should show "hostile intent." When these torpedoings, without visit and search, began, the United States decided to hold Germany to "strict accountability" for the injury or loss of American lives or property by violations of international law[qv], even when those violations were directed against a ship flying, not the American flag, but a foreign flag, even a foreign belligerent flag, even a foreign belligerent flag on an armed merchant ship. Following the peace with Germany of 1921, a mixed claims commission[qv] of the United States and Germany awarded damages to citizens of the United States for these acknowledged violations of international law. Since the war, multilateral treaties have outlawed submarine warfare which did not exercise the right of visit and search and provision for the safety of the crew and passengers, unless the merchant ship should not heed the signal to stop.

Of these treaties the most significant was the London Naval Treaty of 1930[qv], in which the United States, Great Britain and Japan agreed on the following as established rules of international law: (1) In their action with regard to merchant ships, submarines must conform to the rules of international law to which surface vessels are subject; (2) in particular, except in the case of persistent refusal to stop on being duly summoned, or of active resistance to visit or search, a warship, whether surface vessel or submarine, may not sink or render incapable of navigation a merchant vessel without having first placed passengers, crew and ship's papers in a place of safety. For this purpose the ship's boats are not regarded as a place of safety unless the safety of the passengers and crew is assured, in the existing sea and weather conditions, by the proximity of land, or the presence of another vessel which is in a position to take them on board.

The United States, Great Britain and Japan ratified the treaty. The naval treaty of London expired by its own limitation on Dec. 31, 1936. Before then, on Nov. 6, 1936, the United States, Great Britain, France, Italy and Japan signed a special protocol, renewing indefinitely these articles for the regulation of submarine warfare. They invited other powers to adhere. Germany adhered, Nov. 23, 1936, and Russia on Feb. 19, 1937. Though codification of existing law is not necessary to make it law, nevertheless the formal acceptance of these principles by all of the great submarine powers confirms their binding character.

These rules were accepted by the principal naval powers when the European war broke out in September, 1939, and for several months appeared to have been, in general, observed. However, as the struggle for mastery of the seas developed, including British measures of "contraband control" and interception of German exports via neutral states, Germany, on the ground that the Allies were arming their merchant ships, and on the basis of retaliation, paid less and less attention to the accepted rules governing submarine warfare. As in 1914–17 the opposing maritime systems of the belligerents used the pretext of "retaliation" in order to reach for their most deadly weapons of warfare.

[Samuel Flagg Bemis, *A Diplomatic History of the United States; Draft Convention on the Rights and Duties of Neutral States in Naval and Aerial War*, Supplement to Vol. XXXIII (1939) of the *American Journal of International Law.*]

SAMUEL FLAGG BEMIS

Submarine and Torpedo in the Civil War. In 1863–64, the Confederate States[qv], incapable of taking the sea in force, resorted to submarines in an endeavor to break the Union blockade[qv] at Charleston, S. C., and Norfolk, Va. The "David"[qv] class of steam-propelled semisubmersibles were cylindrical in form with conical ends. They carried a spar torpedo having a powder charge of 54 to 132 pounds. The first "David" was 54 feet long by 5½ feet in diameter. The *Hunley,* an improved type, was a hand-propelled submarine. At Charleston, S. C., on Oct. 5, 1863, a "David" damaged the *Ironsides,* and on Feb. 17, 1864, the *Hunley* sank the *Housatonic*. Both attacking vessels were lost. A converted steam pinnace "David" damaged the *Minnesota* at Newport News, Va., April 9, 1864, and escaped. The Union Navy built one submarine, the *Alligator*. Launched November, 1861, she was unsuccessful and sank under tow off Cape Hatteras, April, 1863. Submarines were instrumental in prolonging the war as a rigid anchored blockade was not possible after they were invented.

During the Civil War the term torpedo[qv] was applied to what are now known as mines. Torpedoes were used extensively by the South to protect rivers and harbors. During Farragut's attack on Mobile Bay[qv] the *Tecumseh* was sunk by a torpedo. In all, seven monitors and eleven wooden vessels were sunk by torpedoes during the war. The greatest ingenuity was shown by the Confederates who used barrels, demijohns, old boilers and cans to make torpedoes. Very few vessels were sunk by gunfire during the Civil War while submarines and torpedoes cost the Union nineteen vessels.

[Murray F. Seuter, *The Evolution of the Submarine Boat, Mine and Torpedo.*] COLBY G. RUCKER

Submarines. The first practical submarine was the invention of David Bushnell of Westbrook, Conn. In 1775–76 he developed the famous *Turtle,* a strongly built, egg-shaped vessel, embodying many of the characteristics of the modern submarine. This vessel made three attacks on British men-o'-war at New York, and while all attacks failed through the inexperience of the operator, the excellence of Bushnell's submarine has never been questioned. The next submarine was the *Nautilus*[qv] of Robert Fulton, in 1801. This was the first metal submarine. It was made of copper over iron frames and was 24 feet long by 7 feet in diameter. Fulton successfully blew up a schooner at Brest in August, 1801. The French turning cold, Fulton went to England in May, 1804, where William Pitt was much attracted by Fulton's invention. With Pitt as a witness, Fulton blew up the brig, *Dorothea,* at Walmer, in 1805. The admiralty finally rejected Fulton's plans and he returned to America.

Submarines were used to some extent in the Civil War (*see* Submarine and Torpedo in the Civil War). In 1875 an Irish-American named John Holland, of Paterson, N. J., constructed his first submarine, the *Holland No. 1.* In 1877 he built his experimental *Holland No. 2* for the Fenian Society and in 1879 he built for the same society the famous *Fenian Ram,* or *Holland No. 3.* This vessel, the direct prototype of Holland submarines of the World War period, was stolen from him by the Fenians. In disgust he turned to building submarines with a view to interesting the U. S. Navy. In 1895 the Navy Department accepted *Holland No. 7,* and the Holland Boat Company was formed. This company has sold submarines to nearly every major nation.

While Holland was successful with his single-hull submarine, in 1895 another inventor, Simon Lake, saw his own plans rejected by the Navy Department. He then built a small experimental ship in Baltimore. He obtained capital and built the 59-ton, steel *Argonaut I.* This ship was of double-hull construction. Lake was able to interest Russia, and many vessels were constructed to his plans. In general, his ships were not as satisfactory as the Holland boats, although his double-hull feature permitted the use of ship lines. Eventually the U. S. Navy brought out a type of submarine which combined the Holland and Lake principles, known as the Government type. All modern American submarines are constructed on this principle.

The first disastrous American submarine accident occurred in 1915, when the *F-4* sank off Pearl Harbor, T. H., in 305 feet of water. All hands were lost. Although the boat was raised the cause of the accident was never determined. In 1925, the *S-51* was rammed and sunk by the SS. *City of Rome* off Block Island, R. I. Three of the crew were saved. In December, 1927, the *S-4* was rammed submerged while on the measured mile off Provincetown, Mass., by the Coast Guard destroyer *Paulding.* All hands were lost. In 1939 the submarine *Squalus* sank off Portsmouth, N. H., with the loss of thirty-three men.

American submarines saw little action in the World War, although seven submarines of the L class were stationed at Berehaven, Ireland. On July 10, 1918, *L-2* encountered *U-65,* but before she could fire her torpedoes the *U-65* suffered a terrific explosion of undetermined origin and sank. During the war the U. S. Navy developed the Submarine Chaser, a fast wooden vessel, 110 feet long, and very seaworthy. A large number of these vessels crossed the Atlantic under their own power. They were used principally to back up the Allied antisubmarine barrage across the Straits of Otranto, Italy.

[The U. S. Naval Institute *Proceedings;* Murray F. Seuter, *The Evolution of the Submarine Boat, Mine and Torpedo.*]

COLBY G. RUCKER

Subsidies. The United States has been exceedingly liberal in granting subsidies to various commercial enterprises, despite frequent doubts concerning the constitutionality of such action. Throughout our national history, state and privately owned transportation improvements have been freely subsidized. Between 1825 and 1829 Congress voted to subscribe $235,000 to the Louisville and Portland Canal, $1,000,000 to the Chesapeake and Ohio Canal, $225,000 to the Chesapeake and Delaware Canal, and $80,000 to the Dismal Swamp Canal[qqv]. About the same time land grants were made to aid in the construction of three canals to connect the Great Lakes with the Ohio and Mississippi rivers, and one of these waterways, the Illinois and Michigan Canal[qv], has continued to receive assistance from the State of Illinois to the present time. The Sault Ste. Marie Canal (*see* St. Marys Falls Ship Canal) also received a large land donation from Congress. Railroad promoters likewise sought Federal subsidies, and between 1850 and 1871 over 131,000,000 acres of public lands[qv] were given to them. The first transcontinental railroads, the Union Pacific and Central Pacific[qqv], received not only 20,000,000 acres of public lands but also a loan of $53,000,000.

Mail subsidies to the merchant marine[qv] were generously granted during the years 1845 to 1858, 1864 to 1877, in 1891 and after the World War, but in each case they failed to establish a shipping industry comparable to that of Great Britain. More successful have been the subsidies given to aviation. Between 1926 and 1933, $87,000,000 in mail subsidies were given to various air transport companies and, while excessive in amount and accompanied by corruption, they have been largely responsible for the present far-flung air service. Airplane manufacturers not only profited from this boon to commercial flying but they also received many lucrative contracts for the sale of their machines to the War and Navy Departments.

Newspapers have also enjoyed government subsidies. In the 19th century many newspapers were largely financed by government advertising and when there was a change in administration a goodly number of the old party organs would be forced to suspend because of the loss of patronage (*see* Newspapers as Political Organs). More recently the cheap postage rates on fourth-class matter have served as a subsidy to newspapers and periodicals.

Under the Newlands Reclamation Act of 1902 the Government has expended many millions of dollars on reclamation[qv] projects and the farmers thereon have also received government largesse in the form of frequent credit extensions, cancellations of interest and even of principal. Irrigation[qv] projects necessitate the construction of dams and reservoirs, many of which provide electric power. This power has been sold at low rates to distributing companies which have thus been saved the necessity of undertaking expensive construction work. Electric power companies further benefited by the government land policy which, until recently, permitted them to preempt power sites at little cost.

The establishment of the Reconstruction Finance Corporation and the Public Works Administration[qqv] with their "pump priming" programs marked a new era in government subsidies to business. Not only are loans made to railroads and industrial corporations at low rates but outright grants are offered to state and local governments for permanent improvements such as sewage-disposal plants, waterworks, parks, public schools, municipal buildings and settlement houses. Federal subsidies and grants-in-aid[qv] have assisted agricultural colleges, vocational training schools, state road construction, state forests and parks.

Tariffs[qv], although not strictly speaking subsidies, have the effect of subsidies because they artificially increase the income of producers of protected goods. The very first tariff gave some protection to American manufactures and that protection was progressively increased until 1833 when the free-trade elements succeeded in forcing a compromise which brought rates down to a lower level. But at no time has the policy of indirectly subsidizing business by tariff protection been abandoned. The farmers who have been more hurt than helped by tariffs obtained their subsidy in 1933 in the Agricultural Adjustment Act[qv], which provided for benefit payments to farmers who co-operated with the Government in the adjustment program.

[M. Neufeld, The Government Has Always Paid, in *American Scholar*, Winter, 1937; J. E. Saugstad, *Shipping and Shipbuilding Subsidies;* J. B. Sanborn, *Congressional Grants of Land in Aid of Railways.*]

PAUL WALLACE GATES

Subsistence Homesteads. Prior to 1933 various groups had interested themselves in correcting the deplorable conditions under which stranded miners and residents of rural slums were living. Their plan was to assist these people to settle upon small farms where they might raise a few chickens, keep a cow and a pig and grow sufficient vegetables for their own needs. To provide cash income, part-time crafts work was introduced, such as weaving, furniture and lace making. Henry Ford, who had contributed his share to the centralization[qv] of industry, became convinced that decentralization was desirable both for employer and employee and he relocated some of his plants in small communities where part-time farming could be engaged in by the workers. In 1933 the New Deal[qv] seized upon the plan and allocated $25,000,000 for the establishment of subsistence homesteads in areas of serious unemployment. Demonstration projects were undertaken, lands acquired, improvements constructed and unemployed people settled thereon. Haste in beginning the Federal program seemed essential and some mistakes were made which received more publicity than their importance warranted. Political opposition later forced contraction of the original plan and some of the projects were abandoned. Most successful, perhaps, is the Arthurdale, W. Va., subsistence homestead colony in which a group of stranded miners have been rehabilitated.

[Report of Division of Subsistence Homesteads, in *Annual Report*, Secretary of the Interior, 1934.]

PAUL WALLACE GATES

Substitutes, Civil War. No conscription[q.v.] in the North during the Civil War was absolute. Always there was the opportunity for the drafted man to hire a substitute, if he could afford it. This was first allowed in the militia draft of 1862 on the theory that, so long as each name drawn from the wheel produced a man, it made no difference whether the drafted person or one hired to take his place appeared for muster. The Conscription Act of March 3, 1863, definitely legalized this method of draft evasion, and each later amendment perpetuated it. Until the act of Feb. 24, 1864, the conscript could take his choice between hiring a substitute or paying the Government $300 as commutation of service. Thereafter, substitution alone was permitted, except for conscientious objectors[q.v.]. Furthermore, exemption by furnishing a substitute extended only till the next succeeding draft, when the principal again became liable (*see* Bounty-Jumper). At once the prices of substitutes rose far above the $300 to which the commutation clause had held them. For this reason legal draft evasion became the prerogative of only the unusually well to do. In the last two years of the war 118,010 substitutes were enlisted, as contrasted with 52,067 conscripts.

The Confederacy also allowed a limited substitution system from early days of the war. The first Conscription Act permitted substitutes from men not legally liable to service to the extent of one man a month in each company. Frauds in the supplying of such substitutes approximated those in the North, as did also the cost of such service (in comparative values). The second Conscription Act (Sept. 17, 1862) made men previously furnishing substitutes again liable to service, thus causing much dissension and legal action. The whole system was abolished by the end of the year 1863. The number of substitutes has never been accurately compiled.

[F. A. Shannon, *Organization and Administration of the Union Army;* A. B. Moore, *Conscription and Conflict in the Confederacy.*]

FRED A. SHANNON

Subtreasuries arose from the problem of the care of the Federal Government's funds. After Jackson had the Government's deposits removed (*see* Removal of Deposits) from the Second United States Bank[q.v.], they were placed in so-called "pet banks"[q.v.]. This system not proving satisfactory, an act, approved July 4, 1840, set up an independent treasury. Until June 30, 1843, part of the payments to the Government might be other than specie. The law was repealed Aug. 13, 1841, but was re-enacted in August, 1846, with the intent that receipts and expenditures were to be in specie or treasury notes. Subtreasuries were established at New York, Philadelphia, Charleston, New Orleans, St. Louis and Boston; and later at Chicago, San Francisco and Cincinnati. The gravest trouble came because government surpluses caused a shortage in the money markets. The situation was helped after the establishment of the National Banks[q.v.] in 1863–64, and these banks were made government depositories. Secretary of the Treasury Shaw, in the period 1902 to 1908, used many devices to smooth the effect of treasury operations on the money market. The Federal Reserve Act of 1913 provided that the Federal Reserve Banks[q.v.] might act as fiscal agents for the Government. This made the subtreasuries unnecessary. However, political pressure caused them to be temporarily retained. The last one was abolished Feb. 10, 1921.

[D. R. Dewey, *Financial History of the United States.*]

JAMES D. MAGEE

Suburban Growth. The rapid growth of cities has been an outstanding phenomenon in American national life during the past three quarters of a century. This growth has taken place, in large measure, through the successive development of suburbs in an ever-widening ring around original municipalities. Not infrequently these suburbs are assimilated, one after another, by the central city and become an integral part of it, but more commonly they set up for themselves as independent political units.

Suburban growth is the outcome of a competition for space in the downtown areas, and in the United States it has generally been determined by the degree of congestion there. Mercantile business concentrates toward the center of every city and this region soon becomes the area of highest land values. When the limit of economical expansion by increasing the height of buildings has been reached, the steadily mounting scale of rents is a prime factor in driving occupants out of this high-value zone. Residences go first, then certain types of business which have a small annual turnover, and finally those industries which require extensive facilities in the form of yards and storage space. Meanwhile neighborhood shopping centers are created in the growing suburban community, usually at the intersection of main traffic thoroughfares. Beginning at the four corners the small business center gradually radiates outward until it sometimes becomes the heart of a new downtown area in a satellite city.

The direction of suburban growth is dictated, for the most part, by considerations of topography. Obstacles in the way of a lake, river, mountain range, or tract of marshy land sometimes interfere with the natural direction of overflow. Areas of moderately high land usually become the location of the better residential suburbs while tracts of low or level land are more favored by industries and for the homes of those who are employed in these industries.

The extraordinarily rapid rate of suburban growth in the United States has been due, in considerable measure, to the spectacular development of facilities for transportation—the street railway, motorbus and motorcar. So far as residential suburbs are concerned the motorcar has been the most important of all centrifugal factors during the past generation. But the resultant heavy congestion of traffic in the downtown areas of the larger cities, caused by the in-and-out flow at certain hours of the day, is now tending to weaken somewhat the lure of suburban life.

[H. Paul Douglass, *The Suburban Trend;* William B. Munro, Principles of City Growth, in *Municipal Administration.*]

WILLIAM B. MUNRO

Subversive is a word which has long been used to describe an action having a tendency to overthrow, destroy or ruin anything. Only incidentally has the term been applied to actions directed against a government. In fact the word seems not to have appeared in the indices and guides to legal literature, at least up to 1938. During that year, however, the national House of Representatives created a Committee to Investigate Un-American Activities, with Representative Martin Dies of Texas as chairman. After its creation, this committee zealously pursued its task of uncovering "subversive" activities of all kinds. The frequency with which this so-called Dies Committee received front-page newspaper publicity caused the word "subversive" to become a part of the vocabularies of many Americans.

During the latter part of 1938 and in 1939, the committee listened to testimony by scores of persons who had real or fancied information regarding subversive activities. A particular object of the committee's probing was the Communist party[qv]. A connection was found to exist between this party in the United States and the Communist Third International or Comintern, which was created in 1919 by the Russian Bolsheviks. Evidence was presented to the committee to show that the Communists were placing their members or sympathizers in positions of labor leadership, particularly in the Congress of Industrial Organizations[qv], and various other organizations, such as peace societies, and even in government offices.

The committee also investigated the activities of agencies attempting to propagate "fascist" or "nazi" ideas in the United States. Attention was chiefly centered on the German-American Bund, headed by Fritz Kuhn. This organization was reported to have about 6600 members divided among fifty local units in 1937. The Bund members claimed to be loyal to the United States but witnesses before the committee claimed that the organization was subversive in character.

[*Congressional Record,* Vols. 83 and 84.]

ERIK McKINLEY ERIKSSON

Subways. Street congestion and the consequent slowing down of urban transportation in the larger American cities were becoming intolerable to the American temperament in the latter 19th century, and it was agreed that transit removed from the street level must be accomplished. Elevated railroads[qv] were built in three of the great cities (*see* Transportation, Urban) and found to be nuisances because of their noise, dirt, unsightliness and detriment to property values. Subways had been discussed in New York in 1860, but the idea had been dropped because of the palpably enormous cost. Nevertheless, Boston made an elementary start toward subterranean travel between 1895 and 1900 by removing 1.7 miles of trolley-car tracks from crowded streets in the business district and placing them underground. Later these tunnels were extended and welded into the city's elevated system, first opened in 1901, so arranged that the trains ran underground in the busier portions of the city. New York's first contract for subway building was let in 1900. By that time or shortly thereafter, it was said that a billion paying passengers per year were riding in the street cars of the city, and the crowding and slowness of movement were serious problems. The first subway line, that of the Interborough Rapid Transit Company, up Fourth Avenue and Broadway, was opened in 1904. The company at once began an extension from the Battery to Brooklyn and completed a tunnel under the East River in 1908. Tunnels under the East River to Queens Borough, built 1905–8 by the New York and Long Island Railroad, were taken over by the Interborough, and its lines extended to Astoria and Flushing. Another tunnel was bored under the river at the Battery by 1919. By 1930 the Interborough operated 224 miles of subway and 139 miles of elevated lines, including (under lease) the Manhattan elevated system. Meanwhile the Brooklyn Rapid Transit (later Brooklyn-Manhattan) Corporation had been building a large network of subway and elevated lines in Brooklyn. This company entered Manhattan by two tunnels driven under the East River between 1914 and 1920, and a third was completed in 1924. The company operates 258 miles of subway and elevated lines. A city-owned system of subways was begun in 1924 and opened its first line up Eighth Avenue in 1932; it thereafter built other track until the system was more than 50 miles in extent. The Hudson and Manhattan Tubes, completed 1908–11, connecting New York, Jersey City, Hoboken and Newark, have four notable tunnels under the Hudson (*see* Tunnels). Philadelphia opened the first line of a subway system in 1907, and thereafter extended it several miles. After 1920 several of the large cities began planning to put short sections of their surface-car lines underground; Newark and St. Louis have carried out the idea. Los Angeles in 1924–25 constructed nearly a mile of subway as a part of the Hollywood-Glendale line, through which short trains of interurban surface cars are operated. Between 1900 and 1910 a remarkable system of freight subways was built under downtown Chicago, to carry goods in and out of large stores and warehouses, remove ashes, waste, etc.

ALVIN F. HARLOW

"Suffering Traders," THE, were a group trading to the Western Indian tribes who lost horses, goods and in instances their lives to Indians on foray during Pontiac's War[qv] (1763–64). Their sufferings were set forth as a basis for compensation in the form of a land grant at the Treaty of Fort Stanwix in 1768[qv]. To strengthen the claim another was combined with it: that of an earlier group which had suffered similar losses (1749–54). The claimants received a grant of land from the Iroquois Confederation, the fate of which was bound up with that of the Indiana Company[qv].

[A. T. Volwiler, *George Croghan.*]

SAMUEL C. WILLIAMS

Suffolk, Operations at (1863). In February, 1863, Longstreet's corps (C.) was detached from Lee's army to the vicinity of Petersburg, Va., for better subsistence and to provide against any sudden Federal movement in that locality. Longstreet's command was divided, two divisions being stationed near Petersburg, Longstreet going with the other two divisions into southeastern Virginia to collect much-needed forage and provisions. It was his first independent command. While carrying on his foraging mission, he allowed himself to become involved in a fruitless siege of the Federal headquarters at Suffolk (April, 1863), which so long delayed him that he was unable to rejoin Lee until after the battle of Chancellorsville[qv]. Though he accomplished nothing of consequence, Longstreet's absence greatly jeopardized Lee's safety.

[D. S. Freeman, *R. E. Lee.*]

THOMAS ROBSON HAY

Suffolk Banking System. When the Suffolk Bank was chartered in Massachusetts (1818), it agreed to redeem the notes of any New England bank at par if the issuing bank would keep with it a permanent deposit of $2000 or upward, depending upon the amount of the bank's capital, and, in addition, deposit sufficient funds to redeem any of its notes that might reach Boston through the ordinary channels of trade. It was calculated that the use of the $2000 permanent deposit would compensate the Suffolk Bank for its services. Country bankers were enraged, for the plan threatened to reduce circulation and profit incident thereto. The Suffolk Bank persisted, however, collecting notes of country banks and presenting them for redemption in specie. By 1824 other Boston banks joined with the Suffolk Bank, making the plan effective throughout New England. Specie redemption so elevated the standing of all New England bank notes that they gradually were accepted at par throughout the country. This specie-redemption plan was later incorporated into the National Bank Act[qv].

[Davis R. Dewey, *State Banking before the Civil War.*]

FRANK PARKER

Suffolk Resolves (Sept. 9, 1774). Of the many meetings held in Massachusetts in 1774 to protest the Coercion Acts[qv], the best known was that of delegates from Boston and other towns in Suffolk County, held at Dedham on Sept. 6 and adjourned to Milton on Sept. 9. There Dr. Joseph Warren presented the resolves, which vigorously denounced the actions of England; refused obedience to the recent acts, or to officials created under them; urged weekly militia musters, nonpayment of taxes and nonintercourse with Great Britain; and suggested the need of a provincial congress to meet at Concord in October. The resolves were passed unanimously and taken by Paul Revere to the Continental Congress[qv] at Philadelphia, which by endorsing them moved another step toward independence.

[Richard Frothingham, *Joseph Warren;* A. B. Hart, *Commonwealth History of Massachusetts;* S. G. Fisher, *Struggle for American Independence;* J. T. Adams, *Revolutionary New England.*]

HERBERT W. HILL

Suffrage. *See* Franchise, The; Woman Suffrage; Negro Suffrage.

Suffrage, Exclusions from the. Age, sex, race, residence, citizenship, religious experience, tax payment and education were at one time or another the basis of exclusion from the suffrage in America, but in the course of the years most of these hurdles were lowered or abandoned until in 1938, as contrasted with the 6% who could vote during the Revolutionary period, over 50% of the total population of the United States had the privilege of suffrage. Despite occasional agitation for lowering the age requirement, all persons below twenty-one were excluded. By the 20th century noncitizens were uniformly prohibited in contrast with some 19th-century attempts on the part of states to lure immigrants by enfranchising those who had only declared their intention of acquiring citizenship. Less than a year's residence and inability to pay a poll tax[qv], especially in the South, have also prevented suffrage; and the constitutions of some states have provided for the exclusion of persons mentally unfit or convicted of infamous crimes.

The educational test for voting[qv] has been the most obvious means of exclusion in an age of generally extended suffrage. Prevented from excluding the Negro as such because of the Fifteenth Amendment[qv], many Southern states, beginning with Mississippi in 1890 (*see* Mississippi Plan), required of voters ability to read or interpret understandingly any part of the state constitution. This barred many Negroes who had not already been excluded by failure to pay the poll tax or by some technicality in answering registration questions. By such devices all but about 10% of the adult Negro population of the South had by 1938 been excluded from the registration lists. (*See also* Grandfather Clause.) Permitting the political parties to prescribe additional qualifications for participation in the primaries, such as the Texas "white primary rule," set a precedent by which Negroes as such could be barred from primaries and thus, in the South, from effective political action. An increasing immigrant problem in the big cities of the North led to agitation in the early 20th century to extend the use of literacy tests[qv] there.

[Paul Lewinson, *Race, Class, and Party;* K. H. Porter, *A History of Suffrage in the United States.*]

BAYRD STILL

Sugar, Beet. *See* Beet Sugar.

Sugar Acts, Colonial. The British Empire was dependent upon its West India islands for sugar. The rich sugar planters, residing in England, became politically powerful, and in 1733 secured the enactment of the Molasses Act[qv]. Under this law foreign molasses, imported into any British colony, was subject to an import duty of six pence per gallon. The object was not taxation, but to give the British sugar planters a monopoly of the American molasses market. The law was opposed by the New England merchants, especially Massachusetts and Rhode Island, on the ground that the resultant increased price of rum[qv] would injure both the fishing industry and the trade to Africa (*see* Trade, Triangular). The protests were ineffective and the dire results failed to develop. Opposition to the law died down, especially as there was little systematic effort to enforce it. The sugar planters discovered the Molasses Act was of little value to them and what they most needed was a larger market in Europe, which they got through a rebate of the import duties on sugar exported to the continent. In time the British rum distilleries absorbed the British molasses while there was no market for that from the growing French sugar industry. This situation made French molasses cheap and there developed a well-organized colonial evasion of the import duty.

In 1764 Grenville had enacted a new Sugar Act by which he undertook to end the smuggling trade in foreign molasses and at the same time secure a revenue. The duty on foreign molasses was lowered from six to threepence a gallon, the duties on foreign refined sugar were raised, and an increased export bounty on British refined sugar bound for the colonies was granted. The net result was to give the British sugar planters an effective monopoly of the American sugar market; smuggling of foreign sugar became unprofitable, and the old illicit trade in foreign molasses was disturbed. Americans had been importing large quantities of foreign molasses on which they paid, by collusion, total sums that averaged somewhere between half a penny and a penny a gallon. Most of this money went into the pockets of the customs officials instead of the treasury. Under the act of 1764, the three pence was more than the traffic would bear, if the law was enforced. There were violent protests at first; two years later the duty was lowered to one penny a gallon, applied alike to foreign and British imports, and the protests on the Molasses duty came to an end. At this lower rate it was an important revenue producer and yielded annually from 1767 to 1775 an average of £12,194 per year.

Other phases of the Sugar Act of 1764 were far more irritating than was the lowered duty on molasses. One was a new duty on wine imported from Madeira, which prior to this time had come in duty free and was the main source of profit for the fish and food ships returning from the Mediterranean. This part of the Sugar Act led to few direct protests, but did produce some spectacular attempts at evasion, such as the Capt. Malcolm wine running episode in Boston. The provisions that produced the most irritation were new bonding regulations compelling ship masters to give bond, even when loaded with nonenumerated goods (*see* Enumerated Commodities). The worst feature was a provision that bond had to be given before any article enumerated or nonenumerated was put on board. Under American conditions it was impossible for a shipmaster to give a new bond at a custom house before he took on board every new consignment of freight. The universal practice was to load first, then clear and give bond. Under the Sugar Act any ship caught with any article on board before bond covering that article had been given was subject to seizure and confiscation. The Customs Commissioners made this provision a source of private profit to themselves. The most notorious seizures for technical violations of the bonding provision included John Hancock's sloop *Liberty* and the *Ann* belonging to Henry Laurens of South Carolina.

[F. W. Pittman, *Development of the British West Indies, 1700-1763.*]

O. M. DICKERSON

Sugar Cane, which had been brought to America by Columbus, was cultivated in a small way for making rum and syrup by the early Louisiana colonists. After preliminary failures the latter succeeded in making sugar about 1761, and in 1803 when Louisiana became part of the United States cane was already an established crop. Not long thereafter it was cultivated in small quantities, principally for syrup, along the Gulf Coast and as far north as South Carolina. Though climatic conditions are not as favorable for cane on the mainland as in the West Indies our protective tariff on sugar and molasses encouraged domestic production. About the time of the War of 1812 mills were erected in Georgia and Florida, and Louisiana's sugar output rapidly increased. A new type of cane, introduced in 1825, gave greater sugar yields than previously and was the first of a succession of improved varieties which have periodically given a stimulus to the industry. Meanwhile technical improvements in the manufacture of sugar, some of which are Louisiana inventions, tended to stabilize this branch of farming and to integrate it with sugar factories.

For many years Louisiana was the only cane sugar state. About one third of the country's crop, however, was raised for syrup in South Carolina, Georgia, Florida, Alabama, Mississippi, Texas and Arkansas. The area of cane harvested varies from season to season according to weather but of recent years has ranged between 400,000 and 500,000 acres. Recently a large mill has been erected in Florida which makes nearly 100,000 tons of sugar annually from cane raised by local farmers. The use of cane fiber for celotex has added to the profit from this crop. Nearly 7000 farms in the Gulf States raise cane to sell to sugar mills and some 200,000 farms report cane used for syrup.

The Spanish-American War added Puerto Rico and Hawaii[qqv] to the cane area of the United States. Capt. Cook found sugar cane growing wild in Hawaii when he discovered the islands in 1778 and it was early introduced in Puerto Rico by the Spaniards. Systematic cultivation and commercial sugar production, however, date in both countries from about the middle of the 19th century. At present each has more than a quarter of a million acres under cane and a potential annual output of one million tons of sugar.

[U. S. Census *Reports;* William C. Stubbs, *Sugar Cane, Its History in Georgia, Florida and South Carolina, 1767 to 1900;* George M. Rolph, *Something About Sugar.*]

VICTOR S. CLARK

Sugar House Prisons. There were several sugar refineries, sturdy brick and stone buildings, commonly called sugar houses, in New York City when the American Revolution began—among them Livingston's, Rhinelander's, Cuyler's, Bayard's and Roosevelt's. These were used by the British as prisons, where both captured American soldiers and civilians under suspicion were confined. The most notorious were Livingston's, on Liberty Street, and Rhinelander's, at Rose and Duane streets. Shocking narratives were prevalent of cruelty and privations in these prisons.

[James Grant Wilson, *Memorial History of the City of New York.*]

ALVIN F. HARLOW

Sugar Industry. Until the Louisiana Purchase the only sugar made in the United States was from maple sap for household use and frontier trading. Cane sugar from the West Indies was refined by colonial "sugar bakers" who remelted raw sugar and poured it into moulds topped with wet clay whence water percolated through the mass, washing out impurities and leaving the traditional sugar loaf of our forefathers. About 1810 New Orleans already refined sugar locally and shipped raw sugar for refining to St.

Louis, Louisville and Cincinnati. By 1830 New Orleans had the "largest refinery in the world" with an annual capacity of 6000 tons. With the introduction of steam melting, boneblack clarifying and centrifugal drying about this time plants became larger, so that by 1856 one New York refinery reported an investment of nearly $1,000,000.

Sugar mill improvements before 1850 included steam power to crush cane and vacuum pans and triple effects—an epoch-making Louisiana invention of the 1840's—to evaporate juice. These made mills more expensive and centralized manufacturing, like refining, in larger establishments. In the 1880's unsatisfactory attempts were made to extract juice from cane by the diffusion process, which is universally employed in making beet sugar.

Today both branches of the industry are dominated by big corporations. They require a vast capital for plant investment and to finance their crops, raw sugar purchases and marketing operations. Refineries are situated near large seaport cities with shipping and banking facilities. New York is the country's chief refining center. Recently some cane sugar has been refined in the process of manufacture, a method universal in making beet sugar.

Since 1828 per capita sugar consumption has risen from 12 pounds to 100 pounds per annum. Meanwhile distributing methods have been revolutionized by special packaging for consumers and by varying sugar types for particular uses.

[V. S. Clark, *History of Manufactures in the United States.*]

VICTOR S. CLARK

Sugar Islands was a popular name in colonial times for the sugar-producing islands of the West Indies not including the Greater Antilles. They were occupied shortly before 1650 by English and French colonists and some of them were at first homestead settlements of small farmers. Soon, however, the latter were reinforced by Dutch and Portuguese sugar growers from Brazil forced out of that country by political disturbances. Capital flowed in from Holland and England to finance large plantations and changed their social organization. The islands were important in colonial commerce because the New England and Central colonies sold them codfish, cooperage stock, flour and provisions in exchange for sugar and molasses. They also traded rum distilled from molasses for slaves on the Guinea coast which they sold to island planters, thus supplementing the direct north and south trade by triangular trade[qv] across the Atlantic to the added enrichment of colonial towns.

[Lowell J. Ragatz, *The Fall of the Planter Class in the British Caribbean;* William B. Weeden, *Economic and Social History of New England.*]

VICTOR S. CLARK

Sugar Trust. This term was first applied to a combination of owners of sugar refineries effected in 1887, which was held to be illegal by the New York Court of Appeal (People v. North River Sugar Refining Co.). Thereafter, the term was applied to the American Sugar Refining Company[qv], organized in 1891 under the laws of New Jersey. The earlier trust had taken the form of a small body of trustees to whom various corporations had assigned their stock, giving the trustees authority to vote the stock as they saw fit. The later trust took the form of a distinct corporation, the certificate holders of the earlier trust becoming the stockholders of the American Sugar Refining Company, while the directors and officers of the new trust remained substantially as under the old. Thus, with merely a change in name and in technical legal form, the practical management remained the same. By March, 1892, the trust had obtained a practical monopoly of the business of refining and selling sugar. The combination was prosecuted by the Department of Justice[qv] as a combination in restraint of interstate commerce, prohibited by the Sherman Antitrust Act[qv] of 1890. A majority of the Supreme Court held that the primary business of the American Sugar Refining Company was manufacturing, not commerce; and that the Sherman Act did not prohibit combinations of manufacturers, although the ultimate purpose was to engage in interstate commerce (*see* U. S. v. E. C. Knight Co.).

[E. Jones, *The Trust Problem in the United States;* W. H. Taft, *The Antitrust Act and the Supreme Court;* J. W. Jenks and W. E. Clark, *The Trust Problem;* Industrial Commission, *Report on Trusts and Combinations.*]

P. ORMAN RAY

Sullivan-Clinton Campaign, THE (1779), was planned by Washington in an effort to curb the attacks of the Indians and Tories on the frontiers of New York and Pennsylvania (*see* Cherry Valley Massacre; Wyoming Massacre). Originally planned in 1778 as a westward movement along the Mohawk, the main drive was shifted in 1779 to the Susquehanna. The command, first offered to Gen. Gates and curtly refused, was given Gen. John Sullivan. To hold the eastern tribes of the Iroquois[qv] in check, Gen. James Clinton, who was in charge of the New York wing of the army, sent Col. Van Schaick in April to make a surprise attack on the Onondagas.

The major force of the campaign was mobilized in Easton, Pa. On June 18 Sullivan with about 2500 men under Generals Maxwell, Hand and Poor moved toward Wyoming, Pa. Here, disappointed at not finding the supplies he expected, he delayed for over five weeks while, with difficulty, supplies were collected. On Aug. 11 the army reached Tioga, and the following day the greater part of the troops were pushed forward to attack the Indian town of Chemung. The Indians fled, and being pursued by Gen. Hand ambushed a part of his men, killing six. Sullivan fell back to Tioga, where Fort Sullivan was built as a base for supplies. Here, on Aug. 22, he was joined by Gen. Clinton, with 1500 men, who had proceeded southwestward from Canajoharie on the Mohawk, destroying the Indian villages on the upper Susquehanna. On Aug. 26 Sullivan moved his whole force toward the territory of the Cayuguas and Senecas. At Newtown, near the present city of Elmira, the Indians and Tories made their only stand. The fatalities on both sides were not large. The Indians and Tories were driven from the field. From Newtown the army pushed forward, skirting the eastern shore of Lake Seneca, to old Genesee Castle. Forty Indian villages were burned and 160,000 bushels of corn destroyed. Failing to make a junction with Col. Brodhead, who had left Fort Pitt on Aug. 11 (*see* Brodhead's Allegheny Campaign), Sullivan felt the season was too far advanced to attempt the capture of Niagara as had been planned and returned to Easton.

[A. C. Flick, *The Sullivan-Clinton Campaign in 1779.*]

A. C. FLICK

Sully, Fort, was built by Gen. Alfred Sully in 1863 as a station for the army in the war against the Sioux[qv]. It was first located three miles below Pierre, S. Dak., but in 1866 was relocated twenty-eight miles above Pierre where forage was more abundant for the cavalry. It was abandoned in 1891 when no longer needed for the protection of the region from hostile Indians. No battles were fought in the region. It was a regimental post.

[South Dakota Historical *Collections*, Vol. VIII, p. 81.]

DOANE ROBINSON

Sully's Expeditions. *See* Dakotas, Expeditions of Gen. Sibley and Gen. Sully in.

Sulphur and Molasses is a familiar home remedy, administered as a spring tonic to young and old, white and black, in certain sections of the country. Sulphur is the active ingredient in the combination, molasses being added to make the mixture palatable, especially to children. It is supposed to thin and purify the blood after a winter of inactivity, and to tone up the entire system in preparation for the hot summer season. It serves the same purpose as "bitters," concocted from the roots of certain herbs and the bark of certain trees, and administered as a spring tonic in other sections of the country.

WALTER PRICHARD

Sulus. *See* Moros.

Summer Resorts. *See* Resorts.

Sumner, Fort, named for Col. Edwin V. Sumner, U. S. Army, was a military post in New Mexico established in 1862 at Bosque Redondo[qv] on the Pecos River. About 400 Mescalero Apaches[qv] and nearly 8000 Navajo[qv] Indians were brought there in 1863–64 and held as prisoners of war on the near-by reservation. Due to intertribal difficulties, the Apaches fled from the reservation in 1865 and in 1867–68 the Navajos were removed to the region near New Fort Wingate. Immediately following their removal in 1868, the post was abandoned and the reservation, with the exception of the cemetery of 320 acres, was sold in 1870. (*See also* Goodnight Loving Trail.)

[Hubert Howe Bancroft, *Arizona and New Mexico;* Ralph E. Twitchell, *The Leading Facts of New Mexican History.*]

EDWARD EVERETT DALE

Sumner's Expedition (1857). Depredations by the Cheyenne Indians[qv] in Kansas and Nebraska caused Col. E. V. Sumner to march against them from Fort Leavenworth[qv] with six companies of cavalry and three of infantry. On July 29 the cavalry advance encountered 400 warriors on Solomon Fork of the Kansas River. A pitched battle ensued, Sumner losing eight men, killed or wounded. Leaving one company, which built Fort Floyd, to protect the wounded and sick, with his remaining troops he fruitlessly pursued the Indians. Marching a thousand miles during the campaign, the soldiers returned to Fort Kearny[qv] in August, many barefooted or destitute of clothing.

[Oliver L. Spaulding, *The United States Army in War and Peace;* Thomas F. Rodenbaugh and William L. Haskin, *The Army of the United States.*]

JOSEPH MILLS HANSON

Sumptuary Laws and Taxes, Colonial. The term "sumptuary laws" is usually meant to refer to legal attempts to regulate food, clothing, morals, amusements, church attendance and Sabbath observance. In this respect there were sumptuary laws in all of the colonies. Some of these were general statutes enacted by the colony, others were local regulations, others were applications of what was understood to be the common law applicable to local situations and still others were the fixed customs of the people of the different colonies. Custom and practice are as much a part of the total laws of a community as are the formal statutes, although their enforcement is different. The most discussed collection of such laws is the famous "Blue Laws of Connecticut." These were originally compiled by Reverend Samuel Peters in 1781. For many years people accepted or denounced this account of the Connecticut colonial code. In 1898 Walter F. Prince published in the *Report of the American Historical Association for 1898* a detailed analysis of the Peters laws based upon careful research. He found that one half did exist in New Haven, more than four fifths existed in one or more of the New England colonies, others were inventions, exaggerations, misunderstandings, or the result of copying from other writers on New England history.

The laws against wearing gold decorations, lace, hatbands, ruffs, silks and similar materials when one's station in life did not warrant such expensive clothing were confined mostly to the 17th century and were not peculiar to New England. In 1621 directions were sent to Virginia limiting the right to wear such apparel to members of the Council. Enforcement was usually by fine, although in Massachusetts the wearer might have his assessed valuation raised to £300 in addition to a fine. Connecticut had no definite laws regulating dress, while in Massachusetts the regulations were very detailed. Laws against Sabbath breaking were common to all of the colonies, and, in most of them, church attendance was prescribed by law. Enforcement was probably stricter in New England than elsewhere. In all but the Middle Colonies everybody was taxed to support the local church and its minister. In New England doctrinal uniformity was prescribed by law. Quakers[qv] were punished and driven from Massachusetts and three were hanged for persistent return. Baptists[qv] were also beaten and imprisoned. Alleged witches[qv] were proscribed and several hanged, all in the latter half of the 17th century. Yet with all this reputation for harshness, there were far fewer death penalties provided by law in New England than in the English statutes of the same time.

Laws against sex immorality were similar in all the colonies, although in the South they were directed particularly against amalgamation with the Negroes. Seating at church in accordance with one's rank in the community was common, and students' names in the catalogue of Yale were arranged in a similar way as late as 1767 and at Harvard till 1772.

[T. J. Wertenbaker, *The First Americans, 1607-1690.*]

O. M. DICKERSON

Sumter, Fort. This fortification, situated upon a sand bar at the mouth of the harbor of Charleston, S. C., and commanding the sea approach to the city, draws its significance from the important part it played in the Civil War. On the night of Dec. 26, 1860, following the passage of the Ordinance of Secession[qv] by South Carolina, Maj. Robert Anderson, in command of the Union forces at Charleston, removed his garrison from Fort Moultrie[qv], on Sullivan's Island, to Fort Sumter where he believed that he would be in a better position for defense in the event of hostilities. President Buchanan, whose term of office would expire on March 4, 1861, avoided the momentous decision of whether to recall Anderson, or send an expedition to reinforce him at the risk of provoking war. Upon assuming the office of President, his successor, Abraham Lincoln, met the issue by despatching a fleet to relieve the fort. With this fleet momentarily expected at Charleston, Gen. Beauregard, in command of the Confederate forces, offered Anderson a final opportunity to evacuate. This was not accepted, and at thirty minutes after four on the morning of Friday, April 12, the Confederate batteries opened fire on Fort Sumter. On April 13, after a bombardment of thirty-four hours, Anderson surrendered, and the Civil War had begun.

On April 7, 1863, Fort Sumter, then garrisoned by Confederates and commanded by Col. Alfred Rhett, was attacked by a Federal fleet of nine ironclads[qv] under the command of Admiral S. F. DuPont. This engagement, which lasted only two hours and twenty minutes, was far-reaching in its effects. For, while it inflicted upon the United States one of the greatest defeats in its naval history, it was conducted upon a sufficiently large scale to bring out the strength as well as the weakness of the new type of fighting ship, and inaugurated the era of the modern steel navy.

In August, 1863, the great siege of Fort Sumter, by combined Federal naval and land forces, began and lasted for 567 days. During this period the fortification was subjected to three major bombardments totaling 117 days of continuous fire, day and night. For 280 days it was under fire "steady and desultory." Projectiles to the number of 46,053, weighing 3500 tons, were hurled against it. Casualties (with a normal complement of officers and men of 300) were 53 killed and 267 wounded. After the first bombardment of sixteen days the fort had been pronounced "silenced and demolished." But it was rebuilt under fire by its defenders. This occurred again after both the second and third bombardments.

During this protracted and successful defense, commanding Confederate officers were successively: Col. Alfred Rhett, Maj. Stephen Elliott, Capt. J. C. Mitchell, Capt. T. A. Huguenin. Maj. John Johnson was engineer officer in charge during the entire siege, and much of the credit for the defense was attributed to his skill and resourcefulness. (*See also* Charleston, Siege of, 1861–65.)

Fort Sumter was never surrendered by the Confederates. On Feb. 17, 1865, when the approach of Gen. Sherman's army of 70,000 made the evacuation of the whole Charleston sector inevitable (*see* Carolinas, Sherman's March through the), the fort was closed and abandoned.

Fort Sumter still constitutes a unit in Charleston's defensive system. Reinforced concrete has supplanted the older brick construction, and modern coast-defense guns are mounted upon the ramparts.

[John Johnson, *The Defense of Charleston Harbor;* DuBose Heyward and Herbert Ravenel Sass, *Fort Sumter, 1861-1865.*]

DUBOSE HEYWARD

Sunday Observance. *See* Sabbath, The.

Sunday Schools are generally considered to have had their origin in the movement begun by Robert Raikes, editor of the *Gloucester* (England) *Journal,* in 1780. His attention was called to the deplorable condition prevailing among the children of the Gloucester poor, many of whom, being employed in a pin factory during the week, were turned loose on Sunday, their only holiday, to engage in rough and vicious sport. Thinking that their conduct was largely due to ignorance he conceived the plan of gathering them into schools on Sundays, where they were taught to read and were also given instruction in the catechism. The movement spread rapidly and schools were established in other towns and cities—where John Wesley, in his wide travels, came upon them, gave them his encouragement, and soon introduced them as a feature of his societies.

The situation which gave rise to Sunday Schools in America was quite unlike that which brought them into existence in England. Here the Sunday School was formed solely to give religious instruction, and from the beginning they were closely associated with the church. Some of the New England churches, such as that at Plymouth, early gave instruction to children on Sundays during the intermission between the morning and afternoon services. But this was not a uniform practice. Francis Asbury, with Wesley's encouragement, organized what was probably the first Sunday School in America, in Hanover County, Va., in 1786. Four years later (1790) the American Methodists[qv] officially adopted the Sunday School, stating that the establishment of Sunday Schools in or near the places of worship was to be encouraged—the first official recognition of Sunday Schools in the United States by an ecclesiastical body.

In 1790 Bishop William White of the Protestant Episcopal Church[qv] formed a Sunday School in Philadelphia; and the same year he with Dr. Benjamin Rush and others of Philadelphia organized the First-Day or Sunday School Society, an interdenominational body and the first of its kind. Sunday Schools now began to appear in numerous places: Pawtucket, R. I., in 1797; New York in 1801–4; Pittsburgh in 1809. Though endorsed and adopted by individual churches the early Sunday School movement in the United States was more largely an interdenominational movement, and Sunday School Unions or Societies were numerously formed in many of the larger towns and cities during the first two decades of the 19th century. In 1824 the American Sunday School Union was organized which incorporated many of the previously formed Sunday School Societies as its auxiliaries. The same year the Union began the publication of its *Sunday School Magazine* which marks the beginning of a vast Sunday School literature. In 1830 the Sunday School Union reported 5901 Sunday Schools, 52,663 teachers and 349,202 scholars throughout the United States.

The formation of state and denominational Sunday School Societies now followed in rapid succession; the Massachusetts Sunday School Union, made up of Congregationalists[qv] and Baptists[qv] in 1825; the Sunday School Union of the Protestant Episcopal Church in 1826; that of the Methodist Episcopal Church in 1827. All of these bodies were active in the publication of Sunday School papers and other literature.

The first national convention of Sunday School workers was held in New York in 1832. A great advance was made in Sunday School work in 1866 when Dr. John H. Vincent projected a uniform system of teaching. This bore fruit in the establishment of the *Berean Series* of lessons 1870 and in the *International Series* in 1873. The Chautauqua[qv] Assembly, begun in 1874 under the leadership of Dr. Vincent to bring together Sunday School teachers and workers for systematic training, was soon duplicated in many sections of the country. In 1893 there were in the United States and Canada 11,669,956 Sunday School members. In 1908 a system of graded lessons was adopted. In 1903 the Religious Education Association was formed to raise the teaching standards of Sunday Schools. It has introduced a more definitely Church point of view and has led to an increased efficiency.

[J. H. Harris, *Robert Raikes: The Man and His Work;* H. F. Cope, *The Evolution of the Sunday School;* Marianna C. Brown, *Sunday-School Movement in America;* Edwin Wilbur Rice, *The Sunday-School Movement and the American Sunday School Union, 1780-1917.*]

WILLIAM W. SWEET

Super Market, THE, is a comparatively recent development in mass merchandising of foods and other related items, aiming, through giant, departmentized, self-service operations, to reduce overhead costs, eliminate service and thus lower prices to the consumer. Known on the Pacific coast for some time, these markets made their first appearance in the East in 1932, on Long Island with the King Kullen Markets, and in New Jersey in 1932 with the Big Bear Markets. Although at first labeled by their competitors as "fly by night" schemes, and "outlets for distress merchandise," the super markets won immediate consumer acceptance, and new markets were opened in all parts of the country. By 1940 it was estimated that there were about 6200 super markets in the country, with new openings announced weekly, doing an annual volume of about $1,500,000,000 or approximately 15% of the total food sales of the country.

In addition to the current depression, which inspired the consumer's willingness to forego service for lower prices, several factors have contributed to the growth of the super market. One is the increase of automobile travel, which enables the housewife to travel a considerable distance for more advantageous buying. Practically all super markets provide large free parking space for customers and choose their sites with a thought of accessibility to the motor trade. Another favorable factor is the increase of punitive laws against the chain store*qv* in almost all states, causing the chains to eliminate many smaller service units and concentrate their activities on large self-service markets.

The super markets have evolved from the first "barnlike," poorly equipped buildings, to modern structures with every facility. In operation they vary from the owner-operated market, in which all departments are operated by a single head, to the concession-type market where the owner may operate one or more departments and lease out the other to concessionaires. The markets vary in size from 5000 square feet of selling area to 200,000 square feet; their annual volume per market may range from $250,000 to $2,500,000. They resort generally to much advertising as well as promotions of all kinds and attract anywhere from 25,000 to 150,000 customers weekly.

[M. M. Zimmerman, *Super Market—Spectacular Exponent of Mass Distribution.*]

M. M. ZIMMERMAN

Superior, Lake, the largest body of fresh water in the world, was discovered probably by Étienne Brûlé about 1620. It is thought that Brûlé reached the lake by way of the St. Marys River from Lake Huron*qv*. The Jesuit*qv* missionaries Isaac Jogues and Charles Rambault established a mission at the outlet of the lake in 1641; René Ménard spent the winter of 1660–61 with the Ottawa Indians*qv* on the south shore, and in the summer of 1661 lost his life in an attempt to cross over to the Hurons on Green Bay; Pierre Esprit Radisson*qv* and Médard Chouart discovered the western end and part of the north shore the same year; Claude Jean Allouez reached the lake in the autumn of 1665, and named it Lac Tracy, after the then Viceroy of New France; he founded a mission on Chequamegon Bay*qv*, and explored part of the south shore. Daniel Greysolon DuLhut was in the country around the western end between 1678 and 1682 (*see* Duluth's Explorations). His brother, Charles de Greysolon, Sieur de LaTourette, built trading posts on the north shore between 1678 and 1686. Zacharie Robutel de LaNoüe built a post at the mouth of the Kaministikwia River in 1717, and made his way inland as far as Rainy Lake. Pierre Gaultier de Varennes, Sieur de La Vérendrye*qv* wintered at Fort Kaministikwia in 1731–32, and in the spring explored the Grand Portage*qv* route to Rainy Lake and the Lake of the Woods. In the days of the fur trade*qv* three canoe routes were used from Lake Superior to the West, by way of Grand Portage, the Kaministikwia River, and the St. Louis River at Fond du Lac; and important posts were maintained at Sault Ste. Marie*qv* and Grand Portage, the latter being removed in 1801, by the North West Company*qv*, to Fort William, at the mouth of the Kaministikwia. The search for copper*qv* mines led to the building of the first sailing ship on Lake Superior in 1737; that was the beginning of an immense commerce, and the gradual spread of population particularly along the south shore.

[T. M. Longstreth, *The Lake Superior Country;* George A. Cuthbertson, *Freshwater.*]

LAWRENCE J. BURPEE

Supply, Camp, was a stockade post established on the Canadian River in present northwest Oklahoma by Gen. Alfred Sully in November, 1868, as a base for operations against hostile Cheyenne, Kiowa and Comanche Indians*qqv*. It was from this point that Gen. George A. Custer began his Washita campaign of 1868[qv], and it was important in the Indian war of 1874–5 (*see* Red River Indian War). It was abandoned about 1895.

[W. S. Nye, *Carbine and Lance.*]

PAUL I. WELLMAN

Supreme Court, THE, stands at the head of the judicial system of the United States. It is provided for in the statement in the Constitution that "The judicial power of the United States shall be vested in one Supreme Court and in such inferior courts as the Congress may from time to time ordain and establish." The judges, appointed by the President by and with the advice of the Senate, hold office during good behavior, with compensation not to be diminished during their continuance in office. The number of judges to be appointed, their salaries, the appellate jurisdiction of the Court, and many other matters were left to be prescribed by statute. Subjects over which the Court was to have original jurisdiction were prescribed in the Constitution, and the Court subsequently held that their number could not be enlarged by statute.

The Judiciary Act of 1789[qv] provided that the Supreme Court should consist of a chief justice and five associate justices, who by another statute were granted compensation of $4000 and $3500 respectively. The salaries have been enlarged from time to time down through the years, to the present figures of $20,500 for the chief justice and $20,000 for each of the associate justices. Under the original act two terms were held each year, but by a statute of 1802 the number was reduced to one. The reduction of the number of justices to five by a statute of 1801 was later countermanded. The number was increased to seven in 1807, to nine in 1837 and to ten in 1863. An act of 1866, intended to prevent the appointment of Supreme Court judges by President Johnson, provided that no vacancies on the Court should be filled to make the total number of judges more than seven. The number was restored to nine by an act of 1869, and has remained there since that date.

The determination of the number of Supreme Court judges was influenced by the number of Federal circuits needed. By the original judiciary act the judges of the Supreme Court were required to join with district judges in holding Federal circuit courts. The expansion of the country and the increase in the amount of litigation to be handled led to the creation of new circuits from time to time, and therefore to provision for additional Supreme Court judges. The requirement that these judges hold circuit courts was not merely an economy measure. It was justified on the ground that they could better perform their Supreme Court duties if they traveled throughout the country and familiarized themselves with the varied conditions amid which arose the cases and controversies to be settled before the highest court in the land.

The burden of combining circuit court duties with those of the Supreme Court was great even in the beginning, and the plan was opposed as taking time which might be better spent in adding to knowledge of law. The requirement was removed by a statute of 1801, but was restored the following year. No important step to lighten the burden was thereafter taken until 1869. In the intervening years, and particularly during the later decades of the period, the Supreme Court found it impossible to keep up with its docket, in spite of such assistance as could be rendered by the additional judges appointed. It was questioned, indeed, whether the addition of new judges added to the facility of the Court in disposing of new cases. In 1869 Congress sought to aid both the Supreme Court and the circuit courts by providing for the appointment of a circuit judge for each of the nine circuits, to share circuit work with Supreme Court and district judges. The act required each Supreme Court judge to attend one term of circuit court during every period of two years (*see* Judiciary, The).

The Supreme Court continued to be overburdened, not merely by the circuit duties of its judges, but by the increasing amount of its own business. In 1891 Congress again came to its aid, by providing an additional judge for each circuit, and creating a three-judge circuit court of appeals in each circuit. Supreme Court judges might sit on these courts, but their attendance was not required. The circuit courts of appeals were given final appellate jurisdiction over certain types of cases, thereby reducing somewhat the flow of cases to the Supreme Court. A more drastic measure affecting the work of the Supreme Court was adopted in 1925. It was drafted by a committee of the justices, and was adopted as a result, in part, of the influence of Chief Justice William Howard Taft. It greatly limited the kinds of cases which litigants might of right appeal to the Supreme Court. In exercise of its discretion the Court might select from the cases sought to be appealed those of greatest public significance, refusing to review the remainder. After the enactment of this measure it was possible for the Court to keep up with its docket, by refusing to review more cases than it was able to pass upon.

The importance of the Supreme Court in the

American constitutional system results in large part from the power of judicial review^qv^, the power to determine finally whether state and Federal statutes and administrative rulings can be sustained under the Constitution of the United States. With reference to state laws the power has been used since the establishment of the Court, and with increasing frequency in recent decades. The first decision holding a Federal statute unconstitutional was announced in 1803, in the case of Marbury v. Madison^qv^. It had no successor until the Dred Scott case^qv^, in 1857. Thereafter the power was used with increasing frequency in this field.

The exercise of the power of judicial review by the Court has usually had at least the passive approval of most of the people. There have been sharp criticisms in certain periods in which it appeared that the Court was using its position of authority to substitute for the judgment of the people and the other branches of government its own conceptions of policy. Vigorous criticisms of the Court were made in connection with the Dred Scott case in 1857, the several Legal Tender cases decided just after the Civil War, the Income Tax cases of 1895, the Minimum Wage case of 1923, and a number of so-called New Deal cases^qqv^ decided in 1935 and 1936. Criticisms have been especially sharp when decisions have been arrived at by a closely divided vote. Various remedial proposals have been made from time to time, such as a constitutional amendment authorizing the recall^qv^ of judicial decisions, the requirement of more than a bare majority vote to invalidate a legislative act, the requirement of retirement from the bench at a fixed age, and the outright enlargement and packing of the Court to secure desired decisions (*see* Supreme Court Packing Bills).

Resort to constitutional amendment is a possible means of removing judicial barriers to particular kinds of legislation. It has been used, as in the case of the income-tax amendment, but it is a slow and unwieldy procedure. Experience has shown that if the legislation desired is in harmony with the trends of the times the normal and inevitable changes of court personnel will usually bring about ultimate acquiescence. Although drastic measures have been debated, the only step actually taken by Congress in recent years to hasten personnel changes on the Court is the retirement act of 1937, under which judges of seventy years of age, with ten years of service, may retire without resigning, retaining thereby the constitutional assurance of full compensation.

[Felix Frankfurter and James M. Landis, *The Business of the Supreme Court of the United States;* Charles Warren, *The Supreme Court in United States History.*]

CARL BRENT SWISHER

Supreme Court Decisions, Five to Four. In recent years there has been a general tendency to criticize the Supreme Court^qv^ of the United States for rendering five-to-four decisions. Unquestionably much of the popular dissatisfaction with such decisions has been due to misinformation concerning them. The impression has been created that this is the typical vote of the Court in handing down constitutional decisions. How erroneous this impression is may be seen from an examination of the record, which reveals that, from its establishment in 1789 to June, 1938, the Court held exactly eleven congressional acts unconstitutional by five-to-four votes. Considering that about 26,000 public laws were passed in the same period, one may conclude that the percentage invalidated by bare Court majorities was very minute.

The first five-to-four decision holding a congressional act unconstitutional was handed down in 1867 in the Test Oath Act^qv^ case. Later decisions of this type which attracted wide attention were rendered in 1895 in the Income Tax case^qv^, in 1908 in the first Employers' Liability case and in 1918 in the first Child Labor case^qv^.

In 1937, when the question of Court packing was being argued (*see* Supreme Court Packing Bills), advocates of the measure sought to create the impression that five justices had done much to block the New Deal^qv^. The record shows, however, that only two New Deal measures were invalidated by five-to-four votes. One was the first railroad pension act, ruled out in 1935, and the other was the first municipal bankruptcy act, invalidated in 1936. Both decisions were later circumvented by new legislation.

[Charles Warren, *Congress, the Constitution, and the Supreme Court,* 1935 edition.]

ERIK McKINLEY ERIKSSON

Supreme Court Packing Bills. Originally created with six members in 1789, the Supreme Court has since been changed in size six times. In 1801 the number of Justices was reduced to five; in 1807 increased to seven; in 1837 increased to nine; in 1863 increased to ten; in 1866 reduced to seven; and, finally, in 1869, increased again to nine.

The increases in the number of Justices in 1807 and 1837 cannot be considered as evidences of "court packing." The action of Congress in 1863 in providing for a tenth Justice is explained by a desire to provide a new circuit for the Western states, California and Oregon. The reduction to seven in 1866 was due to a desire to prevent President Johnson, with whom Congress was in disagreement over Reconstruction[qv] policies, from making appointments to the highest tribunal. When Congress again authorized an increase to nine in 1869, President Grant, whose views were satisfactory to the Republican majority, was in the White House. Before he could make the appointments, there came before the Court the case of Hepburn v. Griswold, involving the question of the constitutionality of the Legal Tender Acts[qv] of the Civil War period. By a vote of four to three, the Court, on Feb. 7, 1870, ruled against these acts. By a coincidence, at the very time the Court was announcing its decision, President Grant was submitting to the Senate nominations to fill the two vacancies on the bench. Thereafter, another legal tender case, that of Knox v. Lee, was brought before the Court. On May 1, 1871, by a vote of five to four, the decision in Hepburn v. Griswold was reversed. Since this reversal was made possible by the votes of the two new Justices, the cry arose that the Court had been packed in order to save the Legal Tender Acts. Those who made the charge ignored the fact that President Grant had nominated the Justices before he had learned of the decision adverse to the Legal Tender Acts. It seems clear, however, that the President, in appointing the two men, Joseph P. Bradley and William Strong, was confident from their records that they would support the legal-tender legislation.

Concerning the next court-packing episode there could be no doubt. When President F. D. Roosevelt, on Feb. 5, 1937, sent a surprise message to Congress asking for a drastic reorganization of the highest tribunal, his proposals were generally interpreted as a plan to pack the Court. He had shown marked irritation at the Court's fourteen decisions adverse to his New Deal[qv].

The President's message to Congress and the bill accompanying it proposed to permit the Chief Executive to appoint an additional Justice for each one who failed to retire after reaching the age of seventy, provided the number of Justices should not exceed fifteen. Similar appointments were to be authorized in the case of the lower courts.

President Roosevelt further proposed to limit the authority of the lower courts to issue decisions or injunctions in cases involving constitutional questions. Appeals in such cases, he recommended, should be taken directly to the Supreme Court, where they should take precedence over other cases. He also recommended the creation of a Supreme Court proctor to supervise all Federal-court business and the transfer of judges from district to district to relieve congestion.

The effect of the President's proposals was to precipitate a debate which absorbed the attention of Congress for about six months. On June 14, 1937, the Senate Judiciary committee submitted a report, adopted by a ten-to-eight vote, strongly denouncing the Court packing plan. Finally, on July 22, 1937, the Senate voted, seventy to twenty, to recommit the plan to the Judiciary Committee, thus killing the measure.

An act of March 1, 1937, permitting Supreme Court Justices to retire at the age of seventy; an act of Aug. 25, 1937, reforming the procedure of the lower courts; and a 1939 act creating the office of proctor, it should be mentioned, carried out a part of the President's judicial-reform program.

[Charles Warren, *The Supreme Court in United States History; Congressional Record*, Vol. 81; *American Year Book*, 1937.]

ERIK McKINLEY ERIKSSON

Surgery. *See* Medicine and Surgery.

Surplus, Federal. From 1800 to the beginning of the World War, the Federal surplus presented, almost continuously, a difficult problem. During the first decade, the surplus was small or nonexistent, but in the second it began to grow, ranging in size from $3,000,000 to $8,000,000 a year. By 1835 the national debt had been paid off, and the surplus was estimated at $9,000,000 for the next eight years. Since constitutional objections were raised to the appropriation of the funds to the states, the states were, in 1836, made depositories of the money (*see* Surplus Revenue, Distribution of).

In the period from 1834 to 1846, when the independent treasury was established, the surplus varied from $20,000,000 to nothing at all. From 1846 to 1861 it rose to $18,000,000 in 1854, and rapidly declined to an even larger deficit in the last four years of this period. Needless to say, the deficit continued through the Civil War period. In 1867 and 1870 the surplus suddenly increased to more than $100,000,000, and to over $90,000,000 in 1871 and 1872. From 1880 to 1890, the surplus remained at or near the higher figure. It declined into a sizable deficit from 1894 to 1899, but in 1900 rose to $79,500,000, and continued in substantial amounts until 1913, with the exception of the years 1905, 1908 and 1909, when deficits appeared, due to the Panama Canal[qv].

No surplus has existed since 1913. Large expenditures for military preparedness were followed by those for the war itself, which left a substantial debt. After a depression in the early 1920's, part of the debt was liquidated. In 1939 the Government concluded a decade of annual deficits, and faced a debt the size of which has been practically doubled within the period.

[Thomas H. Benton, *Thirty Years;* Davis R. Dewey, *Financial History of the United States* (bibliography); J. J. Knox, *United States Notes;* Richardson, *Messages and Papers of the Presidents.*]

W. BROOKE GRAVES

Surplus Revenue, Distribution of. In his first two annual messages to Congress, President Jackson recommended a distribution among the states of the surplus in the national treasury, but, by the time he delivered his third annual message, he had changed his mind. He then urged that the governmental revenue be so reduced that, after the necessary expenses of government had been paid and the public debt*qv* retired, there would be no surplus. No action was taken to reduce revenues substantially; so consequently, after the last of the national debt was retired on Jan. 1, 1835, the surplus began to accumulate rapidly, aided by increased receipts from customs and public land sales*qqv*.

Meanwhile, since 1832, Sen. Clay had been trying unsuccessfully to secure the enactment of a bill providing for the distribution to the states of the proceeds of the public land sales (*see* Land Distribution Bill, Clay's). In 1836 Sen. John C. Calhoun assumed the leadership in the movement for distribution (*see* Distribution, or Deposit, Act of 1836). Subsequently there was passed a bill, reluctantly signed by President Jackson on June 23, 1836, which provided that the surplus in the Treasury on Jan. 1, 1837, less $5,000,000, should be "deposited" with the states, "to be returned, when the wants of the government shall require it." In spite of this statement, the general and correct understanding was that the money would never be recalled.

The amount actually available for distribution on "deposit" proved to be $37,468,859.97. Since the distribution was to be in proportion to the electoral vote, New York, with forty-two votes, was apportioned the largest amount, $5,352,694.28 while Arkansas, Delaware and Michigan, each with three votes, were awarded the smallest amounts, $382,335.31 each. Due to the Panic of 1837*qv* only three out of four scheduled installments were paid to the states, or a total of $28,101,644.97. This money was spent in various ways, chiefly for internal improvements or education*qqv*.

[E. G. Bourne, *The History of the Surplus Revenue of 1837.*]

ERIK McKINLEY ERIKSSON

Surrogate's Court or Court of Probate in most states is a county court having jurisdiction over the settlement of the estates of deceased persons. It receives wills for probate, issues letters of administration, supervises the management of the property, hears and allows claims against the estate and decrees distribution in accordance with the probated will or, if no will, the laws of inheritance. In many states such a court also has jurisdiction over guardianships of minors, insane persons, habitual drunkards and spendthrifts.

[15 *Corpus Juris* 690, 1918.]

GEORGE W. GOBLE

Survey Act of 1824, The General. Interest in national internal improvements*qv* increased after Secretary Gallatin's Report on Roads, Canals, Harbors and Rivers*qv* (1808). In an effort to appropriate money for such purposes, Congress passed Calhoun's Bonus Bill*qv*, vetoed by President Madison, and the Toll Gate Bill, vetoed by President Monroe. While favoring the aims of these measures, both Presidents thought an amendment to the Constitution necessary to authorize national expenditures for the construction of roads or canals*qqv*. But Henry Clay, who championed national appropriations for internal improvements, introduced a bill in 1824 which was passed by Congress and approved by President Monroe. Clay argued that Congress had appropriated money for coast and harbor improvements but had "done nothing for the great interior of the country." The act authorized the President, with the aid of army engineers, to conduct surveys of such canal and turnpike routes as would serve an important national interest.

[Edward Frank Humphrey, *An Economic History of the United States.*]

L. W. NEWTON

Survey System, National. *See* Public Lands, Survey of.

Surveyors, Early. One of the first white men to appear in a frontier district was the pioneer surveyor. In the New England colonies he preceded the settlers, ran the township lines and laid out the lots into which the rectangular township*qv* was divided. The New England surveyor followed an orderly system in which tier after tier of townships were surveyed as additional land was required for settlement, but the surveyor was never far from places of abode. In the Southern colonies surveying was done privately for speculators who were locating lands in advance of settlement or for squatters who had preceded the surveyor. There the rectangular system was not adopted and the surveyors' lines had to conform to the squatters' improvements no matter how irregular they were.

Early surveyors operating mostly in uninhabited areas encountered many hardships and risks in the performance of their work. During the winter the heavy snow made walking difficult, food and forage were scarce and it was more difficult to cover up one's tracks to prevent pursuit by unfriendly Indians. In the summer the mosquitoes were intolerable, the heat intense, the underbrush almost impenetrable, numerous streams had to be forded and fever and ague were likely to lay the surveyor low. The danger from the lurking Indian or wild animals was always present and intimidated all but the most intrepid.

Save for the steel tape and the solar compass, surveyors in 1750 had available every basic instrument of modern surveying, including the compass, the bubble level, the telescopic sight, and the chain. But, as a rule, frontier surveyors were supplied with these instruments only in their crudest and most elementary form. The Mason and Dixon Line[qv] was run with wooden rods and the Military Tract[qv] of New York was surveyed by the magnetic compass without due regard for the three degree of declination from the true meridian. The United States surveys were let out on contract, the compensation depending upon the nature of the land. The contract system encouraged "running" of the lines, errors in measurements and calculations, poorly marked corners and outright fraud. When land activity was great and when surveys were being rapidly pushed, many individuals who possessed only the bare rudiments of surveying were able to secure government contracts and it was but natural that errors should be made by them.

Early surveyors like Christopher Gist, James Harrod, Isaac Shelby and Daniel Boone combined exploring and search for fertile land with actual surveying. As they appeared in the Indian country before it was ceded by the Redmen their coming produced conflicts such as Pontiac's Conspiracy and Dunmore's War[qqv]. To many frontiersmen whose principal occupation was exploring and buying and selling land, knowledge of surveying was essential. Among the outstanding Americans who had early experience in surveying were Washington, Jefferson and Lincoln. The first official surveyor and "geographer" of the United States was Thomas Hutchins of New Jersey who, between 1785 and 1789, had charge of the survey of the Seven Ranges[qv] in eastern Ohio. On his staff was Rufus Putnam who later surveyed the tract of the Ohio Company of Associates[qv].

The notebooks of the early surveyors are an invaluable source for a description of the geography, flora and soil of the public land states as they were before settlement entered them.

[J. Bakeless, *Daniel Boone: Master of the Wilderness;* R. B. Buell, *Memoirs of Rufus Putnam;* M. Conover, *The General Land Office, Its History, Activities and Organization;* A. Henderson, *Conquest of the Old Southwest.*]

PAUL WALLACE GATES

Susquehanna Settlers, THE, were sent from Connecticut into the valley of the Susquehanna by the Susquehannah Company[qv]. An exploring party was sent out in 1755 to see if settlement were then feasible, but the French and Indian War[qv] made any further effort at settlement unwise until 1763. In that year a settlement was begun, but it had barely started when a band of Indians massacred all of the inhabitants. In 1769 another group of settlers was sent out by the company under the leadership of Maj. John Durkee and the town of Wilkes-Barre in the Wyoming Valley[qv] was laid out. The Yankee-Pennamite Wars[qv] (1769–72, 1775 and 1784), the threat of Indians, and the uncertainty of land titles were the chief obstacles faced by the settlers. They won the first "war" with the aid of the Paxton Boys[qv], and a comparatively peaceful and orderly settlement began in 1772 which in 1774 was given the protection of Connecticut law. By the beginning of the Revolution there were about two thousand taxables in this region living under Connecticut jurisdiction. In December, 1775, an armed force of about 500 men, acting under Sheriff Plunkett of Northumberland County but financed by a group of Philadelphia land speculators, was met at the lower end of the Wyoming Valley and forced to retire down the river. On July 3, 1778 the loyalists and tories under Maj. John Butler defeated the settlers at the so-called Wyoming Massacre[qv], causing a complete disruption of the settlement. The next year the settlement was renewed but in 1784 the Pennsylvania local authorities brought on the second Yankee-Pennamite War and most of the inhabitants were dispossessed. However, the original settlers in Wilkes-Barre and sixteen other townships were quieted in their titles by the Confirming Act of 1787, which was repealed in 1790 but substantially re-enacted in 1803.

The Susquehanna settlers brought with them the institutions they were familiar with in Connecticut. In particular they introduced into northern Pennsylvania free public schools half a century before the state as a whole adopted the system.

[O. J. Harvey, *History of Wilkes-Barre.*]

JULIAN P. BOYD

Susquehannah Company, THE, was a merging of a number of smaller groups of Connecticut farmers who organized at Windham, Conn., in 1753, for the purpose of settling on lands in Wyoming Valley^{qv} in Pennsylvania, basing their claim on the Connecticut Charter of 1662 (*see* Connecticut's Western Lands). Leading citizens of Connecticut were shareholders in this company, such as Ezra Stiles, Phineas Lyman, Eliphalet Dyer and Jedediah Elderkin, and it was supported by Governors Wolcott and Trumbull, though Thomas Fitch and his followers opposed the company's claims. The company leaders engaged John Lydius to effect a purchase of lands from the Six Nations^{qv}, and this was done at the Albany Congress in 1754^{qv}, though there is reason to believe Lydius used devious means to secure the deed and the Pennsylvania authorities bought a part of the same land from some of the same Indians at the same congress. The Susquehannah Company merged with the First and Second Delaware Companies, started a settlement at Wyoming in 1763 (which was wiped out by Indians), sent Eliphalet Dyer to London in 1764 to obtain a charter for a separate colony, and, after the Treaty of Fort Stanwix (1768)^{qv}, began in 1769 to settle the lands with the establishment of the town of Wilkes-Barre. But the first Yankee-Pennamite War^{qv} interrupted this settlement until 1772 when permanent settlement of the region by Connecticut settlers began. The company laid out townships five miles square throughout the 41st parallel of latitude from a line ten miles east of and parallel to the Susquehanna River to a line 120 west of the river. The jurisdiction of this territory was awarded to Pennsylvania in 1782 (*see* Pennsylvania-Connecticut Boundary Dispute) and at once the second Yankee-Pennamite War broke out, resulting in the dispossession of most of the Connecticut settlers. But under the stimulus of John Franklin's leadership a horde of "half-right" men invaded the upper Susquehanna from Connecticut and in 1786 made an abortive attempt to erect a separate state in this region, with Athens, Pa., as its capital. The next year Pennsylvania, urged on by land operators of Philadelphia who were tired of the conflict, passed the Confirming Act recognizing titles under the Susquehannah Company in seventeen townships which had been settled prior to 1782. This act was repealed in 1790, but the region remained thereafter in comparative quiet until an act of 1803 enabled the holders of Connecticut titles in the seventeen townships to exchange them for Pennsylvania titles. By then John Franklin had ended his twenty-year fight to make a success of the Susquehannah Company's claim and had retired to Athens. The company in its half-century of existence succeeded in populating the northeastern section of Pennsylvania with Connecticut stock and in giving to the heterogeneous population of Pennsylvania a new element which has not been without its influence in the history of the Commonwealth.

[J. P. Boyd, ed., *The Susquehannah Company Papers.*]

JULIAN P. BOYD

Susquehannock, THE, were an Indian tribe of Iroquoian stock first noted in 1608 by John Smith on the lower Susquehanna and its tributaries. These Indians were of an unusually large stature, lived in palisaded towns, and were very warlike. They were finally subjugated by the Iroquois^{qv} in 1676.

[F. W. Hodge, *Handbook of American Indians.*]

JULIAN P. BOYD

Sussex **Case,** THE. On March 24, 1916, the English channel steamer *Sussex* was attacked by a German submarine. Eighty persons were killed or injured, two of the latter being Americans. The United States, regarding this action as a violation of the pledge given by the German government in the *Arabic* case^{qv}, stated in a note of April 18 that unless Germany "should immediately declare and effect an abandonment of its present methods of submarine warfare against passenger and freight-carrying vessels," the United States would sever diplomatic relations with the German Empire. The German government gave the necessary assurances, but with the qualification that the United States should require Great Britain to "forthwith observe the rules of international law universally recognized before the war," i.e., abandon the blockade of Germany. The United States refused to accept the German qualification and asserted that "responsibility in such matters is single, not joint; absolute, not relative." Consequently, when Germany renewed submarine warfare on Feb. 1, 1917, the United States immediately severed relations.

[*Foreign Relations of the United States*, 1916, supplement, *The World War;* Charles Seymour, *American Diplomacy during the World War;* Ray Stannard Baker, *Woodrow Wilson: Life and Letters*, Vol. VI.]

BERNADOTTE E. SCHMITT

Sutler, The Merchant, was a feature of army life until after the Civil War. Because army posts frequently were located at considerable distances from towns, some arrangement had to be made to furnish troops with the simple luxuries and wants which they desired to purchase to supplement regular army rations. Consequently, a civilian was given a contract to keep a store at each army post. The post council determined what he must carry in stock, regulated his prices, and sometimes decreed that a small part of his profit must go to the post fund for social activities. In return, he received a monopoly of the post trade, army protection, and some help in collecting his bills from the soldiers. His business establishment compared favorably with the log cabin, general stores of the smaller towns and his stock of goods sometimes exceeded in value that of ordinary western stores. The modern post exchange[qv] is an outgrowth of the earlier sutling arrangement.

[Marcus L. Hansen, *Old Fort Snelling, 1819-1858.*]

LEWIS E. ATHERTON

Sutro Tunnel. Adolph Sutro, operator of an ore stamp mill at Virginia City[qv], Nev., conceived the idea of a tunnel into the side of Mount Davidson to intercept all the mines on the Comstock silver lode[qv], drain them of water and gases and make ore removal easier. His franchise specified that work must begin in 1866 and be completed in eight years, but the time was later extended because of his difficulty in raising money. He was fought by mine owners and financial interests, and only his indomitable will carried the project through. Ground was broken in 1869. Unable to obtain funds in America, Sutro finally found backers in England. The tunnel broke through into the Savage Mine July 8, 1878, but by that time the best days of the Comstock lode were over. The tunnel property was sold in 1889 to satisfy the English investors' bond mortgage. It was reorganized, but continued a losing venture.

[C. B. Glasscock, *The Big Bonanza.*]

ALVIN F. HARLOW

Sutter's Fort, on the site of what is now Sacramento, Calif., is one of the most familiar names in American history because it was near this stronghold, and on land belonging to the Swiss Capt. John August Sutter, that gold was discovered on Jan. 24, 1848. The fort was erected in 1841 with walls five feet thick and twelve feet high and room for a garrison of a hundred men. Guns and other equipment were moved from the Russian Fort Ross[qv]. Here Sutter lived in baronial style, possessing at one time 4000 oxen, 1200 cows, 1500 horses and mules and 12,000 sheep. His fort was a stopping place for army officers and early California pioneers. Following the discovery of gold in California[qv] an eruption of squatters dispossessed Sutter and most of the movable parts of the fort were carried away.

[J. P. Zollinger, *Sutter: The Man and His Empire;* R. R. Wilson, *Out of the West.*]

CARL L. CANNON

Swamp-Angel, The, was the name given by Federal soldiers to an 8-inch Parrott gun used in the Charleston, S. C., siege, 1863[qv]. It was mounted on a battery constructed on piles driven into the swamp. After firing thirty-six shots, it burst August 23. Later it was mounted in Trenton, N. J.

[F. T. Miller, ed., *The Photographic History of the Civil War,* Vol. V.]

W. B. HATCHER

Swamp Fight. *See* Great Swamp Fight.

Swamp Lands. The public land states[qv] contained great areas of swamp and overflowed lands which were neglected by the early settlers, who could not drain them. Congress, badgered by the states, which wanted to gain control of the Federal lands, and wishing to aid in draining the swamp and overflowed lands, granted them to the states in which they were located. By the Swamp Land Act of 1850, 70,000,000 acres passed into the possession of the states. Florida and Louisiana alone received 20,000,000 and 9,000,000 acres respectively. Great frauds were committed by the state representatives in selecting the lands, and the record of the states in disposing of them is equally bad. Few states made efforts to drain the lands. Illinois and Iowa granted their swamp lands to the counties, which sold them for the benefit of schools, exchanged them for bridge construction or offered them as military bounties[qv] in the Civil War. Michigan, Minnesota and Florida granted large tracts to railroads. Most of the states disposed of their swamp lands in unlimited amounts to capitalist groups and thereby furthered the land monopolization to which Federal policy was effectively contributing.

[B. H. Hibbard, *History of the Public Land Policies.*]

PAUL WALLACE GATES

Swanee River is the popular title given in America to Stephen Collins Foster's "Old Folks at Home," probably the most widely beloved song in the whole world. With the utmost simplicity in melody and harmony, flowing from an exalted inspiration, Foster expresses the homesick yearning over the past and far away which is the common emotional heritage of the human race. The verses have been translated into every European language and into many Asiatic and African tongues. Dozens of composers have woven variations about its melody. In the original draft Foster wrote, "Way down upon the Pedee River." One day in 1851 he entered his brother Morrison's office in Pittsburgh and asked for a "good name of two syllables for a Southern river." Morrison took down an atlas, passed his finger down the page until he came to Suwannee. "That's it, that's it exactly," exclaimed the composer. The river, variously spelled Suwannee and Suwanee, flows through southern Georgia and Florida into the Gulf of Mexico at about latitude 20° 18′ N. Its length is 250 miles. Stephen Foster never rested his eyes upon its rippling surface.

[Morrison Foster, *Biography, Songs and Musical Compositions of Stephen Collins Foster;* H. V. Milligan, *Stephen Collins Foster.*]

HARRY R. WARFEL

Sweatshop, The, is a system of employment using principally the labor of women and children. "Sweating" is the farming out, by competing manufacturers to competing contractors, of materials which are distributed among the workers. The middleman or contractor is the "sweater"; his workers are the "sweated" and the exploited. In the clothing industry, for example, the sweater contracts to make up certain garments at a given price per piece and then hires other people to do the work at a less price, his profit being the difference between the two prices. Thus, there is constant pressure to reduce the price paid to the actual laborers.

Although, in the United States, sweating emerged almost with the advent of the factory system and was protested by organized labor as early as 1830, it became a serious social problem only after the influx of the "new immigrants" from the east and south of Europe, beginning about 1880 (*see* Immigration). This explains why the sweatshop exists chiefly in our congested cities, in which immigrants' families have been exploited.

Two major methods exist for carrying on sweated industry: The sweater may furnish shop-room and machines to his employees, or he may allow others, usually finishers, to take the work to their living and lodging rooms in the tenements. The evils of the sweatshop are everywhere the same—low wages, long hours of work, unsanitary conditions, speeded-up employees, child labor^qv^. While sweating has thrived most in the clothing industry, other lines of manufacturing, such as cigar making and artificial flower making, have been invaded by it. An abundant supply of cheap labor and the adaptability of homework and the small workshop are responsible factors in its development.

Considerable progress has been made toward the elimination of the sweatshop in the United States. The National Consumers' League through the distribution of its "white list" and "label," the Women's Bureau of the United States Department of Labor through its excellent studies of the problems of sweated labor, and organized labor through its fight for collective bargaining and regulatory legislation have contributed largely to the advance of the movement against the sweatshop.

[J. R. Commons and J. B. Andrews, *Principles of Labor Legislation.*]

GORDON S. WATKINS

Sweden, New. *See* New Sweden, The Colony of.

Swedenborgianism. The teachings of Emanuel Swedenborg were brought to America in 1748, and spread gradually among the intellectuals. Seventeen "New Church" Societies united in 1817 to form the General Convention of the Church of the New Jerusalem, and in 1890, as the result of a schism, a second body, the General Church of the New Jerusalem, was founded (headquarters at Bryn Athyn, Pa.). Through indefatigable publishing activity Swedenborgian doctrines became widely disseminated, arousing considerable interest outside the church, especially among the New England Transcendentalists^qv^. Chiefly through Emerson, and Henry James, Senior, they permeated American philosophy, theology and literature to a greater degree than is generally recognized. Also, through an active, though unofficial participation in reform movements such as Fourierism^qv^, Christian Socialism and the Single Tax^qv^, Swedenborgians brought their distinctive ideas into the main stream of 19th century culture. Since 1900, however, Swedenborgianism has declined in numbers, and in influence.

[C. T. Odhner, *Annals of the New Church, 1688-1850;* M. B. Block, *The New Church in the New World.*]

MARGUERITE BECK BLOCK

Swedish Immigration. Leaving out of account the episodic Swedish settlements on the Delaware (*see* New Sweden, The Colony of), the stream of emigration from Sweden began in the fourth decade of the 19th century with the migration, in 1841, of a small party led by Gustaf Unonius to Pine Lake, Wisc. The number increased until 1855, when the movement was checked by conditions similar to those that operated in the case of emigration from other countries (*see* Immigration). In 1863 the movement again took on momentum, declined for a few years after the Panic of 1873^{qv}, and reached its second culmination in 1882, with 64,607, the peak for all time. Except for 1888, the number never again reached 50,000. Following a decline from 1894 to 1900, the third culmination was reached in 1903, with 46,028. Down to 1915 the yearly arrivals never fell below 12,688. After lean years from 1915 to 1922, the fourth culmination came in 1923 and 1924, when the figures were 17,916 and 18,310, respectively. By the acts of 1924 (*see* Immigration Act of 1924) and 1929 Sweden's quotas were 9561 and 3314, respectively, but favorable economic conditions at home kept emigration below those figures.

From 1868 to 1873 the movement assumed the proportions of an exodus, when approximately 100,000 immigrants laid the substantial foundations of Swedish America. Before 1860 the most striking example of group migration was the Eric-Jansonist colony at Bishop Hill[qv], in Henry County, Ill., which was established in 1846. Similar efforts promoted by land and railroad companies and church organizations were episodic and incidental to the flow which was set in motion and accelerated, first, by the impact of agricultural America and, second, by the impact of industrial America. It is estimated that approximately 1,000,000 Swedish immigrants came to the United States.

According to the census of 1930, there were in the United States approximately 1,562,700 persons of Swedish descent of the first and second generations, of whom slightly more than one third were born in Sweden. Although the Swedes are distributed from Maine to California, they are concentrated in the northern Mississippi Valley. Chicago, Minneapolis and St. Paul are the great urban centers.

[A. B. Benson and N. Hedin, *Swedes in America, 1638-1938;* G. M. Stephenson, *The Religious Aspects of Swedish Immigration*, and Letters Relating to Gustaf Unonius, in *Augustana Historical Society Publications*, Vol. VII.]

G. M. STEPHENSON

Sweeping Resolution, THE, of the Ohio General Assembly, January, 1810, declared vacant all judgeships and other state offices filled by appointment by the Assembly for seven-year terms, on the ground that all such terms began with statehood in 1803 and had expired. It cut short the terms of officials appointed to fill vacancies after 1803 even though commissioned for seven years. The purpose was to fill the judgeships with men amenable to the will of the legislature, as impeachment proceedings had failed against two judges who had declared an act of the assembly unconstitutional. The principle of the resolution was repealed in 1812.

[W. T. Utter, Judicial Review in Early Ohio, in *Mississippi Valley Historical Review*, XIV.]

EUGENE H. ROSEBOOM

Swift v. Tyson (16 Peters 1, 1842). The Federal Constitution was adopted in part to establish a central government capable of regulating commercial relations between citizens of different states. Fear of the provincialism of state courts led Congress to give Federal courts jurisdiction over suits between citizens of different states. In Swift v. Tyson the rule was established that in matters of commercial law where the Federal court deemed a uniform rule preferable to separate state rules, it might give its own interpretation of the common law[qv]. On the basis of this decision a considerable body of national common law of commercial relations has grown up. The rule, always a matter of controversy among constitutional lawyers, was reversed in Erie Railroad v. Tompkins[qv] in April, 1938.

HARVEY PINNEY

"Swinging Round the Circle" (Aug. 28–Sept. 15, 1866) was a tour which President Johnson and party made to Chicago to participate in laying the cornerstone of a monument to Stephen A. Douglas. Using the tour to bring his moderate views on Reconstruction[qv] before the people—a congressional election was pending—Johnson was goaded into making some injudicious remarks which probably lost rather than won votes for his policies. Various factors, however, account for the unfavorable election.

[H. K. Beale, *The Critical Year;* R. W. Winston, *Andrew Johnson.*]

WILLARD H. SMITH

Swiss Settlers. The material on Swiss immigrants in the United States is scanty and unsatisfactory; and the immigration statistics are unreliable because the Swiss, speaking German, French and Italian, were confused with immigrants from other lands. In the colonial period Swiss immigrants came singly and in groups; and notable settlements were established in Pennsylvania, North Carolina and South Carolina. Similarly, group settlements were founded in the first half of the 19th century, among them being the colony in Switzerland County, Ind., shortly after 1800, and the colony of New Glarus in Green County, Wis., in 1845. From 1820 to 1924 immigration from Switzerland to the United States amounted to 278,187. Before 1881, the peak year was 1854, when nearly 8000 arrived. The greatest influx was in the years from 1881 to 1883, with more than 10,000 arrivals.

There is a galaxy of distinguished names among the Swiss immigrants and their descendants: Albert Gallatin, Secretary of the Treasury under Jefferson and Madison; William Wirt, Attorney General under Monroe and John Quincy Adams; Philip Schaff, church historian; Henry Clay Frick, steel magnate; Alexander Agassiz, curator of the Museum of Natural History at Harvard; Albert J. Ochsner, well known surgeon; Felix Kirk Zollicoffer, Confederate general; Christopher de Graffenried, founder of the first Swiss colony in America, at New Berne, North Carolina, in 1710.

[*Prominent Americans of Swiss Origin*, a compilation prepared by the Swiss-American Historical Society; Perret Dufour, *The Swiss Settlement of Switzerland County, Indiana;* John Luchsinger, The Swiss Colony of New Glarus, *Collections of the Wisconsin State Historical Society*, Vol. VIII.]

G. M. STEPHENSON

Sycamore Shoals, The Treaty of (1775), was perhaps the most important treaty ever made with a southern Indian tribe. A group of North Carolinians, headed by Judge Richard Henderson, conceived a plan to acquire a vast western domain from the Cherokee Indians[qv]. In 1769 Daniel Boone was employed to make a reconnoissance of the Kentucky country. On Aug. 27, 1774, a company was organized, the name first assumed being the Louisa Land Company (changed in January, 1775, to the Transylvania Company[qv]); and Henderson soon visited the Overhill Cherokees, who deputed their great Chief Attakullakulla to go home with Henderson and continue negotiations. March 14, 1775, was agreed upon as the time and Sycamore Shoals of the Watauga as the place for holding the treaty. On March 17 a treaty was signed which conveyed to the members of the Transylvania Company the vast domain lying between the Kentucky River and the south watershed of the Cumberland River—large portions of the Kentucky and Tennessee countries. The recited consideration was two thousand pounds. A smaller tract was conveyed by a separate instrument called the "Path Deed," because this tract connected the larger territory with the white settlements.

[S. C. Williams, *Dawn of Tennessee Valley and Tennessee History.*]

SAMUEL C. WILLIAMS

Symmes Purchase, THE. *See* Miami Purchase.

Syndicalism, or revolutionary industrial unionism, originated in France as the ideal of the Confederation Générale du Travail (1895). In the United States syndicalism has been identified with the Industrial Workers of the World[qv] (1905). Its aim is the establishment of a producers' co-operative commonwealth, in which industries will be socially owned, but managed and operated by *syndicats* or labor unions[qv]. Syndicalists emphasize the class struggle[qv], and are opposed to militarism, imperialism and patriotism. They adopt "direct action," which consists mainly of sabotage and the general strike. Strikes are regarded as an educative and revolutionary force preparing the workers for the final overthrow of capitalism through the general strike. Opposition to syndicalism in the United States, as expressed through antisyndicalist laws[qv] in several states, develops from the fact that the movement seeks the abolition of political government, tends to condone violence and is uncompromisingly militant.

[P. F. Brissenden, *The I. W. W., A Study in American Syndicalism;* Louis Levine, *Syndicalism in France*, and *Development of Syndicalism in America;* Sydney and Beatrice Webb, *What Syndicalism Means.*]

GORDON S. WATKINS

Synod of Dort, THE (1618), an assembly of delegates from the principal Reformed or Calvinistic churches, at which the Church of England was represented, condemned the doctrine of free will propounded in Holland during the previous two decades by Arminius[qv] and his followers. It published five canons, declaring the approved Calvinist positions concerning innate depravity, irresistible grace, election, reprobation and the perseverance of the saints, which thereafter furnished the standard of orthodoxy for Congregational and Presbyterian churches[qqv] in England and America.

[*The iudgement of the synode holden at Dort*, London, 1619; A. W. Harrison, *The Beginnings of Arminianism.*]

PERRY MILLER

T.V.A. See Tennessee Valley Authority.

Tabernacle, The Mormon, is a large turtle shaped auditorium in Salt Lake City, built by the Mormons[qv] between 1863 and 1867. It is noted for its acoustic properties and the fact that the massive roof is a lattice truss held together by wooden pegs and strips of rawhide. Nails and bolts were not available at the time of its construction. It rests upon forty-four red sandstone piers. The auditorium seats 8000 and the general conferences of the Mormon Church are held in it twice each year. It is also used for civic gatherings and concerts; several Presidents of the United States have spoken from its stand.

[Bureau of Information, *The Great Mormon Tabernacle.*]

J. F. SMITH

Tabloids, The Rise of the, followed the World War, although their antecedents appeared in cheap labor dailies in the 1830's, postbellum penny papers, the diminutive New York *Daily Graphic* (1873–89) pioneer picture paper, and the "yellow journalism"[qv] of the 1890's which had tabloidism's mass appeal philosophy if not its form.

Patterned after Northcliffe's well-established London tabloid, the first successful American venture was Joseph M. Patterson's New York *Illustrated Daily News,* launched June 26, 1919. It was half regular size, which appealed to crowded car riders, and—a significant journalistic development of the war—largely devoted to pictures. An uncultivated audience was reached at once. In two years "this unholy blot against the fourth estate,"as one critic called it, had the largest circulation in New York, and by 1938 issued 1,783,341 copies daily and 3,122,720 Sunday.

The *Daily News'* phenomenal success soon provoked more sensational imitators. Hearst entered the field in 1924 with the *Daily Mirror;* Bernarr Macfadden attempted to build a daily circulation on cheap entertainment instead of news with the *Evening Graphic* (1924–32). About the same time Cornelius Vanderbilt IV undertook a chain of "clean" tabloids which collapsed in 1926–27.

Despite the failures, tabloids, however, had arrived. The twenty-first anniversary (1940) found the country with more than 50 and a combined daily circulation of more than 4,000,000 and upward of 6,000,000 on Sunday. If crime, sex, comics and sports were the main fare of metropolitan tabloids, some, notably Patterson's *News* and the Chicago *Times,* also became popular pleaders, espousing editorial policies proposed in behalf of metropolitan masses.

[S. M. Bessie, *Jazz Journalism;* Silas Bent, *Ballyhoo: The Voice of the Press;* A. M. Lee, *The Daily Newspaper in America;* P. W. Slosson, *The Great Crusade and After.*]

IRVING DILLIARD

Tacna-Arica Controversy. Under the treaty signed in 1883 after the Chile-Peruvian war, Chile was to hold Tacna and Arica for ten years, after which a plebiscite was to determine the ultimate disposition of these formerly Peruvian provinces. It was impossible to agree on the terms of the plebiscite, and the question repeatedly brought the two powers to the verge of war until they agreed in 1922 to submit it to arbitration by the President of the United States. In 1925 President Coolidge decided that the plebiscite should be held under the direction of a commission representing the two countries and the United States. First Gen. Pershing and later Gen. William Lassiter served as chairman. The latter, in June, 1926, voted with the Peruvian commissioner to terminate the plebiscitary proceedings, on the ground that the Chilean authorities had made a free vote impossible. Negotiations were later resumed through the good offices of the United States, and Chile and Peru agreed in 1929 to divide the territory in dispute.

[W. J. Dennis, *Tacna and Arica.*]

DANA G. MUNRO

Taënsa, THE, were a small Indian tribe dwelling at Lake St. Joseph, on the western bank of the Mississippi, midway between present-day Vicksburg and Natchez, when LaSalle[qv] visited them in 1682, Tonti in 1686 and 1690 and Iberville in 1699. Expelled by stronger tribes in 1706, they occupied successively the following sites: Bayou Manchac, 1715; banks of the Mississippi, thirty miles above New Orleans; near Mobile; head of Bayou Lafourche, after 1763; and, finally, lower Red River, until after 1803, when they sold their lands and lost their identity as a separate tribe.

[Isaac J. Cox, ed., *The Journeys of Rene Robert Cavalier, Sieur de la Salle,* I; John R. Swanton, *Indian Tribes of the Lower Mississippi Valley and Adjacent Coast of the Gulf of Mexico,* Bureau of American Ethnology, Bulletin 43; Robert Dabney Calhoun, The Taënsa Indians: The French Explorers and Catholic Missionaries in the Taënsa Country, in *Louisiana Historical Quarterly,* XVII.]

WALTER PRICHARD

Tafia (*taffia, tassia*) was a low-grade rum, originating principally in Louisiana and the West Indies, which served as a staple of trade, and sometimes as a medium of exchange, between the Indians and the French and Spanish in the Mississippi Valley and the Floridas. Observers saw that its use was disastrous to the natives, but efforts to restrict its sale were rarely effective. *Tafia's* popularity survived the withdrawal of the French from North America, but with American settlement the national preference for whiskey[qv] drove it out of use.

PAUL M. ANGLE

Taft Commission, THE (1900), frequently referred to as the second Philippine Commission, supervised the transfer from military to civil government in the Philippine Islands[qv]. The commission of five members assumed legislative authority on Sept. 1, 1900. The president of the commission, William Howard Taft, became civil governor on July 4, 1901. The commission organized the administrative services and passed laws concerning health, education, agriculture, public works, etc. On Sept. 1, 1901, three Filipinos were added and each American member became an executive department head. In the reorganization which went into effect in 1907 the commission became the upper house of the Philippine legislature.

[D. C. Worcester, *The Philippines Past and Present.*]

BENJAMIN H. WILLIAMS

Taft-Katsura Memorandum, THE (July 29, 1905), was a so-called "agreed memorandum" exchanged between Secretary of War William H. Taft, speaking for President Theodore Roosevelt, and Prime Minister Katsura of Japan. It was negotiated on the eve of the Peace of Portsmouth[qv]. The document invoked Japanese-American co-operation "for the maintenance of peace in the Far East." Thus ornamented, it expressed an approval by the United States (that is to say, by the administration of President Theodore Roosevelt) of Japanese suzerainty over Korea, and a disapproval by Japan of "any aggressive designs whatever on the Philippines." President Theodore Roosevelt assured Taft afterward that his "conversation with Count Katsura was absolutely correct in every respect," thus placing his emphatic approval on this effective agreement which remained secret until 1925.

[Tyler Dennett, *Roosevelt and the Russo-Japanese War.*]

SAMUEL FLAGG BEMIS

Taft-Roosevelt Split. At the outset of the Taft administration political observers in Washington noted the existence of adverse criticism of the President by men who had been closely associated with the so-called Roosevelt policies. Also there was disappointment among members of the House of Representatives who hoped for the support of the new President in their program of reform in the rules (*see* Rules of the House). Within a year, in both House and Senate, the Republican party[qv] membership was seriously divided. This division was reflected in public opinion throughout the Western states following Taft's defense of the Payne-Aldrich tariff bill[qv]. Gradually the general issue was drawn between those who supported the President, backed by the party machine in both Senate and House and most of the states, and those who were known as insurgents. In the congressional and state elections of 1910 the Republicans suffered general defeat. Upon his return from Africa, Roosevelt consulted with Taft and in this campaign Roosevelt actively participated. On the surface there was no break with Taft at this time. Insurgents organized the Republican-Progressive League. A coalition of Republicans and Progressives captured control of Congress. The Progressive-Republicans selected Robert M. LaFollette to contest in the primaries with Taft for the presidential nomination (*see* Campaign of 1912). LaFollette's failure to win general support led seven Republican state governors, backed by a great number of former Roosevelt lieutenants, to urge Roosevelt to permit the use of his name in the pre-convention canvass. This campaign was bitterly personal. Regular party leaders, including many former friends of Roosevelt, kept control of the national convention and renominated Taft. Roosevelt bolted and organized the Progressive party[qv].

[E. E. Robinson, *Evolution of American Political Parties.*]

EDGAR EUGENE ROBINSON

Tagliamento River, Italy, Operations on (Nov. 3–4, 1918). The 332d U. S. Infantry, as part of the Italian 31st Division, reached the Tagliamento River near Valvasone, Nov. 3, after four days' forced march. On the morning of Nov. 4 the Americans crossed the river on planks laid over the wreckage of bridges at Ponte della Delizia, beset by severe frontal and flanking machine-gun fire. They advanced to the final objective, Villaroba, which was reached just as fighting ceased on the Austrian front.

[Cablegram Communique No. 189 of General John J. Pershing, War Department records; *Il 332d Reggimento di Fanteria Americana alla Fronte D'Italia*, compiled in the Office of the Italian Ministry of War, Rome.]

ROBERT S. THOMAS

Talking Machine. *See* Phonograph, The.

Talladega, Battle of (Nov. 8, 1813). On the site of this Alabama city, 154 Creeks[qv], friendly to the whites, were beleaguered in a small fort by hostile fellow-tribesmen in the autumn of 1813. Gen. Andrew Jackson marched to their relief and almost annihilated the besieging force, killing at least 300 of them. Jackson's loss was 100.

[James Parton, *Life of Andrew Jackson.*]

ALVIN F. HARLOW

Tallasahatchee, Battle at (Nov. 3, 1813), was an incident of the war with the Creek Indians[qv]. Gen. Andrew Jackson ordered Gen. John Coffee with 1000 men to destroy Tallasahatchee, a Creek village. Coffee's force was accompanied by a number of renegade Creeks. The attack was made in the early morning, and though the Indians fought sturdily, they were overpowered by numbers. Coffee reported that not a warrior escaped; nearly 200 were killed, including some women and children, and 84 squaws and children were made prisoners.

[James Parton, *Life of Andrew Jackson.*]

ALVIN F. HARLOW

Tallmadge Amendment, THE (1819), proposed to so amend the Missouri Enabling Bill, reported favorably by the House Committee on Territories, that further introduction of slavery into Missouri should be forbidden, and that all children born of slave parents after the admission of the state should be free upon reaching the age of twenty-five years. The heated debate in Congress and the agitation of the country at large was the beginning of the sectional controversy over the expansion of slavery. The slave section was convinced of the necessity of maintaining an equality in the Senate. The House adopted the Amendment but the Senate rejected it. The Missouri Compromise[qv] of 1820 settled the issue.

[F. C. Shoemaker, *Missouri Struggle for Statehood, 1804-1821.*]

JOHN COLBERT COCHRANE

Tammany Hall is the headquarters of the New York County Democratic Committee and of the Society of Tammany, or Columbian Order. This oath-bound society was formed, shortly after the signing of the Definitive Treaty of Peace in 1783[qv], to uphold the new experiment in democracy, but was not organized until May 12, 1789. Its name was borrowed from the Sons of St. Tammany, whose patron was Tammanend, or Tammany, a Delaware chief. Its members were allies of the Sons of Liberty[qv] in the prelude to the American Revolution. The society has a ritual patterned on Indian customs, and is governed by thirteen sachems; it has no political test for membership. By 1800 most of its Federalist[qv] members withdrew. On April 9, 1805, it was incorporated as a charitable organization. Now it boasted a fixed meeting place, or wigwam: the long room of Martling's tavern, where Republicans, later called Democrats (*see* Republican Party, Jeffersonian), foregathered. These partisans were known as Martling men[qv] until the close of the War of 1812, when they were dubbed Tammanies.

The enfranchisement of propertyless whites (1822), which Tammany had championed, was the source of its gradual growth of power (*see* Franchise). During the early political struggles for control, the sachems denied the use of Tammany Hall to ambitious factions, and decided disputed nominations. When this usurpation was first challenged (1852), and the sachems were reminded that the society was independent of the party, and incorporated solely for charitable ends, they replied that the society's fame as a political organization was "too extended to need mention."

Until the advent of William M. Tweed as leader (1860), Tammany Hall differed from other urban political organizations only in degree. He made it a smoothly running juggernaut, which has served as a model for most city machines. He controlled the mob by catering to its religious and racial groups, and by gifts to the poor; he managed rival political groups by bribing their leaders. "This population is too hopelessly split into races and factions to govern it under universal suffrage, except by the bribery of patronage, or corruption," said Tweed. He established another tradition by making himself supreme, and glorified in his title of "Boss." Subordination to his will was a prerequisite to appointment or election to office. He raised Tammany to state power when he elected his candidate for governor (1868). Then emerged the Tweed Ring[qv], and the disclosure of its systematized stealings temporarily halted Tammany's pace. This was the first of several major public scandals in which outstanding Tammany leaders have been involved (*see* Nast Cartoons).

Tammany wielded still greater power when Brooklyn, Long Island City and scores of villages, with old New York, were merged into the present metropolis (1898). In 1910 Tammany again elected a governor, and thenceforward ruled the state, both party and government, save for six years, until 1932. In 1928 its *de facto* leader, Alfred E. Smith, was nominated for President. Four years later, Franklin D. Roosevelt, in reprisal for Tammany's refusal to make his nomination for President (1932) unanimous, attempted to control the organization, and failing, reduced it to the status of a county organization.

[J. D. Hammond, *The History of Political Parties in the State of New York;* G. Myers, *The History of Tammany Hall;* D. T. Lynch, "*Boss*" *Tweed.*]

DENIS TILDEN LYNCH

Tammany Societies, apparently patterned after the New York or Philadelphia societies, appeared in several states around 1810, controlling politics in Rhode Island in 1810–11, and playing an active part in the factional struggles of Ohio Republicans, 1810–12, though local societies persisted for some years afterward. The first Ohio "wigwam" was authorized by a dispensation from Dr. Michael Leib, grand sachem of the Philadelphia society, though there is little other evidence of any central organization. The constitution and ritual were those of a patriotic fraternal order of a democratic character.

[W. T. Utter, Saint Tammany in Ohio: A Study in Frontier Politics, *Mississippi Valley Historical Review*, XV.]

EUGENE H. ROSEBOOM

Tampico Affair, THE (1914). *See* Vera Cruz (1914).

Tanks, Military. The tank, a war-baby, was originally conceived and produced by the British. The impregnability of the modern trench-wire-artillery-machine-gun defense was the primary cause of this weapon's introduction into modern war.

Essentially the tank is an armed and armored tractor. Due to the weights of the necessary armor for protection, the ammunition for firepower, the fuel for added cruising radius, and the crew of from one to eleven men for manipulating the weapons and machinery, few successful tanks have been constructed weighing less than six tons. They are classified according to weight—eight tons or less are light or reconnaissance tanks, those around fifteen tons are medium or breakthrough tanks and those over twenty-five tons are the heavies, or combat tanks.

Tanks are armed with one or more machine guns and often one or more larger guns for use against other tanks or heavy matériel. The World War tank had a combat speed of about three miles per hour; recent models have maximum speeds comparable with the modern motor car. The most successful World War tank was of great length in order to cross trenches; it was built heavy to crush wire; and the speed deemed necessary was just enough to keep ahead of the assaulting infantry. The modern tank has a high cross-country speed, a prime necessity for protection as well as for reconnaissance purposes.

The tanks were first used in the battle of the Somme, September, 1916. The British used them thereafter in a number of attacks but without any signal success until the battle of Cambrai in November, 1917, when for the first time they were correctly employed. From then until the end of the war the British major successes were based on the tanks. The French used tanks the first time in April, 1917.

The Americans equipped three battalions with tanks during the war. They operated with fair success in the battles of St. Mihiel, in the Meuse-Argonne[qqv], and on the British front. As a result of World War experience the tank has been adopted as an auxiliary weapon—important for its assistance to the foot soldier and for reconnaissance work.

[Jones, Icks, Rarey, *The Fighting Tanks since 1916.*]

W. L. ROBERTS

Taos, N. Mex., an old Indian-Spanish-American town, is located some seventy miles up the Rio Grande from Santa Fé[qv]. Within three miles of one another stand an old and large Indian pueblo[qv] and a town, begun by Spaniards before 1680, whose life and architecture even now show a strong Indian influence. The pueblo, with its curious pyramidlike dwellings of three and four stories, was discovered in 1540 by some of Coronado's[qv] men. Oñate's[qv] expedition arrived there in 1598 and gave it its present name, though other names were used until an American postmaster in 1884 fixed the name Taos permanently.

The Taos Indians played an important part in the early history of New Mexico. With Taos as headquarters, the Indian leader, Popé, planned and carried out in 1680–82 a general revolt against Spanish rule which succeeded in killing or expelling all Spaniards from the province. When twelve years later DeVargas reconquered Santa Fé and the southern part of the province, he encountered a continued and stubborn revolt among the Taos Indians until he defeated them in 1696 (*see* Pueblo Revolt). Again, in 1847, it was mainly some Indians of Taos with a few Mexicans who scalped and killed Charles Bent, first American governor of New Mexico, while at his home in Taos, and attempted to raise a general revolt against American authority. With the execution of a few leaders, the revolt subsided. The dress and habits of the Taos Indians make them colorful subjects for American artists.

Spaniards came to Taos as missionaries early in the 17th century and later established both a village and a permanent mission. The only newspaper in New Mexico before the American period was issued by a printing press at Taos in 1834. The white population, previously much less than the Indian, was gradually increased after the arrival of American traders, such as LaLande in 1804, William Becknell and associates in the Santa Fé trade[qv] in 1822, Ewing Young and James O. Pattie about 1824 and Kit Carson in 1826. Indians and Spaniards had traded in Taos before this. During most of the 18th century, and perhaps later, annual fairs were held at which goods of various kinds were bartered, since no money was available. Chihuahua traders who sent wagons to Taos seem to have reaped enormous profits. Americans after 1822 made Taos the center of a very active fur trade. Most notable of all these Americans was Kit Carson who at seventeen years of age arrived, in 1826, to make his future home in Taos and to get a reputation as the greatest of American scouts.

The first American artists who were especially attracted by the possibilities of the Taos region were the brothers Edward and Richard Kern from Philadelphia who came there in 1848 with John C. Frémont's[qv] fourth expedition. Today Taos is a mecca for art students and for many thousand tourists annually.

[Blanche C. Grant, *When Old Trails Were New.*]

L. W. NEWTON

Taos Trail, THE, was already called the "Old" Taos Trail when Jacob Fowler traversed it in 1822. It first served as a road for Spaniards going north to the Rockies and for Plains Indians attending the Taos fair. Later the American fur trappers of the Rockies followed the trail south to enjoy the friendliness and hospitality of Taos[qv]. It also served as the westernmost branch of the Santa Fé Trail[qv] and was used as such until 1880. The route of the Taos Trail varied considerably. Roughly it ran north from Taos, crossed the Sangre de Cristo Range at La Veta Pass and followed the Huerfano River to the Arkansas.

[Jacob Fowler, *Journal, 1821-22;* Blanche C. Grant, *When Old Trails Were New*, p. 45.]

BLISS ISELY

Tappan Patent, THE, a tract of wild land located at Tappan on the west side of the Hudson, was purchased on July 1, 1682, from the Indians, with the permission of the governor of New Jersey, by a group of Dutch farmers residing on Manhattan Island. In 1683 some of the shareholders settled on the land. In 1684, however, a boundary dispute arose between New York and New Jersey, and New York ordered the settlers to prove their title. The Indian deeds were produced and on March 17, 1687, a patent was issued by Governor Dongan to the subscribers. In 1704 the land was legally apportioned, each owner apparently being confirmed in the possession of the farm he had settled.

[George Bulke, The History of the Tappan Patent, in *Rockland County Record*, 1931-32.]

A. C. FLICK

Tar was made in the American colonies, as a by-product of land-clearing and as a regular industry, both to supply local shipyards and for export. Some colonies enacted inspection laws to guarantee its quality. Between 1687 and 1704 two groups of English promoters tried to secure from Parliament special charters to manufacture and trade in tar and other naval stores in America. Parliament denied the privileges they requested, which had a somewhat monopolistic character, but in 1705, moved by a desire to lessen the navy's dependence on Sweden for naval stores[qv], established bounties upon those imported from the colonies including one of £4 sterling per ton on tar. Following this law and subsequent acts, annual shipments of pitch and tar from the colonies to Great Britain rose from less than 1000 barrels to more than 82,000 barrels. One hundred years later the Republic's export of these commodities to all countries averaged annually less than 90,000 barrels. Nevertheless the commercial manufacture of tar expanded, especially in North Carolina, and during the era of wooden ships it retained an important place in manufacturing and trade statistics. Today, however, modern methods of wood distillation have largely replaced it by more valuable products.

[Eleanor L. Lord, *Industrial Experiments in the British Colonies of North America.*]

VICTOR S. CLARK

Tar and Feathers. Pouring molten pitch over the body and covering it with feathers was an official punishment in England as early as the 12th century. It was never legal in the United States, but was always a mob demonstration, often directed against a violator of community opinion—as, for example, an occasional abolitionist in the South before the Civil War. The most famous instance in American memory is that of Skipper Floyd Ireson who, according to New England legend, was tarred and feathered by the women of Marblehead because he refused to aid seamen in distress. We hear of a number of Loyalists[qv] so treated at the beginning of the Revolutionary War, among them Judge James Smith of the Court of Common Pleas in Dutchess County, N. Y. On the other hand, British soldiers in Boston tarred and feathered a "rebel" in 1775. During the Whiskey Rebellion[qv] in Pennsylvania in 1794, it is said that more than a score of government agents were given tar and feathers. Wife beaters and highly immoral persons who became a scandal to the community often received this drastic treatment by way of emphatic prelude to banishment. The practice finally vanished in the latter 19th century.

[H. E. Barnes, *The Story of Punishment;* William Hardman, Tar and Feathers, in *Once a Week*, Jan. 24, 1863.]

ALVIN F. HARLOW

Tarascon, Berthoud and Company was composed of Louis A. and John A. Tarascon and James Berthoud, who had fled from France during the French Revolution. They settled in Shippingport on the Ohio, which soon thereafter became a part of Louisville, Ky., and engaged in milling and other commercial activities during the first quarter of the 19th century. Wealthy, aristocratic and public-spirited, they lived in a style seldom seen in frontier towns.

[Lewis Collins, *History of Kentucky.*]

OTTO A. ROTHERT

Tariff history involves not only a record of the leading laws and reasons for their enactment, but the machinery for customs administration, and in recent years, under high protective duties, a study of methods for meliorating to some extent the rigors of the laws, including reciprocity, trade treaties, flexible clauses and the operation of most-favored-nation treatment[qv]. While tariff action has been a feature of American history even from pre-Constitution days the issue has not been continuously before Congress or people. Rather long breaks have occurred in which interest lay dormant only to be called to life by some apparent need, as with business depressions, revenue requirements and occasional revival of political controversy. About eleven years elapsed after the Walker tariff of 1846 before Congress again tackled the tariff problem. For a decade after the enactment of the Dingley tariff of 1897 the issue dropped into the background to be revived again with the controversy preceding the Payne-Aldrich Act of 1909[qqv]. And, if we except minor alterations, the Civil War tariffs remained practically intact until about 1890, although tariff was a political issue during a portion of this period.

During the early years of our Government, income from customs was the mainstay of the treasury. Thus, whatever the state of protective sentiment, the revenue motive was always present. In the two years, 1789 and 1790, customs and tonnage duties, mainly customs, contributed approximately 88% of the total ordinary receipts of the Federal Government; as an annual average from 1801 to 1810 the same sources provided about 92%; in the decade from 1811 to 1820, due to the use of internal revenues during the War of 1812, the amount declined to 77%, but came back again to the old level in most of the years prior to 1860. In fact, as an annual average for the decade ending 1860 customs and tonnage duties contributed about 90% of the total ordinary receipts. The use of certain excises after the Civil War reduced somewhat the importance of customs but this source still remained as one of the two most important general divisions of income until the introduction of more varied domestic taxes after 1915.

Prior to the Civil War Congress passed six major tariff acts. The preamble of the law of 1789, the first of its kind in our history, indicated that the purpose was to "support the government," to "discharge the debts of the United States" and the "encouragement and protection of manufactures." Duties were imposed on a rather long list of commodities. Some were purely revenue items, as with coffee, cocoa, tea and sugar; others combined the purpose of revenue and protection[qv]. The act made use chiefly of specific duties[qv]; *ad valorem* rates were applied to only a few articles. The moderate policy of the act of 1789 was maintained for a number of years, lending color to the statement that the purpose was mainly revenue. Reduced to an *ad valorem* basis the average rates did not exceed 8.5%. But in this connection it may be remarked that the cost of ocean transportation at this time added something to the disadvantages of foreigners selling in American markets. Duties were increased from time to time, mainly to secure more revenue.

Changing business conditions have often supplied the motive for tariff revision. The interruption of foreign trade during early Revolutionary times, similar disturbances during the Revolution, the regime of the Embargo and Nonintercourse acts[qqv], and our own War of 1812 brought forth a new type of enterprise with attention focused less on ocean trading and more on the development of domestic industries. A new type of businessman appeared. Many enterprises were threatened by the large importations of 1815 and 1816. Owners of businesses called for protection. Subsequently, the hard times following the Panic of 1819[qv] added momentum to this movement. The act of 1816 was an expression of a decided change in sentiment in the direction of the protective system. In his message to Congress, Feb. 18, 1815, submitting copies of the Treaty of Ghent[qv], President Madison said: "No subject can enter with greater force and merit into the deliberations of Congress than a consideration of the means to preserve and promote the manufactures which have sprung into existence and attained an unparalleled maturity throughout the United States during the period of the European wars." Similar sentiment was expressed in later messages. Secretary of the Treasury A. J. Dallas submitted an elaborate report in which he made recommendations with respect to protection. The act of 1816 provided a duty on woolens and cottons amounting to 25%, to be reduced to 20% after June 30, 1819. An application was made for the first time of the minimum principle, the effect of which was to increase the rate on lower-priced cotton fabrics. The act imposed a 30% *ad valorem* rate on a number of other commodities.

A general revision of the tariff was made in 1824, among other things granting further protection to wool, iron, hemp, lead, glass, silk, linens and cutlery. Agitation for still higher rates continued. The friends of protection, in convention at Harrisburg in 1827, presented a memorial to Congress urging their point of view. Still higher rates were granted in the act of 1828, but tariff discussion became complicated with political intrigue so that the act was unsatisfactory to many interests. Opponents called it the "tariff of abominations"[qv]. This act marked the culmination of the protectionist movement prior to the Civil War. An interesting aspect of the debates was the change in attitude of Daniel Webster who, because of a shift of industrial interests among his constituents, was forced to reverse the position which he had taken on the act of 1824. The Southern states strongly opposed the act and the revisions of 1832. South Carolina passed a nullification[qv] ordinance declaring the act of 1828, and amendments of 1832, null and void and not binding on its officers and citizens. The outcome was the compromise tariff of 1833[qv] which provided a biennial reduction of rates between 1834 and 1842.

Vigorous protective sentiment was revived again in 1842, but the act of 1846 (Walker tariff) put the issue to rest for a number of years. Under this law imported articles were divided into classes—Class A paying 100%, and grading down with reduced duties for each division to Class I which included a free list. Duties were reduced again by the act of 1857, this time because the income of the Government exceeded its needs.

The Civil War tariff legislation put the country on the course which it has followed to the present. Subsequent to 1890 attempts were made on various occasions to liberalize the laws, or to soften the effects, by reciprocity agreements, trade treaties and bargaining arrangements, but the underlying principle of protection still prevails. As a preparation for war revenue, several tariff acts were passed in 1861, but much more extensive measures were adopted in 1862 and 1864. The internal war taxes supplied a unique reason for an advance in customs duties, namely, the need of defense for domestic industries, which were heavily taxed, against foreign exporters who, without added duties, would not have shared these burdens, and hence would have received an advantage in competing in American markets. This course of protection once established became permanent. During the decade following the close of the war most internal duties were removed, but tariff imposts remained.

Tariff legislation became an active political issue shortly after 1880. In 1882 Congress authorized the appointment of a tariff commission, but failed to accept its recommendations. Some changes were made in the act of 1883. In his message of Dec. 8, 1885, President Cleveland recommended a reduction of the tariff, and two years later devoted a message exclusively to this subject. A bill which largely expressed his views passed the House but failed in the Senate. The tariff question was a dominant issue in the campaign of 1888–89. The McKinley Act[qv] of 1890 was an attempt to carry out campaign pledges. Duties were lowered on certain articles, such as steel rails, iron, and steel plates; some additions were made to the free list; but on other commodities the rates were increased; this class included wool and woolen goods, finer grades of cottons, lawns, linens, cutlery, tinplate, hemp and flax. The average for dutiable articles was about 48%. A unique feature of this act was a grant of bounty of 2 cents a pound on sugar produced in the United States.

A change of political party was responsible for the act of 1894 (*see* Gorman-Wilson Tariff). This law was in force less than three years, being replaced by the Dingley law of 1897, which advanced the rates to the highest level in our history. The rather long period of good times beginning about 1898, and the shift of congressional attention to other domestic problems, turned interest away from the tariff until the political campaign of 1908, when the supposed relations between tariff and trusts came to the fore. The Payne-Aldrich Act of 1909 was designed to make adjustments to new conditions. The general level of duties became about 40%. A tariff board[qv], authorized at this time, with duties to advise Congress with respect to tariffs, disappeared after about three years, because of lack of congressional support. The tariff continued as a political issue. Under Democratic regime was enacted the Underwood tariff[qv] (1913) which brought the average of rates down to about 30%. A subsequent act (1916) created a tariff commission[qv] with powers to investigate and advise. The Emergency Tariff of 1921 was a postwar measure, replaced the following year by the Fordney-McCumber Act[qv], and this in turn by the Hawley-Smoot Act[qv] of 1930. The average rates under this law were about 40%.

From time to time since 1890 Congress has provided devices for modifying somewhat the effects of our high protective tariffs. The act of 1890 recognized the principle of commercial reciprocity. The President was given power to levy duties by proclamation on certain commodities if countries exporting given goods to the United States imposed duties on certain of our products. This policy was directed chiefly to the Central and South American area. It was a part of Blaine's suggestion of a fuller measure of Pan-American union. A number of commercial treaties were negotiated under this arrangement.

Various recent acts have made use of the so-called flexible clause, under which the President is given some latitude in the readjustment of rates without specific action of Congress.

The general advance in tariff rates over the world, and the growth of nationalistic sentiment, since the conclusion of the World War, supplied the occasion for the act of June 12, 1934, which amended the law of 1930. The President was authorized to negotiate reciprocal treaties[qv], the object being to drive a spearhead into the mounting tariff barriers. The Hull treaties were an outcome of this act. This policy is a departure from general tariff revision; it accepts a given tariff as a base, say that of 1930, and by treaty makes readjustments from that level. Meanwhile, the United States has gone over to the European system of "unconditional favored nation treatment" in its trade treaties.

Tariff laws require an extensive machinery for administration. Questions arise with regard to valuation, classification of nonenumerated goods, refunds, conversion of currencies, transportation of goods in bond, appraisals, protest and appeal and a host of others.

[F. W. Taussig, *Tariff History of the United States*, and *Free Trade, the Tariff and Reciprocity;* Percy Ashley, *Modern Tariff History.*]

ISAAC LIPPINCOTT

Tariff Board. The tariff of 1909 (*see* Payne-Aldrich Tariff) required the President to penalize imports from any country whose tariff discriminated against American goods, and authorized him to "employ such persons as may be required" in the performance of this duty. Using this slim authorization, President Taft created a Tariff Board with Prof. H. C. Emery as chairman. The board co-operated with the State Department in the discrimination study, and then proceeded to investigate a large number of industries. The Democrats, regarding the board as a distinctly Republican creation, did not make appropriations for it in 1912 and it ceased to exist after publishing only three reports.

[Joshua Bernhardt, *The Tariff Commission*, Service Monograph No. 5, Institute for Government Research.]

FRANK A. SOUTHARD, JR.

Tariff Commissions. Congress experimented repeatedly with fact-finding agencies to advise it in tariff matters: the Revenue Commission of 1865–66; Commissioner of Revenue David A. Wells, 1866–70; the protectionist Tariff Commission of 1882 whose report had some influence on the tariff of 1883; the Department of Labor (1888–91) and the Bureau of Foreign and Domestic Commerce (1912–17) which made cost of production comparisons; and the short-lived Tariff Board[qv]. But not until 1916 did Congress, urged by President Wilson, create a nonpartisan Tariff Commission. The Fordney-McCumber tariff of 1922 and the Hawley-Smoot tariff of 1930[qqv], whose technical and administrative sections were largely written by Commission experts, enlarged its duties—notably empowering it to recommend duty changes to the President under the "flexible" provision. The Commission played an indispensable role in the reciprocal trade agreements program[qv].

[Joshua Bernhardt, *The Tariff Commission*, Service Monograph No. 5, Institute for Government Research; *Annual Reports*, United States Tariff Commission.]

FRANK A. SOUTHARD, JR.

"Tariff for Revenue Only." The precise phrase was in the Democratic platform of 1880, but it was foreshadowed in the expression in the Democratic platform of 1876: "demand that all custom-house taxation be only for revenue." It represents a clear-cut free-trade position in opposition to the protectionist and the believer in a revenue tariff with incidental protection. A tariff may be for "revenue only," if it is levied on articles not produced within the country, or if it is levied on something produced within the country, by levying an equal internal duty on the goods produced at home.

[Edward Stanwood, *American Tariff Controversies in the Nineteenth Century.*]

JAMES D. MAGEE

Tariff of Abominations (1828). By 1828 tariff had become both a sectional and partisan issue. After the defeat of the woolens bill by the vote of Vice-President Calhoun in 1827, Andrew Jackson's supporters determined to use the tariff to insure Jackson's election to the Presidency. Certain that New England would vote for Adams and the South for Jackson, they framed a tariff bill with such high duties on raw materials that they expected New England to vote with the South and defeat it. Jackson could then appeal to the protectionists of Pennsylvania and other Middle states whose votes, added to those of the South, would secure his election. John Randolph said the scheme related to "manufactures of no sort or kind but the manufacture of a president." Contrary to expectations, enough New Englanders voted for the bill to secure its passage. Generally condemned by the Southern states, the "tariff of abominations" was nullified by South Carolina in 1832 (*see* Nullification).

[William MacDonald, *Jacksonian Democracy;* W. M. Meigs, *Life of John Caldwell Calhoun;* F. W. Taussig, *Tariff History of the United States.*]

FLETCHER M. GREEN

Tariff Powers of the President, THE, under early tariffs were limited to the right to determine when conditions warranted the imposition or removal of discriminatory duties or the negotiation of reciprocity arrangements. In the Fordney-McCumber tariff of 1922 and the Hawley-Smoot tariff of 1930[qqv], Congress granted greater powers, since upheld by the Supreme Court in Hampton v. United States (276 U. S. 394, 1928).

The President, after an investigation by the Tariff Commission[qv] whose findings he is not obliged to follow, may raise or lower the statutory rates not more than 50%, in order to equalize the cost of production in the United States and abroad. If necessary, he can change the basis of valuation of goods charged with *ad valorem* rates from the usual foreign value to the American selling price of a comparable domestic-made article, a change which may result in increasing the duty far in excess of 50%.

The cost-equalization formula of the flexible tariff provisions necessarily tends to keep the law protective, but the Democrats supplemented it in 1934. Their amendment likewise permits 50% changes by the President—but by means of reciprocal trade agreements[qv], the natural tendency of which is to lower rates and to encourage international trade.

The President also can prohibit importations by individuals competing unfairly; penalize countries discriminating against United States commerce; and authorize the free entry of emergency relief supplies and reciprocal agreements to admit advertising circulars duty-free.

[J. D. Larkin, *The President's Control of the Tariff.*]

LAWRENCE A. HARPER

Tarpley Letter, THE (July 9, 1849). Fearing that the South faced submission or secession yet hoping to prevent either, John C. Calhoun wrote Collin S. Tarpley, urging that Mississippi call all those who desired to save the Union and Southern institutions to meet in convention and issue an address on Southern grievances. The Nashville Convention[qv] resulted.

[P. M. Hamer, *The Secession Movement in South Carolina, 1847-1852;* Cleo Hearon, *Mississippi and the Compromise of 1850.*]

FLETCHER M. GREEN

Taverns. The tavern or inn was one of the most important buildings in a colonial town or village: political headquarters and village club; stopping place for travelers, worn, drenched or half frozen from long journeys by stagecoach[qv] or on horseback over fearful roads; likewise a place of warmth and refreshment after long sermons in unheated churches—and it was noticeable in early New England that the tavern was always close to the church. As in England, the taverns were apt to have names, such as the King's Arms, the Bunch of Grapes, the Plow and Harrow or the Dog's Head in the Porridge Pot (New York). In Pennsylvania the word "inn" predominated, but "tavern" was generally preferred in New England, where—especially in the 18th century—some thought "inn" "too English." In Virginia and many parts of the South a hostelry was apt to be called an ordinary. Our friendship with France during the Revolution caused the gradual introduction of the word "hotel," and "tavern" came more and more to be applied to a mere drinking place. Liquors were practically always sold at taverns, and the occasional proprietor who tried to operate one without them often found the going difficult. It was a stipulation of a tavern-keeper's license that he must maintain good order. A good tavern always had a large parlor or lounge with sanded floor and huge fireplace, a bar at one side, plenty of benches and chairs and at least two or three tables where some travelers ate their meals, though the more fastidious might demand their food served in their own bedrooms. The best houses had a separate parlor for ladies. Such taverns, if they had also an affable landlord, good cooking, soft, roomy beds, fires in all rooms in cold weather, warming pans used on the beds at night, these acquired so wide a reputation that travelers went miles out of their way to stop at them. After 1800 dining rooms apart from the bar became more common. On byroads and in the backwoods, the taverns were often small, wretched hovels, dirty and verminous, though rarely unsafe for the stranger. Even on main highways such as the Boston Post Road, travelers complained bitterly of bad food, hard beds with scanty covering and poor, indifferent service at some places. Foreign tourists in the North were astonished, especially after the Revolution, to find white tavern servants too proud to accept tips. Even in villages, the taverns had the honor of entertaining Presidents, statesmen and diplomats. It was in the Indian Queen Tavern[qv] at Philadelphia that Thomas Jefferson, who was stopping there at the time, drafted the Declaration of Independence[qv].

[Elise Lathrop, *Early American Inns and Taverns.*]

ALVIN F. HARLOW

Tax, Income. *See* Income Taxes.

Tax-in-Kind, The Confederate (1863–65), was a 10% levy in the general tax law of 1863 on agricultural products. Collected by the quartermaster in the form of produce or, until March, 1865, in currency, it furnished after September, 1863, most of the army's food. Carrying a limited exemption for planters and being the first heavy tax on small farmers, it was the object of much criticism and probably was a cause for the growing despondency, especially in North Carolina, Georgia and Alabama.

[Ernest A. Smith, *The History of the Confederate Treasury.*] HENRY T. SHANKS

Tax on Corporations. *See* Corporation Tax.

Taxation may be defined as the act of levying an assessment against the citizens or residents of a given tax jurisdiction for the purpose of paying all or a part of the costs of maintaining the government of that jurisdiction. The levy is made without reference to any special benefits conferred upon the individual taxpayer. For example, an individual cannot escape paying taxes for the maintenance of a municipal fire department simply by showing that he makes no use of that department. Payment of taxes is compulsory, and this gives the tax jurisdiction considerable power over the economic life of its residents. The extent of this power was well expressed by Chief Justice Marshall in 1819 when he said that the power to tax was the power to destroy (*see* McCulloch v. Maryland).

In early colonial days taxation was not important because the simple needs of colonial governments could be met largely by fees, by the direct services of the citizens, and to some extent by quitrents[qv]. Later, however, the colonists were subject to varying degrees of taxation, both at the hands of their own governments and at the hands of England. The colonies used a wide variety of taxes, the nature of the taxes used varying from colony to colony. In general, it may be said that the Northern colonies preferred property and poll taxes and various types of taxes on income and occupations. The Southern colonies, with large land-owning populations, made little use of property taxes, preferring instead excise and poll taxes. The Middle colonies showed less uniformity in tax methods, although excise taxes were common and there was some property taxation. All of the colonies made use of import and export duties as a source of revenue. Local communities were supported by voluntary contributions, by compulsory contributions of services, and by fees, fines and various personal and property taxes. Throughout most of the colonial period England made little effort to collect taxes for revenue purposes, but in 1765 Parliament introduced the famous stamp duties[qv]. These raised widespread resentment, partly because they were felt by the citizens of all of the colonies and partly because they involved "taxation without representation"[qv]. The stamp duties were followed by duties on the importation of various commodities, but all of these taxes, with the exception of one on tea[qv], were repealed in 1770 (*see* Townshend Acts).

The burden of organizing and supporting the Revolutionary Army was first met by the individual colonies, the funds for this purpose being secured from already existing revenue sources and by the issuance of paper money[qv]. In 1775 the Continental Congress[qv] took steps to establish a continental army and navy, and for this purpose it had to have some source of revenue. However, the colonies had given the Continental Congress no power to levy taxes, for it was not a constitutional body and to give it the power to tax the citizens of the various colonies would have been contrary to the very principle for which they were fighting. As a result the Continental Congress had to rely chiefly on the issuance of paper money and on foreign and domestic loans. It did, however, call upon the individual colonies to raise funds for its use, and in 1780 it also called for contributions in the form of specific items of food and fodder. These demands on the individual colonies could not be enforced, and met with but little success. The colonies had never found it necessary to levy heavy assessments against their citizens, and they found it difficult to do so now (*see* Revolution, Financing of the).

Under the Articles of Confederation[qv] the central government was not given the right to levy taxes, but its needs were to be met by assessments against the various states, a method of financing that proved wholly unsatisfactory since the states met these obligations but indifferently. In an effort to secure funds to pay interest on the foreign debt and meet the expenses of government, customs duties were proposed but this solution was blocked by Rhode Island in 1781 and by New York in 1783. In general it may be said that the financial position of the central government under the Articles of Confederation was little short of ludicrous.

The impossibility of continuing the situation prevailing under the Articles of Confederation was recognized by the framers of the Constitution[qv], and that document gave the Federal

Congress the right to levy and collect taxes. Certain restrictions, however, were placed on this right. Congress was to levy taxes only to pay the public debt and to provide for the common defense and general welfare; taxes were to be uniform throughout the United States; no taxes on exports were permitted; and all direct taxes[qv] were to be laid in proportion to the population of the various states. In 1796 and again in 1881 the Supreme Court defined direct taxes as poll taxes and taxes on land.

Congress promptly made use of its tax powers by establishing indirect taxes in the form of import duties on various commodities and excise taxes on distilled spirits, carriages and other items (*see* Customs, Colonial; Internal Revenue). An inheritance tax[qv] was adopted in 1798 but repealed in 1802. The first direct tax was set up in 1798 and was assessed against dwellings, lands and slaves, and subsequently, in 1813, 1815 and 1816, similar direct taxes were levied to finance the war with England. However, the constitutional provision with regard to the apportionment of direct taxes made the use of such property taxes by the Federal Government rather unsatisfactory. It was first necessary for Congress to fix the specific amount to be collected and then apportion this amount among the states, each state's share being determined by the size of its population. Thus if a given state contained 20% of the population of the United States, it would have to assess its property owners enough to equal 20% of the total tax levied by the Federal Government. Such a scheme inevitably led to numerous injustices since the size of the population of a given state bears no necessary relationship to the wealth, income, or land area within its boundaries, and individual property owners in some states had to pay far more than those in other states. Because of this difficulty of apportionment, little use was made of direct taxation by the Federal Government, the bulk of Federal revenue coming from import duties and excise taxes.

Civil War finance[qv] was facilitated by the adoption of additional excise taxes, stamp taxes, an inheritance tax, an income tax and a new direct tax on land, buildings and slaves. The latter tax proved ineffective and was the last attempt made by the Federal Government to levy a direct tax on property. After the Civil War the special taxes were abandoned and the Government continued to make use of customs duties and excise taxes, the latter being levied chiefly on liquor and tobacco. In 1894 a new income-tax measure was adopted, but the Supreme Court—which had previously (1881) upheld the Civil War income tax—declared that a tax which fell upon income from land was a direct tax on land and could not, therefore, be levied unless it were apportioned among the states in accordance with their population. During the Spanish-American War an inheritance tax and a wide variety of stamp and occupation taxes were added to the regular sources of income but were abandoned after the war was over.

Up until 1909 it may be said that the Federal Government depended upon customs duties and liquor and tobacco taxes for its revenue, but in that year a new departure in peacetime taxation was taken when Congress levied a tax on corporations[qv]. In 1913 the adoption of the Sixteenth Amendment[qv] made it possible for Congress to levy an income tax[qv] without the necessity of apportioning it among the states, and this was followed in 1916 by an estate tax, an estate tax being a death tax that is levied on the entire estate of the deceased rather than upon the individual bequests as is the case with the inheritance tax[qv].

Participation of the United States in the World War in 1917 inaugurated a new era in American tax procedure. At the outset of a war heavy reliance must be placed upon borrowing because the working out and setting up of an enlarged tax base takes time, and it takes even more time before the new taxes can bring in the increased revenue. However, there is general agreement that the tax base should be broadened as soon as possible and as much revenue as practicable secured from this source. This helps to ease the burden on future generations, reduces the ultimate cost of the war and helps protect the nation from the inflation that may easily accompany large-scale public borrowing. Furthermore, the collection of substantial sums in taxation maintains confidence in the public credit because it indicates ability to meet debt charges after the war is over. In 1917 the United States inaugurated its war fiscal policies with an immediate $2,000,000,000 loan, and public borrowing continued throughout the emergency period. Prompt steps were also taken to increase tax revenues, and in this connection full advantage was taken of the recently adopted corporation, income and estate taxes. The rates on these taxes were sharply increased and to them were added an excess-profits tax, a war-profits tax, a transportation tax, a tax on insurance companies and a host of excise taxes on specific commodities and services. These new taxes brought in substantial revenues, although this increase was offset somewhat by the loss of revenue that followed upon the prohibition[qv] of the sale of intoxicating liquor in 1918. The drop in imports that accompanied the war also had an adverse effect on Federal revenues.

After the war the special war taxes were dropped, and substantial reductions were made in the income-tax rates, these moves being in keeping with the Government's policy of lightening the burden of Federal taxes, but with the depression years the need for revenue to finance unemployment relief necessitated sharp increases in tax rates. In 1926 the maximum surtax was 20%, but in 1932 this was boosted to 55% and in 1934 to 59%, these changes being accompanied with some reduction in exemptions and various attempts to plug loopholes in the income-tax law. In 1934, too, Congress established a corporation excess-profits tax, a capital-stock tax, and a tax on undistributed adjusted net income[qqv]. In 1935 the rates of the estate tax were raised, and a new corporation tax law provided one set of graduated rates on net income and another and higher set on undistributed net income. The tax on undistributed net income was severely criticized because of certain claimed adverse effects on business, and it was virtually abandoned in 1938. In addition to these changes in the existing laws, a gasoline tax, various excise taxes and a number of "nuisance" taxes were adopted.

The recovery program and the New Deal[qv] program of social legislation gave rise to the need for certain new taxes. Under the Agricultural Adjustment Administration[qv] farmers were to receive benefit payments for withdrawing acreage from cultivation, and the funds for making these payments were to be obtained from a tax levied on the first processor of the commodity in question. This tax, however, was abandoned when the A.A.A. was declared unconstitutional in 1936. The Social Security Act[qv] of 1935 brought with it new taxes in the form of a payroll tax on employers for unemployment insurance and a gradually increasing tax on both employers and workers for the purpose of providing relief from old-age dependency.

State and local taxation in the United States followed along the lines laid down in colonial times except for the provision in the Constitution which made it impossible for the states to levy import and export duties for revenue purposes. While the new Federal Government placed early reliance on indirect taxation, the states were able to make effective use of direct taxation in the form of poll and property taxes[qqv], the latter being easily the more important. For years the general property tax, along with direct taxes on business, provided the bulk of the revenue needs of state governments, but after the World War the increasing expenditures for public highways[qv] led the states to place an increasing reliance on motor-vehicle and motor-fuel taxes as a source of revenue. The inheritance tax has long been used by the states and is an important source of revenue in some of the Eastern states and in California. On the whole, however, it has played only a minor role in state revenue systems. The income tax has come into increasing use of late years, but it, too, plays only a minor role. More recently the exigencies of depression financing have brought new tax problems to the states, many of which have attempted to solve their financial difficulties with taxes on specific commodities and with general sales taxes.

Counties, municipalities and other local governing bodies have long relied on the general property tax as a chief source of revenue, although there has been a tendency of late to adopt local sales and gasoline taxes[qqv] as supplementary forms of revenue.

[W. J. Shultz, *American Public Finance and Taxation.*]

R. E. WESTMEYER

Taxation, Concept of. Taxation is frequently used as a generic term to indicate any sort of payment to a governmental unit. Such, however, is far from accurate and a tax must be distinguished from a public price, which is a voluntary payment made for a commercial service; from a fee, which is a payment to legalize some action of benefit to the payee; from a special assessment, which is a levy against property in proportion as the property is benefited from the expenditure of the assessment; and from fines, penalties and gifts. A tax is a compulsory payment, presumably to be expended for the general good, without regard to the benefit to the individual who makes payment.

In the development of the concept of taxation many principles have been considered basic by their sponsors. To levy taxes that will produce revenue; to produce the least objection; to be convenient in payment and certain in amount; to be economical in administration; to fall on the basis of benefit received; to fall on the basis of ability to pay; to attain equality of sacrifice; to secure good to the greatest number: these are but a few of the concepts which have been advanced as a center around which to build a good tax system.

Revenue appears as the *magnum opus* of any tax system. In the use of many taxes, however, the receipt of revenue is given secondary consideration or none at all. The tax machinery, in short, may be used primarily as a regulatory device and the use of taxes for other than revenue has been extensive. The use of the tariff[qv] to prevent the importation of goods and the levy of a tax of 10% upon the circulation of state bank notes are two examples of a Federal tax in which no revenue was expected. The heavy tax levied by many states upon oleomargarine is not primarily to secure revenue but to make it easier for the dairy industry to maintain itself. Taxes may also be used to discourage or prohibit the use of products which may be considered harmful. Some of the taxes upon liquors doubtless fall in this category. The use of taxation for purposes other than to produce revenue has long been important.

In more recent years the use of taxation as an instrument through which to accomplish social and economic change has become more and more important. Congress attempted to regulate the use of child labor[qv] by a tax upon goods entering interstate commerce produced under certain conditions of child labor, but was thwarted by the Supreme Court; to prevent the accumulation of large fortunes, steeply progressive income taxes[qv] are advocated; to break up large fortunes once accumulated, steeply progressive estate or inheritance taxes[qv] are brought forward; to force the payment of dividends, heavy taxes may be levied upon undistributed corporate earnings[qv]; to make marriage more attractive a tax may be levied upon bachelors. Thus, while such taxes may produce considerable revenue, at least a part of the motive for levy is to produce economic or social change.

Whatever the motive, the levy of every tax is regulative and this should be taken into account in its levy. Whether a tax is economically good or bad for those who pay it, or from the social viewpoint, must depend upon the use which would have been made of the funds by the individuals in comparison with the use made of them by the Government. The utilitarian concept of good to the greatest number is a much broader concept of taxation than the earlier one of a device merely to produce revenue.

[H. L. Lutz, *Public Finance.*]

MERLIN H. HUNTER

Taxation, Exemptions from, may be conveniently grouped into several classes, the first and best known being the exemption of religious, charitable, educational and similar institutions from property[qv] and corporation taxes[qv]. In the early days the church was considered a basic social institution which performed such a broad public service that it was in a sense an agent of the Government, and a similar point of view was held toward educational and charitable institutions. With the passage of time, however, some of these exempt institutions acquired property holdings far in excess of their own immediate needs, and a number of states now strictly limit the amount of tax-free property such institutions, particularly churches, may hold.

A second class of exemptions is of a personal nature, such exemptions being designed to ease the lot of the poor. The thought here is that taxes on the poor may easily deprive them of the minimum comforts or even the necessities of life, thus impairing the efficiency of the individual and possibly making him a public charge. This type of exemption also has a practical aspect, for the cost of collecting small sums from a large number of individuals is heavy in comparison with the amount of revenue received.

A number of other types of exemptions may be mentioned. The Supreme Court decision in McCulloch v. Maryland[qv] in effect prevents one political jurisdiction from taxing the instruments of another, and this has been extended to include public employees as well. A given community may offer to relieve prospective industries of the burden of local taxation over a period of years as an inducement to get them to locate in the community. Some exemptions also arise out of a desire to avoid double taxation. Thus bonds and mortgages are frequently exempt from property taxation because they are already taxed in some other fashion.

[C. L. King, *Public Finance.*]

R. E. WESTMEYER

Taxation, Inheritance. *See* Inheritance Tax Laws.

Taxation, Reciprocal Immunity from, was subject to notable delimitation in Graves v. New York *ex rel.* O'Keefe, decided by the Supreme Court of the United States, March 27, 1939. The roots of the doctrine are in McCulloch v. Maryland[qv], wherein Chief Justice Marshall in holding unconstitutional a state tax discriminating against a Federal agency uttered the sweeping generalization that "the power to tax involves the power to destroy." In harmony with this generalization the Supreme Court thereafter developed the principle that the states and the Federal Government might not levy even a nondiscriminatory tax on the instrumentalities of each other without the consent of the government affected. Included in this principle was the exemption of the salaries of the employees of each government from taxation by the other. The operation of the principle has been much criticized on the ground that nondiscriminatory taxation did not necessarily endanger either government, and that because of the immunity set up each government was cut off from important sources of revenue. Finally, in the Graves case, the Supreme Court directly or by implication overruled Collector v. Day[qv] and a number of other decisions, and asserted the right of a state to levy a nondiscriminatory tax on an employee of the Federal Government not exempted from such taxation by Federal statute. The Court similarly asserted the right of the Federal Government to tax salaries of state employees. Nothing was said about reciprocal taxation of state and Federal securities, but the reasoning of the Court suggests approval of such taxation.

[John M. Mathews, *The American Constitutional System.*]
CARL BRENT SWISHER

Taxation in Territories and Possessions. The application of the Constitution to taxation in American territories and possessions depends upon whether the area involved is an "incorporated" or an "unincorporated" territory, a distinction set up by the Supreme Court in 1900 and thereafter in a series of decisions on the so-called Insular Cases[qv]. If Congress designates a certain territory as an incorporated territory, then all parts of the Constitution and the laws and treaties of the United States apply to it, including those constitutional provisions and laws having to do with Federal taxation. In this connection it is worth noting that the citizens of these territories are without representation in Congress and in a very real sense are subject to taxation without representation. At the present time Hawaii and Alaska are formally incorporated territories, and the District of Columbia may be considered to be in the same position.

In the case of those possessions not designated as incorporated territories, Congress and the Supreme Court determine to what extent the Constitution applies. In 1900 in the case of Downes v. Bidwell (182 U. S. 244) the Supreme Court upheld the right of Congress to levy a duty on goods entering the United States from Puerto Rico, and since the Constitution provides that all duties, imposts and excises shall be alike throughout the United States, it may be assumed that uniformity of taxation does not apply to unincorporated territories.

As far as local taxation is concerned the United States Government allows a good deal of local autonomy, even in the unincorporated territories. An exception is the District of Columbia, the citizens of which are subject to taxation at the hands of a board appointed by the President.

[W. R. West, *American Government.*]
R. E. WESTMEYER

Taxation No Tyranny is the title of a political pamphlet written by Dr. Samuel Johnson, probably at the instigation of the British ministry, in 1775. It is an answer to the declaration of the Second Continental Congress[qv] setting forth their reasons for taking up arms. The style is extremely partisan and uncompromising, although some of the most insulting passages are said to have been stricken out by the ministry. Its object was to justify the repressive measures against the colonies. The tone of the pamphlet contributed to end all hopes of compromise and hastened the American decision in favor of independence.

[A. B. Hart, *American History Told by Contemporaries*, Vol. III.]
O. M. DICKERSON

"Taxation without Representation" became an issue in the American colonies when Charles Townshend[qv] (1767) sought to impose taxes on such commodities as glass and tea, and provided means for the enforcement of the taxes. That James Otis, in arguing against Writs of Assistance[qv] in 1761, first used the expression "Taxation without Representation is Tyranny!" may be doubted. The phrase in various forms was in common use during the period preceding the outbreak of the Revolution. The colonists agreed with Camden and with Chatham that in the matter of internal taxation they were free from parliamentary control. External taxes for the regulation of colonial trade could be levied by Parliament but only with the consent of the colonies. Colonial statesmen admitted the authority of Parliament over the colonies but sought to establish the principle that there were some things Parliament could not do. The real grievance of the colonists lay in the defective system of parliamentary representation which permitted the manipulation of the "rotten boroughs" so that there was always a standing majority in support of the ministers.

At first the representation was held to be one of land but was later shifted to the assertion that in Parliament all British subjects find a virtual representation. "We virtually and implicitly allow the institutions of any government of which we enjoy the benefit and solicit the protection," declared Samuel Johnson (*see Taxation No Tyranny*). He denied that in the case of the colonies the disfranchised were unrepresented. "They are represented," he said, "by the same virtual representation as the greater part of England." But the theory of virtual representation was attacked in England and was wholly rejected in the colonies. To the colonists it was identified with political corruption and appeared irreconcilable with the dogma that government derives its just powers from the consent of the governed. Colonial debaters could not believe that a man was represented who stood under a personal incapacity to become an elector. "If every inhabitant of America had the requisite freehold"[qv], said Daniel Dulany, "not one could vote, but upon the supposition of his ceasing to become an inhabitant of America, and becoming a resident of Great Britain." The colonial argument therefore insisted that representation was achieved only through an assembly of men actually elected by the persons they were intended to represent. That is not to say the colonists desired a representation in Parliament. What the colonists desired was the confirmation and continuance of the authority of their local assemblies to legislate, especially in matters of taxation. From external taxation they claimed to be wholly free.

The United States has not deemed taxation without representation to be tyranny in dealing with its territories. Taxes have been levied although representatives are not elected to Congress. But the whole question of the government of territories has been confided to Congress by the Constitution. In formulating a policy for the government of territories, Congress has generally laid down two principles: Either to prepare the territory for admission as a state or to pave the way for ultimate independence, as in the case of the Philippines. With this generous policy in effect, the issue of taxation without representation has not arisen.

[W. S. Carpenter, *Development of American Political Thought.*]

WILLIAM S. CARPENTER

Taxes, Direct and Indirect. From a legal standpoint, direct taxes include taxes on property, income taxes and poll taxes[qqv]. Excise and transfer taxes, on the other hand, are considered as indirect. The Constitution forbids the Federal Government to levy direct taxes unless proportioned to the population of the several states, although the Sixteenth Amendment[qv], ratified in 1913, now permits the National Government to levy taxes on income from whatever source without apportionment in accordance with population.

In spite of the prohibition of direct taxes, a personal income-tax law was passed in 1861 and remained in force until 1872. Later, in 1894, a combined income and inheritance tax law was held unconstitutional as constituting a direct tax. In 1909 an act called a corporation excise law was passed, but, in spite of the name, it was really a corporation[qv] income-tax law and marked the beginning of Federal taxation of corporate income. Since 1913 the National Government has regularly taxed both corporate and personal income.

Direct taxes have always bulked large in state systems, the state and local governments having derived a substantial income from real-estate, personal-property, poll and income taxes.

The economic distinction between direct and indirect taxes is a point on which there is little agreement among economists and need not be elaborated on.

[W. J. Shultz, *American Public Finance and Taxation.*]

FREDERICK A. BRADFORD

Taxes, Property. Property taxation developed in the colonies as soon as there was a need for revenue that could not be met more easily by other means and was used by both the colonial and municipal governments. The tax apparently was the cause of little complaint, probably because the rates were too low to be a serious burden on property owners. In all localities the tax was on specific items of property, such things as land and slaves. After the Revolution, the new states continued to make use of taxes on property as did the various lesser tax jurisdictions within the states. By 1796 every state except Delaware had a tax on land, and in addition the Northern states generally taxed horses, cattle and money; the Southern states taxed slaves and even billiard tables; while the Central states exhibited no great uniformity in the nature of the property they taxed. Four states levied a tax on the whole mass of property owned by their citizens, certain items, however, being exempt. In some cases the assessment was based on quantity of taxable property owned, in others on value, and in still others on estimated earning capacity. The Federal Government levied several property taxes between 1798 and 1816, but the constitutional requirement that such taxes be apportioned among the states in accordance with population made its use of this form of taxation impracticable (*see* Taxation).

The early system of levying taxes on specific items of property proved simple enough and on the whole quite satisfactory, but as the revenue needs of state and local governments increased and as new classes of wealth grew more important it was found desirable greatly to extend the number of items subject to taxation, and in due course the taxation of specific items of property gave way to laws which taxed all property at a uniform rate, exemptions being made in the case of church, school, Federal and certain other properties. In McCulloch v. Maryland[qv] the Supreme Court held that the states could not tax instruments of the Federal Government.

In its original form the property tax was levied against real property and such common articles of personal property as livestock and carriages, but with the passage of time the tax began to take in an increasing amount of property of an intangible nature—such things as currency, stocks and bonds, mortgages, etc. This type of property, which in many places far exceeded the value of real property, was easily concealed, and it came to be said that the only persons who paid the tax were those who were scrupulously honest or who did not know any better. Thus the various tax jurisdictions making use of the property tax lost substantial amounts of revenue, and the tax came to be looked upon as an incentive to dishonesty. In an effort to overcome the loss of revenue arising out of the difficulty of assessing intangibles, some tax jurisdictions have of late years adopted a classified property tax. The classified property tax places a lighter rate on personal property than on real property, apparently in the belief that most holders of personal property will be honest about rendering their property if it does not cost too much. In a few cases the tax on personal property has been abandoned altogether and an attempt made to get at this source of income through the use of an income tax[qv] or some other form of taxation.

The assessment or valuation of real property for tax purposes is carried on by a host of elected or appointed tax assessors, while the declaration of the value of personal property is usually left up to the owner. It is possible to have as many assessors as there are tax districts levying a property tax, but in practice the assessments made by city and county assessors are often accepted by the other jurisdictions. In all cases the state accepts the assessments made by the county or municipal assessors, and the state tax is collected through local officials.

All modern tax authorities hold to the theory that the tax burden should be distributed among the citizens in accordance with the individual taxpayer's ability to pay, and at one time property ownership probably did provide a rough measure of ability to pay. However, the general property tax as administered in the present day complex economy is in no way in accord with this principle. Taxes are levied against the assessed value of land and buildings without regard to the income derived from such property, a particularly serious problem for agriculture during the years following 1920. Furthermore the number of individuals engaged in assessment work leads to wide variations in the way in which a given type of property is assessed and even to the way in which the same piece of property is assessed. Finally, state and Federal securities are exempt from taxation, and other types of securities are easily concealed, yet this is probably a form of property that does represent some ability to pay. Consequently the use of the property tax has been condemned for many years, but it is not likely that it will be abandoned until some other tax scheme equally productive of revenue is worked out.

[R. T. Ely, *Taxation in American States and Cities;* W. J. Shultz, *American Public Finance and Taxation.*]

R. E. WESTMEYER

Taxing Power, Federal. Although the Federal Government has more than two hundred distinct sources of revenue, taxation in varying forms is by all odds the main reliance. The long list of powers specifically granted to Congress in the Constitution starts off with the fundamental power "to lay and collect taxes, duties, imposts, and excises." The power of taxation thus given to the National Government is very comprehensive, but there are certain express and implied limitations upon its exercise. To begin with, Congress is not free to lay and collect taxes for any and all purposes, but only "to pay the debts and provide for the common defense and general welfare of the United States" (Art. I, sec. 8). The phrase "general welfare"[qv] is sufficiently broad and loose to give Congress great latitude. It has, however, been considerably narrowed in recent years by decisions of the Supreme Court, holding that the taxing power may not be employed by Congress to draw to itself control of matters that have been reserved to the states. In other words, the general welfare that may be aimed at must fall within the boundaries marked out for the Federal Government by the Constitution, as that instrument is interpreted by the Supreme Court. Furthermore, direct taxes[qv] (capitation or poll taxes and taxes on land) must be apportioned among the states according to population. Income taxes[qv] were held to be direct taxes in 1895 (Pollock v. Farmers' Loan and Trust Co.[qv]), but the Sixteenth Amendment[qv] (1913) now permits Congress to levy such taxes upon the basis of uniformity. All other taxes are indirect taxes, and must be levied at uniform rates in all parts of the country, except in the case of goods coming from the Insular Possessions[qv]. Export taxes[qv] are definitely prohibited. In addition there are a few implied limitations upon the taxing power: Congress may not tax the essential governmental functions or agencies of the state and local governments (*see* Taxation, Reciprocal Immunity from). Under a decision of the Supreme Court in 1870 (Collector v. Day[qv]), salaries of state and local officials were long included in this exemption. In 1939, however, Congress did away with this exemption and authorized the taxation of salaries of state and local officials, and at the same time permitted the states to tax the salaries of Federal officials, which had previously been exempt. Congress may not, however, tax the securities (or the income therefrom) issued by state and local governments. Whenever Congress has the power to tax at all, the determination of the amount and expediency of the tax rests solely with Congress. Although most tax laws have for their primary purpose the production of revenue for the Government, there are regulatory measures which, although tax laws in form, aim only incidentally to bring in revenue. Most of these have been upheld as a proper means for rendering effective some expressly granted power, e.g., the regulation of commerce. The Supreme Court has, however, denied to Congress authority to employ the taxing power as a means of eliminating child labor[qv] in industry (*see* Bailey v. Drexel Furniture Company), of regulating agricultural production (*see* Hoosac Mills Case), and as a penalty for noncompliance with coal-mining regulations (*see* Carter v. Carter Coal Company), on the grounds that such matters were reserved to the states under the Tenth Amendment[qv]. Serious problems of double taxation have arisen in recent years out of the power of both Congress and the states to tax the same person or property at the same time. Efforts are now being made to bring about an allocation of specific fields for taxation by the National Government on the one hand, and by the state and local governments on the other hand.

[C. J. Bullock, The Origin, Purpose and Effect of the Direct-Tax Clause in the Federal Constitution, in *Pol. Sci. Quar.*, XV, 217-239, 452-484; Veazie Bank v. Fenno[qv]; McCray v. United States; C. T. Crowell, Taxation Not for Revenue, in *Harpers Mag.*, CLXXV, 89-95; M. Philipsborn, Jr., and H. Cantrill, Immunity from Taxation of Governmental Instrumentalities, in *Georgetown Law Jour.*, XXVI; Should State-Local Employees Pay Federal Income Tax? in *U. S. News*, Nov. 29, 1937, p. 9 ff.; A. L. Harding, *Double Taxation of Property and Income;* Interstate Commission on Conflicting Taxation, *Conflicting Taxation; Book of the States*, 3rd ed., pp. 84-91; *ibid.*, II, pp. 76-86.]

P. ORMAN RAY

Taylor System. *See* Industrial Management.

Tea, Duty on. Tea coming to America was subject to British import and excise or inland duties. The import duties were practically fixed at 11 2/3%, and the inland duties varied from four shillings in 1723 to one shilling plus 25% *ad valorem* in 1745. In 1748 a rebate of the inland duty was given on tea exported to the colonies or to Ireland, and in 1767 the Tea Act provided a rebate of the import duty as well as the inland duties, so that tea left England duty free. In the same year the Revenue Act levied an American duty of threepence per pound collected at the American ports. This American duty became the center of a political agitation that finally resulted in actual resistance. The changes made in 1767 lowered costs of tea in America and resulted at first in increased exports, in spite of an organized agitation against the use of tea and an attempted boycott against its importation (*see* Nonimportation Agreements). Apparently Americans would have their tea and, between 1767 and 1774, more than 2,000,000 pounds were imported and paid the regular American duty.

In 1772 a change was made in the law by which the East India Company[qv] was permitted to export tea directly to America and set up wholesale markets on this side. Four centers, Boston, New York, Philadelphia and Charleston were determined upon. Agents were appointed and quantities shipped in accordance with estimates of probable sales. Immediately there was precipitated an agitation in America not unlike that over the sale of stamps (*see* Stamp Act). There had been no change in the tax since 1767, but the tea ships with their loads of taxed freight became a symbol of taxation tyranny. The discussion was not confined to the local ports, but involved the whole country. The tea must be prevented from landing. Efforts were made by the East India Company to arrange for the payment of the American duties in England, ship the tea in bond, and enter it at the local customs house without visible payment of the tax. Both a newspaper and a pamphlet war developed. Tories claimed the tea was coming in without paying any tax. Whigs exposed the subterfuge. It was in this warfare that Alexander Hamilton won his first reputation as a political writer. Every tea ship was turned back, had its tea destroyed, or its cargo was landed under agreement it would not be sold (*see* Boston Tea Party; Tea Parties). After 1774 the Association[qv] enforced an effectual boycott on most English imports. Some tea, however, filtered through, was entered at the customhouses and paid the regular duty. During the life of this duty, 1767–75, taxes on tea totaling £31,768 were collected.

[Edward Channing, *History of the United States*, III.]

O. M. DICKERSON

Tea, Trade in. As an Asiatic product tea could be legally imported into the colonies only from England, where the British East India Company had a legal monopoly of all British importation. Tea was subject in England to high import duties and heavy excise taxes, especially from 1723 to 1745. These taxes invited an active smuggling trade in Dutch tea both in England and in America. There is no positive evidence of the amount of this trade, but it is believed to have been considerable in America during the first half of the 18th century and to have continued much later in England. Some important shipping fortunes in America, including that of John Hancock, are supposed to have been accumulated in the earlier clandestine trade (*see* Tea, Duty on).

The possible profits from an illegal tea trade after 1748 were small and after 1767 were reduced to a maximum of threepence a pound, the amount of the American duty. Boston, New York and Philadelphia were the chief centers of the American import trade and their imports increased with the lowered total duties after 1767. Total British exports of tea to these centers increased from 449,548 pounds in 1764 to 786,314 pounds in 1768. The American attempt to prevent the importation of tea because it carried the new American tax was fairly effective at New York and Philadelphia where tea exported from England decreased from 494,096 pounds in 1768 to 1530 pounds in 1771 and 658 pounds in 1772. However, the exports to New England, mainly Boston, in the same years only decreased from 291,899 in 1768 to 280,825 pounds in 1771, and 151,184 pounds in 1772. Exports to Boston never fell to the level of those at New York and Philadelphia. The figures are from the customs accounts in London; those given by Channing tell a similar story.

The American demand for tea was greater than the patriots could control. After 1768 a trade in tea from England in defiance of the nonimportation agreements[qv] developed; such tea was not smuggled, but entered regularly at the customhouse. Even the Association[qv] in 1774 and 1775 could not wholly stop this traffic. Total British exports of tea to America were 326,615 pounds in 1772; 781,534 pounds in 1773; 131,514 pounds in 1774; and rose to 739,569 pounds in 1775. Newfoundland, Nova Scotia and Barbados became new centers of the export trade. These provinces could not use the increased imports of tea; obviously they were only distributing centers from which it was hoped secretly to supply the continental colonies. There is no satisfactory explanation for the sustained decline in tea imports at New York and Philadelphia. The trade there practically ends with the nonimportation agreements of 1768–69. There are neither exports from England nor receipts at the customs. It is possible that an entire population shifted from tea to coffee and thus destroyed the foundation for the old tea trade at these centers.

[Edward Channing, *History of the United States*, III.]

O. M. DICKERSON

Tea Growing in the South was introduced experimentally at Middleton Barony, S. C., in 1800 by the French botanist François André Michaux and later by agents of the Federal Government. These trials proved that the famous shrub could be grown in the warmer regions of the South but did not lead to its propagation commercially. The bravest attempt of that character was made after 1890 by Charles Upham Shepard, Jr., an enterprising chemist. He established a tea farm of 600 acres at Summerville, S. C., and marketed in a single year as much as 13,155 pounds of its product. When Congress in 1898 imposed a protective duty, an extensive development of tea farms in the Summerville area was planned. But these plans were halted when the duty was repealed five years later. When efforts to re-enact the tax in 1909 failed, the Summerville project was abandoned. Its friends ascribed this action to the competition of cheap Oriental labor. But there were more fundamental causes. They were the absence of heavy rainfalls and high minimum temperatures like those found in the Oriental countries in which the tea plant is most successfully cultivated.

[R. H. True, Tea Culture in the United States, in *Review of Reviews*, XXXIV.]

FRANCIS B. SIMKINS

Tea Parties. The term "tea party" is applicable to several pre-Revolutionary episodes concerning this particular symbol of British taxation. Of these the first (Dec. 16, 1773) was held at Boston[qv]. Previously, citizens of New York had persuaded consignees to refuse to receive any tea; and the first cargo at that port (April, 1774) was turned back. A consignment discovered on board another vessel was, after the Boston precedent, thrown into the river. At Portsmouth, N. H., and Philadelphia tea ships were turned away.

At Annapolis, Md., public resentment against importation included the importer, when unmasked citizens in broad daylight forced the owner of the offending vessel to put it to the torch. This incident has been called the "Peggy Stewart Tea Party"[qv] after the name of the ship that was burned. Edenton[qv], on the coast of North Carolina, held what was known as the "Ladies' Tea Party," so called because the women of the neighborhood met and openly proclaimed their allegiance to the principles of colonial self-government through endorsing the action of the Continental Congress[qv] and passing resolutions against the use of tea until the impost thereon should be repealed. South Carolina held a "tea party" during the Revolution, when a considerable quantity of the proscribed leaf that had been seized at Charleston was sold and the funds used to promote the cause of independence.

[Peter Force, *American Archives.*]

MATTHEW PAGE ANDREWS

Teachers. In early colonial America a teacher held a high social position. The earliest record of a teacher that we have is that of the Boston town meeting of 1636. "It is voted that our brother Philemon Pourmont be entreated to become schoolmaster amongst us." Here we have the social standing of the teacher, the social or group service which he performed, the recognition of his fellow citizens, and the fact that the services are not merely a commodity, all indicated. For the 17th century and much of the 18th century the schoolmaster in New England is addressed as "Mr." or "Sir" though this may be due to the fact that many of the masters were graduates or students at Harvard and hence entitled to the address of "Mr." or "Sir."

By the middle of the 18th century this higher status was lost throughout the colonies. The early laws of the Province of Pennsylvania state as one of the reasons for a founding of a college "that a number of the poorer sort be hereby qualified to act as schoolmasters." This decline in status is also indicated by the many advertisements in colonial newspapers; by the very frequent establishment of private schools also announced in newspaper advertisements; by the introduction of the woman teacher which also accompanies the introduction of the moving, divided (*see* School, District) and of the summer school, especially in New England towns.

The improvement in the status of the teacher during the early 19th century is due to the elevation of teaching into a distinct profession. This in turn was due largely to a new social notion of the importance of education and also to the organization of special schools for the training of teachers, the so-called normal schools. This event followed a long use of academies and a shorter one of teacher institutes to produce these results. The first normal school was founded in Massachusetts in 1839 (*see* Teachers Colleges). The next step in improving the social and professional status of the teacher came during the latter part of the 19th century with the introduction of the study of education as a subject of university investigation and through the professional training of teachers in the university. This latter placed them on a basis with the training in medicine, in law and in engineering and has done much to revive the repute of the profession.

[J. P. Gordy, *The Rise of the Normal School Idea in the United States;* Clifton Johnson, *Old Time Schools and Schoolmasters;* Nobel, *The History of Education in the United States;* Cubberley and Elliott, *State and County Systems of Educational Administration;* Martin, *The Evolution of the Massachusetts Public School System;* H. Updegraph, *The Origin of the Moving School in Massachusetts.*]

PAUL MONROE

Teachers Colleges. The founders of the nation recognized the necessity of a general education widely diffused among its citizens for the successful operation of democratic institutions. The establishment of public schools[qv] demonstrated the need for more competent teachers[qv]. No agency being then in existence which was both able and willing to undertake the function of educating teachers for the elementary schools, new agencies were necessary. New York and Massachusetts led in the establishment of new types of institutions, of which the normal school was the survivor. New York State began in 1834 state grants to the academies for training teachers. The first normal school was opened in Massachusetts at Lexington in 1839. The name was borrowed from France, where the *École Normale* had a respectable academic heritage, but in the United States these schools were more nearly a folk movement, led by intellectuals like Henry Barnard and Horace Mann.

The economic backgrounds of salary and tenure for teachers prevented extended preparation, with consequent limitations upon the curriculum and upon the selection of those entering into the work. The methods course and a review of the elementary subject matter to be taught, with a heavy emphasis upon apprenticeship, were the main characteristics of the curriculum until the first quarter of the 20th century. Local administration and local certification in the public schools enabled young people to secure positions with little or no preparation.

The high school[qv] began to expand about 1890. West of the Allegheny Mountains the normal schools supplied teachers for the high schools and developed curricula and resources appropriate to this field. From its earliest inception in the Middle West the high school was considered an extension of the common school and provision of teachers for it a legitimate state function. This was in contrast to the country east of the mountains where the private arts college performed this function almost exclusively. (The State College for Teachers at Albany, New York, was the notable exception: Normal School founded 1844; Normal College, with right to grant the bachelor's degree, 1890; State College for Teachers, with right to grant higher degrees, 1914.)

Since 1900 the normal school has shared the expansion common to other forms of higher education. By 1920 the change of name to teachers college was well on its way and the name normal school is now little used. Almost all institutions give the bachelor's degree at the end of four-year curricula, entrance to which is based upon graduation from high school. In the eastern part of the country a program of selective admissions is beginning to be enforced. High-school teachers are now prepared in many states in the East by the teachers college where, as in the West, the high school has come to be the common school.

About 1900 the isolation of the normal school began to be broken down by association first of its heads and later by staff members. In 1918 the American Association of Teachers Colleges was formed and in 1923 became the single clearinghouse for all these institutions. In 1927 standards were adopted for an accredited list. The first accredited list was published in 1929. In 1938 there were 199 institutional members, of which 157 were accredited. Of these, 25 granted the master's degree. The period since 1920 has been one of rapid development in resources and administration in all parts of the country.

[Charles A. Harper, *A Century of Public Teacher Education*, published by the American Association of Teachers Colleges, Washington, D. C.]

CHARLES W. HUNT

Teachers' Institute, THE, probably existed at some time in nearly every part of the United States, but its form and purpose varied in different localities. It was especially common in the newly settled areas of the trans-Mississippi West during the last two or three decades of the 19th century. In most cases it was a meeting of the public school teachers of a county or region, lasting from one day to two weeks or more, at which papers dealing with school problems were read and discussed. Time was also given to lectures and informal discussions designed to help teachers in their work, advance education and improve school conditions.

[Everett Dick, *The Sod House Frontier.*]

EDWARD EVERETT DALE

Teachers' Oath. During periods of tension, attempts have been made to assure the loyalty of teachers by requiring an oath to support the Constitution. The laws vary widely in form. Between 1863 and 1867 oaths were prescribed in California, Nevada and West Virginia; in 1917 and 1919 Rhode Island and Ohio required oaths. Four states passed such laws in 1931, six more in 1935, bringing the total, including the District of Columbia, to twenty-four. Such laws have been supported by groups who believe legislation can control teaching. The requirement has become associated with the issue of academic freedom^qv^ and has been opposed on the ground that it is a symbol of intellectual compulsion and official pressure.

[Henry R. Linville, *Oaths of Loyalty for Teachers*, published by the American Federation of Teachers in 1935.]

HENRY M. WRISTON

Teapot Dome Oil Scandal. Teapot Dome, Wyoming, was the second of the Naval Oil Reserves^qv^ leased as a unit. The lease was executed, April 7, 1922, by Secretary of the Interior Albert B. Fall with H. F. Sinclair, president of the Mammoth Oil Co., the lessee, without competitive bidding. Its provisions were generally similar to those of the Elk Hills^qv^ lease, and as in that case the special Federal prosecutors brought a civil suit to cancel the lease, and a suit for criminal conspiracy, against Fall and Sinclair. The Federal District Court of Wyoming held the lease valid, but was reversed by the Circuit Court, and the reversal was upheld by the Supreme Court, Oct. 10, 1927. Sinclair was tried on the conspiracy charge before a jury in the District of Columbia and acquitted April 21, 1928; the indictment against Fall was dismissed in June, 1932, he having been meanwhile convicted on a bribery charge in connection with the Elk Hills lease. The verdict of acquittal of Sinclair was extremely distasteful to the newspapers of the country, which had tried and convicted Fall, Doheny and Sinclair in their columns while the Senate hearings were in progress. But a dispassionate survey of the evidence indicates that there was no conspiracy and that the lease was voided on the technical ground that although Congress had passed legislation permitting the leasing of the Reserves it had not intended it should be done in the way it actually was. Nevertheless Teapot Dome remained a catch phrase to typify graft in government circles.

[Hearings pursuant to Senate Resolution No. 282, beginning Oct. 22, 1923.]

T. T. READ

Technocracy Movement. As in all periods of acute industrial depression, the slump which began late in 1929 stimulated profound misgivings and wide questioning of the salutariness of the current capitalistic organization of industry. The same conditions excited widespread speculation upon alternative modes of organizing the economy, and panaceas were in order. One of these was the technocracy movement which had its birth in the depths of the depression of 1931–32.

The central idea it embodied was somewhat older. In 1923 Thorstein Veblen in a book entitled *The Engineers and the Price System* had elaborated upon the growing discrepancy between the potential productivity of modern mechanized industry and the actual productivity made available under the current method of its control, i.e., business guided by the profit motive. It was Veblen's thesis that only by placing the control of production in the hands of technicians guided by technical considerations could the full efficiency of industrial equipment be realized.

Starting with these ideas, a study group was organized in the early 1930's which focused its inquiry upon a survey of the development of automatic processes and a determination of the actual capacity of industry to turn out goods. Ignoring the value problem, and concentrating upon a calculation of productivity in "weight and tale" terms, it is not surprising that these technicians uncovered much evidence of undercapacity output. They professed even to foresee the elimination, shortly, of all need for manual labor. While no definite program for "taking over" control was propounded, it was clearly suggested that the use of money in the distribution of goods would have to be abandoned and the market displaced. The mystery in which this rather esoteric group enveloped its "findings" was in no small part responsible for the feverish excitement awakened among a perplexed public by its "revelations," and with the dissipation of this mystery the movement quickly subsided.

[Stuart Chase, *Technocracy: an Interpretation.*]

MYRON W. WATKINS

Technological Unemployment is a new term for an ancient problem—the temporary or permanent unemployment which results from technological changes. Printing may have thrown out of employment thousands of monkish scribes; gunpowder made obsolete the skill of the armorsmiths; the power loom in the 18th century led to revolutionary uprisings among the weavers who would have been deaf to the argument that the new invention would ultimately create thousands of jobs for every one it destroyed.

Readjustments in the past have come with industrial expansion and population shifts, so that the impact of change has tended to be obscured. Moreover it seems evident that technology[qv] has created more employment than it has destroyed, although this statement has been challenged in the period since the World War. But readjustments take time, and the problem seems likely to grow rather than to diminish as time goes on.

Perhaps the term technological unemployment reflects the new social attitude toward industry rather than the rate of change, but recent changes have been rapid and continuous and at times they have seemed almost revolutionary. Only 55 men were needed in 1934 to do as much work in manufacturing as 100 men had done in 1920; 74 in railroading; 75 in the telephone service; 81 in mining. During the first third of the 20th century 1,440,000 new patents were taken out in the United States. The number of new inventions shows no tendency to diminish and seems likely to increase.

We read of factories which are so completely mechanized already that no worker is visible. A practical cotton picker, if generally introduced in the South, might eliminate four or five million agricultural workers, and the inventors of one well-known type of picker have (1939) announced their intention of controlling its use so as to prevent any sudden dislocation.

Improvements in method as well as mechanical inventions throw men out of work. This was a reason for the opposition of labor unions when Frederick W. Taylor was introducing scientific management[qv]. Studies of displaced workers indicate that the most highly skilled bear the brunt of technical changes. A sample study also shows that after a year about half the discharged workers were still unemployed and that most of those who had found employment were working at lower rates of pay.

Under certain collective bargaining agreements new machines are not installed until the workers have been retrained, or if actually displaced they are transferred to other jobs. For example, the American Telephone and Telegraph Company[qv] undertook to find employment for its telephone girls before installing the new dial phones. But such farsighted planning is not general or even typical, and its extension is affected by the influence of competitive practices and the place and power of labor organizations.

Some of those who see mechanical inventions and discoveries as disturbers of the social peace propose a moratorium of science to give the world a chance to catch up. This may be fantastic, but planning to anticipate the major consequences of change seems feasible. Great inventions have usually taken about fifty years from the first patent or working model to the time when they made marked changes in the life of the average man. An average lag of some thirty years seems probable, within which to exert a measure of planning and control.

[*Technological Trends and National Policy, including the Social Implications of New Inventions*, U. S. Government Printing Office, June, 1937.]

EDWARD EYRE HUNT

Technology. During the past century and a half, technology has revolutionized western civilization and has completely changed the old world of agriculture and handicrafts (*see* Industrial Revolution). As a result of the innumerable discoveries and inventions which have affected every field of human endeavor our age has become the machine age. Most of the social and cultural changes of modern times have been precipitated by technological changes. Man's problem of adaptation to his machine-made environment is quite different from the problem that confronted primitive man in adapting himself to nature because the machine-made environment is continually and rapidly changing.

The development of mechanical power from coal and petroleum[qqv], and the harnessing of the force of waterfalls for conversion into electrical energy have been outstanding landmarks in the economic advance of civilized man. Steam power, electricity[qqv] and power produced by internal-combustion engines play a most important part in our civilization. The United States leads the entire world in the amount of power available and used. Another aspect of technology is that of the development of machines in manufacturing, agriculture, transportation and even in business and housework. Since the growing, manufacturing and transporting of goods and commodities have been so greatly accelerated, an industrial system has developed, the efficient operation of which depends upon the co-operation of its various parts.

Technology has brought many problems. An equitable system of distribution in an economy of abundance, industrial management[qv] and control, the activities and organization of government, technological unemployment[qv], and a new type of education to meet the needs of the age, are but a few. The constant social and cultural changes brought about by continuous technological advancement constitute another problem. In the United States national committees as well as many writers have suggested policies and guiding principles designed to adjust society to inevitable future changes, while various programs have been advocated to bring about a planned society.

[Stuart Chase, *The Economy of Abundance;* Lewis Mumford, *Technics and Civilization;* National Resources Committee, *Technological Trends and National Policy*, 1937; President's Research Committee on Social Trends, *Recent Social Trends in the United States*, 1933; George Soule, *A Planned Society.*]

ARTHUR C. BINING

Tecumseh, Crusade of (*ca.* 1806–13). By the Treaty of Greenville[qv] the American Government wrested from the Indians most of modern Ohio, while it recognized their ownership of the remainder of the Old Northwest[qv]. Before long, however, fresh cessions of land were demanded and obtained, while the red man was debauched and his means of existence destroyed by his contact with the white race.

These conditions evoked the remarkable crusade of Tecumseh and his brother, the Prophet, to rescue their people from impending doom. For the existing evils two remedies were proposed: to reform the conduct of the warriors, and to recover the lost hunting grounds. To the former end, sweeping social and religious reforms were instituted, involving abstinence from liquor, community of property and adherence to the native way of life. To stay the white advance, Tecumseh sought to organize a tribal confederacy, and to establish the principle that the land was the common property of all the tribes, to be alienated only by their common consent.

Such a crusade could end only in war, and Gov. Harrison determined to strike first. The Tippecanoe campaign[qv] followed, and in 1812 the Indian war merged into the larger struggle between Great Britain and America (*see* War of 1812). Tecumseh perished at the Thames[qv] (Oct. 5, 1813), and with him were buried the hopes of the red race.

[M. M. Quaife, *Chicago and the Old Northwest;* Ethel Raymond, *Tecumseh.*]

M. M. QUAIFE

Tecumseh, Fort. *See* Pierre, Fort.

Tejas Indians was the erroneous Spanish designation of the Hasinai tribes who lived along the upper reaches of the Angelina and the Neches rivers in Texas. Tejas means "friends" and was used by the Hasinai as a form of greeting which the Spaniards who visited the region in 1690 mistakenly assumed to be the name of the tribe.

[F. W. Hodge, *Handbook of American Indians.*]

C. T. NEU

Telegraph, THE. After a century of experimenting, mostly in Europe (though some attempts were made in America and messages actually sent), Samuel F. B. Morse, a painter, at the cost of twelve years of hard work and miserable poverty, produced the first practicable telegraph instrument. With the aid of a $30,000 appropriation by Congress, a line of wire was strung from Washington to Baltimore. While it was under construction, frequent messages were sent from Washington to the end of the line and back, and on May 1, 1844, when it had reached Annapolis Junction, news of the Whig nomination in Baltimore of Henry Clay for the Presidency was telegraphed to Washington, arriving an hour before a train brought the news. On May 24 the line was formally opened to Baltimore, with Morse himself in Washington ticking off the message, "What hath God wrought!"—often erroneously referred to as the first message by wire—and Alfred Vail, his assistant, who had played no small part in developing the instrument, receiving it.

For nearly three years the Government owned this 44-mile line, while Congress was pondering whether to take over the patent and make the telegraph a government agency, as is the post office. For eleven months after the opening, messages might be sent free, but almost no one sent any. Meanwhile, private companies were being organized under Morse patent privileges to build lines throughout the East, always with the proviso that the Government might eventually assume control. However, on April 16, 1847, Congress decided that the telegraph was not destined to be a lucrative business, and so turned the Washington–Baltimore line over to the Magnetic Telegraph Company, organized by two of Morse's partners. But at that very time, enthusiasm for the new device was developing everywhere, notwithstanding the fact that it was so imperfect that there was constant and even furious complaint. Little was known of insulation until the glass insulator was discovered about 1850, and during rainy weather the current was often so feeble that messages could not come through. A line consisted of only a single wire, which might become so crowded that messages were delayed for days. Construction was flimsy, wires frequently attached to trees instead of poles, and broken almost daily. The New York–Boston line was once broken or grounded in 170 places within 30 miles.

Litigation also tormented the business for years. New instruments were being patented: Royal E. House's automatic printing telegraph in 1846; Alexander Bain's chemical telegraph (which made marks on a sort of litmus paper) in 1848; David E. Hughes' printing telegraph in 1855; and all these brought on lawsuits. Henry O'Rielly, a dynamic promoter, built 8000 miles of line in the Middle West and South, but he was accused of violating his contract with the Morse patentees at the very start, and litigation followed, which was fought with much bitterness. In 1848 O'Rielly's line across Kentucky was destroyed by order of a Federal court. With the rise of the Western Union[qv] in the latter 1850's, an era of consolidation began. During the Civil War, the telegraph, as operated by the Federal Government with experts taken over from the great commercial companies, was used by armies in the field for the first time in history. Remarkable feats were performed in setting up lines as the armies moved, sometimes during battle, and in sending messages under fire. The Confederate Army's telegraph was much less mobile than that of the North. The invention of the stock ticker in 1866 was another milestone in telegraph history. After 1900 printing telegraphs began slowly to displace the Morse clicking key, and the coming of the teletype still further depleted its numbers, though a few are still in use.

[Alvin F. Harlow, *Old Wires and New Waves.*]

ALVIN F. HARLOW

Telegraphers' Strike (1883). In 1881 the Brotherhood of Telegraphers of the United States and Canada, embracing all classes of employees, was organized, and by July, 1882, claimed 15,000 members. Its chief grievances were long hours and low pay, especially to women operators, of whom there were many. On July 16, 1883, it approached all the larger companies of the 200 then in business, demanding an eight-hour day, seven-hour night, equal pay for the sexes, a general wage increase of 15% and extra pay for Sunday work. The companies refused to accept the terms, and at noon on the 19th the strike began; but solidarity was lacking and many remained at work, keeping up a partial service. Meanwhile, the companies were filling the strikers' places as rapidly as feasible with new employees. On August 15 the Brotherhood capitulated and asked that the strikers be reinstated, but many who had been most active in the affair were never re-employed.

[James D. Reid, *The Telegraph in America.*]

ALVIN F. HARLOW

Telephone, The. Between 1872 and 1875, Alexander Graham Bell of Boston, a teacher of diction and of the deaf, and Elisha Gray, an electrical inventor of Highland Park, Ill., were both working along similar lines toward the development of a telephone, though both had started with the idea of producing a harmonic telegraph. On Feb. 14, 1876, Gray and an attorney acting for Bell entered the Patent Office in Washington at different hours and filed applications, Bell's being for a patent, while the more cautious Gray merely filed a caveat—a notice that he had his invention well under way. A scandal later arose over this coincidence. The Patent Office maintained that Bell's paper was the first to be filed by two or three hours and therefore had a sole right—while Gray and his supporters charge that he had been first, and that his caveat had been falsely placed after Bell's application. Gray died many years later, firmly convinced that he had been cheated of his rights as the patentee. Bell's patent was granted on March 7, but he did not succeed in transmitting speech over his telephone until March 10, three days later. Improvements followed rapidly, not only by Bell, but by other inventors. James W. McDonough applied for a patent on a complete telephone within a month after Bell's application. Thomas A. Edison invented a carbon transmitter in 1878 which was better than Bell's; and about the same time Emil Berliner, an obscure clerk in a Washington dry goods store, produced another transmitter, which was better still. Other inventors also brought forth devices. Berliner's patent was not granted until 1892, but during almost all of that time, his transmitter had been in use by the Bell companies. By reason of Bell's original priority, his company succeeded in obtaining control of all other inventions of importance.

The telephone quickly gave indication of being the most enormous moneymaker yet invented—even outranking the telegraph. Bell himself and the two men, Gardiner and Hubbard, who backed him during his experiments, were millionaires within a few years. So lucrative a discovery was naturally forced to withstand many attacks. But in a quarter century of litigation (*see* Telephone Cases), the American Telephone and Telegraph Company^qv^, holder of the Bell patent, fought off all claimants. After the patent had expired in 1890, independent companies sprang up all over America; but by that time the Bell system was too firmly ensconced to be deprived of its supremacy. No other invention before the automobile^qv^ so quickly became a popular convenience and then a necessity. By the middle 1880's scarcely any city physician dared be without a telephone. An instrument was installed in the White House during Cleveland's first term (1885–89), and when that number was called, the President himself sometimes answered. Long-distance telephony was rapidly developed. In 1892 service between New York and Chicago was inaugurated, but it took longer to link New York and San Francisco satisfactorily, and this was not accomplished until 1915. Ten years later, speech by radio across the Atlantic was at last made commercially practicable. The assimilation of the teletype into telephone service was the next great triumph of the telephone engineers.

[Alvin F. Harlow, *Old Wires and New Waves.*]

ALVIN F. HARLOW

Telephone Cases, The. No sooner had Bell been granted a patent on the telephone^qv^ in 1876 than other inventors who had been working on the idea came to light. The Western Union Telegraph Company^qv^ organized a subsidiary corporation, which took over the telephone inventions of Prof. Amos E. Dolbear, Edison's transmitter and other devices and began manufacturing and installing telephones. The Bell company brought suit, and on Nov. 10, 1879, the Western Union forces capitulated. But hordes of other inventors and pseudo-inventors sprang up, and during a quarter-century, the holders of the Bell patent had to battle through more than 600 lawsuits. One Daniel Drawbaugh, an obscure Pennsylvania mechanic, who claimed to have had a workable instrument as far back as 1866, came nearest to defeating them; the Supreme Court sustained Bell's claim over him in 1887 by a vote of only 4 to 3. The Government itself sought from 1887 to 1897 to annul the patent, but failed.

[Alvin F. Harlow, *Old Wires and New Waves.*]

ALVIN F. HARLOW

Television is an outgrowth of the sending of drawings and photographs by telegraph^qv^, first demonstrated in 1847. Experiments with television—at first by wire, later by wave—began shortly after 1900. By 1926 several inventors had apparatus which would transmit scenes for short distances. In April, 1927, action was transmitted by wire from Washington to Whippany, N. J., and relayed thence to New York. By late 1929 the scene could be reproduced in its natural colors and viewed by a roomful of spectators instead of only one or two, as formerly. In 1930 two-way television was demonstrated, whereby two persons talking by telephone could see each other.

[Frank C. Waldrop and Joseph Borkin, *Television: A Struggle for Power*.]

ALVIN F. HARLOW

Teller (or Fourth) Resolution, THE (1898), was a disclaimer on the part of the United States of any intention "to exercise sovereignty, jurisdiction or control" over the island of Cuba[qv] when it should have been freed from Spanish rule. It was proposed in the Senate by H. M. Teller of Colorado and adopted as an amendment to the three resolutions demanding that Spain relinquish sovereignty over Cuba (*see* Spanish-American War).

[J. F. Rhodes, *The McKinley and Roosevelt Administrations.*]

JULIUS W. PRATT

Temperance Movement. Although the temperance movement originated in the sporadic attempts to curb the use of intoxicants during the 17th century, the first temperance society in English America was formed in 1808 at Moreau, Saratoga County, N. Y., by Dr. Billy J. Clark, a physician who had been much impressed by Benjamin Rush's *An Inquiry into the Effects of Spirituous Liquors on the Human Mind and Body* (first published in 1784), for it confirmed his own ideas based upon long observation of intemperance among the people to whom he ministered. The forty-four members of the unique society signed a pledge to "use no rum, gin, whisky, wine or any distilled spirits . . . except by advice of a physician, or in case of actual disease." This was no ironclad pledge, but it became the model for other groups opposed to intemperance. More important than the work of Dr. Clark was the influence of Lyman Beecher, pastor at East Hampton, L. I., who was inspired by Dr. Rush's essay to preach a series of sermons in 1810 against the current drinking customs. Entering upon a pastorate at Litchfield, Conn., the following year, Beecher persuaded the political and ecclesiastical leaders of the "standing order," fearful of the tendency of the ungodly to join the Jeffersonian ranks (*see* Jeffersonian Democracy), that it was essential to organize in order to save the state from "rum-selling, tippling folk, infidels and ruff-scruff." From this agitation came the Connecticut Society for the Reformation of Morals (May 19, 1813), which was dedicated to the suppression of drunkenness, gambling and general lawlessness. Meanwhile, the Massachusetts clergy, supported by Federalist[qv] politicians, had organized their campaign against intemperance (February, 1813) under the leadership of Jedidiah Morse and Jeremiah Evarts. Auxiliary societies were soon formed in New England and New York, but for a decade no phenomenal victories were won.

Not until 1825 were the forces of evangelical Protestantism really mobilized for the temperance crusade. In that year Lyman Beecher again stirred his parishioners with powerful sermons which were printed and widely distributed. The response to his appeal quickly took form; on Feb. 13, 1826, sixteen clergy and laymen in Boston signed the constitution of the American Society for the Promotion of Temperance. Their action revealed a new spirit. The temperance reformers were now under divine compulsion to send out missionaries to preach the gospel of total abstinence from the use of ardent spirits. Using an effective system of state, county and local auxiliaries, the Boston society soon claimed to be national. Voluntary contributions enabled it to support agents who visited every part of the country striving to affiliate all temperance groups with the national society. By 1834 there were auxiliaries in every state with which approximately 5000 locals and 1,000,000 pledge signers were affiliated. Two years later there were eleven weekly and monthly journals devoted solely to temperance, while many religious periodicals carried news of the reform. Despite limited financial resources, the reformers printed and distributed millions of tracts. In song and story, in pageant and play, in essay and sermon, the temperance plea was presented to the nation.

In 1836, at the annual convention of the American Temperance Union (sponsored by the American Temperance Society), dissension appeared within the ranks. The delegates wrangled over three proposals: (1) to denounce the antislavery reformers and placate the Southern temperance societies; (2) to sponsor legislation against the liquor traffic; (3) to adopt a pledge of "total abstinence from all that can intoxicate." The convention avoided a decision on the first two proposals, but by a narrow majority adopted the total abstinence pledge. As a result there was a noticeable decline in the membership of the societies affiliated with the A.T.U., for many insisted that abstinence and temperance were not synonymous, and vigorously opposed placing wines and malt beverages under the ban. But the ground thus lost was more than regained during the decade of the 1840's, as the Washingtonian revival brought a remarkable increase in pledge signers. Labeling themselves as reformed drunkards, the Washingtonians in the spring of 1841 began to stage sensational "experience meetings" which aroused the interest of thousands who had not been reached by the literary propaganda of the older societies. The emotionalism of such meetings was contagious, and the most successful temperance lecturer of the day, John B. Gough, soon utilized it in winning converts. While Washingtonianism was at its height, Father Theobald Mathew, whose campaign against intemperance among his Irish fellow countrymen had won world-wide acclaim, undertook a speaking tour through the United States. Between July, 1849 and Nov. 1851, according to the *New York Herald,* he traveled 37,000 miles and administered the pledge to almost 500,000 Catholics.

Beneath the surface the temperance movement had been slowly converted into a campaign for prohibition. A few leaders had long been eager to direct the force of law against the liquor traffic; they had denounced the licensing of retail dealers in intoxicants; they had supported such legislation as the "fifteen gallon law" of Massachusetts (1838) which forbade the sale of spirituous liquors in less quantity than fifteen gallons "and that delivered and carried away all at one time." The demand for statewide prohibition was most ably expressed in Maine[qv], where Neal Dow, a successful merchant of Portland, had committed the temperance groups to the policy of legal coercion. In 1846 the legislature passed an act which prohibited the retail sale of intoxicants. Not satisfied, Dow's followers secured a truly prohibitory statute in 1851. Thereafter, the temperance forces, wearied from the long effort to combat intemperance by persuasion, turned to the "strong arm of the law." Their objective was state-wide, then national, prohibition[qv].

[J. A. Krout, *The Origins of Prohibition;* Daniel Dorchester, *The Liquor Problem in All Ages.*]

JOHN A. KROUT

Ten-Forties, THE, were gold bonds redeemable after ten, payable after forty years. Authorized by Congress (March 3, 1864) to allow greater freedom in financing the Civil War, their 5% interest made them unpopular. Bond sales declined rapidly and forced the Treasury to resort to short-term loans.

[D. R. Dewey, *Financial History of the United States.*]

CHESTER McA. DESTLER

Tenant Farmer. *See* Farm Tenancy.

Tenements are multifamily dwellings, housing three or more families. In the period between 1850 and 1900 with the demand for shelter, particularly for the poor, continually ahead of the supply, the tenement house came into existence. It constituted a simple method of putting a certain number of people in a limited amount of space. New York was the first city in the United States to adopt the tenement house as a means of answering a peculiar problem arising from the fact that Manhattan, the original City of New York, was surrounded by water and, therefore, hindered in the ordinary courses of expansion. Built first to house the poor, uncontrolled and unregulated, with less than the minimum standards of decency and for the maximum of profit, the tenement house soon developed into the accepted mode of living until today about 70% of the city's population live in what is now called the multiple dwelling (*see* Apartment Houses). Other cities throughout the country adopted the tenement house as a method of providing shelter for a part of its population, but not to the same extent as New York nor for the same original reason. Today the tenement house is built, not so much by reason of an inability to expand, but because the present cost of land in our cities makes it economically necessary to crowd that land in order to derive adequate returns therefrom.

The tenement house has therefore developed in three stages: the first arose out of physical necessity due to the rapid growth in population; the second grew out of a realization of the large profits to be made from the crowding of the land; the third represents economic necessity due to the high cost of land. With the standards now set up by law and with the existing high cost of land, tenement houses can be profitably constructed only for the upper income groups representing less than 25% of the population. In the last few years a realization of this has led the governments of city, state and nation to enter the field of housing in an effort to clear the slums of our cities and build with governmental funds the tenement houses which private enterprise can no longer provide for the poor. (*See also* Housing; Slums.)

[James Ford, *Slums and Housing;* Edith Elmer Wood, *Recent Trends in American Housing;* Langdon W. Post, *The Challenge of Housing.*]

LANGDON W. POST

Tennessee, Army of (Confederate), was the designation given, Nov. 20, 1862, by Bragg (C.) to the reorganized Army of Mississippi[qv]. Soon afterward it fought at Stone's River[qv], later engaging in a summer campaign of maneuver in middle Tennessee (*see* Tullahoma Campaign). Reinforced by troops from Virginia, it achieved a brilliant victory at Chickamauga[qv] marred by subsequent indecision and dissension. The fruitless siege of Chattanooga[qv] followed, to be ended by decisive defeat and withdrawal into northern Georgia (*see* Ringgold, Battle of).

Bragg was replaced by Hardee and then by J. E. Johnston, who, outnumbered two to one, vigorously and skilfully opposed Sherman's (U.) advance to Atlanta (*see* Atlanta Campaign). Because of failure to defeat Sherman, Johnston was summarily replaced by Hood (*see* Davis-Johnston Controversy). Severe fighting followed and Hood was forced out of Atlanta (*see* Atlanta, Capture and Burning of). Concentrating his army, Hood soon marched northward into Tennessee (*see* Hood's Tennessee Campaign). Defeated at Franklin and at Nashville[qqv], the army retired southward into Mississippi. Taylor replaced Hood. Later the army was transferred eastward to aid in opposing Sherman (*see* Carolinas, Sherman's March through the) and was included in Johnston's surrender. (*See also* Bentonville, Battle of.)

[*Battles and Leaders of the Civil War.*]

THOMAS ROBSON HAY

Tennessee, Army of the (Union), composed largely of Middle West regiments, was constituted from the forces gathered by Grant (U.) following his capture of Fort Donelson, and, with the Army of the Ohio, fought at Shiloh[qqv]. Later the army was transferred to Memphis and from there began the movement which culminated in the capture of Vicksburg[qv]. Under Sherman (U.), in November, 1863, the army, reduced by transfers, was moved to Chattanooga to reinforce the Army of the Cumberland[qqv].

When Sherman began his Atlanta Campaign[qv], McPherson commanded the army. He was killed in battle at Atlanta, being replaced temporarily by Logan and permanently by Howard.

The army constituted the right wing in Sherman's March to the Sea, was present at the siege of Savannah and on the northward march through the Carolinas[qqv]. It participated in the operations culminating in Johnston's surrender. (*See also* Bentonville, Battle of.) On May 24, 1865, still commanded by Howard, it marched in the Grand Review in Washington, after which it was dispersed and demobilized.

[W. T. Sherman, *Memoirs.*]

THOMAS ROBSON HAY

Tennessee, State of. In 1541 Hernando De Soto[qv] discovered the Mississippi River, presumedly within the bounds of present-day Tennessee at the site of Memphis, and it is also believed probable that he had already crossed the southeastern corner of the state on his journey from Florida. This visit was not followed by Spanish occupation; therefore, it was the English and the French who, more than a century later, became rival claimants for the possession of the region. In 1673 two Virginia traders, James Needham[qv] and Gabriel Arthur, visited the Indians who resided in the southeastern part of Tennessee; and in the same year the two French voyagers, Marquette and Jolliet[qv], touched the western edge of the present state when they landed on the eastern bank of the Mississippi River. Nine years later LaSalle[qv] built Fort Prudhomme at the mouth of the Big Hatchie during his voyage down the Mississippi.

Soon thereafter the English and French traders engaged in bitter rivalry for the trade and friendship of the Indian tribes which occupied or claimed portions of the Tennessee country. For a time the Shawnee lived in the Cumberland Valley, but early in the 18th century they were driven northward across the Ohio River by the Cherokee and Chickasaw[qqv]. The Chickasaw towns were situated south of the Tennessee line in northwestern Mississippi but they claimed possession of the whole of West Tennessee and part of Middle Tennessee. The Cherokee occupied the southeastern part of the state and claimed the remainder of East Tennessee and all of Middle Tennessee. In 1739 the French built Fort Assumption at the site of Memphis within the Chickasaw domain as a part of an unsuccessful effort to destroy that tribe. In an attempt to retain the friendship of the "Over Hill" Cherokee the English in 1756–57 built two forts on the banks of the Little Tennessee River. The more important of these, Fort Loudoun[qv], constructed and garrisoned by an expedition from South Carolina, was for a time the most western English fort in America.

Lured on by the tales of hunters and agents of land companies who had been traversing the western country, the first permanent settlers came into Tennessee from the "back country" of Virginia and the Carolinas about 1769. Under the leadership of William Bean, James Robertson and others, they settled along the Watauga, Nolichucky and Holston rivers in the northeastern corner of the state. Finding themselves outside the bounds of organized government and on Indian land, they set up in 1772 a "home-spun" government called the Watauga Association[qv]. They succeeded in negotiating a lease of their lands from the Cherokee, which they converted into a purchase in 1775 when Richard Henderson and the Transylvania Company[qv] bought an extensive tract of land in Middle Tennessee and Kentucky from the same tribe.

Soon after the outbreak of the Revolution the Wataugans organized the district of Washington[qv], the first local division of government to be named after the commander in chief of the Revolutionary army. In 1777 the district was annexed to North Carolina, which gave the name Washington County to the whole of its territorial claim west of the mountains. During the war the Wataugans not only defended their homes successfully from Indian attacks, but also participated in campaigns east of the mountains, notably at King's Mountain[qv]. They also sent forth the expeditions which founded Nashville[qv] in Middle Tennessee in 1779–80.

When North Carolina ceded her western lands[qv] to the United States in 1784, the settlers in the East Tennessee region organized the State of Franklin[qv], and although the cession act was quickly repealed, they attempted unsuccessfully to maintain themselves as a separate state. Both the Franklinites and the Cumberland settlers[qv] participated in an intrigue with the Spanish in 1788, which was brought to an end by North Carolina's second cession of her western claim in 1789. The region ceded was organized in 1790 as the "Territory South of the River Ohio" with William Blount as governor, and admitted to the Union as a state on June 1, 1796.

Due to the large number of soldiers supplied by Tennessee in the War of 1812 and the Mexican War the state became known as the "Volunteer State." During the middle period of American history it was one of the most prominent states in the Union, contributing three Presidents, Andrew Jackson, James K. Polk and Andrew Johnson, and two presidential candidates, Hugh L. White and John Bell. Following the election of Lincoln in 1860 and the secession of seven Southern states, the people of Tennessee refused to call a convention to consider secession[qv]. With the beginning of hostilities, however, public sentiment rapidly changed, and in June, 1861, the people voted by an overwhelming majority in favor of separation from the Union. Tennessee was the last of the eleven states to leave the Union, and she did so by the unique procedure of declaring her independence rather than adopting an ordinance of secession. Moreover, a majority of East Tennesseans remained loyal to the Union, and the state was represented in both the United States Congress and the Confederate Congress during the first year of the war. Some of the most important campaigns of the war were fought on Tennessee soil, notable among them being the capture of Forts Henry and Donelson, and the battles of Shiloh, Murfreesboro, Chickamauga, Chattanooga and Knoxville[qqv].

From 1862 to 1865 Tennessee was under the military governorship of Andrew Johnson. Under the control of the Reconstruction governor, William G. Brownlow, elected March 4, 1865, Tennessee was the only ex-Confederate state to ratify the Fourteenth Amendment[qv] prior to the forcible establishment of the Negro-carpetbag regimes in the South. In consequence of this action, in July, 1866, Tennessee was immediately reinstated to its position in the Union, and thus escaped the harsh congressional program of military reconstruction applied to the other states of the Confederacy. The Tennessee Reconstruction legislature was predominantly East Tennessean, and although Negroes were allowed to vote and later to hold office, none sat in the legislature until long after the Reconstruction[qv] period had ended. The disfranchisement of ex-Confederates, which included the overwhelming majority of the white population of Middle and West Tennessee, increased materially the evil of sectionalism[qv] which had already seriously divided the people of the state. Ever since the overthrow of the radical regime in the election of 1869, which was preceded by considerable activity on the part of the Ku Klux Klan[qv], which was born in 1866 in the Middle Tennessee town of Pulaski, Tennessee has remained identified with the so-called "Solid South," except for Republican victories in four gubernatorial and two presidential elections.

From a population of 77,262 in 1795, on the eve of admission to the Union, Tennessee has grown to a population of 2,616,556 according to the census of 1930. Although the state has been primarily agricultural throughout most of its history, it has witnessed a considerable growth of industry after the Civil War. The abundance of water power available in the Tennessee River system is now being developed by the Tennessee Valley Authority[qv], which has its headquarters in the city of Knoxville.

[P. M. Hamer, *Tennessee: A History.*]

S. J. FOLMSBEE

Tennessee, THE, a Confederate ram, fitted out and commissioned at Mobile, Feb. 16, 1864, was 209 feet long, 48 feet in beam and carried 6 heavy Brooke rifles in an inclined casemate having 6 inches of armor forward and 4 inches aft. As flagship of Admiral Franklin Buchanan's squadron, after a prolonged and desperate engagement with Admiral Farragut's fleet of four monitors and fourteen wooden warships at the entrance to Mobile Bay[qv] on Aug. 5, 1864, she was captured.

[J. Thomas Scharf, *History of the Confederate States Navy;* Charles Lee Lewis, *Admiral Franklin Buchanan: Fearless Man of Action.*]

CHARLES LEE LEWIS

Tennessee Bond Cases, THE (114 U. S. 663), decided by the Supreme Court in 1885, involved an unsuccessful attempt on the part of certain holders of Tennessee bonds, since they were constitutionally prevented from bringing suit against the state to obtain payment, to enforce in their own behalf a lien which the state had taken on the property of the railroad companies to which the bonds had been issued under the operation of a system of loans in aid of railroad construction instituted in 1852 and extravagantly abused during the Reconstruction period. The Court decided that although the lien had been executed "for the payment of said bonds . . . and for the interest accruing thereon," the state was at the outset and remained the sole debtor bound by the bonds. The decision made certain the acceptance by the bondholders of a settlement arranged by the legislature in 1883 refunding the debt at fifty cents on the dollar.

[P. M. Hamer, *Tennessee: A History.*]

S. J. FOLMSBEE

Tennessee Centennial Exposition, THE, held at Nashville from May 1 to Oct. 31, 1897, celebrated the centennial of the state's admission into the Union. The Exposition cost approximately $1,200,000 and extended over 200 acres. There were twenty main exhibit buildings housing the offerings of other states and foreign nations, but the emphasis was upon Tennessee, her mines, agriculture and manufactures. Influenced by the World's Columbian Exposition[qv] of 1893 the principal feature was an allegedly exact reproduction of the Athenian Parthenon, built upon an elevated plateau.

FRANK MONAGHAN

Tennessee River, THE, formed by the confluence near Knoxville of the Holston, which rises in southwest Virginia, and the French Broad, which has its source in western North Carolina, follows a serpentine course into northern Alabama and thence northward to the Ohio River at Paducah, Ky. The length of the main stream is 652 miles, and the total drainage area is 40,569 square miles. Called for a time the Cherokee River, it was used extensively by Indians on their war and hunting expeditions, especially by the Cherokee[qv], some of whose towns were located along the branches of the river in southeast Tennessee. The Tennessee Valley played an important part in the Anglo-French rivalry for the control of the Old Southwest which culminated in the French and Indian War[qv]; and the river was an important route of migration of settlers into the Southwest following that struggle. The use of the river for navigation purposes was handicapped by the presence of serious obstructions, especially the Muscle and Colbert Shoals at the "Great Bend" in northern Alabama. The Muscle Shoals[qv] region became the scene of numerous land speculative undertakings, beginning as early as 1783. The problem of removing or obviating the obstructions to navigation has been a perennial one, and has received spasmodic attention from the Federal Government as well as from the states of Tennessee and Alabama, including a grant of public lands to Alabama in 1828 for the construction of a canal, and several subsequent surveys and appropriations. In the 20th century the emphasis shifted from navigation to power production and flood control[qv], and the construction during the World War of the Wilson Dam and nitrate plants at the Muscle Shoals initiated a nation-wide controversy over the question of public or private ownership and operation of power facilities. Since 1933 the Tennessee Valley Authority[qv] has been engaged in an extensive program involving navigation and flood control, fertilizer experimentation, the production and sale of electric power and the social and economic transformation of the Tennessee Valley.

[J. H. Alldredge et al., *A History of Navigation on the Tennessee River System*, 75 Cong., 1 Sess., House Document No. 254.]

S. J. FOLMSBEE

Tennessee Valley Authority. Growing out of the original construction by the Federal Government of a dam and nitrate plant at Muscle Shoals on the Tennessee River[qv] in the years of the World War (1917–19), and following years of agitation for further development, the Tennessee Valley Authority was created by Congress in 1933 to provide for the unified development of the entire watershed, an area of approximately 40,000 square miles. The purpose of the Authority is to plan and develop the resources of the entire river for the maximum benefit of the region with respect to all purposes, and as such is a unique experiment in the history of our Government.

The most tangible results of the experiment are seen in the construction of large multipurpose dams on the Tennessee River and its tributaries. The Norris Dam[qv] on the Clinch River was finished first, in 1936, and the Wheeler Dam, just above the Wilson Dam at Muscle Shoals, was completed later in the same year. Three more dams in the main river, Pickwick Landing, Guntersville and Chickamauga, and one on the Hiwassee River, are (1940) completed. In addition, the Gilbertsville Dam, the largest of the program and nearest to the mouth of the river, and the Watts Bar Dam between Chattanooga and Knoxville, are under construction. Plans are being developed for the Coulter Shoals Dam, below Knoxville. A third tributary dam on the Little Tennessee River at Fontana was in the original program. The total cost of all of these projects is estimated at about $500,000,000, half of which amount has been spent up to the present time.

Of the purposes for which these dams are constructed, flood control[qv] is probably the most impressive at present. The Gilbertsville Reservoir will have a storage capacity of 4,600,000 acre-feet for flood control alone, and will reduce flood flows on the lower Ohio and Mississippi rivers by two or three feet. This reservoir is perhaps the most strategically located for flood control of any that can be designed for the Mississippi River. It will be a multipurpose dam, serving the interests of navigation and power development as well as flood control. The value of the entire T.V.A. reservoir system for flood control has been already proved by the operations to withhold water from the Ohio River during the winter flood of 1937, which materially assisted in saving Cairo from flooding. A second purpose of the system, navigation, cannot become fully effective until a longer continuous stretch of the river has attained a standard navigable depth, and while this will not be accomplished for some time there are already indications that industry is availing itself of the more economical water transportation.

In addition to flood control and navigation (*see* Waterways, Inland), the creation of water power[qv] is the third purpose of the system. The dams already finished, together with the existing Wilson Dam, provide an installed electrical capacity of 630,000 kilowatts with a firm power capacity of 350,000 kilowatts. As additional projects are completed these figures will be successively increased. The sale of much of this power has already been contracted for by municipalities and co-operatives and by industries at a low prevailing rate, in spite of many injunctions and a considerable amount of litigation brought by private power utilities. Court decisions have been favorable to the Authority and further progress in the sale of hydroelectric power is to be anticipated. The Authority has also assisted in increasing the consumption of electricity by its program of rural electrification and its experimentation in additional uses for electricity.

One of the most important activities of the Authority is the development of low-priced fertilizer. A new high-grade fertilizer of 60–70% phosphate concentration has been produced in the remodeled munitions plant at Muscle Shoals. This program will have a permanent value in the conservation of phosphates[qv] in the United States, enabling the economical utilization of the low-grade phosphate deposits of the Western states. The program for soil conservation[qv], diversification of agriculture, terracing of hillsides, encouragement of animal husbandry, and the reforestation of denuded areas has proceeded along with the fertilizer program. Other activities include the development of native products and industries, the creation of recreational areas in connection with the construction of the dams, and the encouragement of co-operatives for grading and marketing agricultural products. The experiment has also demonstrated the feasibility of co-operation between local interests and the many Federal agencies, state governments, and local and county governments involved in the development of the region—an experiment which is not yet completed but which is well on its way.

[*Annual Report of the Tennessee Valley Authority for Fiscal Year Ending June 30, 1937*, U. S. Government Printing Office.]

ARTHUR E. MORGAN

Tennis was introduced into this country from England about 1874 and rapidly became a popular game in the fashionable circles of American life. At first a gentle as well as a genteel pastime, played by both men and women, it evolved only slowly into the more active modern game with its hard, overhead service, back court drives and smashes at the net. The formation of the United States Lawn Tennis Association (1881), institution of its annual tournaments at Newport (1881), and the beginning of the Davis Cup matches (1900) marked the important stages of its early growth. By the end of the 19th century a group of outstanding players had emerged from the ranks—R. D. Sears, Robert D. Wrenn, Dwight F. Davis, William A. Larned—and tennis began to be played more and more widely throughout the country. With the new century America began to produce players who could carry off international honors, the most outstanding being William T. Tilden II, and what had originally been the polite pastime of society became a sport for millions. The growth of public courts has further extended the scope of tennis and while tours of professional players are a recent innovation, it remains one of the country's most popular amateur, participant sports.

[John A. Krout, *Annals of American Sport.*]

FOSTER RHEA DULLES

"Tennis Cabinet," THE, was a journalistic description of a group of intimate friends with whom Theodore Roosevelt rode, walked or played tennis for exercise during his Presidency (1901–9). Official matters were often informally discussed, and the President admitted seeking advice from this trusted but unofficial circle.

[T. Roosevelt, *An Autobiography.*]

STANLEY R. PILLSBURY

Tenor, Old and New, is old and new issues of paper money. In colonial times, paper money[qv] was issued without much provision for redemption. When it depreciated a new tenor would be made, the old tenor being redeemed at a discount in the new tenor. Often the new tenor also depreciated.

[Horace White, *Money and Banking.*]

JAMES D. MAGEE

Tenure-of-Office Act, THE, passed by Congress March 2, 1867, over Johnson's veto, was designed to restrict greatly the appointing and removing power of President Johnson. The Senate's consent was required for removals in all cases where this consent was necessary for appointment. At first the design seems not to have been that of protecting any particular Cabinet member—these officers being expressly excepted—but rather Republican appointees in general. But after considerable debate there was substituted for the Cabinet exception a proviso that Cabinet members should hold office during, and for one month after, the term of the President who made the appointment, subject to removal only with the Senate's consent. Violation of the act was made a high misdemeanor. When Johnson attempted to remove Secretary of War Stanton the Radical Republican[qv] Congress proceeded with its long-laid plans for the impeachment and trial of the President (*see* Impeachment Trial of Andrew Johnson). It was shown, however, that, as Stanton was not a Johnson appointee, the act could not apply to him. Passed during, and as part of, the struggle between Johnson and Congress over Reconstruction[qv], the act was virtually repealed early in Grant's first administration and entirely repealed March 5, 1887.

[D. M. Dewitt, *The Impeachment and Trial of Andrew Johnson;* R. W. Winston, *Andrew Johnson.*]

WILLARD H. SMITH

Tepee, Teepee, or Tipi. The Dakota Indian word *tipi,* meaning "where I live," was adopted by frontiersmen to designate a conical skin-covered shelter supported by a framework of poles. An alternate term is lodge. The tipi differs from a pointed tent by possessing an opening at the top through which the poles extend two feet or more. The poles range from 12 to 18 feet in total length and vary from 12 to 15 in number. Generally, the name tepee is applied to any such conical pole structure, covered with skins, mats, bark or cloth. The geographical distribution of the tipi is from Texas to Canada (formerly skin-covered, now using cloth), from Nova Scotia into Siberia (covered with birchbark and occasionally with mats).

[Clark Wissler, *The American Indian,* and Material Culture of the Blackfoot Indians, *Anthropological Papers of the American Museum of Natural History,* Vol. 5.]

CLARK WISSLER

"Terrapin War," THE, was a term of derision applied by the Federalists[qv] during the late spring and early summer of 1812 to the War of 1812.

LOUIS MARTIN SEARS

Territorial Claims of the United States, THE, are bound up with exceedingly controversial questions of national policy and expediency. Only the more obvious bases of claims to our major accessions are here listed.

In the post-Revolutionary negotiations with Great Britain, the American claims to the western lands[qv] outside the boundaries of the original states appear to have been based on the extent of the colonial charter grants rather than on military occupation. Louisiana[qv] was purchased from France (1803), but the American claim that West Florida and Texas were included in the purchase was denied by Spain. West Florida[qv] was forcibly annexed between 1810 and 1812. By the Adams-Onís Treaty of 1819[qv] the United States acquired all of Florida for $5,000,000 and relinquishment of our claim to Texas. Spain in turn relinquished her title to all territory north of latitude 42. This acquired title strengthened our claim to the Oregon country[qv], also claimed by Great Britain. The American claim was also based on the settlement of Astoria[qv] and the explorations of Capt. Gray and of Lewis and Clark[qv]. The present boundary was established by treaty in 1846 (*see* Oregon Treaty), and by subsequent negotiations.

The peaceful annexation of Texas[qv] in 1845 was followed by the acquisition of the Southwest as a result of the Mexican War[qv] (1848). The United States gained all the region west of the

Rio Grande on the basis of conquest plus the payment to Mexico of $15,000,000 (*see* Guadalupe Hidalgo, Treaty of; Gadsden Purchase). Alaska[qv] was purchased from Russia in 1867 for $7,200,000. The Hawaiian Islands[qv] were annexed in 1898 with the consent of the white citizens of the Republic of Hawaii. Puerto Rico, Guam and the Philippine Islands were the fruits of the Spanish-American War in 1898, although the treaty of peace provided for the payment of $20,000,000 for the Philippines[qqv]. The Samoan Islands were acquired by treaty with Germany and Great Britain (1899), the Canal Zone by a combination of annexation and purchase from Colombia and Panama (1903), and the Virgin Islands by purchase from Denmark (1917)[qqv].

[Hunter Miller, *Treaties and Other International Acts of the United States;* S. F. Bemis, *A Diplomatic History of the United States;* E. M. Douglas, *Boundaries of the United States.*]

EDGAR B. NIXON

Territorial Governments are similar to state governments in form but differ essentially in that they are completely subject to Congress. The first territorial government, established for the Northwest Territory by the Ordinance of July 13, 1787[qv], has furnished the prototype for those subsequently organized. As modified in 1789, the Ordinance provided for a governor, secretary and three judges, all appointed by the President with the consent of the Senate. The governor, appointed for three years, was also head of the militia and superintendent of Indian affairs. The secretary, appointed for four years, recorded the territorial laws and served as governor in the latter's absence. The judges, who served during good behavior, had common-law jurisdiction only.

Under the first or temporary stage of government, the governor was authorized to establish townships and counties, appoint their officials, and, in conjunction with the judges, adopt laws for the territory. Laws thus adopted were subject to revision by Congress, and also by the territorial legislature after the organization of the permanent government. This consisted of a house of representatives, elected for two years by the resident freeholders, a council, appointed by the President for five years, and a delegate to Congress, elected by the house and council together. The delegate had the privilege of debate but no vote. The governor had authority to convene, prorogue and dissolve the legislature, and he had an absolute veto over its enactments.

Slavery was prohibited by the ordinance, but this prohibition was not extended to the Southern territories. Otherwise the governments established for the Southwest, Mississippi and Indiana territories, organized in 1790, 1798 and 1800 respectively, differed but little from that described above. Thereafter, however, changes in the original form were made by Congress with increasing frequency, either by the organic acts, by acts applied to specific territories, or by general laws extended to all the territories. In the main, these modifications tended to (1) increase the powers of the legislature, (2) widen the electoral base and increase the powers of the electorate, and (3) extend the jurisdiction of the courts. Innovations adopted for one territory were not always extended to the others, but with the organization of Minnesota Territory in 1849 the evolution of the territorial government was essentially complete. The government of that territory, as established by its organic act and by previously enacted statutes applicable to all territories, illustrates the changes introduced in the preceding half century.

The Minnesota governor, secretary and judges were appointed for four years. The members of the council and the congressional delegate were elected by the territorial electorate for two-year terms. The governor's appointive power was subject to the consent of the council, and his veto was subject to overrule by two-thirds vote of the legislature. The legislature was empowered to apportion its representation, fix the qualifications for suffrage and organize the judicial districts. Acts of the governor and the legislature were subject to the approval of Congress. Most of the township and county officers were elective, and the freehold qualifications demanded of the early territorial voter and officeholder were replaced by residence requirements. The judicial power was vested in supreme, district, probate and justice-of-the-peace courts, with the judges of the supreme and district courts possessing equity and chancery as well as common-law jurisdiction.

The above description is, in general, applicable to the territories organized after 1849. In the later territories the governmental organization becomes more elaborate and more specialized, and the powers and duties of the territorial officers and agencies are described in greater detail in the organic acts. Hawaii and Alaska, organized June 14, 1900, and Aug. 24, 1912, respectively, are the only United States possessions now designated as territories by Congress. In these two governments, a senate, elected for four years, and a house of representatives, elected for two years, have replaced the former council and house.

The territories were administered by the Department of State until 1873; since then they have been under the Department of the Interior.

[F. N. Thorpe, ed., *Federal and State Constitutions*, I-VII; C. E. Carter, ed., *Territorial Papers of the U. S.*, I-VIII.]

EDGAR B. NIXON

Territorial Waters. It is universally recognized that the sovereignty of a state extends somewhat beyond the shore line of its seacoast. While three nautical miles is popularly regarded as the limit of such jurisdiction, states have often asserted larger claims for special purposes. With reference to the claims of other states, the United States Government has generally stood for a strict interpretation of the three-mile limit. The ramifications of, and exceptions to, this position can be followed through a number of diplomatic episodes, the most important and best known of which was the long-drawn-out North Atlantic fisheries[qv] controversy with Great Britain (1783–1910). While generally opposing other states' special claims, the United States Government has itself asserted jurisdictional claims exceeding the three-mile limit. One such claim, put forward during the Napoleonic wars, asserted a right to exclude belligerent vessels from a coastal zone at least twelve miles in width, and possibly extending into the Atlantic as far as the Gulf Stream. A twelve-mile limit was also incorporated in antismuggling legislation patterned on the British "hovering acts." Under this legislation, American revenue cutters exercised the right within a twelve-mile zone, to stop, search and even seize private vessels, regardless of nationality, for violations of the customs laws. And the right to pursue smugglers[qv] still farther out to sea was asserted and exercised. This question became acute following adoption of the Eighteenth Amendment[qv] and the subsequent epidemic of rum running. Only after retaliatory seizure of liquor on board foreign merchant vessels in American ports was a compromise reached, which gave the United States a treaty right to enforce its prohibition laws to a distance of one hour's steaming, or somewhat more than twelve miles out to sea. The most extreme claim was that of a special if not exclusive jurisdiction to prevent unregulated slaughter of fur seals[qv] in Bering Sea (1886). While this claim was subsequently abandoned following an adverse arbitral award (1892), a similar claim is implicit in legislative proposals (1938) for protecting the Alaskan salmon fisheries. These proposals, growing out of a fear that large-scale Japanese fishing operations were exterminating the salmon, were designed to extend United States jurisdiction one hundred miles or more to sea, on the theory that the submerged "continental shelf" was to be regarded as national territory covered by "territorial waters" under national jurisdiction.

[W. E. Masterson, *Jurisdiction in Marginal Seas;* J. B. Moore, *Digest of International Law*, Vol. I, and *Principles of American Diplomacy.*]

HAROLD H. SPROUT

Territories of the United States are parts of the national domain which have been separately organized by Congress. Their governments are similar to those of the states in form but not in authority; they are dependent on Congress for their status and powers, and their chief officers are appointed by the President and the Senate. All the states except the original thirteen and Vermont, Kentucky, Maine, Texas, California and West Virginia have passed through the territorial stage. Most of the territories were formed by the breaking up of the major or parent territorial areas. The successive delimitations through which the territories passed prior to their admission as states are too involved to permit of even approximate description in every case, but the following illustrations are typical.

The territory northwest of the River Ohio, as organized by the ordinance of July 13, 1787[qv], was bounded by the New York and Pennsylvania state lines, the Ohio and Mississippi rivers, a line drawn north from the headwaters of the Mississippi to Canada, and the international boundary. In 1800 that part west of a line drawn north from the mouth of the Kentucky River, on the Ohio, to Fort Recovery[qv], thence north to Canada, was organized as Indiana Territory. From the remaining territory, the State of Ohio, with approximately its present boundaries, was admitted March 1, 1803. Indiana thus comprised all the original Northwest Territory[qv] except Ohio until reduced by the creation of Michigan and Illinois territories, and Michigan was in turn reduced by the formation of Wisconsin Territory. The dates of the acts organizing these territories, and the dates of their admission as states, are: Indiana, May 7, 1800–Dec. 11, 1816; Michigan, Jan. 11, 1805–Jan. 26, 1837; Illinois, Feb. 3, 1809–Dec. 3, 1818; Wisconsin, April 20, 1836–May 29, 1848. Part of Minnesota (March 3, 1849–May 11, 1858) was also originally in the Northwest Territory.

The territory south of the River Ohio was organized May 26, 1790, from the region west of the present states of North Carolina and Georgia to the Mississippi, north of parallel 31. The northern part was admitted as the State of Tennessee, June 1, 1796. The lower third of the remainder was organized as Mississippi Territory[qv],

April 7, 1798, but was later enlarged to comprise what is now included in Mississippi and Alabama. Mississippi was admitted as a state, with its present boundaries, Dec. 10, 1817, and at the same time the remaining eastern half was organized as Alabama Territory. Alabama became a state Dec. 14, 1819.

Louisiana*qv*, purchased from France in 1803, extended from the Mississippi to the western boundary of the Mississippi drainage basin. Orleans Territory*qv*, comprising approximately what is now Louisiana, was organized March 26, 1804, while the rest of the Purchase was established as Louisiana Territory, March 3, 1805. Orleans became the State of Louisiana, April 30, 1812, and in the same year Louisiana Territory was renamed Missouri. The latter became a state Aug. 10, 1821, but the remaining undivided part of the Purchase retained the name Missouri Territory until 1854. In addition to those mentioned, all or part of the following territories were created from this region: Arkansas, March 2, 1819–June 15, 1836; Iowa, June 12, 1838–Dec. 28, 1846; Kansas, May 30, 1854–Jan. 29, 1861; Nebraska, May 30, 1854–Feb. 9, 1867; Colorado, Feb. 28, 1861–Aug. 1, 1876; Dakota, March 2, 1861–Nov. 2, 1889; Montana, May 26, 1864–Nov. 8, 1889; Wyoming, July 25, 1868–July 10, 1890. During this period Florida became a state (March 30, 1822–March 3, 1845), and the great areas of the Northwest and Southwest were organized.

The Oregon country*qv* was held jointly by the United States and Great Britain until 1846, when the northern boundary was fixed at parallel 49. The country south of this line to parallel 42, and west to the Rocky Mountains, was organized as Oregon Territory (Aug. 14, 1848–Feb. 14, 1859), and the remainder as Washington Territory (March 2, 1853–Nov. 11, 1889). Idaho (March 3, 1863–July 3, 1890) was formed from parts of Washington, Dakota and Nebraska. The region acquired from Mexico in 1848 was divided into the territories of Utah (Sept. 9, 1850–Jan. 4, 1896), Nevada (March 2, 1861–Oct. 31, 1864), and parts (*see* Texas Cession of 1850) of New Mexico (Sept. 9, 1850–Jan. 6, 1912), Arizona (Feb. 24, 1863–Feb. 14, 1912), Wyoming and Colorado. California was admitted directly as a state, Sept. 9, 1850.

Alaska*qv*, purchased from Russia, March 30, 1867, was made a territory Aug. 24, 1912. The Republic of Hawaii*qv* was annexed July 7, 1898, and given territorial status June 14, 1900. None of the other possessions of the United States have been designated by Congress as territories, although Puerto Rico*qv* has been given many of the privileges of territorial status possessed by Hawaii.

[Edward M. Douglas, *Boundaries of the United States; Territorial Expansion of the United States*, pub. by U. S. Bureau of Statistics; C. E. Carter, ed., *Territorial Papers of the United States*, I-VII.]

EDGAR B. NIXON

Terry's Texas Rangers was the popular name for a unit of ten companies of volunteer horsemen who were mustered into the Confederate Army as the Eighth Texas Cavalry. Commissioned by the Confederate government to "recruit a regiment of skilled horsemen for immediate service," B. F. Terry and Tom S. Lubbock promptly enrolled at Houston a thousand men, many of whom were former Texas Rangers*qv*. In November, 1861, they joined Gen. A. S. Johnston's force at Bowling Green, Ky. Though Terry was killed in their first engagement at Woodsonville, Ky., his name clung to the organization. It rendered valuable service at Shiloh and in the campaigns around Murfreesboro, Chattanooga, Atlanta, Knoxville and in their last engagement at Bentonville, N. C., in 1865*qqv*. The Rangers furnished their own horses, enjoyed the privilege of acting as an independent unit of the army, and paid their own expenses or lived off the enemy. Seventy-five per cent of the men lost their lives in the war.

[Dudley G. Wooten, *A Comprehensive History of Texas*, Vol. II.]

L. W. NEWTON

Tertium Quids (1806–8) were disaffected Jeffersonian Republicans*qv* who desired Monroe rather than Madison for President. Such Virginia "Old Republicans" as Monroe, John Randolph and John Taylor contended that Jefferson had abandoned original principles, opposed the President's West Florida and Embargo*qv* policies, and criticized him for refusing to submit Monroe's English treaty of 1806 to the Senate (*see* Monroe–Pinkney Treaty). Estranged Republicans in other Southern states sympathized with Virginia *Quids;* an alliance with New York Clintonians was considered (*see Quids*). A minority of the Virginia legislature and three members of the congressional caucus declared for Monroe; strong administration support of Madison led Monroe to withdraw from the contest.

[William C. Bruce, *John Randolph of Roanoke, 1773-1833;* Henry H. Simms, *Life of John Taylor.*]

WENDELL H. STEPHENSON

Test Laws. Political test oaths have been rather uncommon in United States history, except during the Civil War and Reconstruction periods. In order to purge the Union Government of pro-

Confederates, the statute of July 2, 1862, required every Federal officeholder to swear the "ironclad oath"^{qv} that he had never given voluntary aid to or held office in any "pretended government within the United States, hostile or inimical thereto." In 1865 this test was extended to lawyers practising in Federal courts (*see* Garland Case), and in Missouri made a prerequisite for practising various professions, although these applications of the oath were later declared unconstitutional (*see* Test Oath Cases). Nevertheless Congress subsequently (March 23, July 19, 1867) required the ironclad oath of voters and election officials as a means of disfranchising former Confederates and insuring the creation of Republican-controlled governments in the defeated South (*see* Reconstruction Acts). In 1868 and 1871 Congress reduced the oath to the simple pledge of future support and defense of the Constitution and the Union.

[Wm. Russ, Jr., Registration and Disfranchisement under Radical Reconstruction, in *Miss. Vall. Hist. Rev.*, XXI.]

MARTIN P. CLAUSSEN

Test Oath Cases (1867). During the Civil War ex-Confederates and Confederate sympathizers at the North had been excluded from Federal office by the ironclad oath[qv] of 1862. In 1865 Congress extended this test oath to lawyers practising in Federal courts, while Missouri's new state constitution prescribed an equally severe test for clergymen, teachers, lawyers and others. Thus the test oath became a vindictive weapon against defeated Southerners during Reconstruction[qv]. Eventually on Jan. 14, 1867, the Supreme Court by two 5–4 decisions (*see* Cummings v. Missouri; Garland Case) invalidated the test oaths of 1865, without, however, reviewing the original test law of 1862. The oaths as extended were held to be *ex post facto* measures, because they in effect imposed punishments for past acts (e.g. giving aid to a Confederate) which had not been punishable at the time they were committed.

As a result of these decisions the Supreme Court was bitterly attacked for disregarding the will of legislative majorities on "political" questions. Radical Republicans[qv], reading the dissenting opinion of Chief Justice Chase and three colleagues, insisted that Congress had acted properly in preventing "traitors" and "disloyal" lawyers from practising in Federal courts; and various measures were threatened to curtail or abolish the Court's power of judicial review (*see* McCardle, *ex parte*). The Court escaped these threats, however, chiefly because it acquiesced in most of the remainder of the Radical Republican reconstruction program.

[Charles Warren, *Supreme Court in United States History.*]

MARTIN P. CLAUSSEN

Texan Emigration and Land Company, THE, also known as the Peters' Colony Company, introduced 2205 families into north-central Texas between 1841 and 1848 as part of the basic settlement of seventeen present-day counties, in which are included the cities of Dallas, Fort Worth and Wichita Falls. Organized by W. S. Peters and associates of Louisville, Ky., and Cincinnati, Ohio, the company entered into contract with the Republic of Texas[qv] on Nov. 9, 1841. The congress of Texas modified the contract on July 26, 1842, and again on Jan. 20, 1843. In distributing free land on the northern Indian frontier of the Republic of Texas at the measure of one section to each head of a household and one-half section, or 320 acres, to each unmarried man, the company likewise agreed to and did furnish 2100 log cabins, 1800 rifles and muskets and 162,000 rounds of ammunition to its colonists. In exchange, the company was to be allowed to retain alternate sections of land for its own benefit. Acrimonious disputes between agents of the company and settlers developed early. These began when other immigrants, acting on their own initiative, moved into the same 16,000 square miles of land assigned to the company and claimed homesteads by preemption. The only organized opposition in Texas to annexation[qv] in 1845 came from agents of the company, who feared abrogation of their colonization contract. Conflicts waxed after annexation, leading to two armed raids by settlers, in 1848 and 1852, on company headquarters at Stewartsville, Collin County, with the consequent destruction of papers and records. Land titles were quieted finally only after Gov. Peter H. Bell called the Fourth Legislature into special session in 1853 when a law was passed granting each settler rights prior to those of the company on land actually occupied as a homestead. The company was then compensated in part with a tract of unoccupied public land in West Texas.

[*Laws of Texas*, Gammel, Austin, 1898; *Special Joint House and Senate Report*, 4th Legislature, Journal of the House of Representatives, State of Texas; files of the Dallas *Herald* and the Dallas *News;* Claude Elliott, *The Life of James W. Throckmorton*, a doctoral thesis deposited at the University of Texas.]

SAM H. ACHESON

Texan–Santa Fé Expeditions. After Spain's establishment of Santa Fé and San Antonio as centers respectively of New Mexico and Texas, joining the two areas was an enduring frontier objective, but there interposed between them as barriers the uncharted southern end of the Great Plains and the Plains Indians. Small parties led by Pedro Vial and José Mares traveled across the intervening country, 1786–89; in 1808 Capt. Francisco Amangual led 200 men from San Antonio to Santa Fé. Spanish efforts, however, never effected a satisfactory communication.

The Texan–Santa Fé Expedition of 1841 was occasioned by Texas' claim of New Mexican territory and President Mirabeau B. Lamar's desire to divert to Texas the regular Santa Fé trade. Gen. Hugh McLeod commanded a force totaling 321 men, which was harassed by Kiowas and broken up by the adversities and limitations presented by the Great Plains environment, eventually to be captured in sections by New Mexican troops under Gov. Manuel Armijo. The Texans were subjected to many indignities en route to Mexico City, where they became the subject of a heated diplomatic controversy between the United States and Mexico. Most of the prisoners were released in April, 1842. Although generally considered a failure, the expedition stimulated a renewal of interest in Texas within both the United States and Mexico.

[W. C. Binkley, *The Expansionist Movement in Texas, 1836-1850;* H. E. Bolton, *Texas in the Middle Eighteenth Century;* H. B. Carroll, The Route of the Texan-Santa Fé Expedition, ms., University of Texas; F. W. Hodge, ed., *Falconer's Letters and Notes on the Texan-Santa Fé Expedition;* G. W. Kendall, *Narrative of the Texan-Santa Fé Expedition;* W. P. Webb, *The Great Plains.*]

H. BAILEY CARROLL

Texas, Annexation of. By the Adams-Onís Treaty of 1819–21[qv] the United States ceded a legally plausible but historically feeble claim to the territory of Texas as a part of the Louisiana Purchase[qv]. John Quincy Adams, while President, endeavored to obtain from Mexico, which had succeeded Spain in the sovereignty of Texas, a readjustment of the boundary in such a way as to give the United States all of the present State of Texas. Jackson, without success, continued these efforts throughout his two administrations. The Texas Revolution[qv] gave the problem a new turn.

In September, 1836, the Texans voted almost unanimously in favor of annexation to the United States. Congress expressed its readiness to recognize the independence of Texas, and one of Jackson's last official acts was to name a *chargé d'affaires* to Texas, but annexation was another matter. Possibilities of international complications and the violent opposition of the free states to the further extension of slave territory were obstacles not easily overcome. Van Buren definitely declined to consider a Texan proffer of annexation in August, 1837, and the subject dropped from public discussion until 1842. Then it was quickened by fear of English designs to control Texas.

The movement which led finally to annexation was inaugurated by President Tyler in the autumn of 1843. In April, 1844, he submitted to the Senate a treaty that proposed to annex Texas as a territory. This, for reasons hard to determine, the Senate rejected in June. In the meantime, the Democratic National Convention had nominated James K. Polk and pledged the party to the immediate "re-annexation" of Texas. The Democrats won the election in November (*see* Campaign of 1844), and Congress, with little opposition, passed a joint resolution authorizing the President: (1) to offer Texas annexation as a state; or (2) to conclude with Texas a new annexation treaty. Tyler acted upon the first alternative (March 1, 1845); Polk concurred and carried the negotiations with Texas to a successful conclusion. The Texan constitution was accepted by Congress, and Texas was admitted to the Union on Dec. 29, 1845. Recognition of the rising commercial importance of Texas and apprehension growing out of England's friendly intervention in behalf of Texas with Mexico were influential in weakening northern antagonism to southward expansion.

[G. P. Garrison, *Texas;* J. H. Smith, *The Annexation of Texas.*]

E. C. BARKER

Texas, Early Colonization of. The Anglo-American colonization of Texas began under a grant issued by the Spanish government to Moses Austin on Jan. 17, 1821. This contract to introduce 300 families was subsequently confirmed by the National Congress of Mexico, after the establishment of Mexican independence, and was carried out by Stephen F. Austin. Under laws passed by the federal and state governments in Mexico (1824–25), Austin and a score of other *empresarios*[qv] obtained contracts to settle some 10,000 families. In general, the *empresarios* were absentees and made little or no effort to fulfill their contracts, regarding them as a basis for speculation. Austin and several others, notably Green DeWitt[qv], worked faithfully, however, so that the total immigrant population of Texas toward the end of 1835, when the Texas Revolution[qv] began, probably exceeded 25,000.

There was a fair sprinkling of colonists from most of the states of the United States and a few from England, Ireland and Germany; but most of them came from the Southern slave states, a fact that lent a specious plausibility to the assertion that the movement to Texas was a plot of the "slavocracy"[qv] to bring new slave states into the Union. Logic and some documentary evidence indicate that free land and the easy accessibility of Texas were the potent attractions which moved most of the colonists. Late efforts of the Mexican government to colonize Mexicans in Texas as a counterbalance to foreign immigration were a total failure.

[E. C. Barker, *Mexico and Texas, 1821-1835.*]

E. C. BARKER

Texas, Early History of. The history of Spanish Texas divides itself into three periods: (1) discovery and exploration, 1519–1684; (2) Spanish and French colonization of and rivalry for, 1685–1762; and (3) reorganization, and Spanish-United States competition for, 1762–1821.

The period of discovery and exploration was initiated by Alonso de Pineda, who, in 1519, explored for Spain the entire coast of the Mexican Gulf from Florida to Mexico. A period of active exploration followed the first glimpses of the Texas coast by Pineda. The southern and western sections of the state were traversed by such well-known explorers as Cabeza de Vaca[qv] (1528–36); Coronado[qv] (1541); Espejo (1583); Castaño de Sosa (1590); Oñate[qv] (1601); Martín and Castillo (1650); Guadalajara (1654); and Domínguez and López (1684). In East Texas the famous DeSoto[qv] expedition explored probably as far west as the Brazos River in 1542.

The period in which Spain's interest in Texas was undisputed and merely incidental ended about 1684. The next year Spain's title to Texas was formally disputed for the first time by a rival aggressor, France. The ill-fated French expedition under LaSalle[qv] to the Lavaca Bay region brought about the explorations of Alonso de León (1688–90) from the present Eagle Pass region, northeastward, by way of Lavaca Bay, to the region east of the Trinity, and also to the temporary Spanish occupation of East Texas between 1690 and 1693. Renewed aggressions of the French in Louisiana[qv] after 1712 stimulated the Spaniards to establish by 1721 six missions and two *presidios*[qv] between the Trinity and Red rivers; three missions and one *presidio*, save for a two-year period (1719–21), remained there continuously until after 1762. From 1722 until 1773 the capital of Spanish Texas was at Los Adaes[qv], fifteen miles west of the French post of Natchitoches on the Red River. To serve chiefly as a stopping place from Coahuila to East Texas, San Antonio[qv] was founded in 1718, and within less than two decades it had become the principal Spanish settlement in the province. To effect better control over outlying Indian tribes and to consolidate their opposition against Indian allies of the French, temporary Spanish missions and *presidios* were established among the Tonkawas of central Texas (1746–55) and among the Apaches[qv] on the San Sabá River, beginning in 1757. In southeast Texas, chiefly in order to check aggressions of French traders along the Gulf coast, a mission and a *presidio* were maintained for a few years near the mouth of the Trinity River, beginning in 1756. Present Texas south of the Nueces River was never a part of Spanish Texas.

By the Treaty of Fontainebleau[qv] with France in 1762 Spain acquired western Louisiana. As a result, Spain was relieved of problems of frontier defense in the Texas-Louisiana sector. Accordingly, in 1773 the remaining three missions and one *presidio* and several hundred colonists between the Trinity and Red rivers were withdrawn, and the capital of Spanish-Texas was removed to San Antonio. This abandonment proved to be temporary, for by 1790 most of the evicted settlers had returned to their former homes, and Nacogdoches[qv] had been established as the chief Spanish center in East Texas.

Western Louisiana, with indefinite boundaries, was receded by Spain to France in 1800 and three years later it was sold, with the same indefinite boundaries, to the United States (*see* San Ildefonso, Treaty of; Louisiana Purchase). A diplomatic dispute between the United States and Spain at once arose concerning, in part, the western limits of the Louisiana purchase. President Jefferson, as early as 1804, claimed that Louisiana, as purchased by the United States, extended to the Rio Grande; and Spain, on the basis of the occupation and administration of Texas as a separate province since 1721, denied that Louisiana had ever extended farther west than Natchitoches[qv]. Threatened hostilities were averted between the two nations in 1806 by the extra-regular Neutral Ground Agreement[qv]. By this agreement—reached by United States and Spanish military commanders—Americans and Spaniards were to refrain from exercising jurisdiction in the territory between the Sabine River and the Arroyo Hondo, a small stream a few miles west of Natchitoches. Thirteen years later—on the basis of incontrovertible evidence submitted by Spain in the form of a masterful argumentative proof of Spain's title to Texas that had been drafted some years earlier by Father José Antonio Pichardo—the western boundary of Louisiana was formally agreed upon by Spain and the United States (*see* Adams-Onís Treaty). This treaty, which was ratified in 1821, had the effect of fixing the eastern and northern boundaries of the Spanish province of Texas along the Sabine from its mouth to the 32nd parallel, thence north to the Red River, along that river to the 100th meridian, thence north to the Arkansas River and along it to its source, thence north to the 42nd parallel, N. Lat., and west on that parallel to a point due north of the source of the Rio Grande.

[Herbert E. Bolton, *The Spanish Borderlands: A Chronicle of Old Florida and the Southwest,* and *Texas in the Middle Eighteenth Century;* William Edward Dunn, *Spanish and French Rivalry in the Gulf Region of the United States, 1678-1702;* Charles Wilson Hackett, ed., *Pichardo's Treatise on the Limits of Louisiana and Texas: An Argumentative Historical Treatise with Reference to the Verification of the True Limits of the Provinces of Louisiana and Texas . . .,* Vols. I and II.]

CHARLES W. HACKETT

Texas, Financing the Revolution of, was accomplished principally by means of land bounties to soldiers, customs and tonnage duties, gifts and loans.

In November and December, 1835, the General Council granted to each soldier a land bounty of 800 acres or less, varying in amount according to rank and class of service. Customs and tonnage duties were collected, but only a very small amount of money was derived from these sources. Treasury notes were authorized but were never issued. Patriotic Texans and friends in the United States donated about $25,000 in money and goods. Soldiers coming from the United States evidently brought in considerable quantities of equipment.

Loans constituted the most important source of income. In December, 1835, Stephen F. Austin, Branch T. Archer and William H. Wharton were sent as commissioners to the United States to borrow as much as $1,000,000, the subscribers to have the privilege of taking Texas land in payment. The commissioners negotiated loans which yielded about $100,000. It is estimated that the permanent Texas government (*see* Texas, Republic of), organized in October, 1836, inherited a debt of $1,252,000, represented as follows: loans, $100,000; army, $412,000; navy, $112,000; supplies, $450,000; civil and contingent expenses, $118,000; not itemized, $60,000.

[E. T. Miller, *A Financial History of Texas.*]

RUPERT N. RICHARDSON

Texas, Republic of (1836–46), was created during the Texas Revolution[v] by the convention of March, 1836, which declared independence from Mexico, drafted a constitution, and set up a provisional government. With the battle of San Jacinto[v], independence became an established fact, and in October, 1836, the provisional government was superseded by the duly elected constitutional authorities, with Sam Houston as president. Houston's administration devoted its attention largely to problems of insuring economic and political stability, of establishing peaceful relations with Indian tribes, and of obtaining recognition from the United States, with hopes for immediate annexation.

Mirabeau B. Lamar succeeded Houston in 1838 and launched a positive foreign policy with a view to laying a basis for permanent independence. Discussion of annexation was stopped; diplomatic relations were established with France and England; attempts were made to negotiate with Mexico; a program of commercial expansion was undertaken; and efforts were made to strengthen the army and navy. In domestic affairs, aggressive warfare was waged against the Indians; plans were made for developing the natural resources of the country; a new land policy was formulated; the basis was laid for a system of public education; and futile attempts were made to establish a sound financial organization.

Returning to the presidency in 1841, Houston found expenses running far ahead of receipts, treasury notes depreciated to about fifteen cents on the dollar, and the public debt increased to about $8,000,000. He inaugurated a drastic program of retrenchment, in spite of renewed threats from Mexico, and in spite of sectional conflict between East and West Texas over such questions as frontier defense and the location of the capital. In foreign affairs, his interest was centered primarily in reopening the question of annexation. By using England and France as intermediaries between Texas and Mexico he probably contributed toward hastening favorable action in the United States. As a result, Anson Jones, who succeeded him in 1844, was able to present to the Texans a choice between annexation on the terms of the Joint Resolution and continued independence acknowledged by Mexico. With the acceptance of the annexation offer in the summer of 1845 and the installation of state officials in February, 1846, the transition of Texas from a frontier Mexican province to a state of the American Union was completed.

[G. P. Garrison, *Texas;* W. C. Binkley, *Expansionist Movement in Texas;* A. K. Christian, *Mirabeau B. Lamar.*]

WILLIAM C. BINKLEY

Texas, Slavery in, under the Mexican Regime. By strenuous effort Austin succeeded in getting permission for his first 300 colonists to bring slaves into Texas on condition that all slave children born should become free at age fourteen. The Mexican congress passed a law July, 1824, forbidding the further introduction of slavery. The Texas-Coahuila State Constitution of 1827 provided that from six months after its promulgation all introduction of slavery should cease. This provision was practically nullified by a state law in 1828 which legalized, in Texas, contracts made with servants and hirelings in the United States before entry. In September, 1829, the president of Mexico issued an emancipation proclamation for all of Mexico, but it was modified for the State of Texas. A law of April 6, 1830, again forbade any further introduction of slavery, and a state law in 1832 limited the servant contract law of 1828. After this, slavery existed by the merest loophole.

[E. C. Barker, *Texas and Mexico, 1821-1835.*]

J. G. SMITH

Texas, State of (1845 *f.*). Politically, the history of the State of Texas has not been unique. It has preserved in its constitutions the provision, adopted during the Republic, that homesteads shall be exempt from forced sale for debts; it has not been so prone as some Western states to innovations in its constitutions; and it has adopted no new constitution since 1876. Admitted to the Union Dec. 29, 1845, under a Democratic administration, it has continually maintained a Democratic state control except under the Republican administration of E. J. Davis during Reconstruction*qv*.

The immense size of the state caused the insertion of a provision in the annexation resolution (*see* Texas, Annexation of) permitting the state to divide itself into as many as five states. From time to time, either because of hostility between sections or because of political ambition to create more offices, an issue has been made of the subdivision question. No reduction of the state has occurred, however, except that in the Compromise of 1850 Texas was to sell to the United States its lands north of latitude 36° 30′ and that part of the present New Mexico lying east of the Rio Grande (*see* Texas Cession of 1850). With the money received Texas paid its public debts, thus satisfying the chief purpose for which it had been permitted by the annexation resolution to retain its public lands. Even after this reduction, however, Texas had more than 100,000,000 acres of public domain. A little of this was sold, some was given to soldiers, a great deal was granted to early railroads, to educational institutions, for the erection of public buildings, and the remainder was set aside as a permanent endowment for public schools. Both the University of Texas and the public school system are now benefiting from the discovery of oil on their lands.

The population of the state has grown from about 140,000 in 1845 to more than 6,000,000. The percentage of Negroes in the total population has decreased from 27 to less than 15, and the percentage of foreign-born has fallen since 1860 from about 8 to less than 2. In 1860 Galveston was the largest city; Galveston, Indianola and Jefferson were the chief ports; and the population was confined mostly to the coast and timbered areas. Travel had improved by the placing of more than thirty overland stage lines in operation and by the construction of 361 miles of railroad within the state. The famous Butterfield Overland Dispatch*qv* through the northern part of the state and the San Antonio-San Diego Mail and Stage Line through El Paso were the best-known connections with the outside. Not until the Missouri, Kansas and Texas Railway*qv* entered Denison in 1873 was outside rail connection established, and within the next decade a network of railways was in operation.

Since the leading men of property in the state supported slavery and states' rights, Texas became involved in the secession movement of 1860*qqv*. In spite of Gov. Sam Houston's efforts to prevent it, Texas seceded and on March 2, 1861, formally joined the Confederacy*qv*. Houston was forced from office and Lt. Gov. Edward Clark succeeded him. Texas furnished to the Confederacy a number of soldiers estimated at from 50,000 to 65,000, most notable of whom were "Terry's Texas Rangers"*qv*. Valuable supplies were sent from the state, and through it from Mexico, to the Confederate armies in the southeast. Texas suffered little from military engagements on its own soil. Galveston, Brownsville and Matagorda were taken by Federals, but Galveston*qv* was recaptured by a Confederate force in a somewhat spectacular engagement. More famous was the repulse of a Federal Army of 5000 men and the capture of 350 prisoners by Lt. Dick Dowling and his forty-seven men at Sabine Pass.

Reconstruction*qv* began favorably for Texas. Under President Johnson's "ten per cent" plan, A. J. Hamilton, a citizen of Texas formerly honored with high offices, was appointed temporary governor, a new constitution was adopted in 1866, and in the following election a government of Texans headed by Gov. J. W. Throckmorton was chosen. Texas was returning to prosperity and normal order. But the congressional Reconstruction Act of 1867*qv* brought an end to the "loyal" white man's government and replaced it with one of the "carpetbag"^{qv} variety. E. M. Pease was appointed to succeed Gov. Throckmorton, the radical constitution of 1869 was substituted for the constitution of 1866, and in 1870 the Republican party elected the state officers headed by Gov. E. J. Davis. As usual in other Southern state governments of that time, there were despotism, extravagance, mounting state debt and increased taxation. In 1872 the Democrats won a majority in the legislature, and in 1874 they forced the unwilling Davis from office and inaugurated a Texan governor, Richard Coke. With cotton, cattle and lumber aided by an expansion of railroads, Texas began to recover from the blight of reconstruction.

When Texas entered the Union it was considered an addition to the Southern cotton kingdom^{qv}. It has become in recent years the chief cotton growing state. From 1868 to 1890 it took the lead in the cattle industry^{qv}, sending more than 10,000,000 head over the Chisholm, Dodge City, Goodnight^{qqv} and Shawnee trails in the long cattle drives^{qv} to outside markets. Texas still ranks first in the number of cattle, sheep and mules and in the production of wool and mohair^{qv}. By the first of the present century the lumber industry grew to importance in the East Texas pine, oak and hickory region. Due to the development of farming in West Texas since 1900, Texas ranks high in the production of sorghums and small grains. More recently the citrus fruit industry^{qv} of southwest Texas has placed the state in close rivalry with Florida and California. But it is the oil industry^{qv} which gives Texas its chief economic leadership. From the first discoveries at Chireno in 1866, Corsicana in 1895 and Spindletop in 1901 new fields have increased to more than 130. Among these the East Texas field is the greatest in the world, and because of it Texas production of oil exceeds that of any two other states.

[L. W. Newton and H. P. Gambrell, *A Social and Political History of Texas.*] L. W. NEWTON

Texas & Pacific Railway Company, THE, was chartered by Congress on March 3, 1871. It was the outgrowth of a movement in the late 1840's for a transcontinental railroad, and but for the intervention of the Civil War might have been built before the Union Pacific^{qv}. A twenty-four mile line was completed in East Texas in 1857, and extended during the Civil War to Shreveport, La. After incorporation in 1872 the older Texas companies were acquired, and construction toward San Diego, Calif., was commenced; but it was halted between Dallas and Fort Worth by the Panic of 1873^{qv}. In 1879 Jay Gould acquired the company with the idea of rapidly completing the line to the Pacific. In the meantime Collis P. Huntington and associates in the Southern Pacific^{qv} (of California) were building eastward. A railway construction race took place, the crews meeting at Sierra Blanca, 100 miles east of El Paso, Dec. 16, 1881. A truce was declared in the so-called "Gould-Huntington Agreement" of that year whereby the Texas & Pacific agreed not to build farther west in exchange for certain joint track privileges. It has retained its affiliation with the Missouri-Pacific Lines^{qv} since the days of Jay Gould.

[*The Texas Almanac*, 1857-72; files of the *Dallas News.*] SAM H. ACHESON

Texas Centennial Central Exposition, THE, held at Dallas from June 6 to Nov. 29, 1936, and June 12 to Oct. 31, 1937, was the largest of the series of celebrations held throughout the state to mark the centennial of Texan independence. It cost $25,000,000; occupied 200 acres in State Fair Park; and attracted almost 13,000,000 visitors during the two seasons. There was no foreign government participation; it was distinctly a local exposition. There were fifty buildings housing exhibits on the American scene, but the principal feature was the "Cavalcade of Texas," a historical spectacle presenting four centuries of Texan history. FRANK MONAGHAN

Texas Cession of 1850, THE, ended a dispute between Texas and New Mexico over the western and northern boundaries of Texas. The new State of Texas claimed the Rio Grande from mouth to source, thence north on the meridian to the 42nd parallel, thus including more than half of New Mexico, as well as parts of the future states of Oklahoma, Kansas, Colorado and Wyoming (*see* Adams-Onís Treaty). Cession or retention of this region was bound up with the question of slavery restriction or extension, and became a leading issue in the Compromise of 1850^{qv}. When armed collision seemed imminent between forces sent by Texas to assert the state's authority over the disputed New Mexico area and the superior authority of the United States over the territories^{qv}, Congress passed a law, approved Sept. 9, 1850, which proposed to the State of Texas the establishment of her northern and western boundaries, the relinquishment of all territory claimed by her exterior to those boundaries, and of all her claims upon the United States. As compensation, Texas was granted the sum of $10,000,000. The act further provided that the northern boundary should begin at the intersection of the 100th meridian and the parallel 36° 30′, thence run west to the 103rd meridian, thence south to the 32nd parallel, thence on that parallel to the Rio Grande, and down the channel of that rivei to the Gulf of Mexico. This arrangement was promptly accepted by the Texas legislature.

[*U. S. Statutes at Large*, IX, Chap. 49; W. J. Spillman, Adjustment of the Texas Boundary in 1850, in *Texas Historical Association Quarterly*, Vol. VII; E. M. Douglas, *Boundaries, Areas, Geographic Centers and Altitudes of the United States and the Several States*, Government Printing Office, 1932.]

P. ORMAN RAY

Texas Navy, THE. Mountainous wastes and cactus barrens, Monclova, Mexico, to San Antonio, Texas, constituted a serious barrier in 1836 to overland military operations. Santa Anna's best general, Filisola, advised against castigation of the rebellious Texans until a Mexican Gulf fleet had been completed to protect the flow of sea-borne military supplies along the coast, paralleling Santa Anna's military advance.

But Santa Anna would not wait, and in the meantime the Texans, with the four small armed ships, *Liberty, Brutus, Independence* and *Invincible,* were able to seize control of the Gulf. Much of Santa Anna's subsequent troubles, and the complete withdrawal of Mexican armies after San Jacinto*qv*, were largely due to collapse of Mexican supply service.

By the summer of 1837, Mexico acquired supremacy on the Gulf, and Texas, notwithstanding countercruising, suffered the effects of a partial blockade. Many Texans feared reinvasion from the sea. In 1838 France fortuitously blockaded Mexico, destroyed her fleet and relieved Texas of all fear. Alarmed by French withdrawal, 1839, President Lamar committed Texas to a naval program. By 1840 the fleet consisted of an 11-gun steamer, the *Zavala,* a 22-gun flagship, the *Austin,* and five smaller but effective men-of-war—which President Lamar sent on a cruise to strengthen the negotiations of James Treat*qv*. Had Treat followed instructions and traded on the presence of the fleet, he might have been successful. The collapse of the Treat negotiations caused Lamar to enter into a *de facto* alliance with the state of Yucatan, then fighting for independence from the Mexican Union. In this role the squadron, under Commodore Moore, captured Tobasco. As late as the spring of 1843 it fought engagements with new British-built-and-commanded Mexican steam warships off Campeche.

In effect, the Texas fleet was a great factor in keeping Mexico busy with other problems and saving the young Republic from reinvasion. By 1843 annexation was close at hand. Because President Houston thought the squadron was too expensive and was jeopardizing his diplomacy, Commander Moore was recalled and repudiated. After annexation*qv*, such of the fleet as remained became the property of the United States Government.

[Jim Dan Hill, *The Texas Navy.*]

JIM DAN HILL

Texas Public Lands. By the treaty of annexation between the Republic of Texas*qv* and the United States, approved by Congress March 1, 1845, it was stipulated that the State of Texas was to retain control of its public lands.

These lands have since been disposed of in various ways, viz: Donations to settlers, as compensation for war service, as a bonus for construction of railroads and other public works, as payment for the construction of the state capitol and for the encouragement and support of education.

Of the 167,000,000 acres of public land in the state, about 50,000,000 acres was set aside for various educational agencies, about 32,000,000 acres in railroad bonuses and 3,000,000 for the building of the state capitol, and the greater part of the remainder was given to settlers. There is little public lands remaining and that is in small scraps widely scattered.

[Records of State of Texas, General Land Office.]

W. P. RATCHFORD

Texas Rangers. As early as 1826 Texas colonists had from "20 to 30 Rangers in service" against Indians. For years the Texas Rangers were loosely and impermanently organized minutemen. About 1840, while Texas was a republic, a definite corps with esprit developed under Jack Hays and other captains. It ranged out mostly from San Antonio against marauding Indians and Mexicans and made the six-shooter*qv* the weapon of the horseback West. During the Mexican War the Rangers achieved fame. In the 1870's they reached their zenith of usefulness in bringing law and order along the Rio Grande border, holding back the wild Indians across a frontier stretching from Brownsville to the northern edge of the Staked Plains*qv*, and clearing horse thieves, feudists and bad men of all kinds—types that followed the Civil War and flourished during Reconstruction disorders—out of the country.

The Rangers have never been uniformed, the only standardized features of their dress being six-shooter and saddle gun. Range men, expert trailers, tireless riders, for them a slicker and saddle blanket afforded bedding and a "Spanish dinner" (which means taking up the belt a hole) nourishment for more riding. They have never drilled, notched a gun, or learned to salute officers. Their mobility is extraordinary. Their quiet reserve has become a proverb. They have always been picked men.

[J. B. Gillett, *Six Years with the Texas Rangers;* W. P. Webb, *The Texas Rangers.*] J. FRANK DOBIE

Texas Revolution, THE, was the result of complex social, political and economic incompatibilities between the Mexican government and the Anglo-American colonists introduced under Mexican federal and state colonization laws (*see* Texas, Early Colonization of). From 1832 to 1835 there was a more or less active rivalry in Texas between a small group of impatient malcontents and the great mass of the settlers who were content to wait awhile in the hope that time would quiet Mexican disorders and bring them ever-increasing measures of local autonomy. The confidence of the pacifists was shaken by Santa Anna's violent revision of the federal constitution to fit the forms of his dictatorship, and was wholly undone by his evident determination to garrison Texas strongly with federal troops.

Though there had been armed conflicts during 1832, the first clash of the final revolution occurred at Gonzales[q.v.] on Oct. 2, 1835. A few days later the Texans captured Goliad with valuable supplies; and in December the strong Mexican force at San Antonio surrendered. In the meantime, Santa Anna was preparing for an overwhelming invasion. Toward the end of February, 1836, the main column, commanded by Santa Anna in person, began to concentrate around San Antonio, where a Texan force held the Alamo[q.v.]. While a strong force commanded by Gen. José Urrea marched along the coast, Santa Anna took the Alamo by assault on March 6, and put to death all defenders. William B. Travis, James Bowie and David Crockett perished here with 180 followers. Urrea "mopped up" several detachments in the coastal area, and on March 19 captured a force of roughly 400 men near Goliad, commanded by J. W. Fannin. A week later these men, except a few who escaped or were spared by individual intervention, were executed by order of Santa Anna (*see* Goliad, Massacre at).

Fannin's men and most of those who died in the Alamo were recent volunteers from the United States. During March and April, however, a considerable force of old settlers joined Gen. Sam Houston, as he retreated across Texas from Gonzales to the Brazos River. Leaving Houston encamped on the Brazos, Santa Anna rashly crossed the river, with a small division, lower down and marched rapidly to capture the Texan provisional government at Harrisburg. The government escaped to Galveston Island. Santa Anna pursued to the bay shore and on his return found Houston blocking his way at San Jacinto[q.v.]. There the decisive battle was fought on April 21, 1836. Santa Anna was captured, ordered his main army to evacuate Texas, and promised to use his influence to obtain recognition of Texan independence.

The "Consultation" of the provisional government had declared on Nov. 7, 1835, that the Texans were in arms to protect the republican constitution of Mexico. The incidents of the war and failure of Mexican liberals to co-operate with Texas caused a new convention to declare the independence of Texas on March 2, 1836. *De facto* independence was established by Houston's fortunate victory at San Jacinto.

[G. P. Garrison, *Texas;* E. C. Barker, *Readings in Texas History;* W. C. Binkley, *Official Correspondence of the Texan Revolution, 1835-1836.*] E. C. BARKER

Texas v. White (1869). This famous case was begun by the Reconstruction governor of Texas to prevent payment on Federal bonds disposed of by the secession state government in payment of supplies for the Confederacy. The Supreme Court acknowledged the governor's competence to sue on the ground that Texas was now, and had never ceased to be, a member of "an indestructible Union"; hence the ordinance of secession was void. The President's Reconstruction acts were termed "provisional" with permanent authority on this subject vested in Congress. As to the immediate issue, the Court denied the power of the secessionist government to dispose of state property for purposes of rebellion.

[Charles Warren, *The Supreme Court in U. S. History.*] HARVEY WISH

Texian, an official variant of the word Texan which enjoyed wide popular usage during the ten years of the Republic of Texas[q.v.]. Many of the earliest Anglo-American settlers were natives of Missouri, Kentucky, Tennessee, Georgia and the Carolinas. Hence they naturally began to speak of themselves in their new allegiance as Texians. After the Civil War a new generation allowed the old spelling to fall into disuse—much to the disgust of many old Texians.

[*The Texas Almanac*, 1857-72.] SAM H. ACHESON

Textiles. Though imported textiles have always figured prominently in American markets, domestic fabrics have supplied most home consumption. Until the advent of power spinning and weaving in the early years of the Republic, the latter were woven in households and were not articles of commerce. They were made mainly of home-grown flax or hemp and local wool, with some West Indian and southern dooryard cotton. Small quantities of home-grown silk were occasionally spun and woven but rarely for practical use. Domestic fabrics were coarse and durable but of mediocre workmanship and were limited largely to garment materials, sheeting and bagging. New England made some sailcloth.

In late colonial times pattern goods and yarn-dyed fabrics became more common and professional weavers appeared. George Washington's spinning house, for example, made bedticking, birdseye, diaper, striped goods, dimity, counterpane and white and striped plain cloth of cotton; huckaback and plain linen of flax; broadcloth, herringbones, jeans, kerseys, plaids, shalloons of wool and several mixed fabrics of cotton, wool and silk. Serges, baizes and fustians were also woven by custom weavers.

With the advent of automatic spinning and weaving factory goods expanded at the expense of homespuns. Though the latter survived in isolated communities until after the Civil War, power-woven fabrics had virtually displaced them by 1850. Early in the century cotton usurped the former place of flax, domestic wools were improved by the introduction of Merino and Saxony sheep, and imported wool was increasingly used.

The first power manufactures were widely consumed standard fabrics capable of quantity production like sheeting, drills and ticking of cotton, and flannels, cassimeres, broadcloth and blankets of wool. Commercial hand-weaving survived until after 1860—for example, in the Philadelphia area—for colored goods like ginghams and specialties. Between 1824 and 1840 New England loom inventions made it possible to weave automatically pattern fabrics like twills, checks and damasks of cotton and fancy cassimeres of wool. The latter became a standard cloth for men's wear. Almost simultaneously power looms for weaving ingrain and Brussels carpets were perfected in Massachusetts, pointing the way to the automatic weaving of plush and velvets a few decades later. This era of uniquely rapid technical progress vastly cheapened and augmented output, diversified products, and made fashion more important in determining mill programs.

Following improvements in cloth printing and mule spinning about the middle of the century fine print cloths attained the leadership among American cotton fabrics previously held by heavy sheetings or "domestics." Meanwhile improved combing machinery and imported combing wools transformed the wool manufacture so that after the Civil War worsteds largely supplanted carded fabrics like broadcloth and cassimeres for men's wear and ladies' dress goods. Simultaneously the growth of the silk manufacture in America invited a larger use of the Jacquard loom[qv] with its wide pattern possibilities.

From linsey-woolsey[qv] days mixed goods have been among the most common American textiles. In the carded fiber era cotton-warp, wool-weft fabrics like satinets and delaines led mill yardage. Since combed fibers have come into extensive use cotton-warp worsteds have found a popular market. Rayon[qv] entered textile manufacturing via the mixed goods highway. Since 1860 knit-wear has become a major textile item. Kentucky bale-cloth has disappeared but ducks, tire fabrics and kindred adjuncts of industry are articles of large production. As civilization advances and manufacturing technique is refined, cloths rule lighter and finer, are better finished and are more varied in texture and pattern. Today our three leading fabrics quantitatively are print cloth yarn fabrics of which we produce 3.2 billion yards annually, cotton sheetings of which we make 1.6 billion yards annually and silk and rayon broad goods of which we make nearly 3 billion yards annually.

[Victor S. Clark, *History of Manufactures in the United States;* Arthur H. Cole, *The American Wool Manufacture;* The Census of Manufactures, 1937.]

VICTOR S. CLARK

Thames, Battle of the (Oct. 5, 1813). The surrender of Detroit[qv] and Michigan Territory in August, 1812, gave the British control of practically all the region tributary to the Upper Lakes[qv]. Thereafter the American objective was to recover, the British to retain, Detroit and the Northwest; the two outstanding leaders were Gen. Procter (Br.) at Detroit and Amherstburg, and Gen. William Henry Harrison (Amer.). Harrison established Fort Meigs[qv] (above Toledo) as an advanced base, which Procter, carrying the war to the Americans, twice attacked (April-May and July, 1813). Meanwhile Perry built at Erie the fleet which on Sept. 10 won the Battle of Lake Erie[qv]. Loss of naval control rendered Procter's position untenable, and a grim race ensued, Procter seeking to retire to Lake Ontario, while Harrison, convoyed by Perry's fleet, hotly pursued, in the hope of destroying him.

The route of the armies along Lake St. Clair

and the Thames River is closely paralleled by the modern highway from Windsor to Hamilton. The race ended when Procter was brought to bay a few miles east of Thamesville. Harrison's strength was overwhelming and there could be but one issue to the battle. The weary Forty-first Regiment held the British left, while Tecumseh's[qv] Indians occupied the right. Col. Richard Mentor Johnson's mounted regiment charged the hostile line and quickly rode over the British left, which, caught between the cavalry behind and Harrison's infantry in front, promptly surrendered. The Indians fought until Tecumseh fell, when they melted into the forest. After ravaging the near-by Moravian Indian settlement, Harrison returned to Detroit, and his Kentucky levies to their homes. Lake Erie and the Thames restored the American dominance in the Northwest which Hull had lost in August, 1812. The glory won at the Thames proved a potent factor in the subsequent elevation of Harrison to the Presidency and of Johnson to the Vice-Presidency of the United States.

[A. C. Casselman, *Richardson's War of 1812;* Henry Adams, *History of the U. S.*, Vols. VI, VII; Robert B. McAfee, *History of the Late War in the Western Country.*]

M. M. QUAIFE

Thanksgiving Day. After the first harvest of the Massachusetts colonists, Gov. Bradford appointed a day of thanksgiving and prayer. Another in 1623 celebrated a fall of rain after a drought. After 1630 an annual thanksgiving came to be observed after harvest, and other New England colonies took up the practice in desultory fashion (*see* Fast Days). During the Revolutionary War the Continental Congress recommended days of thanksgiving, and decreed a special one in 1784 for the return of peace. President Washington proclaimed one in 1789, at the setting up of the new government, and another in 1795 for general benefits. President Madison in 1815 again asked the nation to give thanks for peace. By 1830 New York had adopted the day as an annual custom, and other Northern states followed its lead. In the South the custom did not appear until 1855, when it was adopted by Virginia, and thereafter by the other Southern states. President Lincoln in 1864 began the practice of a national proclamation, fixing the fourth Thursday (later it came to be regularly the last Thursday) in November, though he had no power to order a holiday in the various states. In 1939 President Franklin D. Roosevelt upset the precedent of several decades' standing by proclaiming Nov. 23. Many governors refused to accept this date, and in their states Nov. 30 was the accepted festival, though a few actually authorized the celebration of both dates.

[Robert Haven Schauffler, *Thanksgiving.*]

ALVIN F. HARLOW

Theater, THE. Religious prejudice prevented for decades the development of the theater in the colonies. There is a record of persons summoned to court in Virginia in 1665 for taking part in a play, apparently an amateur performance. In 1690 Harvard students staged a play written by one of their number. It seems evident that plays were professionally performed in New York around 1700. There were no theaters anywhere then, and plays had to be given in any available large room. Williamsburg, Va., erected what appears to have been the first American theater in 1716. It did not prosper greatly, and in 1745 it became a town hall. Most of the colonies discouraged the drama[qv]. A tumult in Boston in 1750 caused by crowds eager to buy tickets for a play caused Massachusetts to forbid stage performances. Pennsylvania banned them in 1759, Rhode Island in 1762. The first play of record in New York was given Dec. 6, 1732, in a remodeled room in a business building, where this company continued until February, 1734. The seating capacity of such theaters then was seldom above 300, and performances were given twice or thrice weekly. A play was professionally presented in Charleston, S. C., in 1735 and a theater built there within the ensuing year. Plays were acted in Philadelphia as early as 1749 in a sail loft over a warehouse. In 1750 a new theater was built in Williamsburg, and William Hallam, English actor-manager, who brought the first full company from England to America in 1752, played there and at New York and Philadelphia. The famous John Street Theater in New York was opened in 1767; President Washington was a frequent attendant there. In 1792 the law was relaxed in Massachusetts, and in 1794 a theater was opened in Boston.

In 1815 a touring company traveled by wagon from Albany, N. Y., to the headwaters of the Allegheny River, boated down that stream and the Ohio, stopping at Pittsburgh, wagoned overland to Frankfort and Lexington, Ky., then to Cincinnati, where a theater had been opened in 1801. Thence they went by water to Nashville, Natchez and New Orleans (*see* Show Boats). The new French Theater in New Orleans was dedicated in 1818. Mobile's first playhouse was opened in 1824. The first professional performance in St. Louis was seen in 1819. In a two-story frame hotel Chicago saw its first play in 1837; a theater was erected there in 1847. The first company of professional thespians reached the new town of San Francisco in January, 1850, and within a year four theaters were operating.

In the early 19th century the theater became one of the most popular activities in American life. Famous British stars, the Keans, the Kembles, the Booths, the Wallacks and others visited our cities and prospered, and some remained with us. Great actors of our own, such as Edwin Forrest, Charlotte Cushman and Joseph Jefferson were developed. For decades the custom prevailed of having a stock company at each theater, with only the stars or more prominent actors as guest performers. The building of railroads facilitated the movement of whole companies, and promoted the theater in general. Its heyday came probably between 1880 and 1900, when there were more touring companies than at any other period. Towns of as little as 2000 population saw Shakespeare given by professionals, not to mention commoner fare. In many cities cheap but usually clean melodrama and farce were presented in theaters whose admission prices were ten, twenty and thirty cents —known as "the Ten-Twent' and Thirt'." The more vulgar production known as burlesque flourished only in the larger cities. After 1905 the rapidly developing motion picture[qv] began to make inroads upon the stage audience, and presently, theaters in smaller towns were being converted into cinema houses. Costs of traveling and shipping scenery also rose to such heights that eventually only a few of the larger cities in the eastern half of the country were visited by touring companies. New York remained the great stronghold of the drama, and many plays successful there did not appear elsewhere. By 1925 in many parts of the country young people were reaching maturity who had never seen a stage performance with living actors. This condition brought about the Little Theater movement[qv]. After 1935 touring by professionals showed a considerable increase.

[Arthur Hornblow, *A History of the Theatre in America.*]

ALVIN F. HARLOW

Theocracy in New England is the term usually applied to the political regime set up by the founders of Massachusetts Bay and New Haven colonies[qqv]. It is a correct description to the extent that the leaders deliberately intended to create a "Bible Commonwealth"[qv], a society where the fundamental law would be the revealed Word of God, and God regarded as the supreme legislator. Thus John Winthrop announced the program before the settlement, "For the worke wee haue in hand, it is by a mutuall consent . . . to seeke out a place of Cohabitation and Consorteshipp vnder a due forme of Government both ciuill and ecclesiastical," the "due forme" being that enacted in the Bible. John Cotton later argued that the New England colonies, having a clear field before them, were duty-bound to erect a "Theocracy . . . as the best forme of government in the commonwealth, as well as in the Church." Consequently the political theory assumed that the colonies were based upon the Bible and that all specific laws must be required to show Biblical warrant.

In a still more fundamental sense, the governments of the two colonies were true theocracies in that all society was held to be ordained by God as a check upon the impulses of depraved human nature, and therefore that all politics should ideally be directed to the ends prescribed by God. Hence, John Winthrop explained in 1645, after men have entered a body politic they thereafter have freedom not to do what is good in their own eyes, but only that "which is good, just and honest," only that, in other words, which God demands. The purpose of the state was universally agreed among the first settlers to be the enforcement, by all possible external means, of the observance of God's laws on the part of every member of the society.

On the other hand, the term "theocracy" is a misnomer if it is taken, as it often is, to mean that the ministers directly ruled the colonies. It was well recognized that the Bible defined a distinct sphere for the civil government, and the secular authorities in both colonies were jealous of any clerical invasion of their province. The ministers did indeed possess great influence; in doubtful cases or at times of crisis their opinion was asked, though it was not always followed exactly as they desired.

[Perry Miller, *Orthodoxy in Massachusetts;* Perry Miller and Thomas H. Johnson, *The Puritans.*]

PERRY MILLER

Theological Seminaries in America arose as a result of three main causes: first, the cutting off of the Old World ministerial supply due to independence; second, the growing secularization of the colleges in which ministerial education had formerly been stressed; third, the religious destitution of the West and the increasing demand for ministers in new communities on the frontier. The colonial Congregational and Presbyterian ministers had been trained in the colonial colleges, while the Anglican, Lutheran and Reformed bodies[qqv] largely drew their ministerial supply from Europe. The Baptists[qv] and German Sectaries were without a trained ministry.

The oldest American theological seminary was established by the Dutch Reformed body in 1784 as a consequence of the drying up of the Old World supply. Andover Theological Seminary, the next oldest, dates from 1808, and was formed by the Congregationalists when the professorship of Divinity at Harvard was filled by a Unitarian[qv] in 1805. The Presbyterians formed their first seminary at Princeton[qv] in 1812, primarily to meet the growing demands of the West, and thereafter other seminaries were established by the several denominations in rapid succession. Harvard Divinity School opened in 1815; Bangor in 1816; Auburn in 1818; General Seminary in New York in 1819; Alexandria (Virginia) in 1823; the Baptists opened their first seminary at Newton, Mass., in 1824; Union Seminary (Presbyterian) in Richmond, Va., dates from the same year; the German Reformed established Lancaster Seminary in 1825; the Lutherans opened Gettysburg in 1826; Hartford dates from 1834 and Union Seminary in New York from 1836. The first seminary to serve the West was Western opened in Allegheny City in 1827, while the 1830's saw the opening of two seminaries in Ohio, Lane at Cincinnati, and Oberlin. Opposition to theological education delayed the Methodists[qv], and their first seminary was not opened until 1846, which later became the Boston University School of Theology. There are now (1939) 198 Protestant theological seminaries in the United States of which 16 are undenominational, while the Roman Catholics[qv] maintain 162 seminaries for the training of candidates for the priesthood. Many of these, however, are merely preparatory institutions.

[W. W. Sweet, *The Rise of Theological Seminaries in America*, *Church History*, Vol. VI, No. 3; W. O. Shewmaker, The Training of the Ministry in the United States of America before the Establishment of Theological Seminaries, *Papers of the Am. Soc. of Church Hist.*, Second Series, Vol. VI.]

WILLIAM W. SWEET

Theological Writings occupied a prominent place in early New England, where Calvinist Puritans expounded the theory of the inability of man to effect either his own or others' salvation. Both the obvious demonstration of human power in taming the American wilderness and the need for an aggressive revival of spiritual life in the churches militated against this Calvinism, and gave rise to Arminian writings which took a more hopeful view of man. Jonathan Edwards (1703–58) offered a re-interpretation of the freedom of the will and made theological concessions to the power of revival preaching. Samuel Hopkins (1721–1803) reinforced Puritan Calvinism, as did also Timothy Dwight (1752–1815), President of Yale University, who fought against the "infidelism" produced by such Deistic[qv] writings as those of Thomas Paine. In Nathaniel Taylor (1786–1858), however, Calvinistic acceptance of the efficacy of revivals[qv] came to a virtual abandonment of the old Calvinist position. W. E. Channing (1780–1842) was able to capitalize on this reaction from high Calvinism and to assert the worth of man as a basic tenet of Unitarianism[qv]. The Romantic movement found its representatives in America in R. W. Emerson (1803–82) and Horace Bushnell (1802–76). The latter, under the influence of Coleridge, applied the theory of poetic symbolism to theology and thereby helped to free religion from creedal formulas, while his *Christian Nurture* marks a new departure in religious education. This liberating spirit was continued in the work of T. Munger, H. W. Beecher and Phillips Brooks in the last half of the 19th century. The philosophical school of Personal Idealism founded in America by Borden P. Bowne (1847–1910) has had great influence in theological thinking, especially in Methodist circles. The introduction of Darwinian[qv] biology into America produced a vigorous reaction which has continued down to the present day among the Fundamentalists[qv]; while Lyman Abbott, in his *Theology of an Evolutionist* (1908), sought to appropriate Darwinism for theology. With the growing social consciousness produced by the abuses of the Industrial Revolution[qv] and the new study called Sociology there arose a "social gospel" literature written by such men as Washington Gladden (1836–1918), Francis Peabody (1847–1936), Henry C. King (1858–1934) and Shailer Mathews (1863–). The United States made a leading contribution after 1890 in the field of the psychology of religion through Starbuck, Coe, James and Ames. After the World War religious humanism became influential as a movement to free religious idealism from the theological doctrines of Christianity and to preach greater reliance on human intelligence. Its approach is exemplified by the writings of John Dewey, Sellars and Haydon. The conservative tradition has persisted steadily in the theology of such writers as W. G. T. Shedd (1820–74), A. H. Strong (1836–1921), B. B. Warfield (1851–1922) and E. Y. Mullins (1860–1928); while W. N. Clarke (1841–1912) and W. A. Brown (1865–) exercised a mediating role.

Recent theology has been influenced both by the reaction against Spencerian optimism and by Marxist social thought, as may be seen in the writings of Reinhold Niebuhr. No comprehensive history of American theology has ever been written.

[F. H. Foster, *A Genetic History of New England Theology;* J. W. Buckham, *Progressive Religious Thought in America;* W. W. Sweet, *The Story of Religions in America;* H. N. Wieman and B. E. Meland, *American Philosophies of Religion.*]

EDWIN E. AUBREY

Theosophy is defined by its expounders as a religion-philosophy-science brought to America by "messengers of the guardians and preservers of the ancient Wisdom-Religion of the East." Its founder was an eccentric Russian noblewoman, Helena P. Blavatsky, who after a turbulent childhood became a wanderer over the earth. After extensive travels in the Far East, where she claimed to have received instruction from "Sages of the Orient," she came to New York (Nov. 17, 1875) and with William Q. Judge, Henry Steel Olcott and fifteen others formed the first Theosophical Society. The purpose of the organization was to further a universal brotherhood of humanity without distinction of race, color, sex, caste or creed; to further the study of the ancient scriptures and teachings, such as Brahmanical, Buddhist and Zoroastrian; and to investigate the "hidden mysteries of nature," and psychic and spiritual powers latent in man.

At first the Theosophists displayed an interest in Spiritualism[qv], but later repudiated it, stating that spiritistic phenomena "were but a meagre part of a larger whole." Later Madame Blavatsky formed what she termed an "Esoteric Section," which was a select group of promising students gathered to study the profounder teachings of Theosophy. Madame Blavatsky left the United States in 1878 and formed theosophical societies in England and India, which recognized her leadership until her death in 1891.

The teachings of Theosophy stress universal brotherhood to be a fact in nature, upon which is based its philosophy and religion. It proclaims a "Deific Absolute Essence, infinite and unconditioned . . . from which all starts, and into which everything returns." Man has an immortal soul, but the soul is a tenant of many different bodies in many different lives. Every soul must become perfect before the next stage of existence can be entered upon, and those who go forward most rapidly must wait for all. For this many incarnations are necessary. It accepts the miracles of Jesus but denies their supernatural character, holding that they were accomplished through natural laws.

According to the latest statistics (1937) there were in the United States 5900 members of theosophical societies, known as lodges.

[A. B. Kuhn, *Theosophy: A Modern Revival of Ancient Wisdom;* Helena Petrovna Blavatsky, *Isis Unveiled.*]

WILLIAM W. SWEET

Third Parties. The vast majority of American voters have supported one or the other of two great political parties throughout most of the period since the adoption of the Constitution. Since 1825, however, there have been many voters, in the aggregate, who have been temporarily dissatisfied with the principles, policies or leadership of the two major parties, and who accordingly have started independent, or "Third party," movements. The earliest of our third parties was the Anti-Masonic party[qv], which arose suddenly in 1826, and disappeared within a decade. Then came the Liberty party about 1840, and the Free Soil party in 1848, soon to be followed by the Native American or Know-Nothing party of 1852–56[qqv]. In 1854–56 the present Republican party[qv] was first organized as a third party. The campaign of 1872 saw the birth of the short-lived Labor Reform party, the forerunner of the Independent or Greenback party of 1876–84, and of the Prohibition party[qqv], the longest-lived of all our third parties if we except the Republican party. Of much greater importance than any just mentioned was the People's or Populist party[qv], which, although polling two million votes in the presidential election of 1892, soon disintegrated. Of more recent third parties, the most influential have been the National Progressive party of 1912–16, the Socialist party organized about 1897, the Farmer-Labor party of 1920, and the LaFollette Progressives of 1924[qqv]. Of considerably less significance have been the Constitutional Union party of 1860, the Liberal Republicans of 1872, the Anti-Monopoly, Union Labor, and United Labor parties, 1884–88, the Socialist Labor party since 1892, the Communist party[qqv] since 1928, and the Union (Lemke) party of 1936. Other short-lived third parties have appeared from time to time in state and local politics.

Although minor parties polled enough votes in pivotal states to affect the result of presidential elections in 1844, 1848, 1884 and 1912, no third party has risen to a commanding position in national politics since the Republican victory of 1860. In fact, there have been only three presidential elections since that year in which third parties altogether have polled more than

10% of the popular vote: the Populists, in 1892; the National Progressives, in 1912; and the La Follette Progressives, in 1924. At most presidential elections since 1860, not one vote in twenty has been cast for the candidates of all minor parties together; they have elected very few members of Congress; and, except in 1892, 1912 and 1924, have failed to carry any of the states.

[A. N. Holcombe, *Political Parties of Today;* E. M. Sait, *American Parties and Elections;* J. D. Hicks, The Third Party Tradition in American Politics, in *Mississippi Valley Historical Review*, Vol. XX; E. Ellis, The Failure of Minor Parties, in *Current History*, Vol. XXXII.]

P. ORMAN RAY

Third-Term Doctrine. The Convention of 1787[qv] did not place in the Constitution any provision with regard to the eligibility of the President for re-election. When Washington was approaching the completion of his second term in 1796 he refused a third term. In his Farewell Address[qv] he based this refusal on personal reasons only. Thomas Jefferson likewise refused a third term in the year 1808. His successors, James Madison and James Monroe, served for two terms each. Thus there grew up a custom of only two terms by a sort of tacit consent. When Andrew Jackson was completing his second term, in 1836, there was a strong movement for a third one, but he positively refused. He was in favor of a constitutional amendment which would limit the President to a single term. He included such a recommendation in his first annual message to Congress (Dec. 8, 1829) and repeated this recommendation several times in subsequent messages, but no final action was taken.

The third-term question was not discussed again until about the year 1874 when it was found that President Grant, who was serving his second term, was desirous of becoming a candidate for the third time. This aroused such popular opposition that in December, 1875, the House of Representatives passed a hostile resolution by the vote of 234 to 18 which included nearly half of the Republican membership in the majority, although Grant was a member of that party. This resolution declared against a third term as "unwise, unpatriotic, and fraught with peril to our free institutions."

The question was raised again when Theodore Roosevelt became a candidate for nomination in the Republican primaries although his success would not have resulted in three consecutive terms, and he did secure the nomination by the newly formed Progressive party[qv]. Again in 1928, although President Coolidge had given notice that "he did not choose to run," a resolution passed the United States Senate by a vote of 56 to 26 which condemned a third term in nearly the same words as the House resolution of 1875. This is the situation as it stands in May, 1940.

It should be remembered that like the Constitution of Great Britain, although to a much less extent, the Constitution of the United States in reality contains in its working provisions, in addition to the written fundamental law, much of custom which through time and general acceptance has the force of law.

[H. W. Horwill, *Usages of the American Constitution;* W. S. Myers, *The Republican Party.*]

WILLIAM STARR MYERS

Thirst. Before wells and windmills[qv] brought water to the surface of vast areas of the West and mechanical transportation facilitated travel over other areas that will never be watered, man and beast often suffered excruciatingly from thirst and not infrequently perished. The *Jornada del Muerto*[qv]—Journey of the Dead Man—between Albuquerque and El Paso became noted for death through thirst. The Santa Fé Trail[qv] and the Salt Lake Trail were routes of thirst. "Dry drives" such as that between the Concho and Pecos rivers in Texas sometimes resulted in the loss of scores of animals out of a single herd. Thirst gave Death Valley[qv] its name, and precious metals associated with it and similar deserts have lured prospectors to death. In the desert country mirages mock and occasional pools of alkali water betray with poison. Yet a cottonwood, the tree marking seep spring as well as stream, has signaled many a perishing soul to water. The Indians of the Southwest know every *tinaja,* and often keep these natural rock water holes covered.

Frederick Remington's great painting, "The Fight at the Water Hole" and Stewart Edward White's story, *The Emigrants,* tell vividly the torture of thirst and the benediction of a cup of water in the desert. Though tradition has exaggerated the number of deaths on the plains and in the mountains, thirst was the most real and the most awful enemy that threatened early penetrators of these regions.

[J. R. Cook, *The Border and the Buffalo;* G. F. Ruxton, *Adventures in Mexico and the Rocky Mountains;* S. E. White, *Arizona Nights.*]

J. FRANK DOBIE

Thirteenth Amendment, THE, which abolished slavery, was one of the so-called "Civil War Amendments." Although Congress in February, 1861, as a compromise measure before the war began, had adopted a resolution for an amendment which would deny to Congress the power to abolish slavery in any state, as the war progressed both the President and Congress became convinced that the Federal Government must assume power over slavery. By the Confiscation Acts[qv], slaves of disloyal owners were subject to forfeiture to the National Government and could thereby be freed. The Emancipation Proclamation[qv], as a war measure, declared free the slaves in the parts of the Confederacy still unconquered, Jan. 1, 1863. At the end of the war existing laws and proclamations left untouched the slaves of loyal owners and did not apply to the whole of the slave-owning region; they provided for the freeing of the slaves, but did not secure the abolition of slavery[qv] as an institution. While slavery was virtually dead, its legal status was not complete nor was it necessarily permanent. For this purpose it was generally recognized that an amendment to the Federal Constitution was required. Resolutions had been introduced in both houses of Congress as early as December, 1863, in the House by Rep. Ashley of Ohio, and in the Senate by Henderson of Missouri and by Sumner of Massachusetts. In its final form the resolution was reported to the Senate by Trumbull of Illinois, chairman of the Judiciary Committee. The phraseology used was almost identical with the slavery prohibition of the Northwest Ordinance, 1787[qv]. The second section of the Amendment expressly gave to Congress power of enforcement by appropriate legislation.

The resolution passed the Senate, April 8, 1864, by a vote of 38 to 6. In the House it failed at first (June 15, 1864) to secure the necessary two-thirds vote, but passed later, 119 to 56, with 8 not voting (Jan. 31, 1865).

Ratification of the Amendment was required by President Johnson of the former seceded states as part of his reconstruction[qv] program, and eight of these states were counted officially in the three fourths of the states necessary to ratification. These states were among those which were not considered as states in the Union by Congress in the Reconstruction Acts of 1867[qv], but their ratification of the Amendment was not invalidated. The Amendment was proclaimed as ratified, and "valid as part of the Constitution of the United States," on Dec. 18, 1865.

[James Ford Rhodes, *History of the United States, 1850-1877*, Vol. IV; J. G. Randall, *The Civil War and Reconstruction.*]

C. MILDRED THOMPSON

Thomas Amendment, THE, is the popular term for Title III of the Agricultural Adjustment Act of May 12, 1933[qv]. It gave the President power, directly or through the Secretary of the Treasury, (a) to make agreements with the Federal Reserve Board[qv] and Banks for the latter to buy up to $3,000,000,000 of government securities, (b) to issue $3,000,000,000, in United States notes, (c) to devalue the dollar up to 50% and/or re-establish bimetallism[qv] and (d) to receive war debt[qv] payments in silver at 50 cents an ounce up to $200,000,000.

[F. A. Bradford, *Money and Banking.*]

FREDERICK A. BRADFORD

Thornburgh Fight (Milk River, Colo., Sept. 30–Oct. 3, 1878). Maj. T. T. Thornburgh, marching from Fort Fred Steele, Wyo., to the assistance of white persons at the Ute agency on the White River, Colo., was attacked by Ute warriors at the Milk River. Maj. Thornburgh was killed, and his command of 200 men driven back and besieged for three days, with a loss of 12 killed and 43 wounded, before being rescued by a column from Fort D. A. Russell under Gen. Wesley Merritt. The Indian loss was never known.

[P. H. Sheridan, *Record of Engagements with Hostile Indians.*]

PAUL I. WELLMAN

Thoroughbred Horse. The present-day American thoroughbred is from the same stock as the original animal of that name which was produced in England in the latter 17th and early 18th centuries. The American colonists began importing animals of this breed as soon as possible and the evolution of the following two centuries proceeded in both countries along parallel lines. But for many years past the thoroughbred has been an international animal and in consequence America has drawn upon other countries than England for racing and breeding purposes, and, most especially, France, which since the World War has sent over some very important and influential animals. However, the basic elements of the breed as it exists today in the United States are those which go back to colonial times, their enduring merit having been such as to leave them a permanent foundation upon which to build. Fashion is a potent force in breeding, and it has always been strongly prepossessed in favor of constant fresh importations of exotic blood, but despite this the old established so-called "American strains" continue to hold their own; though in 1913 the pages of the English *General Stud Book* were closed to them and they were declared by its sponsors "not thoroughbred." Nevertheless, horses bred in America, or bred abroad from animals with American strains, continue to be prominent upon English and other European courses and to carry off many of their most celebrated events.

For over 100 years past the great majority of American thoroughbreds have been bred and reared in Kentucky, and there have been produced the bulk of the most famous ones of recent times, including such as Man o' War, Equipoise, Gallant Fox, Exterminator, Discovery, Omaha, Flares, War Admiral, Crusader, Seabiscuit, Top Flight, Twenty Grand, etc. About 5000 individuals are now being bred annually, of which the majority are marketed as yearlings, the most select ones being sold at the Saratoga, N. Y., auctions, where as high as $75,000 has been paid. Breeding, however, is really supervised by The Jockey Club of New York, an organization not for profit, composed of the leading metropolitan and other members of the ranks of sportsmen. From its office is published the official *American Stud Book,* now in its 16th volume, and no horse not registered in that work is allowed to race at a reputable meeting. The Jockey Club has also, ever since its organization in 1894, exercised a supervisory influence over other departments of both breeding and racing which has been both vigilant and beneficial. (*See also* Horse Racing.)

[*American Turf Register*, 16 vols., 1829-44; *Spirit of the Times*, 31 vols., 1831-61, and later volumes down to 1902; *Turf, Field & Farm*, 75 vols., 1865-1902; *American Stud Book*, 16 vols., 1873-1936; *Thoroughbred Record*, 127 vols., 1875-1939; *Goodwin's Turf Guide*, 43 vols., 1882-1908; *Daily Racing Form*, 44 vols., 1894-1939; *American Racing Manual*, 41 vols., 1897-1939; *Early American Turf Stock*, 2 vols., 1934-35; *American Trotting Register*, 28 vols., 1871-1932; *Horse Review*, 83 vols., 1888-1932.]

JOHN HERVEY

Three-fifths Compromise. *See* Convention of 1787; Compromises of the Federal Constitution.

Three-Mile Limit. *See* Territorial Waters.

Three Notch Road, The, so called from the manner of marking the trees along its course, was a pioneer road of Mississippi connecting Natchez with St. Stephens[qqv] on the lower Tombigbee. It was first marked after the Choctaw cession of 1805, of which cession it formed in part the northern boundary. Before this date it was a trail running through the Choctaw country and had been commonly known as McClary's Path from the fact that Lt. McClary in 1799 led a detachment of troops over it from Natchez to St. Stephens on the occasion of the American occupation (*see* Southern Boundary, Survey of the). It was, in fact, an old Indian trail, a part of the great road from the Creek country to Mexico. At St. Stephens the Three Notch Road connected with the Federal road leading to Milledgeville. The name Three Notch Road was sometimes applied to the Federal road. It remained throughout the pioneer period the only land communication between Natchez and the Mobile region.

[P. J. Hamilton, *Colonial Mobile.*]

R. S. COTTERILL

Three Rivers, Battle of (June 8, 1776). This American reverse resulted from an attempt of a force of about 2000 men under Brig. Gen. William Thompson to surprise the British garrison of Three Rivers (*see* Canada, American Invasion of). The Americans were misled by a guide and their attack delayed, while the garrison, commanded by Brig. Gen. Simon Fraser, was much stronger than they had believed, and was supported by ships on the St. Lawrence. The attack was a failure; the American loss in killed and wounded was heavy, though unascertained, and the British took 236 prisoners, including Thompson himself. The British loss was eight killed and nine wounded.

[A. L. Burt, *The Old Province of Quebec;* Justin H. Smith, *Our Struggle for the Fourteenth Colony.*]

C. P. STACEY

Threshing Machine, The. The colonial farmer brought to the task of threshing the same primitive methods used throughout the world from ancient times. The first process, that of shelling the kernels from the head, was done with the flail. Among the more well-to-do farmers, horses were sometimes used to trample out the grain on a specially prepared threshing floor. Here a man and four horses might prepare thirty bushels in a single day.

After the threshing the next task was the separation of the straw. This was done by raking off the straw, leaving the grain and the chaff on the threshing floor. Then came the winnowing, that is the separation of the chaff from the grain. The most primitive method was to throw the grain in the air, allowing the wind to blow away the chaff. Sometimes a heavy sheet was used to "fan" the wheat.

As early as 1710 a hand-driven fanning mill had been developed in Scotland. Before the close of the century, such devices were common in America.

The credit for developing a complete thresher, one combining in a single unit machinery for accomplishing all three processes, goes to Andrew Meikle of Scotland, who, in 1788, patented a thresher, in 1789 added a separator, and in 1800, a fanning mill.

Such a machine as this could not be operated by hand. Sometimes water power could be used, but this sacrificed essential mobility. Until the application of the steam engine in farming operations, the only solution was the use of horse power. At first stationary and later portable treadmills and capstanlike sweeps were manufactured.

Because such machines were too expensive for the ordinary farmer, two developments are to be noted. The cheap hand-driven fanning mill became a part of the standard equipment of most farmers. Then, in the early 1820's, Jacob Pope put on the market a cheap hand-operated thresher; in the next decade scores of such machines were patented and sold.

In the 1840's we have the real advance in thresher making. Wheeler and Melick developed a small, cheap thresher-separator, and in 1844 Jerome I. Case began to turn out a similar machine in Racine, Wis. The first American machine to combine the three operations, threshing, separating and cleaning, was built by John and Hiram Pitts of Winthrop, Maine. In 1840 John had established a factory at Albany, N. Y., which was later moved to Buffalo. Hiram Pitts in 1847 began manufacturing threshers in Alton, Ill., moving to Chicago in 1851. Like the plow and the harvester (*see* Farm Machinery), the manufacture of the thresher tended to follow the extension of the wheat-growing area into the Northwest. By the 1860's most of the threshers had a cleaning attachment, and by the 1880's the old hand-driven fanning mill was a museum piece.

The thresher was too expensive for the average farmer to own. The owner of such a machine with its portable "power" moved from farm to farm during the threshing season. Sometimes such an entrepreneur supplied the threshing crew, but more often the "hands" were the farmers in the neighborhood formed into a simple co-operative group.

Up to the late 1870's the horse continued to be the source of power. Then, in the Far West, where wheat growing was carried on, on a large scale, the steam tractor came into general use. Here too the thresher was attached to the harvester, making a single unit, the "combine"[qv]. It was not until the coming of the cheap portable gas engine, however, that the old "horse power" finally disappeared from most American farms.

[P. W. Bidwell and J. I. Falconer, *History of Agriculture in the Northern United States, 1620-1860;* Victor S. Clark, *History of Manufactures in the United States, 1607-1860;* Leo Rogin, *The Introduction of Farm Machinery in Its Relation to the Productivity of Labor in the Agriculture of the United States during the Nineteenth Century.*]

ERNEST S. OSGOOD

Thrift, The Decline of. Thrift is that disposition or habit which will sacrifice a smaller satisfaction in the present in order to secure a larger satisfaction in the future. It depends partly on the ability of the individual to foresee and appreciate future needs, and partly on outward social conditions. It is encouraged where savings and investments are secure. It is discouraged by a state of lawlessness on the part of individuals and by uncertainty as to what a predatory government may do. In other words, where present enjoyment is certain and future enjoyment extremely uncertain, even the prudent person will choose present enjoyment.

The development of a thrifty attitude of mind depends upon a number of factors. In a geographical situation where nature provides food in all seasons of the year, especially where it is difficult to preserve food, there is no survival value in thrift. But where there are long winters or long dry spells, only the thrifty individuals or tribes can survive, and in the course of time a thrifty people is produced.

Morals, religion and education also encourage or discourage thrift, according to their character. Any system of teaching which discourages gluttony, ostentation or any other form of self-indulgence, automatically encourages thrift. One does not need to invent an occult reason why Puritanism encouraged the accumulation of capital[qv], or why an abundance of investible capital made a market for mechanical inventions.

With the development of the mechanical industries, which followed automatically upon the creation of a market for inventions, thrift took on a somewhat new character. Large numbers have come to depend on weekly or monthly wages, and do not see so clearly the need for thrift as do farmers and other self-employed persons. It does not take a great deal of foresight for a farmer to see the need of saving seed for next year's planting, or food and fuel for next winter's consumption. The self-employed person sees also the need for keeping up or replacing his equipment.

Yet the fact remains that thrift is as necessary for the maintenance or growth of the mechanical industries as for that of agriculture or the handicrafts. The real difference lies in the fact of specialization. Some can practise thrift and provide the investible capital which is necessary for industrial expansion, while others can live without thrift, on their daily, weekly or monthly wages or salaries. A part of the population may provide the funds necessary to pay those who build the factories, railroads and other forms of industrial equipment, and the rest of the population may, if they choose, consume their entire incomes.

When the latter element comes to outnumber the former, demagogues are certain to arise who will persuade the thriftless that they are superior persons. Books will appear on the fallacy of saving. Politicians will enact laws to tax those who have for the benefit of those who have not. This, of course, merely substitutes compulsory for voluntary saving. It does not, in any way, decrease the necessity of saving. It only forces those who save to share with those who do not.

Even the coercive communist has to recognize the necessity of saving when he is faced with responsibility. With inadequate accumulations of capital he cannot equip his workers adequately. With inadequate equipment his workers cannot produce much per worker. With a small product per worker real wages must be low.

The reasons for the decline of thrift were anticipated a long time ago by William G. Sumner, who wrote: "If you get wealth you will have to support other people. If you do not get wealth, it will be the duty of other people to support you." *(What the Social Classes Owe to Each Other).* Needless to say, in proportion as these anticipations are realized, in that proportion is thrift discouraged. Those who are disposed to save are discouraged by the fear that their savings will be taxed away. The thriftless are encouraged to think that they will be supported out of the savings of others.

The evidence of a decline of thrift is not found in a scarcity of investible funds. The demand for investible funds comes from the activity of investors who wish to start new enterprises or to expand existing enterprises. The inactivity of investors is mainly the result of the same kind of fear that discourages saving. The decline of thrift is evidenced by the increase of luxury, of gambling and of political spoliation of the thrifty for the benefit of the thriftless.

[An argument against thrift will be found in Wm. T. Foster and Waddill Catchings, *The Road to Plenty.* In favor of thrift consult any standard work on economics under the caption, Capital and its accumulation. For the reasons for the slow growth of thrift, and its frequent decline, see Alfred Marshall, *Principles of Economics.*]

T. N. CARVER

Thrift Stamps. As a means of increasing savings in the United States during the World War, thrift stamps and war savings certificates were created. By way of facilitating the accumulation of small sums of money, the Federal Government issued a small stamp the size of a postage stamp, called a thrift stamp, costing twenty-five cents each but bearing no interest. With the original purchase of a thrift stamp, the purchaser was given a card containing spaces for sixteen thrift stamps, with the expectation that when the card was filled, thus having a value of $4.00, it would be exchanged for a war savings stamp, or as it was sometimes called, a war savings certificate.

The war savings certificates were issued as of Jan. 2, 1918, for $4.12 each, the purchase price advancing approximately at the rate of one cent each month. At maturity, Jan. 1, 1923, the Federal Government promised to pay to the purchaser at any post office, $5.00 for each certificate. The difference between the purchase price and the maturity value of the certificate allowed the investor an interest rate of about 4% a year, compounded quarterly. Certain features of the certificates made them especially attractive investments: they could be registered at any first, second, or third class post office as a precaution against loss, and they could be redeemed at any time before maturity by giving ten days' notice to the post office.

Through the media of the thrift stamps and war savings certificates, coupled with the gospel of thrift that was vigorously preached and publicized throughout the nation, in little more than a year the Federal Government raised more than $1,000,000,000.

[Financing the War, *Annals of the American Academy of Political and Social Science,* January, 1918.]

FRANK PARKER

Ticonderoga, Capture of (1775). The suggestion for reducing this British post has at various times been credited to Will Gilliland, John Brown of Pittsfield, Ethan Allen and Benedict Arnold. The immediate object of the attack was not only to take the dilapidated fort, but also to obtain cannon for the siege of Boston[qv]. The Hartford Committee of Correspondence raised more than fifty men and £300 and urged the "Green Mountain Boys"[qv] to take part in the expedition. It was decided that Ethan Allen should command, and the rendezvous was set for Hand's Cove on the eastern shore of Lake Champlain. Meanwhile, Col. Benedict Arnold had been commissioned by the Massachusetts Committee of Safety to raise 400 men, and with a single servant he arrived at Hand's Cove in time to claim the command. When the "Green Mountain Boys" refused to participate in the expedition without their own officers, it was agreed that Allen and Arnold should enter the fort side by side at the head of the column. Early in the morning of May 10, Allen, Arnold and eighty-three men crossed the lake in two boats. After a harangue by Allen, the expedition passed through the ruined walls and without bloodshed quickly subdued the sleepy garrison, consisting of Capt. Delaplace, Lt. Feltham, and forty-three men.

The ensuing plan of Congress to abandon Crown Point[qv] and Ticonderoga aroused so much opposition in New England and New York that it was finally dropped. Not until the winter of 1775–76 were the Ticonderoga cannon removed to Cambridge. Col. Henry Knox, a young artillery officer of twenty-four, laid the plans for transporting the ordnance. Knox arrived at Ticonderoga on Dec. 5, 1775, and arranged to move 14 mortars and coehorns, 2 howitzers and 43 cannon, weighing a total of 119,900 pounds. The guns were taken in groups by water to Fort George at the southern end of Lake George. On sleds drawn by oxen and horses, they progressed past Fort Edward, Saratoga, Albany and Kinderhook to Claverack. Their route then turned east through the mountains to Springfield, Worcester and Cambridge. Citizens along the way were impressed by the great guns, and one mortar known as the "old sow" was fired off several times for the people to hear its deep roar. By Jan. 24, 1776, the first section of the artillery train was in Cambridge, and Washington was enabled to force the British from Boston.

[A. C. Flick, General Henry Knox's Ticonderoga Expedition, N. Y. State Historical Association *Proceedings*, XXVI; Allen French, *The Taking of Ticonderoga;* John Pell, *Ethan Allen.*]

EDWARD P. ALEXANDER

Ticonderoga, Fort. Begun in October, 1755, by the Marquis de Lotbinière as an outpost for Fort St. Frédéric, the fort was named Carillon by the French. It commanded the route between Lakes Champlain and George and was called Ticonderoga by the English. The fort today belongs to the Pell family, who have restored it.

[H. I. Gilchrist, *Fort Ticonderoga in History.*]

EDWARD P. ALEXANDER

Ticonderoga, Operations at (1758–59). "At Ticonderoga, July Ye 8, for seven hours we fought the French, While we ware all in open field and they within a trench." Thus did a common soldier describe one of the bloodiest battles in the history of British arms. In 1758 Gen. James Abercromby, with more than 15,000 men, opposed Montcalm, the French commander, with only 3600 (*see* French and Indian War). Montcalm, realizing how hopeless was his plight, considered retreat but decided instead to build and defend a strong abatis to the northwest of the fort. Young Lord Howe, Abercromby's second in command, was intelligent, vigorous, personable and a real leader. When he was killed in a preliminary skirmish, the soul went out of the expedition. Abercromby, ignoring his artillery, tried to take the impregnable French position by storm and lost 1944 men to 377 for the French. When he retreated in a panic, he well deserved the epithet, "Nabbycromby," bestowed upon him by the provincials.

During the next summer Sir Jeffery Amherst, methodical and deliberate, led another army against Ticonderoga. He had 11,000 men, and the French under Bourlamaque, about 3500. So thoroughly did Amherst prepare his siege that the French, on July 26, 1759, blew up the fort and retreated.

[Francis Parkman, *Montcalm and Wolfe.*]

EDWARD P. ALEXANDER

Ticonderoga, Taken by Burgoyne (1777). Burgoyne's army[qv] of more than 9000 was opposed by Gen. Arthur St. Clair with about 2500 men. The British dragged cannon up steep Sugar Hill (Mount Defiance), which commanded the fort from the southwest. St. Clair would have been trapped if the British had surrounded Mount Independence, connected with Ticonderoga by a bridge of boats. Shortly after midnight on July 6, St. Clair wisely retreated across the bridge and southward along the eastern shore of Lake Champlain with the British close behind. So exultant was George III over the news from Ticonderoga that he exclaimed, "I have beat them! I have beat all the Americans!"

[Hoffman Nickerson, *The Turning Point of the Revolution.*]

EDWARD P. ALEXANDER

Tide Mills. Early settlers erected tide mills in the northern and central colonies to grind grain. They were confined to flat tidal coast country where other water power was not available. Apparently they were preferred to windmills[qv] though the latter were not uncommon especially in the Dutch settlements. To secure power a dyke was built across the mouth of a marsh or inlet, so arranged that the tide could enter and fill the reservoir thus formed, where it was retained until the receding ocean left a head sufficient to turn for a few hours an undershot water wheel. Their slow propulsion made it necessary—at least in some instances—to double-gear them in order to accelerate the speed of the millstones. Such mills were in operation in eastern Massachusetts as early as 1650. European visitors described similar mills on Long Island and Staten Island in the 18th century. Several were in operation on the lower Delaware in Salem County, N. J.

[Victor S. Clark, *History of Manufactures in the United States;* Barber and Howe, New Jersey Historical *Collections;* Peter Kalm, *Travels into North America.*]

VICTOR S. CLARK

Tidewater is a term commonly used in American history to designate that part of the Atlantic coastal plain lying east of the points in rivers reached by oceanic tides. This region, first occupied by settlers from the Old World, became slowly the habitat of comparative wealth. Merchants and shippers in the towns, and planters growing tobacco, rice, indigo and cotton, dominated the tidewater population. Since in New England the tidewater coastal area is so narrow the terminology is more applicable elsewhere, particularly in the Middle Atlantic and South Atlantic regions of the English colonies and the later states of the Federal Union. First on the ground and earlier established economically, socially and politically, the inhabitants of the tidewater regions secured control of the government. Almost inevitably they used the machinery of government for their own benefit, and in accordance with their traditions and ideals, and resisted any effort to weaken their control. But the later population, composed largely of small farmers, which moved beyond into the Piedmont region[qv], found this tidewater domination of government both unfair and injurious. A serious and long-continued sectional conflict resulted. Sometimes, as in the case of Bacon's Rebellion of 1676 in Virginia, the Paxton riots of 1765 in Pennsylvania, and the Regulator Movement of 1767–71 in North Carolina[qqv], the conflict resulted in open warfare. At times, as a result of manipulation and compromise, violence was kept down. But on all occasions the serious conflict in ideals and interest had to be taken into consideration. The political history of first the colonies, and later the states, can only be interpreted adequately in the light of this conflict.

Control of the government by the tidewater element of the population was maintained largely by a device of disproportional representation which was widely in operation from Pennsylvania to Georgia. Another device was that of restricted suffrage, wherein a heavy property qualification was used to the advantage of the wealthy of the tidewater and to the disadvantage of the poorer inhabitants of the interior. Using these advantages to control the legislatures, the tidewater element pursued policies in regard to the Indians, in regard to debts and in regard to taxes which were most beneficial to the tidewater population and thereby often injurious to the up-country population.

[F. J. Turner, *Sectionalism in American History.*]

ALFRED P. JAMES

Tigre Island. Acquisition of California, 1848, was an immediate stimulus to United States and British rivalry for isthmian advantages, from Tehuantepec to Panama. Tigre Island, strategically located in the Gulf of Fonseca, was a pawn in the game. England illegally seized it. The United States countered by getting a cession treaty of questionable validity. For a time the issue was tense, but it was liquidated in the self-denying clauses of the Clayton-Bulwer Treaty, 1850[qv].

[M. W. Williams, *Anglo-American Isthmian Diplomacy.*]

JIM DAN HILL

Tillmanism, a South Carolina aspect of the agrarian movement[qv], was inaugurated by Benjamin R. Tillman in 1885 by a series of letters to the Charleston *News and Courier* vividly expressing the grievances of the white rural population against the dominant forces of the post-Reconstruction period in that strongly Southern commonwealth. This farmer-agitator accused the merchants of extortionate charges for advances to farmers; the oligarchy under Wade Hampton of greed and of failure to be progressive; the state college of improper expenditure of Federal appropriations for agricultural education; and the Negro of trying to recover his Reconstruction privileges. He set the country against the town; the upcountry against Charleston; the farmer against the lawyer and the businessman; and the common man against the aristocrat. His formula for success was effective appeal to the prejudices of the majority against the minority. Yet he possessed constructive notions, notably the demand for an agricultural college. In 1890, after arousing unparalleled enthusiasm for his person and measures by a canvass of the state, Tillman won complete control of the state government. Notable results followed. Officeholders were supplanted by Tillman partisans; Negro suffrage was destroyed and the white masses, through a wider application of primary elections, gained greater political power; colleges were founded for the vocational education of white boys and girls; corporations were forced to pay a greater share of taxation; and the Dispensary, a state liquor monopoly, was established. Tillman's elevation to the United States Senate in 1895 was followed by an abatement of the partisan and reformist zeal of his movement and by a gradual revival of the forces he had fought. But Tillmanism was not without permanent results. Within definite limitations it gave a progressive tone to events in an otherwise reactionary commonwealth, and it gave a new life to white democracy. It also lowered the quality of the public service, made reactionary attitudes toward the Negro a permanent policy, and made the Blease movement[qv] possible.

[F. B. Simkins, *The Tillman Movement in South Carolina;* W. W. Ball, *The State That Forgot.*]

FRANCIS B. SIMKINS

Timber Culture Act. The principal deterrents to settlement in the plains country were the absence of timber, insufficient rainfall, hot winds and dust storms[qv]. A weather hypothesis of the 1870's was that the presence of growing timber tempered the climate and increased the humidity and perhaps the rainfall of a region. The residents of the plains country, not unnaturally, urged the Federal Government to encourage tree planting in that area in the hope that the climate might be bettered. They also were bedeviled by the fact that after 1870 the government land regulations were made more stringent with the result that homeseekers in Kansas, Nebraska and Dakota could acquire only 320 acres of land. To encourage tree planting and increase the acreage open to entry, Congress adopted in 1873 the Timber Culture Act according to which 160 acres of additional land could be entered by settlers who would set out 40 acres to trees. Ten million acres were donated under this act but much fraud was involved in its administration and little permanent tree growth resulted. Widespread abuse of the act led to its repeal in 1891.

[B. H. Hibbard, *History of the Public Land Policies.*]

PAUL WALLACE GATES

Timber Lands. When America was first settled, almost half of the country was covered with forest. Part of this, especially in the West and Southwest, was not valuable forest from the standpoint of lumber[qv] production. Of the whole territory east of the Mississippi the greater part was wooded, Illinois being the only "prairie" state, and even so, Illinois was about half covered with woods. The great share of this land, though covered with timber, was wanted for farming purposes, and most of it was cleared by the slow pioneer methods during the first 250 years of settlement. From the Atlantic coast to the west line of Indiana trees were, with few exceptions, an encumbrance to the land. Timber was abundant, and cheap, with the result that great quantities of wood were burned on the land on which it had grown in order to make possible the cultivation of cereal, cotton and other crops. The exception to this general rule was found in the coniferous forests of the Appalachian region, the great forests of Minnesota, Wisconsin and Michigan, and considerable areas in the Gulf states, mainly in the lower Mississippi Valley.

While more than half the farms of the United States are located within the eastern forest area, the "timber lands" as related to agriculture are found mainly in the areas above designated, the upper Mississippi Valley and Lake states, and the lower Mississippi Valley. In addition to these areas there is, more recently developed, a considerable district, quite similar in character, in the Pacific Northwest. In these districts, from which the main part of our lumber has come during the past seventy-five years, there have developed serious problems. It was assumed, until rather recently, that "the plow would follow the ax." It had always done so, but more properly the ax had preceded the plow. Soon after the Civil War vastly more lumber was wanted. The soft wood forests of the Lake states were exploited; next the Southern forests came to the front as a source of lumber; a little later dependence on the supplies of the Northwest developed.

For the past few decades the expression "cut-over" lands has been a familiar one. We have at the present time not far from 120,000,000 acres of "noncommercial" forest land, mainly cut-over, on which little or nothing has been done by way of improvement, and which is not producing, as it should be doing, a suitable crop for another harvest. This land is not needed as farm land.

Aside from the "noncommercial" forest land, about equal in area to the combined size of Minnesota, Wisconsin and Michigan, there is much poor wood land included in pastures, and farm woodlots, on the basis of which it has been estimated that noncommercial forest land is greater in extent than the above amount. In 1923 it was reported that the "cut-over" land amounted to 249,000,000 acres (Senate Hearings, March 7 and 8, 1923; Senate Resolution 398). Some of this land has since been rated as commercial.

In general, reforestation is expensive, prohibitively so. No small part of the cut-over timber land is in farms. Such lands are often poor assets to the owner. An ever-increasing quantity of cut-over land is making its way back into public hands, mainly through the avenue of tax delinquency. While some farmers can, no doubt, handle cut-over land successfully, it is plain that for the most part the public will have to assume the responsibility in most instances. The land has at present a low market value, often none. The time required to develop another crop is, in general, long; the danger that taxes will eat up all profits is great; alternative uses for land of this sort are few. It is a problem for governments to face and handle.

[B. H. Hibbard, *A History of the Public Land Policies; A National Plan for American Forestry*, Vol. I, U. S. Printing Office, 1933; Raphael Zon and W. N. Sparhawk, *Forest Resources of the World.*]

BENJAMIN HORACE HIBBARD

Time. In our early history, a community's time was dictated by a town clock in a church steeple or public building, which was set as nearly as possible by the sun. In later years it might follow the time of the railroad running through the town. But among the railroads of the country there were no less than seventy-five systems of time! The resulting confusion became so great that the American Meteorological Society appointed a committee in 1879 to study the subject —with the result that Congress in 1882 authorized the President to call an international conference to select a common prime meridian for reckoning longitude and regulating time throughout the world. Delegates from twenty-six countries met in Washington on Oct. 1, 1884, but could not agree on a prime meridian, though most of them favored that of Greenwich, England. But just before this conference met, the United States and Canada had agreed upon a series of time zones in multiples of 15° corresponding to one hour of sun time difference. For the United States, these were Eastern, centered roughly on 75° west of Greenwich, Central (90° west), Mountain (105°) and Pacific (120°). For several years, many communities still clung to sun time, and often the two systems were found functioning in the same area; but gradually standard time prevailed. (*See also* Daylight Saving.)

[W. F. Allen, *A Short History of Standard Time and Its Adoption in America in 1883.*]

ALVIN F. HARLOW

"Times That Try Men's Souls" (1776) was the short title of the first of thirteen essays published at various periods of the American Revolution by Thomas Paine. These essays, collected under the title *The American Crisis,* were intended to bolster the morale of the American people at critical times. Together with *Common Sense*[qv], also written by Paine, they represent the most effective propaganda written during the Revolution.

[Moncure Conway, *The Life of Thomas Paine.*]

E. H. O'NEILL

Tin Can, THE. As the canning industry[qv] grew in the United States, many improvements were made in the manufacture of the container. The earliest tin cans were laboriously made and sealed by hand. Among the improvements in the manufacture of tin cans, the drop press invented by Allen Taylor in 1847 and the combination press invented by Henry Evans a few years later deserve mention. The lock seamer was invented in 1869 and the automatic soldering of can ends in 1876. The first complete automatic can-making machinery was put into operation in 1885 in Baltimore. There are about sixty-eight separate companies in the United States manufacturing tin cans for sale, in addition to many companies that make cans for their own use. The American Can Company is the leading producer, owning forty-eight plants.

The importance of the tin can in American civilization cannot be overestimated. It has become a necessity in preserving foods of all kinds including meats, fish, poultry, soups, vegetables, milk, jams, fruit juices and beverages. Few foods cannot be preserved in tin cans. Tin containers are also widely used for nonfood products such as oil, polish, tobacco and cigars.

[Bruce W. Gonser, Tin Plate and Tin Cans in the United States, *Bulletin of the International Tin Research Council*, No. 4.]

ARTHUR C. BINING

Tin Pan Alley, a phrase probably coined early in the 1900's, describes the theatrical section of Broadway in New York, where the popular song publishers are located. Most of America's ephemeral ballad and dance tunes originate in Tin Pan Alley, and the term suggests the tinny quality of the cheap, over-abused pianos in the publishers' offices.

[I. Goldberg, *Tin Pan Alley.*]

STANLEY R. PILLSBURY

Tin Plate is thin sheet iron or steel coated with tin. During the late Middle Ages the tin-plate industry was established in Bohemia. Attempts were made to introduce it into England and France in the 17th century, but not until the 18th century was success obtained. The English tin-plate industry was concentrated largely in South Wales, and from this region, even before 1800, tin plate was exported to America and made into utensils by "whitesmiths." A small amount of hammered plate, some of which was tinned, was also produced here at plating mills.

With the exception of the small production at plating mills and also the tinning of Welsh black plate in the United States, all tin plate was imported. Attempts were made to establish the industry after the Civil War. Between 1872 and

1874 three American rolling mills for making tin plate and terne plate (coated with an alloy of lead and tin instead of tin alone) were built by the American Tin Plate Company, Wellsville, Ohio; Rodgers and Burchfield, Leechburg, Pa.; and the United States Iron and Tin Plate Company, Demmler, Pa. Owing to the low duty on tin plate, these companies could not compete with foreign production and the three plants ceased operations before 1878.

The McKinley tariff of 1890[qv] placed a duty of 2.2 cents a pound on imported tin plate, which was to cease after 1897 unless domestic production reached specified amounts. As a result of this protection a new industry was born in the United States. Its growth has been remarkably rapid. By 1912 production equaled that of Great Britain and imports practically ceased. The United States has now (1940) become the leading producer and consumer of tin plate. In 1935, 1,692,380 tons of tin plate and 190,147 tons of terne plate were produced in this country. The latter is used chiefly for roofing, ventilators and many nonfood containers. Tin plate is used in the manufacture of containers and tin cans[qv], as well as kitchen utensils, toys and novelties, merchandising displays, closures, seals, tags and signs.

[Bruce W. Gonser, Tin Plate and Tin Cans in the United States, *Bulletin of the International Tin Research and Development Council*, No. 4; J. H. Jones, *The Tinplate Industry.*]

ARTHUR C. BINING

Tintype, THE, a distinctively American style of photograph, made by the wet process on black japanned metal, was patented by Hamilton L. Smith of Gambier, Ohio, in 1856. Originally introduced as the *melainotype* and the *ferrotype,* it is now universally called by the popular term tintype. Small tintype medals of the presidential candidates widely distributed in the campaign of 1860 first brought national recognition, but the tremendous popularity of the tintype occurred during the Civil War. Small tintypes in oval cutout mounts, known as "gems," have been made in prodigious numbers by itinerant photographers. They are still produced by modern materials.

[Robert Taft, *Photography and the American Scene.*]

ROBERT TAFT

Tinware Peddlers. In 1738 two brothers, Irish tinsmiths, named Pattison, settled in Berlin, Conn., but due to the scarcity of tin plate they practised their craft only with difficulty. About two years later they began the importation of tin plate[qv] from England. The plate was shaped into vessels in the Pattison home and when a stock had been accumulated the brothers sold it from door-to-door. When the local demand had been met they began carrying their wares to near-by settlements. Since the bright and shining vessels were a relief from dull, puritanical pewter the business of the brothers thrived. Others noting this success entered the business and soon, like the Pattisons, they were sending courageous, tricky, keen-witted young men to dispose of tinware to villagers and settlers.

With a cart or wagon loaded with tin vessels the peddlers would start in the autumn on an expedition into the Southern states or whereever they could find settlements. On reaching Richmond, Newbern, Charleston or Savannah they would be met by workmen with a quantity of tin plate who would make a supply of vessels which would stock the peddlers for a journey into the interior. At the beginning of summer they would return to New York, sell their vehicles and horses, and go by water to New Haven. The value of the load of a single horse rarely exceeded $300 or that of a wagon $600.

Following the close of the War of 1812 as many as 10,000 boxes of tin plate a year were made into tinware in the Connecticut village of Berlin. By 1820, however, the peddler began to add other items to his stock; transportation and communication were improved; the low business ethics of the peddler were more generally known; other methods of distribution were more efficient; and the tinware peddler as such was on his way to disappearing.

[Timothy Dwight, *Travels in New England and New York;* Richardson Wright, *Hawkers and Walkers in Early America.*]

FRED M. JONES

Tippecanoe, Battle of (Nov. 7, 1811). The opposition of Tecumseh[qv] to the steady advance of the white race in the Northwest produced a situation which could be resolved only by a test of military might. The crisis came in the summer of 1811, when the Indian leader, after renewing his demands upon Gov. Harrison at Vincennes, departed to rally the tribes of the Southwest to the confederacy he was organizing. Urged on by the frantic frontier settlers, Harrison determined to anticipate Tecumseh's blow by striking first, and the Tippecanoe campaign followed.

The Indian capital was on Tippecanoe Creek, 150 miles north of Vincennes, and Harrison began his northward advance on Sept. 26, with an army of 1000 soldiers, equal in quality, probably, to the best America could produce. Most of October was consumed in constructing Fort Harrison at Terre Haute, to serve as an advance base. On Oct. 29 the march was resumed, and a week later the army was within striking distance of Prophetstown. For several miles it advanced in line of battle, with numerous warriors hovering on its front and flanks; then, with the town in sight, and immediate victory within his grasp, Harrison unaccountably yielded to belated appeals for a conference, and, turning aside, encamped on an elevated site a mile distant from the village. The camp site was like an inverted flatiron and the best the vicinity afforded. Although mutual promises were exchanged that no hostilities would be indulged before the morrow, the soldiers slept on their arms at their appointed stations, in readiness for instant action. Meanwhile the warriors, a mile away, were stirred to frenzy by the Prophet's appeals, and shortly before dawn (Nov. 7), without leaders and largely without a plan, they drove in Harrison's pickets and furiously stormed the still-sleeping camp. The soldiers sprang to action, and the battle raged, either hand-to-hand or at close range, until daylight came, when a series of charges drove the warriors from the immediate field. Following the action, Harrison visited and razed the Indian town, and then began the weary retreat to distant Fort Harrison.

Although Tippecanoe was popularly regarded as a great victory, Harrison's triumph was dearly bought and far from decisive. Under circumstances highly advantageous to himself he had struck an indecisive blow; with almost one fourth of his followers dead or wounded he retreated to Vincennes, where the army was disbanded or scattered, and the frontier became as defenseless as before the campaign. Since Tecumseh's plans were not yet matured, it suited his policy to make light of the Tippecanoe affair, yet it was obvious that the war must be continued to a conclusion, and equally obvious that if war between America and Great Britain should eventuate, the northwestern Indians would make common cause with the British. This came to pass the following summer, when the War of 1812[qv] was declared.

[Elmore Barce, *The Land of the Miamis;* Henry Adams, *History of the United States, 1801-17,* Vol. VI.]

M. M. QUAIFE

"Tippecanoe and Tyler Too!" was the campaign slogan of the Whigs[qv] in 1840, when William Henry Harrison, the hero of the battle of Tippecanoe[qv], and John Tyler were their candidates for the Presidency and Vice-Presidency respectively. The party cry typified the emotional appeal of the Whig canvass. Deliberately avoiding issues, its supporters wore coonskin caps, built campaign log cabins in almost every town of consequence and freely dispensed hard cider to the voters, who were persuaded that Harrison had saved the country from untold Indian atrocities. Few American political slogans have been such unadulterated demagoguery (*see* Campaign of 1840).

[James Truslow Adams, *The Epic of America;* J. H. Denison, *Emotional Currents in American History;* Charles A. and Mary R. Beard, *The Rise of American Civilization.*]

IRVING DILLIARD

***Titanic,* Sinking of the.** This White Star liner, the largest ship in existence at the time, westbound on her maiden voyage, with 2223 persons aboard, struck a partly submerged iceberg at 11:40 P.M. on April 14, 1912, and sank two hours and forty minutes later, with the loss of 832 of her passengers and 685 of the crew. Ocean wireless telegraphy was in its infancy then; many ships carried no radio, others had only a day operator. There was a ship, the *Californian,* only a few miles distant at the time, but her operator was asleep and her instruments silent. However, the eastbound liner *Carpathia,* 56 miles distant, caught the *Titanic's* distress signal, sped to the scene, picked up over 700 survivors and returned to New York. There was bitter criticism of the *Titanic's* construction, of her shortage of lifeboats, of her high speed after receiving iceberg warnings, and of the *Californian,* whose crew admitted seeing rockets from the *Titanic,* but "didn't know what they meant."

[Lawrence Beesly, *The Loss of the Titanic;* Archibald Gracie, *The Truth about the Titanic.*]

ALVIN F. HARLOW

Tithes, Southern Agricultural, were an expedient of the Confederate Congress for securing subsistence for its armies. Because taxes collected in the depreciated currency of the times were not sufficient for this purpose, the levy in kind was adopted on April 24, 1863, to tap the resources of Confederate farms. It was reasoned that one tenth of the products of a population of seven or eight million would support armies less than one tenth as numerous. Complaints against this measure because of alleged class distinctions led to its modification, but it was an important factor in the survival of the Southern armies during the last two years of the Civil War.

[J. C. Schwab, *The Confederate States of America.*]

FRANCIS B. SIMKINS

Tithingmen were town officers of colonial New England, charged with the responsibility of getting out church attendance and maintaining decorous conduct on the Sabbath day. The symbol of office according to tradition was a wand tipped with feathers or a fox tail with which to awaken the drowsy during protracted sermons; while mischievous youngsters were rapped with the hard end.

[D. W. Howe, *The Puritan Republic.*]

W. A. ROBINSON

Titles of Nobility. *See* Nobility, Titles of.

Tobacco, the most important export staple of the colonial period, has always held a major place in American economy.

Encouraged by the success of John Rolfe, who in 1612 began experimenting to develop a tobacco suitable for commerce, his fellow-Virginians adopted the leaf as their chief product and by 1627 annually produced about half a million pounds. From Virginia the culture of tobacco soon spread to Maryland and to North Carolina. Such was the energy applied to the crop that on the eve of the Revolution the yearly exports averaged about a hundred million pounds. Most of the tobacco eventually reached the continent, though as an "enumerated article"[qv] under the mercantile system[qv] it had to be sent first to Great Britain. For the successful marketing of tobacco there evolved in Virginia, and later in Maryland and in North Carolina, inspection systems to guarantee the quality of the exported staple. The problem of controlled quantity was less easily solved, and excessive crops periodically drove the price to profitless levels. Many planters, overestimating the income to be derived from their produce, became hopelessly indebted to British merchants.

During the American Revolution the tobacco industry suffered an inevitable setback. There was temporary recovery about 1790, but international trade difficulties, a new demand for wheat and the rivalry of cotton[qv] postponed a permanent revival until about 1820, when the production of tobacco regained its old levels.

Soon after the War of 1812 tobacco culture expanded into the Mississippi Valley; especially noteworthy were the crops of Kentucky, Tennessee, Ohio and Missouri. By the early 1840's the planters in those states were raising more tobacco than their brethren east of the Alleghenies, and, with a product grown on virgin soil, were displacing in foreign markets the leaf of the older section. The planters of the Atlantic seaboard were forced to improve their technique of production and sale. Fortunately for them they found a home market in the factories of the Virginia and North Carolina piedmont[qv], which by 1860 were manufacturing over 61% of the nation's finished product, other than cigars. In this period before the Civil War the making of cigars evolved into important enterprises centering in New York and Philadelphia.

The staple produced distinctive patterns of slavery on the plantation, where the necessity for intense supervision led to comparatively small slaveholdings, and in the factories, where the initiative of the slave was stirred by relative freedom and a system of bonuses.

Types of tobacco other than the colonial dark fire-cured have been extensively cultivated since the middle of the 19th century. White burley, useful in manufacturing because of its peculiarly absorptive properties, originated in Ohio during the 1860's and from there spread to Kentucky and other states. In the cultivation of cigar leaf, localized in the Connecticut Valley, in Pennsylvania, in Ohio and Wisconsin, a notable innovation after 1875 was the adoption of Havana seedleaf. About 1900 a shade-grown cigar wrapper was introduced in the Connecticut Valley and in Florida. Although bright or flue-cured manufacturing was developed in the ante-bellum period, its culture was restricted to a small area until after the Civil War, when it spread over large parts of piedmont Virginia and North Carolina. The cultivation of bright tobacco extended into the eastern sections of North Carolina and South Carolina about 1890; later into Georgia. Originally used as a wrapper for chewing tobacco, bright tobacco has proved especially adapted for cigarette manufacture. The production of all types of tobacco increased from 434 million pounds in 1859 to 1297 million pounds in 1935.

The annual product of the factories was by 1860 valued at less than thirty-one million dollars; by 1919, at over a billion dollars. This expansion of manufacturing was characterized by the concentration of production into fewer and larger units, the application of machinery to processes formerly carried on by hand, and the energetic pursuit of both domestic and foreign markets.

Around the production of machine-made cigarettes James B. Duke in 1890 organized the American Tobacco Company[qv], which by 1910 had obtained virtual control of all branches of the tobacco manufacturing industry, save cigars. In 1911 the Supreme Court declared the American Tobacco Company a monopoly contrary to the provisions of the Sherman Antitrust Act[qv]. Its properties were divided among sixteen companies, among them being a less powerful American Tobacco Company. The cigar-making industry, with the appearance of efficient automatic equipment since the World War, has evidenced a tendency toward concentration and combination.

Most significant has been the increasing consumption of cigarettes. In the year 1910 the production was 9 billion cigarettes; in 1936, 153 billion. Of the 501 million dollars in internal revenue taxes collected by the Federal Government from tobacco manufacturers for the fiscal year ending June 30, 1936, the cigarette industry contributed 85%.

[Reavis Cox, *Competition in the American Tobacco Industry, 1911-1932;* W. W. Garner et al., History and Status of Tobacco Culture, in *U. S. Department of Agriculture Yearbook, 1922*, pp. 395-468; L. C. Gray, *History of Agriculture in the Southern United States to 1860;* Meyer Jacobstein, *The Tobacco Industry in the United States;* J. C. Robert, *The Tobacco Kingdom.*]

JOSEPH CLARKE ROBERT

Tobacco as Money. Due to the scarcity of metallic money, Virginia, Maryland and North Carolina used tobacco as currency throughout most of the colonial period. In 1619 the Virginia legislature "rated" tobacco at "three shillings the best and the second sort at 18d. in the pound," and a statute of 1642 made tobacco a legal tender. Maryland began to use tobacco for money soon after the founding of that colony, and nearly all business transactions were in terms of tobacco, and all governmental levies, except customs duties, were payable in this commodity. Alsop, writing in 1660, said: "Tobacco is the current Coyn of Maryland and will sooner purchase Commodities from the Merchant, then [sic] money." Oldmixon, writing about fifty years later, said: "Tobacco is their Meat, Drink, Clothing and Money." In 1715 the North Carolina legislature fixed the price of tobacco at 10 shillings per hundredweight. This colony used tobacco as money until the outbreak of the Revolution, though in lesser degree than either Virginia or Maryland.

Overproduction of tobacco led to sharp fluctuations in its market price, in spite of the laws. There was also a tendency to pay debts in inferior tobacco, in spite of numerous inspection laws designed to remedy this evil. It was also found to be impracticable to transfer large quantities of tobacco from hand to hand. Accordingly, Virginia, in 1727, adopted the system of using "tobacco notes," which were certificates issued by the official inspectors of government warehouses. These notes formed a more convenient medium of exchange than the tobacco which they represented and they constituted the most important source of money in Virginia at that time. Apparently Maryland made little use of tobacco notes, though that colony did establish government warehouses in 1747.

Tobacco did not possess many of the qualities of a good money and was never entirely satisfactory as a medium of exchange. It was not easily portable; it had divisibility but lacked homogeneity; and it lacked stability of value due to the uncertainty and variability of production. Nevertheless its use as money proved to be a great boon to colonial Virginia and Maryland.

[C. P. Gould, *Money and Transportation in Colonial Maryland;* Neil Carothers, *Fractional Money.*]

HUGH T. LEFLER

Tobacco Contract, The (1622). After the exemption from customs duties allowed by the Virginia and Bermuda charters had terminated in 1619, it proved difficult to secure satisfactory terms for the importation of colonial tobacco into England. In search of a remedy, Sir Edwin Sandys, whose followers controlled both companies, negotiated with the government in 1622 a contract giving the companies a joint monopoly of all tobacco importations. The terms, ratified by the adventurers on Nov. 27, were none too favorable, and plans to implement the contract by appropriating £2500 for salaries and other costs, with Sandys and his partisans holding all salaried posts, angered many of the more substantial adventurers. An effort under Sir Nathaniel Rich's leadership to reverse the decision in the companies' courts failed, but on appeal to the Privy Council[qv] the contract was set aside in March, 1623. The struggle intensified the factionalism long dividing the adventurers, brought a signal victory to Sandys' opponents in the offer in April of terms more favorable than any enjoyed since 1619, and led directly to a petition for a royal investigation of Sandys' conduct of the affairs of both colonies. The contract is significant largely, therefore, for its contribution to the dissolution of the Virginia Company[qv] in 1624, following the unfavorable report of a commission appointed for this investigation.

[G. L. Beer, *Origins of the British Colonial System;* C. M. Andrews, *Colonial Period of American History*, Vol. I; W. F. Craven, *Dissolution of the Virginia Company.*]

WESLEY FRANK CRAVEN

Tobacco Co-operatives. The earliest known tobacco marketing association operated in Connecticut (1862). The Grangers[qv] maintained tobacco warehouses in Kentucky, Tennessee and Massachusetts (*ca.* 1873–75). About twenty-two warehouse associations sprang up in Wisconsin (1902–4). Under the American Society of Equity, organized by J. A. Everitt of Indiana (1902), dark-tobacco growers of southwest Kentucky (1904) and burley growers (1906) formed pools to control prices. Although legalized by the Kentucky legislature (1908) and temporarily successful in raising prices (1908–9), the pools soon declined, partly because of the criminal activities of the "Night Riders"ᵠᵛ. The oldest existing organization, in Maryland, has operated a sales agency since 1909.

The sharp price decline of 1921 caused Robert W. Bingham, Louisville newspaper publisher, to advocate co-operative marketing. A committee headed by James C. Stone pledged 85% of the burley growers of Kentucky, Ohio, Indiana and West Virginia to sell through the Burley Association for five years (1922–27). Similar organizations were formed in western Kentucky, Virginia and the Carolinas, Connecticut, Wisconsin and Ohio, and controlled nearly half of the American crop (1922–24). But after 1927 the only active groups were in Maryland and Wisconsin. Encouraged by the Federal Farm Board[qv], six new associations were formed (1930–33), but had little success. In 1936 there were fourteen associations, with 91,224 members.

[Federal Farm Board, *Co-operative Marketing of Farm Products;* Charles Kerr, ed., *History of Kentucky.*]

W. C. MALLALIEU

Tobacco Warehouses were authorized by the Grand Assembly meeting at Jamestown[qv], Feb. 1, 1632. Before the following January each planter, except for family use, was required to store all of his crop, not to exceed 1500 stalks, in one of the five designated warehouses. Inspectors burned the unsalable, and repacked for London the marketable, classified as Aronoke, produced in the back settlements and upper Chesapeake Bay, and as sweet-scented, the crop between the James and Potomac rivers. By 1730 Virginia and Maryland had warehouses every fourteen miles. Bonded at £1000 sterling, each inspector received from £25 to £60 as annual salary. Four hogsheads of 950 pounds were considered a ton for London shipment. Crop-notes were issued to planters for such, while transfer-notes were given for less amounts. By 1833 warehouses dotted the Mississippi.

[C. A. Werner, *Tobaccoland.*]

FRANK MARTIN LEMON

Todd's Tavern, Action at (May 7, 1864). As Grant's (U.) army moved to the left at the close of the battles of the Wilderness[qv], Sheridan's (U.) cavalry defeated Stuart's (C.) cavalry at this point on the Brock Road, and drove it almost to Spotsylvania Court House, five miles distant. The loss on each side was nearly 200.

[*Personal Memoirs of P. H. Sheridan.*]

ALVIN F. HARLOW

Tohopeka, Battle at. *See* Horseshoe Bend, Battle of.

Token Money, a term of variable meaning, refers generally to coins of nonstandard character, these coins being made of metal of less value than their value as currency, their circulation maintained by legal-tender[qv] law or promise of redemption or mere acceptance by the people. "Fiduciary coins" is a better term than "token coins." It is current usage to call token coins of silver "subsidiary coins" (*see* Coinage, Subsidiary) and coins of base metals "minor coins."

The colonists had inherited from a European background of royal debasements and universal counterfeiting a strong aversion to token coins, but in practice they had no certain standard money and for two hundred years accepted nondescript token coins of every kind. Hamilton set up the coinage system in 1792 with the avowed purpose of making every coin a standard piece. The silver half-dollar, dime and half-dime were full free-coinage, unlimited legal-tender standard coins. The copper cent and half-cent were given absurdly large weights, so that they were at intervals more valuable as bullion than as currency. They never circulated. The failure of Hamilton's system led the people to use Spanish coins for sixty years, most of them so worn that they were "token" in an extreme sense.

A postal emergency led to the first token coinage, in 1851, in the form of a 3-cent piece, ¾ silver and ¼ copper, made by the Government and sold at a profit, and made legal tender to 30 cents. This was followed in 1853 by the coinage of 5-, 10-, 25- and 50-cent subsidiary silver pieces, legal tender to $5.00 (*see* Coins). The fear of "debasement" was so great that the pieces were "token" only by a fraction, the value of the coins as metal averaging 95 cents to 99½ cents per dollar for many years.

In 1857 the unused copper cents and half-cents were abolished, and the "flying-eagle" cent, 88 parts copper, 12 parts nickel, was created. The nickel was added because of the popular distrust of "debased" coins, but the cost of production was low enough to make them genuine minor coins. This acceptable one-cent piece and the abundant small silver coinage of 1853 led to the withdrawal of hundreds of millions of the Spanish coins which had been the universal currency. With the disappearance of Spanish coins the people suddenly abandoned the accounting in pounds, shillings and pence which had prevailed for two centuries. The creation of token coins for small change thus created a revolution in the thinking habits and business practice of the nation.

In the Civil War period and after, the entire token money system was reorganized. The 3-cent and 5-cent silver pieces and the copper-nickel cent were dropped. Our present-day bronze cent was created. Our present-day five-cent piece, popularly known as the "nickel" but containing 3 parts copper and 1 part nickel, was also introduced. A 2-cent bronze piece and a 20-cent silver piece were tried for a time. The legal tender of the silver coins was set at $10.00, of the 5-cent and 1-cent pieces at 25 cents. Redemption was provided for.

The demonetization of the silver dollar[qv] and the subsequent political drive which forced the Government to buy silver bullion, coin it into dollars, and circulate these dollars at face value made the coin a token currency. The law makes the pretense that it is a standard coin. In actual fact it is an irredeemable token coin which the Government forces on the people at a profit to itself of about 70 cents (in 1939).

Our present token money system consists of the silver dollar, half-dollar, quarter-dollar, and dime, the 5-cent nickel piece and the 1-cent bronze coin. In 1873 Congress gave the half-dollar, quarter, and dime and the 5-cent nickel piece metric weights, not expressible in our English grains, under the delusion that such weights would lead to the circulation of our token coins in Europe.

[Neil Carothers, *Fractional Money.*]

NEIL CAROTHERS

Toledo War, THE, grew out of a boundary dispute between Ohio and Michigan. A strip of land averaging six and one-half miles in width and extending along the northern border of Ohio west of Lake Erie was involved. It included the mouth of the Maumee and the city of Toledo, the projected terminus of the Wabash and Erie Canal[qv].

Michigan's claim was based on the boundary as laid down by the Northwest Ordinance[qv], while Ohio's claim rested on a revision of this line as set forth in the state constitution under which Congress, without either confirming or rejecting the change, had admitted Ohio to the Union.

In 1835 Michigan framed a constitution and elected state officials, without the usual enabling act from Congress. Ohio, in the same year, extended her jurisdiction over the disputed territory by legislative act. Michigan made ready to oppose this action, and armed forces were collected by both sides. There were numerous border brawls, but no one was seriously injured.

On June 15, 1836, Congress offered to admit Michigan to the Union on the condition that the "Upper Peninsula"[qv] be accepted in lieu of the disputed strip. A convention, called in Michigan on July 20 to consider the proposal, voted 28–21 for rejection. Another convention, called without official sanction on Dec. 14, 1836, voted to accept the compromise. On Jan. 26, 1837, Congress voted to admit Michigan to the Union, the preamble to the act stating that the people of the state had given their consent to the proposed boundaries.

[Charles R. Tuttle, *General History of the State of Michigan;* H. M. Utley and B. W. Cutcheon, *Michigan as a Province, Territory and State.*]

WILLIS F. DUNBAR

Tolerance. Although there have been many cases of intolerance[qv], Americans have in general shown a tolerant spirit. In spite of the persecutions of the Baptists and Quakers[qqv] in early Massachusetts the colonies led the world in religious toleration in the 17th century. Especially notable was the policy of Rhode Island as expressed in a letter from the assembly in 1658. The Proprietor of Maryland[qv] planned for complete religious liberty, even though he was a Roman Catholic. Not only was there an unusual amount of freedom in all the colonies, except Massachusetts, but the very fact that various sects were more or less dominant in the different colonies was itself an object lesson and a great experiment. There was no such freedom in European countries. When the first ten amendments to the Federal Constitution, known as the Bill of Rights[qv], were adopted (1791) freedom of religion[qv] was forever guaranteed to all, and it must be remembered that similar Bills had previously been adopted in many of the state constitutions[qv]. Though there has been popular opposition at times to certain religions, notably the Roman Catholic (*see* Nativism) and the Mormons[qv], there have been no government actions against any one on account of his religious beliefs.

Tolerance has also been noteworthy with regard to race, excepting Asiatics. In spite of the fact that the United States contains the greatest racial minority groups in the world, to a considerable extent segregated locally, including 12,000,000 Negroes, they all get along together and there is no such minority problem as plagues some European nations. Although Americans have tended to look upon and even resent the first generation of alien immigrants these have been quickly absorbed and accepted, and there have never been racial riots or feuds except on a small local scale (*see* Race Riots). Speaking generally there has been remarkable racial toleration and acceptance. The equal rights of all races are guaranteed in the Fourteenth and Fifteenth amendments[qqv].

Politically and ideologically Americans have

on the whole shown themselves tolerant except in times of war or unusual emotional excitement (*see* "Reds"). Political tolerance, indeed, has extended far in condoning many evils in our political life. We have shown less tolerance in the realm of ideas which may involve changes in the political or economic systems, in spite of the guarantees of freedom of press, speech and assembly in the Bill of Rights.

Socially, partly due to our being a new country, we are both more and less tolerant than some other peoples. On the one hand, like a crowd of schoolboys, we tend to insist on uniformity of life and ways, but on the other we are much more tolerant of the newcomer in any grade of society as he makes his way upward, and of temporary failure of any sort.

Tolerance is negative, and the motives behind it often difficult to trace. Moreover the term is obviously relative. Without running into anarchy, the state could not tolerate murder or overt treason. The line where tolerance and intolerance meet cannot be a universally accepted one. It depends on the opinions and emotions of individuals. On the whole, however, it may be said that America has been notably tolerant in all the more important departments of its national life, and that toleration is deeply ingrained in its people in spite of occasional indications to the contrary.

JAMES TRUSLOW ADAMS

Toleration Acts. In Rhode Island the code of 1644 granted full freedom of worship, a principle confirmed by the royal charter of 1663 (*see* Rhode Island, Colonial Charters of). In Pennsylvania the great charter of 1682 (*see* Penn's Frame of Government) from the hand of William Penn provided for religious liberty to all who acknowledged God. In 1706 under the pressure of royal authority religious and political liberty was denied to Jews, Catholics and Socinians. In Maryland the Toleration Act of 1649 guided the policy of the proprietors except for the period 1654–58. The royal charter of 1732 creating Georgia confirmed religious liberty for all except papists.

Berkeley and Carteret, grantees of New Jersey[qv], in their concessions of 1665, and the Carolina proprietors[qv] in their proposals of 1663, offered liberty of worship to attract settlers. When the Jerseys came into the control of Quakers and others religious liberty continued, in West Jersey by the law of 1681, East Jersey, 1683.

The Congregational church was legally established in Massachusetts and Connecticut. Taxpayers were required by law to contribute to the support of the Puritan church and ministry. The strong protest of dissenters in Massachusetts found a response in the law of 1731 exempting Quakers from this burden; a few years later Baptists and Episcopalians were relieved. In Connecticut the Toleration Act of 1708 provided freedom of worship but gave no release from paying rates to the established church. However, in 1727–29 Quakers, Baptists and Episcopalians were exempted from this financial exaction.

The Episcopal church was legally established early in Virginia; in Maryland and the Carolinas in the first part of the 18th century; and not till 1758 in Georgia. The church was not strong except in Virginia and South Carolina. In all colonies the dissenters were a growing majority. The church did not invade the religious liberty of others in South Carolina, and in Virginia and Maryland dissenters were granted the benefits of the English Toleration Act of 1689.

The American Revolution, heralding the doctrines of individual liberty, brought the movement for religious freedom to a climax. Most state constitutions[qv] framed in this era sanctioned freedom of conscience in religion in full or qualified manner. The connection of church and state continued in Connecticut until 1818, in Massachusetts until 1833, but in other states it was abolished early. The Ordinance of 1787[qv] extended the principle of liberty of worship to the Northwest Territory. On a national scale the Federal Constitution (Amendment I[qv]) forbade Congress to abridge the free exercise of religion.

[Sanford H. Cobb, *The Rise of Religious Liberty in America.*]

WINFRED T. ROOT

Toll Bridges and Toll Roads grew out of the desire to improve conditions of land transportation, with a minimum burden upon public treasuries. These bridges and roads (turnpikes[qv]) were commonly owned by private corporations and operated for profit. State and colonial governments always determined toll rates and generally provided for reversion to the public at the end of a stated number of years or upon provision of a reasonable return to their proprietors.

Toll bridges antedate toll roads by nearly a century. Whereas the first American turnpike was chartered in Virginia in 1785, Sarah Knight wrote of crossing toll bridges on a journey from Boston to New York in 1704. The first wave of toll bridge construction began about 1730 in the northern colonies and produced several extremely crude and dangerous structures over the smaller rivers. Although land travel was meager, it was concentrated on a very few roads, and well located bridges seem to have earned amounts ample to justify rebuilding after destructive freshets.

The second and more significant wave of bridge building arrived with the turnpikes, about 1800. Turnpike companies, which took over most of the existing highways and constructed many new ones, generally provided necessary small bridges without special toll charges, but many bridge companies were formed to build spans over the more important rivers, such as the Schuylkill and Connecticut. However, although multiplication and improvement of roads by the turnpike companies encouraged investment in toll bridges, the duplication of highway routes spread the traffic to such an extent that in general both roads and bridges were unprofitable investments.

Most roads had become free and public by 1850. Earnings were so small that most proprietors gave them up eagerly. The same is true of toll bridges, although some were situated favorably enough to warrant continued private ownership. Those which in any era have not become free are those which defy duplication on grounds of expensiveness or engineering difficulty.

[Sarah Knight, *Private Journal of a Tour from Boston to New York in the year 1704;* A. Gallatin, *Report on Roads and Canals*[qv], 1808; F. J. Wood, *Turnpikes of New England;* A. B. Hulbert, *Historic Highways;* B. Meyer, *History of Transportation in the United States before 1860.*]

PHILIP E. TAYLOR

Tolls Exemption Act. In anticipation of the opening of the Panama Canal[qv], an act of Congress, Aug. 24, 1912, exempted American vessels in coastwise traffic from the payment of tolls. The Hay-Pauncefote Treaty[qv] of 1901 had provided that the canal should be free and open to the ships of all nations without discrimination in the matter of charges. The congressional enactment therefore involved a serious question, moral and legalistic, as to observance of treaty stipulations. President Wilson on March 5, 1914 made an eloquent plea for repeal both as a matter of sound diplomacy and of international good faith. Elihu Root and other Republicans seconded his efforts, and the act was repealed a few weeks later. Congress, however, expressly denied any relinquishment of the right to grant exemptions to coastwise shipping.

[Charles Seymour, *Intimate Papers of Col. House.*]

W. A. ROBINSON

"Tom Thumb" Locomotive, THE, was built by Peter Cooper for use on the new Baltimore & Ohio Railroad[qv] which, at the beginning, used horses as motive power. In its test, Aug. 28, 1830, the engine, on a double track line out of Baltimore, raced against a car drawn by a horse and would have beaten it had not a pulley belt slipped off.

[Edward Hungerford, *The Story of the Baltimore & Ohio Railroad.*]

ALVIN F. HARLOW

Tomahawk, THE, seems to have been derived from an Algonkin word, to cut. In 1607–9, Capt. John Smith wrote that an English hatchet was a tomahawk, as did Strachey in 1610. In New York, Van der Donck (1650) says the Indians use small axes or tomahawks, instead of warclubs. The early tomahawks made by the English and French had wide chopping blades and at the top a kind of hook. Later, French traders introduced one with a pointed blade, obviously a weapon. By 1700 metal tomahawks were the preferred hand weapons of the Algonkin and Iroquois-speaking Indians.

The history of the pipe tomahawk, one with a hole through the handle and a pipe bowl where the head of the hatchet should be, is obscure, but early in 1700 it displaced other forms. Among the prized types are handsome, engraved blades of bronze. The handles are of wood and usually Indian-made.

Since colonial times the tomahawk has been the symbol of Indian fighting (*see* Hatchet, Burying the). In northeastern United States, throwing a tomahawk was a technique in fighting and an exhibition of skill. Many frontiersmen also became proficient in such use of the tomahawk, but exploits of hurling this weapon were probably more frequent in fiction than otherwise.

[William H. Holmes, The Tomahawk, in *The American Anthropologist*, New Series, Vol. X.]

CLARK WISSLER

Tomahawk Claims. By the blazing of trees encompassing land desired, frontiersmen often asserted irregular claims or "rights" to soil preliminary to survey and possible settlement. The practice existed where lands were taken prior to establishment of legal means for securing title, especially between the Ohio and Muskingum rivers after Pontiac's War[qv]. Colonial land laws sometimes admitted these claims and the "rights" were bought and sold as warrants; the national land system gave them no legal recognition.

[A. C. Ford, *Colonial Precedents of our National Land System;* P. J. Treat, *The National Land System.*]

RAYMOND P. STEARNS

Tombigbee Valley, THE, through which drain the northeast counties of Mississippi and most of west Alabama, played an important part in early Southwest history. France established Fort Tombecbee in 1735 as a base for expeditions against the Chickasaw[qv] allies of the British. Bienville, 1736, attacked these natives at Ackia[qv] with the same disastrous results as befell DeSoto[qv] in 1540. Bernard Romans, a British captain, 1771, explored the region to promote commercial relations with the Choctaws[qv]. After the Revolution, settlers came through East Tennessee, across the highlands south of Bear Creek, at the end of Muscle Shoals, down the valley along the Warrior and Tombigbee rivers. Steamboats began in 1821 to ascend the Tombigbee and, shortly, river navigation went as high up as Cotton Gin Port, Miss. The lands watered by the streams in the valley are rich, and for many years produced large quantities of cotton[qv]. Federal grants to French exiled followers of Napoleon, 1818, started Demopolis at the junction of the Black Warrior and the Tombigbee rivers. The colony was short-lived. The valley embraces much of the lands claimed by the Choctaws prior to the Treaty of 1765 with the British. The name is from the Indian words, "Itombi" and "ikbi," meaning box-maker, literally, "the coffin-maker."

[Peter J. Hamilton, *Colonial Mobile;* Albert J. Pickett, *History of Alabama;* Thomas M. Owen, *History of Alabama.*]

PETER A. BRANNON

Tombstone, a famous silver-mining town of the Southwest, is located in the valley of the San Pedro River of Arizona, some twenty-five miles north of the Mexican boundary. The common tradition is that Ed Schieffelen, a prospector who discovered a large silver deposit there in 1878, gave the location its name because he had been told by scoffers at near-by Fort Huachuca that he would find nothing more than his tombstone in that region. Production of silver on a large scale began in 1880. During the next twenty years the district yielded about $40,000,000 worth of silver and $3,000,000 in gold. Tombstone attained notoriety because of its extravagant social life, its numerous gunmen such as Sheriff Wyatt Earp and his brothers and foes, and the violent feuds among the miners, gamblers and outlaws who made up a considerable part of what was, at one time, said to be a population of 15,000. In the 1890's the mines began to be flooded with underground water, and, despite expensive efforts to drain them, were nearly all abandoned by 1911. From that time Tombstone declined steadily in population and importance, as the mining interests of Arizona were shifted from silver to copper.

[H. H. Bancroft, *History of Arizona and New Mexico;* W. N. Burns, *Tombstone;* T. E. Farish, *History of Arizona;* F. C. Lockwood, *Pioneer Days in Arizona;* J. H. McClintock, *Arizona, Prehistoric, Aboriginal, Pioneer, Modern.*]

RUFUS KAY WYLLYS

Tom's Brook, Engagement at (Oct. 9, 1864). After the battle of Winchester[qv] Sheridan (U.) pursued Early (C.) to Mount Jackson, and then withdrew to Strasburg. Early's cavalry following, Sheridan ordered his own cavalry commander, Merritt, to attack and whip the enemy's mounted troops "or get whipped himself." The Confederates formed behind Tom's Brook, Rosser's (C.) division on the Valley Pike, Lomax's (C.) across the "back road," on Rosser's left. Merritt's division attacked Lomax while Custer charged upon Rosser. The Confederates were routed, fleeing 26 miles through Woodstock to Mount Jackson, losing their artillery and trains. The Federals called the pursuit "Woodstock Races."

[Frederick Whittaker, *A Complete Life of General George A. Custer; Official Records, Union and Confederate Armies,* Vol. XLIII.]

JOSEPH MILLS HANSON

Tondee Tavern, constructed in Savannah by Peter Tondee a few years before the Revolution, became "The Cradle of Liberty" in Georgia. Practically all the early meetings to oppose the king's authority took place here, and when the revolutionary government was set up it made the Tondee Tavern longroom its legislative chamber. In July and August, 1774, revolutionary meetings were held here; beginning in January, 1775 the so-called provincial congresses met here; and in the latter part of December of the same year the Council of Safety made the tavern its permanent meeting place. When the independent state government returned to Savannah in 1782 it first met at Tondee's. Peter Tondee, the owner and builder of the tavern, was a carpenter by trade. After his death in October, 1775, his wife, Lucy, readily lent herself and the tavern to the cause of the Revolution.

[W. B. Stevens, *History of Georgia;* C. C. Jones, Jr., *History of Georgia;* E. M. Coulter, *Short History of Georgia;* L. L. Knight, *Georgia's Landmarks, Memorials and Legends.*]

E. MERTON COULTER

Tonnage Act (1789), the second law passed by Congress under the Constitution, discriminated against foreign ships by taxing them five to eight times per ton more than the six cents per ton levied on American vessels. An even more severe discrimination virtually closed the coasting trade and fisheries[qqv] to foreign-owned ships. Between 1815 and 1830 this policy of encouraging the merchant marine[qv] by discrimination was generally abandoned both by congressional action and by treaties.

[Abraham Berglund, *Ocean Transportation.*]

FRANK A. SOUTHARD, JR.

Tonquin, THE, was the ship used by one division of the expedition which established Astoria*qv* in 1811. After landing its cargo, the vessel proceeded northward on a trading voyage, was attacked by Indians who killed most of the crew, and was finally destroyed by an explosion of gunpowder in the hold.

[Washington Irving, *Astoria.*]

DAN E. CLARK

Tontine Plan, THE (named after a Neapolitan banker, Lorenzo Tonti), combined both lottery and old-age security features as applied in the United States during the late 18th century. A group of persons, in accordance with articles of agreement, would sometimes hold real estate intact with the understanding that it, or the amount for which it sold, would ultimately be divided among certain surviving members. This plan, notably exemplified in the Old Tontine Coffee House, in New York City, became extensively applied to life insurance*qv* policies after 1868 by a number of companies in reacting against annual dividends and surrender values. The Tontine policies received no dividends for a specified period, and, in the event of a lapse, the policyholder received nothing. The Tontine plan eventually developed into the less drastic "deferred dividend" plan—which, in turn, became weakened by the insurance investigation*qv* (1905) and regulatory legislation following it.

[J. B. Maclean, *Life Insurance;* T. O'Donnell, *History of Life Insurance in Its Formative Years.*]

RAY W. IRWIN

"Too Proud to Fight." At Philadelphia on May 10, 1915, three days after the sinking of the *Lusitania*qv, President Wilson, speaking to some newly-naturalized citizens, said, *inter alia,* "The example of America must be a special example. The people of America must be the example not merely of peace because it will not fight but of peace because peace is the healing and elevating influence of the world and strife is not. There is such a thing as a man being too proud to fight. There is such a thing as a nation being too proud to fight. There is such a thing as a nation being so right that it does not need to convince others by force that it is right." The phrase "too proud to fight" was caught up by critics, especially in England, but it revealed the President's mind and probably helps to explain why he did not make the sinking of the *Lusitania* a cause for war.

[N. D. Baker and W. E. Dodd, eds., *The Public Papers of Woodrow Wilson,* Vol. III, 321; Ray Stannard Baker, *Woodrow Wilson: Life and Letters,* Vol. V, 334.]

BERNADOTTE E. SCHMITT

Tookabatchee, the chief town of the Upper Creeks*qv*, was located on the west bank of the Tallapoosa near its junction with the Coosa. It was probably founded by the Shawnee*qv*, some of whom were incorporated in the Creek nation. It was here that Tecumseh*qv* (a Shawnee) held his councils with the Creeks before the War of 1812.

[J. R. Swanton, *Early History of the Creek Indians and Their Neighbors,* Bulletin 73, Bureau of American Ethnology, pp. 277-82.]

R. S. COTTERILL

Topeka Movement and the Topeka Constitution. The movement for statehood, launched by Free State Kansans*qv* in opposition to the proslavery territorial government, was inaugurated in late summer, 1855, and was directed by an executive committee headed by James H. Lane. A "People's" assembly at Topeka, Sept. 19, called an election for members of a constitutional convention on Oct. 9. Fifty-one delegates were chosen but only thirty-seven signed the constitution. The convention was held Oct. 23 to Nov. 12, 1855. Thirteen of the delegates were natives of Southern states, ten of New York and Pennsylvania, eight of the Old Northwest*qv*, four of New England and two of foreign countries. On the basis of former politics, there were twenty-one Democrats, nine Whigs, four Republicans, two Independents and one Free Soiler*qqv*. Lane, an erstwhile popular sovereignty*qv* Democrat who posed as an administration spokesman, was chosen president.

The constitution was not unlike other organic acts in its provisions for the forms and functions of government. A resolution endorsing popular sovereignty, adopted by a majority of two, temporarily revived former political affiliations; the following day it was reconsidered and postponed indefinitely. Sections in the bill of rights prohibited slavery and declared invalid Negro indentures executed in other states. The service of free Negroes in the militia was prohibited, but the fundamental question of admitting them to Kansas was referred to the voters along with the constitution and a general banking law. On Dec. 15 the instrument was ratified, 1731 to 46; the banking law was approved; and a provision to exclude free Negroes was adopted by a majority of nearly three to one. A month later state officials, including Charles Robinson as governor, were chosen. Lane was dispatched to Washington to present Congress with a memorial petitioning admission. On March 4, 1856, the legislature assembled at Topeka and elected United States senators. The House of Representatives passed a bill July 3, 1856, to admit Kansas under the Topeka constitution; five days later the Senate substituted its own measure authorizing a constitutional convention. Practically, the movement terminated with senatorial rejection, although subsequent sessions of the legislature convened, the last on March 4, 1858.

[W. H. Stephenson, *The Political Career of James H. Lane.*] WENDELL H. STEPHENSON

Topographic Mapping of the United States (1600–1900). Early explorations along the coasts of North America (*see* Maps, Coastal) established the New World as a potential source of wealth to European nations. France had visions of a large-scale trade with the Indians. England was interested in establishing colonies and growing silk. Rumors of mines of precious metals were inviting, but the great incentive for exploring and mapping the interior of North America was the probability of finding a northwest passage[qv] to the Orient. The early penetration of the interior by Europeans, led by the French, yielded information which stimulated further exploration. Foremost among 17th-century explorers and observers in America was Samuel (Seur) de Champlain[qv], whose voyages into the interior by way of the St. Lawrence Valley and the Great Lakes from 1603 to 1632 resulted in several important maps and valuable journals. Further intelligence on the St. Lawrence and Acadia was compiled on maps drawn by Marc Lescarbot (1609). Reports were brought in by adventurous *voyageurs*[qv] such as Etienne Brulé, who penetrated the interior beyond Lake Huron (1618?). Jean Nicolet[qv] explored and mapped the interior (1634–35) in the interests of the fur trade[qv], as far west as Sault Ste. Marie, Green Bay and the Wisconsin River. As early as 1650 the five Great Lakes[qv] had been at least partially surveyed, and appeared for the first time on Sanson's map of that year. In 1673 Louis Jolliet[qv] and Father Marquette reached the Mississippi River. Jolliet's map of the river is probably the earliest survey based on actual knowledge. Daniel Greysolon DuLhut, a trader, explored the Sioux country beyond Lake Superior (1678–79) in the region of Mille Lacs, Minn. (*see* Duluth's Explorations). Jesuit and Recollect missionaries[qqv], devoted to the conversion of the Indians, introduced the compass and astrolabe into the interior; they drew maps and made detailed scientific reports on the physical features of the country and the inhabitants. The reports or *Relations* of the Jesuits[qv] (1632–73) are authentic, scholarly records of great value. In 1679 Jean Baptiste Louis Franquelin[qv] began to make maps of the French explorations in New France. These appeared between 1679 and 1684, when he climaxed his efforts on a great map which has been termed "the most remarkable of all the early maps of the interior of North America." Other cartographic records were made by the Baron Lahontan (1683) and by the Recollect missionary, Louis Hennepin[qv], the same year. Westward exploration by the English, Dutch and Swedish settlers along the Atlantic seaboard was limited by the natural barrier of the Appalachian Mountains, and by the French domination of the land beyond this barrier, as far west as the Mississippi River. However, many regional surveys and maps were made by colonial surveyors along the Atlantic seaboard during the 16th and 17th centuries. Two important surveys were made by Capt. John Smith; one of New England (1614) and one of Virginia (1608). The latter was improved and enlarged in 1673 by Augustin Herrman. Detailed maps of the various colonies were made to facilitate the settlement of disputes relative to overlapping boundary claims. Many of these maps were incorporated in the numerous geographical atlases then popular in Europe.

During the 18th century the mapping of the interior was advanced by several able cartographers of the French school. Foremost among these were Guillaume Delisle and Guillaume D'Anville. The former published numerous maps, but his great *Carte de la Louisiane,* 1718, was for many years the basis of all maps of the Mississippi River and the Far West. During the first half of the century maps of the coastal region, "The British Dominions in North America," were enlarged and improved by cartographers of the French, Dutch and English schools. Herman Moll (1729) produced the first postroad map of North America and in 1732 the first large-scale map of North America was published by Henry Popple, English cartographer. Three important maps published in 1755 had a pronounced effect on all later maps of the interior east of the Mississippi. The first was John Mitchell's map[qv] of the British and French dominions in North America. The second, by the colonial surveyor Lewis Evans[qv], treated the "Middle British Colonies." The third, by Joshua Fry and Peter Jefferson, mapped in detail the extensive lands claimed by Virginia, as well as part of Maryland and Pennsylvania. The Treaty of Paris (1763)[qv] activated the further mapping of the French and British claims in the interior. The British territory established by the treaty was surveyed in great detail by army engineers and officers attached to regiments stationed in North America. Prominent among these men were Thomas Hutchins, Phillip Pittman, Bernard Romans, John Stuart and Joseph Purcell. Their maps received widespread attention in Europe, and remained standard throughout the 18th century. The American Revolution emphasized the need of detailed topographic maps of all parts of the "Theatre of War in North America," from Newfoundland to Florida. The colonies were resurveyed, and improved road maps were made. The search for the northwest passage went on sporadically; a few hardy explorers investigated the territory west of the Mississippi. Franciscan monks from Lower California, led by Silvestre Velez de Escalante[qv] and Francisco Domínguez (1776–77), journeyed through New Mexico, Colorado, Utah and Arizona, recording their observations of the country. After the Definitive Treaty of Peace[qv] (1783) between the United States and Great Britain resulting in the birth of the United States, American maps began to appear. In 1784 Abel Buell, Connecticut printer and type-founder, produced the first map of the United States printed in this country, based on all available surveys. Other important American maps of this period were McMurray's map of the United States, 1784, which outlined the ten Jeffersonian states[qv] proposed to be laid out northwest of the Ohio River, and John Fitch's map of the Northwest, 1785. The first series of maps of the individual states appeared in Carey's Atlas of 1795. Discoveries made by the members of the Hudson's Bay Company in the north were recorded on Aaron Arrowsmith's[qqv] important map of the "Interior Parts of North America," 1795 *et seq.*

The purchase of Louisiana[qv] (1803) stimulated the surveying and mapping of the vast region beyond the Mississippi River. The expeditions made by Lewis and Clark[qv] (1804–6) resulted in the discovery of the first overland route to the Pacific. The military reconnaissances of Zebulon Pike[qv] (1805–7) resulted in valuable maps of Louisiana and New Spain. A group of enterprising fur-traders, headed by William Henry Ashley[qv] and Andrew Henry, launched several exploring expeditions which resulted in valuable contributions to the knowledge of the Far West. Under their direction Jedediah Smith[qv] made explorations between 1827 and 1829, and discovered a second overland route to the Pacific Ocean. Joseph C. Brown, leading a United States surveying expedition (1825–27), opened and mapped the Santa Fé Trail[qv]. The first good map of the river system between the Rockies and the Pacific was made by Capt. B. L. E. Bonneville[qv] on expeditions made between 1832 and 1836. The extensive surveys made by John Charles Frémont[qv] (1842–46) beyond the Rockies were incorporated on a map made by his cartographer, Charles Preuss, published in 1848. Capt. Bonneville was one of the first of a long list of military engineers, surveyors and geologists working in the field during the first half of the 19th century. Throughout this period, map publishers exerted themselves to keep up with the new discoveries made by explorers and surveyors. Among the more prominent publishers were Samuel Augustus Mitchell, John Melish, Henry Schenk Tanner and John Disturnell[qv]. In 1853 an act was passed by Congress which aimed to co-ordinate the various government mapping agencies in an effort to survey all possible railroad routes from the Mississippi River to the Pacific Ocean. Four expeditions entered the field, two under the direction of the War Department and two under the direction of the Department of the Interior, making familiar the names of Hayden, King, Powell and Wheeler, their leaders. Five routes were surveyed over a period of seven years. A voluminous report, accompanied by maps, gave a scientific analysis of the country, but the expense of the field work and publications made imperative further economy and co-ordination. (*See also* Emory's Military Reconnaissance; Marcy's Exploring Expedition; Stevens' Railroad Survey.) It was to this end that the United States Geological Survey[qv] was inaugurated by an act of Congress on March 3, 1879. The agency has functioned continuously since that date.

[Justin Winsor, *Narrative and Critical History;* Archer B. Hulbert, *Overland to the Pacific;* Charles O. Paullin, *Atlas of the Historical Geography of the United States;* Wm. R. Shepherd, *Historical Atlas;* U. S. Engineer Dept., U. S. Army, *Report upon United States Geographical Surveys West of the 100th Meridian.*]

LLOYD A. BROWN

Tordesillas, Treaty of (1494). The discovery of America by Christopher Columbus raised a question of claims of Spain and Portugal, respectively, to the newly discovered regions. Pope Alexander VI, a Spaniard, settled the dispute by a series of papal bulls in 1493, which awarded to Spain exclusive dominion and sovereignty over all lands not already belonging to any other Christian prince, discovered and to be discovered "west and south" of a line to be drawn from the North Pole to the South Pole, 100 leagues west of the Azores and Cape Verde

Islands. All lands to the east and south of the demarcation line were to go to Portugal. The kings of Portugal and Spain subsequently agreed by the Treaty of Tordesillas to shift the demarcation line to a point 370 leagues west of the Cape Verde Islands. This treaty received papal approval in 1506. Though the treaty line never was surveyed, in effect it cut off a big eastern triangle of South America. Northern Brazil very roughly derives its claims to sovereignty from the Portuguese share of this ancient treaty.

[Frances Gardiner Davenport, *European Treaties Bearing on the History of the United States and Its Dependencies to 1648.*]

SAMUEL FLAGG BEMIS

Tories. *See* Loyalists, or Tories.

Tornadoes and Cyclones. Lexicographers make no clear distinctions between hurricanes[qv], tornadoes and cyclones; but common practice in America has made the hurricane a marine or West Indian gale, the tornado or cyclone a land storm, usually a gigantic whirlwind. This type of storm has been most prevalent in the mid-Western prairie states and in parts of the South. Destructive winds have often occurred in the East, but the whirling or cyclone type has been very rare east of the Alleghenies. Benjamin Silliman, the scientist, observed one, however, near New Brunswick, N. J., in 1835. The life of a cyclone may be only a few minutes or an hour or so. That which assailed Little Rock, Ark., on Oct. 2, 1894, lasted only three minutes, but in that time did a million dollars' damage, killed four persons and injured many. A cyclone is therefore known usually by the name of one town where it does its worst execution—as, the Grinnell, Iowa, cyclone of 1882, which destroyed nearly all of the town, including the buildings of Iowa College, and killed more than 100 people. Kansas was perhaps the most frequent sufferer from these storms in the 19th century, and it became common practice for farmers and villagers to construct cyclone cellars apart from the dwelling, stoutly roofed and covered with earth, in which the family took refuge when menacing clouds were seen. All the prairie states, including Wisconsin, Illinois and Indiana, have been attacked by these fatal and destructive storms. Early in the 20th century Alabama and Mississippi suffered so much from them that cyclone cellars were built in many neighborhoods. Only rarely have cyclones attacked large cities. St. Paul was considerably damaged by one in 1904. Another killed 170 persons, injured more than 250 and did great damage in Omaha on March 23, 1913. On the evening of March 27, 1890, a tornado passed through Louisville, causing the deaths of more than 100 and destroying many large buildings, including the Union Railway Station. Far more destructive was the cyclone which tore through the south-central portion of St. Louis on the afternoon of May 27, 1896, killing 400 persons, injuring 1200 and inflicting enormous property damage. It crossed the Mississippi River, wrecking a number of steamboats and a part of the city of East St. Louis. On March 18, 1925, a cyclone crossed southern Illinois from Missouri to Indiana, leaving 830 dead and 3800 injured in its wake. Two such storms developed in Georgia in 1936 within four days' time: on April 2 Cordele and on April 6 Gainesville were stricken, with great property losses. At Gainesville 185 were killed and more than 1700 injured.

ALVIN F. HARLOW

Toronto. *See* York (Toronto), Capture and Destruction of.

Torpedoes and Torpedo Boats. The torpedo, the name given by Robert Fulton to an enclosed mass of gunpowder designed to be exploded under hostile vessels, was first invented by David Bushnell of Connecticut. In 1776 Bushnell attempted unsuccessfully to destroy the British warship *Eagle* in New York harbor with a torpedo attached to a hand-propelled submarine[qv]. He made two other attempts against British ships, both unsuccessful. On Aug. 11, 1801, Robert Fulton, who had endeavored to interest Napoleon in torpedoes and submarines, blew up a sloop in Brest harbor, the first vessel ever sunk with a torpedo. In 1805 he destroyed the brig *Dorothea* in England with a torpedo and another vessel was sunk in New York harbor in 1807. Although Fulton failed to interest the United States Navy Department in his plans for harbor defense with torpedoes, his various experiments nevertheless stimulated private enterprise to design torpedoes with which the British blockading fleet was harassed throughout the War of 1812. On June 21, 1813, a line of defensive torpedoes was laid across the Narrows in New York harbor. Samuel Colt in 1842 made several successful experiments at New York and Washington in exploding torpedoes by electricity.

During the Civil War both sides devised many types of torpedoes; the spar, or outrigger; the towing, floating, or anchored, the latter now generally called submarine mines. These torpedoes were responsible for destroying twenty-two Union vessels and six Confederate. The first successful self-propelled torpedo was invented in

1866 by Robert Whitehead, an Englishman. Many other inventions followed.

The torpedo boat, a small, very fast craft, was designed to carry the mobile torpedo. The *Alarm* and the *Intrepid,* both built in 1874, were the first American torpedo boats. During the World War the United States manufactured over 150 torpedoes a month. A torpedo repair station at Queenstown, Ireland, was maintained for destroyer use.

The modern torpedo is cigar-shaped, weighs about three thousand pounds, has about a six-mile range, is equipped with steering apparatus, balance chamber, engines run with compressed air, rudders and propellers, and carries a charge of trinitrotoluol.

[R. B. Bradford, *History of Torpedo Warfare;* J. S. Barnes, *Submarine Warfare, Offensive and Defensive;* William Hovgaard, *Modern History of Warships.*]

LOUIS H. BOLANDER

Torrens System, THE, provides for the registration of titles to land instead of deeds or conveyances of land. Title searches are made by the Government instead of by private abstractors and attorneys and when the title is registered it is insured. Thereafter no title search is necessary and the heavy expense for abstracts under the old system of deed registration is ended. First adopted in Australia, the system has been introduced since 1895 into nineteen American states, but is used very little except in Massachusetts, Illinois, Minnesota and California. The high initial cost of title registration has delayed its wider use.

[D. D. Gage, *Land Title Assuring Agencies in the United States;* H. Russell and A. Bridewell, Systems of Land Title Examination; in *Journal of Land and Public Utility Economics,* Vol. XIV.]

PAUL WALLACE GATES

Torreys' Trading Post was established by Torrey Brothers, George Barnard and others, in 1843, eight miles southeast of the present Waco, Texas. Sam Houston probably owned an interest in it. It was designated by the government of the Republic of Texas[qv] as Trading Post Number Two. Many Indian councils were held there, for it was the main point of contact between the Texan government and the Indians. It lost its importance after Barnard's trading post was established near the present Fort Spunky, in 1849.

[John K. Strecker, The Chronicles of George Barnard . . ., in *The Baylor Bulletin,* Waco, Texas, September, 1928, 5-8.]

RUPERT N. RICHARDSON

Torture among Indians falls under three main heads: (a) ordeals to test guilt, endurance, or bravery; (b) self-torture to win the sympathy of the gods; and finally (c) the torture of captives. Ordeals to determine guilt were weakly developed among the Indians of the United States, but self-torture to win the favor of the supernatural was common. Fasting and abstaining from drink for four days was a common and widespread practice. Then a finger or two might be cut off as an offering to the gods. Bits of flesh, cut away one after the other, were supposed to be highly acceptable to the gods. However, the extreme form of self-torture was practised by the Plains Indians in drawing cords through the flesh and hanging the supplicant to a post until the flesh gave way, first described by George Catlin in 1832.

The colonists found among the Indians of eastern United States an elaborate method of torture for captives. If the captive did not cry out with pain he thereby shamed his captors. In this sense it was an ordeal. White captives were subject to the same tortures. When brought home, all captives ran the gauntlet[qv], but this was preliminary to the real tortures. Lengthy descriptions of such tortures, observed and experienced, are given in the literature of the colonial period. Fingernails were torn off, hair pulled out, firebrands held to the skin, fingers twisted off, sex organs mutilated and finally burning at the stake. Such tortures led to retaliation, and account for some of the atrocities of the whites in Indian warfare.

[R. G. Thwaites, ed., *The Jesuit Relations and Allied Documents,* Vols. XXX, pp. 241-5; XXI, pp. 31-51; XXXIX, pp. 61-77.]

CLARK WISSLER

Totem Poles are tall tree trunks erected in front of their houses by the coast tribes of Indians between Sitka and Puget Sound. Upon the front of these columns, conventionalized representations of animals, birds, fish and human beings are carved in relief, their character emphasized by painting. These carvings symbolize the family histories of the persons dwelling in the house, their mythical ancestors in particular. A similar series of carvings may be found upon the interior massive posts supporting the roof of the house. Wooden columns similar to totem poles were raised over graves as monuments, or memorials. Most of the aboriginal totem poles have disappeared, but in Indian cemeteries carved marble monuments take the place of the former memorial columns. Totem poles were in use when these Indians were first discovered, but the introduction of metal tools gave this art a new impetus, reaching its maximum about 1850.

[William H. Halliday, *Potlatch and Totem;* J. R.

Swanton, *Contributions to the Ethnology of the Haida*, Chapters IX and X, *Memoir* of the American Museum of Natural History, Vol. V, Part I.]

CLARK WISSLER

Toulouse, Fort, an important fortified French trading post on the Coosa River near Wetumpka, Ala., is said to have been built by Bienville in 1714. After the territory was ceded to the English in 1763 (*see* Paris, The Treaty of, 1763) the post was abandoned. It was repaired and rechristened Fort Jackson during the Creek Wars*qv*. Jackson there signed the treaty of peace with the Creeks, Aug. 9, 1814.

[Thomas M. Owen, *History of Alabama*.]

HALLIE FARMER

Touring. In the early days of motoring, around the beginning of the 20th century, the automobile*qv* was primarily a means of urban transportation. Only the more adventurous souls dared the perils of the open road, which included mudholes, irate farmers, lack of fuel supplies and other difficulties. Most of the touring in that era was done by groups of motorists, usually through the sponsorship of a motor club. With flimsy tires and undependable motors, breakdowns were frequent and to the motorists' other trials was added the discomfiture of hearing the bystanders' favorite jeer: "Get a horse!"

Gradually, as improved roads were provided, the touring horizon widened. The day's run into the country became a week-end trip, and finally lengthened into a journey lasting a fortnight or longer. As more and more people became car owners, the annual tide of touring became a veritable migration, leading first into New England, then to Florida, then to Michigan and Wisconsin, and last of all toward the West. Transcontinental travel developed very slowly, due largely to the inadequate roads. Even so late as 1928, travel experts were telling motorists about to start on a transcontinental journey to carry a shovel, tow rope, fuel cans, plentiful supplies of food and water and other paraphernalia.

By 1929 automobile vacationing had become a great national pastime. A fine nation-wide system of roads, ample accommodations at reasonable rates, a much more dependable vehicle, and a network of service facilities along the highway —all acting on the restless, nomadic spirit of the people—brought about the phenomenon of millions of people moving back and forth over the face of their land in search of new scenes and new surroundings. A good deal of the summer motor travel was beginning to push its way into Canada and a few tourists were crossing the border into Mexico. During the depression years following the Panic of 1929*qv*, travel fell off somewhat with tourist expenditures dropping rapidly as motorists sought more economical accommodations. With the return of better times, there was a tremendous resurgence of touring and by 1937 it had reached an amazing peak; one estimate placed the number of motoring vacationists in that year at 47,000,000 with their total touring expenditures in the neighborhood of four and a half billion dollars. More than 15,000,000 people visited the national parks and monuments, 4,500,000 cars traveled to Canada, 30,000 into Mexico, and several thousand cars were shipped abroad for vacation touring along overseas highways. Motor travel had become a national vacation habit.

[The Travel Industry, in *Development of American Industries*, Chap. 39; American Automobile Association, *Americans on the Highway*.]

RICHARD W. TUPPER

Tourist Camps began to appear in substantial numbers along the American roadside early in the 1920's. Usually comprising ten to fifteen cabins, each with two beds, the tourist camps took the place of automobile camps, where the motorist had to pitch his own tent and do his own cooking. Rates varied between $1 and $2 per person, with higher charges prevailing in the western part of the country. They were often run in conjunction with a restaurant and a filling station and catered to a large class of the traveling public unable or unwilling to patronize more expensive accommodations.

Estimates of the number of tourist camps in operation range between 15,000 and 20,000. The 1935 Census of Business surveyed 9848 tourist camps, which had a total of 10,011 active proprietors and 5812 full- and part-time employees, with an annual payroll of $2,465,000 and a total income of $24,300,000. With the advent of the house trailer*qv*, many camps provided special trailer facilities, such as water and electricity connections, while a number of camps catering exclusively to "trailerites" were established, in some cases by municipalities. Originally very crude affairs, many tourist camps have, since 1930, sought to attract the wayfarer by providing more inviting surroundings and more comfortable accommodations.

RICHARD W. TUPPER

Town Government, the most important local jurisdiction within the New England colonies and states, had its precedents in local authorities in rural England dealing with churches, poor relief, highways, schools and other neighborhood concerns. The founders of New England, actuated by their community of interests, settled compactly in villages surrounded by farms, meadows, pastures and woodland. They looked to the General Courts[qv] (the colonial legislatures) for recognition or incorporation of these villages and their environs as towns, privileged to enjoy local autonomy and to be represented in the legislature, usually securing these town privileges only after a probationary period as "plantations." Sometimes a second church "gathered" within a community became the nucleus of a new town; often discontent with local conditions led to a group exodus or petition for a separate incorporation. Most of the adult male inhabitants assembled in town-meetings[qv] to discuss and decide public business, levy taxes, and elect local officials, the most important of whom were the selectmen[qv] who administered affairs along lines determined in town meeting. Constables (peace officers) were elected, and provisions made for public education and local courts. "Town lands" at first were bought from the Indians or bestowed by the General Court upon "town proprietors"; later the legislatures sold colony lands for township sites to secure public revenue. Distributed according to decision in town-meeting, in equal division (sometimes by lot), or according to "ratable estates," or otherwise, early landholdings were sufficiently similar in value to encourage economic and political democracy within the towns. But in the 18th century speculation in "town rights" and town sites by proprietors, often nonresidents, introduced serious evils of absentee ownership[qv]. These proprietors, intent on financial gain, discriminated against settlers with no legal proprietary rights, excluding them from common lands, ignoring them in making new divisions, and seeking drastically to restrict their part in town meetings. Other inequalities, too, appeared. Nevertheless, the town governments retained much of their vitality and on the eve of the Revolution were notably effective in formulating and directing public opinion through Committees of Correspondence[qv] and by instructions to their representatives in the colonial legislatures.

Early in the 19th century President Jefferson felt "the foundation of Government" shaken under his feet "by the New England townships" which relentlessly opposed his Embargo[qv] policy. Impressed by the effectiveness of New England town government, Jefferson advocated a similar form of "elementary republics" to make every man feel "that he is a participant in the government of affairs." But later in this century the industrialization and urbanization of much of New England, and the influx of European immigrants, difficult to assimilate, greatly impaired the community of interests characteristic of the earlier towns. Throughout New England, however, town government survived, although losing some of its functions to larger local jurisdictions and somewhat modernized, as by the introduction of limited town meetings, advisory committees and town managers. Its continued importance is largely due to the fact that, in contrast to the practice in other sections where townships exist, the town government in New England functions as the chief local government for many villages and small urban communities as well as serving the surrounding rural districts. Sometimes claiming powers by long-established right, independent of current statutory provision, sometimes, on the contrary, dubbed "mere agencies of the state," the New England town may be justly termed "a quasi corporation . . . high in the scale of corporate life," which performs numerous services as a political subdivision of the state and at the same time manages corporate property of its own and regulates many matters of local concern.

[Tercentenary Commission of Connecticut Historical Publications, No. VI, *The Settlement of the Connecticut Towns;* J. T. Adams, *Revolutionary New England;* J. A. Fairlie and C. M. Kneier, *County Government and Administration.*]

LOUISE B. DUNBAR

Town Meetings, in their most highly developed form, are assemblies of the voters of the New England towns. With modifications they are reflected in the town and township meetings in the northern tier of central states where westward moving New Englanders carried their institutions with them. Faintly foreshadowed by vestry meetings in rural England, such assemblies are chiefly a product of conditions of settlement in the New England colonies. General participation in local government by the men who shared in the establishment of local settlements seems to have been taken for granted. A system soon developed in which the men dwelling in a town were generally accepted as town freemen regardless of requirements for the colony franchise, and even if they were not among the proprietors to whom the town lands were confirmed by the General Court[qv]. These men assembled in annual town meetings for the election of selectmen[qv], constables and other officers, and, upon due call, attended special town meetings. By majority vote at these assemblies town lands were distributed, local taxes levied, and action taken on other matters of local concern, such as town schools, roads, bridges, trainbands and the local church. Differences of opinion in these meetings were often acute and hotly argued, especially in the 18th century when profiteering proprietors sought to dominate the towns regardless of the nonproprietary interests. The controversial and critical faculties thus exercised were turned against British management of colonial affairs so conspicuously that the Parliamentary Act of 1774 (*see* Massachusetts Government Act) revising the government of Massachusetts decreed that no town meetings should be held without the royal governor's written permit except for election of town officers and representatives to the General Court. Nothing daunted, town meetings continued to voice protests against England and, after Independence, against such state and national policies as displeased any of them.

Despite 19th- and 20th-century factors which have tended to handicap town government (*see* Town Government), town meetings have continued to furnish to hundreds of communities open forums on local affairs. The town government's authority is greatest and town meetings best attended in New England, where they usually serve as the chief local government agency in villages and small cities as well as in rural portions of the townships. Although only qualified voters are summoned by the warrant which calls the meeting and specifies its business, inhabitants in general are admitted and sometimes participate in debate. A date in the spring is most usual for the annual meeting. Called to order by the town clerk, the typical town meeting proceeds to the election of a moderator (often honored by a long series of re-elections), then proceeds to the business stated in the "warning," or call for the meeting. Although some transactions may have been prearranged by informal caucus or special advisory or finance committees, the open discussion is often spirited and effective. Town business is so extensive as sometimes to require adjourned sessions of the annual meeting as well as occasional special meetings. Although fixed within certain limits by state law, it includes a wide variety of subjects, such as maintenance of schools, roads, bridges, waterworks, libraries, cemeteries, parks, poor relief, band concerts, public health, old-home week and the eradication of insect pests.

Some of the larger New England towns have provided "limited town meetings," restricted chiefly to elected members representing subdivisions of the town. In many sections, outside of New England, townships exist only as minor local units, without provision for town meetings. In New York, New Jersey and in more than half of the north central states town meetings are called but generally attract little interest, often being, in effect, only gatherings of township officials.

[J. A. Fairlie and C. M. Kneier, *County Government and Administration.*]

LOUISE B. DUNBAR

Townsend Plan, THE, or the Old-Age Revolving Pension, announced on Jan. 1, 1934, by its originator, Dr. Francis E. Townsend, speedily enrolled millions of supporters in one of the most astonishing social movements of the period. As embodied in a bill endorsed by Townsend the Plan provided that every person sixty years of age and over, who is a citizen of the United States and has been for at least five years, shall on application receive from the U. S. Treasury an annuity "not exceeding $200 per month," provided he "shall not engage in any gainful pursuit," and shall spend within the United States all of each month's annuity during the month it is received or five days thereafter. The $20,000,000,000 a year held by proponents of the Plan to be necessary in financing it is to be raised not by a tax on income or wealth, but by a "duty of 2 per centum upon the gross dollar value of each transaction done within the United States." In effect this would amount to a general sales tax of such proportions, say its critics, that wholesale inflation would result. The authors of the Plan regard it as no mere old-age pension but as a solution for virtually all our economic ills. "This is all we need," states Dr. Townsend, "to create a stabilized prosperity for all sections of the country. . . ."

Combining the American traditions of pressure politics, reform by monetary manipulation, and evangelical utopianism, the Townsend Plan was only one of several such movements produced by the social distress and insecurity following the Panic of 1929[qv]. Eventually it overshadowed the combined strength of all its rivals from Technocracy to Senator Long's Share-Our-Wealth organization[qqv]. Appealing largely to the lower middle class, the leaders defended the profit system as "the very mainspring of civilized progress," and denounced tendencies toward collectivism. Its disciplined voters were instrumental in electing to Congress several outspoken opponents of the New Deal[qv]. Among many benefits expected from their Plan, Townsendites include a balanced budget.

[House Resolution No. 4199 entitled General Welfare Act of 1937; pamphlet by J. W. Brinton, *The Townsend National Recovery Plan.*]

C. VANN WOODWARD

Townshend Acts, THE, take their name from Charles Townshend, Chancellor of the Exchequer and head of the British government at the time they were enacted. There were four acts and all were passed between June 15 and July 2, 1767.

The first, passed on June 15, suspended the New York assembly from further legislative activities until it complied with the provisions of the Quartering Act of 1765 (*see* Billeting) which required colonies to supply barracks, or other shelter; straw for bedding; cooking utensils; firewood for cooking and heating purposes; and the antiscorbutic ration of rum, cider or vinegar. Pontiac's Conspiracy[qv] had just occurred and had demonstrated the danger of leaving the army units scattered in small garrisons throughout the West where they could be attacked and destroyed in detail. Gen. Gage, commander in chief in America, decided to skeletonize the western garrisons and concentrate all available troops in central reserves to be dispatched to any place where they were needed. New York was selected as the best place for the reserves, and troops were ordered there, which imposed an unforeseen financial burden upon that province. Apparently the amount of expenditures would vary, not with the plans of the assembly, but with the whims of the commanding general. The New York assembly made its usual appropriation for a limited number of troops, but refused to appropriate for additional quarters in New York, especially as there was still ample room in the barracks at Albany. The Suspending Act forbade the assembly to carry on any other business until it had met fully the demands of Gen. Gage. As assemblies were summoned, prorogued, and dissolved by order of the governor, representing the crown, this assumption of authority on the part of Parliament created serious concern in America. It was a weapon that might be used to invade other American rights, and enforce other laws that the colonists considered unjust and unconstitutional.

The second and third acts were passed on June 29, 1767. One provided for an American revenue, and the other set up a special board in Boston to collect the revenue.

The Revenue Act levied import duties payable at American ports on white and red lead, painters' colors, various kinds of paper, glass of all kinds, and three pence a pound on tea[qv]. All of these articles were legally importable only from Great Britain. It was the second time in the history of the Empire that commercial regulations affecting the colonies had been adopted for revenue purposes. All other laws, except the Sugar Act of 1764[qv], had been for the purpose of protecting some industry within the Empire. For this reason men like Pitt, Burke, Trecothic and others assailed this law as anticommercial. Instead of encouraging British industry, it discouraged English manufacture, and by taxation encouraged a competing industry in the colonies or discouraged the use of the articles singled out for taxation.

The revenue arising from these new colonial taxes was to go first to the cost of collection, then to support an independent civil establishment in America—that is, judges, governors and other crown employees were paid from this fund instead of being dependent, as they always had been for their salaries, upon annual appropriations of the local assemblies. This use of the money struck at the very foundation of American political liberty. During the past half century the colonies had achieved almost complete local self-government through financial control of the royal officers. To put judges and governors beyond all local control, and at the same time make them dependent upon the Ministry for the tenure of their offices and their pay was to set up what many Americans considered despotic control.

Resistance to a program of political enslavement took the form of agitation, nonimportation agreements[qv], open evasion of the duties in some cases, promotion of American spinning, weaving, glass and paper industries, and open hostility to the enforcing officers.

The new taxes were to be collected by a Board of Customs Commissioners (the third act) stationed at Boston, which was given complete control over all customs in America. They were empowered to revise and reorganize the entire American customs; discontinue old or establish new ports of entry; appoint customs officers, searchers, spies; hire coast-guard vessels, provide them with search warrants, and in general do whatever seemed to them necessary to enforce the revenue laws.

Costs of this new and very costly establishment were to be paid out of the revenue and out of seizures. As the revenue law itself was unpopular and considered by the colonists unconstitutional, the enforcement officers met with resistance in some cases as in the seizure of the *Liberty* and the burning of the *Gaspee*[qv]. The real or fancied opposition led the customs commissioners to ask for troops, and large forces were hurried to Boston in September, 1768, where they were quartered in the city contrary to the Quartering Act. For more than nine months Boston was practically under military rule. There was friction between the people and the soldiers. The people of Massachusetts appealed to other colonies through protests and through *The Journal of the Times,* an ostensible day-to-day account of actual conditions in Boston. This was widely published in American and British papers. Most of the troops were withdrawn in 1769, but two regiments were left. One of these, the Twenty-ninth, was involved in the Boston Massacre^qv^, March 5, 1770, after which all troops were withdrawn. With the repeal of all duties, except those on tea in 1770, the controversy gradually quieted down, until aroused anew by the tea controversy and the Boston Tea Party^qv^ in 1773.

The fourth act repealed the inland duties on tea in England and permitted it to be exported to the colonies free of all British taxes (*see* Tea, Duty on).

It has been said that Townshend sought to raise a revenue in America by enforcing the Navigation Acts^qv^. Such statements are without foundation. The only navigation act that could yield a revenue was 25 Charles II which levied export duties on enumerated products^qv^ shipped from one British colony to another. This was purely regulative and only designed to prevent enumerated products being shipped to Europe in competition with the direct trade from England. The collections under this law after 1767 were not increased; for the fifteen years, 1749–63, the collections had averaged £1395 annually; and for the six years ending with 1774 under the Townshend Acts, they averaged only £778 per year—an actual decrease of more than £600 per annum under the Townshend Acts. The increased revenues came from the Sugar Act and from the Townshend Revenue Act.

[Edward Channing, *History of the United States.*]

O. M. DICKERSON

Township System, The, as provided for in the Ordinance of 1785^qv^, was an adaptation of a system of local governmental units involving a system of land survey, ownership and settlement. The term had been used rather vaguely in England. It was at one time a subdivision of a parish, with certain officers for the subdivision. The words town and township have been, and still are, much confused. In parts of New England a town is a subdivision of a county, likewise in Wisconsin. In other parts of New England the county subdivision is called a township, as is the case over a large part of the country.

Our townships are, with a few exceptions, six miles square, divided into thirty-six square miles, called sections. The sections are numbered, beginning in the northeast corner from east to west, forth and back. In the "Seven Ranges"^qv^, surveyed under the Ordinance of 1785, the numbering of the sections begins in the southeast corner and runs from south to north for all tiers. Ohio has two tracts of townships five miles square.

The township came to be a basic unit in the land system of the country, but of just as much importance, it has become a basic unit of government. Each township, or each "town" (which may be more or less than the congressional township of thirty-six sections of land) is a unit of local government. Varying much from place to place, these local governments have important functions to perform respecting schools and roads, as well as in the more general matters of keeping the peace, and providing poor relief. These local units of government elect tax assessors, and in many states collect the taxes. In New England the town government^qv^ is more significant than the county^qv^. Over most of the country the town functions and responsibility are distinctly subordinate to those of the county. (*See also* Local Government; Political Subdivisions.)

[Thomas Donaldson, *The Public Domain;* B. H. Hibbard, *A History of the Public Land Policies;* Payson J. Treat, *The National Land System, 1785-1820.*]

BENJAMIN HORACE HIBBARD

Towson, Fort, first called "Cantonment Towson," was a frontier military post established by the United States about 1823 in the Indian country^qv^ on Red River, in the southeastern part of the present State of Oklahoma, and named for Col. Nathan Towson, for many years paymaster general of the army. Soon thereafter it was connected by military roads with Natchitoches, Fort Leavenworth and other frontier posts, but it appears to have been abandoned after the annexation of Texas in 1845^qqv^.

[Cardinal Goodwin, *The Trans-Mississippi West,* and John H. Fonda's Explorations in the Southwest, in *Southwestern Historical Quarterly,* Vol. XXIV; *American State Papers, Military Affairs, passim.*]

WALTER PRICHARD

Trace. *See* Buffalo Trails.

Tractor, The, is an agricultural machine which has been developed since the beginning of the 20th century. Because of the success in utilizing steam for transportation, men thought of applying power to agriculture. Although the Otto internal combustion engine of 1876 theoretically solved the problem of developing a tractor, it was not until shortly after 1900 that a successful engine operating on a movable frame was devised. By 1906 the building of tractors was a large-scale industry, and during the World War the business was further stimulated. In 1925 a small lightweight tractor was perfected for general use on small farms. And in the late 1920's the yearly value of tractors produced in the United States approximated $150,000,000. The evolution of concentration in business and the use of tractors in other than agricultural pursuits have done much to increase the scope of the industry. In agriculture there are certain advantages commonly given for widespread use of tractors. These factors are: a reduction of necessary work stock; a decrease of hired help; a larger farmed acreage; and, an increase of crops. However, size of the farm, type of soil, topography of countryside, and extent of fields are all considerations in the possible use of the tractor.

[Cyrus McCormick, *The Century of the Reaper;* U. S. Dept. of Agriculture, *Farmers' Bulletin,* Nos. 1295-1300.]

BENJAMIN F. SHAMBAUGH

Tracts. Colonial newspapers*qv* contained little more than a rehash of European news; also, most early newspapers consisted of but four pages which made it impossible to publish extensive essays—hence the prevalence of political, religious and social tracts from the 17th century to the Civil War. Tens of thousands were issued and eagerly read, many of them being of great importance in shaping public opinion, social conduct and political action. Many of them were controversial, espousing the cause of a certain sect or political party, as Roger Williams' *G. Fox digg'd out of his Burrowes,* 1676; Thomas Paine's *Common Sense*qv and *The Crisis*qv, 1776. Some were used as a means of personal attack, as Isaac Hunt's *A Humble Attempt at Scurrility,* 1765; others were aimed at social reform, including such subjects as slavery, temperance, rights of women, attacks on the theater, card playing and dancing. Tracts reappeared as propaganda literature of the World War. Many long series of noncontroversial religious tracts were issued by the American and New England Tract Societies.

[M. C. Tyler, *History of American Literature.*]

R. W. G. VAIL

Trade, Boards of. *See* Chambers of Commerce.

Trade, Domestic. One difficulty which confronted every new community in the United States was to find something to ship beyond its confines which other communities wanted. Until after 1860 hundreds of settlements scattered over the country were faced with this problem. Thus, in the early years, much of the trade which we call domestic was within towns, villages and growing cities. Trade is based on differences in products and services. Differences of some description must exist for commerce to move. But another factor of great importance is required. This is transportation*qv*. In the commercial development of this country the most significant additions to our trade facilities have been the improvement of waterways, the building of railways, and since 1900 the enormous extension of surfaced roads*qqv*. Widened markets made possible higher prices for the products of forest, fields and mines, while at the same time they made lower prices for goods brought into the communities in return for products shipped out. Improved transportation brought about growing specialization in goods in which the communities had advantages; at all times the favored conditions of domestic trading, unhampered by duties, or other forms of taxes, gave this country an unusual opportunity for the development of its domestic trade. In short, a great free market was open to manufacturers and merchants everywhere.

A few examples will illustrate the importance of adequate means of transport. The Great Lakes region has become one of the most important markets of the country. Prior to the opening of the Erie Canal*qv* in 1825 this was one of our most inaccessible regions. Before that date, wheat from western New York was shipped down the Susquehanna River to Baltimore as the cheapest route. According to a report to the legislature of New York in 1817 the cost of shipment from Buffalo to New York City was $100 a ton, which was three times the usual market value of wheat, six times that of corn, twelve times that of oats. With the opening of the canal the rates to New York ranged from $5.00 to $13.00, and by 1852 from $3.00 to $7.00, depending on the season of the year and the conditions of the traffic. At any time from the first settlement of the interior to about 1825 the charge for transporting a ton of merchandise from Philadelphia to Pittsburgh was from $100 to $150. Before 1817 it cost as much to bring a similar weight upriver from New Orleans. Flatboats*qv*, which were the usual means of conveyance before the advent of the steamboat, were unable to return upstream. Hence, northbound trade was carried in keelboats*qv*, operated by man power. These devices had only a small capacity for freight, and the voyage was intermittent.

The steamboat*qv*, introduced on the Ohio-Mississippi system in 1811, brought relief from these difficulties. A writer of the times estimated the importance of the new facility in the following terms: "It has contributed more than any other single cause, perhaps more than all other causes combined, to advance the prosperity of the West." This statement was borne out by the facts.

The history of domestic commerce has been characterized by the successive opening of new markets. The earliest trading areas[qv] were along the north Atlantic seaboard. Cereals and flour were of some importance in inter-regional trade, with the Middle Colonies being the chief sources of production. In addition to a small export, and to a demand to meet the sailor's trade, limited quantities were sold in New England, and to some extent in the Southern areas. While the fish and lumber and timber products of New England, the tobacco of Virginia, and the rice and indigo[qqv] of Carolina were destined mainly for foreign export they provided the means for purchase of a considerable variety of foreign goods which subsequently became articles of domestic trade. Meanwhile, even in the early years of settlement, some seaboard communities enjoyed trade with the natives which, from their point of view, was important, because it supplied furs[qv] and skins, unique products for export. In the course of time this trade became an important branch of domestic enterprise, and it continued to grow in significance until about 1860. At one time St. Louis was the fur-trading center of a region which ultimately comprised practically all the country west of the Mississippi River to the Pacific. In 1763 Albany and Philadelphia were still fitting out places for trade with the Indians of the interior. Meanwhile, the leading Atlantic cities were becoming the source of supply of hardware and dry goods distributed over the entire interior.

A second important market to receive development was along the Ohio River south of Pittsburgh. This city, along with Cincinnati and Louisville, became manufacturing centers. The output included various articles of iron and steel, machinery, engines for steamboats and for flour and lumber mills, boots, shoes, clothing, packing house and related products. The markets were mainly in the river towns as far south as New Orleans.

A third market area to come into prominence was along the Great Lakes. The introduction of steam navigation on these waters in 1819 and the opening of the Erie Canal were the major contributing factors. Canal transport provided an easy access to the interior not only for human beings but for their belongings. Great migrations moved into the areas which are now tributary to the lake cities. Farming, trading and manufacturing were developed to supply not only local needs, but demands in distant areas. Chicago, Cleveland, Toledo, Buffalo became the leading industrial and commercial cities—gathering points for commodities in the regions roundabout, and points of distribution for goods brought in from a wide area.

The marketing area west of the Mississippi was originally in the hands of merchants of St. Louis. Eventually, with the building of western railroads, Chicago became a competitor for this commerce, particularly in all the area west and north of the great bend of the Missouri River. Trade lines branched mainly in three directions; one to the southwest to the old Spanish town of Santa Fé, and eventually into old Mexico; to the mid-mountain area in the direction of Denver, which city became the marketing center for the new mining camps in Colorado; and to the Far West over the Oregon Trail[qqv].

The southern market, particularly east of the Mississippi, had received attention from merchants and manufacturers of the Ohio River cities as early as 1820. This trade was extended to cover not only the whole area east of the Mississippi but, after 1840, to the regions of Texas. With the development of manufacturing in the South, notably after 1880, with the growth of the lumbering industry, and after 1900 of petroleum production and refining, the whole South became a marketing region of great significance.

The development of trade with the Pacific received its earliest stimulus from the gold rushes, 1848 to 1860, and subsequently to the opening of the first transcontinental railroad in 1869 (*see* Union Pacific Railroad). After 1914 the opening of the Panama Canal[qv] was a further trade advantage. These developments caused an opening of the great nonferrous metal resources of the Rocky Mountains, the timber resources of the Northwest, and agriculture along the Pacific, notably citrus fruit in California and certain cereals in the north Pacific.

Although rather complete records have been kept of foreign commerce even from colonial days, little definite information could be obtained about domestic trade until the census of 1930. In this prior period we are able to obtain information here and there which indicates the magnitude and direction of growth. Commercial journals of the time contain scattered information which is sometimes helpful. We are informed from such sources that the trade of New Orleans with the interior, which had been about $8,700,000 in 1815, became $185,200,000 in 1860, and that about 1852 the total commerce of the Mississippi and its tributaries was about $339,500,000, and that the estimated value of the commerce of the Mississippi Valley was $653,900,000.

Since this was growth from almost nothing in 1790 it is a truly remarkable record of commercial expansion.

From such sources, also, we are informed that the trade west of the Mississippi expanded to considerable proportions, beginning shortly before 1860. In that year the total investment in the trade of the Plains, including wagons, teams, merchandise and wages of men, was estimated at $5,500,000. The merchandise shipped from Missouri River points was said to have been $10,000,000, of which the New Mexican trade took about $3,000,000, the Pikes Peak gold area about $6,000,000, the Utah trade about $500,000, and the remainder was trade with the Indians. Kansas City enjoyed the largest share of this commerce but found competitors in Leavenworth, Atchison, Nebraska City, St. Joseph and Omaha.

The rapid expansion of railroad building brought the whole country into one great market. The operated railway mileage was about 4000 in 1842; it became 30,600 in 1860 and 254,800 in 1934. This development was aided, notably with the lines west of the Mississippi, by Federal land grants[qv] and in some cases by guarantee of certain types of railroad bonds. Mainly since 1900 the development of interurban[qv] electric transport, and the building of surfaced roads, have added enormously to the facilities for moving passengers and freight. In 1930 the total mileage of rural roads was over 3,000,000, of which over 693,000 were surfaced.

The movements of commerce within this country are determined largely by regional specialization of industries, and this in turn is dominated by various factors which go to make up the advantages of carrying on enterprises within given areas. While practically every section contains manufactures of some description, the greater factory industries are in New England, Central Atlantic and Midwest sections. These, in 1929, reported upwards of 75% of the total manufactured values. Raw materials[qv] are obtained from many parts of the country and from abroad. The upper Mississippi Valley is the main source of foodstuffs, the mountain regions of the West of nonferrous metals, the Upper Lakes of iron ore, the South of cotton, lumber and petroleum, the Far West of citrus fruits, among other agricultural products, and of lumber and so on. This division of labor makes possible an extensive inter-regional trade.

The rank of revenue freight carried on our railroads is as follows: coal and coke, manufactured products, the output of mines other than coal, products of agriculture, products of forests, and various miscellaneous freight, all in all, some 2,341,000,000 tons as an annual average for the years from 1926 to 1930.

In 1929 the total distribution of goods at retail amounted to about $53,000,000,000. Of this about 25% was credited to the Middle Atlantic section, 22.9% to the East North Central (including Ohio, Indiana, Illinois, Wisconsin and Michigan), 10.7% to the West North Central (including Nebraska, Kansas, Missouri, Iowa, Minnesota and the Dakotas). New England took 7.7% of the total.

A summary of business in the United States when the census was taken in 1930 reveals the fact that the composition was as follows: manufactured values, $70,000,000,000; wholesale business $70,000,000,000; retail business, $53,000,000,000; value of farm products, $12,000,000,000; output of mines and quarries, $5,800,000,000; hotel business, $1,000,000,000. In addition various other enterprises which might be classified as commercial, such as investment and commercial banking, dealings in real estate, publishing and other information service, contributed large amounts to the total national turnovers.

Meanwhile, the commercial organization has constantly undergone diversification and expansion to meet changing conditions. Such commercial functions as banking in its various divisions, storage, insurance, industrial and commercial research, among others, have been in constant flux under the impact of new trade and industrial developments.

[John H. Frederick, *The Development of American Commerce;* Isaac Lippincott, *The Development of Modern World Trade.*]

ISAAC LIPPINCOTT

Trade, Foreign. The United States is probably less dependent on foreign trade than any other major trading country except, possibly, Russia. Yet this continent was stumbled upon by men seeking new trade routes, and from its first settlement to the present time some sections and some industries have derived much of their livelihood from exporting and importing. In the decade 1791–1800 foreign commerce averaged $106,000,000 per year; from 1926 to 1930 it averaged $8,811,000,000. Whether it provided a larger share of the national income in the first period than in the second probably cannot be determined; certainly the *per capita* figures help very little ($22.75 compared with $71.52) since the national income and the purchasing power of money in the two periods possess unknown disparities.

During the colonial period the only well-developed external trade was that along the Atlantic coast. The Spanish colonies in what is now the United States failed to yield the sought-for treasure and, sparsely settled, carried on only a small, fitful, and largely illegal foreign trade prior to 1800. Fur exports and simple imports to supply the scattered trading posts provided most of the foreign trade in French America. Under English rule fur exports declined and by 1770 amounted to less than $700,000 for all the North American colonies.

In keeping both with the frontier character of their economy and with the colonial system (*see* Mercantilism), the English colonies along the Atlantic coast early developed the export of foods and raw materials and the import of manufactured goods, molasses, slaves and sugar*qqv*. Exports to England occurred soon after settlement: the Pilgrims in 1621 shipped pelts and clapboards and in 1622 Virginia exported tobacco*qv*. The export trade of the Northern colonies was based on fish and whale products, timber and furs*qqv*. By 1765, 350 vessels were used in carrying the better-grade fish to Europe and the poorer grades to the West Indies. New England shipyards and Pennsylvania iron furnaces*qv* also supplied an export market. In the Southern colonies, tobacco was the chief export; cotton was not exported before 1790. In 1706, 300 ships were engaged in the tobacco trade. But in the Carolinas exports consisted largely of rice, indigo and naval stores*qqv* (the last named encouraged by Parliamentary bounty for fifty years after 1705). Manufactures were the most important import both in North and South; they comprised 81% of the total imports from Great Britain in 1768. But from the West Indies came molasses, sugar and rum*qv*; and from the East, directly or via Europe, came spices.

In the decade before the Revolution the foreign trade of the Southern colonies was more than double that of the Northern colonies, and was largely concentrated in the English market. In 1769 from 70% to 85% of Southern exports and from 60% to 90% of Southern imports were to or from Great Britain; while less than half the exports of New York and Pennsylvania and only a fourth of New England's went to England, and England supplied less than half of New York's imports, 40% of New England's, and a very small part of Pennsylvania's. The Northern colonies—and especially New England—chronically had an adverse trade balance with England which was usually settled by export surpluses with the West Indies and Europe. Trade with the English and foreign West Indies (*see* West India Trade; Slave Trade) was an essential link in the voyages of Yankee traders, and was vital to the fisheries, shipbuilding, and rum distilleries of the Northern colonies.

Throughout the colonial period American shippers and merchants carried on foreign trade largely without insurance protection from storms and piracy, and had to accommodate themselves to a constantly shifting mass of mercantilistic legislation which in the aggregate was probably a hindrance rather than a help. The Navigation Acts*qv*, to the extent that they were enforced, hampered the direct trade of the Northern colonies with the foreign West Indies and with Europe. The Molasses Act of 1733 and the Sugar Act of 1764*qqv* in particular put a premium on evasion. The relative moderation of the Stamp Act of 1766 was ended by the new duties imposed by the Townshend Acts in 1767*qqv*; renewed boycotts, particularly in the North, greatly reduced imports of English goods.

During the Revolution, American foreign trade shifted somewhat. Imports naturally increased from France, Holland and Spain despite heavy depredations by the British blockaders. American products even reached England in large quantities; but the trade with the British West Indies was handicapped by both war and law.

Probably the most difficult period in the history of American foreign trade was that from 1783 to 1815. American whale products were excluded from England, and the British West Indies market and carrying trade were closed. Had there been peace in Europe a satisfactory commercial understanding might have been reached with England much sooner. But the Napoleonic Wars subjected American commerce to war-risks in Europe (1500 American ships were seized, 1803–12) and to the restrictions of the Embargo and Nonintercourse Acts, 1807–10*qqv*. Exports declined from $108,000,000 in 1807 to $22,000,000 in 1808. The consequences were disastrous to the tobacco and growing cotton exports of the South and to New England shipping. The War of 1812*qv* added more troubles: the blackest year was 1814, when the carrying (re-export) trade was completely destroyed, and exports of domestic products were less than $7,000,000. However, recovery was abrupt in 1815, and by 1817 exports were again approaching $100,000,000.

From 1820 to 1860 United States foreign trade increased in both quantity and value; during the decade 1851–60 combined imports and exports averaged $533,000,000 annually. But foreign trade *per capita* declined during most of this period of forty years, and even in 1851–60 averaged less than in 1791–1800 ($18.26 compared with $22.75). Domestic development and population growth were rapid; external commerce was lagging. Exports were overwhelmingly composed of crude materials and foods—80% to 85% of the total before 1860—but finished manufactures increased from 6% in 1821 to 15% in 1860, a trend that was to continue almost without interruption down to the present time. Cotton was the largest export, absorbing about three-fourths of the crop; other exports included tobacco, grain, naval stores, hides, furs, leather, wool and fish. Imports consisted very largely of finished manufactures—45% to 57% of the total—and foods, although crude materials and semimanufactures increased from 15% of the total in 1821 to 25% in 1860, paralleling the growth in American manufacturing. Trade was increasingly with Europe; by 1860 that area accounted for three fourths of the exports and three fifths of the imports. As the European and, more modestly, the Canadian markets expanded, the old dependence on the West Indies lessened and in 1860 took less than a tenth of American exports and supplied only 13% of the imports. Average rates of duty declined from 49%, 1821–30, to 24%, 1851–60 (*see* Tariffs; Free Trade; Protection), but *per capita* figures do not reflect any very pronounced stimulus to foreign trade.

Between 1860 and 1915 American foreign trade increased approximately eight times in value ($4,000,000,000, 1911–15) while the trade *per capita* doubled. Under the influence of a shift in the creditor position of the United States, a net excess of exports developed, 1870–80, and has continued to the present, reaching the fantastic level of $3,000,000,000 per year from 1916 to 1920 (*see* Creditor Nation). On the whole, there were no major developments in the external commerce of the United States during this period which were not foretold by the trends visible before 1860. Exports of crude materials grew absolutely, but continued to lose ground relatively. Food exports gained relatively until 1885 and then began the decline which has continued down to the present (1939). In other words, the United States was becoming industrialized: exports of manufactures and semimanufactures were 20% of the total in 1871–75 and 46% in 1911–15. This shift in our domestic economy was hastened by increased tariffs and was reflected in the composition of our imports: crude materials and semimanufactures, largely destined to supply factory and mill, were 52% of the total by 1911–15, while finished manufactures had dwindled to 23%. These changes, coupled with our tariff policy, made inevitable a *relative* decline in the importance of Europe. Of our exports, 81% went to Europe in 1881–85; only 64% in 1911–15. As a supplier of imports Europe suffered a steady decline from the peak of 71% of total imports in 1850 to only 47% in 1911–15. Meantime, Asia, Canada and Latin America had made relative gains in our foreign trade. Large-scale wheat[qv] exports began about 1870 and until after the World War absorbed a third or more of the American crop. Cotton, grain, petroleum, animal products, tobacco, lumber, naval stores, copper and an increasingly important conglomeration of manufactures comprised the bulk of export trade. Foods and materials, largely tropical, were the typical imports: sugar, coffee and wool led the list, but imports of rubber, silk, paper and paper stock were increasing at a rate prophetic of their postwar importance.

The World War up-surge in American foreign trade to an annual average, 1916–20, of almost $10,000,000,000, financed largely by United States Government credits, needs no more than mention. It differed only in degree from our foreign trade in the postwar decade (notably 1926–30), also greatly stimulated by foreign loans (*see* Debts, Foreign). Prewar trends continued during and after the war. Almost 60% of our exports, 1926–30, consisted of manufactures (notably machinery and vehicles) and semimanufactures; by 1937 the percentage had increased to 75. Exports of cattle and meat had become unimportant as had grain exports except in years of large crops and low prices (e.g., 1937). Cotton exports continued large (45%–65% of the crop) but by 1934 began to feel the combined effects of domestic price policy and new foreign competition. Imports of finished manufactures further declined to 18% in 1937. Import trade is still (1940) characterized by foods and materials of great variety: in the period 1926–39 the leading imports were (in 1939 order) rubber, coffee, sugar, silk, newsprint, woodpulp, tin and wool; but they comprised only about one third of total imports. Europe's position continued to decline without interruption; by 1939 she accounted for only 40% of our exports and 27% of imports. Meantime the importance of rubber, silk, tin, etc., had lifted Asia to first place, 1939 (30%), as a source of imports, with North America (Canada, Cuba, Mexico) third (25%) and South America fourth (14%). With Europe still first as an export market, North America was second (25%), Asia third (18%) and South America fourth (10%).

Foreign trade has probably declined somewhat in importance since 1900. In 1899 an estimated 13% of our exportable production was actually exported, by 1929 the percentage was about 10, by 1937 about 7½. In this latter year an estimated 2,400,000 persons, or only 5½% of the total gainfully employed, were engaged in some phase of export trade. But many sections of both agriculture and industry export from 15% to 65% of output (e.g., cotton, tobacco, lard, sardines, linseed, pears, dried fruit, canned fruit, naval stores, lubricants, sulphur, copper, office appliances, aircraft, etc.).

Beset by increased tariffs, exchange restrictions, rapidly changing domestic policies and exclusive trade arrangements abroad, the foreign trade of the United States in the depression years 1931–35 averaged only 45% of the 1923–25 value and 75% of its quantity. Under the stimulus of a program of reciprocal trade agreements*qv* and considerable domestic and world business recovery, our external commerce displayed encouraging recovery in the years 1936 to 1939.

[Harry J. Carman, *Social and Economic History of the United States;* Emory R. Johnson, T. W. Van Metre, C. G. Huebner, D. S. Hanchett, *History of Domestic and Foreign Commerce of the United States;* Department of Commerce, *Foreign Trade of the United States* (annual); National Industrial Conference Board, *Trends in the Foreign Trade of the United States.*]

FRANK A. SOUTHARD, JR.

Trade, Triangular. Unlike the tobacco and sugar colonies, the mainland English colonies north of Maryland did not, from their beginnings, have great staple products readily exportable directly to England in exchange for European goods. Yet, in order to maintain their accustomed European standards of living and to support an expanding economy, their relatively heavy populations demanded large imports of European manufactured wares—hardware, kitchen utensils, furniture, guns, building materials, farm tools, textiles, etc. Thus, from earliest times their imports from England exceeded their direct exports to England; moreover, after 1660, many of their exportable surpluses—fish, cereals and meats—were forbidden in England. As they were unable or forbidden by law to manufacture their needs in the colonies, they were forced to balance their trade by engaging in complex trading enterprises, to dispose of diversified surpluses in non-English markets in order to provide purchasing power in England. One such means to redress the unfavorable English trade balance was the Triangular Trade, sometimes called the "three-cornered," or "roundabout," trade.

The Triangular Trade did not conform to a constant mercantile pattern. In its simplest form, near the mid-18th century, its three "corners" were, in sequence: a port in the Northern colonies (most commonly Boston or Newport, R. I.), the Gold Coast of Africa, a port in the West Indies (often Kingston, Jamaica), and thence home. For example, the brigantine *Sanderson* of Newport sailed (March, 1752) with a crew of nine and a cargo of 8220 gallons of rum*qv*, some short iron bars ("African iron," used as currency among African natives), flour, pots, tar, sugar, shackles, shirts, provisions and water. Reaching Africa, the cargo was exchanged for 56 slaves*qv*, 40 ounces of gold dust and about 900 pounds of pepper. Proceeding to Barbados (June 17, 1753), the captain sold the slaves at £33 to £56 per head and disposed of the gold dust and pepper—with net proceeds of £1324. Of this, £911:17s. was spent for 55 hogsheads of molasses and 3 hogsheads, 27 barrels of sugar; the remainder due the captain was paid in bills of exchange drawn upon Liverpool. The *Sanderson* then returned to Newport.

Cargoes, routes and ports varied. Though the main cargo on the first leg was generally rum and "African iron," it sometimes consisted of cloth or trinkets; the chief cargo on the second leg of the voyage—famous as the horrible "middle passage"*qv*—was slaves, but occasionally it consisted of gold dust, condiments, ivory, or wines purchased en route at the Wine Islands, Spain, or France; and on the homeward voyage, besides molasses and sugar, salt, wines, condiments, cotton, dyewoods, rice, tobacco, silver, bills of exchange and slaves occasionally made up the cargo—any wares, in fact, that could be used at home or sold in England. Another variant of the trade ran as follows: a New England, New York, or Philadelphia vessel carried fish, tobacco, or lumber to Lisbon, Cadiz, Gibraltar, or other Mediterranean ports, exchanged the cargo for European goods, traded in the West Indies for molasses, sugar, silver, or bills of exchange, and returned home.

Roots of the Triangular Trade extended into early Massachusetts commerce, though the trade itself did not flourish until after 1700. In the 1640's New England sales of fish and lumber in Spain and concurrent commerce with the West Indies must have suggested the "roundabout" trade; and in the 1650's New England vessels engaged directly in the African slave trade*qv*. But the monopoly of the Royal African Company*qv* (1672–97) closed to colonial vessels legal slave trade to the West Indies. Meanwhile, New England trade with the sugar colonies reached enormous proportions, and the uses of rum in the Indian trade and in the fisheries came to be widely recognized. Twenty-five years after Parliament threw open the slave trade (1697), rum—increasingly of New England origin—displaced

French brandy in the African slave trade. Rum distilleries arose everywhere in New England after about 1700; Newport alone had twenty-two in 1730, Massachusetts had sixty-three in 1750. To a lesser extent they also developed in New York and Philadelphia. By 1770 three fourths of the imports from the West Indies to Northern colonies consisted of rum, molasses and sugar. After 1715 much of these derived illegally from the French sugar islands, giving rise to English demands for the widely ignored Molasses Act of 1733 and the revolution-provoking Sugar Act of 1764[qqv]. The importation of rum's baser cane equivalents and the growth of distilleries in the colonies were in direct proportion to the growth of the Triangular Trade.

Centered in New England, principally at Newport and Boston, the Triangular Trade extended to New York and Philadelphia, engaged hundreds of vessels before the Revolution, mostly small ships of 100 tons or less. Prominent merchants, notably Peter Faneuil of Boston, took the lead in the business, sold countless slaves in the West Indies, whence most were distributed to Spanish colonies, some to New England, New York, Philadelphia and the Southern mainland. Profits arising from the trade not only materially assisted to balance the colonies' trade with England (adverse to the extent of £1,232,000 in 1770), but also accumulated great private capital surpluses in the colonies, capital of great value in developing subsequent American business enterprise.

[William B. Weeden, *Economic and Social History of New England, 1620-1789;* Emory R. Johnson, T. W. Van Metre and others, *History of Domestic and Foreign Commerce of the United States;* C. P. Nettels, *The Roots of American Civilization;* Edward Channing, *A History of the United States*, Vol. II.] RAYMOND P. STEARNS

Trade Acts. *See* Navigation Acts.

Trade Agreements. *See* Reciprocal Trade Agreements.

Trade and Plantations, Board of. *See* Board of Trade and Plantations.

Trade Areas (or trading areas) are the geographical territories from which an individual seller or group of sellers draws customers. The size and contour of a trading area depends primarily on the facilities for transportation and communication. A secondary factor is the willingness of the buyer to expend time and energy in satisfying his wants; this varies according to the kind of commodity, and is generally greater with shopping or industrial goods than with conveniences. In colonial days and the first half of the 19th century, when roads were few and bad, trade areas were small, even for cities on the seacoast or a navigable river. The country general store[qv] in a small village might have a virtual monopoly of trade in its neighborhood.

The railroads and newspapers widened trade areas, and were largely responsible for the rise of department stores[qv] after the Civil War. Wholesalers usually had wider trade areas than retailers. Some manufacturers regarded the whole country as their market areas. This was also true of the mail-order houses[qv] after the improvement of post office service toward the close of the century.

The automobile, together with paved roads, widened still further the trading areas of retailers in the larger cities and towns, and thus had a centralizing tendency. By 1929 between 600 and 700 municipalities were regarded as important shopping centers. The mail-order houses were constrained to open branch stores in many of these. Later the volume of traffic and the acute parking problem lessened the advantage of metropolitan retailers. Some department stores opened branches in the suburbs, and after 1930 super markets[qv] arose on the outskirts. In recent years much research has been devoted to the definition and analysis of retail and wholesale trade areas, and the study of market areas for manufacturers. Since these seldom conform to city or state lines, the county is the usual unit in charting areas.

[H. E. Agnew, R. B. Jenkins, J. C. Drury, *Outlines of Marketing;* G. B. Hotchkiss, *Milestones of Marketing.*] G. B. HOTCHKISS

Trade Association, THE, in the United States is a generic term that refers to associations of business firms, or their owners and managers, formed in a wide variety of ways and for a wide variety of purposes, although the general object of such associations is to increase the profits of their members. The basis of the trade association lies in the common commercial interests of firms in the same line of business, or of firms in different lines but closely related geographically or in some other way. In the United States modern trade associations began to appear by the middle of the 19th century, though they did not achieve much importance before 1900. The "co-operative competition" and "open price" movement in the second decade of the 20th century, together with the World War, greatly stimulated their formation, as did the passage of the National Recovery Act in 1933[qv].

Trade association activities include such diverse matters as the pooling of credit information, the standardization of products and practices, co-operative advertising and publicity campaigns, and the formation of a united body to bargain with trade unions, railroads and insurance companies^qqv^. Less defensible, perhaps, are the long series of actions taken by trade associations to manipulate the market through coordinated price policies and terms of sale. Many such practices have brought the associations into conflict with the antitrust statutes^qv^, and from one point of view their history is a history of decisions made under these statutes. The movement for "self-government in industry" generally assumes that trade associations or similar bodies will be the means by which this goal will be reached.

[S. N. Whitney, *Trade Associations and Industrial Control;* J. H. Foth, *Trade Associations: Their Service to Industry.*]

CHARLES C. ABBOTT

Trade Commission, Federal. *See* Federal Trade Commission.

Trade Dollar. A special type of silver dollar, weighing 420 grains instead of the standard 412½ grains, was created by the currency law of 1873, ostensibly to encourage trade with China, but more probably to provide a market for domestic silver producers (*see* Crime of 1873). The trade dollar was not excluded from another provision in the law making all silver coins a legal tender^qv^ to $5. Monetary historians have uniformly declared this to have been an inadvertence. It was more probably done with design.

The total coinage was 36,000,000. The bulk of these went to China, but at least 6,000,000 were forced into circulation in this country, despite the fact that after 1876 they were no longer legal tender, and for several years were not even redeemable; while their bullion value was considerably less than one dollar. In many cases they were bought at a discount and paid out at par to ignorant immigrant laborers who were forced to take the loss. At the same time the silver interests resisted government redemption of the coins, as such redemption would have resulted in the Government using the silver for small change and thus, to that extent, limiting the market for new silver. Coinage of the trade dollar was stopped in 1878 and in 1887 redemption was authorized. Some 8,000,000 pieces in the hands of speculators and banks were redeemed. Of these probably 2,000,000 were brought back from China.

[N. Carothers, *Fractional Money.*]

NEIL CAROTHERS

Trade Journalism. Early New York, Boston and Philadelphia newspapers supplied shipping news, commodity prices and bank note tables. In 1795 the Boston *Prices Current* began as a legitimate business paper, although conservative papers continued commercial matter, and in 1822 the Boston *Columbian Centinel* printed market prices for stocks "corrected by two brokers weekly." Of a different sort were Hunt's *Merchant's Magazine* (1839) and Homan's *Banker's Magazine* (1853). Insurance and other fields soon supported their own journals.

After 1870 there was a trend toward specialization, and the modern trade journal appeared. Manufacturers of carriages, drugs, dry goods, hardware, shoes, tobacco and wines soon had periodicals, and after 1880 most other trades were represented. Rapid industrialization produced technical fields which needed such organs as the *American Machinist* (1880) and the *American Journal of Railway Appliances* (1884). The electrical industry brought forth a number of periodicals, as did also mining and oil production. After 1900 new techniques led to such magazines as *Food Industries, Radio Retailing* and *Bus Transportation.* Yet there was still room for the general business paper—e.g. *Industrial Management, System* and the *Magazine of Business.*

Advertising^qv^ was a principal inducement to founding such journals; and an eagerness for information in a new field was a publishing bonanza. Promotional material frequently subordinated editorials and mere reading matter. Some of this crudeness disappeared with greater maturity, or because of competition. Prosperity and expansion made it possible to hire first-rate writers, but a prejudiced point of view came to be associated with the term "trade journal." Able editors frequently wrote on general topics, and interpreted politics for "the trade." Their influence, judging from circulation figures, was considerable, though usually conservative. While often protesting their independence and freedom from commercial pressure, they could not remain unbiased. Furthermore, these papers have forwarded the trend to nation-wide standardization in both products and methods.

[Frederic Hudson, *Journalism in the United States;* F. L. Mott, *History of American Magazines;* J. H. McGraw, Business Papers Grow Up, in *Scribner's Magazine,* Vol. 87; F. Pratt, Cinderellas among Magazines, in *Sat. Rev. of Lit.,* Vol. 18.]

MILTON W. HAMILTON

Trade-marks have always been used by some makers of merchandise in the United States, as in other countries, particularly in fields requiring special skill or artistic merit. The mark might be either a signature or some distinctive symbol or label. As early as 1791 a Boston manufacturer petitioned Congress for the right to register his trade-mark and have it protected against imitation, but it was not until 1905 that a Federal act was passed conferring substantially these rights. In the meantime a number of state laws were passed to protect the public by regulation of marks on goods.

The demand for statutory protection of trade-mark rights was not keen in the first half of the 19th century. Many manufacturers sold only to a local market; others sold unidentified bulk goods which were accepted by consumers on the retailers' recommendation. But as large-scale production developed, and trade areas[qv] widened through the building of railways and the use of advertising[qv], the value of a distinctive trade-mark became greater as a means of securing repeat sales. Manufacturers who were subjected to the unfair competition of imitators sought redress under the common law. The earliest recorded case was in 1837. Altogether sixty-two trade-mark cases tried in the civil courts were reported in Cox's *American Trade-Mark Cases* published in 1871.

The first Federal act permitting trade-mark registration was passed in 1870. Registrations averaged less than 1000 per year for the first ten years, and never reached 2000 in any one year until 1902. The act of 1905 made registration of a trade-mark *prima facie* evidence of ownership. This fact, together with the great changes in marketing brought about by rapid transportation, advertising and the increased use of packaged goods[qv], stimulated greater activity in registering trade-marks, some of which had been in use for many years. In 1906 more than 10,000 marks were registered.

In 1860 the earliest American text on trade-marks, Francis H. Upton's *Treatise on the Law of Trade-marks,* had defined the trade-mark as a mark indicating origin or ownership, but later the conception broadened to include almost any nondescriptive mark of identification which served as a guide to purchasers. Thus a large proportion of modern trade-marks are arbitrary coinages of symbols or words. Some nationally known trade-marks have acquired a good-will value estimated in the millions of dollars, which has had to be protected by restraint of infringing marks. In recent years an increasing proportion of trade-marks have been those of wholesalers and large-scale retailers, the so-called "private brands"[qv].

[E. S. Rogers, *Good Will, Trade-Marks and Unfair Trading;* W. J. Derenberg, *Trade-Mark Protection and Unfair Trading.*]

G. B. HOTCHKISS

Trade Practices. Although the American colonies began with much the same methods of officially regulating trade that were customary in 17th-century England, internal trade was almost entirely freed of restrictions before the formation of the Federal Union. Thereafter for nearly a century competition in trade had little regulation of any kind, and many practices that were unfair to competitors or consumers became prevalent. The first systematic efforts to suppress unfair competition were made by trade associations[qv], a few of which were organized in such industries as brewing, silk, paper and paint, between 1862 and 1890. Several hundred more were organized before 1917, and as they were fostered by the War Industries Board[qv], the number increased to over 2000 by 1919.

Since trade associations were primarily interested in the welfare of their members, and often leaned in the direction of price stabilization and monopolistic (or oligopolistic) control of trade, their activities were subjected to Federal scrutiny in the antitrust movement of the early 20th century. In 1914 unfair competition in interstate commerce was brought partly within the jurisdiction of the Federal Trade Commission[qv]. No exact definition of unfair competition was attempted, but rulings in specific cases gradually built up a body of precedent.

Between 1928 and 1930 the Federal Trade Commission stimulated the self-regulatory activities of the trade associations by a series of Trade Practice Conferences, held in more than 100 industries. Many associations adopted specific codes of fair trade practices. Such codes were further encouraged by the National Industrial Recovery Act of 1933, and when adopted became binding upon the industries. Some were continued voluntarily after the effective life of National Industrial Recovery Administration[qv] was ended. By the Robinson-Patman Act[qv] of 1936 and the Wheeler-Lea Act of 1938 the Federal Trade Commission received enlarged powers for suppressing unfair trade practices, whether unfair to competitors or to consumers.

[G. C. Henderson, *The Federal Trade Commission;* A. R. Burns, *The Decline of Competition.*]

G. B. HOTCHKISS

Trade Routes and Centers, Effects of Shifts in. With the building of canals[qv] (1800 and after), a new element entered into population distribution and urban growth. The Erie Canal[qv] played a major part in making New York the nation's metropolis. Had not Boston been shut off from the upper Hudson Valley by a mountain range, it might have built a canal and captured much of that trade; but as it was, it rapidly fell behind New York in importance. Pennsylvania had by 1832 built her own canal and railroad from Philadelphia to Pittsburgh, and so saved the former's position as one of the nation's major cities. The pioneers who settled in the Ohio Valley, shut off from Eastern markets by mountains, found their market via the rivers in New Orleans (*see* Mississippi River, Free Navigation of). George Washington warned that if trade facilities with the east were not established, these people, though of British stock, might cast their lot with Spain and Louisiana (*see* Western Separatism). The Cumberland Road, and the Erie and Pennsylvania canals, as well as the later railroads, did much to cement this area to the North and so decide the Civil War*qqv*. The Ohio and Erie Canal*qv* also gave Ohio an eastern outlet through Lake Erie, and made the little hamlet of Cleveland*qv*, at the northern terminus of the canal, one of America's great cities. On the other hand, many hopeful towns of early days, left off the course of new canals or railroads, fell into a decline and never recovered. Some flourishing cities, on the great mid-western river system, when the railroads destroyed much of the river traffic, became stagnant, or even declined in population (*see* Dead Cities).

[B. H. Meyer, ed., *History of Transportation in the United States before 1860.*] ALVIN F. HARLOW

Trade Unions. *See* Labor Unions.

Trade with the Enemy Acts. Restriction of trade with the enemy as a means of economic coercion and domestic conservation was governed in the colonial era by England's common law, supplemented by orders-in-council*qv* and acts of Parliament. During the French and Indian War*qv* (1756–63) these prohibitions, with the revival of the Molasses Act*qv*, threatened to disrupt the interdependent commerce between the food-producing English colonies and the sugar- and rum-producing French West Indies. Colonists thereupon evaded the embargoes by fraudulently sailing cargoes of provisions to the enemy's Caribbean ports in "flags of truce," ships which were licensed ostensibly to exchange prisoners; and an indirect trade also developed through neutral ports such as Curaçao, St. Eustatius and Monte Christi, until neutral ships thus involved were captured and condemned under the Rule of War of 1756*qv*. The Revolutionary embargoes and nonconsumption agreements (*see* Associations) against England were more effective, largely because of the energy of local committees directed by the Continental Congress and re-enforced by state embargo laws (*see* Committees of Safety).

During the Franco-American "misunderstanding" (1798–1800) and the War of 1812*qqv* trading with the enemy was proscribed as part of military policy, although imports of war materials from the enemy country were usually opportunistically permitted, and the President was authorized to limit and suspend operation of the law. These restrictions during the War of 1812 provoked anew the opposition of New England mercantile interests (*see* Essex Junto) who had defied and evaded the peace-time embargoes*qv* of 1807–12; and Congress eventually (Jan. 27, 1813) modified the statute to permit the profitable trade with British dependencies in the Orient to be resumed.

In the Mexican War enemy trading was not restricted. When the enemy's ports and customs houses had been captured President Polk not only raised the blockade but encouraged imports into Mexico in order to collect duties to finance the army of occupation.

During the Civil War both belligerents partially employed the commercial weapon. At the North, the Blockade*qv* of Southern ports and an embargo were ordered by statutes and executive proclamations; but the Treasury was at the same time authorized to purchase Southern cotton and license a limited enemy trade (*see* Civil War, Trade in Cotton during the). Meanwhile the Confederacy had prohibited trade with Northerners, and various states ordered further embargoes on cotton exports both to coerce Northern opinion and condition world sympathy (*see* King Cotton). Smuggling followed and laws were passed to penalize it (*see* Blockade Runners, Confederate); but the traffic became so lucrative that North Carolina decided to tax its profits, and toward the end of the war the Confederacy organized a Cotton Bureau to sell to the North through foreigners.

The extensive World War measures to prevent enemy trading and to re-enforce the Allied blockade of Germany included executive proclamations, the Espionage Act*qv*, and the "trading with the enemy act" of Oct. 6, 1917. By the latter act such trade was carefully defined, almost completely prohibited, and severely penalized. Importers and exporters were licensed by the War Trade Board, enemy-alien applications for patents were reviewed by the Federal Trade Commission*qv*, and the Treasury regulated insurance companies with enemy-alien connections.

Restriction of commerce as a coercive weapon was supported by the American delegation to the Paris peace conference in 1919 and included in the League of Nations Covenant as a "sanction"[qqv] against states resorting to war under certain conditions; and in spite of the nonmembership of the United States in the League, a minority of Americans favored such economic cooperation against enemies of world peace, either by governmental action or unofficial boycott.

[G. L. Beer, *British Colonial Policy, 1754-65; U. S. Statutes at Large*, Vols. 1, 2, 4, 9, 12, 13, 30, 40; J. C. Schwab, *The Confederate States of America, 1861-65;* J. W. Garner, *International Law and the World War.*]

MARTIN P. CLAUSSEN

Trader, Indian. *See* Indian Trade and Traders.

Trading Companies played an important part in the early settlement of America after Raleigh's[qv] failure demonstrated that the cost of colonization was beyond the resources of any single individual. There were six incorporated British companies that established settlements: The Virginia Company[qv] (1606); the London and Bristol Company (1610); the Council for New England[qv] (1620); the Bermuda Company[qv] (1622); the Massachusetts Bay Company[qv] (1628), and the Old Providence Company[qv] (1630). Their settlements were at Jamestown, Sagadahoc, Newfoundland, Bermuda, Salem and Old Providence, respectively. The Dutch used a similar organization to plant their settlement in New Netherland[qv] at New Amsterdam. The Hudson's Bay Company[qv] was a trading but not a colonizing company.

Companies were of two well-known types. One was the joint-stock company which was legally incorporated by the crown under the great seal. The document reciting this fact was known as a royal charter and was very expensive to get. Joint-stock companies resembled modern corporations. Stock was sold to whomever would buy, and the stockholder's liability was limited to his specific investment. There was the usual set of officers—a treasurer, and an executive council. The headquarters of the company was named in the charter, at which place the company maintained its main office. Under most conditions there were each year four regular meetings of the stockholders, called "a general court," where business was transacted by those present. The charter gave the company title to a specific territory, granted a legal monopoly to trade in that region, and empowered the company to exercise extensive governmental powers over any settlements that might be made, control over the natives, and authority to defend its settlements and to protect its trade and territory from foreign aggression.

The stockholders controlled the company at home, but the settlers were governed by rules and regulations enacted by the company, together with those made by themselves under the authority of the company. All of the ships, storehouses, goods and livestock, bought from funds supplied by the company, were the property of the joint-stock company. The buildings and other property developed by the planters belonged to the individuals and could be taxed by themselves for plantation purposes. The land was a common stock belonging to the stockholders until disposed of by grant to adventurers or actual immigrants. Practically there was no way a stockholder in England could share in this common stock except by emigrating to the colony. Trading privileges belonged to the stockholders of the home company and not to the planters in America.

Another type of trading company extensively used was less formal than the joint-stock company and was called "Associates." It was somewhat like a partnership but had limited liability for the members. Such companies were not fully incorporated, and their territorial grants came from some legally incorporated company. This device was largely used in the settlement of Virginia by the London Company. Berkeley Hundred and many other regions were settled by groups of men called Associates who, in return for a title to a specified tract of land, agreed to transport a certain number of settlers to a given area and establish them within a limited time. The London Company issued forty-four such grants, including one to the Pilgrims which was never used. The settlement at Plymouth[qv] was made possible by a company of Associates.

One of the most famous companies of Associates was the Dorchester Company[qv] which received a grant of what later became Massachusetts and established a settlement at Salem. This company with its grant was finally merged into the Massachusetts Bay Company which was regularly incorporated by royal charter at a very considerable expense. As no place for the offices and meetings of the company was fixed in the charter, the company and charter were removed to America and became the basis of a commonwealth, with the "general court" of the company the source of all governmental power. The trading feature of the company retained an organization in England with headquarters in London, until after 1638. This action by the Massachusetts Bay Company furnished a model for the later settlements in Rhode Island and Connecticut whose government in form was similar to that of the joint-stock companies, with similar names of "freemen" and "general court"*qqv*. As in the case of the joint-stock company, all power was lodged in the "general court" as created by the charter.

[Charles M. Andrews, *The Colonial Period of American History*, Vol. I.] O. M. DICKERSON

Trading Posts, Frontier. From the establishment of Jamestown (1607) until the end of Indian treaty-making (1871), traders and trading posts have been important factors in border relations. By 1774 Albany and Oswego (N. Y.) were important trade centers for the Iroquois*qv* and other northwestern tribes. At both places Indians would exchange their furs for guns, ammunition, hatchets, scalping knives, kettles and blankets. And during the period of colonial rivalries Spain and France, also, had their strategic trading posts. Mobile (1710), Natchitoches (by St. Denis, 1713), Natchez (by Bienville, 1716), and St. Louis, Mo. (by LaClede and Chouteau, 1764) were only a few maintained in the Mississippi Valley and from New Orleans to Pensacola*qqv*.

After American independence, President Washington proposed, and Congress inaugurated (1796), the setting up of government factories and trading posts, and every border fort became a trade center (*see* Factory System, The Indian). But bitter opposition of individual traders led to the abandonment of the policy in 1822. Moreover, American influence with frontier tribes up to 1814 was hampered by British trader influence. Not until 1795 would England agree to surrender occupied posts within the northern boundary of the United States (*see* Border Forts, The Evacuation of). And English traders at Detroit*qv* continued to sell war supplies to tribes of the Ohio and Mississippi valleys until after 1814.

Shortly after American occupation of the Louisiana Territory*qv* (1804), trading posts were established throughout the trans-Mississippi West. St. Louis was the center for supplying traders and posts within the Pacific northwest and central west, and New Orleans the southwest. Missouri traders had built Fort Lisa*qv* by 1813 and Fort Benton (at the mouth of the Big Horn, not to be confused with Fort Benton*qv* on the Upper Missouri) by 1821, and John Jacob Astor had set up a post at Astoria*qv* on the Columbia River in 1811. Astor's organization encountered severe competition from the Hudson's Bay Company*qv* which had several posts in the same region. Sutter's*qv* post on the American River (1841) in California was the best-known trading station in California; and farther east, Fort Bridger and Fort Laramie*qqv* became well known by the early 1840's.

In the greater Southwest posts were equally important as factors in advancing the frontier. At the three forks of the Arkansas, in present Oklahoma, A. P. Chouteau*qv* and other traders had established their posts by 1815; and Chouteau built another near present Purcell (1835). The best-known trading post in the Southwest during the 1830's was Bent's Fort*qv* on the Arkansas, begun by Charles and William Bent, Ceran St. Vrain, and Benito Vasquez (1828–29). In Texas, posts were established during the days of the republic near modern Waco (Torrey's*qv*), and higher up on the Brazos (the Barnards). From these and others, here and there, went vast quantities of trade goods for furs and buffalo hides taken by the Indians.

[Hiram Chittenden, *The American Fur Trade of the Far West;* Clarence A. Vandiveer, *The Fur-Trade and Early Western Exploration.*] C. C. RISTER

Trail Drivers were cowboys*qv* in the act of moving cattle from a home range to a distant market or another range. The typical herd consisted of around 2500 head of cattle; though the average herd was smaller, herds of 3000 head were not uncommon; one of 5000 was exceptional. To move, water and graze more than 5000 cattle in one herd was virtually impossible.

The typical outfit consisted of a boss, who might or might not be the owner; from ten to fifteen hands, each of whom had a string of from five to ten horses; a horse wrangler (or *remudero*), who drove and herded the cow horses; and a cook, who drove the chuck wagon—or, in the earlier stages of trail driving, carried his kitchen and chuck on pack animals. The wagon carried the bed rolls; tents were considered excess luxury. The men drove and grazed the cattle most of the day, herding them by relays at night. Ten or twelve miles was considered a good day's drive, as the cattle must thrive on the route. Bread, meat, beans with bacon, and coffee comprised most of the fare. Wages were around $40 a month. If stampedes*qv*, bad weather, trouble with thieves or Indians kept the trail drivers in the saddle all night as well as all day, they might rub tobacco juice in their eyes to stay awake and look forward to plenty of sleep next winter. The code presupposed that, no matter what the hazards, hardships or physical torture, a man would stay with his herd as loyally as a captain stays with his ship at sea (*see*

Cattle Drives; Chisholm Trail; Goodnight Loving Trail).

[Andy Adams, *The Log of a Cowboy;* J. Frank Dobie, *A Vaquero of the Brush Country;* J. Evetts Haley, *Charles Goodnight, Cowman and Plainsman;* J. Marvin Hunter, *The Trail Drivers of Texas;* Sam P. Ridings, *The Chisholm Trail;* Charles A. Siringo, *Riata and Spurs.*]

J. FRANK DOBIE

Trail of Tears, THE, was the journey of the eastern Cherokees[qv] to Oklahoma in 1838 (*see* Indian Removal). By the treaty of New Echota[qv], signed by a minority of the tribe in 1835, the Cherokees were to surrender their lands in Georgia and remove west of the Mississippi to the Indian country[qv]. The majority bitterly opposed removal and refused to go until forced to do so by troops under Gen. Winfield Scott. Soldiers drove the Indians into concentration camps, from which they were later released and detachments formed for the journey. In October and November, 1838, over 15,000 started westward, mostly on foot, since wagons were provided only for small children and the old and infirm. Winter came on and cold, rain and poor food brought sickness. Heartbroken at being compelled to leave their old homes, many fell an easy prey to disease. Exact figures cannot be found, but it is probable that nearly 10% of those who started died on this tragic journey.

[Grant Foreman, *Indian Removal;* R. C. Eaton, *John Ross and the Cherokee Indians.*]

EDWARD EVERETT DALE

Trailer, THE. First appearing early in the 20th century in England (where they are known as caravans), house trailers were used only to a small extent in the United States until the onset of the 1929 depression. Thereupon, their popularity grew rapidly and within five or six years had skyrocketed to boom proportions. Scores of trailer factories were established; organizations of trailer travelers were formed, boasting membership running into tens of thousands; special trailer facilities such as running water and electricity connections were installed in tourist camps[qv]. In 1937 the boom suddenly collapsed and the trailer industry began readjusting itself to meet the normal demands of a substantial, but definitely limited, market. The 1938 estimate of trailers in use was 350,000, of which about half were factory-built.

[Charles Edgar Nash, *Trailer Ahoy!*]

RICHARD W. TUPPER

Trails. *See* Buffalo Trails; Indian Paths.

Train Robberies were more frequent in America than anywhere else in the world in the latter half of the 19th century. This was in part due to vast stretches of sparsely inhabited country which permitted the robbers to escape undetected, but was in part due to carelessness and lack of adequate protection. The first train robbery on record was that of an Adams Express[qv] car on the New York, New Haven and Hartford Railroad which was rifled of $700,000 between New York and New Haven in 1866. In the same year occurred the first train holdup by the Reno gang in southern Indiana. They took the express messenger's keys from him at gun point, and robbed the safe of $13,000. Some members of the gang were arrested, but never tried, and a year later another gang repeated the exploit in the same neighborhood. For an arrest of one of the Renos in 1867, the remainder of the gang staged a number of bold-faced bank[qv] and train robberies in southern Indiana and Illinois in 1868. They were traced by the Pinkerton Detective agency, just then coming into prominence, arrested and jailed, but the entire family of brothers, except John, were executed by vigilantes before their cases came to trial. The Farringtons operated in 1870 in Kentucky and Tennessee; and Jack Davis of Nevada started operations at Truckee by robbing an express car of $41,000. He had learned his trade robbing stagecoaches[qv] in California a few years earlier.

The year 1870 marked the climax of train robberies, East and West. An express car was robbed at Albany in that year and the messenger shot. In those days care was not taken to lock the express and baggage end doors and the cars were frequently used for loafing and smoking. The picturesque and daring James gang began to operate in 1873 near Council Bluffs, Iowa. No other train robbers are so well known, and legends and songs cluster about their deeds. For nine years they terrorized the Middle West (*see* Northfield Bank Robbery), and it was only after Jesse was shot by a confederate and Frank retired to run a Wild West show, that trainmen could breathe freely. Sam Bass in Texas, the Dalton Boys in Oklahoma and Sontag and Evans in California are other robbers with well-known records. After 1900 the number of holdups declined conspicuously.

[A. F. Harlow, *Old Waybills.*]

CARL L. CANNON

Training Day in New England was the day for drilling the "trainbands." New England inherited the mediæval custom of a militia periodically drilled; by 1600 the organization in England, outside of London, had fallen into decay and the shire militia in 1640 was little better than a mob, but frontier conditions in New

England made efficient administration necessary. The local militia was organized only for drill or for emergency defense; the actual fighting, as in King Philip's War^qv^, was done by special companies of "troopers," recruited from the various bands and officered by men appointed by the General Court^qv^. The militia on the contrary was largely self-governing, electing its own officers, who had merely to be approved by the court.

On training day all able-bodied men, with the exception of a few professions such as ministers, magistrates, town herdsmen and millers, met to elect officers, drill, and converse. The clerk of the band called the roll and the companies themselves inflicted fines upon absentees. In 1649 the General Court defined the purposes of the day as drilling and fortification; in the 17th century the days were often devoted to constructing palisades, watch houses, and even churches. The day was always opened and closed with prayer and there was often a sermon. In contrast to such occasions in England, the New England days were at first models of propriety, so that John Winthrop could boast that when 1200 men trained on Boston Common no man was drunk, no oath was sworn, and nobody was hurt.

At first captains were required to train the companies every week; in 1636 eight days in every year were ordered; in 1660 the number was reduced to six; in 1679 to four. The town bought arms and supplies and sold them to individuals; the equipment was varied and often not efficient. There were no uniforms. Because the militia organization was an integral part of the community life, the training day became a gathering of the whole town; transactions of every sort were then performed and by the end of the century the day had become a sort of bazaar. By this time the clergy were complaining that it was an occasion for intoxication and quarrels.

[The Militia laws are in *The Laws and Liberties of Massachusetts, 1648*, edited by Max Farrand; a description of a training day in Boston, Aug. 30, 1686, is in *Proceedings*, Massachusetts Historical Society, 2nd Series, XIII, 328 ff.; "Laws and Orders to Keepe Iniquity out of the Camp," *ca.* 1675, in *New England Historical and Genealogical Register*, VII, 60 ff., 1853; there is an unpublished dissertation at Harvard University, by Morrison Sharp, *New England Trainbands in the Seventeenth Century*, 1938.]

PERRY MILLER

Tramps. There were a few itinerant beggars in the earlier days of the United States, but not until the railroads had developed baggage and mail cars with end platforms, on which a man might steal a ride, did the professional vagrant become common. After the Civil War, discharged soldiers, men whose balance had been upset by army life, added to their number, and industrial depressions increased it still more. The typical American restlessness and nomadic tendency was another factor. By 1900 there were many thousands of tramps, the name "hobo" had been coined for them, they had become a sort of loose fraternity, a nuisance to railroads and municipalities, sometimes a dangerous element. For food they counted almost entirely on begging at dwelling house doors. They very early divided into classes. The "blanket stiff" and "bundle stiff," in their current jargon, were the sybarites, the former carrying a blanket or two for comfort in sleeping, the latter some extra clothing, perhaps a razor and toothbrush, in a bandana handkerchief or package. Others had no impedimenta at all. The "gay cats" were those who would work at a trade for a short time, then yield to the wanderlust and disappear; these were and are looked down upon by the real hoboes. The depression following the year 1929 enormously increased the itinerant population of the United States.

[Josiah Flynt, *Notes of an Itinerant Policeman.*]

ALVIN F. HARLOW

Trans-Appalachia is the historical terminology applied to that part of North America lying west of the Appalachian Mountains. Used mainly in reference to late colonial and early national history, it refers particularly to the region drained by the Ohio River and thus includes Kentucky, Tennessee and parts of the Old Northwest^qv^.

ALFRED P. JAMES

Transcendentalism, a philosophical term developed by Kant embodying those aspects of man's nature transcending, or independent of, experience, became the inspiration of a liberal social and cultural renaissance in New England during 1830–45 and received its chief American expression in Emerson's individualistic doctrine of self-reliance. In 1836 Emerson and a radical wing of Unitarians^qv^ formed the Transcendental Club as a discussion group, Margaret Fuller's *Dial* later becoming its leading organ. Experiments in "plain living and high thinking" like Brook Farm and Fruitlands^qqv^ attracted the exponents of a new self-culture; and social utopians, from vegetarian enthusiasts to abolitionists, found a congenial atmosphere within the movement.

[H. C. Goddard, *Studies in New England Transcendentalism.*]

HARVEY WISH

Trans-Mississippi Exposition, THE, held at Omaha, Nebr., from June 1 to Oct. 31, 1898, devoted itself to the products, the industries and the civilization of the states west of the Mississippi River. There were twelve principal buildings, 2,613,408 visitors, and $1,924,078 in receipts. It was reopened the following year as the Greater American Exposition, but this attempt was a failure. FRANK MONAGHAN

Transportation, Federal Co-ordinator of. (*See* Railroad Co-ordinator.)

Transportation, Urban. Before 1800, if one had no vehicle of one's own, the only means of riding about the larger American cities was by one- or two-horse vehicles of various types, individually engaged, for which service there came to be standard rates for various distances. About 1800 a sort of stagecoach or omnibus—usually called "stage"—appeared in the streets of New York, and soon there were several lines. Other cities took them up, and in some places there were so many stages on the streets that their racing and reckless driving were dangerous both to passenger and pedestrian. The early stages were supposed to seat only eight people, but double that many were often crowded into them. The floor was covered with straw, theoretically to keep the passengers' feet warm, and to absorb some of the mud and snow. Fares were paid to the driver through a little trap door in the roof, and there were many complaints by passengers that he "short-changed" them. The first street railway[qv] appeared in New York in 1833, but the development of this form of transit was very slow, and the stages held their supremacy in many cities for many years thereafter. By 1880 in New York, almost the only large city that still maintained them in quantity, they had grown much roomier and more comfortable. When the first streetcar line was built far up Broadway between 1884 and 1890, many of the buses were sold to small-town hotels and transportation companies, some even in the West, where they were used for many years thereafter. As early as 1860 traffic had become so heavy in New York's streets that the question of elevated or underground transit began to be discussed. Toward the close of the century, elevated railways and later subways[qqv] were beginning to provide rapid transit in New York, Boston and Chicago. For individual service, the hackmen persisted in all cities, their vehicles being variously closed carriages, coupés, surreys, victorias, etc. A few years later, with the further development of the automobile[qv] and the beginning of the rise in streetcar fares, some automobile owners, or small companies hastily formed, began running what was called "jitney" service, with a nickel fare, competing with the streetcar. This was soon replaced in the larger cities by the taxicab, a European idea, and later by motorbuses[qv]. On Jan. 2, 1900, the first urban motorbuses in America began running on Fifth Avenue in New York, displacing horse-drawn stages of long service. For two decades buses encroached comparatively little upon tramcars as public carriers, but after 1920 they began displacing the cars rapidly. By 1930 nearly every major city in the country had them. In some cities streetcars had disappeared and in others their entire elimination was planned for the near future. ALVIN F. HARLOW

Transportation, War Time. *See* Railroad Administration.

Transportation Act of 1920, THE (also known as the Esch-Cummins Act). The railroads were in the possession of the United States Government from Dec. 26, 1917, until March 1, 1920. By presidential proclamation, during the period of American participation in the World War, they were administered by the Director General of Railroads, under the Railroad Administration[qv]. The traffic situation in 1917 was alarming, and the step was more or less inevitable. During the period of government operation, the roads were obliged to carry a very heavy volume of traffic, without much attention being given either to replacements or to ordinary maintenance. This was more a result of circumstances than the fault of the Government; nevertheless, the roads were in a deplorable condition when, after a little more than two years, they were returned to private operation. In addition, there had been serious difficulties with labor during 1919.

As a result, some remedial legislation was imperative. The act of Feb. 28, 1920, was the result. The Cummins bill in the Senate and the Esch bill in the House "revealed divergencies so marked in character" that a conference committee was necessary, and the measure when finally adopted was, therefore, a compromise. The act became effective on March 1, a little more than three months after President Wilson's proclamation of Dec. 24, 1919, providing for the return of the railroads to private operation. The act attempted to insure the profitable operation of the roads in the future, by improving their financial condition, and providing more adequate machinery for the settlement of railway labor disputes.

Under the first heading, consolidations were authorized, a six-month guarantee period was established, and extensive loans for a variety of purposes were authorized. Under the second, arbitration without power of enforcement was provided, and provision made for voluntary adjustment boards for the settlement of labor disputes, these provisions to be enforced by a Railroad Labor Board consisting of nine members, and having national jurisdiction. The measure was hotly contested in Congress, and was a subject of controversy for many years thereafter. On the one hand, it was contended that the favorable terms of the act were necessary if a paralysis of the national transportation system was to be avoided; on the other, the claim was made that the railroads and financial interests had dictated terms far more to their advantage than to that of the public.

[Frank. H. Dixon, *Railroads and Government, Their Relations in the United States, 1910-21;* Albert R. Ellingwood and Whitney Coombs, *The Government and Railroad Transportation;* Eliot Jones, *Principles of Railway Transportation;* D. Philip Locklin, *Railroad Regulation since 1920.*]

W. BROOKE GRAVES

Transportation and Travel. People in early colonial times lived near the numerous rivers, inlets and bays adjoining the Atlantic, and water provided the most suitable means of travel and transportation. Brigs, barks, schooners, sloops and numerous other types of sailing vessels (mostly of New England make) carried men and cargoes across the ocean (a six- to eight-week voyage), to the West Indies and to neighboring coastal points. If a farmer lived above a seaport, he nevertheless used water transportation in that he moved his produce—be it logs, wheat, salted pork, corn, rice, cotton, indigo or tobacco—in flatboats*qv*, "fall-boats," rafts and other river-going craft. By necessity the colonial remained close to home; but if for business, education or pleasure he did venture abroad, he found the irregular merchant vessel his only means of transport. On the ocean-going ships both food and quarters were provided; but it was the custom for river craft to tie up for the night near some wayside inn where those aboard reputedly were offered a poor bed and an indifferent bill of fare. The ketch, sloop, bateau*qv* and later the log canoe carried people up and down the many coastal rivers, and it was by this means that at least during the 17th century the great mass of people went to market, to church and made a neighborly call.

At first all land travel was done on foot or horseback. Even governors are recorded as having gone from place to place afoot and as having crossed streams "pick-a-back" with the assistance of Indian guides. And in the remoter hill country of the South, people relied almost exclusively upon foot travel until the close of the Revolutionary War. It was not long, however, before Indian trails became bridle paths—called "trodden paths"—and young and old, men and women alike, made long journeys on horseback. Ladies rode on sidesaddles, and in 1702 one woman is recorded as having traveled in this manner from Boston to Philadelphia and held an infant on her lap the entire distance.

Vehicles were scarce articles during the first century of colonization. While private coaches made their appearance in Boston as early as 1685, it was Philadelphia's boast twelve years later that no more than thirty carts and other wheeled contrivances could be found within her limits. The first two American wheeled vehicles were the chair, a two-wheeled two-passenger cart drawn by one horse, and the chaise which differed from the former in that it had a leather top and was swung on leather braces. The curricle, chariot, stagecoach*qv* and numerous other vehicle types were to follow.

By the turn of the century "trodden paths" of New England widened into rough dirt roads. Due chiefly to the impetus of postal service*qv*, and subsequently due to the spread of civilization to regions where water travel was not expedient, ferries, and even bridges*qqv* (usually of a "floating" type) were built. By the close of the colonial period there existed a veritable network of dirt and corduroy roads throughout the Northern and Central colonies with thoroughfares extending into Maryland, Virginia, the Carolinas and even as far south as Savannah, Ga.

Hand in hand with roadmaking came commercial stagecoach and wagon transportation. The first regular stage line was established March 8, 1759, between New York City and Philadelphia with the use of a springless Jersey wagon. With this event a new era of travel was inaugurated in America, since by the close of the period one could travel by coach in all of the colonies at moderate fare. Ordinaries, or taverns*qv*, became more numerous with the advent of stagecoach travel and before long they could be found in almost every important village. As such they fulfilled a social as well as a practical need.

Just as the stagecoach in part met the needs of travelers, so, too, the Conestoga wagon*qv* partly met the problem of overland freight. The Conestoga was developed in Pennsylvania, and its chief characteristics were its large canoe-shaped bottom where goods could ride at sharp angles, its sturdy running gear, and the fact that

Transportation and Travel

four to twelve horses were required to pull it. Wagons[qv] came slowly. It will be recalled that in 1755 Gen. Braddock secured with difficulty only twenty-five wagons for his expedition against the French. But by the Revolution Conestogas were numerous in the West. "Regulars" made freighting a business, and farmers found in these tough wagons a new way to bring their goods to the nearest port (*see* Wagoners of the Alleghenies).

One of the most striking changes following independence was the amazingly rapid growth and the westward march[qv] of the American people. The first United States census of 1790 revealed that 94% out of a total of 4,000,000 people still lived on the Atlantic seaboard; whereas in 1860 a total of 31,000,000 inhabitants was almost evenly divided between the two areas separated by the Appalachian Mountains. This spread of population into the West was accompanied by a persistent and vociferous demand for improvement in the avenues and the means of transportation to facilitate the marketing of goods, migration and general travel. This was met in part by the construction of the National Road[qv], state and privately owned turnpikes[qv], a veritable network of canals[qv] of which the Erie (1825) and the Ohio (1833) were the most significant achievements, and the discovery, survey and popularization of trails extending from the Middle West to Santa Fé, Utah, California and the Pacific Northwest.

By 1817 a regular stagecoach service was established on the National Road, a route which was already the scene of heavy emigrant traffic, commercial Conestoga wagon freighting, packing, foot travel, and droves of horses, mules, cattle, swine and sheep. And to a less degree the same bustling activity could have been observed on the main road that followed the Shenandoah Valley through Cumberland Gap[qv]. Once across the mountains this traffic "took water" on the westward flowing streams. "If bound to Indiana, Illinois, or Missouri," wrote Timothy Flint, "they build or purchase a family boat. Many of these boats are comfortably fitted up," he continued, "and are neither inconvenient nor unpleasant floating houses." "Within twenty-five years past," bemoaned a contemporary North Carolinian, "more than two hundred thousand of our inhabitants have removed to the waters of the Ohio, Tennessee, and Mobile. . . ." And here one might add that the opening of the Erie Canal[qv] brought additional thousands of emigrants—especially those from above the Mason and Dixon line—into the northern portions of the Old Northwest[qv]. Furthermore, this 363-mile man-made waterway provided a direct commercial artery for the exchange of goods between New York City and the Northwest at rates commensurate with the ordinary pocketbook. Freight rates formerly fixed at $100 per ton between Buffalo and New York City were now reduced to less than $8 per ton. In appearance canal boats were somewhat reminiscent of the Mississippi and Ohio river keelboats and barges; they were about fifty feet long and contained a superstructure or cabin which provided very meagre accommodations for passengers and crew. And, to use the words of Charles Dickens, they resembled "the dwarf's private apartment in a caravan at the fair." Travel on canal boats was slow, monotonous, cramped, somewhat dirty and yet on the other hand it was safe and cheap. Consequently it became a widely used though none-too-popular mode of travel. "I say nothing about 'the good old times,' " wrote one, "but if anyone would recall the good old line-boats, I object."

The application of steam power to transportation was a slow and painful process. During and immediately after the Revolutionary War such men as Denis Papin, James Rumsey and John Fitch experimented in steamboat[qv] building—in fact, commercial service on the Delaware River was advertised in Philadelphia newspapers during 1790—but not until the launching of Robert Fulton's[qv] *Clermont* in 1807 was this form of transportation acclaimed commercially successful. Thereafter, river steamboats became so numerous that by 1820 steamboat companies operated on practically all the navigable rivers and lakes lying between the Atlantic coast and the Mississippi River with as many as ninety-seven such vessels on the Ohio River alone. The advent of the steamboats, partly due to increased speed and partly due to marked increase in tons burden, further lowered freight costs and this was an added boon to those engaged in the upriver trade. Steamboat travel was from the outset thrilling and dangerous. "It has been stated," wrote Zadok Cramer in 1811, that a certain steamboat on the Hudson "goes at the rate of four miles an hour against the wind and tide . . . and frequently with 500 passengers on board. . . . There can be but little doubt of the plan succeeding on our western waters, and providing immense advantage to the commerce of our country." "The flush times" came during the 1850's when, for example, over a thousand steamboats navigated the Father of Waters, and when this river was the scene of cutthroat competition, constant racing and innumerable tragic wrecks and explosions. Today on inland rivers

 Transportation and Travel

cargo boats are relatively scarce, and passenger ships have all but vanished. The launching at St. Louis in June, 1940, of a streamlined passenger ship "for the honeymoon trade" (as one newspaper put it) is in itself a commentary upon what was once America's number one transportation business.

The reason for the decline in river transportation is easy to find. River steamboats were practically foredoomed by the coming of the steam locomotive and the railroad[qv]. The first railroads in the United States appeared during the first decade of the 19th century, but not until the arrival in America of George Stevenson's English-made *Stourbridge Lion*[qv] was it clear that the steam locomotive would successfully displace horse- and sail-drawn railroad cars. In Baltimore on July 4, 1828, the cornerstone was laid for America's first railroad line designed to be a public carrier. It was to be known as the Baltimore and Ohio[qv] and when finally completed twenty years later extended from Chesapeake Bay to Ohio. In 1830 Peter Cooper's *Tom Thumb*[qv] made its first run. "Here was railroading indeed . . ." wrote a Baltimore newspaper. "No longer a mere plaything. . . . What stories all these [passengers] would have to carry home; of the remarkable new Ohio Railroad at Baltimore." This same press comment said of *Tom Thumb,* the locomotive: "Awkward and ridiculous and clumsy as it may seem, it breathes an awesome sense of mystery into the hearts and minds of these Baltimoreans. . . . Off and away. . . . The Railroad to the distant Ohio. . . . The saviour of a goodly American town."

From that day on this novel form of transportation experienced a mushroom growth. Many railroad companies entered the field, among them the still existing Pennsylvania Railroad Company[qv] which linked Pittsburgh with the Atlantic, and the New York Central[qv] which represented a consolidation of several lines operating between New York City and Buffalo. By 1857 one could travel by rail from the Atlantic coast to St. Louis by making only five changes, save for crossing rivers on ferries and by making two short trips on steamboats. And when the Civil War came, there were no less than 30,000 miles of railroads in the country, and one third of this mileage lay in the Old Northwest.

The inrush of population into the trans-Mississippi West began with migrations out to the Willamette Valley, Oregon, during and after 1841, and with the Mormon[qv] migrations to Utah beginning in 1846. Two years later began the California Gold Rush[qv], followed by the spread of the mineral frontier to Nevada, Colorado and other parts of the Far West. Then immediately after the Civil War the range cattle industry swept the great plains. Soon followed the dirt farmers whose advance was so rapid that by 1890 the frontier line ceased to exist.

With regard to the transportation history of the trans-Mississippi West, it is clear that it followed roughly the pattern laid down by the East with the one difference that it appeared to be more spectacular. The Mountain Men[qv] marked the trails; Conestoga wagons now became known as "prairie schooners"[qv] and in them the thousands of immigrants made their way west along the Oregon, California and other trails. In the Far West the stagecoach business achieved gigantic proportions with the establishment between 1858–61 of a semiweekly passenger and mail service over a 3600-mile stage road between St. Louis and Portland, Oreg., via El Paso, Texas, and San Francisco, Calif. A month was required for such a journey and, contrary to many romantic conceptions about stagecoach travel, it was not without its aches and pains; or, to quote Horace Greeley after his transcontinental stage ride: ". . . it is a balm for many bruises to know that I am at last in California."

Perhaps the most unique form of transportation business to develop in the Far West was the express business—the rapid and efficient transportation of goods and mail. The first expressmen, to be sure, appear to have been two bank messengers operating over the Boston and Providence Railroad in 1834, but it was on the Pacific coast that the express business first became important. During the 1850's no one was more anxious to receive news from families and friends than the men in isolated mining camps of California, and since the government mail service was inadequate, express companies—the most important of which were the Adams and Company and the Wells, Fargo and Company[qqv]—organized to carry the mails. Their duties soon included the transportation of gold dust from the mines to designated depositories, and the carrying of small and valuable parcels, as well as the issuing of bills of exchange. By 1860 there were over 264 companies in California alone, and scores of others in other parts of the Far West. The Pony Express[qv] was organized in 1860 to carry mails across the plains and over the mountains between St. Joseph, Mo., and Sacramento, Calif., in eleven days. The experiment proved to be too costly and it was dropped the next year.

The Far West never regarded the stagecoach and the pony express business as anything but stop-gaps until such a time when the transcontinental railroads could be brought to completion. Hardly had the immigrants come to Oregon and California when there issued petitions, newspaper editorials and memorials which voiced the insistent demand of the West for railroads. Then, finally, on July 4, 1864, President Lincoln signed the act which provided for the construction of the Union Pacific–Central Pacific Railroad[qv]. It was to run from a point in Nebraska to Sacramento, Calif., and work was immediately begun at both ends. The Central Pacific Company built from Sacramento eastwardly, the Union Pacific westward from a point out of Omaha, Nebr. The amount of government compensation in the form of land and loans was determined by miles constructed and there accordingly ensued a mad race between these rival concerns (*see* Land Grants to Railways). Finally, on May 10, 1869, at Promontory Point, Utah, Leland Stanford, president of the Central Pacific, drove the last spike which bound the East and West by rails of steel and iron. George Pullman's new golden palace cars now sped across the continent at the rate of twenty-two miles per hour. And as they moved into the West, to quote first hand: "On either side are the prairies, abode of the buffalo, where the eye sees naught but desolation . . . then, looking back through the long aisle, or avenue, one gazes on the supreme achievement of our civilization."

Railroad building continued at a breakneck pace during the remainder of the century: 1882 saw the completion of the Santa Fé–Southern Pacific combination; the next year the Northern Pacific; and 1893 the Great Northern[qqv]. In fact, so great had been construction that when the peak was reached in 1916 there existed 254,037 miles of railroad within the present boundaries of the United States. Since then the number of miles has declined slightly, and this may in part be explained by the advent of automotive transportation. Today many railroads are failing to show a profit, but the time is yet to come when they will take their place in the museum along with the prairie schooner, Concord stagecoach[qv], and other transportation relics of bygone days.

The invention of the internal combustion engine toward the last quarter of the 19th century paved the way for automobile, bus, truck and airplane transportation[qqv], and as such has completely motorized if not revolutionized 20th-century America. Today the horse has all but vanished from the roads and now—with the presence of paved highways everywhere—there are enough automobiles in the country to transport the entire population of the United States. The fact that California's receipts from touring now exceed those of her fruit industry will illustrate the use to which the automobile is put. By 1904 commercial trucking began and today large fleets of multiwheeled motor trucks carry much of the nation's goods that were formerly transported on rails.

The World War did much to promote the use of airplanes, and the fact that today regular commercial aviation is available to all citizens of the country is in itself evidence that the success of aviation as a practical, as well as a speedy, method of transportation is at last assured.

The whole history of American transportation has been one of evolution. Transportation has kept pace with the march of civilization if indeed it has not been the advance agent of what is known as progress. And well might one agree with Emerson Hough who said: "There is in history no agency so wondrous in events, no working instrumentality so great as transportation."

[Seymour Dunbar, *A History of Travel in America;* Agnes C. Laut, *The Romance of the Rails;* Robert E. Riegel, *The Story of Western Railroads;* Charles F. Carter, *When Railroads Were New;* Alvin F. Harlow, *Old Waybills: The Romance of Express Companies;* William Banning and George H. Banning, *Six Horses;* C. R. Gibson, *The Motor Car and Its Story.*]

O. O. WINTHER

Transylvania Company, The, was an unincorporated association composed, at its largest, of nine influential citizens of North Carolina: Richard Henderson, John Williams, Thomas Hart, Nathaniel Hart, David Hart, John Luttrell, Leonard H. Bullock, James Hogg and William Johnston. It was organized to invest in vacant, unpatented wild lands, within the chartered limits of North Carolina and Virginia, to which the Cherokee[qv] were supposed to have some sort of plausible claim.

In the fall of 1774 Capt. Nathaniel Hart, with Judge Henderson and several attendants, paid a visit to the Overhill Cherokee, at their Otari towns, to negotiate for the lease or purchase of an immense tract of land between the Kentucky and Cumberland rivers. Three or more Cherokee returned with Capt. Hart to select or pass upon the goods proposed to be given in payment for the desired cession. This happened shortly after the First Continental Congress had convened in Philadelphia, and close upon the desperate battle at Point Pleasant[qv], both of which events bore witness to the growing ferment and deranged condition of the country, in the midst of which constituted authority was relaxed and the ties of allegiance to government were all but sundered or flouted (*see* Dunmore's War).

At the beginning of the year 1775 new articles of co-partnership (bearing date Jan. 6, 1775) were entered into more clearly to define the terms of the joint venture. It was left in doubt whether the transaction with the Cherokee would be a long-term lease, as suggested by the practice of the Watauga Association[qv], or outright purchase. In the end, the Transylvania partners took from the chiefs of the Cherokee what purported to be an absolute conveyance of the millions of acres in question.

The peculiar proprietary tenure, with its system of quitrents[qv], by which it was planned to hold and dispose of this vast domain, was plainly copied from the modified feudal establishment under which the Granville District[qv], at the northern end of North Carolina, had long been held and administered. In essence it closely resembled the colonial setup of Pennsylvania and Maryland (*see* Proprietary Provinces). The abortive attempt to form a provisional government and enact emergency measures for the infant colony at Boonesborough[qv] in May, 1775, duplicated the experiment of the Watauga Association in 1772. Several of the Transylvania proprietors came to Kentucky, and Judge Henderson and Capt. Nathaniel Hart both visited the Cumberland settlements[qv] in Tennessee; but Capt. Hart was the only one of the entire company who brought his family across the mountains and settled down as a permanent resident of Kentucky.

The attempted purchase from the Indians was publicly denounced by the governors of the two states involved and the scheme was invalidated. Virginia, in 1778, granted the company 200,000 acres at the mouth of Green River in Kentucky (*see* Virginia v. Transylvania Company), and North Carolina, in 1783, granted it an equal amount in Powell's Valley, in East Tennessee, as an equitable recompense for the labor, hazards and outlay incurred, and a fair return for the public advantage gained by extinguishing the putative title of the Cherokee.

[George W. Ranck, *Boonesborough;* Archibald Henderson, *The Conquest of the Old Southwest;* William Stewart Lester, *The Transylvania Colony;* Samuel C. Williams, *Dawn of Tennessee Valley* and *Tennessee History.*]

SAMUEL M. WILSON

Trappers' Rendezvous. An advertisement appearing in the *Missouri Republican* of St. Louis, Mo., in the spring of 1822 read as follows: "To enterprising young men. The subscriber wishes to engage one hundred young men to ascend the Missouri river to its source, there to be employed for one, two or three years. . . . [Signed] William H. Ashley." Out of this recruiting grew an organization of mountain men[qv] destined to institute a unique method of trapping and trade in the beaver country.

Following established practice, Ashley's men (Rocky Mountain Fur Co.[qv]) held to the valley of the Missouri and depended upon Indians and white trappers to come to their forts to trade. Pushed by the competition of the Missouri Fur Company[qv], Ashley relinquished the Missouri Valley and carried his operations to the west side of the Rocky Mountains. Here he dropped the practice of conducting trade from fixed points, and relied upon itinerant parties equipped to trap rather than trade, so obtaining his beaver directly from the streams. Such giants of the fur trade era as Andrew Henry, Jedediah S. Smith, the four Sublette brothers, James Bridger, Thomas Fitzpatrick, Henry Fraeb, Robert Campbell, David Jackson and Étienne Provost, are identified with the expeditions launched by Ashley. The parties penetrated the untapped regions of the Green, the Snake and the Salt Lake basin. The new method of doing business necessitated annual gatherings of the itinerant parties, at which time pack outfits from St. Louis delivered equipment, supplies, trade goods—and liquor—and picked up the product of the trappers' work. Naturally, to these meetings came hordes of savages to participate in the trade and hilarity. These notable fairs in the wilderness became known as annual *rendezvous.* The first one, a mild affair on the Sweetwater (Wyo.) in 1824 was held for the convenience of scattered parties of Ashley's men under Fitzpatrick, who had trapped the Wind River country in 1823–24. In the summer of 1825, Ashley, himself, assembled his parties, joined by a Hudson's Bay Company[qv] group, on Henry's Fork of the Green River. The next year, Ashley met with his company at a site near the present Ogden, Utah. Here, with great profit he disposed of his interests in the Rocky Mountain Fur Company to some of his associates, who continued with the rendezvous method. Succeeding assemblages, in some of which rival companies participated, were held at Bear Lake, Utah, 1827; Ogden, Utah, 1828; Popo Agie, Wyo., 1829, 1830 and 1838; Big Hole near the Salmon River, 1831; Pierre's Hole[qv], Idaho, 1832; Green River at Horse Creek, 1833, 1835, 1836, 1839 and 1840; Green River on Ham's Fork, 1834; and Wind River, Wyo., 1837. Many contemporary accounts of trapper revelry, desperate competition between American companies, international strategy, and bloody combat with Indians have been handed down by participants in the wild mountain fairs, but no comprehensive treatment of the rendezvous episode in western history has been written.

A fair idea of the atmosphere of a trappers' summer assemblage may be gained from the following notes made by Sir William Drummond Stewart, a British nobleman, who for sheer pleasure repeatedly joined the mountain men in annual rendezvous. These comments refer to a meeting on Horse Creek, probably in 1839: "At the rendezvous, where is held that busy fair, where Indians and scarce less savage whites assemble to receive supplies, to bring in the fruits of preceding hunts, and hold wild revelry—the borders of the river are lined for miles with huts and lodges, the extended plain is covered with every species of steed, from the high-bred racer to the faded pack-horse; the sullen mule, whose endurance is well-nigh run out, rolls in the dust with his lacerated hide; the circle of surrounding heights is crowned with mounted videttes, at whose distant signal of alarm the scene of repose is changed and the scattered bands are hurried up in clouds of dust to the nearer protection of the vast encampment. . . .

"Various utensils were carried forth in every direction from the fountain of alcohol which a tent concealed. . . . The sound of mirth and wild music, the triumphant shout of drunkenness, the busy hum of that short carnival, where the labor of the adventurous hunter for the bygone season, and even the hope of the one to come, are held amply recompensed by the wild extravagances that distinguish the days of jubilee from the season of danger and toil. The bright fire everywhere marked the circulating bowl. Occasionally, through the merky gloom, unlit by any blaze, the dark figure of the lover seeks the promised meeting."

[H. M. Chittenden, *The American Fur Trade of the Far West;* H. C. Dale, *The Ashley-Smith Explorations;* L. R. Hafen and W. J. Ghent, *Broken Hand: The Life Story of Thomas Fitzpatrick;* Osborne Russell, *Journal of a Trapper;* F. G. Young, *The Correspondence and Journals of N. J. Wyeth;* Sir Wm. Drummond Stewart, *Altowan,* edited by W. J. Webb; W. A. Ferris, Life in the Rocky Mountains, 1830-35, in *Western Literary Messenger,* 1843-44; Washington Irving, *Adventures of Captain Bonneville;* Frances F. Victor, *The River of the West;* Cecil B. Alter, *James Bridger.*]

CARL P. RUSSELL

Trappers' Trail. *See* Cherokee Trail.

Trapping continues to be a part-time occupation for many rural Americans. Until the middle of the 19th century trapping was a prime factor in the process of westward movement[qv], for professional trappers and traders not only developed a source of wealth for a growing nation but, more important, they explored the rivers, blazed trails through unmapped forests, brought hostile Indians under control, made known the agricultural values of the wilderness, and extended American holdings to the very Pacific itself. The American trapper, as a type, may well be identified as that picturesque mountain man[qv] of the Rocky Mountain region who during the first half of the 19th century worked out of the fur trade center, St. Louis, in a struggle against nature and British antagonists in winning the West for the United States. This American trapper did not, however, arrive ready-made to succeed Lewis and Clark[qv] in further penetration of our western country. He evolved through many stages from the Pilgrim trapper of 1620, from the Dutch trader of the Connecticut and the Hudson, from the Frenchman of Green Bay, from the British North West Company agent, from the Hudson's Bay Company *voyageur,* and from the backwoodsman of Kentucky and Tennessee[qqv]. From some of these, he inherited a psychological character that made him indomitable; from all, he borrowed his technique and his material equipment. The upper Missouri trapper of 1830 (*see* Fur Trade on the Upper Mississippi and Missouri Rivers) was a composite picture of the many types that had dared the wilderness through two hundred years of westward progress. With him he took a method that had its beginnings in the Indian trade on the St. Lawrence and the Potomac, and a paraphernalia that sprang from roots deep in the countries of Europe. Many of his items of equipment and objects of trade had changed not a whit in two centuries of use in America.

In following his profession, the trapper of the upper Missouri traveled with a company of companions employed by one of the established trading firms of St. Louis or worked out of that city as free and independent trappers. Zenas Leonard, writing of his arrival with the Gant and Blackwell party in beaver country at the junction of the Laramie and Platte rivers, Aug. 27, 1831, gives the following description of procedure: "Captain Gant gave orders to make preparations for trapping. The company was divided into parties of from 15 to 20 men, with their respective captains placed over them, and directed by Captain Gant in what direction to go. Captain Washburn ascended the Tiber Fork; Captain Stephens, the Laramie; Captain Gant, the Sweetwater—all of which empty into the River Platte near the same place. Each of these companies were directed to ascend these rivers until they found beaver sufficiently plenty for trapping, or until the snow and cold weather compelled them to stop, at which event they were to return to the mouth of the Laramie River to pass the winter together."

Osborne Russell, who trapped in the Yellowstone Park country in the 1830's and 1840's, wrote: "The trapper extracts this substance (castoreum, the trapper's bait) from the scent glands of the beaver and carries it in a wooden box. He sets his steel trap in the water near the bank about six inches below the surface, throws a handful of mud upon the bank about one foot from the trap, and puts a small portion of the castoreum thereon. After night, the beaver comes out of his lodge, smells the fatal bait 200 or 300 yards distant, and steers his course directly for it. He hastens to ascend the bank, but the trap grasps his foot and soon drowns him in the struggle to escape."

Probably, the only contemporary drawing of a mountain man making his "set" is to be found in the Alfred J. Miller illustrations possessed by the Municipal Museum of Baltimore. These unpublished drawings and paintings were made by the artist Miller in the Green River country, and enroute thereto, in 1837.

Beaver no longer constitutes the chief item in the American fur trade, and St. Louis now (1940) meets competition from the raw fur dealers in Chicago, New York, St. Paul and other large centers from which the trade is conducted. Trapping in the United States today brings largest returns in muskrat, fox, skunk, opossum and raccoon, and the volume of business is far greater than ever it was during the days of the mountain man. The significance of the trapper and trapping in the history of the United States is not to be judged by proportions, however. Their influence upon the course of empire cannot be reflected in bare statistics of commercial returns.

[H. M. Chittenden, *The American Fur Trade of the Far West;* W. F. Wagner, ed., *Adventures of Zenas Leonard;* Osborne Russell, *Journal of a Trapper, 1834-43.*]

CARL P. RUSSELL

Trappist Monasteries. The Trappists, a Catholic religious order of men, derive their name from the abbey of LaTrappe in France, where the Abbot de Rancé (1626–1700) revived the primitive rule of the Cistercians. Officially known as the Order of the Cistercians of the Strict Observance (O.C.S.O.), they follow a markedly austere and self-denying manner of life. The three Trappist monasteries now in the United States are located at Gethsemani, Ky., Valley Falls, R. I., and in the environs of Dubuque, Iowa. A group of refugee Trappist monks from France was in residence for a period (1809–13) alongside the great archæological earthwork outside of East St. Louis, Ill., subsequently known as Monks Mound[qv].

[G. J. Garraghan, *Chapters in Frontier History;* B. J. Webb, *History of Catholicity in Kentucky.*]

GILBERT J. GARRAGHAN

Travel. *See* Transportation and Travel.

Traveling on Sunday. In most of the colonies in the 17th century travel on Sunday other than to and from church was forbidden by law. During the 18th century public opinion relaxed, except in some New England localities where the prohibition lasted until 1800. After 1830 stagecoaches and ferries[qqv] began Sunday operation and after a legislative battle Sunday carriage of United States mails was authorized, the railroads having run on Sunday from the outset, despite protests. With the advent of automobiles[qv], Sunday evolved from the least to the most favored day for travel. (*See also* Sabbath.)

[Leo Markun, *Mrs. Grundy: A History of Four Centuries of Morals in Great Britain and the United States.*]

HARVEY L. CARTER

Traverse des Sioux, The Treaty of (July 23, 1851). By this treaty, signed at Traverse des Sioux on the Minnesota River, the Upper Sioux[qv] ceded to the United States all their lands in Iowa and Minnesota east of a line following the western bank of the Red River through Lake Traverse, thence southwesterly to the Big Sioux River and along the western bank of that river to the Iowa line. The chief consideration to the Indians was an annual interest payment of $68,000 for fifty years, of which $40,000 was to be cash. According to the "Traders' Paper," signed by the chiefs directly after the treaty, $210,000 was designated to liquidate their debts to the traders. The reservation assigned them extended along the upper Minnesota River, ten miles wide on either side. Later, on Aug. 5, the Lower Sioux ceded the same lands in a treaty at Mendota differing essentially from that at Traverse des Sioux only in the amounts of money. Their reservation continued along the Minnesota from the upper reserve nearly to New Ulm. These treaties, ratified at Washington June 23, 1852, with amendments later accepted by the Indians, were proclaimed by President Fillmore, Feb. 24, 1853. Dissatisfaction of the Indians with these treaties and their nonfulfillment culminated in the Sioux War of 1862[qv].

[Thomas Hughes, The Treaty of Traverse des Sioux in 1851, under Governor Alexander Ramsey, *Minnesota Historical Collections*, 12:101-129; W. W. Folwell, *A History of Minnesota;* Charles J. Kappler, *Indian Affairs, Laws and Treaties*, Vol. 2.]

RUTH THOMPSON

Travois. A characteristic method of transportation employed chiefly by plains Indians, consisted of poles, lashed on the back of a horse in such manner that the ends dragged behind. Usually in moving camp these were teepee poles, the teepee cover, food, luggage and even persons, riding on the dragging ends. Sometimes especially constructed travois, consisting of two springy poles and a litter, were employed for transportation of children or aged persons. Dogs were often employed to drag small travois.

[F. W. Hodge, *Handbook of American Indians.*]

PAUL I. WELLMAN

Treason. The Convention of 1787[qv] included in Art. III, Sec. 3 of the Constitution a strict definition of treason, required the testimony of two witnesses to the overt act, or confession in open court, and while authorizing Congress to punish the offense, provided that "no attainder of treason shall work corruption of blood or forfeiture except during the life of the person attainted." These constitutional provisions recognized the right of the National Government to safeguard itself, but at the same time insured against the procedural abuses and inhuman practices which had been all too common in the English state trials. The trial of Aaron Burr[qv] demonstrated that these precautions were wise, as the doctrine of "constructive treason" would have proved a deadly weapon against political opponents. The constitutional provisions apply to treason against the Federal Government only, the states being free to define and punish treason against themselves, subject to the limitations of the Federal and their own constitutions.

[W. W. Willoughby, *The Constitutional Law of the United States.*]

W. A. ROBINSON

Treason: "If This Be Treason, Make the Most of It." There are several versions as to the exact wording of this part of Patrick Henry's Stamp Act speech. Wirt's version reads: "Cæsar had his Brutus, Charles the First his Cromwell, and George the Third—['Treason' cried the Speaker . . .] may profit by their example. If *this* be treason, make the most of it." Since, however, several witnesses, writing independently, included a reference to Tarquin, the most accurate rendition would seem to be the W. W. Henry version: "Tarquin and Cæsar had each his Brutus; Charles the First, his Cromwell; and George the Third"—interrupted here by cries of "Treason!" Henry concluded: "may profit by their example. If *this* be treason, make the most of it."

[W. W. Henry, *Patrick Henry: Life, Correspondence, and Speeches.*]

MATTHEW PAGE ANDREWS

Treason Trials. The United States has nothing comparable to the British series of *State Trials,* and with the exception of the Burr conspiracy[qv], treason cases are few and uninteresting. The Constitution defined treason in Sec. 3, Art. III, and thereby prevented Congress from broadening the scope of the offense and introducing the principle of "constructive treason," which governments have found such a deadly weapon against their enemies. The death penalty for treason was, however, established by an act of 1790. Several obscure participants in the Whiskey Insurrection[qv] were convicted in 1795, and John Fries[qv] was sentenced to death for his share in the Northampton County, Pa., disturbances a few years later. The power of the new Government had been sufficiently demonstrated and all were promptly pardoned. Marshall's rulings in the Burr affair made successful prosecution of treason still more difficult.

The Civil War, regarded by Unionists as "treason and rebellion," apparently offered opportunity for wholesale punishment of "traitors" but there were practical and legalistic obstacles in the way. The contest had most of the attributes of international war and the Confederacy[qv] had abundant opportunity for reprisal. While Congress passed several treason statutes there was little attempt at enforcement (*see* Conspiracies Acts of 1861 and 1862). There were disloyal activities and conspiracies in the North and the Indiana prosecutions were later dealt with by the Supreme Court in the famous *ex parte* Milligan decision[qv]. With the cessation of hostilities there were wholesale indictments of Confederates, including President Davis[qv], but the common sense of the country asserted itself, indictments were dropped and amnesty[qv] extended.

[Francis Wharton, *State Trials of the United States during the Administrations of Washington and Adams;* Charles Warren, What is Giving Aid and Comfort to the Enemy? in *Yale Law Journal*, January, 1918; *see also* Treason under the Constitution of the United States, in *12 Illinois Law Review*, 381; W. W. Willoughby, *The Constitutional Law of the United States.*]

W. A. ROBINSON

Treasury, Department of the, was established by Congress by the act of Sept. 2, 1789. The law provided also for the appointment by the President of a Secretary of the Treasury who was to be the head of the Treasury Department. The Secretary was directed to digest and prepare plans for the management and improvement of the revenue and the support of the public credit. He was also authorized to superintend the collection of revenue, to report budget estimates, etc. The act placed the Secretary in intimate connection with Congress by providing that calls for financial information be made direct to the Treasury without going through the President.

In addition to providing for a Secretary of the Treasury, the law authorized the appointment of a treasurer, comptroller, auditor, register and an assistant secretary, all save the last-named being purely accounting officers with special functions of checking accounts and payments to be sure no unauthorized expenditures were made by the Treasury.

Although the number of officers has been increased from time to time as the business of the Treasury increased, there has been no radical change of functions from those specified in the act of 1789. Since that act, however, a number of bureaus of the Treasury Department have been created. The customs service[qv], established by the act of July 31, 1789, automatically came under the control of the Treasury Department after the passage of the act of Sept. 2. The office of Director of the Mint[qv] was assigned to the State Department by Washington in 1792, but was transferred to the Treasury Department in 1795 at the request of Hamilton. The mint was not legally made a bureau of the Treasury, however, until the act of Feb. 12, 1873.

Collectors of Internal Revenue were first authorized by the act of July 16, 1798, but the existing office of Commissioner of Internal Revenue was not established until July 1, 1862. The National Bank Act[qv] of Feb. 25, 1863 (re-enacted June 3, 1864) established the office of Comptroller of the Currency as a Treasury bureau, and the act of March 3, 1877, established the Bureau of Engraving and Printing. The Bureau of the Budget[qv] was created by an act of June 10, 1921. The Department also has charge of the Coast Guard[qv], the Architect of Federal Buildings, the Public Health Service[qv] and the Secret Service[qv].

Alexander Hamilton was appointed by Washington as the first Secretary of the Treasury on Sept. 11, 1789. He served in this capacity until Jan. 31, 1795, and made a reputation for himself as the outstanding incumbent of this office in the history of the country.

[D. R. Dewey, *Financial History of the United States;* Institute for Government Research, *Service Monographs of the United States Government;* National Monetary Commission, *Laws of the United States concerning Money, Banking and Loans.*]

FREDERICK A. BRADFORD

Treasury Notes, short-term borrowings by the Federal Government, were first used in 1812–15. The term was one year except for those issued in 1815. Except for the small denominations, they bore interest. Over $36,000,000 were issued. Between 1837 and 1843 eight issues of treasury notes were put out, amounting to over $47,000,000 in all. During the Civil War, in addition to the interest-bearing issue, some noninterest-bearing demand notes were issued. Then came the Greenbacks[qv], in 1862 and 1863, with $450,000,000 authorized. To pay for the silver bought under the Sherman Act of 1890[qv], the Treasury Notes of 1890 were issued. They were noninterest bearing and were used as currency. During the World War $51,000,000,000 of short-term issues were put out in anticipation of Liberty loans[qv] and tax receipts. Since then there have always been some outstanding, at first to give flexibility in debt repayment, and, after 1932, to get funds at low rates for deficits. On June 30, 1938, $9,147,000,000 were outstanding. Most were issued for a five-year term.

[D. R. Dewey, *Financial History of the United States.*]

JAMES D. MAGEE

Treat Mission (1839). James Treat, a native of New York, was appointed by the Republic of Texas[qv] as a confidential agent to negotiate with Mexico for peace between the two states, with recognition of Texas independence and the Rio Grande boundary as essentials. Texas was willing to pay $5,000,000 for the liquidation of all Mexican claims. Treat reached Mexico City, Dec. 11, 1839, and obtained a hearing from the Council of State; but the Mexican Congress flatly refused negotiation, and his mission failed. Treat then endeavored to arrange a truce for one, two or three years, but without success. On his return journey, he died on shipboard.

[George Lockhart Rives, *The United States of America and Mexico.*]

ALVIN F. HARLOW

Treaties, Commercial, are negotiated by the President and ratified by the Senate (Constitution, Art. II, Sec. 2); commercial *agreements* with foreign countries are concluded by the President under general executive powers or under congressional authorization and require no ratification. Treaties or agreements may be *special,* concerned with such matters as migration, civil rights, quarantine, taxation, shipping; or *general,* providing for consular rights, national treatment, and most-favored-nation treatment. National treatment, says Culbertson, "has been the central treaty principle in the tendency toward assimilation of rights of aliens to those of nationals; [most-favored-nation treatment] has been the principle which has contributed to the establishment of equal and stable treatment as between states."

Before the American Revolution it was the practice of Western powers to seek equality of commercial relations through an unqualified or *unconditional* pledge of most-favored-nation treatment. But the United States, beginning with its first commercial treaty (with France, 1778), introduced a qualifying or *conditional* proviso making it unnecessary for benefits to be extended to third powers except for "the same compensation." European countries used both forms of most-favored-nation clause[qv] until 1860, but thereafter almost invariably followed the unconditional principle. The United States, with few exceptions, inserted the conditional clause in its commercial treaties and agreements until 1923.

To supplement its commercial treaty system, the United States experimented on several occasions with reciprocity[qv] treaties or agreements involving special tariff concessions. Seven were negotiated before 1890, but only two were ratified: with Canada (1854–65) and Hawaii (1875). The Tariff Act of 1890 provided for penalty duties on certain imports if from countries discriminating against American goods. Under this authority Secretary of State Blaine (1891–92) negotiated ten reciprocal *agreements,* all of which were terminated in consequence of changes in the Tariff Act of 1894 (*see* Gorman-Wilson Tariff). Under authority of the reciprocity provisions of the tariff of 1897, John A. Kasson, agent under McKinley and Roosevelt, negotiated "argol *agreements*" with eight European nations. But the more important "Kasson *treaties*"[qv] which he negotiated in 1899 with seven countries died in Senate Committee although pushed by both Presidents. The Payne-Aldrich tariff[qv] of 1909 terminated all reciprocity arrangements except the Cuban treaty of 1902.

In 1919 the Tariff Commission[qv] concluded that equality of commercial treatment could not be achieved by the *conditional* most-favored-nation system, plus exclusive reciprocity arrangements. Influenced by such opinion, and in accord with Sec. 317, Tariff Act of 1922, Secretary of State Hughes, beginning with Germany in 1925, shifted American commercial treaties to the *unconditional* most-favored-nation principle. By 1936 the United States had general commercial treaties or agreements (including reciprocal trade agreements[qv]) with 52 countries, 37 of which were *unconditional.*

[W. S. Culbertson, *International Economic Policies;* United States Tariff Commission, *Reciprocity and Commercial Treaties.*]

FRANK A. SOUTHARD, JR.

Treaties, Indian. *See* Indian, Treaties with the.

Treaties, Most-Favored-Nation. *See* Most-Favored-Nation Principle.

Treaties, Negotiation and Ratification of. The Constitution provides that the President "shall have power, by and with the advice and consent of the Senate, to make treaties, provided two-thirds of the Senators present concur." These words, now read through the lenses of subsequent practice, were written when the perspective was different. Congress had approved instructions, controlled negotiations, and made treaties. Moreover, discussions in the Constitutional Convention[qv], in the ratifying conventions, and elsewhere show that contemporaries expected treaties to be negotiated in this country where the Senate could follow the negotiations.

In his first treaty negotiation, one with Indians in 1789, Washington got a specific appropriation, submitted the names of his commissioners for approval, and went to the Senate to discuss instructions and bases of negotiation. He viewed the Senate as a "council," and regarded treaties as "of a legislative nature." The attempt to put his ideas into practice broke down. Personal contact between the President and Senate proved uncomfortable to both, and fell into disuse. When the President offered to send a secretary in 1790 the Senate declined the offer. Jefferson, as Secretary of State, knowing the difficulties of earlier procedures, declared in 1790 that "the transaction of business with foreign nations is executive altogether." John Marshall went farther in 1800 to assert, "The President is the sole organ of the nation in its external relations." The economy of language in the Constitution was matched by the brevity of the act establishing the Department of State[qv]; both opened the way for the views of Jefferson and Marshall to prevail. Precedents hardened while Senate participation in negotiations as a "council" was virtually impossible because the only agreement signed in the United States during the first thirty years was an article explanatory of Jay's Treaty[qv].

Practice gradually crystallized. Indian treaties and postal treaties came to be Executive agreements[qv] and the Senate had no part in them. Consent of the Senate before the appointment of a commissioner to negotiate with a foreign nation became the exception, and prior consultation with the Senate regarding the desirability of a negotiation became equally exceptional. In practice the President appoints either a private citizen or an official as negotiator. If the President approves the draft treaty, it is sent to the Senate with appropriate papers and a request for its "advice and consent." The Senate may give or withhold consent; or it may advise changes through "amendments" or "reservations." It has refused approval to only about thirty treaties, but has "amended" or made "reservations" in approximately one sixth of all presented. The President may reject proposed changes, letting the treaty fail, accept them and negotiate their incorporation, or he may negotiate substitute provisions for Senate approval. After the Senate consents, the President ratifies and proclaims the treaty.

This method of procedure having been established by long practice, efforts by senators to alter it have proved unavailing. Effects of the prevailing interpretation have been frequent clashes between the President and Senate over amendments, a record of several treaties not consented to, and embarrassment in conducting negotiations, since the negotiator can give no assurance his views will be accepted by the Senate.

[S. B. Crandall, *Treaties: Their Making and Enforcement;* H. M. Wriston, *Executive Agents in American Foreign Relations;* W. S. Holt, *Treaties Defeated by the Senate.*]

HENRY M. WRISTON

Treaties, Secret. Secret articles have been negotiated five times, twice before the Constitution. An Act Separate and Secret with France, 1778, went into force (*see* Franco-American Alliance). One in the Preliminary Articles of Peace with Great Britain, 1782, was not ratified; supposed to be secret it became known (*see* Definitive Treaty of Peace). A treaty with the Creek Indians[qv], 1790, contained a secret article (*see* McGillivray Incident). In 1829 commissioners to negotiate with Turkey, instructed to include a secret article about customs duties, did so. The Senate rejected it, disapproving its substance, not its secrecy. In the Treaty of Guadalupe Hidalgo[qv], 1848, Nicholas Trist included, without instructions, a secret article regarding ratification. The Senate refused consent, following President Polk's suggestion.

Nothing in the Constitution prevents secret treaties, but barriers are twofold. First, the Senate's secrecy is not to be trusted, having been violated many times. Second, no secret treaty with a foreign nation has been ratified since 1778; precedent and tradition are now so strong as to be virtually decisive. The Creek Indian treaty constitutes no precedent, since Indian treaties came to be regarded as Executive agreements[qv].

[Hunter Miller, ed., *Treaties and Other International Acts of the United States.*]

HENRY M. WRISTON

Treaties with Foreign Nations. Treaty-making by the United States began almost contemporaneously with the founding of the Republic. The alliance with France of Feb. 6, 1778, with the concurrent Treaty of Amity and Commerce, was vital in the establishment of independence (*see* Franco-American Alliance); also of major significance was the peace with Great Britain after the Revolutionary War (*see* Definitive Treaty of Peace, 1783). Other treaties dating before 1789 were with the Netherlands (1782), with Sweden (1783), with Prussia (1785) and with Morocco (1786).

When Washington became President, Great Britain and Spain were our neighbors; France was our ally. The outbreak in 1793 of European conflicts, destined to continue for more than two decades, soon brought the United States near to war with Great Britain; catastrophe was averted by Jay's Treaty[qv] (1794), justly famous for its practical embodiment of the principle of international arbitration[qv]. Relations with Spain were stabilized by Pinckney's Treaty[qv] (1795), a complete success for American diplomacy. With France the situation became more and more acute; there were naval hostilities during the administration of John Adams (*see* Franco-American Misunderstanding); by the Convention of 1800[qv] both countries recognized that the alliance of 1778 was ended; and in 1803 came our first episode in expansion, the purchase of Louisiana[qv].

Important clauses of the treaty of 1794 with Great Britain expired in 1807 without renewal or substitutes, a circumstance not irrelevant to the outbreak of the War of 1812[qv]. The peace, the Treaty of Ghent[qv] of 1814, was essentially the *status quo ante;* soon followed the commercial convention of 1815 (still in force in 1940), the demilitarization of the Great Lakes, 1817 (also in force), and the Convention of 1818 regarding the North Atlantic fisheries, the northern boundary, and for the so-called "joint occupation" of the Oregon Country[qqv]; together these constituted a liquidation of controversy; the peaceful frontier to the north had been created.

The other frontier was with Spain, east and west of the Mississippi. The treaty with Spain of 1819 (*see* Adams-Onís Treaty) added the Floridas to the national domain and gave to the United States, in exchange for Texas, rights of Spain in the Oregon Country north of Spanish California, from the Rocky Mountains to the Pacific. Of relatively minor importance were treaties with Prussia (1799) and Sweden and Norway (1816); and outside of Europe there were agreements for tribute or peace with the corsair states (Algiers, Tunis and Tripoli, 1795–1816; *see* Barbary Wars).

The number of treaties of nearly half a century (to 1821) was small; they had been entered into with only six European powers (apart from

Treaties with Foreign Nations

countries of North Africa); but among those treaties may be counted at least twelve that were fateful and momentous.

During the next forty years the field and scope of treaty-making were extended. Numerous agreements dealing with such varied subjects as claims in Europe and in this hemisphere, extradition, consuls, neutral rights, *droit d'aubaine,* and release of shipping tolls were negotiated. A long series of treaties with other American states began with that with "Greater" Colombia in 1824; the first treaty with Russia, regarding the Pacific, dates from the same year; conventional relations of commerce and navigation now came to be established or renewed with almost all countries of Europe; one to be mentioned is the "temporary" convention with France of 1822, still partly in force (1940); our first treaty with Turkey was made in 1830; the mission of Edmund Roberts to the Far East resulted in treaties of 1833 with Muscat (still in force) and with Siam (revised in 1856); another mission to the Far East had for its result only the treaty with Brunei (Borneo) of 1850; and in the Near East a treaty of 1856 was made with Persia. The United States was among the Western powers to make treaties with China, in 1844 (*see* Cushing's Treaty) and 1858 (*see* Reed Treaty); also in 1858, following the agreement made by Commodore Perry[qv] in 1854, was signed the treaty with Japan which was the basis of relations with that country for four decades; growing interest of the United States in the Pacific was evidenced by the treaty with Hawaii of 1849. Major questions were adjusted with Great Britain; the Webster-Ashburton Treaty[qv] of 1842 ended dispute about the northeastern boundary and was otherwise a global settlement, except for the Oregon Country, which was divided in 1846 by the present line (*see* Oregon Treaty of 1846). In that same year came the beginning of our Panama policy by the treaty with New Granada (*see* Bidlack-Mallarino Treaty of 1846); in 1850 was written the Clayton-Bulwer Treaty[qv] with Great Britain, not abrogated until half a century later; by the treaty of 1854 there was commercial reciprocity[qv] for a decade with Canada. With Mexico (independent from 1821) important treaties were made in 1828 and 1831; Texas became a republic in 1836 and was annexed in 1845[qqv]; the Mexican War ended in 1848 with the Treaty of Guadalupe Hidalgo, by which and the Gadsden Treaty[qqv] of 1853 the present boundary was established.

Within the thirty-six years from the beginning of the Presidency of Lincoln to the close of the second Cleveland administration (1861–97) there was continued increase in the number of agreements, including some with countries not previously appearing as contractors; the list of treaties of commerce and of consular, naturalization and trade-mark conventions is long; the network of extradition conventions became more comprehensive; important claims commissions were set up; conventions with China included those of 1880 and 1894 on immigration (*see* Chinese Exclusion Acts). Famous bilateral treaties of this time were that of 1867 with Russia for the purchase of Alaska[qv]; the Treaty of Washington[qv] of 1871 with Great Britain, which provided for arbitration of the *Alabama* and other claims and of the San Juan water boundary and dealt with the North Atlantic fisheries and the navigation of the St. Lawrence; and the treaty of 1894 with Japan, which ended, on a footing of equality, all restrictive privileges and jurisdiction. The question of the seal fisheries[qv] in Bering Sea was arbitrated under the convention with Great Britain of 1892. Commercial reciprocity with Hawaii was established by the convention of 1875; but with Mexico the reciprocity convention of 1883 failed to become effective. Provisions for the government of Samoa, which proved to be quite temporary, were agreed to with Germany and Great Britain in 1889; and the United States became party to various multilateral instruments such as the Red Cross Convention of 1864, the Industrial Property Convention of 1883, the Submarine Cables Convention of 1884, and the General Act for Suppression of the Slave Trade of 1890.

Expansion overseas began in the McKinley administration with the annexation of Hawaii (1898); the United States, by the Peace of Paris of 1898, acquired from Spain the Philippines, Puerto Rico and Guam, Cuba becoming independent[qqv]; Samoa was partitioned with Germany (Great Britain withdrawing) in 1899; by the Hay-Pauncefote Treaty[qv] of 1901 Great Britain consented to the abrogation of the Clayton-Bulwer Treaty; an American Panama Canal[qv] became a reality following the treaty of 1903 with Panama; the Virgin Islands[qv] were ceded by Denmark in 1916; and policy in the Caribbean[qv] was evidenced by conventions for administration of Dominican customs (1907) and of Haitian finances (1915).

During the period from 1897 to 1917 there were instruments of importance concerning relations with Canada[qv]; to be mentioned are the convention of 1903 for arbitration of the Alaska boundary, the treaty of 1908 for demarcation of the frontier, the Boundary Waters Treaty of 1909 setting up the International Joint Commission[q.v.], the agreement of the same year for arbitration of the North Atlantic fisheries, and the convention of 1911 for the preservation of fur seals, to which Great Britain, Japan and Russia were parties. Along with the growing number of bilateral conventions on subjects of special interest, one feature of these years was the making with various countries of treaties in similar form; arbitration conventions of a rather mild type were entered into quite generally beginning with 1908; and in 1913–14 the Bryan treaties[q.v.] for the advancement of peace were signed with more than a score of states, noteworthy exceptions being Germany and Japan. Among multilateral conventions of significance, by far the most notable were those written at the Hague Conferences[q.v.] of 1899 and 1907, particularly the convention of the first Conference (revised at the second) for the pacific settlement of international disputes; and the United States was party to the General Act of Algeciras[q.v.] of 1906. Pan-American conventions[q.v.] began with those of the second, third and fourth Conferences, held respectively at Mexico City in 1901–2, at Rio de Janeiro in 1906, and at Buenos Aires in 1910.

The nonratification by the United States of the Treaty of Versailles[q.v.] was followed by numerous agreements for liquidation of the World War, including treaties of friendly relations with Germany, Austria and Hungary (1921); with the same powers were made treaties of commerce (Germany, 1923; Hungary, 1925; Austria, 1928). It was now the policy of the United States to include in treaties of commerce an *unconditional* most-favored-nation clause[q.v.]; this reversal of earlier and almost constant practice was first introduced in the treaty with Germany of 1923 (though deleted therefrom in 1935), and is found in a dozen later treaties dating from 1925 to 1934. Postwar conditions brought to an end the regime of extraterritoriality[q.v.] in Siam (1920) and also in Turkey (see treaties of 1929 and 1931); a general convention for the abolition of capitulations in Egypt was signed in 1937.

The results of the Washington Conference of 1921–22[q.v.], during the Harding administration, were deemed at the time to be of high significance; chief among them were the Treaty for the Limitation of Naval Armaments (United States, British Empire, France, Italy and Japan; terminated in 1936); the Four-Power Treaty[q.v.] (United States, British Empire, France and Japan); the Nine-Power Pact[q.v.] (United States, Belgium, British Empire, China, France, Italy, Japan, the Netherlands and Portugal); and a number of resolutions, mostly relating to China.

The London Naval Treaty of 1930[q.v.] terminated in 1936 except for its rules of submarine warfare; the London Naval Treaty of 1936[q.v.], limited in scope and parties, was to be in force until 1942.

The Treaty for the Renunciation of War (*see* Briand-Kellogg Pact), initiated by the United States and France and signed at Paris in 1928, was ratified by nearly all civilized states throughout the world.

The volume of treaty-making during the last two decades precludes detailed analysis; of the bilateral conventions, more than ninety deal with such usual subjects as arbitration, conciliation, extradition and naturalization; a unique group is that of "liquor treaties," made because of the Eighteenth Amendment[q.v.] and beginning with Great Britain in 1924; another group comprises "supplementary" extradition conventions to cover crimes under the bankruptcy law; fishery treaties with Canada were those of 1923 (halibut; revised in 1930 and 1937) and 1930 (salmon); the Senate in 1921 assented to the treaty of 1914 for the payment to Colombia of $25,000,000, and in 1925 to the Isle of Pines Treaty of 1904 with Cuba; there were various claims conventions, including two of importance with Mexico signed in 1923, with later extensions and modifications; under a convention with Mexico of 1933 rectification of the Rio Grande has proceeded; concrete evidences of the "good neighbor" policy[q.v.] were the treaty of 1934 with Cuba abrogating the Platt Amendment[q.v.] and that of 1937 with Mexico terminating the Tehuantepec clauses of the Gadsden Treaty of 1853.

In modern times, and more particularly since the establishment of the League of Nations[q.v.], multilateral or group treaties have grown in number and importance; the sovereignty of Norway over Spitzbergen was recognized in 1920 by treaty to which the United States, Great Britain, Denmark, France, Italy, Japan, the Netherlands, Norway and Sweden were parties; the United States became party (in 1929) to the 1919 convention regarding liquor traffic in Africa, and (in 1934) to the 1919 revision of the General Acts of Berlin of 1885 and of Brussels of 1890, regarding trade and navigation in Africa; subjects of some other recent general treaties are weights and measures, bills of lading, industrial property, sanitation, slave trade, radio, import and export restrictions, safety of life at sea, Red Cross, prisoners of war, aviation, double nationality, load lines, narcotic drugs, whaling and sugar; besides there are Pan-American treaties, concluded at the fifth to seventh Conferences held respectively in 1923 at Santiago, in 1928 at Havana, and in 1933 at Montevideo; those of the Inter-American Conference of 1936 at Buenos Aires (*see* Peace Conference at Buenos Aires) are politically significant in their relation to the policy of "good neighbor," as is also the "Antiwar Treaty" of Rio de Janeiro to which the United States adhered in 1934.

Treaty-making is progressive; during a recent session of Congress twenty-seven instruments were submitted to the Senate, more than were sent to that body during the thirty-two years from 1789 to 1821; treaties made by the United States up to this writing number about 790; their texts in English run to some 5000 pages in a four-volume publication.

Even a summary account of treaties of the United States would be incomplete without reference to Executive agreements, of equal effectiveness and validity as international acts. Some Executive agreements are made by sole authority of the President, but more under statute or joint resolution. They are more numerous than treaties; postal conventions, made under laws dating from 1792, form the largest group; another category comprises settlements of claims of American citizens, directed by the Executive, with precedent as early as 1799; in late years the subjects of Executive agreements have been most varied; a few examples are tariff duties, arbitration, copyright, patents, most-favored-nation treatment, radio, aviation, shipping and measurement of vessels; and in matters of vital concern procedure by way of Executive agreement has at times been adopted for the very reason that the constitutional majority of the Senate for a treaty was not available; after rejection by the Senate of a treaty of annexation, Texas was annexed in 1845 pursuant to joint resolution[qv]; similarly the treaty of 1897 for annexation of Hawaii was laid aside, and annexation under joint resolution followed; the armistice of the Spanish-American War[qv] of 1898 provided for the cession of Puerto Rico and Guam; the protocol of 1901 after the Boxer Rebellion[qv] in China was not submitted to the Senate; funding agreements of the Harding and Coolidge administrations, involving about ten billion dollars principal of war debts[qv], were made with the sanction of Congress; in 1927 World War claims were adjusted with Great Britain by exchange of notes; it was by authority of joint resolution that the United States became a member of the International Labor Organization[qv] in 1934; the silver agreement of 1933 and the currency accords with Great Britain and France of 1936 have their basis in statute; and the reciprocal trade agreements[qv] of the administration of President Franklin D. Roosevelt rest on an act of Congress.

[*Statutes at Large;* Malloy, *Treaties, Conventions . . .* and supplementary volumes; Hunter Miller, *Treaties and Other International Acts; Treaty Series; Executive Agreement Series; List of Treaties Submitted to the Senate, 1789-1934,* and supplements; W. S. Holt, *Treaties Defeated by the Senate;* Wallace McClure, *Democracy in Treaty-Making.*]

HUNTER MILLER

Tredegar Iron Works. Rolling mills rose at Richmond almost as soon as at Pittsburgh. The Tredegar rolling mill, privately built in 1836, was first operated by the Tredegar Iron Company, Jan. 2, 1838. Joseph Reid Anderson, a West Point graduate, the company's third commercial agent, saved it from failing in 1841. In 1843 he leased, and in 1848 bought the works. By 1860 he had enlarged them, and successfully manufactured for a national market nearly every type of iron, including 1200 cannon for the United States Government. Produced largely by skilled slave labor, Tredegar iron, because of its great tensile strength, ranked as one of the three leading charcoal irons of America. Without the Tredegar the Confederacy would have collapsed, since, until 1863, it constituted the government's only source for cannon other than by capture. It served as a laboratory for Confederate military and naval experiment, and a reservoir of munitions; it equipped the army with nearly 1100 cannon; it made mandatory the defense of Richmond, and thus the removal of the capital from Montgomery for psychological reasons. Re-incorporated, after the war, as the Tredegar Company, with Anderson as president, it led in rebuilding the new South. Today, more than a century old, directed by Anderson's descendants, it supplies munitions to the United States Government.

[Kathleen Bruce, *Virginia Iron Manufacture in the Slave Era.*]

KATHLEEN BRUCE

Tree Planting on the Plains (1854–1940). The first settlers entering Kansas and Nebraska, after those territories were opened to settlement in 1854, found that trees diminished as they advanced westward until on the High Plains no timber existed except in scanty fringes beside water courses. Desire for beauty, shade, windbreak and fuel induced the pioneers to set out groves, many of which survive today. An extra inducement to tree planting was the theory that rainfall increases with trees. The theory yet persists. J. Sterling Morton of Nebraska City, editor, farmer, acting territorial governor of Nebraska and later U. S. Secretary of Agriculture in President Cleveland's second Cabinet, is credited with being the originator of Arbor

Day^qv^. The first observance was April 10, 1872, having been designated by the Nebraska state board of agriculture of which Morton was a member. In recognition of Morton's long campaign for trees on the plains, the Nebraska legislature of 1885 changed Arbor Day to April 22, Morton's birthday.

Sen. P. W. Hitchcock of Nebraska introduced the Timber Culture Bill^qv^, which passed Congress in 1873, providing that a settler on public domain^qv^ could acquire title to 160 acres by planting forty acres to trees. The next year the requirement was reduced to sixteen acres and two years of successful tree growth. Most of the groves planted under the Timber Culture Act died, yet some well-planted trees have survived for sixty years. State experiment stations^qv^ on the High Plains, some established in the 1890's, have demonstrated that certain varieties, such as cottonwoods, flowering willow, green ash, honey locust, Russian mulberry, Russian olive, Chinese elm, etc., will thrive as far west as the fifteen-inch rainfall line, which approximates the western Kansas boundary. By diverting rainwater from highways and ravines, experiments have proved the possibility of growing trees with less than fifteen inches.

The Federal Government engaged in wholesale tree planting, commencing with 1934, in selected localities scattered from the twenty-five inch rainfall line west to the Rocky Mountains. Millions of trees have been set out on leased or purchased land and more than half of the plantings were reported as thriving in 1939, some surviving severe drouth years with only eight inches of rainfall but with utilization of drainage water. (*See also* Reforestation.)

[Kansas State Board of Agriculture, *Quarterly Report*, March, 1935, pp. 45-57; U. S. Department of Agriculture, Forest Service, Lake States Forest Experiment Station, *Possibilities of Shelterbelt Planting in the Plains Region*, 1935; Addison Erwin Sheldon, *Nebraska, Land and People.*]

BLISS ISELY

Tree-Ring Dating is a device of American archæologists, developed by A. E. Douglass about 1914, to date ruins in New Mexico and Arizona. The annual rings of trees of the same species vary in thickness in unison with fluctuating rainfall. Excessively wet and dry seasons can be dated by wide and narrow rings, respectively. Beginning with a living tree and matching cross sections with older overlapping logs, a standard scale was established including old beams in ruins. The present standard scale, for northern Arizona and New Mexico, ranges from 350 A.D. to 1937. When beams are found in ruins in the same locality, cross sections are cut from them and matched on the scale. Over a hundred important ruins have been dated, ranging from 354 A.D. to 1370 A.D. For example, the timbers in the large ruin known as Pueblo Bonito, New Mexico, were cut between 919 A.D. and 1130 A.D. which represents the approximate period of occupation. Further, by this method the culture periods in the area, formerly determined by stratigraphy, have been dated as follows: Basket Maker III, ?–700; Pueblo I, 700–900; Pueblo II, 900–1100; Pueblo III, 1100–1300; Pueblo IV, 1300–1700. Thus in this area sections of trees serve as dated documents, revealing changes in climate as well as in human habitat and cultures.

[*Tree-Ring Bulletin*, a Quarterly published by the Tree-ring Society, Tucson, Ariz.; Harold S. Gladwin, *Methods and Instruments for Use in Measuring Tree-rings.*]

CLARK WISSLER

Trelawney Plantation, THE, at Richmond's Island, Maine, was typical of the early fishing and trading posts along the New England coast. Title to the territory was based on a grant by the Council for New England^qv^ to Robert Trelawney and Moses Goodyear, merchants of Plymouth, England, dated Dec. 1/11, 1631. Trelawney, left in sole possession by the death of Goodyear in 1637, never came to America, active direction of the plantation being in the hands of John Winter, who was put in possession, July 21/31, 1632, by Richard Vines, the agent of Gorges^qv^. In addition to fishing, which was the main business, there was a trade with the Indians and white settlers. Agriculture was carried on (twelve acres were devoted to corn, grain and peas in 1639), and pigs, goats and cattle were raised. In 1637 the population was forty-seven. The labor problem was acute, because workers decamped to go into business for themselves. In 1648, after the death of Trelawney (1644) and of Winter (1645), Robert Jordan, Anglican minister, son-in-law of Winter, was awarded the plantation by the general assembly of Lygonia^qv^ as security for a claim which Winter's estate had upon the proprietor. Trelawney's minor heirs never had a hearing, and their intermittent efforts (1677 to 1758) to recover were unsuccessful.

[J. P. Baxter, ed., *The Trelawney Papers*, Maine Hist. Soc. *Documentary History*, Vol. III.]

ROBERT E. MOODY

Trench in American Warfare, THE. In the American colonial wars, where fortifications came into question at all, they were generally in the form, not of field trenches, but of fortresses—permanent works large or small. Serious field operations were maneuvers about a fortress, such as Wolfe's operations on the Montmorency front at Quebec. Sieges were rare, Louisburg[qv] perhaps the only example. Battles in the field did not occur, except in Indian warfare.

With the Revolutionary War a new situation arose—civilized forces facing each other in the field; and instantly began the use of hasty field entrenchments. Bunker Hill[qv] was the first case; a flimsy entrenchment was built, on Gen. Putnam's theory—"an American soldier is not afraid for his head, but terribly afraid for his legs; cover these, and he will fight all day." Washington used trenches continually and freely, and often mentions them in his letters, especially enjoining their habitual use in instructions to detached commanders, like Greene in the South and Schuyler in the North. Trenches were to him a means of keeping his army in the field; he constantly warned against allowing them to become a trap.

Trenches were little used in the War of 1812 and the Mexican War, the occasion for them seldom arising. The art was practically lost during the ensuing period of peace, and at the beginning of the Civil War the soldiers of both sides, like all raw soldiers, resented work on trenches. The light soon broke upon both armies, however. Chancellorsville[qv] was a trench battle, and thereafter both sides acquired great skill and ingenuity; whenever a line halted in the presence of the enemy, each man began to dig without orders.

The ultimate development was Petersburg[qv] in 1864–65. Here we find the completely developed forerunner of the trench warfare of 1914–18 in France. Parallel lines of trenches were created, each side holding them with the minimum force and keeping the maximum force free for maneuver against the exposed flanks. When the line became so long that Lee's weakened army could not hold it, he had to let go of Richmond[qv] and try in vain to escape to the Carolinas. This is what happened in France after the battle of the Marne in 1914; but in this case, the "Race to the Sea," as it is often called, distances were so short and forces so large that the maneuvering flanks reached the English Channel before the trench-holding elements were strained to the breaking point. This is one of the points which the French had in mind when, after the war, they introduced serious study of our Civil War into their École de Guerre.

[Spaulding-Nickerson-Wright, *Warfare*; Oliver L. Spaulding, *The United States Army in War and Peace.*]

OLIVER LYMAN SPAULDING

***Trent* Affair,** The, involved the disputed doctrine of the freedom of the seas[qv]. In the autumn of 1861 the Confederate government selected as diplomats James Murray Mason of Virginia for London and James Slidell of Louisiana for Paris. The commissioners successfully ran the blockade to Havana, Cuba, where they took passage, Nov. 7, 1861, on the *Trent,* a British ship. The next day, without instructions, Capt. Charles Wilkes of the U.S.S. *San Jacinto* stopped the *Trent,* searched the vessel, arrested the two Confederate commissioners and their secretaries, and removed them to the *San Jacinto.* The *Trent* was permitted to continue its voyage, but the commissioners were taken as prisoners to Fort Warren, in Boston Harbor. Capt. Wilkes had made the mistake of searching the ship and seizing the agents on board a neutral vessel at sea instead of bringing the ship into port for adjudication. The *Trent* might have been seized, however, for performing an unneutral service. The ship's "cargo," though, could not be legally condemned except by bringing the vessel before a prize court[qv] and receiving a judicial decree to that effect.

When the news of the *Trent* affair reached the American public, there was naturally great rejoicing in the North because Union victories on the battlefield thus far had been few. In England, however, news of the incident was followed by a wave of indignation. In fact, a demand for war spread through the British Isles. Lord Russell drafted a demand for an apology and for the immediate release of Mason and Slidell. If this demand were not met, Lord Lyons, the British minister at Washington, was to come home. Fortunately, the Prince Consort, who was on his deathbed, softened the British note, and Lyons presented the position of his government as tactfully as possible. The British government rushed 8000 troops to the defense of Canada and forbade temporarily the exportation of arms and ammunition.

A majority of Lincoln's Cabinet had rejoiced with the public, and failed to question Wilkes' act. The House of Representatives even voted Wilkes a gold medal. Lincoln, fortunately, was cautious, and Secretary Seward soon realized that a mistake had been made. Nothing was done, however, prior to the arrival of the British note, except to instruct Charles Francis Adams, American minister to England, to inform Lord Palmerston that Wilkes had acted without instructions.

Upon realizing that the alternative to the surrender of the commissioners must be war with England, Seward, in a communication, Dec.

26, "cheerfully liberated" them because Wilkes had erred in not bringing the ship into port for adjudication, and because he had violated American established policy of freedom of the seas. The dispatch was written to soothe the American public and also to satisfy the British. Although successful in this endeavor, Seward lost for the United States an opportunity to secure British acquiescence in the principle of freedom of the seas.

[W. C. Ford, ed., *A Cycle of Adams Letters;* E. D. Adams, *Great Britain and the American Civil War;* The Diary of Edward Bates, 1859-66, H. K. Beale, ed., in the *Annual Report of the American Historical Association,* Vol. IV; James D. Richardson, *A Compilation of the Messages and Papers of the Confederacy, including the Diplomatic Correspondence;* H. W. Temple, William H. Seward, Secretary of State, in S. F. Bemis, ed., *American Secretaries of State.*]

GEORGE D. HARMON

Trenton, Battle of (Dec. 26, 1776). Following Washington's evacuation of New Jersey, Howe (Br.) had established two unsupported cantonments of 1500 Hessians each, at Bordentown and Trenton. Col. Rall, the commandant at Trenton, scorning the American soldier, refused to fortify the village. To Washington, facing the dissolution of his army and sure the enemy only awaited the freezing of the Delaware to seize Philadelphia, the exposed position of these posts offered an opportunity. He accordingly planned a simultaneous surprise movement against both, with the main blow falling at Trenton.

On Christmas night, with 2500 troops, he crossed the Delaware at McKonkey's Ferry, eight miles above Trenton. Delayed by floating ice and a storm of sleet and snow, it was eight o'clock and broad day when his two columns, under his own and Sullivan's command, reached the village. The Hessians, who, as Washington had foreseen, had spent Christmas night in celebrating, were completely surprised. "They made no regular stand" (Washington); their firing was ineffective as their powder was dampened by the storm; and Rall, who had ignored warnings of the attack, seemed not to know what to do. The Americans, among whom were many expert riflemen, fired from houses, cellars, from behind trees and fences, while their artillery raked the two main streets of the town. In the battle, lasting scarcely forty minutes, the Hessians lost 22 killed (including Rall), 84 wounded and 1000 taken prisoner, while the patriots had only two officers and two privates wounded. Two supporting divisions failed to cross the river until the following day; meanwhile the Hessians at Bordentown safely withdrew.

Coming so swiftly after a succession of bitter defeats, this victory infused new life into the patriot cause, restored confidence in Washington both at home and abroad, strengthened the resolution of Congress and, coupled with Princeton[qv], practically freed New Jersey of British control. "It was a momentous turning point in the Revolution" (Fisher).

[S. G. Fisher, *The Struggle for American Independence;* W. S. Stryker, *The Battles of Trenton and Princeton.*]

C. A. TITUS

Trenton, Decree of (Dec. 20, 1782). Both Pennsylvania and Connecticut (*see* Connecticut's Western Lands) claimed that part of Pennsylvania lying between the forty-first and forty-second parallels. For a number of years intermittent civil war was waged between settlers and official representatives of the two colonies (*see* Pennsylvania-Connecticut Boundary Dispute). Finally, Pennsylvania appealed to Congress, empowered under the Articles of Confederation[qv] to arbitrate in jurisdictional disputes between states. The unanimous decision of the Court of Commissioners, meeting at Trenton, supported Pennsylvania's claim. This decision, known as the "Trenton Decree," terminated a controversy pending since 1757.

[Trenton Historical Society, *A History of Trenton, 1679-1929,* Vol. II.]

C. A. TITUS

Trespass Act (1783), an act contrary to the provisions of the Definitive Treaty of Peace[qv], was passed at the insistence of Gov. Clinton. Primarily designed to benefit the owners of real estate in or about New York City, whose property had been occupied by the British during the Revolution, it permitted the owners of real estate which had been thus used to sue to recover rents and damages. A large number of actions were started under the law. Chief Justice Richard Morris was awarded a judgment of £5000 against Gov. Tryon for damages to a farm worth only a third of that sum. When Mayor James Duane, in the mayor's court of New York City, virtually pronounced the act unconstitutional in the case of Rutgers v. Waddington, the legislature censured him, and some members sought to remove him from office. Alexander Hamilton under the name of "Phocion" wrote a pamphlet in 1784 denouncing the harsh treatment of the loyalists[qv], and appealing to Congress and the states to observe the treaty of peace in respect to them. He was answered by Isaac Ledyard, as "Mentor"; and the controversy continued until 1788, when under the influence of Hamilton, Jay, Schuyler, Duane and

Robert R. Livingston, the legislature repealed all laws contrary to the treaty of peace.

[A. C. Flick, *Loyalism in New York during the American Revolution.*]

A. C. FLICK

Trevett v. Weeden, a decision rendered by Judge Howell of Rhode Island, Sept. 18, 1786, is frequently cited as a precedent for the doctrine of judicial review[qv] laid down by Marshall in Marbury v. Madison[qv]. Acts of the legislature provided heavy fines for those refusing to accept the state's depreciated paper currency at par. The defendant, John Weeden, a butcher, was discharged on the ground that the acts were unconstitutional and void.

[S. G. Arnold, *History of the State of Rhode Island.*]

W. A. ROBINSON

Trevilian Station, Battle at (June 11–12, 1864). Sheridan, commanding 10,300 Federal cavalry, left the Pamunkey, June 7, under Grant's orders to destroy the Virginia Central Railroad and join Hunter at Charlottesville. Hampton (C.), marching from Atlee's with 5000 horsemen, intercepted Sheridan at Trevilian Station, June 11. Torbert's (U.) division, attacking Hampton's right, was struck in rear by Fitzhugh Lee's (C.) division. Custer's (U.) brigade was driven back, but recovered its ground. During the night Hampton retired one mile. Sheridan attacked again next day but, unable to make progress or reach Charlottesville, retired to the York River.

[Edward L. Wells, *Hampton and His Cavalry in '64; Battles and Leaders of the Civil War*, Vol. IV.]

JOSEPH MILLS HANSON

Trials, Famous. The first trial in American history which excited the whole nation was that of the soldiers of the 29th British regiment in the provincial court of Massachusetts charged with the murder of six citizens in the so-called Boston Massacre[qv] in 1770. Ably defended by John Adams and Josiah Quincy, all were acquitted save two who were convicted of manslaughter and given light sentences.

The most talked-of murder trial of the early 19th century was that of Rev. Ephraim K. Avery at Newport, R. I., in 1833 for the murder of Sarah Cornell, a factory worker. The minister was acquitted, but his reputation was ruined. A still more noted case was that of Dr. John W. Webster, professor in a Boston medical college, in 1850 for the murder of a colleague, Dr. George Parkman. Webster was convicted and hanged. Lizzie Borden, of Fall River, Mass., tried–and acquitted–in 1893 on the charge of killing her father and stepmother with a hatchet, became one of the most celebrated figures in our unsolved mystery literature. The trials of several members of the Clan-na-Gael, a secret society, for the assassination of Dr. Philip P. Cronin in Chicago in 1889, excited nationwide interest because of their revelations of the workings of a ruthless cult. Three defendants were given life sentences and three were sent to prison for three years each. The three trials of Caleb Powers (1901–2–3), former Secretary of State of Kentucky, for the murder of William Goebel (*see* Goebel Affair) were notable for the intense political feeling aroused the country over, even national magazines carrying bitter articles and editorials on their alleged unfairness. Powers' death sentence was commuted to life imprisonment and after several years he was pardoned, and entered Congress in 1911. The trial of Harry Thaw at New York in 1907 for the murder of Stanford White, architect, was a cynosure of attention because of the prominence of the parties concerned, the brilliance of the opposing counsel – District Attorney William Travers Jerome against Martin W. Littleton for the defense–and Jerome's famous lengthy hypothetical question. The three trials of Leo Frank at Atlanta (1913–15) for the murder of Mary Phagan aroused racial antagonisms which traveled far. Frank's death sentence was commuted to life imprisonment, but shortly thereafter, on Aug. 26, 1915, he was lynched by a mob. The finding of the bodies of Rev. Edward W. Hall, a prominent clergyman of New Brunswick, N. J., and one of his parishioners, Mrs. Eleanor Mills, near their home city in 1922, finally led to the trial, four years later (November–December, 1926) of Mrs. Hall and two of her brothers, but all were acquitted. The trial of Bruno Hauptmann in 1935 for the Lindbergh kidnapping[qv] and murder attracted throngs which fairly overwhelmed the little town of Flemington, N. J., where it was held; it was followed even in foreign countries, and scathing criticism was evoked by the behavior of the counsel, the press and the spectators.

The trials of the anarchists accused of the bombing in the Haymarket riot, of the Mafia murderers in New Orleans, of the Molly Maguires in Pennsylvania, of Sacco and Vanzetti, of the Scottsboro Negroes and the Gastonia labor rioters, all affairs of great social importance, have been treated in separate articles. The several trials of the members of the Tweed Ring and the Whiskey Ring[qqv] were high spots in the turbulent judicial history of the 1870's; but they attracted no more attention than, if as much as, that of the suit of Theodore Tilton against the Rev. Henry Ward Beecher, noted pastor of Plymouth Church, Brooklyn, charging adultery with Mrs. Tilton and asking $100,000 damages. The trial was drawn out through six months in 1874–75, and the jury, after nine days of deliberation, were unable to agree, nine voting for the defendant and three for the plaintiff. Another sensational case was the suit of Madeline Pollard against William C. P. Breckinridge, congressman and noted political figure, for breach of promise in 1893. There were noted civil trials of the 19th century, each the subject of special articles, such as the Wheeling Bridge, Charles River Bridge and Dartmouth College cases[qqv]—the last-named most notable because of the eloquent participation of Daniel Webster—which have set precedents still invoked in the 20th century. The Dred Scott Case[qv] was ominous as one of the last fatal steps toward Civil War. Judge Kenesaw M. Landis, in disintegrating the Standard Oil Company[qv] in Federal Court in 1907, also startled the country by imposing the largest fine on record—$29,240,000; which, however, was set aside by the Supreme Court.

[Faculty of Yale Law School, *Two Centuries of Growth of American Law;* Edmund L. Pearson, *Instigation of the Devil.*]

ALVIN F. HARLOW

Triangle Fire (1911). The Triangle Waist Company, occupying the three top floors of a ten-story loft building in New York City, suffered a disastrous fire on March 25, 1911, in which 147 lives, mostly those of women and girl workers, were lost. More than 50 jumped from the windows to the street; the others were burned or trampled to death. The cause of the fire was unknown; perhaps a lighted cigarette or match was dropped into inflammable waste. It was found that little provision had been made for fighting fire; that there was only one narrow fire escape, that some of the doors through which the women might have fled were habitually kept locked and stairway entrances were cluttered with boxes and rubbish. The elevator men did their best, but could not work rapidly enough. The proprietors of the business were indicted and tried, but acquitted. Public opinion had been aroused, however, and the disaster led to sweeping reforms in building and factory laws, especially as to precautions against fire.

[*The Outlook,* Vol. 97, pp. 754, 851, 949, and Vol. 100, p. 8; *Collier's,* Vol. 51, pp. 7, 8.]

ALVIN F. HARLOW

Triangular Trade. *See* Trade, Triangular.

Tribal Courts, Indian, often called "Courts of Indian Offenses," have existed on many western reservations since 1883 when an order for their establishment was issued by the Secretary of the Interior. Authority for them, therefore, rests upon an executive order rather than any act of Congress, though that body makes appropriations for their support. Such a court usually consists of one, two, or three Indian judges appointed by the reservation superintendent, who also has power to approve, disapprove, or modify every decision. Most cases have to do with petty offenses, minor civil disputes, or domestic relations. Procedure is informal, but grave, deliberate, and dignified. Decisions rendered are based upon equity and a spirit of fair play rather than upon statutory law and are characterized by justice and wisdom. Before their governments were abolished, the Five Civilized Tribes[qv] also had courts commonly called tribal, but these were entirely unlike the courts of Indian offenses.

[Laurence F. Schmeckebier, *The Office of Indian Affairs;* Lewis Meriam and others, *The Problem of Indian Administration.*]

EDWARD EVERETT DALE

Triborough Bridge, THE. Construction on this project was begun by the City of New York in 1929, and halted by the business depression early in 1932. The Triborough Bridge Authority was then incorporated, funds were borrowed from the Public Works Administration[qv], work resumed in 1933 and completed in July, 1936. The "bridge" is really an elevated highway, a series of bridges and viaducts crossing two islands, linking Manhattan, Bronx and Queens boroughs, and including a suspension span of 1380 feet over the East River.

[Triborough Bridge Authority, *The Triborough Bridge.*]

ALVIN F. HARLOW

Tribute. To avert the loss of commercial vessels and the enslavement of American seamen, the United States for many years followed the example of other Christian powers in dealing with the piratical governments of Morocco, Algiers, Tunis and Tripoli. These Barbary governments regarded the Mediterranean as their private property, for the use of which they demanded that other nations pay them a fixed annuity or give them many valuable presents.

The unwillingness of the United States to comply with these demands resulted in the confiscation of numerous American vessels and the enslavement of several hundred American seamen by Algiers alone prior to the concluding of a peace treaty in 1795. This treaty, the only one with the Barbary States stipulating the payment of annual tribute, cost the United States more than $900,000 by the time it was concluded. Treaties with Morocco (1786 and

1795), with Tripoli (1796) and with Tunis (1797) also proved so expensive that by 1802 the United States had paid more than $2,000,000 to the four powers.

The rapacity of the North African governments increased with each concession, and finally resulted in indecisive hostilities (1801–5) between the United States and Tripoli (*see* Barbary Wars). In 1815, after a renewal of Algerine aggressions, Commodore Stephen Decatur[qv] compelled Algiers to abandon all claims to tribute from the United States, and soon thereafter collected indemnity from Tunis and Tripoli for illegal seizures.

Until the middle of the 19th century the United States continued to give occasional presents to Barbary officials, but the payment of tribute, in any strict sense of the word, ceased in 1812. Although some features of American policy with respect to Barbary exactions now seem disgraceful, it may well be remembered that the United States led all other nations in opposing what amounted to international subsidizing of piracy.

[H. Adams, *History of the U. S. during the Administrations of Jefferson and Madison;* G. W. Allen, *Our Navy and the Barbary Corsairs;* R. W. Irwin, *Diplomatic Relations of the United States with the Barbary Powers.*]

RAY W. IRWIN

Tripartite Agreement, THE (Sept. 25, 1936), was an international monetary agreement entered into by France, England and the United States for the purpose of stabilizing their currencies both at home and in the exchange. Following suspension of the gold standard[qv] by England (1931) and the United States (1933), a serious disequilibrium developed between their currencies and that of the gold bloc countries, particularly France. At the same time the controversy between "sound money" advocates, urging stabilization, and those favoring complete demonetization of gold and a managed currency, became acute in both England and America. Likewise, the gold bloc countries urged stabilization of the sterling and dollar, due to the adverse influence of their fluctuating values on the exchange value of gold bloc currencies. As devaluation had raised import and lowered export prices in England and America, the gold bloc countries would eventually have to devaluate unless international stabilization was agreed upon by leading monetary powers. The franc was devalued practically simultaneously with the announcement of the Tripartite Agreement.

By this informal, relative, and provisional agreement the three powers were pledged to refrain from competitive depreciation, and to attempt to maintain currencies at existing levels provided it did not interfere seriously with internal prosperity.

[Paul Einzig, *World Finance, 1935-1937;* C. R. Whittlesey, *International Monetary Issues.*]

KENNETH POTTER

Tripoli, War with. *See* Barbary Wars.

Trist Mission, THE. As the Mexican War[qv] drew to a close, Nicholas P. Trist, Chief Clerk of the Department of State, was designated to negotiate the peace, but was recalled when the administration decided upon harsher terms than the instructions given Trist. No longer an executive agent[qv], Trist nevertheless remained in Mexico, where on Feb. 2, 1848, he was the sole American negotiator of the Treaty of Guadalupe Hidalgo[qv]. Indignant though it was with Trist, and strongly tempted to disavow his work, the United States Government nevertheless ratified the treaty.

[Louis Martin Sears, Nicholas P. Trist, A Diplomat with Ideals, in *The Mississippi Valley Historical Review,* Vol. XI.]

LOUIS MARTIN SEARS

Troup and Clark Parties were the names attached to the two factions in Georgia state politics, following the disappearance of the Federalists[qv] early in the 19th century. They reached their greatest virulence from 1819 to 1825, during which time George M. Troup and John Clark, the political enemies who gave their names to the parties, were each elected governor twice. Though differing little in principles, the Troup party tended to represent the aristocratic states'-right[qv] tradition and the Clark party the frontier nationalistic group.

[U. B. Phillips, *Georgia and State Rights;* E. M. Coulter, *Short History of Georgia.*]

E. MERTON COULTER

Truax v. Corrigan (257 U. S. 312, 1921). In this case the Supreme Court, in a five to four decision, held unconstitutional the Anti-Injunction Law of Arizona (1913). Conspiracy and illegal picketing and boycott were alleged. The majority opinion held that the action of the strikers was coercive, a violation of the plaintiff's right of property, and a denial of free access of employees, owners and customers to the place of business. The Court held that the Arizona law deprived the owner of property without due process[qv] of law; was invalid under the Fourteenth Amendment[qv]; and conferred class privilege.

[Gordon S. Watkins, *Labor Problems.*]

GORDON S. WATKINS

"Trust-Busting." This term originated during the administration of Theodore Roosevelt, which marked the turn from an apathetic policy in enforcement of the Sherman Antitrust Law[qv] to one of energetic prosecution of Big Business[qv]. In the phrases of the period, trust-busting might be defined as "wielding the Big Stick" upon "malefactors of great wealth."

[Walter Lippman, *Drift and Mastery.*]

MYRON W. WATKINS

Trusts. Authorities on trusts agree that the term has been so broadly used that a precise definition is impossible. Eliot Jones limits it to an industrial monopoly, and that is the general practice, although banking combines have been known as "money" trusts, public utilities have been called "power" trusts, and railroad companies and labor organizations have been prosecuted under the Federal antitrust laws[qv]. The attempt or even the ability to control a large portion of the market is what makes a concern a trust.

The monopolistic tendency on a national scale first became apparent in American industry after the Civil War and took the form of pooling agreements limiting production, fixing prices, centralizing selling, and setting quotas, but since these were unenforceable under the common law, they were often broken. The first trust was the Standard Oil[qv] whose form of organization, secret in 1879 but amended and publicized in 1882, originated the name. The stockholders in numerous refining, pipe line and other companies assigned their stock to a board of nine trustees at a stipulated price and received trust certificates. The trustees had legal and voting rights in the stocks; and the stockholders received the profits. This ingenious system was shortly copied by other industries; the American Cotton Oil Trust was set up in 1884, the National Linseed Oil Trust in 1885, and the Distillers and Cattle Feeders Trust, known as the "whiskey trust," in 1887.

Public agitation over the size and power of these giant organizations led to the testing of their legality in state courts, which decided that entering into such agreements was beyond a corporation's powers. Congress passed the Sherman Antitrust Law[qv] July 2, 1890, section 1 of which states that "Every contract, combination . . . or conspiracy in restraint of trade or commerce among the several states . . . is . . . illegal." Between 1891 and 1897 there were only fifty combinations of over a million dollars formed, most of them of the property-holding type. The depression covering much of this period was, of course, also a discouraging factor.

The antitrust legislation was not effective for long. The Supreme Court seemed to draw the teeth of the Sherman Act in 1895 in the Knight case (*see* U. S. v. E. C. Knight Co.) by ruling that the control of 98% of the sugar refining in the country was not illegal because it took the form of manufacturing in one state and not commerce between states. Said the Court, "Commerce succeeds to manufacture, and is not a part of it." In addition a satisfactory substitute for the trustee device was found when New Jersey in 1889 and 1893, then Delaware, Maine and other states, authorized corporations receiving charters from them to hold stock in other corporations, a right previously not enjoyed. The holding company[qv] thus made possible differed from the trustee system in that ownership was substituted for trusteeship.

Between 1898 and 1903 trusts were formed in rapid succession. The census of 1900 showed 185 industrial combinations, 73 of them capitalized at $10,000,000 or more, turning out 14% of the industrial products of the nation; 1901 witnessed the founding of the billion-dollar United States Steel corporation[qv]; and by 1904, 318 trusts controlled two fifths of the manufacturing capital of the country. The "rich man's panic" of 1903 brought the movement to a close.

Meanwhile the Government had won a few minor cases with the Sherman law, Theodore Roosevelt had become President, and a fever of reform had begun to sweep the nation. The "trust busting"[qv] movement began with the Supreme Court decision of March 14, 1904, against the Northern Securities Company[qv], a holding company formed to unite two great competing railroad systems in the Northwest. Suits were brought against forty-four trusts and combinations in Roosevelt's administration and against ninety more under President Taft.

The trusts became better behaved. Ruthless extermination of rivals that had characterized the oil and cash-register trusts gave way to a more tolerant system of letting the independents live if they would adhere to the trust's price policy and so keep business stable and profits at a maximum. These milder tactics bore fruit in 1911 when the Supreme Court announced in an *obiter dicta* in the Standard Oil and American Tobacco cases[qqv] that these trusts were being dissolved because they were acting in "unreasonable" restraint of trade. The implication of this renowned "rule of reason"[qv] was that "good" trusts would not be broken up in the future. The following year the Court went a step farther in the Terminal Railroad Association case (224 U. S.

383) and contended that even a trust which had acted in restraint of trade should be tolerated, if it could be used for legitimate purposes.

In 1912 Woodrow Wilson popularized his "New Freedom"[qv] whose keynote was the restoration of free competition in trade and industry, and in 1914 his administration secured the Clayton and Federal Trade Commission acts[qqv]. The Clayton Act condemned such business practices as local price discrimination, tying contracts, interlocking directorates and even the acquisition by one corporation of the stock of another in the same business, if the consequences were monopolistic. The Federal Trade Commission act forbade "unfair methods of competition in commerce," a broad term which it was left to the commission to enforce and the courts to continue to interpret. But the "New Freedom," handicapped by greater judicial tolerance of trusts and by the outbreak of the World War, died young.

There are several explanations for the public's less hostile attitude toward trusts after the World War armistice[qv]. The war taught businessmen in all lines the advantages of concerted action; it showed the public that a rising price level was probably caused more by monetary factors than by monopoly exploitation; and it bred a cynical attitude toward reform. The Webb-Pomerene Act of 1918 and the Merchant Marine Act of 1920 permitted American concerns to combine to some extent in their foreign business. When the Supreme Court did not dissolve the U. S. Steel Corporation in 1920 (251 U. S. 417), despite its control of over half the steel output, and such evidence as a price of $28 a ton for steel rails maintained for ten years, a new trust movement got under way. The merger was now the chief method of combination because the Clayton Act virtually forbade large-scale commercial combination by stock purchase. However, public utility[qv] empires were built with the holding company device. It has been estimated that there were over 500 combinations in the Coolidge administration alone. During the prosperous 1920's businesses in the same line were permitted to an increasing degree to compare recent statistical information, basing point systems grew in popularity, and finally, in the Appalachian Coal Case (288 U. S. 344) in 1933 a joint sales agency, including producers of 75% of the output, was judged not contrary to the antitrust laws.

The great amount of price-cutting that took place during the depression after 1929 led to criticism of the predatory character of competition and to considerable talk of the need for a more planned economy. The F. D. Roosevelt administration under the National Industrial Recovery Act[qv] of 1933 permitted trade associations[qv] and other industrial groups to control prices, and determine production, and encouraged them to draw up codes of fair competition, promising that any action taken in compliance with an approved code would not subject them to prosecution under the antitrust laws. The Federal Trade Commission was to enforce these codes. Within the first month over 400 of the eventual total of 677 were filed, and many were too hastily approved. Code groups were allowed to do many things the antitrust laws forbade, and this was especially true of the soft coal, petroleum, lumber and cleaning and dyeing businesses. The suspension of over forty years of antitrust legal precedents left the courts bewildered. However, the Supreme Court's adverse decision in the Schechter case[qv] in May, 1935, brought this experiment in industrial self-government to an end.

Two subsequent laws slightly altered antitrust legislation. The Robinson-Patman Act[qv] (1936) attempted to define more clearly the types of wholesale price discrimination that were prohibited. The Miller-Tydings Act (1937) gave force in interstate commerce to the resale price maintenance laws most states have, and represented a lessening of competition.

The recession of 1937 saw a renewal of trust prosecutions, proceedings against the Aluminum Company of America and the Federal Trade Commission's attack on the cement industry's basing point system being particularly notable. Then on June 16, 1938, Congress by joint resolution authorized the appointment of the Temporary National Economic Committee (the T.N.E.C.), Sen. Joseph C. O'Mahoney of Wyoming chairman, to discover some method of reconciling existing antitrust law and the growing concentration of economic power and eventually to recommend legislation to Congress. Judged by its hearings, which began on Dec. 1, 1938, the committee is especially concerned over monopolistic practices and profiteering. Some believe the committee's findings will be used to inaugurate a new "trust busting" era; others foresee their employment to justify a new N.R.A.

Antitrust legislation has been criticized on several scores. It is presumed that the public benefits by competition, yet some of the most effective competition, from abroad, is inoperative because of our high-tariff[qv] policy. Dissolutions have not been very successful, partly because of the framework of laws within which the courts must function, and partly because the courts have shown less interest in this aspect of the problem. In the Standard Oil case and several others the Court simply ordered the stock of subsidiary companies distributed pro rata among the stockholders of the parent company, which meant that stockholders prominent in the trust remained prominent in presumably competing successor companies. The third criticism is that some large industries, like steel, have such enormous overhead costs that to force price competition in depression times would bankrupt costly plants certain to be needed again later. As our economy becomes increasingly complex, this is becoming true of more industries. The solution to this problem remains to be found.

[E. L. Bogart, *Economic History of the American People;* F. A. Fetter, *The Masquerade of Monopoly;* Eliot Jones, *The Trust Problem in the U. S.;* G. M. Modlin and A. M. McIsaac, *Social Control of Industry;* H. R. Seager and C. A. Gulick, *Trust and Corporation Problems;* Ida Tarbell, *Standard Oil Company;* M. W. Watkins, *Industrial Combinations and Public Policy;* M. R. Thompson, *Trust Dissolution;* The Background of the Anti-Monopoly Investigation, in *Business Week*, Dec. 24, 1938.]

DONALD L. KEMMERER

Tryon's Line. William Tryon, as royal governor of North Carolina, in pursuance of agreements made with the Cherokee[qv] on Oct. 20, 1765, and June 13, 1767, caused to be run a line between North Carolina and the Cherokee hunting grounds. Under instructions from London, this line was run in the summer of 1767 as a part of the line referred to in the Proclamation of 1763[qv]. Tryon named three commissioners who ran the line from Reedy River, where the North Carolina–South Carolina line terminated, to the top of Tryon Mountain of the Blue Ridge; thence by a straight course to Chiswell's Mine[qv] (the present Austinville, Va.) on New River. Tryon then issued a proclamation forbidding any purchase of land from the Indians and the issuance of grants beyond and within a strip one mile east of the line. (*See also* Hard Labor, Treaty of.)

[*North Carolina Colonial Records*, Vol. VII.]

SAMUEL C. WILLIAMS

Tubac, the first settlement founded by Spaniards in Arizona, lies about twenty miles north of the Mexican border, on the Santa Cruz River. Visited by missionaries as early as 1691, the site was probably not permanently occupied by whites before 1750. A rebellion of Pima Indians[qv] in the following year led to the establishment of a Spanish military presidio at Tubac in 1752, chiefly for the protection of the Jesuit missions[qv] of San Cayetano del Tumacácori and San Xavier del Bac. Tubac was from 1764 to 1774 under the command of Juan Bautista de Anza[qv], leader of the colonial expedition from Compostela to found a presidio and mission at San Francisco Bay in 1776, being one of Anza's points of departure on that journey. The presidio was moved from Tubac to Tucson in 1776, but small Spanish, Pima and Mexican garrisons were stationed there for varying periods after 1784, until the time of the Mexican War in 1846.

[H. H. Bancroft, *History of Arizona and New Mexico;* H. E. Bolton, ed., *Anza's California Expeditions;* E. R. Forrest, *Missions and Pueblos of the Old Southwest.*]

RUFUS KAY WYLLYS

Tuberculosis. The Quaker lady, Elizabeth Sandwith Drinker, who kept a Diary (1758–1807), left for posterity a description of the tuberculosis of her son William, and of the treatment he endured. The foremost figure in colonial medicine, the dominating Benjamin Rush, taught his pupils and contemporaries that pulmonary consumption was not contagious; that rheumatic pains, abscesses in the armpits, and early spitting of blood were favorable signs; that a sea voyage was beneficial, but sea air on the shore was dangerous (baneful effects of mixed land and sea air); that the consumptive should live on horseback like a Tartar; that remedial measures were vigorous labor, swinging, running, dancing and military hardships in the army; that treatment consisted in blisters, setons, nitre, mercurial salivation and bloodletting. Every one of these propositions is wrong.

The junior James Jackson of Boston was the first to describe the prolonged respiratory sound heard in incipient phthisis (1833); William Wood Gerhard of Philadelphia established the anatomico-clinical basis of tuberculosis meningitis (1833); the treatise (1843) of William Adair McDowell of Kentucky was modern both in its protest against bloodletting, purging and vigorous exercise, and in its plea for plenty of food, outdoor life and graduated exercise; Austin Flint introduced the term cavernous respiration, and wrote a monograph on phthisis (1875) which was standard before the bacteriological period; Edward Gamaliel Janeway was the earliest in this country to teach the contagiousness of tuberculosis (1882); Hermann Michael Biggs was the first to induce a health department to declare tuberculosis a communicable and preventable disease (1889), and for being ahead of his time was sharply rebuked by the New York Academy of Medicine; Nathan Straus, the apostle of pasteurization, was the first to open depots where the masses could obtain pure milk (1893), and founded the first Tuberculosis Preventorium for Children; Theobold Smith, demonstrating that nature evolved two races of the microbe from a common ancestor, was the first to differentiate the tubercle bacillus of man and of cattle (1896).

The most glamorous name in our tuberculosis history is Edward Livingston Trudeau, himself a victim, who erected on the hills of Saranac a cross of hope to which thousands have clung—the first sanatorium for the consumptives of America (1884), and the first laboratory for the study of tuberculosis (1894). As the communicability, anatomical unit, stethoscopic diagnosis, animal transmission, bacteriological etiology, tuberculin reaction, and sanatorium treatment of tuberculosis were demonstrated in other lands, no discoveries of fundamental importance were made by American investigators. Nevertheless, in America the retreat of the tuberculosis death rate has been more marked than in any other industrialized nation.

[Victor Robinson, Autobiography of the Tubercle Bacillus, in *Medical Review of Reviews*, 1917, 79-83.]

VICTOR ROBINSON

Tukabatchi, Council at. *See* Tookabatchee.

Tule Lake, Battles of. The first serious attempt to dislodge Capt. Jack and his Modocs[qv] from caves in the Lava Beds south of Tule Lake on the California-Oregon boundary was made by Lt. Col. Frank Wheaton, Jan. 16 and 17, 1873, without success. After Maj. Gen. E. R. S. Canby was killed, April 11, fighting continued in the same area until April 20, a major attack being made by Col. A. C. Gillem, April 15, 16 and 17, after which the Indians fled to another part of the Lava Beds.

[A. B. Meacham, *Wigwam and Warpath;* Cyrus Townsend Brady, *Northwestern Fights and Fighters.*]

DON RUSSELL

Tullahoma Campaign, THE (June-August, 1863). After the battle of Stone River, Bragg (C.) retired southward to Tullahoma in middle Tennessee. Rosecrans (U.) occupied Murfreesboro[qv]. Some Confederate re-enforcements were detached to Vicksburg to oppose Grant (U.). As soon as the weather and roads permitted, Rosecrans, on June 24, 1863, reorganized and enforced, moved to maneuver Bragg out of Tennessee and to occupy Chattanooga[qv]. By July 3, 1863, through skilful employment of his numerical superiority and with only minor engagements at Liberty and Hoover gaps, Rosecrans had forced Bragg to the vicinity of Chattanooga. These successes, coinciding with Confederate defeats at Gettysburg and Vicksburg[qqv], marked the turning point of the war. Much fighting followed, but except for the "barren" victory at Chickamauga[qv], the Confederate Army of Tennessee[qv] thenceforward fought on the defensive.

[*Battles and Leaders of the Civil War.*]

THOMAS ROBSON HAY

Tunis. *See* Barbary Wars, The.

Tunnels. The first American tunnel of record was the 400-foot bore near Pottsville, Pa., through which the Schuylkill Canal passed, constructed in 1820–21. The second, 729 feet in length, conveyed the Union Canal[qv] through a hill near Lebanon, Pa., and was completed in 1827. The third, 901 feet in length, completed 1833, was on the Portage Railroad[qv]. The difficulty of achieving these works with hand-drilling and common gunpowder can scarcely be comprehended by later generations. Railroads dug many tunnels thereafter, with a rapid increase in length. Between 1850 and 1860 (not to mention numerous smaller ones) six were bored, from 4800 to 5800 feet long. The Hoosac Tunnel[qv], completed in 1875, was the most noted tunnel project of the century, though the 4½-mile Sutro Tunnel[qv] was an equally difficult undertaking. The public heard little of New York's New Croton Aqueduct, opened in 1888, 31 miles long and nearly all tunnel.

The first discoverable suggestion to tunnel under water is found in 1834. A railroad was planned, running eastward from Albany, N. Y., but it was deemed impossible to bridge the Hudson, so a tunnel under the river was proposed, but as funds were not available even the railroad project was abandoned for several years. The first attempt to tunnel under the Hudson at New York was begun in 1874, but a disaster in 1880, in which twenty men were killed, ended the project. It was begun again in 1888, halted in 1902, and finally opened in 1908 as the Hudson and Manhattan Railroad. Other tunnels in this system, connecting New York, Jersey City, Hoboken and Newark, were completed in 1909–10–11. Meanwhile, the Michigan Central Railroad[qv] parallel tunnels, 2⅓ miles long, under the Detroit River (opened 1910), were being constructed as huge concrete tube sections 260 feet long and 23 feet in diameter, molded on land, floated to the site in pairs on great pontoons and sunk in position, 74 feet below the surface. Between 1904 and 1910 the Pennsylvania Railroad[qv] completed tunnels (over 13,000 feet in all) giving it an entrance to New York City and continuing under Manhattan Island and the East River into Long Island, to give the subsidiary Long Island Railroad access to the city. The subways[qv] of New York, though mostly built on the cut-and-cover plan, have some remarkable tunnels under the city's hills and under the East and Harlem rivers. In fact, subterranean New York is a honeycomb of tunnels—railroads, subways, large bores carrying water, electric cables, gas, etc. The Catskill Aqueduct, opened 1915, passes under the Hudson near Cornwall by a siphon tunnel reaching a depth of 1114 feet below the river surface, and in reaching the five boroughs of New York, traverses an 18-mile tunnel, often from 200 to 750 feet below the surface. The great tunnel carrying water from the Hetch-Hetchy Valley to San Francisco, opened 1934, is 25.2 miles long. By a tunnel nearly four miles long through the Continental Divide in Colorado, completed in 1935, waters flowing westward are diverted to irrigate lands 250 miles down the Arkansas Valley to eastward. The largest tunnels in existence, four 56-foot passages for carrying water around Boulder Dam[qv] on the Colorado, were completed in 1936. San Diego in 1931–32 built four tunnels for pedestrians under busy street intersections, thus adding another use for the subterranean passage.

ALVIN F. HARLOW

Tupelo, Battle at (July 14, 1864). Following Sturgis' (U.) defeat at Brice's Cross Roads, A. J. Smith (U.), with 14,000 troops near Memphis, undertook to prevent Forrest (C.), who had 12,000 men, from interrupting Sherman's (U.) rail communications in Tennessee (*see* Atlanta Campaign). Smith marched southward and on July 14 sent Grierson's cavalry division to Tupelo, Miss., to destroy the Mobile and Ohio Railroad. Following with his two infantry divisions, Smith was attacked by Forrest one mile west of Tupelo. The Confederates were defeated in four assaults, losing 1326 men killed and wounded. Smith, who had lost 650, though gaining the field, retreated to Memphis, where he arrived July 23, followed all the way by Forrest.

[John A. Wyeth, *Life of General Nathan Bedford Forrest; Battles and Leaders of the Civil War*, Vol. IV.]

JOSEPH MILLS HANSON

Turbine, The. Water turbines, invented in France, were known in America by 1790, but being less efficient than breast wheels were not commonly used. Nevertheless, 300 patents were granted for them before 1843 when successful installations near Philadelphia and Fall River, Mass., commanded attention. The following year they began to displace pitchback wheels at Lowell, Mass., soon adding one fourth to the effective water power at that city, Lawrence, and other mill centers. Their epochal application, however, was to hydroelectric generation fifty years later, when 5000 horsepower turbo-generators at Niagara marked a half-century's advance from the 75 horsepower turbine installed at Lowell in 1844. Today (1940) ten to thirteen times the 1894 capacity is not uncommon.

Steam turbines, likewise foreign inventions, were perfected in America about 1893 and invaded the fields of both water turbines and reciprocating steam engines. They help account for the fact that steam power now outranks water power as a source of electric energy. During the last years recorded, the number of reciprocating engines driving electric generators has declined nearly two thirds while the number of turbines so employed has increased more than tenfold, and the amount of current generated by steam approaches twice the amount generated by water.

[James B. Francis, *Lowell Hydraulic Experiments;* Victor S. Clark, *History of Manufactures in the United States.*]

VICTOR S. CLARK

"Turf and Twig." This expression refers to a ceremony of a somewhat primitive nature in vogue in England down to, and during, the time of the early American settlements, as a tangible and visible part of the "livery of seizin"[qv]. It was close kin to "seizin by hasp and staple," an old Scotch ceremony in which the buyer or heir of a house took hold of the hasp, entered the building and locked himself in as a sign of rightful possession.

The "turf and twig" ceremony of transfer was used in several of our colonies, for example, in Pennsylvania, Delaware and Maine. On Oct. 25, 1682, at New Castle, Del., William Penn, Esq., took possession of the town of New Castle "by virtue of an instrument of Indenture signed and sealed by his Royal Highness James, Duke of York, and did there demand possession and seizin of John Moll, Esq., and Ephraim Harman Gentlemen Attornies." The ceremony of delivery was consummated "by giving him the key thereof to lock upon himself alone the door, which being opened by himself again, we did deliver also unto him one turf with a twig upon it, a porringer with river water and soil in part of all what was specified in the said indenture, or deed of enfeoffment. . . ."

[Deed Record G., p. 410, also B. 9, pp. 407-412, of New Castle County, Delaware Book B.; Samuel Hazard, *Annals of Penn.*, p. 597 and 607; Thomas Holcomb, *History of Immanuel Church*, p. 39; Amelia C. Ford, Colonial Precedents of Our National Land System As It Existed in 1800, in *University of Wisconsin Bulletin 352, History Series.*]

BENJAMIN HORACE HIBBARD

Turkey Island Battle, The, occurred Sept. 4, 1763, when several hundred Indians in canoes attacked by night the schooner *Huron,* manned by twelve men, becalmed in Detroit River near the island. The defenders fought desperately with hatchets and spears. When all seemed lost the command was given to blow up the ship, whereupon the savages fled.

[Francis Parkman, *Conspiracy of Pontiac.*]

M. M. QUAIFE

Turkey Town, so named for its chief, was a Cherokee village founded in 1770 on the west bank of the Coosa River opposite Center, Ala. Occupied by both Cherokee and Creeks[qqv] it was the center, 1780–95, for raiding expeditions against the Cumberland settlement[qv]. Its site was claimed by the Creeks and the two tribes had many disputes over it. After the Revolution the Cherokee councils were often held here.

[Publications of the Alabama Historical Society, *Miscellaneous Collection,* I, 420.]

R. S. COTTERILL

Turkeys, Wild, were originally found in great flocks from the Atlantic to the Rocky Mountains and from the Gulf of Mexico to latitude 44° N. Their wide distribution and numbers made them an important article of food for travelers, pioneers and later for soldiers at army posts, cattlemen and even for city dwellers after the construction of western railroads. The unwillingness of the turkey to take to its wings and its preference for hiding, after a short flight, in bush or high grass made it a comparatively easy prey and large numbers were obtained in a short time by skilful hunters in new territory. Some were even run down by horse and dog on the prairies. The wild turkey cock often weighed 25 to 30 pounds and its popularity is shown by the fact that Audubon's[qv] drawing of it is the most sought after of all the plates in his celebrated volume. Persistent hunting has practically exterminated this splendid game bird so that few now exist save in remote and inaccessible parts of the country. Like the passenger pigeon and the buffalo[qv] it disappeared in the path of the advancing white man. Most Indian tribes, for superstitious reasons, declined to eat it and its prolific characteristics account for the immense number of flocks originally found.

[R. I. Dodge, *Plains of the Great West;* W. T. Hornaday, *American Natural History.*]

CARL L. CANNON

Turner, Nat, Insurrection. *See* Nat Turner's Rebellion.

Turnpikes were roads on which tolls were collected from users to meet the costs of construction and maintenance. The idea of thus financing highways was imported, toward the end of the 18th century, from England, where the turnpikes were publicly owned and administered by trustees. In America, however, they were generally built with private capital and operated by corporations for profit under state regulation, although outside New England public funds were sometimes so invested.

The greatest activity in company organization and road construction occurred between 1795 and 1810. The growth of commerce, which called for road betterment, and an easing of capital combined to encourage this activity. One hundred seventy active turnpike companies were chartered in New England between 1792 and 1810. They invested over $5,000,000 in building or improving nearly 3000 miles of road. By 1807 New York had 88 different operating companies, representing a capital investment of over $5,500,000 and operating over 3000 miles of road; Pennsylvania had 88 companies operating 1807 miles by 1821.

Costs of construction varied in New England between $200 and $13,000 per mile. Companies which built entirely new roads, especially those in metropolitan areas, invested heavily in land. Other companies simply took over old public roads without purchase. Those roads built in tidewater areas often required an artificial roadbed, while others required only clearing and grading. The number of bridges[qv] required affected costs of construction significantly, as did the type of road surface desired. Turnpikes in New England were rarely surfaced, since the sand content of its soil is generally high. In New York, Pennsylvania and some of the Southern states, however, an artificial gravel surface was common.

Turnpike corporations were responsible for a decided improvement in road conditions generally. Cities and villages were brought closer together. The extensive business done by stage lines and the rapid increase in the number of privately owned traveling vehicles between 1800 and 1830 attest to the encouragement of travel by turnpikes. In freight carriage they were important as feeders to water transportation facilities, but ineffective as competitors with water routes (*see* Canal Building).

In spite of this stimulus to land travel and transportation[qv], especially the former, as business enterprises the turnpikes were miserable failures. By 1825 turnpike stocks were generally worthless, since maintenance charges were only slightly, if any, less than toll receipts. During the turnpike era, 1800–1840, probably not over a dozen turnpike roads paid their proprietors even reasonably well. An overwhelming majority lost the whole amount of original investment. The trouble lay in overbuilding. Naturally well-situated roads should have been built less expensively and less well-situated roads should not have been turnpiked at all. The inherent inefficiency of horse-drawn vehicles for long-distance travel or hauling could not be overcome by the expensive multiplication or improvement of highways.

[F. J. Wood, *Turnpikes of New England*; A. Gallatin, *Report on Roads and Canals, 1808*, Appendix; U. P. Hedrick, *History of Agriculture in the State of New York;* W. C. Plummer, *Road Policy of Pennsylvania*.]

PHILIP E. TAYLOR

Turpentine, Trade in. As early as 1700, turpentine was being exported in small quantities from the various English colonies to the mother country. Although this trade increased considerably after the middle of the 18th century, tar and pitch remained the most important "naval stores"[qv] during that period. It was not until about 1820 that American turpentine exports became significant, and it was not until about 1850 that they amounted to as much as $200,000 a year. By 1860 they had increased to $1,916,289, 90% of which came from the two Carolinas. The industry declined materially during the next decade, and it was not until about 1873 that it reached the 1860 level. Meantime the industry was expanding southward, and by 1890 Georgia had become the leading producer—a position now held by Florida. From 1870 to 1900 the average annual exports of turpentine amounted to about $3,000,000; from 1900 to 1920, to about $7,000,000. From 1870 to 1920 the United States exported over $260,000,000 worth of this product to some thirty different countries. Great Britain has been the largest purchaser, taking over one third of the total turpentine exports, with Germany, Belgium and Holland being the next largest purchasers. In recent years there has been an increasing trade with South America. Of course, there is a tremendous home market for turpentine, which is used in the manufacture of paint, varnish, soap, shoe polish, disinfectants and a hundred other articles.

[Thomas W. Gamble, ed., *Naval Stores: History, Production and Consumption*, Savannah, Ga., 1921.]

HUGH T. LEFLER

Tuscarora War, THE (1711–13), was fought in eastern North Carolina. The lower Tuscarora Indians, led by Chief Hancock, were moved to attack their English neighbors chiefly because of the vicious practices of white traders and alarm at settlers' encroachments on their hunting grounds. A sudden massacre (September, 1711) almost overwhelmed the colony. New York officials persuaded the warlike Seneca[qv], related to the Tuscarora, not to enter the fray. Virginia aided by overawing the upper Tuscarora into neutrality and, later, nominal alliance. South Carolina's assistance was more apparent. Col. John Barnwell led a relief expedition of about fifty whites and over 350 Indian allies. Although his campaign (January–April, 1712) weakened the enemy, it ended in a poorly observed truce. A second South Carolina expedition was commanded by Col. James Moore; it consisted of thirty-odd whites and almost 1000 Indian warriors. The main body of the enemy took refuge in Fort Nohoroco, near present Snow Hill. A three-day engagement resulted in its capitulation (March, 1713) and in Tuscarora acceptance of a drastic treaty of peace. Most of the Tuscarora trekked northward and joined their kindred; thereafter the Five Nations[qv] were known as the Six Nations[qv]. Native opposition having been shattered, North Carolina's westward expansion began in earnest.

[W. Clark, Indian Massacre and Tuscarora War 1711-13, in *The North Carolina Booklet*, Vol. II, 1902-3, No. III.]

W. NEIL FRANKLIN

Tuskegee Institute, THE, was established by the Alabama legislature in the post-Reconstruction period. Its first session began with thirty students, July 4, 1881, under Booker T. Washington. His plan of education included the correlation of academic courses with industrial training. His successors, Robert Russa Moton and Frederick Douglass Patterson, with a Negro faculty and friends North and South, co-operated in making Tuskegee one of the Negro's achievements. Its graduates number 30,000; the annual student enrollment totals 2000; the faculty of 250 is in 10 schools; and the plant contains 132 buildings.

[Anson Phelps Stokes, *Tuskegee Institute, The First Fifty Years;* Booker T. Washington, *Up from Slavery*.]

CHARLES H. WESLEY

Tutorial Instruction, System of. The first American university to adopt and adapt the traditional English use of "dons" and tutors was Princeton[qv]. In 1905 Woodrow Wilson secured an appropriation wherewith to add to the faculty fifty young men to be known as preceptors, whose function was not to hold classes but, by meeting students informally and more or less individually, to supplement the conventional work of the classroom. For fifteen years other institutions surveyed the Princeton experiment, then in 1920–22 Harvard, Smith and Swarthmore Colleges modified it by introducing "honors courses"—informal instruction for superior students in the two upper classes. By 1930 more than a hundred colleges had followed suit. In 1931 the University of Buffalo went considerably farther by accepting as upper classmen only those able to profit by this highly individual form of instruction. In most of the colleges which have adopted either honors courses as at Swarthmore or the tutorial method of Buffalo (and the former type is more popular, partly on account of the lesser expense) the capstone of the system is the comprehensive examination, which tests the knowledge and applications not of one or more courses but of the whole college experience in the candidate's field. The doctrine departs radically from the conventional system of required attendance, courses and credit hours which had grown up in the half century preceding 1920, and for these substitutes, in short, the principle that the best education is self-education.

[Ray Stannard Baker, *Woodrow Wilson;* Robert C. Brooks, *Reading for Honors at Swarthmore;* Julian Park, *The Evolution of a College;* Edward S. Jones, *Comprehensive Examinations in American Colleges;* W. S. Gray, ed., *Recent Trends in American College Education.*]

JULIAN PARK

Tutuila Island Naval Station. The Samoan^{qv} Treaty of 1878 permitted the United States to establish a naval station in Pago Pago Bay. On Feb. 19, 1900, three days after Samoan partition had been proclaimed, President McKinley signed an order placing Tutuila under command of the Navy Department, to be used as a naval base. The U. S. Naval Radio Station at this base maintains direct schedules with naval radio stations at Honolulu, San Francisco, Washington, etc.

[*American Samoa—A General Report by the Governor,* Navy Department, Washington, 1927; G. H. Ryden, *The Foreign Policy of the United States in Relation to Samoa.*]

J. W. ELLISON

Tweed Ring, THE, robbed the New York City treasury of a minimum of $30,000,000 in the thirty months ended July 31, 1871. Another audit estimated that the Tweed Ring proper, which began in 1869, and its immediate forerunner, looted the city of between $45,000,000 and $50,000,000 in the three years and six months beginning Jan. 1, 1868. An aldermanic investigation (1877) raised this figure to $60,000,000. Matthew J. O'Rourke, a journalist who, while county bookkeeper, bared the frauds, reckoned $200,000,000 as the total stealings of the Ring and the lesser Tweed rings from Jan. 1, 1865, to July 31, 1871. This included fraudulent bond issues, the sale of franchises, tax reductions and other official favors, of an approximate worth of $125,000,000.

When the Ring came into being on Jan. 1, 1869, it seemingly had nothing to fear. Tweed's man, John T. Hoffman, had that day been inaugurated governor of the state; and in the metropolis, Tweed was sovereign. He controlled the police, the district attorney, the courts and most of the newspapers. A Democrat, he silenced the Republican party by putting scores of its leaders on the payroll—his own or the taxpayers'. He took over the city's lone reform organization in like manner.

The Ring members were Mayor A. Oakley Hall, surnamed "The Elegant One"; City Comptroller Richard B. Connolly, alias "Slippery Dick"; City Chamberlain Peter Barr Sweeny, otherwise "Bismarck," or "Brains"; William M. Tweed, president of the Board of Supervisors and leader of Tammany Hall^{qv}.

The Ring's methods called for unscrupulous contractors, merchants and others who dealt with the municipality. The original plan called for mulcting the city out of one dollar for every two paid out. The Ring's share was gradually increased until, drunk with avarice, checks were drawn to imaginary individuals, firms, hospitals and other charitable institutions.

The Ring's recklessness and the magnitude of its thefts shoved the city to the verge of bankruptcy. This, coupled with a struggle between Tweed and Samuel J. Tilden for party control, led to the Ring's undoing.

Promises to publish a complete list of the Ring's beneficiaries and to sue them all were broken because too many influential ones were involved. Three of the Ring judges, George G. Barnard, John H. McCunn and Albert Cardozo, were impeached. The first two were removed. Cardozo resigned. Tweed, reputedly worth $12,000,000 at the peak of his power, was made the scapegoat. He made a partial confession. His offer to tell all if permitted to die outside prison walls was spurned. He died in Ludlow Street jail (1877).

[Denis Tilden Lynch, *Boss Tweed,* and *The Wild Seventies.*]

DENIS TILDEN LYNCH

Twelfth Amendment. The Constitution originally provided that "the person having the greatest number of votes shall be President, if such number be a majority of the whole number of electors appointed; and if more than one have such a majority, and have an equal number of votes, then the House of Representatives shall immediately choose by ballot one of them for President." It soon became evident that this arrangement was not satisfactory. The almost inevitable result was a lack of harmony between the President and Vice-President, since two candidates from the same party would not normally be at the top of the list. In case of the death of the President, a change of party control in the middle of the four-year term would result, without any mandate from the people.

In 1800 an acute situation developed. Jefferson and Burr not only received the largest number of votes, but the same number; it was, therefore, necessary for the House of Representatives to break the tie. While provision had been made for this contingency, its actual occurrence almost precipitated a crisis. The Federalists[qv] were restrained only with difficulty from frustrating the expressed will of the electorate, and throwing the election to Burr (*see* Jefferson-Burr Election Dispute). Steps were promptly taken to prevent the recurrence of such a situation.

The Twelfth Amendment, having passed the Senate on Dec. 2, 1803, was proposed by Congress on Dec. 9, following its passage by the House. There were seventeen states in the Union; the approval of thirteen was necessary for ratification. The legislature of New Hampshire, by its approval of the amendment on June 15, 1804, made that state the thirteenth to ratify. However, the governor vetoed the action, and if his veto was valid—which it probably was not—then the ratification by Tennessee on July 27, 1804, was decisive. Formal notice of ratification was made by Secretary of State Madison on Sept. 25, 1804, in time for its provisions to be effective in the presidential election of 1804[qv].

[Herman V. Ames, The Proposed Amendments to the Constitution of the United States, in *Annual Report* of the American Historical Association, 1896; Charles K. Burdick, *The Law of the American Constitution;* G. J. Schulz, Election of the President of the United States by the House of Representatives, 68th Cong., 2 Sess., *Sen. Doc. No. 227,* 1925; Edward Stanwood, *History of the Presidency;* W. W. Willoughby, *Constitutional Law of the United States.*]

W. BROOKE GRAVES

Twelve-Mile Limit. *See* Territorial Waters.

Twentieth Amendment. *See* "Lame-Duck" Amendment.

Twenty-first Amendment, THE, providing for repeal of the Eighteenth Amendment[qv] was proposed by Congress in February, 1933, ratified by the 36th state within ten months, and proclaimed to be in effect Dec. 5, 1933. At the time only eleven states had provisions in their constitutions concerning prohibition[qv] but among these were some curious ones, Kentucky, e.g., permitted liquor to be used medicinally, the patient prescribing the dosage for himself. The Twenty-first Amendment apparently permits states to levy an import tax on alcoholics, operative against goods produced in other states, thereby modifying the provision of Article I of the Constitution[qv] prohibiting state imposts; or to bar importation altogether.

ROBERT G. RAYMER

Twenty-one Gun Salute, THE, dates from the early times when seven guns was the recognized British national salute. Early British regulations provided that ships should fire but seven guns, but that forts could fire three shots for every shot afloat. At that time powder made from sodium nitrate was easier to keep ashore than on shipboard. When gunpowder was improved by using potassium nitrate the sea salute was made equal to the shore salute of twenty-one guns. The British finally proposed that the United States should return their salutes "gun for gun." Accordingly the United States adopted the twenty-one gun salute and the "gun for gun" return, Aug. 18, 1875.

[L. P. Lovette, *Naval Customs, Traditions and Usage.*]

LOUIS H. BOLANDER

Twightwees, THE. *See* Miami, The.

Twin Cities, THE, St. Paul and Minneapolis, are situated at the head of navigation on the Mississippi River. Pierre Parrant staked a claim on the site of St. Paul in 1838, and in the summer of 1840 a group of Catholic French-Canadians settled in what is now the heart of that city. Father Lucian Galtier built a log chapel there in October, 1841, which he dedicated to St. Paul, and from it the city received its name. The settlement thus established was designated the capital when Minnesota was organized as a territory in 1849, and was incorporated as a city in 1854.

Minneapolis, about ten miles north and west of St. Paul, was originally two communities—St. Anthony[qv] on the east bank of the Mississippi, and Minneapolis on the west. St. Anthony was settled in the 1840's and Minneapolis grew up after 1849. The two were united in 1872 and by 1880 had a population of 46,887. The older community of St. Paul had already fallen behind with 41,473 inhabitants. In 1930 Minneapolis had a population of 464,356, and St. Paul, 271,-616. Protestant New Englanders and Scandinavians predominated in the population of Minneapolis, while in the settlement of St. Paul there were many French, Irish and German Catholics.

From early times, St. Paul developed as a commercial metropolis and Minneapolis as an industrial center. Steamboats connected St. Paul with points downstream, and trade developed with the Red River^qv settlements. The city became an important market for furs, livestock and farm products, and a wholesale distributing point in the 1850's and 1860's, decades when industrial plants, particularly lumber and flour mills^qv, were growing up about the Falls of St. Anthony in Minneapolis. In addition to developing as the marketing, manufacturing and wholesale distributing point of the Northwest, the Twin Cities have become the financial, cultural and educational center of a wide region.

[M. L. Hartsough, *The Twin Cities as a Metropolitan Market;* W. W. Folwell, *A History of Minnesota;* J. F. Williams, *A History of the City of Saint Paul.*]

T. C. BLEGEN

"Twisting the British Lion's Tail." This phrase first began to be seen in print about 1885, though the custom had been popular since the end of the Revolutionary War. Early Fourth of July^qv orators lost few opportunities to voice the boast that we had whipped England twice, and could and would do it again upon any provocation. For Irish politicians and others desirous of winning the Irish vote, this was a favorite exercise. Incidents such as the Maine and Northwest boundary disputes, the Fenian raids, British aid to and recognition of the Confederacy as a Civil War belligerent and the Venezuelan boundary controversy^qqv each caused new flare-ups of swashbuckling spirit and oratory.

[The History Circle, *British-American Discords and Concords;* J. D. Whelpley, *British-American Relations.*]

ALVIN F. HARLOW

Two-Party System, THE. The United States is said to have a two-party system because during most of the history of the country since the formation of the Federalist and Anti-Federalist parties^qqv soon after the Constitution was adopted two parties have dominated the political campaigns and have been supported by most of the voters. Especially has this been the situation since the formation of the Republican party in 1856. Since that time the Republican and Democratic parties^qqv have dominated the political scene without serious challenge by other parties. This dominance is shown by the fact that with but few exceptions these two parties have divided the entire electoral vote between them (*see* Voting, Regularity in). The outstanding exceptions since 1856 were: in 1912 when the Progressive party^qv, with Theodore Roosevelt as its candidate for the Presidency, carrried six states; in 1924 when the Progressive party, with Robert LaFollette, Sr., as its candidate, carried one state; and in 1892 when the Populist party^qv secured the electoral vote of six states.

This same dominance of two parties holds true for the popular vote as well, with only a small percentage of the total vote being polled by the minor parties, in most cases less than 5%. On only one occasion since the Civil War, in 1892, has the total vote of the minor parties exceeded 10% of the total popular vote. In that election (*see* Campaign of 1892) the Populist party polled its largest vote, 1,041,028, the Prohibition party^qv polled 264,133, the Socialist-Labor party 21,164, a total vote of 1,326,325 compared with the total vote of all parties, 12,059,351.

There are a number of reasons for the continuing dominance of the political scene by two major parties. In the first place the overwhelming majority of the voters are attached to one or other of the two parties by inheritance, for social or business reasons, on account of the political environment, for political purposes, and others. And then the two major parties have built up elaborate organizations reaching down to all the counties and to nearly all of the precincts, and are usually well financed. To compete, a third party must build similar structures and to do so requires tremendous effort and—most important—heavy financing. The presidential system, with the election of one man, as compared with the cabinet system, helps to maintain two parties, one in power and one in opposition. Added to these are barriers in state laws in the form of petition requirements, filing fees and requirements for recognition as parties.

The two-party system among the nations is the exception rather than the rule. In most other countries the multi-party system exists with several strong parties competing.

[E. Stanwood, *A History of the Presidency;* E. B. Logan, ed., *The American Political Scene.*]

EDWARD B. LOGAN

Two Penny Act, THE (1755), enacted by the Virginia assembly in anticipation of a shortage in the tobacco crop, permitted payment, over a ten-months period, of obligations due in tobacco at a commutation rate of 2d. per pound. In 1758 a similar act of one-year's duration was passed. Among those affected, the clergy of the established church, whose salaries were fixed in terms of tobacco, raised the principal objection. Securing a royal disallowance^qv of the act, they sought then to collect, for the period of its operation, the difference between 2d. and the market price. Of the court actions resulting, the most celebrated was the so-called "parson's cause"^qv.

[H. J. Eckenrode, *Separation of Church and State in*

Virginia; H. L. Osgood, *American Colonies in the 18th Century,* Vol. III.]

WESLEY FRANK CRAVEN

Two-Thirds Rule, The. At the Democratic convention in Baltimore in May, 1832, the committee on rules reported the following resolution: "Resolved that each state be entitled in the nomination to be made of a candidate for the vice-presidency, to a number of votes equal to the number to which they will be entitled in the electoral colleges, under the new apportionment, in voting for President and Vice-President; and that two thirds of the whole number of the votes in the convention shall be necessary to constitute a choice." Thus originated the two-thirds rule which was followed by all Democratic conventions in making nominations until the convention at Philadelphia in June, 1936, at which convention the rule was abolished and a majority vote substituted. Numerous attempts had been made to remove the rule, but it had always been strongly defended by the southern group of states, which, with the rule in effect, could control nominations. A fight on the question in the Philadelphia convention was avoided by the adoption of a resolution designed to secure a new method of apportioning delegates among the states which would take into account the Democratic strength within each state.

[E. Stanwood, *A History of the Presidency.*]

EDWARD B. LOGAN

Tydings-McDuffie Act, The (1934). In January, 1933, Congress passed the Hawes-Cutting Act over President Hoover's veto. It provided for the independence of the Philippine Islands[qv] and for trade relations with the United States effective ten years after the inauguration of the authorized Commonwealth government. On account of tariff and immigration provisions this act was rejected by the Philippine legislature. The Tydings-McDuffie Act of March 24, 1934, eliminating certain objectionable provisions of the Hawes-Cutting Act, was passed and ratified by the Philippine legislature, May 1, 1934, and the new government was shortly inaugurated. In order to cushion the economic effects of this act and to facilitate independence in 1946, the Philippine Economic Adjustment Act was passed in 1939.

[G. L. Kirke, *Philippine Independence;* G. M. Stephenson, *American History since 1865.*]

THOMAS ROBSON HAY

Type Founders. Type was cast by Christopher Sower at Germantown, Pa., in 1735 and by Benjamin Franklin and other colonial printers[qv]. Before 1800 commercial founderies existed in Philadelphia and New York. In 1811 David Bruce of the latter establishment improved hand-casting. In 1831 his son patented the first successful type-casting machine.

[Albert S. Bolles, *Industrial History of the United States;* James Leander Bishop, *A History of American Manufactures.*]

VICTOR S. CLARK

Typewriter, The. Beginning with a patent for a "writing machine" issued in 1714 to Henry Mill, an engineer of London, numerous variations of the typewriting principle appeared in France, England and the United States in contrivances frequently using embossed letters intended primarily for the blind. Thus, in 1829 William A. Burt of Detroit patented a boxlike device with type arranged on a segment of a circle. Other inventions before 1867, however ingenious, usually proved to be too slow in operation or to involve costs that were prohibitive.

The invention of the first practical typewriter has been attributed to the work of Christopher L. Sholes, editor and politician of Milwaukee, and his associates, S. W. Soule and Carlos Glidden. Influenced by the "Pterotype," an English invention, they patented in 1867 a machine that was both accurate and rapid, although crude, which they called "the type-writer." In 1873 Sholes and Glidden concluded a historic contract for the manufacture of typewriters with E. Remington and Sons, famous gunmakers of Ilion, N. Y. The first users of this machine were court reporters; then came lawyers, editors, authors and clergymen. Once the union of the typewriter and stenography was consummated the success of the invention was assured. By 1923 the typewriter served 84 language groups in every portion of the globe. The pioneer Model 1 Remington, printing solely in capital letters, was replaced in 1878 by Model 2 which added the shift key and had two letters mounted on each type bar.

Although Sholes had turned over his royalty rights to a partner, he felt gratified to witness the social revolution wrought by his machine in the status of women. The typewriter aided materially in giving that sex economic emancipation and opportunity for greater participation in public life.

[Herkimer County Historical Society, *The Story of the Typewriter.*]

HARVEY WISH

Tyranny. The American temperament has been practical rather than philosophical, with the result that the meaning of such concepts as "freedom"[qv] and "tyranny" has been determined by the circumstances and interests of the day. "Taxation without representation is tyranny"*qv* became a slogan of the Revolution; and the Declaration of Independence*qv* is an inclusive summary of what Americans considered the tyranny of British rule. As safeguards for the future, they incorporated in our fundamental law the principles of popular election, short terms, constitutional limitations on governmental power, and a separation of powers*qv* which would guarantee "a government of laws and not of men." Enumerated powers and elaborate checks and balances*qqv*, it was hoped, would prevent the new Federal system from becoming tyrannical; but in 1798 the Alien and Sedition laws*qv* constituted tyranny in the eyes of the Republicans (Jeffersonian), and the commercial policies of the latter were tyranny to the Federalists of the Hartford Convention*qqv*. A century later Woodrow Wilson wrote, "By tyranny, as we now fight it, we mean control of the law, of legislation and adjudication by organizations which do not represent the people, by means which are private and selfish." Within a quarter century the administrative agencies*qv* established to control these private organizations were denounced as combining the functions of lawgiver, judge and executioner, with tyranny the inevitable result (*see* Quasi-Judicial Agencies).

W. A. ROBINSON

U-Boats. *See* Submarines.

Uintah, Fort (Utah), a fur-trading post, was built by Antoine Robidoux on the banks of the Uintah River above the mouth of the DuChesne in 1831. Frémont*qv* passed it in 1844 and recorded later that the fort had been attacked by the Utah Indians and all the garrison killed.

[H. M. Chittenden, *History of the Fur Trade of Far West;* Charles Kelley and M. L. Howe, *Miles Goodyear.*]

CARL L. CANNON

Unalaska, an important Aleutian island, is situated 135 miles southwest of the Alaskan peninsula. Unalaska village, on Dutch Harbor, serves as port of call for the Bering Sea region. The island, acquired from Russia by the United States in 1867, is considered a feasible site for a naval and aerial base in the North Pacific.

[H. H. Bancroft, *History of Alaska;* J. P. Nichols, *History of Alaska.*]

KENNETH POTTER

"Uncle Sam" is a nickname of the United States Government. Arising in the War of 1812, and coming into notice in the autumn of 1813, the term was first applied somewhat derisively to customhouse officers and then to soldiers by those opposed to the war, but was avoided by the "war hawks"*qv*; and, as contemporary newspapers show, was doubtless a jocular expansion of the letters U. S. on uniforms and government property.

[*Proceedings of the American Antiquarian Society,* XIX, 21-65.]

ALBERT MATTHEWS

Uncle Tom's Cabin; or, Life among the Lowly, by Harriet Beecher Stowe, was published serially in the Washington *National Era* (June 5, 1851–April 1, 1852) and appeared in book form March 20, 1852. Mrs. Stowe came into intimate contact with the bitter criticism of the Fugitive Slave Law*qv* in New England and determined to write an account of slavery as she had known it in Cincinnati. She intended to condemn the system, not the slaveholder, and expected a favorable hearing in the South. Based on fact, the book was not, however, an accurate picture of the system, although it did show both the strength and weakness of Southern society. The book had a popular reception never before accorded a novel. Three hundred thousand copies were sold the first year and more than one million by 1860. Dramatized and produced on the stage, it reached millions who never read the book. Northern people were incensed and aroused against the inhuman system. Many Southerners read the book; some wrote ineffectual replies; others forbade its circulation. Measured by its emotional appeal and lasting influence the book ranks high as reform propaganda. Most potent of all accounts of slavery, it lighted a new torch in the North and was a contributing cause of the Civil War*qv*.

[J. F. Rhodes, *History of the United States from the Compromise of 1850;* Anne B. Stewart, *A Critique of Uncle Tom's Cabin;* C. E. and L. B. Stowe, *Harriet Beecher Stowe;* H. B. Stowe, *Uncle Tom's Cabin,* 1888 edition.]

FLETCHER M. GREEN

Uncompahgre cantonment or agency was located on the Uncompahgre River in west Colorado to supervise the Utes*qv* collected there. An uprising of the Utes in 1879, due in part to pressure from the settlers for lands, resulted in the establishment of Fort Crawford in 1880 on the west bank of the river, about four miles north of the Los Pinos agency and eight miles south of the present town of Montrose. It was abandoned in 1890.

[J. H. Nankivell, Fort Crawford, Colo., in *Colorado Magazine,* March, 1934.]

CARL L. CANNON

"Unconditional Surrender" was the most popular of several nicknames bestowed on Gen. U. S. Grant after the capture of Fort Donelson*qv*, in 1862. The Confederate commander, Simon B. Buckner, proposed an armistice to discuss terms or further fighting. Grant replied that no armistice would be accepted, but only unconditional surrender. The words were carried North and became his popular given name.

[G. E. Shankle, *American Nicknames.*]

CARL L. CANNON

Underground Railroad, THE, was an informal, secret system of aiding fugitive slaves[qv] to attain freedom in the free states and Canada. It was operated, generally at night, by Quaker, Negro, Covenanter, Wesleyan Methodist, and other antislavery people, who, using all sorts of hiding places, and sometimes disguising their passengers, passed the fugitives from station to station. Slaves first heard of Canada from veterans of the War of 1812. They sang of that "promised land" and learned from friendly whites of the north star as their guide. A master losing trace of his chattel at Ripley, Ohio, is said to have been the first to apply the name of "underground road" to the method of escape. The system developed until it extended through fourteen Northern states from Maine to Kansas and Nebraska, inclusive. Networks of routes ran northward through eastern and western Pennsylvania, all of Ohio and Indiana, and eastward through southern Michigan. Another network extended eastward through southern Iowa and northeast through Illinois. Numerous routes ran through eastern Massachusetts and New Hampshire and through western Massachusetts and Vermont. Hundreds of fugitives came to New England as stowaways from Southern ports, and some were shipped to New Brunswick, Nova Scotia and England. From the coast towns of Lakes Ontario, Erie and Superior thousands entered Ontario. The Underground's business increased until 1861, and was probably used by 75,000 slaves.

[W. H. Siebert, *The Underground Railroad from Slavery to Freedom, The Underground Railroad in Massachusetts,* and *Vermont's Anti-Slavery and Underground Railroad Record.*]

WILBUR H. SIEBERT

Underprivileged, THE, is a designation applied by the philanthropist and social worker and, to a less extent, the politician, to those persons who live near or on the subsistence level. It is generally loosely used and more often with reference to children than adults. It suggests that those who are below the normal standard of living are victims of social injustice. Even if the existence of the underprivileged is an indictment of society's indifference and neglect, it is also true that these unfortunates, as a class, are handicapped by physical, psychic and social defects sometimes the results of inheritance but more often of environmental misfortune.

ERNEST R. GROVES

Underwood Act. The Democrats, who had complained that the Republican tariff raised the cost of living and helped trusts, had a tariff bill ready when President Wilson called a special session of Congress, in March, 1913. It passed the House in early May, the Senate in late September, and became a law on Oct. 3, 1913. It was called a "competitive tariff" and reduced rates generally. The reductions were not particularly effective since the ensuing World War was equivalent to a prohibitive tariff.

[F. W. Taussig, *Tariff History of the United States.*]

JAMES D. MAGEE

Undistributed Corporation Profits Tax. The Federal revenue acts of 1913, 1916 and 1917 provided for a tax on that portion of corporate earnings not declared as dividends but retained as surplus. Reintroduced in 1921, the tax was in effect until 1939. Prior to 1936 the tax presumably was a penalty instrument, designed to prevent deliberative accumulations of surplus to assist stockholders in income-tax avoidance. In 1936 this concept was changed; a surtax (progressive for most corporations) was levied upon undivided profits regardless of the purpose of retention. Revenue, recovery and reform were advanced as reasons for the new interpretation.

[A. G. Buehler, *The Undivided Profits Tax;* P. F. Gemmill and R. H. Blodgett, *Current Economic Problems;* H. L. Lutz, *Public Finance;* G. F. Luthringer and others, *Money, Credit and Finance.*]

W. B. LOCKLING

Unemployment has traditionally been viewed in America as a problem in personal adjustment. In colonial times an abundance of land provided a ready employment opportunity for every man willing to pioneer. Under such conditions unemployment was identified with unemployability. Following English precedents the colonial authorities distinguished between "impotent beggars" and "sturdy beggars." The former, consisting of the ill, the physically and mentally defective, together with the aged and children, were cared for by outdoor relief or in almshouses, while the latter were dealt with as vagrants, indentured, flogged, put in the stocks and sometimes branded or mutilated. During periods of depressed business, the self-sustaining colonial economy enabled the population for the most part to continue to produce and distribute the basic means of subsistence. Indian wars and the vicissitudes of the seasons were more important factors in the well-being of the masses than general economic trends.

The modern view of unemployment as a problem in industrial organization presents a sharp contrast to this earlier conception. Many authorities now refuse to include idleness due to personal characteristics of the worker within the definition of unemployment at all, and limit the term to lack of economically remunerative work on the part of persons of working age who are able and willing to work but can find no opportunity to do so on account of maladjustments within a given industry, or within the general economic organization of society. The former are problems for social case work; the latter are the concern of industrial reorganization.

Little is known of the extent of unemployment in this sense until recent years. As long as the daily routine of toil in shop, store and field changed but little from generation to generation, the gradual emergence of the phenomenon was not noted. But after the Civil War the rapid development of industry brought with it extreme division of labor, marked changes in occupations and a system of production dominated by price, profit and the market, and the working population became dependent for jobs and income upon the steady flow of goods for exchange, and hence upon the maintenance of the purchasing power of consumers. Even agriculture became dependent on the exchange system, and farmers began increasingly to suffer from crises which left them unaffected as producers, but bankrupted them as merchants.

Mass unemployment now appeared, and in 1890 the United States Census for the first time took cognizance of the fact. From these and other data it is estimated that for the past half century unemployment has varied from 5% in good years to upward of 20% in bad. At the depth of a depression in 1933, it affected from twelve to fifteen millions, approximately one third of the working population.

Economists recognize that an irreducible minimum of normal unemployment, affecting 1% or 2% of the working population, is unavoidable in a free market, where workers are at liberty to leave their jobs and seek other employment in whatever locality it is to be found. Normal unemployment was much greater in the United States than in western Europe before the World War, and since this type of unemployment rises in areas where economic expansion is declining, it has substantially increased in many countries during the postwar period.

Seasonal unemployment (*see* Labor, Migratory) is characteristic of certain trades in which the weather conditions production, as in agriculture, lumbering, fishing and the construction industry, or in which climatic changes or annually recurring conventions and customs influence consumer demand, as in coal mining and the garment and luxury trades.

Technological unemployment[qv] is the displacement of workers either by improved machinery or by more efficient methods of business organization and management. Although it has been generally acknowledged to affect the total volume of employment favorably in the long run, its dislocation of workers within certain industries has often been severe.

Cyclical unemployment, or the increase of joblessness due to recurrent business crises, is, however, the most serious aspect of mass unemployment. Fourteen such cycles have been identified in the period from 1885 to 1939. The most serious of these from the standpoint of unemployment were in 1893–95, 1903–4, 1907–8, 1913–14, 1920–22 and 1930–37.

Prolonged unemployment results in underfeeding, overcrowding, greater susceptibility to disease, denial of educational opportunity, the breaking up of homes, the increase of children in institutions, and of destitute and demoralized migratory youth, both boys and girls, the loss of morale among older workers, and general deterioration in the physical and social welfare of its victims.

There is little agreement as to the cause of depressions, and still less as to their prevention. The remedies proposed for unemployment are therefore chiefly palliatives to lessen its ill-effects. The chief measures are unemployment insurance, public employment agencies, public works, dovetailing of seasonal industries which have their slumps at different times of the year, manufacturing for stock so as to spread labor throughout the year, vocational guidance, reeducation of technologically displaced workers and resettlement of the unemployed in more favorable localities.

[John Maynard Keynes, ed., *Unemployment as a World Problem;* Paul Howard Douglas and Aaron Director, *The Problem of Unemployment;* Corrington Gill, *Wasted Man Power, the Challenge of Unemployment.*]

HOWARD E. JENSEN

Unemployment, Technological. *See* Technological Unemployment.

Unemployment Census, The National (Nov. 16–20, 1937), was taken pursuant to an act of Congress approved Aug. 30, 1937. It was a voluntary registration of totally unemployed and partly unemployed persons and of persons on emergency work, effected through the use of Unemployment Report Cards distributed by the Post Office Department in the forty-eight states, the District of Columbia and the territories of Hawaii and Alaska. The census was to provide information ". . . to aid in the formulation of a program for re-employment, social security and unemployment relief for the people of the United States. . . ."

[*Census of Partial Employment, Unemployment and Occupations, 1937.*] MEREDITH B. GIVENS

Unemployment Insurance. *See* Insurance, Unemployment.

Unicameral Legislatures. Colonial assemblies[q.v.], with only two or three exceptions, originated as unicameral bodies. Charters and patents vested the management of affairs in a governor and a small council or board of directors and granted, vaguely or expressly, for the purpose of consultation and advice, a voice to the freemen[q.v.] through their chosen deputies. These two groups, governor and council on the one hand and the locally elected deputies on the other, developed sharp differences of opinion over matters of taxation, internal policy of government and status of civil rights, a prolonged conflict in which the deputies, as the representatives of the freemen, ultimately gained a coequal voice in lawmaking. At the beginning of the 18th century only two colonies, Delaware and Pennsylvania, had one-house legislative bodies. When state governments were formulated during the Revolutionary period, all except two, Georgia and Pennsylvania, adopted bicameral legislatures[q.v.]. When Vermont became a state in 1777, its constitution provided for a unicameral lawmaking body. Georgia's one-house legislature was in operation only twelve years and gave way to a bicameral body under the second constitution, adopted in 1789. The unicameral legislature of Georgia was one house in name only since a board of censors acted practically as a second house. In Pennsylvania also a board of censors so thwarted the rights and prerogatives of the legislature that the latter assumed the responsibility of calling a constitutional convention. The new constitution provided for a bicameral legislature. Vermont retained its unicameral legislature until 1836 when the force of example of the other states and of the national Congress influenced the vote of the people. The unicameral idea did not assume importance again until the second decade of the 20th century when it was considered in several states. In 1934 Nebraska[q.v.] adopted a one-house legislature.

JOHN P. SENNING

Uniforms of the American Army (1775–1940). *Period 1775–1810.* The popular conception that Washington's Continental Army was uniformed in buff and blue has little foundation in reality. It is true that in 1779 Washington designated dark blue as the army color with different facings for the several states, but dark-blue cloth was hard to procure and uniforms were made from any available material. The uniform most generally worn throughout the war was the hunting shirt and overalls, which were cheap and comfortable and in Washington's own words carried "no small terror to the enemy who thinks every person so dressed a complete marksman." At the close of the Revolution one regiment of infantry and two companies of artillery were retained in the service; they were garbed in the continental pattern during the war: dark-blue coats, white small clothes and cocked hats; the artillery wore scarlet facings, the infantry white.

Period 1810–20. In 1810 the uniform was changed to the single-breasted, swallow-tailed coat and long trousers. The bell-crowned plug hat was worn, to be replaced in 1812 by the "tar-bucket," still worn for full dress by the corps of cadets; the present West Point full dress, in fact, is practically the uniform of this period except that high collars reaching the tip of the ear were in vogue. Dark blue was the prescribed color but, as during the Revolution, dark-blue cloth was scarce and the army appeared mostly in gray. In honor of Lundy's Lane[q.v.] and other victories won by regiments in gray, the corps of cadets was put into gray in 1819; this color remained popular with national guard units until the state troops adopted the regular army uniform in the 1880's.

Period 1820–60. During the Mexican War a short shell jacket and trousers of a light sky-blue mixture appeared. The jacket had a high collar trimmed with white for the infantry, scarlet for the artillery, and green, yellow or orange for the cavalry. Officers wore a dark-blue frock coat with shoulder straps. In 1847 chevrons designating rank among noncommissioned officers were ordered. These were worn above the elbow with points up at first but were soon inverted and were worn with the points down until 1901. In the same year the trimmings of the infantry uniform were changed to light blue, to become white again in 1885. In 1855 French military fashions became the vogue. Frock coats were worn by both officers and enlisted men; the shako and pompom became the full-dress hat.

Period 1860–70. During the Civil War period the high collars of officers and enlisted men were cut very low. A blouse with rolling collar was introduced and the sack coat with lapels was often worn. Shoulder straps were always worn instead of the epaulettes. Pictures of this period show a great variety of headgear; felt hats, high and low, straw hats and chasseur caps were all worn.

Period 1870–95. In 1874 a uniform order was published which applied with few changes until 1901. The shako again became full dress; officers wore a double-breasted coat with high-standing collar and the shoulder knot replaced the epaulette on all ranks below brigadier general. The following year the bugle, long the infantry ornament, was replaced by the cross rifles. In 1895 a comfortable cap with flat top and gently sloping vizor was introduced. The branch insignia was changed from the hat to the coat collar and a U. S. was added to distinguish Regulars from National Guardsmen.

Period 1895–1900. Khaki-colored cotton uniforms were first introduced during the Spanish-American War. Originally they were faced with the color of the branch on the collar, shoulder straps and cuffs, but this was soon changed and the facing remained only on the shoulder strap.

Period 1900–1940. In 1901 a uniform board, convened in Washington, adopted the olive drab uniform for service wear, retaining the blue for dress. During the World War the blue was discarded and the olive drab served on all occasions. In 1921 the Sam Browne belt was added and in 1925 the roll collar with lapels replaced the straight, high collar. The present, 1940, tendency is toward a return of blue uniforms for all dress occasions and a new field-service uniform of olive drab shirts and trousers which will be more comfortable and practical than the blouse and breeches.

Insignia (1780–1917). Insignia designating rank evolved gradually. In 1780 Washington prescribed two stars for the major general and one for the brigadier. Other grades were determined by the size, length of fringes and manner of wearing the epaulettes. In 1832 the spread eagle appeared on the colonel's epaulette and in 1836, with the adoption of the shoulder strap for informal occasions, the silver leaf, gold leaf, double silver bar and single silver bar were adopted to designate the ranks of lieutenant colonel, major, captain and first lieutenant, respectively. The second lieutenant's gold bar was not introduced until 1917. The seniority of silver over gold may be traced to the fact that on the gold epaulettes silver insignia was more visible.

[L. A. Curtis, *Uniform of the Army;* U. S. Quartermaster Department, *Uniform of the Army of the United States, 1774-1889.*]

C. A. WILLOUGHBY

Union, Fort (N. Dak.), was built on the northerly side of the Missouri River, just above the mouth of the Yellowstone, by Kenneth McKenzie in 1829 for the American Fur Company[qv]. It was in longitude 104° 02′ 07″, which location is within the boundaries of the present State of North Dakota. This was the most important and pretentious fort of the company, palisaded with poplar logs and stone bastions. The *chevaux-de-frise* was quite 20 feet high and had towered blockhouses 24 feet square, with embrasures for cannon, rising from the southwest and northeast corner to a height of 30 feet. Around the second stories were balconies for observation purposes and along the inside of the enclosure was a raised walk for shooting firearms over the top in case of attack. The enclosure was about 60 feet north of the river bank, the fort proper having a front of 220 feet and depth of 240 feet. In the fort were some 8 or 10 log houses, stores, kitchen, council rooms and a powder magazine of fifty thousand pounds capacity. There were accommodations for more than 150 horses. The fort was built for trading with the Assiniboine Indians[qv] and as a central depot to the scattered outposts, from which unification it derived its name. Fort Union was not completed for several years, although functioning meanwhile. This accounts for varying descriptions by different visitors to the place from time to time. On Feb. 3, 1832, a fire broke out in the west quadrangle 24 x 120 feet in size, where clerks, interpreters, mechanics, *engagés* and their families were quartered. These buildings with large stores of building materials, furs, etc., were destroyed. McKenzie said that the whole fort would have been destroyed if the wind had blown otherwise than from the east. In 1834 the fort was finally completed and continued in existence until 1867, when it was bought by the United States, wrecked, and the materials used to complete Fort Buford about two miles down the Missouri. Many celebrated persons were entertained at Fort Union while it reigned in splendor as the king of trading forts. Fort Union was never Fort Floyd, as some writers have supposed. These forts were coexistent in 1830 as shown by a letter of McKenzie, dated Fort Union, May 5, 1830.

[H. M. Chittenden, *American Fur Trade in the Far West;* Frank B. Harper, *Fort Union and Its Neighbors on the Upper Missouri;* Charles Larpenteur, *Forty Years a Trader on the Upper Missouri;* Lt. Gouverneur K. Warren, *Explorations in the Dakota Country in the Year 1855;* Chouteau Collections; Fort Union Letterbook, mss. Mo. Hist. Soc.]

STELLA M. DRUMM

Union, Fort (N. Mex.), located north of the present Watrous, Mora County, was established by Col. E. V. Sumner during the summer of 1851 to help protect the inhabitants of New Mexico from hostile Ute and Apache Indians[qqv]. It was one of the most important military establishments in the Southwest, frequently serving as headquarters of the Department of New Mexico. During the Civil War the Confederates aimed to capture it, but just fell short of their objective in April, 1862 (*see* Rio Grande, Sibley's Operations on). Evacuated by the army in 1891, the post gradually fell into ruins, which can still be seen.

[J. H. Vaughan, *History and Government of New Mexico.*]
RALPH P. BIEBER

Union and Loyal Leagues. *See* Loyal Leagues.

Union Canal, THE, connecting the Schuylkill and Susquehanna rivers, was suggested by William Penn in 1690. In 1762 the course was surveyed from Reading to Middletown, but the canal was not completed until 1828. Handicapped at first by its small size, it was enlarged in 1850, but never prospered thereafter, and was finally abandoned in 1885.

[Alvin F. Harlow, *Old Towpaths.*]
ALVIN F. HARLOW

Union Colony, THE, was organized in New York City in December, 1869, by Nathan C. Meeker, agricultural editor of the New York *Tribune,* in order to plant a settlement in Colorado. Within four months there were about 450 members, two thirds of whom were from New England, New York, Pennsylvania and Ohio, and all of whom were characterized by high standards and temperance principles. On the site chosen in the Cache la Poudre Valley north of Denver the town of Greeley was established in 1870, named for Horace Greeley, friendly editor of the *Tribune*. In return for fees which varied from $50 to $200, members received farming land and the right to buy lots in the colony town. The success of this semi-co-operative venture stimulated similar undertakings. Group settlement, which had been common in colonial New England and occasional west of the Alleghenies, seemed especially appropriate at the base of the Rockies because of the need for reducing the cost of migration to the more distant frontier and for community action in the installation of irrigation systems.

[J. F. Willard, *The Union Colony at Greeley, Colorado.*]
COLIN B. GOODYKOONTZ

Union Democrats during the Civil War[qv] supported the war aims of the conservative Republicans to preserve the Federal Union and not interfere with slavery[qv]. This coalition of conservatives in a Union party[qv] was vigorously supported by such representative Democrats as Sen. Stephen A. Douglas and Gov. John Brough in the North, and by minorities of Democrats in the South; and in the election of 1864, a Union Democrat, Andrew Johnson, ran for Vice-President as President Lincoln's running-mate.

[Samuel S. Cox, *Three Decades of Federal Legislation, 1855-1885;* E. C. Kirkland, *The Peacemakers of 1864.*]
MARTIN P. CLAUSSEN

Union Labor Party, THE, was organized at Cincinnati, Ohio, Feb. 22, 1887, in an attempt to unite the remnants of the Greenback Labor party with wage earners made articulate by the industrial conflicts of the period. Organized labor, however, received little recognition in the platform or state and national tickets of 1888. Alson J. Streeter of Illinois, presidential nominee, received but 147,000 votes, the bulk of which came from the agricultural South and West (*see* Campaign of 1888).

[F. E. Haynes, *Third Party Movements since the Civil War.*]
CHESTER McA. DESTLER

Union Pacific Railroad. Early in the railroad era visionaries like Asa Whitney dreamed of a transcontinental railroad which would span the continent from the Atlantic to the Pacific. Whitney petitioned Congress in 1845 for a charter and a grant of land sixty miles wide from the Great Lakes to the Pacific coast to aid in financing the project, but he only succeeded in obtaining publicity for it. The acquisition of California and Oregon brought the need for a Pacific railroad more sharply to public attention and from 1850 to the outbreak of the Civil War it shared the spotlight with slavery, the public land and territorial questions[qqv]. As few people thought that more than one trans-American railroad could ever be built there was keen rivalry between the Old Northwest and the South, and between cities in each section, for the eastern terminus and this rivalry delayed Federal assistance. Finally, with the South out of the Union, Congress, in 1862, incorporated the Union Pacific Railroad Company for the construction of a railroad by the central route from the western border of Iowa to the California-Nevada line where it was to meet the Central Pacific Railroad[qv] and thus connect with San Francisco. For each mile of completed railroad Congress offered 6400 acres of public lands and a loan of $16,000 to $48,000—depending on the terrain—which was to be a first mortgage on the railroad.

Despite this subsidy, the most liberal yet offered to a railroad, capitalists continued to regard the Union Pacific as a questionable speculation until 1864 when Congress doubled the land grant and made the financial subsidy a second lien on the property. The chances for profit-making in the construction of the railroad, if not in its operation after completion, now seemed promising, capital was forthcoming and construction work was pushed ahead under the forceful direction of Gen. Grenville M. Dodge. The Central Pacific was permitted by the act of 1864 to build 150 miles east of the California-Nevada line and in 1866 it was authorized to advance eastward until it met the westward moving Union Pacific. This led to the historic race between the two railroads which culminated in their dramatic union at Promontory Point[qv], Utah, in 1869.

Charter restrictions and the continued difficulty of raising adequate capital induced the promoters of the Union Pacific to assign construction contracts at enormously inflated costs to the Crédit Mobilier[qv]—a railroad construction company which was controlled by Thomas C. Durant, Oakes Ames and other insiders of the Union Pacific. To the Crédit Mobilier was transferred most of the liquid assets of the railroad and they in turn were paid out to the former's stockholders. Members of Congress and other influential people were assigned stock in the construction company, partly, it seems, to win their aid against the frequent attacks which were directed at the Union Pacific. During Grant's administration the whole sordid story was unearthed by a congressional committee and many political reputations were badly besmirched.

The Union Pacific Railroad was of great importance to the growth and development of such commonwealths as Nebraska, Colorado, Wyoming, Nevada and California. It brought in immigrants to settle upon the railroad and public lands, it helped to end the migrations of the plains Indians, it provided marketing facilities for the cattle, lumber, mining and farming industries of the Great Plains and Interior Basin, and it brought the West coast into closer political, economic and social contact with the East.

Poor and costly construction, high rates, unfortunate financial management and the other evils characteristic of railroad management in the late 19th century forced the Union Pacific into bankruptcy during the Panic of 1893[qv]. Subsequently, Edward H. Harriman secured control of the railroad. He added many branch lines, rebuilt the roadbed, improved the rolling stock, and made of the Union Pacific one of America's premier railroads.

[J. P. Davis, *The Union Pacific Railway;* J. R. Perkins, *Trails, Rails and War: the Life of Grenville Dodge;* N. Trottman, *History of the Union Pacific.*]

PAUL WALLACE GATES

Union Party (1861). After the defeat of Bull Run[qv], July 21, 1861, many leaders urged that all Union men, regardless of party, stand together for the preservation of the Union. Consequently a Union party ticket, pledged to the prosecution of the war, appeared in most of the important state elections in the fall of 1861. In general the Union ticket represented a coalition of Republicans and "War Democrats"[qv]. Separate Democratic tickets were common and in some states the Republicans also nominated candidates.

[J. B. McMaster, *A History of the People of the United States during Lincoln's Administration.*]

GLENN H. BENTON

Union Prisons. *See* Prison Camps, Northern, in Civil War.

Union Rights Party, more properly Union and Southern Rights party or, later, Constitutional Union party, was organized largely under Whig[qv] leadership in Georgia in 1850 following the enactment of the legislation which precipitated a secession movement upon the part of the Southern Rights forces. A similar cleavage had developed over the question of participation in the Nashville Convention[qv]. The Constitutional Union party then undertook to control the state convention called by Gov. George W. Towns. Its success and its program were revealed in the "Georgia Platform"[qv] adopted by that convention. It continued its existence through the state elections of 1851. Similar movements were in evidence in Mississippi and Alabama and there was talk of organizing a National Union party. (*See also* Southern Rights Movement.)

[A. C. Cole, *Whig Party in the South;* R. H. Shryock, *Georgia and the Union.*]

ARTHUR C. COLE

Union Sentiment in the South (1861–65) was widespread throughout the Civil War, but was strongest in the mountainous parts of Virginia, North Carolina, Tennessee, Georgia and Alabama. In these states, and to a lesser extent in others, there lived a number of individuals, like W. G. Brownlow of Tennessee (*see* Parson Brownlow's Book), who were sincerely attached to the Union and viewed with dismay the secession[qv] of their commonwealths. Thus at the very beginning of the conflict the Confederacy[qv] had within its borders a number of citizens who thought their first allegiance was due to the old Union. These Unionists constantly increased their numbers as the war progressed. After the passage and enforcement of the conscription, impressment and tax-in-kind laws[qqv], a large number of previously loyal Confederates acted in concert with the Unionists and participated in activities designed to obstruct Confederate policies. They had no particular love for the Union, but as the enforcement of these laws became more rigorous, they began to prefer it to the Richmond administration. William W. Holden[qv], of North Carolina, is a good example of this type of Unionist.

Throughout most of the Southern states, the Unionists organized themselves into peace societies in order to accomplish their objects. The "Peace and Constitutional Society" prevailed in Arkansas; the "Peace Society" was very strong in Alabama and extended into Georgia, Mississippi and probably Florida; and the "Heroes of America" attained great strength in North Carolina, east Tennessee and southwest Virginia. All these secret organizations had similar passwords, grips and oaths, and their main objects were identical: to provide mutual protection; to render aid to the Federals; and to weaken the Confederate forces. By burning bridges, encouraging desertion, and transmitting military information to the enemy, the members of these peace societies greatly embarrassed the Confederate government and compelled it to use a part of its strength in controlling its own disaffected citizens.

[Georgia Lee Tatum, *Disloyalty in the Confederacy.*]

RICHARD E. YATES

Unionist Sentiment in Border States was the outgrowth of strong nationalist feeling which had previously been expressed in the compromises sponsored by Henry Clay and others. In the winter of 1860–61 the border states[qv] urged schemes of compromise and conciliation. After the outbreak of war public opinion appeared to hesitate, as if awaiting assurances that Lincoln's objective was chiefly the preservation of the Union. By June a large majority of the people of Maryland, western Virginia and Missouri rallied to the Federal cause, and by September, Kentucky ceased to be neutral. Unionist sentiment was strongest in the cities and in communities accessible to railroads and navigable rivers. Generally it was stronger in mountainous and comparatively barren regions, where Jacksonian Democrats[qv] had been most numerous, than in sections with rich soils worked by slaves. Many communities were secessionist. Though much harassed by Confederate raids and guerrilla bands, the border states contributed heavily in men to the Union armies.

[Edward Conrad Smith, *The Borderland in the Civil War.*]

E. C. SMITH

Unions, Craft and Industrial, are the two chief American types of labor organization. The earliest unions were organized by crafts, each organization including those in a particular trade; such unions as the Molders (1859), Bookbinders (1892), Carpenters (1891), Plasterers (1864) illustrate this type. The American Federation of Labor[qv] (1886) was made up predominantly of craft unions.

The industrial union embraces all workers in a given industry regardless of craft or skill, including skilled, semiskilled and unskilled workers, such as the United Mine Workers[qv] (1890) and the Brewery Workers (1896). Left-wing elements have favored the industrial union, as illustrated by the Industrial Workers of the World[qv] (1905). The conservative industrial union group is represented by the Congress of Industrial Organizations[qv] (1938).

[C. R. Daugherty, *Labor Problems in American Industry;* J. R. Commons and associates, *History of Labor in the U. S.*]

HERBERT MAYNARD DIAMOND

Unions, Labor. *See* Labor Unions.

Unit Rule, The, is the practice followed by the Democratic party in its national conventions, whereby the entire vote of each state delegation must be cast as a unit for the candidate preferred by the majority of that delegation. The delegates in the Republican convention, on the other hand, may vote either according to their individual preferences or the instructions received from their local or state conventions. In order to meet requirements in state presidential primary laws under which delegates may be definitely pledged to support particular candidates, strict enforcement of the unit rule has been deviated from. The national Democratic convention modified its traditional practice in 1912 by providing that the unit rule shall be enforced only where the state convention has the power to instruct its full delegation.

[R. C. Brooks, *Political Parties and Electoral Problems.*]

FRANK B. HURT

Unitarians. From the English Presbyterian Unitarians the name, originating in Poland and Transylvania about 1600 A.D. among the Socinian disciples of Erasmus, was transferred to a group of about 125 of the old Puritan churches of New England. Their members, under the leadership of the great Boston preacher, William Ellery Channing, came in 1819 to an open break with the Calvinist tenets of the Trinity, predestination, total depravity, biblical inerrancy. They believed that Christ taught none of these doctrines but saved souls by the simple truths of the universal Fatherhood of God, salvation through integrity and charity of life, and the eventual brotherhood of Man in the kingdom of God on earth, of which Christ was the appointed Messiah. To such beliefs Harvard College had been won in 1805, although the erstwhile Anglican King's Chapel in Boston had become virtually Unitarian in 1785; Rev. Joseph Priestly, the discoverer of oxygen, a leader of British Unitarianism, had founded a Unitarian society in Philadelphia in 1796. The American Unitarian Association was formed in 1825.

In 1838 Ralph Waldo Emerson, a disciple of Channing and a former Unitarian minister of Boston, in his Harvard Divinity School Address, enlarged Channing's liberal Christianity into a Transcendentalist version of the ethical theism of Plato, the Stoics and Kant, co-ordinated with the nascent evolutionist science of the day and the newly explored mysticism of the ancient East. This new religious philosophy, as construed and applied by the Boston preacher Theodore Parker and other disciples of Emerson, included the other great ethnic faiths with Christianity in a universal religion of Humanity and through its intellectual hospitality operated to open Unitarian fellowship to evolutionists, monists, pragmatists and humanists.

In 1900 the American Unitarian Association undertook the organization of the International Association of Liberal Christian and Religious Freedom, a world-wide fellowship of over fifty liberal religious bodies, committed to universal ethical theism, with a constituency of about twenty million members, and headquarters at Utrecht, Holland.

In 1939 there were about 125,000 Unitarians in the United States and Canada.

[G. W. Cooke, *Unitarianism in America;* E. M. Wilbur, *Our Unitarian Heritage.*]

CHARLES LYTTLE

United Americans, The Order of, was a nativistic[qv] benevolent association, formed in New York in 1844 and quickly attaining national membership. American laborers, who were alone admitted, were promised old-age benefits, but the society was principally important as an agency to disseminate anti-Catholic, antiforeign propaganda. Its secret methods and elaborate ritual were copied by the Know-Nothing party[qv] a decade later.

[R. A. Billington, *The Protestant Crusade.*]

RAY ALLEN BILLINGTON

United Brethren, The Church of the, dates from 1800. Philip William Otterbein and Martin Boehm were its joint founders. Otterbein came to America in 1752 as a German Reformed missionary, becoming pastor of a congregation at Lancaster, Pa. A deep personal religious experience caused him to become a zealous evangelist. Coming into contact with Martin Boehm, a Mennonite[qv] minister of like views, they united their efforts and carried on extensive evangelistic work among the Germans of Pennsylvania, Maryland and Virginia. In 1774 Otterbein became the minister of an independent congregation in Baltimore where he continued his revivalistic work. Others joined in this work and in 1800 Otterbein and Boehm with eleven others formed the Church of the United Brethren in Christ. Otterbein was a close friend of Francis Asbury the Methodist bishop and the new church became Methodistic in both polity and doctrine, Otterbein and Boehm being chosen the first bishops. The new church expanded into the Middle West following German settlement. The present membership of 377,436 is centered in Pennsylvania, West Virginia, Ohio, Indiana and Illinois. The church maintains seven colleges and one theological seminary and expends more than $600,000 yearly for missionary and benevolent enterprises.

[A. W. Drury, *History of the Church of the United Brethren in Christ.*]

WILLIAM W. SWEET

United Colonies of New England, THE, was a confederation consisting of the four colonies of Massachusetts, Plymouth, Connecticut and New Haven[qqv], from which Rhode Island and Maine were excluded because of their political and religious uncongeniality. Suggested as early as 1637, it gradually evolved after the outbreak of the Puritan Revolution from a complexity of motives, chief of which was defense. The infant colonies realized that they would be particularly exposed to danger of attack from other countries while England's attention was taken by troubles at home, while the menace of the Indians was increasingly apparent after the Pequot War[qv]. Perhaps also they may have feared being drawn into the vortex of civil war in England. In addition to defense, they had in mind the wellbeing of their state religion and the spread of the gospel according to its doctrines; and there were many intercolonial problems such as control of runaway servants and prisoners for which the need of united action was felt.

According to the articles of agreement adopted, the confederation government consisted of a board of eight commissioners, two from each member colony, and a vote of six was necessary to make action legal. If six could not agree, the business in question was then to be referred to the General Courts[qv] of the four constituent colonies. The commissioners were to meet annually and oftener if necessary. Although a permanent center was projected for the future, for the time being the confederation was to be itinerant, meeting twice out of every five times at Boston. The commissioners had power to make ordinances concerning general matters of a civil nature and to act as a sort of court of arbitration in the settlement of conflicts between members or with foreign countries or colonies. In case of war, offensive or defensive, the burden of expense and of soldiers was to be borne in proportion to the size of the male population between the ages of sixteen and sixty. Provision was made for emergency action in case of sudden invasion, but even though help of member colonies had been thus invoked, the confederation was not to bear the expense if upon examination the colony or colonies concerned were at fault in the action provoking the war.

Equal representation and proportional support contained an element of unfairness to Massachusetts, but there was no other way to prevent her exercising a preponderance of influence in the affairs of New England. As it was, she sometimes defied the confederation when she disapproved of its decisions, and there was no way of coercing her to obedience.

In spite of its inherent weaknesses, the confederation performed a very real service for New England during its first twenty years. Although it lost prestige and influence after Connecticut's absorption of New Haven in 1662, it continued to exist until the new order of things following the annulment of the Massachusetts charter in 1684.

[H. L. Osgood, *The American Colonies in the Seventeenth Century*, Vol. I.]

VIOLA F. BARNES

United Empire Loyalists was the name applied to those inhabitants of the thirteen colonies who remained loyal to the British crown at the time of the Revolution, and particularly to those who migrated to what is now Canada. In 1783 and 1784 the United States lost between fifty and sixty thousand refugees, who became the backbone of pioneer settlement in Canada. They went mainly from New York, Massachusetts and Connecticut to Nova Scotia, New Brunswick and Prince Edward Island, in 1783, and to Upper and Lower Canada, now Ontario and Quebec, in 1784.

[C. H. Van Tyne, *Loyalists in the American Revolution.*]

LAWRENCE J. BURPEE

United Mine Workers, THE, was an industrial labor union, organized Jan. 25, 1890, at Columbus, Ohio, as an affiliate of the American Federation of Labor[qv], from various local, state and district Knights of Labor[qv] unions, to present a united labor front both in the bituminous and anthracite[qqv] fields. Small and weak in the beginning, the U. M. W., through constructive leadership and general observance of agreements, grew to power and strength in its struggle for recognition and for higher wages, shorter hours and better working conditions. Its first considerable strike in 1894 almost destroyed the union, but faith and devotion to a program and the direction of able men like John Mitchell, preserved and strengthened the union. By a strike in the bituminous field in 1897 it won valuable concessions; in 1902 it won a five-month strike in the anthracite field and the first successful union of immigrant labor from Eastern and Southern Europe demonstrated its power. Eventually, the anthracite miners won the eight-hour day, the checkoff[qv] and union recognition. Wage and working conditions in the bituminous field were likewise gradually improved. The U. M. W. became the strongest, the largest and the richest affiliate of the A. F. of L., with thirty-one district organizations. In 1936 it made the largest single contribution to President Franklin D. Roosevelt's campaign for re-election; became one of a number of powerful pressure groups[qv]; and was able to secure passage of the Guffey coal acts[qv]. In October, 1937, it seceded from the A. F. of L. to become the foundation stone of the Congress of Industrial Organizations[qv] and to dominate the movement.

[John R. Commons and associates, *History of Labor in the United States.*]

THOMAS ROBSON HAY

United Press, a world-wide news agency designed to offer independently gathered news in competition with the older and more conservative Associated Press[qv], was formed in 1907 by Edward Wyllis Scripps and Milton Alexander McRae. The former Scripps-McRae Press Association, operating west of Pittsburgh since 1897, and the Publishers' Press, formed 1904 to cover the eastern field, were amalgamated into the United Press Association. The new "UP," second of its name, discarded the exclusive franchise practice of the Associated Press, allowing any newspaper to become a member upon application. Developing primarily the South American and Japanese fields as its foreign interests, the United Press gained general recognition for its liberal policies, for its interest in labor, for its "human-interest" features and for the brightness of its writing.

[Gilson Gardner, *Lusty Scripps;* Victor Rosewater, *History of Co-operative Newsgathering in the United States.*]

HARRY EMERSON WILDES

***United States,* THE** (frigate), 44-guns, designed by Joshua Humphreys of Philadelphia and launched from his shipyard on May 10, 1797, was the first vessel of the newly organized United States Navy[qv]. During the Naval War with France[qv], as the flagship of Capt. John Barry, she took seven prizes. In 1800 she carried the peace commissioners to Europe. On the cessation of hostilities, the frigate was laid up until the War of 1812[qv]. Under Capt. Stephen Decatur, Jr., on Oct. 12, 1812, she captured the British 38-gun ship *Macedonian*[qv]. Returning safely home, she was blockaded at New London, Conn., for the remainder of the war.

During 1815–18 under various commanders, she aided in keeping the Barbary[qv] powers subdued and thereafter saw service on many foreign stations. On April 21, 1861, she was burned at the Norfolk Navy Yard to prevent her falling into the hands of the Confederate troops.

[W. B. Clark, *Gallant John Barry;* Theodore Roosevelt, *Naval War of 1812;* D. D. Porter, *Naval History of the Civil War.*]

MARION V. BREWINGTON

United States Bank. *See* Bank of the United States, First and Second.

United States Housing Authority. *See* Housing.

United States Military Academy. *See* Military Academy, The United States.

United States Naval Academy. *See* Naval Academy, The United States.

United States of America (origin of the name). Our national name was first used officially in the Declaration of Independence[qv], where, however, it merely took the place of "United Colonies," etc., hitherto employed, although in varying forms. The "United Colonies of New England"[qv] was the name of the so-called New England Confederation, and it was therefore quite natural that "United Colonies" should be used to designate the new union. The earliest official use of the designation in the Revolutionary period appears to have been in a communication of the Massachusetts convention, May 16, 1775, embodied in the *Journals of the Continental Congress*[qv] under June 2. The term was used by Congress itself in a resolution of June 7, 1775, again in a resolution of June 10, then definitely in Washington's commission, June 17, and in his instructions, June 20. Thereupon, both officially and unofficially, "The United Colonies," in variant forms, came into general use. Among the earlier forms used were, "all the English colonies on this continent" (the fast-day proclamation of June 12), "all the colonies from Nova Scotia to Georgia" (pledge of support to Gen. Washington, June 17), and "associated colonies" (committee report, June 19). In official documents thereafter the name was usually "The United Colonies of America," or "of North America" (more often the latter), and frequently with "twelve" or "thirteen," as the case might be, prefixed, sometimes also preceded by the word "English." For instance, the imprint of the Rules for the troops, June 30, 1775, names the governing authority as "the Twelve united English Colonies of North-America."

As the idea of independence grew and the term "colony" came to connote a status of dependence, writers came more and more to employ the term "states" to designate the American political entities. The term was accordingly used in the Virginia resolutions of May 15, 1776, whence came the resolution proposed in Congress June 7, "That these United Colonies are, and of right ought to be, free and independent States." It was therefore a matter of course that, in the Declaration of Independence, the name "United Colonies," etc., should give place to "The United States of America." From the Declaration the name was taken over into the Articles of Confederation (1777) and thence into the Constitution (1787)[qqv].

Curiously enough, for a brief period the name of this nation was "The United States of North America." The prevailing inclination to use "North America" had found official expression in the Declaration on Taking Arms (July 6, 1775), and again (probably through Franklin's preference for that form, as witness his proposed articles of confederation, July 21, 1775) in the treaty with France (Feb. 6, 1778)[qv], in which the name is set down as "the thirteen United States of North America." Thereupon (May 19, 1778) Congress adopted "the Stile of the Treaties of Paris" (letters of President Laurens May 19, 20, 23); but, on July 11 following, that action was rescinded, and the word "North" dropped from the name.

[Edmund C. Burnett, The Name "United States of America," in *American Historical Review*, XXXI, 79-81; John C. Fitzpatrick, The "United States of America" and the "U. S. A.," in *Daughters of the American Revolution Magazine*, LIV, 17; also in *The Spirit of the Revolution; Journals of the Continental Congress*, Library of Congress edition, Vols. II-VI, including Bibliographical Notes.]

EDMUND C. BURNETT

United States Shipping Board Emergency Fleet Corporation. *See* Emergency Fleet Corporation.

United States Shipping Board Merchant Fleet Corporation. *See* Merchant Fleet Corporation.

United States Steel Corporation. At the close of the 19th century, enormous mergers were taking place, especially in the metal-working industries. In 1900 Andrew Carnegie and Henry C. Frick combined their interests, including steel and coke plants, coal and iron ore lands and a controlling interest in the Pittsburgh, Bessemer & Lake Erie Railroad. Eight other mergers with their dates were these: American Bridge Company, uniting several smaller concerns in 1900; American Tin Plate Company, involving thirty-nine plants, 1898; National Steel Company, 1899; American Steel Hoop Company, merging nine factories, 1899; American Sheet Steel Company, 1900; National Tube Company, a union of thirteen manufacturers of wrought steel pipe, 1899; American Steel and Wire Company, taking in most of the country's wire mills, 1899; and Federal Steel Company, uniting four steel plants and a railroad, 1898. Elbert H. Gary, president of the last-named company, saw advantages for all in a giant consolidation, and at his urging and that of Carnegie, who wished to retire, the elder J. Pierpont Morgan arranged and financed the deal, which was completed in February, 1901, the Lake Superior Consolidated Iron Mines, a Rockefeller property, being added to the nine corporations already mentioned. The ten companies had an aggregate capital of $867,550,394; owned 149 steel plants of various kinds, 84 blast furnaces, more than 500,000 acres of coal lands, more than 1000 miles of railroad, 112 vessels on the Great Lakes, not to mention iron ore, natural gas and limestone lands. The authorized capital of the new U. S. Steel Corporation was $1,404,000,000 which, as even friendly commentators have admitted, was at least half "water." The assets, however, were later built up to and beyond that figure. The corporation in 1907 absorbed the Tennessee Coal, Iron and Railroad Company, with huge plants and mineral lands around Birmingham, Ala., the Atlas Portland Cement Company in 1929, the Columbia Steel Company of San Francisco and the Oil Well Supply Company in 1930 and the Virginia Bridge Company in 1936. The "Steel Trust," as it is called, was twice investigated by the U. S. Commissioner of Corporations, and in 1911–12 by a committee of the House of Representatives. In 1911 the Department of Justice filed suit for its dissolution, but was defeated in the lower court, and in 1920 by the U. S. Supreme Court in a 4-to-3 verdict, two justices not voting. From its organization to the end of 1939 the corporation dispensed $10,943,000,000 in wages and salaries, $1,937,000,000 in dividends and $1,630,000,000 in taxes.

[Arundel Cotter, *United States Steel;* Ida M. Tarbell, *Life of Elbert H. Gary.*]

ALVIN F. HARLOW

U. S. v. Butler. *See* Hoosac Mills Case.

U. S. v. Clark. In this case a Federal circuit court in Michigan in 1887 asserted that by enlistment a soldier surrenders his liberty, waives some civil rights*qv*, and subjects himself to more rigid punishment rules. The Supreme Court (In re Grimley, 137 U. S. 147) in 1890 adopted this view, holding that "enlistment changes the status" (*see* Enlistment).

[U. S. v. Clark, 31 Fed. 710; In re Morrissey, 137 U. S. 157; W. Winthrop, *Military Law and Precedents.*]

ELBRIDGE COLBY

U. S. v. Cruikshank (92 U. S. 542, 1876) involved the 1870 Force Act*qv* provision forbidding interference with constitutional rights. The Supreme Court held that the Constitution does not grant the rights of assembling peaceably and bearing arms; it merely forbids Congress to infringe upon them. The Fourteenth Amendment's due process and equal protection clauses*qqv* guarantee the citizen against encroachment by the states, but not against encroachment by another citizen.

[C. Warren, *The Supreme Court in United States History.*]

RANSOM E. NOBLE, JR.

U. S. v. E. C. Knight Co. (156 U. S. 1, 1895) was the first Supreme Court case involving the Sherman Antitrust Act*qv*, which forbade combinations restraining interstate commerce. The American Sugar Refining Company*qv* purchased four independent concerns, giving it control of 98% of the country's output. The Court held that the acquisition of refineries and the business of sugar manufacturing within a state bore no direct relation to interstate commerce, and hence were not in violation of the act. The decision stimulated the formation of trusts*qv*.

[E. Jones, *The Trust Problem in the United States;* A. H. Walker, *History of the Sherman Law.*]

RANSOM E. NOBLE, JR.

U. S. v. Harris (106 U. S. 629, 1883). The Supreme Court held unconstitutional the 1871 Ku Klux Act*qv* provision which penalized conspiracy to deprive any person of equal protection of the laws. It was broader than the Thirteenth Amendment warranted, and neither the Fourteenth nor

Fifteenth Amendment[qqv] authorized Congress to legislate directly upon the acts of private persons.

[C. Warren, *The Supreme Court in United States History.*]

RANSOM E. NOBLE, JR.

U. S. v. Lanza (260 U. S. 377, 1922). In this case culminated events marking increased centralization[qv] of government. Previous decisions had indicated in Ohio (1847, 1850) and Illinois (1852) that concurrent jurisdiction by Federal and state systems over counterfeiting and fugitive slave offenses might be enforced by either without violating the Fifth Amendment's "double jeopardy" clause. The Eighteenth Amendment[qv] in 1919 gave Congress concurrent powers with the states over prohibition enforcement. Federal courts in Alabama, Connecticut, New Hampshire, North Dakota, Ohio and New York upheld the right of Federal agents to try offenders already tried in state courts. In the Lanza case in the State of Washington that right was denied. On appeal to the Supreme Court, Chief Justice Taft held that a second trial might be had, saying: "The defendants committed two different offenses by the same act, the offense against the State and a different offense against the United States," and denied the double jeopardy plea.

[Fox v. Ohio, 5 How. 410; U. S. v. Marigold, 9 How. 560; Moore v. Illinois, 14 How. 13; Grafton v. U. S., 206 U. S. 333; U. S. v. Bostow, 273 Fed. 535; U. S. v. McCann, 281 Fed. 880; U. S. v. Regan, 273 Fed. 727; U. S. v. Holt, 270 Fed. 639; U. S. v. Ratagizak, 275 Fed. 558; N. Y. *Herald*, Feb. 21, 1923.]

ELBRIDGE COLBY

U. S. v. Lee (106 U. S. 196, 1882). In 1857, upon the death of George Washington Parke Custis, the Arlington House estate passed to his daughter, Mrs. Robert E. Lee, for the term of her natural life. By the will of Custis the property was to pass to his eldest grandson, George Washington Custis Lee, upon the death of Mrs. Lee.

During the Civil War the estate was seized by agents of the United States for delinquent taxes, offered for sale and bid in by an army officer for a national cemetery and military post. A friend of Mrs. Lee appeared at the sale and offered to bid in the property, but the bid was rejected.

After the death of Mrs. Lee, her son Custis brought an action to eject the superintendent of Arlington Cemetery on the grounds of trespass. The United States pleaded the immunity of a sovereign to suit. In 1882, however, the Supreme Court held that the United States was not in lawful possession of the estate. The doctrine of immunity did not extend to the misuse of authority by agents of the Government. Eventually the matter was settled by the Government paying for possession.

[R. E. Cushman, *Leading Constitutional Decisions.*]

LEONARD C. HELDERMAN

U. S. v. Reese (92 U. S. 214, 1876). The Supreme Court declared that the Fifteenth Amendment[qv] authorized Congress to prevent denial of the franchise only because of race, color, or previous condition of servitude. Parts of the 1870 Enforcement Act[qv] which provided punishment for obstructing citizens from voting, were unconstitutional because not limited to this type of discrimination.

[C. Warren, *The Supreme Court in United States History;* E. S. Bates, *The Story of the Supreme Court.*]

RANSOM E. NOBLE, JR.

U. S. v. Texas (143 U. S. 621, 1892). By an act of Congress, May 2, 1890, the Attorney General was instructed to enter suit in the Supreme Court to decide the true boundary between United States territory and Texas. Texas demurred on grounds of no jurisdiction because of the particular wording of the act authorizing the suit. The case was argued Dec. 9, 1891, and Mr. Justice Harlan delivered the opinion Feb. 20, 1892. The demurrer was overruled and the Court assumed jurisdiction (*see* Greer County Dispute).

J. G. SMITH

U. S. v. Trans-Missouri Freight Association (166 U. S. 290, 1897) involved the attempt of eighteen western railroads to fix freight rates by mutual agreement. The Government brought suit to dissolve the association on the ground that it violated the Sherman Antitrust Act[qv]. By a five-to-four decision, the Supreme Court held that the Sherman Act did apply to railroads, and that it prohibited *all* contracts in restraint of interstate or foreign commerce, not merely those in which the restraint was unreasonable. Justice White's dissenting opinion, that *reasonable* contracts do not contravene the act, became substantially the majority view fourteen years later in the Standard Oil and American Tobacco cases[qqv].

[A. H. Walker, *History of the Sherman Law.*]

RANSOM E. NOBLE, JR.

U. S. v. Wong Kim Ark (169 U. S. 649, 1898) was a most important interpretation of that clause in the Fourteenth Amendment[qv] declaring that "all persons born or naturalized in the United States and subject to the jurisdiction thereof, are citizens of the United States and of the State wherein they reside." Wong Kim Ark was an American-born Chinese laborer, his parents ineligible to citizenship under the naturalization laws. On returning to this country from a visit to China, an attempt was made to debar him from entry under the Chinese Exclusion Acts[qv]. Claiming that his birth in San Francisco conferred citizenship, Wong Kim Ark secured a writ of habeas corpus[qv] and when his case eventually reached the Supreme Court, that tribunal, two justices dissenting, upheld his contention. The principle laid down in this decision has also served to protect Orientals born in this country against discriminating state legislation.

W. A. ROBINSON

"United We Stand, Divided We Fall," favorite toast, in varying forms, of political orators from Franklin to Lincoln, gained currency from John Dickinson's "Liberty Song," published July 18, 1768, in the Boston *Gazette,* containing the lines:

Then join hand in hand, brave Americans all—
By uniting we stand, by dividing we fall!

Renewed popularity came three quarters of a century later with the appearance of G. P. Morris' "The Flag of our Union," which quoted the sentiment as given above, from the motto of Kentucky, adopted in 1792.

IRVING DILLIARD

Universal Service. *See* Conscription; Draft.

Universalists. Opposition to the preaching of eternal torment and the predestination of the elect had been growing in England and New England during the 17th and 18th centuries, but it was not effectively preached in this country until the arrival of the Rev. John Murray from London in 1770. Murray's preaching in Gloucester, Mass., and vicinity was paralleled in Philadelphia by the Rev. Elhanan Winchester and in New Hampshire by the Rev. Caleb Rich. In 1790 these three movements united in a general convention in Philadelphia. After 1805 the Rev. Hosea Ballou of Massachusetts, who opposed both eternal damnation and the doctrine of the Trinity, became denomination leader for the next fifty years.

Universalism spread into New York State and the Middle West, although the majority of its churches have always been in New England. About 52,000 persons (1939) in the United States and Canada belong to the Universalist General Convention.

[Richard Eddy, *History of Universalism.*]

CHARLES LYTTLE

Universities, State. In the state university system the United States has made a distinctly American contribution to educational history. The state university was, in effect, a new interpretation of those liberal educational concepts developing in the United States after the Revolution, formulated in the Ordinance of 1787[qv] and the subsequent allocation of two townships in every state within the Northwest Territory[qv] "for the purpose of a university." This was the charter of the great expansion of public education in the Middle West.

The first state universities, however, were established in the South. North Carolina University, chartered in 1789, opened its doors in 1795. The University of Tennessee was first chartered as a territorial college in 1794; Georgia and South Carolina, chartered in 1785 and 1801, began teaching in 1801 and 1805 respectively; while the University of Virginia was established in 1819. Meanwhile Vermont had opened its University in 1800, while Ohio University, first in the Northwest Territory, came in 1804; Indiana University, chartered in 1820, opened in 1824. Most of these institutions, it may be said, maintained a precarious existence and were actually academies and secondary schools, rather than colleges—much less universities—and were regarded as private, rather than public, corporations.

In 1817 the territorial government of Michigan set up an elaborate state system of instruction known as the "Catholepistemiad of Michigania," which soon proved impracticable, but its conception of an educational program survived and was incorporated in Michigan's constitution, under which the present University was organized in 1837 and opened in 1841. Within eight years Michigan's full academic course was supplemented by a medical department and the institution became a true university. It grew rapidly, and its success led to general recognition of the principle of state education and a strengthening of institutions already established. The University of Wisconsin opened its doors in 1849; Minnesota was founded in 1851; Iowa, founded in 1847, first began teaching in 1855; Washington in 1861; Kansas was organized in 1864; Illinois was incorporated in 1867; California in 1868; and Oregon in 1876—all infused with a liberal spirit and a readiness to experiment.

In most of the state universities control lies with a board of trustees, or regents, appointed by the governor or the legislature, sometimes jointly. In 1850 Michigan made its eight regents an elective body, a co-ordinate part of the state administrative system. Similarly, Minnesota, California and Idaho have made their universities constitutionally independent corporations. In most states, however, the regents remain an appointive body and subject to legislative control. At the present time forty states maintain universities. Aside from the original land grants[qv], in many cases carelessly administered, financial support for state universities was for many years uncertain, but in recent years most states have given generous support. This has come through legislative appropriation or, in some cases, through making a certain proportion of a mill a university tax assessed upon all taxable property, thus providing a flexible income which constantly increases with the growth of the commonwealth.

[Nicholas Murray Butler, ed., *Monographs on Education;* Clarence Stephen Marsh, ed., *American Universities and Colleges;* Edward C. Elliott and M. M. Chambers, *The Colleges and the Courts;* Norman Foerster, *The American State University;* Wilfred B. Shaw, *A Short History of the University of Michigan.*]

WILFRED B. SHAW

Unknown Soldier, Tomb of the, in Arlington National Cemetery, near Washington, D. C., was dedicated in 1921 as a memorial to all American soldiers and sailors who lost their lives in the World War. The body within was selected with great care to avoid future identification. The present tomb was designed by Thomas Hudson Jones and Lorimer Rich and erected in 1931 on the site of a former uncompleted monument. A perpetual military guard is maintained.

FREDERICK P. TODD

Unofficial Observer is an executive agent[qv] of a type appointed in considerable numbers by all Presidents since Washington. Payment could be made from the President's "contingent" fund (1790 and thereafter) or from other funds if available. The practice is coterminous with government under the Constitution but the phrase "unofficial observer" became common after the World War. Domestic political differences, senatorial attempts to limit executive power, and international exigencies required the use of a large group of liason agents between the executive department of the United States Government and the Allied and Associated Powers in liquidating war questions, particularly through such agencies as the Reparations Commission[qv] and various international conferences.

[H. M. Wriston, *Executive Agents in American Foreign Relations.*]

HENRY M. WRISTON

Unreasonable Searches and Seizures. According to John Adams, the American Revolution began in 1761 when James Otis delivered his famous arguments against the writs of assistance[qv]. These general warrants permitting revenue officers to search for smuggled goods were regarded as a gross violation of the common law rights of Englishmen[qv]. These rights, the colonists argued, were in full force in America. In drafting the Revolutionary constitutions, care was taken to protect private dwellings, papers, etc., from arbitrary invasion by government agents. The Fourth Amendment[qv] provided similar protection against Federal authority, prohibiting "unreasonable searches and seizures" and defining the procedure by which legal searches and seizures could be made. Earlier court decisions tended to hold government officers to strict observance of the constitutional limitations, and evidence illegally secured was in some instances held equivalent to self-incrimination forbidden by the Fifth Amendment[qv]. The implications of the Fourth Amendment are, however, that reasonable searches and seizures are proper and the courts have, therefore, an important responsibility in defining "unreasonable" (*see* Wire Tapping Cases).

[W. W. Willoughby, *The Constitutional Law of the United States.*]

W. A. ROBINSON

Upper and Lower Lakes. The French, who first explored the Great Lakes, reached them via the St. Lawrence, the Ottawa River and Lake Nipissing route to Georgian Bay (Champlain, 1615). From here they extended their explorations to lakes Huron, Michigan and Superior (Nicolet, 1634, Jogues and Raymbaut, 1641, et al.); the adjoining country was known as the Upper Country, and the three lakes as the Upper Lakes. Direct access from Lower Canada, via the Upper St. Lawrence River to Lake Ontario and Lake Erie, was gained only much later, following the humbling of the Iroquois[qv]. In time, the name Lower Lakes was employed to distinguish Erie and Ontario from the remaining, or "Upper" Great Lakes.

The terms "Upper" and "Lower" have been loosely used at different times. Thus, in negotiating the Rush-Bagot Agreement (*see* Great Lakes, Agreement for Disarmament on the), Lake Erie was obviously included among the "Upper" Lakes.

M. M. QUAIFE

Upper Peninsula of Michigan. The addition of this region to Michigan resulted from the prolonged dispute over the Ohio-Michigan boundary[qv]. The Ordinance of 1787[qv] directed that three states be created for the Northwest Territory[qv], and authorized Congress to form one or two additional states north of the east and west line through the southern extreme of Lake Michigan. In fixing the boundary separating the three southern states from the two northern ones this provision was ignored in every instance. Ohio demanded—and got—a boundary which gave the Maumee River and Bay to that state. Public opinion in Michigan was outraged, leading to the creation of a state government which functioned out of the Union for a year and a half. As a substitute for her loss of territory to Ohio, Congress forced upon Michigan the remote and undesired Upper Peninsula. The experience of a century has dismally failed to confirm the wisdom of this measure, which forcibly united two distinct and widely different geographical areas.

[Standard histories of Ohio, Michigan and Wisconsin; monographs on boundaries of Michigan in *Mich. Pioneer and Hist. Colls.*, Vols. XI, XXVI, XXVII, XXX and XXXVIII.]

M. M. QUAIFE

Upper Sandusky, in present Wyandot County, Ohio, referred to also as Sandusky[qv], became a headquarters of the Wyandot Indians[qv] in the period of the American Revolution. Located in the "Sandusky Plains," a nearly treeless prairie, the Wyandot towns served as a convenient base of operations for British-Indian forays and a center to which captives and plunder were brought. Crawford's retaliatory expedition[qv] ended disastrously and the Wyandots remained under British influence until Wayne's victory[qv]. Thereafter they were loyal to the United States, Gen. Harrison erecting Fort Ferree at Upper Sandusky in the War of 1812. Indian treaties in 1817–18 ceding northwestern Ohio to the United States Government reserved a considerable part of present Wyandot County and a portion of Crawford County for the Wyandots and Delawares[qv]. Not until 1842 was the last reservation ceded to the United States. In 1843 the Federal Government laid out the town of Upper Sandusky on a tract of 619.47 acres including the site of the last Wyandot village.

[E. O. Randall and D. J. Ryan, *History of Ohio;* C. E. Sherman, Original Ohio Land Subdivisions, in *Ohio Co-operative Topographic Survey*, Final Report, Vol. III.]

EUGENE H. ROSEBOOM

Urban Drift, The. The United States, more than 95% agrarian in 1790, had become predominantly urban by 1930. Of her population 56.2% lived in cities of 2500 or over; and cities of 100,000, nonexistent until 1820, numbered 93. The census of 1880 disclosed a city of one million; there were five such by 1930. This drift to the city and the consequent emergence of the metropolis were almost revolutionary developments in American life between 1880 and 1930.

Despite the trek to the West, expansion in manufacturing, canals and railroads[qqv] led to urban concentration between 1840 and 1850. In the 1860's this resulted from the check upon westward settlement imposed by the Civil War and the great increase of manufacturing during and after it. City promotion, the demands of urban industry, and the replacement of manual labor by farm machinery[qv] combined with a psychological factor to bring in the 1880's a "flight to the city" which was deemed the "phenomenon" of the age. The lure of the city began to outshine the former attraction of the "sunset regions"; the city rather than the frontier[qv] was fast becoming the pivot of American life.

Stimulating migration from 1900 to 1930 were opportunities in centers associated with the rapidly expanding automobile[qv] and electrical industries and in the new cities of the industrial South, Florida and California. The World War shook men loose permanently from rural moorings and brought increased calls for workers in urban wartime industries. The decline following quota restrictions on immigrants—for some years now primarily urban dwellers—was counterbalanced by the movement of Negroes from Southern farms to Northern cities. The mechanization of agriculture and the shrinking of its world market continued to diminish the demand for farm laborers. The urban drift was checked temporarily by a "back to the farm" movement attendant upon the economic depression of the early 1930's. At the same time, suburbs were expanding at the expense of "downtown" sections and rural areas were increasingly dominated by the near-by metropolis.

Significant results of this urban drift were the transfer of wealth and talent from country to city, the extension of economic and social specialization, the emergence of problems springing from the physical hazards and interdependence of city life, and, most important, the appearance of a pervasive metropolitan influence and urban habit of mind which increasingly affected social patterns and exerted political influence in American life.

[A. F. Weber, *The Growth of Cities in the 19th Century;* A. M. Schlesinger, *The Rise of the City;* J. M. Gillette and G. R. Davis, Measure of Rural Migration and Other Factors of Urban Increase in the United States, in *Am. Statistical Assn. Quar. Publs.*, XIV, 642-52; Carter Goodrich et al., *Migration and Economic Opportunity*, 676-99; O. E. Baker, Rural-Urban Migration and the National Welfare, in *Annals of the Assn. of Am. Geographers*, XXIII, No. 2, June, 1933, 59-126; R. D. McKenzie, The Rise of Metropolitan Communities, in *Recent Social Trends*, 443-96; W. S. Thompson and P. K. Whelpton, *Population Trends in the U. S.*, 18-32.]

BAYRD STILL

Ursuline Convent (Charlestown, Mass.) Burned (Aug. 11, 1834). This was a landmark in the American nativistic movement[qv]. The Ursuline convent school had been established in 1818 but attracted little attention until the early 1830's when the clergy, the press and a self-proclaimed "escaped nun," Rebecca Theresa Reed, began spreading tales of its immorality and proselytizing efforts. A growing excitement was climaxed in 1834 when a member of the order, temporarily deranged, fled to the near-by home of her brother. She later returned voluntarily but rumors that she was being forcibly retained brought a mob together; the sisters and pupils were driven out, and the convent burned. Popular approval of this act, as shown by the prompt acquittal of the mob leaders, the refusal of the state to reimburse the Ursuline order, and the thinly veiled satisfaction voiced by the press, led to a nation-wide campaign against Catholicism in the following decades.

[R. A. Billington, The Burning of the Charlestown Convent, in *New England Quarterly*, Vol. X; R. A. Billington, *The Protestant Crusade.*]

RAY ALLEN BILLINGTON

Ursulines, The, were a prominent order of French nuns. On Sept. 13, 1726, the order signed a contract with the Company of the Indies[qv], which then controlled Louisiana, to send a group of their members to New Orleans to take charge of the hospital and to establish a school for girls. With Marie Tranchepain de St. Augustin as Mother Superior, the group arrived in 1727. In 1770 they were relieved of their duties in connection with the hospital, but the convent and school for girls which they established, the first of its kind in the Mississippi Valley, is still in existence in New Orleans.

[Charles Gayarré, *History of Louisiana;* C. F. Richardson, A Note on the Organization of the Oldest School for Girls in the Mississippi Valley, in Mississippi Valley Historical Association *Proceedings*, VIII; Heloise Hulse Cruzat, The Ursulines of Louisiana, in *Louisiana Historical Quarterly*, II; H. C. Semple, *The Ursulines in New Orleans and Our Lady of Prompt Succor: A Record of Two Centuries, 1727-1925;* Henry Renshaw, The Louisiana Ursulines, in Louisiana Historical Society *Publications*, II, Part 4.]

WALTER PRICHARD

Useful Manufactures, The Society for Establishing, was founded by Alexander Hamilton to show America the way to independence of European manufactures by establishing an emporium of great factories producing a variety of products for common use. A perpetual charter granted by the New Jersey legislature (Nov. 22, 1791), authorized the Society to engage freely in manufacturing and selling, to acquire real estate, improve rivers, dig canals, collect tolls on improvements, and to incorporate a municipality at the site chosen, to be called Paterson, in honor of Gov. William Paterson. Seven hundred acres were purchased (May, 1792) at the Great Falls of the Passaic River where a small cotton factory was built. Since 1796, when manufacturing was abandoned due to financial reverses, the Society's chief business has been to lease sites, furnish water and electric power and capital to establish useful manufactures by others. Repeated efforts to break the Society's charter and to terminate its tax immunity have failed. Its property was recently (1938) valued at $1,500,000.

[John Whitehead, *The Passaic Valley, New Jersey.*]

C. A. TITUS

Utah, the 45th state of the Union, was named for the Ute[qv], or Eutaw, Indians. The eastern portion is traversed by mountain ranges running north and south, excepting the Uintah Mountains, running east and west, the only range so situated in the United States. The western half of Utah is in the Great Basin[qv], or bed of Lake Bonneville, the remnant of which is Great Salt Lake[qv], the largest body of salt water in America, holding in solution more than 20% of salts. The average rainfall is about twelve inches, making irrigation[qv] necessary in all parts of the state. The tillable land is extremely productive and the climate healthful, the mean temperature of Salt Lake City in January being 31° and in July 73°, with colder temperatures in the higher plateaus and a semitropical climate in the Rio Virgin Valley in the south. The first white men known to have entered Utah were soldiers in the army of Coronado[qv], who in 1540 came searching for the mythical Seven Cities of Cíbola. In 1776 two Spanish friars, Escalante and Dominguez, from Santa Fé[qv] entered Utah seeking a direct route to California but were unsuccessful and returned. Next came the trappers of the early 19th century. The first permanent settlers were the Mormons[qv], religious outcasts driven from Illinois after the slaying of their leaders Joseph and Hyrum Smith. Brigham Young, who succeeded Joseph Smith as president of the Mormon Church, led his people to the Salt Lake Valley, the first company arriving July 24, 1847. The Mormons planted colonies in all parts of the desert, and to them more than to any others is due the redemption of the arid West. Their industry made the desert blossom and the Great Basin habitable. Upon the arrival of the Mormons, a provisional government was set up and in 1849 Congress was petitioned to accept that government as the

State of Deseret. This petition was denied, but in 1850 Congress created the Territory of Utah. Brigham Young, who was acting as governor in the provisional government, was appointed governor and served two terms. Near the close of his second term friction arose between Utah and the Federal Government based upon false reports made by Utah Federal officers. They said the territorial records had been burned and the people were in rebellion. Without an investigation President Buchanan sent an army to suppress the supposed rebellion and to install Alfred Cumming of Georgia as governor to succeed Brigham Young. This army under Albert Sidney Johnston entered Salt Lake City in 1858, but moved forty miles south and established Camp Floyd where they remained for a considerable time (*see* Mormon Expedition). The true condition eventually became known in Washington and the troops were withdrawn. Gov. Cumming was received and loyally supported by the Mormon people. From that time forth, while Utah remained a territory, Federal appointees, who were men from other states, with few exceptions were unfriendly to the Mormons. Many attempts were made to obtain statehood, but due to the internal strife, and the question of polygamy as practised by the Mormons before 1890, these failed until Jan. 4, 1896.

[O. F. Whitney, *History of Utah;* H. H. Bancroft, *History of Utah;* A. Jenson, *Church Chronology.*]

JOSEPH FIELDING SMITH

Utes, The, are Indians belonging to the Shoshonean linguistic family. Their country once included eastern Utah, central and western Colorado, and part of northern New Mexico. Formerly there were thirteen or more Ute tribes or bands, seven in Utah being organized into a confederacy. By 1870 there were probably about 4000 Utes; there are now (1940) about 2000, on reservations in Utah and Colorado. They were nonagricultural and warlike. Before 1700 the Spaniards in New Mexico felt their strength and during the 19th century Anglo-Americans frequently clashed with them. Their first treaty with the United States was made in 1849.

[F. W. Hodge, *Handbook of American Indians.*]

RUPERT N. RICHARDSON

Utrecht, Treaty of (1713), concluded Queen Anne's War[qv]. The terms of peace pertinent to American history were included in treaties between France and Great Britain (April 11, 1713), and between Spain and Great Britain (July 13, 1713). France restored to Great Britain Hudson Strait and Bay within boundaries to be defined by commissioners; and the English Hudson's Bay Company[qv] was to be indemnified for losses incurred through French action in times of peace. France conceded to Great Britain the island of St. Christopher, Acadia[qv], Newfoundland and its adjacent islands; but retained Cape Breton and the islands of the St. Lawrence. French fishermen retained the right of drying fish, caught off Newfoundland, on shores between Cape Bonavista and Point Riche. Frenchmen in newly acquired British territory might exercise the Roman Catholic religion so far as British laws allowed. France acknowledged British sovereignty over the Five Nations of Iroquois[qv]; and both parties agreed not to interfere with Indians under their respective influence. For her part Spain pledged that no portion of Spanish America would ever be transferred to any foreign power. Spain granted to Great Britain, for thirty years, the *Asiento*[qv], together with a depôt on the Rio de la Plata and the right of sending an annual ship to trade with Spanish America.

[F. G. Davenport, *European Treaties;* G. M. Trevelyan, *England under Queen Anne;* G. M. Wrong, *Rise and Fall of New France.*]

E. B. GRAVES

Vacations. Customs varied widely among educational institutions in earlier days, but the vacations were always short, and summer was not considered as necessarily a recreation season. At Norwich College in Vermont before 1828 the only vacation of the year consisted of four weeks in December. At Union College, Schenectady, at the same time, there were three vacations yearly—three weeks at Christmas, six weeks in May–June, and three weeks in autumn. Commencements at Harvard and some other colleges did not take place until August (sometimes as late as the 25th); but as the 19th century advanced, one finds Commencement moving slowly back into June, and the summer vacation lengthening to three months, with perhaps ten days more covering Christmas and New Year, and a week around Easter. City public schools in general followed college practice in most particulars.

Vacations for business and working people were unknown before 1850 save by rare special favor; but during the "flush period" following the Civil War, a fortnight's vacation became almost a perquisite for office workers. At first it was granted without pay; but toward the close of the century, pay began to be continued during the vacations of the better-salaried office workers and executives. After 1900 this grew to be an expected thing in the case of persons on monthly or yearly salaries. The 20th century, especially after the development of the automobile[qv], saw the various businesses catering to the needs of vacation tourists assuming enormous proportions; play assumed an importance in social life in startling contrast to the hard-working creed of the previous century.

[*Atlantic Monthly*, December, 1869, p. 824; *Nation*, Aug. 7, 1873, p. 90.]

ALVIN F. HARLOW

Vaccination, Introduction of. The copy of Edward Jenner's *Inquiry into the Causes and Effects of the Variolæ Vaccinæ* (1798), which John Coakley Lettsom of London forwarded to Benjamin Waterhouse of Boston, was the earliest to reach this country. Waterhouse, the first professor of theory and practice at Harvard, read with interest the thin quarto, bound in boards, selling for 7s. 6d., and reviewed it in a newspaper (*The Columbian Sentinel,* March 12, 1799) under the title, "Something Curious in the Medical Line." After repeated efforts, Waterhouse succeeded in obtaining vaccine virus from Jenner's stock, with which he vaccinated his offspring (July 8, 1800), starting with Daniel Oliver Waterhouse (the first vaccinated American). Waterhouse then exposed his children in William Aspinwall's private Smallpox Hospital at Brookline, where smallpox[qv] matter was inserted by punctures into one of these children, and an infected thread passed through his skin. The dreaded smallpox did not develop, and Aspinwall, who had made a fortune through the old inoculation, acknowledged the superiority of the new inoculation. Waterhouse's experiment on his family removed the *variolous papule* as the most appalling menace on the American continent.

[William M. Welch of Philadelphia (frequently confused with the more famous William H. Welch of Baltimore), *The Jenner of America*, 1885.]

VICTOR ROBINSON

Valcour Island, Battle of (Oct. 11, 1776). Benedict Arnold with fifteen hastily constructed vessels manned by 700 men, mostly soldiers, disputed the control of Lake Champlain with Capt. Thomas Pringle, who commanded twenty-five vessels and 700 experienced sailors. Defeated at Valcour Island, Arnold slipped past the British at night and during the next two days kept up a running fight. When he arrived at Crown Point[qv], he had lost ten of his ships and nine tenths of his men, but his determined resistance had delayed British invasion for another year.

[A. T. Mahan, *The Major Operations of the Navies in the War of American Independence*.]

EDWARD P. ALEXANDER

Vallandigham Incident (May, 1863). Clement L. Vallandigham, Dayton, Ohio, Copperhead[qv] leader and ex-congressman, was arrested on May 5 for violating Gen. Burnside's "General Order No. 38"[qv] in a speech at Mount Vernon, Ohio, on May 1 in which he appealed from Order No. 38 to Order No. 1, the Constitution (*see* Arrest, Arbitrary, during the Civil War). Tried by military commission at Cincinnati, sentenced to imprisonment for the duration of the war, Lincoln commuted the sentence to banishment beyond the Federal lines, which was done on May 25. Passing through the Confederacy to Canada, Vallandigham, now Democratic candidate for governor of Ohio, conducted an unsuccessful campaign against John Brough.

In February, 1864, Vallandigham appealed through counsel to the U. S. Supreme Court for revision of the sentence of the military commission. His petition was denied for lack of jurisdiction. Vallandigham returning to the United States in June, 1864, to take part in the political campaign, was not further molested by the Federal authorities.

[George H. Porter, *Ohio Politics during the Civil War Period.*]

CHARLES H. COLEMAN

Valley Campaign, Jackson's (1862). *See* Jackson's Valley Campaign.

Valley Forge, the encampment ground for the Continental army from Dec. 19, 1777 until June 19, 1778, is situated on the west bank of the Schuylkill River, in Montgomery and Chester counties, Pa., twenty-two miles northwest of Philadelphia.

After the Americans had been defeated at Brandywine, Paoli and Germantown[qqv], and after the British had occupied Philadelphia (then the National Capital) Washington led 11,000 regular troops to Valley Forge from Whitemarsh to take up winter quarters. The site was chosen for strategic reasons. Its high ground commanded the roads from Philadelphia to the ironworks, gunneries and powder mills of Warwick and Coventry in northern Chester County. Valley Forge also lay close to the great road, now called the Lancaster Pike[qv], which tapped the interior of Pennsylvania, and the site dominated the route from the South that led through Coryell's Ferry to West Point and New England. Valley Forge was in easy reach of the fertile farm lands of the pro-Revolutionary Pennsylvania Germans, and it was only eight miles distant from a famous health resort at Yellow Springs which could readily be adapted for hospital use. Du Portail, French fortification engineer with the army, believed that the sloping hills, flanked by the Schuylkill and supported on the rear by the high, winding, wooded gorge of Valley Creek, could be made impregnable against attack. As a further safeguard, picket parties were detached to watch the movement of the British.

Washington's plans were well drawn and his staff was efficient in carrying out their duties, but negligence and mismanagement on the part of others, particularly in the commissary department and in the transport service, almost destroyed the Continental army during the encampment. An unexpectedly early winter, with heavy snows and abnormally freezing weather in Christmas week, prevented the receipt of regular supplies. A January thaw brought mud so deep upon the roads that hundreds of army wagons had to be abandoned. Even when transport was available, however, the neglect of the army by the Continental Congress[qv] and the failure of the commissary officers to forward food, clothing and supplies by the most available routes, increased the sufferings of the men. On several occasions, Washington expressed his fears that only extraordinary efforts could prevent the army from disbanding. Camp fever, probably of the type now called typhus, and smallpox were epidemic during the army's stay at Valley Forge. Medical supplies were lacking. Hundreds of men died and were buried in unmarked graves.

During the encampment period, however, much constructive good was accomplished, particularly in the restoration of morale and in the insistence upon proper discipline. Baron Steuben introduced efficient drilling. The Franco-American Alliance[qv], known in camp about May Day, brought new supplies of money and especially of adequate arms and clothing. Ten days after the army left Valley Forge, it met the British army withdrawing from Philadelphia, and fought with it on equal terms at Monmouth[qv].

[Harry Emerson Wildes, *Valley Forge;* Henry Woodman, *The History of Valley Forge.*]

HARRY EMERSON WILDES

Valverde, Battle of (Feb. 21, 1862). Early in the Civil War, Confederate troops invaded New Mexico and in February, 1862, Brig. Gen. Henry H. Sibley, with 2000 men, attacked Fort Craig, where most of the Regular Army garrisons of the territory had been assembled under Col. E. R. S. Canby, who had been joined by a number of New Mexico volunteers (one regiment being commanded by Kit Carson) and a company from Colorado Territory, his total being 3810. Sibley attempted to cross the Rio Grande[qv] at Valverde, but was opposed, the fight centering about an improvised regular battery commanded by Capt. Alexander McRae, which eventually was captured. Canby then withdrew to the fort, but declined to surrender. Sibley advanced to Albuquerque and Santa Fé. Subsequent fighting at Apache Cañon and Glorieta[qv] resulted in the defeat of Sibley and his retreat. Losses at Valverde were: Union, 3 officers, 65 enlisted men killed; 3 officers and 157 enlisted men wounded; 1 officer, 34 enlisted men captured; Confederate, 40 killed, 200 wounded.

[*Official Records of the Union and Confederate Armies*, Series I, Volume 9; *Battles and Leaders of the Civil War*, Volume II; W. C. Whitford, *Colorado Volunteers in the Civil War.*]

DON RUSSELL

Van Ness Convention (Feb. 17, 1834), negotiated at Madrid, by Cornelius P. Van Ness and José de Herédia, settled American claims against Spain subsequent to 1819 (*see* Adams-Onís Treaty), arising principally from irregular seizures of American property in the course of Spanish operations against the rebellious colonies. After unsuccessfully pressing claims for $2,500,000 for a decade, the United States accepted an offer for the equivalent of $600,000 in 5% perpetual Spanish bonds and mutual cancellation of claims. The bonds were finally redeemed in cash by Spain in 1907.

[John Bassett Moore, *History of International Arbitrations*, Vol. V.]

CHARLES C. GRIFFIN

Van Zandt, Free State of, is a common designation given to an East Texas county created from Henderson County, March 20, 1848, and was named for Isaac Van Zandt, a prominent diplomat of the Republic of Texas. The origin of the term "Free State" is uncertain and has developed as a form of folklore. One legend is that the citizens in the Van Zandt end of Henderson County refused to pay taxes to the county and declared themselves free. Another is that a slave owner from Louisiana, hunting a place of refuge for his slaves during the Civil War, declared to a Van Zandt editor he would just as soon take them to a free state as this county. Still another explanation is that a group of citizens of this county refused to accept the terms of the surrender at Appomattox[qv] and declared themselves free from the Confederacy. From an obscure, uncertain origin the term has grown to common use by citizens of this section of Texas.

[Wentworth Manning, *Some History of Van Zandt County.*]

J. G. SMITH

Vancouver, Fort (located on the north bank of the Columbia about 100 miles from its mouth, at the present site of Vancouver, Wash.), was the western headquarters of the Hudson's Bay Company[qv] from 1825 to 1845. Under the direction of George Simpson, American governor of the company, the site was selected in 1824. The buildings were dedicated in March, 1825 and replaced Fort George as the chief western post with Dr. John McLoughlin as chief factor.

The first location was almost a mile from the river; but in 1829 the fort was rebuilt on the banks of the river. With the declining importance of fur trade in the Columbia region, combined with fear of unfriendly relations with incoming American settlers, the principal western headquarters were transferred to Victoria on Vancouver Island in 1845.

Old Fort Vancouver and its lands were later purchased by the United States Government and the site used for a military post.

[Charles H. Carey, *A General History of Oregon prior to 1861.*]
ROBERT MOULTON GATKE

Vancouver's Exploration (1791–95). To carry out the terms of the Nootka Sound Convention[qv] Capt. George Vancouver was sent to meet the Spanish commissioner at Vancouver Island. His expedition consisted of the sloop-of-war *Discovery* and the armed tender *Chatham,* with the equipment and personnel for scientific research. He sailed from England in January, 1791, with instructions to survey the American shore line from 30° to 60° North Latitude. He was especially instructed to see if there might be interlocking river systems opening communication into the interior of the continent.

Vancouver reached the American coast off California on April 17, 1792. He skirted the northern California and southern Oregon coast rather far out, naming Cape Orford and noting only a few major landmarks. He observed the mouth of the Columbia River[qv] but mistook its true nature. Giving the coast to the north a more minute survey, he noted the Strait of Juan de Fuca and sailed into the great waterways opening into it. Puget Sound[qv] was explored in detail. Principal geographical features were named, many of the names becoming established in permanent usage.

During his subsequent months of exploration Vancouver and his officers gave detailed examination and made charts of the coast from California to 60° N., including the lower hundred miles of the Columbia River which had been recently discovered by Capt. Robert Gray. The charts were accurate enough to be readily compared with the ones in use at the present time. He ended his four years of exploration in 1795.

[Charles H. Carey, *A General History of Oregon prior to 1861.*]
ROBERT MOULTON GATKE

"Vandalia Colony" was the term applied to a project for a settlement on the Ohio River, sponsored in the early 1770's by the Grand Ohio Company[qv], often referred to as the Walpole Company. While the colony never materialized, the movement behind it was typical of the great land speculation schemes which were so numerous in England and America in the 18th century. This particular project had a long and extremely complex history and counted among its backers many persons of prominence on both sides of the ocean. It became deeply involved in politics in both England and America.

The plan had its origin in a grant of land known as "Indiana," made at Fort Stanwix[qv] on Nov. 3, 1768, by the Six Nations, representing certain dependent tribes, to a group of Pennsylvania traders, in order to reimburse the latter for losses sustained in 1763 (*see* Pontiac War). Samuel Wharton and William Trent proceeded to England early in 1769 to receive royal confirmation of the grant (*see* Baynton, Wharton and Morgan). When it was not immediately forthcoming, a company was organized in London which petitioned the crown for a considerably larger grant of 2,400,000 acres. After a preliminary hearing before the Board of Trade[qv], this group was reorganized on Dec. 27, 1769, as the Grand Ohio Company, which petitioned to be allowed to purchase a vast tract of some 20,000,000 acres, bounded roughly as follows: on the northwest by the Ohio River, on the west by a line extending southward from the mouth of the Scioto to Cumberland Gap[qv], and on the south and east by the Cumberland and Allegheny Mountains and the western boundaries of Maryland and Pennsylvania. The proposed limits were later extended still farther to the southeast.

The plan contemplated the establishment of a new colony with a separate government of the royal type, with ownership of most of the land vested in the proprietors of the Grand Ohio Company. Though many of the proprietors were Englishmen holding high official positions, the project encountered strong opposition from influential British quarters and from rival speculative interests in Virginia (*see* Ohio Company of Virginia). In 1773 the grant appeared about to materialize but there were further delays, and the outbreak of hostilities in America in 1775 ended all hope of success. In 1781 Wharton and certain other Americans who were interested tried to persuade Congress to recognize the abortive Vandalia grant, but the opposition was too strong and the enterprise finally lapsed.

[T. P. Abernethy, *Western Lands and the American Revolution;* C. W. Alvord, *The Mississippi Valley in British Politics;* A. T. Volwiler, *George Croghan and the Westward Movement, 1741-1782.*]

WAYNE E. STEVENS

Vanderbilt Cup Race. *See* Yacht Racing.

Vanhorne's Lessee v. Dorrance (2 Dallas 303, 1795) was one of the earliest cases in which a Federal court asserted the right to disregard a state law that was held to be in conflict with the state constitution. Justice Paterson instructed a jury in the Federal circuit court to consider a Pennsylvania law divesting one person of property and vesting it in another as inconsistent with the Pennsylvania constitution and the Constitution of the United States, and therefore unconstitutional and void (*see* Judicial Review).

[Charles Warren, *The Supreme Court in United States History,* and Earliest Cases of Judicial Review of State Legislation by Federal Courts, in *Yale Law Jour.,* XXXII, 15-28.]

P. ORMAN RAY

Vare Case, The. In 1926 William S. Vare, Philadelphia Republican organization leader, defeated George Wharton Pepper and Gifford Pinchot in the Pennsylvania Republican primaries for nomination to the United States Senate. Investigation of campaign expenditures resulted in the Senate's refusal to accept Vare's certificate of election even after he had defeated William B. Wilson, Democratic nominee, in the subsequent general election. The investigation was launched by a senatorial resolution of May 17, 1926, and was concluded with a vote of the Senate on Dec. 6, 1929. The verdict was 58 to 22 rejecting Vare's claim to a seat on the ground that corrupt practices[qv] and exorbitant expenditures had been employed in obtaining the nomination; this despite the fact that Vare's major competitor, George Wharton Pepper, had spent at least twice as much in the same campaign.

[Senate Report 1197, 69 Cong., 2 Sess., Pt. 2; Senate Report 1858, 70 Cong., 2 Sess.; Senate Report 47, 71 Cong., 2 Sess.]

FRANCES L. REINHOLD

Vaudeville. Songs, dances and acrobatic turns were seen in small concert halls and "museums" in the early 19th century. They grew in popularity, became known as "variety," and by 1860 there were theaters devoted to such programs in all the larger cities. Many noted legitimate actors first appeared in variety. It was late in the 19th century that the French word vaudeville appeared. B. F. Keith, who first began managing a music hall in Boston in 1883, acquired a number of vaudeville theaters, and combining with a rival, F. F. Proctor, in 1906, became the leading figure of the vaudeville world. Sullivan & Considine, Orpheum, Marcus Loew, Pantages and others were operating large vaudeville circuits in those years. But between 1910 and 1930 the motion picture[qv] so supplanted the stage in popular patronage that after 1930 vaudeville acts were but little seen save as parts of the program at the larger picture theaters.

[M. B. Leavitt, *Fifty Years in Theatrical Management.*]

ALVIN F. HARLOW

Veazie Bank v. Fenno (8 Wall. 533, 1869). In 1866 Congress imposed a 10% tax on the notes issued by state banks[qv] in order to drive them out of circulation. In 1869 the Supreme Court in Veazie Bank v. Fenno upheld the constitutionality of the enactment on the ground that this destructive use of the taxing power was for an object clearly within the constitutional powers of Congress—the power to regulate the currency of the nation.

W. A. ROBINSON

Vehicles, Colonial. Among the first colonial contrivances for land carriage were sledges hewn from a forked tree of which the branches served as runners and the stem as tongue. Somewhat similar plank stoneboats survive today. Bobsleds and sleighs[qv] were from the first familiar winter vehicles. Homemade farm carts often had solid wheels sawed from tree trunks coupled by a hickory or oak axle. Spoke wheels were frequently imported though wheelwrights appear among the first generation of colonists. By 1669 New Englanders had built roads and "cart bridges" permitting vehicle transport beyond the farm and its immediate neighborhood, but sometimes forbade using iron tires in towns to spare the pavements. Progress was slower in the plantation colonies. In Virginia and Maryland tobacco was sometimes "rolled" in heavy-hooped hogsheads to points of water shipment though carts—still known as tumbrils—were not uncommon. The supreme land freighter in colonial America was the Conestoga wagon[qv], a long hammock-bodied vehicle developed in Pennsylvania about 1730 to connect the inland settlements with tidewater trading centers.

"Riding carriages"[qv] were often imported, were used mostly in towns, and were regarded as luxuries which were occasionally taxed for the benefit of the poor. The most elaborate were coaches and chariots, heavy enclosed vehicles drawn by four or six horses. The earliest stagecoaches^{qv} were little more than lumber wagons with seats and awning. Lighter two-wheeled vehicles, the covered chaise and the open chair, were in general use in the 18th century. Before the Revolution the calash, consisting of an open seat on a pair of low heavy wheels, became popular. About the middle of the 18th century the tax records of Charlestown, Mass., list 6 coaches, 11 chariots, 326 chaises and 970 chairs. Westmoreland County, Va., however, reported in its wheel-tax returns for 1782 not more than 50 "riding carriages."

[W. B. Weeden, *Economic and Social History of New England;* J. L. Bishop, *History of American Manufactures;* P. A. Bruce, *Economic History of Virginia in the Seventeenth Century.*]

VICTOR S. CLARK

Venango was the early name, in turn, of Indian village, trading post, fort and frontier settlement at the junction of French Creek and the Allegheny River in northwestern Pennsylvania. Long inhabited by Indians, the site first gets into the records in connection with the fur trade and the establishment there of a post by John Frazer, a fur trader and gunsmith. In the struggle between the French and English for control of the Ohio Valley, Venango became important. Céloron[qv] passed by in 1749. The expedition of Marin drove out Frazer in 1753. Washington visited the French there in that autumn (*see* Le Bœuf, Fort, Washington's Mission to). Fort Machault[qv] was erected in 1754. Much enlarged in 1758, it was abandoned and burned at the time of the British attack on Niagara[qv]. Fort Venango, built by the British in 1760, was in turn destroyed by the Indians in 1763 (*see* Pontiac War). After the Revolutionary War, Fort Venango was replaced by Fort Franklin, which for a decade remained a haven for frontiersmen threatened by Indians. The dramatic period of old Venango was at an end by 1795.

[C. A. Babcock, *Venango County, Pennsylvania.*]

ALFRED P. JAMES

Venezuela, Blockade of. In 1902 the German, British and Italian governments decided to take joint action to compel President Castro to settle claims for defaulted debts and for injuries suffered by their nationals during several years of internal disorder in Venezuela. The German government had previously informed the United States of its purpose, giving assurances that no permanent occupation of territory was contemplated; and Secretary Hay had replied that the Monroe Doctrine[qv] did not guarantee any state against punishment for misconduct, provided that there was no occupation of territory by a non-American power. A formal blockade was established in December, several Venezuelan gunboats were seized, and fortifications on the coast were bombarded. Within a few days Venezuela made a proposal for arbitration, which was supported by the United States and accepted by the blockading powers. The claims involved were subsequently settled either by direct agreement or by mixed commissions, which after investigation awarded only a small portion of the amounts demanded.

The American minister at Caracas[qv], who represented Venezuela in negotiating the settlement, resisted the contention of the blockading powers that their claims should be paid before those of states which had not taken part in the intervention. This question was submitted to the Hague Court[qv], which decided in 1904 in favor of the blockading powers.

President Theodore Roosevelt some years later asserted that he had compelled the German government to agree to arbitration by threatening to send a fleet under Admiral Dewey to the Venezuelan coast. Just what he did in this connection is not clear from the written record, and scholars who have investigated the matter have concluded that Mr. Roosevelt's recollection of the matter was not entirely accurate.

[H. C. Hill, *Roosevelt and the Caribbean.*]

DANA G. MUNRO

Venezuela, Perry's Mission to (1819), was an example of the use of naval officers in American diplomacy. John Quincy Adams, dissatisfied with earlier special agents, and unwilling to arouse hopes of formal recognition, ordered Capt. Oliver H. Perry to Venezuela and to Buenos Aires to explain the United States' policy of neutrality in the Spanish-American revolution and to protest against unwarranted acts of rebel agents and privateers. Perry interviewed Bolívar, but died of fever near Angostura, his mission uncompleted.

[A. S. Mackenzie, *Life of Commodore Oliver Hazard Perry.*]

CHARLES C. GRIFFIN

Venezuela Boundary Controversy. When Great Britain annexed the territory of British Guiana (1814) there was no definite boundary along the western side. Negotiations took place from time to time with Venezuela but no agreement was reached nor was any serious effort made on the British side to secure one. In 1840 a British agent, Robert Schomburgk[qv], surveyed a line to the westward of the British settlements and the government, after a few years, adopted this as its definite claim. Against this Venezuela made a counterclaim, covering two thirds of the British colony, manifestly as a basis for compromise. The United States Government became gradually involved, owing to the constant pressure of the Venezuelan government, and from 1876 began, as a friend to both parties, to urge a settlement by arbitration. The British refused to agree to any plan which did not guarantee the continuance under their flag of all British settlements. From this position they never varied.

In 1885–86 the British authorities suddenly extended their claims to include some 30,000 square miles to the westward of the Schomburgk line, in a region where gold was reported. The Venezuelan government protested hotly, and securing no satisfaction broke off relations. The United States then began to exert increasing pressure for a settlement by arbitration, meeting invariably the British refusal to endanger existing settlements. Finally in June, 1895, Secretary Richard Olney[qv] injected a new note by demanding a settlement, under the authority conferred upon the United States by the Monroe Doctrine[qv], which he interpreted as equivalent to a virtual protectorate over the western hemisphere. When the Marquis of Salisbury refused to accept this interpretation of the Doctrine and reiterated the refusal to accept unrestricted arbitration, President Cleveland, in great indignation at the "grab" of 1886, asked Congress for authority to determine and maintain the legal boundary, under the Monroe Doctrine. This step, which involved a flat defiance of Great Britain, stirred great excitement in both countries, but in England the matter was almost immediately overshadowed by the greater excitement caused by the Jameson raid and the Kruger telegram. Salisbury not only did not resent the American demand but, expressly waiving the Monroe Doctrine, offered to discuss the problem with Secretary Olney as the representative of Venezuela, being pushed to this by the overwhelming pressure of British public and parliamentary opinion. In the negotiations which followed, the British still refused any form of unrestricted arbitration and no progress was made until Olney suggested that settlements in existence for sixty years be guaranteed. After reducing sixty years to fifty, Salisbury accepted this solution and a treaty was signed in 1897. Olney's provision enabled the arbitrators in 1899 to award to Venezuela the land "grabbed" in 1885–86, the rest of the boundary following approximately the Schomburgk line. Usually described as a British triumph, the award did, in fact, accomplish the main purpose that Cleveland and Olney desired, the blocking of the 1886 seizure. The extreme language of both men about the Monroe Doctrine served to stir American feeling but did not affect the outcome.

[H. James, *Richard Olney;* A. Nevins, *Grover Cleveland.*]

THEODORE CLARKE SMITH

***Vengeance-Constellation* Fight.** *See Constellation-Vengeance* Fight.

Vera Cruz (1914). When Victoriano Huerta seized the Mexican presidency in 1913, the United States refused to recognize him. Early in 1914, when Tampico was under martial law, some United States marines were arrested there, but quickly released and apologies made. President Wilson, however, insisted that a salute of twenty-one guns to the American flag also be fired. When this was not forthcoming, he ordered a fleet to Vera Cruz. Troops were landed on April 21, and, aided by bombardment, the city was taken with an American loss of seventeen killed and sixty-three wounded. Continued American political pressure forced Huerta out in July, and he fled to Jamaica.

[Edith O'Shaughnessy, *A Diplomat's Wife in Mexico.*]

ALVIN F. HARLOW

Vera Cruz, The Siege and Capture of (1847). With 10,000 troops and a siege train, Gen. Winfield Scott, during the Mexican War[qv], landed on the beach near Vera Cruz, March 9, 1847. Without serious opposition intrenchments were dug, the city completely invested, and, on the 13th, summoned. Gen. Juan Morales, with 1200 soldiers in San Juan de Ulúa castle and 3800 in the town, refused to capitulate. Scott opened the bombardment on the 22nd. Naval guns, borrowed and manned from the fleet, planted 800 yards from the walls, opened breaches and partially destroyed the city. Ulúa was undamaged, but pressure from the terrified populace induced Morales to yield. He relinquished command to Gen. Landero, who, on the 29th, raised the white flag. American losses were 19 killed, 63 wounded; Mexican, 80 military casualties and 100 civilians killed. Landero and his troops were paroled; the city was cleaned and garrisoned by Scott. Thereafter, throughout the war, it served as the port base of the invading army.

[Justin H. Smith, *The War with Mexico;* G. L. Rives, *The United States and Mexico.*]

CHARLES WINSLOW ELLIOTT

Verendrye Explorations, The. In 1728 Verendrye (Pierre Gaultier de Varennes) was stationed by the French government of Canada at a small outpost on Lake Nipigon. Here he heard from the Indians of a river flowing west into a salt sea. He knew nothing of the Rocky Mountains and he conceived the idea of an overland commerce between Lake Superior and the Pacific Ocean to bring the goods of the Far East to France by way of Montreal. The cost of this route could, he was sure, be defrayed from the profits of his fur trade.

Obtaining from the governor general of Canada a trade monopoly in this vast territory, he established a line of posts westward from Lake Superior to Lake-of-the-Woods and Lake Winnipeg, and up the Red and Assiniboine rivers. On the latter stream he built Fort La Reine, now Portage La Prairie, at the point where the old Indian trail from the Great Plains led across the river northward to York Factory on Hudson's Bay. In 1738, in search for the westward-flowing river, he led a party south from this point to Star Mound in Canada. This was the First Mountain mentioned in his journal and was the site of an abandoned Hidatsa village on the old trail. He next records passing Turtle Mountain on the north side and from this point his guides led him far out of his course to an ancient Hidatsa site on Antler Creek. From this point he went directly south to a fortified Hidatsa village he called Fort La Butte, recently identified as near Minot, N. Dak. While here he sent his son to a second Hidatsa village, a day's journey distant, located on the Missouri at Old Crossing at the present site of Sanish, and he reported that he had found there a westward-flowing river.

The identification of these sites as Hidatsa rests upon such evidence as the typical arrangement of their houses in the villages, the primitive form of their fortifications and the testimony of the various Indians in the vicinity.

In 1742 Verendrye sent his two sons from Fort La Reine across the Missouri River at Old Crossing. From the account in their journal, the party traveled west and southwest until they came within sight of the Big Horn Mountains, west of the Black Hills. Here, on the banks of the North Platte River (erroneously called by their guides the Missouri), they buried a lead plate inscribed with the date and the names of three of the party (*see* Verendrye Plate). How this lead plate came to be found in 1913 on the west bank of the Missouri River at Fort Pierre, S. Dak., may be explained from the lively curiosity of the Indians where the plate was originally buried and from the naïveté of the Verendrye sons, who appeared to believe they had successfully concealed the plate under a pile of stones on a bluff overlooking the river.

From their own account the party returned by the same route over which they had already traveled. It is worthy of note that after crossing the Missouri again they spoke of Fort La Butte as being a day's journey from Old Crossing.

[O. G. Libby, Verendrye's Visit to the Mandans in 1738-39, *Collections* of the State Historical Society of North Dakota, 1908, Vol. II, 502; O. G. Libby, *Mississippi Valley Historical Review*, Vol. III, No. 2, Some Verendrye Enigmas, and No. 3, Additional Verendrye Material; Francis Parkman, *A Half Century of Conflict.*]

O. G. LIBBY

Verendrye Plate. A sheet of lead, seven inches by eight inches in size, buried upon the hill at the junction of Bad River and the Missouri in Fort Pierre, S. Dak., March 30, 1743, by the Verendrye brothers, to certify the French claim to the upper Missouri Valley, was recovered by a party of school children on Feb. 17, 1913. (*See* comment on this location in article on Verendrye Explorations.) Upon the obverse is incised an inscription relating to the then existing French and Canadian governments. On the reverse are scratched the names of those present when the plate was deposited. It is now in possession of the South Dakota Historical Society, Pierre.

[Brymner, *Canadian Archives;* L. J. Burpee, *Journals and Letters of La Verendrye;* South Dakota Historical *Collections*, Vol. VII, p. 90; F. Parkman, *Half Century of Conflict;* P. Margry, *Découvertes et Etablissements des Français*, Vol. VI.]

DOANE ROBINSON

Vermont was discovered in 1609 by Samuel de Champlain. Decades of predatory warfare and organized battle followed, making settlement uncertain and transient. In 1666 the French built Fort St. Anne on Isle La Motte. In 1724 the English built Fort Dummer[qv] near Brattleboro. Both were military outposts and marked a definite approach of the two nations that was to result inevitably in a major clash for control of the strategic Champlain Valley. In 1731 the French, advancing farther south, erected Fort St. Frédéric.

Lake Champlain now became the key to rival campaign strategy. On the English side Winthrop's campaign (1690) and Nicholson's first and second campaigns (1709, 1711) all ended in failure. The French gained an advantage by throwing up Fort Carillon (1756), later Ticonderoga[qv], at the southern end of the lake, which, with its advanced position, backed up by Fort St. Frédéric (1731), served as an operative base for raids and as a constant threat to the northern colonies in any concerted campaign. French attacks on Vermont during this period included Bridgman's Fort, Fort Massachusetts[qv], Number Four[qv] across the Connecticut, and Hobbs Fight.

Blocking further French progress, the English had Fort William Henry[qv] (1755) at the southern end of Lake George, where it faced off against Carillon, being backed up by Fort Edward (1755) as Carillon was backed by Fort St. Frédéric. In the valleys of Lake George and Champlain armies of thousands of men were now on the move. Then came Amherst (1759), driving the lilies of France down Champlain into their Canadian strongholds (*see* French and Indian War).

In 1749 Benning Wentworth, governor of New Hampshire, had made the first official grant of land in the territory now known as Vermont, but it was not until the capture of Fort Frédéric, or Crown Point[qv], by Gen. Amherst ten years later and the subsequent destruction of the St. Francis Indians[qv] in lower Canada that settlement on an extensive scale began. The territory was now called the New Hampshire Grants[qv], and the classic controversy arose between New Hampshire and New York as to which had jurisdiction over it. The claim of New York, based on a grant made by Charles II to the Duke of York[qv] in 1664, was sustained by the crown, and New York immediately began chartering townships within the Grants. Some of these conflicted with charters already granted by Gov. Wentworth, and when an effort was made to enforce the New York claim the settlers stood on what they considered their rights, appealing to the New York courts for protection. The courts decided in favor of the New York claimants. Deprived of legal defense, the settlers sent Samuel Robinson to England to present their grievance. The crown issued an injunction restraining New York from making grants, pending his Majesty's pleasure, but New York, putting its own interpretation on the injunction, continued its former practice, and the settlers, resorting to physical measures, organized the "Green Mountain Boys"[qv] and other protective bodies to safeguard their interests.

The controversy was interrupted by the outbreak of the Revolution, which again brought war upon the settlements. On March 10, 1775, Ethan Allen and his "Green Mountain Boys" took Ticonderoga. The Battle of Hubbardton[qv] was fought July 7, 1777, under Warner. Vermont arms were prominent at the important Battle of Bennington[qv], Aug. 16, 1777.

It was in 1777 that Vermont, threatened with invasion by Burgoyne on the one hand and dismemberment by three neighboring colonies on the other, declared herself an independent commonwealth and set up the machinery of government which became operative in 1778 with a unicameral legislature and Thomas Chittenden as the first governor (*see* Vermont, Republic of). Political differences with the neighboring states and Congress, in which Vermont played a lone and victorious diplomatic hand, continued until 1791, when the conflicting claims of all parties were satisfactorily settled and Vermont was admitted into the Union (March 4, 1791) as the fourteenth state.

Hardly was the new state substantially under way, with its population rapidly increasing, when over its stormy course swept the War of 1812, renewing a military and naval activity that reached its climax in the Battle of Plattsburg and Macdonough's victory[qqv] off Cumberland Head.

The turbulent course pursued by the young state had produced a spirit of self-reliance and liberalism in its people. Free manhood suffrage, complete religious tolerance and the abolition of Negro slavery had all been written into her constitution. Until 1800 radical political and religious philosophies were at war with the established order and raised the louder voice. Intemperance as a scourge, recognized as early as 1806, was a concomitant of the condition of the times, and a great temperance crusade swept the state from the 1820's to the passing of the state prohibition law in 1850. For nearly a decade, from 1827 to 1836, the antimasonic storm flared hotly in the rural districts, and for four successive years captured the government of the state. Running abreast of the temperance and antimasonic reform movements was the antislavery movement[qqv], which, accompanied by bitter controversy, strongly influenced both the religious and political order of the state.

Erected on such a tempestuous past, with a steady occupational background as an offset, has risen the Vermont of today, so unchanging as steadfastly to follow one party, the Republican, for decades, yet so revolutionary as rebelliously to refuse to be swallowed up as a Federal park. It is an agricultural state of more cows than people, known for its maple sugar, its marble, its granite and its summer homes.

[W. H. Crockett, *History of Vermont;* R. E. Robinson, *Vermont;* H. F. Wilson, *The Hill Country of Northern New England;* M. B. Jones, *Vermont in the Making;* D. M. Ludlum, *Social Ferment in Vermont.*]

LEON W. DEAN

Vermont, Republic of (1777–91). An agrarian controversy between New York and New Hampshire in which the "Green Mountain Boys"[qv] took a prominent part, led in 1777 to the erection of the New Hampshire Grants[qv] into the state of Vermont. The opportunistic founders sought to validate their disputed land titles, make careers for themselves, and have Vermont admitted as one of the United States. From the outset most Vermonters supported the American Revolution. Vermont's contribution to the victory at Bennington[q.v.] besides Ethan Allen's earlier seizure of Ticonderoga[q.v.] attracted wide attention and placed the Continental Congress under obligation to the state. But Congress could not admit Vermont when New York, New Hampshire and the large Southern states were opposed. Twice ruin faced the state through the threatened secession of the Vermont townships near Connecticut River. In 1778 and again in 1781 Vermont met the crisis by temporarily annexing a strip of New Hampshire (first and second Eastern Union). In 1781 she temporarily annexed a strip of New York between southern Vermont and the Hudson (Western Union). The disinclination of Congress to admit Vermont, the resentment of the neighboring states, and the danger of British invasions from Canada, caused Vermont in 1780 to enter into the Haldimand negotiations[q.v.]. Great Britain thereby sought to detach Vermont from the American cause by offering the self-governing status that Congress denied. Ira and Ethan Allen deplored the abandonment of the Eastern and Western Unions in 1782, while there was a chance of Vermont's joining Great Britain and having them included in a greater Vermont.

The end of the war found Vermont a robust, frontier republic, unconnected constitutionally with the United States but within it territorially. In 1790 Vermont settled her dispute with New York for $30,000 and in 1791 Congress admitted her as the fourteenth state.

[W. H. Crockett, *Vermont the Green Mountain State.*]

CLARENCE W. RIFE

Versailles, Treaty of, 1783 (Sometimes so called). *See* Paris, Peace of, 1783; Definitive Treaty of Peace.

Versailles, Treaty of. Signed on June 28, 1919, by the United States, the British Empire, France, Italy and Japan, and twenty-three other Allied and Associated Powers, and Germany, it consisted of 15 parts comprising 440 articles. Part I was the Covenant of the League of Nations[q.v.]. Part II defined the boundaries of Germany in Europe: she lost Alsace-Lorraine to France, West Prussia and Posen to Poland, and two small areas to Belgium; she surrendered the Saar and Danzig to the League of Nations, and Memel to the Allied Powers; she agreed to plebiscites in North Slesvig, Allenstein and Marienwerder, and Upper Silesia. Part IV deprived Germany of her overseas possessions, which were made mandated territories under the League of Nations, and of various rights and interests in China, Siam, Liberia, Morocco, Egypt, Turkey and Bulgaria. In Part III Germany consented to the abrogation of the neutrality of Belgium and Luxembourg and to the exclusion of the latter from the German Customs Union. She acknowledged and promised to respect the independence of Austria. She accepted the demilitarization of the Rhineland and a zone extending 50 kilometres east of the Rhine. She ceded to France the coal mines of the Saar as compensation for the destruction of French mines during the war.

Part V provided for the disarmament of Germany, "in order to render possible the initiation of a general limitation of the armaments of all nations." Her army was limited to 100,000 men, recruited by long-term enlistment; the general staff was abolished; military and naval air forces were forbidden. The manufacture of munitions was limited, their import forbidden; poisonous gases were also forbidden. Her navy was restricted to a small number of old ships. Inter-Allied commissions were established to supervise the execution of these clauses.

Part VI dealt with prisoners of war and graves. In Part VII William II, the former Emperor, was indicted for "a supreme offense against international morality and the sanctity of treaties," and he was to be tried by the five Principal Powers. Germany also promised to deliver any of her nationals who might be accused by the Allies of having violated the laws and customs of war.

Part VIII dealt with reparation, beginning with the famous Article 231: "The Allied and Associated Governments affirm and Germany accepts the responsibility of Germany and her allies for causing all the loss and damage to which the Allied and Associated Governments and their nationals have been subjected as a consequence of the war imposed on them by the aggression of Germany and her allies" (the purpose of this article was, not to assess a moral judgment, but to establish the legal liability of Germany for reparation, to which she had agreed in the Armistice[q.v.] of Nov. 11, 1918). Germany undertook to make compensation for "all damage done to the civilian population" of the Allies "by land, by sea and from the air," which was defined in a manner large enough to include military pensions and separation allowances; Germany had furthermore to reimburse Belgium, with interest, for all sums borrowed from the Allies. A reparation commission[q.v.] was to determine, by May 1, 1921, the amount which Germany should pay; in the meantime, Germany was to pay in gold, commodities, ships, securities or otherwise $5,000,000,000. Elaborate clauses provided in great detail for the delivery of goods in kind. The Allied Powers reserved the right to take whatever measures they deemed necessary in the event of "voluntary default" by Germany. Part IX was concerned with financial clauses. Part X dealt with tariffs, business contracts and the like; in particular the Allies obtained the right to seize German private property in their territories on account of reparation. Many of these financial and economic clauses were of a temporary character. Part XI had to do with aerial navigation. In Part XII, which dealt with ports, waterways and railways, international control of the Rhine, Oder and Elbe was established in the interest of land-locked states. The Kiel Canal was opened to all nations. Part XIII established the International Labor Office[qv] as an autonomous branch of the League of Nations.

Part XIV provided for guarantees. The Allies were to occupy the Rhineland and its bridgeheads for 15 years, certain zones to be evacuated at the end of 5 and 10 years. Article 430 empowered the Allies to reoccupy the region at any time thereafter if Germany defaulted on reparation payments. Germany was to pay the cost of the armies of occupation. Part XV dealt with miscellaneous items.

By the treaty Germany did not become a member of the League of Nations or the International Labor Office, although in time she might be eligible to both. She lost more than 25,000 square miles of territory and more than 6,000,000 inhabitants in Europe, besides many valuable resources abroad. The Treaty of Versailles was regarded by German opinion as a *Diktat* (a dictated peace) and a violation of the Fourteen Points[qv], on the basis of which Germany had surrendered and the Allies had promised to make peace. In Allied countries, the treaty was considered as just punishment to Germany for the war which she had brought on the world in August, 1914. In the United States, the treaty was received with mixed feelings.

The treaty was promptly ratified by Germany and more slowly by the Allied Powers. It came into force on Jan. 10, 1920, without being ratified by the United States, and it was rejected by the Senate on March 19, 1920. The war between the United States and Germany was formally ended in 1921 by the Treaty of Berlin[qv].

[Carnegie Endowment for International Peace, *The Peace Treaties of 1919-1923;* Harold Temperley, ed., *A History of the Peace Conference of Paris*, Vols. II and III.]

BERNADOTTE E. SCHMITT

Vesey Rebellion, THE (1822), was a Negro plot intended to completely annihilate the white population of Charleston, S. C. The leader of the conspiracy, Denmark (corruption of Telemaque) Vesey, had been brought from Africa at the age of fourteen in 1781. In 1800 he won $1500 in the East Bay Street lottery in Charleston and with $600 purchased his freedom. The fact that his children, born of a slave mother, were the property of her master aroused his resentment. For several years he worked quietly, but sometime around Christmas 1821–22 the plot took concrete form. It was planned to seize the arms and ammunition stored in the city and massacre the white population. July 14 was first set for the attack, which date was subsequently advanced to June 16. It is said that from 2000 to 3000 slaves were involved. The plot was betrayed to the authorities and Vesey and others of the chief conspirators were tried and executed.

[A. H. Grimke, *Right on the Scaffold or Martyrs of 1822.*]

A. C. FLICK

Veterans, Disabled, of the United States include two groups—those disabled as a result of service in the armed forces and those disabled from other causes. The Federal Government by congressional enactments provides benefits for veterans and their dependents and many states have laws which afford additional assistance. The nature and extent of the Federal benefits are changed by law from time to time but they are now available in three forms: monetary (compensation or pension); medical (hospitalization and treatment); and domiciliary (care in a Federal Home). These are administered by the Veterans' Administration through its central office at Washington, D. C., and its field stations, comprising regional offices, hospitals and homes so distributed throughout the country that an applicant may apply for and receive service from a station near his home. After each war the benefits first provided have been generally limited to veterans disabled by service and their dependents, but after the lapse of a period of years (varying for different wars) laws have been passed to grant benefits to all honorably discharged veterans. Legislation granting money payments to World War veterans for disabilities not incurred in service has been limited principally to total and permanent disabilities. Persons who have served in time of peace and have been honorably discharged are entitled to pension for service-incurred disabilities of degree required by law, and to hospital treatment and domiciliary care if discharged from service for disability incurred in line of duty or if receiving pension.

Total disbursements for the relief of persons who have served in the armed forces of the United States, and their dependents, from the inception of our Government to Jan. 31, 1938, exceeded twenty-two billions of dollars. On this date there were in all 596,838 living veterans receiving monetary benefits from the Federal Government, as well as the dependents of 244,120 deceased, at a total annual cost of nearly $400,000,000. Besides these strictly financial benefits, 50,440 veterans of all wars were being maintained by the Veterans' Administration in government hospitals and 15,255 in government homes.

[*Federal Laws Relating to Veterans of Wars of the United States*, 1932, Superintendent of Documents, Washington, D. C.]

FRANK T. HINES

Veterans' Administration. *See* Soldiers' Homes.

Veterans' Organizations have continued the comradeship of the campaigns, assisted in the care of needy veterans and lobbied for pensions. The pace was set by the formation, in 1783, of the Society of the Cincinnati[qv], whose constitution was drafted by Gen. Henry Knox. Eligible to membership were officers of the revolutionary army, their eldest male posterity, "and in failure thereof the collateral branches who may be judged worthy of becoming its supporters."

The National Association of Veterans of the Mexican War encountered sectional prejudice as late as the 1880's because so large proportion were Southerners. Out of the secessionist struggle came the Grand Army of the Republic[qv] in 1866; also a group of similar Confederate societies which, in New Orleans on June 10, 1889, merged to form the United Confederate Veterans of whom 7800 remained in 1937. Several times Congress has lent necessary tenting, bedding and other equipment for their annual encampments, a practice later extended to other veterans' societies. The Veterans of Indian Wars of the United States was organized in Philadelphia, April 23, 1896. Its membership consisted of three classes: (1) commissioned officers; (2) lineal male descendants of the same; and (3) non-commissioned officers and soldiers who received some distinction for service.

The war against Spain gave rise to several societies. The Spanish-American War Veterans, organized Dec. 14, 1899, failed to survive, but the earlier (1898) United Spanish War Veterans boasted 106,494 members, about 40% of total number engaged, as late as 1937. Modeled somewhat after the Cincinnati was the Naval and Military Order of the Spanish-American War, founded Feb. 2, 1899, whose membership passes to eldest male descendant. This order had 1000 members in 1938. The Veterans of Foreign Wars of the United States is a society formed in 1913 by a merger of the American Veterans of Foreign Service (1899) and the Army of the Philippines. It has approximately 3500 local posts. Out of the World War came the American Legion[qv], largest of this type of society and with a political influence greatly out of proportion to its numbers (830,000). Another product of this war was the Disabled American Veterans of the World War, which received Federal incorporation in 1921. About one fourth of those wounded in the war were members of this group in 1937, an increase of 10,000 in six years.

ROBERT G. RAYMER

Veto, Royal, of Colonial Acts. *See* Royal Disallowance.

Veto Power of the President and the Senate, THE, combine the activities of two Federal agencies. Both are authorized by the Constitution[qv] to restrict the effective action of the originating agency and to require a two-thirds majority to overcome the negative intent. The former fortifies the President in his relations with Congress on legislative policies. The latter serves the Senate in its relations with the President on treaty ratifications. Bills and legislative resolutions passed by Congress must be presented to the President for approval. Disapproval constitutes exercise of the veto power. Eight Presidents have not utilized it. Two had no opportunity, W. H. Harrison and Garfield. One, Taylor, experienced only one congressional session. The remaining five served in the formative years when exercise was considered either unnecessary or inappropriate. Up to 1865, nine Presidents disapproved only thirty-six measures. Since 1865, however, the veto has been consistently used to control the legislative product. From 1792 to June, 1938, message vetoes totaled 771, and only 55 returned measures were repassed. No veto President up to Johnson disapproved more than twelve measures. No President since Cleveland, except Harding, disapproved less than thirty-seven. Thirty-six distinctive subjects or subject headings inspired the veto messages of twenty-three Presidents. The most consistent subject was special relief. The motives for disapproval have expanded. Constitutional objections were considered the chief basis for action by early Presidents, although every veto President, except Monroe, disapproved one or more measures on other grounds. The most persistent reason given was impropriety. In later years, questions of expediency, economy, public policy and precedent have been consistently raised. Early Presidents stressed belief in the veto as an extraordinary weapon. All veto Presidents since Johnson have used it as part of their regular equipment for guiding Congress. In recent administrations it has been applied to more measures of major importance and national significance. The threat of its use has been sufficient at times to suspend normal congressional procedure on specific legislation. Its potency cannot be ignored in the consideration of any proposal not having administration endorsement.

Treaties negotiated by the President must be submitted to the Senate for its consent to ratification. Two thirds of the senators present must approve. Failure of formal approval constitutes negative action of the Senate. Less than seventy treaties have failed of Senate approval. Insistence on amendments or reservations for over one hundred fifty caused executive readjustment and ratification. More than four fifths of all treaties presented to the Senate have been approved unconditionally. The negative action has been consistent on only one type of subject, the pacific settlement of disputes. The power of the Senate over treaties lies in the potential threat of one third of its membership obstructing a proposed foreign policy. This has prevented some negotiations or caused resort to executive agreements. Its merits have been questioned, and proposals have been advanced to curb the power by requiring for consent a simple majority of the Senate membership or a simple majority of both Senate and House of Representatives.

[E. C. Mason, *The Veto Power; Record of Veto Messages, 1889-1935*, Office of the Secretary of the Senate of the United States, 1935; D. F. Fleming, *The Treaty Veto of the American Senate.*]

GEORGE C. ROBINSON

Vial's Road was traced by Pedro Vial and two companions from New Mexico to St. Louis in 1792. Indians robbed them on the journey and although they left Santa Fé[qv] in May they did not reach St. Louis until October. The governor who ordered the expedition intended to use it as a route for trading with the French at St. Louis, but the pathfinding venture was never followed up.

[E. D. Branch, *Westward.*]

CARL L. CANNON

Vice-Presidency, THE, of the United States is an office under the Constitution[qv] requiring the same qualifications as the Presidency. The formal duties are explicit. The Vice-President presides over the Senate (*see* Congress, The United States) and casts the deciding vote when the Senate is equally divided. He receives the Electoral College[qv] lists and in the presence of the Senate and House of Representatives opens all the certificates. Nearly all Vice-Presidents have had the opportunity to vote. John Adams holds the record with twenty-nine. The time and manner of election and term of office correspond to the provisions for the President, except that in case of failure of a majority vote in the Electoral College, the Senate, instead of the House, elects one of the two highest candidates for Vice-President, and that no filling of a vacancy in the office is authorized. One Vice-President, Richard Johnson, was elected by the Senate in 1837. Vacancies may result from death, resignation, succession, conviction on impeachment, or inability. Fourteen of thirty-two Vice-Presidents have caused vacancies. Seven died in office. One resigned. Six succeeded to the Presidency. Three of the deaths and five of the successions occurred in the first two years. For more than one fifth of the time the office has been vacant. General duties and functions have developed a dual personality. As president of the Senate, the Vice-President becomes informed on proposed legislation, conduct of foreign relations, and personnel problems of administration. He acquires an appreciation of a legislative body by directing its procedure. He prepares himself for an understanding of national problems and national legislators. As a nationally elected officeholder, he may view the course of administration with unhampered judgment—sympathetic to general objectives and aloof from local and sectional interests. His counsel can be of great value, and recent Presidents have encouraged their Vice-Presidents to participate in Cabinet sessions.

[L. C. Hatch and E. L. Shoup, *A History of the Vice-Presidency of the United States.*]

GEORGE C. ROBINSON

Vick Estate, THE (Newitt Vick, 1819), included the site of Vicksburg; Vicksburg claimed the "Commons" (Levee Street) as public property; Vick's male heirs sold their claims to Seargent S. Prentiss, to whom Vicksburg lost in Mississippi's courts, 1837. Female heirs established their claim in a United States Supreme Court decision (3 Howard 464, 1845) which impoverished Prentiss.

[Joseph D. Shields, *Life and Times of Seargent S. Prentiss.*]

MACK SWEARINGEN

Vicksburg, Miss., on the high eastern bank of the Mississippi at the Yazoo's mouth, occupied an old, important site; near by the French built Fort St. Pierre (1715); there Spaniards built Fort Nogales (1791); Spain's American successors (1798) called it Walnut Hills, its name under

England; Fort Nogales became Fort McHenry.

Settlement began with Newitt Vick, Virginia Methodist preacher, about 1812. He set aside (1819) 200 acres for a town site. Settlers thereon incorporated as the town of Vicksburg (1825). Although property was somewhat disturbed by Vick Estate litigation, prosperity followed opening the Mississippi-Yazoo Delta for settlement after removal of Choctaws by the Treaties of Doak's Stand (1820) and Dancing Rabbit Creek (1830)[qqv]. The Delta was fabulously fertile cotton country; Vicksburg stood at the junction of the rivers bounding it; thus Vicksburg began to rival Natchez[qv] as Mississippi's center of wealth and political power. Its population in 1860 was 4600 (Natchez, 7100).

Famous in Vicksburg was an "under the hill" section surpassing in disrepute that at Natchez. Outraged citizens in 1835 lynched five gamblers in a batch.

Vicksburg depended on river traffic; the decline of steamboating reduced its importance after the Civil War, though population continued to increase. (*See also* Vicksburg in the Civil War.)

[M. J. Mulvihill, *Vicksburg and Warren County, Mississippi;* Dunbar Rowland, *Mississippi*, Vol. II.]

MACK SWEARINGEN

Vicksburg in the Civil War. Until after the fall of New Orleans[qv] in April, 1862, Vicksburg was practically undefended and probably could have been easily captured. In May, however, Vicksburg's importance as an obstacle to Union control of the Mississippi River had become evident. At the direction of Gen. Mansfield Lovell (C.) construction of fortifications was rushed. On June 28, 1862, several ships from Farragut's squadron (U.), under cover of heavy bombardment, went upstream past the Vicksburg batteries and anchored. On July 15 the Confederate ram *Arkansas*[qv] steamed out of the Yazoo River and down the Mississippi past the Union fleet to safety under the batteries. In the last days of July the Union fleet returned to New Orleans, and Vicksburg was free of any menace until the following year (*see* Baton Rouge, Battle of).

In October, 1862, Gen. Earl Van Dorn (C.), who had succeeded Lovell, was replaced by Gen. J. C. Pemberton (C.). Early in December, 1862, Gen. U. S. Grant (U.) began his campaign against Vicksburg, his troops moving from Memphis through northern Mississippi. The advance, under Sherman (U.), was decisively beaten at Chickasaw Bluffs[qv]. Four subsequent unsuccessful attempts to reach Vicksburg culminated in the burning of the Union supply depot at Holly Springs, Miss.[qv] The Union troops had floundered about in the water and morass of the numerous bayous without coming near to their objective. In a final desperate effort, Grant decided to abandon his base at Memphis, move down the west bank of the Mississippi, live off the country, cross below Vicksburg and try to get at the city by coming to it from the east through the back door. By skilful leadership and earnest determination on the part of the troops, the plan was successful.

The Confederate commander, governed by events, waited on the man of action. Unexpectedly Grant's army was across the Mississippi, but only a small force opposed it. Within three weeks Vicksburg was in a state of siege (*see* Port Gibson, Raymond, Jackson, Champion's Hill and Big Black River, Battles of). Though nearly cut off from supplies and re-enforcements and with Union ships in control of the river, Pemberton might still have escaped and joined forces with Gen. J. E. Johnston, near Jackson, before Grant surrounded Vicksburg. Divided counsel, long-distance control and personal antagonisms prevented.

The Confederate soldiers fought bravely against odds of superior strength and vacillating leadership. Aided by bombardment from the river fleet under Porter, Grant assaulted the Vicksburg lines three times on May 22. Each attack was repulsed with heavy loss. In spite of numerical superiority it now became evident to Grant that Vicksburg could only be taken by siege operations. Dwindling food and ammunition, mounting casualties, sickness and the hopelessness of re-enforcement or relief finally induced Pemberton to open surrender negotiations. On July 4, 1863, he capitulated, officers and men being paroled as prisoners of war. Port Hudson[qv], 300 miles down the river, surrendered July 9. The Mississippi flowed "unvexed" to the sea. Vicksburg thenceforth became a Union base of operations.

[*Battles and Leaders of the Civil War.*]

THOMAS ROBSON HAY

Vicksburg Riots, THE (Dec. 7 *et seq.*, 1874), were a Reconstruction[qv] incident characteristic of the period after Grant's hesitancy to use the military in the South became apparent. White citizens of Vicksburg and Warren County organized and sought legal redress; rebuffed by the proper agencies of government, they became desperate. When Federal authorities refused requests of Reconstruction officials for troops, disturbances began. Two whites and twenty-nine Negroes were killed.

[J. W. Garner, *Reconstruction in Mississippi.*]

MACK SWEARINGEN

Victory Loan of 1919. (*See also* Liberty Loans.) The act of Congress which authorized this loan provided for the issue of two series of 3–4 year 4¾% and 3¾% convertible gold notes, in a total amount of $4,500,000,000, dated May 20, 1919. Bearer notes were issued in denominations ranging from $50 to $10,000, registered notes from $50 to $100,000. The maturity date was May 20, 1923, but either or both series were callable for redemption in whole or in part on June 15 or Dec. 15, 1922, on four months' notice. Victory 3¾'s were called on June 15, Victory 4¾'s on December 15, and the balance matured on May 20, 1923.

[Treasury Circular, No. 133, of April 21, 1919; The Liberty Loans, Liberty Bonds and Victory Notes, a four-page release of the Commissioner of the Public Debt, dated Sept. 17, 1937.]

W. BROOKE GRAVES

Vieux Carré ("Old Square") is the name commonly applied to the old French and Spanish section of New Orleans. It is bounded by the Mississippi River in front, Rampart Street in the rear, Canal Street above, and Esplanade Avenue below. Retaining much of its antique European atmosphere, it possesses a peculiar attraction for present-day visitors to New Orleans.

[Lyle Saxon, *Fabulous New Orleans;* S. C. Arthur, *Old New Orleans: A History of the Vieux Carré, Its Ancient and Historical Buildings.*]

WALTER PRICHARD

Vigilantes. Western vigilance committees operated in border communities before law courts were organized and peace officers were elected. In 1844 an English traveler in Texas noted that settlers had a "primitive system of administering justice." Since state and county service could not be had, substantial citizens sought by mass action to drive desperadoes from their midst. The best example of the employment of such corrective measures was the work of the San Francisco Vigilance Committee (1851). The inrush of thousands of people following gold discovery in January, 1848, brought many outlaws (*see* California Gold Rush). Soon outlaw rule made unsafe the life and property of all residents, and a band of thugs actually crossed the bay and raided Berkeley in open day. But soon the vigilantes began the weeding out of outlaw leaders by summary executions, and others scattered to other parts of the West.

Desperadoes who fled from the California vigilantes found only temporary tenure in Arizona and Nevada. California had been successful with its committees; other Rocky Mountain communities took up the movement. In some instances action was little more than that of a mob; in others it was deliberate and well planned. Missourians in June, 1854, set up near Leavenworth, Kans., the Squatters' Claim Association*qv* which included a committee of thirteen pledged to protect the rights of slaveholders; others were organized in Linn County, Council City and elsewhere. An early publicist, A. D. Richardson, found a vigilance committee in Denver, and other Colorado towns caring adequately for their outlaw problem. In Montana (1864) a large outlaw gang, headed by Sheriff Henry Plummer*qv*, terrorized the citizens in the mining communities until the vigilantes broke it up. During the month of January, 1864, twenty-one desperadoes were hanged. John X. Beidler from Pennsylvania is said to have presided at many of these trials.

Much effective vigilance committee work was done in Texas, New Mexico and Kansas after the Civil War. That of the committee at Fort Griffin, Texas, is best known. The Dallas *Herald* (April 23, 1876) comments that here a "vigilance committee is now astonishing the authorities . . . by the off-hand way it does business." And the Denison *News* (March 23, 1874) speaks of a "neck or two stretched" when thugs had congregated there after the Missouri, Kansas and Texas Railroad*qv* had reached the Red River. The Topeka *Commonwealth* (July 14, 1875) indicated that Kansas was keeping stride with Texas by announcing that a vigilance committee had been organized at Dodge City*qv* to rid the Arkansas Valley of "a bold gang of horse thieves." Like California, all the Western states and territories broke up organized bands of cutthroats by vigilance committee operations.

[Mary Floyd Williams, History of the San Francisco Vigilance Committee of 1851, in University of California *Publications in History*, XII; H. H. Bancroft, *Popular Tribunals;* C. C. Rister, Outlaws and Vigilantes of the Southern Plains, 1865-85, in *Mississippi Valley Historical Review*, XIX.]

C. C. RISTER

Vikings. *See* Norsemen in America.

Villa Raid at Columbus, THE (March 9, 1916). Mexican depredations against American persons and property on both sides of the border culminated on the night of March 8–9, 1916, with Villa's raid on Columbus, N. Mex. Units of the 13th U. S. Cavalry, totaling 12 officers and 341 enlisted men, stationed at Columbus, were quickly aroused and drove the Mexicans, variously estimated as from 500 to 1000 men, back across the border. American losses were: seven soldiers killed, five wounded, eight civilians killed, two wounded; Mexicans: approximately 190 killed or wounded. This raid marked the zenith of

Villa's career and was directly responsible for Pershing's Punitive Expedition into Mexico[qv].

[Frank Tompkins, *Chasing Villa*.]

C. A. WILLOUGHBY

Villages. When a portion of a township or county becomes more thickly settled than the rest and begins to take on a semiurban aspect, the inhabitants usually demand more in the way of special public services than the township or county authorities care to undertake. The community therefore seeks incorporation as a village, and thus is enabled to undertake these special services, to borrow money and levy taxes, and to have its own village government distinct from that of the township and county. Villages, of which there are more than 10,000 in the United States, are found in all parts of the country, the greater number being in the North Central states.

[J. A. Fairlie, *Local Government in Counties, Towns and Villages;* K. H. Porter, *County and Township Government in the United States;* F. G. Bates, Village Government in New England, in *American Political Science Rev.*, Vol. VI.]

P. ORMAN RAY

Villasur Expedition (1720). In the summer of 1720 Don Pedro de Villasur left Santa Fé with forty-two soldiers and sixty Indian allies for a reconnaissance of the French thrust from the east into Spanish territory, which had been going on for several years. On Aug. 13 the party was attacked and routed by a band of Pawnee Indians[qv], allies of the French, the scene of the battle being on the south side of the North Platte River, in the vicinity of the present town of North Platte, Nebr. The killed, forty-four in number, included Villasur, the Franciscan chaplain, Father Juan Minguez and the interpreter, Juan de l'Archevêque, erstwhile companion of LaSalle.

[A. B. Thomas, *After Coronado: Spanish Explorations Northeast of New Mexico, 1696-1727*.]

GILBERT J. GARRAGHAN

Villere's Plantation, Battle at (1814). After defeating the inferior American fleet on Lake Borgne[qv], the British landed their troops and marched them through the swamps to Villere's plantation on the eastern bank of the Mississippi, a few miles below New Orleans. Here Jackson attacked and repulsed the British forces on the foggy night of Dec. 23, 1814, after which the enemy retired until their full strength could be brought to bear against the Americans in the decisive battle of Jan. 8, 1815 (*see* New Orleans, Battle of).

[Charles Gayarré, *History of Louisiana;* Alcée Fortier, *History of Louisiana*.]

WALTER PRICHARD

Vincennes. The French government, in order to protect its claim to territory in the New World reaching from Quebec to New Orleans, early in the 17th century began the erection of a chain of fortified posts. One was built at Detroit[qv] (1701). An Indian village on the east bank of the Wabash River, 150 miles above its mouth, was selected as a suitable site for another such fort, and around this post a permanent settlement grew up. The date of the settlement is uncertain, but fur traders probably made this important Indian village their headquarters as early as 1700. It was visited by missionaries about the same time.

François Morgane Sieur de Vincennes with a considerable body of French troops was stationed there in 1736. The promotion of actual settlement by the French government followed the surrender by the Company of the Indies[qv] of their charter (1732) granting them exclusive control of the fur trade in the Illinois and Indiana country. From the Indians the Vincennes settlers received a large tract of land on both sides of the Wabash River. Five thousand acres of this grant were laid off as common fields and enclosed with pickets. Adjoining the village were the narrow, ribbonlike strips of land, from one half to a mile long and varying in width from ten to forty rods, common to French settlements. The *habitants* cultivated these fields, which were plowed, sowed and reaped according to rules agreed upon in the public assembly made up of all males of military age. It was at the door of the church, after Mass, that the assembly met, and the Syndic was the official elected to carry out the will of the assembly.

Most of the settlers came originally, with their families, from Canada. Some of them married Indian wives. Vincennes was a typical French village of the period. Thomas Hutchins, the geographer, who visited the village before the close of the Revolution, wrote that it consisted of sixty settlers and their families. "They raise Indian Corn, wheat, and tobacco of an extraordinary good quality. . . . They have a fine breed of horses and large stocks of Swine and Black Cattle. The settlers deal with the natives for Furs and Deer skins to the amount of £5000 annually."

Influenced by the victory of George Rogers Clark[qv] (1779), immigrants from Kentucky and Virginia with land warrants for service in the Revolution began coming to Vincennes. Before his return to Kaskaskia, Clark set up a form of government at Vincennes by appointing Capt. Leonard Helm as civil and military commandant.

In 1790 Knox County, the first organized government in Indiana, was formed with Vincennes as the county seat. Its jurisdiction embraced an area larger than the present State of Indiana. Ten years later (1800) Indiana Territory, which included practically all of the Northwest Territory[qv], excluding Ohio, was created by an act of Congress. On Jan. 10, 1801, William Henry Harrison arrived at Vincennes, which had been made the capital—then a town, including the area in and around it, of some 2500 inhabitants. Gov. Harrison's duties as Superintendent of Indian Affairs occupied the greater part of his time and from 1802 to 1809, six of the eight treaties by which the Indians were driven from their domain in Indiana were conducted at Vincennes.

By an act of the Territorial Assembly, March 11, 1813, after a bitter contest, the capital was located at Corydon because of its more central situation within Indiana Territory. Vincennes continued to be an important trade center.

[Lee Burns, Life in Old Vincennes, in *Indiana Historical Society Publications*, Vol. VIII; Logan Esarey, *A History of Indiana from Its Exploration to 1850.*]

JAMES ALTON JAMES

Vincennes, French Defection at (1797), was caused by local intrigues against the United States fomented by British and Spanish sympathizers. The "defection" was supported by a ten-year accumulation of complaints. Some of the leaders, men of means, held slaves which the Ordinance of 1787[qv] prohibited; likewise, the provisions of the Land Act of 1796[qv] caused dissatisfaction. Gov. Sargent personally adjusted many of the land claims, extended civil rights and privileges previously withheld or denied and made delayed appointments of civil and militia officers, thus averting serious trouble and conciliating local leaders.

[C. E. Carter, ed., *Territorial Papers of the United States.*]

THOMAS ROBSON HAY

Vincennes, Treaty of (1803). Next to his victory at Tippecanoe[qv], William Henry Harrison is best known for his thirteen successful Indian treaty negotiations. Appointed governor of the newly created Indiana Territory in 1800, Harrison was instructed by the Federal Government to gain title to Indian lands in the area, in order to remove the source of constant friction between traders, settlers and Indians. After a preliminary conference in the fall of 1802, in which he had difficulty reconciling the jealousies of the chieftains, Harrison succeeded in getting a formal treaty signed at Fort Wayne, June 7, 1803. This provided for the cession by nine tribes (Shawnees, Potawatomis, Miamis, Weas, Eel Rivers, Delawares, Piankashaws, Kaskaskias and Kickapoos) of the land about Vincennes, extending along the Wabash River from the mouth of the White River about twenty-five miles north and from twelve miles west of that river to seventy-two miles eastward. By a supplementary treaty signed at Vincennes (Aug. 7, 1803) several tracts were ceded for way-stations from Clarksville to Kaskaskia[qv] via Vincennes.

[Homer J. Webster, William Henry Harrison's Administration of Indiana Territory, in *Indiana Historical Society Publications*, IV, No. 3; Logan Esarey, *History of Indiana.*]

ELIZABETH WARREN

Vinland. It is impossible with certainty to determine the location of Vinland. Besides the northern limit of wild vines the *Tale of the Greenlanders* gives this clue: "The days and nights there were of more nearly equal length than in Greenland or Iceland. On the shortest day of winter the sun was up between 'eyktarstad' and 'dagmálastad'." By astronomers this has been calculated as indicating the most northerly latitude of 49°, but it could be farther south. The *Tale* also says that there was no lack of salmon there; accordingly it could not lie beyond the southern limit of this fish, which is Long Island Sound. Hence Vinland is probably to be sought somewhere on the coast of New England.

[A. M. Reeves, *The Finding of Wineland the Good;* J. E. Olson and E. G. Bourne, eds., *The Northmen, Columbus and Cabot;* H. Hermannsson, *The Problem of Wineland.*]

HALLDÓR HERMANNSSON

Virgin Islands, THE, are Saint Thomas, Saint Croix and Saint John, with about 50 adjacent islets and rocks, formerly known as the Danish West Indies. They are located about 40 miles east and south of Puerto Rico[qv], and have a total area of 138 square miles with a population (1930) of 22,012, 95% of which is Negro. Since 1927 the inhabitants have been citizens of the United States, and under the Organic Act of 1936 all who can read and write can vote, if of age. A governor is appointed by the President. Two municipal divisions have been formed, each with a colonial council. These form the legislative bodies and meet yearly. The islands are under the general jurisdiction of the Secretary of the Interior. Governmentally they are not yet (1940) self-supporting. Saint Thomas has an excellent harbor, said to be large enough to hold the whole fleet of the United States. Its splendid location, 1440 miles from New York, 1020 miles from Colon and 500 miles from LaGuaira, Venezuela, makes it a port of great value to American commerce, especially since the construction of the

Panama Canal[qv]. The chief exports from the islands are sugar and rum.

Long owned by Denmark, the value of these islands to the United States as a naval station was, during the Civil War, recognized by President Lincoln and Wm. H. Seward who started negotiations for their purchase. Denmark, in need of cash because of defeat in the war with Prussia and Austria, was willing to sell. A treaty was agreed upon, and a plebiscite was held in the islands, which showed that the inhabitants were overwhelmingly in favor of the transfer, but political conditions connected with Reconstruction[qv], led the Senate to refuse ratification (1870). This put the United States in a peculiar situation because of the Monroe Doctrine[qv]. If Denmark should want to dispose of the islands, the United States would either have to allow another nation to purchase them, or change her mind on purchasing them herself. Attempts to secure the islands were made in 1893 and 1902 but they failed, the last time by the act of the Danish *Landsthing*. The consideration at that time was $5,000,000. Many Danish people felt that the islands were a financial burden to their country and favored sale to the United States. The outbreak of the World War (1914) created a new situation. It was believed that Germany, if victorious, would insist on obtaining the islands in order to secure a foothold in the Caribbean. It was undoubtedly to forestall such a possibility, as well as to secure the Saint Thomas harbor for the United States, that negotiations for the purchase were taken up for the fourth time. Robert Lansing, Secretary of State, and Constantin Brun, Danish Ambassador to the United States, concluded a treaty, Aug. 4, 1916, which was duly ratified by the Senate and the Danish *Rigsdag*. A plebiscite was held in the islands which showed that the inhabitants still favored the transfer. Ratifications were exchanged Jan. 17, 1917, and the formal transfer took place March 31, 1917. The purchase price was $25,000,000.

[S. P. Fogdall, *Danish-American Diplomacy, 1776-1920;* W. Westergaard, *The Danish West Indies, 1671-1917.*]

S. P. FOGDALL

Virginia, Army of Northern. On June 1, 1862, after the wounding of Gen. J. E. Johnston (*see* Fair Oaks, or Seven Pines, Battle of), President Davis personally placed Robert E. Lee in command of the Confederate Army and officially designated it the Army of Northern Virginia. Henceforth, until the surrender at Appomattox[qv], nearly three years later, this most famous and best known of Confederate armies was commanded by Lee. During this period he established his reputation as one of the most skilful of American generals. Likewise, the Army of Northern Virginia became one of the most effective fighting weapons ever constituted. Jackson's foot cavalry, Longstreet's and A. P. Hill's fighters, "Jeb" Stuart's horse, and Pelham's, Pegram's and other batteries were among its famous personnel. The army, its members varying in age from fifteen years to sixty-five, many of them often marching and fighting barefooted and hatless in slacks and shirt, was the embodiment of faith and determination. It included many world-famous soldiers among its leaders. Always it fought against numerical odds. It won battles with skill and lost only to try again in the hope of better luck. As an army, its personnel was truly representative of the Southern Confederacy. Leaders and men in the ranks alike came from Virginia, from the Border and Gulf states, from the Eastern seaboard and from the Deep South. At Gettysburg nearly one half of the regimental organizations and of the corps and division commanders were from the lower South, the remainder being from Virginia and North Carolina.

Originally organized in divisional form, after the Second Bull Run[qv] it was divided into two corps under Longstreet and Jackson. Following Jackson's death after Chancellorsville[qv] it was reorganized into three corps under Longstreet, Ewell and A. P. Hill. This division was preserved for the remainder of the war. Its effective battle strength was at a maximum in the Seven Days' Battles[qv] when it exceeded 90,000. From this time it declined, after each battle, until at Appomattox, decimated by deaths, desertions, absentees and from other causes, only 8000 men were in line.

The bogs of the Chickahominy, the stone wall at Sharpsburg, the sunken road at Fredericksburg, Jackson's flank marches at the Second Bull Run and at Chancellorsville, Pickett's charge at Gettysburg, the fire and smoke of The Wilderness, the Bloody Angle at Spotsylvania, the Crater at Petersburg, the wall of fire from the Cold Harbor trenches, the thin gray line at Five Forks and the tattered remnant at Appomattox are memorable events in the history of the Army of Northern Virginia.

[D. S. Freeman, *R. E. Lee.*]

THOMAS ROBSON HAY

Virginia, Colony of. After Raleigh's[qv] attempts at Roanoke Island, a permanent settlement was established in 1607, following the issuance of a charter to the Virginia Company of London[qv] in

Virginia, Colony of

1606. The first colonists of about one hundred men and boys were sent out in the *Sarah Constant,* the *Goodspeed* and the *Discovery,* all being under the command of Christopher Newport. On May 24 (N. S.) the settlers disembarked on a site which they named James Fort, or Jamestown[qv].

Besides Newport, a number of these pioneers were men who had acquired reputations for distinguished service in England, in transatlantic exploration, or in foreign countries. Outstanding leaders were Capt. Bartholomew Gosnold, Edward Maria Wingfield, Capt. George Percy, Gabriel Archer, Capt. John Martin, Capt. John Smith, Capt. John Ratcliffe; and the Rev. Robert Hunt, who ministered to the spiritual welfare of the settlers. The entire group, from the highborn Percy to the lowliest laborer, represented a cross section of contemporary English life.

The settlement began happily as all went to work "every man to somewhat." Sentinels were placed down the river to warn of threatened attacks by the Spaniards, while fortifications and palisades were erected for protection against the Indians, who very shortly made a fierce night assault.

Several causes soon brought the colony to desperate straits. Neighboring swamps bred mosquitoes with consequent malaria, so that disease alone is believed to have carried off from one half to two thirds of all new settlers during several summer seasons, unless by chance the newcomers sought high ground on which to build. Again, the colonists were required to hold supplies and produce in common, so that the poorer sort lived at the expense of the industrious in a "comunitie" plan, that was later attempted at Plymouth with similar ill results, until four years later success was forecast when Sir Thomas Dale (1611–16) allowed private ownership of property. Shortly thereafter, John Rolfe discovered a method of curing tobacco[qv] which made "the weed" a profitable commodity for export.

In 1622 the Indians executed a widespread surprise attack in which several hundred settlers were slain. This "Great Massacre"[qv] cut short an extensive plan to convert and civilize the savages, for whom schools and a college were under construction, with George Thorpe, scholar and philanthropist, in charge.

In 1609 and again in 1612 the Virginia Company in London had secured charters which transferred matters of colonial government from the crown to the company. These patents led in 1618 to what has been called a constitution for self-government; so that in the summer of 1619 the first legislature in the New World met at Jamestown under Gov. Sir George Yeardley. In the same year the first Negroes[qv] were brought to Jamestown in a noncommissioned English-manned Dutch frigate. Since records of release from service have been found, it seems clear that these Negroes were indentured[qv] for a term of years, much as many white immigrants whose services were "sold" in payment for their transatlantic passage. In 1624 James I procured the dissolution of the London Company, whereupon Virginia became a royal colony[qv].

Under the lead of Gov. Sir William Berkeley, Virginia was strongly royalist and, despite the triumph of Oliver Cromwell, declared for the exiled Prince, afterwards Charles II. The Civil War that had thus ended in England seemed about to break out in Virginia. Cromwell's commissioners, however, offered liberal terms of agreement and Berkeley retired. Virginia was subsequently awarded the complimentary title of the "Old Dominion,"[qv] with the status of a "fifth kingdom." Restored to power after the fall of Cromwell's Commonwealth, Berkeley became tyrannical, and dissatisfaction broke out in open rebellion (1676) under the leadership of Nathaniel Bacon[qv]. At the height of the uprising, with Berkeley driven across the Bay, Bacon died of fever, and the rebellion collapsed.

Despite the oft-quoted expression of thanksgiving by the despotic Berkeley that there were no free schools in Virginia, a few had been established by private endowment. Throughout the colonial period after the Berkeley regime a great number of tutorial schools were maintained. These were small, for Virginia remained almost wholly agricultural, with few towns, even in the tidewater section. A college for the colony, first projected in 1620, was finally realized in the establishment of William and Mary[qv] in 1693.

From the beginning many of the colonists were given to writing, as may be seen from the first return voyage of Admiral Newport in 1607, which bore a "report" on Virginia; a "Relatyon"; Tindall's "Journal" and map; and narrative letters addressed to the Prince of Wales, the Earl of Salisbury and other notables. A few years later, the first English literature in America was written by George Sandys in a translation of Ovid's *Metamorphoses,* published in London in 1626.

The establishment of the capital at Williamsburg[qv] (1699) was followed by the "Golden Age" of Virginia colonial history, in which Gov. Spotswood played a prominent role. He it was who turned general attention to the "Great Valley" beyond the Blue Ridge (*see* Knights of the

Golden Horseshoe); and in 1749 Thomas Lee recorded the accustomed English claims in the statement that the western boundary of Virginia was "the Great South Sea, including California." When the clash came with the French for the control of the transmontane region, the Shenandoah Valley[qv] had become peopled not only by eastern Virginians, but by Scotch-Irish, Irish and Germans[qqv]. The tidewater planters had always in mind western expansion. This ambition led in 1748 to the formation of the Ohio Company[qv]. Subsequently, the concern of the Virginians over the prospective shutting off of this western development (*see* Proclamation of 1763) was shared by Gov. Dunmore (1771–75); and clashes with the Indians led to a war under Dunmore's administration in which George Washington and his lordship saw eye to eye in opposition to British policy (*see* Dunmore's War).

During this period of the French and Indian War[qv], Virginia was developing a number of political philosophers who were largely instrumental in setting forth the colonial attitude toward the policies of the mother country and the subsequent shaping of the principles that were to guide the creation of independent states and the Federal Republic. The first or foremost of this group of political pamphleteers was Richard Bland, who, as early as 1764, announced the doctrine that England and her various colonies were co-ordinate entities under the crown.

In resisting the Stamp Act[qv] and other revenue measures enacted by Parliament, the Virginia leaders made it clear that their opposition was not based on "taxation without representation"[qv] in the British Parliament, which representation they did not want, but on the principle of "taxation without the consent" of the colonial assemblies[qv]. Again, while Virginia immediately and wholeheartedly took up the cause of Massachusetts in the matter of the Intolerable Acts[qv] that brought on the clash of arms, the Old Dominion was directly concerned with the Quebec Act[qv], which aimed to cut off the western territory she long regarded as her own. Chance only prevented in Virginia a clash of arms simultaneously with that at Lexington and Concord[qv]. Lord Dunmore took refuge on the *Fowey,* whence he issued a proclamation of emancipation with a view to arousing the Negroes, some of whom were enlisted. The royal navy controlled the sea, but after the bombardment of Norfolk[qv] and neighboring towns, the British did not descend upon Virginia in force until the closing year of the war. Virginia was then an independent state and had strengthened its claim to the Northwest[qv] by authorizing the expedition of George Rogers Clark[qv], who, supplied by Virginia men and money, defeated the British and took possession in the name of the Commonwealth.

As Virginia turned from her colonial status, she called upon her ablest leaders to prepare the constitution of the independent commonwealth; and George Mason drafted that portion of the instrument known as the Declaration of Rights[qv], which was to become a model for other states and ultimately of the United States. The constitution that formally created the state was adopted June 29, 1776, several days before the Continental Congress[qv] approved the Declaration of Independence[qv].

[Alexander Brown, *The Genesis of the United States;* Matthew Page Andrews, *Virginia, The Old Dominion.*]

MATTHEW PAGE ANDREWS

Virginia, State of. On June 29, 1776, the Commonwealth was launched. Her constitution, partly written by Mason, included his model Declaration of Rights[qv]. Starting with an empty treasury, her successive legislatures created larger and larger issues of paper money[qv], permitted planters to pay debts to British merchants in depreciated paper of the state, confiscated Tory property; but also, led by Jefferson, revised civil and criminal law, abolished entail and primogeniture, and passed the bill for Establishing Religious Freedom, thus attaining legislative achievement rarely paralleled in American history.

Economic benefit from war and separation were only partly realized. The state was ravaged by both armies; she was first to cede her Western lands[qv] to Congress; she suffered by having no delegate to plead her interest at the Paris peace table, where commercial not agrarian rights were defended. Though Washington presided over the Federal Convention of 1787[qv], and though Virginians contributed the basic plan of the strong central government on which was grounded the Constitution, Virginia in part tried to defeat the Constitution which, when finally ratified, enabled the courts to order planters to settle with British merchants (*see* British Debts). By 1800 economic, religious, social and political revolution had turned "the stronghold of aristocracy" into "the bulwark of republicanism." But manhood suffrage was delayed until 1851.

To waning tidewater lands, European war markets brought, in the early years of the 19th century, fictitious prosperity. Jefferson's Embargo[qv] pricked the bubble; in 1814 the post-Revolutionary march westward was resumed (*see* Westward Movement). But research shows that Virginian decline, 1800–60, stressed by many scholars, was relative, not absolute. Though the

Virginian dynasty^qv^ ended, it is fallacious to pronounce in decline a state where virile agricultural reform, expansion of higher education, and the rise of rolling mills and factories were occurring, and where land values leaped from eighty or ninety millions in 1829 to $371,761,661 in 1860. Roots of Virginian history lie in the debates of the constitutional convention of 1829–30. By maintaining property representation against the largely nonslaveholding piedmont^qv^ demand for manhood suffrage, tidewater^qv^ slaveholders entrenched slavery, strengthened conservatives, defeated a potential railroad to the Ohio which might have forestalled war, and made inevitable West Virginian secession. Though the piedmont won manhood suffrage in 1851, all sections east of the Alleghenies had become proslavery. By 1860 industrialists were Southern nationalists, and aided planters in seceding and sweeping Virginia into the Confederacy. Compelled probably to create a popular reason for defending the Confederate state which constituted almost the only native source of coal, and of munitions industries such as the Norfolk Navy Yard, Harpers Ferry Armory, and Anderson's Tredegar Iron Works^qv^, Confederate authorities removed the capital from Montgomery to Richmond, whereupon Virginia led as in the Revolution.

War and Reconstruction^qv^, which ended economic and social revival and injected the Negro into politics, paralyzed Virginia. The state managed to evade carpetbagger^qv^ control. But the census shows her acres in cultivation, when she returned "reconstructed" to the Union in 1870, less by two million than in 1860, her tobacco production only one third, and her wheat and corn about one half. The state debt incurred before 1860 (with interest, $45,000,000) produced the Readjusters^qv^ who advocated scaling the debt, and economic and social reforms; split the Democrats; and reinjected the Negro into politics. The Readjuster, Mahone, in the United States Senate "traded his commanding vote for offices and committee assignments," and built a political machine, of which he was boss, that dominated the Republican party in Virginia, though ostensibly Mahone was a Democrat. Forced into greater liberalism, the conservatives demolished Mahone in 1889; and in 1892 banished the debt from politics by enabling the state to reach an agreement with bondholders. Disfranchising^qv^ the Negro in large numbers, the constitutional convention called in 1901 to revise the Radical Republican^qv^ Underwood Constitution of 1868 removed the race question. Henceforth politics involved economic and social issues.

The World War accelerated industry. Roanoke, Virginia's third largest city, a village in 1880, and Newport News testify to the urban trend. But in 1930, 67.4% of the population of 2,400,000 was rural. About one fourth only of Virginia's workers are normally employed in manufacturing industries. Thus Virginia's problems are still agrarian: her raw produce, which constitutes the people's wealth, flows out to contribute to other regional surplus; and her factories are financed mainly by outside capital. Rich and wasteful in human and physical resources, her economy is tributary, while approximately one half of her white rural and three fourths of her Negro rural folk are marginal in income, property holdings, living standards and educational levels.

[W. M. Gewehr, *The Great Awakening in Virginia, 1740-1790;* I. S. Harrell, *Loyalism in Virginia;* L. G. Tyler, *History of Virginia*, Vol. II: *The Federal Period, 1763-1861;* R. L. Morton, *History of Virginia*, Vol. III: *Virginia since 1861;* K. Bruce, *Virginia Iron Manufacture in the Slave Era*, and Virginian Agricultural Decline to 1860: A Fallacy, in *Agricultural History*, Vol. VI, No. 1; A. Craven, *Edmund Ruffin, Southerner; Reports*, 1933-39, Virginia Agricultural Station, Blacksburg, Va.]

KATHLEEN BRUCE

Virginia, THE, first steamboat to navigate the Upper Mississippi above the Des Moines Rapids, reached Fort Snelling^qv^ May 10, 1823, twenty days out of St. Louis. Built at Wheeling in 1819, the 109-ton stern-wheeler had Lawrence Taliaferro and Giacomo Beltrami aboard, the latter chronicling the voyage. The boat was snagged and sunk below St. Louis in the fall of 1823.

[W. J. Petersen, *Steamboating on the Upper Mississippi.*]

WILLIAM J. PETERSEN

Virginia, THE. *See Monitor* and *Merrimack*, Battle of the.

Virginia, The Army of (Union), constituted June 26, 1862, consisted of Frémont's, Banks' and McDowell's corps, with Gen. John Pope as commander (*see* Headquarters in the Saddle). Pope was ordered to drive Lee out of Richmond (*see* Seven Days' Battles). The Confederate Army marched northward to oppose Pope. McClellan's Army of the Potomac^qv^ was ordered to Pope's aid. The combined Union armies were defeated in the Second Bull Run campaign^qv^ and retreated into Washington. Pope was relieved. The Army of Virginia was broken up and dispersed.

[John C. Ropes, *The Army under Pope.*]

THOMAS ROBSON HAY

Virginia, The Old Regime in. At the apex of society stood the planter class which came to a fine flowering in the 18th century. At the base were the Negro slaves whose labor supported the social structure. In 1724 the Negroes were one fourth of the population, thirty years later over 40%. The aristocratic nature of society was the result of forces operating within the colony. In general the gentry sprang from middle-class English stock. The Byrds, Blands, Carys and Ludwells traced their English ancestry to the merchant class. Tobacco[qv] gives the chief key to Virginia history. Soil and climate favored its culture. England and Europe offered a good market. Land was cheap and plentiful, Africa supplied adequate labor. Men of brawn, brain and persistence grasped the opportunity and laid the foundations of family wealth. Succeeding generations expanded their holdings of land and labor.

The estates were extensive. The average plantation was about 5000 acres, but some were greater. For example, William Byrd I left upward of 15,000 acres which William Byrd II increased probably tenfold. Robert Carter, founder of a famous line, held thirty-three slaves on his home plantation and seven hundred on outlying estates in several counties. Freed from toil, possessed of leisure and wealth, the gentry enjoyed the opportunity for self-expression and decorous lives.

The planters shipped their tobacco to English ports as purchasing power for the trappings of fine living, furniture, silverware, linen, clothes, books, pictures, coaches. They built stately and spacious homes. With leisure to read, they collected libraries. Connection with England was intimate. The Anglican Church was the established order and from England came the parish priests. Eminent lawyers, such as Byrd II, Peyton Randolph, Arthur Lee, were trained in the Inns of Court in London. Children were schooled under tutors at home and some sons were sent to English schools. William and Mary College[qv] sent forth a distinguished list of leaders.

The plantations were large and far apart. Travel was difficult and the great estates were isolated and each a little community unto itself. In addition to the field hands, each plantation had a quota of skilled workers, coopers, tailors, smiths. For the most part commerce was carried on directly from the plantation. The many creeks, rivers, inlets floated the seagoing ships of that age and a plantation had its own wharf. This little world molded and colored the character of the gentry. It developed the power to command; it created a spirit of pride and importance. Out of this class came that galaxy of eminent leaders in the history of Virginia and the nation.

Although isolated by reason of the plantation, yet the planter aristocracy was well integrated. It was closely allied by marriage ties. The Carters, Fitzhughs, Lees, Washingtons, Stuarts, Ludwells and Corbins were intermarried. They gathered in the great homes for house parties and for the sports of hunting and racing. They formed a ruling political group. They met in the governor's council or the assembly at Williamsburg. They served in the local districts as sheriffs, justices of the peace and vestrymen. (*See also* Plantation System of the South.)

[T. J. Wertenbaker, *Patrician and Plebeian in Virginia;* J. T. Adams, *Provincial Society.*]

WINFRED T. ROOT

Virginia, The University of, founded and architecturally designed by Thomas Jefferson, was given statutory existence in 1819. Developed from an academy charter of 1803, its buildings were started in 1817 and eight schools were opened in 1825. Its foundation was one of the landmarks in the development of higher public education in America (*see* Universities, State). Jefferson spoke of himself as its "father," and in writing the inscription for his tombstone, mentioned his connection with its foundation as one of the three achievements of his life by which he wished to be remembered.

The University's specific contributions to American education have been the secularization of scientific thought; the installation (in 1842 by Henry St. George Tucker and his colleagues along lines suggested by Jefferson in 1818) of a system of student self-government; and the establishment, as part of larger tenets of freedom in teaching and learning, of an elective system of study.

Outstanding features are its beautiful grounds, its neoclassical columns, its Honor System and its association (on its governing body) with Jefferson, Madison and Monroe, and (among its students) with Edgar A. Poe, Woodrow Wilson and Walter Reed.

[Philip Alexander Bruce, *History of the University of Virginia.*]

JOHN COOK WYLLIE

Virginia and Kentucky Resolutions, THE, were resolutions passed by the legislature of Virginia, Dec. 24, 1798, and of Kentucky, Nov. 16, 1798 and Nov. 22, 1799. The first two are those usually referred to and are the more important, though the word "Nullification"[qv] first appears in the third. The Kentucky Resolutions were written by Thomas Jefferson, though the authorship long remained unknown, and the Virginia one by James Madison. The immediate occasion was to protest against the passage of the

Alien and Sedition Acts[qv] by the Federalist administration, but the problems considered were much wider in scope, having to do with the nature of the Federal Union. Both sets of Resolutions took the sound position that the Federal Government was one of limited and delegated powers[qv] only. But there was the further question, who should judge whether the central government was overstepping its rightful powers or not.

Jefferson stated that the National Government could not be the final judge of its own powers, and that the states—perhaps even one state—should be. Madison's words were less emphatic, but all three resolutions, unless we are very careful to interpret political terms and philosophy in their contemporary significance, can easily be made to appear as advocating the doctrines of state sovereignty, nullification and secession as those doctrines were later developed. We have to consider, however, the prevailing theory of divided sovereignty; and in 1828 when Calhoun[qv] was preaching his versions of state sovereignty and nullification, Madison pointed out that the Union was a Constitutional one, not a mere League, and that his Virginia Resolution of 1798 could not be considered as affording a basis for Calhoun's interpretation. In the earlier year, the Government was facing unsolved problems. If it appeared illogical that a central government of merely delegated powers should be the judge of whether it had overstepped them, the other horn of the dilemma, that of making the states judges, offered equal practical difficulties.

The resolutions, as passed in 1798 and 1799, were forwarded for comment to the legislatures of the other states, which proved cool to the suggestions made, and in a number of cases replied that states could not decide on the constitutionality of Federal laws because that power belonged to the judiciary[qv]. There, in the course of our development, it was finally to be lodged, but the resolutions may have helped by bringing the problem to a head and causing John Marshall to develop his theory of the functions of the Supreme Court[qv]. Later, the resolutions were used to buttress the doctrines of states' rights[qv] as promulgated particularly in the South, and their political influence was great. By many, the resolutions came to be considered as almost a part of the Constitution, and to have a legal authority which in fact they never possessed.

[A. C. McLaughlin, *A Constitutional History of the U. S.;* E. D. Warfield, *The Kentucky Resolutions of 1798;* G. Hunt, *Life of James Madison.*]

JAMES TRUSLOW ADAMS

Virginia Capes, The Battle of (Sept. 5, 1781), was an indispensable factor in the Yorktown Campaign[qv]. In close harmony with Washington and Rochambeau, the French Admiral de Grasse had brought from Haiti to the Chesapeake all the troops and ships available. Anchored in Lynnhaven Bay, his fleet of twenty-four ships of the line was soon confronted by a British fleet of nineteen ships commanded by Admiral Graves. Standing out to sea, de Grasse prepared to give battle. The British delayed to bear down until center might oppose enemy center, and van enemy van; their rear (Hood's division of seven ships) never got into the fighting. The British suffered greater losses, but at the end of the day the issue was still undecided. For four days the two fleets sailed along parallel courses without renewing the battle. Meanwhile de Barras, with a fleet and siege guns from Newport[qv], had slipped into the Chesapeake to augment the French forces. Relief and reinforcements being barred from the British, Cornwallis the following month was forced to surrender.

[A. T. Mahan, *The Major Operations of the Navies in the War of American Independence.*]

CARROLL S. ALDEN

Virginia City, the largest and most famous of Nevada's early mining towns, came into existence in 1859. It had every characteristic of a frontier mining community: huts, shacks and tents of every description; a cosmopolitan population, with few women; and numbers of lawless characters. By 1861 it was a town of importance with a population of more than 3000. Soon it had hotels, churches, banks, an opera house and an Odd Fellows hall. It declined in the 1880's when the ores of the great Comstock[qv] mining region failed.

[C. H. Shinn, *The Mine.*]

RUPERT N. RICHARDSON

Virginia Company of London, THE (1606–24). The individual effort at the close of the mediæval period that revealed itself in other phases of economic development was especially prominent when, in 1606, the Society of Adventurers to trade in Virginia was organized by letters patent of that year "to Sir Thomas Gates, Sir George Somers and others, for two several Colonies and Plantations, to be made in Virginia, and other parts and Territories of America. [Dated] April 10, 1606." Articles IV and V of the document specify two colonies, called "the first Colony" and "the second Colony" (*see* Plymouth, The Virginia Company of). The "first Colony" included "any place upon the said coast of Virginia or America" between latitudes

34° and 40°. The second colony allowed Thomas Hanham and others "of the town of Plimouth in the county of Devon or elsewhere" to begin a plantation between latitudes 38° and 40°, but neither one was to "plant" itself within 100 miles of the other. Article VII provided that each colony should have a council to "govern and order all matters and causes, which shall arise" within the colony. To investors were left the privileges of raising funds, furnishing supplies and sending out expeditions. However, affairs were to be conducted by the king through a council in England called "our Council of Virginia," created by himself, and responsible to himself, resembling private companies for trade based on ancient charters. It was a modification of this form of management to which the government of the London Company reverted after its dissolution in 1624, and again at the end of the century when royal colonies[qv] were substituted for proprietary and corporate forms throughout America.

From 1606 to 1609 the body of undertakers had little influence even in commercial interests. Business management was left to joint-stock companies and the magazine was controlled by a treasurer and two clerks elected by the president and council in the colony. But the government of the colonies and of the territory of Virginia was reserved to the crown through the Council of Thirteen for Virginia, which was to be appointed by the king and to reside in England. It nominated to the king persons to whom lands were to be granted and appointed the first council in Virginia.

In 1609 a "Second Charter" was granted to the company, erecting it into a corporation and body politic "for . . . enlargement . . . of the said Company and first Colony of Virginia. . . ." It was to be "called and incorporated by the name of, The Treasurer and Company of Adventurers and Planters of the City of London for the first Colony in Virginia." The "limits of the colony" were expressed in terms of distance from "Cape or Point Comfort," 200 miles to northward and 200 miles to southward and from "sea to sea, west and northwest." The undertakers, with Sir Thomas Smith as treasurer, became distinctly proprietary, retaining the commercial responsibilities but assuming governmental functions in place of the king. The investors desired more authority. They feared that desire to placate Spain, or religious consideration, might lead the crown to abandon the scheme. Certain it is that "petitioners" wished to secure more direct authority and larger investments. The council of the company in London chosen by the adventurers therefore acted as a standing committee for them and exercised controlling authority in place of the king.

The charter of 1612 erected a commercial company and made it overlord of a proprietary province[qv]. Matters of importance were decided in the quarter courts. A system for joint management of land and trade to extend over a period of seven years promised dividends to the adventurers and support to the planters.

After 1619 Virginia was still a proprietary province with a commercial company as overlord and the company was still the immediate source of government in the colony. It adopted "Orders and Constitutions" to secure legality of action and they were read at one quarter court each year. The forms and usages followed in other commercial companies, in other corporate bodies and in Parliament greatly influenced the decisions of the company. Through reward or by purchase an individual might own land and not purchase stock, but he might secure the latter within three years by "planting" or peopling his land. Ownership of land and possession of freedom of the company were not always coexistent. Each involved the possibility of the other. The company, domiciled at London, was thus a body of adventurers that had gained the freedom of the company by payment of money, by rendering of service or by settlement of land in Virginia. It was presided over by a treasurer chosen by itself at will and conducted all of its business through its regularly elected officers or committees or by special committees. According to the "Orders and Constitutions," it kept a complete record of its actions in the courts and compelled its committees to do the same.

Between 1619 and 1622 factions developed in the company due to the administration of Samuel Argall, deputy governor of the colony, under whom both the lands and trade of the company were recklessly exploited for his own benefit and that of his friends. The incident resulted in an administration under the Earl of Southampton, Lord Cavendish, Sir Edwin Sandys and John and Nicholas Ferrar. No radical change in policy took place. Gradually certain developments occurred. Emigration by laborers, artisans and apprentices was encouraged to attain production of grain and to install industry. As stated by Osgood, "introduction of free tenancy and the development of private plantations in addition to the company's land was all the time . . . preparing the way for its transition from the plantation to the provincial type."

Doubtless in 1622 the catastrophe of the Indian

massacre (*see* Great Massacre) added to complications in the colony and in England. Also, political difficulties arose. The Sandys-Southampton party supported parliamentary opposition in England and the king and Sandys were bitterly hostile.

On April 17, 1623, a committee headed by Lord Cavendish was summoned before the Privy Council[qv] to defend the company against the "grievances of Planters and Adventurers." As a result, the first blow was struck at the liberty of the company when the Privy Council announced that a commission had been appointed to inquire into the state of the Virginia and Somers Island plantation. On Nov. 4, 1623, the writ of *quo warranto* was issued out of the Court of the Kings Bench. Judgment was rendered on May 24, 1624, and the Virginia Company was thereby dissolved. The patent roll, dated July 15, 1624, records appointment of "the commission and certain others" to supplant the Virginia Company and establish the first royal province in America. The commission was composed of the lords of the council and "certain others," and the council register seems to indicate that it was usually the council sitting as a commission. Papers, letters and instructions, and commissions to the councilors and to governors of the colony passed the Privy Seal and were engrossed on the patent roll, and the letters or papers from the colony were addressed to the council.

Although advice of the company was sought by the king on questions affecting the government of the colony, Sir Edwin Sandys was unsuccessful in his attempt to secure new letters patent. The *Discourse of the Old Company* was issued later in reply. A new charter for the company was never granted and its function as a trading organization ceased.

The mass of materials that form the records between 1619 and 1624 is much greater than in the earlier decade. The minutes comprise two volumes of the "court book" and fill 741 large manuscript pages. Between November, 1623, and June, 1624, Nicholas Ferrar was busily engaged in having these documents transcribed. These transcripts were secured by Thomas Jefferson and are now in the Library of Congress.

[*The Records of the Virginia Company of London*, edited with an Introduction by Susan Myra Kingsbury.]

SUSAN MYRA KINGSBURY

Virginia Constitutional Convention (1829–30) was a response to the liberal tendencies of the period and to demands of transmontane Virginia for a redress of long-standing grievances primarily with respect to representation in the general assembly, suffrage and local government. The convention is of historical importance, chiefly because of its contributions to the ideas regarding the respective rights of property and persons in government. It resulted in the adoption of arbitrary bases in representation in the general assembly, the suffrage was slightly extended, but little change was made in the local governments.

[C. H. Ambler, *Sectionalism in Virginia, 1776-1861*, and *History of West Virginia.*]

C. H. AMBLER

Virginia Declaration of Rights, THE, was formulated by George Mason and adopted by the Virginia Convention, June 12, 1776, preceding by seventeen days the adoption of the constitution that made Virginia an independent state. It furnished a model for similar declarations in other state constitutions (*see* Bills of Rights, State), as also for the first ten amendments to the Federal Constitution, or the Bill of Rights[qv].

[Kate Mason Rowland, *The Life of George Mason.*]

MATTHEW PAGE ANDREWS

"Virginia Dynasty" was a term applied to the succession of Virginia Presidents, especially from 1809 to 1825. In 1824 the legislature of Tennessee in nominating Andrew Jackson referred to the habit of Virginia Presidents in selecting fellow Virginians as secretaries of state and thus guaranteeing their succession to the Presidency.

[J. W. Burgess, *The Middle Period.*]

JAMES ELLIOTT WALMSLEY

Virginia Exiles, THE, were a score or more of Philadelphia Quakers, including the most prominent in Pennsylvania, who were exiled to Winchester, Va., for seven months in 1777–78. Accused of showing "a disposition inimical to the cause of America" during the Revolution, they were banished without even being granted a hearing. Undoubtedly some of the group were British sympathizers, but nearly all were conscientious objectors[qv] upon religious grounds to all war and revolution. Their attempt to follow a policy of strict neutrality amid the passions of war very naturally laid them open to suspicion.

[T. Gilpin, ed., *Exiles in Virginia.*]

RUSSELL H. SEIBERT

Virginia Indian Company (1714–17). The early sweep of the Virginia Indian trade was southwestward, reaching the Tuscarora[qv] by 1650, the Catawba[qv] soon after, and the Cherokee[qv] as a result of a remarkable journey by James Needham[qv] and Gabriel Arthur in 1673. Gen. Abraham Wood and Col. William Byrd I were, successively, giants in the peltry traffic. Subsequently, the business fell into the hands of several unenterprising persons of limited means. In order to delimit French activities in the West, Gov. Francis Nicholson throughout the 1690's urged the creation of a strong trading concern. Not, however, until the project was taken over by Gov. Alexander Spotswood did it bear fruit. Authorized by provincial statute, the Virginia Indian Company was given exclusive control over traffic with natives. Stock subscriptions netted about £10,000. The organization supplied tributary tribes, reopened trade with the Catawba and Cherokee and sponsored the discovery, made in the spring of 1716, of a passage through the Blue Ridge Mountains at or near Swift Run Gap. The act creating the corporation was disallowed by the English Privy Council[qv] on the ground that the enterprise constituted a monopoly. The history of the Old Dominion affords no other example of a private stock company being given complete control of Indian trade.

[L. Dodson, *Alexander Spotswood;* W. N. Franklin, Virginia and the Cherokee Indian Trade, in East Tenn. Hist. Soc. *Pubs.*, IV.]

W. NEIL FRANKLIN

Virginia Military Reserve in Ohio, THE. In ceding her land claims north of the Ohio (*see* Western Lands), Virginia reserved the district between the Little Miami and Scioto rivers for her Revolutionary War veterans of the Continental establishment, in case sufficient good lands could not be found for them in Kentucky. Her generosity far exceeded that of Congress or any other state, and grants were found necessary north of the Ohio, the first survey being made in 1787. Land warrants were issued by the state, but when each survey was completed and recorded, the patent was issued by the Federal Government upon proper certification. Many war veterans assigned their warrants to speculators, who came to control large tracts (*see* Land Speculation). The time limit for grants was extended finally to Jan. 1, 1852, for entries and surveys, and March 3, 1857, for titles. The Virginia legislature, Dec. 6, 1852, released all further claims on such lands. Total grants on military bounties in the region amounted to 4,334,800 acres. Ungranted lands (76,735.44 acres) were turned over to the State of Ohio in 1871 and given by the state to the Ohio Agricultural and Mechanical College (later Ohio State University). The Virginia system of indiscriminate surveys caused much litigation over titles and boundaries, while difficulty in locating the source of the Scioto left part of the western boundary unsettled until about 1830. The first settlement in the district was Massie's Station (later Manchester, Adams County), founded in 1791 by Nathaniel Massie. This part of Ohio long reflected the Virginia origin of its early population.

[C. E. Sherman, Original Ohio Land Subdivisions, in *Ohio Co-operative Topographic Survey, Final Report*, Vol. III; W. E. Peters, *Ohio Lands and Their History.*]

EUGENE H. ROSEBOOM

Virginia Path, THE, often incorrectly called a trail, was the route taken by hunting parties of Indians through Virginia from the Potomac to the Carolinas. As early as 1662 the General Assembly of Virginia rightly forecast that, used by hostile tribes, the path would "prove of dangerous consequence." Entering Virginia approximately at the mouth of the Monocacy, the path ran east of the Blue Ridge and ended at the island of the Occaneechees in the Roanoke River below the junction of the Dan and Staunton. Later it became known as the Carolina road and is not followed, in part, by the Southern Railway[qv].

[*Landmarks of Old Prince William*, authorship ascribed to Fairfax Harrison.]

MATTHEW PAGE ANDREWS

Virginia Plan, THE. *See* Convention of 1787.

Virginia Resolutions, THE (1847), first official state pronouncement against the Wilmot Proviso[qv], served as a model for other Southern protests, and thereafter became the symbol of Virginia's stand on congressional interference with slavery in the territories. Unanimously adopted by the General Assembly, the resolutions pledged resistance "at all hazards" to the enforcement of the Proviso.

[Henry T. Shanks, *Secession Movement in Virginia, 1847-1861.*]

HENRY T. SHANKS

Virginia Resolves, THE (1769), were the first American protests against the Townshend Acts of 1767[qv] and the treatment of Massachusetts for resenting these acts. The Virginia resolves besought the king, "as the father of his people however remote from the seat of his empire," to quiet the minds of Virginians and avert from them threatened dangers to their lives and liberties. Among the burgesses approving these resolves were Patrick Henry, Thomas Jefferson and Richard Henry Lee, each of whom sat for the first time. Adoption of the Virginia resolves led to similar adoptions by each of the other colonial assemblies.

[George E. Howard, *Preliminaries of the American Revolution.*]

C. H. AMBLER

Virginia v. Transylvania Company. The Transylvania Company[qv], shortly after the organization of a government in the Kentucky country, met with determined opposition on the part of a considerable portion of the settlers, who claimed that the land company was asking exorbitant prices for lands the Cherokee title to which was none too secure in view of the acceptance by the British crown of the cession made by the Iroquois Confederation in the Treaty of Fort Stanwix (1768)[qv]. A petition of grievances was sent to the legislature of Virginia. The enterprising George Rogers Clark was soon at the head of those in revolt. He called a meeting of the settlers which was held, June 6, 1776. It resulted in Clark and Gabriel Jones being sent to a constitution convention, at Williamsburg, to which Richard Henderson had presented a memorial for the recognition of his company's claims. On July 4, 1776, the convention appointed commissioners to take proof in behalf of Virginia. A session of the general assembly, which followed the adjournment of the convention, organized Kentucky County[qv]—an assertion of jurisdiction as against the Transylvania government. Both sides took depositions and the final decision of the general assembly, Nov. 4, 1778, was that the Transylvania title was void. A consolation grant of 200,000 acres was awarded to the Transylvania Associates.

[W. S. Lester, *The Transylvania Colony.*]

SAMUEL C. WILLIAMS

Virginia v. West Virginia. When Congress admitted West Virginia[qv] to the Union in 1863, her constitution contained provision for assumption of an "equitable" portion of the undivided state's debt. After early futile attempts at adjustment through commissions, West Virginia became neglectful and Virginia, attempting to secure relief alone, in refunding operations gave to creditors certificates representing what she declared to be West Virginia's obligation to them. This arrangement having proved unsatisfactory, Virginia by acts of 1894 and 1900 took steps which resulted in her bringing suit in the United States Supreme Court in 1906. In 1915 the Court decreed that West Virginia should pay $12,393,929, which was to go to certificate holders in final settlement. The Court, proceeding as a friendly arbitrator, had found West Virginia's obligation to be 23.5% of the old state's debt less the same percent of the old state's assets which Virginia had disposed of or was still profiting by plus interest at varying rates since the old state's division. In 1918 the Court asserted its power to enforce its decision but postponed further action in the belief that West Virginia would now discharge her plain duty. Thereupon West Virginia paid.

[J. G. Randall, The Virginia Debt Controversy, in *Political Science Quarterly*, Vol. 30; C. H. Ambler, *A History of West Virginia.*]

C. C. PEARSON

Virginian Railway Co. v. System Federation No. 40 (300 U. S. 515, 1937) challenged the constitutionality of provisions in the Railway Labor Act[qv] (1926, amended 1934) requiring a carrier in labor disputes to treat with the agent certified by the National Mediation Board as the proper bargaining representative of its employees. The carrier argued this was compulsory bargaining, depriving it of liberty and property without due process[qv] of law. Furthermore, the employees concerned were engaged solely in intrastate commerce. The Supreme Court's decision (March 29, 1937) held that the act compelled only the preliminary steps to agreement and not agreement itself and this was not inconsistent with the Fifth Amendment[qv]. Also since 97% of the railroad's business was interstate in character, the activities of repair shop employees had such a close relation to interstate commerce that they were to be regarded as part of it.

[Railway Labor Act Declared Constitutional, *Monthly Labor Review*, 44:1197-1201, May, 1937.]

W. B. LOCKLING

***Virginius* Affair,** THE. News reached the United States Nov. 5, 1873, of the capture in British waters by a Spanish gunboat of the *Virginius,* a ship of American registry engaged in carrying arms to Cuban rebels. Two days later information followed that four of the captives had been executed, one of them an American. On November 12, confirmation arrived that Capt. Fry of the *Virginius* and thirty-six men had been executed as "pirates" by Gen. Juan Burriel, the governor of Santiago.

The case against Spain was thus extremely serious. The *Virginius* was of American registry and her pursuit and seizure on the high seas, with the ensuing massacre, not only violated international law[qv] but excited public resentment in the United States. Weakening these claims, however, was the fact that registration papers had been fraudulently obtained, the vessel's actual owners being Cubans. Both governments understood the weakness in their respective cases. But in the first wave of indignation Secretary of State Hamilton Fish drafted a virtual ultimatum, which lost nothing in its presentation by Gen. Sickles, American minister at Madrid, whose maladroit maneuvers appear to have been motivated by a personal desire for war.

Transferring the negotiation to Washington, Secretary Fish and Admiral Polo, the Spanish minister, achieved a compromise. The attack upon the *Virginius,* whatever her defects of registry, was an injury. The *Virginius,* then, and her survivors, must be restored to the United States, from Spanish waters, and with the American flag at mast. On the vexing question of punctilio concerning a salute to the flag, opportunity was granted for further research into conflicting claims.

The *Virginius* was surrendered on Dec. 16, 1873, but foundered before reaching port. As Fish wrote shortly afterward, there was no *"unnecessary* war undertaken for a dishonest vessel."

[Allan Nevins, *Hamilton Fish.*]

LOUIS MARTIN SEARS

Visible Admixture Law, THE, enacted by the Ohio General Assembly in 1859, provided that all persons having "a distinct and visible admixture of African blood" should be denied the franchise. Hitherto persons more than half white had been regarded as eligible to vote under the term "white" in the state constitution. Democratic charges that voters of mixed blood had decided the state election of 1857 account for the passage of this law by a Democratic legislature. A Republican supreme court in February, 1860, declared the act unconstitutional on the ground that the settled construction of the constitution could not be altered by an act of the Assembly.

[G. H. Porter, Ohio Politics during the Civil War Period, in *Columbia University Studies in History, Economics and Public Law,* Vol. XL.]

EUGENE H. ROSEBOOM

Visit and Search is a well-established device employed by maritime nations for the control or police of the high seas. It is ordinarily associated with war, but it has also been widely used in peacetime.

As a belligerent right[qv], the rules respecting it crystallized during the Napoleonic Wars, only to be revolutionized a century later in the World War. A belligerent warship may stop and search *on the high seas* a neutral merchantman (a) for proof of the latter's neutral nationality, and (b) for contraband[qv]. These rules the United States recognized, with the exception of search for impressed persons (*see* Impressment of Seamen). Early in the World War England abandoned the practice of search *at sea* in favor of search *in port,* and compelled neutral vessels accordingly to deviate from their course. She searched *mails* as well as cargo for contraband, and she gave a new twist to the supposedly dead impressment issue by removing persons of enemy nationality from the decks of American vessels (*see China* Incident). On their side, the Germans, by the submarine campaign, utterly rejected the principle of visit and search. Legally the United States has not moved from its position in the Napoleonic Wars, but the Neutrality Acts of 1937 and 1939[qqv], if permanent, are bound to affect the principle.

In peacetime visit and search has been used in connection with the following matters: (1) the British crusade against the African slave trade, (2) Spanish arrests of filibustering[qv] expeditions dispatched from the United States in aid of Cuban revolutions, and (3) the American police of the North Pacific in the early 1890's for the protection of Alaskan seals[qv].

Of these the British antislave trade crusade presented the most difficult questions. Through a system of mutual right of search treaties England sought to establish an international maritime police, comprised mainly of her own vessels, against the traffic. Since the United States alone of the maritime nations refused such a treaty, slavers made fraudulent use of the American flag. To cope with them England in 1841 attempted to separate *visit* from search, asserting a *right of visit* in order to determine nationality of the vessel by inspecting her papers. This was akin to applying the law of piracy[qv], particularly since under the American law slave trading was piracy. By such means England circumvented American protests, though not without numerous irritating controversies. A mutual right of search treaty, agreed to by Seward in April, 1862, laid the matter to rest and made possible the eventual suppression of the slave trade.

[Charles Cheney Hyde, *International Law Chiefly as Interpreted and Applied by the United States;* Hugh G. Soulsby, *The Right of Search and the Slave Trade in Anglo-American Relations, 1814-1862.*]

RICHARD W. VAN ALSTYNE

Vital Statistics. Actuarial science in America was born when the theologian, Edward Wigglesworth, analysing sixty-two bills of mortality, published *A Table Showing the Probability of the Duration, the Decrement, and the Expectation of Life, in the States of Massachusetts and New Hampshire* (1789). This contribution was America's earliest life-table, and its author is the father of vital statistics in this country. The following year, as ordered by the Constitution, saw the taking of our first decennial Census[qv] (1790), inaugurating the modern era in the statistics of a nation. American contributions of the 19th century include Ezekiel Brown Elliott's logarithm of the probabilities of life (1856); James Wynne's important monograph on the vital statistics of the United States (1857); Sheppard Homan's classic survey of American mortality (1859); John Shaw Billings' introduction of mechanical aids in counting statistical data (1880), adopted by the U. S. Census; and Samuel Warren Abbott's model registration reports of births, marriages and deaths in Massachusetts (1886–96). Our contributions to biometrics include Charles Benedict Davenport's application of statistical methods in biological variations, and Raymond Pearl's logistic curve of population-growth. It is now recognized that vital statistics comprise the alphabet of sanitary science, and that bookkeeping is as essential in modern hygiene as in the industrial world.

[E. M. East, *Mankind at the Crossroads.*]

VICTOR ROBINSON

Volstead Act. The Eighteenth Amendment[qv] needing a law to enforce it, the National Prohibition Act, introduced by Andrew J. Volstead of Minnesota, was passed through Congress in October, 1919. It was vetoed by President Wilson (October 27), repassed by the House the same day and by the Senate the following day. It construed intoxicating liquor as that containing as much as one half of one percent of alcohol by volume. It fixed penalties for liquor sales, provided for injunctions against and the padlocking of hotels, restaurants, etc., found to be selling liquor, contained a search and seizure clause, and oddly enough, continued the taxation of a product which had been outlawed. It permitted the retention of private stocks of liquor bought before the act went into effect, and likewise the manufacture of beer by brewers, on condition that they reduce the alcoholic content to one half of one percent before sale.

[D. Leigh Colvin, *Prohibition in the United States.*]

ALVIN F. HARLOW

Volunteers. In spite of the present accepted idea of a nation-wide obligation for military service to be made effective by conscription[qv], volunteer service has been the rule in the United States in peace and war save when great emergencies have required the draft[qv]. Compelled service in the militia[qv] has been considered a state affair, and local town militia units with only annual muster days[qv] gradually disappeared. The growing efficiency of permanent citizen volunteer state militia units, with frequent drills and the lack of need for strictly local defense as in Indian days, put practical military training on a volunteer basis. Until 1917 all presidential militia calls were made through the state-quota method, filled by individual volunteering in state units, as for the War of 1812, the Civil War and Mexican Border defense in 1916[qqv]. Under the National Defense Act of 1920[qv], such peacetime volunteers now take dual (state and Federal) oaths and are subject to direct Federal calls.

For overseas operations in Mexico (1846), Cuba and the Philippines (1898), state units went as national volunteers. During the Civil War such volunteering was numerous enough to reduce materially state militia and draft quotas. During the World War[qv] volunteering was early replaced by "selective service."

Peacetime regular army service, following British practice, has been voluntary. Compulsory universal military service, common in 19th and 20th century Europe, was proposed in 1916 and 1920 but not adopted in the United States. In war this nation has maintained a dual system, so that our battlefields have seen, fighting side by side, the Continental Army and militia (1775–81), regular army and militia (1812–14, 1861–65), and regulars and national volunteers (1846–48, 1898).

For both regulars and militia, volunteering has sometimes been stimulated by bounties[qv]. The navy has been throughout a volunteer force. (*See also* Enlistment.)

[War Department, *The Organized Militia of the United States*, 1896; War Department, *Organization of the Land Forces of the United States*, 1912; Military Training, Compulsory or Volunteer, *Proceedings of the Academy of Political Science*, July, 1916; T. Cross, *Military Laws of the United States;* J. T. Dickinson, *The Building of an Army.*]

ELBRIDGE COLBY

Voodooism is a modification of primitive serpent worship brought from the African jungles to the United States via the West Indies. Though widely prevalent among Negro slaves in the antebellum South, it flourished most in New Orleans whither numerous practitioners and believers had come from Haiti. Its chief instrumentalities were weird and mystical incantations, accompanied by licentious dances and wild orgies, and the use of charms (called "gris-gris") to which Voodoo Kings and Queens pretended to transmit the power to cast "spells" over intended victims, thus harming the enemies of the initiated, or influencing others whose actions they desired to control. Meetings were held at midnight in secluded spots, and knowledge of the membership and activities of the cult were carefully guarded from the uninitiated. Superstitious Negroes and whites still occasionally seek aid of voodoo "doctors"; and in spite of persistent efforts to eradicate the cult, the use of "gris-gris" is still practised in New Orleans.

[Lyle Saxon, *Fabulous New Orleans;* H. C. Castellanos, *New Orleans As It Was.*] WALTER PRICHARD

Voter, The. Article I, Section 2 of the Constitution[qv] uses the term "electors" in reference to those who choose members of the House of Representatives, leaving to the several states power to determine their qualifications. The "right to vote" appears in the Fourteenth Amendment[qv] (1868), which sought to penalize exclusions for any reason except participation in rebellion or crime; in the Fifteenth Amendment[qv] (1870) prohibiting discrimination "on account of race, color, or previous condition of servitude"; and again in the Nineteenth Amendment[qv] (1920), prohibiting discrimination "on account of sex." Left to their own devices in this field, apart from these three negative amendments, the states have developed fairly uniform requirements. Eager for settlers, fifteen Western states permitted aliens to vote as late as 1894; since 1900, however, this hoary relic of pioneer conditions has been wiped out and citizenship[qv] is now required in all states. Earlier exclusions based on property qualifications, debt, or religious affiliations[qqv] have been abandoned. On the other hand, tax-paying (*see* Poll Tax) and literacy[qv] qualifications have been continued or added by a number of states. Both are used largely in the South, reducing the number of Negro voters considerably. During the first half century of our national history distinction was sometimes made on property or tax-paying bases as to the elections in which voters might participate, higher qualifications being required for the more important offices. Women were enfranchised first in local, particularly school board and municipal, and in territorial elections, later gaining the right to vote in state and national elections. Age twenty-one is now everywhere required. Beginning in 1866 personal registration has been adopted in some form by more than forty states. Over large areas predominantly of one-party faith the vote in primaries is much more important than in elections. With few exceptions primary laws are of the "closed" type, requiring declaration of party membership. Provisions of this character have also been employed by Southern states to exclude Negroes. Residence requirements likewise show a tendency toward uniformity; they now vary from three months to two years, one year being the rule in thirty-two states. (*See also* Franchise, The.)

[K. H. Porter, *History of Suffrage in the United States.*] ROBERT C. BROOKS

Voters, Registration of. See Registration of Voters.

Voting. In American history the election of public officials by popular vote dates back almost to the beginning of the colonial period. Originally the process of voting, particularly in the royal colonies[qv], was an adaptation of the contemporary English practices, always *viva voce*—acclamation, "ereccion" of hands, or individual announcement. The most common procedure was to require each voter to face the election officials and openly state his choices, which, while the favored candidates bowed and murmured their appreciation, were entered upon the books. Concomitant applause, mingled with jeers, enlivened the occasion.

The first signal departure from English precedent came in New England. As early as 1634, Massachusetts set up the innovation of using a paper ballot[qv]. Other states gradually followed her example, though in some localities a preference was shown for beans or kernels of corn, black for one candidate and white for the other. By 1800 almost all the states had adopted the paper ballot, at least for some purposes. Oral voting, however, long persisted in parts of the South, Kentucky (1890) being the last state to give up the practice.

The paper ballots were unofficial, each person furnishing his own. Shortly after the beginning of the 19th century, therefore, political parties[qv] began to capitalize on the situation by supplying their own tickets for the convenience of the voter. To make identification possible, each party printed tickets of a separate color. "Vest-pocket" ballots they were termed, from the puzzled voter standing in the presence of the clerk, fumbling in his vest pockets for the missive he intended to have recorded. That voting was politically controlled, is evident from the expression, "straight-arm voting," which described the common spectacle of lines of persons being marched to the polls holding their colored ballots above their heads to show that they were observing orders or fulfilling promises.

By the time of the Civil War, election processes everywhere in the United States were falling into disrepute. Violence, intimidation and bribery were prevalent, especially in the cities; and although statutes were enacted, it was difficult to suppress the train of evils so long as each person could discern how the others were voting.

The importation of the Australian ballot, late in the 19th century, provided the necessary element of secrecy. Now the citizen came to the polls, gave his name, and received the official ballot, which he marked in the shelter of a booth. Where the precinct adopted the voting machine[qv], the citizen was protected by curtains. Everywhere today the statutes make it illegal to campaign close to the polls, to divulge how one has voted, to bet on the election results, to offer bribes or threats, or to create election disturbances. The purpose of this legislation is to preserve the secrecy and freedom of the franchise[qv].

[J. P. Harris, *Election Administration in the United States;* C. Seymour and D. P. Frary, *How the World Votes.*]

ROBERT PHILLIPS

Voting, Educational Tests for, have been devised as a means of excluding from suffrage primarily Negroes and immigrants whose vote was deemed a menace to dominant groups in the states in which they resided. Literacy[qv] qualifications were uncommon before the middle 19th century. In 1857 a Massachusetts act required that all voters must read English but exempted voters in the year of its adoption. Other Northern states followed suit, motivated by opposition to the immigrant vote and its receptiveness, in the large cities, to boss control. Southern states, goaded by the post-Civil War excesses of legislatures controlled by Negroes, "carpetbaggers," and "scalawags"[qqv], found in the educational test a way to deprive the Negro of power without violating the Fifteenth Amendment[qv]. In 1890 Mississippi's constitution demanded, in addition to other qualifications for voting, ability to read or interpret understandingly any part of the state constitution (*see* Mississippi Plan, 1890). Other states quickly adopted this means of keeping many Negroes from the polls. In 1895 South Carolina excused temporarily from the educational test all men who were voters or descendants of those who had voted on Jan. 1, 1867. Variations of this "grandfather clause"[qv], appearing in other Southern states, proved an expedient to prevent the literacy tests from disenfranchising untutored whites.

[K. H. Porter, *A History of the Suffrage in the United States.*]

BAYRD STILL

Voting, Regularity in. The American voter may criticize his political party in off-years, split his ticket in local elections, but presidential campaigns find him regular on election day. States are often classified as normally Republican or normally Democratic; this classification holds true for most counties and even for townships. The rural counties of New England and up-state New York, all but a dozen counties of Pennsylvania, several unbroken blocks of Ohio and Indiana, all of Michigan, northern Illinois, and most of Iowa, Nebraska and Kansas have been as regularly Republican as the solid South[qv] has been Democratic. Most of the mountain counties of Virginia, West Virginia, North Carolina, Kentucky and Tennessee are steadily Republican. In the deep South, Fannin County, Ga., Winston County, Ala., and Gillespie County, Texas, were Republican even in the Democratic landslide of 1936. By contrast, in that year Horry and Lancaster counties, S. C., returned not a single Republican vote. Indiana, a pivotal state, shows 48 Republican and 44 Democratic counties, with 3 Republican and 4 Democratic counties that have withstood all landslides[qv] in the twenty-one elections, 1856–1936. Dubois County, Ind., with a total Democratic excess of 42.6% is the strongest Democratic county in the North; an example of inconsistency is Clinton County, Ind., which has gone Democratic 11 times and Republican 10 times but shows a slight Republican excess. An analysis of Pennsylvania, Ohio, Indiana and Illinois (1856–1936), Kentucky (1864–1936), Tennessee and West Virginia (1868–1936), shows 314 Republican and 301 Democratic counties. Of these, 61% are "stand patters" with 0 to 3 defections, 23% are "steady" with 4 to 6 defections, only 16% are "weak," showing 7 or more defections from the favored party. County political patterns were established as early as the Jacksonian period, but some were modified at the time of the Civil War (*see* Churches, Split of, by the Slavery Issue). Strong Republican counties were usually Whig in the earlier days. Political regularity is remarkably persistent in rural counties, but is modified somewhat by urban conditions. Thorough study reveals that religion, economic interest, geographical location and migration have been strong factors in establishing traditional political patterns. (*See also* Immigrants in Politics.)

[C. O. Paullin, *Atlas of the Historical Geography of the United States;* F. J. Turner, *The Significance of Sections in American History;* Election returns may be found in the *Whig Almanacs*, the *New York Tribune Almanacs* and the *New York World Almanacs.*]

HARVEY L. CARTER

Voting Machines. Thomas A. Edison devised a crude model of a voting machine as early as 1869, but it was never employed in an actual election. The first practical use of machines of this type was made by Rochester, N. Y., in 1899. Since then they have been installed widely throughout the country, adoptions having been particularly numerous during the last decade. At present voting machines are authorized by law in twenty-five states: New York, Indiana and Montana make their use mandatory under certain conditions. Particularly suited to urban needs, some 3500 cities and towns now conduct elections with machines. In 1936, 9,000,000 out of a total of 45,000,000 votes were cast in this way. The chief advantages attributed to voting machines are that they make voting quick and easy, facilitate rapid and accurate counting, and prevent a number of fraudulent practices common when ballots are used. Hence their unpopularity with crooked politicians. The chief objection made to voting machines is their high initial cost. In the long run, however, quite considerable savings may be effected by their use.

[Peter H. Odegard and E. Allen Helms, *American Politics: A Study in Political Dynamics*, pp. 709-12.]

ROBERT C. BROOKS

Voyageurs, or *engagés,* in American and Canadian history, were a class of men employed by fur traders[qv]—especially by the North West, the American, and the Hudson's Bay companies[qqv]—to paddle their canoes[qv] and perform other menial tasks connected with the securing of furs and the maintenance of posts in the interior. They begin to be mentioned as such by French writers about the middle of the 17th century when it became necessary to travel (*voyager*) long distances into the interior in order to get furs. From that time until the third quarter of the 19th century these men formed a rather distinct class that was recognized as such by their contemporaries. Most of the canoemen were born in parishes along the lower St. Lawrence, but in time their descendants in the fur country were also recognized as *voyageurs,* in so far as they followed their ancestors' calling. Perhaps 5000 was an average number for the *voyageurs* to be found in Canada and the United States in any one year of the late 18th and early 19th century.

These men had a distinct dress, their own customs, peculiar methods of building houses in the interior, a distinct vocabulary, and a whole repertoire of songs that were heard wherever *voyageurs* were to be found. They were usually short men with heavy shoulders of great strength, very tractable, mercurial and lighthearted. Their great service to their continent was the exploring of its rivers and lakes, the naming of these and other topographical features, and the establishment of many settlements, some of which, like St. Paul and Winnipeg, have grown to great cities.

They were generally divided into two classes: (1) according to experience, the pork-eaters and the winterers; and (2) according to skill, the guides, middlemen and *bouts.* The pork-eaters (*mangeurs de lard*[qv]) were the novices; the winterers had spent at least one winter in the interior. The guides were the men capable of directing the course of a brigade of canoes. The middlemen (*milieux*) sat in the middle of the canoe and merely propelled it in unison without attempting to guide its course, which was governed by the *bouts* (the two men who stood in the prow and stern respectively), i.e., by the *avant* in the prow, and the steersman (*gouvernail)* in the stern. In the interior the *voyageurs* at the posts helped construct them, cut shingles and made canoes, fished and hunted, went out among the natives, and generally were more or less versatile. They even served their countries during the American Revolution and the War of 1812 as soldiers, certain companies, especially in the Canadian armies, being composed and named by them.

[Grace Lee Nute, *The Voyageur.*]

GRACE LEE NUTE

W. C. T. U. *See* Woman's Christian Temperance Union.

Wabash, St. Louis and Pacific Railroad v. Illinois (118 U. S. 557, 1886). This railway was charged by the State of Illinois with a gross discrimination in freight rates between two shippers. The penalty was a $5000 fine, and the aggrieved party was entitled to recover heavy damages. The railway company demurred, but was defeated by both the lower court and the state supreme court. The case reached the United States Supreme Court in 1886, which reversed the state courts' ruling, deciding in favor of the railway company (*see* Granger Cases).

[J. B. Thayer, *Cases on Constitutional Law.*]

ALVIN F. HARLOW

Wabash and Erie Canal. This great waterway, the object of such fond hope in early Indiana, planned to follow the Maumee and Wabash rivers from Lake Erie to the Ohio River, was agreed upon by the states of Ohio and Indiana in 1829 (*see* Indiana State Canals). State lands were sold in Indiana to raise money; $200,000 was borrowed; and in 1832 that state began excavation. Ohio was to build eastward from the Indiana line, but delayed action for several years. Progress in Indiana was slow. By 1841 the canal was in operation only from Fort Wayne to Logansport, and the panics of 1837–39, plus mismanagement, graft and unexpectedly high costs, had well-nigh ruined the state's finances. In 1843 Ohio completed the eastern section of the canal, and some real prosperity now came to the Maumee and upper Wabash valleys. In 1844 the fastest canal packet service in the country was operating between Toledo, Fort Wayne and LaFayette. The canal was opened to Terre Haute in 1849; but flood damage and the competition of railroads[qv] being built parallel to its course foreshadowed its end. In 1856 it reached Evansville, 452 miles from Toledo, making it the longest canal in the United States—but it was already dying. The portion below Terre Haute was closed in 1860, and the last short stretch near LaFayette was abandoned in 1875.

[Logan Esarey, *Internal Improvements in Early Indiana.*]

ALVIN F. HARLOW

Wabash Land Company. *See* Illinois and Wabash Company.

Wabash Towns, Expeditions against (May and August, 1791). Indians operating from their towns on the Wabash and Eel rivers in northern Indiana, encouraged by Harmar's defeat[qv], constantly raided across the Ohio into Kentucky. The frontier leaders, chafing at apparent indifference by the newly constituted Federal Government, were anxious to "wipe away the stain" of Harmar's defeat. Accordingly, in the spring of 1791, Gen. Charles Scott was authorized to lead an expedition against the Kickapoo Eel River villages. He destroyed towns and crops and took prisoners. In August Col. James Wilkinson, who had been Scott's second in command, led a second expedition against the Indians in the vicinity of L'Angville (present Logansport), repeating the destruction of the previous spring. These expeditions, "more brilliant in appearance than destructive," accomplished nothing of particular benefit beyond infuriating the Indians, who eagerly joined the expedition that several months later accomplished St. Clair's defeat[qv].

[R. M. McElroy, *Kentucky in the Nation's History.*]

THOMAS ROBSON HAY

Wachovia. *See* Betharaba.

***Wachusett* Affair.** On Oct. 7, 1864, the U. S. S. *Wachusett* captured the Confederate cruiser *Florida*[qv] in the Brazilian port of Bahia, despite the attempted interference of Brazilian naval forces. The *Florida* was taken to Hampton Roads. At the demand of the Brazilian government, the *Wachusett's* commander was court-martialed, and the American consul at Bahia, who had been implicated in the affair, was dismissed. The crew of the *Florida* was released. The Brazilian government had also demanded the return of the vessel to a Brazilian port, but this was impossible because she had sunk at Hampton Roads as the result of a leak. On July 23, 1866, the U. S. S. *Nipsic* made further reparation by saluting the Brazilian flag at Bahia.

[J. B. Moore, *Digest of International Law,* Vol. VII.]

DANA G. MUNRO

Wade-Davis Bill, THE, passed by Congress July 2, 1864, provided that the government of a seceded state could be reorganized only after a majority of the white male citizens had taken the oath of allegiance, and a constitution acceptable to the President and Congress was adopted. Henry W. Davis and Benjamin F. Wade, sponsors of the bill, and other Radical Republicans[qv] believed that Reconstruction[qv] was the prerogative of Congress rather than of the President. Lincoln's pocket veto[qv] of this bill, which was the response of Congress to Lincoln's plan of Reconstruction[qv], angered the Radicals and presaged the contest over Reconstruction between Johnson and Congress.

[E. G. Scott, *Reconstruction during the Civil War in the United States;* Charles McCarthy, *Lincoln's Plan of Reconstruction.*]

WILLARD H. SMITH

Wadsworth Agreement, THE (May 25, 1923), was an executive agreement signed between the United States and the principal powers allied against Germany in the World War. It provided that the net cost ($255,544,810.53) of the American Army of Occupation[qv] in the Rhineland should be paid out of allied reparation cash receipts from Germany in twelve annual installments. The schedule of payments, subsequently was stretched out by agreements between the United States and Germany, and defaulted after the collapse of reparations[qv] in 1932.

[*British White Paper,* Cmd. 1973, of 1923.]

SAMUEL FLAGG BEMIS

Wages and Hours of Labor largely determine workers' living standards. With varying periods of loss and gain money and real wages have steadily tended to rise, but marked occupational and sectional wage differences obtained from the start.

The hours issue has been agitated unceasingly; the ten-hour movement of the 1820's, the eight-hour drive of the 1860's and the thirty-hour week proposals of the 1930's are noteworthy episodes. Beginning with twelve- and thirteen-hour days early in the century, by 1890 industry had moved toward a ten-hour day—and a fifty-eight to sixty hour weekly basis. Unionized workers in important instances had gained the eight-hour day prior to the World War, but industry in general had not yielded shorter hours. During the World War period the shorter work day and work week gained substantially. But even in the postwar decade the sixty-hour week was not unknown. The steel industry retained the twelve-hour shift until 1923. The depression decade of 1930 witnessed a sharp reduction in working hours.

The shorter work day and work week for women and children, however, were the objects of much legislative solicitude. In 1842 Massachusetts endeavored to regulate hours of child labor[qv]. The first enforceable hours law was enacted by Massachusetts in 1879. Subsequently, and largely after 1900, legislation by the states has regulated length of the work day, the work week, night work, rest periods, etc. for women. In 1908 the Oregon ten-hour law for women was upheld by the United States Supreme Court (Oregon v. Muller) and in 1915, in Miller v. Wilson, the California eight-hour law.

The legal regulation of hours of labor for men follows a different course. For public employees a long series of legislative provisions should be noted. States and municipalities have pursued similar policies. The Adamson Act[qv] (1916) established a legal work day for railway employees. For miners, limitation of working hours was held constitutional in Holden v. Hardy, 1898. In Lochner v. New York[qv] (1905) the Supreme Court invalidated a ten-hour statute for bakery workers; but in Bunting v. Oregon (1917) a general ten-hour statute was upheld. Men's hours were regulated generally only in specified occupations under state and Federal statutes. The National Industrial Recovery Act[qv] in 1933 endeavored by industrial codes to fix maximum hours and minimum wages for each industry. In the Schechter case[qv] (1935) the Supreme Court held the code system unconstitutional.

The minimum-wage[qv] movement for women and children began with Massachusetts in 1912, followed by the laws of several states to 1923. The Supreme Court by a four-four vote in Stettler v. O'Hara upheld the Oregon minimum-wage statute in 1917; but in 1923, in Adkins v. Children's Hospital[qv], the Court held the District of Columbia statute invalid and raised doubt as to the validity of the state acts. Such legislation thereafter remained at a standstill until the depression of the 1930's. The revival of sweat shops, the appearance of fly-by-night employers, and a demoralized labor market after 1929 revived a demand for minimum-wage laws; several states enacted such statutes. In the Morehead case (1936), however, the Supreme Court, holding to the Adkins' precedent, found a New York statute unconstitutional; in 1937, in West Coast Hotel v. Parrish[qv], the Supreme Court reversed its view and upheld the Washington state minimum-wage law. With the way now clear, many states enacted minimum-wage laws for women and minors.

In 1938 the Federal Fair Labor Standards Act[qv] was enacted providing minimum wages and maximum hours for all classes of workers in industries affecting the flow of interstate commerce, thus reattempting the type of Federal control earlier projected by the National Recovery Act.

[A. G. Taylor, *Labor Problems and Labor Laws;* D. D. Lescohier and E. Brandeis, *History of Labor in the United States,* Vol. III; J. R. Commons and J. B. Andrews, *Principles of Labor Legislation.*]

HERBERT MAYNARD DIAMOND

Wages and Prices are among the key indices of standards of living[qv]. Modern economists include other factors. Comparison of these elements, either separately or in conjunction, from period to period is unsatisfactory because workers in our early history were not dependent wholly on wages for their support. In many instances they produced their own garden stuff and animal fats. Household work for the ordinary run of people provided fabrics, clothing, soap, candles, medicaments, among many others. Moreover, a comparison of hourly rates is rendered difficult by the fact that out-of-door workers, and sometimes others, labored from sunrise to sunset. Comparison is further complicated by the existence of indentured servants[qv] who, at some time during their career, received some kind of compensation. In terms of present levels, colonial wages seem to have been unusually low. For example, in Massachusetts in 1640 common laborers received 1s 6d per day. In 1666 mowing paid 2s 2d per day; common laborers got 2s per day and £10 a year. In 1694 seamen's wages were, for masters, £6 per month and for ordinary seamen £3 per month. During much of the colonial period wheat sold for about 5s per bushel, and corn, rye and oats for lower amounts. Wages gradually advanced with the coming of the industrial system. These were affected by the region in which the worker was employed and by the nature of his skill. In the iron business at Pittsburgh about 1837 "good" moulders received from $10.00 to $12.00 a week; common laborers from 75 cents to $1.00 a day. Writers of this period often stated that with the savings from their annual income thrifty laborers could lay by enough to acquire a farm of 80 acres. At this time board was about $2.50 a week. The introduction of power machinery and the progress of invention[qv] contributed gradually to a great increase in productivity of both men and machines. Laborers were among the beneficiaries. Taking the average wage for 1923-25 as the base (100) the hourly rate in 1840 was 14.9. Prior to 1870 it never exceeded 30. Between 1870 and 1900 it lingered in the neighborhood of this figure, but rose thereafter by steady stages. It was 41.9 in 1910, 50 in 1916, and during the period of war prosperity (1920) rose to 105.4. In the prosperous times from 1923 to 1928 it ranged from about 100 to 105, dropping to 80.2 in the early 1930's, and with the subsequent revival of business, rose to 93.2 in 1935. Over most of our history since 1840 the earnings per hour have increased more rapidly than the cost of goods purchased, which signifies that, as a rule, wages have kept in advance of prices. The wages of farm labor have moved at a slower rate. Stated in terms of actual income the monthly rate for farm labor in 1866 with board was $10.09; without board $15.50. In 1928 the wage with board was $34.66; without board $48.65. Wages in the skilled trades reveal considerable differences and these in turn are influenced by sectional conditions. The wage-hour law[qv] which went into effect in October, 1938, provided for the establishment of minimum-pay standards of 25 cents an hour and maximum hours of 44 per week with various exemptions.

[W. B. Weeden, *Economic and Social History of New England; Statistical Abstract of the United States* (any year); S. Perlman, *A History of Trade Unionism in the United States.*]

ISAAC LIPPINCOTT

Wages-Hour Act (1938). *See* Fair Labor Standards Act.

Wagner Act (1935). *See* National Labor Relations Act.

Wagner Battery, Attack on (July 10–Sept. 6, 1863). "Battery Wagner," originally known as "Neck Battery," was first built as an open work on Morris Island, 2600 yards from Fort Sumter[qv] —part of the defenses of Charleston[qv]. Intended for eleven guns, it was never completely armed. Yet, for fifty-eight consecutive days, men, artillery and sand here beat off the combined efforts of Union land and naval forces, finally succumbing to Gen. Quincy A. Gillmore, at that time the outstanding engineer officer in the Federal army. A total of nearly 10,000 projectiles were hurled against the battery during the siege.

[*War of the Rebellion—Official Records of the Union and Confederate Armies; Battles and Leaders of the Civil War.*]

ROBERT S. THOMAS

Wagon Box Fight (Aug. 2, 1867). Sioux[qv] under Red Cloud attacked a wood-cutting detail under Capt. James Powell near Fort Phil Kearny[qv], Wyo. Thirty-two white men retreated to a corral built of wagon boxes from which they repulsed all attacks of the Sioux. Lt. J. C. Jenness and six men were killed. Powell estimated the Indian loss at 180 killed and wounded.

[Cyrus Townsend Brady, *Indian Fights and Fighters.*]

PAUL I. WELLMAN

Wagon Manufacture. Horse-drawn wagons replaced oxcarts in America gradually, first on highways and later on farms. Local shops built those used in the 18th century to carry freight between inland towns and seaports, to carry army supplies to Gen. Braddock[qv], and to meet later demands due to the opening of highways parallel with the coast during British blockades and the movement of population across the Alleghenies. Soon after 1800 some custom shops became factories manufacturing for the local market and plantation trade. Government orders for army wagons of uniform construction promoted this development by encouraging a practice previously borrowed by New Haven carriage makers from neighboring clock factories of using power machinery to produce in quantity standard spokes, hubs and other parts (*see* Interchangeable Parts). The great growth of wagon making, however, occurred in the West where the tide of settlement across the plains and into California called into being the prairie schooner, a successor of the Conestoga wagon[qqv]. By the time of the Civil War the Studebaker Brothers of South Bend, Ind., who date back to 1813, were the largest wagon makers in the world. Since 1900 mechanical traction has lessened wagon output. Nevertheless, over 100,000 horse-drawn wagons and trucks, valued at nearly $6,000,000, are made annually.

[J. L. Bishop, *History of American Manufactures;* C. M. Depew, *One Hundred Years of American Commerce;* United States *Census of Manufactures.*]

VICTOR S. CLARK

Wagon Train Charge (Nov. 8, 1874). Leading a mixed infantry and cavalry detachment from Gen. Miles' Indian Territory Expedition, Lt. Frank D. Baldwin launched a charge against Grey Beard's camp at McLellan's Creek on the Staked Plain[qv] of Texas. Twenty-three 6-mule wagons, loaded with infantry, slashed through the Indian camp, routing all therein and recapturing two white children, Adelaide and Julia Germaine[qv], who, with two older sisters, had been held captive since the preceding September.* Lt.

* In the article on the Germaine Girl Captives (Vol. II, p. 382) the date of the recapture of the two girls is given as Nov. 8, 1875. It appears from the War Department Records that the correct date is 1874 as given above.

Baldwin received his second Congressional Medal of Honor for the success of his brilliantly conceived, unorthodox use of wagons as weapons of offense.

[Quartermaster *Review*, November-December, 1921; Pampa *Daily News*, May 22, 1932.]

ROBERT S. THOMAS

Wagon Trains. For purposes of protection and efficiency, California, Oregon, Santa Fé and other traders and emigrants of the trans-Mississippi West before 1880 customarily gathered their wagons into more or less organized caravans or trains. There is some doubt as to who first used wagons of the "prairie schooner"[qv] or canvas-covered type over the transmontane trails to the Far West, but apparently William L. Sublette, one of the partners in the reorganized Rocky Mountain Fur Company[qv], conducted a ten-wagon, mule-drawn train over the Oregon Trail[qv] from St. Louis as far as the company's Wind River rendezvous between April 10 and July 16, 1830, arriving back at St. Louis on October 10. To Capt. Benjamin L. E. Bonneville's[qv] fur-trading expedition is usually ascribed the distinction of first taking wagons through South Pass[qv], when in July of 1832 his twenty-wagon train, drawn by oxen and mules, reached the Green River by that route. It was not until 1843 that the celebrated "cow column" Oregon emigrant party of about 1000 persons under Peter H. Burnett, Jesse Applegate and Dr. Marcus Whitman brought most of its 120 wagons over the trail to arrive near the Columbia River on October 10, the first wagon train to reach Oregon. Separating from the main emigration of 1843 at Fort Hall[qv], Joseph B. Chiles left Joseph R. Walker to guide a portion of his party with three wagons and reach California after abandoning their wagons just east of the Sierra Nevada at Owen's Lake. The so-called Stevens-Murphy-Townsend party of some fifty persons in October–December of the following year, with five of its original eleven ox-drawn vehicles, is claimed to have been the first group to bring wagons all the way from Missouri and through the Sierras by the California Trail, Donner Lake and Truckee Pass, guided by Caleb Greenwood. William Becknell, a Missouri merchant, took the first wagon train, of three wagons, to Santa Fé in May–July, 1822; and the first wagon trail from Santa Fé on to southern California seems to have been marked during the Mexican War by Lt. Col. Philip St. G. Cooke with his Mormon Battalion[qv] (Oct. 19, 1846–Jan. 29, 1847), by way of Guadalupe Pass and the Gila River and Colorado Desert to San Diego. The eastern section of the Old Spanish Trail, from the Wasatch Mountains through Utah, Colorado and New Mexico to Santa Fé, seems to have been seldom if ever traversed by wagons, although Mexican pack trains had used it at least as early as 1830. The western section of this trail, however, through southwestern Utah and across Nevada and California to the vicinity of Los Angeles, was used frequently during the gold rush days (*see* California Gold Rush) by wagon trains of emigrants turning southward from Salt Lake City. A number of well-marked wagon routes ran across Texas from its coast towns and from Louisiana, Arkansas and the Indian Territory to El Paso or other points on the Rio Grande, whence connections could easily be made with the Gila Trail.

The number of wagons making the overland journey annually from 1843 to 1848 is difficult to determine with accuracy. But some idea of the increased emigration by wagon train, after the news of the California gold discovery was confirmed in the East, may be gathered from the report, dated June 23, 1849, that already that year 5516 wagons had passed Fort Kearny[qv] on the Platte River, bound for California or the Columbia Valley. In 1865, when the "prairie schooners" were beginning to carry rather more freight than passengers, from thirty to fifty canvas-topped wagons, each capable of transporting from 4000 to 7000 pounds, and drawn usually by five or six yoke of oxen, urged on by "bullwhackers"[qv], were said to make up an ordinary train, and trains five miles in length were occasionally reported.

The organization and daily routine of a wagon train depended upon the danger expected from Indians, the nature of the country to be traversed and the number and character of the parties composing the train. Some trains, such as those of the Mormon migrations, had a semimilitary formation, others were very loosely bound together. It was customary to elect a "captain" as central authority, and several "lieutenants" were put in charge of assigned sections of the train, their duties being chiefly to execute the commands of the captain, to keep order in their sections and to place them properly in designated positions when the train paused for its encampments. One function of the captain was usually to select each night's camping site in accordance with the advice of a guide or the reports of horsemen sent out in advance during the day. At night the wagons were commonly drawn up in a circle or square, end to end, so as to form a corral for at least the more valuable horses, mules and cattle, as well as a fortress for the passengers. Frequent causes for these precautions were Indian thefts, buffalo herds, storms and other alarms which might stampede the domestic draft animals. Horse- or mule-drawn wagons could make as a rule from ten to fifteen miles a day, the more dependable ox-drawn trains seldom more than ten, under average conditions of travel.

After the completion of the Union Pacific-Central Pacific[qqv] transmontane railway line in May of 1869, wagon trains tended to decrease in size, save in the case of freighting lines. The establishment of stagecoach lines[qv], the conquest of the Rocky Mountain and Great Plains Indians, the practical extermination of the buffalo, and the building of other far western railways in the 1880's, all combined to make the wagon train a means of freighting heavy goods rather than of carrying passengers, and it was increasingly safe for an emigrant family of the poorer type to make its way westward in a single "covered wagon"[qv].

[H. H. Bancroft, *History of California*, Vols. VI-VII, and *History of Oregon*, Vol. II; K. Coman, *Economic Beginnings of the Far West;* O. C. Coy, *The Great Trek;* R. L. Duffus, *The Santa Fé Trail;* Seymour Dunbar, *A History of Travel in America;* W. J. Ghent, *The Road to Oregon;* Josiah Gregg, *Commerce of the Prairies;* L. W. Hastings, *The Emigrant's Guide to Oregon and California.*]

RUFUS KAY WYLLYS

Wagon Yard, The, was the descendant of the Old World caravansery and the ancestor of the later automobile camp. It was common throughout the Prairie West during the last three decades of the 19th century. Ordinarily it consisted of a great hollow square enclosed on three sides by sheds divided into stalls. The fourth side was occupied by a grocery and feed store and a wide gate. In the center stood the camp house where travelers cooked, ate and slept, and near by were a well and watering trough. Charges for a wagon team and driver were usually fifteen to twenty-five cents a night.

[E. E. Dale, Tales of a Wagon Yard, ms. in University of Oklahoma Collections.]

EDWARD EVERETT DALE

Wagoners of the Alleghenies transported merchandise from the ports of the East to the entrepôts of the West and returned with agricultural products; they rose to prominence during the second decade of the 19th century, but finally succumbed to the competition of the railroads. Their chief routes were the Pennsylvania Road (*see* Forbes Road) from Philadelphia to Pittsburgh and the Cumberland Road[qv] from Baltimore to Wheeling. Their wagons, referred to as Conestoga[qv] or Pittsburgh wagons, were about twenty feet long, bending up in front and back, and six to eight feet wide. Over their rounded wooden bows white canvas was stretched; the lower sides were blue, and the removable sideboards were red. An average load consisted of 6000 pounds (referred to as 60 hundred), although in 1844 the largest load recorded on the Cumberland Road was one of 12,000. The price of carriage varied from $4.25 per hundred for a western trip to the Ohio to $1.25 per hundred for the return journey, depending upon destination, load and merchandise. Teams of six or eight horses were usually employed and many of these teams had bells on the lead horse (*see* Baltimore Bell Teams).

There were two classes of wagoners—regulars and sharpshooters. Regulars engaged in hauling the year around; sharpshooters were farmers who, when freight rates were high, undertook hauling for short periods. Sharpshooters paid higher tolls because their ordinary farm wagons had narrow-rimmed wheels, whereas the regulars' wagons had broad-rimmed wheels which cut up the road less and so were charged lighter tolls.

Wagoners traveled about fifteen miles a day, although sharpshooters might make twenty or more. They stayed overnight at taverns[qv] along the road and by the end of the period it was said that there was a tavern every mile from the Atlantic to the Ohio. At night the men wrapped blankets around themselves and spread in a semicircle on the floor in front of the tavern fireplace. Their horses were rarely stabled but simply rested in the tavern's yard, although in severe weather blankets might be thrown over them.

The number of wagons was enormous; in 1822 a congressman estimated that 5000 wagons had passed over the southern road that year, and in 1836 during a period of five weeks thirty wagons passed daily over the northern road. Rivalry with canals[qv] caused the wagoners to form associations or to join transportation lines; and competition from the railroads[qv] forced the wagoners out of a large share of the business shortly before the Civil War.

[Thomas B. Searight, *The Old Pike, A History of the National Road, with Incidents, Accidents and Anecdotes Thereon.*]

JOHN W. HARPSTER

Wakarusa War, The (December, 1855), was an episode in the rivalry between Free State and proslavery forces in Kansas. The murder of an antislavery settler and threatened retaliation loosed pent-up tension, and 1200 proslavery Missourians and Kansans assembled at Franklin on the Wakarusa River for an attack upon Lawrence. Charles Robinson and James H. Lane prepared to defend the town against attack. To prevent bloodshed, Gov. Wilson Shannon hastened to the scene, signed a "treaty" with Lane and Robinson, conferred with proslavery leaders, and secured their reluctant acquiescence. Both parties disbanded their forces without a resort to arms.

[W. H. Stephenson, *The Political Career of General James H. Lane.*] WENDELL H. STEPHENSON

Wake Island. This small coral island lies in latitude 19° 10′ North and longitude 166° 35′ East, on the cable route between San Francisco and Manila, 2325 miles west of Honolulu and 1505 miles east-northeast of Guam. It was discovered in 1796, acquired for the United States in 1898 by the second Philippines expedition, and formally occupied in 1900. It is about three square miles in area and, until recently, uninhabited. Since 1935 it has been one of the important ports of call for the transpacific clipper ships of the Pan-American Airways.

[*Stewart's Handbook of the Pacific Islands;* Wm. B. Miller, Flying the Pacific, *National Geographic Magazine*, LXX, No. 6.] KENNETH POTTER

Wakefield, birthplace of George Washington, a plantation on the Potomac, in Westmoreland County, Va., was bought by Augustine Washington in 1718, adjoining lands of his grandfather, John Washington, who came to America in 1656. The house, burned in 1780, was not rebuilt. The Government erected a monument on the site in 1881. In 1923 the Wakefield National Memorial Association was organized by Mrs. H. L. Rust to build on the old foundations a duplicate of the birth-house, to restore the neglected graveyard in which five generations of Washingtons are buried, and to recreate the physical conditions of the original estate. On Feb. 11, 1932, the Association conveyed its 367 acres to the United States, to be maintained as the George Washington Birthplace National Monument.

[C. A. Hoppin, *The Washington Ancestry;* Charles Moore, *Wakefield, Birthplace of George Washington.*] CHARLES MOORE

Waldenses, THE, an heretical Christian sect dating from 1170, owed their origin to Peter Waldo, rich merchant of Lyons, France. After 1665 thousands of them fled to the Protestant countries of Europe and to the English colonies in America. In 1893 a colony of Waldenses from the Cottian Alps, led by Matteo Prochett and Charles Tron, purchased 5000 acres of land in the North Carolina foothills six miles from Morganton, and founded the town of Valdese. For a few years this settlement operated on a communal basis, but this proved unsatisfactory and was soon abandoned. Subsequently they developed a thriving wine industry, hosiery mills, cotton mills, lumber plants, a bakery and a macaroni factory.

[*News and Observer*, Raleigh, N. C., Jan. 29, 1922.] HUGH T. LEFLER

Waldo Patent, THE, embraced all the land from the Muscongus to the Penobscot River in the District of Maine equal in area to a tract thirty miles square. Included in the original grant of James I to the Council for New England[qv] in 1620, it was transferred in 1629 to John Beauchamp and Thomas Leaverett whose heirs admitted, in 1719, The Ten Proprietors and The Twenty Associates into partnership in order to develop the resources of the country and hasten its settlement. When the rights of the Associates were challenged in 1729 by Daniel Dunbar, the king's surveyor, they granted Brig. Gen. Samuel Waldo one half of their claim for successfully defending their title before the king. Waldo increased his share by inheritance and purchase to more than a half million acres and had it set off from the rest in 1732 by a deed of partition. By generous and attractive offers he lured the Scotch-Irish to St. Georges (Thomaston), the English to Medumcook (Friendship), and the Germans to Broad Bay (Waldoborough). Blockhouses were built for protection against Indian attacks. At the death of Samuel Waldo in 1759 the Patent was inherited by two sons and two daughters with a double portion for the eldest son. After the Revolution four fifths were purchased by Gen. Henry Knox whose wife had inherited one fifth from her mother. He resigned from Washington's Cabinet and moved to Maine to develop the lime and lumber industries and sell farms. When he died in October, 1806, the Patent was divided among his creditors and broken up into small lots for sale.

[Cyrus Eaton, *History of Thomaston, Rockland & South Thomaston, Maine, from the First Exploration A.D. 1605,* and *Annals of the Town of Warren in Knox County, Maine, with the Early History of St. George's, Broad Bay, and the Neighboring Settlements on the Waldo Patent;* John L. Sibley, *A History of the Town of Union, in the County of Lincoln, Maine;* William D. Williamson, *A History of the State of Maine from Its First Discovery, A.D. 1602, to the Separation, A.D. 1820, Inclusive.*]

THOMAS MORGAN GRIFFITHS

Walk-in-the-Water was the first steamboat to navigate the Upper Great Lakes. Built by

Noah Brown, it was launched May 28, 1818, at the Black Rock shipyard at the mouth of Scajaquada Creek (now Buffalo, N. Y.). On August 23, she left port on her maiden voyage, commanded by Job Fish, and continued in service until wrecked off Buffalo, Nov. 1, 1821.

[Robert W. Bingham, *The Cradle of the Queen City.*]
ROBERT W. BINGHAM

Walker Expedition, The J. R. (1832–33). Capt. Benjamin L. Bonneville dispatched a party of sixty men, under the leadership of J. R. Walker, from the Green River (Wyoming) rendezvous, July 24, 1833, to trap and explore the region between Great Salt Lake and the Pacific. Walker, experienced in the Santa Fé and Missouri trades, was a capable leader. From the Great Salt Lake, he led his expedition down the Humboldt River to the Carson Sink and Walker Lake in western Nevada, thence over the Sierras through a pass that took him into the present Yosemite National Park. In his descent of the western slope, he passed "some trees of the redwood species, incredibly large." This was the discovery of the California Big Tree (*see* Sequoia, The). Members of the party also came to the edge of a precipice "from a quarter to a half mile high," which in all probability was the discovery of the Yosemite or Hetch Hetchy valleys. Descending to the San Joaquin Valley, Walker continued westward to the coast. Diverting hosts at Monterey gave the party a Merry Christmas and provided riotous entertainment until February, 1834, when the eastward journey was started. The Sierras were crossed near their southern extremity through a gap since known as Walker's Pass. Turning north, Walker reached his old trail near Carson Sink and continued eastward, rejoining Capt. Bonneville on the Bear River in Utah. The Walker party was the first American trapping expedition to cross the Sierra Nevada proper *into* California. Walker and a number of his followers later became guides for parties that crossed the Sierras.

[Douglas S. Watson, *West Wind: Life of Joseph Reddeford Walker;* Zenas Leonard, *Narrative of Adventures;* Washington Irving, *The Rocky Mountains: Journal of Capt. Bonneville;* H. H. Bancroft, Vol. XX, p. 41, n. 14: George Nidiver's Journal; H. M. Chittenden, *The American Fur Trade of the Far West.*]
CARL P. RUSSELL

Walker Expeditions, The William. *See* Filibustering.

Walking Delegate, THE, has been an important factor in the development of American trade unionism[qv]. He may be either a union organizer or business agent. As an organizer, his function is to persuade nonunion employees to join the union and demand union standards of wages, hours and conditions of employment. As a business agent, his responsibility is safeguarding the terms of the trade agreement and adjusting grievances which arise in its interpretation and application.

[G. G. Groat, *Organized Labor in America.*]
GORDON S. WATKINS

Walking Purchase. In Indian land sales the extent of the purchase was sometimes determined by the distance a man could walk within a specified time. In 1686 the Delaware Indians[qv] deeded to William Penn a tract in the fork of the Delaware and Lehigh rivers, in depth "as far as a man can go in a day and a half"—forty miles as walked by Penn. When, in 1737, the Delawares agreed to a new release of this tract, Thomas Penn employed experts, one of whom, starting near Wrightstown meetinghouse in the head line of the deed of 1682, and walking in a northwesterly direction over a prepared route, reached the Poconos, a distance of 66½ miles, within the allotted time. The land thus obtained, about 1200 square miles, and extending northeastward to the Delaware, included portions of the present Bucks and Carbon counties, nine tenths of Northampton and about a fourth of Monroe and Pike counties. When the Delawares complained of the manner and extent of the walk Penn called in the Iroquois[qv] who expelled them from the purchase. Charging fraud and unjust dispossession they then allied themselves with the French and made war upon the province. Penn later relinquished to the Six Nations the northern half of the purchase (1758) while the colony settled with the Delawares for £400 (1762).

[C. P. Keith, *Chronicles of Pennsylvania, 1688-1748,* Vol. II.]
C. A. TITUS

Wall Street, since the early 19th century, has been synonymous with high finance in the United States, as Lombard Street has been still longer in England. Its beginnings as a center of speculation in securities trace back even farther, to around 1790, when Hamilton's funding scheme (*see* Assumption of, and Funding of, Revolutionary Debt) and the incorporation of several banks, including the first Bank of the United States[qv], gave occasion for the establishment of a regular market for stocks. Some twenty-four brokers, operating around the lower end of Wall Street, introduced an informal organization of their business in 1792, a development which seems to have been connected with a wild flurry of speculation followed by America's first panic, in that year. But at this period Philadelphia was the chief financial center of the country and it was there that the first stock exchange was formally organized in 1802. The New York Stock Exchange was established in 1817.

Many factors contributed to raising Wall Street to its pre-eminent position as a capital market and center of security speculation. In the first place it was less handicapped than State Street in Boston or Chestnut Street in Philadelphia by the "climate of opinion" or prevalent moral standards of provincial society. Speculative profit-making from trade or industry, in which something at least in the way of a tangible *quid pro quo* was given in exchange, might be tolerated, even held in esteem, but profiting from the mere purchase and sale of paper claims smacked too much of usury to be indulged in by upright Quakers or acquiesced in by the New England conscience. As a matter of fact, these scruples, holding over from colonial times and still nurtured in the Middle West, account for no small part of the traditional suspicion and disesteem of Wall Street in the country at large.

A second factor which helped to make Wall Street the leading financial market of America was the advantage given to the commerce of New York by the completion of the Erie Canal[qv]. Of similar import was the superior natural accessibility of New York, on the one hand, to the interior of the country through rail connections, and on the other to foreign ports via steam navigation. The mounting commercial ascendancy of New York was connected with the growing financial supremacy of Wall Street in two ways. The size of a security market, like any other market, is conditioned by the volume of demand and by the volume of supply there coming into conjunction. The demand for capital funds in enterprises of any considerable scope now centers in Wall Street, coming from every part of the country and indeed to an extent from abroad; but originally the market there grew up because of the demands for capital locally and in the development of immediately tributary regions. Correspondingly the increasing commerce and industry of New York yielded profits which provided a supply of funds for investment. Through the reciprocal action of these forces Wall Street was enabled to outdistance all rivals as a focal point for the assembly and distribution of capital.

Undoubtedly another factor in the rise of Wall Street has been the comparative ease and impunity with which it has been possible there for clever and not too scrupulous operators to filch innocent "lambs" of their funds by the manipulation of the prices of securities. There are many ways in which at various times this has been done, from "wash sales," or fictitious transactions, to large-scale pools, or cornering operations. From the days of the Livingstons, to those of Drew, Fisk, Sage, Gould, Keene and their successors, "rigging the market" has been one of the favorite pathways to fortune. But perhaps more important from the standpoint of the general economy has been the persistent tendency toward the assumption of prerogatives of industrial control by financiers over the manufacturing, commercial and transportation enterprises which depend upon the New York capital market for funds. The ultimate interconnection in Wall Street between the investment banking houses, which act as merchants of securities, the great commercial banks, which provide the "money market," and the brokerage firms, which buy and sell securities for the account of customers, has at times undoubtedly facilitated a perversion of its functions from those of a genuine capital market.

Though suspicions of these developments have long been prevalent, and the popular opprobrium has been particularly acute at times, it was only subsequent to the disillusionment which followed the Panic of 1929[qv] that active measures were taken to bring "Wall Street" under effective regulation, as expressed in the Banking Act of 1933[qv], the Securities Act of the same year and the Securities Exchange Act of 1934[qv].

[O. G. Villard, *Early History of Wall Street;* S. S. Pratt, *The Work of Wall Street*, 3rd ed.; J. S. Lawrence, *Wall Street and Washington;* I. R. Warshow, *The Story of Wall Street.*]

MYRON W. WATKINS

Wall Street Explosion, The, occurred in Wall Street near the corner of Nassau Street, New York City, Sept. 16, 1920; and was believed to have been caused by a bomb carried in a ramshackle, one-horse wagon which witnesses later remembered having seen near the spot. Horse and wagon were entirely destroyed. Forty persons in the street were killed. The perpetrator was never discovered.

[*World Almanac, 1921.*]

ALVIN F. HARLOW

Walla Walla Settlements, The, began with the establishment of the Indian trading post, Fort Nez Percé, in 1818 by Donald MacKenzie and Alexander Ross for the North West Company[qv] on the east bank of the Columbia at its junction with the Walla Walla River. This post was often called Fort Walla Walla. A farm was maintained in connection with it.

Waiilatpu, the Whitman mission, twenty miles up the river from the post, built in October, 1836, was the next white settlement. Agriculture was carried on there. It served (quoting Mrs. Whitman) "as a resting place for weary travelers." This settlement was destroyed when the Indians killed Dr. and Mrs. Whitman[qv] and some twelve other men, women and children, temporary immigrant and missionary residents, Nov. 29, 1847. Later, a new settlement sprang up near by, known as Whitman or French Town, made up of Catholic French-Canadians and half-breeds.

A few white families had settled in the Walla Walla Valley by 1855 at the time of the Indian uprising in eastern Washington (*see* Yakima Indian Wars). These were ordered out by the United States Indian agent. He also forced Fort Nez Percé to be abandoned at the same time. A new Fort Walla Walla, a United States military post, was erected in November, 1856, about twenty-eight miles up the river of that name.

Walla Walla County was created by the Washington territorial legislature in 1854. By 1859, with the close of the Yakima Indian Wars, 2000 white settlers were located in this valley. In 1862 the city of Walla Walla was incorporated and Wallula at the mouth of Walla Walla River was laid out as a town. A railroad connecting these two points was completed in the early 1870's. These towns were very prosperous during the period of the rush to the gold mines in eastern Oregon and western Idaho, 1860 and afterward.

[C. W. Drury, *Marcus Whitman;* H. H. Bancroft, *History of Washington, Montana and Idaho.*]

R. C. CLARK

Wallace, Fort (Kans.), one of the most important posts of Indian days in the West, was built in September, 1865, at the junction of Pond Creek and the south fork of the Smoky Hill River, about two miles south of the present town of Wallace. It was named in honor of Gen. W. H. L. Wallace who was killed at Shiloh. It was important during the building of the Union Pacific Railroad[qv] and the Cheyenne raids, but was abandoned in 1882 as unnecessary.

[F. H. Blackmar, *Kansas.*]

CARL L. CANNON

Walloons were people of Celtic stock in northeast France (present-day Belgium), French speaking, who became Protestant in large numbers at the Reformation. Many, exiled to Holland, England and Germany, emigrated to America. They were the first colonizing settlers in New Netherland[qv] (first called Nova Belgica): at Manhattan (called New Avesnes), at Fort Orange (Albany), at Wallabout (Brooklyn) and at Boompjes Hoek on the Delaware River (Gloucester, N. J.); later on Staten Island and in the Walkill Valley. They brought seed, fruits and cattle. The first white children born in Middle Colonies were Walloons. Continued immigration increased their numbers, and as they intermarried with Dutch and Huguenots their descendants are often confused with Huguenots[qv] because of the French names.

[W. E. Griffis, *The Story of the Walloons.*]

AUGUSTUS H. SHEARER

Walnut Hills. *See* Vicksburg, Miss.; Nogales, Treaty of.

Walpole Grant. *See* Grand Ohio Company; Vandalia Colony.

Walsh-Healy Act, THE, approved June 30, 1936, established minimum standards for work on Federal contracts. Every contract involving a Federal purchase of supplies in an amount exceeding $10,000 was required to contain an agreement on the part of the contractor that he would conform to the standards prescribed by the act. The contractor was required to pay prevailing wages as determined by the Secretary of Labor, establish an eight-hour day and forty-hour week; employ no male under sixteen, or female under eighteen, and utilize no convict labor. Such contractors were required to be manufacturers of, or regular dealers in, such materials and supplies.

The purpose of the law was to confine bidding for government contracts to established concerns in the trade, and to prevent competitive bids from employers whose labor policies failed to conform to established standards.

[U. S. Monthly *Labor Review*, Vol. 42, No. 3.]

HERBERT MAYNARD DIAMOND

Wampum is an Indian word meaning a string of shell beads. When the whites settled along the northern Atlantic seaboard certain shell beads were highly prized by the Iroquois[qv] and their neighbors. The former exacted tribute in wampum of the tribes they conquered. It had, in addition, a ceremonial value (*see* Wampum Belt). From the beginning the Dutch and English accepted wampum from the Indians as money. In 1640 Massachusetts made it legal tender. According to Roger Williams six white and three black beads were equivalent to a penny; 360 white and 180 black beads were considered a fathom, valued at 5 shillings. The term "string of wampum" at one time signified strung wampum, about one foot in length, and was rated at twelve and one half cents. In Virginia the use of wampum began early, but glass beads were imported as a cheap substitute and in 1621 a glass furnace was built to manufacture them at home. Adulteration eventually set in among the Dutch and in New England, causing wide fluctuations in the value of wampum. Machines were built to turn out wampum beads in quantity. Two such factories are known to have existed, one in Hackensack, N. J., the other in Babylon, L. I. In 1650 the Council of New Netherlands attempted to fix the value of wampum, but counterfeiting continued on such a scale that the use of wampum as currency declined, vanishing at the end of the 17th century. However, the Indians continued to value it for gifts, peace pledges and ceremonial purposes well into the 19th century.

After the middle of the 17th century beaver skins began to rival wampum in the Indian trade and soon became legal tender. For a time beaver skins and wampum were equated, as one beaver to two fathoms of white and one fathom of black wampum, but later we find a different quotation, two strings of wampum for one beaver. In the Canadian trade the value of a beaver was rated in goods directly, and not in terms of wampum, as may be noted in the reports of the Hudson's Bay Company[qv].

[J. W. Barber and H. Howe, *Historical Collections of the State of New Jersey.*]

CLARK WISSLER

Wampum Belt, THE, was an Indian symbol of a message of good will, peace or war, often between individuals but sometimes between tribes or confederacies. The use of such belts was highly characteristic of the Iroquois[qv]-speaking tribes, especially the Six Nations, but to a less degree among all the tribes of northeastern United States. None of the belts in collections is believed to be of great age for most of the beads in them are of Dutch and English manufacture. All the belts known are made of cylindrical or tubular shell beads, the wampum of colonial times, strung or woven in bands two to four inches wide and of varying length. When a treaty was made belts were exchanged as symbols or pledges. The tradition is that the Iroquois declared war by sending a belt painted red, but that this was more than figurative language is uncertain. On the other hand a belt was sometimes carried by a messenger to call out warriors from the allied or subject tribes of the Six Nations. The colors of wampum beads varied with the natural color of the shells used, the prevailing colors being white, black (dark blue) and shades of purple. Simple designs were formed by arranging beads of these colors. In most cases these designs were geometric but in a few existing belts there are crude figures of houses and of men holding hands. The so-called reading of the belts seems to have been little more than a verbal narrative of the occasion and the reasons for presenting the belts in question, the differences in design and size serving to identify them.

[Frank G. Speck, The Functions of Wampum among the Eastern Algonkin, *Memoirs of the American Anthropological Association*, Vol. VI, No. 4; L. H. Morgan, *League of the Iroquois.*]

CLARK WISSLER

Wanderer, THE, a ship owned by Charles A. L. Lamar and other Southerners interested in reopening the African slave trade[qv], landed a cargo of some 450 young African Negroes near Brunswick, Ga., in December, 1858. The ship was seized, condemned and sold by Federal authorities, but the owners escaped punishment. The Negroes were sold to planters in Georgia and Mississippi.

[Frederic Bancroft, *Slave Trading in the Old South;* J. R. Spears, *The American Slave Trade; The Wanderer: The Speech of Hon. Henry R. Jackson of Savannah, Ga.*]

FLETCHER M. GREEN

War: Antiwar Organizations. The first American organizations primarily to oppose war were apparently formed just after the War of 1812, one of them being the Friends of Peace. In 1828 the American Peace Society[qv], the oldest antiwar organization in the country, was founded by William Ladd[qv]; but, though at first uncompromising toward war, it did not remain consistently so, for it supported the North in the Civil War and the United States Government after it entered the World War. In an effort to keep out of the world conflict other groups were organized, among them the American Union against Militarism and the Women's Peace party, the latter founded under the leadership of Jane Addams. Subsequently the Peace party became the United States Section of the Women's International League for Peace and Freedom. The latter and the National Council for Prevention of War—started in 1921 as a clearinghouse for various peace organizations—were perhaps the strongest antiwar groups of the 1920's and 1930's. Among other groups of importance were the Fellowship of Reconciliation, largely under Quaker influence, the War Resisters, completely pacifist[qv], the National Committee on the Cause and Cure of War, and the Committee on Militarism in Education. In the early 1930's was formed the somewhat communistic[qv] American League against War and Fascism, soon renamed the

American League for Peace and Democracy. (*See also* Peace Movement.)

[Merle Curti, *Peace or War, the American Struggle, 1636-1936.*] MARY WILHELMINE WILLIAMS

War, Articles of. *See* Articles of War.

War, Declaration of. The framers of the Federal Constitution vested in the Congress, as representatives of the people, the power to declare war. Their action, withholding from the Federal Executive this phase of the war-making power, was fully consistent with America's newly evolved concept of democracy. How far they recognized the inherent hazards, in particular the possibility that Congress might not be in session at a time of national emergency, is not clear. In any event, by giving the President the initiative in the field of foreign relations, and by designating him commander in chief of the army, navy and of the militia[qqv] of the states when called into Federal service, they accorded him ample power to maintain the constitutional safeguards for the United States, its foreign possessions, its nationals wherever located, and its rights.

The states individually were denied the power to wage war "unless actually invaded or in such danger as will not admit of delay." The development of means of communication since 1789 and the fact that the invasion of a state constitutes *per se* a violation of national sovereignty practically preclude the necessity of independent military action by an individual state.

The historical development of the war-making powers vested in the executive and legislative branches indicates a gradual gravitation of preponderant authority toward the President in the determination of any issue for peace or war. In fact Congress has never formally declared war; it has only recognized the existence of a state of war. Moreover, in three of the seven instances of America's international clashes, Congress went no farther than to authorize the necessary defensive measures to repel foreign aggression. These were the undeclared naval war with France in 1798, and the troubles with Tripoli (1801–5) and with Algiers (1815)[qqv]. In the two latter cases Tripoli and Algiers formally declared war against the United States.

In 1812, following a long series of aggressive acts by Great Britain, President Madison in a message to Congress, declared "We behold, in fine, on the side of Great Britain a state of war against the United States, and on the side of the United States a state of peace toward Great Britain." Congress, declaring the existence of a state of war, granted the President authority and means for armed resistance. (*See* War of 1812.) In 1846 a dispute between the United States and Mexico as to the ownership of the strip of land lying between the Nueces and Rio Grande rivers led to a Mexican attack on American troops operating in the disputed area. The joint resolution of Congress, May 13, in response to President Polk's message declared that "by the act of the Republic of Mexico a war exists between that Government and the United States." (*See* Mexican War.)

The war with Spain in 1898 was preceded by a joint resolution of Congress declaring Cuba independent and authorizing armed intervention to secure the independence of Cuba. When Spain characterized that step an act of war, Congress in turn declared the existence of a state of war. (*See* Spanish-American War.) The last sequence of this kind occurred April 2, 1917, when President Wilson, after stigmatizing Germany's unrestricted submarine warfare as "war against all nations," requested of Congress "that it formally accept the status of belligerent[qv] which has thus been thrust upon it." The joint resolution of Congress passed April 6, 1917, employed the President's identical language. (*See* World War.)

The War Department's archives record more than a hundred "wars" in addition to those cited above. A considerable proportion of these represent the suppression of hostile Indian tribes. Such wars, and similarly our Civil War, entailed no declaration of war. These were domestic difficulties. The constitutional powers of the President have always been ample for the initiative of military measures without resort to Congress, even though Congress' control of the purse strings gives the legislative branch a potent voice in the determination of policies in any major emergency.

There remains one class of the use of American armed forces without declaration of war: intervention in the affairs of foreign nations. The seizure of the port of Vera Cruz in 1914[qv], Gen. Pershing's punitive expedition into Mexico[qv] in 1916, and the various occasions in which American marines were employed to restore order in the Caribbean area are typical examples. Historians generally regard such acts as the normal offspring of the policy enunciated by President Theodore Roosevelt in 1904 and 1905, the so-called "corollary of the Monroe Doctrine"[qv], asserting the necessity of using a police power to correct conditions in instances where, under the Monroe Doctrine, we could not permit European powers to obtain by force the redress of wrongs suffered.

Recent years have witnessed a determined effort to curb the war-declaring powers of the

President and Congress. Resolutions have been introduced in both branches of Congress for an amendment to the Constitution providing that, except in the case of invasion of the United States by a foreign Power, the authority should not become effective until confirmed by a nationwide referendum. The most notable of these is the resolution introduced by Rep. Louis Ludlow[qv], of Indiana, Jan. 14, 1935. Reintroduced by Rep. Ludlow, Feb. 5, 1937, it received nine days later sufficient signatures on a discharge petition to obtain consideration by the House. On a vote to discharge the Committee on Judiciary from further consideration, the motion was lost, 209 to 188.

[S. F. Bemis and G. G. Griffin, *Guide to the Diplomatic History of the United States;* J. H. Latané, *American Foreign Policy.*]

HERMAN BEUKEMA

War, Economic and Social Effects of. The patterns of postwar periods have remarkable similitude regardless of general conditions. Thus at the close of the American Revolution we had no banking and credit system, no steam, electricity, modern transportation, mass production, and so on, as contrasted with the close of the World War. Yet the resemblance of the postwar patterns is close. Peace was made in 1783. About two years of prosperity followed and then two years of intense depression. Next came some years of wild speculation, ending in 1791 in our first great panic. In the case of the World War, peace was made in 1919 and we had a boom for about two years. Then came the primary depression of two years, followed by about seven years of wild speculation, when came the great postwar depression, as always five to seven years, or so, after peace. While the graph varies somewhat in other cases, in general the line is the same.

The relief from war brings a feeling that the old life has come back and prosperity will begin. Hence the first burst of enthusiasm, while psychological reasons equally control the pattern for the ensuing cycle. But things are never the same after war as before. Capital has been destroyed and must be replaced with pain and saving. Normal business has been dislocated. Because of the inevitable inflation[qv] in war, and unusual demand for some kinds of goods, especially food products, prices have been inflated, debts incurred, and an extravagant way of living engendered. The reverse from war to peace meets falling prices and lessened demand, with natural consequences. Farmers and labor are always hard hit and resentful. Demands for continued inflation always occur. There is social unrest. Socially, also, the breakdown of customary habits and restraints brings about a hectic period in manners. Economic and political scandals usually develop. Business difficulties and social discontent call for a stronger government, leading to the adoption of a Constitution or a New Deal[qqv]. Gradually debts are cleared off, wages and prices are readjusted, the new rich settle down, the "young generation" grows up, capital is replaced, the wild panaceas are abandoned, an era of conservatism returns. Art and literature, which fare badly in war, are likely to have a period of bloom in the generation following. Although history never repeats itself in all details this seems to be the standard pattern for postwar periods, and we appear to have repeated the pattern closely with regard to main trends.

[J. T. Adams, *New England in the Republic, 1776-1850;* Allan Nevins, *The Emergence of Modern America, 1865-1878;* L. M. Hacker and B. B. Kendrick, *The United States since 1865.*]

JAMES TRUSLOW ADAMS

War, Laws of. In 1863 the War Department issued, as General Orders No. 100[qv], a set of "Instructions for the Government of Armies of the United States in the Field," especially prepared for such publication by Dr. Francis Lieber (*see* sketch in *Dictionary of American Biography,* Vol. XI); and by this action, America took the leadership of the world with regard to the rules of land warfare. These instructions formed a practical analysis and adaptation of customs and practices, courtesies and disciplines which had been hitherto dealt with in full only by publicists, or in fragmentary fashion by commanders. Many of these had been in existence for centuries; some had been practised in the United States, as, for example, the paroling and exchange of prisoners during the American Revolution (*see* Prisoners of War), the formalities regarding surrenders at Saratoga and Yorktown[qqv], and British respect for private property in Washington in 1814. This was their first full formulation and official adoption in America, if not indeed in the world. Considering the usually bitter and brutal character of most internecine conflicts, it is especially significant that the United States should have promulgated these rules in the midst of a Civil War to suppress rebellion.

In spite of the traditional militia principle of American military action, these regulations clung to the philosophical distinctions of such writers as Grotius and Vattel who had attempted to formulate doctrines for periods when wars were fought by armies largely professional and when clear distinctions were made between combatants and noncombatants, soldiers and civilians. These rules defined and limited the jurisdiction of military commanders, provided for the protection of properties and the safety of citizens, and regulated matters concerning deserters, prisoners of war, hostages, reprisals, armistices, capitulations, flags of truce, spies and informally armed bands.

Although by practice and law, war is basically ruthless, with each citizen of one country the enemy of each citizen of the other (Lamar v. Browne, 92 U. S. 187; Brown v. U. S., 8 Cranch 110), this strict rule was qualified early in American history by the treaty with Prussia[qv] in 1785. Also, in addition to being what Prof. Holland calls "the first Power to attempt the codification of the laws of war on land" (*Letters on Neutrality,* 3rd ed. 1921, p. 23), the United States continued to exert its influence toward humanizing combat. In 1864 and in 1906, the United States participated in the Geneva conventions[qv] for ameliorating the conditions of the wounded. In 1899 and 1907, they participated in the Hague Conventions[qv] concerning the laws and customs of wars on land. Since, under the Constitution (Article VI), treaties approved by the Senate become the "supreme law of the land," the doctrines were completely binding in America (Ware v. Hilton, 3 Dallas 199). In 1898, for the Spanish-American War, the Government reissued the Lieber instructions to its forces. In 1914 it prepared and published a complete compilation of "Rules of Land Warfare" for the army, embodying the best practices to date. It took a leading part in the drafting of the abortive aircraft convention drawn up at the Hague in 1923 and not yet ratified, and in the formulation of restrictions on the use of poison gas and submarines proposed in Washington in 1922 but not yet adopted by any other nation.

On the whole the attitude of the United States from the beginning has been a reflection of the most advanced European philosophies of the 18th century, with their emphasis on fundamental law and the natural rights of men and nations, even when these might be engaged in combat. It has been steadily held that certain definite formalities must be observed, that belligerency should affect only fighting personnel, and that prisoners and wounded should be spared distress and damages and private property considered inviolate—all in so far as the main war necessities and purposes are not obstructed (Tect v. Hughes, 229 N. Y. 222). The course steered has been generally humane, although tinged with characteristic American practicality. At the Hague, Admiral Mahan, under instructions from his own Government, refused to acquiesce in a prohibition against gas projectiles, saying (shortly after the *Maine*[qv] had been sunk in Havana harbor) that it would scarcely seem reasonable to forbid choking a man with asphyxiating gas when all will admit the propriety of destroying a ship and choking a man to death with water. However, when actual experience with war gases had showed needless torture and sentiment had generally condemned their use, the United States was quick to support the more humane contentions. The United States Army in 1922 put into immediate effect in its own forces the prohibitions against aggressive chemical warfare[qv] included in a treaty of 1922 which still stands unratified and ineffective.

In addition, occupation of Mexican territory in 1846–48 (Fleming v. Page, 9 How. 603) and of Cuba, Puerto Rico and the Philippines in 1898 by United States troops (McLeod v. U. S., 229 U. S. 416), of Detroit and Castine by British during the War of 1812 (U. S. v. Rice, 4 Wheat. 246), and of rebellious Confederate states between 1861 and 1865 (Coleman v. Tennessee, 97 U. S. 509; Dow v. Johnson, 100 U. S. 152) developed in court decisions and in administrative documentary precedents a definitive body of accepted law regarding military government and the rights of residents of occupied territories, which is far more humane than traditional imperialistic conquest or current modern seizures in totalitarian war.

[C. C. Hyde, *International Law as Interpreted and Applied by the United States;* Q. Wright, *Enforcement of International Law through Municipal Law in the United States;* J. B. Moore, *Digest of International Law*, Vol. VII; General Orders No. 100, War Department, 1863; Rules of Land Warfare, U. S. Army, 1914; J. B. Moore, *International Law and Some Current Illusions;* Instructions for the Navy of the United States Governing Maritime Warfare, 1917; W. E. Birkhimer, *Military Government and Martial Law;* H. A. Smith, *Military Government;* D. Y. Thomas, *Military Government;* Magoon's *Reports;* E. Colby, Occupation under the Laws of War, in *Columbia Law Review*, November, 1925-February, 1926, and The Occupation of Michigan, in *Michigan Law Review*, April, 1924.]

ELBRIDGE COLBY

War, Prisoners of. *See* Prisoners of War.

War Amendments is the name by which the Thirteenth, Fourteenth and Fifteenth Amendments[qqv], certified as adopted on Dec. 18, 1865, July 20, 1868, and March 30, 1870, respectively, are known. They represent the effort of the Radical Republicans[qv] in Congress to guarantee certain rights and privileges to the Negro: freedom, by the Thirteenth Amendment; citizenship, by the Fourteenth; and the privilege of voting, by the Fifteenth.

[A. Capterton Braxton, *The Fifteenth Amendment;* Charles K. Burdick, *The Law of the American Constitution;* Charles W. Collins, *The Fourteenth Amendment and the States;* Richard T. Ely, *Property and Contract in Their Relation to the Distribution of Wealth;* Horace E. Flack, *The Adoption of the Fourteenth Amendment;* Ernst Freund, *Police Power;* William D. Guthrie, *Lectures on the Fourteenth Amendment of the Constitution of the United States;* Lucius P. McGehee, *Due Process of Law under the Federal Constitution;* John M. Mathews, *Legislative and Judicial History of the Fifteenth Amendment;* Charles H. Maxson, *Citizenship;* Rodney L. Mott, *Due Process of Law;* Samuel P. Orth, *Readings on the Relation of Government to Property and Industry;* Hannis Taylor, *Due Process of Law and the Equal Protection of the Laws;* Christopher G. Tiedeman, *The Unwritten Constitution;* W. W. Willoughby, *Principles of Constitutional Law of the United States*, Second Edition; Walter Wilson, *Forced Labor in the United States.*]

W. BROOKE GRAVES

War and Ordnance, The Board of, was authorized by the Continental Congress[qv], June 12, 1776, to assume administrative control of the army previously exercised by congressional resolutions. The Board personnel consisted of five members of Congress and a paid secretary. Included among its duties were control of all military supplies and munitions, supervision of the raising, equipping and despatching of troops, keeping a register of officers, recording accounts of the condition and disposition of troops, etc.

It was soon evident that congressional responsibilities interfered with Board membership duties. On Oct. 17, 1777, the Board was reconstituted to consist of three members, no one of whom was a member of Congress. Gen. Gates served for a short time as president. In this period the Board membership became involved in the notorious Conway Cabal[qv].

On Oct. 29, 1778, two members of Congress were added to the Board, any three members to constitute a quorum. On Feb. 7, 1781, a Department of War[qv] was authorized and Nov. 26, 1781, Gen. Benjamin Lincoln was appointed Secretary. The Board of War theoretically ceased to exist. Lincoln resigned, effective Nov. 29, 1783. No successor was immediately appointed, though Baron von Steuben is reported to have desired the position. Finally, Gen. Henry Knox was appointed, March 4, 1785.

During its existence Richard Peters, serving with few interruptions as Secretary, and Timothy Pickering carried the burden of the administrative duties.

[*Journals of the Continental Congress;* W. H. Carter, *The American Army.*]

THOMAS ROBSON HAY

War and the Constitution. The Convention of 1787[qv], with the disasters of the Revolution fresh in mind, conferred on the National Government ample "war powers," financial and military, and concentrated executive control in the President as commander in chief. The power "to raise and support armies," liberally interpreted, put the entire man power of the country and all its material resources at the command of the Government. The machinery created in 1787 proved its effectiveness in four foreign and one domestic struggle, but gave rise to serious issues involving conflict between the war powers[qv] and other sections of the Constitution—above all, the Bill of Rights[qv]. To what extent does military necessity justify interference with freedom of speech, of assembly, of the press[qqv], or suspension of the ordinary procedure of the courts? In the War of 1812 and the Mexican War there was widespread and bitter criticism of the Government with a minimum effort at suppression. The desperate nature of the Civil War created a more serious situation in which civil rights[qv] were frequently abused by the suspension of the writ of habeas corpus, arbitrary arrest[qqv], and suppression of newspapers, for which the Lincoln administration was denounced as "tyrannical." To the historian, however, it seems to have been remarkably tolerant, and after the conclusion of the war the Supreme Court (in *ex parte* Milligan[qv]) struck a powerful blow for the supremacy of the civil over the military arm of the Government in regions not actually involved in warlike operations. The World War was accompanied by restrictions unknown in the earlier contests and the Espionage Acts[qv] of 1917–18 created a series of new offenses against the Government. The modern concept of "the nation in arms," a realization of the vital bearing of industrial and agricultural production on military success and of the importance of psychological factors in the civilian population, created an entirely different situation. Harsh sentences were imposed on persons whose utterances were held to have come under statutory prohibitions on "inciting resistance," "promoting the cause of the enemy," "obstructing the sale of United States bonds," etc. In the words of Justice Holmes (Schenk v. U. S.[qv]), "the question in every case is whether the words used are used in such circumstances and are of such a nature as to create a clear and present danger that they will bring about the substantive evils that Congress has a right to prevent. It is a question of proximity and degree." Obviously, war involves a vast increase in the discretionary powers of executive officers, prosecutors and judges in interpreting "proximity and degree" and is entirely incompatible with ordinary constitutional guaranties of civil rights.

[Zechariah Chaffee, *Freedom of Speech;* A. C. McLaughlin, *Constitutional History of the United States;* J. G. Randall, *Constitutional Problems under Lincoln.*]

W. A. ROBINSON

War Bonnet Creek, Fight on (July 17, 1876). The Fifth Cavalry, Col. Wesley Merritt, at War Bonnet Creek (now Hat Creek at Montrose, Nebr.), intercepted a band of Cheyennes^qv^ fleeing from the Red Cloud Agency, Camp Robinson, and prevented them from joining Sitting Bull. William F. Cody ("Buffalo Bill") opened the fight by killing "Yellow Hand" (Hay-o-wei, or Yellow Hair). The Indians fled before a cavalry charge and were driven back to the reservation.

[Charles King, *Campaigning with Crook;* Chris Madsen Finds the Spot, in *Daily Oklahoman*, Nov. 4, 1934; Don Russell, The Duel on the War Bonnet, in *Journal of the American Military History Foundation*, Vol. I, No. 2.]

DON RUSSELL

War Claims Act, The Settlement of (1928), was an act of Congress for the windup and payoff of claims and awards of the nationals and the Government of the United States and nationals of Germany, arising out of the World War.

It created a pool or special German deposit fund in the Treasury of the United States composed of: (1) an appropriation by the Government of the United States of approximately $86,800,000 to satisfy the awards of the War Claims Arbiter as provided for in the Settlement of War Claims Act as compensation for German ships, etc., 50% of which appropriation was to be initially used toward the satisfaction of the awards made by the Mixed Claims Commission to American nationals; (2) 20% (approximately $33,300,000—the remaining 80% totaling about $133,000,000, was immediately returned to the former owners) of the proceeds of enemy property sequestered during the war, excluding amounts under $10,000 which had been theretofore released to the former owners; (3) the unallocated interest (approximately $21,000,000) accruing prior to 1924 on German enemy property sequestered; (4) moneys received from Germany under the Paris Agreement^qv^ of Jan. 14, 1925, on account of reparations^qv^ (deducting certain sums earmarked for the payment of occupation costs of the United States Army in the Rhineland) which amounted to approximately $32,200,000; (5) the proceeds of German bonds, approximately $21,200,000, deposited with the Treasury Department under the Debt Funding Agreement of June 23, 1930 (Germany is now in arrears in meeting these bonds to the amount of approximately $100,000,000. The total face value of the bonds so deposited is approximately $505,000,000 gold); and (6) certain earnings, profits and other miscellaneous items totaling approximately $10,800,000 arising out of alien property funds. The act also provided for an American arbiter to adjudicate the claims of German nationals, Austrian nationals and Hungarian nationals against the Government of the United States.

By 1939 all but approximately $35,900,000 (exclusive of accumulating interest and of the awards entered by the Commission, Oct. 30, 1939, in the sabotage claims involving the explosions at Black Tom, N. J., and at Kingsland, N. J.) of awards to nationals of the United States against Germany had been paid off; and all but approximately $43,400,000 (exclusive of accumulating interest) of awards of the War Claims Arbiter to German nationals had been paid off.

The Mixed Claims Commission under date of Oct. 30, 1939, handed down awards against Germany in the 153 sabotage claims in the total amount of approximately $31,400,000, stated as of Jan. 1, 1928. There is a balance in or available to the German Special Deposit Account sufficient to pay American nationals (on whose behalf these sabotage awards were made) amounts sufficient to place them on a parity with the other award holders as required by the Settlement of War Claims Act. Such payments, however, were not effected by the Secretary of the Treasury due to certain litigation that has been instituted for the purpose of upsetting such awards.

No payments have as yet been made on account of the awards of the Commission to the United States on its own behalf approximating, as of Jan. 1, 1928, $61,200,000.

The settlement of the financial obligations of Germany on account of the awards of the Mixed Claims Commission was complicated by the failure of Germany since 1934 to meet her obligations under the Debt Funding Agreement.

The awards of the Tripartite Commission on behalf of American nationals having claims against Austria and Hungary have been satisfied, as is likewise the case of the awards of the War Claims Arbiter against the United States in favor of Austrian and Hungarian nationals.

[Samuel Flagg Bemis, *A Diplomatic History of the United States.*]

SAMUEL FLAGG BEMIS
H. H. MARTIN

War Claims Agreement between Great Britain and the United States (1927). The United States had accumulated certain claims against Great Britain for spoliations on neutral commerce of American citizens during the period 1914–17. Although the United States did not altogether adopt British belligerent maritime practice during the World War^qv^, its association with the European allies against Germany weakened the moral, if not the technically legal, support of these claims. On the other hand, Great Britain had certain claims against the United States for supplies furnished during the period of common belligerency. By the War Claims Agreement of May 29, 1927—an executive agreement[qv], not a treaty—the United States agreed reciprocally not to claim damages or demand arbitration of damages to its nationals growing out of the "war measures" of Great Britain. Great Britain, on the other hand, relinquished certain of her claims. Each government retained its right to maintain in the future its own interpretation of the legality or illegality of the measures which had given rise to the claims.

[*State Department, Treaty Series, No. 756.*]

SAMUEL FLAGG BEMIS

War Debts (World War). The total indebtedness of foreign governments to the United States in January, 1937, amounted to almost 12.7 billions of dollars. The loans were made both during and after the World War[qv], the money loaned in turn being borrowed by the United States Government from the people of the United States. The accepted and generally applied principle upon the basis of which the loans were made was that they should be used only for the purpose of meeting payments due in the United States. Payments were for such purposes among others as munitions, foodstuffs, other supplies, exchange and cotton purchases and miscellaneous items.

Practically all of the original demand loans were funded by agreement following negotiations with the respective debtors. The Debt Funding Commission, created by act of Congress in February, 1922, prior to the expiration of its five-year term, entered into funding agreements with our several European debtors, the principal ones of which were Great Britain, France, Italy and Belgium. These funding agreements possessed certain common characteristics, namely, financial clauses which fixed the total amount of the funded indebtedness, the interest rate, and the annuities the debtor government would be required to pay; the distribution of these annuities over a period of sixty-two years; and the use of bonds payable to the United States by the debtor government.

In making these agreements the Commission operated upon the basis of the principle of capacity to pay, reducing in the aggregate, but with varying treatment of the different debtors, by about one half the sum represented by principal and interest of the original debts. The amount of the debt prior to funding compared with the present value of the settlements as made, extending over the sixty-two years, gives the amount of the reduction. Calculated upon a 4¼% basis, the United States relinquished claims varying from about 20% for Great Britain and several other countries to 53% for France and Belgium, 70% for Yugoslavia and 75% for Italy. The extent of reduction for all debtors combined was 43%.

By 1931 economic conditions resulted in the Hoover moratorium[qv] upon all intergovernmental debts for a period of one year. The President, in presenting this proposal, which was accepted by all the important creditor governments, had said: "The fabric of intergovernmental debts, supportable in normal times, weighs heavily in the midst of this depression." Payments, however, were not resumed at the close of the moratorium period. Defaults began with the payments due in December, 1932. Great Britain paid at this time but in doing so remarked that the payment was not to be regarded as a resumption of the annual payments contemplated by the existing agreement and that the amount being paid would be regarded as a capital sum of which it was proposed to take account in any final settlement. At the time of the June, 1933, payments $144,000,000 were due from the debtor governments. The Treasury actually received $11,374,000 of which $10,000,000 was paid by Great Britain and $1,000,000 by Italy. Similarly in December, 1933, of $153,000,000 payable on debt funding and moratorium agreements, the Treasury actually received slightly less than $9,000,000. From 1933 to 1938 there were no debt payments of consequence.

The explanation of this impasse was largely economic. Great Britain's position was typical. She argued that the exchange or transfer difficulty remained an obstacle; that if payments were resumed, steps would have to be taken to swing the balance of Anglo-American trade in her favor; that payment in gold would involve serious inroads upon gold reserves; that due to the fall in prices, the debt represented in goods not less than twice the amount that was borrowed; and that there was a connection between war debts and reparations[qv] which by implication was admitted when the United States proposed the moratorium. In 1933 there occurred discussions for several weeks in Washington between representatives of Great Britain and the United States. The British apparently emphasized the Balfour Note diplomacy of 1922, unacceptable to the United States. President F. D. Roosevelt, in his war-debt message to Congress of June 1, 1934, stated: "These discussions made clear the existing difficulties and the discussions were adjourned."

In this same message were restated certain basic principles of the debt relationships as viewed by the United States. "These debts were actual loans," not joint contributions to a common cause; "each government has been and is to be considered individually. . . . In no case should we deal with the debtor governments collectively"; "debt settlements made in each case take into consideration the capacity to pay of the individual debtor nations"; and "the indebtedness . . . to our government has no relation whatsoever to reparations payments made or owed to them." These principles have been shorn of much of their significance and potency. Certainly, whether the debts were actual loans has become in the course of time a matter of inconsequence. These principles constitute, contends one observer, "the dogmatic debris of the postwar muddle."

The economic arguments for debt revision have been numerous and important. A moderate view has been that a reasonable adjustment promised far greater material benefits to the American people than the direct income from payment in full. A more extreme view suggesting outright cancellation maintains that, "Economic analysis leads unmistakably to the conclusion that the restoration and maintenance of world prosperity will be rendered much easier if the disorganizing effects of the war-debt payments are eliminated once and for all."

Settlement of the war-debt problem awaits the future.

[H. G. Moulton and L. Pasvolsky, *War Debts and World Prosperity.*]

MARVEL M. STOCKWELL

"War Democrats," THE, represented the wing of the Democratic party in the North which supported President Lincoln and the Union cause during the Civil War. They were opposed by the regular Democrats and the "Peace Democrats." Stephen A. Douglas and Andrew Johnson were leading "War Democrats."

[Edward Stanwood, *A History of the Presidency from 1788 to 1897.*]

GLENN H. BENTON

War Department, THE, is the executive department which, under the direction of the Secretary of War, administers the military establishment of the United States. It is essentially civil in character and distinguishable from the army, although the chiefs of most of its offices are *pari passu* the chiefs of arms or services of the army.

During the Revolutionary War the military establishment was administered successively by an unstable system of congressional committees, a congressional Board of War and Ordnance[qv] (1776–77), a mainly noncongressional Board of War (1777–81), and a Secretary at War (1781–89) at the head of a small War Office. This office was in effect continued by the act of Aug. 7, 1789, establishing a Department of War under the Constitution. A permanent system of staff departments was not envisaged and provided for by Congress until 1816, for reasons of economy and since the heads of such departments were traditionally considered to belong to the staff of the commanding general in the field. When their offices became fixed at the seat of government they gradually came to be regarded as bureaus of the War Department. As perfected by Secretary Calhoun (1817–25) the system survived with but little change until the end of the 19th century, except for necessary expansion and supplementation during and after the Civil War.

Throughout its existence the Department has administered certain civil matters including Indian affairs (to 1849), pensions (to 1849), river and harbor improvements (since 1824), and reconstruction in the South (1865–72)[qqv].

The Spanish-American War demonstrated that the old system, with its almost independent staff departments, had become inadequate. In 1903, therefore, a General Staff Corps[qv] was created to co-ordinate the activities of all branches of the service under direction of a Chief of Staff definitely subordinate to the Secretary of War, and the office of Commanding General of the Army was abolished. The staff succeeded only in becoming a superbureau of amorphous character and indefinite function until after the World War, when it was reorganized (1922) upon the lines of the A. E. F.[qv] general staff, which had been adapted from European models.

The World War found the Department in the process of change after the National Defense Act of 1916[qv] and left it widely altered in a new direction. To cope with the immense problems of industrial mobilization an Assistant Secretary of War was appointed with wide powers over procurement of munitions of war and a number of civil co-ordinating agencies were established independent of the Department. Following the war the planning functions of these agencies were given to the Assistant Secretary. As a result, all of the fighting arms and civilian components, as well as the technical and supply services, have obtained representation in the Department.

[Raphael P. Thian, *Legislative History of the General Staff of the Army of the United States;* Lurton D. Ingersoll, *A History of the War Department of the United States;* Lloyd M. Short, *The Development of National Administrative Organization in the United States.*]

FREDERICK P. TODD

War Finance Corporation, The, was created by Congress, April 5, 1918, to aid in the prosecution of the World War^qv^. Its chief purpose was to facilitate the extension of credit to vital war industries, primarily by making loans to financial institutions. During the six months of its wartime existence, it advanced $71,387,222. In 1919 it gave substantial financial assistance to the Director General of Railroads and to railroad companies, and until 1920 it served as the chief agency through which the Treasury purchased government obligations. With the return of peace, amendments to the corporation's charter greatly expanded its activities. In 1919 it became interested in financing American exports, particularly agricultural products, and in 1921 it initiated a nation-wide system of loan agencies for the benefit of the agricultural and livestock industries. As a result of the passage of the Agricultural Credits Act in 1923, the active life of the corporation was terminated in 1924, after it had loaned $700,000,000. In many respects the corporation was the forerunner of the Federal Intermediate Credit Banks and the Reconstruction Finance Corporation^qqv^.

[John McDiarmid, *Government Corporations and Federal Funds;* Harold Archer Van Dorn, *Government-Owned Corporations.*]

CHARLES C. ABBOTT

"War Hawks" was the term applied to those members of the Twelfth Congress (1811–13) whose advocacy of war with Great Britain brought on the War of 1812^qv^. Their leaders, among whom were Clay and Johnson of Kentucky, Porter of western New York, Grundy of Tennessee and Calhoun of South Carolina, came chiefly from the West and South, the regions least affected by British interference with "free trade and sailors' rights." Their enthusiasm for war may be attributed partly to their youthful exuberance—they were nearly all young men; but as spokesmen for their sections they envisioned concrete advantages as the fruit of war. Men of the Northwest commonly held the British responsible for their troubles with the Indians (exemplified in the activities of Tecumseh and the bloody encounter at Tippecanoe^qv^, Nov. 7, 1811) and expected to end these difficulties by driving the British from Canada. Southerners planned to conquer Florida from Spain, Great Britain's ally. Thus the "war hawks" represented the expansionist aims of the frontier.

[J. W. Pratt, *Expansionists of 1812.*]

JULIUS W. PRATT

War Industries Board, The, was a wartime agency of 1917–18 which grew out of the efforts to co-ordinate American industry to war purposes. The Committee of National Defense set up in 1916 enjoyed only advisory powers and could not compel any governmental or private agency to accept its advice. There were five procurement agencies in the War Department^qv^ and they frequently competed for the same materials and manufacturing facilities. The lack of planning in the program of war industries led to a serious congestion in the New England area, since the procurement agencies gave most of their contracts to firms in that area and had new factories built there. Shortages of transportation, labor and material resulted in a serious slow-up of the war program in the winter of 1917–18.

The War Industries Board was formed on July 17, 1917, out of the General Munitions Board of the Committee of National Defense, but it was as powerless as the other agencies had been. When the extremely limited production of military equipment in the United States was discussed in Congress early in 1918, the aim of many leaders was the establishment of a munitions ministry on the English model. In order to forestall this thinly veiled censure of his administration, President Wilson, on March 4, 1918, appointed Bernard Baruch as Chairman of the War Industries Board with greatly augmented powers based on an executive order. This grant of authority enabled the War Industries Board to utilize all the agencies of the old Committee of National Defense, to mobilize industry, and to force the adoption of its orders by the various procurement agencies of the War Department. This board had control of all available resources and manufacturing facilities. It fixed prices, raised the volume of munitions^qv^ produced, and brought order out of industrial chaos. It was terminated by executive order on Jan. 1, 1919. (*See also* World War: Economic Mobilization for.)

[*Minutes of the War Industries Board; Final Report of the War Industries Board.*]

H. A. DeWEERD

War Labor Board. The National War Labor Board (1918–19) consisted of joint chairmen representing the public, chosen respectively by national associations of employers and employees, and five representatives of each of these two groups. The members of the Board were appointed by the Secretary of Labor. The creation of the Board was approved and affirmed by President Wilson in his proclamation of April 8, 1918, in which he summarized its powers, functions and duties. The function of the Board was to secure voluntary, peaceful arbitration^qv^

of industrial disputes. Because the Board was a nonstatutory body, its decisions were not enforceable at law; reliance for enforcement was placed principally upon the patriotic co-operation of employers and employees and on public opinion. However, because many of the large contracts for war supplies contained a clause requiring arbitration of disputes and adherence to awards, and because union recognition in a number of industries was established on the same grounds, an element of compulsion entered into the action of the Board.

Among the major principles governing the Board's adjustments were: abandonment of strikes and lockouts during the war, recognition of the right of collective bargaining, adjustment of disputes by conciliation and mediation, maintenance of maximum production, determination of wages and hours in accordance with prevailing local standards, and the recognition of the right to a living wage. By the middle of April, 1919, the number of cases docketed aggregated 1244, only 33 of which had not been disposed of.

[G. S. Watkins, *Labor Problems and Labor Administration in the United States during the World War.*]

GORDON S. WATKINS

War of 1812: Blockade of U. S. Seaboard. Although Congress declared that a state of war existed with Great Britain on June 18, 1812, the British government delayed giving orders for a blockade of the United States until November, when it instructed Admiral Warren to blockade rigorously Chesapeake and Delaware bays. The blockaded areas were gradually extended to include New York, Charleston, Port Royal, Savannah and the mouth of the Mississippi in the spring of 1813; Long Island Sound in November, 1813; and the entire eastern seaboard (including New England, previously exempt because of pro-British sentiment in that section), in May, 1814.

To enforce the blockade, the British Admiralty maintained off the American coast at least ten ships-of-the-line (necessitated by the superiority of the American 44-gun frigates over the British "thirty-eights") and a large number of frigates and sloops-of-war. So effective was their work that only rarely was a swift American vessel able to steal through, and maritime trade practically ceased. This was true of coastwise no less than of foreign trade; even the sounds and inland channels of the southern coast were penetrated by the ubiquitous blockading ships.

The effect was disastrous upon both private business and government revenues. Only from Georgia, by way of Spanish Florida, and from New England up to the summer of 1814, could American produce be exported. Exports from Virginia fell from $4,800,000 in 1811 to $17,581 in 1814. New York and Philadelphia suffered almost as heavily. The destruction of exports, ruinous to the farmer, forced the suspension of specie payments by all banks south of New England by the early fall of 1814. Imports, likewise, practically ceased, save through the favored New England ports, and import duties fell proportionately. Revenue from this source, over $13,000,000 in 1811, declined to less than $6,000,000 in 1814, and from the ports south of New England fell close to the zero mark. Economic ruin and governmental bankruptcy were averted only by the timely termination of the war (*see* Ghent, Treaty of).

[Henry Adams, *History of the United States;* A. T. Mahan, *Sea Power in Its Relations to the War of 1812.*]

JULIUS W. PRATT

War of 1812, The, was provoked by Great Britain's maritime policy in her war with Napoleon and by her overfriendly relations with the Indian tribes of the American Northwest; its advent was facilitated by the desire of the West and South to secure possession of Canada and Florida.

Neither England nor France, in their life-and-death struggle (1793–1801, 1803–15), paid much heed to the rights of neutrals[qv]. While Napoleon, through a series of decrees, issued at Berlin, Milan and elsewhere (*see* Napoleon's Decrees), sought to exclude neutral ships from all trade with Great Britain, British Orders in Council[qv] forbade neutral ships to trade with France or with French dependencies except after touching at English ports. Thus American ships conforming to the demands of one belligerent were subject to confiscation by the other. Meanwhile, Great Britain insisted upon the right of her naval officers to "impress"[qv] from American ships on the high seas deserters from the royal navy or other British subjects liable to naval service, and bona fide American citizens were frequently the victims of this practice.

The dispute over British practices became acute in 1806 and reached a climax in 1807, when the British frigate *Leopard* fired upon the U.S.S. *Chesapeake*[qv] and removed four sailors, three of them American citizens. Finding it impossible to adjust the disputes with the belligerents by negotiation, and unwilling to resort to war, Jefferson experimented with a policy of "peaceful coercion." At his request Congress passed the Embargo Act of 1807[qv], forbidding the departure from American ports of both American and foreign vessels, except those American ships engaged in the coastwise trade. When the Embargo proved more injurious to the United States than to its intended victims, France and England, it was repealed (March, 1809), and in its place a Nonintercourse Act[qv] merely forbade trade with the offending powers. This in turn gave way to a new measure (May, 1810), which reopened trade with all the world, but promised that if either England or France would revoke its obnoxious measures, nonintercourse would be revived against the other.

Napoleon, through a pretended revocation of the Berlin and Milan Decrees, inveigled President Madison into reinstituting nonintercourse against Great Britain (November, 1810), and when the British government, nevertheless, refused, until too late (June, 1812, when the Orders in Council were in fact repealed), to modify its policy toward the United States, Madison called Congress a month ahead of time and on Nov. 5, 1811, recommended that that body prepare the country for hostilities.

The Twelfth Congress, which received Madison's bellicose message, proved to be dominated by the "War Hawks"[qv]. This group of young men, chiefly from the West and South, resented the injuries inflicted on the country by Great Britain and wished to avenge them. In their eyes, British crimes were not confined to the high seas. While western agriculture, like that of other sections, suffered from the British blockade of France, the West had peculiar grievances which were not felt along the seaboard. On the northwestern frontier, in Ohio and in the territories of Indiana, Illinois and Michigan, the Indians, led by the enterprising Shawnee chief, Tecumseh, were showing a new disposition to unite in opposition to further encroachments upon their lands. It was no secret that British agents in Canada were sympathetic toward Tecumseh and his policy. It was known that the Indians received British arms and ammunition, and it was believed (somewhat unjustly) that the British were actively inciting the Indians to hostilities against American settlers. Even as Congress met, a western army under Gen. William Henry Harrison, governor of Indiana Territory, suffered severe losses in an attack by the Indians near the village of Tippecanoe[qv]. Almost with one voice, the Northwest held England responsible for this bloodshed and demanded the expulsion of the British from Canada as the only remedy for Indian troubles.

The northwestern demand for Canada was balanced by a southwestern and southern demand for the conquest of East and West Florida[qqv]. These Spanish provinces were coveted because of their strategic position, their navigable rivers draining American territory, and the harborage which they gave to hostile Indians and runaway slaves. The United States had long claimed a portion of West Florida as part of the Louisiana Purchase[qv], and had begun absorbing it piecemeal (*see* Baton Rouge, Seizure of, 1810). The fact that Spain was an ally of Great Britain offered a plausible excuse for seizing the remainder of both provinces in the event of war.

These frontier grievances and ambitions occupied a prominent place in the war debates in Congress. It is impossible to disregard them in estimating the causes of the war. On the whole, it seems safe to say that it required a combination of the maritime and the frontier grievances to bring about war with Great Britain; that neither set alone would have been sufficient. Certain it is that it was the hope of the "War Hawks," as one of them phrased it, "not only to add the Floridas to the South, but the Canadas to the North of this empire."

Unfortunately, the Congress which on June 18, 1812, approved war by an ominously close vote (19 to 13 in the Senate, 79 to 49 in the House) had spent seven months in debating without making adequate military, naval or financial preparation for war. The consequence of congressional trifling, of insufficient and ill-trained troops, of military incompetence in high command and of defective strategy was a series of military disasters which, had not England's hands been tied in Europe, might have spelled national calamity. The first year of war witnessed the surrender of Gen. Wm. Hull at Detroit[qv], the failure of Generals Van Rensselaer and Smyth on the Niagara River (*see* Niagara Campaigns) and of Dearborn at the foot of Lake Champlain[qv]. Eighteen-thirteen saw the recovery of Detroit and the defeat of the British at the Thames[qv] by Gen. Harrison, but closed with the complete failure of Gen. James Wilkinson's campaign against Montreal[qv], and with the capture of Fort Niagara[qv] and the burning of Buffalo by the British. By the summer of 1814, the competent hands of Generals Jacob Brown and Winfield Scott had imbued the northern army with excellent discipline and a fighting spirit, but British veterans were now present in such force that the Americans could hope for nothing more than to hold their own. The hard fighting at Chippewa, Lundy's Lane and Fort Erie[qqv] demonstrated the prowess of the United States army but failed to conquer any territory.

Meanwhile, a British army landed on the shores of Chesapeake Bay, burned Washington*qv*, but failed to take Baltimore*qv*. Another, advancing from Montreal, reached Plattsburg*qv*, on Lake Champlain, but retreated hastily when the accompanying fleet was destroyed (*see* Macdonough's Fleet on Lake Champlain). At New Orleans*qv* on Jan. 8, 1815 (two weeks after the signing of the peace treaty), Andrew Jackson inflicted upon a British army under Gen. Pakenham the most crushing military defeat of the war.

Meanwhile, the United States Navy had given a good account of itself. The victories on Lake Erie (September, 1813) and Lake Champlain (September, 1814)*qqv* gave the United States control of those important waterways. The numerous single-ship actions on the high seas proved the mettle of the navy, but failed to diminish the overwhelming superiority of the British fleet, which gradually tightened its blockade upon the American coast (*see* War of 1812, Blockade of U. S. Seaboard).

As an indirect result of an offer of mediation by the Czar of Russia, American and British peace commissioners met at Ghent in the summer of 1814. The Americans (Gallatin, J. Q. Adams, Clay, Bayard and Jonathan Russell) were in no position to ask for territory and soon found it necessary to drop even their demands for concessions in regard to neutral rights and impressments. The British commissioners, in their turn, abandoned their demands for boundary readjustments and for a permanent Indian barrier state*qv* in the Northwest and at length accepted the American ultimatum of peace on the basis of the *status quo ante bellum* as to territory. The British right to navigate the Mississippi and the American right to engage in inshore fishing on the coasts of British North America, both provided in the Definitive Treaty of Peace of 1783*qv*, were allowed to lapse. The fact was that both nations were war-weary, and the British government was advised by the Duke of Wellington that it could not hope for better terms without an expenditure of energy which it was unprepared to make.

The Treaty of Ghent*qv*, signed Dec. 24, 1814, though it gained not one of the ends for which the United States had gone to war, was joyously received in this country and unanimously ratified by the Senate. It nipped in the bud a rising sectional opposition to government policy which had appeared rather ominously in the Hartford Convention*qv*.

Although, measured by military achievement or by the terms of the treaty of peace, the war was a failure, it is not wholly correct so to regard it. Through it the West and South, although indirectly, achieved their principal objectives. Canada was not conquered, but the war shattered British prestige among the Indians, ended British interference in their affairs, and left them powerless to check the American advance. In the South, though efforts to seize Florida were blocked by northern opposition, Jackson's campaign against the Creek Indians*qv* (1813–14) opened for settlement an enormous area in Georgia and Alabama and started the train of events which ended with Spain's surrender of Florida by the Adams-Onís Treaty of 1819*qv*. The cessation of impressments and of interference with neutral trade, though due almost entirely to the termination of the war in Europe, doubtless contributed to the feeling that the war, though ill-fought, had not been wholly devoid of profit.

[Henry Adams, *History of the United States;* A. T. Mahan, *Sea Power in Its Relations to the War of 1812;* J. W. Pratt, *Expansionists of 1812.*]

JULIUS W. PRATT

War of 1812 in the West. When the War of 1812 was approaching, the Sioux*qv* of the Mississippi, having long had their trade with the English, were strongly favorable to the English cause. The Sioux of the Missouri having had American trade with St. Louis*qv* favored the Americans. The Yanktonais, ranging from Big Stone Lake to the Missouri, had been won to English support through the marriage of the sister of their chief to Robert Dixon, the British agent in the West. In 1811 Manuel Lisa was upon the upper Missouri (*see* St. Louis Missouri Fur Company) and discovering the likelihood of an alliance of the Yanktonais, Hidatsa and Mandans of North Dakota in opposition to the American interest returned to St. Louis to lay the matter before Capt. Clark, then western commissioner of Indian affairs. The latter sent Lisa back to the upper Missouri with about 100 men, directing him to build a post at a point where the semihostile Indians could be best controlled. Lisa reached a point just below the 46th parallel, where he built a post, strongly stockaded, which he had ready for occupation late in October, 1812. From the first, the English Indians were unfriendly and difficult, and this situation became more and more critical until about March 10, 1813, when the united enemy tribes fell upon the fort, burned it and killed 15 of Lisa's men, he getting away with the remnant of his men and some of his wares, and at Cedar Island, below the present Pierre, established a camp where he made an asylum for the old and destitute Sioux, taught them agriculture, purchased their furs and kept the Sioux of the Missouri friendly and comfortable. Due to the burning of the files of the Indian office in Washington by the British (*see* Washington Burned) in the summer of 1814, this phase of the war was unknown to historians until the 20th century. In 1918 Miss Stella Drumm of St. Louis unearthed the diary of John Luttig, Lisa's chief clerk, which revealed the activities of Clark and Lisa on the Missouri.

[Luttig's Diary, in Missouri Historical Society; South Dakota and the War of 1812, in *South Dakota Historical Collections*, Vol. XII.]

DOANE ROBINSON

War Powers of President. A common and oft-repeated subject of reproach to democratic forms of government, and one especially prevalent among dictators of the present day, is that of lack of efficiency or ability to meet a crisis when an emergency may arise. This is in large part true and the charge can only be met upon other political and social grounds. Yet the makers of the United States Constitution, knowingly or unknowingly, provided the means for meeting this difficulty at least in time of war, through the so-called war powers of the President. The bestowal of these powers is contained in the following provisions of the Constitution. "The President shall be Commander in Chief of the Army and Navy of the United States, and of the militia of the several States when called into the actual service of the United States . . ." (Article II, Section 2, Par. 1); and "he shall take care that the laws be faithfully executed" (Section 3). These provisions have been vastly extended by the acts of such Presidents as Abraham Lincoln and Woodrow Wilson, by statute law passed by Congress, and by various court decisions.

The powers of the President as Commander in Chief are those of military command in war time. He possesses all the powers allowed a military commander against the persons and property of enemies of the United States encountered within the field of military operations as recognized by the Law of Nations (E. S. Corwin). The Emancipation Proclamation[qv] of President Lincoln (Sept. 22, 1862) is an illustration of the use of such power. It was a war measure effective only for the duration of the war and within the field of military operations.

The provision which charges him with the duty of caring that the laws be faithfully executed may justify him in assuming any power that in his discretion he may think necessary in order to meet any emergency in time of war. This was even extended at the time of the depression of 1933–35 to justify the use of great powers by President F. D. Roosevelt upon the ground of emergency although not in a time of war. The President has the right to take any measures which are not forbidden by the Constitution or by statute law to protect the interests which are entrusted to the National Government under the terms of the Constitution.

[James Bryce, *American Commonwealth;* E. S. Corwin, *The Constitution and What It Means Today.*]

WILLIAM STARR MYERS

War Prizes. *See* Prizes.

War Trade Board, The, was created by President Wilson through an executive order dated Oct. 12, 1917. The order was issued under the authority of the Trading-with-the-Enemy Act[qv]. Control over both imports and exports was vested in the agency. The Board members were representatives of the Secretaries of State, the Treasury, Agriculture, and Commerce, and of the Food Administrator and the Chairman of the United States Shipping Board, with Vance McCormick as the chairman. By an executive order the duties and functions of the Board were transferred to the Department of State on July 1, 1919.

[L. E. Van Norman, *War-Time Control of Commerce;* W. F. Willoughby, *Government Organization in War-Time and After.*]

ERIK McKINLEY ERIKSSON

Ward Leader, The, organizes and manages the party machine in his district, which may be a ward, assembly district, or precinct. Since organization is essential to the winning of elections, this is a key post. The leader must be a master of organization, willing to devote unlimited time and energy to the smooth functioning of the party machine[qv]. Political experience, physical energy and financial backing are essential to success. Ward leaders are either elected in the primary or appointed by some party body. In the latter case, the committee is likely to be the leader's creation, selected in advance. He has to make his own position; no one gives it to him. He holds the job because he has strength to hold it—in the form of political support—and for no other reason.

[Robert C. Brooks, *Political Parties and Electoral Problems;* Edward M. Sait, *American Parties and Elections.*]

DONALD G. BISHOP

Ware v. Hylton (3 Dallas 199, 1797) determined a basic principle in our Federal system. The immediate question was whether a Virginia statute sequestrating debts owed to the

British or allowing their payment in depreciated currency took precedence over a treaty with Great Britain. Essentially at stake was the authority of the National Government to regulate foreign affairs^qv^. Debts in the millions of dollars were involved and partisan feeling ran high. The Court recognized the issue's "uncommon magnitude," but the five sitting Justices of the United States Supreme Court agreed that a national treaty stood above state law.

[Charles Warren, *The Supreme Court in United States History.*]

IRVING DILLIARD

Warehouse System and Acts. The development of a carefully and uniformly regulated warehouse system, involving the storage in public and private warehouses of such items as household goods, general merchandise, agricultural commodities and cold storage products, came about slowly in the United States. One of the most important of the earlier steps in this direction was taken in 1846 with the passage of "An Act to Establish a Warehousing System," whereby the Federal Government sought to encourage commerce by providing more adequate storage facilities for imports, and more generous terms with respect to the payment of customs duties prior to the placing of stored goods upon the market. This early form of public storage, which was eventually extended to private "bonded" warehouses, also came to include the depositing of liquors, tobacco and other taxable products pending their sale and payment of the tax.

The growth of commerce, the accumulation of goods, and the need for improved marketing facilities, have led to great expansion and specialization of the warehousing industry; also to the enactment of a large amount of Federal and state legislation relative to it. Particularly noteworthy in those respects have been the Hepburn Act^qv^ of 1906, designed to eliminate flagrant and long-standing abuses in transportation and storage; the Federal Warehousing Act of 1916, providing for Federal licensing and bonding of warehousemen in an effort to secure greater responsibility on their part than had been achieved under a system of state regulation and inspection; and the gradual adoption throughout the United States of a Uniform Warehouse Receipts Act, which is generally applicable to all warehouses.

[H. A. Haring, *Warehousing.*]

RAY W. IRWIN

Warren, Fort Francis E., at the northwest edge of Cheyenne, Wyo., was established in 1867 to protect the Union Pacific Railway^qv^ and lines of travel north and south against Indian attacks. The Fifth Cavalry operated from the fort against Cheyennes, Nez Percés and Sioux^qqv^ in the 1860's, 1870's and 1880's. It had the name of D. A. Russell, in honor of the Civil War general, until 1929 when the name was changed to honor Francis E. Warren, U. S. senator from Wyoming.

[Frances B. Beard, *Wyoming.*]

ALFRED LARSON

Warren's Trading Posts. Abel Warren established at least three trading posts on Red River. The first, located in 1836 but soon abandoned, was in northwest Fannin County, Texas; the second, established in 1837 (?) and maintained until 1848, was near the mouth of Walnut Creek, in the present Love County, Okla.; and the third, established in 1848, was maintained for a short while near the mouth of Cache Creek, in the present Cotton County, Okla. In the vicinity of the two locations last named Holland Coffee had maintained trading posts at an earlier date. Warren's trading operations with the prairie Indians of Texas and Oklahoma evidently attained considerable volume.

[R. W. Strickland, History of Fannin County, Texas, 1836-1843, in *Southwestern Historical Quarterly*, XXXIII.]

RUPERT N. RICHARDSON

Warriors Path, Great, was the war road between the northern and southern Indians, that is, between the Shawnee and Wyandot of the Ohio country and the Catawba and Cherokee of western North Carolina^qqv^. The road ran from opposite the mouth of Scioto River along the eastern portion of what is now Kentucky, past the Upper Blue Licks and the Red River branch of the Kentucky to the Cumberland Gap^qv^; thence it passed down Powell's Valley, crossed the New River and the north fork of the Holston. There it divided, the eastern end going on to the Catawba towns, the western across Nolichucky and the French Broad rivers to the heart of the Overhill Cherokee Indian towns.

The Great Warrior Path was mentioned in 1750 by Dr. Thomas Walker in his western explorations (*see* Loyal Land Company). It was plainly marked in Powell's Valley when Boone and Finley came out in 1769. Except at the Cumberland Gap it was avoided by explorers, because of danger from passing Indians.

It was shown on the map of Lewis Evans^qv^ in 1755; on that of Thomas Hutchins in 1778. On Filson's map^qv^ of Kentucky, 1784, there are two branches, one direct from the Scioto mouth, the other passing westward, crossing the Ohio at Cabin Creek and proceeding to the Mingo towns on a branch of the Scioto.

[Archibald Henderson, *Conquest of the Old Southwest.*]

LOUISE PHELPS KELLOGG

Wars: Cost of Major United States Wars. Estimates of war costs depend on what expenses are considered chargeable to war costs and there is no agreement on this matter. Appropriations made for the operation of the military and naval forces during a war may be counted as a direct war cost, yet smaller appropriations are required even during peace time and the difference between the two constitutes the real war cost. A large proportion of army and navy expenditures are used in feeding, clothing, lodging and otherwise caring for personnel, which would have to be done by some one even if no conflict were in progress but in this case most of the men could care for themselves and produce a surplus. Property damage is a proper charge against the cost of war but has not been satisfactorily estimated for wars of the United States. The economic value of the lives lost in war has been estimated by calculating the difference between what an average man would have produced and what he would have consumed during his lifetime, had he not been killed, and multiplying the amount obtained by the number of deaths. Disability costs have been calculated in a similar manner but figures obtained in both instances are inconclusive and will not be included in this study. Estimates have been made of the cost to the nation of the disruption of its economic system, because of war, involving the balancing of booms against depressions; in this case, also, the figures obtained are unsatisfactory. Interest on the public debt and pensions are sometimes counted as war costs but these fiscal transfers merely shift funds from the nation's taxpayers to its bondholders and veterans, have nothing to do with the conduct of wars, and should not be charged against war costs. Finally, comparative war cost figures are misleading because the purchasing power of the dollar varies between periods of war.

Estimates of what may be termed the direct costs of major United States wars appear below. The figure given for the cost of the Revolutionary War includes the amounts of the debts of Congress and the states after the war and the amount of currency issued during the war. The costs of the War of 1812, the Mexican War, the Spanish-American War and the World War are estimated by combining the military and naval expenditures directly related to each of these wars, no deduction being made for what the normal peace-time expenses would have been. The cost of the Civil War to the Union is given as stated in an official estimate, with the addition of the amount the northern states were reimbursed for their war expenditures. The estimate of the cost to the Confederacy is derived from a summary of the military appropriations by the Confederate Congress. Expenditures by states and individuals, disproportionately heavy in the South, cannot be estimated accurately, nor can the tremendous property damage and the several-billion-dollar loss of slave property. The war debts*qv* of foreign nations to the United States, which may never be paid, are not included in estimating the cost to the United States of the World War.

Estimates of the costs of the major wars are as follows:

Revolutionary War*qv*		$370,000,000
War of 1812*qv*		112,912,543
Mexican War*qv*		97,705,860
Civil War*qv*:		
Union	$4,486,198,881	
Confederacy	1,520,033,632	
Total		6,006,232,513
Spanish-American War*qv*		444,599,343
World War*qv*		20,737,493,826
Total		$27,768,944,085

GEORGE FREDERICK ASHWORTH

Wars: Loss of Life in Major United States Wars. Statistical data on loss of life, as well as on numbers engaged, in wars are often unreliable. This is particularly true of the earlier wars waged by the United States and of the statistics relating to the Confederate Army. One difficulty, in estimating numbers of men in armies, which must be done if loss of life figures are to appear in true perspective, is encountered in making a proper allowance for so-called multiple enlistments, which occurred when individuals re-enlisted on the expiration of terms of service and sometimes repeated this process again and again during a war. The inefficient and expensive policy, which allowed short enlistments, renders accurate estimates of numbers of men engaged in United States wars, prior to the World War, very difficult.

About 250,000 men served during the Revolutionary War. Multiple enlistments swell the total for the War of 1812 to 527,654 and it is reasonably certain that 111,347 fought in the Mexican War. Civil War statistics are complicated by multiple enlistments in the Union forces and loss of Confederate rolls and other records but estimates of 2,250,000 and 900,000 for the two armies, respectively, will be approximately correct. Two hundred eighty thousand five hundred sixty-four served during the Spanish-American War but only 45,590 of these left the United States. Four million men were enlisted during the World War; 2,086,000 went overseas and 1,390,000 engaged the enemy.

Estimates of losses of life given in the table below are based on the most authoritative sources available but many of them depend on incomplete returns. Those given for the Revolutionary War and the War of 1812 seem low and the numbers of deaths from disease and "other" causes are not known. All of the figures given for the Confederate Army are probably low, particularly that for disease losses. The Confederate deaths listed under "other" causes are accounted for by 5569 who died of wounds and 25,591 of disease in Union prisons. The total number of Confederate Army deaths given is probably more than 100,000 below the real number:

Cause of Death	*Battle*	*Disease*	*Other*	*Total Known Deaths*
Revolutionary War	4,044			4,044
War of 1812	1,877			1,877
Mexican War	1,721	11,155	361	13,237
Civil War: Union	110,070	224,586	24,872	359,528
Civil War: Confederacy	74,524	59,297	31,160	164,981
Civil War: Total Known Deaths	184,594	283,883	56,032	524,509
Spanish-American War	700	5,423	349	6,472
World War	50,510	62,670	6,776	119,956
Total Known Deaths	243,446	363,131	63,518	670,095

[Department of War, Adjutant General's Office; F. B. Heitman, *Historical Register and Dictionary of the United States Army;* T. L. Livermore, *Numbers and Losses in the Civil War in America, 1861-1865;* L. P. Ayres, *The War with Germany - A Statistical Summary.*]

GEORGE FREDERICK ASHWORTH

Wars and Campaigns, Indian. Classification of Indian hostilities into wars and campaigns must be largely arbitrary, and initial and terminal dates are not capable of exact definition. Prior to the Civil War, convenient grouping is not practicable but after that conflict Indian hostilities fall into three broad classifications, (1) Indian Wars of the Great Plains, including adjacent regions of the Rocky Mountains and Texas, (2) Indian Wars of the Southwest, in Arizona, New Mexico and adjacent regions, and (3) Indian Wars in the Northwest and adjacent regions.

In many instances given below, action was local but regular troops were involved and the engagements and campaigns were prosecuted under Federal authority. Reduced to chronology, the more important wars and campaigns are listed as follows:

1790–95, Northwestern Indian War (Ohio); 1811–13, Northwestern Indian War (Indiana); 1812, Florida or Seminole War; 1813, Peoria War (Illinois); 1813–14, Creek War (Georgia, Alabama, Mississippi, Tennessee); 1817–18, Florida or Seminole War (Florida and Georgia); 1823, Arickaree and Blackfeet War (Missouri River region and Dakota Territory); 1832, Black Hawk War; 1835–42, Florida or Seminole War (Georgia and Alabama); 1836–37, Creek War (Georgia and Alabama); 1836–37, Sabine or Southwestern Indian War (Louisiana); 1847–48, Cayuse War (Oregon); 1849–61, Campaigns against Navajos, Comanches, Cheyennes, Lipans and Kickapoos (Texas and New Mexico); 1850–53, Utah Indian War; 1851–52, California Indian War; 1851–56, Rogue River War against Yakimas, Klikitats, Klamaths and Salmon River tribes (Oregon and Washington); 1855–56, Campaign against the Sioux, Cheyennes and Arapahos; 1855–58, Florida or Seminole War; 1857, Campaign against Sioux (Minnesota and Iowa); 1858, Campaign against Northern Indians (Washington Territory); 1858, Campaign against Spokane, Cœur d'Alene and Paloos Indians (Washington Territory); 1858, Campaign against Navajos (New Mexico); 1858–59, Campaign against Wichitas (Indian Territory); 1861–90, Apache Wars, including campaigns against Victorio and Geronimo; 1862–67, Sioux War (Minnesota and Dakota); 1863–70, Campaigns against Cheyennes,

Arapahos, Kiowas and Comanches (Kansas, Colorado and Indian Territory); 1865–68, Northwestern Indian War (Oregon, Idaho, California and Nevada); 1867–81, Campaigns against Lipans, Kiowas, Kickapoos and Comanches; 1872–73, Modoc War (Oregon); 1874–75, Campaigns against Cheyennes, Arapahos, Kiowas, Comanches and Sioux (Kansas, Colorado, Texas, New Mexico and Indian Territory); 1874–79, Campaigns against the Sioux and the Cheyennes (Wyoming, Nebraska, Dakotas, Nevada, Montana, Indian Territory and Kansas); 1877, Nez Percé War (Utah); 1878, Bannock War: Bannocks, Piutes, Shoshones or Snakes (Idaho, Washington and Wyoming Territories); 1878, Campaign against Utes (Colorado); 1879, Campaign against Sheepeater Indians (Idaho); 1879–80, Campaigns against Utes (Colorado and Utah); 1890–91, Sioux Campaign (South Dakota); 1895, Campaign against Bannocks; 1898, Campaign against Chippewas (Leech Lake, Minnesota).

[Francis B. Heitman, *Historical Register and Dictionary of the United States Army;* C. K. Gardner, *Dictionary of the United States Army; Reports of the Secretary of War;* N. A. Strait, *Alphabetical List of Battles; Weekly Statistical Report No. 137, Office of the Chief of Staff,* War Department—April 10, 1920; *Chronological List of Actions with Indians from January 1, 1866, to January, 1891*—Office Memorandum, Adjutant General's Office, War Department, Washington, D. C.; *Record of Engagements with Hostile Indians within the Military Division of the Missouri,* Government Printing Office, Washington, D. C., 1882; G. F. Brimlow, *The Bannock Indian War of 1878;* J. C. Riddle, *Indian History of the Modoc War.*]

ROBERT S. THOMAS

Wars of the United States. Excluding those operations which are covered herein under the heading "Wars and Campaigns, Indian," the following would constitute a listing of the wars of the United States:

April 19, 1775–April 11, 1783, Revolutionary War; July 9, 1798–Sept. 30, 1800, War with France (Naval); June 10, 1801–June 4, 1805, War with Tripoli (Naval); June 18, 1812–Feb. 17, 1815, War of 1812; March 3, 1815–Aug. 9, 1815, War with Barbary pirates (Naval); April 24, 1846–May 30, 1848, Mexican War; April 15, 1861–Aug. 20, 1866, Civil War; Feb. 15, 1898–April 11, 1899, Spanish-American War; Feb. 4, 1899–July 4, 1902, Philippine Insurrection; May 29, 1900–Sept. 7, 1901, China Relief Expedition; 1902–12, Operations in the Philippines (including pacification of Moros, fighting on Island of Samar and on Island of Leyte); April 6, 1917–Aug. 25, 1921, World War (*see* Berlin, The Treaty of).

[Francis B. Heitman, *Historical Register and Dictionary of the United States Army;* C. K. Gardner, *Dictionary of the United States Army; Reports of the Secretary of War;* N. A. Strait, *Alphabetical List of Battles;* R. S. Ripley, *The War with Mexico; Weekly Statistical Report No. 137, Office of the Chief of Staff,* War Department—April 10, 1920; J. R. M. Taylor, *Philippine Insurrection against the United States;* M. F. Steele, *American Campaigns;* Justin Smith, *The War with Mexico; War of the Rebellion—Official Records of the Union and Confederate Armies;* Oliver L. Spaulding, *United States Army in War and Peace.*]

ROBERT S. THOMAS

Warships. The first warships used by the United States Navy[qv] in the Revolutionary War[qv] were merchant vessels purchased or chartered and equipped with guns. But on Dec. 13, 1775, Congress provided for the construction of thirteen frigates[qv], three-masted vessels mounting from twenty-eight to fifty guns. Eighteen such frigates were built or purchased during the war. One ship-of-the-line[qv], the *America,* was also built. Seventy-three war vessels of all descriptions were used by the Revolutionary Navy. After the war every remaining ship was sold, but by 1794 the depredations of the Barbary[qv] pirates on American merchantmen forced Congress to authorize the construction of six frigates, one of which was the famous *Constitution*[qv]. In 1798 when war threatened with France[qv] Congress authorized twelve ships of thirty-two guns, twelve of from twenty to twenty-four guns, and six not to exceed eighteen guns. In 1803 fifteen small gunboats[qv] were built, and in succeeding years, at President Jefferson's insistence, one hundred seventy-six more were built for coast and harbor defense. In the War of 1812[qv] these gunboats were practically useless. When this war broke out the navy was equipped with but eighteen seagoing vessels, seven of which were frigates. Yet with these frigates American seamen won a series of brilliant victories in single-ship actions. During the war four ships-of-the-line were authorized, of which three were completed, and in 1816 nine more such ships were authorized of which seven were completed.

But the navy had been so rapidly built up during the war that by 1817 it possessed one hundred eleven vessels, including ships-of-the-line, frigates, sloops, brigs, schooners and one steam frigate, the *Demologos*[qv], or *Fulton the First,* the first steam warship in the world. At the beginning of the Mexican War[qv] the number of ships had dropped to seventy-six, including nine steamers. In 1861, at the outbreak of the Civil War[qv], the navy possessed but ninety-one warships of all types, thirty-eight of which were steamers. The experiences of the Civil War proved conclusively the superiority of steam-driven ironclad warships[qv] over old-fashioned wooden sailing vessels, so that in 1865 of the six hundred eighty-one warships then in the navy, five hundred seventy-two were steamers, and of these steamers seventy-one were ironclad.

After the Civil War the navy was neglected. In 1881, of its one hundred forty vessels, twenty-five were tugs and but few were seaworthy. President Arthur, in 1881, demanded "A thorough rehabilitation of the Navy." Four steel cruisers, the first of the "white squadron"[qv], were authorized in 1883, and two cruisers and two gunboats in 1885. In 1890 Congress authorized the first American battleships, the *Indiana, Massachusetts* and *Oregon*. In 1905 the dreadnoughts[qv] *South Carolina* and *Michigan* were authorized, and fifteen others of this type were built prior to the World War. To combat the torpedo boat[qv] and to act as torpedo-carriers, destroyers, very fast sea-going vessels of about seven hundred tons, were designed. The first American destroyers were launched in 1909. On Jan. 1, 1938, the navy possessed in and out of commission and in process of building seventeen battleships, six aircraft carriers, eighteen heavy cruisers, nineteen light cruisers, two hundred forty-two destroyers and one hundred one submarines.

[G. F. Emmons, *The Navy of the United States from the Commencement, 1775 to 1853;* William Hovgaard, *Modern History of Warships;* G. R. Clark and others, *A Short History of the United States Navy.*]

LOUIS H. BOLANDER

Warwick, R. I. *See* Shawomet, R. I.

Warwick Commission, The (1643–49), was established by Parliament for control of colonial affairs after the outbreak of the Puritan Revolution in England. It was headed by the Earl of Warwick, who was also appointed Governor in Chief and Lord High Admiral of the colonies. Though endowed with extensive powers of appointment and administration, the commission interfered very little with the government of the colonies. It appeared willing to recognize a practical autonomy in New England under the Confederation (*see* United Colonies of New England) by refusing to become involved in boundary disputes and by an agreement not to receive appeals from New England malcontents, but was opposed to the domination of Massachusetts. Against that colony's theocratic tendencies the commission supported liberty of conscience and set a check to its aggressive expansion by granting Rhode Island a charter. Shortly after the establishment of the Commonwealth in England the powers granted to the commission were revoked.

[C. M. Andrews, *The Colonial Period in American History*, Vol. I.]

VIOLA F. BARNES

Warwick Patent. *See* Connecticut, The Old Patent of.

Washakie, Fort, near Lander, Wyo., was an army post (1869–1909) maintained for the protection of the Shoshone Indians on the Wind River reservation. The post was known as Camp Augur (1869), Camp Brown (1870) and after 1878 as Fort Washakie in honor of Washakie, Shoshone chief and great friend of the whites.

[Grace R. Hebard, *Washakie.*]

ALFRED LARSON

Washing Machines. The first American patent for washing machines was issued in 1797 and was followed by 330 others before 1860. These included family and laundry machines and apparatus for bleacheries, dye works and textile factories. Subsequent improvements were largely determined by the introduction of electric motors and larger use of rustless metal in place of wood. Today some sixty factories, principally in New York, Illinois and Ohio, make about 2,000,000 washing machines annually.

[James Leander Bishop, *A History of American Manufactures; U. S. Census of Manufactures.*]

VICTOR S. CLARK

Washington, D. C. Congress located the permanent seat of government of the United States on the Potomac River and accepted the cession of ten miles square from Maryland and Virginia (*see* District of Columbia). Over this territory the Constitution gave to Congress exclusive authority in order to prevent such indignities as the Continental Congress had suffered in the nine cities in which it successively assembled. Boundaries and the planning were left to President Washington, as was also the selection of three Commissioners to survey and mark the district and to provide buildings for Congress, the President and the public offices. The City of Washington in the Territory of Columbia was the name chosen by the Commissioners in consultation with Jefferson and Madison.

President Washington (1791) sent Andrew Ellicott (experienced in running state and international boundaries) to survey an area ten miles square, to include Georgetown in Maryland and Alexandria in Virginia, prospective centers of western commerce. He accepted the proffered services of Maj. Pierre Charles L'Enfant to design the city plan. L'Enfant, trained as an architect and engineer, came to America in 1777 as a French lieutenant. He suffered the privations of Valley Forge, was wounded, captured and exchanged at Savannah, and was commissioned major in the Continental Army. He established a reputation as an arbiter of taste, designed the insignia of the Order of the Cincinnati, and remodeled Federal Hall in New York (where Washington was inaugurated), reputed the finest building in the country.

During 1791 Ellicott and L'Enfant worked as companions. Ellicott was thirty-seven and L'Enfant the same age. Riding over the ground, Washington and L'Enfant selected commanding sites for the Capitol and the President's House; the two men consulted at Mount Vernon as the plans progressed. Putting aside Jefferson's sketch for a town one third the size of L'Enfant's, with a gridiron street plan, Washington readily responded to L'Enfant's enthusiasm for a city area as extensive as that of the Paris of their day, with public buildings connected by broad avenues arranged to create fine vistas, open spaces for landscape effects, and with canals and fountains to provide embellishments such as L'Enfant had been familiar with in the gardens LeNôtre had made at Versailles and Fontainebleau for Louis XIV. The plans for the extension of Paris were still only on paper (the Tuilleries Gardens a stone quarry and the Place d'Etoile an apple orchard) when L'Enfant drew his plan for that park connection between "the Federal House" and "the Presidential Palace" which (prolonged to the Potomac in the plan of 1901) forms the central composition of Washington.

L'Enfant regarded (with some reason) the plan as his personal property; his drawing (now in the Library of Congress) the President sent to Congress for information, and when L'Enfant refused to encourage speculation by yielding it to the Commissioners, Ellicott prepared for publication the L'Enfant plan with minor changes approved by Washington. With characteristic extravagance and disregard of private rights, L'Enfant proceeded to open streets beyond the financial ability of the Commissioners, whose funds came from the sale of the moiety of city lots divided with the proprietors. After a year of strenuous labors, L'Enfant's service was ended with the President's reluctant assent. Refusing what he regarded as inadequate payment and declining a professorship (in 1812) at West Point, L'Enfant, importunate and embittered, lived in poverty with compassionate friends until his death in 1825.

Inherent excellence caused the plan to persist in spite of many serious mutilations. Notably the Mall (the park between the Capitol and the President's House) was dismembered; railway tracks bisected it; axial relations, dear to both Washington and L'Enfant, were destroyed in the casual location of the Washington Monument[qv]. Like all other American cities during the 19th century the National Capital had a haphazard growth. Then came the Chicago World's Fair of 1893 to reveal the value of orderliness, convenience and beauty in planning cities.

In 1901 Sen. James McMillan secured Senate sanction for plans to develop the park system of the District of Columbia and for the location of future public buildings and monuments. For the task he selected the designers of the Chicago Fair, D. H. Burnham, C. F. McKim, Augustus Saint-Gaudens and F. L. Olmsted, Jr., recommended by the American Institute of Architects. After a visit to European capitals and a study of the sources of L'Enfant's inspiration (particularly in LeNôtre's gardens), the Senate Park Commission presented plans restoring the authority of L'Enfant's plan, curing mutilations of it and extending it to comprise the entire District of Columbia. The McMillan plan (officially so called) is the L'Enfant plan brought up to date; it has guided the development of Washington since 1902. Tardily, fittingly, on March 28, 1909, the remains of L'Enfant, recovered from a casual grave on the Diggs farm, were borne in honor to the Capitol and thence to Arlington National Cemetery, to find sepulture among his fellow soldiers of the Republic.

The rapid growth and diversification of government functions, beginning with the Spanish-American War (1898), caused an imperative demand for departmental buildings; also for the removal of the Supreme Court from the Capitol to a home of its own. On the initiative of President Coolidge, Congress in 1926 began a public-building program more extensive than ever before undertaken by any nation, and still in progress. Washington (now coextensive with the District of Columbia) has grown to a city of over half a million people within the seven miles square to which it was reduced by the retrocession of Virginia's portion in 1846. Naturally the political center of the country, government service (supplemented by the Smithsonian and Carnegie institutions[qqv]) has gathered a great body of scientists; the Library of Congress[qv] compares with leading libraries of the world both in size and richness; the National Gallery of Art has in the Mellon collection world masterpieces of sculpture and painting: all contributions to cultural life, wherein our capital has previously lagged. Park extensions now under way will cause the Potomac to flow through a continuous park for thirty miles from Great Falls to Mount Vernon. Washington never will be finished; it will continue to progress with the Republic.

[W. B. Bryan, *History of the District of Columbia;* Elisabeth S. Kite, *L'Enfant and Washington;* Gaillard

Hunt, ed., *The First Forty Years of Washington Society;* G. Hunter Bartlett, *Andrew and Joseph Ellicott;* Coast and Geodetic Survey reproductions of L'Enfant and Ellicott plans; Jonathan Elliot, *Historical Sketches of the Ten Miles Square;* W. V. Cox, *National Capital Centennial; Senate Report 166, 57th Congress, 1st Session, 1902;* The Capital of Our Country, *National Geographic Society*, 1933; *Century Magazine*, February and March, 1902; Development of the United States Capital, *House Document 35, 71st Congress, 1st Session, 1929; Reports of the National Commission of Fine Arts, 1910-37.*]

CHARLES MOORE

Washington, Fort (N. Y.), built during the early days of the Revolution, was located on the Hudson at the upper end of Manhattan Island, and is described as a "pentagonal bastioned earthwork, without a keep, having a feeble profile and scarcely any ditch, supported by batteries, redoubts and intrenched line." It mounted eighteen guns and was thought able to defend a territory within a radius of three miles. It was intended, with the co-operation of Fort Lee[qv] on the opposite bank of the Hudson, to guard the river and prevent the ascent of the British. On Nov. 16, 1776, the fort was surrendered to the British, with 2634 prisoners and 43 pieces of artillery.

[J. G. Wilson, *Memorial History of the City of New York.*]

A. C. FLICK

Washington, Fort (Ohio), was built in the fall of 1789 at Cincinnati, to protect the rapidly growing settlements in the Miami Purchase[qv]. Late in December, Gen. Harmar arrived with a garrison of about 300 men, and Fort Washington took the place of Fort Harmar[qv] as the most advanced American post on the north bank of the Ohio. Commanding the important trails northward up the Miami and the Little Miami valleys, it became the base for expeditions against the hostile Indians around the headwaters of the Wabash and the Maumee. The first important one, under Gen. Harmar[qv] in the fall of 1790, was directed against the Miami stronghold near Fort Wayne. A year later came the unfortunate expedition under Gov. St. Clair[qv] which was so badly defeated at Fort Recovery[qv]. More fortunate was the expedition under Gen. Wayne which, after a preliminary training in the neighborhood of Fort Washington, decisively defeated the Indians at the Battle of Fallen Timbers[qv], Aug. 20, 1794. After this, the importance of Fort Washington rapidly declined, and in 1804 it was abandoned. The fort had greatly aided the early development of Cincinnati[qv], as the source of a very considerable amount of trade, as well as a stronghold to protect the inhabitants.

[Charles T. Greve, *Centennial History of Cincinnati*, Vol. I; R. R. Jones, *Fort Washington at Cincinnati, Ohio.*]

BEVERLEY W. BOND, JR.

Washington, Naval Treaty of (1922), also known as the Five-Power Naval Treaty[qv], was one of a group of treaties signed at the Washington Conference on the Limitation of Armaments[qv]. The United States, Great Britain, France, Japan and Italy ratified the treaty, which was limited to ten years, but which, extended five years at the London Naval Conference of 1930[qv], finally expired on Dec. 31, 1936. Japan was unwilling to continue the treaty after that date. The treaty limited the tonnage of capital ships of war (battleships, aircraft carriers, heavy cruisers) according to this ratio: United States 5, Great Britain 5, Japan 3, France 1.7, Italy 1.7, subject to certain replacements; and limited fortifications by the respective powers in the region of the Pacific Ocean as follows:

"The United States, the British Empire and Japan agree that the *status quo* at the time of the signing of the present Treaty, with regard to fortifications and naval bases, shall be maintained in their respective territories and possessions specified hereunder:

"(1) The insular possessions which the United States now holds or may hereafter acquire in the Pacific Ocean, except (a) those adjacent to the coast of the United States, Alaska and the Panama Canal Zone, not including the Aleutian Islands, and (b) the Hawaiian Islands;

"(2) Hongkong and the insular possessions which the British Empire now holds or may hereafter acquire in the Pacific Ocean, east of the meridian of 110° east longitude, except (a) those adjacent to the coast of Canada, (b) the Commonwealth of Australia and its Territories, and (c) New Zealand;

"(3) The following insular territories and possessions of Japan in the Pacific Ocean, to wit: the Kurile Islands, the Bonin Islands, Amami-Oshima, the Loochoo Islands, Formosa and the Pescadores, and any insular territories or possessions in the Pacific Ocean which Japan may hereafter acquire.

"The maintenance of the *status quo* under the foregoing provisions implies that no new fortifications or naval bases shall be established in the territories and possessions specified; that no measures shall be taken to increase the existing naval facilities for the repair and maintenance of naval forces, and that no increase shall be made in the coast defenses of the territories and possessions above specified. This restriction, however, does not preclude such repair and replacement of worn-out weapons and equipment as is customary in naval and military establishments in time of peace."

[Samuel Flagg Bemis, *Diplomatic History of the United States;* A. Whitney Griswold, *Far Eastern Policy of the United States.*]

SAMUEL FLAGG BEMIS

Washington, Pa., as Tinigoocqua's Camp, or Catfish Camp, was an Indian site, located on an extension of Nemacolin's path. Sold in 1771, by the Hunter family to the Hoge family, it was surveyed and named Bassett Town, alias Dandridge. Resurveyed in 1784, it was named Washington, probably the fourth town so named. Thanks to its location on a favorite path, it became a noted way station of the westward movement*qv*.

[Earle R. Forrest, *History of Washington County, Pa.*]

ALFRED P. JAMES

Washington, State of, was, until 1844, inhabited largely by some 25,000 Indians: Chinooks, Flathead, Nez Percé, Cayuse and others. Probably the first white man to sight the Washington shore was the Spaniard Juan Perez, who in 1774 discovered the Nootka Sound and Mt. Olympus. In 1775 the Spaniard Bruno Heceta landed on Washington soil at 47½°, barely missing the discovery of the Columbia River*qv*.

English and Americans followed. In 1778 Capt. Cook sojourned at Nootka, recorded native words, which later became the Chinook jargon*qv*, and opened the Northwest fur trade*qv*. Spain's and England's controversy over Nootka*qv*, in 1790, ended in favor of the latter. In 1792 George Vancouver mapped Puget Sound, named Hood Canal, Mt. Ranier and Puget Sound. On May 11, 1792, Robert Gray sailed over the bar into the river which he named Columbia in honor of his ship, thus giving America her first claim to the Oregon country*qv*. This claim was strengthened when Lewis and Clark*qv* crossed the continent and reached the Pacific, November, 1805.

The British and Americans raced for the possession of "Oregon." David Thompson explored and mapped the Columbia Valley in 1810. In 1811 John Jacob Astor of the American Fur Company*qv* founded Astoria, which was taken over by the British in 1812, but restored in 1818. Spain and Russia surrendered their claims to this region in 1819 and 1824, respectively (*see* Adams-Onís Treaty). Between 1824–46 Dr. John McLoughlin of the Hudson's Bay Company*qv* ruled the Northwest firmly and wisely from Fort Vancouver, controlling the Indians and helping American settlers. In 1818 England and the United States agreed to hold the territory for ten years (*see* Convention of 1818), and in 1827, joint occupancy*qv* was extended indefinitely. Meanwhile, newly arrived American settlers organized a provisional government in Oregon in 1843, and the slogan of the Democratic party "Fifty-four forty or fight"*qv* added to the other factors influenced England in 1846 to accept the 49th parallel as her southern boundary (*see* Oregon Treaty of 1846).

Until 1853 "Washington" was part of the Oregon Territory. Encountering the difficulty of traversing the distance to the capital at Salem, the settlers north of the Columbia petitioned Congress to organize the Territory of Columbia. Supported by the Oregon Legislature, Congress created Washington Territory, March 2, 1853.

From 1853 to 1889 Washington as a territory developed many typically American institutions. Mining booms in the eastern section and in British Columbia in 1855–84 brought prosperity, population and Indian troubles (*see* Yakima Indian Wars). In 1854–55 Gov. Isaac Stevens entered into treaties with the Indians, but encroachments upon Indian lands led to rebellions which were not crushed by Federal troops until 1858, 1878. In 1885–86 labor agitators instigated mobs who expelled Chinese from many communities. Riots in Tacoma and Seattle were quelled by Federal troops when martial law was declared. In 1921 Washington passed an anti-alien land act, aiming at the Japanese.

When Oregon became a state in 1859 Washington acquired the eastern territory, including Idaho, parts of Montana and Wyoming. In 1863, when the Idaho Territory was created, Washington was given her present eastern boundary. From 1863 to 1889 the Washington legislature resisted schemes for detaching parts of the eastern section to be annexed to Oregon, or to form an Inland Empire Territory. From 1867 to 1889 Washington conducted a campaign for statehood. After defeating propositions to call constitutional conventions in 1869, 1871 and 1873, the people approved in 1876. A constitution was drafted in 1878, but despite numerous bills and memorials, it was not until Feb. 22, 1889, that Congress passed the enabling act and admitted Washington into the Union, Nov. 11, 1889.

Since 1889 Washington has prospered. In 1892 the Great Northern Railroad*qv* was completed. In 1897 the Klondike*qv* mining rush started. Seattle became the gateway to Alaska and the Orient. By 1935 Washington's population reached 1,500,000. In the production of lumber and fruit, Washington leads the country. Politically Washington has been Republican since the Civil War except during the campaigns of 1896, when it voted for the Fusion party; 1912, for the Progressive; and in 1916, 1932 and 1936 for the Democratic. Washington takes rank in social and liberal legislation: workmen's compensation law (1911); Mother's Pension Law (1913); woman suffrage (1910); Direct Primary (1907); the initiative, the referendum and the recall (1912).

[H. H. Bancroft, *History of Washington, Idaho and Montana*, and *History of the Northwest Coast;* George W. Fuller, *A History of the Pacific Northwest;* H. T. Lewis and S. I. Miller, *The Economic Resources of the Pacific Northwest;* Edmond S. Meany, *History of the State of Washington;* C. W. Smith, *Pacific Northwest Americana;* Clinton A. Snowden, *History of Washington.*]

J. W. ELLISON

Washington, The Treaty of, was concluded May 8, 1871, between the United States and Great Britain for the amicable settlement of the Alabama Claims[qv] and other differences between the two nations. Much of the groundwork for it had been discreetly laid by Secretary of State Hamilton Fish in 1869–70. During 1870 British reluctance to negotiate was removed by the Franco-Prussian War and the ensuing denunciation of the Black Sea agreement by Russia, which threatened European complications; by pressure from financial interests; and by the appointment of the conciliatory Lord Granville as Foreign Secretary. The reluctance of some American elements to negotiate was modified by difficulties with Spain; pressure from American bankers; and general realization that the hope of peaceable annexation of Canada was vain. When John Rose, recently a Canadian statesman and now a London financier, came to Washington in January, 1871, Fish and he readily made arrangements with the British minister, Sir Edward Thornton, for submission of the various disputes to a Joint High Commission. This had been Fish's desire since taking office. The British Commissioners (Earl de Grey and Ripon of the Gladstone Cabinet, Sir Stafford Northcote, Prof. Mountague Bernard of Oxford, Sir John MacDonald, Prime Minister of Canada, and Thornton) were soon at work in Washington with the American Commissioners (Fish, Rockwood Hoar, Robert C. Schenck, Justice Nelson of the Supreme Court and Sen. George H. Williams). The principal questions at issue were the Alabama Claims, the rights of American fishermen in Canadian waters, and the water-boundary between British Columbia and the State of Washington. The fisheries question was settled by agreement that a mixed commission should sit at Halifax and determine the relative value of certain reciprocal privileges granted each other by the two nations. The northwestern or San Juan boundary dispute was submitted to the German Emperor. Most important of all, the first eleven of the forty-three articles of the treaty provided that the Alabama Claims should be adjudicated at Geneva by five arbitrators, appointed respectively by the Presidents of the United States and Switzerland, and the rulers of Great Britain, Italy and Brazil.

The treaty was distinguished by two unprecedented features. One was the British confession of wrongdoing incorporated in the preamble, where the imperial commissioners expressed regret for the escape of the *Alabama*[qv] and other cruisers. The other was agreement upon three rules of international law[qv] for the guidance of the Geneva Tribunal in interpreting certain terms used in the treaty. The chief of these rules asserted that "due diligence" to maintain absolute neutrality "ought to be exercised by neutral governments" in exact proportion to the risks to which belligerents[qv] were exposed by breaches. The other two made explicit the impropriety of letting a vessel be constructed, equipped and armed under such circumstances as attended the building of the *Alabama;* and dealt with the use of neutral territory by belligerent vessels. The compact was defective in only one particular. It failed to touch on the so-called "indirect claims" of the United States for prolongation of the war by the cruisers, an evasion of a delicate question which almost wrecked the Geneva Arbitration. But the treaty remains a great landmark in the history of peaceful relations between Britain and America. Credit for it belongs chiefly to Fish, but in some degree also to Rose, Thornton and Lord Granville.

[Allan Nevins, *Hamilton Fish;* John Bassett Moore, *International Arbitrations;* Caleb Cushing, *The Treaty of Washington;* Bancroft Davis, *Mr. Fish and the Alabama Claims.*]

ALLAN NEVINS

Washington and Lee University, at Lexington, Va., grew out of the Scotch-Irish[qv] migration into the Valley of Virginia in the 18th century, and its early history was closely identified with that of Princeton College. Originally known as Augusta Academy, thought to have existed as early as 1749, it was called Liberty Hall Academy in 1776 and formally chartered under that name in 1782. After Washington's gift of his shares in the James River Company[qv] the name was changed to Washington Academy in 1798 and to Washington College in 1813. Robert E. Lee became president after the Civil War, and following his death the name was changed to Washington and Lee University in 1871.

[L. C. Helderman, *Washington—Patron of Learning.*]
L. C. HELDERMAN

Washington Benevolent Society, THE, was founded in New York in 1808 for the purpose of popularizing and strengthening the Federalist party[qv]. It spread into New England in the following three years and attained its greatest strength in that region, especially during the War of 1812. It performed the usual functions of such auxiliary party bodies, observing the anniversaries of Washington's birth and inauguration and endeavoring to inculcate sound principles in a rising generation exposed to the pernicious doctrines of Democracy. It also cared for needy brethren and was charged with corrupting elections by gifts or intimidation. It was discredited by disloyal criticism of the Madison administration and disappeared in the "Era of Good Feelings"[qv].

[W. A. Robinson, The Washington Benevolent Society in New England, in *Proceedings, Mass. Hist. Soc.*, 2nd Series, Vol. XLIX; H. H. Ballard, A Forgotten Fraternity, in *Coll. Berkshire Hist. and Scientific Society*, Vol. III.]
W. A. ROBINSON

Washington Burned (Aug. 24, 1814). The capture and burning of Washington, by British forces under the command of Maj. Gen. Robert Ross and Rear Admiral Sir George Cockburn was a major episode in the series of Atlantic seaboard operations authorized by Vice Admiral Sir Alexander Cochrane as a response to American depredations in Canada, and as a means of demoralizing the general Government of the United States (*see* War of 1812).

In executing a slowly formed plan to seize the National Capital, the seasoned British regulars quickly routed the raw, poorly organized and badly led militia opposing them at Bladensburg[qv], near Washington—although a detachment of American sailors and marines commanded by Commodore Joshua Barney displayed great bravery under assault. This engagement took place during the afternoon of August 24. That evening, without encountering further opposition, the invaders took possession of Washington, where the wildest confusion had prevailed during the afternoon and early evening as the progress and outcome of the fighting had become known, and as many of the city's inhabitants had fled with whatever valuables they could convey to safety.

That night a detachment of British troops, headed by Ross and Cockburn, began their work of destruction by burning the Capitol, the White House and the Treasury building. Temporarily interrupted by a terrific thunderstorm, they renewed their incendiary activities the following morning, and by noon had laid in ruins the buildings housing the Departments of State, of War, some private dwellings, two ropewalks, a tavern, several printing establishments including the office of the *National Intelligencer*[qv], and such naval structures and supplies as the Americans had not themselves destroyed. So sweeping was the havoc wrought by the invaders before their retirement from the ravaged city on the night of August 25 that even in England the extreme ruthlessness displayed by Ross and Cockburn found few defenders.

[H. Adams, *History of the United States during the Administrations of Jefferson and Madison;* J. B. McMaster, *History of the People of the United States;* G. R. Gleig, *Narrative of the Campaigns of the British Army at Washington, Baltimore and New Orleans;* Wm. M. Marine, *British Invasion of Maryland, 1812-1815.*]
RAY W. IRWIN

Washington Conference on the Limitation of Armaments, THE (1921–22), was called on Anglo-American initiative in November, 1921, for the purpose of adjusting the international problems of the Pacific Ocean and Eastern Asia in accordance with a schedule of limitation of naval armaments. The following nations participated: the United States, Great Britain and the Dominions, Japan, France, Italy, the Netherlands, Portugal, Belgium and China. Germany, ejected from the Far East by the results of the World War, and Russia, paralyzed by revolution, were not invited. The conference arrived at a peaceful adjustment of existing problems—notably in the Far East—by a network of treaties, principally multilateral, accompanied by a Sino-Japanese treaty (for the evacuation of Shantung) and an American-Japanese treaty (for regulation of Yap Island[qv]). A perpetual Nine-Power Treaty[qv] bound all the powers to the principle of the Open Door[qv] and the integrity of China and pledged the signatories not to take advantage of disturbed conditions in China to seek special concessions or favors for themselves. A ten-year (later extended to fifteen years) naval treaty (*see* Washington, Naval Treaty of) brought naval tonnage in capital ships of the five naval powers down to a ratio of 5 (United States)—5 (Great Britain)—3 (Japan)—1.7 (France)—1.7 (Italy), with limitation of island fortifications to the existing *status quo* in certain regions of the Pacific. A Four-Power[qv] (United States, Great Britain, France, Japan) consultation treaty in effect replaced the Anglo-Japanese Alliance; the Lansing-Ishii Agreement of 1917[qv] was abrogated as a result of the Nine-Power Treaty.

The result of the treaties was to leave Japan

as a preponderant naval and military power in the Far East in return for her pledges not to take advantage of conditions in China for further special privileges for herself. This was the fallacy of the settlement, to expect a power like Japan to hold to this pledge in the face of a national revival of China. In 1931 Japan, taking advantage of the economic prostration and political divisions of the Occident, brushed all treaty restrictions aside, began her conquest of China, and bolted the protesting but impotent League of Nations[qv]. The naval limitations treaty expired Dec. 31, 1936.

The Washington conference saved the peace for ten years in the Orient, and in the Occident for fifteen. It can be interpreted to have relieved the United States from the sole sponsorship of the doctrine of the Open Door and the integrity of China, an embarrassing legacy of American diplomacy stemming from the acquisition of the Philippines[qv].

[Samuel Flagg Bemis, *A Diplomatic History of the United States;* A. Whitney Griswold, *The Far Eastern Policy of the United States.*]

SAMUEL FLAGG BEMIS

Washington District. The settlers in the Tennessee country on the Watauga and Nolachucky rivers, when the Revolutionary War seemed almost a certainty, in the latter part of 1775 followed the examples of Virginia and North Carolina in the organization of a Committee of Safety[qv]. They assumed for their region the name of Washington District—the first territorial division in America to be named for Gen. Washington. Early in 1776 they constructed rude forts on the frontier toward the Overhill Cherokees, that tribe being then under British influence and a menace to Virginia as well as to themselves. The inhabitants sent a petition to the legislature of North Carolina praying to be received under the protection of that state. The document was signed by over 100 settlers in July, 1776. On Aug. 22, 1776, the petition was granted and the western folk were granted a county form of government and asked to send delegates to the succeeding provincial congress[qv]. Four delegates were elected and seated. A curious fact is that the district covered a part of the present area of North Carolina, west of the Blue Ridge. That state repented its generosity the following year and Washington County was established to succeed the District, its eastern boundary being then fixed at the Allegheny range. Thus Tennessee lost a large portion of "The Land of the Sky."

[*N. C. State Recs.*, X-XI.]

SAMUEL C. WILLIAMS

Washington Elm, THE, under which Washington took command of the American Army, July 3, 1775, on Cambridge Common, fell in 1924 despite all efforts at preservation. Its estimated age was 203 years. An inscribed circular granite marker was placed on the site in 1926.

[J. R. Simmons, *Historic Trees of Massachusetts.*]

FRANCES DORRANCE

Washington Monument, a towering marble shaft of great beauty, erected in Washington, D. C., to commemorate the Father of His Country, is focally located on the Mall between the Capitol and the Lincoln Memorial. Its completion in 1884, after many years of effort, represented a great engineering as well as an artistic achievement. Rising to a height of 555 feet, 5 inches, it was until recent years the highest masonry structure in the world. Elevators within the shaft carry hundreds of tourists daily to the 500-foot level from where views may be had over the capital city and near-by Virginia and Maryland. At night the shaft is illuminated. The movement to erect the memorial was led by the Washington National Monument Society, a private organization founded in 1833, which tried by various expedients to raise sufficient funds. Congress in 1848 granted the site, and the cornerstone was laid on July 4 the same year. Construction proceeded slowly until 1860, when the structure had reached 156 feet, and then stopped entirely with the Society's funds exhausted. Work was not resumed until 1876 when Congress appropriated funds. The capstone was set in place on Dec. 6, 1884.

[Frederick L. Harvey, *History of the Washington National Monument and Washington National Monument Society.*]

OLIVER W. HOLMES

Washington Peace Convention (1861). *See* Border Slave State Convention.

Washington's Eight Months Army. When the minutemen[qv] and militia besieged Boston[qv] after Concord Fight[qv], the Massachusetts civil authorities, seeing them beginning to disperse, began to enlist a new army with appointive officers under Artemas Ward. The province endeavored to enlist 13,600 men, asking the other New England provinces for enough men to make up 30,000. Many of the Massachusetts men were enlisted in camp; the remainder came from home, and by strenuous efforts an army was kept before Boston until twenty-five regiments were commissioned, the total less than 12,000 men. New Hampshire enlisted two regiments mostly in camp, and after Bunker Hill sent a third. The Rhode Island and Connecticut men, having left camp, were enlisted at home. Late in May Rhode Island sent three regiments, 1390 men, under Nathaniel Greene. Connecticut sent only two regiments and a few companies to the siege, under Joseph Spencer and Israel Putnam. At no time, however, did the total of the army exceed 20,000 men.

It was this army which fought Bunker Hill[qv] battle before Washington reached camp. Meanwhile, New England had been appealing to the Continental Congress[qv] for supplies, pay and a general. The Congress "adopted" the army, and on June 15 named Washington as commander in chief, with Ward, Charles Lee, Philip Schuyler and Israel Putnam as major generals, and eight brigadiers. Arriving in camp July 2, Washington took over the command. Under him the army blockaded Boston during the remainder of 1775, and detachments, on board ship, manned Washington's little navy.

The Connecticut enlistments expired December 10, the remainder on the 31st. In advance, Washington enlisted a new army chiefly from the old, keeping it on paper until January 1. Most of the Connecticut men went home in spite of appeals, there to enlist afresh. The remaining troops were held together until the last day of the year, when the new army was established.

[Lexington Alarm Lists, *Massachusetts Archives;* Proceedings of New England Provincial Congresses and Committees of Safety, most easily found in Force's *American Archives*, series 4, Vols. 1 and 2; H. P. Johnston, ed., *Record of Service of Connecticut Men in the War of the Revolution; New Hampshire State Papers*, Vol. 7, 14; *Rhode Island Historical Society's Collections*, Vol. 6; Allen French, *The First Year of the American Revolution*, Chaps. 5, 6, 7, appendices 2 to 7.]

ALLEN FRENCH

Washington's Farewell Address (Sept. 19, 1796) had for its main purpose the elimination of himself from the third presidential election. He had hoped to evade his second election and had roughed out a declination at that time; but political pressure and the critical state of our foreign relations forced a change of purpose. Reasons for the inclusion of other matters than a simple declination of candidacy are to be found in Washington's habit of mind and honest love of his country. The first part of the address gives his reasons for retiring; the second, and most important part, presents his reflections on the necessity of a strong union of the states and the principles upon which permanent domestic contentment could be maintained and foreign respect compelled; the third, and briefest part, justified his neutrality toward France and England (*see* Neutrality, Proclamation of), and merged that justification into the more important principles of the address, which flowered from his deeply rooted, personal experiences in managing a revolutionary army for eight years of disheartening war, and directing an untried form of republican government for eight years of difficult peace. The unselfish honesty of his hope that the address would be of some occasional good in moderating the fury of party spirit, of warning against foreign intrigue, and guarding against the impostures of pretended patriotism does not entirely conceal the deep wound inflicted on his sensibilities by the malignant and unscrupulous political enemies of his administration; but the address is, nevertheless, one of the world's remarkable documents. After one-hundred and fifty years it still remains a wholesome political guide to the people of the nation to whom it was addressed. It was never publicly read by Washington, and was first published in the Philadelphia *Daily American Advertiser*. The senseless controversy over authorship credit is now recognized as a mixture of egoistic pedantry and ignorant partisanship.

[Victor H. Paltsits, *Washington's Farewell Address.*]

JOHN C. FITZPATRICK

Washington's Mission to the French (1753). *See* LeBœuf, Fort, Washington's Mission to.

Washington's Western Lands. As advertised at various times both before and after the Revolution, George Washington owned about 45,000 acres of land west of the Allegheny Mountains. More than half of this acreage, including a tract of 10,990 acres on which he, in 1775, made a settlement, was in the Great Kanawha Valley. Four tracts along the Ohio River, one at Round Bottom a little south of the mouth of Grave Creek; another at Washington Bottom about ten miles below the mouth of the Little Kanawha River; another at present Ravenswood; and still another at near-by Millwood, aggregated 9744 acres. Three tracts in southwest Pennsylvania, including one of 234 acres, embracing the site of Fort Necessity[qv], aggregated 4695 acres. Washington owned also a tract of 5000 acres on Rough Creek, Kentucky, and one of 3051 acres on the Little Miami River near Cincinnati, Ohio. Ownership of still other tracts, some of them large, was not definite and determined.

Much has been said, both in America and abroad, about Washington's purposes in acquiring and holding large quantities of land in the Ohio Valley. Most of his acreage was for services in the French and Indian War[qv]. He acquired the remainder through purchases of claims of officers and soldiers for the same service. Whatever his motives as a young man may have been in acquiring these lands, as the "Father of his Country," Washington was much concerned in the uses to be made of the public domain[qv]. In 1785 he suggested to Richard Henry Lee, President of the Confederation Congress[qv], that it should have made a map of the western country with a view to reserving "all mines, minerals, and salt springs" for public uses. Following his death his western lands were inherited by his numerous heirs, who in time sold them to other persons, so that none are owned by the descendants of his heirs.

[R. B. Cook, *Washington's Western Lands;* C. H. Ambler, *George Washington and the West.*]

C. H. AMBLER

Washita, Sheridan's Operations on (1868–69). Early in August, 1868, Cheyenne, Comanche and Kiowa Indians[qqv] began raids which, within sixty days, resulted in the death or capture of 124 settlers in Kansas, Colorado and Texas. Gen. P. H. Sheridan was ordered to punish the Indians.

He at once garrisoned the abandoned post, Fort Cobb[qv], on the Washita River, Indian Territory, and ordered Gen. Alfred Sully to establish Camp Supply[qv] on Beaver Creek to the north. From the latter post, Gen. G. A. Custer marched late in November and destroyed the Cheyenne camp of Black Kettle on the Washita, November 27, killing 103 and capturing 51 Indians, with a loss of 35 officers and men killed or wounded.

Maj. A. W. Evans, December 25, defeated a Comanche-Kiowa band at Soldier Spring, south of the Wichita Mountains, later going to Fort Cobb where Custer maintained winter headquarters.

Sheridan himself established Fort Sill[qv], on Cache Creek, south of Fort Cobb, completing a line of posts in the Indian country. Under energetic military pressure, the hostile bands began to surrender, Custer securing the submission of many of the Cheyennes the following spring, while Gen. Eugene A. Carr pursued one group under Tall Bull, as far north as Summit Springs, Colo., where he crushed them, May 13, 1869.

[P. H. Sheridan, *Record of Engagements with Hostile Indians;* George A. Custer, *My Life on the Plains;* W. S. Nye, *Carbine and Lance.*]

PAUL I. WELLMAN

Washoe, The Rush to. *See* Comstock Lode.

***Wasp,* The** (sloop-of-war), commanded by Master-Commandant Jacob Jones, on Oct. 18, 1812, about 500 miles east of the Chesapeake Capes, captured the British brig *Frolic,* Capt. Thomas Whinyates, escorting a convoy of six vessels. During a furious action of forty-three minutes at close quarters, the Americans had five killed and five wounded and the British suffered ninety casualties. Both vessels were severely injured in spars and rigging, and the British ship-of-the-line *Poictiers,* appearing soon after the action, captured the *Wasp,* which was unable to flee, and took her to Bermuda.

Wasp, The Second (sloop-of-war), commanded by Master-Commandant Johnston Blakely, sailed from Portsmouth, N. H., on May 1, 1814. Capturing eight prizes on the voyage to her station off the English Channel, early on the morning of June 28 she fell in with the British brig *Reindeer,* Capt. William Manners. After two hours of skilful maneuvering for position, the *Wasp* secured the advantage and raked the *Reindeer,* repelled an attempt to board, and then boarded the enemy, who surrendered after an action of only nineteen minutes. The British lost twenty-five killed, including Capt. Manners, and forty-two wounded; the American loss was five killed and twenty-one wounded. In men and armament the *Wasp* had the advantage by about three to two.

After making six more prizes during a second cruise, on the evening of September 1, Blakely destroyed the British brig *Avon,* Capt. James Arbuthnot, after an engagement of forty-five minutes. The *Avon* lost nine killed and thirty-three wounded; the *Wasp,* two killed and one wounded. Sailing with dispatches for Savannah, the *Wasp* captured the *Atlanta* off the Madeiras and was last seen about 900 miles farther south. The fate of the little man-of-war is one of the mysteries of the sea.

[Theodore Roosevelt, *Naval War of 1812;* Alfred T. Mahan, *Sea Power in Its Relations to the War of 1812.*]

CHARLES LEE LEWIS

Watauga Settlement and Association. Into the Treaty of Fort Stanwix, 1768[qv], bordermen in Virginia and North Carolina willingly read permission to venture their fortunes in the farther West notwithstanding the claim of the Cherokees[qv] to the region. Following the collapse of the first phase of the Regulation in North Carolina a few of the Regulators[qv] moved to the Holston and Watauga; but William Bean of Pittsylvania County, Va., became in 1769 the first permanent settler in Tennessee, on the Watauga. Soon there gathered around him relatives and friends from that Virginia county. Another nucleus of settlers was farther up the

Watauga under James Robertson; and gradually the gap between the two was filled by immigrants. For protection against horse thieves and outlaws, they formed, in 1772, a government under written articles known as the Watauga Association. The Brown Settlement, begun in 1771 on the Nolachucky, later (1775) adhered to this government, which existed until Washington District[qv] was established. In 1772 the people of Watauga took a ten-year lease of all lands on that stream from the Cherokees. A court of five men, with legislative powers, was their governmental body. The laws of Virginia were taken as guide "so near as the situation of affairs would admit." Wataugans joined their brethren of the Holston Settlement[qv] in the campaign of 1774 against the Indians on the Ohio and fought in the battle of Point Pleasant[qv].

These two settlements in the Tennessee country were the seed-plot of the civilization of the Old Southwest. The founders, or their descendants, aided in establishing the Transylvania government[qv] in Kentucky. James Robertson led fellow settlers to the Cumberland[qv] where was established the nucleus of Middle Tennessee. They furnished the first governors of Tennessee, Kentucky, Missouri and Arkansas, and the first senators in Congress of Tennessee, Missouri, Indiana and Arkansas. At the breaking out of the Revolutionary War, these settlements "were the advance guard of civilization, on the farthest border yet pushed out into the western wilderness" (Thwaites); and during the war they swarmed into the farther West to have and to hold against Great Britain and the Indian allies of that power.

[S. C. Williams, *Dawn of Tennessee Valley and Tennessee History.*]

SAMUEL C. WILLIAMS

"Watchful Waiting" was a phrase coined to describe the policy pursued by President Wilson in dealing with revolutionary governments in Mexico from 1913 to 1917. While sympathizing with the efforts of Mexicans to improve their lot, he frequently became exasperated with the dilatory tactics of revolutionary leaders and resorted to "Watchful Waiting" for satisfactory results.

[S. F. Bemis, *Diplomatic History of the United States.*]

KENNETH POTTER

"Water Cure" was a form of torture brought into public notice during the Philippine Insurrection[qv]. A contemporary of that period, Gen. Frederick Funston, describes it: "The method was merely to throw a native on his back, hold his nose with one hand, and pour water down his throat from a canteen or other vessel. It occasioned nothing more than a few moments of strangling and never resulted fatally." Antiadministration newspapers of the period heaped unwarranted calumny on the army for the supposedly general use of this method of handling stubborn *insurrectos,* entirely neglecting to publicize the barbarous character of the warfare waged by the natives of the Philippine jungles.

[*The Outlook*, March 22 and April 26, 1902; *The Independent*, May 15, 1902; *Senate Documents No. 166 and 331, First Session, 57th Congress; Senate Document 213, Second Session, 57th Congress.*]

ROBERT S. THOMAS

Water Holes. In the arid sections of the West, water was a constant preoccupation of travelers, and the discovery of drinking places regulated in large measure the direction of the great trails as well as the settlements.

The Santa Fé Trail[qv] followed the Arkansas River to the mountains and turned south across the Raton Pass[qv], until Jedediah Smith discovered a path to reach the Cimarron River, which shortened the trail by many days. The California Trail, leaving the Oregon Trail[qv] at Soda Springs, Idaho, traversed the Nevada desert by sticking to the Humboldt River and taking advantage elsewhere of a series of small lakes and tanks. Similarly, the old Spanish Trail[qv], running west out of Santa Fé, went hundreds of miles out of its way to the northwest, in order to cross successively the Rio Grande, San Juan, Colorado, Green and other rivers, turning south in middle Utah along the line of the Sevier and Virgin rivers and crossing southern California by way of small water holes to the Mojave River, thence to Los Angeles.

The remarkable knowledge they possessed of every water hole, stream and spring in their habitat enabled the hostile Apaches[qv] to hold out for many years against superior white forces, and it was not until Gen. Nelson A. Miles established, in 1886, a policy of putting guards over all known watering places in Arizona that those Indians were brought to submission.

So valued were watering places that some of them, such as the Hueco Tanks in Texas, show primitive paintings and other indications that they were places of religious veneration.

[LeRoy R. Hafen and W. J. Ghent, *Broken Hand.*]

PAUL I. WELLMAN

Water Law in United States history was important only west of the ninety-eighth meridian of longitude, where irrigation[qv] was necessary for crops, and streams were necessary for watering livestock. The old English law which was applied in eastern United States giving the owner of the banks of a river or brook unrestricted use of the water passing through his property, was modified by necessity to the use of a "reasonable amount" of this water for the purpose of irrigation. If this had not been so the water would all have been appropriated by the dwellers in the upper reaches of a river, and those below would have been deprived. The breakdown of the common law[qv] regarding water usage in the western states is one of the most remarkable modifications of English law in American jurisprudence. The Indians and Spanish predecessors of American settlers had already recognized the need of distributing water rights.

[W. P. Webb, *Great Plains;* C. S. Kinney, *Law of Irrigation.*]

CARL L. CANNON

Water Mills. One of the first things to be provided in a pioneer community was the mill to grind grain for flour and meal. With the exception of a few windmills and horse treadmills, America depended entirely upon water for its machine power until the early 19th century. Water not only ground grain, but it made cider, sawed and planed lumber, turned lathes, operated the numerous small paper and textile mills which sprang up, ground plaster and cement rock, helped to make starch and gunpowder (the first DuPont mills were water-operated), did rolling and slitting of iron and whatever else was done with machinery. In early Virginia every plantation of consequence had its water mill. Most of the early mills had overshot wheels, some of them of enormous size, thirty feet and more in diameter. Turbines did not come in until later, save in the southern Appalachians, where there were (and still are some) tiny turbine mills of a primitive type found in the Shetland Islands and of unknown antiquity. Undershot wheels were mostly in the tide mills, some of which still exist along the Atlantic coast. Here an estuary was dammed, the water gate was closed at high tide, impounding the water, which was allowed to flow under the wheel at low tide and thereabouts. On Midwestern streams in pioneer days might be seen an occasional floating mill, like that devised by Belisarius when besieged in Rome by the Goths in 535; a hull containing the mill was moored or anchored in the stream and the wheel was turned by the passing current.

[Marion Rawson, *Little Old Mills.*]

ALVIN F. HARLOW

Water Power. In pioneer days a man dammed a small stream and located his water-driven grist or sawmill on it without asking for governmental permission or franchise. There are still many small water mills[qv] in the southern Appalachian region for which no public authority has ever been granted. But power rights even on small streams soon became a governmental concern in New England. There is a series of small factories along a steeply falling brook at Winsted, Conn., whose power rights date back to the incumbency of Sir Edmund Andros, Governor of New England, 1686–89. Nothing was done in the way of corporate development of larger streams with a view to the sale of power until the latter 18th century. The power of the Blackstone River at Pawtucket, R. I., was the first development of importance, this in 1790. In like manner the first utilization of the Great Falls of the Passaic, in New Jersey, in 1791, made a large industrial center of Paterson (*see* Useful Manufactures, The Society for Establishing). So also was Fall River given its start in 1813, and Lowell—where a city was created out of nothing—in 1822. In these early developments, a canal was built around the falls, and the water (or portions of it) passed successively over the wheels or through the turbines of mill after mill, each at a lower level than the preceding one. Other notable early power developments were those at Nashua, N. H. (1823), Cohoes, N. Y. (1826), Norwich, Conn. (1828), Augusta, Maine (1834), Manchester, N. H. (1835), Lawrence, Mass. (1845), Augusta, Ga. (1847), Holyoke, Mass. (1848), Lewiston, Maine (1849), Columbus, Ga. (1850), Rochester, N. Y. (1856), St. Anthony's Falls at Minneapolis (1857), Turner's Falls, Mass. (1866), Fox River, Wis. (1866), Bangor, Maine (1876). Many of the early transportation canals[qv] were able to sell power produced at their locks. In 1849, 721,000 horsepower was being supplied by water in the United States; by 1859 the figures had risen to 1,111,000. The first attempt to derive power from Niagara Falls[qv] by canal in 1853 was a failure. Another project was completed in 1861. In 1894 the first tunnel there for electric power[qv] was completed. The far Northwest began to tap its enormous power resources at Spokane, Wash., in 1887, and at Great Falls, Mont., in 1890. In 1891 the St. Marys River Ship Canal[qv] began producing power.

Water was of great aid to the early gold seekers in the West, in ground sluicing, hydraulic mining, and for power purposes in the development of quartz mines. After the invention of the incandescent electric light in 1879 (*see* Lamp, Incandescent), water first began to be envisioned as "white coal" for supplying city lighting; and the first central station for this purpose was installed at Appleton, Wis., in 1882. Then engineers realized that a fall of water which would turn only one mill wheel or turbine would, if utilized to turn generators, operate several mills. This brought about an enormous increase in power use, jumping from 8,076,000 horsepower in 1889 to 17,930,000 in 1899. Many of the noted old power systems, such as those at Paterson, Cohoes, Rochester, Turner's Falls and others, were now converted into hydroelectric plants. The improvement of transmission lines was a great factor. At first, power could not be sent more than 15 or 25 miles from the generator. When in 1900, with all conditions favorably prepared, a dynamo was turned 153 miles from the generator at Snoqualmie Falls, Wash., it was considered a marvelous performance. Within a few years this had become a commonplace. In the early years of the present century, water power development was enormous. In the southern Appalachians, private interests built numerous plants on the upper waters of the Tennessee and Cumberland river systems, and of those flowing south and east through Alabama, Georgia and the Carolinas. Larger rivers were harnessed. The 4278-foot dam across the Mississippi at Keokuk, Iowa, completed in 1913, was long considered one of the most remarkable low-head power projects in existence. Both there and at Cedar Rapids, Iowa, 100,000 horsepower was developed. By additional tunnels, Niagara's production finally reached 300,000 horsepower. The Muscle Shoals project[qv] was begun by the Government in 1916. In 1928 Government embarked in the public power business when Congress authorized the Hoover (later Boulder[qv]) Dam. President Franklin D. Roosevelt's administration, which came into office in 1933, launched a vast Federal power program, arousing much antagonism because of its competition with and in some cases actual elimination of private utilities. Among its nineteen major projects, costing variously from $1,559,000 up to $180,000,000 and producing, all told, 6,000,000 horsepower, were the several plants of the Tennessee Valley Authority, those at Bonneville and Grande Coulee on the Columbia River, Passamaquoddy Bay, Fort Peck, Mont., on the Missouri River[qqv], the Parker Dam on the Colorado River and the Shasta Dam on the Sacramento.

[*Scientific American*, 1851-1938.]

ALVIN F. HARLOW

Water Power Conservation. A systematic study of our water resources was begun by order of Congress by the United States Geological Survey[qv] in 1889. By acts of 1895 and 1902 the Government reserved from settlement certain watersheds, thinking, however, of water supply rather than power. All water power was originally owned by the states; but from time to time, the power of certain streams was handed over to private interests, which, by 1900, had acquired many of the most valuable watersheds and power sites. At the suggestion of Gifford Pinchot, President Theodore Roosevelt called a conference of governors, members of Congress and others at the White House, May 13–15, 1908, and there the movement for the conservation[qv] of our natural resources, including water power, had its beginning. An act was passed in 1910, authorizing the President to set aside public lands for water power or irrigation[qqv]. Most of the states also appointed water power conservation commissions of their own. The Federal Water Power Act of 1920 provided that no lease or grant of Federal water power should be made for more than fifty years, arranged for rentals and payment of excess profits to the Government, and stipulated that neighboring states or cities should have the first call on power sites.

[U. S. Chamber of Commerce, *National Aspects of Water Power Development;* American Institute of Electrical Engineers, *Proceedings*, Vol. 29, p. 1335.]

ALVIN F. HARLOW

Water Supply for Cities. In America as in Europe the development of large cities has greatly complicated the problem of obtaining an ample and clean supply of water. Our growing cities have demanded quantities of water which have taxed the ingenuity of engineers. To this demand must be added the necessity of obtaining water satisfactory to medical officers. In the early days water was drawn from a well upon the property of the individual. Soon, however, cities grew sufficiently large to require water from purer sources. Springs in the hills were sometimes tapped and the water brought into town through wooden pipes. In 1652 Boston developed a water supply system for the city. Other towns followed her example. In 1800 the Manhattan Bank Company, the first large water supply company of New York City, delivered water to 1400 homes. By 1830 New York City had set up a public well which piped water through seven miles of mains. In the first systems the water was carried through wooden pipes; indeed as late as 1909, Denver had 100 miles of such pipes. Philadelphia introduced cast-iron pipes and these and pipes of other composition ultimately replaced those of wood.

The growing demands of the cities required larger supplies than wells and springs could furnish. In 1801 Philadelphia began pumping water from the Schuylkill River. New York's problem was more serious; by 1830 the increased population required more water, while epidemics[qv] made the people suspicious of the city's supply. To solve its difficulties the first Croton Dam (1842) was built and water was piped forty miles and, after crossing the Harlem River on a bridge, stored in the artificial reservoir at what is now 42nd Street and Fifth Avenue. Boston followed suit by piping water from Lake Cochituate. Subsequently other cities chose far-distant sources of pure water, Los Angeles today going 235 miles from the city. New York has constantly sought new supplies. In 1927 the city was using 867,000,000 gallons of water daily. Increasing demands have led to further construction in the Delaware and Hudson valleys ultimately to furnish 750,000,000 additional gallons. Again, on the Pacific Coast, San Francisco has built the highest dam to store water, the O'Shaughanessy Dam.

While these cities have built up large reservoirs and piped their water by gravitation, others have relied upon wells, rivers or lakes. Great Lakes cities pump or tunnel their water from the lakes, Chicago, for instance, tunneling several miles beyond the shore line to avoid sewage. Cities relying upon rivers have been forced to develop methods of purifying water. Sand filters have become common since Poughkeepsie introduced them some sixty years ago. Other cities such as St. Louis store the water in large storage tanks while the mud is precipitated out and the bacteria exposed to the sun. Whatever the methods, most cities supply their own water. If the system is large, it is invariably a civic project.

However efficient the general system of water supply may be, emergencies do occur. In 1911 ice obstructed the intake pipes of the St. Louis system. After heroic efforts and a fortuitous warm spell, operation was resumed just as the 400,000,000 gallon reserve was exhausted. Other cities have made provision for similar contingencies. The O'Shaughanessy Dam serves this purpose for San Francisco. The Kensico Reservoir in New York has a 30,000,000,000 gallon reserve, enough to last New York City for several weeks. These figures dramatically demonstrate the changes which have affected our cities. In 1800 the Manhattan Bank Company distributed water to 1400 houses; by 1938 billions of gallons of water would serve the same city only a few weeks.

[Hope Holway, *The Story of Water Supply;* J. J. Cosgrove, *History of Sanitation.*] HENRY BURNELL SHAFER

Waterways, Inland. Inland water transportation was very important to the early settlers as the rivers furnished the best means of transportation. There were no important inland settlements away from the rivers, as nothing but a self-sufficing economy could exist. As a result, the rich resources located away from their banks were not utilized.

Prior to the Revolution, intercolonial commerce was very small. The British government had discouraged this trade as it desired each colony to trade directly with the mother country. Except in densely populated areas, roads[qv] were few and poor. As a result, the short streams flowing into the Atlantic were of vital importance. The first settlers to migrate westward, about 1720, settled in the Appalachian Mountain valleys in Pennsylvania where the Susquehanna River cut through the mountain ranges.

It was not until the end of the Revolution that the settlement of the West began and not until the Constitution was accepted and a strong National Government created, that it reached large proportions. By 1800 the frontier had expanded so rapidly that its population stretched along both banks of the Ohio and parts of the Mississippi, Tennessee and Cumberland rivers[qqv]. This advance of the frontier[qv] was contrary to Washington's advice, as he wanted it to proceed in an orderly manner. However, it proceeded along the lines of most attraction and least resistance.

From a national standpoint, the early history of our inland transportation was concerned largely with plans to break through the Appalachian Mountain ranges. Sectionalism was rampant and commercial intercourse between the East and West had to be established. However, the mountain wall proved to be a formidable barrier for several decades. During this period, the frontiersmen found the route down the Ohio and Mississippi to New Orleans their best avenue of transportation for their surplus production. These river systems accounted for the westward spread of the population, but they served to isolate still further the two sections of the country (*see* Western Separatism).

But this route was not without its handicaps. River travel was dangerous, difficult and hazardous. Until the invention of the steamboat[qv] in 1807, it was mostly a one-way route, as man power only could bring boats up against the current (*see* Keelboats). Spain controlled the mouth of the Mississippi River and for several years it refused the Americans official permission to use New Orleans as a place of deposit[qv], largely because of the frontier disputes in Florida. In 1795, however, the Federal Government obtained a treaty which allowed the use of this port (*see* Pinckney's Treaty), but this permission was withdrawn again in 1802 when Spain secretly ceded the Louisiana territory to France (*see* San Ildefonso, Treaty of). As this treaty did not designate another place of deposit as required, the United States realized that its westward expansion was seriously threatened. Jefferson suggested an alliance with Great Britain to fight France whenever war should break out between the two countries. However, Napoleon's ill-fated expedition to crush a revolt in Santo Domingo caused him to drop his project of a western empire and in 1803 he sold the entire territory to the United States, thus creating a free outlet for western commerce (*see* Louisiana Purchase).

The War of 1812[qv] emphasized the weakness of river transportation and the lack of good roads for troop transportation. This factor combined with a greater desire to settle in the West created a strong demand for improved inland water transportation. Many rivers and lakes throughout the United States were canalized and a few artificial waterways were constructed (*see* Canals). The longest were built by New York, Pennsylvania and Maryland, and of these the Erie Canal[qv] exerted the strongest influence in reducing transportation costs, facilitating commercial intercourse between the East and West, and relieving somewhat the ever-present problem of sectionalism. By 1840 the active period of canal construction was concluded as the supremacy of the railroad[qv] was recognized. By this time over $100,000,000 had been spent to create about 3300 miles of improved waterways and practically all of it was lost as the railroad net spread over the country.

It was not until the advent of the 20th century that interest in these waterways was revived. Its revival then was due to the desire to conserve natural resources[qv], control floods[qv], create a more adequate national transportation system, set up a competitor to railroads and secure a cheaper form of transportation. While local governments and private capital financed most of the early projects, the Federal Government is now chiefly responsible for their construction. Between 1824 and 1906 the latter spent less than $184,000,000 on inland waterways, but since 1906 about $750,000,000 has been expended, mostly on the Mississippi River system.

Traffic on the nation's inland waterways has been increased. In 1920 over 125,000,000 tons of freight, not including that carried on the Great Lakes, were transported. In 1936 this traffic, adjusted also to eliminate all known duplications, has increased to a new peak of 276,000,000 tons, having an estimated value of almost $4,700,000,000.

[*Economic Survey of Inland Water Transportation in the United States*, Bureau of Railway Economics; E. R. Johnson and collaborators, *History of Domestic and Foreign Commerce of the United States;* B. H. Meyer, *History of Transportation in the United States before 1860; Inland Waterways Commission, Report of.*] HOBART S. PERRY

Waterways Treaty, THE, was negotiated by Elihu Root and James Bryce, and signed at Washington on Jan. 11, 1909. Its principal purpose was to make provision for the International Joint Commission[qv]. One of its articles limits the diversion of water on each side of Niagara Falls; and another provides for equal and similar rights in the use of boundary waters, and sets up an order of precedence in their use: domestic and sanitary purposes, navigation, power and irrigation. Navigation of Lake Michigan and of all canals connecting boundary waters is guaranteed to Canada and the United States.

[J. M. Callahan, *American Foreign Policy in Canadian Relations; Papers Relating to the Work of the International Joint Commission.*] LAWRENCE J. BURPEE

Watling's Island, Columbus' landfall, is a small island eighteen miles long, located in the Bahamas, in the British West Indies, lying in 24° 06′ N. Lat. and 74° 06′ W. Long., and being 220 miles northeast of Cuba. On Oct. 12 (o. s.), 1492, Columbus landed at an island, which the natives called Guanahani, and which he renamed San Salvador (Holy Saviour). The exact location of his landfall has been a matter of controversy and several islands among the Bahamas have been assigned that honor, but most modern historians maintain that Watling's Island, with its large lagoon near the center, conforms to the description which Columbus gave of San Salvador.

[C. R. Markham, *The Life of Christopher Columbus;* J. B. Thacher, *Christopher Columbus.*]

HUGH T. LEFLER

Wauhatchie, Battle of (Oct. 28–29, 1863), was fought at the foot of Lookout Mountain during Grant's advance on Chattanooga[qv]. A portion of Hooker's Federal division under Gen. John W. Geary was attacked at night by a Confederate force under Col. John Bratton, and a hotly contested action of two hours or more took place in the darkness. Hooker ordered Howard's corps, which was three miles away, to reinforce Geary. Howard, groping his way to the field, came near enveloping Bratton, who hastily withdrew. This action saved the supply line from Nashville for the Federal Army. The Union loss was 420, the Confederate, 356.

[*Battles and Leaders of the Civil War.*]

ALVIN F. HARLOW

Wawayanda Patent, The, was granted March 5, 1703, to John Bridges and eleven associates, by Lord Cornbury and confirmed by Queen Anne. Located in Orange County, N. Y., it consisted of 150,000 acres and was bounded on the east by the Highlands of the Hudson, on the north by the division line between Orange and Ulster counties, and on the south by the division line between New York and New Jersey. It was the occasion for a number of disputes and was unoccupied until 1712.

[R. Headley, *History of Orange County.*]

A. C. FLICK

Wax Portraits. The first American wax modeler, Patience Wright, made portraits of Washington and Franklin. Later, just after the Revolution, itinerant modelers traveled the northern Atlantic coast. Johan Christian Rauschner and George M. Miller made many miniatures in varicolored wax, often jeweled, which show the more prominent local worthies and their wives. Daniel Bowen copied Patience Wright's Washington moderately well. Robert Ball Hughes (Boston) modeled delicately in white wax. Giuseppi Volaperta made reliefs of three Presidents in red wax. Reuben Moulthorpe (Connecticut) moulded heads in the round, and made wax works.

[E. S. Bolton, *Wax Portraits and Silhouettes,* and *American Wax Portraits.*]

ETHEL STANWOOD BOLTON

Waxhaws is a section of South Carolina on the eastern side of the Catawba River on and near Waxhaw Creek and extending into North Carolina. Near the border line, probably in South Carolina, was born Andrew Jackson, March 15, 1767. In the southern part of the Waxhaw Settlement was the site of the Revolutionary battle of Hanging Rock[qv]. (*See also* Waxhaws, Battle of.)

[Marquis James, *Life of Andrew Jackson.*]

JAMES ELLIOTT WALMSLEY

Waxhaws, Battle of (May 29, 1780). At the time of the capture of Charleston[qv] by the British, May 12, 1780, Col. Buford, with 380 Virginia troops, was marching to its assistance; but hearing of its fall, he retreated rapidly northward. Lord Cornwallis sent Tarleton with nearly 300 cavalry in pursuit of him. Tarleton overtook the Americans at the Waxhaws, near the North Carolina line. He first sent an officer ahead to demand capitulation. This Buford refused. But when his wearied men on foot were attacked by cavalry, most of them threw down their arms in offer of surrender. Little quarter was given them, however; 113 were slain outright, 150 were so badly maimed that they could not be moved, and only 53 prisoners were carried off by the British. Col. Buford and some of his mounted men escaped. The British loss was only 20. "Tarleton's quarter" thereupon became a common expression for butchery.

[George Bancroft, *History of the United States;* Sydney George Fisher, *The Struggle for American Independence.*]

ALVIN F. HARLOW

Wayne, Fort, built by Gen. Wayne at the junction of the St. Joseph and St. Marys, commanding the strategic Maumee-Wabash portage, was named by Col. John F. Hamtramck, its commandant, at its dedication, Oct. 22, 1794. The place had been an important Indian trading center and French and English forts (to 1763) had once occupied the site. The American fort, moved to a new location in 1800, was the scene of important Indian treaties (1803, 1809[qv]) negotiated by Gov. William Henry Harrison of Indiana Territory, and was a center for distributing annuities and supplies. In August, 1812, Indians under British influence besieged the garrison of seventy or eighty men but Harrison relieved the fort Sept. 12. The loss of Forts Dearborn and Detroit[qqv] made the retention of Fort Wayne important to American defense of the Northwest. It was abandoned as a military post, April 19, 1819.

[Bert J. Griswold, ed., Fort Wayne, Gateway of the West, 1802-13, in *Indiana Historical Collections,* Vol. XV.]

EUGENE H. ROSEBOOM

Wayne, Fort, Treaty of (Sept. 30, 1809), was one of the most important treaties made by the United States with the Indians. Concluded by William Henry Harrison, then governor of Indiana Territory, with the Delaware, the Potawatomie, the Miami[qqv] and the Eel River tribes, the treaty ceded to the United States three tracts of land containing over two and a half million acres on the upper Wabash River. Ancillary treaties confirming the Fort Wayne purchase were made with the Wea and the Kickapoo[qv] tribes on Oct. 26 and Dec. 9 (1809), respectively.

The Fort Wayne Treaty aroused bitter opposition among the Indians. Tecumseh[qv] (who, with his brother, the Prophet, had since 1807 been organizing a confederation of the Indians of the Old Northwest) denounced it violently. He denied the validity of the purchase, asserting that the Indian chiefs had no right to alienate land because all the Indian tribes owned the land in common. He openly declared his intention of uniting the Indians in order to check the encroachments of the white men. He so stirred up the Indians that during 1810 and 1811 the frontier was kept in a state of alarm and tension. This strengthened Gov. Harrison's suspicions as to the designs of Tecumseh and the Prophet, and led to his attack against the Prophet's encampment on Tippecanoe Creek, November, 1811[qv]. The Treaty of Fort Wayne was thus a factor in precipitating hostilities against the Indians of the Northwest, and contributed to their decision to join the British against the United States in the War of 1812[qv].

[D. B. Goebel, *William Henry Harrison.*]

DOROTHY BURNE GOEBEL

Wayne Campaign (1792–95). Since the northwestern Indians were determined to retain, and the white settlers to possess, the region northwest of the Ohio River, the Indian warfare of 1790–95 may be said to have been inevitable. The failure of two successive armies (led by Harmar and St. Clair[qqv]) to conquer the savages induced President Washington, early in 1792, to assign the task to Gen. Anthony Wayne, who had made a brilliant record in the Revolution.

Wayne moved deliberately to organize an army competent to his task, and almost two years were consumed before he brought it to the scene of combat. Not until the spring of 1793 did he advance to Fort Washington[qv] (modern Cincinnati), where months of further drill and seasoning ensued. In the autumn he advanced to Greenville[qv], eighty-one miles north of Cincinnati, and from here sent a detachment to build Fort Recovery[qv], on the scene of St. Clair's slaughtered army.

Another winter of drill and preparation followed. The savages now took the initiative, and on June 30, 1794, 2000 warriors began a two-day assault on Fort Recovery. Defeated, the northern or "Lake" warriors returned to their homes, abandoning their southern allies to their fate. This failure and desertion marked the turning point in the five-year war. Following it, Wayne resumed his own advance northward. At the junction of the Glaize and the Maumee, where his hope of striking a decisive blow was defeated by the withdrawal of the Indians, he built Fort Defiance[qv]. From here, on Aug. 15, he resumed his pursuit of the savages, who had retreated eastward down the Maumee. At Fallen Timbers[qv], where a tornado had uprooted the trees, they made their stand, and here on Aug. 20 were decisively defeated.

The fleeing warriors were pursued to the walls of British Fort Miamis[qv], where Wayne engaged in a spirited exchange of notes with the commandant. Several score of Detroit militia had fought in the Indian ranks, and the general conduct of the British fell barely short of open alliance with them. After thoroughly razing the property of both Indians and British traders, Wayne marched up the Maumee to the Wabash Portage, the objective of Harmar and St. Clair, and there built Fort Wayne[qv]. From here he returned to Greenville, where he awaited the fallen foemen to dictate terms of peace. The treaty of Greenville[qv], signed Aug. 3, 1795, gave southern and eastern Ohio to the United States, recognized the Indian title to the remainder of the Northwest, subject to the condition that they could sell it only to the United States, and gave to the latter sites for forts at numerous strategic points, together with the free passage of the rivers and portages connecting them.

Wayne's achievement was of epochal importance in the history of America. He terminated a generation of warfare in the Ohio Valley, during which thousands of settlers had been slain or carried into a captivity frequently worse than death. The peace dictated at Greenville endured until the conditions which had evoked it passed away, being broken only by the belated movement of Tecumseh[qv] for Indian independence.

[General Wayne's Orderly Book, in *Mich. Pioneer and Hist. Colls.*, XXXIV; *Am. St. Pap., Ind. Aff.*, I, *passim;* E. O. Randall and D. J. Ryan, *History of Ohio.*]

M. M. QUAIFE

Wayne-Wilkinson Quarrel, THE (1792–96), grew out of Wilkinson's disappointment at not being appointed commander of the western army (*see* Wayne's Campaign). Wilkinson intrigued constantly against Wayne, but there is no evidence that Wayne's preparation of his army was interfered with seriously. The two men when together were friendly, but criticized each other when apart. The army was split into pro-Wilkinson and pro-Wayne factions. Finally, Wilkinson preferred charges against Wayne and the latter returned the compliment. The Indians were decisively defeated at Fallen Timbers[qv], Wayne died and the charges were forgotten.

[James R. Jacobs, *Tarnished Warrior.*]

THOMAS ROBSON HAY

Ways and Means, Committee on. This powerful standing committee of the House of Representatives was established in 1795. It has jurisdiction over public financial matters, the most important today being tariff and taxation legislation. Its present twenty-five members are approved by respective party caucuses, with due regard to geographical and political factors, and, since 1911, formally elected by the House. The committee is one of the two "political" or partisan committees, the chairman, an important agency of party strategy, being frequently also the floor leader[qv]. The committee is privileged to report at any time. Majority and minority members usually prepare separate bills in financial legislation.

[D. S. Alexander, *History and Procedure of the House of Representatives;* P. D. Hasbrouck, *Party Government in the House of Representatives;* L. G. McConachie, *Congressional Committees.*]

THOMAS S. BARCLAY

Wayside Markets, virtually unchanged from colonial times, were markedly affected by the automobile and hard roads*qq.v.*. Market operators moved close to highways, at intersections or on the far side of curves when possible, and placed their fruit, vegetables, pottery, furniture, quilting, handicraft and other wares in view of occupants of speeding motor cars. As automobiles increased such markets multiplied rapidly to eliminate middlemen in a producer-to-consumer distribution of many products with a large annual value.

[Caroline B. Sherman, *Roadside Markets,* U. S. Dept. of Agriculture Leaflet No. 68.]

IRVING DILLIARD

"We are coming, Father Abra'am, three hundred thousand more" was the refrain of one of the most popular Civil War songs. The poem, written by the Quaker abolitionist, James Sloan Gibbons, was first printed anonymously, July 16, 1862, in the New York *Evening Post* after President Lincoln's call (July 2) for 300,000 more volunteers following McClellan's defeat at Richmond. Several composers set the words to music, including Stephen C. Foster, but the most popular setting was by Luther Orlando Emerson (1820–1915).

[B. Matthews, *Pen and Ink,* "The Songs of the Civil War," reprinted from the *Century Magazine* for August, 1887; B. E. Stevenson, ed., *Poems of American History;* M. and A. Oberndorfer, *A Century of Progress in American Song.*]

STANLEY R. PILLSBURY

"We have met the enemy and they are ours." On defeating, spectacularly and decisively, the British fleet under Robert H. Barclay in the Battle of Lake Erie*q.v.*, Sept. 10, 1813, Oliver Hazard Perry, commander of the American fleet, dispatched one of the most famous messages in military history to Maj. Gen. William Henry Harrison, commander of the western army at nearby Seneca town. Written in pencil on a soiled envelope for delivery by a midshipman, it read: "Dear Gen'l: We have met the enemy, and they are ours, two ships, two brigs, one schooner and one sloop. Yours with great respect and esteem. O. H. Perry."

[C. J. Dutton, *Oliver Hazard Perry;* State of New York, *Report of the Perry's Victory Centennial Commission.*]

IRVING DILLIARD

"We the People" are the opening words of the United States Constitution*q.v.*. During the American Revolution the United States were under a national government created by the "Articles of Confederation*q.v.* and perpetual Union between the states of," etc., which Articles were agreed upon by the Continental Congress*q.v.* on Nov. 15, 1777. This agreement created a league or confederacy which was entered into by the existing state governments.

In contrast to this, the Constitution of the United States begins with the statement, "We the people of the United States, in Order to form a more perfect Union . . . do ordain and establish this Constitution for the United States of America." It has been a matter of controversy for years as to whether this introduction meant all the people of the ratifying states considered as one political body, or whether it meant the people as organized in the several state communities. Of course, this controversy was fundamental to the discussions leading up to the Civil War and the attempted secession*q.v.* of the Southern states. The framers of the Constitution of the Southern Confederacy*q.v.* (1861) tried to make plain their position by stating in the preamble "We, the people of the Confederate States, each State acting in its sovereign and independent character, in order to form a permanent federal government . . . do ordain and establish this Constitution for the Confederate States of America." It would seem that the successful outcome of the Union cause established the truth of the doctrine that the people acting in their original sovereign capacity entered into a fundamental Union which resulted in the creation of a new national state. While the individual states today retain those sovereign powers not delegated to the National Government (*see* Reserved Powers of States), yet aside from grammatical considerations it would seem to be right to say that "The United States *is* a nation" rather than "The United States *are* a nation."

[W. W. Willoughby, *The Constitutional Law of the United States.*]

WILLIAM STARR MYERS

Wealth, Distribution of, in America, as everywhere else, has been governed by changing laws and social customs. And while the American people, opening up a new continent and dedicating themselves to the production of wealth, may seem to have come tardily to the problems of its distribution, the two have gone hand in hand. The Pilgrims*q.v.* (1620) began with an experiment in communism, after the example of the early Christians who "had all things common," and the conflicts of the colonial period between the royal governors and judges and those whom they were attempting to govern had to do primarily with efforts of Great Britain to control the distribution of wealth and to intervene in the relations of debtors and creditors, of agriculture and business enterprise (*see* Colonial Policy, The British).

The American Revolution had important effects upon the distribution of wealth as well as the distribution of political power in the former colonies. Western lands[qv] were thrown open as the prohibition upon free settlement became a dead letter; crown domains fell into the hands of the state legislatures; the rights of the proprietary[qv] families, the Penns and Baltimores, were extinguished; and Tory estates worth all the way from $15,000,000 to $40,000,000, were seized, divided up, and sold to patriots without compensation to the original owners (*see* Loyalists). The "leveling democracy" which inspired the Declaration of Independence[qv] did not climb into power for another half century, but its economic foundations were greatly strengthened by the outcome of the Revolution.

As Madison, "the father of the Constitution," wrote in the tenth number of *The Federalist*[qv]: "The most common and durable source of factions has been the various and unequal distribution of property. . . . A landed interest, a manufacturing interest, a mercantile interest, a moneyed interest, with many lesser interests, grow up of necessity in civilized nations and divide them into different classes actuated by different sentiments and views." It was, he declared, "the regulation of these various and interfering interests [which] forms the principal task of modern legislation and involves the spirit of party and faction in the ordinary operations of the government." The familiar struggle between creditors and debtors, employers and employees, industrialists and agriculturalists, figured in the debates over the adoption of the Constitution[qv] and in the new national system associated with the name of Alexander Hamilton.

The sectional[qv] conflicts of the next century marked further stages in the use of political power for the conquest of economic power. From 1828 down to the Civil War the "Sable Genius of the South," as John Quincy Adams called slavery[qv], held the balance of power in the nation in alliance with the agriculturalists of the South and West. When war broke that power the industrial capitalists took command. They maintained the new national banking system[qv] set up to aid in the prosecution of the war, the protective tariff[qv] system, and payment of the war debts in gold specie. They encouraged subsidies and land grants[qv] to the Pacific railway and its successors, and although the ex-slaves were returned to the political control of their ex-masters in 1876 (*see* Home Rule, Restoration of, in the South), the South did not regain its former standing.

The 19th and 20th centuries witnessed attacks on private property[qv] from many directions. The abolition of chattel slavery without compensation to the slave-owners was only one of these. Communistic experiments and various third-party movements were attempted[qqv]. Communities such as the Moravians and Rappites were held together by a common religious faith, like the monastic orders; others like Robert Owen's group at New Harmony and those at Brook Farm and the Fourierite Phalanxes were secular[qqv]. The American followers of the German socialist Karl Marx repudiated religion altogether. Economic determinism, the class struggle, the "inevitable" disappearance of the middle class, and the growing concentration of wealth—these were economic dogmas which owed little to moral precepts. But in practice the socialists[qv] used much the same arguments as the moralists. The share taken by the capitalist belonged "of right" to the laborer; labor was "exploited"; private property was "theft." The single-taxer[qv] Henry George also held that private property, at least private property in land, was "a bold, bare, enormous wrong, like that of chattel slavery." The Prohibition party[qv] set out to destroy the liquor interest, with or without compensation. The Populist[qv] and other agrarian and labor parties set out to destroy monopoly.

The reforms of the first third of the 20th century stemmed from these movements and others which marked the advance of industrial capitalism. The frontier[qv] was gone after 1890. Already the value of manufactured goods had outstripped that of agriculture. Industrially the nation had gone through "the most amazing economic transformation that the world has ever known." But after 1900 industrial progress accelerated. When the century began the yearly value of manufactures was $4,831,000,000; in 1916 it was $9,878,-000,000; in 1929 it was $31,783,000,000.

Kuznets states that comparative studies seem to show that inequality in income is less conspicuous in younger industrial countries, such as the United States, than in older ones, such as the United Kingdom; that differences are greater in the case of property incomes than in the incomes of labor; and finally that the personal distribution of income where it has been measured over a considerable time seems to show increasing inequality among the recipients. In the United States since 1850 wages and salaries account for a slightly rising proportion of the national income, entrepreneurial income shows a marked decline, and the share of interest and dividends shows considerable stability.

Changes in price levels, double counting, the inclusion of doubtful items and the like make estimates of the national wealth and income doubtful at best. But in 1800 the national wealth of every kind probably did not exceed $1,800,000,000, equal to $328 per person, including Negro slaves. In 1850, according to estimates of the U. S. Bureau of the Census, it was $7,136,000,000; in 1900, $88,517,000,000, or $1162 per person; in 1922, $320,804,000,000, or $2920 per person.

According to the National Industrial Conference Board the nation's wealth increased two and one-half times, or from $192,000,000,000 to $489,000,000,000, between 1914 and 1920, and even with the decline in the price level after 1920 it stood at the enormous total of $362,000,000,000 in 1929. Mills says that under prewar conditions "a doubling of the annual share theoretically available for distribution to every inhabitant of the country would have required 63 years. . . . Between 1922 and 1929 rates of population and production changes were such that the doubling of the individual's portion would have required only 29 years." No estimates are available to indicate what, if any, changes have occurred since the beginning of the world depression in 1929. The report of President Herbert Hoover's Committee on Recent Social Trends (1933) points out that there is little evidence that any striking change in the distribution of wealth has occurred for several decades.

[W. I. King, *The Wealth and Income of the People of the United States;* Frederick C. Mills, *Economic Tendencies in the United States; Recent Social Trends.*]

EDWARD EYRE HUNT

Weather Bureau, THE. Weather observations in the United States were first taken by Josiah Meigs, Commissioner-General of the General Land Office, who in 1817 started a system of tri-daily observations in the land offices. In 1819 similar observations were instituted by the Surgeon-General of the Army at military posts. In 1841 the Patent Office and in 1847 the Smithsonian Institution[qqv] began to record observations. It was not until 1849, however, that Joseph Henry of the Smithsonian Institution inaugurated the first published weather forecasts, based on simultaneous telegraphic observations. Twenty years later Cleveland Abbe, director of the Mitchell Astronomical Observatory, paved the way for regular forecasts by collecting observations from thirty stations by telegraph and preparing a chart of weather forecasts.

The weather service was first established as part of the United States Army Signal Service, later the Signal Corps, by Joint Resolution of Congress, Feb. 9, 1870 (16 Stat. L., 369), for the benefit of navigation along the seacoast and on the Great Lakes. The value of its services, however, was soon realized by commercial, agricultural and industrial interests. The service was expanded in an effort to meet these wide demands, but the need for a new organization with more real scientific apparatus was apparent and by act of Congress Oct. 1, 1890 (26 Stat. L., 653) the Weather Service of the Signal Corps was transferred to the Department of Agriculture[qv], effective July 1, 1891.

At the present time the country is divided into six forecast districts and each state, with a few exceptions, is a climate unit. At 7:30 A.M. and 7:30 P.M., seventy-fifth meridian time, simultaneous observations are taken at 372 stations throughout the country and Alaska, with supplementary reports coming from Canada, Mexico, Central America, the West Indies and from ships at sea. These observations cover the readings of the barometer, the dry and wet bulb thermometers, the anemometer, the wind vane, the rain and snow gages and the condition of the sky. These reports are immediately telegraphed to the central office and other forecast centers and within two hours forecasts are ready for distribution. In addition to the daily forecasts there is a weekly temperature and weather forecast and special warnings are issued when necessary. Storm warnings by means of storm flags and lanterns are displayed at more than 300 points on the Atlantic, Pacific and Gulf coasts, and the Great Lakes. Cold wave warnings are distributed by telegraph, telephone and mail service and also by cold wave flags. Frost warnings, fire weather warnings and special forecasts for industries particularly dependent on weather and temperature are all part of the regular service.

In addition to the stations with paid employees there are more than 4500 co-operative observers, who take one observation a day, and many co-operating navigators. This climatological data is used primarily for establishing the weather characteristics of each locality and is of great service to other agencies in the control of erosion, prevention of floods and forest fires[qqv], improvement of land-use system and agricultural production. Summaries of all observations are published in the *Climatological Data.* To aid farmers the Bureau publishes local bulletins during crop seasons as well as the *Weekly Weather and Crop Bulletin;* and maintains a horticultural protection service which gives advance warning of dangerous temperatures. A special river and flood service gives warnings of impending floods.

[E. B. Calvert and Henry E. Williams, *The Weather Bureau*, Government Printing Office, Washington, 1926; Gustavus A. Weber, *The Weather Bureau, Its History, Activities and Organization*, Institute for Government Research, Service Monograph No. 9, New York, 1922.]

T. R. SCHELLENBERG

Webb Export Act, The (1918), freed exporters from antitrust laws[qv] sufficiently to permit combination in selling agencies. In 1924 the Federal Trade Commission[qv] ruled that Webb Associations could confine their activities to price fixing and alloting export orders, although the act clearly specifies that they must be actually engaged in export trade. The number and size of associations promptly increased. There was evidence, in 1940, that the Commission was interpreting more strictly the activities to be permitted to Webb Associations.

[Leslie T. Fournier, Webb-Pomerene Law, *American Economic Review*, March, 1932.]

FRANK A. SOUTHARD, JR.

Webb-Kenyon Act (1913). In order to promote the more effective enforcement of state prohibitory liquor laws, Congress passed the Webb-Kenyon Act, which prohibited the transportation in interstate commerce of liquor intended to be received, sold, or used in violation of the law of the state to which it is sent. The act was vetoed by President Taft on the ground that it delegated to the states an exclusively Federal power. It was repassed, however, and upheld by the Supreme Court. The substance of the law was later included in the Twenty-first Amendment[qv] to the Constitution.

[*Code of the Laws of the U. S.*, 1934, p. 1223; Clark Distilling Co. v. Western Maryland Railway Co., 242 U. S. 311, 1917; *Congressional Record*, XLIX, Pt. 5, p. 429, Feb. 28, 1913.]

P. ORMAN RAY

Webster-Ashburton Treaty (1842). This treaty, and accompanying exchanges of notes, made great headway in the settlement of a number of vexing Anglo-American issues of the middle of the century. Of these, boundary disputes were the most prominent. The dispute over the northeastern boundary[qv] (Maine and New Brunswick) had brought nationals of the two countries to the verge of armed hostility (*see* Aroostook War); this was settled by what then appeared to be a wise compromise of territorial claims which provided the present boundary line. Actually it was a concession which knowledge of Franklin's "Red-Line Map"[qv], discovered in 1932, would have made unnecessary. The boundary was also rectified at the head of the Connecticut River, at the north end of Lake Champlain, in the Detroit River, and at the head of Lake Superior. There was a useful extradition article, and another providing for the free navigation of the St. John River. Exchanges of notes covering the slave trade[qv] assured the United States against "officious interference with American vessels," and the protection of "regularly-documented ships" by the flag they flew. The famous McLeod case[qv] was laid to rest, following McLeod's acquittal by New York courts, at Webster's insistence.

[Samuel Flagg Bemis, *A Diplomatic History of the United States;* Hunter Miller, *Treaties and Other International Acts of the United States*, Vol. IV.]

SAMUEL FLAGG BEMIS

Webster-Fairbank Trials, The (1844–45), involved Calvin Fairbank and Delia A. Webster for abducting the slaves, Lewis Hayden and family, from Lexington, Ky., to an Underground Railroad[qv] station at Hopkins, Ohio, in September, 1844. Tried separately, Miss Webster served two years in the penitentiary, while Fairbank was pardoned Aug. 23, 1849, by Gov. John J. Crittenden after serving nearly one third of his fifteen years' sentence.

[*The Rev. Calvin Fairbank, during Slavery Times*, edited from his Manuscript; W. H. Siebert, *The Underground Railroad from Slavery to Freedom;* Rufus R. Wilson, Exploits of Calvin Fairbank, in *Illustrated Buffalo Express*, Jan. 20, 1893.]

WILBUR H. SIEBERT

Webster-Hayne Debate, The (January, 1830), was one of the most significant constitutional debates ever held in Congress; in it the two opposing philosophies of American government —nationalism and states' rights[qqv]—were clearly enunciated and forcefully championed. It started over public lands; ranged over tariff, slavery, local patriotism, and sectionalism; and finally narrowed down to a discussion of the Constitution and the nature of the American Union. Samuel A. Foote of Connecticut introduced a resolution in the Senate (Dec. 29, 1829) looking toward the restriction of the sale of public lands. Thomas Hart Benton of Missouri attacked the resolution (Jan. 18, 1830) as a manifestation of Eastern hostility to the West and called upon the South to protect the West. Robert Y. Hayne of South Carolina, seeking to strengthen the alliance between the South and West and thus defeat the protectionist forces, responded (January 19), denouncing the "selfish and unprincipled" attitude of the East and expressing the fear that consolidation tendencies in the Federal Government threatened the independence of the sovereign states. Daniel Webster of Massachusetts defended the East (January 20) and cleverly led Hayne to expound and champion the states' rights philosophy and nullification spirit of Calhoun's *Exposition*[qv]. Webster was thus enabled to meet Hayne on his own chosen field, and Foote's resolution was soon forgotten. Hayne added little to Calhoun's theory but fell into an error in stating that the Federal Government was a party to the compact between the states. Webster's reply was one of the greatest speeches ever delivered in Congress. Largely ignoring Hayne's economic arguments, he centered his fire upon his theory of the Constitution. He showed the fallacy of twenty-four separate states interpreting the Constitution; maintained that the Constitution was the work of the people; and that "liberty and Union" were "one and inseparable." Hayne was correct in his historical arguments but Webster's was the new, growing spirit of nationalism.

[Frederic Bancroft, *Calhoun and the South Carolina Nullification Movement;* C. M. Fuess, *Daniel Webster;* T. D. Jervey, *Robert Y. Hayne and His Times;* H. C. Lodge, *Daniel Webster;* William MacDonald, *Jacksonian Democracy;* M. M. Miller, *Great Debates in American History,* Vol. V.]

FLETCHER M. GREEN

Webster-Parkman Murder. John White Webster, a professor at Harvard College and lecturer at the Medical School, was convicted April 1, 1850, after a trial lasting eleven days, of the murder of Dr. George Parkman, wealthy benefactor of the School and prominent citizen of Boston, and was hanged Aug. 30, 1850. The chief witness against him was Ephraim Littlefield, janitor, who found parts of the dismembered body (later identified by the dental work) in a waste disposal vault at the Medical School where the murder had been committed in Webster's quarters. Webster, who lived beyond his means, was in debt to Parkman and had dishonestly sold property pledged as security. After his conviction, Webster confessed to the crime and attributed it to a fit of anger brought on by Parkman's attempts to deal with the situation.

[Edmund Pearson, America's Classic Murder, in *Murder at Smutty Nose and Other Murders;* George Dilnot, ed., *The Trial of Professor John White Webster.*]

ROBERT E. MOODY

Webster's Blue-Backed Speller is the affectionate name, derived from the blue paper covers, of Noah Webster's *The Elementary Spelling Book,* published continuously since 1783. The first edition appeared as *A Grammatical Institute of the English Language, Part I: A New and Accurate Standard of Pronunciation.* In 1788 the nationalistic author, who contended in this book for an American language and an American standard of pronunciation, altered the title to *The American Spelling Book.* In 1829, for reasons of copyright, the final title was adopted. The work also appeared after 1843 as *The Pictorial Elementary Spelling Book.* Southern editions, removing or altering Northern sentiments, were prepared in 1862. Probably the Holy Bible has been the only book more widely circulated in the United States; nearly a hundred million copies have been printed. Webster originally taught a form of simplified spelling, but after 1807 he developed conservative principles. To the Speller and to the author's dictionaries[qv] the United States owes much of its amazing uniformity in pronunciation.

[H. R. Warfel, *Noah Webster: Schoolmaster to America.*]

HARRY R. WARFEL

Webster's Dictionary, a name now generally given to many small compilations of definitions and, with additional descriptive words, to some large books, honors the achievement of Noah Webster (1758–1843), American lexicographer, whose *An American Dictionary of the English Language* (1828) became the first edition of an authoritative reference book continuously edited and improved. On June 4, 1800, Webster announced a plan for three dictionaries, one for businessmen, one for elementary schools and one for scholars. The first, *A Compendious Dictionary,* appeared in 1806; a year later came the school book. In the twenty succeeding years, perfecting his knowledge of etymology by a study of twenty different languages, Webster formulated a theory of the relationship of words through consonantal groupings. In his great dictionary he used Dr. Samuel Johnson's *Dictionary* (1755) as a base, but everywhere improvements were evident in the fulness of the vocabulary of 70,000 words, in the perspicuity of the definitions and in the accuracy of the etymologies. The author's nationalistic bias led to the use of many illustrative sentences drawn from the writings of his compatriots and to the inclusion of many American words. The first edition in two volumes numbered 2500 copies and sold for $20 a set. When Samuel Converse, the publisher, failed, Webster, unwilling to let his work remain out of print, mortgaged his home at the age of eighty and issued a corrected edition in 1841.

Upon the lexicographer's death in 1843,

George and Charles Merriam purchased the remaining copies and made the sale and publication of this work their sole business activity. They engaged Chauncey A. Goodrich, a Yale professor and Webster's son-in-law, to edit an edition in 1847. This work, marketed in one volume at $6, established the vogue of the book; it was adopted as standard equipment in the schools of several states. In 1864 Dr. Noah Porter, later president of Yale, edited the *Unabridged,* to which supplements were occasionally added, a device now generally adopted during the interim between revisions. In 1890 came *Webster's International Dictionary* with a vocabulary of 175,000 words and with encyclopædic appendices. In 1909 appeared *Webster's New International Dictionary,* and in 1934 came the *Second Edition,* the latest revision, a work containing 600,-000 entries.

Meantime there have been many abridgments of the large work, the latest being *Webster's Collegiate Dictionary, Fifth Edition* (1936). Dozens of other dictionaries bear Webster's name; in the United States "Webster" and "dictionary" are synonymous words.

[H. R. Warfel, *Noah Webster: Schoolmaster to America.*]

HARRY R. WARFEL

Weehawken. The dueling-ground at Weehawken was located two and one-half miles north of Hoboken, just beyond the ravine where the Awiehawken rushed down the cliffs to join the Hudson. The site may no longer be precisely identified. Here, where the palisades rose to 150 feet, was a grassy shelf about six feet wide by thirty-five feet long, and only some twenty feet above high water, accessible only by boat. This spot, outside the jurisdiction of New York, easily reached and as easily left, was, for forty years, the favorite resort of those who must settle affairs of honor. The duels[qv] fought here have been numbered in the hundreds, not a few stemming from the bitter political rivalry culminating in the fatal combat between Hamilton and Burr[qv] (July 11, 1804). John B. Church (1799), Philip Hamilton (1801), DeWitt Clinton (1802) and Commodore Oliver H. Perry (1818) fought here. A monument to Hamilton, on the site, was torn down by antiduelists (*ca.* 1820). The last recorded duel here occurred Sept. 28, 1845.

[C. H. Winfield, *History of the County of Hudson, New Jersey.*]

C. A. TITUS

Weeks Act, The, was sponsored by Rep. John W. Weeks of Massachusetts and approved by President Taft in March, 1911. It authorized (1) interstate compacts[qv] for the purpose of conserving forests and water supply; (2) Federal grants to states to aid in the prevention of forest fires upon watersheds of navigable waters; (3) acquisition of land by the Federal Government for the protection of watersheds, to be held as national forest land; and (4) the grant to states of a percentage of proceeds derived from national forests located within their boundaries, to be used for schools and public roads.

[*United States Statutes at Large,* XXXVI, Part I, Chap. 186, pp. 961-63; A. F. Macdonald, *Federal Aid.*]

P. ORMAN RAY

Welcome, The, was a 300-ton vessel, Robert Greenway, Master, which sailed from Deal, England, Sept. 1, 1682, with William Penn and his party, about 100 in all, who landed at New Castle[qv], October 27 (O.S.). This was the first of twenty-one vessels which in the next few months brought Penn's emigrants to Pennsylvania. One third of the *Welcome's* passengers are said to have died of smallpox on the voyage, and two births occurred. No authoritative list of passengers is at present known.

[Henry Darrach, *Voyage of William Penn in the Ship Welcome, 1682.*]

JULIAN P. BOYD

Welland Canal, The, between Lake Erie and Lake Ontario, originally opened in 1829 (depth six feet), has, because of the steadily increasing volume of American and Canadian produce seeking a market via this canal and the St. Lawrence, been twice completely reconstructed, in 1874 (fourteen feet) and 1929 (twenty-seven feet). The British tariff (1843–46) provided for special rates for American grain milled in Canada. The Reciprocity Treaty (1854–66) and the Washington Treaty (operative since 1871)[qqv] have secured equal treatment for American and Canadian shipping utilizing the Great Lakes, canals and St. Lawrence. Tolls were abolished by the Dominion in 1903. Since that date from one to three million tons of American freight have moved through the canal annually.

[J. L. McDougal, *Welland Canal to 1841,* M. A. thesis, Univ. of Toronto Library; H. A. Innis and Lower, eds., *Select Documents in Canadian Economic History,* pp. 154-85, 250-51, 470-83.]

J. S. PRENTICE

Wells, Fargo & Company. The founders of the American Express Company[qv], Henry Wells, William G. Fargo and associates, organized this new company in 1852 to function as a western ally of the American. The two companies were to divide the continent approximately at the Mississippi and Missouri rivers. Wells, Fargo &

Company at once installed ocean service between New York and San Francisco via Panama, erected a fine office building in San Francisco and began to operate, not only in the gold region of California, but over the entire Pacific coast. In less than ten years it had either bought out or eliminated nearly all competitors and become the most powerful company in the Far West. It was the chief dependence for letter-carrying of citizens in remote mining camps where the mails had not yet penetrated; and, even after the mails came, was often preferred as being more dependable. It spread rapidly through the entire Rocky Mountain region. It carried more gold, silver and bullion by many millions than any other agency. It took over the famous Pony Express[qv] after the failure of the original projectors. It extended its operations to western Canada, Alaska, Mexico, the West Indies, Central America, Hawaii, and for a short time even carried letters to China and Japan. Later, it pushed its service eastward to the Atlantic coast. Along with all the other expresses, it was merged with the American Railway Express Company in 1918, but as a separate corporation continued to function on 14,000 miles of railway in Mexico and in Cuba.

[Alvin F. Harlow, *Old Waybills.*]

ALVIN F. HARLOW

Welsh, THE, were among the first settlers in the American colonies. Many of them followed the movement of westward expansion into the Ohio and Mississippi valleys and to the Pacific coast. They were firm advocates of political and religious liberty and held important posts in the colonies, in the Revolutionary armies, in the Continental Congress, in the Constitutional Convention, and in the Federal Government. While hundreds settled on farms others preferred industry through factories, mills and mines. Many have engaged in journalism, law, teaching, preaching and other professions. Their talent for music has gained world recognition through the Eisteddfod, their great festival. St. David's Society was organized among them for benevolent and social purposes. Educational institutions have received generous support from them. They are widely scattered over the country today with large centers of Welsh population in New York, Pennsylvania, Ohio, Wisconsin, Illinois, Iowa and Missouri.

[C. H. Browning, *Welsh Settlement in Pennsylvania;* E. Edwards, *Welshmen as Factors in the Formation and Development of the U. S. Republic;* T. A. Glenn, *Welsh Founders in Pennsylvania;* I. Gwynedd, *History of the Welsh in America;* H. M. Jenkins, *Historical Collections relating to Gwynedd, a Township of Montgomery County, Pennsylvania;* A. Jones, *Cymry of '76;* A. Jones, *Hanes Cymry America;* H. B. Lewis, *Welsh Society in Philadelphia;* R. Rhys and D. Jones, *The Welsh People;* D. J. Williams, *Welsh Community in Waukesha County; The Cambrian; Y Deych.*]

THOMAS MORGAN GRIFFITHS

Werowance was the title of Indian chiefs as used in Virginia and Maryland, e.g., the "great werowance Powhatan." In Maryland the principal chieftains were called werowances, the lesser ones, tayacs.

[M. P. Andrews, *Virginia, the Old Dominion.*]

MATTHEW PAGE ANDREWS

West, THE. Literally a direction, more broadly and adequately speaking a region, the West as a concept in American history is much more than either: it is a set of conditions obtaining and constantly changing in the land beyond the settled East. It is distinct from the Westward Movement[qv] since the latter term indicates a process. The West is the *raison d'être* of the Westward Movement. It is more than the frontier[qv], since the frontier, or zone of the edge of settlement, was a local phenomenon. The West was the sum total, at any given time, of the various zones of advance: the impermanent activities of explorers, traders and cattle rangers, the frontier of settlement, and finally the conditions existing between the frontier and the East, where the rigors of pioneering were partly overcome and the comforts of life had in part penetrated. The West included the whole series stretched in a rough gradation from the definitely established region where people had achieved satisfaction with their mode of life, out to the spaces known only by the reports of transient visitors.

The explorers and hunters and traders did not pin down and hold a line of advancing civilization; they merely passed through the region and came back to tell their story. They belonged to the West, however, and their part was important because it brought to the edge of settlement and to the East two things: a lure that induced further movement of the frontier and a knowledge of paths and conditions to guide such advance. The waves of progress that followed the frontier—material development and cultural and æsthetic achievements—are more like the westward march of the frontier. It is probably more sound, however, to regard them as the gradual reassertion of basic elements of civilization inhibited by hardships and the demands of the frontier and emerging in modified forms when those demands are lightened.

The West everywhere presented (1) relatively unfettered political and social conditions, and (2) powerful forces to be overcome. Into it came people with well defined ideas of life. The result was that original ideals and *mores* were modified both by the freedom and by the resistant nature of the primitive environment. At first the West forced the pioneer to put a portion of his civilization aside. Wisely he adjusted himself to the situation. But as rapidly as possible he introduced what he had held in abeyance, and always with alterations due to his new surroundings and experiences. This modified culture in turn affected the East and its leaven continually helped to make the whole people different from the older East of Europe.

The West has been so comprehensive, however, that despite this persistent tendency it has never been homogeneous. It has always included varying conditions and people of different aims. The purposes of the trader and settler were antithetical. The squatter and the land speculator[qqv] were natural enemies. In the North and the South, in the wooded trans-Allegheny and on the western plains the frontier itself showed widely divergent aspects. The Western war-hawks[qv] of 1812 were a coalition, as were the expansionists[qv] of 1844. Jefferson Davis' state of Mississippi in the 1850's was as much a part of the West as Lincoln's Illinois. And different elements joined in the Western protests between 1872 and 1912.

That the West was constantly changing is obvious. The first West was not easily distinguishable from the seacoast settlements. The piedmont[qv] West and the transmontane West were progressively different stages. The colonial West as a whole was made up of individual and largely unrelated elements, affecting the East in local issues such as that of Nathaniel Bacon in Virginia, the Paxton Boys in Pennsylvania, and the Regulators in North Carolina[qqv]. But one cannot fail to notice the prevalent outcropping of a democratic spirit.

After the Revolution the West centered in the trans-Allegheny region, with the far side of the Mississippi calling to such souls as Thomas Jefferson and Philip Nolan, and the people of the cis-Allegheny West trying to level the obstacles that lay between the Atlantic and the Ohio. Western democracy became intensified and contributed largely to Jefferson's victory (*see* Campaign of 1800). Separatism was rampant beyond the mountains in this period (*see* Western Separatism); nevertheless, nationalism[qv] sprang from the very existence of the West as a common possession of the diversely minded states. Unity was further advanced by treaties favorable to the West with England and Spain (*see* Jay's Treaty; Pinckney's Treaty) and by the acquisition of statehood in Kentucky and Tennessee and in Ohio—first fruit of an ordinance representing old institutions changed to suit new conditions (*see* Ordinances of 1784, 1785 and 1787).

With the Purchase of Louisiana[qv] and the subsequent crumbling of foreign competition from St. Augustine to Puget Sound the West assumed heroic proportions. It called to fur companies, farmers and miners. Migration became a tide and with numbers came power. Nationalistic spirit was more clearly a possession of the West with the greater participation of Westerners in national politics, and because of the rapidity of expansion which fostered and was fostered by the idea of manifest destiny[qv]. Southerners went westward with cotton, and Northerners with grain. In the end the West gave with unequal generosity to the two sides, and having prolonged the existence of slavery by its early promises, had a great part in its destruction.

After the middle of the 19th century, with national territorial limits practically determined, the emphasis changed from expansion to utilization. The frontier still existed—a vital westward moving zone—and following it came the transforming ideas of more settled life, reasserting the old but partaking of the new. The West still contained a reservoir of resources and free land (*see* Public Domain), giving opportunity and mobility to the speculator and to the man without funds. This had tended to postpone monopoly and tight class struggle. But now the inevitable industrial advance brought economic unrest and typical Middle Western reactions (*see* Granger Movement), possibly accentuated by a realization that the Far Western offer of mobility was decreasingly effective. In 1890 the Superintendent of the Census announced that the frontier was gone, whereupon Turner began interpretative writings which form the soundest basis of our study of the frontier and the West.

The West, however, did not disappear with the frontier. Each decade has shown the persistence of the westward movement of people. Certain improvident accompaniments of the process of subjugation have made the West a region of new problems which will have to be solved. The absence of a frontier and free land, and the development of a new industrial order have changed the dominant aspect of our national life. But the earlier transforming forces have not been erased. Since 1890 the marked characteristic has been the establishment of the comforts and refinements of life. The motivating spirit has been discontent, and the continuing virile effect of the West is shown in various modified forms of education, literature and the arts. When satisfaction with a mode of life has crossed the country, permeating every part, the distinction between East and West will be gone; but as long as there is a region of incomplete development, where a younger spirit and fresher and more open conditions are changing old ideas into new forms, there will still be the West.

[F. J. Turner, *The Frontier in American History* and *The Significance of Sections in American History;* F. L. Paxson, *When the West Is Gone;* D. R. Fox, ed., *Sources of Culture in the Middle West;* J. C. Parish, The Persistence of the Western Movement, in *The Yale Review*, April, 1926, and Reflections on the Nature of the Westward Movement, in *Proceedings* of the Pacific Coast Branch of the American Historical Association, 1930.]

JOHN C. PARISH

West Coast Hotel Company v. Parrish (300 U. S. 379, 1937) was a decision by the Supreme Court of the United States involving the constitutional validity of a Washington statute creating a commission with power to fix minimum wages[qv] for women in the state. The court thought that the close division by which the case of Adkins v. Children's Hospital[qv] (holding a similar act unconstitutional) had been decided, and changed economic conditions since that case, called for a fresh consideration of the validity of minimum-wage legislation. The question was: Does minimum-wage legislation constitute an undue infringement of the freedom of contract[qv] guaranteed by the "due-process" clause[qv] of the Fourteenth Amendment of the Constitution? Chief Justice Hughes, speaking for the Court (Justices Brandeis, Stone, Roberts and Cardozo concurring), contended that the fact that both parties were of full age and competent to contract, did not mean that the state could not interfere, where it appeared that the parties were not equal in bargaining power, or where public health required that the weaker party be protected against himself.

The Court pointed out that the health of women is peculiarly related to the vigor of the race, that women are easily overreached, and that denial to them of a living wage is not only detrimental to their health and well being, but casts a burden on the community to support them. The enactment of a minimum-wage law for women, therefore, said the Court, was not a taking of "liberty" without "due process of law," and the Adkins case, being wrongly decided, should be overruled. Justices Sutherland, Van Devanter, McReynolds and Butler reiterating the arguments of the Adkins case, dissented.

[Roscoe Pound and others, *The Supreme Court and Minimum Wage Legislation.*]

GEORGE W. GOBLE

West Florida, established as a British province by the Proclamation of 1763[qv], was bounded on the east by the Appalachicola River, on the south by Lake Pontchartrain and the Gulf of Mexico, on the west by Lakes Pontchartrain and Maurepas and the Mississippi, and on the north by 31°. In 1764 the northern boundary was changed to 32° 30′ to include the Mississippi settlements. After the Definitive Treaty of Peace, 1783[qv], a dispute arose between the United States and Spain over the northern boundary. It was settled at 31° by the Pinckney Treaty[qv], 1795. West Florida was eliminated when the United States gained possession of it (*see* West Florida, Annexation of; Adams-Onís Treaty). The region east of the Perdido was joined to East Florida[qv] to make the Territory of Florida in 1822. The area west of the Perdido was joined to the Mississippi Territory and became the southern portions of Mississippi and Alabama. (*See also* Florida, British.)

KATHRYN T. ABBEY

West Florida, Annexation of (1810–11). In 1810 the inhabitants of that part of West Florida[qv] nearest the Mississippi River revolted against Spain, proclaimed statehood, seized the fort at Baton Rouge[qv], and requested annexation to the United States (*see* Mobile Act). By proclamation, Oct. 27, 1810, Madison asserted the right to West Florida by virtue of the Louisiana Purchase[qv] and ordered Louisiana's territorial governor, W. C. C. Claiborne, to extend authority over the district, but Claiborne actually occupied only the region west of the Pearl River. Following Britain's protest, Congress, in secret session Jan. 15, 1811, passed, at Madison's request, a resolution asserting authority over this territory.

[I. J. Cox, *The West Florida Controversy, 1798, 1813: A Study in American Diplomacy.*]

W. B. HATCHER

West Florida Controversy. The area between the Iberville and Perdido rivers[qqv] on the Gulf of Mexico coast was included in Spain's claims by discovery from 1492 on, but from 1695 to 1763 France occupied it as part of Louisiana. Great Britain held it, with an enlarged Florida boundary, from 1763 (*see* Paris, The Treaty of) until the Definitive Treaty of Peace of 1783[qv] provided for its return to Spain. After 1803 the United States claimed it as part of the Louisiana Purchase[qv], coveting it for commercial control of rivers rising in the Southwest Territory[qv]. Spain refuted the claim due to the separation of the area from Louisiana in 1763, but could not defend it. Congress by the Mobile Act[qv] of 1804 authorized the President to assume control, but nothing definite was done then. Frontiersmen from the United States, who had settled the Baton Rouge district, rebelled against Spain in 1810, whereupon this country seized that portion of the province which was included in the new state of Louisiana in 1812 (*see* West Florida, Annexation of). The remainder was added to Mississippi Territory*qv* in 1813 (*see* Mobile Seized). United States troops made the occupation permanently effective in 1814. Spain relinquished all claim in the Adams-Onís Treaty*qv* of 1819, but the negotiators of that agreement intentionally failed to state who had owned West Florida before.

[Isaac J. Cox, *The West Florida Controversy, 1798-1813*; S. F. Bemis, *The Diplomatic History of the United States.*]

PHILIP COOLIDGE BROOKS

West India Trade, THE, was a triangular commerce between the American colonies, Africa and West Indies. This exchange of commodities, which became the backbone of New England prosperity, grew up easily and naturally for three reasons. First, there was geography; lying in the shape of a rough crescent in the Caribbean Sea, the West Indies, whether under the French, Dutch, or British flags, formed the most accessible market for colonial merchandise. Secondly, each major partner in the trade, the American merchants and the West Indian sugar planters, desired the others' produce, as the commodities of the temperate zone were needed in the West Indies, while the islands in turn supplied the mainland colonies with sugar and molasses*qqv*. Finally, both France and England unconsciously fostered the intercourse by discouraging the importation of anything which competed with home products.

In this trade the New Englanders became the most active, both because their very diverse merchandise was more needed by the tropical islands than the products of the agricultural South, and also because nature, endowing the Northern colonies with magnificent forests and excellent harbors, seemed to have designed to build there a race of seafaring men.

The commerce soon developed a regular course which came to be known as the triangular trade. Colonial ships laden with a miscellaneous cargo of soap, candles, buttons, provisions, sheep and hogs, lumber, horses, rum and the thousand and one other articles of home manufacture sailed first for the coast of Africa. There, Negro slaves were secured in return for rum*qv* and perhaps some few knicknacks. Plowing back across the Atlantic, the shipmasters headed for the West India ports where the Negroes and the rest of the cargo were traded for sugar and molasses. After the return to America, the sugar and molasses were distilled into New England rum, which was sent to ready markets along the seacoast, and to the hinterland of New York and Pennsylvania for the Indian trade*qv*. Thus, the two great branches of the West India trade —the rum traffic and the slave trade*qv*—supported not only the merchants who owned the ships and the farmers who adventured their slender crops, but an army of artisans of many trades, shipbuilders, sailmakers, cordwainers and metal workers. The shipmasters and their crews, the lumbermen in the New England forests, the fishermen off the Grand Banks, the sugar planters and their slaves, even the distant African tribes were all bound up in the fortunes of the West India, three-cornered traffic.

Up to approximately the middle of the 18th century the commerce was allowed to develop almost without restrictions. In 1733, however, in spite of bitter opposition from the American merchants, England passed the Molasses Act*qv* which imposed a duty of five shillings per hundredweight on sugar, nine pence per gallon on rum, and six pence per gallon on molasses imported into the colonies from the French and Dutch islands. Thus, although trading with the foreign islands was not expressly forbidden, the extremely high duties were intended to make it prohibitive. Notwithstanding this act, trade with the French and Dutch continued to flourish, although in a clandestine manner. Little attempt was made to obey a law bitterly hated as economically unsound, since colonial merchants were thoroughly convinced of their dependence on wider markets than those of the British West Indies. For the rest of the colonial period the West India trade operated under difficulties which bred deep-rooted resentment both in the American colonies and in the mother country. As the years passed, this resentment slowly sharpened the diverging interests which became the background of the American Revolution.

[Frank S. Pitman, *The Development of the British West Indies.*]

MARGUERITE APPLETON

West Indies, Danish. *See* Virgin Islands.

West Jersey. In 1674 Edward Byllynge, a Quaker*qv*, possibly acting for his Society, purchased Lord Berkeley's interest in New Jersey*qv*. John Fenwick, another Quaker, agreed to manage the property for a share in it. Dissatisfied with his share, Fenwick asked William Penn to arbitrate and accepted a one-tenth interest. Becoming involved in debt, Byllynge assigned his rights in trust to Penn and two other Quakers.

Inequity of the division, and Penn's desire to have a free hand to test his ideas of government, led to the execution of the "quintipartite deed" of 1676. By this deed a line running from Little Egg Harbor northwesterly to a point on the Delaware River at the forty-first parallel of latitude divided the province, Carteret receiving the eastern portion, henceforth called East Jersey[qv], and the Quaker associates the remainder, West Jersey. In 1675 Fenwick founded a colony in his "tenth," at Salem. Two years later, 1677, Burlington was founded and became the chief port and capital of the province. West Jersey was governed by the most liberal charter drawn up to this time, the "Concessions and Agreement"[qv]. About 1691 the province passed into the hands of the West Jersey Society which governed it until the surrender to the crown in 1702.

[C. M. Andrews, *Colonial Self-Government, 1652-1689,* being Vol. V of The American Nation Series.]

C. A. TITUS

West Point, N. Y. The swift collapse of the Hudson River defenses in October, 1777, when in a fortnight Gen. Sir Henry Clinton brought under British control the entire area from Manhattan Island north to Kingston, impressed on the Continentals the need of a proper defense. Moved to action by the urgent pleas of Gen. Washington, the Provincial Congress of New York initiated a new survey of the Highlands[qv], with the result that West Point was chosen as the site of the citadel for a strong system of defenses. The location was ideal. A plateau, of about forty acres, lying more than 100 feet above the river level, formed a peninsula which dominated the water of a double right-angled bend of the river, as well as the river approaches, north and south, within cannon range. Moreover, the crests of two ridges west of the plateau could be fortified to meet a land attack.

The original plans were largely those of a French engineer officer, Lt. Col. de la Radiere. In their execution, a brigade under Gen. Samuel H. Parsons began breaking ground Jan. 20, 1778. Weather conditions could not have been worse (it was the Valley Forge[qv] winter). In spite of extreme suffering among the men, the construction of gun emplacements at the river's edge and of a stone fortress at the nose of the peninsula, Fort Arnold (later, Clinton) was pressed vigorously. In March, 1778, Tadeusz Kosciuszko, appointed by Washington engineer in charge, took over the construction work which continued to the end of the war.

Washington, who referred to West Point as the "key to America," made his headquarters there for the four months following July 28, 1779. He was impelled to take charge by the urgencies of Baron Von Steuben who, writing of British plans of campaign, declared: "Whatever means they employ, I am positive their operations are directed exclusively to getting charge of this post and of the river as far as Albany. . . . On their success depends the fate of America." It proved to be the year of greatest activity, with some 2600 men, aside from the garrison troops, engaged in the work. In April of the previous year a great sixty-ton chain had been stretched across the stream to Constitution Island, closing it to navigation (*see* Hudson River Chain). Protective water batteries on both sides, including the remodeled fortifications of Constitution Fort[qv], effectively barred the channel. On the first ridge west of the plateau, Forts Webb, Wyllys and Putnam protected the land approaches. These in turn were covered by four redoubts on a ridge lying west and south. The strongest of these, and the fort into which Benedict Arnold was to have admitted the British, was Fort Putnam. Its possession by the British would have destroyed American resistance in the Highlands, with consequences already described. The seizure of West Point was always present in the British plans of campaign after 1777. Except for Arnold's treason[qv] and Gen. Clinton's nibbles at the Highlands when he twice seized Stony Point[qv], it was never threatened.

A Corps of Invalids (Veterans) created by act of Congress, June 20, 1777, was transferred four years later to West Point, with the intention of using them as a *cadre* for the instruction of candidates for commissions. The germ of the idea which ultimately produced the United States Military Academy[qv] existed in that plan. However, in June, 1784, Congress declared that "Standing armies in time of peace are . . . dangerous to the liberties of a free people," and accordingly reduced the army to 80 men, of which 55 were detailed to guard stores at West Point.

When domestic violence and foreign embroilments later forced Congress to increase the army, West Point became the garrison station of a corps of artillerists and engineers. Finally, in 1802, Congress took the step which legally established the United States Military Academy at West Point. That step ensured the fact that it was to be the oldest United States military post over which the country's flag has continuously flown.

[E. C. Boynton, *History of West Point; The Centennial of the United States Military Academy,* U. S. M. A. Association of Graduates, 1902; J. R. Simms, *Frontiersmen of New York; History of West Point*, Department of Economics, Government and History, U. S. M. A.; *George Clinton Papers*, Vol. III.] HERMAN BEUKEMA

West Virginia, the thirty-fifth state in the Union, was originally a part of Virginia and shares her early traditions. The first white settlement of record in present West Virginia was made by Morgan Morgan in 1731 near Bunker Hill, Berkeley County, but recently discovered church records indicate the possibility of earlier settlements. First settlers were Scotch-Irish[qv] and Germans (Pennsylvania Dutch[qv]) with sprinklings of English, Welsh and Dutch. Most of the English settlers came from eastern Virginia, Maryland and New Jersey. The others came mostly from Pennsylvania in search of cheap lands. Among all of them there were many dissenters in church and state who, together with their descendants, favored religious liberty and American independence.

With the termination of the Indian wars in the Upper Ohio Valley following the American Revolution and the purchase of Louisiana[qv], the inhabitants of present West Virginia tended to particularism in things political, but with the awakened interest of trans-Allegheny in industry, internal improvement and banking following the War of 1812, inhabitants of northwest Virginia developed a decided trend to nationalism[qv]. This tendency was quite pronounced about 1830, when eastern and western Virginia were said to be at the parting of the ways. These sectional differences were reconciled somewhat by the influence of the Abolition agitation[qv], by the reforms of 1830 and 1851 in the state government, and by concessions which eastern Virginia made meanwhile in such things as internal improvements, appointive and elective officers, and free public schools, but the safeguards considered necessary by the east for the protection of slave property caused an irreparable breach between the two sections.

As a consequence of this difference the adoption of the Virginia Secession Ordinance was seized upon by northwest Virginia as sufficient cause to assert nationalism in the form of loyalty to the Union (*see* Secession of Southern States). The Virginia state government was, therefore, restored on a loyal basis with its capital at Wheeling, and when the Civil War which followed did not end quickly as expected, the Virginia Restored Government gave its consent to the formation of West Virginia which became a separate state on June 20, 1863, in accord with an act of Congress signed by the President on Dec. 31, 1862.

Although West Virginia is still largely rural, it is best known as an industrial state. This development was a part of the awakening following the Civil War due to extension of oil and gas production, railroad building, coal mining and the usual enterprises which accompany such developments. In 1936 the coal production reached 117,925,706 short tons and employed 111,468 miners; the oil production for 1938 was 3,734,750 barrels, while that of gas for the preceding year was 163,000,000,000 cubic feet; in 1936 there were 7300 miles of railroad, which were assessed at $289,500,000; and excluding plants with production values of less than $5000, there were 1042 industrial establishments which employed 77,317 persons and paid $80,105,045 in wages.

Since well before her separate statehood, West Virginia has been interested in free public schools, primarily on the primary and elementary levels. For the year 1938–39 there were 11,334 elementary and 4838 high schools which in 1939–40 shared a total state fund of $14,075,000. The free public schools are administered by a state superintendent, elected by the people, and by fifty-five county boards of education, one board for each county operating under a county unit plan. The state supports eight teacher-training colleges with a total enrollment in 1936–37 of 3270, and a state university with a total enrollment for the same year of 2683.

Since her separate statehood West Virginia has had two state constitutions—that of 1862 and that of 1872. The long ballot is in use and most terms of county and state officials are for four years each. The governor is ineligible to succeed himself for a consecutive term, and the state legislature, which meets biennially in odd years, is composed of a senate of thirty-two and a house of delegates of ninety-four members. Since May 1, 1885, Charleston has been the state capital. Following the destruction by fire, Jan. 21, 1921, of the "Old Capitol," a new capitol building designed by Cass Gilbert, was dedicated on June 20, 1932.

[C. H. Ambler, *West Virginia, The Mountain State;* J. M. Callahan, *History of West Virginia, Old and New;* Phil Conley, *West Virginia Encyclopedia.*] C. H. AMBLER

West Virginia: Constitutional Aspects of Its Formation. After studying the West Virginia statehood bill during the full time allowed under the Constitution and meanwhile referring it to his Cabinet which stood three for to three against, President Lincoln signed the bill. His decision was determined largely by political expediency and consideration for West Virginians, but it was sustained also on the ground that loyal

Virginians were the only ones who, under the circumstances, counted and that a majority of them had approved the bill in a popular referendum. In 1870 and later these points were sustained by the courts, but in accord with a theory of Thaddeus Stevens the admission of West Virginia was "under our absolute power which the laws of war give us in the circumstances." Admission was under an act signed by the President on Dec. 31, 1862, and was conditioned upon acceptance of the so-called Willey Amendment which provided for the gradual abolition of Negro slavery.

[J. G. Randall, *Constitutional Problems under Lincoln;* C. H. Ambler, *Francis H. Pierpont: Union War Governor of Virginia and Father of West Virginia* and *History of West Virginia.*]

C. H. AMBLER

Western, Fort, was built in 1754 on the Kennebec River at Cushnoc's ancient trading post (Augusta, Maine) to protect traders and promote trade with the Indians. From a high elevation a large rectangular enclosure commanded the river for more than a mile. Blockhouses 24 feet square and "watch-boxes" 12 feet square guarded opposite corners, and within stood a two-story main house 100 x 32 feet. After 1769 Fort Western fell into decay. In 1919 the buildings were restored.

[William D. Williamson, *The History of the State of Maine from Its First Discovery, A.D. 1602, to the Separation, A.D. 1820, Inclusive;* John W. North, *The History of Augusta from the Earliest Settlement to the Present Time, 1870;* George F. Dow, *Fort Western on the Kennebec.*]

THOMAS MORGAN GRIFFITHS

Western and Atlantic Railroad, THE, was begun by the State of Georgia in 1836 at a point south of the Chattahoochee (which later became Atlanta) where railroads from Augusta and Macon were to meet and was constructed to Ross' Landing (present-day Chattanooga) on the Tennessee River, a distance of 138 miles. It was opened to traffic in 1851. The road was designed to draw the commerce of the West through Georgia to the southeastern states and to the sea. Being state-owned, it was also state-managed until 1870, when it was leased to a group of financiers and politicians for a period of twenty years for a rental of $25,000 a month. With the expiration of this lease in 1890 it was leased to the N. C. & St. L. R. R. Co. until 1919, for $420,012 per year. In 1917 it was re-leased to the same company until 1969 at a rental of $45,000 monthly. During the Civil War Sherman's army destroyed much of it and during the latter part of Radical control in the state the road was plundered by political adventurers (*see* Reconstruction).

[U. B. Phillips, *History of Transportation in the Eastern Cotton Belt to 1860;* J. H. Johnston, *Western Atlantic Railroad of the State of Georgia;* E. M. Coulter, *Short History of Georgia;* A. Johnson, *Georgia as Colony and State.*]

E. MERTON COULTER

Western Boundaries, THE (1783–98). The Definitive Treaty of Peace of 1783[qv] with Great Britain laid down the boundary, in general conforming with the present one (which has been rectified and delineated since then), on the north as far as the Lake of the Woods. From the Lake of the Woods the north boundary line was to continue due west until it struck the Mississippi River; thence it was to follow down that river as far as 31° N. Lat., eastward on that line to the Chattahoochee River; down, or up, the Chattahoochee to its junction with the Flint; thence by a straight line to the headwaters of the St. Marys River and down that river to the Atlantic Ocean. To secure the integrity of American territory within these boundaries was the principal task of American diplomacy to 1798.

In the North, Great Britain refused to evacuate strategic frontier posts within American territory at Michilimackinac, Detroit, Niagara, Oswego, Oswegatchie, Pointe-au-fer and Dutchman's Point (*see* Border Forts, The Evacuation of). Her professed reason for this was alleged previous violation by the United States of the treaty of peace by putting obstacles in the way of recovery of pre-war debts to British creditors (*see* British Debts). Historical research has demonstrated that the real reasons were to keep the Canadian fur trade, which reached far south into American territory, and to retain the loyalty of former Indian allies who might turn against their old masters if left deserted within American territory. In the southwest, Spain never recognized the boundary of the Anglo-American treaty of peace, in the negotiation of which she was not consulted although she had just conquered Florida, which was ceded to her by the contemporaneous Anglo-Spanish treaty of peace. Spain retained military posts well within American territory at Memphis, Vicksburg, Natchez, Fort St. Stephens and Fort Confederation on the Tombigbee River in present Alabama.

During the period of the Confederation[qv], 1783–89, the weakness of the Government made it impossible to cope with these territorial questions. The new energy of the Federal Government inaugurated by President Washington under the Constitution, coupled with the distresses of Great Britain and Spain in the European wars of the French Revolution, made it possible for the United States to redeem its territorial integrity. The Northwest was evacuated in 1796 according to the terms of Jay's Treaty of 1794 with England, and the Southwest was freed of Spanish troops in 1798, as a result of the execution of Pinckney's Treaty of 1795 with Spain[qqv].

The line due west from the Lake of the Woods to the Mississippi proved to be impossible geographically because that river has its source 150 miles south of such a latitude. This left a serious boundary gap. Jay's Treaty appointed a mixed commission to settle the northwest boundary, but it was never acted upon. Various proposals to close the gap were made before the War of 1812, but they were never ratified, nor was it possible to do so in the Treaty of Ghent[qv]. The boundary gap finally disappeared in the Convention of 1818[qv] with Great Britain. This treaty provided that a line should be drawn from the northwesternmost point of the Lake of the Woods to the 49th parallel north latitude and that the boundary between British North America and the United States should continue west on that parallel as far as the "Stony Mountains."

[Samuel Flagg Bemis, *A Diplomatic History of the United States.*]

SAMUEL FLAGG BEMIS

Western Company, The (Compagnie de L'Occident). *See* "Mississippi Bubble."

"Western Design," The, was a plan of the English Protector, Oliver Cromwell, to replace the power of Spain in the Caribbean with that of England. In part he was inspired by hatred of Spain and Catholicism, in part by Thomas Gage's *English-American* (1648), which described the wealth and defenselessness of Spanish America, in part by desire for plunder, and in part by dreams of colonial expansion. A powerful naval and military force was prepared in the latter part of 1654 under command of Admiral Penn and Gen. Venables and sailed on Christmas Day under sealed orders which directed them "to assault the Spaniards in the West Indies" wherever, after consultation with those who had "a particular knowledge of those parts," seemed most advantageous. The expedition reached Barbados in January, spent two months there seeking information and volunteers, and thence sailed by way of Antigua, Montserrat, Nevis and St. Christopher's to St. Domingo, which it reached on April 13, 1655, landing about thirty miles west of the city. After a further delay of ten days, the army of some 7000 men under Venables attacked the city and on April 25 was "shamefully repulsed," owing to lack of leadership, discipline, supplies and communications. Thence the expedition sailed to Jamaica, which it reached on May 10, and the next day took possession of the virtually undefended town. The island was surrendered by the Spanish authorities a week later and, on June 27, Penn sailed for England, leaving Goodson in command. In the course of the following twelvemonth Goodson sacked and burned Santa Marta, but found Cartagena too strong to be attacked and returned to Jamaica. Meanwhile Penn and Venables were sent to the Tower on their return to England but presently released. Every effort was made to disguise the failure of the expedition, which was in some measure masked by the success of Blake and Stayner in 1656 against the Spanish treasure ships at Cadiz and Santa Cruz. The new colony of Jamaica, failing to induce immigration from the British Isles or New England to any great degree, was reinforced by prisoners and deportees from Great Britain and Ireland, and with the progress of sugar planting and rum manufacture rose to importance in the 18th century.

[S. R. Gardiner, *History of the Commonwealth and Protectorate;* F. Cundall, *History of Jamaica;* A. P. Watts, *Histoire des Colonies Anglaises aux Antilles;* G. Penn, *Memorials of . . . Sir William Penn; Narrative of Gen. Venables . . .,* ed., C. H. Firth, *Camden Society,* N. S. 61.]

W. C. ABBOTT

Western Electric Company. Enos M. Barton, a small manufacturer of electric and telegraph supplies, and Elisha Gray, an inventor, formed the manufacturing firm of Gray & Barton in Chicago in 1872. Gray invented a crude telephone almost simultaneously with Bell, but the latter was first to obtain a fundamental patent, which gave him the advantage (*see* American Telephone and Telegraph Company). Gray and Thomas A. Edison having invented other telephonic devices, these were purchased by the Western Union Telegraph Company[qv] and early in 1878 Gray and Barton, whose firm name had now been changed to Western Electric Company, began manufacturing telephones under these patents for the Western Union. The triumph of the Bell patent in the courts in November, 1879, deprived Western Electric of this business, and in 1881 the Bell organization obtained control of the company, which, however, retained its name and Barton as its head. Thereafter, the Western Electric plant was the great central laboratory for telephonic invention. Charles E. Scribner, one of its engineers, took out more than 600 patents on the switchboard alone.

[Herbert N. Casson, *The History of the Telephone.*]

ALVIN F. HARLOW

Western Engineer, the first steamboat to ascend the Missouri to Council Bluffs (above

Omaha), was built on the Allegheny near Pittsburgh for the S. H. Long expedition^qv^ of 1819. Four privately chartered boats failed to conquer the Missouri. In 1820 this thirty-ton government-owned craft made the first ascent of the Upper Mississippi to the Des Moines Rapids.

[W. J. Petersen, *Steamboating on the Upper Mississippi.*]

WILLIAM J. PETERSEN

Western Exploration. The activities of French and English explorers, hunters and traders had made the portion of the United States east of the Mississippi River well known by 1783, when that area, north of Florida, was included within the boundaries of the new nation. On the other hand, the region west of the Mississippi was comparatively unknown to Americans when the Louisiana Purchase^qv^ was made in 1803.

Fifty years later this entire area was so well known that substantially accurate maps could be published. This accomplishment was the result of the explorations, observations and writings of a large number of individuals and groups. While the official explorations directed and financed by the Federal Government receive principal attention in the following summary, it must be remembered that important contributions to geographical knowledge were made by fur traders, scientists, adventurers and surveyors of possible routes for railroads to the Pacific (*see* Explorers, Unofficial).

The expedition of Lewis and Clark^qv^ to the Pacific coast brought to fulfilment a dream of western exploration long cherished by Thomas Jefferson. Starting from St. Louis in May, 1804, the party proceeded up the Missouri River and wintered among the Mandan Indians. The following year they explored the Missouri to the headwaters of the Jefferson Fork, crossed the Bitter Root Mountains, descended the Columbia River, and reached the Pacific early in November. The return journey was accomplished between March and September, 1806.

Contemporaneously with Lewis and Clark several other exploring expeditions were sent into the region west of the Mississippi River. During the winter of 1804–5 William Dunbar and Dr. George Hunter explored the lower Red River and the Ouachita. In 1806 Thomas Freeman ascended the Red River about 600 miles. After returning in 1806 from an exploration of the Upper Mississippi, Zebulon M. Pike^qv^ received instructions from Gen. James Wilkinson to explore the country drained by the Arkansas and Red rivers. Setting out in the summer of 1806 Pike led his party westward into the present Colorado, crossed the Sangre de Cristo Range, and found himself on the Conejos, a small tributary of the Rio Grande. Here he and his men were captured by a company of Spanish soldiers, held prisoners for a time, and finally conducted to the Louisiana frontier and released. Pike's report stimulated American interest in the Spanish town of Santa Fé^qv^, and laid the groundwork for the myth of the Great American Desert^qv^.

Twelve years now elapsed before there was another governmental expedition into the Far West. In the interval, John Shaw, John Bradbury, Henry M. Brackenridge, Henry R. Schoolcraft and Thomas Nuttall made private ventures west of the Mississippi, most of which resulted in published reports or journals of considerable value.

In 1819 Stephen H. Long^qv^ was directed by the War Department to lead a small party to the Rocky Mountains for the purpose of discovering the sources of the Platte and Red rivers, exploring the upper Arkansas, and gathering scientific data regarding the country. Long reached and explored portions of Colorado and went as far south as the Canadian River. A section of his party descended the upper Arkansas River. The report of Long's expedition reinforced Pike's statements concerning the unsuitability of much of the country traversed for habitation by white men.

Thus far all the official explorations of the Far West, with the exception of the Lewis and Clark expedition, had been confined to the country east of the Rocky Mountains. Fur traders, however, became familiar with the vast region between the Rockies and the Pacific coast. For instance, there is reason to give Jedediah Smith^qv^ and Thomas Fitzpatrick credit for discovering the South Pass^qv^ in 1824; while between 1826 and 1829 the former made two trips into California, traversed almost the entire length of California, and crossed the present State of Oregon. Capt. B. L. E. Bonneville and Joseph Walker also made important expeditions in the Great Basin and the Northwest^qqv^.

With the growth of interest in the Oregon country^qv^ early in the 1840's, the Government decided that more detailed information should be secured regarding the country beyond the Rockies. John C. Frémont^qv^ was selected to lead expeditions with this object in view. In 1842 he went as far as the region around the South Pass. His most famous expedition (1843–44) took him into Colorado, northward to the South Pass, southwestward to the Great Salt Lake, and then over the route of the Oregon Trail^qv^ to The Dalles on the Columbia River. At this point he turned south and traveled across central Oregon, into Nevada, across the high Sierras into California, south nearly as far as Los Angeles, then eastward by the old Spanish Trail[qv]. He visited Utah Lake, re-entered the Colorado region, descended the Arkansas some distance, and then struck off across the prairies to St. Louis. On his last official expedition in 1845 Frémont journeyed to California by a more central route. His published reports were widely read and contributed greatly to the spread of knowledge regarding the Far West.

[E. W. Gilbert, *The Exploration of Western America, 1800-1850;* Cardinal Goodwin, *The Trans-Mississippi West, 1803-1853.*] DAN E. CLARK

Western Federation of Miners, organized 1893 and at first affiliated with the American Federation of Labor, brought on the Cripple Creek strike of 1894, and others in the Cœur d'Alene district in 1896 and 1897[qqv]. There was much bloodshed and violence in these troubles, as in that which the Federation called at Colorado City, Colo., 1903–4. The W. F. of M. allied itself with the Industrial Workers of the World[qv] in 1905, but seceded in 1907 and rejoined the A. F. of L. in 1911 (*see* Haywood-Moyer-Pettibone Case).

[Selig Perlman, *A History of Trade Unionism in the United States.*] ALVIN F. HARLOW

Western Land Schemes (18th century) were projected in great numbers by individual land speculators and by duly established companies for the purpose of effecting settlements in the region between the Appalachian Mountains and the Mississippi River. The second half of the century was particularly productive of such schemes because of many complex and interrelated reasons. The fact that the more valuable land east of the mountains was occupied by actual settlers or controlled by speculators necessitated plans for settling the more remote transmontane region. The motives behind the land schemes were engendered by the desire for personal economic gain and by political situations, both intercolonial and international. In addition, there was the ever present Indian menace which the seaboard settlers wanted removed to the distant hinterland.

The desire to obtain land for speculative purposes was obviously an important motive in stimulating the Ohio Company[qv] which was composed of Virginia planters in 1747. They were interested in trade with the Indians and settlers and relied on the London merchant, John Hanbury, a member of their company, to provide the articles of commerce. The grant of 200,000 acres of land near the Forks of the Ohio[qv] in 1749 served as a fine vehicle to bring the English and French forces into conflict in 1753, thus introducing a political phase of international scope (*see* French and Indian War). Apparently, the organization of the Mississippi Company[qv] in 1763, by practically the same group of Virginians to procure a grant of land at the junction of the Ohio and Mississippi rivers, was for the same purposes of land speculation and trade. In addition, the actual occupation of the land by settlers, under the auspices of either the Ohio Company or the Mississippi Company, would have strengthened Virginia's claim to the western lands[qv].

The land companies formed by Pennsylvania colonists and their associates were motivated by the same economic and political factors, though probably not in the same order of importance. Merchants were dominant in the land schemes originating in the Quaker colony. George Croghan and his partner, William Trent, and the mercantile firm of Baynton, Wharton and Morgan[qv], Benjamin Franklin and his son William, governor of New Jersey, were associated and sympathetic with these merchants. Apparently, western settlements would aid their commercial activities. Losses suffered by these traders at the hands of the Indians led to the forming of companies to procure compensation through grants of land. The Burlington Company[qv] formed in 1763 by Croghan, Trent, William Franklin and others met with no success in securing a grant. In the Treaty of Fort Stanwix, 1768[qv], the Indians made restitutions for despoiling the Wharton-Trent group by granting them land lying between the Allegheny Mountains and the Ohio and Little Kanawha rivers. This was known as the Indiana grant and its grantees formed the Indiana Company[qv]. Wharton, in England, neglected Morgan's interests and became involved with English merchants in the Vandalia Company[qv], which sought a grant that overlapped the Indiana grant. In these negotiations in England the Franklins aided the merchants, even proposing a colony in the Illinois country, possibly for the purpose of frustrating Virginia's claims to western lands. In both colonies land for the purpose of speculation, commerce and intercolonial rivalry motivated the land schemes.

[Thomas Perkins Abernethy, *Western Lands and the American Revolution.*] R. J. FERGUSON

Western Lands. When the thirteen colonies declared their independence of Great Britain seven of them had overlapping and conflicting claims to western lands which were based on royal grants and charters. These claims, which extended to the Mississippi River, had been cut off by the Proclamation of 1763 and the Quebec Act of 1774[qqv], but with independence the states revived them and Virginia undertook a campaign to recover her territory. Virginia had the largest claim, which included present Kentucky and West Virginia and the territory north of the Ohio and east of the Mississippi. Cutting across this northwest territory of Virginia were the claims of Massachusetts, Connecticut and New York. South of Virginia were the claims of North and South Carolina and Georgia which included the land between their present boundaries and the Mississippi.

The ownership of such vast areas by a few states aroused jealousy and ill-feeling among the small states which had no western lands. It was feared that the western lands would give the states owning them too great power in the Confederacy, and Maryland refused to ratify the Articles of Confederation[qv] until the landowning states should surrender their claims to the new government. The Continental Congress[qv] urged the states to cede their land claims to the central government and promised that the territory so ceded would be erected into new states having full equality with the old. Thus assured, New York and Virginia ceded their claims, the latter, however, with qualifications which were not acceptable. New York's claims rested on Indian treaties of doubtful legality but the cession by this state was of importance in starting the movement. By 1781 Maryland had become sufficiently convinced that other states would follow this example and her delegates therefore ratified the Articles of Confederation.

In 1783 Virginia again offered to cede its lands north of the Ohio on condition of being allowed to reserve for itself the Military District[qv] between the Scioto and Little Miami rivers in the present State of Ohio to satisfy military grants made during the Revolution. This offer was accepted. Virginia also retained its land south of the Ohio which was organized as the State of Kentucky and permitted to enter the Union in 1791. In 1785 Massachusetts ceded its claim to a belt of land extending across present Michigan and Wisconsin, and in the following year Connecticut ceded its western lands. Connecticut reserved to itself a tract of 3,800,000 acres in northeastern Ohio—called the Western Reserve[qv]—a part of which was set aside for the relief of Connecticut sufferers whose property had been destroyed by the British during the Revolution (*see* Firelands) and the remainder was sold to the Connecticut Land Company[qv]. South Carolina ceded its narrow strip of land in 1787 and North Carolina transferred its western lands in 1790. After long delay Georgia was induced to make a satisfactory cession in 1802 but not until it had sold vast tracts in the Yazoo Valley to land speculating companies. These sales had been revoked by a later legislature, but the Yazoo Land Companies claimed they were valid despite the notorious fraud involved in them, and demanded from the state or Federal Government restitution of the lands or compensation for the losses sustained. The Yazoo[qv] land question embroiled the political waters for a generation before relief was granted by Congress.

These cessions of western lands gave to the Confederation a vast public domain[qv] in which it owned the land and over which it had governmental jurisdiction. Within present Kentucky and Tennessee, however, the soil had already been granted to Revolutionary War veterans, settlers and land companies by Virginia and North Carolina and the Confederation received no land but only political jurisdiction. Some 221,987,000 acres of the public domain resulted from the land cessions. In 1785 a Land Ordinance was adopted by the Confederation to provide a method of disposing of the vast territory and in 1787, in response to demands of the Ohio and Scioto Land Companies[qqv], which were negotiating for the purchase of large tracts of land north of the Ohio, the Northwest Ordinance (*see* Ordinances of 1784, 1785 and 1787) was adopted to provide a form of government for what came to be known as the "Old Northwest" (*see* Northwest Territory). The land and government systems were not extended to the territory of the Southwest[qv] until later.

[B. A. Hinsdale, *The Old Northwest;* B. W. Bond, *Civilization of the Old Northwest;* B. H. Hibbard, *History of the Public Land Policies;* For maps showing claims, cessions and reservations see W. R. Shepherd, *Historical Atlas.*]

PAUL WALLACE GATES

Western Merchant and the Indian Trade. Large concerns like the American Fur Company[qv] dominated the Indian trade in the West, but small storekeepers obtained much business from the same source. Merchants in river towns like Independence[qv] and Lexington, Mo., purchased horses and mules for the fur companies, furnished wagons at times to haul furs to St. Louis[qv], supplied rush orders to trading posts, and sometimes recruited men for company work. Because of the difficulty involved in shipping farm produce to outside markets, merchants found occasional sales of farm crops to the fur companies very helpful. J. M. D. Burrows of Davenport, in Iowa Territory, thus sold a twelve months' collection of produce to the American Fur Company. Furthermore, government agents with the Indian tribes often disliked fur-company traders, and sometimes attempted to divert purchases of Indian supplies to western storekeepers. Church missions also bought much of their goods from local Western merchants, James Aull at Lexington, Mo., often furnishing Harmony Mission to the South with sugar, coffee, tea, pepper, tar, shot and agricultural implements. The removal of Indian tribes west of the Mississippi River in the Jackson administration (*see* Indian Removal) brought a temporary but profitable business of supplying rations to the emigrant parties, and many merchants obtained government contracts for such business.

[Lewis E. Atherton, James and Robert Aull—A Frontier Missouri Mercantile Firm, in *Missouri Historical Review*, XXX, 1935.]

LEWIS E. ATHERTON

Western Reserve, a part of northeastern Ohio lying along the south shore of Lake Erie and once belonging to Connecticut, may be roughly described as a somewhat irregular quadrilateral with Conneaut, Youngstown, Willard and Port Clinton at the corners. The charter which the Connecticut River Towns[qv] obtained from Charles II in 1662 fixed the colony's boundaries North and South by parallels extending westward to the South Sea. With royal disdain for the inconveniences of geography King Charles granted parts of the same region to the Duke of York and to William Penn, while King James had already given Virginia a basis for a claim to all the territory included in Connecticut's boundaries beyond Pennsylvania. The thirteen states faced for the future serious territorial disputes. Confederation[qv] during the Revolution was delayed by the small states without western lands[qv], particularly Maryland, loath to enter a union with great inequalities in public lands. Congress pointed the way out by proposing that the states cede their western lands, all or part, to the Confederation, promising to use such for the benefit of the whole and the admission of the territories formed therefrom as new states on equal terms with the original thirteen. The states accepted the plan and the Confederation was launched. In 1786 Connecticut ceded its lands west of Pennsylvania, except a portion, the Western Reserve, attempting by the reservation to secure for itself some compensating advantage for its relatively small size, and proceeded at once to plan for an advantageous disposal of its western estate. In 1792 a half million acres from the western end were assigned to the inhabitants of the Connecticut towns along the Sound as compensation for losses inflicted by raids of the British Army during the Revolution. "The Sufferers' Lands" or "The Firelands"[qv], as the region was called, drew in after years a steady stream of immigrants from Connecticut. In 1795 the remaining portion of the Western Reserve, supposed at the time to amount to more than three million acres, was sold to the Connecticut Land Company[qv], a body composed of thirty-five Connecticut landowners who sought to enlarge their estates by a western speculation. Each shareholder gave a mortgage on his Connecticut real estate, due in five years, interest to begin after the second year. Moses Cleaveland, one of the purchasers, general agent of the company, went west in 1796 to supervise a survey and other preparations for sale and settlement. History has not been concerned with the struggle of the speculators to dispose of their lands or their losses or gains in the end. Conditions were long unfavorable for extensive sale of the heavily forested area along the south shore of Lake Erie. The absence of any form of local government was also for many years a barrier to settlement. In 1800 Connecticut and the United States arranged by a joint agreement that the Western Reserve should be attached as a county to the newly formed Ohio Territory. Gov. St. Clair gave it the name Trumbull County and proceeded to organize local government. In later years as conditions in the new West became favorable, particularly after the completion of the Erie Canal[qv] (1825), the population grew and Trumbull County was divided and redivided into many counties. The term Western Reserve ceased to have any territorial meaning, and lingered merely as a memory of the old settlers or as a local name for various enterprises, mercantile, banking and the like. Only in such instances as the Western Reserve Historical Society and the Western Reserve University has the phrase survived to puzzle a larger public. But Connecticut's Western Reserve by the process of development became an extension of New England into the West. Names of families and towns, architecture and social customs carried evidence of this transfer of population, and marked Western Reserve apart from other parts of the country until industrialization and a new immigration blurred origins and made the name wholly meaningless to all but the historically minded few.

[Charles Whittlesey, *Early History of Cleveland;* S. P. Orth, *History of Cleveland; Western Reserve Historical Society Tracts No. 96.*]

ELBERT J. BENTON

Western Reserve, Early Religion in the (1795–1837). Settlement of the Western Reserve[qv] under the auspices of Connecticut, and the religious responsibility assumed for it by the New England churches gave to its early religion a distinctive character, compounded of conservatism toward the vagaries of religious revivalism and radicalism in theology. The Congregational General Association of Connecticut and the General Assembly of the Presbyterian Church, under the Plan of Union[qv] (1801), sent missionaries, chiefly Congregationalists from Connecticut and Massachusetts. But the superior organization of the Presbyterians eventually claimed most of the churches. Although Unitarianism[qv] made but slight headway, a modified Arminianism[qv] developed, under the influence of Charles G. Finney, among the Congregational churches of the "Oberlin Association" (1836). New School Arminianism among the Presbyterian churches was largely responsible for the excision of the Western Reserve Synod (1837) from the Presbyterian Church.

Immigration from western Pennsylvania soon undermined the early leadership of cold New England mysticism, by bringing susceptibility to the warmer emotionalism of the Great Revival[qv]. Methodists and Baptists[qqv], who showed little strength in the Reserve before 1825, grew rapidly thereafter, although many Baptists were diverted into the antidenominationalism and Christian primitivism of Alexander Campbell, and the Baptist Mahoning Valley Association surrendered to the Disciples[qv] in 1830. The first significant American establishment of Mormonism[qv] was at Kirtland in the Reserve (1831), and Universalism, Spiritualism, Shakerism and Millerism[qqv] soon appeared there. After 1830–40 the religious history of the region was assimilated to that of the whole Midwest.

[H. E. Davis, Religion in the Western Reserve, 1800-25, *Ohio Archæological and Historical Quarterly*, XXXVIII, 1929; L. K. Mathews, *Expansion of New England.*]

HAROLD E. DAVIS

Western Sea, The Search for the. The first voyages to the West from Europe were designed to find a new route to Asia, and it was assumed for some time that the new lands discovered were part of that continent. Then, as the belief grew that they intervened between Europe and Asia, they expanded, in the minds of men and on their maps, from scattered islands into a comparatively narrow barrier, and, finally, into a formidable new continent. Through, or around, or across this continent, generations of explorers tried to find a way. This was the long search for the western sea. It embraced such widely different expeditions, in time and place, as those of Columbus, John Cabot, Magellan, Henry Hudson, Jacques Cartier, La Vérendrye, Lewis and Clark and Alexander Mackenzie. It included the quest of a Northwest Passage[qv]; and, from another point of view, it was interwoven with such diverse interests as colonization, conquest and the fur trade.

In attempts to find a way across the continent to the Pacific—and that is what is generally understood by the search for the western sea—the discovery and exploration of many lakes and rivers were involved, and to a large extent it was the existence of these waterways that made success practicable, for they spread like a great network over the continent of North America, and extend, with occasional portages[qv], from the Atlantic to the Pacific and from the Gulf of Mexico to Hudson Bay and the Arctic Ocean. The Missouri and the Columbia, used by Lewis and Clark, formed one of the thoroughfares of exploration to the Pacific; and the Colorado comes to some extent into the story; but the water system that more than any other had to do with the search for the western sea is that of the St. Lawrence and the Great Lakes[qv]. French explorers, all more or less with this object in mind, gradually carried discovery to the western end of Lake Superior. Vérendrye[qv], very definitely with the same aim, followed the lakes and rivers that now form the international boundary from Lake Superior to the Lake of the Woods, and from there to Lake Winnipeg and the Saskatchewan. Alexander Henry, Peter Pond and others, in the latter part of the 18th century and the beginning of the next, ascended both branches of the Saskatchewan to their sources in the Rockies, and discovered and explored the Athabaska River, Lake Athabaska and Peace River. Alexander Mackenzie, by way of the Peace, the Fraser, the Blackwater and the Bella Coola rivers, reached the Pacific in July, 1793. Lewis and Clark[qv] ascended the Missouri in 1804 and arrived at the mouth of the Columbia in 1805. Simon Fraser, in 1808, descended the river that bears his name to the sea. David Thompson, having already made important discoveries east of the Rockies, spent parts of the years 1807 to 1811 in surveying the Columbia[qv] and the Kootenay from source to mouth.

[L. J. Burpee, *The Search for the Western Sea;* N. M. Crouse, *In Quest of the Western Ocean.*]

L. J. BURPEE

Western Separatism. While the thirteen colonies along the seaboard struggled for unification and adjusted themselves to the conditions of independence, new commonwealths were springing up on the trans-Allegheny frontier. These western districts in Kentucky and Tennessee labored under the same grievances—disputed boundaries, uncertain land titles, inefficient and insufficient military and judicial protection, remoteness from the seat of government and eastern control of legislatures. Repeated petitions and overtures to the mother states of Virginia and North Carolina fell on deaf ears.

The coming of the land-hungry hordes to the fertile Western river valleys went hand in hand with the great speculative orgy that followed the Definitive Treaty of Peace of 1783[qv], and this in turn was the by-product of the sudden expansion of Eastern capital. Land became the stable commodity of the West and as population increased and credit facilities enlarged, a new optimistic speculative psychology permeated the whole frontier. With land the very basis of its existence, the West interpreted progress in terms of rising land values, increasing population, and above all, in accessible commercial outlets. Since Eastern markets were too remote, and with Spain astride the Mississippi in the New Orleans area, the frontiersman was faced with rotting crops and heavy financial loss. A feeling of resentment grew up which turned into hatred and revenge as Spanish officials, fearing the expansive and democratic habits of these adventurous Americans, restricted trade privileges and deprived the Westerner of what he considered his natural and inalienable right—the free navigation of the Mississippi River[qv].

When news of Jay's proposed compromise treaty (*see* Jay-Gardoqui Negotiations) came, by which Spain was to make certain concessions to Eastern commerce, in return for closing the Mississippi to the Americans for a period of 30 years, this smouldering discontent threatened to break out in insurrection. The West, realizing that it could not expect any help from the Federal Government, was desperate, and listened eagerly to the proposals of the clever intriguer, James Wilkinson, who had just returned from New Orleans with word that Spain would treat with the Western regions, on condition that they would withdraw from any connection with the East.

Intrigue and negotiation with Spain (*see* Spanish Conspiracy), with France (*see* Genêt Mission), and with England (*see* Blount Conspiracy), leading to possible separation, followed in the Kentucky and Tennessee districts. Calmer judgment prevailed, however, for Kentucky entered the Union in 1792; while Tennessee joined in 1796. With the ratification of the Jay Treaty in 1795 and the Pinckney Treaty[qqv], the following year, the major causes of Western discontent vanished.

[Albert P. Whitaker, *The Spanish-American Frontier*, and *The Mississippi Question, 1795-1803;* E. Wilson Lyon, *Louisiana in French Diplomacy, 1759-1804.*]

ELIZABETH WARREN

Western Town Life. The little Western town of Franklin, Mo., in the 1820's covered two thirds of a square mile and centered around the village square with its public well. The residential district consisted of some 120 single-story log houses, several frame dwellings of two stories and two of brick. Thirteen mercantile shops, four taverns, two smiths' shops, two large team-mills, two billiard rooms, a courthouse, a log prison of two stories, a post office, and a printing establishment were the chief features of the business section. Manufacturing was represented only by skilled workmen, such as shoemakers, saddlers, cabinetmakers and potters; merchandising had not developed beyond the general store. Lawyers, doctors and preachers practised their calling in Franklin, although in the early days preaching was held in the courthouse or in private homes. Itinerant teachers and one academy constituted the educational system. Other Western towns were similar in structure, though most were less well developed.

Social activities in such villages consisted of public banquets on the Fourth of July[qv] and similar occasions, membership in volunteer fire companies, commencement day at the academies, preaching services, gossip in post office and general store—heavily political in nature—perhaps membership in a Masonic lodge, horse racing, drinking, gambling, hunting and exercises on militia day.

[Jonas Viles, Old Franklin: A Frontier Town of the Twenties, in *The Mississippi Valley Historical Review*, IX, 1923.]

LEWIS E. ATHERTON

Western Union Telegraph Company, THE, was the outgrowth of a company organized in 1851 by Hiram Sibley and Samuel L. Selden of Rochester, N. Y., to use the House printing telegraph[qv] instrument. Sibley saw opportunities for great expansion in the Middle West, and reorganized the company as the Western Union in 1856. It absorbed smaller companies rapidly, and by 1860 its lines reached from the Atlantic to the Mississippi River, and from the Great Lakes to the Ohio River. Its progress during the next few years was well-nigh fantastic. Its capitalization rose from $385,700 in 1858 to $41,000,000 in 1867. Now top-heavy with stock issues, it was also threatened by rival companies, among them the Atlantic & Pacific, of which Jay Gould obtained control in 1874. In 1881 Gould sold this and another company to the Western Union on terms which raised the latter's capital stock to $80,000,000 and gave him control of it. Its position as the chief telegraph power on the continent was never thereafter seriously menaced.

[Alvin F. Harlow, *Old Wires and New Waves.*]

ALVIN F. HARLOW

Westinghouse Electric and Manufacturing Company, THE, was organized in 1886 with a force of 200 men to make electrical machinery. Expanding business soon compelled it to move from its original shop in Pittsburgh to an extensive plant in East Pittsburgh. It absorbed several kindred enterprises and soon shared with the General Electric Company[qv] dominance in the growing electrical industry of the country. About 1896 incessant patent litigation between these two companies was terminated by a pooling agreement which left General Electric relatively more interested in lighting and Westinghouse in transmission and traction. In the middle 1890's the Westinghouse Company built the 50,000-horsepower hydroelectric plant at Niagara, carried out the early electrification program of the Pennsylvania Railroad[qv] and began to manufacture steam turbo-generators. In 1899 a British Westinghouse Electric and Manufacturing Company, Ltd., took over the corporation's business in Great Britain, but it still owns subsidiary companies in Australia, South Africa, India, Japan, Chile, Cuba and elsewhere. Besides machinery for power generation and distribution and lighting it now (1940) manufactures the consumer appliances including radios[qv] that characterize the latest development of the industry. It has 35,000 employees engaged in manufacturing and net sales approaching $125,000,000 annually.

[Victor S. Clark, *History of Manufactures in the United States;* Westinghouse Electric and Manufacturing Company, *Annual Reports.*]

VICTOR S. CLARK

Westminster, Treaty of (Feb. 9/19, 1673/74), was a treaty of peace between the Netherlands and Great Britain, providing for the return of the colony of New Netherland to England and renewing the Treaty of Breda of 1667[qqv]. It also provided for a mixed commission for the regulation of commerce, particularly in the East Indies, between the contracting parties.

[Frances Gardiner Davenport, *European Treaties Bearing on the History of the United States and Its Dependencies to 1648.*]

SAMUEL FLAGG BEMIS

Westminster Confession, THE, is the doctrinal formula prepared by the Westminster Assembly of Divines (1643–49), and is the strongest and most logical statement of the Calvinistic doctrine. Though at once adopted by the Church of Scotland, it has been modified from time to time in the interest of a more liberal position. The American Congregationalists incorporated the Confession in their Cambridge Platform[qv] (1648), with the exception of that part which deals with polity and discipline. The Synod of Philadelphia (1729) adopted the Confession and since that time it has remained the doctrinal basis of American Presbyterianism, though not without modification.

[Philip Schaff, *Creeds of Christendom;* B. B. Warfield, *Significance of the Westminster Standards as a Creed.*]

WILLIAM W. SWEET

Westminster Massacre, THE. Lt. Spaulding had been jailed at Westminster in the New Hampshire Grants[qv], now Vermont, on a charge of high treason. The settlers forcibly set him free. The royal authorities sought to punish the jail breakers and a court was called at Westminster. The people of the Grants took possession of the courthouse. To gain admittance the New York officers fired into the building, killing William French and severely wounding others. The people, aroused by the action, drove the king's party out of town, and much agitation followed throughout the Grants. The incident, occurring in 1774, has been called the first bloodshed of the Revolution[qv].

[R. E. Robinson, *Vermont.*]

LEON W. DEAN

Weston's Settlement (1622–23) was a private undertaking of Thomas Weston, the English merchant who had been active in helping finance the Pilgrims[qv]. After the founding of Plymouth[qv] he became alienated from that enterprise and attempted to establish a separate settlement and rival trading center. His colonists, under the leadership of Andrew Weston, landed at Plymouth in June, 1622, where they remained for some time as unwelcome guests of the Pilgrims. Having found a suitable location they moved on to Wessagusset, now Weymouth, to begin a plantation of their own. Lacking effective leadership and the strong motivation of the Pilgrims, the enterprise never prospered. Starvation led the colonists to beg and steal from the Indians, who turned on them with intent to destroy not only their settlement but also the Plymouth colony. The Weston settlers appealed to Plymouth for aid and Capt. Standish hastened to Wessagusset. The punishment meted out to the savages eliminated further danger from that source, but the settlement in spite of this timely aid was too weak to survive. The colonists drifted elsewhere and the plantation was abandoned in 1623.

[C. M. Andrews, *The Colonial Period in American History*, Vol. I.]
VIOLA F. BARNES

Westport, Battle of (Oct. 21–23, 1864), was a decisive struggle in Gen. Sterling Price's[qv] third invasion of Missouri during the Civil War. Price, with 9000 men of the Confederate Army of trans-Mississippi, was opposed by Gen. A. S. Pleasanton with 6500 men and Gen. S. R. Curtis with 15,000 men. The three-day battle began with fighting in Independence, Mo., October 21. On the following day Shelby's division of Price's command drove Curtis' forces across the Big Blue River into prepared fortifications about Kansas City. The third day of the battle saw Marmaduke's Confederate division fight a losing battle against Pleasanton's army at the Big Blue, while Curtis' heavy force slowly forced back the rest of Price's army from the valley of Brush Creek, facing Westport, Mo. By evening of October 23, the Confederates were in full retreat. Losses on both sides totaled about 1000 dead and severely wounded. The battle, called "the Gettysburg of the West," ended any further invasions of Missouri by the South.

[Paul B. Jenkins, *The Battle of Westport;* John N. Edwards, *Shelby and His Men.*]
PAUL I. WELLMAN

Westport, Mo. In 1831 Rev. Isaac McCoy, a Baptist missionary, purchased land in western Missouri about four miles south of Chouteau's[qv] warehouse on the Missouri River. John C. McCoy, his son, erected a store on the land to trade with near-by Indians and settlers, and in 1833 laid out the town of Westport at that place. Other trading houses were soon established there. Westport's Indian trade, at first only local, eventually extended to the Great Plains and Rocky Mountains. During the late 1840's and early 1850's, together with Kansas City, it superseded Independence[qv] as an outfitting and starting point for Santa Fé traders[qv], trappers, emigrants and explorers. Its period of greatest prosperity was between 1854 and 1860. During the Civil War its trade decreased. After that conflict, with the advent of railroads and growth of Kansas City, the town declined in importance. It was annexed to Kansas City in 1899.

[Union Historical Company, *History of Jackson County, Missouri.*]
RALPH P. BIEBER

West's Steamboat (1794–1802). At Lexington, Ky., Edward West, a Virginia immigrant, exhibited in 1794 his steamboat to a throng of citizens. This early boat was a miniature, the engine being a mechanical curiosity which lacked a flywheel or a counterbalance of any kind. In order to overcome the inertia of dead center, the pistons were equipped with brackets which came in contact with springs that kept the engine in motion. On July 6, 1802, West secured a patent for his steamboat, which, however, never got beyond the experimental stage.

[George Ranck, *History of Lexington;* Richard Collins, *History of Kentucky.*]
T. D. CLARK

Westsylvania was a proposed province or fourteenth state to be erected in the territory between the Allegheny Mountains and the Ohio River, and extending from the Indian boundary line of 1768 (about Kittanning, Pa.; *see* Stanwix, Fort, Treaty of, 1768) to a line drawn from the mouth of the Scioto River to the Cumberland Gap[qv]. A movement for a meeting of the settlers to consider the project in June, 1776, probably never materialized. By August 1, however, a petition was in circulation in the region requesting the erection of a new state. The inhabitants supporting the petition were weary of the Pennsylvania-Virginia contest[qv] for that region and objected to the taxes levied by either state. Furthermore, the capitals of both states were several hundred miles distant. The Continental Congress[qv], to which they presented their petition, was unwilling to offend either Virginia or Pennsylvania and refused to act favorably upon the petition.

[Boyd Crumrine, ed., *History of Washington County, Pennsylvania.*]
R. J. FERGUSON

Westward Movement, The. The movement of people which resulted in the settlement of America constitutes one of the most fascinating and significant topics in the history of the United States. In character, volume and rate of progress the westward movement in America is not fully paralleled elsewhere in world history. Invading armies have swept over many lands. There have been numerous colonial projects, fostered by governments and rulers. Nowhere else has an area of equal size been settled in so short a time almost entirely as a result of the initiative of individuals and small groups.

Treated fully, the history of the westward movement might well include the establishment of the English colonies in America. It is true also that there is still a considerable movement of people westward even in the 20th century. In general usage, however, the westward movement is considered to have begun with the first expansion from Atlantic tidewater[qv] settlements into the interior. In most respects the movement lost its typical characteristics around the closing years of the 19th century, when there could no longer be said to be a frontier[qv] line.

Thus limited, the story may well begin in 1635, when a group of Massachusetts Bay[qv] colonists, led by Roger Ludlow, moved westward into the Connecticut Valley (*see* River Towns of Connecticut). Windsor, Hartford, Wethersfield and Springfield soon appeared, and thereafter settlers pushed up the Connecticut as far as Deerfield and Northfield. King Philip's War[qv] (1675–76) temporarily checked expansion, and during the series of struggles between the French and the English the New England frontier settlements suffered from frequent Indian raids (*see* Colonial Wars). It speaks volumes for the hardihood, courage and persistent land hunger of the New England pioneers that by 1754 the frontier had been extended well into Vermont, New Hampshire and Maine.

The settlement of interior New York was long delayed, because of geographical obstacles, hostility of the Iroquois Indians[qv], exposure to French attack, but especially because of the unenlightened land policy of the colony. The only notable activity before the French and Indian War[qv] was that of German immigrants, fleeing from the desolation of the war-ridden Palatinate[qv]. Beginning in 1710 they settled on both banks of the Hudson near Saugerties. A few years later some of these Germans made homes for themselves along the Schoharie River; and still later others went far up the Mohawk and established the settlement known as the German Flats[qv].

Pennsylvania presented a striking contrast. The religious toleration, liberal land policy, and widespread advertising of that colony attracted a host of immigrants who rapidly moved into the interior. By 1750 the frontier settlements extended along the foot of the mountains from Easton southwestward to the Maryland line. This westward expansion was largely the work of Germans and Scotch-Irish[qqv], with a mingling of Swiss Mennonites[qv], who began pouring into Pennsylvania by the thousands in the early decades of the 18th century.

South of Pennsylvania, frontier expansion was the achievement of two streams of settlers: one which pushed westward from the tidewater regions, and the other which flowed southward from Pennsylvania. Virginia was well occupied as far west as the "fall line"[qv] by 1700. During the first quarter of the 18th century the settlement of the country between the fall line and the Blue Ridge was in full swing, as small farmers were crowded out of the tidewater section by large plantation owners. The Shenandoah Valley[qv] received some settlers from eastern Virginia, but its settlement was accomplished mainly by Germans and Scotch-Irish moving southward from Pennsylvania between 1730 and 1750. The occupation of the piedmont[qv] and mountain regions in the Carolinas came a little later and in about the same manner, with Scotch-Irish, Germans, and others from the North pioneering the way in the upland back country.

Thus, by 1750 settlements extended far into the interior of New England, there were agricultural outposts up the Mohawk in New York, and from Pennsylvania southward settlers were living close up against the Appalachian barrier and there were scattered cabins on westward-flowing streams. Here the advance was halted by the French and Indian War, and the frontier line even receded temporarily.

No sooner, however, had Fort Duquesne[qv] and the other Western posts of France been captured in 1758 and 1759 than the westward march was resumed and the frontier crossed the mountains in complete disregard of the royal Proclamation of 1763[qv]. By Braddock's Road[qv] settlers from Maryland and Virginia moved inland as far as the Forks of the Ohio[qv], where they were joined by others coming across Pennsylvania by Forbes' Road[qv]. In Virginia, the Carolinas and Georgia cabins appeared farther and farther up the streams flowing into the Atlantic and even in Powell's Valley and on such westward-flowing rivers as the Cheat, the Holston[qv], the Clinch and the French Broad. About 1769 pioneers from Virginia began to settle along the Watauga River[qv], in what is now southeastern Tennessee, and after 1771 they were joined by discouraged "Regulators"[qv] from North Carolina. Before the beginning of the Revolutionary War numerous settlements were made in West Florida[qv]. By this time also settlements had been established in central Kentucky around Boonesborough[qv].

This was the situation at the close of the Revolutionary War, when the new American nation came into existence. The small stream of settlers that had begun to trickle over the mountain passes now swelled to an ever-increasing torrent that spread with amazing rapidity over the great interior valley, and within scarcely more than a half-century deposited outposts of settlement on the Pacific coast (*see* Astoria). The decennial reports of the Federal census[qv], beginning in 1790, are valuable sources for the study of this great westward movement of land-hungry settlers. The dates of the creation of territories and the admission of states are other indications of the volume and direction of the movement. A series of shaded maps, in the *Report of the Eleventh Census,* 1890, showing population density and the spread of settlements by decades, tells the story even more graphically. But to gain an intimate, first-hand view of the process by which our country was settled one must go to the letters, diaries, journals of travel, newspapers and other writings of those who saw the movement when it was in progress.

These latter sources tell of roads crowded year after year, during the months from early spring to late fall, with settlers moving westward, singly, by families, or in groups. The typical migrating unit was the family, moving to a new home in the West with their belongings in a single covered wagon[qv] and with perhaps a cow or two. There is frequent mention, however, of well-equipped cavalcades of well-to-do farmers or plantation owners. On the other hand, a two-wheeled cart, pulled by a horse or an ox, was the only vehicle of many; while others made the journey on horseback or on foot.

Thousands of settlers placed their possessions, often including livestock, on flatboats[qv] on the upper Ohio and floated down that great highway to their destination in the West, or on down the Mississippi. Similarly the canal boats on the Erie Canal[qv], after its completion in 1825, were often crowded with emigrants on their way to western New York or to Michigan and northern Ohio, Indiana and Illinois. Steamboats[qv] later played a large role in transporting settlers upstream to lands along the Mississippi and the Missouri.

The close of the Revolutionary War was followed by a great outpouring of people, principally from Virginia and North Carolina, into central Kentucky and Tennessee. Across the Ohio River there also appeared the vanguard of the stream of emigrants who soon transformed that region into a land of homes and farms and towns. The principal effects of the westward movement down to 1810 were seen in Ohio, Kentucky and Tennessee. The next decade witnessed the so-called "Great Migration" following the War of 1812, when the entire frontier moved westward. So many settlers poured into the Old Southwest[qv] that Mississippi and Alabama were admitted into the Union before the close of the decade. The movement into the Old Northwest[qv] resulted in the creation of the States of Indiana and Illinois. Across the Mississippi the influx of settlers set the stage for the great struggle over the admission of Missouri (*see* Missouri Compromise). By 1830 not only had all the Western states received large accessions of population, but the tide of settlers was moving into the territories of Michigan and Arkansas, and there were probably 20,000 Americans in Texas, which still belonged to Mexico.

During the decade of the 1830's the movement to Michigan and Arkansas, especially to the former, reached such large proportions that two new states were admitted. Illinois nearly trebled in population and two new territories (Wisconsin and Iowa) were created. The "fabulous forties" were notable years in the history of the westward movement. Not only was the frontier expansion into Wisconsin and Iowa so vigorous that there were two additions to the roster of states, but thriving American settlements appeared on the Pacific coast. Early in this decade there began the movement of pioneers over the long Oregon Trail[qv] to the Pacific Northwest. In 1846 and 1847 the Mormons[qv] made their famous hegira from Nauvoo[qv] to their new home in Utah. Then just at the close of the decade came the mad rush of thousands of people of every description to the newly discovered gold fields in California[qv].

During the decade of the 1850's migration to Oregon, California and Texas continued unabated. New converts swelled the population of the Mormon colony in Utah, and the Territory of New Mexico attracted thousands of settlers. The struggle for Kansas (*see* Kansas-Nebraska Act) brought streams of zealous emigrants from the North and the South into that turbulent territory, which had a population of more than 100,000 in 1860. But in many respects the most significant phase of the westward movement of this decade is to be found in the fact that the population of the eight states of the upper Mississippi Valley increased by more than 3,350,000, or more than 167%. This growth, due partly to natural increases but mainly to the westward migration of Americans and hosts of foreign immigrants[qv], definitely established the numerical and economic superiority of the North and had profound political effects.

The Civil War naturally checked the westward movement. And yet, even during those troubled years, there was a surprisingly large migration to the Far West, for this was the period of constantly recurring gold and silver discoveries in Colorado, Nevada, Oregon, Idaho and Montana. For instance, an observer writing in 1863 stated that the road at Omaha was "covered most of the time with the wagons of those bound for Colorado, California and Oregon; one train of nine hundred wagons was noted, another of twelve hundred. On the Kansas route this year a traveler from Colorado, sixteen days on the road, met on an average five hundred wagons a day going to Colorado and California." After the close of the war the movement to the Far West was greatly augmented, and was notable in the South as well as in the North, and particularly in the Border States[qv] where large numbers of southern sympathizers left their homes for the West.

It was during the decades of the 1870's and the 1880's that the Great Plains[qv]—the last American frontier—received the greatest number of westward-moving settlers. This was the region long known as the Great American Desert[qv]. Then it became the scene of an extensive range-cattle industry[qv]. But steadily and inexorably the settlers moved westward and the great cattle range disappeared. By 1890 Kansas and Nebraska were populous states and the newly admitted states of North and South Dakota had substantial populations. Just at the close of the decade of the 1880's the dramatic rush to Oklahoma[qv] recalled scenes which had been witnessed many times when Indian lands were opened to settlement.

With the closing decade of the 19th century the story of the westward movement in America may well close. The farmers' frontier had advanced into some part of almost every section and region, and the pioneer phase of the occupation of the land within continental boundaries of the United States, excluding Alaska, was finished.

[Dan E. Clark, *The West in American History; Report of Population of the United States at the Eleventh Census, 1890*, Pt. I.]

DAN E. CLARK

Wethersfield, Conn. *See* River Towns of Connecticut.

Whalebacks were first constructed in the 1880's at Duluth, Minn., by a Capt. McDougall. These ships were both passenger and freight vessels, although only one of the former—the *Christopher Columbus*—was built. This passenger ship was 360 feet long and was first used in 1892. It was scrapped in 1934. Whaleback freighters were smaller, measuring from 250 to 325 feet in length; they were also different in that the machinery was placed aft, whereas in the *Christopher Columbus* it was placed amidships. The freighters of this class were so designed that the greatest possible clear open-hold space was provided for carrying bulk cargoes. Whereas old freighters had numerous beams to strengthen the sides of the ships, the arch of the side of the whaleback made such beams unnecessary. Underwater, the bodies of most whalebacks were shaped at the ends like ordinary freighters, but others were like a cigar, with the round point forward. Whalebacks are being replaced by still more modern ships. These latter vessels have retained the arch used in whalebacks, thus leaving the space in the hull entirely open for bulk freight.

[Manitowoc Shipbuilding Company, *Engineering*, London, July 31, 1891.]

CHARLES B. SWANEY

Whaling in the 18th and 19th centuries was a staple industry that provided oil for lamps and spermaceti for the candles of a nation. It had likewise a marked influence upon the territorial expansion of the United States and the management of diplomatic relations. Largely because of the activities of American whalemen an envoy was sent to South America before the War of 1812, Capt. David Porter doubled the Horn in the first American navy vessel to sail the Pacific, Lt. Charles Wilkes[qv] explored the coast of California and the South Seas, Commodore Perry[qv] opened Japan to occidental trade, and Hawaii and Alaska[qqv] became American territories.

Whaling was early pursued by the settlers of southeastern Massachusetts and Long Island. Nantucket became the great whaling port of the world. Important fishery grounds were Davis' Strait, the Gulf of St. Lawrence and the Strait of Belle Isle. Between 1770–75 the industry expanded to an extent theretofore unparalleled. At the outbreak of the Revolution colonial ships had ventured south of the equator. The war seriously crippled American whaling. Hundreds of Nantucket seamen emigrated from New England to sail under the French or English flags. A Nantucket captain in a British ship had the distinction of first exploiting the rich Australian grounds. The first whaleship to round Cape Horn[qv] was English fitted (cleared London, 1797), manned by a crew of Nantucket sailors. The mate, an American, killed the first sperm whale known to have been taken in Pacific waters.

The Pacific fishery grew rapidly and, after the War of 1812, was a virtual American monopoly for nearly one hundred years. By 1846 America had more than 700 ships at sea. New Bedford became the greatest whaling port the world has ever known, sending ships to the Pacific by way of Cape Horn or the Cape of Good Hope. Yankee captains discovered many tiny islands, at first considered worthless, but which discoveries have since perfected the right of American sovereignty to lands necessary for the development of transpacific airplane routes.

The Arctic Ocean grounds were discovered

(1846) when an American ship in a dense fog drifted northward through Bering Straits. Adjacency to the new grounds and the advent of steam whalers (1879–80) promoted San Francisco to first rank as a whaling port, although many ships that outfitted there were owned and registered at New Bedford. The long four- or five-year voyages of the 1840's and 1850's from Atlantic ports were now reduced to less than one year out of San Francisco. In 1889 the *Nicoline* made the experiment of wintering in the North. After two years it returned to San Francisco without the capture of a single whale. The *Grampus* and *Mary D. Hume* wintered at Herschel Island at about the same time, with rich success. The latter ships were owned by a firm of Western capitalists who ventured the construction in San Francisco of large works for the treatment of oil. Prior to this experiment oil and bone had been shipped East, first around the Horn from San Francisco or Hawaii, or across the Isthmus of Panama. With the advent of the transcontinental railroad, oil and, especially, bone were commonly shipped by rail to Eastern centers of industry. In the early days of Pacific whaling captains frequently sold their oil in Australia.

American whaling came to a virtual end during the first decade of the 20th century. The discovery of petroleum[qv], the development of electricity[qv] and the scarcity of whales were attributes which contributed to its decline. Considering physical risks and pecuniary hazards, the whaling industry was never extremely, nor consistently, profitable.

[Alexander Starbuck, History of the American Whale-Fishery, etc., in *Report of the Commissioner of Fish and Fisheries for 1875-76.*]

LLOYD C. M. HARE

Wheat, in the United States, was first planted in Virginia in 1618. Subsequently both spring and winter wheats were introduced into the colonies. New England attempted raising wheat, but was forced to give up its culture. In the South, only Virginia and Maryland used it as a cash crop. But the Middle Colonies became famous for their wheat, especially after "the blast" of 1664 drove the grain first into western Massachusetts and Connecticut, thence into the Genesee country of New York, the limestone region of Pennsylvania and the Shenandoah Valley of the South.

Production reached 84,000,000 bushels by 1839, with Ohio, Pennsylvania, New York and Virginia producing 60% of the nation's wheat. After the second westward movement (1859), the North Central Region became the national granary, harvesting 173,104,000 bushels of wheat.

Until 1879 the old Middle West was still the great producing area because wheat was the great cash crop, withstood transportation better and had a world market. But the Great Plains, supreme in 1889, never again relinquished first place in national production. The final transition westward occurred after 1890 when the Columbia Valley produced wheat for the Orient.

Meanwhile America kept the old Common White Wheat and introduced four new classes: (1) Soft Red Winter (1840); (2) Hard Red Spring (1860); (3) Hard Red Winter (1873); and (4) Durum (1892). Of these, Hard Red Spring and Hard Red Winter are best for bread flour; while Soft Red Winter, Common White and Durum mill the pastry and macaroni flours. Of these it is variously estimated that the United States produces 250 to 275 varieties.

Moreover, production of wheat reached 886,470,000 bushels by 1930 and the acreage 62,614,000, while costs of production increased slowly but steadily. The harvesting and marketing centered around three great factors: the country elevator[qv], the primary or terminal market, and the board of trade. Upon these depended the purchasing power of the West.

Therefore, wheat has been very important in the growth of our nation. It stimulated interstate and international migration into the West. Its changing varieties alone made possible the economic revaluation of the Great Plains. Its new methods made the American family the world's greatest producing unit. It hastened the shift from self-sufficiency to commercial agriculture. It revived large-scale farming. It revolutionized the whole milling process. It caused the rise of storage systems. It created new divisions of labor. It brought about organizations of farmers. It inspired basic economic changes in tractive power from oxen to horses to steam and gas engines (*see* Farm Machinery). It prompted the organization of the Wheat Pit[qv]. It brought in its train the building of turnpikes, canals and railroads[qqv]. It made America the granary and the bread basket of Europe.

Furthermore, it hastened bankruptcy and tenancy[qv] among the older regions of the United States and Europe. It fostered land butchery and temporarily flouted scientific agriculture. And it demanded government regulation from the Massachusetts Assize of Bread (1696) to the formation of the Agricultural Adjustment Act[qv] and Wheat Crop Insurance of 1938.

[L. B. Schmidt, The Internal Grain Trade of the United States, 1860-90, in *Iowa Journal of History and Politics*, XIX, 197-245, 414-445; Charles B. Kuhlmann,

The Development of the Flour-Milling Industry in the United States; Lyman Carrier, *The Beginnings of Agriculture in America;* M. M. Cleworth, Twenty Years of Brown County Agricultural History, 1880-99, in *S. Dak. Historical Collections,* XVII; John Lee Coulter, Industrial History of the Valley of the Red River of the North, in *Collections of the State Historical Society,* III; P. T. Dondlinger, *The Book of Wheat.*]

MARC M. CLEWORTH

Wheat, Turkey Red, and the Mennonites. Little Mennonite children, selecting seed in their fathers' bins in the Crimea in 1874, gave Turkey Red wheat to the Southwest Plains. Our story begins when the German states were instituting compulsory military service. The Mennonites[qv], most of whom lived in Germany, were and are pacifists[qv]. Part of them fled to America to become the Amish[qv]. Others accepted an invitation in 1783 of Catherine the Great of Russia to settle in Crimea, which she had taken from Turkey. She promised exemption from the army for one hundred years. Her hope was that the industry of the Mennonites would be an example to her shiftless Tatar subjects.

Ninety years later the Mennonites, realizing that their century of exemption would soon end, began a migration to the United States and Canada. Three scouts sent out in 1873 returned to induce 500 families to move to central Kansas. The first band of twenty-four families migrated to Kansas in 1874 and the others soon followed. While in Crimea the Mennonites had found the Turks growing a dark, hard wheat of desirable strength for bread baking. They improved it by seed selection and named it Turkey Red. Each family bound for Kansas took a small quantity of the Turkey wheat as seed. Since they could carry very little with them, they hand-picked it, a grain at a time, to insure that none but the finest was taken to the new land.

This tedious task was assigned to little children, for the elders had the heavier work to do. Anna Barkman, who as an eight-year-old child selected a peck of seed for her father, recollected in her old age that it required a week to pick a peck. She examined each individual grain for hardness and the dark red color, an appalling task when we know that about 250,000 grains are needed for a peck.

Turkey Red did so well in Kansas where no other wheat had been successful that the neighbors bought seed from the Mennonites. It has spread over the Southwest Plains states and to the Argentine. Kanred, Blackhull and some lesser varieties are derived direct from Turkey, and Tenmarq is a cross of Kanred and Marquis. Because of the high-protein content of Turkey and its offspring, they are blended with low-protein wheat to bring up baking strength. Today 45% to 50% of the wheat grown in the United States, and 25% of that of the Argentine is descended from the seed brought to Kansas by the Mennonites.

[*Wichita Beacon,* May 15, 1927, Town Crier Sec., p. 5; *Yearbook of U. S. Department of Agriculture,* 1914, pp. 397-405.]

BLISS ISELY

Wheat Markets. *See* "Pit," The.

Wheeler Compromise (1876) was an agreement effected between two antagonistic political factions in Louisiana under the auspices of a congressional investigating committee composed of G. F. Hoar, W. F. Wheeler, W. P. Frye and S. S. Marshall. It stipulated that Gov. W. P. Kellogg should complete his term unmolested, and that twelve Democratic members of the state legislature, excluded by the Kellogg faction, should be reinstated. The committee's formal report was submitted February 23. A caucus of the Conservative (Democratic) party ratified the agreement, and a special session of the state legislature accepted it in March.

[*House Reports,* 43 Cong., 2 Sess., No. 261; J. D. Richardson, *Messages and Papers of the Presidents,* VII, 311 ff.]

JOHN S. KENDALL

Wheeler-Howard Act, The (June 18, 1934), gave the Indian tribes on reservations the right to adopt by a majority vote a constitution for local self-government; or, if one third of the adult Indians living within a reservation petitioned for a charter of incorporation, the Secretary of the Interior could issue one to become effective upon approval by the Indians at a special election.

To promote self-respect, initiative and education, the Indians who qualified for administrative positions, maintained by the Indian Office, were to receive preference in making appointments. The sum of $250,000 might be spent annually to educate promising young Indians in vocational and trade schools, high schools and colleges. To encourage the economic development of the tribe and individuals, $250,000 annually might be used to pay for organizing Indian chartered corporations. A revolving fund of $10,000,000 was established to make loans to such corporations.

To conserve, develop and enlarge tribal lands, the act prohibited future allotments in severalty. The surplus lands hitherto opened to sale were restored to tribal ownership. Annually, $2,000,000 might be spent to enlarge the tribal land holdings. Land titles thus acquired "shall be taken in the name of the United States in trust for the Indian tribe or individual Indians."

[*Hearings before the Committee on Indian Affairs*, United States Senate, 73rd Congress, 2nd Session, Part 2, Washington, 1934; *United States Statutes at Large*, Vol. 48, Part I, Public Law No. 383, Washington, 1934.]

GEORGE D. HARMON

Wheeling, W. Va. The name "Wheeling," in a modified form, is older than the West Virginia city of that name. According to an Indian legend "Weeling" was "the place of the skull" and was so named because a party of whites was murdered there and their heads left on poles as a warning to other palefaces. As "Wheeling Island" and "Wheeling Creek" were each indicated on the Evans Map[qv] of 1755, the Indian legend regarding the name of Wheeling was of early origin. The "h" is supposed to have been suggested by the circuitous windings of Wheeling Creek.

The site of Wheeling was first settled in 1769 by Ebenezer Zane. Five years later Fort Fincastle, named for Lord Dunmore, was built thereon, but early in the Revolutionary War it was renamed Fort Henry[qv] for Patrick Henry, governor of Virginia. Fort Henry was attacked by Indians on Sept. 1, 1777, and again by British and Indians on Sept. 10, 1782, in what historians claim was "the last battle of the American Revolution." Following the Revolution a village grew up about the fort. In 1795 this village was first established as a town which was incorporated by an act of the general assembly bearing date of Jan. 16, 1806.

Following the coming of the steamboat[qv] in 1811 and the completion of the Cumberland Road[qv] to the Ohio River in 1818, Wheeling grew rapidly. Red-letter days in its history were Nov. 15, 1849, when the Wheeling Suspension Bridge was dedicated; Jan. 12, 1853, which witnessed celebration of the completion of the Baltimore and Ohio Railroad[qv] to the Ohio River at Wheeling; and May 13, 1861, date of the meeting of the "First Wheeling Convention." Wheeling was the seat of the Virginia Restored Government from June 19, 1861, to June 20, 1863, when it became the first capital of West Virginia[qv]. April 1, 1870, the capital was moved to Charleston, but on May 23, 1875, it was returned to Wheeling, where it remained until May 1, 1885, when it was returned to Charleston.

Wheeling is an industrial center. As the "Gateway to the West," it was long an important boatbuilding and wagonmaking center. For one hundred years it has been known as the "Nail City." Most of the friction matches used in the world are made there, and it is a center for the tobacco, glass, queensware, packing and brewing industries.

[J. L. Wilde, *History of Wheeling during the Past Forty Years;* C. H. Ambler, *History of Transportation in the Ohio Valley*, and *History of West Virginia.*]

C. H. AMBLER

Wheeling Bridge Case (1849–52) grew out of the efforts of Pittsburgh to prevent the construction of a suspension bridge over the Ohio River at Wheeling[qv] on the ground that it would interfere with navigation. The Supreme Court sustained the contentions of Pittsburgh, but they were nullified by an act of Congress, which declared the Wheeling Bridge a post road and required steamboats using the waters under it to adjust their smokestacks to existing conditions.

[C. H. Ambler, *History of Transportation in the Ohio Valley;* J. M. Callahan, *Semi-Centennial History of West Virginia.*]

C. H. AMBLER

Whig Party, THE, was an opposition party that took form in the early 1830's to challenge the achievements of a triumphant Jacksonian democracy[qv]. Charging executive tyranny against "King Andrew," the representatives of the vested property interests of the North and the South recurred to an 18th-century formula that promised to be effective in rallying his opponents. Originally used (in 1832) by the antitariff leaders of South Carolina in close association with the "principles of 1798"—the Virginia and Kentucky Resolutions[qv]—the term, "Whig," soon came to be applied to all elements which found themselves opposed to the Jackson or Democratic party[qv]. Jackson's proclamation against nullification[qv] resulted in Henry Clay's co-operation with the nullifiers and their sympathizers in enacting the "Compromise Tariff"[qv] of 1833, which was dictated by the antitariff forces. Jackson's war on the Bank of the United States[qv] brought new recruits to the opposition, both from the South and from the North. His promotion of Martin Van Buren for the presidential succession alienated another group, the supporters of the aspirations of Judge Hugh L. White of Tennessee. Even before this most of the former National Republicans and the remnants of the Anti-Masonic party[qqv] had joined the opposition. Van Buren's subtreasury policy brought an accretion of Democratic "conservatives" and the "Log Cabin" campaign of 1840[qv] for William H. Harrison added important strength in the back country, which had previously seen little attraction in Whiggery.

The Whig success of 1840 imposed upon it the obligations of a temporarily dominant majority charged with the responsibilities of power. Clay promptly laid down a nationalistic program[qv] to which the majority of the party rallied, despite President Tyler's insistence in continuing what were to him the true Whig traditions of the 1830's. Read out of the party, the President watched in dismay the acceptance of the Clay formula by the vast body of Whigs. The issue of the annexation of Texas[qv] and of the extension of slavery into the territories in time proved a menace to solidarity of the party. The election of 1844[qv] showed the loss of expansionist forces that had in 1840 yielded to the lure of "Hard Cider." The conservative property interests of leading Whigs, however, made them opponents of the Mexican War and of expansion[qqv]; the "no territory" resolutions which they supported were largely sponsored by their Southern leaders. While some of the Northern element were antislavery men (Conscience Whigs[qv]), others were sufficiently proslavery to earn the label, "Cotton Whigs." In the crisis of 1850–51 the Southern element was prominent among the Union forces that fought secession (*see* Compromise of 1850). By 1852 the logic of sectional allegiance was so strong that the party began to disintegrate and suffered a defeat which marked the beginning of the end.

[A. C. Cole, *The Whig Party in the South;* D. R. Fox, *The Decline of Aristocracy in the Politics of New York.*]

ARTHUR C. COLE

Whip, Party, is a party officer in Congress, whose duties are particularly to see that members of his party are present for important roll calls and that they vote right. This kind of officer has been used in the English Parliament at least since 1836, but was first formally introduced into our House of Representatives in 1899, when Rep. James E. Watson of Indiana was designated as whip by the House Republican caucus, and into the Senate in 1913, when Sen. James Hamilton Lewis of Illinois was similarly designated by the Senate Democrats. Since that time whips have been regularly chosen by each party in each house, and their work has become of increasing importance, so much so that the Democrats in the House recently provided for fifteen assistant whips chosen by geographical districts, and required at least four to be on the floor of the House at all times.

[Paul D. Hasbrouck, *Party Government in the House of Representatives;* James Hamilton Lewis, Duties of the "Whip" in Congress, in *Congressional Record,* Vol. 80, pp. 7044-46, May 12, 1936.]

CLARENCE A. BERDAHL

Whipping Post, THE, stood in every colonial court town beside the pillory or stocks[qqv], ready to entertain those offenders whose crimes merited more than these but less than the gallows. The whipping post was busy, for jails were places of detention for those awaiting trial, not places for punishment by imprisonment. It was sometimes painted red, probably less to conceal the blood of its visitors (as tradition has it) than to impress the waywardly inclined by its silent warning between court days. The whips used by the civil officers at the post were far more merciful than the frightful cat-o'-nine-tails of the navy, and the flaying to death which resulted from heavy sentences common in all armed forces even at a much later date was rarely inflicted by the civil courts.

The use of the whipping post has been discontinued in the United States except in Delaware, where it has served as a deterrent to crime since its institution during the period of colonization, and in Maryland where its use has been revived in recent years.

C. K. SHIPTON

Whipple, Fort (Virginia). *See* Myer, Fort.

Whipple's Expedition in 1853–54 was an army survey of the West ordered by Congress. Lt. A. W. Whipple traced the thirty-fifth parallel beginning at Fort Smith[qv] on the Arkansas River in July, 1853. Crossing Oklahoma and the Panhandle he reached Albuquerque in November. From here, guided at times by Indians, he crossed the Sierra Madre and later, by the Mormon Road, the desert and the Sierra Nevadas. Los Angeles was reached in the spring of 1854. Unknown territory had been explored, and the route of the Santa Fé railroad indicated.

[G. L. Albright, *Official Explorations for Pacific Railroads, 1853-55.*]

CARL L. CANNON

Whiskey. The whiskey used in the earlier years of the colonies was imported from Great Britain. Among the early settlers were many Irish and Scotch, who were acquainted with the art of distilling whiskey, principally from malt, though rye, wheat and even potatoes were sometimes used in early American stills. Many of the Irish and Scotch settled in western Pennsylvania which, in the early 18th century, became a center of rye whiskey making (*see* Whiskey Insurrection), and Maryland began producing it about the same time. Whiskey became the leading spirituous drink for the entire country (*see* Indian and Liquor; Liquor, Use of, in the Fur Trade) outside of New England, where rum[qv] remained the favorite tipple for more than a century. Appalling excesses in the use of these two drinks brought about the Temperance Movement[qv]. There was a still in Kentucky as early as 1789. Here it was found that whiskey could be produced from Indian corn, and this eventually became America's leading spirituous product, exceeding in volume the rye whiskeys of Maryland and Pennsylvania. In 1792 there were 2579 small distilleries in the United States. By 1810 Kentucky alone had 2000, some of which shipped whiskey even to the East via New Orleans, by flatboat down the rivers and thence by ocean vessels. Some enormous distilling plants grew up in Kentucky, manufacturing sour mash, sweet mash, Bourbon—so called from the Kentucky county of that name—and a small percentage of rye. Other states in the Corn Belt, such as Ohio and Illinois, also developed large distilling industries. During the period from 1901 to 1919 there were withdrawn from bonded warehouses after payment of tax a yearly average of 60,000,000 gallons of whiskey. The Prohibition[qv] era worked enormous changes in the business, destroying many long-established companies whose distilleries, if reopened at all after the repeal of the law, were in many cases under other ownership. Kentucky in 1935 produced 197,000,000 gallons of whiskey.

[Daniel Dorchester, *The Liquor Problem in All Ages;* Thomas D. Clark, *History of Kentucky.*]

ALVIN F. HARLOW

Whiskey Insurrection. The American back country in the 1790's was intensely democratic in its views and resented the way in which Alexander Hamilton's fiscal policies concentrated power in the hands of the upper classes. Other grievances accentuated Western resentment, notably the failure to open the Mississippi to navigation[qv], the dilatory conduct of the Indian war (*see* Harmar's Expedition; St. Clair's Defeat), the speculative prices of land, arduous and ill-paid militia duty, scarcity of specie and the creation of a salaried official class. The excise law of 1791 which taxed whiskey, the chief transportable and barterable Western product, furnished a convenient peg on which to hang these grievances, and for three years the opposition to this measure increased.

The fact that non-complying distillers from western Pennsylvania had to go to York or Philadelphia for trial (a procedure that would cost the value of the average Western farm) formed so legitimate a grievance that in May and June, 1794, Congress passed a measure making such offenses cognizable in state courts. While the bill was in Congress the U. S. District Court of Pennsylvania issued a series of processes returnable to Philadelphia. The fact that these processes were not served until July, six weeks after the easing measure was passed, angered the citizens of the southwestern counties. A Federal marshal was attacked in Allegheny County while serving a process and on July 17 several hundred men, led by members of a local "Democratic society," attacked and burned the home of Gen. John Neville, the regional inspector of the excise.

The attackers would probably have stopped with this action but certain leaders robbed the mail and found in the stolen letters expressions that they used in stirring up the people to attack Pittsburgh. A muster of the southwestern militia was called at Braddock's Field for Aug. 1. The citizens of Pittsburgh were so alarmed that they exiled the odious townsmen and thus averted the wrath of the recalcitrants. The militia march on Pittsburgh on Aug. 2 was carried through without violence.

On Aug. 14–15 delegates from the Monongahela country met at Parkinson's Ferry, but were prevented from drastic measures by the parliamentary tactics of the moderates. A committee appointed by Washington met with a Western committee and arranged that the sentiment of the people of the western counties concerning submission be taken on Sept. 11. The vote was unsatisfactory and Washington set in motion the militia army which had meanwhile been gathering in the East. The western counties were occupied during November and more than a score of prisoners sent to Philadelphia. All of them were acquitted, pardoned, or dismissed for lack of evidence.

The result of the insurrection was simply to strengthen the political power of Hamilton and the Federalists[qv], and circumstantial evidence seems to indicate that Hamilton promoted the original misunderstanding and sent the army West solely for that purpose. It is likely also that the defeat of the democrats encouraged investors to accelerate the economic development of the region which they had already begun.

[Leland D. Baldwin, *Whiskey Rebels.*]

LELAND D. BALDWIN

Whiskey Ring. Subsequent to becoming Secretary of the Treasury in Grant's Cabinet in June, 1874, Benjamin H. Bristow procured the indictment and conviction of three government officials and a journalist in St. Louis, Mo., and of a government official in Washington. The charges involved conspiracy between Internal Revenue officials and whiskey distillers, located chiefly in St. Louis, and accomplices in Washington to divide certain illegal abatements of taxes on whiskey. The facts revealed would have been of little historical importance had not allegations been made that the illegal abatements of taxes were to raise funds for the Republican party[qv], especially to procure a second and third term for Grant and that the improprieties involved not only Grant's private secretary, but in a measure the President himself. All of this made the matter a political scandal of the first water. While the private secretary was acquitted and the nation as a whole gave slight credence to the charges reflecting upon Grant himself, the revelations undoubtedly had an effect upon public sentiment in the ensuing presidential campaign.

[James F. Rhodes, *History of the United States;* J. McDonald, *Secrets of the Great Whiskey Ring.*]

JOHN FRANCIS, JR.

Whiskey Towns grew up about saloons established just outside the borders of Indian lands, or other areas where the sale of liquor was prohibited. In most of these the sale of whiskey was the chief business since they were in many cases founded only a mile or two from long-established and flourishing towns located in dry territory. One such example was Lexington, built in Oklahoma Territory just across the river from Purcell, Indian Territory[qv]. Many towns and cities just beyond the boundaries of prohibition states have developed a large liquor business, but are not properly called whiskey towns unless established for that purpose.

[C. N. Gould, *Oklahoma Place Names.*]

EDWARD EVERETT DALE

Whispering Campaigns have been a feature of American life during much if not all of its history. Teachers and clergymen have been the object of innuendoes and reports of outright scandal circulated from mouth to mouth until an entire community has seethed with excitement. The stock markets have witnessed the drop or rise of prices as a result of calculated whispers. Cosmetic manufacturers have found their products unsalable because of widespread rumors started by competitors claiming poisonous ingredients. However, it has been in the field of politics that whispering campaigns have perhaps reached their climax in the United States. Scarcely a presidential, a state, or a local election occurs without one or more of these undercover campaigns being launched.

The unsavory gossip that constitutes the ammunition of whispering campaigns is of many different types. Charges of illegitimacy, illicit sexual relations, domestic difficulties, venereal disease and mixed blood are common. Alleged crimes are bruited about; religious, social, or political unconventionalism may be sensationally portrayed. Often there is no actual basis for such reports; sometimes there may be some substance along with gross exaggeration; in a minority of instances the real situation is represented.

The history of whispering campaigns in politics is very involved, but it is apparent that some of the techniques accompanied if they did not antedate the birth of political parties. Alexander Hamilton, Andrew Jackson, Abraham Lincoln and Grover Cleveland are a few of the national figures against whom whispers were directed. During the 20th century the use of such a device has probably become more extensive, among other reasons because of the more effective libel and slander laws. During this period Woodrow Wilson, Warren G. Harding, Alfred E. Smith and Franklin D. Roosevelt received considerable inimical attention from whisperers. The Ku Klux Klan[qv] depended very heavily upon such a weapon in controlling state and local elections during the 1920's.

[Alfred E. Smith, *Up to Now;* P. H. Odegard and E. A. Helms, *American Politics.*]

HAROLD ZINK

White Caps, THE, were an anti-Negro, night-riding organization in south-central Mississippi, around 1900. Centered chiefly in Lincoln County, they were credited with crimes of violence against Negroes. They were broken up by prosecution in Gov. James K. Vardaman's administration, 1904–8.

MACK SWEARINGEN

White-Collar Class, THE, has become in the American vocabulary an expressive phrase referring to clerks and the like who earn their living without soiling their hands, usually of the lower middle class, and who identify themselves with the economically successful even though living on a low income and in relative insecurity. In expectation they ally themselves with capitalism and business interests, looking forward to higher standards of living either for themselves or their children. They resent the encroachment of organized labor[qv] as a menace to their own status and do not easily unite in economic self-protection. Their lack of organization leaves them open to the economic hazards of business cycles, technological advances, changing fashions and customs, and depressions. Their wage income tends to be lower than that of the well-organized skilled laborers and their employment less secure. As a consequence of their experiences, they are as a class discontented and restless, but, because of their feeling of alliance with the well-to-do, they lean toward political and economic conservatism even though frequently radical in their attitudes toward other human interests. Of late, because of economic pressure, they have been more inclined toward organization than formerly and more critical of industrial and commercial leadership. As a class they marry late and have a low birth rate.

ERNEST R. GROVES

White House, THE, was familiarly so called from early times, because the Aquia Creek sandstone of which it was built was painted white. Originally named the President's House, in President Lincoln's day it was officially The Executive Mansion and so continued until President Theodore Roosevelt adopted the commonly used appellation. President Washington and Maj. L'Enfant selected for the Capitol[qv] and the White House two commanding sites in the city of their planning (*see* Washington). The fact that the locations were a mile and a half apart was welcomed by the courtly L'Enfant as conducing to ceremonial intercourse, and by the practical President as mitigating the importunities of legislators, a waste of time he suffered in New York and Philadelphia. As the result of a competition in which nineteen designs were submitted (including an anonymous one by Jefferson) the commissioners selected that of James Hoban, architecturally trained in Dublin. Washington approved the choice as combining elegance with simplicity and dignity; and it appealed to Jefferson by its adherence to classical precedents. In fact Hoban designed a gentleman's house of his period.

In October, 1800, Mrs. John Adams found an unfinished and unfurnished White House in which to spend an uncomfortable winter. President Jefferson, coming five months later, gave to the furnishings a French touch that has persisted.

After Washington was burned[qv] by the British in 1814 Hoban superintended the repairs. The east and west terraces, and the south and north porticoes were added by B. H. Latrobe prior to 1824.

During the century, the combination of President's office and residence in one building resulted in mutilations to the house and unspeakable discomforts to its occupants. In 1902 Congress charged President Theodore Roosevelt with drastic renovations. He selected McKim, Mead and White as architects. Between May and November, 1902, the interior was entirely rebuilt and refurnished, reverently restoring and preserving the architecture of the historic White House while giving to the interior all the facilities of elegant and comfortable living and entertaining. The President's offices were removed to an inconspicuous building at the end of the west terrace. Designed to be but temporary, the offices have been thrice enlarged and still await a permanent building.

[*Restoration of the White House, Report of the Architects, with Plans, Drawings and Photographs*, 57th Congress, Second Session, Senate Document 197, 1903; Ethel Lewis, *The White House.*]

CHARLES MOORE

White House of the Confederacy. At Richmond, Va., on the brow of steep Shockoe Hill across the wide ravine from old Church Hill, rises a stately Doric-columned mansion of the period of the Greek Revival. Bought by the city of Richmond on June 11, 1861, it was furnished and presented to the Confederate President. When he refused the gift, the Confederate Government rented it. As the Executive Mansion, it was occupied by President Davis as his official and private residence, until he was forced to leave it forever on that fateful April 2, 1865. In her *Memoir*, Mrs. Davis notes the garden terraced down the steep hillside, the Carrara marble mantelpieces, the great high-ceilinged rooms, the well-staircases. On April 3, 1865, the Union commander, Godfrey Weitzel, made the Mansion his headquarters. After the Federal Government returned it in 1870, the city used it as a public school. On June 12, 1894, the city deeded it to the Confederate Memorial Literary Society, as a memorial to President Davis and for a Confederate museum.

[Richmond Hustings and Chancery Deeds; Confederate Museum Leaflet.]

KATHLEEN BRUCE

White League, THE, organized in Louisiana in 1874 in consequence of the political troubles there, first appeared at Opelousas in April, and then spread rapidly throughout the state. Except in New Orleans, it consisted of "ordinary political clubs, neither secret nor armed," with little or no connections between the different units. Its object was to protect the white race "from the daily increasing encroachments of the Negro," eliminate from public office "a horde of miscreants," and "proscribe socially" all those who "united with the Republicans." The so-called "Coushatta Massacre" (Aug. 30) is sometimes attributed to the League, but there was no serious clash between it and the state authorities until the uprising in New Orleans on Sept. 14. The New Orleans League, which was responsible for the latter affair, was organized in June, and sixty days later claimed to have more than 3000 members. Having attained its object when the Radical state government was overthrown, the League declined, and, after 1877, disappeared.

[*House Reports*, 43 Cong., 2 Sess., No. 101; *Louisiana Historical Quarterly*, XVIII.] JOHN S. KENDALL

White Oak Swamp, Battle at (June 30, 1862). McClellan's (U.) cattle herd and train of 3600 wagons passed the swamp on June 29 (*see* Seven Days' Battles). Franklin's corps (U.) remained behind to guard the crossing. Jackson (C.), pursuing, shelled the Federals vigorously but did not attempt to cross the swamp. Lee's attacks at Frayser's Farm[qv] having meanwhile been repulsed, Franklin that night retired safely to Malvern Hill[qv].

[G. F. R. Henderson, *Stonewall Jackson; Official Records, Union and Confederate Armies*, Vol. XI.]

JOSEPH MILLS HANSON

White Plains, Battle of (Oct. 28, 1776). After the Battle of Harlem Heights[qv] both the American and British armies were inactive for about three weeks. The next military movement came from Howe. With the main part of his army he moved up the East River in order to get in the rear of the Americans and at the same time cut off communication with Connecticut and the other New England states. So slowly did he advance, however, that he did not reach New Rochelle until Oct. 21. His delay gave Washington time to move north and take up a strong position across the roads leading up the Hudson and to New England. Strongly entrenched on the high ground northwest and northeast of the village of White Plains he waited for Howe's next move. On Oct. 28 Howe was ready to attack. The action was short, sharp and creditable to the Americans. Avoiding a direct attack on Washington's front, Howe sent a detachment to gain Chatterton Hill, a rocky eminence west of the Bronx River, and near the village. The British were forestalled, however, by Gen. McDougall, who gained the hill first and held it until British reinforcements forced a retreat to the village. During the night Washington drew back his line and strengthened it. Howe waited for reinforcements before continuing the attack. On the night of the 31st, however, Washington withdrew into the "Hills" five miles to the northwest.

[H. B. Dawson, *Battles of the United States.*]

A. C. FLICK

White-Slave Traffic. The term "white slavery" originated in the United States as a synonym for compulsory prostitution[qv]. Various investigations in the early period of the 20th century showed that although there were few cases of victims being forced against their will into prostitution, there was a considerable organization of persons who enticed young women into a life of vice and distributed them not only from state to state but from nation to nation. As a result of an investigation by the Immigration Commission in 1907–09, the White Slave Traffic Act of 1910 was passed, placing severe penalties on interstate or foreign transport of women or girls for immoral purposes (*see* Mann Act). In addition, by 1915 forty-five states had passed laws prohibiting third persons from profiting from prostitution. Various attempts at international co-operation for the suppression of the white-slave traffic preceded the World War. That conflict emphasized the need of more effective methods of protecting women and children.

In 1919 the League of Nations[qv] was given general supervision over the carrying out of agreements made between nations for the stamping out of the traffic. Its study of conditions and the reports it has published have done much to limit the activity of the procurers, although its service has been hampered by the domestic policy of some nations regarding prostitution.

[Chicago Committee of Fifteen, *Annual Report*, 1915; League of Nations, *Report on Traffic in Women and Children*, Parts I and II, 1927.] ERNEST R. GROVES

"White Squadron," THE, so called because painted white, comprised the first modern American steel vessels (*Atlanta, Boston, Chicago* and *Dolphin*) to be completed (1887–88) after the naval decay following the Civil War. The policy of modernizing the navy was adopted by Congress in 1882 and the use of steel of domestic manufacture was legally specified.

[F. M. Bennett, *The Steam Navy of the United States.*]

DUDLEY W. KNOX

White Woman of the Genesee was a term applied to Mary Jemison who was captured at an early age by the Iroquois Indians[qv] and continued to reside with them for seventy-two years on the banks of the Genesee River. At the time of Sullivan's expedition[qv] against the Six Nations in 1779 she escaped with the Indians, but later returned and reared a large Indian family. Her story was told to James E. Seaver who first published it in 1856 and has proved so popular that it has since gone into almost fifty editions.

[J. E. Seaver, *Life of Mary Jemison.*]

CARL L. CANNON

Whitehall, The Treaty of (1686), provided for the cessation of hostilities in America between Great Britain and France and a mutual abstention from illicit commerce. Its most significant provision, however, was the clause embodying the principle of the "two spheres": armed clashes in America were not to be considered as causes of war between France and Great Britain in Europe, and a European conflict between them was not to be considered a cause for war in America; should such a European conflict take place, the colonies were to remain neutral. The treaty was supplemented by the appointment of commissioners, in 1687, to adjust the Anglo-French disputes in America and to arrange a boundary between their respective possessions there. The work of the commissioners came to naught, however, by reason of the English Revolution of 1688 and the outbreak of the War of the League of Augsburg in 1689.

[Frances G. Davenport, *European Treaties Bearing on the History of the United States and Its Dependencies*, Vol. II, pp. 309-29.]

MAX SAVELLE

Whitemarsh, a township adjacent to Philadelphia on the northwest, was the site of Washington's encampment from Sunday, Nov. 2, until Thursday, Dec. 11, 1777. While here, Washington learned of the Conway Cabal^qv^ (Nov. 9), and of the fall of the water defenses protecting Philadelphia (Nov. 23). The Battle of Edge Hill^qv^ was fought (Dec. 5–7) and here Lydia Darragh is supposed to have sent word of an impending British attack.

[Harry Emerson Wildes, *Valley Forge*.]

HARRY EMERSON WILDES

Whites, The Poor. *See* Poor Whites.

"Whitewash," with the meaning to free from debt through bankruptcy, was a common expression in the English colonies. It was applied politically by 1800, the Philadelphia *Aurora* (July 2, 1800) referring to a "whitewash" for Adams. This adaptation, meaning to give misconduct an appearance of good character through superficial examination, was common by 1839 when Rep. Duncan castigated "the committee to whitewash the black frauds and corrupt practices of Swartwout. . . ."

[*Congressional Globe*, Jan. 17, 1839; R. H. Thornton, *An American Glossary*.]

IRVING DILLIARD

Whitman Massacre (Nov. 29, 1847). Growing trouble between Dr. Marcus Whitman and the Indians to whom he ministered as a missionary doctor at Waiilatpu (near the present city of Walla Walla^qv^, Wash.) led to a treacherous attack which resulted in the death of Dr. and Mrs. Whitman and twelve others. Until ransomed by the Hudson's Bay Company^qv^ fifty-three women and children were held captives by the Indians during which time the women and girls were subjected to serious abuse.

Distrust by the Indians had been aroused by the increasing numbers of white settlers entering the country, a distrust aggravated by stories of the white man's domination told by eastern Indians and mixed-bloods employed in the fur trade. Dr. Whitman's apparent greater success in treating the diseases of the whites than of the Indians (who had developed no degree of immunity) increased the Indian suspicion that they were being cleared away to make room for the whites. The age-old Indian custom that gave the relatives of a deceased person the right to take vengeance against the medicine man may well have played its part.

The massacre was the direct cause of the Cayuse War^qv^, one of the most serious of the Indian wars of the Pacific Northwest.

[Clifford M. Drury, *Marcus Whitman, M.D., Pioneer and Martyr*.]

ROBERT MOULTON GATKE

Whitman Mission. *See* Walla Walla Settlements.

Wichita, starting as a trading post for the Wichita Indians in 1864, became a white man's village and cowboy trading town (*see* Cow Towns) on the Chisholm Trail^qv^ in 1868. When the railroads passed the new town by, the boosters laid their own track twenty-six miles north to Newton in 1872 and connected with the Santa Fé. This made Wichita the railhead of the Texas cattle drive^qv^ and brought 350,000 cattle for shipment and $2,000,000 in business the first season. It made Wichita the metropolis of southern Kansas, a leadership she held even after losing the Texas cattle trade to Dodge City^qv^.

[Joseph G. McCoy, *Historic Sketches of the Cattle Trade of the West and Southwest*.]

BLISS ISELY

Wickersham Commission, The, officially known as the National Commission on Law Observance and Enforcement, was appointed by President Hoover in May, 1929, with George W. Wickersham, attorney and former Cabinet member, as its chairman. Judges, lawyers and educators predominated in its personnel, all parts of the country being represented. Eleven subcommittees were created, and the findings were published in fourteen lengthy reports in 1931. The first and most widely discussed was that on Prohibition^qv^. Some others covered methods of dealing with juvenile delinquency, the cost of law enforcement, the "third degree," lawless practices in law enforcement and the belief that criminals were mostly foreign born.

[A Committee with a Herculean Task, *Literary Digest*, June 1, 1929, pp. 5-7; National Commission on Law Observance and Enforcement, *Reports*, 1931.]

ALVIN F. HARLOW

Wickyup. This term, from an Algonkin Indian[qv] word, a variant of wigwam, came into use in the early years of the 19th century to designate a rude brush shelter, usually temporary. In recent years the tendency has been to restrict its use to the conical brush-covered homes of the Great Basin Indians in Utah and Nevada. The type structure is a tripod of forked poles covered with brush.

CLARK WISSLER

"Wide-Awakes" was a name first used by an antiforeign, anti-Catholic organization which flourished around 1850 (*see* Nativism). In the campaign of 1860[qv], Republican marching clubs under this name arose everywhere. The first, in Hartford, wore black cambric capes when marching as protection against torch-drippings. These they later replaced with oilcloth capes, which, with glazed hats, became the official Wide-Awake garb.

[Meade Minnigerode, *Presidential Years, 1787-1860.*]

ALVIN F. HARLOW

Wigwam is an Abnaki Indian[qv] word meaning "dwelling," but similar forms of the word are found in most Algonkin[qv] languages. Wickyup[qv] is a variant of the same term. The English settlers adopted the word from the first, thus giving it a definite place in English speech. The wigwam in New England was a dome-shaped structure or a similar elongated form, covered with bark—birch-bark whenever available. In some cases the winter covering was of mats or thatch. However, the English extended the name wigwam to all Iroquois[qv] and Algonkin dwellings, thus covering the area from the Atlantic to the Mississippi, and north of Carolina and Tennessee into Canada. Later, the term wigwam was applied to tepees[qv]. In modern literature the tendency is to use wigwam for oval and elongated bark houses and tepee for conical structures of the tepee type.

CLARK WISSLER

"Wigwam," THE, headquarters of Tammany Hall[qv], is so called because of the pseudo-Indian organization of the society. The name was first applied to the building erected opposite the City Hall in 1810. The most famous Wigwam was that on Fourteenth Street, where, between 1868 and 1928 (when a new building was completed on Union Square), the famous succession of "bosses," Tweed, Kelly, Croker and Murphy, ruled.

[M. R. Werner, *Tammany Hall.*]

ALVIN F. HARLOW

Wild Life, Destruction of, by Settlement. Civilized man has constantly modified and altered his environment. When he thus changed his environment, he has revamped the composition of his animal associates. Some have been forced out or virtually extinguished while others have been introduced and encouraged. Some have been encouraged consciously while others have been attracted and fostered by the mere process of the change of the environment without conscious effort on the part of man. Thus on the North American continent, where wild life was once more abundant than in any other part of the world, the process of settlement has been the major force in the destruction of that life, and this extermination of certain of the species has been virtually independent of the curtailment of the supply by the hunter and the trapper.

Perhaps the most potent factors in this shift have been the process of deforestation and the destruction of the natural grazing lands. The colonial farmer, laboring in the shadow of the forest, "girdled" the trees and substituted cultivated land, which may be viewed as the creation of an artificial steppe. This steppe, which would have encouraged the development of grass-feeding animals, was dominated by man who took steps to see that the larger of the animals, at least, did not molest his handiwork. The principal fur-bearers of the New England and the Middle Colonies, the beaver, the otter, the mink, the marten, the bear, the raccoon and the fox were all affected. The marten, once an important animal in the fur trade[qv], deprived of his habitat became exceedingly rare. The fondness of the beaver for orchards and cornfields, in lieu of his natural food supply, led the farmer to complete the process of virtual extinction.

South of Maryland, where the white-tailed deer was to be found in such abundance that for a time the leather industry was centered there, the encroachments of the farmer, and later the lumberman and fire, threatened extinction of the species. Yet, in spite of all this, in those regions where the wilds remained and still remain untouched, the deer still hold their own. In the South, where the process moved more slowly, wild life remained longer. South Carolina, until well near the end of the 18th century, still had an abundance of wild life. In the whole area, the trapper usually moved westward before the advent of the settler, and when the increasing wariness of the game made its total destruction unprofitable.

As settlement moved westward to the plains area, the natural grasses that had been the source of food and the grazing lands of the herbivorous animals began to be turned under and in their place came the cultivated grains of civilized man. The vast herds of buffalo[qv], estimated when the continent was first discovered at between thirty and sixty million, began to move their habitat and then to diminish. With the settlement east of the Mississippi River, they gradually moved westward to the plains of rich grasses, once referred to as the Great American Desert[qv]. The buffalo, like all grazing animals, needed vast stretches of territory for pasturage. The severe winters, particularly on the high plains, made it imperative that they be allowed to roam, but man again upset the balance. With the building of the transcontinental railroads[qv] and the attendant rise of the cattle industry[qv], the days of the bison were numbered. As long as the cattle industry was based upon open pasturage it was merely a question of the survival of the fittest. Barring ruthless slaughter, the buffalo might have competed upon somewhat even terms with the cattle for survival. The advent of the barbed-wire[qv] fence threatened, for a time, the extinction of both the buffalo and the cattle. Neither could protect themselves from the relentless winters. But man, the environment changer, adjusted his procedure to protect the cattle. Artificial shelters and winter feeding with storage foodstuffs protected the cattle, but left the buffalo to their own devices. When to this there was added the virtual dependence of the Indian upon the buffalo for meat, shelter and clothing, and the apparently insatiable demand of the white man for robes and sport, the final chapter of one of the most picturesque phases of aboriginal life in America was written. And, with the passing of the buffalo, almost in retribution, it would seem, came the dependence of the Indian upon the white man for his food, shelter and clothing.

Withal, however, many forms of wild life were not destroyed by settlement. Indeed, they seemed to be encouraged and profited by making adjustment to the new environment created by man. Portions of the weasel family, *Mustelide*, particularly the common skunk (genus *Mephitis*) have had a peculiar fondness for the vicinity of man. Man's cultivation of fowl and his unwilling encouragement of the rodent, along with his shelters, made for the skunk an environment as beneficial, if not more so, than that before the advent of man. So, too, the raccoon, in spite of all man's hunting and his occupation of the land, was able to maintain himself. The green corn of the bottomland field and the refuse of man, made this scavenger able to survive where others failed. No less persistent, despite years of persistent warfare against it, the coyote not only held his original range but moved eastward. The process of settlement, which destroyed the game, merely made the coyote turn for food to poultry and livestock. Because of this a bounty rests upon his head. So, too, the lowly cottontail has enjoyed the rich fields resulting from the labors of man and has increased, and become a pest.

It is apparent, then, that settlement had a marked effect upon animal life. Apparently, no place other than a desert was more destructive of large mammalian life than the cultivated fields of civilized man. But at the same time those forest margin forms, like the small and moderate-sized rodents, found in man's increasing habitat in his westward march an environment not unlike that of the original steppe but far more suitable. So, too, the creation of an urban environment had its effect. In the region of Chicago, where a hundred and fifty years ago there were fifty-three known species of mammals, there have disappeared the "Virginia deer, American elk, American bison, beaver, eastern cougar, Canada lynx, bobcat, gray fox, timber wolf, otter, American badger, marten, fisher and black bear." Thirty-nine other species still remain but these almost without exception are of the rodent or scavenger type.

Birds and fish have also had their environments altered by man. More important than the constant fishing by man has been the pollution of the streams. Birds, while they suffered from the process of urbanization, profited by the increase in grain. With birds and fish the process was the same. Those able to adjust or profit from the change increased while the others became virtually extinct or diminished in number. (*See also* Game, Wild, Early Abundance of.)

[Richard Hesse, W. C. Allee and Karl P. Schmidt, *Ecological Animal Geography.*]

JOHN T. GANOE

Wild Rice (*Zizania aquatica*) is of significance in American history chiefly because it conditioned to a great degree the life of certain Indian tribes in the so-called wild-rice district, i.e., most of Wisconsin and a part of eastern Minnesota. It grows, however, in practically every state east of the Rocky Mountains. It belongs to the family of grasses and is a beautiful, single-stem annual growing in the soft ooze of glacial lakes and ponds and in the alluvial beds of slow-flowing streams. Among the Indians who were largely dependent on it for their food supply during a part of the year were the Chippewa, the eastern Sioux and the Menominee; and, to a lesser degree, the Sauk and Fox, Winnebago, Potawatomi and Assiniboin[qqv] found it necessary to their economy. Not only did it of itself afford food, but it drew thousands of ducks and geese to places where it grew and so supplied other food to the natives. It is worthy of note that the great struggle for territory between the Siouan and the Algonquian tribes occurred in the wild-rice district; and that that district probably sustained an Indian population equal to all the rest of the so-called Old Northwest[qv]. The plant gave its name to hundreds of places where it grew, to the Menominee Indians, to native words for the months of August and September, and to feasts occasioned by its harvesting. It seems also to have made for a superior physical stock among the tribes of the district where it was plentiful. It flowered in June, ripened in August, and was harvested and prepared for storage in September. It was usually prepared for eating by boiling or parching. Today its presence accounts in large measure for wild fowl in the districts where it grows.

[Albert E. Jenks, The Wild Rice Gatherers of the Upper Lakes, in *19th Annual Report of the Bureau of American Ethnology*, part 2, 1900.] GRACE LEE NUTE

Wild West Show, THE, is an original American entertainment featuring exhibitions typical of the life of cowboy[qv], Indian and soldier. The first was the "Wild West, Rocky Mountain and Prairie Exhibition" of William F. Cody ("Buffalo Bill") and Dr. W. F. Carver, opening at Omaha, Nebr., May 17, 1883, with Maj. Frank North, Gordon W. Lillie ("Pawnee Bill") and Capt. A. H. Bogardus in the cast. It was reorganized in 1884 by Cody, Bogardus and Nate Salsbury. Annie Oakley, "Little Sure Shot," joined in 1885 and Sitting Bull was with the show that season. "Buffalo Bill's" Wild West toured Europe in 1887, 1889–92 and 1902–7. At the Chicago World's Fair in 1893 (*see* World's Columbian Exposition) a "Congress of Rough Riders of the World" was featured. Carver, Lillie and Buck Taylor were also in the field. "Buffalo Bill" merged with "Pawnee Bill" in 1908 and with the Sells-Floto circus in 1913; his last appearance was with the Miller Brothers "101 Ranch Wild West Show" in 1916. Financial troubles were attributed to motion-picture competition. Zach T. Miller failed to repeat Cody's 1893 triumph with the 101 Ranch at the Chicago World's Fair of 1933 (*see* Century of Progress International Exposition) and Col. Tim McCoy's attempt to revive the Wild West Show in the grand manner in 1938 was a quick failure. The rodeo[qv] is a closely related form of entertainment.

[Richard J. Walsh and M. S. Salsbury, *The Making of Buffalo Bill;* Ellsworth Collings and Alma Miller England, *The 101 Ranch;* Luther Standing Bear, *My People, the Sioux.*] DON RUSSELL

"Wildcat" Money was currency issued by "Wildcat" banks. The name calls attention to the practice of banks of locating where it would be difficult for noteholders to present notes for payment. They flourished in the period 1830–60. Often they were started with specie borrowed only long enough to show the banking commissioners. They created a confusion in the currency and gave point to Chase's demand for a national bank currency (*see* Banks, National).

[H. White, *Money and Banking.*] JAMES D. MAGEE

Wildcat Oil Drilling. Hardly had Edward L. Drake[qv] completed his oil well on Oil Creek, Pa., late in August, 1859, than others seeking like fortune set to drilling near by with spring poles. Thus was born that romantic American figure, the wildcatter, who has fairly overshadowed the prospector in color, in wild hopes and rosy dreams of quick wealth. From Pennsylvania he has led the way across the continent, hazarding his all and often that of his supporters on the point of an ever deepening drill. Frequently dry holes or a host of dupes were the only fruit of his gamble. Again discovering oil[qv] in the most unexpected places, he has made paupers into millionaires overnight. Proration may check him and conservation impede his operations, but human nature being what it is, he and his hopes will not die. Against him, largely, must be charged the uneconomical development of the nation's petroleum resources. On the other hand the oil companies depend upon his explorations and to him in part, at least, must be credited the swift development of our petroleum resources.

[Ida M. Tarbell, *History of the Standard Oil Company;* C. G. Gilbert and J. E. Pogue, *America's Power Resources.*] JOHN FRANCIS, JR.

Wilderness, Battles of the (May 5–7, 1864). On May 4 Grant's (U.) army was across the Rapidan River, preparing to attack Lee's (C.) army. The move had been anticipated. Instead of attacking the Union troops in the act of crossing, as might have been expected, Lee preferred to engage Grant in The Wilderness where the Union two-to-one superiority in numbers and artillery would be somewhat neutralized. Grant directed his main movement at Lee's right, hoping to get clear of The Wilderness before effective resistance could be offered. Lee, however, moved rapidly to check this attempt. Road divergence separated his two wings; Longstreet (C.), expected to support either wing, was late in arriving. On May 5 Grant attacked. Ewell (C.) on the left and A. P. Hill (C.) both held firm. Night ended the fighting.

The next day Grant resumed his attack. Hill's troops were driven in confusion. Lee personally rode among the fleeing men to rally and lead them back into battle. As the cry, "Lee to the rear" rose on every side, Longstreet's tardy command arrived and struck with suddenness and fury, driving Grant's men back. Ewell, on Lee's left, repulsed all attacks. In the midst of success, Longstreet was wounded by his own men, as Jackson had been at Chancellorsville[qv]. Soon afterward fighting ceased for the day.

It is doubtful if Longstreet's wounding had any important effect on the outcome of the day's fighting. The troops on both sides were much disorganized, the hour was late and little more could have been accomplished. During the 7th the two armies faced each other from behind their hasty breastworks. The two days had seen bitter fighting in a region difficult either to receive or deliver battle. Thousands of acres of tangled forest, interlaced undergrowth and scrub trees were on every hand with here and there only narrow roads, some of them mere paths. Cavalry was useless and artillery hardly less so. Vision was limited to short distances and once the fighting began, control passed to local commanders. The brush caught fire and many wounded were burned to death. Dense smoke filled the air. The Wilderness became a tract of doom and over all was the shadow of death.

Perceiving the uselessness of again assaulting Lee's lines, Grant decided to move by the flank toward Richmond, thus forcing Lee to come and meet him. The goal was Spotsylvania Courthouse[qv]. As Grant's advance troops reached this objective Lee's men were in position to meet the threat. The first act of a campaign, bitterly fought and replete with brilliant strategical and tactical movements, was completed (*see* Richmond, Campaign against).

[*Battles and Leaders of the Civil War;* F. B. Maurice, *Robert E. Lee: The Soldier;* E. P. Alexander, *Military Memoirs of a Confederate.*]

THOMAS ROBSON HAY

Wilderness Road, The, ran from eastern Virginia (where it linked up with the Maryland and Pennsylvania roads from the north and the Carolina and East Tennessee roads from the south) through the mountain pass, known as Cave or Cumberland Gap[qv], to the interior of Kentucky and thence to the Ohio and beyond. A rudimentary road already existed when, in March, 1775, Daniel Boone and a party of about thirty woodsmen undertook to clear and mark out a trail from the Indian treaty-ground at Fort Watauga, in what is now East Tennessee, by way of Cumberland Gap and through the rugged mountains and rolling canelands of Kentucky, to the mouth of Otter Creek, on the Kentucky River, a site chosen for a fortified town and forthwith named Boonesborough[qv]. Later the road forked at the Hazel Patch, in Laurel County, one branch leading by the Crab Orchard and Danville to the Falls of the Ohio[qv] at Louisville. This primitive road, made up in large part of a succession of irregular woodland paths trodden down and worn bare by wandering herds of buffalo and roving Indian hunters or war parties, was blazed by Boone at the instance of the Transylvania Company[qv]. Its total length was close to 300 miles, and fully two thirds of the distance had to be opened and marked to guide an endless train of plodding pioneers who followed in the wake of Boone and his fellow road builders. At first little more than a footpath or pack-horse trail, spasmodic but insufficient measures were taken by the Virginia government to enlarge and improve the crowded thoroughfare, but a score of years elapsed before it was passable by wagons. After Kentucky became a separate state, renewed efforts to grade, widen and reinforce the road were put forth. Sections of the road were leased to contractors who, in consideration of materials and labor furnished to maintain the road, were authorized to erect gates or turnpikes across it and collect tolls[qv] from travelers. In legislation on the subject, the road was generally called "The Wilderness Turnpike Road." Blockhouses were erected and manned at intervals along the way to protect travelers against marauding Indians and other outlaws. For more than half a century after Boone blazed the way in 1775, the Wilderness Road was a principal avenue for the movement of immigrants and others to and from the early West. The Ohio River afforded the only alternative route; and over these converging highways to the great inland empire of the new nation, thousands upon thousands of Americans of the pioneer period passed and repassed in a never-ending procession. The Wilderness Road is still an important interstate arterial roadway and constitutes a part of U. S. Route 25, otherwise known as the "Dixie Highway."

[Thomas Speed, *The Wilderness Road;* A. B. Hulbert, *Boone's Wilderness Road;* W. A. Pusey, *The Wilderness Road to Kentucky.*]

SAMUEL M. WILSON

Wilkes Exploring Expedition (1838–42). By an act approved May 14, 1836, Congress authorized the President "to send out a surveying and exploring expedition to the Pacific Ocean and South Seas." This expedition, commanded by Lt. Charles Wilkes, of the United States Navy, sailed from Hampton Roads, Va., in August, 1838. After exploring the American quadrant of the Antarctic, Wilkes sailed for Australia, arriving off Sydney harbor on the night of Nov. 29, 1839. No pilot was available but Wilkes had charts and entered safely. Great was the surprise of the people of Sydney when they awakened to find the United States war vessels riding at anchor. Subsequently, upon his second visit to Sydney, Wilkes announced in the *Sydney Morning Herald,* March 13, 1840, his discovery of an Antarctic continent in the Australian quadrant.

In addition to the Antarctic Wilkes surveyed islands in the Pacific and 800 miles of coast and streams in the Oregon country. While in Oregon he investigated, by special order of the United States Government, a dispute between American missionaries and the Hudson's Bay Company[qv]. He reported that the discontent of the former arose from the refusal of the company to allow their participation in the fur trade. The complaint against the Hudson's Bay Company, reported Wilkes, "comes with an ill grace from the members of a mission who are daily receiving the kindest attentions and hospitality from its officers."

Wilkes' *Narrative of the United States Exploring Expedition* was published in Philadelphia in six volumes in 1844. The scientific reports, in many volumes, appeared at intervals until 1874, when Congress refused to finance further publication.

Scarcely had Wilkes returned when a controversy broke forth that still continues. Wilkes invariably observed mountains—and always in the distance. Other explorers sailed over "mountains" charted by Wilkes. Yet it was impossible for Wilkes to have lied. His officers, at the time, wrote letters home, which were published in American newspapers; each letter affirmed the discovery of land in the Antarctic. If Wilkes had perpetrated a wilful fraud his officers, with whom he quarreled, would have revealed it in Wilkes' trial by naval court-martial. The probable explanation is that advanced by T. W. Edgeworth David, who wrote: "it is very easy to mistake, in the distance, grounded bergs for table-shaped mountains."

[Autobiography of Wilkes, ms. in the Library of Congress, Washington, D. C.; relative to the Antarctic explorations of Wilkes, see articles by Sir Douglas Mawson and Frank E. Ross, respectively, in the *Proceedings of the Royal Geographical Society of Australasia, South Australian Branch,* Vols. XXXIV and XXXV; and by W. H. Hobbs in the *Geographical Review,* October, 1932, and in the *Geographical Journal,* June, 1933.]

FRANK EDWARD ROSS

Wilkes Fund Dispute. A fund of £17,000 was raised in Europe and America to pay the debts of and defend John Wilkes, English editor, charged with libeling King George III in 1763. The South Carolina house of commons voted £1500 for the fund in 1769. The crown denied its right to do this, the commons defended it, and the controversy continued until the beginning of the Revolutionary War.

[David Duncan Wallace, *History of South Carolina.*]

ALVIN F. HARLOW

Wilkinson, Fort, named for Gen. James Wilkinson and situated on the Oconee River near Milledgeville, Ga., was constructed about 1797. June 16, 1802, Gen. Wilkinson here negotiated a treaty with Creek Indians[qv] as initial fulfilment of the Georgia Compact[qv]. Troops soon afterward were withdrawn.

[*American State Papers, Indian Affairs,* Vol. I, pp. 669–672, 693.]

THOMAS ROBSON HAY

Willamette Valley Settlements, The, began about 1830 when French-Canadian employees of the Hudson's Bay Company[qv] took up farms on the French Prairie, the region within the great bend of the Willamette River below Salem. These were followed by the Methodist missionaries led by Jason Lee who settled beside the French-Canadians in 1834. Americans, some of them Mountain Men[qv] and others unconnected with fur companies or missions, but who had been trappers in the Rockies, joined these settlers. By 1841, before the beginning of large immigrations, there were settled in the lower Willamette Valley 9 missionary, 65 American and 61 French-Canadian families. Some Americans and French-Canadians had formed attachments with Indian women.

On May 3, 1843, the American settlers in the valley elected officers and on July 5 adopted a constitution, thus setting up a provisional government. The following year the French-Canadians joined this government and in 1845 it was expanded to include the officials of the Hudson's Bay Company.

The overland immigration to the Willamette Valley began in 1841 when some 70 people arrived. The immigration of 1842 numbered about 120 and that of 1843 some 900. In each year, until California[qv] gold (1849–50) proved the greater attraction, increasing numbers of settlers arrived. By the end of 1845 the population of the valley numbered about 6000. The first census, 1850, showed 11,631 valley settlers out of a total of 13,294 for the entire Oregon Territory.

The Donation Land Law^qv^, passed by Congress in 1850 giving each married settler in Oregon 640 acres of land, speeded up settlement. The immigration of 1850 was about 2000. Settlement advanced up the valley and by 1847 had reached the neighborhood of Eugene near the junction of the three forks of the river. Lane, the most southern of the valley counties, was organized in 1851.

[R. C. Clark, *A History of the Willamette Valley.*]

R. C. CLARK

William and Mary, College of. The third attempt to establish a college in Virginia was successful when King William and Queen Mary granted to Rev. James Blair a charter and endowment Feb. 8, 1693. The Wren building, erected 1695, used for classes and dormitories, was rebuilt after a fire in 1705. An Indian school was supported by part of the income from a fund bequeathed for philanthropic purposes by the distinguished physicist, Hon. Robert Boyle. The grammar, philosophy and divinity schools, modeled on English predecessors, were fully established by 1729. Many of the alumni were leaders in the American Revolution, including Thomas Jefferson, James Monroe, Richard Bland, Peyton Randolph, Edmund Randolph and Benjamin Harrison. The buildings were damaged by Revolutionary troops and the endowment was seriously impaired as a result of the war. In 1776 the Phi Beta Kappa Society^qv^ was organized by a group of students. In 1779 the grammar, Indian and divinity schools were replaced by schools of modern languages, medicine and law. In 1859 the Wren building was burned a second time and rebuilt; it was burned a third time in 1862. The College was closed from 1861 until 1865, when instruction was resumed and continued until 1881. In 1888 a small grant from the state enabled the College to reopen. In 1906 the property of the College was deeded to the State of Virginia. It became coeducational in 1918. The Wren building, President's house, and Brafferton Hall were restored in 1929 by Mr. John D. Rockefeller, Jr.

[L. G. Tyler, *Williamsburg, The Old Colonial Capital;* E. G. Swem, *Virginia Historical Index.*]

E. G. SWEM

William and Mary, Fort. The leading radicals of Portsmouth^qv^, N. H., were warned by Paul Revere on Dec. 13, 1774, that Gen. Gage might take over the military stores at the fort, located in Newcastle, an island at the mouth of the harbor. Several hundred men under John Langdon and Pierse Long crossed over the next day, received the brief fire of the garrison of six without harm, seized the fort, and removed about 100 barrels of powder. On the 15th John Sullivan with another party took the muskets and some of the cannon; further action was blocked by the arrival of a naval vessel. There was no serious attempt to apprehend the participants in what was probably the first armed attack of the Revolution on the military forces of the crown.

[L. Mayo, *John Langdon;* C. L. Parsons, Capture of Fort William and Mary, in *Proceedings of the N. H. Hist. Soc.*, Vol. IV.]

HERBERT W. HILL

William Henry, Fort, Massacre at (Aug. 10, 1757). The Marquis de Montcalm, the French commander, with an army numbering more than 8000 including 2000 Indians, laid siege to the British fort at the head of Lake George early in August. Lt. Col. Monro with fewer than 2500 men bravely defended the post, while Col. Webb, at Fort Edward^qv^, cravenly refused to lead his 4000 troops to the rescue. Monro was finally forced to surrender on the 9th, though Montcalm allowed him fair terms and agreed to give the garrison safe conduct to Fort Edward. However, the French Indians treacherously killed the wounded British, plundered the fort and camp, and at last began a general massacre. Montcalm and his chief officers were able to restrain the Indians only with the greatest difficulty and at the risk of their own lives. "Kill me, but spare the English who are under my protection," exclaimed Montcalm. Though some accounts put the number massacred as high as 1500 persons, the best evidence shows that only about fifty were killed, though six or seven hundred were carried off, stripped and otherwise mistreated. The massacre served for long as an "atrocity story" and has often been called a blot on Montcalm's record. (*See also* Lake Champlain in the French and Indian War.)

[Francis Parkman, *Montcalm and Wolfe.*]

EDWARD P. ALEXANDER

Williams v. Mississippi was a test by a Negro, Henry Williams, of Mississippi's constitution of 1890 and code of 1892, under the Fourteenth Amendment^qv^, claiming a denial of the equal protection of the law to Negroes in the franchise provisions, in that they invited discriminatory administration. The Supreme Court decided (April 25, 1898) that mere possibility of discrimination did not invalidate the provisions.

Mississippi's ingenious exclusion device thus was upheld and Negroes are still disfranchised under it.

[Henry Williams v. the State of Mississippi, United States Reports, Cases Adjudged in the Supreme Court, Vol. XXI, Wallace, 170.] MACK SWEARINGEN

Williamsburg, Battle of (May 5, 1862), was the most important incident in the retreat of the Confederates under Gen. Joseph E. Johnston from Yorktown to the Chickahominy and their pursuit by the Federals under Gen. George B. McClellan. On the eastern outskirts of Williamsburg swampy terrain both to the north and the south of the highway and the existence of strong redoubts commanding the roads brought pursuit to a halt on May 4. Determined attacks upon these defenses on May 5 constituted the battle. It was an interlude in the retreat and pursuit, which continued the following day. Union losses in the battle were 2239. The Confederate losses were not much smaller.

[*War of the Rebellion, A Compilation of the Official Records,* Vol. XI.] ALFRED P. JAMES

Williamsburg, Va., had its origins in a central section of Middle Plantation, a palisaded outpost established between the James and York rivers in 1633 against the Indians. The town received its present name in 1699 in honor of William III, the then reigning British monarch, at which time it became the second capital of the colony of Virginia[qv]. The College of William and Mary[qv] had been established at this point six years prior to that time. From 1699 to 1779 Williamsburg remained the economic, educational, religious and social, as well as the governmental center of the colony. Being the urban center for a large and dispersed civilization, this city of one or two thousand inhabitants became a metropolis of five or six thousand persons during court seasons and other "public times."

Williamsburg was the scene of much political activity in the period immediately preceding the American Revolution and toward the end of that struggle was occupied in turn by British and American forces. Owing to the exigencies of the war and to the desire for a more central capital on the part of an expanding population, the seat of government was removed to Richmond[qv] in 1779. Until the 20th century, except for intervals during the Civil and World wars, Williamsburg remained a quiet county seat and college town. During the Battle of Williamsburg[qv] in 1862, Federal troops occupied the town and remained there until 1865. As a result of naval and military activities on the Virginia peninsula during the World War, Williamsburg was somewhat altered and tended to lose the marked 18th-century character it had retained up until that time. (*See also* Williamsburg Restoration.)

[L. G. Tyler, *Williamsburg, The Old Colonial Capital;* Rutherfoord Goodwin, *Williamsburg in Virginia;* M. P. Andrews, *Virginia, the Old Dominion.*]

HUNTER D. FARISH

Williamsburg Restoration, THE, at Williamsburg, Va., is the realization of "an endeavor to restore accurately and to preserve for all time the most significant portions of an historic and important city of America's colonial period." This undertaking, envisaged by the Rev. W. A. R. Goodwin, Rector of the Bruton Parish Church in Williamsburg, was made possible through the generosity of John D. Rockefeller, Jr. The work has been achieved through an exhaustive study of archæological, architectural and documentary material of the 17th and 18th centuries, both in America and in England and France. The selected areas have been restored to their 18th-century aspect and comprise Duke of Gloucester Street, the principal thoroughfare of the colonial city, and certain adjacent squares and greens upon which were located the colonial Capitol, the "Governor's Palace," the colony Gaol and other public buildings and numerous private residences. The more important of the public edifices, including the Governor's Palace and the Capitol, both of which had burned to the ground, have, with the exception of their brick foundations which remain, been entirely reconstructed. Numerous buildings required only slight alterations to restore them to their 18th-century appearance. Altogether in the restored area, 507 buildings were demolished, 21 were moved away, 122 were reconstructed, and 67 have been restored and repaired. The educational purpose of the Restoration has been emphasized at all times.

[L. G. Tyler, *Williamsburg, the Old Colonial Capital;* Rutherfoord Goodwin, *Williamsburg in Virginia,* and *A Handbook for the Exhibition Buildings of Colonial Williamsburg, Incorporated;* M. P. Andrews, *Virginia, the Old Dominion.*]

HUNTER D. FARISH

Williamson Purchase. *See* Pulteney Purchase.

Willing, THE (1779), was a large Mississippi boat, armed with cannon and manned by forty-six men, which George Rogers Clark sent from Kaskaskia to Vincennes[qqv] to co-operate in the reduction of the latter place. Despite Clark's "great dependence in the vessel," she arrived too late to participate in the assault upon the British fort (*see* Clark's Northwest Campaign).

[M. M. Quaife, *The Capture of Old Vincennes;* James A. James, *Life of George Rogers Clark.*] M. M. QUAIFE

Willing Expedition, THE (1778–79), sanctioned by the Commerce Committee of the Continental Congress[qv] and commanded by James Willing of Philadelphia, was apparently a military project for the purpose of despoiling British property and trade on the lower Mississippi. Willing, with a party of about thirty men, left Fort Pitt[qv] on Jan. 10, 1778, in an armed boat, the *Rattletrap,* and arrived in Natchez on Feb. 19, intimidating British subjects and seizing their property on the way. With the co-operation of volunteers from New Orleans including Oliver Pollock[qv] and his nephew, Thomas Pollock, Willing continued to attack the settlers in British Florida[qv] and their ships on his journey from Natchez to New Orleans[qv]. There he was cordially received by Gov. Galvez, who attempted to preserve the status of neutrality between the British and American belligerents. Willing's rapacity and British threats of retaliation caused not only Gov. Galvez but Oliver Pollock to seek the departure of Willing and his men, as early as May 16. His men returned by way of the Mississippi but Willing himself sailed for Philadelphia later in the year, only to be captured by the British and incarcerated at New York. The expedition disrupted enemy commerce as planned but stimulated an increased opposition of Floridians to the American cause.

[John Caughey, Willing's Expedition Down the Mississippi, 1778, in *The Louisiana Historical Quarterly*, XV, No. 1.]

R. J. FERGUSON

Wills Creek Post. *See* Cumberland, Fort.

Wilmington Riot (Nov. 10, 1898). On Nov. 9, 1898, a mass meeting of white citizens was held at Wilmington, N. C., in an effort to redeem the city from Negro rule, most of the offices being held by Negroes, who outnumbered the whites 17,000 to 8000. It was demanded that the editor of the Negro newspaper remove himself and his press by 7 o'clock the next morning. When this demand was not met, 600 armed whites destroyed the printing material, and the building "took fire" and burned to the ground. A race riot followed, with some ten Negroes being killed and three whites wounded. The coroner ruled that the Negroes came to their death by gunshot wounds at the hands of unknown parties. All of the city officials resigned and were superseded by white Democrats.

[Hugh T. Lefler, *North Carolina History Told by Contemporaries.*]

HUGH T. LEFLER

Wilmot Proviso. Soon after the Mexican War[qv] began, President Polk requested $2,000,000 from Congress with which to negotiate peace, it being understood that territory would be acquired from Mexico. Aug. 8, 1846, a bill to appropriate the sum was moved in the House. David Wilmot, a Democrat from Pennsylvania, hitherto identified with the administration, proposed the following amendment to the bill: "Provided, That, as an express and fundamental condition to the acquisition of any territory from the Republic of Mexico by the United States, by virtue of any treaty which may be negotiated between them, and to the use by the Executive of the moneys herein appropriated, neither slavery nor involuntary servitude shall ever exist in any part of said territory. . . ." This amendment became famous as the Wilmot Proviso. It precipitated a bitter debate over the question of slavery in the territories.

An effort was made in the House to amend the Wilmot Proviso by limiting its application to the region north of the Missouri Compromise line[qv], but this was defeated. The appropriation bill carrying the Wilmot Proviso was then passed by the House by a vote of 87 to 64. The bill as amended was then sent to the Senate; but the Senate adjourned for the session before a vote was taken.

In the next Congress, a bill to appropriate $3,000,000 for peace negotiations was introduced in the House, and Wilmot again moved his Proviso. The bill as amended was carried in the House, Feb. 1, 1847, by a vote of 115 to 106. The Senate refused to consider the amended bill, but passed one of its own appropriating the desired sum. After bitter debate the House concurred in the Senate bill, and the $3,000,000 became available to President Polk, without Wilmot's conditions.

In the meantime debates over the Proviso had aroused the country, North and South. State legislatures and other public bodies approved and condemned the principle incorporated in the Proviso. Sectional animosity was heightened. The principle of the Proviso, contained in other legislation, continued to provoke sectional debate. The modern Republican party[qv] was later founded on this principle, and Abraham Lincoln was elected on a platform pledged to carry it out.

Modern historical scholarship recognizes that more is involved in the Wilmot Proviso than meets the eye. Polk was unpopular with Northern Democrats in 1846 because of his recent settlement of the Oregon question[qv], the Walker tariff of 1846, and his recent veto of a rivers and harbors bill. Votes for the Wilmot Proviso were calculated to embarrass the President. The motive of David Wilmot, an administration Democrat, has been puzzling. The usual theory is that he merely served as an accommodating mouthpiece for an antiadministration Democrat, Jacob Brinkerhoff. Some historians now maintain that Wilmot, not Brinkerhoff, was the real author of the plan, and that his motive was not unconnected with a desire to regain the support of his Pennsylvania constituency, alienated by his recent tariff vote.

[Charles B. Going, *David Wilmot, Free Soiler;* Richard R. Stenberg, Motivation of the Wilmot Proviso, in *Mississippi Valley Historical Review*, March, 1932.]

HAYWOOD J. PEARCE, JR.

Wilson-Gorman Tariff Act. *See* Gorman-Wilson Tariff.

Wilson's Creek, Battle of, was fought Aug. 10, 1861, between Federal troops under Gen. Nathaniel Lyon and an army of the Missouri State Guard under Gen. Sterling Price, co-operating with a force of Confederates from Arkansas under Gen. McCulloch. Lyon had 5400 men and Price and McCulloch had nearly 11,000. Lyon attacked the combined force at Wilson's Creek, Mo., ten miles southwest of Springfield, at 5 o'clock in the morning. He sent Gen. Franz Sigel to make a flank attack but McCulloch defeated him and both armies turned on Lyon. At the critical moment Lyon was killed. The Federal army retreated toward Rolla. The total casualties, about equally divided between the two armies, were 2544 or nearly 16% of all those engaged. This was the first success of the Confederates in Missouri.

[E. M. Violette, *History of Missouri.*]

W. FRANCIS ENGLISH

Winchester, Battle of (May 25, 1862). The disaster to Kenly's forces at Front Royal, Va., placed the command of Gen. N. P. Banks at Strasburg, consisting of some 10,000 Federal troops and 16 guns, in grave peril from Confederate forces operating in the Valley of Virginia under Generals "Stonewall" Jackson and R. S. Ewell. Reluctant to retire, Banks delayed starting for Winchester until he was all but outflanked. With Jackson striking at his flank and rear and Ewell striving to intercept him, he finally reached Winchester late in the afternoon of the 24th and took position south, west and east of the town. There at dawn on the 25th, Banks was attacked by Ewell, soon reinforced by Jackson, their combined troops and guns double his own. Against these odds Banks retreated five or ten miles beyond Winchester, where the Confederates, unable to break his columns, allowed him to proceed unmolested to the Potomac River. Rejoined there by his wagon trains, he crossed the river at Williamsport next day.

[G. H. Gordon, *Brook Farm to Cedar Mountain.*]

JOHN FRANCIS, JR.

Winchester, Battle of (Sept. 19, 1864). On Aug. 7, 1864, Gen. P. H. Sheridan (U.) was placed in command of all troops in the Shenandoah Valley, was given both authority and means and was directed to halt the offensive operations directed by Gen. J. A. Early (C.), and to drive the Confederates from the Valley (*see* Shenandoah Campaign, The, 1864). With reinforcements from Grant's (U.) army, Sheridan forced Early up the Valley and when the latter was also reinforced, Sheridan withdrew northward. Early, following in pursuit, divided his force about the same time that his reinforcements were recalled by Lee (*see* Petersburg, Siege of). Sheridan with superior force attacked the Confederates and forced them back. Reinforced by concentrating detachments, Early halted, attacked and drove the Federals back. He then took position behind Opequon Creek to the westward and in front of Winchester. Sheridan, again reinforced, counterattacked, on Sept. 19, 1864, using his cavalry effectively. After severe fighting, which lasted throughout the day, the Confederate left was turned and Early's troops were forced back in some confusion. After dark, the Confederate Army retired southward through Winchester, finally halting at Fisher's Hill[qv].

[G. E. Pond, *The Shenandoah Valley.*]

THOMAS ROBSON HAY

Windmills were known before the time of Don Quixote, but they did not become a feature of Western American life until after the Civil War. The occupation of lands beyond the belt of regular rain, springs, streams and shallow underground water tapped by hand-dug wells—wells drawn from by the "old oaken bucket"—made windmills a necessity. Well-drilling machinery and practical mills afforded by the Industrial Age made them a possibility. Popularized in the 1870's, they came to dot villages, farms and ranches of the prairie states, Texas, and rough, arid or semiarid lands beyond, before the gasoline engine as an economic substitute—in certain cases only—had been invented. They came to supply family water, stock water and often irrigation for garden patches. At first the wind-catching staves, or spokes, in the windmill wheel were made of wood—flat slats; curved steel blades supplanted these with more power.

The windmill became common only after barbed wire[qv] had made the control of waterings by private owners possible. It redeemed tens of millions of acres of waterless land from desert idleness. It made possible plots of green, garden patches, a few trees for shade and fruit even during the most parching drouths. It brought running water into houses located out in a land once characterized as a place where "you have to climb for water" (go *up* gravelly canyons for water lost below in the sands) "and dig for wood" (roots of mesquites[qv] and other bush growth).

[W. P. Webb, *The Great Plains.*]

J. FRANK DOBIE

Windsor, Conn. *See* River Towns of Connecticut.

Wine. Unsuccessful efforts to use the abundant native grapes as a source of wine forced the colonists to import this luxury. As early as 1694 South Carolina had offered a bounty for the production of the beverage, and a century later (1769) Virginia gave a French *vigneron* a hundred acres of land, with house and slaves, that he might attempt to introduce a new industry. In 1764 England had laid upon the wines of Madeira and other Atlantic islands, when imported directly, a tax of £7 per 252-gallon tun, upon the wines of Portugal and Spain, when imported through Great Britain, a tax of 10s, and had forbidden the import of French wines (4 Geo. III cap. 15). South Carolina added to this tax a further impost of £8. On May 9, 1768, the *Liberty,* owned by John Hancock, was alleged to have attempted an illegal entry at Boston of a cargo of Madeira; a riot and prosecution ensued.

The census of 1810 reported an annual American production of 11,755 gallons, made largely from currants, but this probably overlooked a considerable amount privately made and consumed. Large-scale production was begun in 1825 by Nicholas Longworth at Cincinnati, using the native Catawba grape; after forty years, this enterprise was ended by the destructive effect of black rot in the vineyards. When the California wineries came under American sovereignty the industry received new impetus. In 1870 three million gallons, of which 60% was Californian, were produced, all the states reporting some yield. A half century of progress increased domestic manufacture to 27¼ million gallons, supplemented by an importation of 5½ million gallons. The Prohibition Era[qv] forced the closure of the commercial wineries and increased private manufacture, as shown by the greatly augmented sale of fresh grapes and raisins. Repeal of the Eighteenth Amendment[qv] found a larger market; importation in 1935 was 2,771,000 gallons and domestic production 92 million; the next year increasing to 170,876,000 gallons.

[John H. Garber, American Wine, in *The Making of America,* Vol. V; Statistical Abstract; *Proceedings,* Massachusetts Historical Society, LV, 239-284.]

ROBERT G. RAYMER

Winnebago, Fort, was the third military post built in Wisconsin after the American occupation. It stood at the portage of the Fox-Wisconsin waterway[qv], and was central in the territory of the Winnebago Indians[qv]. After the uprising of this tribe in 1827 known as the Red Bird or Winnebago War[qv], Maj. David E. Twiggs of the First United States Infantry was sent in 1828 to begin this post. Lt. Jefferson Davis, just from West Point, cut timber for the fort and assisted in its building. During the Black Hawk War[qv] of 1832 Fort Winnebago was a center for supplies and feared an attack of the hostiles, which was averted by the Indian agents, especially John H. Kinzie. The garrison was maintained until 1845, when the troops were ordered to abandon the post. The property was sold in 1853, under direction of Jefferson Davis, then Secretary of War.

[Mrs. John H. Kinzie, *Wau-Bun, or the Early Day,* ed. of 1930.]

LOUISE PHELPS KELLOGG

Winnebago, THE, were an offshoot of the Siouan family[qv], closely akin to the Iowa, Oto, etc. They called themselves Otchungras, "people of the parent speech." When discovered by the French in 1634 they occupied all of southern Wisconsin. Their numbers declining, because of wars with the Illinois[qv], they permitted the intrusion of the Algonquian[qv] tribes. They were most closely allied with the Sauk and Foxes and the Menominee[qqv]. They were allies of Tecumseh[qv], and their chief, Caramaunee, was with him when he died. The Winnebago opposed the advent of the Americans (*see* Winnebago War), but in 1828, 1832 and 1840 were forced to make treaties, ceding all their Wisconsin lands. Transferred to Minnesota, they were in 1862 carried away to the upper Missouri, where they had a reservation with the Omaha. About half the tribe now live in Wisconsin, on lands which they have purchased.

[F. W. Hodge, *Handbook of American Indians.*]

LOUISE PHELPS KELLOGG

Winnebago War, THE (1827). Traditionally friendly with the French and British, the Winnebago long opposed the Americans, and over their resentment of the coming of white settlers to southwestern Wisconsin, the uprising called the Winnebago War developed. The vigorous measures of Gov. Cass and the army snuffed out the "war" before it really got started, but for several weeks the Illinois-Wisconsin area was in turmoil. Highlights of the affair were the remarkable thousand-mile canoe journey of Gov. Cass, the dramatic conduct of Red Bird, and the rescue of infant Chicago by the hilarious Danville militia. Among consequences of the war were the establishment of Fort Winnebago[qv], the restoration of garrisons at Chicago and Prairie du Chien, and the ultimate expulsion of the tribe from Wisconsin.

[*Wis. Hist. Colls., passim;* M. M. Quaife, *Chicago and the Old Northwest, 1673-1835.*]

M. M. QUAIFE

Winona Speech. In the fall of 1909 President Taft made a tour of the Middle West in order to defend his policies. Sept. 17 at Winona, Minn., Taft defended the Payne-Aldrich Bill[qv] as the best tariff ever passed. The furore created by this defense of the tariff overshadowed the constructive features of the speech and widened the breach between Insurgents and Standpatters.

[R. V. Harlow, *Growth of the United States;* Mark Sullivan, *Our Times.*]

THEODORE G. GRONERT

Wire-Tapping Cases. The difficulty of reconciling the constitutional safeguards of the Fourth and Fifth Amendments[qqv] with the necessities of what Mr. Justice Sutherland described as "the deadly conflict constantly being waged between the forces of law and order and the desperate criminals who infest the land" is apparent in two leading decisions of the Supreme Court. In Olmstead v. United States (277 U. S. 438, 1928) the Court ruled by a five-to-four vote that the actions of prohibition agents (*see* Volstead Act), who tapped a defendant's telephone line and submitted records of conversations in court, did not constitute an unreasonable search and seizure[qv]. Furthermore, although the state where the tapping occurred made it a misdemeanor, under common law[qv] such evidence was still admissible until Congress by express enactment should declare otherwise. A requirement of "nice ethical conduct" by enforcement officers would merely aid criminals. In a dissenting opinon Mr. Justice Holmes castigated the Government for engaging in such "dirty business." Lawless conduct by officials promoted contempt for law by everybody. In 1937 in Nardone et al. v. U. S. (302 U. S. 379), a similar question was involved. The Communications Act of 1934, however, had forbidden interception, publication, etc., of all communications, unless authorized by the sender. Despite the fact that Congress in the intervening years had refused to pass specific legislation debarring evidence secured by wire tapping, the Court held that the Communications Act applied to all persons, including the agents of the Government. The defendants had been convicted on evidence improperly admitted. Justices Sutherland and McReynolds in a vigorous dissent declared that the act in question did not include the Government or affect its rights. The decision would enable "the most depraved criminals to further their criminal plans over the telephone, in the secure knowledge that, even if these plans involve kidnapping and murder, their telephone conversations can never be intercepted by officers of the law and revealed in court." An appeal from a second conviction resulted in another decision by the Supreme Court, Nov. 11, 1939, making a still more drastic prohibition on evidence secured in violation of the above statute. The use of intercepted telephone conversations as evidence was not only forbidden but prosecutors were not free to use such "proscribed evidence" in other ways.

[*Readers' Guide to Periodical Literature.*]

W. A. ROBINSON

Wireless Telegraphy. Marconi's patent on wireless in England was only three years old when a wireless set was installed on the American liner *St. Paul* (1899), though its range was less than 75 miles. By 1901 a message was received on the liner *Philadelphia* from 500 miles' distance. Several American inventors, R. A. Fessenden, Lee deForest, E. F. W. Alexanderson, Edwin H. Armstrong and others, devised a number of improvements between 1900 and 1915, including deForest's Audion Tube (1906), one of the epochal inventions of wireless. The Marconi Company built a station on Cape Cod which succeeded in sending a message across the Atlantic in January, 1903, but was not adequate for commercial telegraphy. It placed another station on Cape Breton Island, which began public service in 1908. Meanwhile, deForest had built five large stations for the U. S. Navy in Florida and the West Indies. Ships were slowly being equipped with wireless, and in January, 1909, the first important SOS call was sent out when the liner *Republic* received its death blow in a collision off Nantucket. The sinking of the *Titanic*[qv] in 1912 and the rescue of 712 of its passengers through SOS calls constituted a milestone in wireless history. There was so much chaos on the air from conflicting calls, many of them by private, amateur sets, that the Government took over the licensing and regulating of wireless in 1912. In October, 1915, radio telephony across the Atlantic was first accomplished. (*See also* Radio.)

[Alvin F. Harlow, *Old Wires and New Waves.*]

ALVIN F. HARLOW

Wisconsin. The topographical location of Wisconsin, between the two upper Great Lakes and the Mississippi River, has conditioned its history. It was discovered by the French in 1634 when Champlain sent Jean Nicolet[qv] to explore for a route to the Western ocean and to the Orient. In 1671 all this region was formally annexed to the Kingdom of France by a ceremony at Sault Ste. Marie[qv]. In 1673 its chief waterway, the Fox-Wisconsin, was opened by Jolliet[qqv] and Marquette who discovered the Mississippi. The Indian name for its principal river gave its name to the state.

The French regime lasted for over a century, when Wisconsin's lakes and waterways were visited by French explorers, missionaries and soldiers. Forts were built at Green Bay, LaPointe on Lake Superior, and at several sites on the upper Mississippi. Missions were maintained at the forts and a central Jesuit mission at DePere. Settlements were begun at Green Bay, LaPointe and Prairie du Chien[qqv]. During the Fox wars[qv] of the early 18th century French expeditions invaded Wisconsin in 1716 and in 1728. During the French and Indian War, Indians from Wisconsin, led by Charles de Langlade, helped defeat Braddock, 1755, and served under Montcalm, 1759[qqv].

The cession of all interior North America to Great Britain and the withdrawal of the French garrisons from LaPointe and Green Bay put an end to the control of what is now Wisconsin by the French government (*see* Paris, Treaty of, 1763). Nevertheless, the French language persisted, and French methods of conducting the fur trade[qv] endured during all the British regime. The British built Fort Edward Augustus at Green Bay in 1761, but the garrison was withdrawn during Pontiac's conspiracy[qv] (1763), and never reinstated. The period of British supremacy was the time of the greatest development of the fur trade. Great companies were organized such as the North West Fur Company[qv], and Wisconsin Indians were encouraged to hunt and bring furs to the trading posts. The region of the upper Mississippi, the south shore of Lake Superior, and the interior lakes had many fur-trading posts. During the American Revolution the fur trade was disorganized; emissaries of the British, Americans and even of the trans-Mississippi Spanish visited the Indian villages (*see* Sauk Prairie, 1778). Milwaukee village was strong for the American cause.

At the close of the Revolution Wisconsin became nominally a part of the Northwest Territory[qv]. In reality, as the British refused to surrender the Northwest posts, the fur trade regime continued under British control (*see* Border Forts, The Evacuation of). While a part of the Northwest Territory, Wisconsin became part of Indiana Territory in 1800; of Illinois Territory in 1809; of Michigan Territory in 1818.

When the War of 1812[qv] broke out, the Indians and few settlers of Wisconsin all sided with the British. In 1814 an expedition from St. Louis mounted the Mississippi and built an American post—Fort Shelby—at Prairie du Chien, which raised the first American flag in Wisconsin. A month later a British force from Mackinac[qv] captured this fort, the only military clash on Wisconsin soil between Great Britain and the United States. The next year, after the treaty of peace, the British evacuated Prairie du Chien and the American regime began in Wisconsin with the building in 1816 of Fort Howard[qv] at Green Bay and Fort Crawford[qv] at Prairie du Chien.

The military occupation of Wisconsin continued until the organization of the territory in 1836. In 1825 a great treaty was held at Prairie du Chien[qv] to induce the Indians to keep the peace. In 1827, however, the Winnebago War[qv] occurred, occasioned largely by the trespass of lead miners on the lands of this tribe. When it was suppressed by the surrender of Red Bird, Winnebago chief, mining rapidly increased, and there was a rush to the southwest that built the settlements of Platteville, Potosi, Mineral Point, Dodgeville, Shullsburg and others. In 1827 Henry Dodge of Missouri settled with his family and freed slaves near the present Dodgeville.

Fort Winnebago[qv] was built in 1828 at the Portage to control the Indians and to safeguard the Fox-Wisconsin waterway. During the Black Hawk War[qv] of 1832, the miners of southwest Wisconsin "forted" at numerous small forts, and Dodge raised a troop of rangers that aided in defeating Black Hawk at the Battle of Wisconsin Heights[qv].

After this last Indian war immigration increased rapidly. The Indian claims south of the Fox-Wisconsin were extinguished, American settlers came in at the Lake Michigan ports, land offices were opened and southern Wisconsin had by 1836 over 12,000 population. That year Wisconsin Territory was organized from what had been a part of Michigan, Dodge was appointed governor, Madison was chosen the capital, and Wisconsin became an American commonwealth.

The twelve years of territorial life saw enormous gains in population, chiefly from the New England states and New York. The census for 1840 was 30,000. Foreigners, mostly Germans, began coming by 1838 and continued with accelerated rate. Norwegians, Belgians, Swiss, as well as English-speaking foreigners came in also during the territorial period. In 1848 Wisconsin, after rejecting one constitution and accepting a second, entered the Union as a state. Its boundaries had been decreased at the south by the inclusion of a large portion in Illinois; on the northeast by the setting off of the northern peninsula for Michigan; on the northwest by the erection of Minnesota Territory. However, Wisconsin comprises 56,066 square miles of territory; it has a large lake shore on Lakes Michigan and Superior; and borders on the upper Mississippi to the St. Croix River.

As a pioneer state having a population of over 300,000 in 1850, political struggles led to the formation in 1854 of the Republican party[qv], at a schoolhouse in Ripon, known as the "birthplace."

The state was carried for the Republicans in 1856, and in 1860 Wisconsin rallied for the Civil War, sending over 90,000 men into the Union ranks. At the close of the war lumbering and manufactures began on an increasing scale, the northern portion was settled, and agriculture changed from an exclusively wheat-raising type to diarying and animal husbandry. The political situation was dominated after 1900 by the Progressives led by Robert M. LaFollette[qv], Sr. In the World War Wisconsin furnished its full quota of men, was the first state to report its selective draft[qv], and the first to organize a Council of Defense.

Since the World War the state has attained an equilibrium in agriculture and industry. Its Progressive policies have expanded under the Wisconsin "idea"[qv]; while in education, led by the Wisconsin University, the state has attained an international reputation. Its population in 1930 was 2,939,006. Its pseudonym—The Badger State—was not acquired because of the unusual numbers of these animals, but because in early lead-mining days some miners dwelt in holes in the rocks like badgers.

[L. P. Kellogg, *The French Régime in Wisconsin and the Northwest*, and *The British Régime in Wisconsin and the Northwest;* Joseph Schafer, *History of Agriculture in Wisconsin;* William E. Raney, *Wisconsin: A Story of Progress*, 1940.]

LOUISE PHELPS KELLOGG

Wisconsin et al. v. Illinois and Chicago Sanitary District. *See* Chicago Sanitary District Case.

Wisconsin Heights, Battle of, occurred July 21, 1832, between Black Hawk's[qv] retreating forces and the troops under Col. Henry Dodge and Maj. J. D. Henry. Black Hawk made a stand near the Wisconsin River, about twenty-five miles northwest of Madison, in order to permit his women and children to cross the river. His strategy was commended by professional soldiers. He held off the whites until dark, and during the night he and all his forces escaped.

[R. G. Thwaites, The Story of the Black Hawk War, in *Wisconsin Historical Collections*, XII, 1892, pp. 217-265.]

LOUISE PHELPS KELLOGG

Wisconsin Idea, THE, is a term given to the coöperation between the experts in the University of Wisconsin and the administration of the state under the Progressive party. The reforms advocated by the Progressives, in the early 20th century, under the leadership of Robert M. LaFollette[qv], Sr., were embodied for the most part in commissions, such as the Tax, Railway (later Public Utilities), Insurance, Civil Service, Industrial, Conservation, Highway, etc. The preparing of the laws erecting these commissions was done in the Legislation Reference Bureau, headed by Charles McCarthy. The aid of University specialists was often evoked, as when Professor D. O. Kinsman was called in, in 1911, to draw the income tax law. On the erection of the several commissions, University professors such as Thomas S. Adams, John R. Commons, Balthasar H. Meyer, and others were frequently appointed members. Sometimes they combined these administrative duties with University work; more frequently they were given leave of absence during their services.

[Charles McCarthy, *The Wisconsin Idea.*]

LOUISE PHELPS KELLOGG

Wisconsin Railroad Commission v. Chicago, Burlington & Quincy Railroad Company (257 U. S. 563, 1922). Congress, by the provisions of the Transportation Act of 1920[qv], undertook to guarantee to the railways "a fair return upon a fair valuation." Previously, the Wisconsin Railroad Commission had entered into an agreement with the defendant railroad, by which intrastate transportation of persons was to be provided at the rate of two cents a mile; after the passage of the Federal act, the state commission sought to compel the continuance of the agreement. The railway contended that at such a rate, it could not earn the fair return contemplated in the law. The Supreme Court accepted this view, and emphasized also the fact that the Interstate Commerce Commission[qv], under the Federal act, had valid power and the duty to raise the level of intrastate rates when such rates were so low as to discriminate against interstate commerce, and unduly to burden it. This decision—together with the similar and companion case of New York v. New York Central Railroad Company—was the last step in a process by which the earliest rate cases were completely reversed (Peik v. Chicago & Northwestern Railroad Company, 94 U. S. 164, 1876; Wabash Railway Company v. Illinois^qv^, 118 U. S. 557, 1886; Houston, East & West Texas Railway Company v. United States, 233 U. S. 342, 1914, commonly known as the Shreveport Case^qv^; Minnesota Rate Cases, 230 U. S. 352, 1913).

[S. Daggett, *Principles of Inland Transportation;* Frank H. Dixon, *Railroads and Government;* Albert R. Ellingwood and Whitney Coombs, *The Government and Railroad Transportation;* D. Philip Locklin, *Railroad Regulation since 1920;* F. D. G. Ribble, *State and National Power over Commerce;* G. C. Reynolds, *The Distribution of Power to Regulate Interstate Carriers between the Nation and the States;* Charles C. Rohlfing, Edward W. Carter, Bradford W. West and John G. Hervey, *Government and Business;* G. Lloyd Wilson, ed., The Railroads and Government, the *Annals* of the American Academy of Political and Social Science, January, 1936.]

W. BROOKE GRAVES

"Wise, and Good and Rich, The." The Federalists, with their distrust of democracy and the common man, laid great stress on aristocratic and propertied influence in government. John Adams, writing before the adoption of the Constitution, speaks of "the rich, the well-born, and the able." On the other hand the aristocratic idea was unpopular with those who came to be identified as the Republican party (Jeffersonian)^qv^. The words *rich,* and even more, *well-born,* antagonized many and were discussed in the conventions called to ratify the Constitution. Hamilton took notice of the phrase in the *Federalist*^qv^. Fisher Ames of Massachusetts, one of the ablest leaders of the Federalist party^qv^, gave the expression perhaps its best known form when, in 1802, he advised concentrating party strength in the state governments, making "State justice and State power a shelter of the wise, and good and rich from the wild destroying rage of the Southern Jacobins"—reference of course to the predilections of the Jeffersonian party for revolutionary France.

[John Adams, *Works;* C. M. Walsh, *The Political Science of John Adams;* Seth Ames, ed., *Works of Fisher Ames.*]

W. A. ROBINSON

Wise, Fort. *See* Lyon, Fort.

Wistar Parties were organized in Philadelphia in 1818, as an outgrowth of the Saturday evening salons at the home of Dr. Caspar Wistar, Fourth and Locust Streets, where members of The American Philosophical Society^qv^ entertained distinguished scientists, diplomats, travelers. The Civil War interrupted the Wistar party as an organization, but it was revived in 1886, headed by a Dean and an executive committee of three. The engraved invitation card has been used since 1835.

[Hampton L. Carson, *The Centenary of the Wistar Party.*]

JULIAN P. BOYD

Witchcraft has been a pet delusion of mankind always, but the Bull of Pope Innocent gave it the authority of the Catholic Church in 1484, and the *Malleus Maleficarum* published in 1489 became the great textbook of its manifestations. The superstition spread over the Western World and many thousands of victims were hanged and burned in Europe in the 16th and 17th centuries. The conduct of Sir Matthew Hale at the Suffolk Assizes in 1664 rather fixed the subsequent procedure for English courts.

Undoubtedly belief in witchcraft was universal and sincere, and came to America with the colonists. Margaret Jones was executed for witchcraft in Boston in 1648. Soon after Mary Parsons of Springfield was indicted for witchcraft, but actually executed for murdering her child. Mrs. Anne Hibbins was hanged in Boston, June 19, 1656. Other accusations, some of them with fatal results, occurred in scattered points in New England and the other colonies. Even William Penn presided over the trial of two Swedish women for witchcraft, but the acquittal of Bridget Bishop in 1680 in Salem, and the execution of a woman named Glover in Boston in 1688, largely on the evidence of a Goodwin child thirteen years old, whose case was studied by Cotton Mather, most closely paralleled the Salem hysteria. The latter probably made Mather the champion of the witchcraft persecution.

In the spring of 1692 in Salem Village, now Danvers, a group of young women and girls, who had been amusing themselves during the long winter listening to the lurid tales of Tituba, an old Negro slave of the minister, Rev. Samuel Parris, showed signs of hysteria. These "afflicted children" presently began to accuse persons of bewitching them. They fell down in fits supposed to be caused by the alleged witches, who were also accused of pinching them and sticking pins into them. The local physician could not see that the children had any malady, so Mr. Parris called in other ministers to confer on the strange manifestations. A powerful and inflammatory sermon was preached at the village by a visiting clergyman against the machinations of the devil. The civil magistrates entered the case. A special court to try the cases was appointed by the governor, and between May and September, 1692, several hundred persons were arrested, nineteen were hanged and many imprisoned. The cases were tried in Salem in an atmosphere of terror and tense excitement. No one knew who would be accused next and condemned on charges by the "afflicted children." Resistance to the delusion, at first terrorized into silence, grew rapidly, however, and by October the people came to their senses. Many strong characters exhibited high courage in resisting the excitement at the risk of their lives. Early in the next year all those arrested had been released with or without trial and the episode was over.

No witch was ever burned in Salem. Giles Corey, who was pressed to death (*see* Pressing to Death), was so treated under an old English law for refusing to plead to the indictment, not for witchcraft. Nowhere except in Massachusetts did the participants in such a delusion have the courage to publicly confess their errors. The General Court passed a resolution to that effect Dec. 17, 1696. Judge Sewall handed to his minister a confession to be read in his meeting house while he stood in his pew, and the twelve jurymen signed a statement admitting their error and asking forgiveness.

While a few later cases of witchcraft persecution occurred in Virginia in 1706, in North Carolina in 1712, and perhaps in Rhode Island in 1728, this fiery outbreak at Salem Village practically ended witchcraft in America.

[Samuel G. Drake, *Annals of Witchcraft;* J. D. Phillips, *Salem in the Seventeenth Century;* G. L. Kittredge, *Witchcraft in Old and New England.*]

JAMES DUNCAN PHILLIPS

"With malice toward none; with charity for all" are the opening phrases of the last sentence of Abraham Lincoln's second inaugural address, March 4, 1865. By many Americans these words, with the sentiments of tolerance and sympathy which follow them, are accepted as the perfect expression of Lincoln's nobility of character.

PAUL M. ANGLE

Withlacoochee River, Battles at (Dec. 31, 1835; Feb. 27, 28, 29 and March 5, 1836). Practically the first engagement of the Florida War*qv* occurred near Fort Drane when Gen. Clinch fought the Seminoles*qv* under Alligator and Osceola at a Withlacoochee River ford, Dec. 31, 1835. Clinch gained no decisive victory. Two months later, Gen. Gaines, returning to Fort Brooke, encountered Osceola's force of 1500 Indians and Negroes and was held up at the river ford from February 27 to March 6. Gaines and Clinch left Florida shortly thereafter, having scored no appreciable success over the Seminoles.

[Henry B. Dawson, *Battles of the United States;* C. K. Gardner, *Dictionary of the Army of the United States;* N. A. Strait, *List of Battles, 1754 to 1900.*]

ROBERT S. THOMAS

Wolff Packing Co. v. Court of Industrial Relations (262 U. S. 522, 1923). Following serious labor disorders in 1920 the Kansas legislature passed an act declaring that the manufacture of food and clothing, mining, public utilities and transportation were businesses affected with a public interest*qv*. A three-judge industrial court was empowered to fix wages and labor conditions whenever the public peace or health was endangered. In 1923 a unanimous decision of the U. S. Supreme Court dealt the Kansas industrial court a deathblow by declaring the fixing of wages in a packing plant a deprivation of property and a denial of the freedom of contract guaranteed by the Fourteenth Amendment*qv*. State regulation of industrial and labor relations was administered a significant check in consequence of this decision.

[A. E. Ragan, *Chief Justice Taft;* The Kansas Industrial Court, in *American Bar Association Journal,* IX; *New York Times,* June 12, 1923, 1.]

ALLEN E. RAGAN

Wolves were originally found throughout the continent of North America, from central Mexico to the Arctic. Several local varieties may be distinguished, differing more or less in color and size, but these variations do not in general represent any real differences in species. The two main species most commonly referred to are the gray or timber wolf (*canis occidentalis*) and the prairie wolf or coyote*qv* (*canis latrans*). The timber wolf is somewhat larger than the coyote and is distinguished by its howl, which is quite different from the high-pitched dirge of the coyote. The coyote is found principally in the Great Plains and Rocky Mountain area, while the gray wolf is more widely distributed.

Wolves have always been present in considerable numbers along the American frontier and the accounts of early western travelers contain innumerable allusions to them and their deep-throated nocturnal howling. These travelers are likely to be inaccurate in their descriptions and in the names which they apply to different varieties. Still, there is a remarkable unanimity in their accounts of the habits of the wolf and the great nuisance involved in its presence. From the very beginning of settlement the wolf was a problem. It preyed upon livestock and in winter would hover in the vicinity of farms and ranches, seeking its victims. While wolves often hunted in packs during the winter, there are few authenticated instances where they attacked man. The settlers from the start waged a war of extermination against wolves and as early as the 1630's bounties seem to have been offered for wolf scalps in Virginia and Massachusetts. The aid of Indians was sometimes enlisted in the war upon them. With the rise of sheep and cattle ranches in the trans-Mississippi West, the wolves constituted a serious economic problem. Most of the Western states and territories resorted to the bounty system while professional "wolfers" were sometimes engaged to hunt the animals. Traps and poisons were imported in an effort to eradicate the pest. Bounties are still paid in some localities but expert opinion differs as to the effectiveness of this method of exterminating wolves. Lack of conformity of bounty laws has led to abuses of the system while the "counterfeiting" of wolf scalps has even been resorted to. The gradual extension of settlement has been more effective than any laws. Wolf skins have always constituted an item in the North American fur trade, although they do not have a relatively high value. From the accounts of early observers it appears that the Indians were fond of wearing wolf heads and skins in ceremonial dances, and the wolf played its part in their folklore. Wolves have practically disappeared from the region east of the Mississippi and south of the Great Lakes, although even in recent years wolf drives have not been unknown in certain localities in the Middle West. Notwithstanding its destructiveness to game and livestock, the wolf seems to have served at least one useful purpose as a carrion-eater and scavenger.

[Ernest Thompson Seton, *Life Histories of Northern Animals;* William T. Hornaday, *The American Natural History;* W. P. Webb, *The Great Plains;* T. S. Palmer, Extermination of Noxious Animals by Bounties, in U. S. Department of Agriculture, *Yearbook*, 1896; John James Audubon and John Bachman, *The Quadrupeds of North America.*]

WAYNE E. STEVENS

Woman Movement. On March 31, 1776, Abigail Adams wrote to her husband, John Adams, then in the Continental Congress[qv], and urged him "to remember the ladies and be more generous to them than your ancestors," in the new code of laws. "Do not put such unlimited power into the hands of the husbands," she wrote, or the women will rebel. This instruction went unheeded, however, and women remained in the inferior legal position in which tradition and English common law[qv] placed them.

The threatened rebellion did not take place until the 1830's, after Sarah and Angelina Grimké had begun to speak in public against Negro slavery[qv]. Since platform appearances of women were then almost unheard of outside of Quaker[qv] meetings, the two sisters were denounced as unwomanly and brazen. This led them to work for emancipation of their own sex as well as of black bondmen. Within the next ten years others began to campaign for women's rights. One of the most prominent, Lucy Stone, a distinguished orator, married Henry Blackwell, but failed to take his name, thus setting precedent for the Lucy Stone Leaguers, women who retain their own names after marriage. Two other early feminists were Elizabeth Cady Stanton and Lucretia Mott, a noted Quaker preacher. Their resentment over the exclusion of the women delegates from the World Antislavery Congress, held in London in 1840, led them finally to call the Seneca Falls Convention[qv] of 1848, the first woman's rights gathering of modern times. Here was launched the organized woman's rights movement. While seeking to remove all injustices, the reformers emphasized woman suffrage[qv] as the best means for securing other rights; and in 1920 an amendment giving women the vote was written into the Federal Constitution (*see* Nineteenth Amendment).

Gradually, women had become better qualified for their reform work through being better educated. Improvement of secondary schools for girls, especially through the efforts of Emma Willard, Mary Lyon and Catherine Beecher, helped encourage college training for women; and Vassar, the first women's college equal to the best for men, was opened in 1865. Others of high quality followed, and state colleges and universities in larger numbers opened their doors to women. But it was not until the 1890's that, largely through the aid of M. Carey Thomas, president of Bryn Mawr, and Mary Garrett, who, through a large gift of money to the Johns Hopkins Medical School, opened that institution to women, that opportunities for first-class graduate study were made available. The industrial revolution[qv], through helping free women from domestic drudgery, multiplied their numbers in colleges and universities. By the early 20th century women had won distinction for scholarly work in many fields.

Their new leisure also influenced the growth of women's clubs[qv], which got a strong start in 1868, through the simultaneous organization of the New England Woman's Club, largely sponsored by Julia Ward Howe, and the Sorosis Club of New York, under leadership of Jane

Cunningham Croly. These, especially the Sorosis, became models for hosts of others which soon appeared. The programs of the organizations varied greatly, but most of them aimed at the self-improvement of their members and at social service. In 1890 was formed the General Federation of Women's Clubs, which by the 1930's had about 2,000,000 members. This was indicative of the co-operation and solidarity among women.

Toward the middle of the 19th century, likewise, women began to enter professions formerly closed to them. The first woman to receive a medical degree in modern times was Elizabeth Blackwell, who, in 1849, was granted a diploma from the medical school of Geneva (N. Y.) University. Antoinette Brown, who, after a theological course at Oberlin, was ordained in the Congregational ministry in 1852, was apparently the first woman trained in the profession who was licensed to preach. The law was more conservative, but Arabella M. Mansfield, the pioneer in this field, was admitted to the bar in Iowa in 1869. Other women followed in these and other professional fields, and also entered new doors opened in the business world.

In the latter part of the 19th century women began to fill political offices in the Western states where they had the vote, many being elected superintendents of schools or to state legislatures. In 1917 the first woman was elected to Congress, Jeannette Rankin of Montana. In 1933 the first Federal Cabinet position was given to a woman, when Frances Perkins was made Secretary of Labor.

The National Woman's party[qv] continues to work for an equal rights amendment to the Federal Constitution, which would remove the hundreds of legal discriminations still remaining against women.

[Inez Haynes Irwin, *Angels and Amazons, A Hundred Years of American Women.*]

MARY WILHELMINE WILLIAMS

Woman Suffrage. Under England a few of the colonies, notably New York, permitted women of property to "vote their estates," but with Independence such suffrage as women had was taken away, except in the case of New Jersey. That state, by its constitution of 1776 and by subsequent laws, gave qualified "inhabitants" the right to vote; but, owing to irregularities in the elections, in which Negroes as well as women voted, in 1807 suffrage was limited to free white men.

On the insistence of Elizabeth Cady Stanton woman suffrage was included in the program adopted at the Seneca Falls Convention[qv] in 1848. Efforts to secure votes for women in connection with the enfranchisement of the Negro by the Fourteenth and Fifteenth Amendments[qqv] failed, and in 1869 a split over policy in the recently formed American Equal Rights Association somewhat weakened the reform movement. But the resulting American Woman Suffrage Association, led by Lucy Stone and Julia Ward Howe, and the National Woman Suffrage Association, championed by Elizabeth Cady Stanton and Susan B. Anthony, reunited twenty years later as the National American Woman Suffrage Association. Though bitterly opposed by the conservative element and by the liquor interests and the leaders in the underworld, the suffragists widened their influence, through press and platform, circulating petitions, lobbying in legislative halls and speaking at hearings before congressional committees.

Gradually some of the states gave women limited suffrage, usually for municipal elections, on educational questions, or on bond issues. Then, in 1869, when Wyoming organized as a territory she gave women the vote and when admitted as a state in 1889 the right was retained. In 1893 Colorado gave women the suffrage; in 1896, Utah and Idaho; in 1910, Washington State; in 1911, California; in 1912, Arizona, Kansas and Oregon; in 1913, Alaska Territory; and, the same year, Illinois, by statute, gave them presidential and municipal suffrage; in 1914 Nevada and Montana granted them full suffrage; and in 1917, impelled by changes produced by the World War, the powerful State of New York granted women the suffrage.

Many years before this the early suffrage leaders had died and the brunt of the responsibility for the movement was being borne by others, notably Anna Howard Shaw and Carrie Chapman Catt. But some of the younger women, impatient with the slow gains made by work with state legislatures, had decided to concentrate on securing passage of the proposed amendment to the Federal Constitution, named for Susan B. Anthony. Led by Alice Paul and Lucy Burns, in 1913, they began to bring pressure on the Wilson administration, using militant methods, which the National American Woman Suffrage Association disapproved. Consequently the radicals reorganized separately, as the Congressional Union, and later, as the National Woman's party[qv], and continued their militant tactics.

In January, 1918, President Wilson came out for the amendment, which passed Congress the next year, and was ratified in time for the national election of 1920 (*see* Nineteenth Amendment). Its most noticeable early results were laws in behalf of child welfare and of more rights for women.

[E. C. Stanton, S. B. Anthony, M. J. Gage and I. H. Harper, *The History of Woman Suffrage;* Edward Raymond Turner, *Women's Suffrage in New Jersey;* Carrie Chapman Catt and Nettie Rogers Shuler, *Woman Suffrage and Politics, the Inner Story of the Suffrage Movement.*]

MARY WILHELMINE WILLIAMS

Woman's Christian Temperance Union, The, had its origin in the Woman's Temperance Crusade of 1873–74. Inspired by a temperance[qv] address delivered by Dr. Dio Lewis, noted health advocate at Hillsboro, Ohio, in December, 1873, the women of the town began a praying crusade against the saloon[qv]. Hymns were sung and prayers offered within and without the saloons. The liquor traffic was swept from some 200 towns in a score of states in less than two months. Realizing the possible temporary effects of the crusade because the saloon enjoyed the protection of the law, and sensing the need of a permanent organization to complete the victory, the leading church women of Chautauqua, N. Y., called a national convention of temperance women. Delegates from seventeen states attended these meetings at Cleveland, Ohio, Nov. 18–20, 1874, at which the Woman's Christian Temperance Union was founded.

The new organization grew rapidly and became a real force in public affairs. By the turn of the century every state required scientific temperance instruction in its public schools. The prohibition[qv] victories of the next two decades may be traced to voters educated as children concerning the evil effects of alcohol. The Anti-Saloon League[qv], formed in 1893, was mainly a result of the work of the W. C. T. U. Based on high ideals of good morals and clean living, the Union worked to convince the American people that drinking was morally wrong. It mercilessly fought the saloon as the destroyer of the home and the ally of corrupt politics and crime.

To the energetic leadership and guidance of Frances E. Willard the Woman's Christian Temperance Union owes the scope of its program. With fifty distinct departments of work headed by experts, working principally through schools, churches, press, politics, contests and petitions, it has exerted a potent influence for good. It has advanced the cause of prison reform, moral education, Sabbath observance, Christian citizenship, woman suffrage, purity in literature and art, armament reduction, international arbitration and world peace, and has relentlessly combated child labor, juvenile delinquency, white slavery[qqv] and legalized vice.

The Woman's Christian Temperance Union is organized in every state, territory and dependency of the United States. But six presidents have served the "white ribbon" cause during its long history: Mrs. Annie Wittenmyer, 1874–79; Miss Frances E. Willard, 1879–98; Mrs. Lillian M. N. Stevens, 1898–1914; Miss Anna A. Gordon, 1914–25; Mrs. Ella A. Boole, 1925–33; and Mrs. Ida B. Wise Smith, since 1933. Largely through the efforts of Miss Willard, the World Woman's Christian Temperance Union was founded in 1883.

[Harold U. Faulkner, *The Quest for Social Justice;* Allan Nevins, *The Emergence of Modern America;* Arthur M. Schlesinger, *The Rise of the City.*]

GLENN H. BENTON

Woman's Party, National. In 1914 the radical wing of the National American Woman Suffrage Association, led by Alice Paul, seceded and organized the Congressional Union, which in 1917 was renamed the National Woman's party. Using militant methods, the party concentrated on getting a woman suffrage amendment written into the Federal Constitution. After the Nineteenth Amendment[qv] was adopted it worked everywhere to remove discriminations against women, but campaigned especially for a Federal amendment giving women equal rights with men.

[Inez Haynes Irwin, *Angels and Amazons, A Hundred Years of American Women.*]

MARY WILHELMINE WILLIAMS

Women, The Citizenship of Married. Until 1855 marriage had no effect on United States citizenship, and the woman enjoyed independent citizenship in her own right. By the act of Feb. 10, 1855, the alien woman who married an American citizen gained American citizenship as the result of marriage. Whether the American woman who took an alien husband was divested of her American citizenship as a result of marriage remained a moot question until the act of March 2, 1907. This act provided that such woman should take the citizenship of her husband. Unquestionably, from this date until the Cable Act of Sept. 2, 1922, marriage determined the citizenship of the married woman. Beginning with the Cable Act and including amendatory acts of July 3, 1930, March 3, 1931, and the Equality Citizenship Act of May 24, 1934, the legislation of the United States has evolved to the presentday regulations by which the citizenship of the married woman is again independent of marriage; she gains or loses her citizenship by virtue of acts entirely apart from marriage.

[Luella Gettys, *The Law of Citizenship in the United States;* Waldo E. Waltz, *The Nationality of Married Women.*]

WALDO E. WALTZ

Women, The Education of. Colonial settlements paid homage to a hoary, traditional conception of woman's subjection. By the law of God, no less by the laws of men, she was held inferior. In the interval from that day to this, a veritable, yet bloodless, revolution for woman's independence and equality has been fought and, in large measure, won: in the world of everyday work she can labor and collect wages; on the holy ground of the highest professions she has planted her feet; in politics she has a voice; before the laws she helps make, she is man's equal. In this metamorphosis the education of woman has been conditioned by changes in the economic order; in turn, education has been a powerful auxiliary in transforming her economic, social and political status.

Education of girls was limited in all colonies. Though little girls attended "dame schools"[qv], New England "town schools" excluded them, generally, at first, as "inconsistent with the design thereof." New Netherland and Quaker communities admitted girls to elementary schools.

In 18th-century cities, southern, central and northern, "venture" schools arose, reflecting increased stability and material welfare, willingness of private teachers to supply more varied, practical education than town and church-controlled institutions were ready to offer, and increasing liberality on the part of burghers toward the education of daughters. Private agencies, competing for fees, were ready to receive girls as well as boys; some opened to girls only. Out of "venture" schools, female seminaries, or academies[qv], arose. The first to receive official sanction, the Female Academy at Philadelphia, was chartered 1792. Though popular, female seminaries lacked public financial support generally, and gave way to public high schools, established at Worcester (Mass.), 1824, in New York and Boston, 1826. The high school's curriculum differed little from the seminary's; but as a public institution, it tended to accept the principle of coeducation. Thus, through these institutions, was woman's title to equal secondary education made clear. In a secondary school enrollment of over six million in 1936, girls outnumbered boys slightly.

As the seminary broadened horizontally, through the high school, to include all girls who had completed elementary schooling, it deepened its foundations of "solid studies" and extended vertically to form the woman's college. Though not all the institutions they established, or furthered, became colleges, Emma Willard, Catherine Beecher, Mary Lyon, Amos Eaton, George F. Pierce, Z. C. Graves blazed the collegiate trail, later graced by Elmira (1855), Vassar (1865), Smith (1875), Bryn Mawr (1885), each competent to be considered a "college like a man's." Facilities for higher education[qv] broadened with the admission of girls to collegiate coeducation at Oberlin (1837), a policy that gained popularity with the growth of state universities; and through the opening of affiliated colleges, Barnard, Radcliffe, Sophie Newcomb, near the close of the century. Of 594,575 enrolled in collegiate education in 1936, women constituted 45%.

Such a colossal change was accomplished despite dire anticipations. Were colleges to contest what God had wrought, what Paul had advised, what Blackstone had set forth with the assurance of immutable law? Girls' gossamer intellects would crack; their bodies would not stand the strain. If some, indeed, survived the ordeal, who would marry them, anyway? Despite the fact that many of the best educated women were opposed, or indifferent, to the suffrage movement, higher education was popularly associated with it. In derision, some parodied the couplet:

"Then whom will you marry, pretty maid?
"Advanced women don't marry, Sir, she said."

Fears proved unfounded. First the pragmatic test, then scientific studies, showed girls' minds equal to the studies of college men; physical health increased; and *amor's* arrows found Alumna's heart as readily as those of girls of like economic and social status who did not go to college.

A few women taught rudimentary schools in colonial days, but special training for women's first significant public profession began with normal schools[qv], instituted (1839) to meet demands of the common schools. From an insignificant fraction, then, women came (1934) to furnish 80.9% of public elementary and secondary teachers.

Although a few colonial women knew something of healing arts, practised midwifery, and were invited to attend lectures by Dr. Shippen of Philadelphia, medical schools opened to women only after Elizabeth Blackwell struggled to gain entrance to Geneva (N. Y.) College, 1847. Dr. Samuel Gregory admitted women to medical lectures, Boston (1848), an event which led to the New England Female Medical College (1852), later merged with Boston University. The Female Medical College, Philadelphia, was incorporated in 1850. Fifty years later, there were 1456 women medical students and 23,757 men. Women physicians constitute 4% of the profession today.

Ada Kepley received the first law degree from Union College of Law in 1870; Washington University's Law School, open to both sexes (1867), issued their first degree to a woman in 1871. Only 205 women law students were reported in 1909 in a total of 19,567; in 1920 there were 1171 in an aggregate of 20,992; 179 law degrees were awarded to women; 3094 to men. From 1920 to 1930 women in law increased 100%; but they represent only 2% of the profession today.

Women in the ministry are still an inconspicuous fraction, though Quakers, requiring no scholastic qualification, permitted them to preach in the 17th century. By the mid-19th century, improvement of general education and a new liberalism made it possible for women to study sacred theology. Antoinette Brown Blackwell won her degree at Oberlin, 1851; Olympia Brown Willis entered the theological department of St. Lawrence University, 1860; at the century's close, 181 women theological students were reported in a total of 8009.

Though doubts as to female competence for original research were entertained by many, the myth vanished as did the belief that college Greek and mathematics would impair female minds. Bryn Mawr, led by M. Carey Thomas, fresh from graduate study abroad, emphasized its facilities for research. By 1893 resident women students in graduate schools numbered 390, about one seventh of all. Women graduate students increased from 1719 in 1900 to 18,185 in 1930; men, from 4112 to 29,070. Of graduate degrees conferred in 1930, 36% were to women, compared with 16% in 1900; of Ph.D. degrees, women won 16%, compared with 6% in 1900.

Change in professional status of women has been noteworthy (*see* Women in Public Life, Business and Professions). From 1890 to 1920, while population increased 68%, and the ratio of men to women remained the same, women in professional services increased 226%, men 78%. Of 8,202,901 gainfully employed women in 1920, 13.3% were in leading professions, compared with 6.4% in 1870. Of all occupations listed by the Census Bureau (1920) women were unrepresented in 33.

[W. Goodsell, *The Education of Women;* T. Woody, *A History of Women's Education in the United States.*]

THOMAS WOODY

Women in Public Life, Business and Professions. In colonial days most women who worked outside the home were seamstresses, dressmakers, or milliners; teachers in elementary schools or in the few girls' academies; nurses or midwives, neither class being scientifically trained; or innkeepers, shopkeepers, or printers and publishers, usually as associates or successors of male relatives.

With the coming of the industrial revolution[qv], early in the 19th century, girls and women flocked into factories, usually being given the most poorly paid work. Later, especially after the typewriter[qv] came into general use in business, women began to be in demand for office work. Meanwhile, an increasing number of sales positions were being filled by them, and they were becoming writers of commercial advertisements, professional buyers for stores, and heads of departments in them. Toward the close of the 19th century they began to supplant men in telephone service, usually as operators, and by 1927 they constituted two thirds of the workers in telephone establishments. Also, women were selling real estate and insurance; some were manufacturers and many were retail merchants. An increasing number were employed in banks, usually in inferior positions; but by the 1930's one bank official in every fifteen was a woman.

As women were admitted to higher educational institutions (*see* Women, The Education of), teaching positions in them became available for women likewise, but even in the fourth decade of the 20th century the presidents of some leading women's colleges were men; women usually held only the inferior positions on the faculties of coeducational colleges; and they were practically unheard of on the faculties of men's colleges, though a considerable fraction of the best-paid teachers in women's colleges were men.

The tradition of women in journalism, established in the colonial era, continued, and many women held important positions as reporters, columnists and editors. Conspicuous among them in the late 19th century were Jane Cunningham Croly (Jennie June) of the New York *World* and Kate Field of the New York *Tribune,* and, in the early 20th century, Dorothy Thompson.

In the middle of the 19th century the learned professions, apart from teaching, began to be opened to women, first, medicine, then, the ministry, then, the law. Elizabeth Blackwell, who received her medical degree from Geneva (N. Y.) University in 1849, was the first licensed woman physician in the United States. The first woman preacher, educated in theology and regularly ordained, seems to have been Antoinette Brown (Blackwell), who was ordained in 1852 by a Congregational church and later occupied a number of pastorates. Later, the Universalist, Unitarian, Methodist and Baptist churches as well as some other progressive denominations authorized women to preach. Arabella M. Mansfield, who studied privately and was admitted to the bar in Iowa in 1869, was the first woman lawyer of the country. The next year the first woman was graduated from a law school, Ada Kepley, from Union College, Chicago.

By 1940 women were engaged in most occupations open to men. Some of the statistics given for women in public life by the census of 1930 are as follows: architects, 379; clergy, 3276; dentists, 1287; lawyers, judges, justices, 3385; physicians, surgeons, osteopaths, 8388; photographers, 8366; trained nurses, 228,737; teachers, 880,409, including 20,131 in collegiate positions. But in numerous ways women were discriminated against in business and the professions, most commonly through being paid smaller wages or salaries than men for the same work.

[Elizabeth Anthony Dexter, *Colonial Women of Affairs;* Inez Haynes Irwin, *Angels and Amazons, A Hundred Years of American Women;* Sophonisba P. Breckinridge, *Women in the Twentieth Century.*]

MARY WILHELMINE WILLIAMS

Women's Clubs grew out of the increasing freedom of women in the 19th and 20th centuries. Some of these organizations were purely cultural. Others were established for humanitarian reasons or to promote social reform.

While there were some women's clubs from early times, the club movement did not begin until the 19th century. At that time it was largely a philanthropic and reform movement. Examples of such clubs are The Female Society for the Relief and Employment of the Poor (1798); The Daughters of Temperance (1840); and The Philadelphia Female Anti-Slavery Society (1833).

A little later cultural clubs appeared. Minerva was organized at New Harmony, Ind., in 1859; and Sorosis, organized in New York in 1868, is still in existence.

After the Civil War a movement arose to perfect national organizations for these clubs. The religious groups formed such organizations as the Women's Home Mission Board (1877) and the Young Women's Christian Association[qv] (1906). The Daughters of Temperance became the Woman's Christian Temperance Union[qv] (1874) and the cultural clubs united to form the General Federation of Women's Clubs (1889).

To clubs of the type already mentioned must be added such secret societies as the Order of the Eastern Star (1876), patriotic organizations such as the Daughters of the American Revolution[qv] (1890) and the Colonial Dames of America[qv] (1890).

As colleges were opened to women, sororities appeared and were brought together in the National Pan-Hellenic Association (1891).

It is not possible to make any accurate estimate of the number of women in these clubs, but certainly the number is large enough to make them an important influence on the cultural and political life of the country.

[Mrs. Jane Cunningham Croly, *The History of the Woman's Club Movement in America.*]

HALLIE FARMER

Women's Rights. *See* Married Women's Property Rights.

Wood Engraving. In America, prior to 1800, only a few small crude illustrations from wood blocks were produced. The portrait of Richard Mather (1596–1669) which was cut by John Foster (died 1681) is considered one of the first. In the next hundred years there were few woodcuts. Benjamin Franklin is credited with one. The reason for this scarcity of illustrations from relief blocks was that intaglio engraving was in vogue because it produced much finer results.

After the formation of the United States, the wood engravers followed the lead of the Englishman, Thomas Bewick (1753–1828), who used boxwood cut across the grain. His most distinguished American follower, Dr. Alexander Anderson (1775–1870), was the first to use boxwood exclusively for his blocks. Prior to 1770, both here and abroad, all prints from wood blocks were from wooden planks cut with the grain. The Bewick method made possible much more detailed results with tone and values. From 1800 to about 1850 nearly all the illustrations were small and many were crude. The best will be found in Harper's *Bible,* in Chapman's *Drawing Book,* 1847, and as illustrations in nature books and religious tracts. From 1850 for twenty years the sizes increased but with little improvement in quality. The next ten years, however, saw the development of what is now called the "New School of Wood Engraving" which lasted for about thirty years. Examples of the work produced will be found in such publications as *Harper's New Monthly Magazine, The Art Journal, Aldine, Scribner's,* and other important magazines of the day. Upon the best work will be found such names as Cole, Closson, Davis, Juengling, Kruel, W. J. Linton, Marsh, J. H. Whitney, Wolf and those few others who made this school famous.

After 1900 the demand for wood engravings almost ceased, due to the perfection and speed of the photomechanical processes. Most of the wood engravers turned to other artistic pursuits, but a few such as Henry Wolf and Timothy Cole continued until their death. Wood engraving in the United States is an art which is now dead for the reproduction of pictures, but it is being used by numerous American artists as a medium by which to produce their own original ideas. In this artistic work much is produced from linoleum.

[W. J. Linton, *History of Wood-Engraving in America;* Frank Weitenkampf, *How to Appreciate Prints,* and *American Graphic Arts;* Samuel Abbott Green, *John Foster, The Earliest American Engraver and the First Boston Printer;* Walter J. Phillips, *The Technique of the Wood-Cut;* E. Morley Fletcher, *Woodblock Printing;* Hesketh Hubbard, *Colour Block Print Making from Linoleum Blocks.*]

R. P. TOLMAN

Wood Lake, Battle of (Sept. 23, 1862). Foragers from Col. H. H. Sibley's[qv] camp near Wood Lake, Minn., on the morning of Sept. 23 stumbled upon Little Crow's warriors, lying in ambush to attack the main army. Quickly reinforced, Sibley's men decisively defeated the Sioux, with white losses of forty-one killed and wounded.

[W. W. Folwell, *A History of Minnesota.*]

WILLOUGHBY M. BABCOCK

Wooden Indian, THE. All through the 19th century the gaudily painted effigy of an Indian carved from wood, sometimes with tomahawk uplifted, sometimes peacefully proffering a bundle of cigars to the passer-by, was a familiar figure beside the doors of tobacco shops in America. Occasionally the figure was that of an Indian woman. The first small images of this sort were seen in England in the 17th century, and one representing Pocahontas is known to have stood in Boston in 1730. Some carvers of the effigies attained high reputation. After 1900 the spread of chain cigar stores and municipal ordinances against blocking the sidewalks gradually eliminated the familiar figure.

[J. L. Morrison, Passing of the Wooden Indian, in *Scribner's Magazine,* October, 1928.]

ALVIN F. HARLOW

Woods, Influence of, on Settlements. The original settlers in America were not forest dwellers in their native England, but everywhere they landed they encountered the fringe of a forest which stretched from Maine to Florida and from the Atlantic to west of the Mississippi. They learned a forest technique of clearing land, and used wood for fuel and building. In 1750 the western frontier line was fairly even, but in the next century it changed, over the mountains, into "bulges and streamers." This was due in part to the fact that the western movement[qv] followed river lines of transport, but also to the fact that the western forest fringe likewise changed into "streamers." In the two centuries of settlement and expansion Americans had so learned their forest technique that they knew no other, and the rich lands of the prairies afforded neither fuel nor building material. The pioneers followed the forests, until they learned anew how to deal with open lands. For long the forest area held and consolidated population. Among influences of the forest technique, early learned and making its deep impress, may be noted that on architecture. America, even in such sections as New England where stone material abounds, has remained largely a land of wooden houses.

JAMES TRUSLOW ADAMS

Woodward Plan, THE. *See* Detroit, Woodward Plan of.

Wool. Sheep were brought to America by English, Dutch and Swedish settlers between 1609 and 1663, and colonial laws were passed to encourage wool growing. At first wolves[qv], dogs, foul pastures and disease checked their increase. Nevertheless, favored points like the Nahant Peninsula near Boston, the Narragansett Bay islands and Hempstead Heath on Long Island had commercial flocks, and wool was an article of local trade. For over 150 years, however, no recorded effort was made to improve colonial breeds. Consequently fleeces were small and native wool was coarse and curly. Yet it made strong homespuns and by 1700 colonial farmers sheared enough wool for family use.

After the Revolution Merino sheep were imported from Europe. The invention of power carding and spinning created a mill demand for fine wools suitable for broadcloths and other carded fabrics which encouraged the extension of Merino and crossbred flocks, especially in the hill country of New England and New York. Vermont and the Berkshires were for a time famous sheep centers. Coarser wool sheep developed from English importations were more popular along the coast and in the bluegrass country of Kentucky, which became a center for Cotswold and Leicester crossbreeds. Ohio attained the position it long held as the chief wool growing state of the Union during the first half of the 19th century. The annexations that followed the war with Mexico brought under the American flag vast grazing regions already possessing small Spanish flocks. These ranges, from Texas to California, were the first great source of "territorial wools," a distinction they now share with the north Rocky Mountain and north Pacific states.

During the period of comparable census records the nation's annual wool clip has increased from about 36 million pounds in 1840 to 438 million pounds in the banner year of 1933. Total clip has grown faster than sheep population because breeding and better care have increased the weight of fleeces. At no time in the nation's history, however, has it produced enough wool for domestic consumption. Roughly the country's factories use two pounds of imported wool for every three pounds raised at home. Some of these foreign wools are varieties not economically produced in the United States. They include fine clothing wools from Australia and the Argentine and coarse wools suitable only for rugs and carpets from half wild flocks in Africa and Asia. Originally, combing wools were imported and the first worsted manufacturers of America got their raw materials from Canada and abroad. Improvements in combing machinery, however, have now made domestic wool available for this branch of manufacturing.

Since the time of Henry Clay's "American system"[qv] of protecting domestic industry so that the country's factories might make markets for its farmers' crops, wool has played an important part in American tariff[qv] policies. Efforts to adjust duties upon wool manufactures and raw wool respectively so that mill owners and sheep men are equally favored have seldom satisfied all parties. Consequently wool schedules have been among the most debated items in the country's tariff history.

For several years the per capita consumption of wool in the United States has declined. This is partly because of the substitution of other fibres and partly because lighter clothing meets the needs of modern life. Meanwhile, however, sheep raisers have turned increasingly to mutton breeds to help feed a growing urban population. At present the number of sheep in the country seems to be about stationary. No new areas comparable with those opened to grazing during the last century are now in prospect. The relative importance of wool in the national economy may have passed its maximum.

[Chester W. Wright, *Wool-Growing and the Tariff.*]

VICTOR S. CLARK

Woolly-Heads was a term of derision applied in various regions after the late 1840's to Northerners, usually Whigs[qv], of antislavery propensities who presumably championed the rights of the Negro; often a synonym for Conscience Whigs[qv].

ARTHUR C. COLE

Worcester v. Georgia (6 Pet. 515) was a decision of the United States Supreme Court handed down in 1832 in the controversy between Georgia and the Cherokee Indians[qv], in which John Marshall held that the Cherokees were a nation under the protection of the United States and free from the jurisdiction of Georgia. The case arose over the arrest of Samuel A. Worcester and ten other missionaries for having violated a Georgia law forbidding white men to reside in the Cherokee country without first taking an oath of allegiance to the state and securing a permit. Sentenced to four years in the penitentiary, nine accepted a pardon, but Worcester and Elizur Butler appealed their case, which resulted in Marshall's decision. Georgia spurned an appearance in court and refused to obey the decision. President Jackson, who liked neither Marshall nor the Indians, allowed the decision to go unenforced.

[U. B. Phillips, *Georgia and State Rights;* A. Bass, *Cherokee Messenger;* C. Warren, *The Supreme Court in United States History;* A. J. Beveridge, *The Life of John Marshall.*]

E. MERTON COULTER

Working Man's Party, The, grew out of the demands of the workers of New York City, in 1829, for an effective lien law for laborers on buildings and the abolishment of imprisonment for debt, and their protest against the threat to lengthen the ten-hour working day. Under the leadership of Fanny Wright and her young protégé, Robert Dale Owen, the movement for a time spread rapidly, and a demand for universal education was added to the party platform. In 1830 Erastus Root, speaker of the Assembly, packed the local and state conventions of the "Workies" with his own men and secured his nomination by them for governor. This nomination was denounced by Owen and Miss Wright and another convention of bona fide delegates of the Working Man's party met and named their own candidate. The heyday of the party's influence, however, was passing. The agnostic teachings of Owen and Miss Wright antagonized many people, and the abandonment of the Tammany[qv] opposition to the mechanic's lien law and to the repeal of imprisonment for debt, together with the formation of the Whig Working Men's party in New York City, hastened its end.

[A. C. Flick, *History of the State of New York,* Vol. VI.]

A. C. FLICK

Workmen's Accident Compensation. The mechanization of industry has created employment hazards with which the employee, acting alone, cannot cope. The common law[qv] and the employer's liability acts of the 19th century neither reduced the number and severity of accidents, nor adequately compensated the employees. The employee was helpless in the face of the employer's legal defenses, and of high court costs. General dissatisfaction with these conditions led states to pass Workmen's Compensation laws, placing the responsibility of compensation upon the employer. European countries had passed such legislation as early as 1883. In 1902 Maryland enacted the first compensation law, but this and other state laws of that decade were declared unconstitutional. The compensation movement was given great impetus when a Federal law (1908), covering certain Federal employees, was upheld. Between 1910 and 1920 forty-two states and three territories passed similar compensation laws; and by 1940 all but one state had such laws. During 1937 thirty-eight states revised and broadened their laws by increasing the weekly and death benefits; shortening the waiting period; widening the coverage; including more liberal provisions regarding occupational diseases, dental, nursing, hospital treatment, artificial appliances and rehabilitation.

States differ widely regarding the provisions and the administration of these laws. Because of the exclusion of certain occupations and of exemptions, nearly half of those gainfully employed are not covered by these laws. Those covered by these laws are only partially compensated for loss of wages. A few states are beginning to compensate for occupational diseases[qv].

[H. A. Millis and Royal E. Montgomery, *Labor Risks and Social Insurance;* Walter F. Dodd, *Administration of Workmen's Compensation;* Barbara N. Armstrong, *Insuring the Essentials;* Clarence W. Hobbs, *Workmen's Compensation Insurance.*]

JOSEPH H. FOTH

Works Progress Administration. This Federal emergency agency for relief of unemployment[qv] was created by executive order May 6, 1935, under authority of the Emergency Relief Appropriation Act of 1935. In 1935 and 1936 appropriation acts allocated a total of more than six billion dollars with which to finance more than 100,000 projects throughout the country. Construction work was given major emphasis; and this included building or repair of highways, renovation or construction of public buildings (especially schoolhouses), and other improvements of public property—Federal, state and local. In 1939 the name was changed to Works Projects Administration, and the Administration became a part of the new Federal Works Agency.

[*Report on Progress of the Works Program, October 15, 1936,* Washington, 1936; C. Gill, W. P. A., in *Current History,* January, 1938; J. D. Millett, *The Works Progress Administration in New York City.*]

P. ORMAN RAY

World Court, THE (Permanent Court of International Justice), was established by a Statute of 1920 framed under authorization of Article 14 of the Covenant of the League of Nations by a commission of jurists appointed by the Council of the League. The provisions covering election of judges were suggested by Elihu Root, who was a member of the commission. Adherence to the Protocol of Signature was endorsed by both major political parties in the United States and by the American Bar Association. The House of Representatives resolved 303 to 28 in 1925 in favor of adherence. Submitted by President Harding to the Senate in 1923, the Court Statute was lengthily debated. The opposition came from those senators most antagonistic to the League of Nations[qv]. To them the Court was a League agency, as indeed it is. Their inference was that adherence to the Court would involve the United States intimately in the League. Sen. Borah, though a strong legalist, led the fight against the Court, being supported by Senators Hiram Johnson, Pepper, Moses and others.

The Senate, by a vote of 76 to 17, advised and consented to American adherence on Jan. 27, 1926. But this apparently overwhelming approval was qualified by five reservations, the only significant one being the fifth. This was prepared by John Bassett Moore, a World Court judge from 1921 to 1928. It provided that there be notice and hearing in the procedure for advisory opinions and that without the consent of the United States the Court should not entertain a request for an advisory opinion upon any issue in which the United States had or claimed to have an interest. At a conference of Signatory states this reservation was found acceptable subject to the determination, by practice, that it did not place the United States in a favored position. To accommodate divergent views Mr. Root in 1929 reformulated the Senate's reservation and added procedures for its execution. This was embodied with the other reservations in a Protocol of Accession which was accepted by nearly all states members of the Court and by President Hoover.

The Protocol admits the United States to participation in elections of judges and amendment of the Statute upon an equality with League states. It provides that the United States shall be consulted by the Council or the Assembly before an advisory opinion is requested; also that the Court shall notify the United States of any request for an advisory opinion, staying proceedings until an exchange of views between the Council or Assembly and the United States has taken place. Thereupon, if the United States is unwilling to support the request, it may withdraw its adherence to the Protocol of Signature without imputation of an unco-operative attitude. The Senate rejected this instrument, 52 to 36, in 1935.

[Manley O. Hudson, *The World Court, 1921-1938.*]

HAROLD S. QUIGLEY

World Economic Conference, THE (1933), was significant as demonstrating: first, that the United States development had reached a point where American decisions drastically influenced international economy and politics; second, that the F. D. Roosevelt administration had abandoned internationalism for nationalism for recovery purposes. Projected with President Hoover's endorsement, and provided with an agenda largely perfected in conferences between President Roosevelt and foreign delegations visiting him at Washington in May, 1933, the conference met at London on June 10. There Europe, especially France, proposed immediate agreement upon currency stabilization under a gold standard*qv*. America had proposed first to effect tariff reduction; she refused to renounce freedom to devalue the dollar, insisting that its purchasing power, not its gold content, needed stabilizing. Secretary of State Hull carried a difficult position with dignity. Sen. Pittman of Nevada collected signatures to an agreement pledging America to support of the silver market. The conference adjourned July 28, a failure.

[D. B. Woodward, *The London Economic Conference;* League of Nations, *Agenda, Silver Memo.*]

JEANNETTE PADDOCK NICHOLS

World Power, The United States as a. This phrase has had an enticing appeal to American journalism and even to historiography. What does it mean? We may define a world power as a state which exercises power throughout the world, whose attitude is taken into consideration in the settlement of major problems of diplomacy. Such a state need not have colonies: nobody would seriously dispute that Germany and Russia are world powers though without colonies. We may even go so far as to say that a world power is a state which exercises appreciable power outside its own continent, Italy, for example.

The United States began to exercise power beyond its own continent in the 1880's when it secured a dominant position in Hawaii and Samoa*qqv*. Since 1898 it has been a world power in the fullest sense of the phrase. The unpremeditated acquisition of the Philippine Islands*qv*, followed by the pronouncement, as a major policy, of the Open Door Doctrine*qv* and the Integrity of China, catapulted American diplomacy beyond the widest and safest of oceans into the Far East, and then into Asia, the "back door of European politics." The Spanish-American War also, of course, clinched American power in the Caribbean and projected it beyond into northern South America. In these areas of this hemisphere the United States had a vital interest, strategically and economically. In Asia, American interests were not then, and have not been since, vital. Only in Africa are they less.

In the ensuing decade, before the World War, it was the habit of the professors, the journalists and the platform orators to extol the phrase world power and to inflate its significance. The American people, intoxicated with the headiest prosperity of their fortunate continental position and its unexampled economic advantages, responded to the echo of this appeal. John Hay became the most popular Secretary of State the United States ever had, although his work today is not popular. Theodore Roosevelt was the most popular President the United States had possessed up to his time, perhaps excepting Andrew Jackson. With typical cowboy vigor and skill, President Roosevelt rode the champing steed of world power into diplomatic ventures in Asia and in Africa. He asserted later that his diplomacy in the Far East (on the eve of the Russo-Japanese War) and in Africa (Morocco, 1904–5) had saved the peace of the world—and he even mediated (at the request of Japan) to bring peace between Russia and Japan (*see* Portsmouth, The Treaty of). Scholars who today place the first Roosevelt's adventures in world power beneath the lenses of historical investigation find little profit for the heavy risks which that President took beyond his own continent in regions where unwittingly he became the cat's-paw of other more experienced diplomatists.

The World War projected American power into the European cataclysm of 1914–18, because of Woodrow Wilson's insistence in holding Germany responsible for violations of international law*qv* suffered by American citizens under foreign belligerent flags on the high seas, and because of other complex factors impossible to examine here. But the United States, in refusing the Treaty of Versailles and the League of Nations[qqv], recoiled cautiously and instinctively back to its continental position, despite the powerful arguings of people beyond the seas, and a chorus at home, who flatteringly told us we had now "become of age," as before the war we were told that we were now a world power, and that therefore we could not help "playing our part."

Since Versailles the United States has been a more prudent world power. It has clarified its foreign policy by further withdrawals from sovereignty in the Philippines (after 1946) and from active diplomacy, much less intervention, in the raging international politics of Asia. There is today a tendency to follow George Washington's advice for aloofness from Europe (and Asia) and Henry Clay's enthusiasm for a peaceful and defensive inter-American system.

[Alfred Vagts, *Deutschland und die Vereinigten Staaten in der Weltpolitik;* Samuel Flagg Bemis, *A Diplomatic History of the United States;* A. Whitney Griswold, *Far Eastern Policy of the United States.*]

SAMUEL FLAGG BEMIS

World War: American Relief in Europe extended from 1914 through 1923, but several agencies continued special projects after 1923. During the war, relief was mainly in Allied countries by organizations for aid to the wounded, refugees, children, war widows, etc., and this work continued during reconstruction. But, except for the Commission for Relief in Belgium[qv], the period of mass relief was after the Armistice[qv] when government finance, cash sales, and benevolence poured millions of tons of supplies into Central and Eastern Europe where 200,000,000 people were in need. This pacific American intervention contributed greatly to the rehabilitation of Europe and particularly to the establishment of the new states formed by the peace treaties. "Benevolence," through the American Relief Administration alone, amounted to $134,000,000 after the Armistice, and total supplies to over $1,000,000,000. About $6,000,000,000 worth of American food and other supplies were sent to Europe, 1914–23. United States Government subsidies and loans for supplies were $624,000,000 during the Armistice, and $81,000,000 in reconstruction and the Russian famine.

The American Relief Administration was created early in 1919 to administer a congressional appropriation of $100,000,000 for European relief, to be partially repaid by the countries aided. Herbert Hoover, United States Food Administrator, went to Europe in November, 1918, to study the need and initiate relief, and was soon appointed Director-General of Relief for the Allies under the Supreme Economic Council. He formed and directed the A.R.A., to carry out the American share of the program. The needs were so appalling that financing by all governments was necessary, but 80% of the supplies came from the United States and were distributed by the A.R.A., Allied commissions, foreign governments and private agencies. The A.R.A. used the machinery for purchase and transport created by the Food Administration[qv] but formed local committees for distribution, with final control in American hands, and encouraged both governments and citizens to donate services. In all, over 4,000,000 metric tons were sent to twenty-one countries. The original United States appropriation excluded enemy countries, but their condition was such that special finance was immediately found (Joint Allied Finance, United States loans to Allies, cash payments by enemy States, etc.) and after the Allied blockade was relaxed, from February through July, 1919, $282,000,000 worth of supplies went to Germany and $98,000,000 to Austria. The A.R.A. instituted child-feeding; transported or allocated food for private agencies; and transmitted $6,000,000 in cash from individuals or groups in the United States to persons in Europe. At liquidation of the Armistice program on June 30, 1919, the A.R.A. had delivered 1,728,000 metric tons of supplies at an operating cost of 53/100 of one per cent of sales value, and returned $84,000,000 of the congressional appropriation to the United States Treasury in foreign government obligations.

Thereafter, the A.R.A. operated as a private agency, though it administered three other congressional appropriations: one (1920) for sale of flour on credit, and two (1921–22) for famine and medical relief in Russia. It co-operated closely with other agencies and, 1920–21, with eight others (European Relief Council) raised $29,000,000 in the United States for children's relief. It fed some 8,000,000 children, entered refugee work, the control of epidemics, relief to special groups, and delivered $22,000,000 worth of food purchased in America for persons or groups in Europe. In 1921 it made an agreement with the Soviet government for famine relief, under which most of the American agencies worked, and at the peak of this relief, 1921–23, fed some 10,000,000 Russians, delivered large shipments of seed grain, food packages and bulk sales, and operated a medical unit which inoculated 8,000,000 persons in epidemics and delivered $3,000,000 worth of Red Cross supplies to 14,000 Russian hospitals and institutions.

The American Red Cross[qv] spent overseas 56 cents on each dollar collected, 1914–19, and some $200,000,000 altogether in Europe, 1914–23. Its greatest work was naturally medical relief, health service and control of postwar epidemics, but it also engaged in child-care and refugee work, allocated funds or supplies (clothing or medical) to other agencies, and had units in twenty-four countries in 1919. It worked in Russia and Siberia, 1917–18, and in the famine of 1921–23 it contributed the $3,000,000 worth of medical and hospital supplies mentioned above.

The American Friends Service Committee (Quakers) was organized on our entry into the war, but American Quakers had previously worked with British Quakers in war relief. They sent small units wherever the need was greatest and were among the first to reach enemy territories. The American Friends' greatest achievement was child-feeding in Germany, 1919–22, where they distributed $9,000,000 worth of relief, about $6,000,000 allocated by the A. R. A. or European Relief Council. The Friends raised over $1,000,000 from German-Americans, and when they withdrew, 1922, helped to provide another $4,000,000 for child-feeding by Germans through 1924. They were also active in Poland, Austria, Serbia, Jugoslavia and Russia.

The Jewish Joint Distribution Committee was formed, November, 1919, to distribute relief funds for American Jewish societies, and at the end of 1926 had spent $69,000,000 abroad. They distributed through other organizations until 1920, and worked closely with the A. R. A. through 1923, sending a vast number of food packages and bulk sales to Poland, Austria and Russia. In 1920 the Jewish Distribution Committee began its own medical work and reconstruction, and in 1921, refugee and child-care, repatriation, and cultural work in twelve European countries besides Palestine, continuing much of this after 1923.

Near East Relief derived from a committee organized, 1919, by Henry Morgenthau, United States Ambassador to Turkey, for Armenian-Syrian relief, and distributed most of the American relief in Near East countries. The A. R. A., Red Cross and others made large allotments to Near East Relief, which, 1919–23, distributed some $28,000,000 in supplies—$16,000,000 from government credits and the rest from benevolence. It did refugee and resettlement work, child-care and child-placing, especially of orphans, and continued after 1923, raising funds by its own American campaigns.

Other organizations, notably Young Men's Christian Association and Young Women's Christian Association[qqv], gave large amounts of relief to all European countries, often for special groups, such as students or the intelligentsia. The Federal Council of Churches, Knights of Columbus[qqv], and National Catholic Welfare Council were members of the European Relief Council, and three foundations—Rockefeller Foundation[qv], Laura Spelman Rockefeller Memorial, and Commonwealth Fund—made large gifts to the A. R. A. and other agencies for children's relief or special purposes.

[Frank M. Surface and Raymond L. Bland, *American Food in the World War and Reconstruction Period;* H. H. Fisher, *The Famine in Soviet Russia;* H. H. Fisher and S. Brooks, *America and the New Poland;* and reports of organizations named.]

PERRIN C. GALPIN

World War, Economic Mobilization for. The vast armies placed in the field by the various belligerents from 1914–18 made new methods for supply and maintenance necessary. When the vision of a short war faded at the Marne in 1914, preparations had to be made for a war of attrition. This called for the mobilization of economic resources as well as man power. Germany was the first country to realize the importance of an economic mobilization for war. Early in the war Dr. Walter Rathenau foresaw the pressure of the Allied blockade and urged the creation of a section in the War Ministry to control the supply of raw materials (*Kriegsrohstoffabteilung*). By November, 1916, the *Kriegsamt* had virtual control of the entire economic resources of Germany. In England and France the progress toward this goal was slower and took the form of a munitions ministry.

In the United States some progress was made toward the mobilization of industry prior to 1917, but, with the system of free enterprise firmly entrenched, little could be done in the direction of economic mobilization until the war emergency called for extreme measures. The Committee of National Defense established in 1916 was charged with providing economic and industrial preparations for defense. Steps were taken in 1917 for this committee to act with the various industries through one man, but the Committee of National Defense lacked authority to compel adherence to its decisions. When Congress declared war in April, 1917, it pledged the entire resources of the United States to its prosecution, but no effective attempt was made to mobilize all the economic resources of the nation until March 4, 1918, when the War Industries Board[qv] was given wide powers by executive order of the President.

Once fortified with power, the various committees of the War Industries Board carried out an economic mobilization unprecedented in American history. The ancient rights of free enterprise were annulled and all resources and manufacturing facilities came under the orders of this agency. The immense work of this board was divided between many subcommittees. A requirements division attempted to reconcile the needs of the military services with the available material and facilities. When additional manufacturing facilities were required, this agency planned their construction with a view to labor, transportation and other considerations. This tended to reduce the dangerous congestion of manufacturing establishments in the New England area, which had caused a virtual breakdown of transportation in the winter of 1917–18. A conservation committee reduced waste in materials and nonessential services. Prices were fixed by one committee (*see* Price Fixing) and the distribution of each important commodity was entrusted to a committee made up of members of the Board and members of the trade.

The result of these changes was "a systematic scheduling of production in practically all industrial plants in the United States in accord and synchronization with the war program." Within a few months America achieved a mobilization of resources and industry. The mobilized industry of America was described by Mr. Bernard Baruch as a "weapon of offense or defense more potent than anything the world has ever seen, more terrible, I think, than the mind of any man has ever imagined." So carefully was the distribution of all commodities supervised that it was impossible to purchase a ton of steel in the United States after March, 1918, without the approval of the War Industries Board. The wartime experience of the United States in the realm of economic mobilization has been incorporated in the Revised Industrial Mobilization Plan of 1933.

[J. H. Beals, *Economic Planning and National Defense; Final Report of the War Industries Board.*]

H. A. DEWEERD

World War, Financing of. After entering the World War, the United States Government decided to finance its participation by borrowing approximately two thirds of the required amount and by raising the remaining third through taxation. Three methods of borrowing were employed. Through the use of certificates of indebtedness, the Treasury borrowed for short periods from the Federal Reserve banks^qv^, retiring the certificates as income was received. A more permanent form of borrowing was through the sales of Liberty Bonds (*see* Liberty Loans). To reach those of small means, war-savings certificates were issued. These held twenty war-savings stamps, each of which had a maturity value of $5.00. Thrift stamps were also sold for twenty-five cents. Sixteen of these could be exchanged for a war-savings stamp.

To provide the needed taxes, Congress enacted special revenue laws on Oct. 3, 1917, and Feb. 24, 1919. These acts greatly increased the income-tax^qv^ rates, imposed war excess profits taxes, and provided for many other special taxes. From April 6, 1917, to June 30, 1919, a total of $9,384,278,708 was received from taxes. This amount, together with $21,432,918,450 received from five bond issues and $1,116,076,438 realized from the sale of war saving certificates and thrift stamps, made up the war revenues of the United States.

[Ernest L. Bogart, *War Costs and Their Financing;* A. D. Noyes, *The War Period of American Finance; Report of the Secretary of the Treasury, 1920.*]

ERIK McKINLEY ERIKSSON

World War: Interference with the Mails. Beginning December, 1915, England treated mail en route between America and Europe as contraband, compelling mail ships, like cargo vessels, to deviate from their course and submit to search in British ports. American popular resentment was stirred with reference to the general principle of the inviolability of the mails, but the Government admitted that parcel and even letter mail might contain contraband^qv^. Thus its ground of protest was restricted to the issues concerning contraband, viz., detention and search *in port,* and had little reference to the alleged inviolability of the mails. The controversy, though keen, ended in a stalemate, being overshadowed by the greater issues with Germany.

[Charles Cheney Hyde, *International Law Chiefly as Interpreted and Applied by the United States.*]

RICHARD W. VAN ALSTYNE

World War: Peace Conference (1919). In May, 1917, preliminary steps preceded a request by President Wilson to Col. House (September, 1917) which produced The Inquiry^qv^, an organization of nongovernmental experts under Sidney E. Mezes which explored ethnic, historical, economic and other phases of issues opened by the war. Neither Inquiry nor State Department, not always working together harmoniously, planned procedure, as had the British, or had a program, hence Americans were hampered during the negotiations. Furnished with results of the investigation and accompanied by the experts, the American delegation (Wilson, House,

Lansing, Bliss and White) reached France Dec. 13, 1918. Delays, partly due to British, French and Italian desire to counteract Wilson's personal popularity and to disparage his Fourteen Points[qv], prevented the Conference's formal meeting till Jan. 18, 1919, although already the Supreme War Council (Wilson, Lansing and Allied premiers) had roughly outlined procedure. The Council of Five (Supreme War Council and Japan) was instituted (Jan. 19) with the understanding that other Allied belligerents should be consulted on issues affecting them and neutrals might be called in. The Council of Ten (executive heads plus foreign ministers) was an inner cabinet which made final decisions until March when the Council of Four (Wilson, Clemenceau, Lloyd George and Orlando) functioned alone.

Closest to Wilson's heart was a proposed League of Nations[qv], approved in principle by the second plenary Conference (Jan. 25), and he was made chairman of the Commission to formulate its constitution. The next day Clemenceau, president of the Conference, appointed committees to work on such things as Reparations, Responsibility, Waterways, Labor Legislation and other questions before the Conference. Each committee with its experts worked almost exclusively on its own problem so that nowhere, except belatedly in the Council of Four, were the cumulative effects of the treaty realized.

The League Commission completed its draft of the Covenant which Wilson presented to the Conference Feb. 14, the day he left Paris for the United States. In his absence Allied delegates, especially the French, regretted their tentative approval, and in the United States Wilson found a disposition to question the project. This, on his return, brought reopening of the subject and modifications including a safeguard of the Monroe Doctrine[qv]. Before leaving Paris, Wilson had been asked by the Jugoslavs to mediate the Adriatic question, but the Italians refused his services. In March, after his return, the Italians threatened to leave the Conference unless they got Fiume, and on April 28, after Wilson's conference with them and his appeal to the Italian people, they returned to Rome where they were upheld by their Parliament and people. It was at this time that Wilson himself threatened to leave Paris on account of the intransigeant attitude of French and Italians.

On May 7, the Italians having returned, a treaty was ready to present to German delegates who (May 29) protested terms which stripped them of much territory including colonies, disarmed them, obligated them to indefinite reparations[qv] and provided sanctions[qv] until compliance. Earlier there was an intention of the Allies, following customary procedure, to draft demands and then work out a treaty with German delegates. Fear that their own ranks might split, impatience of their peoples spurred by a press kept in the dark, and a desire not to rework the treaty made it a unilateral affair. German protests, emphasizing the Fourteen Points, were generally unavailing and the Treaty of Versailles[qv] was signed June 28. Americans and their associates knew it was imperfect and harsh, but Wilson, having seen his Fourteen Points emasculated or ignored, counted on the League to rectify injustices.

[James T. Shotwell, *At the Paris Peace Conference;* Ray Stannard Baker, *Woodrow Wilson and World Settlement.*]

L. B. SHIPPEE

World War: Private Loans. *See* Debts, Foreign.

World War, THE (1914–18), took wholly by surprise Americans who considered Sarajevo and its immediate consequences just another European war scare. Although believing war would be short-lived, Americans felt the effects immediately: travelers abroad were repatriated with difficulty; stock markets crashed and exchanges closed; markets abroad were disrupted and business depression made the winter of 1914–15 one of hardship. Soon, however, war orders from the Allies, who controlled the seas, started a boom which lasted until after the Armistice.

Issuing a proclamation (Aug. 4, 1914) warning citizens to observe wartime regulations and abstain from participation in hostilities, Wilson later called for neutrality[qv] of spirit as well as act, but opinion rapidly took sides, stimulated by propaganda from all belligerents[qv]. Sentiment afforded the Allies better opportunity except in parts of the West. Sentiment worked with economic interest of those profiting by increased trade or having bought bonds floated by J. P. Morgan, who became purchasing agent for all the Allies.

Immediately diplomatic issues arose from neutral trade and from a blockade attempting to isolate Germany and her associates. American precedent from Civil War times made a basis for extension of continuous voyage[qv] doctrine through ultimate destination to ultimate consumption, thus affecting European neutrals as well as belligerents. The contestants were asked whether the Declaration of London[qv] (1909) would be observed, but while Germany, standing to gain, agreed if the others would, the Allies refused to be bound and gradually limited the free list until it was negligible. Complaints about seizures and diversions mounted, while interference with mails (*see* World War: Interference with the Mails) and establishment of a blacklist irritated, until in 1916 many feared a breach with England. But Wilson, believing a German victory would be calamitous, though authorizing vigorous protests, did not push the issue to a breaking point. In Congress an attempt to embargo munitions, favorable to the Central Powers, was blocked by Wilson who asserted a change of rules during the war would be unneutral.

Attention was diverted from neutral trade by Germany's submarine warfare (starting February, 1915) and, when the *Lusitania*[qv] was sunk (May 7) with loss of 124 Americans, Wilson so strongly demanded apology, reparation and promise to desist that Bryan resigned as Secretary of State and Lansing succeeded him. Bryan had contended Americans should be warned from belligerent merchantmen and that defensively armed vessels should be denied American ports, maintaining this was a practice, antagonistic to Germany, which would lead the United States into war. After the *Arabic*[qv] was sunk (August, 1915) Germany modified its policy and the issue was quiescent until revived by the *Sussex* case[qv] (March 24, 1916) when another series of notes brought a promise not to sink without warning.

Meantime submarine warfare[qv] raised the question of American preparation for possible war. Many agreed with Secretary of War Garrison in demanding increase of armed forces, but opposition was voiced by those who held the United States was not menaced and arming would incite to belligerency. In late 1915 Wilson swung to limited preparedness but not far enough for Garrison who resigned to be replaced by Baker. Preparedness[qv] had a prominent part in the presidential campaign of 1916[qv] as did Wilson's policy toward the World War and toward Mexico (*see* Mexico, Punitive Expedition into). The narrow Democratic victory was attributed by many to belief Wilson had kept the United States out of war, as indeed he tried, for he sought opportunity to help to peace through mediation, utilizing Col. House who, however, never quite understood or sympathized with the President. In December, 1916, with contestants apparently deadlocked, Germany hinted at American mediation although making clear her ambitions in Central and Eastern Europe. Risking the charge of pro-Germanism, Wilson asked the belligerents to state their aims, which the Allies did somewhat more explicitly than Germany. This offered Wilson opportunity to state (Jan. 22, 1917) the position of America if drawn in: he proposed a negotiated peace guaranteed by world organization. Meantime German navalists had persuaded the Kaiser that France and England could be crushed by unrestricted submarine warfare before America could be effective, and announced through Ambassador Bernstorff, who opposed the step, intention to start the policy Feb. 1. Bernstorff was dismissed and Gerard recalled from Germany. Then was published (Feb. 24) the Zimmermann Note[qv] inviting alliance with Mexico, whence Pershing's expedition had just been withdrawn, and co-operation with Japan, holding out to them a prospect of securing American territory. Two days later Wilson asked power to arm American merchantmen[qv], and, Congress failing to act, proceeded under an old law. Armed forces were increased. After reports of sinking American vessels Wilson called together the new Congress (April 2, 1917) to read his War Message and four days later signed the resolution declaring its existence. Strongly in support of the action was sentiment among Americans who had been keyed up by the war in general and especially by atrocity[qv] stories, submarine operations and real or suspected subversive acts by German agents in the United States.

Allied missions visited the United States to plan co-ordination of effort, secure credits and facilitate flow of war materials. Congress immediately started a legislative basis for participation. A Selective Service Act (May 10, 1917), inaugurating compulsory service, caused enrollment of 10,000,000 men of whom some 4,000,000 were drafted[qv]; the regular army was strengthened, the National Guard[qv] brought under stricter Federal control and a great navy program started. A token force under Pershing (*see* American Expeditionary Forces) was sent to France (June 10) although it was not till a year later that significant numbers were abroad to help stop the German advance. Russia's defection through revolution, Italy's retreat, Rumania's collapse, and yielding of the Western Front made the situation so desperate that in December, 1917, Pershing, seconded by House who relayed the Allies' pleas, stated that without effective aid a German victory was imminent. Stimulated thus and by American impatience for action, men were rushed over until by July, 1918, a million had reached France; by the Armistice two million were there and as many more preparing to follow. At first Americans were brigaded with French and British, but Pershing, backed by Wilson, insisted on a separate American army.

German determination to break the Western

Front brought in 1918 four drives which were not stopped until after enormous gains, and Paris was threatened. After June increasing American aid helped stem the rout; it figured at Cantigny, Chateau Thierry, Belleau Wood and elsewhere; it participated in a counter-drive (St. Mihiel, Argonne), and, with a second army, was ready to drive toward Metz in the spring, but the Armistice (Nov. 11) made this unnecessary[qqv]. Some aid in Italy and participation in the North Russian expedition and in Siberia were among American activities. The navy aided principally in convoys and patrolling sea lanes (*see* World War, The Navy in).

To keep the army in the field and support the Allies necessitated organization on the home front. A Council of National Defense (August, 1916) set up committees from which emerged the War Industries Board[qv] which, especially after the Overman Act (May 20, 1918), centralized control of production, apportioned materials with preference for war industries, advised on prices and, through its divisions, practically dominated key industries. Herbert Hoover as Food Administrator[qv], especially after the Lever Act[qv] (August, 1917), by persuasion and without recourse to rationing, enormously stimulated food production. Fuel[qv] was under Harry A. Garfield. The transportation system by autumn, 1917, threatened to break down and McAdoo (Treasury) was put in charge of all railways and later of express companies (*see* Railroad Administration). Telegraphs were co-ordinated under the Postmaster General. The United States Shipping Board, organized in 1916 to stimulate the merchant marine, created the Emergency Fleet Corporation[qv] which, after a period of dissension, by building, purchase, lease and by confiscation of German interned bottoms, built up a fleet of ten million tons by the end of the war, although the "cost-plus" system[qv] had encouraged waste and extravagance. The War Trade Board[qv] (October, 1917) co-operated with the Shipping Board to control commerce through licensing, while the Alien Property Custodian[qv] took over and turned to American use German properties and patents. Labor, being scarce, necessitated co-ordination provided by a National War Labor Board working under policies framed by a War Labor Policies Board.

Opinion was guided by the Committee on Public Information[qv], while opposition to the war and its conduct, never very serious, was restricted by the Espionage (June 15, 1917) and Sedition (May 6, 1918) Acts which went farther than ever before in curtailing expression of opinion[qqv]. State and local Committees of Public Safety, while often doing effective work, sometimes exceeded legitimate objects and left a memory of unjust repression in many communities. No formal censorship[qv] existed but its ends were achieved by pressure, while prosecution of objectors (*see* Conscientious Objectors), sometimes sustained by the Supreme Court, brought a good many convictions for political crimes.

Some two thirds of war expenses, including loans to Allies, were met by bond issues widely oversubscribed; taxation was heavy and vexatious, but even at the time some, usually in silence, regretted that more emphasis had not been placed on taxation and less on borrowing (*see* World War, Financing of). While there was in general less waste and corruption than in the Civil War there could not fail to be some; perhaps the greatest scandal rose from the failure of an ambitious airplane program where hundreds of millions were spent and almost no planes sent abroad.

In the winter of 1917–18 there was popular and congressional criticism of America's delay in getting an effective force into France, with Secretary Baker the principal target. In Congress there was agitation for an investigation, probably looking to a war cabinet, which Wilson interpreted as indicating lack of confidence. He demanded and obtained defeat of the proposition and then Congress bestowed upon him (Overman Act, May 30, 1918) almost unlimited power to reorganize, co-ordinate and centralize governmental functions. Thereafter there was little vocal objection to the conduct of the war, although when, before the congressional elections (November, 1918) Wilson appealed for return of a Democratic majority, he lost support and incurred opposition for what was interpreted as a reflection upon the loyalty of Republicans.

Throughout the war, as before America's entrance, Wilson looked for openings leading to peace, but, as time went on, he envisaged a peace based upon complete defeat of the Central Empires. He emphasized drawing a distinction between the German people and their government which, he maintained, was based upon Prussian militarism. From time to time he defined his country's position and objectives and, on Jan. 8, 1918, enunciated his Fourteen Points[qv] as a basis upon which lasting peace, maintained by a League of Nations, might be established. A month later he discussed before Congress the replies of the Allies and the Central Powers, again laying blame upon German militarism. In August the Pope's offer of mediation was declined both by Allies and the United States. In

September, with German armies in retreat and Austria-Hungary on the verge of collapse, the latter put out feelers for a conference, but Wilson said there could be no bargaining for peace. A suggestion from Germany brought questions whether the old military clique was still in power and whether Belgium and France would be evacuated. What seemed a favorable response was rejected by the President who seemed to be affected by the sweep of opinion in the United States that Germany must be completely defeated and humiliated; hence it was not until a new German government, after the Kaiser fled to The Netherlands, sued for an Armistice that firing stopped on Nov. 11, 1918.

[Charles C. Tansill, *America Goes to War;* Charles Seymour, *Woodrow Wilson and the World War;* James G. Harbord, *The American Army in France, 1917-1918;* Preston Slosson, *The Great Crusade and After.*]

L. B. SHIPPEE

World War, The Navy in. The United States Navy's notable contribution to Allied victory lay in services against submarines[qv] and in transporting troops and their supplies across the Atlantic Ocean. Allied defeat was imminent in the spring of 1917 because more than 850,000 tons of essential shipping was being sunk per month by German submarines. Reinforcements of American destroyers, yachts and gunboats made possible a system of convoys[qv] that cut shipping losses nearly two thirds by November, and thereafter held them at safe levels. Our overseas escorting vessels were based principally at Queenstown, Brest and Gibraltar, all forces in Europe being commanded by Vice-Admiral W. S. Sims with headquarters in London. Approximately 18,600 ships were escorted. Another major antisubmarine effort was a huge mine barrage across the North Sea from the Orkney Islands to Norway. Of a total of 70,263 mines, 56,611 were planted by ten large American mine-layers in thirteen expeditions. This project under Admiral Joseph Strauss was not quite complete at the Armistice[qv] but had sunk possibly eight submarines besides damaging others, and its moral effect was great (*see* Northern Mine Barrage).

A method of hunting submarines by underwater sound detection devices was developed for use on destroyers and "sub-chasers," a special type of craft of only eighty-five tons displacement. Of the latter 120 crossed the Atlantic and served in northern waters or the Mediterranean, manned principally by Naval Reserves. A group of eleven under Commander Nelson screened British and Italian heavy ships during their bombardment of Durazzo on Oct. 2, 1918. Sound detection devices were installed on American submarines and seven of them sent to Europe under Capt. Hart. In four attacks on enemy submarines one was destroyed.

Naval aviation was also employed on an extensive scale in patrolling for and attacking submarines, in assisting convoys and in bombing submarine bases. At the Armistice overseas aviation personnel had expanded to 16,000 and equipment to 500 planes, 3 dirigibles and 50 kite balloons. Twenty-two thousand war-flights had been made from 27 operating bases covering 1,000,000 miles.

The British Grand Fleet, reinforced by a squadron of American battleships under Admiral Hugh Rodman, gave general protection to antisubmarine and convoy operations against possible attack by the German main fleet. Toward the war's end the Germans sent six submarines successively to the American coast as a diversion. They laid mines and attacked single ships and were combatted by "sub-chasers," destroyers and airplanes while our convoys sailed uninterruptedly.

The foregoing antisubmarine measures saved enough merchant shipping, which, together with new construction, made possible the transatlantic transport of nearly 2,000,000 American troops and their supplies—in addition to meeting Allied demands. Despite great obstacles the Transport Force under Admiral Albert Gleaves grew to nearly 50 troopships, and 450 supply ships were also organized under the Navy. By midsummer of 1918, 300,000 troops were being transported per month. The margin of American troops prevented imminent defeat in early 1918 and brought unexpected victory by November. American naval vessels transported 911,000 troops and escorted many more moving in foreign ships. The *Leviathan* alone carried 96,804 soldiers to France. The principal debarkation port at Brest was under Admiral H. B. Wilson who also directed special destroyer escorts for troops convoys. A few transports were torpedoed while homeward bound and nearly empty and the troops losses at sea were inconsiderable. About 30,000 Marines reinforced the Army in combat operations in France and a Naval Railway Battery of five 14-in. long-range guns also saw action ashore.

[D. W. Knox, *A History of the U. S. Navy.*]

DUDLEY W. KNOX

World War Propaganda and Undercover Activities. The outbreak of the World War in August, 1914, was followed by an intense competition between the Allies and the Central Powers for the support of American public opinion. Allied propaganda was facilitated by pre-existing linguistic, cultural and financial ties with the United States, by Allied control over European news services and cables, and by the mistakes and difficulties of the Central Powers. In September, 1914, the British established a propaganda bureau at Wellington House, 8 Buckingham Gate, London, under the direction of Charles F. G. Masterman. Sir Gilbert Parker, in charge of one of its divisions, undertook to mold public opinion in the United States. This division made weekly reports to the British cabinet on the state of American public opinion, kept in close touch with American newspaper correspondents and assisted them in arranging interviews with prominent Englishmen, supplied 360 American newspapers with a weekly news service, and inspired the preparation of vast quantities of books, pamphlets, articles and motion pictures for distribution in the United States. In 1917 Wellington House as a propaganda center was supplanted by a Department of Information under the direction of John Buchan, assisted by an Advisory Committee headed by Lord Northcliffe. In June, 1917, Lord Northcliffe brought a special mission to the United States which resulted in the establishment of the British Bureau of Information in New York City. A further reorganization of British propaganda took place in February, 1918, with the creation of a Ministry of Propaganda under Lord Beaverbrook.

The principal agents of German propaganda in the United States were diplomatic and consular officials, notably Ambassador J. H. von Bernstorff and Capt. Franz von Papen; representatives of German banks and shipping companies; German-American associations and societies such as the National German-American Alliance under the presidency of Dr. J. C. Hexamer; as well as numerous sympathizers in the academic and journalistic fields. An important center of German propaganda in the United States was the office of Dr. Bernhard Dernburg in New York City, under whose direction a press bureau was established and a weekly periodical, *The Fatherland,* devoted to the idea of fair play for Germany and Austria-Hungary. The propaganda[qv] activities of the Central Powers were less skilfully executed than those of the Allies and ultimately culminated in exposures that led to the imprisonment or expulsion from the United States of some of their agents.

On April 14, 1917, subsequent to the entry of the United States into the war, the President by executive order established a Committee on Public Information[qv] composed of the Secretaries of State, War and Navy with George Creel as chairman. This famous Creel Committee, under the vigorous leadership of its chairman, soon became a mammoth propaganda agency enlisting the services of more than 150,000 persons. From the time of its creation until its disestablishment on June 30, 1919, it operated at a cost of $4,912,553. As it finally took shape the Committee comprised two main sections, domestic and foreign. The domestic section, with fifteen divisions, supervised the dissemination of governmental news; issued an official daily newspaper; assembled the artists of America for the production of posters; mobilized the advertising forces of the country; planned various types of war exhibits; organized and directed societies and leagues of foreign language groups; created a nation-wide network of speakers' bureaus; distributed motion pictures; gathered together leading novelists, essayists and publicists; arranged special kinds of propaganda activities designed to appeal to the women of the country; and interpreted war aims to the public through pamphlets and books prepared by outstanding scholars. One of the most extraordinary activities of the domestic section was the creation of an organization of Four-Minute Men[qv] which commanded the volunteer services of 75,000 speakers operating in 5200 communities.

The foreign section, with three divisions, operated a world-wide news service, a foreign mail press service, and distributed propaganda films throughout the world. It had offices in practically every neutral and Allied country.

The work of the Creel Committee, and for that matter the effectiveness of Allied propaganda generally, was greatly enhanced by the speeches and writings of President Wilson, such as his address to Congress on April 2, 1917; the Flag Day address of June 14, 1917; the message to Congress on Dec. 4, 1917; the Fourteen Points[qv] speech on Jan. 8, 1918; and the speeches on Feb. 11, 1918; April 6, 1918; and July 4, 1918. They proved to be unparalleled weapons for propaganda purposes. It was only necessary for the Creel Committee to translate and publicize Wilsonian principles and statements into popular terms.

World War propaganda greatly affected the subsequent history of propaganda. It gave the word a more invidious connotation. It stimulated the rise of state propaganda machines and influenced the propaganda techniques of unofficial economic, political and social groups. The growing interest in the study and analysis of public opinion and propaganda is traceable in large part to propaganda activities during the World War.

[Johann Heinrich, Graf von Bernstorff, *My Three Years in America;* Committee on Public Information, *Complete Report of the Chairman of the Committee on Public Information,* 1917, 1918, 1919, Washington, D. C., Government Printing Office, 1920; George Creel, *How We Advertised America;* Guy Stanton Ford, America's Fight for Public Opinion, *Minnesota History Bulletin,* 3:3-26, 1919; Henry Hamilton Fyfe, *Northcliffe: An Intimate Biography;* Harold Dwight Lasswell, *Propaganda Technique in the World War;* Ralph Haswell Lutz, Studies of World War Propaganda, 1914-33, *Journal of Modern History,* 5:496-516, December, 1933; Sir Gilbert Parker, The United States and the War, *Harper's Magazine,* 136:521-31, 1918; Friedrich Schonemann, *Die Kunst der Masseneinflussung in den Vereinigten Staaten von Amerika;* James Duane Squires, *British Propaganda at Home and in the United States from 1914 to 1917;* George Sylvester Viereck, *Spreading Germs of Hate.*]

HARWOOD L. CHILDS

World's Columbian Exposition, THE, celebrating the four-hundredth anniversary of the discovery of America by Columbus, was held in Chicago from May 1 to Oct. 30, 1893. The Exposition cost more than $20,000,000; forty-six foreign nations and virtually all the American states officially participated; admissions totaled 27,539,000. The official historian reported it a financial success, but the balance sheet is now curiously difficult to check. This Exposition was the first to introduce a separate amusement area, "The Midway Plaisance"; it was here that "Little Egypt" first won a place in the heart of the public. A charming innovation was the Ferris Wheel[q.v.]. The Exposition was notable for its many congresses and conferences: 5978 addresses were made before audiences that numbered more than 700,000. The most significant influence of the Exposition was its lasting effect upon American architecture[q.v.], the modern period of which can be said to have begun at Chicago in 1893. The Exposition embodied the new classicism of the American Renaissance; here the classical style won a lasting victory for the formal ideal. The Columbian Exposition represented the greatest and most harmonious group effort thus far achieved in America; it was a fitting symbol of progress and achievement.

[Hubert Howe Bancroft, *The Book of the Fair.*]

FRANK MONAGHAN

World's Fairs. *See* under separate titles; also list of Expositions.

World's Industrial and Cotton Centennial Exposition, THE, opened in New Orleans, La., on Dec. 1, 1884. The two-million-dollar exposition celebrated the centenary of the export of six bags of cotton from the United States in 1784. A dominant theme of the Exposition was the improvement of educational appliances and conditions and the relation of education to industrial progress. The grounds covered 247 acres; the attendance reached almost 10,000,000. Eleven foreign governments and thirty-two states and territories officially exhibited.

FRANK MONAGHAN

Wormley Conference was the name given to the series of conferences by which the conflict between Republicans and Democrats over the disputed election of 1876[q.v.] was settled. The name grows out of the fact that the final conference was held at Wormley's Hotel in Washington, Feb. 26, 1877. This conference resulted in the "Wormley Agreement" that the Democrats would permit the counting of the electoral votes which would make Hayes President of the United States and that in return the Republicans would withdraw Federal troops from the Southern states, thus consenting to the overthrow of the carpetbag[q.v.] governments in these states (*see* Home Rule, Restoration of, in the South).

[E. P. Oberholtzer, *History of the United States since the Civil War.*]

HALLIE FARMER

Wounded Knee, The Battle of (Dec. 29, 1890), last important clash of Indians with United States troops, climaxed the Ghost Dance[q.v.] trouble. Big Foot's band of Sioux, which fled into the Badlands[q.v.] after the killing of Sitting Bull (*see* Messiah War), Dec. 15, 1890, was captured by the 7th Cavalry at Wounded Knee Creek, S. Dak., December 28. Col J. W. Forsyth, the following day, ordered the Indians disarmed. When a few resisted, general firing began in which more than 200 Indian men, women and children were slaughtered, including Big Foot. The white losses were 29 dead and 33 wounded. Many wounded Indians, left on the field, froze to death in a blizzard the next night.

[James Mooney, *The Ghost-Dance Religion and the Sioux Outbreak of 1890.*]

PAUL I. WELLMAN

Writs of Assistance were general search warrants issued to the customs officers by the superior courts of the various colonies. They were first issued in Massachusetts in 1751. Neither the issue nor the use of such writs seems to have excited controversy prior to 1761. In that year new writs were applied for as the old ones were expiring. These were opposed as unconstitutional by some merchants through their attorney, James Otis. There was some delay but the writs were issued (1762) after instructions had been received from England supporting their legality. That closed the controversy in Massachusetts.

The Townshend Revenue Act[qv] (1767) authorized writs of assistance, but did not specify any form. A form was prepared by the customs officers similar to the one that had been granted in Massachusetts. Every customs officer in America was sent a copy of the desired writ and directed to request the Attorney General of his colony to secure such writs from the superior court. This action made writs of assistance an issue in the superior court of every province in America. The form of the writ was novel to the judges and seemed to encroach upon important rights of citizens. The term "writ of assistance" as used in the law was a common legal expression used to designate a search warrant. It was difficult, however, to convince the judges that such words meant general search warrants. There was delay in most of the courts and the issue dragged through 1768 to 1772, resulting in a direct refusal by the courts of Connecticut, Rhode Island, New York, New Jersey, Pennsylvania, Maryland, Virginia and North Carolina, although the judges offered to issue "writs of assistance," in particular cases, "as directed by law." In some cases the refusals stated the forms presented to the judges were novel and unconstitutional. Finally in 1772 the customs officers reported that they had secured writs in East Florida, West Florida, South Carolina, Bahama, Bermuda, New Hampshire, Nova Scotia and Quebec. It is obvious that the controversy over writs of assistance was not a Massachusetts affair only, and it was not the speech of Otis that made their issue a cause of the Revolution, especially as his speech did not become generally known until long after the Revolution was over. It was the raising of the issue in every superior court in America, dragged through five years, that made writs a common grievance as stated in the Declaration of Independence. (*See also* Unreasonable Searches and Seizures.)

[Information concerning Writs of Assistance in colonies other than Massachusetts has not been published, but it can be found in the Treasury Papers in London. Chief printed sources are William Macdonald, *Select Charters* and A. B. Hart, *American History Told by Contemporaries*, Vol. II, 374-78; O. M. Dickerson, Essay on Writs of Assistance, in *The Era of the American Revolution*, edited by R. B. Morris.]

O. M. DICKERSON

Wyandot Indians. *See* Hurons, The.

Wyandotte Constitution, THE. The present constitution of Kansas was drafted at Wyandotte (now Kansas City, Kans.) by the first territorial convention in which Republicans and Democrats, as such, participated, July 5–29, 1859, and was adopted by popular vote October 4. It followed the constitution of Ohio as a model, prohibited slavery, and reduced Kansas to its present boundaries. (*See also* Lecompton Constitution.)

[F. W. Blackmar, *Kansas, A Cyclopedia of State History.*]

SAMUEL A. JOHNSON

Wyoming. Mystery cloaks the first entry of the white man into the area now included in Wyoming. The Verendrye[qv] brothers, French-Canadian fur traders, may have penetrated to the central part of the Wyoming country in the winter of 1742–43, but it seems probable that they did not go farther west than the Black Hills[qv] of South Dakota. Early in the 19th century came trappers and traders: John Colter who passed through the Yellowstone Park region in 1807; Andrew Henry, the Western partner of Manuel Lisa[qv], who entered western Wyoming in 1809; Jacques La Ramie, employee of the North West Company[qv]; Jim Bridger, one of the partners in Ashley's Rocky Mountain Fur Company[qv], who explored much of Wyoming; and many others.

Capt. Bonneville[qv], on leave of absence from the army, led a fur-trading expedition of 110 men into the Wyoming region in 1832, taking the first wagons over the Continental Divide, on the way to Pierre's Hole[qv]. Lt. John Frémont[qv] explored the country for the Government, 1842–43. On the heels of the trappers and explorers came missionaries: Whitman, Spalding, DeSmet and White.

The Oregon Trail[qv] became the great highway across Wyoming in the 1840's: for Whitman[qv], who led a thousand settlers with 200 wagons over the Trail to Oregon in 1843; for Brigham Young who led a party of Mormons[qv] over the Trail in 1847; for those who participated in the Gold Rush to California[qv] in 1849 and after. The opening of the Overland and Bozeman Trails[qqv] provided new courses for population flow. The telegraph reached Wyoming in 1861; the Union Pacific[qv], in 1867.

The first permanent settlers in Wyoming were a party of Mormons who came to Fort Bridger[qv] in 1853. Gold discovery at South Pass[qv] in 1867 led to the foundation of mining towns and to the establishment of Carter County with the approval of the Dakota Legislature in December, 1867.

Wyoming contains lands obtained from the Louisiana Purchase, Texas Annexation, the

Oregon Treaty and the Mexican Cession of 1848[qqv]. Parts of the Wyoming country were included in the Unorganized Country, 1834–54; Oregon Territory, 1848–53; Utah Territory, 1850–68; Washington Territory, 1853–63; Nebraska Territory, 1854–63; Dakota Territory, 1861–63, 1864–68; and Idaho Territory, 1863–68. Wyoming Territory, with the same boundaries that the state was to have, was created July 25, 1868, from portions of Dakota, Idaho and Utah territories. Territorial government was organized in 1869. Woman suffrage[qv] was granted in the Territory, Dec. 10, 1869; in 1870 a woman served as justice of the peace and women served on juries.

The numerous Indian tribes of the region caused much trouble for the whites who first traversed, explored and settled Wyoming. Government commissioners met the several tribes in council at Fort Laramie in 1851[qv], outlined tribal boundaries, and promised annuities. Increased traffic along the trails, particularly along the Bozeman Trail, opened in 1863, and the arrival of stage lines, pony express, telegraph and railroad[qqv] provoked Indian attacks which led to military retaliation. In the late 1860's and 1870's all of the tribes except the Shoshone and Arapahoe were removed from the Territory. The Shoshones and Arapahoes were placed on the Wind River Reservation in west central Wyoming where they still remain.

Between 1870 and 1890 the population of Wyoming Territory increased tenfold. Statehood was achieved July 10, 1890, Wyoming entering as the 44th state of the Union. Hostilities between cattlemen and settlers marred the early days of statehood (*see* Rustler War). Much of the state's recent history has been concerned with cattle, sheep, oil, irrigation and "dude ranches." Much of the Old West has been faithfully preserved in daily life and in annual celebrations, such as Frontier Days at Cheyenne. Cultural problems have been those of a small population scattered over a large area.

[Frances B. Beard, *Wyoming*.]

ALFRED LARSON

Wyoming Massacre (July 3–6, 1778), the "surpassing horror of the Revolution," included the Battle of Wyoming, July 3, and subsequent atrocities.

Unlike Indian raids, this battle between Butler's Rangers, with Tories and Iroquois, and the Connecticut settlers in the Wyoming Valley[qqv], Pennsylvania, under Col. Zebulon Butler, had a definite line of attack and defense.

The able-bodied men of the settlement were with Washington's army, but Zebulon Butler, home on furlough, gathered the families in Forty Fort[qv], upon the British approach, June 30. On July 3, overruled by rash counsel, Butler led the small garrison, about three hundred, against a force four times their number. The thin line held, then, overwhelmed by the Indians, broke into confusion. The wounded were ruthlessly killed, or slain later by the half-breed Queen Esther.

Barely sixty escaped to surrender on July 4. Butler lost control of the Indians, who disregarding the capitulation terms destroyed the settlers' possessions.

A pivotal battle of the Revolution, stimulating the patriots to activity and union, the Wyoming massacre decided Washington to send the Sullivan Expedition[qv] (1779) to destroy the Iroquois, while it created English opposition to the policy of employing Indians.

[O. J. Harvey, *History of Wilkes-Barre and Wyoming Valley;* C. H. Van Tyne, *The American Revolution.*]

FRANCES DORRANCE

Wyoming Valley, Settlement of, was the cause of many conflicts, involving the governments of Pennsylvania and Connecticut, the British government, the Continental Congress, the Yankees from Connecticut, the Pennamites of Pennsylvania, and the Indians. According to Connecticut's Charter of 1662[qv], her territory reached straight across the continent in a narrow strip from Narragansett Bay to the "South Sea." But Charles II granted part of the same area to his brother, the Duke of York[qv], in 1664, and still another part to William Penn in 1681 (*see* Pennsylvania). However, in the early 1750's the Connecticut General Assembly received several petitions from persons who wished to purchase from the Indians and settle on the reputedly better lands to the west, within Connecticut's charter limits (*see* Connecticut's Western Lands). In 1753 the Susquehannah Company was formed, at Windham, Conn., to buy land, colonize, and evangelize the natives. The section chosen, called Wyoming Valley, is located within the present Commonwealth of Pennsylvania, and is about 21 miles long and 3 or 4 miles wide, with the Susquehanna River running through the middle. In 1754 the Company purchased a large tract from the Six Nations[qv], and in the same year the General Assembly gave approval to the plan for settlement, because it saw the possibility of preventing French encroachments, increasing Indian trade, and befriending the Indians.

The French and Indian War[qv], together with

the intervention of Pennsylvania and Sir William Johnson, interfered with settlement until 1762, when the first white settlers were sent out by the Susquehannah Company to build and plant. They returned to Connecticut for the winter, but went back to the Valley the next spring and built more houses near the site of the present Wilkes-Barre. The Indians drove them out in October, 1763, and no further attempt at settlement was made till 1769, when forty picked men arrived to settle and defend the land. There followed many years of strife, called the "Pennamite War," with the Yankees and the Pennamites alternately in control, but the population continued to grow, nevertheless (*see* Yankee-Pennamite Wars).

Public opinion, in general, seems to have been behind the Connecticut settlers. Even many Pennsylvanians sided with and aided the Yankees, because they appreciated the great advantages of some of their practical ideas, for example: the allodial land system (whereby land was actually owned by the settlers, free from rent or service, as opposed to the Pennsylvania system of absentee ownership by proprietors, of manors, quitrents[qqv], etc.); also, the co-operative town organization[qv], imported intact from New England, with free public schools, churches, and town officers elected by and from the shareholder-settlers.

The whole collection of settlements (with a population of 1922) was officially set up as the town of Westmoreland in Litchfield County, in 1774, and two years later, declared to be a separate county of Connecticut, with its own county court, which of course conflicted with the Pennsylvania jurisdiction. One of the last acts of the Pennsylvania proprietary government, aided by the British ministry and Philadelphia Tories, was the unsuccessful invasion of the Valley by 700 militia in December, 1775.

The Wyoming settlers supplied many men for the Connecticut Line in the Continental Army during the Revolutionary War. This so depleted the number of able-bodied men at Wyoming that there was very little protection against Indians and Tories. The Wyoming massacre[qv], July, 1778, virtually put an end to Connecticut's power in Pennsylvania.

In December, 1782, five impartial commissioners, appointed by Congress to settle the land-title controversy by arbitration, decided in favor of Pennsylvania. The 5000–6000 settlers who held land through the Susquehannah Company were loath to be dispossessed, and more fighting ensued. Finally, the Pennsylvania legislature passed the Compromise Act of 1799, by which Pennsylvania claimants in the Wyoming Valley were paid off, and titles in the seventeen Connecticut townships established before 1782 were confirmed to the Connecticut settlers on payment to Pennsylvania of a certain sum per acre. The Wyoming people became valuable citizens of Pennsylvania and contributed to her development in many ways.

[J. P. Boyd, ed., *The Susquehannah Company Papers, 1750-1772; Public Records of the Colony (and the State) of Connecticut; Pennsylvania Archives*, 2d series, Vol. XVIII; Charles Miner, *History of Wyoming.*]

MARJORIE E. CASE

XYZ Affair, THE, was the most dramatic incident in the bitter dispute between the French Directory and the United States. Incensed at our negotiation of Jay's Treaty[qv] with Great Britain, France issued decrees against American shipping and refused to receive Charles Cotesworth Pinckney, the newly appointed American minister. President John Adams held to a pacific course and sent a mission to Paris composed of Pinckney, then in Holland, John Marshall and Elbridge Gerry, the first two southern Federalists, the last a Massachusetts Republican.

The American ministers arrived just after their supporters in the French legislature had been destroyed by the *coup d'état* of Sept. 4, 1797. The Directory's armies were victorious in Italy and the Rhineland, and Talleyrand, the new foreign minister, thought he could take advantage of the bitter feud between Federalists and Republicans (Jeffersonian)[qqv] in the United States and embarrass the Federalist administration without running any risk of war. Reports from the United States showed the Republicans were gaining ground, and even Jefferson had suggested to the French consul general that France would profit by temporizing.

Talleyrand received the envoys unofficially on Oct. 8, 1797, and stated that they would have an audience with the Directory as soon as a report could be prepared on American affairs. Weeks of official silence ensued. Meanwhile, three unofficial agents of the foreign minister, Hottinguer, Bellamy and Hauteval, called on the Americans suggesting a gratuity of $250,000 for Talleyrand, a loan to France, and an indemnity for Adams' criticism of France in his speech to Congress on May 15, 1797. The ministers were willing to consider a payment to Talleyrand after a treaty had been signed, and they even proposed that one of them return to confer with Adams regarding a loan, provided the Directory would cease its attacks on American shipping and negotiate with the two ministers who remained. Not even these concessions could secure the reception of the ministers by the Directory.

On Jan. 17, 1798, Pinckney, Marshall and Gerry presented a dignified statement of the American position, defending Jay's Treaty, offering France the same privileges Britain enjoyed under that document and demanding compensation for the losses of American shipping. Talleyrand deferred his reply until March 18 when he made an insulting proposal to treat with Gerry alone, characterizing him as the only one of the ministers friendly to France. Although Gerry refused to negotiate with Talleyrand, he remained in Paris after the departure of his colleagues, in the honest but erroneous belief that his presence there prevented war.

The publication of its ministers' despatches by the American Government created such a stir in this country that the affair acquired a unique place in the popular mind. The incident was given a mysterious quality by the substitution of the letters X, Y, and Z for the names of Talleyrand's agents. The Federalists made political capital of the situation, and Congress abrogated the treaties of 1778 (*see* Franco-American Alliance), suspended commercial relations with France, authorized the seizure of *armed* French vessels and strengthened the nation's naval and military forces. Talleyrand, thoroughly alarmed, sought valiantly to prevent a declaration of war (*see* Franco-American Misunderstanding). The wise policy he and President Adams then pursued led to the Convention of Sept. 30, 1800[qv], which ended the misunderstanding.

[Samuel Flagg Bemis, *A Diplomatic History of the United States;* S. E. Morison, Elbridge Gerry, Gentleman, Democrat, in *New England Quarterly,* II, 3-33; Albert J. Beveridge, *Life of John Marshall;* E. Wilson Lyon, The Directory and the United States, in *American Historical Review,* XLIII, 514-32.]

E. WILSON LYON

Yacht Racing in America had its beginning about 1835, although sailing for pleasure had, since 1812, been indulged in by members of several New England and New York families whose interests lay in the sea and commercial shipping. Such men as George Crowninshield and Robert Bennett Forbes of Boston, and John C. Stevens of New York, did much to encourage the sport and the first recorded yacht race is said to have been sailed in Massachusetts waters August, 1835, between the schooners *Sylph* and *Wave,* owned by the two last-named gentlemen.

With the formation of yacht clubs, such as the New York Yacht Club (1844), organized yacht racing grew in popularity. Members of this organization, headed by John C. Stevens, built the schooner *America*[qv] (1851) and sent her to England where she sailed the first international races in which American yachts participated, and won from the Royal Yacht Squadron a cup which her owners gave to the New York Yacht Club as a permanent trophy for international competition of the highest class, and which has since been known as the America's Cup. The defense of this trophy in sixteen matches since 1870 has had a marked effect on the development of American yachting, especially in the larger boats. The first matches for this cup, 1870–71–76, were sailed between schooners, since then in sloops or cutters. The designing of these successful defenders brought fame to some of the leading American naval architects—A. Cary Smith, Nathanael Herreshoff, Edward and W. Starling Burgess. *Ranger,* 1937 defender, the work of W. Starling Burgess and Olin J. Stephens, was probably the fastest yacht to windward built up to that time.

Until about 1880 American yachting was carried on chiefly in large yachts sailed with professional crews. With the formation of the Seawanhaka Yacht Club (1871) at Oyster Bay, N. Y., later called the Seawanhaka-Corinthian Y. C., the racing of yachts by their owners and amateurs was encouraged and small boat racing became popular. By 1920 most of the racing in America was in yachts under 50 feet in length. The growth of the racing fleets was such that at the principal yachting centers on the Atlantic Coast, Marblehead and Long Island Sound, as many as 350 to 400 yachts now participate in the more important regattas. The growth of one-design classes, such as the Stars, New York Thirty-Foot and others, added much to the popularity of the sport and size of the fleets.

[W. P. Stephens, *American Yachting.*]

HERBERT L. STONE

Yadkin River Settlements, The. The Yadkin River Valley of North Carolina was not settled until after 1740, though Henry McCulloh, Arthur Dobbs, and several other prominent men received an extensive grant of land in that region in 1737. In 1746 a few families removed from the Cape Fear region of southeastern North Carolina "to the west of the Yadkin where they joined others who had already broken into that wilderness." About 1750 there were a few German settlers along the Yadkin, and in 1753, Moravians[qv] from Bethlehem, Pa., planted the Wachovia Colony and founded three towns,

Betharaba[qv], Bethania and Salem. From that date to the outbreak of the American Revolution, thousands of Scotch-Irish and Germans[qqv] moved from Pennsylvania to the Yadkin River Valley of North Carolina, coming down the "wagon road," the terminal points of which were Lancaster, Pa., and Salisbury, N. C. The latter town was begun about 1755.

[R. D. W. Connor, *North Carolina: Rebuilding an Ancient Commonwealth.*] HUGH T. LEFLER

Yakima Indian Wars (1855–58). The Yakima Indians, in alliance with the Klickitats, started this war which finally involved the principal tribes of the Pacific Northwest. Before the Indians were forced to submission the conflict had ranged over what is now eastern Washington and northern Idaho, reaching the coast at Puget Sound, and being stopped in its threatened invasion of western Oregon at the Cascades of the Columbia. Throughout, the leading spirit and organizer of the Indians was the remarkable chieftain, Kamiakin, of the Yakimas.

In August, 1855, parties of prospectors passing through the Yakima country were attacked by the Indians. When the Indian agent, A. J. Bolon, went alone to confer with Kamiakin, he was killed. A small detachment of regulars under Maj. Granville O. Haller left The Dalles to arrest the murderers, but was forced to retreat before superior numbers of hostiles. All regulars from the western posts were put into the field and companies of volunteers were called from Oregon and Washington. The Federal military officers were generally critical of the volunteers, and Maj. Gen. John E. Wool, in command of the department of the Pacific, became involved in a bitter quarrel with the territorial authorities of both Oregon and Washington, needlessly prolonging the struggle.

Regulars under Maj. Gabriel J. Rains and volunteers under J. W. Nesmith jointly invaded the Yakima country during November and December, 1855. Although there was no decisive engagement they swept the hostiles from the country.

During the time of the action in the Yakima section, Lt. Col. James K. Kelly conducted a campaign in the Walla Walla Valley where he became involved in a winter campaign, ending, for the regulars, after a four-day battle in early December, which drove the Indians across the Snake River; but the poorly equipped and provisioned volunteers endured a severe winter in the Indian country.

The war had many outcroppings in widely separated regions. The regular army was aroused from its indifferent handling of the Indian war by a defeat suffered under Lt. Col. Edward J. Steptoe in the Spokane country (May, 1858). The military authorities then accepted the territorial view of the seriousness of the situation and pushed the war rigorously. Col. George Wright, in charge of the campaign in the Spokane country, finally broke the power of the Indians and forced them to submission in the early fall of 1858.

[George W. Fuller, *A History of the Pacific Northwest.*] ROBERT MOULTON GATKE

Yale Band, THE, is the name given to the group of seven students from the Theological Department of Yale College, who on Feb. 21, 1829, signed an agreement expressing their readiness to go to the State of Illinois for the purpose of establishing a seminary of learning. Part of them were to engage in teaching, the others in preaching in surrounding territory. As a result of their labors Illinois College was established at Jacksonville (1829) and numerous Presbyterian and Congregational churches[qqv] were formed. Theron Baldwin and J. M. Sturtevant were perhaps the two most conspicuous members of this heroic band.

[Charles H. Rammelkamp, *Illinois College: A Centennial History, 1829-1929;* J. M. Sturtevant, Life of Theron Baldwin, in *Congregational Quarterly*, April and July, 1875.] WILLIAM W. SWEET

Yale University was founded in October, 1701, as the "Collegiate School within his Majties Colony of Connecticot." In that year, so runs tradition, ten Congregational ministers met at the Rev. Samuel Russel's parsonage in Branford, each with a gift of books. Classes were first taught at Killingworth, now Clinton, in the house of the first Rector, the Rev. Abraham Pierson. Upon Pierson's death in 1707 the College moved to Saybrook, and in 1716 to New Haven, whose citizens had outstripped other communities in subscribing sums toward a building. Two years later help came from Elihu Yale, a retired East India merchant, New England born, then living in London. He sent nine bales of East India goods, which brought at sale for the College, £562 12s., and the institution, in gratitude, took his name. The philosopher, George Berkeley, afterward Bishop of Cloyne, gave the College his farm in Rhode Island and a collection of valuable books in 1731–33.

The first brick building, Connecticut Hall (still standing), was built in 1752; the first professorship, a chair in divinity, was established in 1755; others in mathematics, physics and astronomy were added in 1771.

The University now comprises twelve schools: Yale College (1701); the Sheffield Scientific School (1854); the School of Engineering, long a part of the Sheffield Scientific School (1932); the Freshman Year (1919), which is common to all three preceding; the Graduate School (1847); School of Medicine (1813); Divinity School (1822); School of Law (1824); School of the Fine Arts (1866); School of Music (1894); School of Forestry (1900); School of Nursing (1923). Yale had the first gallery of fine arts among American colleges (1832), and conferred the first degree of Doctor of Philosophy in America in 1861.

The *Yale Literary Magazine* is the oldest literary periodical in this country; the *Yale Daily News* the oldest college daily paper.

Today (1940) Yale is a university of about 5200 students, of whom 3100 are in the undergraduate schools. Upperclassmen in these schools live in groups of about 200 in any one of ten undergraduate colleges: Berkeley, Branford, Calhoun, Davenport, Timothy Dwight, Jonathan Edwards, Pierson, Saybrook, Silliman and Trumbull. The undergraduate college plan was made possible by the gift of Edward S. Harkness, '97.

The Faculty numbers about 900. The University Library contains over 2,000,000 volumes.

[Edwin Oviatt, *The Beginnings of Yale, 1701-1726;* Franklin Bowditch Dexter, *Sketch of the History of Yale University*, and *Documentary History of Yale University.*]

CARL A. LOHMANN

Yamasee War, The (1715–16), was waged in southeastern South Carolina. Possibly instigated by Spaniards, the Indians certainly were incensed at land encroachments and at numerous evils incident to their extensive peltry traffic with Carolinians. At dawn, April 15, 1715, about ninety traders and their families were slain. Subsequently, Yamasee bands raided plantations, burning and murdering. Most of the Indian nations between Saint Augustine and Cape Fear[qqv], and some in the interior, allied themselves with the Yamasee, but usually did not go beyond the murdering of traders in their towns. Aided by supplies from New England and a few troops from North Carolina and Virginia, South Carolina gradually gained the upper hand; in the autumn the Yamasee were driven far southward into Florida. For its persuasive effect, a force of 300 Carolinians was sent among the powerful Cherokee[qv], wavering between peace and war. That nation chose peace (January, 1716), while the Lower Creek[qv], openly hostile, migrated westward to obtain protection of the French at Mobile[qv]. Thus the far-reaching conspiracy against Carolina collapsed. Although costly in men, money and trade, the war facilitated the subsequent establishment of Georgia[qv] and ushered in a long period of generally peaceful relations between South Carolina and its Indian neighbors.

[V. W. Crane, *The Southern Frontier, 1670-1732.*]

W. NEIL FRANKLIN

Yankee, The, was a famous privateer[qv] brig from Bristol, R. I., with 18 guns and 120 officers and men, which during the War of 1812[qv] cruised off Halifax and in the South Atlantic and took eighteen prizes worth nearly a million dollars. In two later voyages under Elisha Snow she cruised off Ireland and in the Atlantic with success, one prize (the *San Jose Indiano*) netting a half million dollars and paying over a thousand dollars to a Negro waiter as his share (*see* Prize Money). In six voyages she captured British ships worth $5,000,000. One million of this actually reached Bristol.

[E. S. Maclay, *History of American Privateers.*]

WALTER B. NORRIS

"Yankee Doodle" is our most popular national air or march, easy to remember, adaptable to fife and drum, and with an appeal to the sense of humor. The origin of the tune, like that of the words, is uncertain. It probably was derived from an old air, possibly Dutch, and in its English form said to have been called "Nancy Dawson," "Lucy Locket," or "Kitty Fisher." It is supposed to have been introduced to the colonies by an English fife-major of the Grenadier Guards about 1750, played in a Philadelphia ballad opera in 1767 and by English bands in America as early as 1768. It seems to have first appeared in print in Aird's *Scotch, English, Irish and Foreign Airs* about 1782 and to have been first published in America in 1794. The words originated probably after 1764 and with many variations were probably embodied in their present form

Yankee Doodle came to town,
Riding on a pony,
Stuck a feather in his cap
And called him [or "it"] Macaroni.

about 1775, probably from the pen of a Tory or Briton. The early versions of the song with many and various verses, running into scores, were obviously composed at various times by various individuals. The origin of these was probably a satirical ballad, *The Yankee's Re-*

turn from Camp, printed between 1810 and 1813. These verses are obviously the product of Americans.

[The whole of this difficult and obscure question is treated fully and competently in O. G. T. Sonneck's *Report on the Star Spangled Banner, Hail Columbia, America, and Yankee Doodle,* Government Printing Office, 1909.]

WILBUR C. ABBOTT

Yankee Notions. In the early years of the 18th century, a large number of small articles such as brooms, pots, pans, tongs, roasting ovens, brass and copper utensils, clocks, spinning wheels, wooden bowls, plates, etc., were made in New England during the winter months when farming was impossible. As soon as roads were passable in the spring, pedlars would start out with one-horse carts full of the winter's accumulation of these things on journeys which often lasted six months. The arrival of the "Yankee Pedlar" in the far South or on the Western frontiers was an event of great importance especially as he brought with him not only goods but news and gossip. The fame of the "Yankee Notions" spread thus throughout the country and because these small wares seemed to backwoodsmen and plantation dwellers to have been contrived with special cunning, the term "Yankee ingenuity" became widespread and New Englanders were believed to be peculiarly gifted with inventive skill.

It is probably true that the manufacture of brass and copper, clocks, cheap watches, small domestic machinery and so on which later developed such large industries in the river valleys of Massachusetts and Connecticut grew originally out of just such tinkering and whittling on the farms. It must be remembered that, in this early period, farming was an almost universal occupation in America, outside of the seaports, and that in New England, where the farming season was short, such artisan manufacture was a necessary avocation in the long winters. Also, on the subsistence farm, an institution sharply differentiated from the staple crop plantation of the South as well as the surplus farm of the Middle States, it was necessary for the farmer to be a jack-of-all-trades, competent to make and repair his own tools, implements, utensils, furniture and, in earlier days, even leather, clothing and shoes. It is natural therefore that the notions, forerunners of the modern "gadgets," should have been Yankee specialties.

[R. Burlingame, *March of the Iron Men;* R. Wright, *Hawkers and Walkers in America;* V. S. Clark, *History of Manufactures in the U. S.*]

ROGER BURLINGAME

Yankee-Pennamite Wars, THE, occurred in 1769–72, 1775 and 1784 when settlers under Connecticut titles and those under Pennsylvania disputed their private claims by force while the Pennsylvania-Connecticut Boundary Dispute[qv] was pursuing its official and legal course (*see* Wyoming Valley, Settlement of). In 1769 the Pennsylvanians dispossessed Maj. Durkee from the blockhouse and fort at Wilkes-Barre. The next spring the Connecticut settlers, led by Lazarus Stewart and his Paxton Boys[qv], recaptured the fort. In 1771 Stewart, or one of his party, killed an attacking Pennamite and the leader of the Paxton Boys fled to Connecticut where he was shielded by the Susquehannah Company[qv] and even, it appears, by Gov. Trumbull. By the summer of 1772 the Connecticut people had gained permanent possession of the region and peaceful settlement began. There was a threat of renewal of the war in December, 1775, when Sheriff Plunkett of Northumberland County led a "posse" (in reality a militia troop of 500 men) against the Wyoming settlements, but he was repulsed in a brief engagement at the lower end of the valley. In 1784 the second so-called Pennamite-Yankee War broke out when local authorities of Pennsylvania, acting in close co-operation with Pennsylvania claimants, dispossessed those holding Connecticut titles. These "wars" were conducted by disciplined companies acting under military leaders, forts were built and besieged, articles of capitulation were drawn up and signed, and in general the formal rules of 18th-century warfare were observed. Some bloodshed, some misery and a great deal of lasting bitterness resulted. But in general the "wars" were carried on by private persons unsupported by governmental authority. (*See also* Connecticut's Western Lands.)

[O. J. Harvey, *History of Wilkes-Barre.*]

JULIAN P. BOYD

Yap Mandate, THE. When the mandates[qv] system was established in 1919 (*see* Versailles, Treaty of), Japan was given the mandate over those former German possessions in the Pacific lying north of the equator. This included the Marshall, Mariana, or Ladrone, and Caroline islands, and among the last group was the small island of Yap, in which the United States was particularly interested because of its proximity to Guam and the Philippines[qqv] and its position as the connecting link for cable communication to and from the Far East (*see* Pacific Cable).

Although agreeing to a Japanese mandate over these Pacific islands, President Wilson had on several occasions during the Peace Conference[qv] made reservations against the inclusion of Yap, desiring instead that it be put under special international control as a cable station. Formal and energetic protest was made by the United States against this feature of the mandate to Japan, to the other principal Allied Powers and to the League of Nations[qv] Council. The controversy was finally settled during the Washington Conference[qv], a special treaty between the United States and Japan being signed on Feb. 11, 1922, and made effective on July 13, under which the United States formally agreed to the terms of the Japanese mandate, including expressly the island of Yap, and obtained from Japan those rights which are accorded to members of the League of Nations, complete equality with respect to the cables, together with some additional rights.

[Charles Noble Gregory, The Mandate over Yap, in *American Journal of International Law*, Vol. XV, pp. 419-427; Walter R. Batsell, The United States and the System of Mandates, in *International Conciliation*, No. 213; Quincy Wright, *Mandates under the League of Nations;* Paul H. Clyde, *Japan's Pacific Mandate.*]

CLARENCE A. BERDAHL

"Yardstick." Meaning a basis or standard of comparison, this term has been widely used in discussions of proposals to set up enterprises owned and operated by the National Government to compete with similar privately owned enterprises. Government generation and distribution of electric power by the Tennessee Valley Authority[qv], for example, is commonly defended on the ground that it will provide a "yardstick" by which to judge the fairness of rates charged for electricity by privately owned utilities.

[B. R. Powell, *Compilation and Analysis of Congressional Debates on the Right of the Federal Government to Operate Electric Power Projects;* S. C. Wallace, *The New Deal in Action;* W. L. Willkie, The New Deal Power Program Challenged, and H. L. Ickes, In Defense of the New Deal Power Program, in *N. Y. Times*, Oct. 31 and Nov. 7, 1937; C. E. Troxel, The T.V.A. Potpourri, in *Public Utilities Fortnightly*, XVIII, 231-240.]

P. ORMAN RAY

Yazoo-Chattahoochee Line, THE, running east-west between the rivers named, at about 32° 26′ N. Lat., was the northern limit of British West Florida[qv] by Order in Council, March, 1764. Important as a factor in Spain's boundary dispute with the United States, 1783–95, which was settled by Pinckney's Treaty[qv], it became the first northern boundary of Mississippi Territory, 1798.

[S. F. Bemis, *Pinckney's Treaty;* A. P. Whitaker, *The Spanish-American Frontier.*] MACK SWEARINGEN

Yazoo Fraud. In 1795 the legislature of Georgia passed a law granting the greater part of the territory now making up Alabama and Mississippi to four land companies for the sum of $500,000. These companies, bearing the names Georgia, Georgia-Mississippi, Upper Mississippi and Tennessee, received varying amounts, the first-named receiving the most. They were composed of people in all walks of life and from various parts of the country, including even a sprinkling of the legislators who passed the law. In this fact and also in the light of proof that all who voted for the law, with one exception, were bribed in one way or another to support the measure, grew up the charge of fraud. With the wrath of the Georgians fanned by William H. Crawford and James Jackson, who resigned from the United States Senate to return to Georgia and fight the fraud, a new legislature was elected in 1796 which rescinded the act. To show further indignation, the legislature in a solemn formal meeting burned the Yazoo act and all papers relating to it; and the state constitutional convention of 1798 inserted a clause ratifying the rescinding act and declaring the land in question inalienable.

The fraud received its name from the Yazoo River which ran through a part of the territory sold, and it had as an important element in its background the dispute of ownership of these western lands[qv]. Georgia claimed them as coming within her colonial limits; the United States claimed them as part of the spoils of the Revolution; Spain claimed, until 1795, all south of 32° 28′ (*see* Pinckney's Treaty); and various tribes of Indians claimed and occupied them. Surrounded with these uncertainties, Georgia had sold most of this land in 1789 to three companies, who, failing to comply with all the terms of the law, lost their rights. Finally in 1802 Georgia sold all her claims west of the Chattahoochee River to the United States for $1,250,000 (*see* Georgia Compact).

The Yazoo claimants denied Georgia's right to rescind the sale and sought a remedy from Congress. For years this body debated the subject, and after the United States Supreme Court had decided in the Fletcher v. Peck case[qv] that the rescinding law was unconstitutional, Congress paid the claimants, in 1814, $4,282,151.12½.

[U. B. Phillips, *Georgia and State Rights;* W. B. Stevens, *History of Georgia;* C. S. Haskins, *The Yazoo Land Companies;* E. M. Coulter, *Short History of Georgia.*]

E. MERTON COULTER

Yazoo Pass Expedition, THE (Feb. 6–April 12, 1863). Failing in their frontal attack on Vicksburg (*see* Chickasaw Bluffs, Battle of), the Federal forces sought to turn Vicksburg's[qv] right flank. Opposite the Federal base at Helena, Ark., the levee was blasted and an amphibious expedition comprised of six gunboats and transports with 800 troops set out across the flooded upper Yazoo Delta, hoping to reach the high ground east of the Yazoo River. After extricating themselves from frequent log jams in the old pass, and chopping their way through overhanging branches along the Coldwater and the Tallahatchie, they were blocked just short of their objective by an improvised Confederate battery behind cotton bales, "Fort Pemberton." Grant (U.) hastily dispatched a force to save them from capture, while Admiral Porter and Gen. W. T. Sherman launched a much larger expedition into the waterways of the lower Yazoo Delta as a diversion. (*See also* Steele's Bayou Expedition; Vicksburg in the Civil War.)

[*Official Records of the Union and Confederate Navies in the War of the Rebellion*, Series I, Vol. XXIV; Richard S. West, Jr., *The Second Admiral, A Life of David Dixon Porter, 1813-91.*]

RICHARD S. WEST, JR.

Yellow Creek Massacre. *See* Cresap's War.

"Yellow-Dog Contract," THE, technically the antiunion contract, is an agreement not to join unions, exacted by employers from a worker. In the 1870's and 1880's the "iron clad," as it was then known, was a common antiunion weapon. Later the term "yellow-dog" stigmatized the conduct of the individual willing to be bound by such an agreement. Endeavors by state and Federal governments to prohibit employers from exacting such contracts were invalidated by the Supreme Court in Adair v. U. S. (1908) and Coppage v. Kansas (1915)[qqv]. The most telling reinforcement of the "yellow-dog" appeared in Hitchman Coal v. Mitchell (1917)[qv] when the Court restrained a labor organizer from an endeavor to induce workers to break their contracts and join a union.

Numbers of workers were alleged to have been held by such agreements after the World War. Public sentiment against the "yellow-dog contract" resulted in the Norris-LaGuardia Act[qv] of 1932 which declared the "yellow-dog contract" contrary to public policy. Several states adopted similar legislation; these agreements are now practically nonenforceable in the courts. The terms of the later National Labor Relations Act[qv] of 1935 which bar antiunion discrimination by employers appear to have ended the long effort to outlaw the "yellow-dog."

[J. R. Commons and J. B. Andrews, *Principles of Labor Legislation;* A. G. Taylor, *Labor Problems and Labor Law.*]

HERBERT MAYNARD DIAMOND

Yellow Fever. In that indispensable sourcebook, John Winthrop's *History of New England,* we find the first reference to yellow fever (1647), referring to yellow fever from the West Indies (Barbadoes Distemper). The effort of the Court on this occasion to exclude the crew and the cargo from Massachusetts was this country's initial enforcement of quarantine. The British ships that sailed from Boston to capture Martinique returned without the island, but with an epidemic of yellow fever (1694). Despite its endemic focus on the African coast, yellow fever emerged as a peculiarly American disease (the "American plague"). If syphilis is the Indian's revenge on his white captors, malaria and yellow fever are the Negro's retaliation, as these two diseases spread through America with the African slave trade. With the single exception of smallpox[qv], the most dreaded verdict on the lips of a colonial physician was yellow fever, and long after immunity was secured from smallpox, there was no protection against yellow fever. The summer or autumn that brought the Yellow Jack to America heard the death-carts through the streets, and the never-forgotten cries of the grave-diggers, "Bring out your dead! Bring out your dead!"

The outstanding epidemic of yellow fever, which doomed the supremacy of Philadelphia among American cities, was described by an eyewitness, the bookseller and publisher, Mathew Carey (1793): "People uniformly and hastily shifted their course at the sight of a hearse coming towards them. Many never walked on the foot-path, but went into the middle of the street, to avoid being infected in passing houses wherein people had died. Acquaintances and friends avoided each other in the streets, and only signified their regard by a cold nod. The old custom of shaking hands fell into such general disuse that many shrunk back with affright at even the offer of the hand. A person with crape or any appearance of mourning was shunned like a leper. And many valued themselves highly on the skill and address with which they got to windward of every person whom they met." The tragedy of this behavior lies in its utter uselessness, since yellow fever can never pass from man to man.

Benjamin Rush, the medical oracle to whom all turned for succour, was relentless in his insistence on bloodletting, calomel and jalop. Rush's reign of blood, and his mercurial thunderbolts did not stop the epidemic. Rush, after noting a meteor, a dead cat, and that mosquitoes were numerous ("the usual attendants of a sickly autumn"), decided the yellow fever was caused by spoiled coffee on a wharf. Many years were destined to pass before the *Ædes ægypti* was proved guilty.

The prevention of yellow fever depends upon the elimination of the yellow-fever mosquito. Walter Reed, an army doctor from Virginia, tracking pestilence in Cuba with his devoted associates, demonstrated that the female mosquito carries the unknown parasite of yellow fever. The work of Walter Reed, James Carroll, the martyred Lazear, and the immune Aristide Agramonte sent William Crawford Gorgas, of Alabama, on his quest of the mosquito. Handicapped for years at Panama by uncomprehending officials ("Do you know, Gorgas, that every mosquito you kill costs the United States Government ten dollars?"), he hunted the wriggling larvæ on that narrow strip of jungle, transforming the death-trap of the tropics into a health resort. The United States was able to break the barrier between the Atlantic and the Pacific (*see* Panama Canal), because this modern Theseus slew two mosquitoes—the devouring Minotaurs of malaria and of yellow fever.

[For the earliest publication of the United States Army Yellow Fever Commission, which solved the mosquital transmission of the disease, see Walter Reed, James Carroll, Aristides Agramonte, Jesse William Lazear, The Etiology of Yellow Fever, in *Philadelphia Medical Journal*, 1900, pp. 790-96.]

VICTOR ROBINSON

"Yellow Journalism." James Gordon Bennett was the first American publisher to introduce the sensational manner in presenting news, but it was not until the 1880's that the term "Yellow Journalism" was applied to this type of news presentation. In this decade the development of pulp paper and the increase in advertising made possible a general reduction in newspaper prices and a consequent extension of the field for subscribers.

Advertising[qv] paid a large share of the publishing costs and since space rates were based on distribution, there was constant pressure for increase in the number of subscribers. Joseph Pulitzer, of the New York *World,* used high-pressure methods to accomplish this end. One of his innovations was a Sunday edition, carrying special articles and comic strips[qv]. One of these strips featured a "Yellow Kid" and it was from this character that the name "Yellow Journalism" was derived. This type of journalism gained a new recruit in William Randolph Hearst, publisher of the San Francisco *Examiner,* who in 1895 acquired the New York *Morning Journal* and began a subscription war with the *World.* This struggle resulted in an intensification of the methods of "Yellow Journalism."

The Cuban question was made to order for the sensational methods of the two publishers. Typical of the journalistic activities of the period were the propaganda methods used in reporting the concentration camps, the DeLome letters and the sinking of the *Maine*[qv].

At the turn of the century the scare head, the scandal section, the sob sister and the elaborate Sunday features had become permanent features of the sensational press.

Some newspapers never adopted the extreme methods of the Yellow Journal press, but a considerable number of the metropolitan papers used some if not all of the innovations that appeared in the newspapers of the 1880's.

[W. G. Bleyer, *Main Currents in the History of American Journalism.*]

THEODORE G. GRONERT

"Yellow Peril," THE. This expression grew out of the ethnocentric, hypernationalistic attitude of Americans toward Oriental immigrants, combined with a high degree of provincialism and frontier sensitivity. The fears of economic competition and the racial barrier to assimilation[qv] worked in favor of treaties and laws which served to discriminate against, restrict and eventually exclude the immigration of aliens "ineligible for citizenship"; namely, of Oriental extraction (*see* Chinese Exclusion Acts; Japanese Exclusion Acts). The idea had its genesis in the early contacts between Americans of European ancestry and Chinese immigrant laborers on the Pacific coast.

Of all immigrants to America, except the Negro slaves, the Oriental presented the greatest racial contrast to Americans of Caucasian ancestry. This fact, combined with their widely different cultural habits and reputed inscrutability and cunning, provided a fertile background for an highly emotional campaign against them characterized by fear, mob violence, fantastic tales and finally unreasonable legal restraints against those already in the United States.

Following the treaty of 1882 with China and the subsequent laws restricting immigration the Chinese population decreased (*see* Chinese Immigration and Labor). However, late in the 19th and early 20th centuries the Japanese came to America in increasing numbers due to the urgent request of Hawaiian sugar planters and Pacific coast interests who clamored for a cheap labor supply. The "Yellow Peril" bogey now became more definitely associated with Japanese immigrants. The attendant friction led to discriminatory local and state legislation and finally to the "Gentlemen's Agreement" of 1907, restricting their immigration by mutual agreement. Following the close of the World War the increasing fear of Japan's ascendancy in the Far East and the Pacific, and increasing suspicion of her motives regarding our Pacific coast led to another emotional reaction under the banner of "Yellow Peril" culminating in the exclusion laws of 1920 and 1924.

[Brown and Roucek, *Our Racial and National Minorities.*] KENNETH POTTER

Yellow Tavern, Battle at (May 11, 1864). With Torbert's, Gregg's and Wilson's divisions, 10,000 horsemen, Sheridan (U.) on May 9 left Grant's army near Spotsylvania[qv] and rode for Richmond via Beaver Dam. Stuart (C.), pursuing with 5000 cavalry, by an exhausting march headed the Federals at Yellow Tavern, six miles north of Richmond. Stuart placed Lomax's brigade on his left and Wickham's on his right and was attacked by Torbert and later by Wilson. Lomax's line was finally broken and here, about 4 P.M., Stuart, gallantly steadying his men, was mortally wounded. He died May 12. Though defeated, his stand saved Richmond, giving the garrison time to man the fortifications. Sheridan's column passed east to Malvern Hill, where he contacted Butler's army.

[John W. Thomason, Jr., *Jeb Stuart; Official Records, Union and Confederate Armies*, Vol. XXXVI.] JOSEPH MILLS HANSON

Yellowstone, the first steamboat to navigate the upper Missouri between Omaha and Fort Union[qv], was built at Louisville for the American Fur Company[qv]. In 1831 she reached Fort Tecumseh (Pierre[qv]) after a difficult trip. The following year, with George Catlin[qv] aboard, she steamed to Fort Union, averaging 100 miles per day downstream on her return. In 1833 she again ascended to the mouth of the Yellowstone.

[H. M. Chittenden, *The History of the American Fur Trade of the Far West*, and *Early Steamboat Navigation on the Missouri River.*] WILLIAM J. PETERSEN

Yellowstone National Park. The wonders of hot spring and geyser activity, together with the phenomena of lasting wilderness and big-game herds, have made Yellowstone well known to the entire world. It is distinguished, too, in that within its boundaries the National Park[qv] idea was conceived, an idea which has influenced the recreation and conservation programs of many nations. When, in 1870, the Washburn-Langford-Doane expedition ventured into the little-publicized wilds of the volcanic upper Yellowstone country, all of America was electrified by the resulting authentic accounts of the natural wonders of the region, and in 1872 Congress gave favorable action to the party's proposal to hold the area in government ownership "for the benefit and enjoyment of the people." Great travertine terraces; more geysers than are found in all of the rest of the world (3000 hot springs and geysers); brilliantly colored canyons; fossil forests; Yellowstone Lake, twenty miles long and 7730 feet above the sea; buffalo herds; thousands of elk and deer; bands of antelope and mountain sheep; the famous Yellowstone grizzly bear and its more common cousin, the black bear; and an abundance of trout—cutthroat, loch leven, brown, eastern brook, mackinaw and rainbow—constitute features which each year attract some 500,000 visitors to this wonderland in the northwestern corner of Wyoming. A park superintendent is in immediate charge of the reservation, 3437 square miles in area, which falls under the administration of the National Park Service, Department of the Interior.

[C. Max Bauer, *The Story of Yellowstone Geysers;* Vernon Bailey, *Animal Life of Yellowstone Park;* W. B. McDougall and Herma A. Baggley, *Plants of Yellowstone National Park;* J. E. Haynes, *Haynes' Guide to Yellowstone National Park.*] CARL P. RUSSELL

Yellowstone River Expeditions, THE (1819–25), were planned by John C. Calhoun, Secretary of War, to overawe British fur traders and the Indians of the upper Missouri. As a means of impressing the Indians five steamboats were commissioned to ascend the Missouri, where no steamboat had ever been, and carry the expedition of 1100 men commanded by Gen. Henry Atkinson. Unfortunately the steamboats were unsuited for Missouri navigation. Two turned back at the start and only one reached Council Bluffs, half way to the Yellowstone, after voyaging the entire summer of 1819. The expedition failed for lack of funds, except that Maj. Stephen H. Long[qv] led an overland party to the Rockies.

Continued Indian attacks on fur traders resulted in a second expedition in 1825 with 476 men under Atkinson, accompanied by Benjamin O'Fallon, Indian agent. Among subordinate officers were Henry Leavenworth, Stephen W. Kearny and Bennett C. Riley, western soldiers, whose names are perpetuated in Forts Leavenworth, Riley and Kearny[qqv]. Atkinson's party voyaged in eight keelboats[qv], arrived at the Yellowstone in August and returned the same season. The Indians were so impressed by the show of force that O'Fallon and Atkinson were able to conclude treaties with fifteen tribes.

[Hiram Martin Chittenden, *The American Fur Trade*

of the Far West; Atkinson's report, *19th Congress, first session, House Document No. 117,* Vol. VI.]

BLISS ISELY

Yerba Buena. *See* San Francisco.

York, Maine, Attack on (1692), was perhaps the "greatest tragedy of colonial times in New England." Led by Madockawando, 150 Abnaki[qv] warriors attacked the frontier town, Monday morning, Jan. 25, 1691/92. Of a total population of 500, about 50, including the minister, Shubael Dummer, were killed, and about 80 made captives. Sixteen or more houses were burned, all north of the York River, leaving only Alcock's and Preble's garrisons, the church, and probably two or three other houses. Retreating along the coast to Sagadahoc, the Indians waited there for friends of the captives, who shortly redeemed 36 of them. Some of the rest were ransomed later while others spent the rest of their lives in Canada.

[C. E. Banks, *History of York, Maine.*]

ROBERT E. MOODY

York, Pa., was the capital of the United States from Sept. 28, 1777, to June 27, 1778. As the British, under Howe, occupied Philadelphia, Congress deemed it wise to move west of the Susquehanna River. During this period, John Hancock resigned the presidency of Congress and Henry Laurens succeeded him, the Articles of Confederation[qv] were drawn up, Burgoyne surrendered[qv], and Lafayette and Von Steuben joined the American forces.

[George R. Prowell, *Continental Congress at York, Pennsylvania.*]

JULIAN P. BOYD

York (Toronto), Capture and Destruction of (1813). Acting in accordance with a plan of campaign outlined by Secretary of War John Armstrong in February, Commodore Isaac Chauncey's fleet, with a force under Gen. Zebulon Pike, sailed from Sackett's Harbor on April 25 to attack York. The Americans landed about a half mile west of Fort Toronto, on the morning of the 27th.

The riflemen under Maj. Benjamin Forsyth were the first ashore, and advanced to attack the enemy composed of 750 regulars and about 100 Indians under Gen. R. H. Sheaffe. The main body of troops led by Gen. Pike soon followed and forced the British to retreat to the shelter of their works. As the Americans advanced, they captured one of the batteries and were a short distance from the main works when the magazine was exploded, killing 100 Americans and 40 of the enemy. Gen. Pike was mortally wounded. Gen. Sheaffe and his regulars, after firing their stores, retreated toward Kingston. The remaining defenders capitulated. On May 8 the post was evacuated by the Americans, and soon was reoccupied by the British.

The American forces under Chauncey and Scott recaptured the fort without opposition, July 31, destroying the barracks, stores and storehouses.

[Benson J. Lossing, *Pictorial Field-Book of the War of 1812;* John Brannan, *Official Letters of the Military and Naval Officers of the United States, during the War with Great Britain in the Years 1812, 13, 14 and 15.*]

ROBERT W. BINGHAM

York's, Duke of, Proprietary (1664–85) had its origin in the new nationalism of the Restoration Period. The passing of the Navigation Acts[qv] and the program to draw the colonies into a closer relationship with the mother country in the interests of mercantilism[qv] demanded the elimination of the Dutch as competitors on the American continent, where they had established themselves on lands which had been granted by the English crown to the Council for New England[qv]. The king decided to conquer New Netherland[qv] and to bestow it upon his brother the Duke of York. After purchasing the claims of the Stirling heirs (*see* Long Island), which included also northern Maine, the king conveyed to the Duke, in March, 1664, several months before the conquest, New Netherland and other scattered territories, a proprietary[qv] stretching from the Connecticut to the Delaware River and Bay, including the near-by islands of Martha's Vineyard, Nantucket and Long Island, and the region north of Gorges' Maine[qv], between the St. Croix and the Pemaquid.

The Duke's charter created him lord proprietor with complete authority to rule his province unchecked by a representative assembly. In him was vested all legislative, executive and judicial power, subject only to appeal to the king. He delegated his authority to governors whom he carefully instructed as to policy. Though he had no faith in democratic government, he expected his governors to consider the well-being of the people. Regions preponderantly English like Long Island were governed by laws of neighboring colonies, drawn up in a code called the Duke's Laws[qv]. Liberty of conscience prevailed throughout the province. Two features of his government the people found hard to bear, his inordinate interest in revenue from the province and the absence of a representative assembly. Though he at first denied petitions for representation, he finally instructed his governor, Andros, to call an assembly, which met for a few sessions in 1683–85 and adopted a Charter of Liberties[qv]. The new institution came to an abrupt end with the ripening of plans for the Dominion of New England[qv].

Rival claims and failure of the Duke to appreciate the potentialities of his new proprietary as a unit resulted in periodic dismemberment of the once princely domain. Even before the conquest of New Netherland, the Duke leased to his friends, Berkeley and Carteret, the rich farm lands of the Jerseys[qv]. Another piece was soon to go to Connecticut[qv] whose charter of 1662 overlapped the Duke's grant, since it gave jurisdiction over the west bank settlements (*see* River Towns of Connecticut), including those of the former New Haven colony[qv]. Long Island was likewise included in both grants. The Nicolls commission[qv] settled the dispute in 1667 by assigning Long Island to New York, but surrendering to Connecticut the lands west of the river to within twenty miles of the Hudson. The Duke, however, did not accept this decision as final. When his province was restored to him in 1674, after the Dutch conquest, he reopened the issue by instructing Gov. Andros to assume jurisdiction over western Connecticut. Andros marched to Saybrook with an armed force and asserted the Duke's authority there. Connecticut refused to recognize these claims and the matter hung fire until 1687 when Connecticut with its boundaries of 1667 was incorporated into the Dominion of New England.

The Duke's possessions on the west bank of Delaware Bay were given to William Penn in 1682, probably in deference to the Duke's regard for Penn's father, Admiral Penn. To these lands the Duke had no strict legal title. They were not included in his charter, but from the time of the conquest of New Netherland, the Duke considered himself possessor by right of conquest of all lands taken from the Dutch, including those which they in turn had taken from the Swedes. Gov. Andros introduced the Duke's Laws there in 1676 and a little later created three counties, New Castle, Kent and Sussex (*see* Delaware). Penn, after receiving Pennsylvania[qv], realized that he might be shut out from the ocean by the possessor of the territory to the south, along the west shore of the river and bay, and he therefore applied to the Duke for a grant. After some hesitation the Duke finally agreed. In 1682 he executed two leases, one for New Castle[qv] and the land within a radius of twelve miles (*see* Delaware Circle), and the other for the land to the south as far as Cape Henlopen. The Duke then made an effort, perhaps at Penn's instigation, to obtain a royal grant, and received one on March 22, 1683. Though this charter appears on the patent rolls, it apparently was incomplete. Doubt as to its validity prompted James, after his accession to the throne, to grant Penn a royal charter, but he was prevented by his abdication.

The last sizable outlying section of the Duke's proprietary to go was Pemaquid[qv], which, as the County of Cornwall, was added to the Dominion of New England in June, 1686. James, now king, apparently had no further interest in preserving the scattered pieces of his proprietary intact, but turned his attention to experimenting with dominion rule throughout the English provinces. In the belief that a more satisfactory colonial policy could be maintained by organizing the colonies into a few large units, the New England colonies were combined into a dominion, but, before a middle group of colonies could be formed into another unit, danger from French attack suddenly decided the king and the Lords of Trade in 1688 to add New York and New Jersey to the Dominion of New England. After the overthrow of the dominion in 1689 by revolutions in Boston and New York City, New York became a royal province of the regular type with the representative government which its people had so long desired (*see* New York, Colony of).

[C. M. Andrews, *The Colonial Period in American History*, Vol. III.]

VIOLA F. BARNES

Yorktown. The land along York River on which Yorktown stands was patented by Nicholas Marteau or Martiau, a Walloon, soon after his first appearance in Virginia in 1621. York County, then called Charles River County (the name was changed in 1642), was one of the eight original shires of Virginia, and was set up in 1634. Court was held in three different places before Yorktown was made the county seat. In 1691 Benjamin Reade, a grandson of Marteau, sold to the colony for 10,000 pounds of tobacco fifty acres of his ancestral tract, on which a port was to be located. The town thus founded quickly became the county seat, and in 1697 a courthouse was built which stood until demolished in the Peninsular Campaign[qv] in 1862. The first customhouse in America was built in Yorktown in 1706 and still stands. Yorktown's importance as a port was destroyed by the Revolutionary War. At the time of the Yorktown Campaign[qv] it had about 60 houses and 400 inhabitants.

[J. Luther Kibler, *The Cradle of the Nation.*]

ALVIN F. HARLOW

Yorktown Campaign (1781). Lord Cornwallis, retreating to Wilmington, N. C., after the Battle of Guilford Court House[qv], decided to move into Virginia and add the forces of Arnold[qv] and Phillips to his own (*see* Southern Campaigns, 1780–81). He left Wilmington April 25, 1781, and on May 20 reached Petersburg, Va., where he met the Arnold and Phillips troops, giving him about 5000 men. Lafayette, who had been sent by Washington to watch Arnold, was then at Richmond with 3000 men, two thirds of them green troops. Cornwallis tried to persuade Sir Henry Clinton to abandon New York and concentrate on Virginia, but the latter refused. Cornwallis then moved against Lafayette, who retreated north of the Rapidan, where new accretions increased his force to more than 4000. He now blocked a raid by Tarleton and became so threatening that Cornwallis thought it wise to place himself nearer the coast. He retired to Richmond, and on June 20 moved farther down the Peninsula to Williamsburg. Lafayette, now reinforced by Steuben with 1000 more men, was close upon his heels, and had a brush with him on July 6, losing 145 men. In the first week in August, Cornwallis settled himself in Yorktown, and added the Portsmouth, Va., garrison to his force, giving him an army of 7000. Lafayette paused at Malvern Hill. On Aug. 31 Admiral DeGrasse arrived in Chesapeake Bay with a powerful squadron (*see* French Fleet in American Revolution, Aid of), and disembarked 3000 troops under St. Simon, who were added to those of Lafayette. The latter, on Sept. 7, drew his line, now numbering 8000, across the Peninsula at Williamsburg, thus blocking Cornwallis' possible escape. Meanwhile, DeGrasse had beaten off the English fleet on Sept. 5 (*see* Chesapeake Capes, Battle of).

Cornwallis, with his seasoned veterans, might still have broken through Lafayette's militia and ill-equipped regulars, and returned to the Carolinas; but he was relying on the British fleet and he was unaware that Washington, kept constantly informed by Lafayette, had conceived the daring plan of shifting his and Rochambeau's forces (*see* French Army, March of Rochambeau's) from New York to Virginia, some 400 miles, to overwhelm Cornwallis. Keeping Clinton at New York, still fearful of an attack upon him, Washington left the Hudson River on Aug. 19, five days after hearing that DeGrasse was heading for the Chesapeake, marched through Philadelphia to the head of the bay and began embarking his troops on Sept. 6. Washington himself reached Lafayette's headquarters on the 14th and assumed command, and his army arrived in detachments between the 18th and the 26th. A few days later, the full force, 16,000 strong, was drawn in a semicircle around Yorktown and began its bombardment with seventy cannon. On Oct. 6 the first parallel of works was opened by Gen. Lincoln. On the 11th the second parallel, only 300 yards from the British works, was opened by Baron Steuben. On the 14th two British redoubts were stormed by American and French troops under Alexander Hamilton and Baron DeViomenil. A British sortie on the 15th failed, and on the 17th Cornwallis asked for terms, the surrender of his 7247 men being completed on the 19th. Although not so regarded at the time by either side, this was really the death blow to the British cause in America. There was no more fighting of consequence thereafter.

[Sydney George Fisher, *The True History of the American Revolution;* Claude H. Van Tyne, *The American Revolution, 1776-83;* Rupert Hughes, *George Washington.*]

ALVIN F. HARLOW

Yosemite National Park. The Yosemite Valley, eight square miles in extent, has been world-famed for its beauty since its discovery in 1851, but the Valley itself is but one feature of the 1176 square miles of Sierra wonderland embraced within the National Park. The Yosemite back-country is characterized by lofty granite domes and peaks (Mt. Lyell, 13,090 ft.), glaciers and everlasting snows, a thousand icy streams, hundreds of snow-bordered lakes, polished pavements and rounded valleys on glaciated mountain slopes, vertical cliffs and plunging waterfalls, magnificent forests climaxed by three groves of Big Trees, and abundant wildlife population. Glacier Point, on the rim of Yosemite Valley, commands a magnificent view of domes, pinnacles, waterfalls and the seldom-visited crest of the High Sierra, while 3254 feet directly below lies the flat forested floor of the Valley.

[François E. Matthes, *Geologic History of Yosemite Valley;* Joseph Grinnell and Tracy I. Storer, *Animal Life in Yosemite;* Carl P. Russell, *100 Years in Yosemite;* Ansel F. Hall, *Yosemite Valley, An Intimate Guide.*]

CARL P. RUSSELL

"Young America" was a popular and widespread figure of speech culturally generic to the period 1840–50 and designating anything that exhibited the youthful spirit of energy and enterprise characteristic of the times; historically, a concept related to ideas of capitalistic progress and romantic individualism. Also an aggressively nationalistic term, it combined Young Europe's democratic universalism, imported by scholars and refugees, with the manifest destiny[qv] espoused by elements in the Democratic party after 1844, notably George Nicholas Sanders. A more elevated nationalistic interpretation was best stated by Emerson (1844). Intermingling with these sources was political Young Americanism, beginning with Edwin DeLeon (1844), influenced by younger party leaders and by George Henry Evans (1845 ff.), and culminating in the amorphous Young America Democratic faction (1851–56). The latter, headed by Sanders and the *Democratic Review* (1852), sought to revitalize its party by uniting all sections on a platform of free trade, foreign markets, a subsidized merchant marine, annexation southward and the encouragement of republican movements abroad. Fundamentally an attempt to construct issues apart from sectional controversy, this premature experiment had no lasting effects. After finding scattered literary and political expression, Young Americanism gradually disappeared, having made chiefly a contribution to native democratic idealism.

[Merle E. Curti, "Young America," in *Amer. Hist. Rev.*, XXXII; Siert F. Riepma, "*Young America*": *A Study in American Nationalism before the Civil War*, ms. in Western Reserve University Library, with bibliography.]

S. F. RIEPMA

Young Men's Christian Associations. The first such organizations in America were formed in Montreal and Boston in 1851, following the plan of a society organized in England in 1844. Forty more units were organized within the next three years, and an international convention was held at Buffalo in 1854. Thereafter, annual conventions took place until the Civil War disrupted the movement considerably, the surviving organizations working mostly among the soldiers in the field. After the war a period of rapid growth ensued, and buildings which steadily developed into residential hotels as well as religious, cultural and recreational centers were erected in all the larger cities. During the World War the Y.M.C.A. operated in every place where Americans trained or served, and handled nine tenths of the welfare work among the American forces in Europe. Just before the Armistice in 1918 it had 1397 stations in France, and operated 2029 stations during the following winter when the troops were awaiting orders to return to America. During the five years following the war, it gave educational assistance to more than 100,000 ex-service men studying in schools and colleges. On Dec. 31, 1937, it had 1,184,722 members in the United States.

[Richard C. Morse, *History of the North American Young Men's Christian Association.*]

ALVIN F. HARLOW

Young Plan, The, is the popular name of a plan recommended by a committee of experts, in its report of June 7, 1929, for the final settlement of the German reparation[qv] problem. This plan was largely adopted by the governments concerned. Its popular name was derived from the fact that Owen D. Young, one of the American experts, was elected chairman of the committee.

The Young Plan set forth a schedule of annuity payments by Germany which, it was felt, would be within the capacity of that country to pay, and established the machinery for transferring such payments in the form of the Bank for International Settlements[qv]. This institution not only had the function of transferring reparation payments from Germany to the Allied powers, but was given important banking powers in dealing with central banks. The bank is still in operation, although Germany has ceased to make reparation payments.

[D. P. Myers, *The Reparation Settlement, 1930;* E. Dulles, *The Bank for International Settlements at Work; Annual Reports of the Bank for International Settlements.*]

FREDERICK A. BRADFORD

Young Women's Christian Associations. In 1858 the Ladies' Christian Association was organized in New York City, "to labor for the temporal, moral and religious welfare of self-supporting young women." In 1866 the Young Women's Christian Association of Boston was established, with employment and boarding directory bureaus as adjuncts, and two years later it set up a boarding house of its own. Associations were formed in other cities, and in 1871 an International Conference of Women's Christian Associations was held at Hartford, Conn. The first college unit was formed at the Normal University, Normal, Ill., in 1873. In 1886 a National Association of Y.W.C.A.'s was formed, and reorganizations took place in 1891–94 and in 1906. Upon the entrance of the United States into the World War the Association raised a large war fund, erected hostess houses in army camps, provided emergency housing for women and girls in newly created military and industrial centers, also hospitality and aid for native and foreign-born women affected by the war. It set up industrial clubs for women in France and Russia, and social centers for American nurses in France. Its work extended during that period into eight countries of Europe and to the Near East.

[Elizabeth Wilson, *Fifty Years of Association Work among Women;* Genevieve M. Fox, *An Idea that Grew.*]

ALVIN F. HARLOW

Youth Administration, The National, formerly a division of the Works Progress Administration[qv], now a division of the Federal Security Administration, was created by executive order of President F. D. Roosevelt on June 26, 1935, for special services to young persons sixteen to twenty-five years of age. It continues the Federal Student Aid Program conducted by the Federal Emergency Relief Administration[qv], whereby capable young people are provided with part-time employment enabling them to pursue further academic, vocational, technical or professional studies, and are at the same time kept out of the general labor market. It also provides apprenticeship training and work projects for young people not in school, and promotes vocational guidance and placement, and the extension of educational and recreational facilities for young persons in neglected areas.

[Betty and Ernest K. Lindley, *A New Deal for Youth: The Story of the National Youth Administration.*]

HOWARD E. JENSEN

Youth Movements. In the United States autonomous, self-conscious organizations of youth have arisen since the late 19th century, reflecting youth's increasing economic inequality and psychological readjustment. While their idealism relates to the tradition of juvenescent national character, as epitomized by "Young America"[qv], they are in their new, spontaneous approach to social problems essentially distinct from movements sponsored by elders. Confined largely to an educated, collegiate minority, they have protested heretofore against the authority of age mostly through student bodies and by espousing advanced attitudes toward international and domestic politico-economic affairs. This insurgency was early expressed by Randolph Bourne (1913) and by the Intercollegiate Socialist Society (1905). The war emphasized the strength of American youth, greatly revivified its political interests, particularly in the cause of peace, and established international ties. There eventually resulted the National Student Federation of America (1925) and various local groups. In the 1930's economic depression brought forth the more united and radical American Youth Congress (1934) and American Student Union (1935), ideologically connected with the labor as well as the peace movements[qqv]. Noteworthy among other recent youth manifestations is a religious phase, exemplified in the Christian Youth Council of North America and the Oxford (Buchmanite) group.

[Besides official reports of organizations, items in the New York *Times*, and publications by the National Youth Administration, see Randolph Bourne, *Youth and Life;* James H. S. Broussard et al., *The Prospect for Youth;* Stanley High, *The Revolt of Youth;* Kingsley Davis, *Youth in the Depression;* Ivison S. Macadam, *Youth in the Universities;* Richard M. Whitney, *The Youth Movement in America.*]

S. F. RIEPMA

Youth's Companion, THE. *See* Children's Magazines, American.

Ypres-Lys Operation (Aug. 19–Nov. 11, 1918). In July the pressing need of the British for troops caused the American 27th (O'Ryan) and 30th (Lewis) divisions, breaking their training period, to be placed in line near Ypres with the 2nd British Army (Plumer). Later Plumer attacked and the American divisions from August 31 to September 2 advanced some 2000 yards, capturing Lankhof Farm and Voormezeele and occupying Vierstraat Ridge and parts of Mount Kemmel and Wytschaete Ridge.

In October the 37th (Farnsworth) and 91st (Johnston) divisions were withdrawn from the American 1st Army and sent to reinforce the French 6th Army (de Boissoudy), advancing toward Brussels, in Belgium. October 30–November 4 the 37th Division, attacking east, cleared Cruyshautem Ridge and crossed the Scheldt River at Eyne and Heurne. On its right the 91st Division flanked and captured Spitaals-Bosschen and took Audenarde. Returning to line November 9, the 91st crossed the Scheldt and both divisions progressed some distance east of it by November 11. Each division suffered about 1600 casualties in the Belgian operations.

[*Order of Battle of the United States Land Forces in the World War;* J. M. Hanson, History of the American Combat Divisions, in *The Stars and Stripes.*]

JOSEPH MILLS HANSON

Yucatan. Early in 1848 a revolt of the Maya Indians threatened to destroy altogether the upper class in Yucatan. As the state government was at odds with the central government of Mexico, it appealed for help to the United States, Great Britain and Spain, offering sovereignty over Yucatan to any power which might respond.

On April 29, 1848, in a message to Congress, President Polk asked authority to send help and stated that the United States could not consent to the transfer of Yucatan to any European power. This declaration against a transfer of territory even by voluntary action of its inhabitants involved a new interpretation of the Monroe Doctrine[qv], which has been referred to as the "Polk Doctrine"[qv]. A measure providing for a temporary occupation of Yucatan was introduced in the Senate but met with much opposition and was withdrawn. Neither Great Britain nor Spain showed any inclination to accept the annexation proposal. The Indian revolt was eventually suppressed with the help from the Mexican government.

[D. Perkins, *The Monroe Doctrine, 1826-1867;* M. W. Williams, Secessionist Diplomacy in Yucatan, in *Hispanic American Historical Review*, 9:132.]

DANA G. MUNRO

Yukon, THE, rises as the Lewes, in the mountains east of Skagway (lat. 59°) within a score of miles of the Pacific. At the confluence of the Lewes and the Pelly at Selkirk the river takes the name Yukon. Joined by numerous tributaries on its northward course, it enters Alaska 90 miles north of Dawson about latitude 65°. At the Arctic Circle, where it is joined by the Porcupine, it bends and flows southwestward discharging through numerous channels over an immense delta into Bering Sea. The Yukon is the largest river in Alaska, fifth largest in North America, draining an area of 330,000 square miles. About 1600 of its 2300 miles are navigable for large steamboats.

In 1842 the Russian Zagoshkin explored part of the river. In 1850 Robert Campbell of the Hudson's Bay Company[qv] descended the river from Fort Selkirk to Fort Yukon, proving the identity of the Yukon and the Kwikpak. In 1866 Robert Kennecott surveyed a route for the Western Union Telegraph Company for a line by way of Alaska and Siberia to Europe. The plan was abandoned with the death of Kennecott. In 1873 gold seekers began to arrive. The Klondike gold rush[qv] in 1896, and after, influenced conditions in the Yukon region. In 1898 the United States Geodetic Survey mapped the delta of the Yukon.

[H. W. Clark, *History of Alaska.*]

J. W. ELLISON

Yuma, Fort. From the late 18th century the Yuma Indians operated a crude ferry service at the confluence of the Colorado and Gila rivers for traders and travelers between California, Sonora and Santa Fé. After the Treaty of Guadalupe Hidalgo[qv], United States boundary surveyors and their military escort camped on the California side at this Indian ferry, and in 1849 John Glanton and other Americans are said to have seized the ferry from the Indians and operated it for emigrants. The hostile conduct of the Yumas toward the ferrymen and westbound emigrants, particularly the massacre of about fifteen Americans at Glanton's ferry on April 23, 1850, led to the establishment of a permanent military camp at this point on Nov. 27, 1850. Maj. S. P. Heintzelman, in charge of United States troops brought from San Diego, named the new post Camp Independence, but in March, 1851, the name became Camp Yuma. Abandoned in December, 1851, it was reoccupied on Feb. 22, 1852, as Fort Yuma. Across the river in what is now Arizona, a town site laid out after the completion of the Gadsden Purchase[qv] in 1854 was variously known as Colorado City, Arizona City and the present Yuma. Fort Yuma flourished as a station on early stagecoach lines beginning in 1857. The lands included in the military reservation of Fort Yuma lay at first partly in California, partly in Arizona; this was changed on June 22, 1874, the land on the Arizona side being given to the Department of the Interior. The fort, on the California side, was turned over to the same department on June 9, 1884, for use as an Indian school, located at the center of what is now the Yuma Indian Reservation. Meanwhile, in 1877, the Southern Pacific Railroad[qv] had built across the reservation into the town and across the river, supplanting gradually the old stage route eastward. The importance of Fort Yuma was thereafter for many years determined more by the flow of railway traffic than by any other factor, especially after steamboat navigation on the Colorado River declined.

[H. H. Bancroft, *History of Arizona and New Mexico;* F. C. Lockwood, *Pioneer Days in Arizona;* J. H. McClintock, *History of Arizona.*]

RUFUS KAY WYLLYS

Zane's Trace and Grants. In 1796 Congress authorized the President to contract with Ebenezer Zane, whose home was on the south branch of the Potomac River in Maryland, to build a "trace"[qv] through Ohio. This was first a bridle path from the Ohio River at Wheeling[qv] by way of the sites of Zanesville, Lancaster and Chillicothe to Limestone (Maysville), Ky. The path east of Zanesville later was developed into the National Road[qv], and the trace became one of the most important pioneer highways in the state. For locating and building the trace, Congress gave Zane the privilege of locating military warrants[qv] upon three sections of land amounting to 1920 acres. The first of these was at the crossing of the Muskingum River, the second at the Hockhocking River and the third at the Scioto River crossing. At the Scioto, Zane was obliged to locate his warrant on the east side of the river opposite Chillicothe, as the western shore lay within the Virginia military grant[qv].

[E. O. Randall and D. J. Ryan, *History of Ohio;* Henry Howe, *Historical Collections of Ohio.*]

HARLOW LINDLEY

Zarah, Fort, was built in September, 1864, by Gen. S. R. Curtis on the left bank of Walnut Creek, about four miles east of the present town of Great Bend, Kans. Its purpose was to furnish the army a base for operations against hostile Kiowas and Comanches[qqv]. It was abandoned in 1869 and the sandstone used in its construction appropriated by settlers.

[F. H. Blackmar, *Kansas.*]

CARL L. CANNON

Zenger Trial (Aug. 4, 1735). From his arrival in 1732 William Cosby, colonial governor of New York, provoked controversy. His prosecution of the interim governor, Rip Van Dam, and his removal of Chief Justice Lewis Morris, stirred up an opposition party. This group established John Peter Zenger as printer of the *New York Weekly Journal* (Nov. 5, 1733), the first newspaper in America to be the organ of a political faction. Strictures published in this paper led the governor to have Zenger arrested and put in jail. His cause became that of the people, and when the governor arbitrarily debarred his New York counsel, Andrew Hamilton of Philadelphia, the most distinguished advocate in the colonies, consented to serve.

The printer was charged with seditious libel. Hamilton admitted the publication, but denied that it was a libel unless false, and sought to prove the truth of the statements. The court held that the fact of publication was sufficient to convict, and excluded the truth from evidence. Hamilton made an eloquent appeal to the jury to judge both the law and the fact, and the verdict was "Not guilty." Zenger was released, and the Common Council voted Hamilton the "Freedom of the Corporation." It was a notable victory for the freedom of the press[qv], and set a precedent against judicial tyranny in libel suits. (*See also* Croswell Libel Suit.)

[Livingston Rutherfurd, *John Peter Zenger.*]

MILTON W. HAMILTON

Zimmermann Note, The (January, 1917), was a telegram from Herr Zimmermann, German secretary for foreign affairs, to the German minister to Mexico. Declaring that unrestricted submarine[qv] warfare would begin on February 1, and fearing the United States would not remain neutral, Zimmermann directed that an alliance be formed with Mexico and that Japan be detached from the Entente. Mexico was to attack the United States on its southwestern border and recover Texas, New Mexico and Arizona. This telegram was intercepted by the British and delivered to the United States Government. Its publication strengthened President Wilson's position and caused popular indignation against Germany to mount even higher (*see* World War).

[B. J. Hendrick, *The Life and Letters of Walter H. Page.*]

RICHARD E. YATES

Zinc Industry, The, in America had its practical origin at the time of the Civil War, when the demand for the metal in connection with war materials manufacture afforded a stimulus to its domestic production. Although zinc minerals were known to exist in the eastern United States they were not early worked, as the brass-fabricating industry of Connecticut was based on imported brass until after 1850. When the Government standard set of weights and measures were made from brass, in 1838, zinc metallurgists were brought over from Belgium to make enough metal for that purpose, and were then returned home. The zinc ores of New Jersey were worked for the production of zinc oxide, not metal; the latter first coming from the ores of Friedensville, Pa., after 1856. Production soon began in the Mississippi Valley, where zinc is associated with lead, and that became the dominant region. The output grew rapidly, reaching 100,000 tons annually in 1897 and 350,000 in 1914. It reached 670,000 tons in 1917 because of the effect of the World War in Belgium. The United States has produced about half of the world's supply of zinc.

[G. C. Stone, Development of Zinc Smelting in the United States, Paper No. 191, Transactions, International Engineering Congress, San Francisco, 1915.]

T. T. READ

Zion, known as Zion City until 1919, is a theocratic city in Lake County, Ill., founded by John Alexander Dowie, General Overseer of the Christian Catholic Apostolic Church in Zion, for the practice of literal Biblical Christianity. The site was quietly acquired in 1898–99; leases were offered for sale in 1901; on March 31, 1902, the City of Zion was incorporated. Its population was then about 2000.

Ownership of land in Zion was vested in God; only long-term leases were sold. All industries and commercial establishments were owned by the church and controlled by the General Overseer. Under Dowie, extravagance and unwise management led to a receivership in 1906, but by 1910 Dowie's successor, Wilbur Glenn Voliva, had regained control of Zion's industries. Under his aggressive and efficient management Zion's stores and factories expanded steadily. In 1927 their value was certified to exceed $4,000,000.

With the economic collapse of 1929, business in Zion began a decline which resulted in receivership in 1933. In local elections in 1934 and 1935 Voliva suffered the first political defeats of his career, and his complete downfall was freely predicted. However, he continued to hold his position as General Overseer of the Church, and in 1935 he was appointed president of Zion's reorganized industries.

Through provisions in leases and city ordinances, the moral and social ideas of the founder have been made effective in Zion since its establishment. The sale or use of pork or swine products, alcoholic liquor, tobacco, drugs and medicines is prohibited; dancing, theatrical performances and secret societies are not allowed.

[John J. Halsey, *A History of Lake County, Illinois; Literary Digest,* May 23, 1936; Correspondence with residents.]

PAUL M. ANGLE

Zoar Society, THE (1817–98), was organized by German Separatists who emigrated from Wurttemberg in 1817 under the leadership of Joseph Michael Bimeler. They founded Zoar, Tuscarawas County, Ohio, in December, 1817, and on April 15, 1819, they formed the Society of Separatists of Zoar. All property was communally owned, and the farms, shops and factories were managed by regularly elected trustees. The Society attained its greatest prosperity in the 1850's when it owned over 10,000 acres of land and was worth approximately $1,000,000. Declining income and a dissatisfied membership forced a dissolution of the Society, Sept. 1, 1898.

[Charles Nordhoff, *The Communistic Societies of the U. S.;* E. O. Randall, *History of the Zoar Society.*]

EDGAR B. NIXON

Zollverein Treaty, Wheaton's. Henry Wheaton, minister to Prussia, 1835–46, labored for eight years to negotiate a commercial reciprocity treaty between the United States and German Zollverein, composed of Prussia (the spokesman state) and eighteen German inland states. The basis of the treaty was a reciprocal lowering of tariffs, particularly on American tobacco and lard by Germany, and on specialties of German manufacture by the United States. After finally securing the assent of all the Zollverein to the treaty, it was signed on March 25, 1844. The Committee on Foreign Relations of the Senate reported, June 14, 1844, against ratification. The rejection of the treaty was due to a combination of causes: resentment of Congress at having tariff rates fixed by treaty rather than by legislation; influential opposition in the United States by representatives of England and the Hanse Towns, which would have been injured by the arrangement; absence of the Prussian minister from the United States; opposition to President Tyler; and conflicting mercantile interests within the United States.

[Elizabeth Feaster Baker, *Henry Wheaton, 1785-1848;* W. S. Holt, *Treaties Defeated by the Senate.*]

SAMUEL FLAGG BEMIS

Zoning Ordinances. Cities had long exercised a limited police power*qv* over building construction, but during the present century the scope of such legislation has been greatly broadened and now goes far beyond such elementary objectives as the prevention of fire hazards or nuisances. An increasingly common type of ordinance regulates the type and use of buildings in specified districts, as for example, the creation of areas for single family residences in which apartment houses or business establishments—neither of which are nuisances *per se*—are prohibited. Obviously zoning ordinances involve a collision with the "due process" clauses*qv* of the Constitution, but in Euclid v. Ambler Realty Company (272 U. S. 365, 1926) the Supreme Court upheld a drastic zoning ordinance as necessary under conditions of modern urban life. A great mass of expert evidence had been gathered by commissions and boards, the Court pointed out, showing that "the segregation of residential, business, and industrial buildings" worked out for the common good of the community.

[T. Adams, *Outline of Town and City Planning;* W. B. Munro, *Municipal Administration;* A. F. Macdonald, *American City Government and Administration.*]

W. A. ROBINSON

Zouaves, distinguished by a drill and uniform derived from the Zouaoua tribe in French service in Algeria (*ca.* 1830), were popularized in the United States by Elmer E. Ellsworth*qv* and others after the Crimean War. In the Civil War Ellsworth's 1st New York Fire Zouaves (11th New York Infantry) attracted much attention, but was mustered out a year after the death of its colonel. The Zouave idea was soon abandoned under field conditions. Among other regiments were: Hawkins' Zouaves (9th New York); National Guard Zouaves (10th New York); D'Epineuil's Zouaves (53d New York); Anderson Zouaves (62d New York); 2d Duryea's Zouaves (76th New York); Fire Zouave Regiment (72d Pennsylvania); Keystone Zouaves (76th Pennsylvania); Collis' Independent

Company of Pennsylvania Zouaves d'Afrique; and Missouri Zouaves (9th Missouri, later 59th Illinois). Ellsworth's two companies of Chicago Zouaves were incorporated in the 19th Illinois.

[Charles A. Ingraham, *Elmer E. Ellsworth and the Zouaves of '61;* Elmer E. Ellsworth, *Manual of Arms ... Arranged for the U. S. Zouave Cadets.*] DON RUSSELL

Zuñi, THE, a tribe of village-dwelling Indians in New Mexico south of Gallup, were discovered in 1539 by Fray Marcos and the Negro Estevan, a survivor from the ill-fated expedition of Cabeza de Vaca[qv]. A story was current in Mexico that seven cities, rich in gold, lay in a country to the north, called Cíbola[qv]. Seven Zuñi towns were found by the Fray Marcos party, but Estevan, leading the advance, was killed, whereupon Fray Marcos turned back. The next year Coronado[qv] led an army into the country, which found no difficulty in capturing the Zuñi towns. The Spanish exercised intermittent control over them until their subjugation was complete. At the end of the Mexican War the Zuñi came under the control of the United States (*see* Guadalupe Hidalgo, The Treaty of).

In 1680 they numbered 2500, occupying three villages instead of seven. They now reside in a single village, numbering less than 2000. In mode of life, economics, architecture, social organization, etc., they resemble the Hopi, Acoma and other pueblo Indians[qqv]. Their speech is a distinct language, but bears a vague resemblance to Shoshoni and Aztec.

[F. W. Hodge, *Handbook of American Indians.*] CLARK WISSLER

Zwaanendael Colony, or "Valley of Swans," was founded on the west shore of the Delaware Bay near present Lewes in 1631. Samuel Godyn, Samuel Blommaert and Kiliaen Van Rensselaer obtained privileges from the Dutch West India Company[qv] for the establishment of this colony and secured the services of David Pieterzen deVries, an experienced navigator, by making him a partner. Capt. Pieter Heyes, hired by deVries to make a settlement and engage in whaling, landed at the present Lewes Creek in the spring of 1631 in the ship *Walvis* (Whale) with twenty-eight men and supplies. Following the erection of a palisaded building called Fort Optlandt and the planting of crops, the *Walvis* returned to Holland in the fall of that year. While deVries himself was making preparations to sail to the South (Delaware) River in the spring of 1632 news was received that all in the settlement had been massacred by the Indians. Upon arriving at Zwaanendael, deVries found that the settlers had been killed and the colony destroyed because of a misunderstanding with the Indians.

[David Peterson deVries, Voyages from Holland to America, 1632-44, translated by Henry C. Murphy, in *Collections of the New York Historical Society,* 2d series, Volume 3, part 1, pages 22-35; Benjamin Ferris, *A History of the Original Settlements on the Delaware.*]

LEON DEVALINGER, JR.

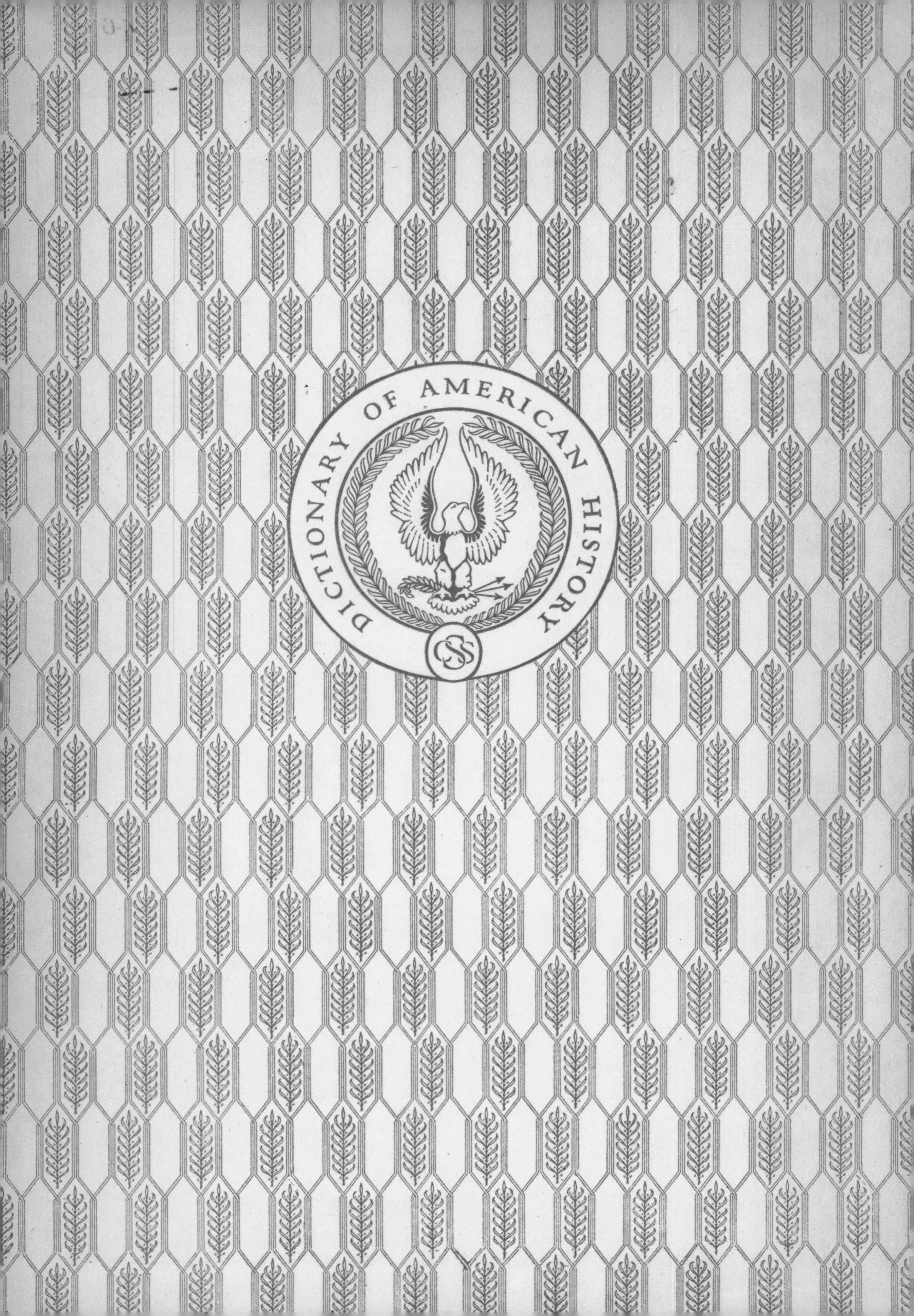
DICTIONARY OF AMERICAN HISTORY
CSS